CASES AND MATERIALS ON
CONTRACTS: MAKING AND DOING DEALS

Third Edition

. . .

By

David G. Epstein

George E. Allen Chair Professor of Law
University of Richmond

Bruce A. Markell

United States Bankruptcy Judge
District of Nevada
Senior Fellow, Bankruptcy and Commercial Law
William S. Boyd School of Law
University of Nevada, Las Vegas

Lawrence Ponoroff

Dean of the College & Samuel M. Fegtly
Chair in Commercial Law
The University of Arizona
James E. Rogers College of Law

AMERICAN CASEBOOK SERIES®

WEST®

A Thomson Reuters business

Mat #41098008

© 2011 Thomson Reuters
    610 Opperman Drive
    St. Paul, MN 55123
    1–800–313–9378
Printed in the United States of America

ISBN: 978–0–314–27238–6

PREFACE TO THE THIRD EDITION

Although this is the third edition of MADD, it is the first one to be published by West; the first two editions having been out by a different publisher. It is still, however, very much the same book that has become a beloved classic (at least in our minds!) over the past eight or nine years.

For prior users of MADD, the object of the third edition has been to make the book even more useable (and we hope enjoyable) for both students and instructors. To this end, we made a number of changes, including:

- moved a couple of chapters around (third-party interests and restitution);
- split one chapter ("Is it a Deal the Law will Enforce") into two (What Is "Consideration" and Why Is It Still an Important Part of Contract Law (or is Consideration Still an Important Part of Contract Law?)) and (Is the Agreement Unenforceable Because of Flaws in the Agreement Process or Problems with the Language of the Agreement?);
- trimmed in a several places and added in just a few;
- replaced some cases from the second edition with cases that we believe are better teaching vehicles, or, if no better, are at least shorter;
- reorganized the remedies chapter in a fashion that we hope will make the sequencing of the material more logical and accessible for students;
- added some new problems and expository material for topics that we thought needed a better explanation; and
- eliminated all references to Revised Article 2, other than a mention in the introductory chapter of its abysmal lack of success insofar as adoption in any of the states is concerned.

Overall, however, we tried to maintain, just as we did with the second edition, the overall organizational structure of the book and the conversational tone. We even injected some new attempts at what Epstein believes qualifies as humor. Ponoroff is not so sure, and Markell is just glad that his reappointment decision is still several years away.

Unlike the first two editions, the manuscript for the third edition was not prepared in camera-ready form. Therefore, while we may have to take responsibility for bad puns, we blame West for any errors or mistakes you may find. Trust us, however, those errors would have been a lot worse but for the superlative efforts of Jean Janisse, Judge Markell's assistant, who did a careful and thorough proof reading of the manuscript under a very tight timeline, and Mona Railan, a second year law student at the University of Richmond Law School who not only was able to work with Epstein but was also able to do an incredible amount of work of the highest quality.

It may bear mentioning that since the second edition, we have continued in our personal inability to hold a job. So, Epstein has moved from SMU to the University of Richmond Law School, and Ponoroff has moved from Tulane to the James E. Rogers College of Law at the University of Arizona. This time, it's Markell who has demonstrated professional stability.

As always, our first hope is that you have fun using the book (or at least as much fun as one can have in law school), and, secondarily, that you, the student, maybe even learn a little something about contract law, and making and doing deals, in the process.

AS ALWAYS, WE WISH YOU A WONDERFUL FIRST YEAR.

DAVID G. EPSTEIN
BRUCE A. MARKELL
LAWRENCE PONOROFF

Richmond, Las Vegas, and Tucson
March 2011

Summary of Contents

———

	Page
Preface to the Third Edition	v
Table of Cases	xxi

Chapter One. What Are We Going to Be Doing in This Course? **1**
1: What Is a Contract? — 1
2: Why Do Lawyers and Law Students Need to Know About Contracts and Contract Law? — 5
3: Where Does Contract Law Come From? — 6
4: What Is the Lawyer's Role in Contract Law? — 16
5: What Is a First Year Course in Contracts? — 18
6: The Lawyer's Role in Contract Law Revisited—Commercial Arbitration — 32

Chapter Two. Has Your Client Made a Deal? — **36**
1: Determining Mutual Assent — 37
2: Offer — 66
3: Destroying the Offer — 83
4: Preserving the Offer — 96
5: Modes and Methods of Acceptance — 106
6: Deficient Agreements: Insufficient, Inadequate, and Postponed Terms — 180

Chapter Three. What Is "Consideration" and Why Is It Still an Important Part of Contract Law (or Is Consideration Still an Important Part of Contract Law?) — **225**
1: Bargain and the Legal Concept of Consideration — 226
2: Promise to Pay for Something That Happened Before the Promise: Moral Obligations — 264
3: Reliance and the Legal Concept of Promissory Estoppel — 278

Chapter Four. Is the Agreement Unenforceable Because of the Flaws in the Agreement Process or Problems With the Language of the Agreement? — **323**
1: Contract Law Reasons for Not Enforcing Agreements: Statutes of Fraud — 323
2: Contract Law Reasons for Not Enforcing Agreements: Fraud, Fraudulent or Material Misrepresentations and Nondisclosure — 343
3: Contract Law Reasons for Not Enforcing Agreements: Defendant's Lack of Capacity — 356
4: Contract Law Reasons for Not Enforcing Agreements: Duress and Undue Influence — 362

Page

5: Contract Law Reasons for Not Enforcing Agreements: Illegality and Public Policy --------- 381

6: Contract Law Reasons for Not Enforcing an Agreement: Unconscionability -------- 403

7: Contract Law Reasons for Not Enforcing Agreements: Mistake -------- 416

Chapter Five. What Are the Terms of the Deal? -------- **434**

1: Terms of the Contract That Are Not Words of the Parties: Trade Customs and Usage -------- 434

2: Words of the Parties That Are Not in the Final Written Version of the Deal: The Parol Evidence Rule -------- 439

3: Using Parol Evidence and Other Extrinsic Evidence to Discover the Meaning of the Terms Used in the Written Contract -------- 470

4: Terms Added by the Courts -------- 510

5: Terms Added by Legislatures -------- 534

6: Warranties and the U.C.C. -------- 535

Chapter Six. When Is Someone Who Made an Enforceable Deal Excused From Doing What She Agreed to Do? -------- **579**

1: Conditions: Non–Occurrence of Something That Contract Expressly Provided Must Occur as an Excuse for Not Doing What You Agreed to Do -------- 579

2: Modification, Waiver, or Estoppel as an Excuse for Not Doing What You Agreed to Do -------- 599

3: Impossibility, Impracticability, Frustration of Purpose: Occurrence of Something Not Provided for in the Contract as an Excuse for Not Doing What You Agreed to Do -------- 612

4: "Anticipatory Repudiation": Other Guy's Unambiguous Indication of an Unwillingness or Inability to Perform as an Excuse for Not Doing What You Agreed to Do -------- 636

5: Material Breach: Other Guy's Improper Performance as an Excuse for Not Doing What You Agreed to Do Under a Common Law Contract -------- 649

Chapter Seven. How Does the Law Enforce a Deal? -------- **686**

1: The Problem Examined -------- 686

2: Specific Performance -------- 687

3: Agreed Remedies -------- 698

4: Judicial Determination of Money Damages -------- 711

Chapter Eight. What Are the Alternatives to Contracts and Contract Law? (Quasi–Contract and Restitution) -------- **800**

1: Nature and Origins of Quasi–Contract -------- 800

2: Elements of a Quasi–Contractual Claim -------- 803

3: Promissory Restitution -------- 829

4: Other Remedies for Unjust Enrichment -------- 830

Page

Chapter Nine.   When Do You Have Rights and/or Duties Under a Contract That You Did Not Make? ---------------------------------- **835**

1: Third Party Beneficiaries -- 835

2: Assignment and Delegation --------------------------------------- 856

INDEX -- 877

TABLE OF CONTENTS

	Page
PREFACE TO THE THIRD EDITION	v
TABLE OF CASES	xxi

Chapter One. What Are We Going to Be Doing in This Course? **1**

1: What Is a Contract? 1
    E. Allan Farnsworth, Changing Your Mind: The Law of Regretted Decisions ... 3
2: Why Do Lawyers and Law Students Need to Know About Contracts and Contract Law? 5
3: Where Does Contract Law Come From? 6
    A. English Common Law Origins and the Evolution of Assumpsit 7
        E. Allan Farnsworth, The Past of Promise: An Historical Introduction to Contract 7
    B. Classical Era of American Contract Law 9
        Lawrence M. Friedman, Contract Law in America 9
    C. Demise of Classical Principles of Contract Law 10
    D. Sources of Modern Contract Law 12
4: What Is the Lawyer's Role in Contract Law? 16
5: What Is a First Year Course in Contracts? 18
    R.R. v. M.H. 23
    Questions, Note, and Connections 29
6: The Lawyer's Role in Contract Law Revisited—Commercial Arbitration 32

Chapter Two. Has Your Client Made a Deal? **36**

1: Determining Mutual Assent 37
    Lucy v. Zehmer 37
    Questions and Notes 44
    Leonard v. Pepsico, Inc. 47
    Questions 54
    Gleason v. Freeman 55
    Questions 57
    Smith v. Boyd 58
    Questions, Note, and Connections 62
    Note on the Intention to Be Legally Bound 64
    Problems on Mutual Assent 65
2: Offer 66
    Lonergan v. Scolnick 66
    Questions 69
    Maryland Supreme Corp. v. Blake Co. 70
    Questions and Notes 75
    Note on U.C.C. Article 2 77
    Leonard v. Pepsico, Inc. 78
    Questions, Notes, and Connections 80
    Problem on Implied–in–Fact Contract 82

	Page
3: Destroying the Offer	83
A. Rejection	84
B. Revocation	84
1. Direct Revocation	84
2. Indirect Revocation	85
Dickinson v. Dodds	85
Questions, Note, and Connections	89
C. Lapse	90
Minnesota Linseed Oil Co. v. Collier White Lead Co.	90
Questions and Notes	93
D. Death (or Incapacity) of the Offeror (or Offeree)	94
Problems	95
Note on Termination by Supervening Incapacity	96
4: Preserving the Offer	96
Beall v. Beall	97
Questions, Notes, and Connections	100
Board of Control of Eastern Michigan University v. Burgess	101
Questions, Note, and Connections	103
Note on Option Contracts and Firm Offers	104
Problem	105
Note on Option Contracts and Reliance	105
5: Modes and Methods of Acceptance	106
A. Offeror's Control Over the Manner of Acceptance	106
La Salle National Bank v. Vega	107
Ever–Tite Roofing Corp. v. Green	110
Note on Required Form of Acceptance	113
Questions About Lasalle and Ever–Tite	114
Introduction to Davis v. Jacoby	115
Davis v. Jacoby	116
Questions and Notes	121
Maryland Supreme Corp. v. Blake Co.	123
Connections	124
B. Effectiveness of Promissory Acceptance	124
Introduction to Hendricks	124
Hendricks v. Behee	124
Questions	126
Introduction to Adams v. Lindsell	127
Adams v. Lindsell	128
Questions and Notes	129
Problems Concerning Application of the "Mailbox Rule"	131
C. Effectiveness of Acceptance by Performance	132
Carlill v. Carbolic Smoke Ball Co.	133
Questions and Notes	136
Marchiondo v. Scheck	138
Questions	141
Problems on Acceptance by Promise, Performance, and Part Performance	142
D. Acceptance by Silence or Inaction	143
Laredo National Bank v. Gordon	143
Questions, Notes, and Connections	145
E. Imperfect Acceptances	146
Gresser v. Hotzler	147
Questions and Notes	152
Dorton v. Collins & Aikman Corporation	155
Questions and Notes	161
Introduction to Klocek and Hill	164

Page

5: Modes and Methods of Acceptance—Continued
    Klocek v. Gateway, Inc. 165
    Questions and Notes 170
    Hill v. Gateway 2000, Inc. 172
    Questions, Notes, and Connections 175
  F. Electronic Acceptances 178
6: Deficient Agreements: Insufficient, Inadequate, and Postponed Terms 180
Introduction 180
  A. Problems of Misunderstood, Incomplete, and Indefinite Terms 181
    Introduction to Mutual Misunderstanding of a Contract Term—Raffles 181
    Raffles v. Wichelhaus 182
    Questions 184
    Problem on Mutual Misunderstanding of a Contract Term 185
    Introduction to Indefinite and Incomplete Terms—Varney 185
    Varney v. Ditmars 186
    Questions 191
    Community Design Corporation v. Antonell 192
    Questions, Notes, and Connections 193
    Note on Long–Term Agreements and Relational Contracts 195
    Note on U.C.C. Gap Fillers 196
  B. Problems of Postponed Agreement 198
    Walker v. Keith 198
    Questions 204
    Moolenaar v. Co–Build Companies, Inc. 204
    Questions and Notes 209
    Problem: "Love in the Time of Faxes" 211
    Budget Marketing, Inc. v. Centronics Corporation 214
    Questions, Notes, and Connections 221

Chapter Three.   What Is "Consideration" and Why Is It Still an Important Part of Contract Law (or Is Consideration Still an Important Part of Contract Law?) 225
1: Bargain and the Legal Concept of Consideration 226
  A. Consideration: "Bargained For" 228
    California Civil Jury Instructions (BAJI) 229
    Reed v. University of North Dakota and the North Dakota Association for the Disabled, Inc. 230
    Questions 231
  B. Consideration and Family Agreements 232
    Kirksey v. Kirksey 232
    Questions and Notes 233
    Hamer v. Sidway 236
    Questions and Notes 239
    Schnell v. Nell 241
    Questions 244
  C. Consideration: One Promise as Consideration for Another Promise 245
    Problems 245
    Hooters of America, Inc. v. Phillips 248
    Questions and Notes 251
  D. Consideration and Contract Modification 253
    Alaska Packers' Ass'n v. Domenico 254
    Questions and Note 256
    Angel v. Murray 257
    Questions and Note 261

Page

2: Promise to Pay for Something That Happened Before the Promise:
    Moral Obligations --- 264
    Harrington v. Taylor -- 265
    Mills v. Wyman --- 266
    Questions and Notes -- 268
    Webb v. McGowin --- 271
    Webb v. McGowin --- 274
    Questions, Notes, and Connections ---------------------------------- 275
3: Reliance and the Legal Concept of Promissory Estoppel --------------- 278
    A. Overview -- 278
    B. Historical Development --- 279
        Ricketts v. Scothorn --- 279
        Questions and Notes --- 282
    C. Contemporary Applications of the Doctrine ----------------------- 284
        Dargo v. Clear Channel Communications, Incorporated --------- 284
        Questions and Note -- 286
        Fortress Systems, L.L.C. v. Bank of the West ------------------- 287
        Questions and Connections --------------------------------------- 296
        Note on Promissory Estoppel in Employment and Retirement Agreements 296
        Problem on Promissory Estoppel ---------------------------------- 298
        Note on Promissory Estoppel and Pre–Contract Negotiations ---- 299
        Introduction to Pavel Enterprises -------------------------------- 301
        Pavel Enterprises, Inc. v. A. S. Johnson Company, Inc. --------- 302
        Questions, Notes, and Connections ------------------------------- 314
    D. Remedial Considerations -- 315
        Edward Yorio & Steve Thel, The Promissory Basis of § 90 ------ 315
    E. The Diminishing Importance of Reliance ------------------------- 317
        Salsbury v. Northwestern Bell Telephone Company -------------- 317
        Questions --- 321

Chapter Four. Is the Agreement Unenforceable Because of the Flaws in the Agreement Process or Problems With the Language of the Agreement? ------------------------------ **323**

1: Contract Law Reasons for <u>Not</u> Enforcing Agreements: Statutes of
    Fraud --- 323
    Radke v. Brenon -- 325
    Questions, Notes, and Connections ---------------------------------- 328
    DF Activities Corporation v. Brown --------------------------------- 331
    Questions and Notes and Connections ------------------------------ 334
    McIntosh v. Murphy -- 335
    Questions, Notes, and Connections ---------------------------------- 341
2: Contract Law Reasons for <u>Not</u> Enforcing Agreements: Fraud, Fraudulent or Material Misrepresentations and Nondisclosure ------------ 343
    Halpert v. Rosenthal --- 344
    Questions and Notes -- 348
    Swinton v. Whitinsville Savings Bank ------------------------------ 349
    Questions and Notes -- 350
    Weintraub v. Krobatsch -- 352
    Questions -- 355
3: Contract Law Reasons for <u>Not</u> Enforcing Agreements: Defendant's
    Lack of Capacity -- 356
    Kiefer v. Fred Howe Motors, Inc. --------------------------------- 357
    Questions and Notes -- 361
4: Contract Law Reasons for <u>Not</u> Enforcing Agreements: Duress and
    Undue Influence --- 362
    P.S. Atiyah, An Introduction to the Law of Contract -------------- 363
    Austin Instrument, Inc. v. Loral Corporation --------------------- 364

Page

4: Contract Law Reasons for Not Enforcing Agreements: Duress and
   Undue Influence—Continued
   Questions --- 367
   Totem Marine Tug & Barge, Inc. v. Alyeska Pipeline Service Company ---------- 367
   Questions, Notes, and Connections ----------------------------------- 373
   Odorizzi v. Bloomfield School District ------------------------------- 374
   Questions and Notes --- 379
5: Contract Law Reasons for Not Enforcing Agreements: Illegality and
   Public Policy --- 381
   Problem -- 381
   R.R. v. M.H. --- 382
   Questions and Note --- 389
   Hanks v. Power Ridge Restaurant Corp. ------------------------------ 390
   Questions and Notes -- 394
   Valley Medical Specialists v. Farber ------------------------------- 396
   Questions and Notes -- 401
6: Contract Law Reasons for Not Enforcing an Agreement: Unconscion-
   ability --- 403
   Williams v. Walker–Thomas Furniture Company ----------------------- 404
   Williams v. Walker–Thomas Furniture Company ----------------------- 405
   Questions and Notes -- 407
   Brower v. Gateway 2000, Inc. -------------------------------------- 410
   Questions, Note, and Connections --------------------------------- 415
7: Contract Law Reasons for Not Enforcing Agreements: Mistake -------- 416
   Sherwood v. Walker -- 417
   Questions and Notes -- 422
   Estate of Nelson v. Rice --- 424
   Questions -- 428
   Grenall v. United of Omaha Life Insurance Company ---------------- 429
   Questions, Note and Connections --------------------------------- 431

Chapter Five.   What Are the Terms of the Deal? ----------------- 434
1: Terms of the Contract That Are Not Words of the Parties: Trade
   Customs and Usage --- 434
   Threadgill v. Peabody Coal Co. ---------------------------------- 435
   Questions and Note -- 438
2: Words of the Parties That Are Not in the Final Written Version of
   the Deal: The Parol Evidence Rule -------------------------------- 439
   A. Common Law -- 440
       Nelson v. Elway --- 441
       Questions and Note -------------------------------------- 448
       Rogers v. Jackson --------------------------------------- 449
       Questions --- 453
   B. Uniform Commercial Code ------------------------------------ 454
       Simmons Foods, Inc. v. Hill's Pet Nutrition, Inc. ------- 455
       Questions and Note -------------------------------------- 459
   C. Exceptions --- 460
       Problems on Parol Evidence ------------------------------ 460
   D. A World Without Parol Evidence—The Convention on the Inter-
       national Sale of Goods ------------------------------------ 461
       MCC–Marble Ceramic Center, Inc. v. Ceramica Nuova D'Agostino, S.p.A. 462
       Questions --- 469
3: Using Parol Evidence and Other Extrinsic Evidence to Discover the
   Meaning of the Terms Used in the Written Contract --------------- 470
   Frigaliment Importing Co., Ltd. v. B.N.S. International Sales Corp. --- 471
   Questions, Note, and Connection ----------------------------- 477

3: Using Parol Evidence and Other Extrinsic Evidence to Discover the
  Meaning of the Terms Used in the Written Contract—Continued
  A. Course of Performance, Course of Dealing and Trade Usage
    (Again) 478
    Problems on Trade Usage and Course of Dealing 479
  B. Ambiguity in Contract Terms—Is It Important, and, If So, When
    Does It Exist? 480
    Random House, Inc. v. Rosetta Books LLC 480
    Questions and Notes 487
    Trident Center v. Connecticut General Life Ins. Co. 489
    Questions, Note, and Connections 495
  C. The Use of Rules, Maxims and Extrinsic Evidence to Construe
    Contract Language 497
    Edwin W. Patterson, The Interpretation and Construction of Contracts 498
    Problems on Construction of Contracts 500
  D. Special Interpretive Rules for Contracts of Adhesion 501
    Meyer v. State Farm Fire & Cas. Co. 501
    Questions 504
    Lauvetz v. Alaska Sales and Service d/b/a National Car Rental ... 504
    Questions and Note 509
4: Terms Added by the Courts 510
  A. Terms Implied by Courts to Effectuate Assumed Intent 510
    Wood v. Lucy, Lady Duff-Gordon 510
    Questions, Note, and Connections 512
    Daniel Wm. Fessler, Teaching Notes for Fessler & Loiseaux's Contracts:
      Morality, Economics and the Marketplace 513
    Billman v. Hensel 515
    Questions and Connections 516
  B. Terms Implied by Courts to Effectuate Public Policy—The Im-
    plied Duty of Good Faith and Fair Dealing 518
    Locke v. Warner Bros., Inc. 518
    Questions and Notes 525
    Hobin v. Coldwell Banker Residential Affiliates, Inc. 529
    Questions and Note 533
5: Terms Added by Legislatures 534
  Connections 534
  Problems on Terms Implied by the U.C.C. 535
6: Warranties and the U.C.C. 535
  A. Introduction 535
  B. Express Warranties 536
    Daughtrey v. Ashe 537
    Questions, Notes, and Connections 541
    Problem on Express Warranty 544
  C. Implied Warranties Generally 544
  D. Implied Warranty of Merchantability 545
    Webster v. Blue Ship Tea Room, Inc. 545
    Questions and Notes 549
    Note on Causation 550
    Problems on Merchantability 551
  E. Implied Warranty of Fitness for Particular Purpose 552
    Leal v. Holtvogt 553
    Questions 558
    Singer Company v. E.I. du Pont de Nemours and Company 559
    Questions, Notes, and Connections 565
  F. Disclaimers of Warranties 567
    Office Supply Co., Inc. v. Basic/Four Corporation 568
    Questions, Notes, and Connections 575

Page

Chapter Six. When Is Someone Who Made an Enforceable Deal Excused From Doing What She Agreed to Do? ----------------------- 579

1: Conditions: Non–Occurrence of Something That Contract Expressly Provided Must Occur as an Excuse for Not Doing What You Agreed to Do --- 579

   A. Occurrence of Express Conditions and Strict Compliance ------------- 580

      Luttinger v. Rosen --- 580

      Questions and Connections -- 582

   B. Recognizing Language of Express Condition ----------------------------- 583

      Peacock Const. Co., Inc. v. Modern Air Conditioning, Inc. --------- 583

      Questions and Connections -- 586

   C. Excusing Conditions (i.e., Eliminates the Excuse) ----------------------- 587

      1. Avoidance of Forfeiture as a Reason for Eliminating a Condition --- 587

         Acme Markets, Inc. v. Federal Armored Express, Inc. ---------------- 588

         Questions --- 592

      2. Prevention as a Reason for Eliminating an Express Condition 592

         Moore Brothers Co. v. Brown & Root, Inc. ---------------------------- 593

         Questions and Connections -- 597

      3. Waiver as a Reason for Eliminating a Condition ------------------- 598

2: Modification, Waiver, or Estoppel as an Excuse for Not Doing What You Agreed to Do -- 599

   Dynamic Machine Works, Inc. v. Machine & Electrical Consultants, Inc. -------- 599

   Questions --- 602

   May Centers, Inc. v. Paris Croissant of Enfield Square, Inc., et al. ---------------- 603

   Questions --- 607

   Clark v. West --- 607

   Questions --- 611

3: Impossibility, Impracticability, Frustration of Purpose: Occurrence of Something Not Provided for in the Contract as an Excuse for Not Doing What You Agreed to Do --- 612

   Taylor v. Caldwell -- 612

   Questions and Notes -- 615

   Wisconsin Electric Power Co. v. Union Pacific Railroad Co. -------------- 616

   Questions, and Connections --- 621

   Krell v. Henry --- 623

   Questions and Note --- 627

   Mel Frank Tool & Supply, Inc. v. Di–Chem Co. ------------------------------- 628

   Questions and Note --- 633

4: "Anticipatory Repudiation": Other Guy's Unambiguous Indication of an Unwillingness or Inability to Perform as an Excuse for Not Doing What You Agreed to Do --- 636

   A. Statement as Anticipatory Repudiation ------------------------------- 636

      Hochster v. De La Tour --- 637

      Questions --- 640

   B. Repudiation Based on Conduct --------------------------------------- 640

   C. Failure to Give Adequate Assurance of Future Performance as Like Unto Repudiation --- 641

      Norcon Power Partners, L.P. v. Niagara Mohawk Power Corp. ----------- 642

      Questions and Notes -- 648

Page

5: Material Breach: Other Guy's Improper Performance as an Excuse for Not Doing What You Agreed to Do Under a Common Law Contract 649
  A. The Material Breach Concept 649
  B. "Material Breach" and "Constructive Conditions" and "Substantial Performance"; The Conceptual Basis for the Material Breach Doctrine 651
    1. A Short History of Constructive Conditions 651
       Nichols v. Raynbred 651
       Kingston v. Preston 652
    2. Constructive Conditions of Exchange in Current Practice 654
       Pullman, Comley, Bradley and Reeves v. Tuck-it-away, Bridgeport, Inc. 654
       Questions 657
    3. The Interplay Between Constructive and Express Conditions ... 658
  C. What Constitutes a Material Breach 660
     Jacob & Youngs, Incorporated v. Kent 660
     Questions and Notes 665
     O. W. Grun Roofing & Construction Co. v. Cope 667
     Questions and Note 671
  D. Divisible Contracts 672
     Problems on Divisible Contracts 673
  E. "Perfect Tender" 674
     Alaska Pacific Trading Company v. Eagon Forest Products, Inc. 674
     Questions and Connections 675
  F. Material Breach and Election of Remedies 676
     ESPN, Inc. v. Office of the Commissioner of Baseball 676
     Questions 683
     One More Note on "Substantial Performance" (a/k/a "Partial Breach") and "Material Breach" (a/k/a "Total Breach") 684

Chapter Seven. How Does the Law Enforce a Deal? **686**
1: The Problem Examined 686
2: Specific Performance 687
   Van Wagner Advertising Corp. v. S & M Enterprises 688
   Questions and Notes 691
   Walgreen Co. v. Sara Creek Property Co., B.V. 693
   Questions and Note 696
3: Agreed Remedies 698
  A. Liquidated Damages 699
     O'Brian v. Langley School 699
     Questions 701
     Kvassay v. Murray 702
     Questions and Note 706
     Problems on Liquidated Damages 708
  B. Limitation of Remedies to Repair, Replacement, or Return of Money Paid 709
4: Judicial Determination of Money Damages 711
  A. The General Measure of Money Damages: "Expectation Interest" (Receipt of the Benefit of the Bargain) 711
     Hawkins v. McGee 713
     Questions and Notes 716
     Panorama Village Homeowners Ass'n v. Golden Rule Roofing, Inc. 718
     Questions and Connection 720
     Groves v. John Wunder Co. 721
     Questions 725
     Peevyhouse v. Garland Coal & Mining Co. 726
     Questions and Note 733

Page

4: Judicial Determination of Money Damages—Continued
B. Money Damages Under the U.C.C. ------ 734
  Basic Problems on Buyer's Damages Under the U.C.C. ------ 734
  KGM Harvesting Co. v. Fresh Network ------ 735
  Questions and Note ------ 741
  Basic Problems on Seller's Damages Under the U.C.C. ------ 743
  Rodriguez v. Learjet, Inc. ------ 743
  Questions and Connection ------ 747
  Problem: Another Lost Profits Recovery Scenario ------ 748
C. Limitations on Money Damages Awards ------ 749
  1. First Limitation on Money Damages: Avoided Costs ------ 749
    Leingang v. Mandan Weed Board ------ 749
    Questions and Note ------ 752
  2. Second Limitation on Money Damages: Avoidable Loss ------ 752
    Parker v. Twentieth Century–Fox Film Corp. ------ 753
    Questions and Notes ------ 759
    R. R. Donnelley & Sons Co. v. Vanguard Transp. Systems, Inc. ------ 760
    Questions ------ 763
  3. Third Limitation on Money Damages: Foreseeability ------ 764
    Hadley v. Baxendale ------ 765
    Questions and Notes ------ 768
  4. Fourth Limitation on Money Damages: Certainty ------ 771
    Manouchehri v. Heim ------ 771
    Questions ------ 777
    ESPN, Inc. v. Office of the Commissioner of Baseball ------ 777
    Questions ------ 783
D. The Reliance Interest as an Alternative Measure of Damages ------ 783
  Hollywood Fantasy Corporation v. Gabor ------ 784
  Questions and Notes ------ 788
E. Restitution Interest as an Alternative Measure of Damages ------ 790
  United States v. Algernon Blair, Incorporated ------ 791
  Questions and Notes ------ 794
  Britton v. Turner ------ 795
  Questions and Note ------ 798

Chapter Eight. What Are the Alternatives to Contracts and Contract Law? (Quasi–Contract and Restitution) ------ **800**
1: Nature and Origins of Quasi–Contract ------ 800
  Henry Sumner Maine, Ancient Law ------ 801
2: Elements of a Quasi–Contractual Claim ------ 803
  A. In General ------ 803
    John W. Wade, Restitution for Benefits Conferred Without Request ------ 803
    Questions, Note, and Connections ------ 804
    Patterson v. Patterson ------ 804
    Questions ------ 806
  B. At the Request of the Defendant ------ 806
    Schott v. Westinghouse Electric Corporation ------ 806
    Questions and Note ------ 811
  C. Not at the Request of the Defendant ------ 812
    Cablevision of Breckenridge, Inc. v. Tannhauser Condominium Association ------ 812
    Questions ------ 816
    Watts v. Watts ------ 816
    Problem: The Good Samaritan and the Greedy Doctor ------ 820

                                                                        Page

2: Elements of a Quasi–Contractual Claim—Continued
    D. At the Request of a Third Party ------------------------------- 820
        Flooring Systems, Inc. v. Radisson Group, Inc. ------------- 820
        Questions and Note -- 824
        Problem on Third Party Benefits --------------------------- 825
    E. Breach of Fiduciary Duty ----------------------------------- 825
        George E. Palmer, Law of Restitution ---------------------- 825
        Wiener v. Lazard Freres & Co. ----------------------------- 825
3: Promissory Restitution-- 829
    Webb v. McGowin -- 829
4: Other Remedies for Unjust Enrichment------------------------- 830
    Pull v. Barnes -- 831
    Questions and Notes -- 833
    Britton v. Turner--- 834

**Chapter Nine.   When Do You Have Rights and/or Duties Under a
    Contract That You Did Not Make?** ------------------------- **835**
1: Third Party Beneficiaries ----------------------------------- 835
    Lawrence v. Fox -- 836
    Questions and Note-- 840
    A. When a Third Party Is a "Third Party Beneficiary" -------- 842
        Ex Parte Stamey -- 842
        Questions -- 845
        *Midwest Grain Products of Illinois, Inc. v. Productization, Inc. and CMI
            Corp.* --- 846
        Questions -- 848
    B. Cancellation and Modification of the Rights of the Third Party
        Beneficiary and Defenses Against the Third Party Beneficiary 849
        Olson v. Etheridge --------------------------------------- 849
        Questions -- 854
2: Assignment and Delegation----------------------------------- 856
    A. Introduction to Assignment and Delegation: What Are They? ----- 856
    B. Consequences of an Assignment and Delegation: Who Can Sue
        Whom? -- 857
        1. Assignee Can Sue Obligor ----------------------------- 857
            Problems -- 857
        2. Obligee Can Sue Delegator ---------------------------- 857
            Problems -- 859
    C. Limitations on Assignment and Delegation ------------------ 859
        Macke Co. v. Pizza of Gaithersburg, Inc.------------------ 860
        Questions -- 862
        Rumbin v. Utica Mutual Insurance Co. --------------------- 864
        Questions and Note --------------------------------------- 867
        Sally Beauty Co., Inc. v. Nexxus Products Co., Inc.------- 868
        Questions and Connection --------------------------------- 875
        Final Note From the Authors ------------------------------ 876

INDEX-- 877

TABLE OF CASES

The principal cases are in bold type. Cases cited or discussed in the text are in roman type. References are to pages. Cases cited in principal cases and within other quoted materials are not included.

***

Acme Markets, Inc. v. Federal Armored Exp., Inc., 437 Pa.Super. 41, 648 A.2d 1218 (Pa.Super.1994), **588**

Adams v. Lindsell, 1817 WL 2056 (KB 1818), **128**

Addie v. Kjaer, 2009 WL 2584833 (D.Virgin Islands 2009), 791

Agnew v. Great Atlantic & Pacific Tea Co., 232 Ga.App. 708, 502 S.E.2d 735 (Ga.App.1998), 81

A. Kemp Fisheries, Inc. v. Castle & Cooke, Inc., Bumble Bee Seafoods Div., 852 F.2d 493 (9th Cir.1988), 496

Akers v. J. B. Sedberry, Inc., 39 Tenn.App. 633, 286 S.W.2d 617 (Tenn.Ct.App.1955), 94

Alaska Pacific Trading Co. v. Eagon Forest Products, Inc., 85 Wash.App. 354, 933 P.2d 417 (Wash.App. Div. 1 1997), **674**

Alaska Packers' Ass'n v. Domenico, 117 F. 99 (9th Cir.1902), **254**

Algernon Blair, Inc., United States v., 479 F.2d 638 (4th Cir.1973), **791**

Allegheny College v. National Chautauqua County Bank of Jamestown, 246 N.Y. 369, 159 N.E. 173 (N.Y.1927), 283

Angel v. Murray, 113 R.I. 482, 322 A.2d 630 (R.I.1974), **257**

Architectural Metal Systems, Inc. v. Consolidated Systems, Inc., 58 F.3d 1227 (7th Cir. 1995), 77

A/S Apothekernes Laboratorium for Special-praeparater v. I.M.C. Chemical Group, Inc., 873 F.2d 155 (7th Cir.1989), 221

ATACS Corp. v. Trans World Communications, Inc., 155 F.3d 659 (3rd Cir.1998), 791

Austin v. Burge, 156 Mo.App. 286, 137 S.W. 618 (Mo.App.1911), 145

Austin Instrument, Inc. v. Loral Corp., 29 N.Y.2d 124, 324 N.Y.S.2d 22, 272 N.E.2d 533 (N.Y.1971), **364,** 371

Barnes v. Treece, 15 Wash.App. 437, 549 P.2d 1152 (Wash.App. Div. 1 1976), 51

Bayliner Marine Corp. v. Crow, 257 Va. 121, 509 S.E.2d 499 (Va.1999), 549

Beall v. Beall, 45 Md.App. 489, 413 A.2d 1365 (Md.App.1980), **97**

Billman v. Hensel, 181 Ind.App. 272, 391 N.E.2d 671 (Ind.App. 3 Dist.1979), **515**

Blackhawk Heating & Plumbing Co., Inc. v. Data Lease Financial Corp., 302 So.2d 404 (Fla.1974), 210

Blinn v. Beatrice Community Hosp. and Health Center, Inc., 270 Neb. 809, 708 N.W.2d 235 (Neb.2006), 297

Board of Control of Eastern Michigan University v. Burgess, 45 Mich.App. 183, 206 N.W.2d 256 (Mich.App.1973), **101**

Borg–Warner Corp. v. Anchor Coupling Co., 16 Ill.2d 234, 156 N.E.2d 513 (Ill.1958), 213

Brangier v. Rosenthal, 337 F.2d 952 (9th Cir. 1964), 94

Bridgestone/Firestone Inc. Tires Products Liability Litigation, In re, 205 F.R.D. 503 (S.D.Ind.2001), 543

Briggs Tax Service, L.L.C. v. Detroit Public Schools, 485 Mich. 69, 780 N.W.2d 753 (Mich.2010), 423

Britton v. Turner, 6 N.H. 481 (N.H.1834), **795,** 834

Broadnax v. Ledbetter, 100 Tex. 375, 99 S.W. 1111 (Tex.1907), 137

Brower v. Gateway 2000, Inc., 246 A.D.2d 246, 676 N.Y.S.2d 569 (N.Y.A.D. 1 Dept. 1998), 175, 177, **410**

Budget Marketing, Inc. v. Centronics Corp., 927 F.2d 421 (8th Cir.1991), **214**

Cablevision of Breckenridge, Inc. v. Tannhauser Condominium Ass'n, 649 P.2d 1093 (Colo.1982), **812**

Caldwell v. Cline, 109 W.Va. 553, 156 S.E. 55 (W.Va.1930), 94

Carlill v. Carbolic Smoke Ball Co, 1892 WL 9612 (CA 1892), **133**

Carnes Co. v. Stone Creek Mechanical, Inc., 412 F.3d 845 (7th Cir.2005), 640

Cate v. Dover Corp., 790 S.W.2d 559 (Tex. 1990), 576

Cipollone v. Liggett Group, Inc., 893 F.2d 541 (3rd Cir.1990), 542

Clark v. West, 193 N.Y. 349, 86 N.E. 1 (N.Y. 1908), **607**

Coastal Aviation, Inc. v. Commander Aircraft Co., 937 F.Supp. 1051 (S.D.N.Y.1996), 105

Colfax Envelope Corp. v. Local No. 458–3M, Chicago Graphic Communications Intern. Union, AFL–CIO, 20 F.3d 750 (7th Cir. 1994), 46

Community Design Corp. v. Antonell, 459 So.2d 343 (Fla.App. 3 Dist.1984), **192**

Continental Laboratories, Inc. v. Scott Paper Co., 759 F.Supp. 538 (S.D.Iowa 1990), 63

Copeland v. Baskin Robbins U.S.A., 117 Cal. Rptr.2d 875 (Cal.App. 2 Dist.2002), 223

Courteen Seed Co. v. Abraham, 129 Or. 427, 275 P. 684 (Or.1929), 76

Crisan's Estate, In re, 362 Mich. 569, 107 N.W.2d 907 (Mich.1961), 820

Crothers by Crothers v. Cohen, 384 N.W.2d 562 (Minn.App.1986), 544

Dadourian Export Corp. v. United States, 291 F.2d 178 (2nd Cir.1961), 478

Dalton v. Educational Testing Service, 87 N.Y.2d 384, 639 N.Y.S.2d 977, 663 N.E.2d 289 (N.Y.1995), 528

Dargo v. Clear Channel Communications, Inc., 2008 WL 2225812 (N.D.Ill.2008), **284**

Daughtrey v. Ashe, 243 Va. 73, 413 S.E.2d 336 (Va.1992), **537**

Davis v. Chase Bank USA, N.A., 2008 WL 4832998 (9th Cir.2008), 32

Davis v. Jacoby, 1 Cal.2d 370, 34 P.2d 1026 (Cal.1934), **116**

Defontes v. Dell Computers Corp., 2004 WL 253560 (R.I.Super.2004), 177

DF Activities Corp. v. Brown, 851 F.2d 920 (7th Cir.1988), **331**

Dick v. United States, 113 Ct.Cl. 94, 82 F.Supp. 326 (Ct.Cl.1949), 130

Dickinson v. Dodds, 1875 WL 16757 (CA 1876), **85**

Dorton v. Collins & Aikman Corp., 453 F.2d 1161 (6th Cir.1972), **155**

Dynamic Mach. Works, Inc. v. Machine & Elec. Consultants, Inc., 444 Mass. 768, 831 N.E.2d 875 (Mass.2005), **599**

Earhart v. William Low Co., 158 Cal.Rptr. 887, 600 P.2d 1344 (Cal.1979), 811

Eastwood v. Kenyon, 1840 WL 4390 (KB 1840), 270

Edward J. Gerrits, Inc. v. Astor Elec. Service, Inc., 328 So.2d 522 (Fla.App. 3 Dist.1976), 584

Envirodyne Industries, Inc., Matter of, 29 F.3d 301 (7th Cir.1994), 497

ESPN, Inc. v. Office of Com'r of Baseball, 76 F.Supp.2d 416 (S.D.N.Y.1999), **777**

ESPN, Inc. v. Office of Com'r of Baseball, 76 F.Supp.2d 383 (S.D.N.Y.1999), **676**

Ever–Tite Roofing Corp. v. Green, 83 So.2d 449 (La.App. 2 Cir.1955), **110**

Ex parte (see name of party)

Feinberg v. Pfeiffer Co., 322 S.W.2d 163 (Mo. App.1959), 297

Ferrofluidics Corp. v. Advanced Vacuum Components, Inc., 968 F.2d 1463 (1st Cir.1992), 402

Filet Menu, Inc. v. C.C.L. & G., Inc., 94 Cal. Rptr.2d 438 (Cal.App. 2 Dist.2000), 672

First Nat. Bank in Oshkosh v. Scieszinski, 25 Wis.2d 569, 131 N.W.2d 308 (Wis.1964), 359

Flooring Systems, Inc. v. Radisson Group, Inc., 160 Ariz. 224, 772 P.2d 578 (Ariz. 1989), **820**

Floss v. Ryan's Family Steak Houses, Inc., 211 F.3d 306 (6th Cir.2000), 252

Fondedile, S.A. v. C.E. Maguire, Inc., 610 A.2d 87 (R.I.1992), 262

Fortress Systems, L.L.C. v. Bank of the West, 2008 WL 64690 (D.Neb.2008), **287**

Frigaliment Importing Co. v. B.N.S. Intern. Sales Corp., 190 F.Supp. 116 (S.D.N.Y.1960), **471**

Gittings v. Mayhew, 6 Md. 113 (Md.1854), 283

Gleason v. Freeman, 2008 WL 2485607 (W.D.Tenn.2008), **55**

Glover v. Jewish War Veterans of United States, Post No. 58, 68 A.2d 233 (D.C.Mun. App.1949), 138

Goldstick v. ICM Realty, 788 F.2d 456 (7th Cir.1986), 194

Goode v. Riley, 153 Mass. 585, 28 N.E. 228 (Mass.1891), 471

Gossels v. Fleet Nat. Bank, 69 Mass.App.Ct. 797, 876 N.E.2d 872 (Mass.App.Ct.2007), 351

Green v. American Tobacco Co., 304 F.2d 70 (5th Cir.1962), 549

Grenall v. United of Omaha Life Ins. Co., 80 Cal.Rptr.3d 609 (Cal.App. 1 Dist.2008), **429**

Gresser v. Hotzler, 604 N.W.2d 379 (Minn. App.2000), **147**

Groves v. John Wunder Co., 205 Minn. 163, 286 N.W. 235 (Minn.1939), **721**

Hadley v. Baxendale, 1854 WL 7208 (Ex Ct 1854), **765**

Halpert v. Rosenthal, 107 R.I. 406, 267 A.2d 730 (R.I.1970), **344**

Hamer v. Sidway, 124 N.Y. 538, 27 N.E. 256 (N.Y.1891), **236**

Hanks v. Powder Ridge Restaurant Corp., 276 Conn. 314, 885 A.2d 734 (Conn.2005), **390**

Harrington v. Taylor, 225 N.C. 690, 36 S.E.2d 227 (N.C.1945), **265**

Harris v. Provident Life and Acc. Ins. Co., 310 F.3d 73 (2nd Cir.2002), 533

Hawkes & Uxor v. Saunders, 1782 WL 95 (KB 1782), 269

Hawkins v. McGee, 84 N.H. 114, 146 A. 641 (N.H.1929), **713**

Hendricks v. Behee, 786 S.W.2d 610 (Mo. App. S.D.1990), **124**

Hill v. Gateway 2000, Inc., 105 F.3d 1147 (7th Cir.1997), **172**

Hobin v. Coldwell Banker Residential Affiliates, Inc., 144 N.H. 626, 744 A.2d 1134 (N.H.2000), **529**

Hochster v. De La Tour, 1853 WL 7479 (QB 1853), **637**

Hoffman v. Red Owl Stores, Inc., 26 Wis.2d 683, 133 N.W.2d 267 (Wis.1965), 299

Hollywood Fantasy Corp. v. Gabor, 151 F.3d 203 (5th Cir.1998), **784**

Hooters of America, Inc. v. Phillips, 39 F.Supp.2d 582 (D.S.C.1998), **248**

Hotchkiss v. National City Bank of New York, 200 F. 287 (S.D.N.Y.1911), 47

Hubbs v. Joseph Enterprises, 198 A.D.2d 757, 604 N.Y.S.2d 292 (N.Y.A.D. 3 Dept.1993), 551

Hughes v. Stusser, 68 Wash.2d 707, 415 P.2d 89 (Wash.1966), 351

Hydraform Products Corp. v. American Steel & Aluminum Corp., 127 N.H. 187, 498 A.2d 339 (N.H.1985), 765

In re (see name of party)

Jacob & Youngs v. Kent, 230 N.Y. 239, 129 N.E. 889 (N.Y.1921), **660**

J.F. v. D.B., 116 Ohio St.3d 363, 879 N.E.2d 740 (Ohio 2007), 30

Johnson v. Waters, 108 U.S. 4, 1 S.Ct. 1, 27 L.Ed. 630 (1882), TEST

Kashmiri v. Regents of University of California, 67 Cal.Rptr.3d 635 (Cal.App. 1 Dist. 2007), 83

Katz v. Danny Dare, Inc., 610 S.W.2d 121 (Mo.App. W.D.1980), 297

Kaufman v. Byers, 159 Ohio App.3d 238, 823 N.E.2d 530 (Ohio App. 11 Dist.2004), 658

Kenco Homes, Inc. v. Williams, 94 Wash.App. 219, 972 P.2d 125 (Wash.App. Div. 2 1999), 748

KGM Harvesting Co. v. Fresh Network, 42 Cal.Rptr.2d 286 (Cal.App. 6 Dist.1995), **735**

Kiefer v. Fred Howe Motors, Inc., 39 Wis.2d 20, 158 N.W.2d 288 (Wis.1968), **357**

Kim v. National Indem. Co., 6 P.3d 264 (Alaska 2000), 510

Kingston v. Preston, 2 Doug. 689, 99 Eng. Rep. 437 (K.B.1773), **652**

Kirksey v. Kirksey, 8 Ala. 131 (Ala.1845), **232**

Klocek v. Gateway, Inc., 2000 WL 1372886 (D.Kan.2000), 171

Klocek v. Gateway, Inc., 104 F.Supp.2d 1332 (D.Kan.2000), **165**

Koellmer v. Chrysler Motors Corp., 6 Conn.Cir. Ct. 478, 276 A.2d 807 (Conn.Cir.A.D.1970), 567

Krell v. Henry, 1903 WL 12966 (CA 1903), **623**

Kvassay v. Murray, 15 Kan.App.2d 426, 808 P.2d 896 (Kan.App.1991), **702**

Laidlaw v. Organ, 15 U.S. 178, 4 L.Ed. 214 (1817), 351

Lake River Corp. v. Carborundum Co., 769 F.2d 1284 (7th Cir.1985), 706

Langer v. Superior Steel Corporation, 105 Pa.Super. 579, 161 A. 571 (Pa.Super.1932), 298

Laredo Nat. Bank v. Gordon, 61 F.2d 906 (5th Cir.1932), **143**

La Salle Nat. Bank v. Vega, 167 Ill.App.3d 154, 117 Ill.Dec. 778, 520 N.E.2d 1129 (Ill. App. 2 Dist.1988), **107**

Lauvetz v. Alaska Sales and Service, 828 P.2d 162 (Alaska 1991), **504**

Lawrence v. Fox, 20 N.Y. 268 (N.Y.1859), **836**

Leal v. Holtvogt, 123 Ohio App.3d 51, 702 N.E.2d 1246 (Ohio App. 2 Dist.1998), **553**

Leingang v. City of Mandan Weed Bd., 468 N.W.2d 397 (N.D.1991), **749**

Leister v. Dovetail, Inc., 546 F.3d 875 (7th Cir.2008), 769

Lenawee County Bd. of Health v. Messerly, 417 Mich. 17, 331 N.W.2d 203 (Mich.1982), 423

Leonard v. Pepsico, Inc., 88 F.Supp.2d 116 (S.D.N.Y.1999), **47, 78**

Locke v. Warner Bros., Inc., 66 Cal.Rptr.2d 921 (Cal.App. 2 Dist.1997), **518**

Lonergan v. Scolnick, 129 Cal.App.2d 179, 276 P.2d 8 (Cal.App. 4 Dist.1954), **66**

Lucy v. Zehmer, 196 Va. 493, 84 S.E.2d 516 (Va.1954), **37**

Luttinger v. Rosen, 164 Conn. 45, 316 A.2d 757 (Conn.1972), **580**

Lynch v. Deaconess Medical Center, 113 Wash.2d 162, 776 P.2d 681 (Wash.1989), 825

Macke Co. v. Pizza of Gaithersburg, Inc., 259 Md. 479, 270 A.2d 645 (Md.1970), **860**

Manouchehri v. Heim, 123 N.M. 439, 941 P.2d 978 (N.M.App.1997), **771**

Manwill v. Oyler, 11 Utah 2d 433, 361 P.2d 177 (Utah 1961), 270

Marchiondo v. Scheck, 78 N.M. 440, 432 P.2d 405 (N.M.1967), **138**

Marvin v. Marvin, 134 Cal.Rptr. 815, 557 P.2d 106 (Cal.1976), 64

Maryland Supreme Corp. v. Blake Co., 279 Md. 531, 369 A.2d 1017 (Md.1977), **70, 123**

Matter of (see name of party)

Maughs v. Porter, 157 Va. 415, 161 S.E. 242 (Va.1931), 234

May Centers, Inc. v. Paris Croissant of Enfield Square, Inc., 42 Conn.Supp. 77, 599 A.2d 407 (Conn.Super.1991), **603**

MCC–Marble Ceramic Center, Inc., v. Ceramica Nuova d'Agostino, S.p.A., 144 F.3d 1384 (11th Cir.1998), **462**

McCormick v. Union Pacific R. Co., 983 P.2d 84 (Colo.App.1998), 501

McGee v. United States Fidelity & Guaranty Co., 53 F.2d 953 (1st Cir.1931), 717

McIntosh v. Murphy, 52 Haw. 29, 52 Haw. 112, 469 P.2d 177 (Hawai'i 1970), **335**

Mel Frank Tool & Supply, Inc. v. Di–Chem Co., 580 N.W.2d 802 (Iowa 1998), **628**

Meyer v. State Farm Fire and Cas. Co., 85 Md.App. 83, 582 A.2d 275 (Md.App.1990), **501**

Midwest Energy, Inc. v. Orion Food Systems, Inc., 14 S.W.3d 154 (Mo.App. E.D.2000), 299

Midwest Grain Products of Illinois, Inc. v. Productization, Inc., 228 F.3d 784 (7th Cir.2000), **846**

Miller v. LeSea Broadcasting, Inc., 87 F.3d 224 (7th Cir.1996), 692

Mills v. Wyman, 20 Mass. 207 (Mass.1825), **266**

Minneapolis & St. L. Ry. Co. v. Columbus Rolling–Mill Co., 119 U.S. 149, 7 S.Ct. 168, 30 L.Ed. 376 (1886), 153

Minnesota Linseed Oil Co. v. Collier White Lead Co., 17 F.Cas. 447 (C.C.D.Minn.1876), **90**

Moolenaar v. Co–Build Companies, Inc., 354 F.Supp. 980 (D.Virgin Islands 1973), **204**

Moore Bros. Co. v. Brown & Root, Inc., 207 F.3d 717 (4th Cir.2000), **593**

Moses v. Macferlan, 1760 WL 4 (KB 1760), 802

MXL Industries, Inc. v. Mulder, 252 Ill.App.3d 18, 191 Ill.Dec. 124, 623 N.E.2d 369 (Ill. App. 2 Dist.1993), 658

Nebraska Seed Co. v. Harsh, 98 Neb. 89, 152 N.W. 310 (Neb.1915), 76

Nelson v. Elway, 908 P.2d 102 (Colo.1995), **441**

Nelson v. Rice, 198 Ariz. 563, 12 P.3d 238 (Ariz.App. Div. 2 2000), **424**

Nichols v. Raynbred, 1614 WL 298 (KB 1614), **651**

Norcon Power Partners, L.P. v. Niagara Mohawk Power Corp., 92 N.Y.2d 458, 682 N.Y.S.2d 664, 705 N.E.2d 656 (N.Y. 1998), **642**

Northern Fabrication Co., Inc. v. UNOCAL, 980 P.2d 958 (Alaska 1999), 373

O'Brian v. Langley School, 256 Va. 547, 507 S.E.2d 363 (Va.1998), **699**

Odorizzi v. Bloomfield School Dist., 246 Cal.App.2d 123, 54 Cal.Rptr. 533 (Cal.App. 2 Dist.1966), **374**

Office Supply Co., Inc. v. Basic/Four Corp., 538 F.Supp. 776 (E.D.Wis.1982), **568**

Olson v. Etheridge, 177 Ill.2d 396, 226 Ill. Dec. 780, 686 N.E.2d 563 (Ill.1997), **849**

Oppenheimer & Co., Inc. v. Oppenheim, Appel, Dixon & Co., 86 N.Y.2d 685, 636 N.Y.S.2d 734, 660 N.E.2d 415 (N.Y.1995), 666

O. W. Grun Roofing & Const. Co. v. Cope, 529 S.W.2d 258 (Tex.Civ.App.-San Antonio 1975), **667**

Panorama Village Homeowners Ass'n v. Golden Rule Roofing, Inc., 102 Wash. App. 422, 10 P.3d 417 (Wash.App. Div. 1 2000), **718**

Parker v. Twentieth Century–Fox Film Corp., 89 Cal.Rptr. 737, 474 P.2d 689 (Cal. 1970), **753**

Pathology Consultants v. Gratton, 343 N.W.2d 428 (Iowa 1984), 218

Patterson v. Patterson, 59 N.Y. 574 (N.Y. 1875), **804**

Patton v. Mid–Continent Systems, Inc., 841 F.2d 742 (7th Cir.1988), 697

Pavel Enterprises, Inc. v. A.S. Johnson Co., Inc., 342 Md. 143, 674 A.2d 521 (Md. 1996), **302**

Peacock Const. Co., Inc. v. Modern Air Conditioning, Inc., 353 So.2d 840 (Fla. 1977), **583**

Peevyhouse v. Garland Coal & Min. Co., 382 P.2d 109 (Okla.1962), **726**

Performance Motors, Inc. v. Allen, 280 N.C. 385, 186 S.E.2d 161 (N.C.1972), 544

Pitts v. McGraw–Edison Co., 329 F.2d 412 (6th Cir.1964), 297

Pull v. Barnes, 142 Colo. 272, 350 P.2d 828 (Colo.1960), **831**

Pullman, Comley, Bradley and Reeves v. Tuck-it-away, Bridgeport, Inc., 28 Conn. App. 460, 611 A.2d 435 (Conn.App.1992), **654**

Radke v. Brenon, 271 Minn. 35, 134 N.W.2d 887 (Minn.1965), **325**

Raffles v. Wichelhaus, 1864 WL 6161 (KB 1864), **182**

Random House, Inc. v. Rosetta Books LLC, 150 F.Supp.2d 613 (S.D.N.Y.2001), **480**

Random Stationers, United States v., (S.D.Fla. 1984), 146

Real Estate Co. of Pittsburgh v. Rudolph, 301 Pa. 502, 153 A. 438 (Pa.1930), 103

Reed v. University of North Dakota, 589 N.W.2d 880 (N.D.1999), **230**

Reybold Group, Inc. v. Chemprobe Technologies, Inc., 721 A.2d 1267 (Del.Supr.1998), 550

Richard F. Kline, Inc. v. Shook Excavating & Hauling, Inc., 165 Md.App. 262, 885 A.2d 381 (Md.App.2005), 586

Ricketts v. Pennsylvania R. Co., 153 F.2d 757 (2nd Cir.1946), 47

Ricketts v. Scothorn, 57 Neb. 51, 77 N.W. 365 (Neb.1898), **279**

Roanoke Hospital Ass'n v. Doyle & Russell, Inc., 215 Va. 796, 214 S.E.2d 155 (Va.1975), 769

Rockingham County v. Luten Bridge Co., 35 F.2d 301 (4th Cir.1929), 753

Rodriguez v. Learjet, Inc, 24 Kan.App.2d 461, 946 P.2d 1010 (Kan.App.1997), **743**

Rogath v. Siebenmann, 129 F.3d 261 (2nd Cir. 1997), 542

Rogers v. Jackson, 804 A.2d 379 (Me.2002), **449**

Roth v. Garcia Marquez, 942 F.2d 617 (9th Cir.1991), 212

R.R. v. M.H., 426 Mass. 501, 689 N.E.2d 790 (Mass.1998), **23, 382**

R.R. Donnelley & Sons Co. v. Vanguard Transp. Systems, Inc., 641 F.Supp.2d 707 (N.D.Ill.2009), **760**

Rumbin v. Utica Mut. Ins. Co., 254 Conn. 259, 757 A.2d 526 (Conn.2000), **864**

RW Power Partners, L.P. v. Virginia Elec. and Power Co., 899 F.Supp. 1490 (E.D.Va.1995), 671

Salem Engineering and Const. Corp. v. Londonderry School Dist., 122 N.H. 379, 445 A.2d 1091 (N.H.1982), 764
Sally Beauty Co., Inc. v. Nexxus Products Co., Inc., 801 F.2d 1001 (7th Cir.1986), **868**
Salsbury v. Northwestern Bell Telephone Co., 221 N.W.2d 609 (Iowa 1974), **317**
Schnell v. Nell, 17 Ind. 29 (Ind.1861), **241**
Schonholz v. Long Island Jewish Medical Center, 87 F.3d 72 (2nd Cir.1996), 298
Schott v. Westinghouse Elec. Corp., 436 Pa. 279, 259 A.2d 443 (Pa.1969), **806**
Schwanbeck v. Federal–Mogul Corp., 31 Mass. App.Ct. 390, 578 N.E.2d 789 (Mass.App.Ct. 1991), 222
7200 Scottsdale Road General Partners v. Kuhn Farm Machinery, Inc., 184 Ariz. 341, 909 P.2d 408 (Ariz.App. Div. 1 1995), 633
Shaw v. State Farm Mut. Auto. Ins. Companies, 19 P.3d 588 (Alaska 2001), 510
Sherwood v. Walker, 66 Mich. 568, 33 N.W. 919 (Mich.1887), **417**
Shreve v. Cheesman, 69 F. 785 (8th Cir.1895), 11
Shuey v. United States, 92 U.S. 73, 2 Otto 73, 23 L.Ed. 697 (1875), 90
Simmons Foods, Inc. v. Hill's Pet Nutrition, Inc., 270 F.3d 723 (8th Cir.2001), **455**
Singer Co. v. E. I. du Pont de Nemours & Co., 579 F.2d 433 (8th Cir.1978), **559**
Smith v. Boyd, 553 A.2d 131 (R.I.1989), **58**
Specht v. Netscape Communications Corp., 306 F.3d 17 (2nd Cir.2002), 179
Stamey, Ex parte, 776 So.2d 85 (Ala.2000), **842**
Swinton v. Whitinsville Sav. Bank, 311 Mass. 677, 42 N.E.2d 808 (Mass.1942), **349**

Taylor v. Caldwell, 1863 WL 6052 (KB 1863), **612**
Texaco, Inc. v. Pennzoil, Co., 729 S.W.2d 768 (Tex.App.-Hous. (1 Dist.) 1987), 223
The Countess of Rutland's Case, 1604 WL 140 (KB 1604), 440
Thomas v. Bryant, 639 So.2d 378 (La.App. 2 Cir.1994), 276
Threadgill v. Peabody Coal Co., 34 Colo. App. 203, 526 P.2d 676 (Colo.App.1974), **435**
Totem Marine Tug & Barge, Inc. v. Alyeska Pipeline Service Co., 584 P.2d 15 (Alaska 1978), **367**
Trident Center v. Connecticut General Life Ins. Co., 847 F.2d 564 (9th Cir.1988), **489**

United American Life Ins. Co. v. Zions First Nat. Bank, 641 P.2d 158 (Utah 1982), 282
United States v. _____ (see opposing party)
United States Bank Nat. Ass'n v. Ables & Hall Builders, 696 F.Supp.2d 428 (S.D.N.Y. 2010), 753

Valley Medical Specialists v. Farber, 194 Ariz. 363, 982 P.2d 1277 (Ariz.1999), **396**
Van Wagner Advertising Corp. v. S & M Enterprises, 67 N.Y.2d 186, 501 N.Y.S.2d 628, 492 N.E.2d 756 (N.Y.1986), **688**
Varney v. Ditmars, 217 N.Y. 223, 111 N.E. 822 (N.Y.1916), **186**
Vastoler v. American Can Co., 700 F.2d 916 (3rd Cir.1983), 321
Victoria Laundry (Windsor) v. Newman Industries, 1949 WL 10461 (CA 1949), 768

Walgreen Co. v. Sara Creek Property Co., B.V., 966 F.2d 273 (7th Cir.1992), **693**
Walker v. Keith, 382 S.W.2d 198 (Ky.1964), **198**
Watts v. Watts, 137 Wis.2d 506, 405 N.W.2d 303 (Wis.1987), **816**
Webb v. McGowin, 232 Ala. 374, 168 So. 199 (Ala.1936), **274**
Webb v. McGowin, 27 Ala.App. 82, 168 So. 196 (Ala.App.1935), **271**
Webster v. Blue Ship Tea Room, Inc., 347 Mass. 421, 198 N.E.2d 309 (Mass.1964), **545**
Weiner v. McGraw–Hill, Inc., 57 N.Y.2d 458, 457 N.Y.S.2d 193, 443 N.E.2d 441 (N.Y. 1982), 241
Weintraub v. Krobatsch, 64 N.J. 445, 317 A.2d 68 (N.J.1974), **352**
Wholesale Sand & Gravel, Inc. v. Decker, 630 A.2d 710 (Me.1993), 641
Wiener v. Lazard Freres & Co., 241 A.D.2d 114, 672 N.Y.S.2d 8 (N.Y.A.D. 1 Dept.1998), **825**
Williams v. Walker–Thomas Furniture Co., 350 F.2d 445, 121 U.S.App.D.C. 315 (D.C.Cir.1965), **405**
Williams v. Walker–Thomas Furniture Co., 198 A.2d 914 (D.C.App.1964), **404**
Willis Min., Inc. v. Noggle, 235 Ga.App. 747, 509 S.E.2d 731 (Ga.App.1998), 549
Wisconsin Elec. Power Co. v. Union Pacific R. Co., 557 F.3d 504 (7th Cir.2009), **616**
Wood v. Lucy, Lady Duff–Gordon, 222 N.Y. 88, 118 N.E. 214 (N.Y.1917), **510**
W. R. Grimshaw Co. v. Nevil C. Withrow Co., 248 F.2d 896 (8th Cir.1957), 371

Zamore v. Whitten, 395 A.2d 435 (Me.1978), 253

CASES AND MATERIALS ON

CONTRACTS:
MAKING AND DOING DEALS

Third Edition

CHAPTER ONE

WHAT ARE WE GOING TO BE DOING IN THIS COURSE?

■ ■ ■

SECTION 1: WHAT IS A CONTRACT?

People often use the word "contract" to refer to the writing that embodies the agreement or deal. For example, Epstein, Markell, and Ponoroff each has a piece of paper signed by them and signed by the lovely Pamela Siege Chandler on behalf of West Academic Publishing Company in which Epstein, *et al.* agree to write a wonderful Contracts book for West and West agrees to pay them $60 for each copy of the book sold.[1] People think of such a piece of paper as being a "contract."

But the piece of paper is not a "contract." At least it is not a "contract" as we will be using the word "contract." At most, the piece of paper is a memorialization of the contract between Epstein, Markell, and Ponoroff, on the one hand, and West, on the other.

In law school (and usually in the practice of law), a contract is a promise or set of promises that the law will enforce. Epstein, *et al.*, promise to write a book; West promises to pay royalties. That is the contract.

To state the obvious (we hope), there are thus two key elements to the existence of a contract:

(1) a promise or promises, AND

(2) enforcement.

Let's briefly consider "promise" first. A "promise" is a commitment as to the happening or non-happening of some future event: "I promise I will paint your house" or "I promise I will not sell my 1973 Cadillac to anyone else for ten days."

"Enforcement" means legal enforcement—an award of damages or some other order by a court of law. Not all promises are legally enforce-

---

[1.] That is why your law school casebooks are so expensive—obscenely high royalties paid to professor/authors.

1

able. In some instances, the making of a promise creates a moral obligation but not a legal obligation.

Because there can be no promise unless there is also someone to whom the promise is made, any contract inevitably involves a legal relationship between at least two parties. Moreover, more often than not, each of the parties will be bound by reciprocal promises to one another. This is because the only reason A may have made a promise to B—was willing to give up $10,000—was that B promised in return to sell her car to A. Therefore, most contracts involve *exchange* relationships where A's promise was motivated by the return promise from B, which, in turn, was induced by A's promise. We will, in this course, be concerned primarily with *exchange transactions*. This is because under the English common law system, from which our own law of contracts evolved, courts are (except in special circumstances) unwilling to enforce a promise unless something is given or promised in return. More technically put, an enforceable promise must be supported by *consideration*.

The promise, "I'll sell you my car for $10,000," if accepted, is enforceable. The promise, "I'll give you my car next Tuesday," is not, because nothing was given or promised in return and the *nudum pactum* (naked promise) is not enforceable under traditional principles of contract law. As should be obvious to you, contract law, and the doctrine of consideration, derive from and, in turn, serve the needs of trade and commerce. A market-driven economy relies heavily on direct, bilateral exchanges between private parties to allocate economic resources, and our law of contracts developed to facilitate these transactions. It is not as if contract law is irrelevant or indifferent to promises made in non-commercial settings, such as social or familial situations, but it is true that contract law is less concerned with those promises and, as we will see, contract law operates less elegantly when applied in those non-commercial settings.

At bottom, contract law exists to satisfy the basic impulse—to which most people subscribe—that the reasonable expectations excited by a promise, if and when disappointed without legal excuse, are entitled to recompense in a court of law. Nevertheless, because not all promises can be enforced, there is considerably less agreement today on when, and, in particular, the reasons *why*, the coercive power of the state should be brought to bear to enforce certain broken promises.* Is it to ensure fairness and promote justice; because of the moral obligation attendant to the making of any promise; or simply to promote commerce and aggregate social wealth? No one can answer this question for you, but how *you* answer the question has enormous implications for deciding which promises ought to be enforced and which not. Consider these thoughts from Professor Farnsworth about wanting to make a commitment and regretting being committed.

----

* *See generally* Randy Barnett, *A Consent Theory of Contract,* 86 COLUM. L. REV. 269 (1986) (reviewing competing theories of contractual liability).

E. ALLAN FARNSWORTH, CHANGING YOUR MIND: THE LAW OF REGRETTED DECISIONS

13–14, 16–18, 24, 26–27 (1998)

[T]he function of promising is usually very different from the function of resolving. While you make a resolution with a view to self-control, you most often make a promise with a view toward self-interest. You make it in order to get what you want from someone else whose self-interest is in having your commitment in return. You make it as part of an exchange in which you swap your commitment for something that you want. * * *

Complete freedom to renege on your promises would make it difficult for you to deal with others by lowering your worth in their eyes. Keeping your resolutions may be of little concern to others, but keeping your promises is an altogether different matter. Who would swap for your promises if you were free to renege on them?

To be sure, even if the law imposed no restraints you might honor your promises because of extralegal restraints. Some of these restraints are external: You might fear diminished standing among peers, harm to reputation, impairment of relationships, or loss of future opportunities. * * * Other restraints are internal: you might be moved by a sense of integrity, acquired by upbringing, education, or introspection. Why else do we use the word "honor" in this connection? * * *

For the law the question is not *why* do you honor your promises but *when* should you be restrained from reneging on your promises. Since extralegal restraints cause some promisors to honor their promises quite without regard to what the law requires, the law has an impact in restraining promisors only to the extent they would otherwise renege.

Even though you wanted to be committed at the time you made your promise, you may in hindsight wish you were not. Rare is the promisor who has never felt regret—the sensation that comes from such hindsight. * * *

Promises are made in the face of an uncertain future. Even if your promise reflected your existing preferences, so that you had no cause for regret, you might nevertheless have cause for regret after the passage of time. For this there are two possible reasons.

First, because you were poor at predicting external circumstances, you may find that they have changed and you made an improvident decision. Because contracts are devices for dealing with uncertainty by allocating risks of future changes, courts have tended to be markedly less paternalistic [i.e., intervene to allow you out from your promise] when faced with excuses based on improvident decisions than when confronted with excuses based on uninformed decisions. * * *

Second, because you were poor at predicting your preferences, you may find they have changed even though external circumstances have not, and that you have made an obsolete decision. * * *

Country-music star, Willie Nelson, when asked about his four marriages, replied, "I've changed. I'm not the same guy that was married to this person or that person. * * * [E]ach of my wives was married to a different person."[37] But contract law is not so forgiving. Even a financial disaster that not only alters one's preferences but leaves one unable to perform is dismissed as mere "subjective impossibility, that is, impossibility that is personal to the promisor and does not inhere in the nature of the act performed" and so is no excuse.[38]

* * *

To sum up, only rarely will a court allow you to change your mind and renege on a binding promise, though there is a trend toward tolerance of reneging and in this sense toward paternalism.

———

Professor Farnsworth's comments underscore the reasons why, once each party has voluntarily made a promise to the other, the law holds the parties to their promises, regardless of what might happen in the future that makes one of those promises more burdensome or less advantageous than originally contemplated. This idea is what we mean when we use the phrase "freedom of contract"—expressing the policy that parties are free to bargain about the terms of their deal, but once the deal is struck there is no turning back. But how far does this principle of freedom of contract extend? Consider that question often as you read the cases in this book. But before reading the cases in the book (or any more of this introductory stuff), please consider the following questions:

WHICH OF THE FOLLOWING LOOKS LIKE A CONTRACT AS OF THE TIME INDICATED TO YOU, A LAW STUDENT WHO HAS NOT YET HAD EVEN ONE DAY OF CONTRACTS?

1. Subaru Sales, Inc. (S) and B sign a document that provides, *inter alia*, that "S, party of the first part, is hereby selling and B, party of the second part, is hereby buying a 2010 Subaru Legacy for $25,000." S delivers the car and title to B, and B writes a check for $25,000.

2. Same facts as #1 above, except that the document does not include the word "hereby" or the phrases "party of the first part" and "party of the second part."

3. On September 9, the partners of X law firm and the partners of Y law firm sign a document that provides that the two firms will merge, effective October 10, with the new firm to be called XY.

4. S asks F if he wants to buy her 2009–2010 contracts notes for $100. F responds that he does if he can get the notes before Friday. S says that she will deliver the notes by Friday.

---

37. 60 Minutes, April 20, 1997 (CBS).

38. *B's Co. v. B.P. Barber & Assocs.*, 391 F.2d 130, 137 (4th Cir. 1968).

5. O, a Tucson resident who owns a second home in Las Vegas, sends the following e-mail to P, a house painter in Las Vegas. "Will pay you $1,000 for painting my house in Las Vegas, with the work to be completed by November 25." P responds immediately by e-mail, "Great. Will paint your house and will complete the work before November 25."

6. Same facts as #5 above, except that P does not respond by email but instead paints O's house and completes the work by November 25.

7. T's lease with L expires next month. L sends T the following fax transmission: "I will renew the lease for two more years, with no increase in rent."

SECTION 2: WHY DO LAWYERS AND LAW STUDENTS NEED TO KNOW ABOUT CONTRACTS AND CONTRACT LAW?

In a free market economy, contracts and contractual relationships permeate almost every aspect of day-to-day life. Perhaps nobody has put it quite so well as Sir Henry Maine who, at the end of the nineteenth century, observed that, "The movement of the progressive societies has hitherto been a movement from status to contract."* We each make numerous contracts of every stripe every year; for example, when we lease an apartment, open a checking account, buy a car, subscribe for cellular phone service, or sign our student loans. Not surprisingly, therefore, contract law and enforcement touch virtually every field of legal practice, from intellectual property to labor law to real estate. For this reason, every lawyer must be conversant with, and every law student must have exposure to, the basic rules and principles of contract law.

Ultimately, however, contract law is economic in focus and orientation. Business and commercial dealings and relationships in this country and, for that matter, throughout the free world are fundamentally contractual in nature. "Contracts" is the area of law that facilitates trade and commerce by setting forth the rules governing economic exchanges and enforcement of commercial obligations. It is important to recognize that businesspeople and companies relate to the rest of the world through their contracts, including contracts with employees, customers, suppliers, lenders, and many others. Indeed, most forms of business transaction, whether a big corporate merger or the routine purchase of office supplies, involve at their core a *contract* between two or more parties; that is to say, each of these parties has undertaken a legally binding performance obligation to the other in order to secure some desired reciprocal performance in return.

---

* HENRY SUMNER MAINE, ANCIENT LAW 141 (New Universal Library ed. 1905).

As should be apparent to you already, the law of "contracts" applies to an exceedingly wide array of transactions in an equally wide variety of settings. Having said this, however, it is also important to point out that certain types of contracts involve special rules because of the unique nature of the relationship involved. For example, if you plan to study labor law, there is a complex statutory framework governing labor/management agreements that you will have to master. Likewise, insurance contracts, government contracts, and consumer credit contracts are the subject of detailed regulatory schema that address the special concerns and issues that arise in each of those areas. However, even the special rules governing these particular kinds of contracts are built upon the basic principles of common law contracts and, in many instances, rely on those principles to fill the gaps where the applicable legislation is silent. Thus, it is the study of those basic rules and principles that this course and book are devoted to because no lawyer worth her salt, whatever her area of expertise, can function effectively in ignorance of them.

SECTION 3: WHERE DOES CONTRACT LAW COME FROM?

Contract law has a long history. Ancient Rome had its own form of contract law. Roman contract law influenced the development of contract law in England in medieval times. And, English contract law, in turn, influenced the development of American contract law.

Even today, lawyers and judges continue to use terms and concepts derived from Roman law and early English common law, such as *quantum meruit*, *assumpsit*, etc. Obviously, the particular problems and more general policy concerns in 21st century America are different from those in ancient Rome, or medieval England or even 18th century America. Thus, there are challenges in adapting long-accepted contract concepts to 21st century deals involving matters such as e-commerce, technology licensing or (as in our very first case) surrogate parenting agreements. The first step, however, is to develop an appreciation for the historical antecedents of contemporary American contract law.

A. ENGLISH COMMON LAW ORIGINS AND THE EVOLUTION OF *ASSUMPSIT*

E. ALLAN FARNSWORTH, THE PAST OF PROMISE: AN HISTORICAL INTRODUCTION TO CONTRACT

69 Colum. L. Rev. 576, 592–98 (1969)

The view that promises are not generally enforceable, which started from the premise of Roman law that a mere agreement did not beget an action, was held by the common law. Its choice was scarcely surprising. It accorded well with the procedural niceties of common law courts, where recovery was not to be had unless the claim could be fitted within one of the established forms of action; and it suited the status-oriented society of the Middle Ages, which was anything but conducive to the flowering of promise. Furthermore, there was no great pressure for enforceability as contracts were not a significant part of the business of the common law courts. * * *

The challenge that faced [the courts in developing a general basis for the enforcement of promises] was to work within the framework of the forms of action, first to develop exceptions as the Romans had done, and then to so fashion these exceptions as ultimately to achieve what the Romans had never achieved—a general theory of contract. This challenge was met by the common law courts in the course of the fifteenth and sixteenth centuries. * * * The achievement was all the more remarkable in view of the fact that when this development began, the English law of contracts was little more advanced than that of many primitive societies. How was it brought about?

The common law courts found the answer in the law of torts. They had already recognized that liability in tort arose when a person undertook (*assumpsit*) to perform a duty and then performed it in such a way as to cause harm. Suit could be brought on the special variety of trespass on the case that came to be known as assumpsit. At the beginning of the fifteenth century it was available only where there had been misfeasance in performance of the undertaking. This example was given in 1436: "If a carpenter makes a covenant with me to make me a house good and strong and of a certain form, and he makes me a house which is weak and bad and of another form, I shall have an action of trespass on my case."[74] In such cases of misfeasance it was not hard to justify liability in tort. But might not the same remedy lie when there had merely been nonfeasance, a failure to perform the undertaking? At first the answer was no. In 1410 it was said: "Certainly it would lie [if the carpenter had built the house badly], because he would then answer for the wrong which he had done, but when a man makes a covenant and does nothing under that covenant, how can you have an action against him without a deed?"[75]

---

74. Y.B. 14 Hy. VI, at 18. 3 W. Holdsworth [A History of English Law] 430 [(4th ed. 1936)].

75. Y.B. Mich. 11 Hy. IV, pl 60, 3 W. Holdsworth, *supra* note [74], at 433–34.

Nevertheless, by the second half of the fifteenth century there was a growing tendency among the common law judges to make the first major extension in the action of assumpsit by enforcing such promises even where there had been only nonfeasance. * * * But some limits had to be placed on what promises would be enforced, for the judges were not about to allow "that one shall have trespass for any breach of covenant in the world."[76] The courts were therefore forced to find a test to distinguish instances where nonfeasance was actionable from those where it was not. Since the misfeasance cases that had originally given rise to the action in assumpsit were characterized by a detriment incurred by the promisee in reliance on the promise, it was natural to formulate an analogous test and to allow enforcement where the promisee had changed his position on the faith of the promise, and had been consequently damaged by its nonperformance.

* * *

As the sixteenth century drew to a close, however, the common law courts, conscious of the expanding jurisdiction of Chancery and anxious to preserve their own powers, made a second major extension of the action of assumpsit. Thus it was held that a party who had given only a promise in exchange for the other's promise had, nonetheless, suffered a detriment by having his freedom of action fettered, since he was in turn bound by his own promise. * * *

On this ground the extension of the action of assumpsit to include the mere exchange of promises can be justified.

The action was to experience yet one more important extension. The procedure in actions of assumpsit, in which the plaintiff was entitled to a jury trial, was more favored by creditors than that in actions of debt, in which the defendant could resort to wager of law.* The next step in the common law's development of the law of contract was to permit assumpsit to supplant debt. By the middle of the sixteenth century, it had been recognized that an action in assumpsit could be brought against a defendant who, being already indebted (*indebitatus*), expressly undertook (*assumpsit*) to pay a particular sum. This action was called one in "*indebitatus assumpsit*", to distinguish it from the older "special assumpsit." Toward the end of the century, it began to be held that a debt alone, without a subsequent express promise, would support such an action. The final triumph of this view came at the beginning of the seventeenth century in Slade's case in which, on a jury finding that "there was no other promise or assumption, but only the said bargain,"[83] all the judges

---

76.   Y.B. Hil. 3 Hy. VI, pl. 33, 3 W. HOLDSWORTH, *supra* note [74], at 435.

    * The debt form of action permitted the defendant to invoke the archaic "wager of law" as the method of trial, instead of trial by jury. Under this system, the party accused of owing a debt could avoid liability by reciting a scripted oath, in effect swearing he did not owe such debt, and supporting his own oath with those of certain hired "oath sayers" who, for a price, would swear that the defendant's testimony was unperjured. The plaintiff was not permitted to cross-examine the oath sayers, meaning that if the defendant was prepared to lie under oath, he could in fact get away with it. Eds.

83.   Slade's Case, 4 Co. Rep. 92 b, 76 Eng. Rep. 1074 (Q.B. 1602).

of England resolved "that every contract executor imports in itself an assumpsit."[84] The creditor was at last assured of the benefits of jury trial in place of wager of law and was freed of the technicalities of pleading in debt.

———

B. CLASSICAL ERA OF AMERICAN CONTRACT LAW

LAWRENCE M. FRIEDMAN, CONTRACT LAW IN AMERICA
17–18, 20–22 (1965)

Quite clearly, Anglo–American law now pays more attention to contract than medieval English law ever did. The rise of contract to legal prominence is fairly recent. Blackstone's classic exposition of the common law was written shortly before the American Revolution; in it, only a few short sections include contract, while the special doctrines of real-property law fill almost the whole of one of the four books of the *Commentaries* and color much of the rest. * * * The nineteenth century was very different. Even in the lawyer's narrow sense, the law of contract swelled into one of the main branches of legal learning. There were no important treatises on the law of contracts published until the nineteenth century; the appearance then of such works was a sure sign that the lawyers saw bread-and-butter importance to the field. When Christopher Columbus Langdell [Dean of the Harvard Law School] in the 1870s undertook to reform legal education and to establish the case method of instruction, he began the career of the law school case-book with a volume on contracts. In the mid-twentieth century the subject remains an immutable pillar of the first-year curriculum of every law school.

* * *

The law of contract is, therefore, roughly coextensive with the free market. Liberal nineteenth-century economics fits neatly with the law of contracts so viewed. It, too, had the abstracting habit [of removing from the realm of concern all particularities concerning persons and subject-matter]. In both theoretical models—that of the law of contracts and that of liberal economics—parties could be treated as individual economic units which, in theory, enjoyed complete mobility and freedom of decision. * * * The correspondence between law and economic theory was never exact. Contract law was not a book written by Adam Smith. Nobody purposely sat down to turn contract law into an applied branch of liberal economics. But a free market developed, and grew; the law of contract was the legal reflection of that market and naturally took on its characteristics. Con-

---
84. *Id.* at 1077.

tract was abstract; the free market was abstract; and the two institutions directed behavior along similar channels.

C. DEMISE OF CLASSICAL PRINCIPLES OF CONTRACT LAW

"Classical contract law," of which Professor Friedman speaks, flourished more or less from 1850 through 1940, holding at its core the first principle of *freedom of contract* and the corollary of that principle, *pacta sund servanda* (promises are to be kept). But what do we mean by "freedom of contract"? The phrase encompasses the notion that private bargains, freely and voluntarily entered into, should be enforced without reservation and certainly blind to the identities of the parties or the relative equities of their positions under the contract. This judicial "hands-off" approach reflected the bias, consistent with the pervading economic theory of the day, that the good of the economy, and ergo society as a whole, would best be served by allowing tough, rugged individualists to bargain it out in the marketplace free from interference or regulation by the state except in extreme cases of fraud, duress, or illegality.

Under the classical principles of contract law, it was not perceived as the role of the courts to review, rewrite, or evaluate the underlying fairness of the deal; the role of the courts was simply to ensure that a bargain had been struck and, if so, to enforce it; nothing less and certainly nothing more. This ensured the stability, predictability, and certainty on which business relied and efficient commercial relations depended. Of course, these principles only existed in idealized form; the reality of contract law and enforcement was always a more complex and nuanced phenomenon. Nevertheless, as you will see, the principles that govern contractual relations today bear only the faintest resemblance to the principles that exemplified classical contract law just over a hundred years ago.

In the main, the second half of the twentieth century witnessed a number of changes in contracts doctrine, but none more important than the removal by both legislative and judicial intervention of various issues that had previously been left to the realm of private bargain of the parties. In effect, as to these matters, freedom of contract has been, if not eliminated, at least curtailed. Professor Grant Gilmore, in his famous work titled THE DEATH OF CONTRACT 95–96 (1974), neatly summed up the reasons for this evolution in contract law theory and doctrine as follows:

> As we look back on the nineteenth century theories, we are struck most of all, I think, by the narrow scope of social duty which they implicitly assumed. No man is his brother's keeper; the race is to the swift; let the devil take the hindmost. For good or ill we have changed all that. We are now all cogs in a machine, each dependent on the

other. The decline and fall of the general theory of contract and, in most quarters, of laissez-faire economics may be taken as remote reflections of the transition from nineteenth century individualism to the welfare state and beyond.

There are any number of social, cultural, and economic factors and attitudes that can be identified as contributing to the demise of classical contract law and the erosion of unbridled freedom of contract. Among the most significant, however, has been the increasing complexity and interde- pendency of our economic system. The growth of large, powerful corporations and other commercial enterprises, coupled with the perfection of the "standard printed form," has meant that the relative equality in bargaining strength and position that was the unstated assumption on which the principle of freedom of contract was predicated no longer reflects the reality of many exchange transactions in contemporary society. This has led courts to take a much more activist role in monitoring the fairness of contractual relationships, particularly where there is a significant disparity in bargaining power between the parties. The hard and fast rules of contract doctrine that tended to confine the discretion of the court in earlier times has in general given way to more open-ended and flexible standards that leave significant room for courts to do particularized justice in individual cases.*

A drawback, arguably, of this trend in the law has been some loss in the certainty, predictability, and stability of contractual relationships. Unlike the era when the policy of freedom of contract reigned supreme, parties can no longer be sure that their bargains, freely and voluntarily entered into, will be enforced. Business and commerce rely on clear rules, as much if not more than they do on the content of those rules. Consider the court's statement in *Shreve v. Cheesman*, 69 F. 785, 791 (8th Cir. 1895): "It is universally conceded that it is often more important that rules [affecting property rights] should be certain and changeless than that they should be right. Men engaged in active business buy and sell in reliance on them." Do you agree with this statement? How much certainty should be sacrificed in the interests of justice? Need one always come at the expense of the other?

Regulation of bargain relationships, and the waning deference to private autonomy, goes far beyond post hoc judicial review of the fairness of existing contracts. Congress and the state legislatures have also gotten into the act, wholly removing certain types of contracts from the realm of general principles of contract law. As we noted earlier, today, labor contracts, insurance contracts, consumer credit agreements, and others are the subject of comprehensive statutory enactments that regulate in detail the form and terms of the contract, as well the permissible scope of what the parties may or may not bargain over by private agreement.

Other statutes create rights in one party to the agreement that the party did not himself bargain for. For example, recognizing that people

---

* *See generally* P.S. ATIYAH, THE RISE AND FALL OF FREEDOM OF CONTRACT (1979).

caught unaware in their homes by a slick, experienced salesman might end-up agreeing to buy something (encyclopedias or a vacuum cleaner) that they really didn't want, the Federal Trade Commission, acting under authority of a federal law, adopted a regulation (an administrative rule) giving consumers in door-to-door sales transactions a three-day "cooling off period" during which they retain the right to cancel the deal even though they signed a "binding contract." 16 C.F.R. § 429 (effective June 7, 1974). In still other cases, a statute may limit the permissible scope of negotiations. For instance, today, parties are free to negotiate over and reach agreement on the rate of interest that one party will have to pay the other in a loan transaction, but only to a point because their agreement is subject to applicable state (or federal) law governing usury. Therefore, even though knowingly and voluntarily agreed to, a promise to pay a usurious rate of interest will simply not be enforced. Likewise, some states restrict the ability of employers to negotiate for and include non-competition covenants in an employment contract upon the employee's termination from service. Unlike many of the rules of contract law which can be "contracted around" if the parties so choose,* these legislative prescriptions cannot be altered by the parties. This is because they represent a form of external regulation of the exchange relationship, typically imposed because of social judgments about either the need to protect parties to contract relationships or the need to protect society as a whole from certain types of conduct.

Despite these legislative incursions into the law of private bargain in certain transactions, our focus in this book remains largely on the general body of principles comprising "contract law" that have been developed over several hundred years by courts employing the common law style of reasoning and analysis. We believe this is appropriate because, even with respect to statutory law, the courts still play a pivotal role in the development of the law. Unlike the application of legislative codes in civil law jurisdictions, where judicial decisions tend to have little impact or effect except upon the litigants to the particular case under decision, in a common law system when a court decides a specific case by interpreting and applying a governing statutory provision, it may also be placing its own *gloss* on that rule. Often, that gloss becomes part of the law and, thus, may affect the interests of litigants in future cases.

D. SOURCES OF MODERN CONTRACT LAW

For most of our history the basic rules and principles of contract law derived and evolved from a wide variety of cases decided by the English

---

* Because it is impossible for the parties to address every aspect of their relationship in detail, an important function of contract law is to supply the rule that will apply in the absence of specific agreement of the parties. These rules are sometimes called "default" rules to contrast them from other kinds of rules which are mandatory or "immutable." *See generally* Richard Carswell, *Contract Law, Default Rules, and the Philosophy of Promising*, 88 MICH. L. REV. 489 (1989).

common law courts with some but relatively few statutory modifications. Of course, the common law courts did not act wholly without structure. They were, in the first instance, guided by the principle of *precedent* and influenced to a considerable degree by other bodies of law such as Roman law, Canon Law and, particularly, The Law Merchant, which was a separate system of rules that developed (reaching its heyday during the sixteenth century) in England to govern commercial transactions, largely administered by local mercantile authorities. The law of contracts that was imported into the American legal system was essentially this common law of contracts as it existed at the end of the eighteenth century.

Beginning early in the twentieth century, however, a trend developed, which continues to the present day, to *codify* our laws, including the law of contracts. The first major codification effort was the Uniform Sales Act, patterned on its English predecessor of 1893, which was approved by the National Conference of Commissioners on Uniform State Laws (the NCCUSL) in 1906. Professor Samuel Williston, also the author of a major treatise on contract law, was the principal draftsperson of the Uniform Sales Act, which was eventually adopted by over thirty states.

The Uniform Sales Act was eventually replaced by the Uniform Commercial Code (the U.C.C.), a much more comprehensive statute governing a wide range of commercial transactions. Contracts involving the sale of goods are the subject of Article 2 of the U.C.C. The U.C.C., the first official text of which was approved in 1952, was the product of a joint effort by the NCCUSL and the American Law Institute (the ALI). The U.C.C. has enjoyed near-universal acceptance in the states (Louisiana, the only civil law jurisdiction in the U.S., has now adopted most of the U.C.C., although not Article 2). Since its inception, the U.C.C. has been the subject of continuing revision and modernization. In 1987, for example, a whole new Article dealing with personal property leases, Article 2A, was approved and has received widespread adoption.

In 2001, a ten-year project to revise Article 2 was completed. However, final approval from the ALI and NCCUSL did not occur until 2003, at which point Revised Article 2 was sent to the states for adoption. So far, none have accepted the invitation, making the future of Revised Article 2 problematic to say the least. Needless to say, all the cases in this book that refer to Article 2 are referring to the non-revised version. Although Revised Article 2 is increasingly looking like a dead-letter, where the revision would change the analysis in any significant respect, we'll let you know.

The Code's Permanent Editorial Board, established by the joint sponsors of the U.C.C. in 1961 to promote uniform state enactment and interpretation of the Code, is responsible for evaluating the operation of the Code in the various states and determining when revisions to the various Articles may be appropriate. With each such revision, a new official text of the uniform version of the Code is promulgated. The most current official text, and the one we refer to when citing to Code provisions (except for Article 2) in this book, is the 2008 Official Text.

The primary architect of the U.C.C., and the principal draftsperson of Article 2, was Karl Llewellyn. The statute very much reflects his normative view of law, and those of a generation of legal scholars roughly classified together as *Legal Realists*. The realists were decidedly pragmatic. They rejected the idea of law as a "science." Instead they believed that the law was a tool to serve societal and economic interests and, therefore, legal rules should be crafted to conform to people's expectations of how the law *ought* to work. The realist attitude about the role of the commercial law is evident in section 1–103(a) of Article 1 of the Code, which broadly sets forth the purposes of the U.C.C. as intending "to simplify, clarify, and modernize the law governing commercial transactions; to permit the continued expansion of commercial practices through custom, usage and agreement of the parties; and to make uniform the law among the various jurisdictions."

The U.C.C. has been very influential even in transactions that do not fall within its broad scope. Article 2 supplies the governing law only if the subject matter of the contract involves a transaction in goods. Nevertheless, Article 2 has had a profound effect upon the development of contract law in non-sale of goods cases, such as contracts involving real estate or services of one kind or another. This is because courts will frequently look to the provisions of Article 2, and even apply those provisions by analogy, in deciding non-sale of goods cases.

The second major development in contract law in the last century has been the *Restatements of Contracts*, developed under the aegis of, and published by, the American Law Institute. The American Law Institute was founded in 1923 "to promote clarification and simplification of the law and its better adaptation to social needs, to secure the better administration of justice, and to carry on scholarly and scientific legal work." Its membership is composed of distinguished judges, lawyers, and law teachers.* Work on the first *Restatement of Contracts* began in 1923, and the final version was approved in 1932. Professor Williston was the Reporter for the project. Among his advisors was Professor Arthur Corbin, the author of another major treatise on contract law. Professors Williston and Corbin's views about, and approach to, contract law are frequently contrasted. Williston was much inclined to see the law as fixed and immutable. Sometimes described as a *positivist* view of law, Williston tended to regard law as a closed system of rules that could be consistently applied to resolve any fact situation. Professor Corbin's approach to contract law was much less mechanical and formalistic. A principal figure in the legal realist movement, Corbin was willing to accept a much greater degree of indeterminacy in the law than Williston in order to assure a just or fair result. Corbin felt that the hard and fast rules of contract law needed to

---

*As all three of your authors are members of the ALI, it also includes some less than distinguished law teachers.

be applied much more flexibly, tempered by the prevailing norms, mores, and attitudes of the social and economic milieu in which the rules operated. Thus, Corbin was open to incorporating into the law broad, open-ended considerations of ethics and justice.

The enormous pace of new developments in contract law in the quarter century following adoption of the first *Restatement* led to the decision in the early 1960s to begin work on the *Restatement (Second) of Contracts*, with Professor Robert Braucher serving as Reporter. Professor Alan Farnsworth replaced Professor Braucher in 1971, after Braucher was appointed to the Supreme Judicial Court of Massachusetts. Work on the *Restatement (Second)* was finally completed in 1981. Heavily influenced by Corbin's perspective on the law, as well as by the U.C.C., the *Restatement (Second)* took a decidedly conscious turn from its predecessor, placing a much greater emphasis on protecting parties' detrimental *reliance* on promises and forsaking bright-line rules for more flexible, open-ended standards.

It is important to realize that the *Restatements*, unlike the U.C.C., do not have the force of law. No state legislature has enacted a *Restatement*. Instead, they reflect a systemic distillation of the prevailing rules and principles of the common law of contracts, albeit sometimes with a deliberative normative twist, into a single code-like document. Thus, while very influential in judicial decision making because of the prestige of the American Law Institute and the individuals selected to work on these projects, a court is not bound to apply the *Restatement* if it believes the applicable rule is wrong or, more likely, not in accord with the common law in that jurisdiction.

While contract law is predominantly state law, there are federal laws relating to specific matters of federal concern, such as interstate commerce or the procurement of goods and services by federal governmental units and agencies. Moreover, the trend toward codification of the law of contracts has not been limited to domestic law. In 1980, the United Nations Commission on International Trade submitted a draft of the *Convention on Contracts for the International Sale of Goods (CISG)*, which governs in the case of contracts between citizens of ratifying nations. The United States formally ratified *CISG* in 1986, and it came into force on January 1, 1988 after being ratified by 11 countries.* Finally, in 1994, the International Institute for the Unification of Private Law (UNIDROIT) announced its *Principles of International Commercial Contracts*, reflecting rules derived from both civil and common law legal systems that might desirably apply to international contracts. Not a formal treaty, which would require adoption by member-nations, the *UNIDROIT Principles* are more like a *Restatement*, although they may be made applicable to a transaction by agreement of the parties. They can also be referred to by

---

* Today, more than 70 nations have ratified the CISG.

an international tribunal as an authoritative source of rules for resolving a dispute between parties from different countries.

SECTION 4: WHAT IS THE LAWYER'S ROLE IN CONTRACT LAW?

Two parties considering entering into a contractual relationship are initially under no obligation to, and have no rights against, one another. Instead, unlike in most areas of law, they have the opportunity, subject only to relatively minimal restriction, to define by agreement what their rights and obligations will be. That is to say, the essence of contractual liability is that it is a consensual form of liability. This notion is reflected in that still core contract law principle of *freedom of contract*. Freedom of contract means that the parties are free to establish their corresponding rights and duties by private bargain. By the same token, the principle of freedom of contract implies its corollary, namely, the principle of freedom *from* contract, which means that neither party is obligated to conclude a deal with the other. Thus, either party may elect to break off negotiations at any point prior to the formation of a binding contract. How does the lawyer fit into this dynamic?

The permutations are innumerable. In the case of large, sophisticated business parties, the lawyer's role tends to be more purely legal; giving advice relating to legal issues and considerations, and drafting the definitive documentation of the transaction. With smaller business clients and individuals, the lawyer will perform these functions as well, but in addition often will also be consulted on the business points of the deal. In both instances, the role of the lawyer is predominantly a *planner* and not an *adversary*. Moreover, while the lawyer is always looking out first and foremost for the interests of her client in the transaction, in many contractual settings there is a substantial identity of interests between the parties and a common or shared desire to achieve a mutually satisfactory accommodation of those interests. This is particularly so in situations where the parties anticipate a long-term mutually advantageous relationship, such as, for example, a partnership arrangement. In some of these cases, with the consent of the parties, the lawyer may actually represent both parties. This will, however, preclude the lawyer's representation of either party individually should there be a falling out in the future because such representation would constitute a conflict of interest and a violation of the lawyer's ethical obligations. However, even when the parties approach one another at arms-length and have their own separate counsel, the lawyers' objectives are often to reach reasonable accommodation on the key points of negotiation rather than solely to maximize their respective client's interests at the expense of the other party. In short, the role is much more collaborative in nature than is ordinarily true of the lawyer's role in representing a party once a dispute has broken out under a contract.

It is also important to recognize that lawyers encounter contracts in virtually all aspects of practice. "Contracts" does not itself represent a discrete area of legal practice in the same way, for example, we might speak of a criminal or a personal injury law practice. Rather, contract law and contractual relationships transcend many different areas of practice, but, in particular, form the foundation of the commercial law. Whether the transaction being handled by the lawyer at any particular moment involves a real estate conveyance, a corporate combination, a financing arrangement, or an employment or agency relation, more often than not the key to the deal is an acceptable contractual arrangement. Thus, the "hired gun" image typically associated with the lawyer in the traditional litigation model is simply inaccurate (if not inappropriate) in the contract negotiation and formation stage of the deal.

Perhaps the most critical lawyer responsibility at this stage is the responsibility for *drafting* the actual written terms of the transaction. Even when contracts are "custom drafted," the lawyer will inevitably begin by retrieving an agreement from a prior deal to use a form. This is because most contracts will contain what has come to be referred to as *boilerplate*. The term boilerplate is used to refer to contractual provisions and language that are routinely included as part of any agreement. There is nothing wrong with boilerplate if it fits, but the draftsperson who includes boilerplate from a form without consciously considering its applicability and appropriateness in the current transaction runs the risk of doing her client a grave disservice.

On other occasions, the lawyer will be faced with a contract where there is no opportunity to participate in the drafting of the proposed agreement. This is because the client will have been presented with a "take it or leave it" deal. In the area of consumer transactions, for example, since World War II businesses have increasingly come to rely upon the standard printed form, representing the only basis on which the merchant will do business with a prospective customer. If you'd like to test this assertion, go down to a new car dealership. Decide on the make and model you'd like and negotiate a price. Then tell the salesperson that you'll draft the contract up that evening and be back in the morning. Now, watch his or her reaction. But what's wrong with you drafting the contract rather than using the dealership's form? In truth, nothing's "wrong" with it, it just "ain't gonna happen."

If you're forced to do business on the dealer's form, how valid is the principle of freedom of contract in these circumstances? Should the courts take a different attitude toward enforcement in consumer cases? As a practical matter, how many of these kinds of contracts do you suppose are actually reviewed by lawyers before they're signed? We haven't actually counted, but we think bloody few.

Even in the non-consumer or commercial setting, oftentimes the parties will not approach one another from a position of equal bargaining strength. In these situations, the party in the superior position may insist the deal be done on its terms or not at all. For instance, how much opportunity do you suppose that the average worker has to negotiate the terms of his or her employment arrangements? In these cases, a lawyer counseling a client plays a somewhat different role. Because there will be very little opportunity to control the terms of the contract, the lawyer's job is to help the client understand the risk so that the client can intelligently decide whether to take the job or look for one that offers greater security.

All of the cases in this book consist of deals that went bad. That's why there was lawsuit. We think it might be useful for you to ask yourself from time-to-time what you, as the lawyer for one of the parties to the deal, might have done differently to have, if not avoided the problem, at least, better protected your client's interest. Remember, freedom of contract means not only considerable freedom for the party to the contract to affect the terms and conditions of the deal, but considerable freedom for the party's lawyer to help structure the transaction in a manner that best serves the client's interest.

SECTION 5: WHAT IS A FIRST YEAR COURSE IN CONTRACTS?

Contracts will be your easiest first year subject. Part of what makes contracts the easiest first year course is that you have already done contracts—apartment leases, automobile purchases, employment agreements, etc. And, part of what makes contracts the easiest first year course is that it only covers eight somewhat related, overlapping* questions:

1. Is there a deal?
2. Was there the necessary consideration or consideration substitute?
3. Is there some reason based on the agreement process or the terms of the agreement not to enforce the agreement?
4. What are the terms of the deal?
5. When is someone who made an enforceable deal excused from doing what she agreed to do because of some post-agreement occurrence or non-occurrence?
6. How does the law enforce a deal?
7. What are the alternatives to contracts and contract law?

---

* In the world of practicing law, most of your work assignments will involve more than one of these eight questions. In the world of learning law, we will, to the extent possible, consider these questions in this order, one question at a time.

8. When can someone assert legal rights because of a deal made by others?

Indeed, contract law is so easy that, when you get out of law school, you will re-learn (learn?) everything that you need to know about contracts for the bar exam in six to nine hours of lecture in a bar review course.

Why then do law schools spend four to nine months on contracts instead of just six to nine hours? The six to nine hours of bar review coverage of contract law helps prepare you for two days of fairly predictable contract law questions from bar examiners. The four to nine months of law school coverage of contracts helps prepare you for a career of unpredictable contracts questions and assignments from clients, judges, and other lawyers in your law firm—a career of writing contracts so as to minimize if not eliminate later problems, and a career of resolving those problems that contract drafting did not eliminate.

As a part of that preparation, your teacher will regularly ask unpredictable questions—questions different from the questions in the book, and different from the questions that you anticipated. And, you will find that most of your professors' questions in law school (like most of the questions from clients, judges, and other lawyers in the "real world") do not have simple answers—or even answers at all.

In dealing with these questions, you will discover the importance of:

1. *Knowing vocabulary*

    Contract law has its own vocabulary. This vocabulary includes familiar words with new meanings. For example, a "contract" is more than just an agreement; an "offer" is similar but not identical to a proposal; "acceptance" is a special form of response to an offer; and "consideration" has a meaning that is even more "special." And it is a vocabulary with lots of new terms and phrases, such as "rescission," "impracticability," "executory contract," "parol evidence," and "promissory estoppel."

2. *Understanding cases and the "case method"*

    Most contract law in law school comes from the written opinions of judges in decided cases. This is commonly called "common law."

    American courts, with the partial exception of state courts in Louisiana, follow the English common law tradition. Louisiana and most of the rest of the world operate under a civil law system. In a civil law system, the legislature makes the laws and courts basically interpret and apply these legislative enactments. Legislatures in a common law system also enact laws, like U.C.C. Article 2, which are interpreted and applied by courts.

    The essential difference between a common law system and a civil law system is that in a common law system courts also make law. A common law court's decision not only resolves the specific dispute between the parties but also becomes a part of the law in that court that is to be applied when similar disputes arise in the future.

In other, new, words, a common law system is based on *"stare decisis,"* i.e., judicial adherence to past decisions that are "precedents." A law dictionary defines "precedent" as "a decided case that furnishes a basis for determining an identical or similar case that might arise later, or a similar question of law."*

A big part of the practice of law is reading judicial opinions to determine which cases are "precedent" that will affect how the court will decide "your" case. And so, learning to read cases is a big part of law school. This is sometimes referred to as the "case method," and we largely follow that approach in this book.

The case method is not, however, without its limitations. To begin with, lawyers don't decide cases, judges do. Therefore, by just reading appellate opinions you do not learn a great deal about the lawyering process. Furthermore, the appellate decision is just the tip of the iceberg in what was a real dispute between real parties that eventually ended up in litigation, *i.e.*, having to be resolved by a judge or jury. However, the reality is that in the vast majority of settings in which lawyers act, they serve as problem-solvers, not progenitors. The true measure of a good lawyer is the ability to plan in advance and in a manner that avoids or at least minimizes the likelihood of problems arising in the future. Therefore, throughout this book we also consider the role of the lawyer and ask you not only how you might have handled the case, but also what you might have done differently to avoid the problem in the first place.

The other major problem with the case method is that it tends to inculcate in students new to the area the false impression that most rules of contract law are ambiguous and that most contract disputes are resolved by trial. In fact, the vast majority of contractual obligations are simply performed without incident. This is in part because many of the rules of contract law and liability are in fact clear and unambiguous. Moreover, when disputes do occur, the vast majority of those are settled amicably by the parties either without the necessity for litigation or prior to trial if suit is actually filed. Finally, as we discuss at the end of this chapter, contract disputes are increasingly resolved by private arbitration, mediation, and other forms of alternative dispute resolution. While the pivotal role that a lawyer plays in the formal adjudicatory process is well-known and understood, the advice and assistance of counsel is often equally critical in the negotiation of private settlements or resolution through informal dispute resolution mechanisms.

---

* BRYAN A. GARNER, A DICTIONARY OF MODERN LEGAL USAGE 680 (2d ed. 1995).

3. *Distinguishing the role of trial courts and appellate courts*

This book is filled with cases, mostly appellate decisions. A lawsuit begins in a trial court. The trial court hears testimony from the witnesses and arguments from the attorneys as to what the relevant facts are, what the relevant law is, and how the law should be applied to the facts. The trial court then makes a decision.

After the trial court has made its decision as to who "wins" and who "loses," the losing party makes a decision as to whether to incur the additional costs of an appeal. In making that decision, the losing party's attorney knows that an appellate court will reverse the trial court's decision if, through her briefs and oral argument, she can convince a majority of the judges on the appellate court that the trial court got the law "wrong". That is to say, an appellate court does *de novo* review of questions of law. ✳

Appellate review of a factual basis for the trial court's decision is much more limited. Since an appellate court does not hear new testimony or consider new evidence, it will generally defer to the factual findings made by the trial court. The trial court's resolution of factual disputes will be reversed on appeal only if "clearly ✳ erroneous". Accordingly, most appeals and most appellate court opinions focus on questions of law.

Think about what this means about the cases that you will be studying in law school. The cases in this book and your other casebooks involve questions of law sufficiently close and unclear that someone was willing to incur the costs of litigating the questions in a trial court and then again on appeal.

Virtually all of the cases in the book have been edited by us, your authors. That is to say, we have omitted certain portions of the courts' discussion from the actual decisions that we considered extraneous or simply not relevant for our purposes. Indeed, sometimes we edited a case simply to make it more readable for you. In any event, whenever you see three asterisks ("* * *"), that is our signal to you that we have deleted some material from the opinion as actually reported.

4. *Recognizing what you are supposed to learn in this class*

Here is what Professor Clark Byse, the inspiration for Professor Kingsfield in the movie *The Paper Chase*, told his contracts students at Harvard (and later Boston University) in their very first class meeting:

On the first day of the class on Contracts, there is a temptation to lecture because, as Adlai Stevenson said when he was the speaker at a college commencement, "This is a wonderful opportunity, for there is so much that I, a man in his fifties, have learned in my lifetime that would be of great value to you in your early twenties."

At this point, Mr. Stevenson paused, shook his head slightly, and said in a mournful tone, "But it would do no good for me to tell you those things, for what is important and lasting in life must be learned—by action, by participation, rather than by passive absorption." So never forget that the emphasis in this class is on what and how you think, not on what some judge or treatise writer or your instructor thinks. My function is to assist you to develop your lawyerly skills and understanding of the institution of Contract and of the legal process and the role of law in our society. Developing those skills and understanding can and will be an exciting experience for some. For others, the experience at times may be frustrating, even unpleasant. Some will enjoy being called on and speaking in class. For others, speaking in front of 100 hearers may be embarrassing, even painful—something to be avoided at all costs. To those who dread being called on, I say, Relax. We are all in this together, to learn, to improve ourselves. Of course, mistakes will be made. This is why there are erasers on pencils. There is nothing wrong about making a mistake. What would be wrong is not learning from one's mistakes.

Clark Byse, *Introductory Comments to the First–Year Class in Contracts*, 78 B.U. L. REV. 59 (1998).

5. *Considering competing policies*

While our common law system is based on judicial adherence to precedent, courts can and do avoid following earlier cases. Often, courts "distinguish" earlier decisions, meaning they conclude that the earlier case was sufficiently dissimilar to the present case that its precedent is not controlling. Less often, a court decides in a later case that the rule it established in an earlier decision should no longer be followed.

In such instances, courts turn to "policy." For example, contract law should be fair. **Equitable.** Contract law should apply even-handedly to all members of society. **Consistent.** Contract law should be certain so that businesses and individuals can act accordingly. **Predictable.** Contract law should reflect our free market economy. **Freedom of contract.**

While most of us would have trouble challenging any of these policies in the abstract, all of us will have trouble this year in reconciling these policies in particular situations. Such is the situation in our first case.

Our first case involves the question whether a surrogate parenting agreement that grants custody of the child to the father and his wife is enforceable. The Probate and Family Court judge's answer is that the agreement is enforceable. On appeal, the justices on the Supreme Judicial Court of Massachusetts decide that the Probate and Family Court judge (a law school graduate whom we can assume knows a hell of a lot more law than you do) came up with the *wrong* answer. The Supreme Judicial

Court of Massachusetts's opinion in *R.R. v. M.H.*, edited and reproduced below, explains the reasons that the Supreme Judicial Court of Massachusetts concludes "the surrogacy agreement is not enforceable."

In reading this judicial opinion (and all of the other "cases" in the book), you should be asking yourself, "Self, why am I reading this case"? If, after reading *R.R v. M.H.* your answer to that question is, "Self, I was reading this case to learn that in Massachusetts, surrogate parenting contracts are unenforceable," then: (1) your answer is too broad, and (2) your answer is too narrow, and (3) you should not ask the registrar of your law school whether you can just skip first year law school courses and get to the second and third year courses where professors don't "cold call" on students and the grades are all "A" or "A–" with only the occasional "B+".

R.R. v. M.H.

Supreme Judicial Court of Massachusetts
426 Mass. 501, 689 N.E.2d 790 (1998)

WILKINS, CHIEF JUSTICE.

* * * [W]e are concerned with the validity of a surrogacy parenting agreement between the plaintiff (father) and the defendant (mother). Both the mother and the father are married but not to each other. A child was conceived through artificial insemination of the mother with the father's sperm, after the mother and father had executed the surrogate parenting agreement. The agreement provided that the father would have custody of the child. During the sixth month of her pregnancy, and after she had received funds from the father pursuant to the surrogacy agreement, the mother changed her mind and decided that she wanted to keep the child.

The father thereupon brought this action and obtained a preliminary order awarding him temporary custody of the child. * * * The judge's order granting the preliminary injunction is before us on her report of the propriety of that order which was based in part on her conclusion that the father was likely to prevail on his assertion that the surrogacy agreement is enforceable. * * * This court has not previously dealt with the enforceability of a surrogacy agreement.

The Facts

The baby girl who is the subject of this action was born on August 15, 1997, in Leominster. The defendant mother and the plaintiff father are her biological parents. The father and his wife, who live in Rhode Island, were married in June 1989. The wife is infertile. Sometime in 1994, she and the father learned of an egg donor program but did not pursue it because the procedure was not covered by insurance and had a relatively low success rate. Because of their ages (they were both in their forties), they concluded that pursuing adoption was not feasible. In April 1996, responding to a newspaper advertisement for surrogacy services, they consulted a Rhode Island attorney who had drafted surrogacy contracts for both surrogates and couples seeking surrogacy services. On the attorney's advice, the father and his wife consulted the New England Surrogate Parenting Advisors (NESPA), a for-profit corporation that helps infertile couples find women willing to act as surrogate mothers. They entered into a contract with NESPA in September 1996, and paid a fee of $6,000.

Meanwhile, in the spring of 1996, the mother, who was married and had two children, responded to a NESPA advertisement. She reported to NESPA that her family was complete and that she desired to allow others less fortunate than herself to have children. The mother submitted a surrogacy application to NESPA. The judge found that the mother was motivated to apply to NESPA by a desire to be pregnant, in order to earn money, and to help an infertile couple.

In October, Dr. Angela Figueroa of NESPA brought the mother together with the father and his wife. They had a seemingly informative exchange of information and views. The mother was advised to seek an attorney's advice concerning the surrogacy agreement. Shortly thereafter, the mother, the father, and his wife met again to discuss the surrogacy and other matters. The mother also met with a clinical psychologist as part of NESPA's evaluation of her suitability to act as a surrogate. The psychologist, who also evaluated the father and his wife, advised the mother to consult legal counsel, to give her husband a chance to air his concerns, to discuss arrangements for contact with the child, to consider and discuss her expectations concerning termination of the pregnancy, and to arrange a meeting between her husband and the father and his wife.[2] The psychologist concluded that the mother was solid, thoughtful, and well grounded, that she would have no problem giving the child to the father, and that she was happy to act as a surrogate. The mother told the psychologist that she was not motivated by money, although she did plan to use the funds received for her children's education. The mother's husband told the psychologist by telephone that he supported his wife's decision.

The mother signed the surrogate parenting agreement and her signature was notarized on November 1. The father signed on November 18. The agreement stated that the parties intended that the "Surrogate shall be inseminated with the semen of Natural Father" and "that, on the birth of the child or children so conceived, Natural Father, as the Natural Father, will have the full legal parental rights of a father, and surrogate will permit Natural Father to take the child or children home from the hospital to live with he [sic] and his wife." The agreement acknowledged that the mother's parental rights would not terminate if she permitted the father to take the child home and have custody, that the mother could at any time seek to enforce her parental rights by court order, but that, if

---

2. Her husband had had a vasectomy in 1994 and did not have sexual relations with the mother after October 1996.

she attempted to obtain custody or visitation rights, she would forfeit her rights under the agreement and would be obligated to reimburse the father for all fees and expenses paid to her under it. The agreement provided that its interpretation would be governed by Rhode Island law.

* * *

The agreement provided for compensation to the mother in the amount of $10,000 "for services rendered in conceiving, carrying and giving birth to the Child." Payment of the $10,000 was to be made as follows: $500 on verification of the pregnancy; $2,500 at the end of the third month; $3,500 at the end of the sixth month; and $3,500 at the time of birth "and when delivery of child occurs." The agreement stated that no payment was made in connection with adoption of the child, the termination of parental rights, or consent to surrender the child for adoption. The father acknowledged the mother's right to determine whether to carry the pregnancy to term, but the mother agreed to refund all payments if, without the father's consent, she had an abortion that was not necessary for her physical health. The father assumed various expenses of the pregnancy, including tests, and had the right to name the child. The mother would be obliged, however, to repay all expenses and fees for services if tests showed that the father was not the biological father of the child, or if the mother refused to permit the father to take the child home from the hospital. The agreement also provided that the mother would maintain some contact with the child after the birth.

The judge found that the mother entered into the agreement on her own volition after consulting legal counsel. There was no evidence of undue influence, coercion, or duress. The mother fully understood that she was contracting to give custody of the baby to the father. She sought to inseminate herself on November 30 and December 1, 1996. The attempt at conception was successful.

The lawyer for the father sent the mother a check for $500 in December 1996, and another for $2,500 in February. In May, the father's lawyer sent the mother a check for $3,500. She told the lawyer that she had changed her mind and wanted to keep the child. She returned the check uncashed in the middle of June. The mother has made no attempt to refund the amounts that the father paid her, including $550 that he paid for pregnancy-related expenses.

Procedure

Approximately two weeks after the mother changed her mind and returned the check for $3,500, and before the child was born, the father commenced this action against the mother seeking to establish his paternity, alleging breach of contract, and requesting a declaration of his rights under the surrogacy agreement. Subsequently, the wife's husband was added as a defendant. The judge appointed a guardian *ad litem* to represent the interests of the unborn child. Proceedings were held on aspects of the preliminary injunction request (now resolved) and on the mother's motion to determine whether surrogacy contracts are enforceable in Massachusetts.

On August 4, 1997, the judge entered an order directing the mother to give the child to the father when it was discharged from the hospital and granting the father temporary physical custody of the child. She did so based on her determination that the father's custody claim was likely to prevail on the merits of the contract claim, and, if not on that claim, then on the basis of the best interests of the child. The mother was granted the right to frequent visits.

On August 13, 1997, the judge reported the propriety of her August 1 order which, as we have said, was based in part on her conclusion that the surrogacy contract was enforceable. * * *

Other Jurisdictions

A significant minority of States have legislation addressing surrogacy agreements. Some [state statutes] simply deny enforcement of all such agreements. Some States have simply exempted surrogacy agreements from provisions making it a crime to sell babies. * * * A few States have explicitly made unpaid surrogacy agreements lawful. * * *

There are few appellate court opinions on the enforceability of traditional surrogacy agreements. * * * The best known opinion is that of the Supreme Court of New Jersey in *Matter of Baby M.*, 109 N.J. 396, 537 A.2d 1227 (1988), where the court invalidated a compensated surrogacy contract because it conflicted with the law and public policy of the State. The *Baby M* surrogacy agreement involved broader concessions from the mother than the agreement before us because it provided that the mother would surrender her parental rights and would allow the father's wife to adopt the child. The agreement, therefore, directly conflicted with a statute prohibiting the payment of money to obtain an adoption and a statute barring enforcement of an agreement to adoption made prior to the birth of the child. The court acknowledged that an award of custody to the father was in the best interests of the child, but struck down orders terminating the mother's parental rights and authorizing the adoption of the child by the husband's wife. The court added that it found no "legal prohibition against surrogacy when the surrogate mother volunteers, without any payment, to act as a surrogate and is given the right to change her mind and to assert her parental rights."

Discussion

1. *The governing law.* The agreement before us provided that "Rhode Island Law shall govern the interpretation of this agreement." No party has argued that Rhode Island law has any application to the issues before us.[7] We are, in any event, not concerned with "the interpretation of this agreement," but rather with the legal significance, if any, of its

---

7. It appears that Rhode Island does not have statutes similar to those in Massachusetts which, as will be seen, provide us guidance.

provisions. The child was conceived and born in Massachusetts, and the mother is a Massachusetts resident, all as contemplated in the surrogacy arrangement. The significance, if any, of the surrogacy agreement on the relationship of the parties and on the child is appropriately determined by Massachusetts law.

2. *General Laws c. 46, § 4B.* The case before us concerns traditional surrogacy, in which the fertile member of an infertile couple is one of the child's biological parents. Surrogate fatherhood, the insemination of the fertile wife with sperm of a donor, often an anonymous donor, is a recognized and accepted procedure. If the mother's husband consents to the procedure, the resulting child is considered the legitimate child of the mother and her husband. G.L. c. 46, § B. Section 4B does not comment on the rights and obligations, if any, of the biological father, although inferentially he has none. In the case before us, the infertile spouse is the wife. No statute decrees the consequences of the artificial insemination of a surrogate with the sperm of a fertile husband. This situation presents different considerations from surrogate fatherhood because surrogate motherhood is never anonymous and her commitment and contribution is unavoidably much greater than that of a sperm donor.[10] * * *

3. *Adoption statutes.* Policies underlying our adoption legislation suggest that a surrogate parenting agreement should be given no effect if the mother's agreement was obtained prior to a reasonable time after the child's birth or if her agreement was induced by the payment of money. Adoption legislation is, of course, not applicable to child custody, but it does provide us with some guidance. Although the agreement makes no reference to adoption and does not concern the termination of parental rights or the adoption of the child by the father's wife, the normal expectation in the case of a surrogacy agreement seems to be that the father's wife will adopt the child with the consent of the mother (and the father). Under G.L. c. 210, § 2, adoption requires the written consent of the father and the mother but, in these circumstances, not the mother's husband. Any such consent, written, witnessed, and notarized, is not to be executed "sooner than the fourth calendar day after the date of birth of the child to be adopted." That statutory standard should be interpreted as providing that no mother may effectively agree to surrender her child for adoption earlier than the fourth day after its birth, by which time she better knows the strength of her bond with her child. Although a consent to surrender custody has less permanency than a consent to adoption, the legislative judgment that a mother should have time after a child's birth to reflect on her wishes concerning the child weighs heavily in our consideration whether to give effect to a prenatal custody agreement. No private agreement concerning adoption or custody can be conclusive in

---

10. A situation which involves considerations different from those in the case before us arises when the birth mother has had transferred to her uterus an embryo formed through in vitro fertilization of the intended parents' sperm and egg. This latter process in which the birth mother is not genetically related to the child (except coincidentally if an intended parent is a relative) has been called gestational surrogacy.

any event because a judge, passing on custody of a child, must decide what is in the best interests of the child

Adoptive parents may pay expenses of a birth parent but may make no direct payment to her. *See* G.L. c. 210, § 11A; 102 Code Mass. Regs. § 5.09 (1997). Even though the agreement seeks to attribute that payment of $10,000, not to custody or adoption, but solely to the mother's services in carrying the child, the father ostensibly was promised more than those services because, as a practical matter, the mother agreed to surrender custody of the child. She could assert custody rights, according to the agreement, only if she repaid the father all amounts that she had received and also reimbursed him for all expenses he had incurred. The statutory prohibition of payment for receiving a child through adoption suggests that, as a matter of policy, a mother's agreement to surrender custody in exchange for money (beyond pregnancy-related expenses) should be given no effect in deciding the custody of the child.

4. *Conclusion.* The mother's purported consent to custody in the agreement is ineffective because no such consent should be recognized unless given on or after the fourth day following the child's birth. In reaching this conclusion, we apply to consent to custody the same principle which underlies the statutory restriction on when a mother's consent to adoption may be effectively given. Moreover, the payment of money to influence the mother's custody decision makes the agreement as to custody void. Eliminating any financial reward to a surrogate mother is the only way to assure that no economic pressure will cause a woman, who may well be a member of an economically vulnerable class, to act as a surrogate. It is true that a surrogate enters into the agreement before she becomes pregnant and thus is not presented with the desperation that a poor unwed pregnant woman may confront. However, compensated surrogacy arrangements raise the concern that, under financial pressure, a woman will permit her body to be used and her child to be given away.

There is no doubt that compensation was a factor in inducing the mother to enter into the surrogacy agreement and to cede custody to the father. If the payment of $10,000 was really only compensation for the mother's services in carrying the child and giving birth and was unrelated to custody of the child, the agreement would not have provided that the mother must refund all compensation paid (and expenses paid) if she should challenge the father's right to custody. Or would the agreement have provided that final payment be made only when the child is delivered to the father? We simply decline, on public policy grounds, to apply to a surrogacy agreement of the type involved here the general principle that an agreement between informed, mature adults should be enforced absent proof of duress, fraud, or undue influence.

We recognize that there is nothing inherently unlawful in an arrangement by which an informed woman agrees to attempt to conceive artificially and give birth to a child whose father would be the husband of an infertile wife. We suspect that many such arrangements are made and carried out without disagreement.

If no compensation is paid beyond pregnancy-related expenses and if the mother is not bound by her consent to the father's custody of the child unless she consents after a suitable period has passed following the child's birth, the objections we have identified in this opinion to the enforceability of a surrogate's consent to custody would be overcome. Other conditions might be important in deciding the enforceability of a surrogacy agreement, such as a requirement that (a) the mother's husband give his informed consent to the agreement in advance; (b) the mother be an adult and have had at least one successful pregnancy; (c) the mother, her husband, and the intended parents have been evaluated for the soundness of their judgment and for their capacity to carry out the agreement; (d) the father's wife be incapable of bearing a child without endangering her health; (e) the intended parents be suitable persons to assume custody of the child; and (f) all parties have the advice of counsel. The mother and father may not, however, make a binding best-interests-of-the-child determination by private agreement. Any custody agreement is subject to a judicial determination of custody based on the best interests of the child.

The conditions that we describe are not likely to be satisfactory to an intended father because, following the birth of the child, the mother can refuse to consent to the father's custody even though the father has incurred substantial pregnancy-related expenses. A surrogacy agreement judicially approved before conception may be a better procedure, as is permitted by statutes in Virginia and New Hampshire. A Massachusetts statute concerning surrogacy agreements, pro or con, would provide guidance to judges, lawyers, infertile couples interested in surrogate parenthood, and prospective surrogate mothers.

We do not reach but comment briefly on the mother's argument that the agreement was unconscionable. She actively sought to become a surrogate and entered into the surrogacy agreement voluntarily, advised by counsel, not under duress, and fully informed. Unconscionability is not apparent on this record.

A declaration shall be entered that the surrogacy agreement is not enforceable. Such further orders as may be appropriate, consistent with this opinion, may be entered in the Probate and Family Court.

So ordered.

QUESTIONS, NOTE, AND CONNECTIONS

1. Questions about the facts of this case
    1.1. What was the mother's "best" fact; that is, the fact that you would emphasize if you were representing the mother?
    1.2. What is the father's best fact?

1.3. Was the agreement process in *R.R. v. M.H.* fair? Was that relevant to the court's decision? Should it be?

1.4. Show me the money! Did the agreement require the genetic father to make payments to the mother? Was that relevant to the court's decision? Should it be?

1.5. Show me the kid! Was it in the best interests of the child to remain with her birth mother? Was that relevant to the specific question the court answered; i.e., the enforceability of the surrogacy agreement? Should it be? What happened to the kid?

2. Questions about the law

2.1. Do adoptions involve contracts? Did this case involve an adoption? If not, why did the court discuss adoption statutes?

2.2. Will the court's opinion in *R.R. v. M.H.* be helpful to the next attorney who draws up a surrogacy parenting contract involving a surrogate mother who is a Massachusetts resident? Do you think that there will even be such a "next" surrogate parenting contract involving a surrogate mother who is a Massachusetts resident?

2.3. The court noted that "surrogate fatherhood, the insemination of the fertile wife with the sperm of a donor, often an anonymous donor, is a recognized and accepted procedure." Assume that Epstein enters into an artificial insemination agreement whereby: (i) he provides sperm,* (ii) Lisa Cuddy pays Epstein $10,000, and (iii) Lisa Cuddy will have custody of any child that results from her artificial insemination. Epstein later changes his mind about relinquishing custody rights. Would this court find such a surrogacy agreement unenforceable?

2.4. Another medically-accepted surrogacy procedure involves implanting the embryo created by the egg and sperm of a man and woman in another woman. To illustrate, eggs from J.R. were artificially inseminated with sperm from J.F. and then implanted in D.B. who subsequently gave birth. J.R., the "egg donor" was paid $2,500 and D.B., the gestational surrogate, was paid $20,000 by J.F. and his wife. If the agreements for such a gestational surrogacy arrangement were similar to the agreement in *R.R. v. M.H.*, would the Supreme Judicial Court of Massachusetts find the agreements unenforceable? How about if the agreement between J.F. and D.B. provided that "D.B. will not attempt to form a parent-child relationship with any child conceived pursuant to the contract, and will institute proceedings upon the birth of any child to terminate her parental rights"? *See*** *J.F. v. D.B.,* 116 Ohio St.3d 363, 879 N.E.2d 740 (2007).

---

* We understand that Epstein is old; *really* old. And, yes, there is a contracts' concept that you may have learned about in an undergraduate Business Law course that undergraduate Business Law teachers call "impossibility." We will deal with that concept later, but for now, forget about it so it doesn't interfere with the question we are currently posing.

** "See" does not mean that you are really supposed to go see these cases. "See" is an "introductory signal" that indicates that "the cited authority directly states or clearly supports the proposition." *See* (sic) THE BLUEBOOK: A UNIFORM SYSTEM OF CITATIONS R. 1.2(a) at 22–23

3. Note

> According to Professor Gillian Hadfield of University of Southern California Law School, "contract pregnancy" raises two difficult policy questions.
>
> The first is a public-law question and is concerned with whether, as a society, we should permit individuals to contract for the conception of a child and the allocation of parental status. This question raises the specter of commodification, and feminists grapple with the implications for children, women and sexuality of the use of market mechanisms to structure childbirth and parenting. The second question is a private-law contract puzzle. It is concerned with whether in a given case in which the birth mother refuses to relinquish her parental status and in the absence of public-law prohibition, contract law should find that the birth mother has a contractual obligation to release the child. Further, the second question asks whether any breach of this obligation should be remedied with an order of specific performance as opposed to an order for compensation.
>
> Gillian K. Hadfield, *An Expressive Theory of Contract: From Feminist Dilemmas to a Reconceptualization of Rational Choice in Contract Law*, 146 U. PA. L. REV. 1235, 1240 (1998). Professor Richard Epstein of University of Chicago Law School has answers for Professor Hadfield's policy questions: unless there is fraud or duress, there should be "full contract enforcement" for surrogacy contracts. Richard A. Epstein, *Surrogacy: The Case For Full Contractual Enforcement*, 81 VA. L. REV. 2305 (1995).
>
> We will reconsider *R.R. v. M.H.* and Professor Hadfield's questions and the other Professor Epstein's answer when we consider contract law reasons for not enforcing an agreement in Chapter 3 and how courts enforce contracts in Chapter 6.

4. Connections:

> Before *R.R. v. M.H.* we asked you to ask yourself, "Why am I reading this case"? Throughout the book, as you read new cases, we also want you to ask yourself, "Self, how does this case relate to other cases I've read"? Obviously, you can't answer the latter question now because *R.R. v. M.H.* is the only case you've read.
>
> The reason we suggest you do this, beginning after you read another case and from then on, is that, at the end of the semester when you take the final exam (on which your grade in the course and probably your entire future will depend), what your professor will want to see

---

(Columbia Law Review Ass'n et al. eds., 18th ed. 2005). All of you will actually see "the Bluebook" in your first year of law school (and your second and third years of law school if you "make law review"). A law professor with a typical law professor-like sense of humor once described the Bluebook as the "Bible of citation form" or even the "Kama Sutra of legal citation." It is at once "Divine Word" and Divine Comedy, holy writ and sexual manual rolled in one. (Yes, that is why they say "Make love, not law review"). Gil Grantmore, *The Death of Contra*, 52 STAN. L. REV. 889, 890 (2000) (The use of the phony name, Gil Grantmore, is another example of what passes for humor in stuff written by law professors; it is a "spoof" of the name of a "famous," and dead, law professor, Grant Gilmore who (while still alive) wrote a book entitled THE DEATH OF CONTRACT.)

is not whether you can simply regurgitate the rules of contract law, but rather whether you can *integrate* the materials covered over the course of the semester and apply them in a thoughtful and coherent manner. In other words, although we have tried to edit the cases and other materials so that you are learning contracts one concept at a time, what you will be expected to do on the final is combine and synthesize these materials. We hope our occasional "connections" sections will assist you in this endeavor.

Now, you think you have finally gotten all of this "introductory stuff" out of the way, and you almost have, but before we move on to Chapter 2 and all of the great cases to come, we want to say one more word about the lawyer's role in contract law, which entails how parties sometimes attempt to avoid the formal litigation process entirely.

SECTION 6: THE LAWYER'S ROLE IN CONTRACT LAW REVISITED— COMMERCIAL ARBITRATION

The remainder of this book is filled with cases that arose when one party sued another in court. This is where much of our law of contracts has traditionally been, and will continue to be, made—in decided and published judicial decisions. However, it is important to realize that most actual contract disputes are disposed of by other means. It has always been the case that, on many occasions, the parties will "settle" their dispute by some form of negotiated agreement reached either before a lawsuit is filed, or after filing but before a final judgment is rendered by a court. Recent decades, however, have also witnessed the rise of so-called "alternative dispute resolution" (ADR) mechanisms whereby the parties will agree to have their disputes resolved by submittal to a private legal regime instead of instituting a lawsuit in court.

Arbitration provisions are frequently utilized by businesses in standard printed form consumer contracts to deprive the computer purchaser, cell phone user, bank or brokerage customer, etc. of effective recourse to a court of law in the event the consumer is aggrieved in some fashion by the vendor's conduct. This has resulted in considerable criticism over the use of so-called "mandatory arbitration clauses".* Increasingly, however, parties to complex commercial deals, who enjoy significant mutual bargaining power, will agree voluntarily in their contract to submit any disputes to

---

* *See, e.g., Davis v. Chase Bank USA, NA,* 299 Fed.Appx. 662, 2008 WL 4832998 (9th Cir. 2008) (refusing to enforce an arbitration provision in a consumer contract of adhesion in a setting in which the party with superior bargaining power has carried out a scheme to deliberately cheat large numbers of customers out of individually small sums of money).

private adjudication through arbitration in lieu of suit in a public court. Unlike other forms of ADR, such as conciliation and mediation, arbitration is typically "binding." This means that the parties have agreed to live with the private arbitrators decision and forego virtually any opportunity for judicial review of the arbitrator's decision.

Why are sophisticated commercial parties so eager to eschew conventional civil litigation in favor of private arbitration? Most commonly, large companies express the conviction that arbitration represents a more cost effective and expeditious way for resolving their disputes. Reasons for this include more limited discovery than in typical judicial proceedings and avoidance of crowded dockets. Other characteristics of arbitration—frequently cited by proponents as to why that form of conflict resolution produces more predictable and satisfactory results—include having the matter: (1) resolved by expert decision makers rather than a judge who may have no background in the subject matter of the dispute; (2) decided in a proceeding that is basically confidential rather than available as a matter of public record; and (3) determined solely on the substantive merits of the dispute without concern about the precedential effect of the decision on future litigants.

Arbitration clauses are particularly common in international transactions, and the use of arbitration in these contracts is facilitated by a number of international conventions, such as the Convention on the Recognition and Enforcement of Foreign Arbitral Awards (the "New York Convention"). Rather than face dispute resolution in a foreign tribunal with unknown procedures and of uncertain reliability, parties to these deals often prefer the ability to select a neutral forum in a prescribed location for arbitration conducted in accordance with established and understood rules and procedures.

On the other hand, arbitration is not without its critics. Some contend that, as it has grown more formalized, arbitration has become nearly as inflexible, costly, and time-consuming as going to court. There is also concern over the availability of good commercial arbitrators, the accountability of private arbitrators, and the perceived tendency of many arbitrators to avoid "all or nothing" judgments in favor of "cutting the baby in half" or "compromise" decisions. It has also been pointed out that the limits on discovery posited as an advantage of arbitration can also deprive parties of the opportunity to investigate and establish valid claims.

In the United States, federal and state arbitration statutes establish broad policies favoring enforcement of written agreements to arbitrate. The Uniform Arbitration Act, originally approved in 1955, was eventually adopted by 49 states. That Act was revised in 2000 by its sponsoring agency, the National Conference of Commissioners on Uniform State Laws, and the Revised Uniform Arbitration Act has already been adopted by 15 states and approval is pending in another half dozen or so. Section 6 of the Revised UAA provides:

An agreement contained in a record to submit to arbitration any existing or subsequent controversy arising between the parties to the agreement is valid, enforceable, and irrevocable except upon a ground that exists at law or in equity for the revocation of a contract.

The Federal Arbitration Act ("FAA"), 9 U.S.C. §§ 1–15 was enacted by Congress in 1925. It governs arbitration agreements in maritime transactions and contracts involving interstate commerce. Section 2 of the FAA holds that such agreements "shall be valid, irrevocable, and enforceable, save upon such grounds as exist at law or in equity for the revocation of any contract." The FAA further provides that "[a] party aggrevated by the alleged failure, neglect, or refusal of another to arbitrate under a written agreement for arbitration may petition any United States district court * * * for an order directing that such arbitration proceed in the manner provided for in such agreement." *Id.* § 4. The court should then "stay the trial of the action until such arbitration has been had in accordance with the terms of the agreement." *Id.* § 3.

 When determining whether to compel a party to arbitrate a dispute under the FAA, a district court may not review the merits of the dispute, but instead must limit its inquiry to: 1) whether a valid agreement to arbitrate exists, and, if it does, 2) whether the agreement encompasses the dispute at issue. Moreover, like the Revised UAA, the FAA broadly endorses the enforceability of agreements to arbitrate future as well as existing disputes. Finally, the FAA has been interpreted to preempt state laws that would limit the enforcement of an arbitration provision in a contract subject to the FAA.

The concomitant to the broad enforceability of private arbitration agreements is strict statutory limitations on judicial review of arbitration awards. By and large, an arbitration award will only be overturned if it can be shown that there was some fundamental unfairness in the process. In other words, a review on the merits for errors of fact or law is rare. This deference to the arbitrator's award is seen as necessary to ensure the values of speed and respecting party autonomy in the choice of decision makers. It does, however, also mean that the traditional mechanism for addressing serious errors on appeal at the trial level that exists in the case of conventional litigation is scarified when the parties agree to adjudication in an extra-legal adjudicatory process through a private arbitrator or panel of arbitrators.

This final point has important implications for lawyers advising clients in the planning, negotiating, and drafting stages of a contract. To what extent do the actual or perceived advantages of arbitration—rapidity, cost, privacy, and less formality—outweigh the risks of placing so much authority for conflict management and resolution in a private arbitrator? Can these risks be controlled to some extent by designating the timing, duration, and procedure that will govern in the event arbitration of a dispute under the contract becomes necessary? These are not questions that we can answer here nor is there any single "right" answer in every case. Rather, working with his or her client, and carefully assessing that client's needs in the particular transaction at issue, these are issues lawyers must think about, because good lawyering entails not only the ability to respond to conflict after it arises, but also the skill to prospectively manage conflict resolution at the onset of the deal.

Chapter Two

Has Your Client Made a Deal?

■ ■ ■

The first of the eight general questions that we will be considering in this course is whether your client has made an agreement—whether there is a deal. It is in the very nature of our system of contract law that an individual can decline to deal with another, and even walk away from unconcluded negotiations, without liability. So, how do you know whether and when your client has made a deal?

In most situations there will be little doubt that an agreement was reached *or* that it was not. For example, in our first case, *R.R. v. M.H.*, there was no dispute over the fact that the parties had made a deal. Rather, the issue in that case was whether it was an agreement the court should enforce.

Remember, then, from *R.R. v. M.H.*, that just because we have an *agreement* does not mean we have a *contract*—an agreement that the law recognizes by way of enforcement. The question of which agreements are enforceable and which not is one we take up in Chapters 3 and 4. Later chapters explore how we determine and enforce the terms of the deal. But, if there is no agreement, there's not much point in talking about anything else. Let's begin by considering the question of how you know whether your client has made a deal.

The question of whether there was an agreement typically arises in situations in which there have been various conversations and negotiations between two persons, one of whom now contends that an agreement was reached, and the other of whom disagrees. We need to read the cases in this chapter to gain an understanding of when parties cross the line from "mere negotiations"—from which either party may walk away without liability—to "agreement"—which may commit the parties to mutual performance obligations.

———

SECTION 1: DETERMINING MUTUAL ASSENT

It is frequently said that an agreement is formed when there is a "meeting of the minds" between the parties on all of the essential terms of the proposed transaction. But that phrase is a misnomer. Hopefully, the phrase "meeting of the minds" will never be uttered by you, because, in fact, there is really no way to determine whether there was a meeting of the minds.

As we'll see in the next four cases, the question of whether the parties have made a deal is determined not by ascertaining whether there was this so-called "meeting of the minds," but rather by answering the question of whether there was a manifestation of *mutual assent*. In reading these four cases, ask yourself, "Self, what are the policy considerations which explain or justify this approach?"

LUCY v. ZEHMER

Supreme Court of Virginia
196 Va. 493, 84 S.E.2d 516 (1954)

BUCHANAN, J.

This suit was instituted by W. O. Lucy and J. C. Lucy, complainants, against A. H. Zehmer and Ida S. Zehmer, his wife, defendants, to have specific performance of a contract by which it was alleged the Zehmers had sold to W. O. Lucy a tract of land owned by A. H. Zehmer in Dinwiddie county containing 471.6 acres, more or less, known as the Ferguson farm, for $50,000. J. C. Lucy, the other complainant, is a brother of W. O. Lucy, to whom W. O. Lucy transferred a half interest in his alleged purchase.

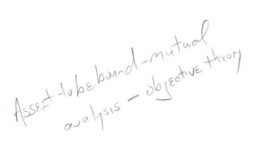

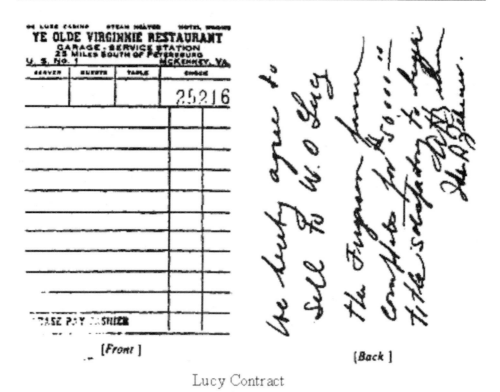

Lucy Contract

The instrument sought to be enforced was written by A. H. Zehmer on December 20, 1952, in these words: "We hereby agree to sell to W. O. Lucy the Ferguson Farm complete for $50,000.00, title satisfactory to buyer," and signed by the defendants, A. H. Zehmer and Ida S. Zehmer.

The answer of A. H. Zehmer admitted that at the time mentioned W. O. Lucy offered him $50,000 cash for the farm, but that he, Zehmer, considered that the offer was made in jest; that so thinking, and both he and Lucy having had several drinks, he wrote out "the memorandum" quoted above and induced his wife to sign it; that he did not deliver the memorandum to Lucy, but that Lucy picked it up, read it, put it in his pocket, attempted to offer Zehmer $5 to bind the bargain, which Zehmer refused to accept, and realizing for the first time that Lucy was serious, Zehmer assured him that he had no intention of selling the farm and that the whole matter was a joke. Lucy left the premises insisting that he had purchased the farm.

Depositions were taken and the decree appealed from was entered holding that the complainants had failed to establish their right to specific performance, and dismissing their bill. The assignment of error is to this action of the court.

W. O. Lucy, a lumberman and farmer, thus testified in substance: He had known Zehmer for fifteen or twenty years and had been familiar with the Ferguson farm for ten years. Seven or eight years ago he had offered

Zehmer $20,000 for the farm which Zehmer had accepted, but the agreement was verbal and Zehmer backed out. On the night of December 20, 1952, around eight o'clock, he took an employee to McKenney, where Zehmer lived and operated a restaurant, filling station and motor court. While there he decided to see Zehmer and again try to buy the Ferguson farm. He entered the restaurant and talked to Mrs. Zehmer until Zehmer came in. He asked Zehmer if he had sold the Ferguson farm. Zehmer replied that he had not. Lucy said, "I bet you wouldn't take $50,000.00 for that place." Zehmer replied, "Yes, I would too; you wouldn't give fifty." Lucy said he would and told Zehmer to write up an agreement to that effect. Zehmer took a restaurant check and wrote on the back of it, "I do hereby agree to sell to W. O. Lucy the Ferguson Farm for $50,000 complete." Lucy told him he had better change it to "We" because Mrs. Zehmer would have to sign it too. Zehmer then tore up what he had written, wrote the agreement quoted above and asked Mrs. Zehmer, who was at the other end of the counter ten or twelve feet away, to sign it. Mrs. Zehmer said she would for $50,000 and signed it. Zehmer brought it back and gave it to Lucy, who offered him $5 which Zehmer refused, saying, "You don't need to give me any money, you got the agreement there signed by both of us."

The discussion leading to the signing of the agreement, said Lucy, lasted thirty or forty minutes, during which Zehmer seemed to doubt that Lucy could raise $50,000. Lucy suggested the provision for having the title examined and Zehmer made the suggestion that he would sell it "complete, everything there," and stated that all he had on the farm was three heifers.

Lucy took a partly filled bottle of whiskey into the restaurant with him for the purpose of giving Zehmer a drink if he wanted it. Zehmer did, and he and Lucy had one or two drinks together. Lucy said that while he felt the drinks he took he was not intoxicated, and from the way Zehmer handled the transaction he did not think he was either.

December 20 was on Saturday. Next day Lucy telephoned to J. C. Lucy and arranged with the latter to take a half interest in the purchase and pay half of the consideration. On Monday he engaged an attorney to examine the title. The attorney reported favorably on December 31 and on January 2 Lucy wrote Zehmer stating that the title was satisfactory, that he was ready to pay the purchase price in cash and asking when Zehmer would be ready to close the deal. Zehmer replied by letter, mailed on January 13, asserting that he had never agreed or intended to sell.

Mr. and Mrs. Zehmer were called by the complainants as adverse witnesses. Zehmer testified in substance as follows:

He bought this farm more than ten years ago for $11,000. He had had twenty-five offers, more or less, to buy it, including several from Lucy, who had never offered any specific sum of money. He had given them all the same answer, that he was not interested in selling it. On this Saturday night before Christmas it looked like everybody and his brother came by there to have a drink. He took a good many drinks during the afternoon and had a pint of his own. When he entered the restaurant around eight-thirty Lucy was there and he could see that he was "pretty high." He said to Lucy, "Boy, you got some good liquor, drinking, ain't you?" Lucy then offered him a drink. "I was already high as a Georgia pine, and didn't have any more better sense than to pour another great big slug out and gulp it down, and he took one too."

After they had talked a while Lucy asked whether he still had the Ferguson farm. He replied that he had not sold it and Lucy said, "I bet you wouldn't take $50,000.00 for it." Zehmer asked him if he would give $50,000 and Lucy said yes. Zehmer replied, "You haven't got $50,000 in cash." Lucy said he did and Zehmer replied that he did not believe it. They argued "pro and con for a long time," mainly about "whether he had $50,000 in cash that he could put up right then and buy that farm."

Finally, said Zehmer, Lucy told him if he didn't believe he had $50,000, "you sign that piece of paper here and say you will take $50,000.00 for the farm." He, Zehmer, "just grabbed the back off of a guest check there" and wrote on the back of it. * * *

After Zehmer had, as he described it, "scribbled this thing off," Lucy said, "Get your wife to sign it." Zehmer walked over to where she was and she at first refused to sign but did so after he told her that he "was just needling him [Lucy], and didn't mean a thing in the world, that I was not selling the farm." Zehmer then "took it back over there * * * and I was still looking at the dern thing. I had the drink right there by my hand, and I reached over to get a drink, and he said, 'Let me see it.' He reached and picked it up, and when I looked back again he had it in his pocket and he dropped a five dollar bill over there, and he said, 'Here is five dollars payment on it.' * * * I said, 'Hell no, that is beer and liquor talking. I am not going to sell you the farm. I have told you that too many times before.' "

Mrs. Zehmer testified that when Lucy came into the restaurant he looked as if he had had a drink. When Zehmer came in he took a drink out of a bottle that Lucy handed him. She went back to help the waitress who was getting things ready for next day. Lucy and Zehmer were talking but she did not pay too much attention to what they were saying. She heard Lucy ask Zehmer if he had sold the Ferguson farm, and Zehmer replied that he had not and did not want to sell it. Lucy said, "I bet you wouldn't take $50,000 cash for that farm," and Zehmer replied, "You haven't got $50,000 cash." Lucy said, "I can get it." Zehmer said he might form a company and get it, "but you haven't got $50,000.00 cash to pay me tonight." Lucy asked him if he would put it in writing that he would sell him this farm. Zehmer then wrote on the back of a pad, "I agree to sell the Ferguson Place to W. O. Lucy for $50,000.00 cash." Lucy said, "All right, get your wife to sign it." Zehmer came back to where she was standing and said, "You want to put your name to this?" She said "No," but he said in an undertone, "It is nothing but a joke," and she signed it.

She said that only one paper was written and it said: "I hereby agree to sell," but the "I" had been changed to "We". However, she said she read what she signed and was then asked, "When you read 'We hereby agree to sell to W. O. Lucy,' what did you interpret that to mean, that particular phrase?" She said she thought that was a cash sale that night; but she also said that when she read that part about "title satisfactory to buyer" she understood that if the title was good Lucy would pay $50,000 but if the title was bad he would have a right to reject it, and that that was her understanding at the time she signed her name.

On examination by her own counsel she said that her husband laid this piece of paper down after it was signed; that Lucy said to let him see it, took it, folded it and put it in his wallet, then said to Zehmer, "Let me give you $5.00," but Zehmer said, "No, this is liquor talking. I don't want to sell the farm, I have told you that I want my son to have it. This is all a joke." Lucy then said at least twice, "Zehmer, you have sold your farm," wheeled around and started for the door. He paused at the door and said, "I will bring you $50,000.00 tomorrow. * * * No, tomorrow is Sunday. I will bring it to you Monday." She said you could tell definitely that he was drinking and she said to her husband, "You should have taken him home," but he said, "Well, I am just about as bad off as he is."

The waitress referred to by Mrs. Zehmer testified that when Lucy first came in "he was mouthy." When Zehmer came in they were laughing and joking and she thought they took a drink or two. She was sweeping and cleaning up for next day. She said she heard Lucy tell Zehmer, "I will give you so much for the farm," and Zehmer said, "You haven't got that much." Lucy answered, "Oh, yes, I will give you that much." Then "they jotted down something on paper * * * and Mr. Lucy reached over and took it, said let me see it." He looked at it, put it in his pocket and in about a minute he left. She was asked whether she saw Lucy offer Zehmer any money and replied, "He had five dollars laying up there, they didn't take it." She said Zehmer told Lucy he didn't want his money "because he didn't have enough money to pay for his property, and wasn't going to sell his farm." Both of them appeared to be drinking right much, she said.

She repeated on cross-examination that she was busy and paying no attention to what was going on. She was some distance away and did not see either of them sign the paper. She was asked whether she saw Zehmer put the agreement down on the table in front of Lucy, and her answer was this: "Time he got through writing whatever it was on the paper, Mr. Lucy reached over and said, 'Let's see it.' He took it and put it in his pocket," before showing it to Mrs. Zehmer. Her version was that Lucy kept raising his offer until it got to $50,000.

The defendants insist that the evidence was ample to support their contention that the writing sought to be enforced was prepared as a bluff or dare to force Lucy to admit that he did not have $50,000; that the whole matter was a joke; that the writing was not delivered to Lucy and no binding contract was ever made between the parties.

It is an unusual, if not bizarre, defense. When made to the writing admittedly prepared by one of the defendants and signed by both, clear evidence is required to sustain it.

In his testimony Zehmer claimed that he "was high as a Georgia pine," and that the transaction "was just a bunch of two doggoned drunks bluffing to see who could talk the biggest and say the most." That claim is inconsistent with his attempt to testify in great detail as to what was said and what was done. It is contradicted by other evidence as to the condition of both parties, and rendered of no weight by the testimony of his wife that when Lucy left the restaurant she suggested that Zehmer drive him home. The record is convincing that Zehmer was not intoxicated to the extent of being unable to comprehend the nature and consequences of the instrument he executed, and hence that instrument is not to be invalidated on that ground. * * * It was in fact conceded by defendants' counsel in oral argument that under the evidence Zehmer was not too drunk to make a valid contract.

The evidence is convincing also that Zehmer wrote two agreements, the first one beginning "I hereby agree to sell." Zehmer first said he could not remember about that, then that "I don't think I wrote but one out." Mrs. Zehmer said that what he wrote was "I hereby agree," but that the "I" was changed to "We" after that night. The agreement that was written and signed is in the record and indicates no such change. * * *

The appearance of the contract, the fact that it was under discussion for forty minutes or more before it was signed; Lucy's objection to the first draft because it was written in the singular, and he wanted Mrs. Zehmer to sign it also; the rewriting to meet that objection and the signing by Mrs. Zehmer; the discussion of what was to be included in the sale, the provision for the examination of the title, the completeness of the instrument that was executed, the taking possession of it by Lucy with no request or suggestion by either of the defendants that he give it back, are facts which furnish persuasive evidence that the execution of the contract was a serious business transaction rather than a casual, jesting matter as defendants now contend.

* * *

If it be assumed, contrary to what we think the evidence shows, that Zehmer was jesting about selling his farm to Lucy and that the transaction was intended by him to be a joke, nevertheless the evidence shows that Lucy did not so understand it but considered it to be a serious business transaction and the contract to be binding on the Zehmers as well as on himself. The very next day he arranged with his brother to put up half the money and take a half interest in the land. The day after that he employed an attorney to examine the title. The next night, Tuesday, he was back at Zehmer's place and there Zehmer told him for the first time, Lucy said, that he wasn't going to sell and he told Zehmer, "You know you sold that place fair and square." After receiving the report from his attorney that the title was good he wrote to Zehmer that he was ready to close the deal.

Not only did Lucy actually believe, but the evidence shows he was warranted in believing, that the contract represented a serious business transaction and a good faith sale and purchase of the farm.

In the field of contracts, as generally elsewhere, "We must look to the outward expression of a person as manifesting his intention rather than to his secret and unexpressed intention. 'The law imputes to a person an intention corresponding to the reasonable meaning of his words and acts.' " *First Nat. Bank v. Roanoke Oil Co.*, 169 Va. 99, 114, 192 S.E. 764, 770.

At no time prior to the execution of the contract had Zehmer indicated to Lucy by word or act that he was not in earnest about selling the farm. They had argued about it and discussed its terms, as Zehmer admitted, for a long time. Lucy testified that if there was any jesting it was about paying $50,000 that night. The contract and the evidence show that he was not expected to pay the money that night. Zehmer said that after the writing was signed he laid it down on the counter in front of Lucy. Lucy said Zehmer handed it to him. In any event there had been what appeared to be a good faith offer and a good faith acceptance, followed by the execution and apparent delivery of a written contract. Both said that Lucy put the writing in his pocket and then offered Zehmer $5 to seal the bargain. Not until then, even under the defendants' evidence, was anything said or done to indicate that the matter was a joke. Both of the Zehmers testified that when Zehmer asked his wife to sign he whispered that it was a joke so Lucy wouldn't hear and that it was not intended that he should hear.

The mental assent of the parties is not requisite for the formation of a contract. If the words or other acts of one of the parties have but one reasonable meaning, his undisclosed intention is immaterial except when an unreasonable meaning which he attaches to his manifestations is known to the other party. Restatement of the Law of Contracts, Vol. I, § 71, p. 74.

"* * * The law, therefore, judges of an agreement between two persons exclusively from those expressions of their intentions which are communicated between them. * * *" Clark on Contracts, 4 ed., § 3, p. 4.

An agreement or mutual assent is of course essential to a valid contract but the law imputes to a person an intention corresponding to the reasonable meaning of his words and acts. If his words and acts, judged by a reasonable standard, manifest an intention to agree, it is immaterial what may be the real but unexpressed state of his mind. * * *

So a person cannot set up that he was merely jesting when his conduct and words would warrant a reasonable person in believing that he intended a real agreement. * * *

Whether the writing signed by the defendants and now sought to be enforced by the complainants was the result of a serious offer by Lucy and a serious acceptance by the defendants, or was a serious offer by Lucy and an acceptance in secret jest by the defendants, in either event it constituted a binding contract of sale between the parties.

Defendants contend further, however, that even though a contract was made, equity should decline to enforce it under the circumstances. These circumstances have been set forth in detail above. They disclose some drinking by the two parties but not to an extent that they were unable to understand fully what they were doing. There was no fraud, no misrepresentation, no sharp practice and no dealing between unequal parties. The farm had been bought for $11,000 and was assessed for taxation at $6,300. The purchase price was $50,000. Zehmer admitted that it was a good price. There is in fact present in this case none of the grounds usually urged against specific performance.

* * *

The complainants are entitled to have specific performance of the contracts sued on. The decree appealed from is therefore reversed and the cause is remanded for the entry of a proper decree requiring the defendants to perform the contract in accordance with the prayer of the bill.

Reversed and remanded.

QUESTIONS AND NOTES

1. Questions about the facts of this case

    1.1. Do you think there was a "meeting of the minds" in *Lucy*? Did Mr. Zehmer really intend to sell the farm to Lucy or was he joshing? How about Mrs. Zehmer?

    1.2. Did Lucy believe that his neighbor was joking?

    1.3. Remember Zehmer's contention that he was "high as a Georgia pine"? Did the court think that either Lucy or Zehmer was intoxicated? Should that matter? Can you enter into a legally binding contract when you're drunk? This is a question of "capacity" to contract, a topic we take up in Chapter 4.

    1.4. If you were representing Zehmer, what facts would you emphasize? If you represented Lucy, what facts would you emphasize?

    1.5. Remember the court's mentioning that the next day Lucy hired an attorney to examine title and arranging with his brother for financing? Are these important facts? If these are not important facts, why did Justice Buchanan mention them? Do you think Justice Buchanan is related to Pat Buchanan? How about Edgar Buchanan?

2. Questions about the law

2.1.   Does the court in *Lucy* take an objective or subjective approach to contract formation? What is the difference between the two?

2.2.   How would the case have been decided if Lucy believed that Zehmer was joking?

2.3.   Of what relevance was Zehmer's refusal to accept the $5 that Lucy offered after the "guest check" had been signed? Was acceptance of the payment necessary to seal the deal? If the rationale for the objective theory is to protect the reasonable expectation of parties, for how long was Lucy reasonable in his belief (i.e., expectation) that Zehmer intended to be bound? Should it make a difference at what stage the offeror tells the offeree he's not serious? Is there a "magic moment" that "will last forever; forever til the end of time"* for determining mutual assent, and that what happens after that moment is irrelevant to determining whether there is an agreement?

2.4.   Even accepting the court's explanation in *Lucy* for how the existence of contractual assent is to be ascertained by the courts when there is a dispute between the parties, is it clear that a reasonable person in Lucy's position would have understood from Zehmer's outward manifestations an intent to sell the farm for $50,000? Is it appropriate to look only at the words used? If not, what other factors were relevant in *Lucy* that were arguably overlooked by the Virginia Supreme Court. Even if the Supreme Court correctly concluded that the trial court had applied the wrong legal standard for determining intention to be bound, was it appropriate for the Supreme Court, as a matter of law, to decide that Lucy "wins"; i.e., that Lucy was entitled to judgment for specific performance?

2.5.   Can you now articulate the legal standard for ascertaining mutual assent? Can you define "offer," "acceptance," "specific performance," or "remand"? If not, don't worry, it's still early in the semester, so just keep reading (perhaps more carefully and with Black's Law Dictionary by your side)!

3.   Notes

3.1.   In ascertaining the existence of a binding contract, the courts examine and give legal effect to the outward manifestation of the parties, regardless of what either party may have privately or secretly intended. The question then is not what the offeror may have actually meant by what she said, but the reasonable impression created in the mind of the offeree by the words used and the conduct engaged in by the offeror. This is known as the *objective theory* of contract formation.

Consider this statement from an opinion by Judge Richard Posner of the United States Court of Appeals for the Seventh Circuit: "The

---

* "This Magic Moment" http://www.lynchnet.com/lh/magic.html Regardless of whether "This Magic Moment" is helpful to you in your efforts to make sense of contracts, Epstein claims that it was helpful to him in his efforts to "make out" in the '60's. We don't know whether Epstein is referring to the 1960's or his sixties.

premise—that a 'meeting of the minds' is required for a binding contract is strained. Most contract disputes arise because the parties did not foresee and provide for some contingency that has not materialized—so there was no meeting of the minds on the matter at issue—yet such disputes are treated as disputes over contractual meaning. * * * So a literal meeting of the minds is not required for an enforceable contract, which is fortunate, since courts are not renowned as mind readers." *Colfax Envelope Corp. v. Local No. 458–3M*, 20 F.3d 750, 752 (7th Cir. 1994). Judge Posner is really smart and writes a lot of opinions, law review articles, and books—stuff that is not always easy to understand. If a literal meeting of the minds is not required to establish a contract, what is required? A figurative meeting of the minds? Is Judge Posner's dictum in *Colfax* consistent with the objective theory of contract formation?

3.2.   "The objective theory of contracts provides that mutual assent to a contract is determined by reference to external acts and manifestations, not by evidence of subjective, internal intention. Stated more simply, contract formation depends on what is communicated, not merely what is thought." Wayne Barnes, *The Objective Theory of Contracts*, 76 U. CINN. L. REV. 1119–20, (2008).

The notion that the law of contracts is not concerned with the parties' undisclosed intent and ideas is traditionally regarded as a relatively new concept. Throughout most of the nineteenth century, courts viewed contractual liability as arising from the conscious, *subjective* agreement on the same undertaking. Hence the origins of the term *meeting of the minds. See* LAWRENCE FRIEDMAN, CONTRACT LAW IN AMERICA 87 (1965) (suggesting that the shift from subjective to objective theory of contract formation was a response to the law's concern around the turn of the last century with reducing business risk and enhancing the predictability of market transactions); *but see* Joseph M. Perillo, *The Origins of Objective Theory of Contract Formation and Interpretation*, 69 FORDHAM L. REV. 427, 428–30 (2000) (arguing that objective approaches predominated in the common law of contracts from "time immemorial"). Subjective theory would certainly be consistent with the nineteenth century's general emphasis on free will and individualism. The objective theory of mutual assent obviously places a higher priority on one party's right to rely on the reasonable expectations created by an apparent agreement of the other, a priority perceived as also assuring the need in the marketplace for certainty and predictability.

Although not without its critics, objective theory ultimately triumphed, thanks, in large measure, to the support of its greatest advocate, Professor Samuel Williston, Reporter for the first *Restatement of Contracts*. Objective theory also found its way into the Second Restatement. *See Restatement (Second) of Contracts* § 24.

It is important to recognize that the objective theory of assent has two components, only one of which is purely objective: (1) would a reasonable person in the position of the offeree understand from the offeror's words and conduct an intent to be bound; and (2) did the offeree in fact so believe? Recall Justice Buchanan's statement: "Not only did Lucy actually believe, but * * *"

3.3. In a frequently-quoted passage from his opinion in *Hotchkiss v. National City Bank of New York*, 200 F. 287, 293 (S.D.N.Y. 1911) the distinguished jurist Learned Hand wrote:

> A contract has, strictly speaking, nothing to do with the personal, or individual, intent of the parties. A contract is an obligation attached by the mere force of law to certain acts of the parties, which ordinarily accompany and represent a known intent. If, however, it were proved by twenty bishops that either party when he used the words intended something else than the usual meaning which the law imposes on them, he would still be held [liable]. * * *

> Is this view consistent with *Lucy*? Thirty-five years after *Hotchkiss* was decided, Judge Jerome Frank, actually concurring in an opinion written by then Second Circuit Judge Hand, criticized the "objectivists" as having gone too far. He complained:

> The objectivists transferred from the field of torts that stubborn anti-subjectivist, the 'reasonable-man'; so that, in part at least, advocacy of the 'objective' standard in contracts appears to have represented a desire for legal symmetry, legal uniformity, a desire seemingly prompted by aesthetic impulses. * * * At any rate, the sponsors of complete 'objectivity' in contracts largely won out in the wider generalization of the Restatement of Contracts and in some judicial opinions.

> *Ricketts v. Pennsylvania R. Co.*, 153 F.2d 757, 761 (2d Cir. 1946).

3.4. If contract law is distinguished from tort law as being consent rather than fault-based, think about whether Judge Frank makes a fair point. And, in light of Judge Frank's statement, think about the "aesthetic impulses" that accounted for Professor Williston's wholesale adoption of objective theory in the first *Restatement of Contracts*.

LEONARD v. PEPSICO, INC.

United States District Court for the Southern District of New York
88 F. Supp. 2d 116 (1999), aff'd, 210 F.3d 88 (2d Cir. 2000)

WOOD, DISTRICT JUDGE

Plaintiff brought this action seeking, among other things, specific performance of an alleged offer of a Harrier Jet, featured in a television advertisement for defendant's "Pepsi Stuff" promotion. Defendant has moved for summary judgment pursuant to Federal Rule of Civil Procedure 56. For the reasons stated below, defendant's motion is granted.

I. Background

This case arises out of a promotional campaign conducted by defendant, the producer and distributor of the soft drinks Pepsi and Diet Pepsi. The promotion, entitled "Pepsi Stuff," encouraged consumers to collect "Pepsi Points" from specially marked packages of Pepsi or Diet Pepsi and redeem these points for merchandise featuring the Pepsi logo. Before introducing the promotion nationally, defendant conducted a test of the promotion in the Pacific Northwest from October 1995 to March 1996. A Pepsi Stuff catalog was distributed to consumers in the test market, including Washington State. Plaintiff is a resident of Seattle, Washington. While living in Seattle, plaintiff saw the Pepsi Stuff commercial that he contends constituted an offer of a Harrier Jet.

A. The Alleged Offer

Because whether the television commercial constituted an offer is the central question in this case, the Court will describe the commercial in detail. The commercial opens upon an idyllic, suburban morning, where the chirping of birds in sun-dappled trees welcomes a paperboy on his morning route. As the newspaper hits the stoop of a conventional two-story house, the tattoo of a military drum introduces the subtitle, "MONDAY 7:58 AM." The stirring strains of a martial air mark the appearance of a well-coiffed teenager preparing to leave for school, dressed in a shirt emblazoned with the Pepsi logo, a red-white-and-blue ball. While the teenager confidently preens, the military drumroll again sounds as the subtitle "T–SHIRT 75 PEPSI POINTS" scrolls across the screen. Bursting from his room, the teenager strides down the hallway wearing a leather jacket. The drumroll sounds again, as the subtitle "LEATHER JACKET 1450 PEPSI POINTS" appears. The teenager opens the door of his house and, unfazed by the glare of the early morning sunshine, puts on a pair of sunglasses. The drumroll then accompanies the subtitle "SHADES 175 PEPSI POINTS." A voiceover then intones, "Introducing the new Pepsi Stuff catalog," as the camera focuses on the cover of the catalog.

The scene then shifts to three young boys sitting in front of a high school building. The boy in the middle is intent on his Pepsi Stuff Catalog, while the boys on either side are each drinking Pepsi. The three boys gaze in awe at an object rushing overhead, as the military march builds to a crescendo. The Harrier Jet is not yet visible, but the observer senses the presence of a mighty plane as the extreme winds generated by its flight create a paper maelstrom in a classroom devoted to an otherwise dull physics lesson. Finally, the Harrier Jet swings into view and lands by the side of the school building, next to a bicycle rack. Several students run for cover, and the velocity of the wind strips one hapless faculty member down to his underwear. While the faculty member is being deprived of his dignity, the voiceover announces: "Now the more Pepsi you drink, the more great stuff you're gonna get."

The teenager opens the cockpit of the fighter and can be seen, helmetless, holding a Pepsi. "Looking very pleased with himself," the teenager exclaims, "Sure beats the bus," and chortles. The military drumroll sounds a final time, as the following words appear: "HARRIER FIGHTER 7,000,000 PEPSI POINTS." A few seconds later, the following appears in more stylized script: "Drink Pepsi—Get Stuff." With that message, the music and the commercial end with a triumphant flourish.

Inspired by this commercial, plaintiff set out to obtain a Harrier Jet. Plaintiff explains that he is "typical of the 'Pepsi Generation' * * * he is young, has an adventurous spirit, and the notion of obtaining a Harrier Jet appealed to him enormously." Plaintiff consulted the Pepsi Stuff Catalog. The Catalog features youths dressed in Pepsi Stuff regalia or enjoying Pepsi Stuff accessories, such as "Blue Shades" ("As if you need another reason to look forward to sunny days"), "Pepsi Tees" ("Live in 'em. Laugh in 'em. Get in 'em."), "Bag of Balls" ("Three balls. One bag. No rules."), and "Pepsi Phone Card" ("Call your mom!"). The Catalog specifies the number of Pepsi Points required to obtain pro- motional merchandise. The Catalog includes an Order Form which lists, on one side, fifty-three items of Pepsi Stuff merchandise redeemable for Pepsi Points. Conspicuously absent from the Order Form is any entry or description of a Harrier Jet. The amount of Pepsi Points required to obtain the listed merchandise ranges from 15 (for a "Jacket Tattoo" ("Sew 'em on your jacket, not your arm.")) to 3300 (for a "Fila Mountain Bike" ("Rugged. All-terrain. Exclusively for Pepsi.")). It should be noted that plaintiff objects to the implication that because an item was not shown in the Catalog, it was unavailable.

The rear foldout pages of the Catalog contain directions for redeeming Pepsi Points for merchandise. These directions note that merchandise may be ordered "only" with the original Order Form. The Catalog notes that in the event that a consumer lacks enough Pepsi Points to obtain a desired item, additional Pepsi Points may be purchased for ten cents each; however, at least fifteen original Pepsi Points must accompany each order.

Although plaintiff initially set out to collect 7,000,000 Pepsi Points by consuming Pepsi products, it soon became clear to him that he "would not be able to buy (let alone drink) enough Pepsi to collect the necessary Pepsi Points fast enough." Reevaluating his strategy, plaintiff "focused for the first time on the packaging materials in the Pepsi Stuff promotion," and realized that buying Pepsi Points would be a more promising option. Through acquaintances, plaintiff ultimately raised about $700,000.

B. Plaintiff's Efforts to Redeem the Alleged Offer

On or about March 27, 1996, plaintiff submitted an Order Form, fifteen original Pepsi Points, and a check for $700,008.50. Plaintiff ap- pears to have been represented by counsel at the time he mailed his check; the check is drawn on an account of plaintiff's first set of attorneys. At the bottom of the Order Form, plaintiff wrote in "1 Harrier Jet" in the "Item" column and "7,000,000" in the "Total Points" column. In a letter accompanying his submission, plaintiff stated that the check was to purchase additional Pepsi Points "expressly for obtaining a new Harrier jet as advertised in your Pepsi Stuff commercial."

On or about May 7, 1996, defendant's fulfillment house rejected plaintiff's submission and returned the check, explaining that:

> The item that you have requested is not part of the Pepsi Stuff collection. It is not included in the catalogue or on the order form, and only catalogue merchandise can be redeemed under this program.

> The Harrier jet in the Pepsi commercial is fanciful and is simply included to create a humorous and entertaining ad. We apologize for any misunderstanding or confusion that you may have experienced and are enclosing some free product coupons for your use.

Plaintiff's previous counsel responded on or about May 14, 1996, as follows:

> Your letter of May 7, 1996 is totally unacceptable. We have reviewed the video tape of the Pepsi Stuff commercial * * * and it clearly offers the new Harrier jet for 7,000,000 Pepsi Points. Our client followed your rules explicitly. * * *

> This is a formal demand that you honor your commitment and make immediate arrangements to transfer the new Harrier jet to our client. If we do not receive transfer instructions within ten (10) business days of the date of this letter you will leave us no choice but to file an appropriate action against Pepsi * * *

This letter was apparently sent onward to the advertising company responsible for the actual commercial, BBDO New York ("BBDO"). In a letter dated May 30, 1996, BBDO Vice President Raymond E. McGovern, Jr., explained to plaintiff that:

> I find it hard to believe that you are of the opinion that the Pepsi Stuff commercial ("Commercial") really offers a new Harrier Jet. The use of the Jet was clearly a joke that was meant to make the Commercial more humorous and entertaining. In my opinion, no reasonable person would agree with your analysis of the Commercial.

* * *

II. Discussion

* * *

C. An Objective, Reasonable Person Would Not Have Considered the Commercial an Offer

Plaintiff's understanding of the commercial as an offer must also be rejected because the Court finds that no objective person could reasonably have concluded that the commercial actually offered consumers a Harrier Jet.

1. Objective Reasonable Person Standard

In evaluating the commercial, the Court must not consider defendant's subjective intent in making the commercial, or plaintiff's subjective view of what the commercial offered, but what an objective, reasonable person would have understood the commercial to convey. *See Kay–R Elec. Corp. v. Stone & Webster Constr. Co.*, 23 F.3d 55, 57 (2d Cir. 1994) ("We are not concerned with what was going through the heads of the parties at the time [of the alleged contract]. Rather, we are talking about the objective principles of contract law."). * * *

If it is clear that an offer was not serious, then no offer has been made:

> What kind of act creates a power of acceptance and is therefore an offer? It must be an expression of will or intention. It must be an act that leads the offeree reasonably to conclude that a power to create a contract is conferred. This applies to the content of the power as well as to the fact of its existence. It is on this ground that we must exclude invitations to deal or acts of mere preliminary negotiation, and acts evidently done in jest or without intent to create legal relations.

Corbin on Contracts, § 1.11 at 30. An obvious joke, of course, would not give rise to a contract. *See, e.g., Graves v. Northern N.Y. Pub. Co.*, 260 A.D. 900, 22 N.Y.S.2d 537 (App. Div. 4th Dept. 1940) (dismissing claim to offer of $1000, which appeared in the "joke column" of the newspaper, to any person who could provide a commonly available phone number). On the other hand, if there is no indication that the offer is "evidently in jest," and that an objective, reasonable person would find that the offer was serious, then there may be a valid offer. See [*Barnes v. Treece*, 15 Wash.App. 437, 549 P.2d 1152, 1155 (1976)] ("If the jest is not apparent and a reasonable hearer would believe that an offer was being made, then the speaker risks the formation of a contract which was not intended."); *see also Lucy v. Zehmer*, 196 Va. 493, 84 S.E.2d 516, 518, 520 (Va. 1954) (ordering specific performance of a contract to purchase a farm despite defendant's protestation that the transaction was done in jest as " 'just a bunch of two doggoned drunks bluffing' ").

2. Necessity of a Jury Determination

Plaintiff also contends that summary judgment is improper because the question of whether the commercial conveyed a sincere offer can be answered only by a jury. Relying on dictum from *Gallagher v. Delaney*, 139 F.3d 338 (2d Cir. 1998), plaintiff argues that a federal judge comes from a "narrow segment of the enormously broad American socio-economic spectrum," and, thus, that the question whether the commercial constituted a serious offer must be decided by a jury composed of, inter alia, members of the "Pepsi Generation," who are, as plaintiff puts it, "young, open to adventure, willing to do the unconventional." Plaintiff essentially argues that a federal judge would view his claim differently than fellow members of the "Pepsi Generation."

Plaintiff's argument that his claim must be put to a jury is without merit. Gallagher involved a claim of sexual harassment in which the defendant allegedly invited plaintiff to sit on his lap, gave her inappropriate Valentine's Day gifts, told her that "she brought out feelings that he had not had since he was sixteen," and "invited her to help him feed the ducks in the pond, since he was 'a bachelor for the evening.'" *Gallagher*, 139 F.3d at 344. The court concluded that a jury determination was particularly appropriate because a federal judge lacked "the current real-life experience required in interpreting subtle sexual dynamics of the workplace based on nuances, subtle perceptions, and implicit communications." This case, in contrast, presents a question of whether there was an offer to enter into a contract, requiring the Court to determine how a reasonable, objective person would have understood defendant's commercial. Such an inquiry is commonly performed by courts on a motion for summary judgment. * * *

3.   Whether the Commercial Was "Evidently Done In Jest"

Plaintiff's insistence that the commercial appears to be a serious offer requires the Court to explain why the commercial is funny. Explaining why a joke is funny is a daunting task; as the essayist E.B. White has remarked, "Humor can be dissected, as a frog can, but the thing dies in the process * * *"[11] The commercial is the embodiment of what defendant appropriately characterizes as "zany humor."

First, the commercial suggests, as commercials often do, that use of the advertised product will transform what, for most youth, can be a fairly routine and ordinary experience. The military tattoo and stirring martial music, as well as the use of subtitles in a Courier font that scroll terse messages across the screen, such as "MONDAY 7:58 AM," evoke military and espionage thrillers. The implication of the commercial is that Pepsi Stuff merchandise will inject drama and moment into hitherto unexceptional lives. The commercial in this case thus makes the exaggerated claims similar to those of many television advertisements: that by consuming the featured clothing, car, beer, or potato chips, one will become attractive, stylish, desirable, and admired by all. A reasonable viewer would understand such advertisements as mere puffery, not as statements of fact, * * * and refrain from interpreting the promises of the commercial as being literally true.

Second, the callow youth featured in the commercial is a highly improbable pilot, one who could barely be trusted with the keys to his parents' car, much less the prize aircraft of the United States Marine Corps. Rather than checking the fuel gauges on his aircraft, the teenager spends his precious preflight minutes preening. The youth's concern for his coiffure appears to extend to his flying without a helmet. Finally, the

---

11.   Quoted in Gerald R. Ford, Humor and the Presidency 23 (1987).

teenager's comment that flying a Harrier Jet to school "sure beats the bus" evinces an improbably insouciant attitude toward the relative difficulty and danger of piloting a fighter plane in a residential area, as opposed to taking public transportation.

Third, the notion of traveling to school in a Harrier Jet is an exaggerated adolescent fantasy. In this commercial, the fantasy is underscored by how the teenager's schoolmates gape in admiration, ignoring their physics lesson. The force of the wind generated by the Harrier Jet blows off one teacher's clothes, literally defrocking an authority figure. As if to emphasize the fantastic quality of having a Harrier Jet arrive at school, the Jet lands next to a plebeian bike rack. This fantasy is, of course, extremely unrealistic. No school would provide landing space for a student's fighter jet, or condone the disruption the jet's use would cause.

Fourth, the primary mission of a Harrier Jet, according to the United States Marine Corps, is to "attack and destroy surface targets under day and night visual conditions." United States Marine Corps, Factfile: AV–8B Harrier II (last modified Dec. 5, 1995) <http://www.hqmc.usmc.mil/ /factfile.nsf>. Manufactured by McDonnell Douglas, the Harrier Jet played a significant role in the air offensive of Operation Desert Storm in 1991. The jet is designed to carry a considerable armament load, including Sidewinder and Maverick missiles. As one news report has noted, "Fully loaded, the Harrier can float like a butterfly and sting like a bee—albeit a roaring 14–ton butterfly and a bee with 9,200 pounds of bombs and missiles." Jerry Allegood, Marines Rely on Harrier Jet, Despite Critics, News & Observer (Raleigh), Nov. 4, 1990, at C1. In light of the Harrier Jet's well-documented function in attacking and destroying surface and air targets, armed reconnaissance and air interdiction, and offensive and defensive anti-aircraft warfare, depiction of such a jet as a way to get to school in the morning is clearly not serious even if, as plaintiff contends, the jet is capable of being acquired "in a form that eliminates [its] potential for military use."

Fifth, the number of Pepsi Points the commercial mentions as required to "purchase" the jet is 7,000,000. To amass that number of points, one would have to drink 7,000,000 Pepsis (or roughly 190 Pepsis a day for the next hundred years—an unlikely possibility), or one would have to purchase approximately $700,000 worth of Pepsi Points. The cost of a Harrier Jet is roughly $23 million dollars, a fact of which plaintiff was aware when he set out to gather the amount he believed necessary to accept the alleged offer. Even if an objective, reasonable person were not aware of this fact, he would conclude that purchasing a fighter plane for $700,000 is a deal too good to be true.

Plaintiff argues that a reasonable, objective person would have understood the commercial to make a serious offer of a Harrier Jet because there was "absolutely no distinction in the manner" in which the items in the commercial were presented. Plaintiff also relies upon a press release highlighting the promotional campaign, issued by defendant, in which "no mention is made by [defendant] of humor, or anything of the sort." These arguments suggest merely that the humor of the promotional campaign was tongue in cheek. Humor is not limited to what Justice Cardozo called "the rough and boisterous joke * * * [that] evokes its own guffaws." *Murphy v. Steeplechase Amusement Co.*, 250 N.Y. 479, 483, 166 N.E. 173, 174 (1929). In light of the obvious absurdity of the commercial, the Court rejects plaintiff's argument that the commercial was not clearly in jest.

* * *

III. Conclusion

* * *

In sum, there are three reasons why plaintiff's demand cannot prevail as a matter of law. First, the commercial was merely an advertisement, not a unilateral offer. Second, the tongue-in-cheek attitude of the commercial would not cause a reasonable person to conclude that a soft drink company would be giving away fighter planes as part of a promotion. * * * [The third reason related to the absence of a "writing" as required under a contract law doctrine known as the "Statute of Frauds."*]

For the reasons stated above, the Court grants defendant's motion for summary judgment. The Clerk of Court is instructed to close these cases. Any pending motions are moot.

SO ORDERED.

_____

QUESTIONS

1. Questions about the facts of this case

     1.1. You can, of course, see the Pepsi/Harrier Jet commercial on Youtube, http://www.youtoube.com/watch?v=ZdackF@H7Qc. After watching, do you agree with Judge Wood's description of the commercial? What do you think you would have understood had you seen the Pepsi promotion commercial when it was first aired?

     1.2. Are there facts that tend to show that John Leonard regarded the commercial as a serious offer by Pepsi? Does that matter?

     1.3. Before John Leonard's attorney made the tactical decision to argue that a jury, unlike Judge Wood, would be "young, open to adventure, willing to do the unconventional," should he have known more facts about Judge Wood—facts such as her consistently being voted #1 "Superhottie" of the female federal judiciary. *cf* http://underneaththeirrobes.blogs.com/main/2004/07/female_superhot.html, and her briefly training to be Playboy bunny before attending Harvard Law School. http://www.nydailynews.com/archives/news/1995/08/06/1995-08-06_quite_an_other_woman_brill.html?

_____

* We will come back to this doctrine in Chapter 4. Eds.

2. Questions about the law

    2.1. Pepsi contends that it was only joking, and the court concludes it did not make an offer. Zehmer contends that he was only joking, and the court concludes that he did make an offer. Are *Leonard* and *Lucy* inconsistent?

    2.2. If a federal judge lacks "the current real-life experience required in interpreting subtle sexual dynamics of the workplace based on nuances, subtle perceptions, and implicit communications," how can that same judge, coming from a "narrow segment of the enormously broad American socioeconomic spectrum," relate to how a member of the "Pepsi Generation" might perceive the commercial? Just who is this "reasonable person" that Leonard's attorney has in mind? That Judge Wood is talking about?

    2.3. When is the question of whether a promise conveys an offer a question for the jury, and when should it be decided by a judge? Should Judge Wood have at least let this question go to a jury of Mr. Leonard's peers? Are *Gallagher* (one of the cases on which Leonard's attorney relied) and *Leonard* inconsistent?

GLEASON v. FREEMAN

United States District Court for the Western District of Tennessee
2008 WL 2485607

Jon P. McCalla, District Judge.

* * *

I. Background

This case arises from the failed negotiations for the sale of the former home of Elvis Presley following its auction online at eBay.com ("eBay"). On April 14, 2006, Defendants Michael Freeman and Cindy Hazen listed an auction for their historic home, formerly owned by Elvis Presley, at 1034 Audubon Drive, Memphis, Tennessee ("Defendants' house"), on eBay. Defendants hired Stephen Shutts to act as their agent for the auction. Plaintiffs Peter Gleason, Uri Geller, and Lisbeth Silvandersson formed a partnership to participate in the auction using Gleason's eBay account to pre-qualify and bid on Defendants' house.

Before participating in the real estate auction, Plaintiffs consented to eBay's terms and conditions of use, which stated in part that "eBay Real Estate auction-style advertisements of real property do not involve legally binding offers to buy and sell. Instead, eBay Real Estate's auctions are simply a way for sellers to advertise their real estate and meet potential buyers" Shutts added the following statement to Defendants' auction page: "[p]lease note that bidding on eBay is a legally binding contract in which the winner commits to following through on the purchase." When

Defendants asked Shutts about this language, he told them that it was used to deter frivolous bidders. Defendants never asked Shutts to remove this language from the auction posting.

* * *

During the auction and before Plaintiffs' final bid, Shutts informed Gleason that Hazen planned to keep possession of the house for sixty days after closing. On May 14, 2006, bidding ended, and Plaintiffs received an automated email from eBay notifying them that their bid of $905,100.00 was the winning one. * * *

On May 16, 2006, Kathleen Webb, Defendants' real estate attorney, sent the parties a "proposed sales contract" that she had used on previous real estate auctions. The "proposed sales contract" had a blank space for the parties to insert the deposit amount and a clause giving Plaintiffs possession immediately after the closing. The parties negotiated a deposit amount of $5,000.00 from each of the three buyers, and Kathleen Webb sent a new "proposed sales contract" on May 21, 2006, with those amounts and the sixty day possession term included. On May 24, 2006, Gleason returned the signed contract with the time of possession provision crossed out, along with a check in the amount of $5,000.00 to be held in escrow as a deposit on the house. Kathleen Webb then sent out an email to all the parties informing them that Gleason would like to talk to the sellers about the sixty day provision. The parties had no further contact.

On May 27, 2006, Mike Curb [made an offer to defendants] to buy the house for $1,000,000.00. Mike Curb and Defendants signed a contract for the sale of the house on May 30, 2006. Plaintiffs filed this action on July 17, 2006, claiming breach of contract, fraud, and negligent misrepresentation.

* * *

III. Analysis

A. Breach of Contract

In Tennessee, a plaintiff must prove three elements to succeed in an action for a breach of contract: (1) the existence of a contract, (2) breach of the contract, and (3) damages which are a result of the breach.

The expression of the parties' intent to be bound and the definitiveness of the terms of the agreement determine the existence of a binding contract. The parties' intent is presumed from the words of the contract, interpreted according to their usual and customary usage. Courts determine the intent behind the words of the contract by examining the meaning that a reasonable person would have derived in the same situation. However, when the words of the contract leave the intent of the parties in doubt, courts must take into account "the situation, acts, and the conduct of the parties, and the attendant circumstances." *APCO Amusement Co. v. Wilkins Family Rests. Of Am., Inc.,* 673 S.W.2d 523, 527 (Tenn. Ct. App. 1984) (quoting 17 Am. Jur. 2d Contracts § 25 (1964)).

Plaintiffs contend that the close of the auction created a binding contract. Plaintiffs assert that the "legally binding contract" language that Defendants added to the auction overrode the contradictory language found in eBay's terms and conditions, which allowed parties to add terms to their auctions but described eBay real estate auctions as "non-binding." Defendants argue that the "legally binding contract" language only obligated the highest bidder to negotiate an eventual sales contract in good faith.

The eBay terms and conditions are silent as to whether or not a term of the agreement may be overridden by contradictory language in an auction posting. However, the terms and conditions state, four times, that eBay real estate auctions are only "auction-style advertisements." Therefore, eBay's terms and conditions are unambiguous in their intent not to make the auction a binding sales agreement.

Even if the eBay terms and conditions were ambiguous and allowed sellers to create a binding contract for sale, there is no evidence of a manifestation of an intent to form a binding contract by the parties in this case. When the words used create a doubt as to the parties' intention to be bound, the Court looks to "the situation, acts, and the conduct of the parties, and the attendant circumstances." *APCO Amusement Co., 673 S.W.2d at 527.* The record shows that Defendants added additional terms to scare off potentially fraudulent bidders, not to create a binding contract. Plaintiffs demonstrated that they too did not intend to be bound to the sale by their high bid when they continued to negotiate the terms of the sale. First, Plaintiffs negotiated a $15,000.00 deposit amount, which was well below the customary 10%, after the end of the auction. After receiving a final sales contract containing both those terms negotiated during and following the online bidding, Plaintiffs rejected the sixty-day possession provision to which they had previously agreed. This continued negotiation manifests Plaintiffs' intent not to be bound to a sales contract for the house simply by bidding on it.

The evidence in the record leaves no genuine issue as to any material fact that the parties did not intend to create a binding contract for the sale of Defendants' house through their participation in the eBay auction. Therefore, the Court DENIES Plaintiffs' Motion for Partial Summary Judgment and GRANTS Defendants' Motion for Summary Judgment as to the breach of contract claim. * * *

QUESTIONS

1. Questions about the facts of this case

   1.1. Are the Defendants arguing that they were just joking or that the auction was just a joke? If the auction was not just a joke and Defendants are arguing that the auction was not a contract, what was the auction?

1.2. Reconsider [or, more honestly, consider] the words that Defendants' agent added to Defendants' auction page: "[p]lease note that bidding on eBay is a legally binding contract in which the winner commits to following through on the purchase." Do we know what Defendants intended by these words? Did the court care what the Defendants intended by these words? Should the court have cared? Do we know the Plaintiffs' understanding of these words? Did the court care what the Plaintiffs understood by these words? Should the court have cared? (Was it perhaps relevant that one of the Plaintiffs, Uri Geller, is a professional mind reader so perhaps the court assumed that Plaintiffs knew what the Defendants intended by this language? *See* 2009 WLNR 12955274.) You are a reasonable person. What do you think those words mean?

2. Questions about the law

2.1. Reconsider [or, more honestly, consider] the words of the court: "when the words of the contract leave the intent of the parties in doubt, courts must take into account 'the situation, acts, and the conduct of the parties, and the attendant circumstances.'" What does that statement mean? What if the words added by the Defendants' agent to the bottom of their eBay page had been "the conclusion of this auction will result in a contract between the Defendants and the high bidder, and we really mean it"! [Speaking of words, should the court have used the words "of the contract"? Isn't the question whether there is a contract?] What (1) "situation" or (2) "acts" or (3) "conduct of the parties" or (4) "attendant circumstances" did the court take into account in this case?

2.2. What is the relevance to the court of the fact that "they continued to negotiate the terms of the sale"? Should subsequent conduct be part of the analysis? What about "This Magic Moment" from the notes after *Lucy*?

SMITH v. BOYD

Supreme Court of Rhode Island
553 A.2d 131 (1989)

Murray, Justice

This case is an appeal by the defendants James F. and Virginia Boyd, and the defendant-intervenors, Philip and Patricia Durigan. The case was tried in the Superior Court by a justice sitting without a jury. The trial court judgment permanently enjoined the Boyds from selling their Narragansett realty to the Durigans, and required them to convey instead to the plaintiffs. We reverse.

The record contains the following pertinent facts. The Boyds own a Cape Cod house on Boston Neck Road in the town of Narragansett. The Boyds decided to sell their house. On January 28, 1988, they listed the home for $325,000 with a real estate broker, Joan Carter. The Boyds discussed with Carter their willingness to include various appliances with the house. They received a written offer to purchase their home by prospective buyers, the Duxburys, but the sale was never completed.

On February 21, 1988, the Smiths viewed the Boyd's house accompanied by their realtor, Gerald Connors. Later that day, Joan Carter called the Boyds and told them that the Smiths were interested in purchasing the house and certain items of personalty for $325,000. The items of personalty were the refrigerator, stove, washer, dryer, dining room draperies, and bedroom curtains. The Smiths and Boyds negotiated over these items through their respective brokers. The parties agreed on a possible closing date of April 25, 1988. Joan Carter filled out a standard purchase-and-sales-agreement form. She filled in the blanks with the items of personalty and the closing date, and the Smiths signed the form.

Meanwhile, the Durigans had visited the Boyds' home with their realtor, Muriel Sullivan. The Durigans decided that they would like to purchase the house. They did not request to purchase any personalty. Sullivan made up a purchase-and-sales-agreement form. She filled out the blanks in the form and filled in April 25, 1988 as the date of closing. The Durigans signed the form.

Joan Carter delivered the two purchase-and-sales-agreement forms to the Boyds simultaneously. She told them that they could accept either or reject both. The Boyds decided to accept the Durigans' offer, and reject the Smiths'. The Boyds signed the Durigans' purchase-and-sales-agreement form. The Smiths then commenced an action seeking specific performance of their alleged oral contract to purchase the Boyds' home.

This case presents the issue of whether the trial justice erred in finding that the discussions between the Boyds and the Smiths progressed beyond negotiations to form a contract. We believe that a contract was never formed. * * *

A contract is a consensual endeavor. Farnsworth, § 3.1 at 106. To form a valid contract, each party to the contract must have the intent to promise or be bound. * * * Farnsworth, § 3.1 at 106. In general, assent to be bound is analyzed in two steps: offer and acceptance. Farnsworth, § 3.3 at 108. Under traditional contract theory, an offer and acceptance are indispensable to contract formation, and without such assent a contract is not formed. * * *

There are two types of intent to contract: objective and subjective. Farnsworth, Contracts § 3.6 at 113. In general, it is a party's objective intent that will be considered as creating either an offer or acceptance. * * * That is, this court shall look to an external interpretation of the party's or parties' intent as manifested by action. * * *

Hence, in order for an offer or acceptance to occur, the party must manifest an objective intent to promise or be bound. Sometimes, however, the individual or subjective intent of a party will be indicative of objective intent. Thus, although it is objective intent that controls in contract formation, subjective intent may be one of the factors which comprises objective intent.

There are instances in which a party intends that his agreement to terms of a contract will have no legal consequences. In this situation, there is no intent to be bound. Farnsworth, § 3.7 at 116–17. In general, courts will honor such intent not to contract if the other party has reason to know of it. *Id.* One instance in which parties may not wish their assent to particular terms to form a contract is when a written instrument is contemplated. The Supreme Court of Maine has held:

"If the party sought to be charged intended to close a contract prior to the formal signing of a written draft, or if he signified such an intention to the other party, he will be bound by the contract actually made, though the signing of the written draft be omitted. If on the other hand, such party neither had nor signified such an intention to close the contract until it was fully expressed in a written instrument and attested by signatures, then he will not be bound until the signatures are affixed." *Mississippi & Dominion Steamship Co. v. Swift*, 86 Me. 248, 258, 29 A. 1063, 1066–67 (1894) * * *

Thus, where the parties understand that a written instrument is to be executed, whether an oral contract is formed may turn upon whether the party denying the contract manifested an objective intent to be bound before signing the written instrument. We hold that when the parties to an agreement understand that the agreement is to be reduced to writing, and extensive preparation or performance has not begun, the burden of proof to show an objective intent to be bound before execution of the written contract is on that party who wishes to enforce the alleged oral contract.

An important policy underlies today's holding. Business transactions require that parties to a contract be able to negotiate without fear that they will be bound by mere discussion. In circumstances where the parties understand that the agreement is to be reduced to writing, and extensive preparation or performance has not begun, the parties to a contract need autonomy to determine whether a bargain will be struck before or upon the execution of such written contract.

In determining whether a party's objective intent was to be bound before or upon execution of the written contract, one must examine the particular case. We shall consider, among other things, the practice of the trade or profession, the prior practice between the parties, whether the written contract was to be drawn up by persons other than the parties, and statements made during the negotiations. Most persuasive will be the fact that at the time of negotiation, a party states that he or she does not intend to be bound contractually until the written agreement is executed.

The findings of a trial justice sitting without a jury are accorded great deference and will not be disturbed unless the trial justice misconceived material evidence or was otherwise clearly wrong. * * * Moreover, this principle applies to inferences and conclusions drawn by the trial justice with respect to the ultimate issues of fact derived from the testimony and evidence. * * * In the case at bar, we believe that the trial justice misconceived material evidence in determining that Dr. Boyd manifested an objective intent to enter into a binding contract before signing a purchase-and-sales agreement.

Applying the above-enunciated considerations to the case at bar, we note that it is a widespread real estate practice that an offer to purchase realty is made in writing by the purchaser's signature on a purchase-and-sales-agreement form, and a contract formed by the seller's countersignature on the same document. Indeed, Joan Carter did not believe the Smiths and Boyds had entered into a binding contract.

As far as the prior practice of at least the Boyds, Doctor Boyd testified that Carter was retained to solicit offers to buy the Boyds' house. This was also Joan Carter's understanding of her role. Prior to the Smiths' and the Durigans' offers, the Boyds received a written offer from other prospective buyers, the Duxburys. Thus it is logical for the Boyds to assume and intend that offers to buy would be made in writing, and that a deal would be consummated only upon their signing a purchase-and-sales agreement. In regard to the preparation of the purchase-and-sales agreement, Doctor Boyd testified:

"I have been involved in * * * several real estate transactions with Mrs. Carter, and I know that at some point in the transaction, when the prospective buyer is going to make an offer and put down a check, at that point an agreement is produced by somebody."

That is, Dr. Boyd believed that the offer would be made by the buyer executing the purchase-and-sales-agreement form. We believe Dr. Boyd's understanding of the transaction was a reasonable and objective view.

We note that as the written contract was to be drawn up by the realtors, the parties and their realtors had to discuss what was to be stated in the written agreement. The purchase-and-sales-agreement form is a standardized document, but nevertheless a real estate agent must fill in the blanks. To fill in the blanks, the appropriate information must be discussed by the parties and their agents. We are convinced that such discussion, considered alone, does not manifest an objective intent to contract before the written agreement is executed.

As far as the statements made during the negotiations, it is true that the Boyds and the Smiths did engage in some very specific discussion in regard to appliances, draperies, and the date of closing. In the complaint, the Smiths stated that:

"5. Plaintiffs on said date agreed to all of the terms of the sale, each term having been defined, and agreed to by the Defendants, and accepted by the Defendants."

Paragraph 4 of the defendants' answer admitted to the allegations in paragraph 5 of the complaint. However, that the terms of the sale were agreed to does not necessarily mean that the Boyds intended to be bound by such agreed-upon terms before they executed the written document. On the contrary, there is much evidence that the Boyds did not intend to contract before signing a written purchase-and-sales-agreement form.

We reverse the judgment below and its order of permanent injunction. The defendants' appeal is sustained, and the papers in this case are remanded to Superior Court.

QUESTIONS, NOTE, AND CONNECTIONS

1. Questions about the facts of this case

    1.1. Did the Smiths and Boyds agree to all of the terms of the sale on February 21, 1988? If not, did they agree on more terms than Lucy and the Zehmers had agreed to on December 20, 1952.

    1.2. Did Dr. Boyd believe that he had agreed to sell the house to the Smiths on February 21, 1988? Was that relevant to the court? Do you recall whether the Zehmers believed that they had agreed to sell the farm? Was that relevant to the court in *Lucy*? What did the Smiths believe? Was that relevant to the court? Were the Smiths reasonable in their belief that the Boyds intended to be bound on February 21, 1988?

    1.3. What did the trial court believe about the parties' intent on February 21, 1988?

2. Questions about the law

    2.1. What "material evidence" was "misconceived" by the trial court judge?

    2.2. What does the court mean by the statement, "Sometimes, however, the individual or subjective intent of a party will be indicative of objective intent"?

    2.3. Why exactly were the Smiths not reasonable in their belief that the Boyds intended to be bound when the parties appeared to reach agreement on February 21, 1988? Was it because the Boyds were joking? Can you reconcile the result in *Smith* with the result in *Lucy*? How about with *Leonard*?

    2.4. Do you understand (misunderstand?) the holding in *Smith* to mean that when the parties intend ultimately to memorialize their agreement in a written instrument, there can be no binding agreement until both parties have signed that written contract? Did the Plaintiffs and Defendants in *Gleason* intend ultimately to memorialize their agreement in a written instrument? Was that relevant to the court? Should it have been?

3. Note

Observe that in *Smith* the plaintiffs were seeking to enforce an *oral* contract. While some wags have insisted that an oral contract is not worth the paper it's written on, in fact, oral contracts, if proven, are perfectly enforceable. However, by virtue of a law (known as the "Statute of Frauds") first enacted by the English Parliament in the seventeenth century, some agreements, in order to be enforceable, must be evidenced by a written note or memoranda "signed by the party to be charged." Recall that the Statute of Frauds issue also came up in *Leonard*.

We will examine the Statute of Frauds at some length in Chapter 4. For now, it's sufficient to point out that among these agreements required to be in writing are contracts involving the sale of any interest in real estate.

An exception to this writing requirement is recognized where the defendant admits under oath all of the elements necessary to a contract. Thus, in *Smith*, the issue boiled down to whether the Boyds, who acknowledged that all of the terms of sale had been agreed upon, also admitted the elements necessary to the existence of a contract.

Obviously, the Supreme Court of Rhode Island concluded that the Boyds had not; can you identify what element(s) was missing? If you're still confused, take a look at *Restatement (Second) of Contracts* § 27, cmt. c, and see if that helps. *See also Continental Laboratories v. Scott Paper Co.,* 759 F.Supp. 538 (S.D. Iowa 1990), *aff'd*, 938 F.2d 184 (8th Cir. 1991) (applying the cited *Restatement* provision).

4. Connections

In *Gleason*, the court indicates that when the words of the contract leave a party's intent in doubt, courts must take into account the situation, the acts of the parties, and the surrounding circumstances. Did the court do that in *Lucy*? If not, was it because the words used by the parties were not ambiguous? Should evidence of surrounding circumstances be taken into account only when the parties' verbal expressions are unclear? How do you think the court in *Leonard* would answer that question? How about the court in *Smith?*

Are the courts' expressions in the last four cases of how objective theory works consistent? How about the courts' application of that standard? Who should decide what a reasonable person in the position of the offeree would infer from the words and actions of the offeror? Who decided in these four cases? Judges, that's who! Markell is a judge! Does that make him a "reasonable person by definition?* How do *you* now understand objective theory to work in determining mutual assent? Can you think of a better test?

---

* Maybe, but Epstein and Ponoroff have their doubts and so will you when get to the parts of the book that Markell prepared!

NOTE ON THE INTENTION TO BE LEGALLY BOUND

Did you notice that in the first four cases none of the defendants made any reference in their alleged contracts to an *intention* to assume a legally binding obligation? And yet, the decisions seem unconcerned with this point in analyzing whether a contract may have been formed. This is because, ordinarily, such an express manifestation of intent to be bound is not required in order for a promise to bind the promisor; rather, it is inferred from the very act of making the promise. However, should an express manifestation of intention *not* to assume a legal obligation affect the enforceability of a promise? Can you justify a distinction under objective theory? Often, in sophisticated business transactions, such as corporate mergers and asset acquisitions, the deal will entail several individual points of agreement that cannot be arrived at simultaneously, but which, together, may be critical to the willingness of one or both of the parties to proceed with the transaction. Assume you represent one of these parties. Once agreement in principle has been reached on some but less than all of the deal points, how would you propose to protect your client's interests? We will consider this question in greater detail in Section 7 of this chapter.

As we saw in *Lucy*, the law does not require, as a condition of enforceability, that a promise be accompanied by an express statement of the promisor acknowledging her intention to be legally bound by her promise. Just the opposite is generally true, however, in the context of promises made in a social or familial setting. Why is this the case?

Suppose one of your new classmates invites you out to dinner, "Dutch treat," promising an evening of good food and good fellowship, but then reneges. Do you have a valid claim for breach of promise? If not, why not? If so, what are your damages? Does your answer (or perhaps your inability to fashion a satisfactory answer) to the last question begin to reveal some of the reasons for the presumption against the enforceability of social and familial contracts? Would it change your answer if your new classmate had said: "I intend this to be a legally enforceable promise? If not, what is it about this relationship as a matter of policy, as distinguished say from an arms-length promise to sell particular goods, that makes the promise unenforceable?

Notwithstanding the law's bias against treating promises among family members as enforceable obligations, in recent years, courts have begun to enforce promises between non-married cohabitants even in the absence of an express statement of the promisor's intent that the promise should be regarded as creating a legally enforceable obligation. For example, in the famous case of *Marvin v. Marvin*, 18 Cal.3d 660, 134 Cal.Rptr. 815, 557 P.2d 106 (1976), the court enforced an oral promise made by actor Lee Marvin (of *Cat Ballou* and *The Dirty Dozen* fame) to his cohabitant of seven years, Michelle Marvin, that they would share equally any property acquired during the course of their relationship. Can you distinguish these cases from other kinds of social and domestic promises where there is a general presumption of non-enforceability unless the parties manifest an express intention that legal consequences should attach to a breach of promise?

Professor Melanie Leslie has argued that the traditional distinction drawn in contract law between "self-interested" market-activity and "altruistic" family relations is misguided. *See* Leslie, *Enforcing Family Promises:*

Reliance, Reciprocity, and Relational Contract, 77 N.C. L. REV. 551 (1999). She maintains that while personal considerations frequently prevent parties in family and personal situations from casting their understandings in bargain terms, "the ability to make gratuitous transfers, and, more importantly, to promise to make such transfers, is a tool that the donor uses to obtain desired intangible 'goods' and 'services' for which there is no comparable market substitute." *Id.* at 568–69. If this is so, should the law's bias against enforcing family promises be reconsidered? Are there other considerations, beyond intention, that make enforcement problematic?

PROBLEMS ON MUTUAL ASSENT

1. Ponoroff offers to sell his car to Epstein for $20,000, but Ponoroff actually misspoke. He meant to say $22,000. Before Ponoroff could correct the error, Epstein promptly accepted. Who bears the risk of Ponoroff's mistake? What if Epstein was aware that Ponoroff had misspoken when Ponoroff offered the car for $20,000? Would it make a difference if Ponoroff had instead erroneously first said he would sell Epstein the car for $2,000? What additional facts would you like to know before giving an answer?

2. Markell had a written employment contract with Epstein's Construction Co. which expired on December 15. Before the agreement expired, Markell had tried without success to arrange a meeting with the president of the company, Epstein, to discuss renewal of his contract. Two days before Christmas, at the height of Epstein's busy season, Markell finally met with Epstein and advised him that unless satisfactory arrangements for a new one-year contract were worked out he would have no choice but to quit on the spot and seek another job. Epstein replied: "Go ahead, you're all right; get your men out and don't let that worry you." Markell assumed this meant that his contract was renewed for another year and, therefore, did not seek alternative employment. However, on March 1 of the next year, Epstein advised Markell that Markell's position was being terminated and that, in two weeks, he would be let go by the company. Markell sued for breach of contract claiming that a contract for an additional year was created during the course of the conversation on the previous December 23. At trial, Epstein testified that he had no recollection of ever making the "you're all right" statement and that, in any event, he was in a hurry during this conversation and had no intention at that point to renew the contract. Instead, his intent was to defer the issue until after the busy season. The trial judge instructed the jury that in order to return a verdict for Markell "you must find not only that the conversation occurred as Markell claimed, but that both parties intended by that conversation to contract with each other for Markell's employment for an additional year on the same terms as his prior agreement." The jury returned a verdict for Epstein. Markell has now appealed, claiming that the trial court erred by giving the jury this instruction. You are a law clerk to the court of appeals judge who has been assigned to

write the opinion on appeal. The judge has asked you to advise her as to how she should rule in this case and why. What will you tell her?

SECTION 2: OFFER

We observed in Section 1 that the courts employ objective theory in deciding whether or not the parties assented to be bound. An objective manifestation of assent can occur in numerous ways. As a practical matter, in most instances, assent occurs simply by mutual concurrence and understanding of the parties. For example, two people are negotiating and at some point in these negotiations one says to the other, "Do we have a deal"? The other responds, "Yes, we have a deal." It is not necessary to determine who made the "offer" and, in fact, it may not even be possible to identify who made the "offer."

In first year Contracts classes, however, the method generally used to illustrate mutual assent is the more formalized, two-step process consisting of an *offer* and an *acceptance*. And, so, it becomes necessary to determine who made the "offer," and, in order to do so, to learn exactly what the heck an "offer" is in the first place.

As you should have already figured out, an offer is the manifestation of assent by the "offeror" that essentially says to the offeree, "I commit to a deal on these terms. You now have the power to seal the deal with your assent to these terms." Look (hopefully, again) at what the *Restatement (Second) of Contracts* § 24 says about an "offer":

> *An offer is the manifestation of willingness to enter into a bargain, so made as to justify another person in understanding that his assent to that bargain is invited and will conclude it.*

Consider the *Restatement's* statement about offers as you read the cases in this section.

LONERGAN v. SCOLNICK

Court of Appeal of California
129 Cal.App.2d 179, 276 P.2d 8 (1954)

BARNARD, J.

The complaint alleged that on April 15, 1952, the parties entered into a contract whereby the defendant agreed to sell, and plaintiff agreed to buy a 40–acre tract of land for $2,500; that this was a fair, just and reasonable value of the property; that on April 28, 1952, the defendant repudiated the contract and refused to deliver a deed; that on April 28, 1952, the property was worth $6,081; and that plaintiff has been damaged in the amount of $3,581. The answer denied that any contract had been entered into, or that anything was due to the plaintiff.

By stipulation, the issue of whether or not a contract was entered into between the parties was first tried, reserving the other issues for a further trial if that became necessary. The issue as to the existence of a contract was submitted upon an agreed statement, including certain letters between the parties, without the introduction of other evidence.

The stipulated facts are as follows: During March, 1952, the defendant placed an ad in a Los Angeles paper reading, so far as material here, "Joshua Tree vic. 40 acres, * * * need cash, will sacrifice." In response to an inquiry resulting from this ad the defendant, who lived in New York, wrote a letter to the plaintiff dated March 26, briefly describing the property, giving directions as to how to get there, stating that his rock-bottom price was $2,500 cash, and further stating that "This is a form letter." On April 7, the plaintiff wrote a letter to the defendant saying that he was not sure he had found the property, asking for its legal description, asking whether the land was all level or whether it included certain jutting rock hills, and suggesting a certain bank as escrow agent "should I desire to purchase the land." On April 8, the defendant wrote to the plaintiff saying "From your description you have found the property"; that this bank "is O.K. for escrow agent"; that the land was fairly level; giving the legal description; and then saying, "If you are really interested, you will have to decide fast, as I expect to have a buyer in the next week or so." On April 12, the defendant sold the property to a third party for $2,500. The plaintiff received defendant's letter of April 8 on April 14. On April 15 he wrote to the defendant thanking him for his letter "confirming that I was on the right land," stating that he would immediately proceed to have the escrow opened and would deposit $2,500 therein "in conformity with your offer," and asking the defendant to forward a deed with his instructions to the escrow agent. On April 17, 1952, the plaintiff started an escrow and placed in the hands of the escrow agent $100, agreeing to furnish an additional $2,400 at an unspecified time, with the provision that if the escrow was not closed by May 15, 1952, it should be completed as soon thereafter as possible unless a written demand for a return of the money or instruments was made by either party after that date. It was further stipulated that the plaintiff was ready and willing at all times to deposit the $2,400.

The matter was submitted on June 11, 1953. On July 10, 1953, the judge filed a memorandum opinion stating that it was his opinion that the letter of April 8, 1952, when considered with the previous correspondence, constituted an offer of sale which offer was, however, qualified and conditioned upon prompt acceptance by the plaintiff; that in spite of the condition thus imposed, the plaintiff delayed more than a week before notifying the defendant of his acceptance; and that since the plaintiff was aware of the necessity of promptly communicating his acceptance to the defendant his delay was not the prompt action required by the terms of the offer. Findings of fact were filed on October 2, 1953, finding that each and all of the statements in the agreed statement are true, and that all allegations to the contrary in the complaint are untrue. As conclusions of law, it was found that the plaintiff and defendant did not enter into a contract as alleged in the complaint or otherwise, and that the defendant is entitled to judgment against the plaintiff. Judgment was entered accordingly, from which the plaintiff has appealed.

The appellant contends that the judgment is contrary to the evidence and to the law since the facts, as found, do not support the conclusions of law upon which the judgment is based. It is argued that there is no conflict in the evidence, and this court is not bound by the trial court's construction of the written instruments involved; that the evidence conclusively shows that an offer was made to the plaintiff by the defendant, which offer was accepted by the mailing of plaintiff's letter of April 15; that upon receipt of defendant's letter of April 8 the plaintiff had a reasonable time within which to accept the offer that had been made; that by his letter of April 15 and his starting of an escrow the plaintiff accepted said offer; and that the agreed statement of facts establishes that a valid contract was entered into between the parties. In his briefs the appellant assumes that an offer was made by the defendant, and confined his argument to contending that the evidence shows that he accepted that offer within a reasonable time.

There can be no contract unless the minds of the parties have met and mutually agreed upon some specific thing. This is usually evidenced by one party making an offer which is accepted by the other party. Section 25 of the Restatement of the Law on Contracts reads:

"If from a promise, or manifestation of intention, or from the circumstances existing at the time, the person to whom the promise or manifestation is addressed knows or has reason to know that the person making it does not intend it as an expression of his fixed purpose until he has given a further expression of assent, he has not made an offer."

The language used in *Niles v. Hancock*, 140 Cal. 157[,73 P. 840], "It is also clear from the correspondence that it was the intention of the defendant that the negotiations between him and the plaintiff were purely preliminary," is applicable here. The correspondence here indicates an intention on the part of the defendant to find out whether the plaintiff was interested, rather than an intention to make a definite offer to the plaintiff. The language used by the defendant in his letters of March 26 and April 8 rather clearly discloses that they were not intended as an expression of fixed purpose to make a definite offer, and was sufficient to advise the plaintiff that some further expression of assent on the part of the defendant was necessary.

The advertisement in the paper was a mere request for an offer. The letter of March 26 contains no definite offer, and clearly states that it is a form letter. It merely gives further particulars, in clarification of the advertisement, and tells the plaintiff how to locate the property if he was interested in looking into the matter. The letter of April 8 added nothing in the way of a definite offer. It merely answered some questions asked by the plaintiff, and stated that if the plaintiff was really interested he would have to act fast. The statement that he expected to have a buyer in the next week or so indicated that the defendant intended to sell to the first-comer, and was reserving the right to do so. From this statement, alone, the plaintiff knew or should have known that he was not being given time in which to accept an offer that was being made, but that some further assent on the part of the defendant was required. Under the language used the plaintiff was not being given a right to act within a reasonable time after receiving the letter; he was plainly told that the defendant intended to sell to another, if possible, and warned that he would have to act fast if he was interested in buying the land.

Regardless of any opinion previously expressed, the court found that no contract had been entered into between these parties, and we are in accord with the court's conclusion on that controlling issue. The court's construction of the letters involved was a reasonable one, and we think the most reasonable one, even if it be assumed that another construction was possible.

The judgment is affirmed.

QUESTIONS

1. Questions about the facts of this case

    1.1. What is the specific communication that the plaintiff points to as the defendant's offer to which the plaintiff contends his April 15 communication accepted?

    1.2. Remember that on April 17 the plaintiff started an escrow and placed $100 in the hands of the escrow agent. Was that fact significant to either the trial court or the court of appeals? [By the way, just what is an "escrow" anyway?]

2. Questions about the law

    2.1. The court of appeals affirms the judgment of the trial court in *Lonergan*. Nevertheless, did the two courts take a different legal journey in reaching the same destination?

    2.2. If the plaintiff's letter of April 15 was not an acceptance, what was it?

    2.3. Quoting from the appellate court opinion in *Lonergan:* "There can be no contract unless the minds of the parties have met and mutually agreed upon some specific thing." Immediately after making that statement, the court went on to quote the following from Section 25 of the first *Restatement of Contracts*:

       A manifestation of willingness to enter into a bargain is not an offer if the person to whom it is addressed knows or has reason to know that the person making it does not intend to conclude a bargain until he has made a further manifestation of assent.

Notice the *Restatement's* (and, in a sense, the court of appeals') phrase "reason to know." Do we know whether the plaintiff actually knew that the defendant was not making an offer with the April 8th letter? Do we know whether the plaintiff had "reason to know"?

MARYLAND SUPREME CORP. v. BLAKE CO.

Court of Appeals of Maryland
279 Md. 531, 369 A.2d 1017 (1977)

ORTH, J.

Maryland Supreme Corporation (Supreme) sued Blake Company (Blake) in general assumpsit in the Circuit Court for Washington County claiming $6,000 damages. Blake filed a counterclaim against Supreme for $12,590.24 as damages for breach of contract. The court, sitting without a jury, found that Supreme owed Blake $6,590.24 and a judgment was entered under the counterclaim in favor of Blake against Supreme in that amount with costs. Supreme appealed to the Court of Special Appeals. We granted a writ of certiorari before decision by that court.

We are called upon to decide whether there was a contract for sale of goods between Supreme and Blake, and if there was, the extent to which it was enforceable.

I.

The controversy stemmed from the construction of the Western Heights Middle School. In such a building project there are basically three parties involved: the letting part, who calls for bids on its job; the general contractor, who makes a bid on the whole project; and the subcontractors, who bid only on that portion of the whole job which involves the field of its specialty. The usual procedure is that when a project is announced, a subcontractor, on his own initiative or at the general contractor's request, prepares an estimate and submits a bid to one or more of the general contractors interested in the project. The general contractor evaluates the bids made by the subcontractors in each field and uses them to compute its total bid to the letting party. After receiving bids from general contractors, the letting party ordinarily awards the contract to the lowest reputable bidder.

II.

From the evidence adduced, it is manifest that the usual method of operation in the construction industry was followed in the construction of the Western Heights Middle School. The letting party, the Board of Education, advertised for bids for the construction of the School. Blake was one of the general contractors who responded. Supreme, a manufacturer of ready mixed concrete, learned through a trade journal what general contractors had bid on the job. After examining the specifications relating to concrete for the project, Supreme, as a subcontractor, wrote the interested general contractors with reference to supplying the concrete required. Its letter to Blake, dated 11 March 1975, read:

> *The Blake Company*
> *P. O. Box 47*
> *Hagerstown, Maryland 21740*
>
> *Attention: Mr. Vernon Tetlow*
>
> *Re: Western Heights Middle School*
>
> *Dear Sirs:*
>
> *We are pleased to submit a quotation on ready mix for the above mentioned project.*
>
> *Please take note that the price will be guaranteed to hold throughout the job. 3,000 p.s.i. concrete $21.00 per yard, net.*
>
> *Hope that you are successful in your bid and that we may be favored with your valued order.*
>
> > *Yours very truly,*
> >
> > *MARYLAND SUPREME*
> > *CORPORATION*
> > */s/ Ben Wicklein*
> > *Sales Representative*

Blake was the successful bidder. About 24 May 1975, fifty-nine days after the bids were opened, it was informed that it had been awarded the job as the general contractor. There was no written notification by Blake to Supreme that Supreme would supply the concrete. Vernon L. Tetlow, Blake's Engineering Manager, testified that he notified subcontractors "as soon as we get a contract that they are going to get one." He verbally notified Benjamin F. Wicklein, Supreme's salesman, that Supreme was to furnish the concrete for the job. "Ben' always asked me "Are we good on that job? Are we going to furnish that job?" I said, "Yes, give me a mix design. Like we always do." That was the way he had notified Supreme on other jobs for which Supreme was to supply the concrete.

On 27 May a quality control engineer of Supreme wrote Blake, at Wicklein's request, submitting a concrete mix design and test data in order to obtain the approval of the concrete by the architect as required by the specifications. Wicklein said that he knew when the test data was submitted that Blake was the general contractor for the project. The specifications for the project included a provision that within forty-eight hours after the bids were opened the three lowest bidders must submit a list of subcontractors to the Board of Education. Thereafter, the successful bidder had to obtain the approval of the Board of Education before changing any subcontractor, and, in the case of concrete, new test data would have to be submitted and approved. In complying with the requirement to name its subcontractors, Blake gave Supreme as the supplier of the concrete, and Supreme was so listed in the contract to build the School.

The Engineering Manager for Blake, Tetlow, explained why there was no formal written contract with Supreme. With some subcontractors, for example the electrical subcontractor, Blake "would furnish * * * a finite-to do all the electrical work complete for 'X' amount of dollars" and enter into a written contract. This cannot be done, said Tetlow, with suppliers of material like stone on the slab, rough lumber or concrete. There is never a written contract covering all the concrete to be furnished "(b)ecause there is no finite amount of money that I can write it for, because we are working with a variable on the quantity of the concrete that's going to be delivered; the same way with rough lumber or stone." He explained that you work it on "a neat yardage, but some would spill over, so I couldn't write a purchase order (to over the entire job)." Therefore, according to Kenneth Lee Wilson, Supreme's Sales Manager, and Wicklein, the procedure in ordering concrete was that "the job superintendent would order what he needed for the next day either by calling our ready mix mispatcher for 10 yards or 20 yards or whatever" or, when Wicklein was on the job site, the superintendent would tell Wicklein.

For a time all went well. Supreme began delivering concrete to the job on 11 July 1975, and it is obvious that the procedure outlined by Wilson and Wicklein was followed. As shown by Supreme's ledger sheets listing invoices to Blake, deliveries were made a number of times a day on various days to supply the concrete to be poured from time to time.[1] Supreme billed Blake at the rate of $21 per yard in accordance with its letter of 11 March 1975, and the parties were apparently content.

Trouble brewed in late October. On 24 October 1975 Supreme wrote Blake: "Due to numerous increases in the cost of cement and other raw materials absorbed by our company since our last increase, we are forced to raise our ready mix prices effective November 1, 1975. * * * We regret we are unable to give any protection on jobs in progress." The price of the kind of concrete required for the School was increased to $27 per yard. The letter was signed for Supreme by its Sales Manager, and he testified that it was a form letter sent to all of Supreme's customers. Blake responded. Under date of 12 November 1975, its Engineering Manager wrote Supreme:

> *I have received your form letter dated October 24, 1975. I assumed then and will continue to assume that this was meant for projects that you have not made a commitment and not, therefore, Western Heights Middle School for which the concrete price is guaranteed for the project duration.*
>
> *If this is incorrect, correspond directly by letter to our office that you intend to default your contract.*

---

1. Through 29 October 1975 some 132 deliveries of various amounts of concrete were made covering about 13 days. Each delivery was represented by a separate invoice.

As a result of the letter of 12 November, Russell R. Reed, Jr., President of Supreme, called on M. William Dutton, Jr., President of Blake "to further amplify the fact that we were forced to raise our prices and to indicate to him that we would be most delighted to deliver concrete to the * * * School at the price of $27.00". Dutton testified that Reed explained to him the necessity for the increase in price, intimating that otherwise Supreme might have to discontinue business. Dutton told Reed that Blake could not accept the increase "because we had bid the job on firm prices." With 2000 to 2500 yards of concrete yet to pour, the $6 per yard increase represented a considerable amount, and there was talk "in the field" that the price "might even go to $29.00." During Reed's testimony, the court asked him: "(W)hen you raised the prices, was it that you felt * * * there was no guarantee or that under the law you were advised that you could any way?" Reed replied: "Our increase, it wasn't because of any legal inquiry that we had made, sir, we just had high costs and we raised the prices." He added: "And, we felt like there was no contractual obligation in a long term on this project." On cross-examination, however, he was referred to the letter of 11 March 1975 to Blake from Wicklein, who, Reed conceded, was authorized to "quote projects," which quoted the price of $21 per yard. Pointing out that the letter said that the price was "guaranteed to hold throughout the job," counsel for Blake asked: "Now, Mr. Reed, you've been in this business and you've dealt with the Blake Company for a number of years on many projects, what does that mean to you?" Reed replied: "It would normally mean that you would do it for the whole job."

As of 1 November 1975, Supreme charged Blake $27 a yard for concrete delivered to the job. Supreme's last delivery was on 13 November. Blake purchased concrete thereafter from two other firms. The evidence is undisputed, however, that it could do so only upon first obtaining the approval of the architect for the Board of Education after submitting new test data on the concrete to be so purchased. Blake received the necessary approval. Even though the concrete to finish the job was purchased at the lowest price obtainable, it cost Blake $12,590.24 more than it would have cost at the original price of $21 a yard. Blake withheld $6,000 from the amount Supreme claimed was due for the concrete which it delivered.

III.

Supreme advances [the following] contentions on appeal:

(1) There was no offer made by Supreme.

(2) Assuming there was an offer, there was no acceptance by Blake.

(3) Assuming there was an offer and an acceptance, there was no valid contract.*

* * *

_____

* At this point, we will only be considering the first contention. The portion of the opinion relating to the second contention appears in § 5 of this Chapter, and we will discuss the third contention in § 6. There was also a fourth argument on appeal; namely, that the contract was

The Offer

It is manifest that what was involved here was a sale of goods within the contemplation of the Maryland Uniform Commercial Code–Sales (hereinafter cited as UCC) Maryland Code (1975), Commercial Law, Title 2. "Offer," however, is not defined in the UCC, and with respect to it we look to the common law and the law merchant.UCC § 1–103.

"An essential feature of every contract is the parties' mutual assent. * * *" Thus, it is usually necessary for one of the parties to propose to the other a promise which he will make for a certain consideration, or to state the consideration which he will give for a certain promise. The promise is an offer. "An offer necessarily looks to the future. It is an expression by the offeror of his agreement that something over which he at least assumes to have control shall be done or happen or shall not be done or happen if the conditions stated in the offer are complied with. Unless the statement gives to the person to whom it is addressed an assurance that, on some contingency at least, he shall have something, the statement is not an offer." Williston on Contracts, s 24A (3rd ed. Jaeger 1957) (hereinafter cited as Williston). So, an offer is always a conditional promise and it may become a contract. It is distinguished from other conditional promises "only because the performance of the condition in an offer is requested as the agreed exchange or return for the promise or its performance, thereby giving the offeree a power, by complying with the request, to turn the promise in the offer into a contract of sale". Williston, § 25.

An offer must be definite and certain. To be capable of being converted into a contract of sale by an acceptance, it must be made under circumstances evidencing an express or implied intention that its acceptance shall constitute a binding contract. Accordingly, a mere expression of intention to do an act is not an offer to do it, and a general willingness to do something on the happening of a particular event or in return for something to be received does not amount to an offer. Thus, a mere quotation or a statement of a price or prices and an invitation to enter into negotiations, are not offers which may be turned into binding contracts upon acceptance. Such proposals may be merely suggestions to induce offers by others. See Williston, §§ 31–33: What this all boils down to is expressed in 17 Am.Jur.2d, Contracts s 33 (1964):

From the nature of the subject, the question whether certain acts or conduct constitute a definite proposal upon which a binding contract may be predicated without any further action on the part of the person from whom it proceeds, or a mere preliminary step which is not susceptible, without further action by such party, of being converted into a binding contract, depends upon the nature of the particular acts or conduct in question and the circumstances attending the transaction. It is impossible to formulate a general principle or criterion for its determination.

Price quote is not an offer

only partially enforceable under the Statute of Frauds, a subject we examine in the next Chapter. Eds.

Therefore, in its final determination, the question of whether an offer was made seems to be one dependent on the intention of the parties, and, being such, it depends on the facts and circumstances of the particular case. The UCC changes none of these principles of law.

Supreme's proposal was evidenced by its letter of 11 March 1975 to Blake. Supreme would now have it be merely a price quotation, and claims that did not contain many of the essential terms of an offer "such as the quality and quantity of the product to be supplied, the number and dates of the deliveries, the terms of payment, the costs of shipment and the time for performance." We do not agree. Considered in light of the facts and circumstances, the trial court could have found, as it obviously did, that the letter of 11 March 1975 constituted a definite and certain offer with the intent that, if accepted, it would result in a contract. By the letter, Supreme proposed to furnish Blake with ready mix 3000 p. s. i. concrete at $21 per yard, net, in such quantity as Blake required for the Western Heights Middle School project. The language in the letter stating the quotation was "on ready mix for the above mentioned project (Western Heights Middle School)," and asserting that "the price will be guaranteed to hold *throughout the job*" (emphasis supplied) may be considered as measuring the quantity of the concrete by the requirements of the buyer, as recognized in UCC § 2–306(1). The contingency was that Blake be the successful bidder. If Blake were awarded the general contract for the construction of the School and accepted Supreme's offer, there would be a binding contract. When viewed with reference to the method of operation of the construction industry and the prior course of dealings between Supreme and Blake, it is manifest that Supreme's letter was no mere price quotation or invitation to negotiate. It gave Blake the assurance that if Blake were the general contractor on the School project Blake could obtain from Supreme the concrete necessary for the job at $21 per yard. Thus, it was an offer, and the trial court did not err in so considering it.

* * *

QUESTIONS AND NOTES

1. Questions about the facts of this case

   1.1. What facts were most pivotal to the court's conclusion in *Maryland Supreme* that Supreme's March 11 proposal was an offer rather than "merely a price quotation"?

   1.2. How significant was Mr. Reed's testimony on cross-examination?

   1.3. Is it true that the March 11 letter was not a "price quote"?

2. Questions about the law

   2.1. In deciding whether certain acts or conduct constitute a definite proposal on which a binding contract may be predicated, the court in *Maryland Supreme* stated: "It is impossible to formulate a general principle or criterion for its determination". Do you agree? Wouldn't it be more helpful to parties (not to mention law students), if we could articulate a "rule"?

2.2.   What is the meaning (and relevance) of the court's statement, "[t]he question of whether an offer was made seems to be one dependent on the intention of the parties * * *"?

2.3.   The court states that this case is governed by Article 2 of the UCC, but nonetheless looks to the common law and the Law Merchant to determine the definition of an offer. Was this appropriate? By the way, what is the "Law Merchant"?

3.   Notes

3.1.   In *Nebraska Seed Co. v. Harsh*, 98 Neb. 89, 152 N.W. 310 (1915), the defendant sent a letter to plaintiff in which he stated he had about 1,800 bushels of millet seed, of which he was mailing plaintiff a sample. He further stated: "I want $2.25 per cwt. for this seed f.o.b. Lowell." Upon receipt of the letter the plaintiff replied in part: "Sample and letter received. Accept your offer." The defendant refused to deliver and the plaintiff brought suit for such non-delivery. The court ruled that the defendant's letter was not an offer but was an invitation for offers, quoting in part:

> If a proposal is nothing more than an invitation to the person to whom it is made to make an offer to the proposer, it is not such an offer as can be turned into an agreement by acceptance. Proposals of this kind, although made to definite persons and not to the public generally, are merely invitations to trade; they go no further than what occurs when one asks another what he will give or take for certain goods. Such inquiries may lead to bargains, but do not make them. They ask for offers which the proposer has a right to accept or reject as he pleases.

Id. at 91, 152 N.W. at 311. Some decisions suggest that the reason for the general rule that a price quote is not an offer is that the price quote lacks sufficient words of commitment, such as "agree" or "offer." *See Courteen Seed v. Abraham,* 129 Or. 427, 275 P. 684 (1929). Is that a sufficient explanation? Does it explain the difference in the outcomes in *Maryland Supreme* and *Nebraska Seed*? Identify the interests of the merchant who makes the quote and those of the prospective buyer who reads it, and see if that helps to sharpen the focus.

3.2.   Should it make a difference whether the quote is in response to a particular inquiry? How important are the contextual circumstances in which the price quote is made? What other problems do you see with treating a price quotation as an offer? What if the quote is not made to the buyer but to the public at large? Does that help or hinder the argument for making the case that the price quote is an offer? Perhaps the next case will shed some light for you on this last question.

NOTE ON *U.C.C. ARTICLE 2*

Because *Maryland Supreme* involved a transaction in goods, Article 2 of the Uniform Commercial Code applies. Section 2–204 is the Article 2 provision that addresses the formation of a contract. It is plain to see from that section that the U.C.C. takes a fairly liberal approach to contract formation, recognizing any manner of assent as sufficient to show agreement of the parties. In turn, U.C.C. § 1–201(3) defines the term *agreement* broadly to mean the parties *bargain in fact*, derived not only from what was spoken between them but also "from other circumstances, including course of dealing or usage of trade or course of performance."

The inclusion of all three of those concepts as part of the agreement of the parties in fact is consistent with the Code's general philosophy of bringing the law into line with prevailing commercial reality and expectation. Judge Posner put it this way: "The Uniform Commercial Code, its draftsmen mindful of the haste and sloppiness, and disregard for lawyerly niceties, that characterize commercial dealing, tolerates a good deal of incompleteness and even contradiction in offer and acceptance." *Architectural Metal Systems v. Consolidated Systems*, 58 F.3d 1227, 1230 (7th Cir. 1995). The test for an offer, according to Judge Posner, is whether it induces a reasonable belief in the recipient that his acceptance is all that is necessary to seal the deal. Thus, the statement "I would like to buy your hamster" is not intended to empower the recipient of that solicitation to reply: "My price is $1 million. We have a contract." *Id.* at 1229.

Article 2's incorporation of course of dealing, usage of trade, and course of performance into the parties' bargain-in-fact means that if a party to a commercial transaction does *not* want a particular prior course of dealing or trade usage to become part of a new contract she must affirmatively say so in the new agreement. In a manner of speaking, this reverses the usual presumption that the terms of the contract consist only of those matters which the parties deliberately chose to *include*. Does this violate the principle of freedom of contract or *freedom from contract*? How did course of dealing and usage of trade evidence influence the court in *Maryland Supreme*? Moreover, the definitions of "agreement" and "contract" in, respectively, § 1–201(b)(3) & (12) make clear that the object is to ferret out as precisely as possible what the parties actually agreed to, whether discovered in the words they used or inferred from other circumstances.

LEONARD v. PEPSICO, INC.

United States District Court for the Southern District of New York
88 F. Supp. 2d 116 (1999), *aff'd*, 210 F.3d 88 (2d Cir. 2000)

Wood, District Judge

[In *Leonard,* you'll recall that John Leonard sued for a Harrier Jet based on a commercial that had been run suggesting the military jet could be had for 7,000,000 Pepsi Points. Earlier, we considered the portion of Judge Wood's opinion focusing on whether the commercial could have been construed as an offer under objective theory. Judge Wood also addressed in her opinion the question of whether a binding offer can originate in a public advertisement. The portion of the opinion containing this discussion follows.]

B. Defendant's Advertisement Was Not An Offer

1. Advertisements as Offers

The general rule is that an advertisement does not constitute an offer. The Restatement (Second) of Contracts explains that:

Advertisements of goods by display, sign, handbill, newspaper, radio or television are not ordinarily intended or understood as offers to sell. The same is true of catalogues, price lists and circulars, even though the terms of suggested bargains may be stated in some detail. It is of course possible to make an offer by an advertisement directed to the general public (see § 29), but there must ordinarily be some language of commitment or some invitation to take action without further communication.

Restatement (Second) of Contracts § 26 cmt. b (1979). Similarly, a leading treatise notes that:

It is quite possible to make a definite and operative offer to buy or sell goods by advertisement, in a newspaper, by a handbill, a catalog or circular or on a placard in a store window. It is not customary to do this, however; and the presumption is the other way. * * * Such advertisements are understood to be mere requests to consider and examine and negotiate; and no one can reasonably regard them as otherwise unless the circumstances are exceptional and the words used are very plain and clear.

1 Arthur Linton Corbin & Joseph M. Perillo, Corbin on Contracts § 2.4, at 116–17 (rev. ed. 1993) (emphasis added); *see also* 1 E. Allan Farnsworth, Farnsworth on Contracts § 3.10, at 239 (2d ed. 1998); 1 Samuel Williston & Richard A. Lord, A Treatise on the Law of Contracts § 4:7, at 286–87 (4th ed. 1990). New York courts adhere to this general principle. * * *

An advertisement is not transformed into an enforceable offer merely by a potential offeree's expression of willingness to accept the offer through, among other means, completion of an order form. In *Mesaros v.*

United States, 845 F.2d 1576 (Fed.Cir.1988), for example, the plaintiffs sued the United States Mint for failure to deliver a number of Statue of Liberty commemorative coins that they had ordered. When demand for the coins proved unexpectedly robust, a number of individuals who had sent in their orders in a timely fashion were left empty-handed. The court began by noting the "well-established" rule that advertisements and order forms are "mere notices and solicitations for offers which create no power of acceptance in the recipient." * * * *Restatement (Second) of Contracts* § 26 ("A manifestation of willingness to enter a bargain is not an offer if the person to whom it is addressed knows or has reason to know that the person making it does not intend to conclude a bargain until he has made a further manifestation of assent."). The spurned coin collectors could not maintain a breach of contract action because no contract would be formed until the advertiser accepted the order form and processed payment. Under these principles, plaintiff's letter of March 27, 1996, with the Order Form and the appropriate number of Pepsi Points, constituted the offer. There would be no enforceable contract until defendant accepted the Order Form and cashed the check.

The exception to the rule that advertisements do not create any power of acceptance in potential offerees is where the advertisement is "clear, definite, and explicit, and leaves nothing open for negotiation," in that circumstance, "it constitutes an offer, acceptance of which will complete the contract." *Lefkowitz v. Great Minneapolis Surplus Store*, 251 Minn. 188, 86 N.W.2d 689, 691 (1957). In *Lefkowitz*, defendant had published a newspaper announcement stating: "Saturday 9 AM Sharp, 3 Brand New Fur Coats, Worth to $100.00, First Come First Served $1 Each." Mr. Morris Lefkowitz arrived at the store, dollar in hand, but was informed that under defendant's "house rules," the offer was open to ladies, but not gentlemen. The court ruled that because plaintiff had fulfilled all of the terms of the advertisement and the advertisement was specific and left nothing open for negotiation, a contract had been formed.

The present case is distinguishable from *Lefkowitz*. First, the commercial cannot be regarded in itself as sufficiently definite, because it specifically reserved the details of the offer to a separate writing, the Catalog. The commercial itself made no mention of the steps a potential offeree would be required to take to accept the alleged offer of a Harrier Jet. The advertisement in *Lefkowitz*, in contrast, "identified the person who could accept." *See* Farnsworth, *supra*, at 239 ("The fact that a proposal is very detailed suggests that it is an offer, while omission of many terms suggests that it is not."). Second, even if the Catalog had included a Harrier Jet among the items that could be obtained by redemption of Pepsi Points, the advertisement of a Harrier Jet by both television commercial and catalog would still not constitute an offer. As the *Mesaros* court explained, the absence of any words of limitation such as "first come, first served," renders the alleged offer sufficiently indefinite that no contract could be formed. *See Mesaros*, 845 F.2d at 1581. "A customer would not usually have reason to believe that the shopkeeper intended exposure to the risk of a multitude of acceptances resulting in a number of contracts exceeding the shopkeeper's inventory." Farnsworth, *supra*, at 242. There was no such danger in *Lefkowitz*, owing to the limitation "first come, first served."

The Court finds, in sum, that the Harrier Jet commercial was merely an advertisement. * * *

QUESTIONS, NOTES, AND CONNECTIONS

1. Questions about the facts of this case

    1.1. What facts does Judge Wood emphasize in this part of the opinion?

    1.2. Do you recall the words of the Pepsi advertisement? Were the words of the Pepsi advertisement important to Judge Wood's concluding that the advertisement was not an offer?

2. Questions about the law

    2.1. If Epstein places an ad in his local newspaper offering to pay a reward to anyone who returns his lost ferret, Chico, and Ponoroff returns Chico the next day, is Ponoroff entitled to the reward? If so, how is Epstein's ad different from the ad in *Leonard*? By the way, make a note to reconsider this question after your class considers the famous *Carbolic Smoke Ball* case later in this chapter.

[handwritten margin note: Yes, very specific]

    2.2. Why is the general rule that "an advertisement does not constitute an offer"? What, if anything, does your understanding of objective theory suggest to you about this issue?

    2.3. If a merchant displays an item with a price, is that an offer or invitation to offer? What does your common sense tell you?

3. Notes

    3.1. In the famous case of *Lefkowitz v. Great Minneapolis Supply Store, Inc.* (which is discussed by Judge Wood in *Leonard*), the defendant actually placed advertisements in a local newspaper on *two* consecutive weeks offering certain expensive items of apparel for one dollar each *"First Come, First Served."* On *both* occasions, the plaintiff was the first to show-up and indicated a readiness to pay the dollar, but the defendant refused to sell the merchandise to him, citing the "house rule" that the offer was intended for women only. The court ruled that "because the ads in question were "clear, definite, and left nothing open for negotiation," an offer had been made which the plaintiff accepted when he successfully managed to be the first person to appear at the defendant's store and tendered the stated purchase price. The court quickly dispatched of the defendant's further argument that the offer had been modified by the "house rule" since the ad itself contained no such restriction. Was the court's holding in *Lefkowitz* concerning the undisclosed house rule consistent with objective theory? Even if so, could you draw a distinction between the first and second transactions based on the existence of this rule?

3.2. Because of the general rule that advertisements are not offers, contract law doctrine and remedies often proved of little help to consumers who were "taken in" by a false or misleading ad. Recognizing the need for additional protection, Section 5 of the Federal Trade Commission Act proscribes certain "deceptive" trade practices, including the notorious "bait and switch" advertising. 16 C.F.R. § 238. The bait and switch was used by unscrupulous merchants to lure customers into their stores with "promises" of deals too good to be true. When the consumer showed to take advantage of the deals, they would be told that the advertised merchandise (the bait) was no longer available, and then be steered into a higher priced product (the switch). However, because the Federal Trade Commission Act provides for only administrative remedies, such as cease and desist orders, many states have promulgated their own false or deceptive advertising laws that permit for a monetary recovery, including attorney's fees, by aggrieved consumers.

[handwritten margin note: Not contract law]

[handwritten margin note: must have damages due to misleading ad]

For example, Georgia's Fair Business Practice Act, OCGA § 10–1–390 *et seq.* provides a private right of action in favor of any person who suffers an injury or damages as a result of consumer practices in violation of the Act. In *Agnew v. Great Atlantic & Pacific Tea Co.,* 232 Ga.App. 708, 502 S.E.2d 735 (1998). Gary Agnew, a lawyer, saw a large sign in front of a grocery store which read: *"Nobody's Gonna Beat Us Now. Buy One Get One Free. 1=2 Sale. All This Week. Single Purchases Will be Charged Regular Retail Price, Second Item Free."* The sign contained no additional limitations. Agnew entered the store, selected two bags of sugar, two boxes of Rice–A–Roni, and two boxes of crackers. The cashier rang up his purchases but no discount appeared. When Agnew inquired about the promotional sale he was told it only applied to certain items, not including those he had selected. Agnew paid full price for his purchases, but then filed a complaint under the Georgia Fair Business Practice Act against the grocery store claiming that the sign caused him injury when he paid full price for the six items. The court concluded that because he purchased the items with knowledge that the sign did not mean what it said, his deliberate choice, and not the misleading sign, was the proximate cause of his injury. Therefore, the court sustained the trial court's dismissal of his claim. Would Agnew have been better off suing for breach of contract? How would you analyze such a claim?

3.3. We've noted that an offer involves some *manifestation* by the offeror of a willingness to be bound upon assent by the offeree. But does that assent have to be expressed in either spoken or written words? The answer is clearly not.

What must be *manifested* is assent, but this manifestation of assent can be found (or *implied*) from conduct. Courts sometimes use the phrase "express contracts" to describe contracts based solely on words, and "implied-in-fact contracts" to describe contracts based at least in part on conduct. There is no legal difference between the two. Both are contracts in the strict sense of the word.

Thus, if you are passing a hot dog vendor who holds out a sandwich that you take and consume, it should be fairly clear that there is an obligation to pay for it. While purely implied-in-fact contracts may be somewhat rare, many, if not most, contracts are partially express and partially implied-in-fact.

For example, when a lawyer expressly agrees to handle a new client's case, there is an implied understanding that the client will pay for those services even if nothing is said about fees (although we hasten to add that we personally think that it is always advisable to have an express agreement concerning fees; the point being, however, that it often doesn't happen that way). However, in situations involving family members or parties who otherwise have an intimate relationship, courts have generally been reluctant to find the existence of a binding obligation to pay for the services. Should it matter, insofar as contractual liability is concerned, whether the client is a stranger or the lawyer's spouse? How about the lawyer's father-in-law? Try to couch your answer in terms of objective theory.

4. Connections

What do the three cases in this section, all dealing with when a communication rises to the level of an offer; *i.e.,* place the power of acceptance on the offeree, have in common? How do they relate to the cases in the last section dealing with the method courts use to determine mutual assent? Suppose Ponoroff sends a letter addressed to both Epstein and Markell stating, "I'm selling my autographed Dirty Harry DVD collection for $100." If Markell calls Ponoroff the next day and says, "I accept" has a contract been formed?

Is it possible for a contract to come into existence without a specific, identifiable "offer" being made? Consider the problem that follows.

PROBLEM ON IMPLIED-IN-FACT CONTRACT

On October 1, 2009, Mongo Markell applied for admission to the Las Vegas State Law School ("LVS") and was accepted for the fall 2012 class. At the time of his application and his enrollment, the catalogues for LVS stated that, in addition to tuition, each student would be charged a Professional Development Fee (the "PDF"). The catalogue went on to state that: "The PDF is one component of the total fee for JD students. For students entering in 2012 the PDF is $4,000 per year, and it will remain at the same level for the three years of the J.D. program." In other words, any increase would be applied to new students only. LVS's catalogues also contained general language in numerous places to the effect that fees and policies were subject to change and that "LVS reserves the right to add, amend, delete or otherwise modify its policies. This includes, but is not limited to, modifications of its degree programs, courses of study, the academic calendar, and its fees, tuition, or other charges.''

On July 23, 2012, LVS's Board of Trustees voted to increase the PDF by 20% for continuing as well as newly enrolling students for the forthcoming year. Mongo complained to his uncle, a federal judge in Nevada, pointing out that based on what he learned in contract law, LVS could not increase the PDF for members of his class. Mongo's uncle was sympathetic, but pointed out to him that there was no formal contract and that the university's promulgated guidelines could only constitute a contractual obligation if the parties had expressly agreed that the guidelines would govern their relationship. Because there was no formal contract, Mongo's uncle told him he thought he was out of luck.

Outraged, Mongo replied, "I bet you wouldn't be taking this position if you were using some of the royalty money you get from your Contracts casebook to help me pay for law school instead of making me take out student loans for the full cost of my education." He went on, stating, "by the act of matriculation, together with payment of the required charges, I believe a contract was formed between LVS and me, which included the express promise not to raise the PDF, and I'm not going to let those flabby-assed administrators get away with this." True to his word, Mongo, along with a number of his classmates, filed suit against LVS. How should the court rule on this claim? *See Kashmiri v. Regents of the University of California,* 156 Cal.App.4th 809, 67 Cal.Rptr.3d 635 (2007).

SECTION 3: DESTROYING THE OFFER

Even though we cannot point you to a case that you have read so far that explicitly says this, we know (and so expect you to know) that an offer, once communicated by the offeror to the offeree, creates in the offeree the power of acceptance. We also know that a Dragon lives forever (Peter, Paul, and Mary (http://www.youtube.com/watch?v=3OiOlnoyljk, more stuff that we know and so expect you to know)), but how long does an offer live for? Can it be killed? What does it take to kill an offer? Kryptonite?

Actually, there are four ways to "kill" or, more delicately put, to terminate an offer: rejection, revocation, lapse, death or incompetence of the offeror. We examine each in this section.

[Throughout this section on termination of offer we must assume that the offeree has not exercised the power of acceptance. Once acceptance occurs (something we have not yet examined but will soon), there is no more offer to terminate. Instead, at that point the offer has been subsumed into the contract. Kind of like a caterpillar becoming a butterfly.]

A. REJECTION

Contract law, like life, is rich with rejection. If you can't handle rejection, we suggest you skip this subsection—and maybe law school.

The first way (at least in the order of our treatment of them) in which an unaccepted offer may be terminated is rejection by the offeree. This occurs, for example, when Markell offers to sell his Kinky Friedman CD collection to Epstein for $500, and Epstein replies, "Hell no!" That is a rejection. The offer is terminated; dead.

What do you think is the basis for this rule?

Suppose Epstein comes to his senses and quickly calls Markell back and says, "I don't know what I was thinking, I accept your offer, I'd love to buy your Kinky CDs for the price you quoted." If Markell says "no," can Epstein sue and recover? Hell no! Epstein already rejected, at which point the offer was terminated. Dead. Dead forever. Not even in the deepest, most Fundamentalist, most Republican parts of the South, is there any such thing as a "born again offer."

In the example above, Epstein initially told Markell that he wasn't interested. In other words, Markell made an offer and Epstein said, in a less polite fashion, "no thanks." This is what we call an "express" rejection.

Like ice cream or jello, however, rejections come in more than one flavor. In Section 5(E) below we will take up the topic that we have termed "imperfect acceptances." When we do, you'll be introduced to another form of rejection; namely, "indirect" rejections.

For example, when the offeree, rather than turning down the offer, makes a "counteroffer," he is rejecting the offer. If Epstein replies to Markell's offer above by saying, "I'll buy your Kinky collection for $450," he is indirectly rejecting the offer.

For now, we suggest only that you appreciate that an offer, once rejected, whether expressly or impliedly, is terminated; dead as a doornail. So, in a sense, the making of an offer not only creates the power of acceptance in the offeror, it also creates in the offeree the power to destroy the offer through rejection.

B. REVOCATION

1. Direct Revocation

The offeror also has the power to destroy the offer, but the offeror's power is not called "rejection." Rather, the term used to describe the offeror's termination of her offer is "revocation." The offeror's right to revoke her offer derives from the fact that, until acceptance, the offeror retains full control and mastery over her offer including the right to modify or terminate the offer.

Suppose Markell offers to sell to Epstein his entire collection of Kinky Friedman CDs for $500. Epstein may well be very excited and eager to accept. If, however, before Epstein is able to communicate his acceptance to Markell, Markell calls Epstein and says, "I changed my mind. I don't want to sell my Kinky collection to you," the offer is gone—terminated; killed; or, more technically put, revoked. There's nothing for Epstein to accept.

This squares with objective theory because Epstein would no longer be reasonable in assuming that his assent will seal the deal once Markell has taken the offer off the table. This is a direct revocation. If Epstein nevertheless tells Markell, "No, wait, I'll buy your Kinky Friedman collection for $500," what is the proper legal characterization of that communication? Suppose after Markell pulls the offer, a stunned and deeply disappointed Epstein says, "No, please don't change your mind, I'll pay $750." Is there a contract? Why or why not, and if not, where do the parties stand?

---

2. Indirect Revocation

A direct revocation is easy to identify and understand. It is an affirmative statement by the offeror to the offeree expressly withdrawing the offer. What other kind of communication is sufficient to revoke an offer, who may it come from, and when is it effective? These are some of the questions that are addressed in the next case.

We also should let you know that this case will expose you for the first time to the doctrine of consideration—although at a sufficiently low dosage so as not to pose any hazard to your health. We also know that we (and you) haven't yet considered consideration and, in fact, will not formally do so until the next chapter. However, in order to understand this case, as well as some other aspects of contract formation that come up in Section 4 *infra*, you need to know a little about—have a little exposure to—consideration. So consider our consideration of consideration in this chapter as just an appetizer and we'll bring on the main course later. We hope you're hungry. * * *

DICKINSON v. DODDS

Court of Appeal, Chancery Division
2 Ch. Div. 463 (1876)

On Wednesday, the 10th of June, 1874, the Defendant John Dodds signed and delivered to the Plaintiff, George Dickinson, a memorandum, of which the material part was as follows:

I hereby agree to sell to Mr. George Dickinson the whole of the dwelling-houses, garden ground, stabling, and outbuildings thereto belonging, situate at Croft, belonging to me, for the sum of £800. As witness my hand this tenth day of June, 1874.

£800   /signed/ John Dodds

P.S.—This offer to be left open until Friday, 9 o'clock, A.M. J.D. (the twelfth), 12th June 1874.

/signed/ J. Dodds

The bill alleged that Dodds understood and intended that the Plaintiff should have until Friday 9 a.m. within which to determine whether he would or would not purchase, and that he should absolutely have until that time the refusal of the property at the price of £800, and that the Plaintiff in fact determined to accept the offer on the morning of Thursday, the 11th of June, but did not at once signify his acceptance to Dodds, believing that he had the power to accept it until 9 a.m. on the Friday.

In the afternoon of the Thursday the Plaintiff was informed by a Mr. Berry that Dodds had been offering or agreeing to sell the property to Thomas Allan, the other Defendant. Thereupon the Plaintiff, at about half-past seven in the evening, went to the house of Mrs. Burgess, the mother-in-law of Dodds, where he was then staying, and left with her a formal acceptance in writing of the offer to sell the property. According to the evidence of Mrs. Burgess this document never in fact reached Dodds, she having forgotten to give it to him.

On the following (Friday) morning, at about seven o'clock, Berry, who was acting as agent for Dickinson, found Dodds at the Darlington railway station, and handed to him a duplicate of the acceptance by Dickinson, and explained to Dodds its purport. He replied that it was too late, as he had sold the property. A few minutes later Dickinson himself found Dodds entering a railway carriage, and handed him another duplicate of the notice of acceptance, but Dodds declined to receive it, saying, "You are too late. I have sold the property."

It appeared that on the day before, Thursday, the 11th of June, Dodds had signed a formal contract for the sale of the property to the Defendant Allan for £800, and had received from him a deposit of £40.

The bill in this suit prayed that the Defendant Dodds might be decreed specifically to perform the contract of the 10th of June, 1874; that he might be restrained from conveying the property to Allan; that Allan might be restrained from taking any such conveyance; that, if any such conveyance had been or should be made, Allan might be declared a trustee of the property for, and might be directed to convey the property to, the Plaintiff; and for damages.

The cause came on for hearing before Vice–Chancellor Bacon on the 25th of January, 1876.

[Vice Chancellor Bacon declared that Allan had no interest in the property and entered a decree of specific performance in favor of Dickinson, from which Dodds and Allan appealed]

JAMES, L.J., after referring to the document of the 10th of June, 1874, continued:—

The document, though beginning "I hereby agree to sell," was nothing but an offer, and was only intended to be an offer, for the Plaintiff himself tells us that he required time to consider whether he would enter into an agreement or not. Unless both parties had then agreed there was no concluded agreement then made; it was in effect and substance only an offer to sell. * * * There was no consideration given for the undertaking or promise, to whatever extent it may be considered binding, to keep the property unsold until 9 o'clock on Friday morning; but apparently Dickinson was of opinion, and probably Dodds was of the same opinion, that he (Dodds) was bound by that promise, and could not in any way withdraw from it, or retract it, until 9 o'clock on Friday morning, and this probably explains a good deal of what afterwards took place. But it is clear settled law, on one of the clearest principles of law, that this promise, being a mere *nudum pactum*, was not binding, and that at any moment before a complete acceptance by Dickinson of the offer, Dodds was as free as Dickinson himself. Well, that being the state of things, it is said that the only mode in which Dodds could assert that freedom was by actually and distinctly saying to Dickinson, "Now I withdraw my offer." It appears to me that there is neither principle nor authority for the proposition that there must be an express and actual withdrawal of the offer, or what is called a retraction. It must, to constitute a contract, appear that the two minds were at one, at the same moment of time, that is, that there was an offer continuing up to the time of the acceptance. If there was not such a continuing offer, then the acceptance comes to nothing. Of course it may well be that the one man is bound in some way or other to let the other man know that his mind with regard to the offer has been changed; but in this case, beyond all question, the Plaintiff knew that Dodds was no longer minded to sell the property to him as plainly and clearly as if Dodds had told him in so many words, "I withdraw the offer." This is evident from the Plaintiff's own statements in the bill.

    * * *

It is to my mind quite clear that before there was any attempt at acceptance by the Plaintiff, he was perfectly well aware that Dodds had changed his mind, and that he had in fact agreed to sell the property to Allan. It is impossible, therefore, to say there was ever that existence of the same mind between the two parties which is essential in point of law to the making of an agreement. I am of opinion, therefore, that the Plaintiff has failed to prove that there was any binding contract between Dodds and himself.

MELLISH, L.J.:

I am of the same opinion. * * * He [Dodds] was not in point of law bound to hold the offer over until 9 o'clock on Friday morning. He was not so bound either in law or in equity. Well, that being so, when on the next day he made an agreement with Allan to sell the property to him, I am not aware of any ground on which it can be said that that contract with Allan was not as good and binding a contract as ever was made. Assuming Allan to have known (there is some dispute about it, and Allan does not admit that he knew of it, but I will assume that he did) that Dodds had made the offer to Dickinson, and had given him till Friday morning at 9 o'clock to accept it, still in point of law that could not prevent Allan from making a more favorable offer than Dickinson, and entering at once into a binding agreement with Dodds.

Then Dickinson is informed by Berry that the property has been sold by Dodds to Allan. Berry does not tell us from whom he heard it, but he says that he did hear it, that he knew it, and that he informed Dickinson of it. Now, stopping there, the question which arises is this—If an offer has been made for the sale of property, and before that offer is accepted, the person who has made the offer enters into a binding agreement to sell the property to somebody else, and the person to whom the offer was first made receives notice in some way that property has been sold to another person, can he after that make a binding contact by the acceptance of the offer? I am of opinion that he cannot. The law may be right or wrong in saying that a person who has given to another a certain time within which to accept an offer is not bound by his promise to give that time; but, if he is not bound by that promise, and may still sell the property to some one else, and if it be the law that, in order to make a contract, the two minds must be in agreement at some one time, that is, at the time of the acceptance, how is it possible that when the person to whom the offer has been made knows that the person who made the offer has sold the property to someone else, and that, in fact, he has not remained in the same mind to sell it to him, he can be at liberty to accept the offer and thereby make a binding contract? It seems to me that would be simply absurd. * * * If the rule of law is that a mere offer to sell property, which can be withdrawn at any time, and which is made dependent on the acceptance of the person to whom it is made, is a mere *nudum pactum*, how is it possible that the person to whom the offer has been made can by acceptance make a binding contract after he knows that the person who has made the offer has sold the property to some one else? * * * I am clearly of opinion that * * * once the person to whom the offer was made knows that the property has been sold to some one else, it is too late for him to accept the offer, and on that ground I am clearly of opinion that there is no binding contact for the sale of this property by Dodds to Dickinson, and even if there had been, it seems to me that the sale of the property to Allan was first in point of time. However, it is not necessary to consider, if there had been two binding contracts, which of them would be entitled to priority in equity, because there is no binding contact between Dodds and Dickinson.

QUESTIONS, NOTE, AND CONNECTIONS

1. Questions about the facts of this case

    1.1. If you'll excuse the expression, Dodds dodged the bullet in this case because of the court's holding that the offer was revoked once Dickinson learned through Berry that Dodds was no longer of a mind to sell the property to him. How much did Dickinson really know, however, about the dealings between Dodds and Allan?

    1.2. The court obviously considered Berry to be a reliable messenger. Why was that fact important to the court? Do you agree with the court's judgment?

2. Questions about the law

    2.1. Is the holding in *Dickinson* consistent with objective theory of contract formation? Suppose Berry was mistaken in what he told Dickinson. Is the offer still revoked? What if Berry was not just mistaken, but deliberately lying to Dickinson? Does that change the analysis?

    2.2. The court states that although Dodds promised that his offer would be held open until Friday morning, this promise was unenforceable *even though* both parties probably believed that Dodds was bound by that promise. Why was this so? How could this promise have been made binding? We will take up the subject of when offers will be regarded as irrevocable in the next section of this chapter. For the time being, accepting the court's statement of the law as true, how would you have advised Dodds to proceed once he decided that he might be interested in selling the property to Allan?

    2.3. Suppose that even though Dodds entered into an agreement with Allan for the sale of the property, Dickinson did not learn of this fact, directly or indirectly, until after he had accepted the offer. This is the problem that Lord Judge Mellish says at the end of his concurring opinion that the court does not have to address. If, however, the court were faced with those circumstances, would a contract have been formed with Allan? Would a contract also be formed between Dickinson and Dodds? Is it possible to have *two* contracts for the same property? If so, and both purchasers sue for specific performance, who gets the property? What does the other party get? Is there any way in which a person in Dickinson's position can protect himself against an intervening contract buyer?

    2.4. Suppose the facts in *Dickinson* had been different so that Dodds learned from a reliable source on the afternoon of Thursday, June 11, that Dickinson was not interested in buying his property and, in fact, was actively negotiating with someone else for the purchase of another parcel of land. Would the offer then be terminated by indirect rejection? But suppose that information was inaccurate and, before 9 a.m. on Friday, Dickinson accepts. Would Dodds be obligated to sell? Would there be an "indirect" rejection?

3. Note

   In a case where an offer is made by a public advertisement, does the offeror retain the power to revoke the offer? If so, how is it done? Does the offeror have to personally contact everyone that might have read the advertisement? *See Shuey v. United States*, 92 U.S. 73 (1875), involving an attempt to collect a reward that had been offered for the apprehension of John H. Surratt, an alleged accomplice of John Wilkes Booth in the murder of President Lincoln.

4. Connections

   Think back to the cases in the last section about what constitutes an offer. Ok, now that you've refreshed your recollection, ask yourself, "Self, what is it about what turns a communication into an offer that justified the court's conclusion in *Dickinson* that Dodd's offer died when Berry told Dickinson on Thursday, June 11, that Dodds was knoodling with Allan?"

C. LAPSE

With the subsection entitled "Rejection," we considered the possibility of termination of an offer because of actions by the offeree. And with the subsection entitled "Revocation," we considered the possibility of termination of an offer because of the actions of the offeror. Now, with this subsection entitled "Lapse," we consider the possibility of termination of an offer because of *inaction*.

MINNESOTA LINSEED OIL CO. v. COLLIER WHITE LEAD CO.

Circuit Court, District of Minnesota
17 F. Cas. 447 (1876)

* * * The plaintiff seeks to recover the sum of $2,151.50, with interest from September 20, 1875—a balance claimed to be due for oil sold to the defendant. The defendant, in its answer, alleges that on August 3d, 1875, a contract was entered into between the parties, whereby the plaintiff agreed to sell and deliver to the defendant, at the city of St. Louis, during the said month of August, twelve thousand four hundred and fifty (12,450) gallons of linseed oil for the price of fifty-eight (58) cents per gallon, and that the plaintiff has neglected and refused to deliver the oil according to the contract; that the market value of oil after August 3d and during the month was not less than seventy (70) cents per gallon, and therefore claims a set-off or counter-claim to plaintiff's cause of action. The reply of the plaintiff denies that any contract was entered into between it and defendant.

* * * The contract is alleged to have been made by telegraph.

The plaintiff sent the following dispatch to the defendant: *"Minneapolis, July 29, 1875. To Alex. Easton, Secretary Collier White Lead Company, St. Louis, Missouri: Account of sales not enclosed in yours of 27th. Please wire us best offer for round lot named by you—one hundred barrels shipped. Minnesota Linseed Oil Company."*

The following answer was received: *"St. Louis, Mo., July 30, 1875. To the Minnesota Linseed Oil Company: Three hundred barrels fifty-five cents here, thirty days, no commission, August delivery. Answer. Collier Company."*

The following reply was returned: *"Minneapolis, July 31, 1875. Will accept fifty-eight cents (58c), on terms named in your telegram. Minnesota Linseed Oil Company."*

This dispatch was transmitted Saturday, July 31, 1875, at 9:15 p.m., and was not delivered to the defendant in St. Louis, until Monday morning, August 2, between eight and nine o'clock.

On Tuesday, August 3, at 8:53 a.m., the following dispatch was deposited for transmission in the telegraph office: *"St. Louis, Mo., August 3, 1875. To Minnesota Linseed Oil Company, Minneapolis: Offer accepted—ship three hundred barrels as soon as possible. Collier Company."*

The following telegrams passed between the parties after the last one was deposited in the office at St. Louis: *"Minneapolis, August 3, 1875. To Collier Company, St. Louis: We must withdraw our offer wired July 31st. Minnesota Linseed Oil Company."*

Answered: *"St. Louis, August 3, 1875. Minnesota Linseed Oil Company: Sale effected before your request to withdraw was received. When will you ship? Collier Company."*

It appeared that the market was very much unsettled, and that the price of oil was subject to sudden fluctuations during the month previous and at the time of this negotiation, varying from day to day, and ranging between fifty-five and seventy-five cents per gallon. It is urged by the defendant that the dispatch of Tuesday, August 3d, 1875, accepting the offer of the plaintiff transmitted July 31st, and delivered Monday morning, August 2d, concluded a contract for the sale of the twelve thousand four hundred and fifty gallons of oil. The plaintiff, on the contrary, claims, 1st, that the dispatch accepting the proposition made July 31st, was not received until after the offer had been withdrawn; 2d, that the acceptance of the offer was not in due time; that the delay was unreasonable, and therefore no contract was completed.

NELSON, DISTRICT JUDGE.

It is well settled by the authorities in this country, and sustained by the later English decisions, that there is no difference in the rules governing the negotiation of contracts by correspondence through the post-office and by telegraph, and a contract is concluded when an accep-

tance of a proposition is deposited in the telegraph office for transmission.
* * *

The reason for this rule is well stated in Adams v. Lindsell, 1 Barn. &
Ald. 681. The negotiation in that case was by post. The court said: 'That if
a bargain could not be closed by letter before the answer was received, no
contract could be completed through the medium of the post-office; that if
the one party was not bound by his offer when it was accepted (that is, at
the time the letter of acceptance is deposited in the mail), then the other
party ought not to be bound until after they had received a notification
that the answer had been received and assented to, and that so it might go
on ad infinitum.' * * * In the case at bar the delivery of the message at
the telegraph office signified the acceptance of the offer. If any contract
was entered into, the meeting of minds was at 8:53 of the clock, on
Tuesday morning, August 3d, and the subsequent dispatches are out of
the case. * * *

This rule is not strenuously dissented from on the argument, and it is
substantially admitted that the acceptance of an offer by letter or by
telegraph completes the contract, when such acceptance is put in the
proper and usual way of being communicated by the agency employed to
carry it; and that when an offer is made by telegraph, an acceptance by
telegraph takes effect when the dispatch containing the acceptance is
deposited for transmission in the telegraph office, and not when it is
received by the other party. Conceding this, there remains only one
question to decide, which will determine the issues: Was the acceptance of
defendant deposited in the telegraph office Tuesday, August 3d, within a
reasonable time, so as to consummate a contract binding upon the
plaintiff?

It is undoubtedly the rule that when a proposition is made under the
circumstances in this case, an acceptance concludes the contract if the
offer is still open, and the mutual consent necessary to convert the offer of
one party into a binding contract by the acceptance of the other is
established, if such acceptance is within a reasonable time after the offer
was received.

The better opinion is, that what is, or is not, a reasonable time, must
depend upon the circumstances attending the negotiation, and the character of the subject matter of the contract, and in no better way can the
intention of the parties be determined. If the negotiation is in respect to
an article stable in price, there is not so much reason for an immediate
acceptance of the offer, and the same rule would not apply as in a case
where the negotiation related to an article subject to sudden and great
fluctuations in the market.

The rule in regard to the length of the time an offer shall continue,
and when an acceptance completes the contract, is laid down in Parsons
on Contracts (volume 1, p. 482). He says: "It may be said that whether the
offer be made for a time certain or not, the intention or understanding of
the parties is to govern. * * * If no definite time is stated, then the

inquiry as to a reasonable time resolves itself into an inquiry as to what time it is rational to suppose the parties contemplated; and the law will decide this to be that time which as rational men they ought to have understood each other to have had in mind." Applying this rule, it seems clear that the intention of the plaintiff, in making the offer by telegraph, to sell an article which fluctuates so much in price, must have been upon the understanding that the acceptance, if at all, should be immediate, and as soon after the receipt of the offer as would give a fair opportunity for consideration. The delay here was too long, and manifestly unjust to the plaintiff, for it afforded the defendant an opportunity to take advantage of a change in the market, and accept or refuse the offer as would best subserve its interests.

Judgment will be entered in favor of the plaintiff for the amount claimed. The counter-claim is denied. Judgment accordingly.

<hr>

QUESTIONS AND NOTES

1. Questions about the facts of this case
    1.1. Why is the party who is alleged to have breached the contract the *plaintiff* in this action instead of the defendant?
    1.2. Can you identify the key fact that, in the court's estimation, made the August 3 transmission untimely as an acceptance?

2. Questions about the law
    2.1. If a prompt acceptance was critical to the plaintiff in this case, why didn't plaintiff's telegram say so? Was it proper for the court to read a time limitation into the offer that the plaintiff had neglected to include of its own accord?
    2.2. Can you justify the court's decision under objective theory?
    2.3. The parties seemed to be in agreement in *Minnesota Linseed Oil* that if the offer were still open, a contract would have been completed when the defendant's August 3 telegraph was deposited for transmission. Is this rule consistent with objective theory? If you're confused, you ought to be, but keep the faith because we return to the issue of when an acceptance is effective in Section 5 of this chapter. For purposes of this case, however, it didn't matter when the acceptance would have been effective—transmission or receipt—because of the court's conclusion that the offer *lapsed* prior to either of those events.

3. Notes
    3.1. *Minnesota Linseed Oil* suggests that an offer for an unstated period lapses after a *reasonable* time. If Epstein approaches Markell and offers him employment for a specific wage and Markell does not respond during that conversation but instead sends notice of acceptance the next day, is there a contract between Epstein and Mar-

kell? *See Akers v. J.B. Sedberry, Inc.*, 39 Tenn.App. 633, 286 S.W.2d 617 (1955). If not, what is the proper legal characterization of Markell's notice of "acceptance"? *Compare Restatement (Second) of Contracts* § 70, *with* Art. 21(2), *United Nations Convention on Contracts for the International Sale of Goods* and Article 2.9(1), *UNIDROIT Principles of International Commercial Contracts* (both providing that a late acceptance may be effective as an acceptance if the offeror gives notice to that effect without undue delay). Does it change your answer if, during the conversation, Markell replies, "Alright, I accept, but you really should pay me more"? See *Brangier v. Rosenthal*, 337 F.2d 952 (9th Cir. 1964), involving a so-called "grumbling acceptance."

3.2.   As illustrated by *Dickinson v. Dodds, supra,* an offer for a stated period of time ("will give you eight days to accept") remains open, unless earlier revoked, for the time stated in the offer. But when does that time period begin to run when there is a delay between the date the offer is made and the date it is received? *See Caldwell v. Cline*, 109 W.Va. 553, 156 S.E. 55 (1930). Which party is in the best position to avoid the ambiguity? Should that affect the determination? If so, and you are drafting an offer for a client intended to be good for eight days, how will you express this intention?

D.   DEATH (OR INCAPACITY) OF THE OFFEROR (OR OFFEREE)

Obviously, if the offeree dies after an offer is made to her but before she accepts the offer, she cannot still accept the offer. She is dead. And so the offer also is dead.

It needs to be equally obvious that if the offeror dies after making an offer but before the offer is accepted that not only is he dead but his outstanding (i.e. unaccepted) offers die with him. Section 48 of the *Restatement (Second) of Contracts* provides: "An offeree's power of acceptance terminates when the offeree or offeror dies or is deprived of legal capacity to enter into the proposed contract." Here's how one court justified the rule:

> In the making of a contract there must be two minds, at least, concurring at the moment of its completion. But this cannot occur if there be but one of the contracting parties in existence. Hence, the death of a party who had the right of revocation or withdrawal of an offer to contract renders the completion impossible and terminates the negotiations or proceedings at the very point where they were when he died. So, an acceptance by the optionee or the other party subsequent to that event is ineffectual to close the bargain. Therefore, the death of a party while a contract is being made, even though only a single act remains to

be done, renders the completion of the contract impossible. * * *
New Headley Tobacco Warehouse Co. v. Gentry's Ex'r, 307 Ky.
857, 212 S.W.2d 325 (Ky Ct. App. 1948).

"Two minds"? Is this court out of its mind? Is the above statement
consistent with the objective theory? Is the Restatement consistent with
the objective theory?

Restatement (Second) of Contracts § 48 has been criticized on the
ground that, under the modern view of the formation of contracts, it is not
the actual meeting of the minds of the contracting parties that is the
determining factor, but rather the apparent state of mind of the parties
embodied in an expression of mutual consent; so that the acceptance by an
offeree of an offer, which is apparently still open, should result in an
enforceable contract notwithstanding the prior death of the offeror unknown to the offeree. Although the rule that the death of the offeror
terminates the offer regardless of notice to the offeree is retained in the
Restatement (Second) of Contracts, comment (a) to § 48 suggests that it is
without much support. Why do you think the drafters retained the rule?

Even if the "termination by death" rule didn't raise conceptual
problems, do you have problems with its application? Try the following
problems:

PROBLEMS

Case #1. Markell offers Epstein's sons a ten-year lease on one of the
many pieces of commercial real estate he owns in Las Vegas, and at which
Epstein's sons plan to open a branch of their wonderful Charlottesville,
Virginia restaurant named "Eppie's" (http://eppiesrestaurant.com/).* Before
accepting Markell's offer, Epstein's sons want to be sure that they can obtain
the necessary financing from Family Finance. Upon being assured about the
financing a couple of days later, they plan to accept. Before doing so, however,
they read in the newspaper that Markell choked on a piece of fillet while
dining in a fancy Las Vegas restaurant and died. Is it too late for the
Epsteins** to accept Markell's offer?

Case #2. Same facts as #1 above, but the Epsteins do not read of
Markell's earlier death until after they have sent Markell both an e-mail and
a letter communicating their acceptance. Can the Epsteins enforce the lease
agreement against Markell's estate?

Case #3. Same facts as #2, except Markell does not die until six months
after the Epsteins' acceptance. Can Markell's estate terminate the lease?

---

* I can't believe that Markell and Ponoroff made me wait until page 95 to promote my sons'
restaurant. More of you guys need to eat at Eppie's more often. If not, when your kids go to law
school, they, too, will be using casebooks that I co-authored. DGE

** Not to be confused with "The Epstein," http://www.myspace.com/theepstein.

Case #4. Same facts as #2, except that the Epsteins had not only arranged for financing, but entered into long-term contracts for the delivery of various foodstuffs to the new restaurant. Does that change your answer?

Note on Termination by Supervening Incapacity

At common law, the offeror's supervening mental incapacity, as established by an adjudication of incompetence or appointment of a guardian, has the same effect on the offeree's power of acceptance as the offeror's death. Professor Arthur Corbin, never a fan to begin with of the rule that the death of the offeror automatically terminates the offeree's power of acceptance, opined that the case for terminating an offer on the subsequent insanity of the offeror without the knowledge of the offeree is "even more doubtful than the rule as to the offeror's death." 1 Corbin, Contracts § 54, at 231.

Why do you suppose Corbin felt that way? Bear in mind that we are speaking of incapacity occurring *after* the offer has been made, and, of course, before it is accepted.

Mental incompetence at the time the offer is made raises a different issue, namely *capacity* to contract, a subject we take up in the next chapter. As you will see, such a contract is voidable at the instance of the mentally incompetent party.

That means that if Epstein offers to sell his Lexus to Ponoroff for $100 before he loses his mind, the issue of whether Ponoroff can enforce his deal will turn on whether Epstein's dementia occurs before or after Ponoroff accepts the offer, regardless of what Ponoroff knows about Epstein's condition at the time he accepts. On the other hand, if Epstein was already around the bend at the time the offer is made, he (or his guardian) can avoid the contract. Is that logical or does Professor Corbin's position make more sense to you?

SECTION 4: PRESERVING THE OFFER

Sometimes, even though an offer is attractive to the offeree, the offeree may not be ready to commit to the deal. For example, the offeree may need time to be sure he can arrange necessary financing or order his other affairs (locate customers, suppliers, etc.) in a manner that ensures that the proposed contract will be a beneficial one. If the offeree simply accepts the offer now, he assumes the risk if the contingencies creating the uncertainty do not occur. On the other hand, if he doesn't accept now, he runs the risk that the offer may be withdrawn or that some other event may occur that terminates the offer.

The logical course of action, therefore, is to request the offeror's agreement to hold the offer open—make it irrevocable—for a specified period of time. If the offeror agrees, in effect, a separate, ancillary promise has been made under the terms of which the offeror surrenders his right to revoke the offer for the principal contract for the agreed period of time. But what has the offeror received in return? If the offeror receives nothing in return, can this ancillary promise be enforced? Obviously, in *Dickinson v. Dodds* the court answered that question in the negative unless the ancillary promise is supported by a separate consideration. The cases and materials collected in this section address the issue of when a promise of irrevocability may become binding on the offeror and also examine the consequences of irrevocability as they relate not only to revocation by the offeror, but also to other circumstances that ordinarily terminate an offer.

BEALL v. BEALL

Court of Special Appeals of Maryland
45 Md.App. 489, 413 A.2d 1365 (1980), *rev'd on other grounds*, 291 Md. 224, 434 A.2d 1015 (1981)

MOORE, J.

This appeal concerns an alleged option agreement and a suit by Carlton G. Beall for the specific performance thereof. The Circuit Court for Prince George's County (Melbourne, J.) found the agreement unsupported by consideration and dismissed plaintiff's bill of complaint pursuant to Maryland Rule 535. From that order, he appeals to this Court.

I

In 1968, the plaintiff, Carlton G. Beall, purchased a farm in Prince George's County from Pearl Beall. At that time, the property was farmed by Pearl's son, Calvin Beall. The record discloses that Carlton, the plaintiff, and Calvin were second cousins. Calvin was married to Cecelia M. Beall, the defendant herein. Carlton agreed that Calvin could continue to farm the property if he would pay the annual property taxes. Calvin and Cecelia owned and resided on a parcel of about one-half acre that was bordered on three sides by the farm bought by the plaintiff; and it is that parcel that is the subject of this dispute.

On the day that plaintiff contracted to buy Pearl's farm, he obtained a three-year option to purchase Calvin's and Cecelia's parcel for $28,000.00. The option recited a consideration of $100.00 which was paid by check. In 1971, the parties executed a new option, for five years, but on the same terms and reciting an additional $100.00 consideration.

This 1971 option was never exercised by the plaintiff, but prior to its expiration the following language was appended at the bottom of the page:

"As of October 6, 1975, we, Calvin E. Beall and Cecelia M. Beall, agree to continue this option agreement three more years—Feb. 1, 1976 to Feb. 1, 1979.

/s/ Calvin E. Beall

/s/ Cecelia M. Beall."

It is this purported extension that forms the basis for plaintiff's bill of complaint seeking specific performance of the agreement. Calvin died in August 1977, and Cecelia now holds the fee simple title by right of survivorship. In letters dated May 24, 1978 and September 14, 1978, the plaintiff advised Cecelia that he was electing to exercise the option. He scheduled settlement for October 5, 1978. As the chancellor found:

> "It is undisputed in this case that Mr. Carlton Beall did eventually hire attorneys to search the title, set a settlement date, attend the settlement, and was ready, willing and able to perform the contract."

Cecelia refused to attend settlement, and this suit for specific performance ensued.

At trial, after plaintiff presented his evidence, Cecelia moved to dismiss the bill of complaint. The chancellor granted the motion because she felt that the option agreements were not supported by consideration in that "no benefit * * * flowed to Cecelia Beall." In addition, as to the 1975 alleged option, the chancellor ruled:

> "[T]here is no consideration recited in that extension or purported extension of the original option contract. And the one extension that had occurred in the interim, even then would also fail because there is no consideration stated in the extension. It is clear that consideration must pass for the extension each time, in some form of consideration. None is stated within the written four lines."

On appeal, the plaintiff contends that the chancellor erred in dismissing the bill of complaint and in excluding certain testimony relative to oral transactions with Calvin, the deceased husband of the defendant.

II

Under Maryland law it is clear that "an option is not a mere offer to sell, which can be withdrawn by the optionor at any time before acceptance, but a binding agreement if supported by consideration." *Blondell v. Turover*, 195 Md. 251, 256, 72 A.2d 697, 699 (1950). In other words, an option is an agreement to keep an offer open that requires consideration to give it its irrevocable character. * * * Once the option is exercised by the optionee a binding contract is created that may be enforced through a decree commanding specific performance. * * * It is apparent, then, that an option must be supported by consideration in order to be irrevocable for the period provided in the option.

When, however, the consideration allegedly supporting an option fails or is nonexistent, the option is no longer irrevocable but rather it becomes "a mere offer to sell, which can be withdrawn by the optionor at any time before acceptance. * * *" *Blondell v. Turover, supra*, 195 Md. at 256, 72 A.2d at 699. The failure of consideration destroys the irrevocability of the option; it nonetheless retains its essential characteristic as an offer to buy or sell for the period stated in the option or until revoked. It has been recognized that equity will enforce a resulting contract despite lack of consideration for the option:

> "While the rule that equity will enforce a contract consummated by the acceptance of an option within the time and upon the terms of the option is often stated in such a way as to suggest or imply the necessity of consideration for the option, all that is meant in most cases is that a consideration is necessary to prevent the defendant from asserting his withdrawal of the option before its acceptance by the plaintiff and before the expiration of the time fixed in the option within which acceptance could be made."

71 Am. Jur. 2d, Specific Performance § 143 (1973) (footnotes omitted). See 1A Corbin on Contracts § 263 (1963). See generally *Kahn v. General Development Corp.*, 40 Del. Ch. 83, 92, 174 A.2d 307, 312 (1961) (failure of consideration "destroyed the irrevocability of the option"). * * *

Assuming, arguendo, that the 1975 option was unsupported by consideration, it remained as an offer to sell the parcel for $28,000. The offer was open until February 1, 1979, but it was revocable at any time by action of Calvin and Cecelia Beall. As stated in the case of *Holifield v. Veterans' Farm & Home Board*, 218 Miss. 446, 450, 67 So. 2d 456, 457 (1953):

> "It is well settled that an option is not binding as a contract where there is no consideration, unless it is accepted within the time limit and before the offer is withdrawn. Since there was no consideration paid by the Veterans' Farm and Home Board and Mauldin for the option, it could have been revoked by the Holifields at any time before the Veterans' Farm and Home Board and Mauldin notified them that they intended to buy the land; *but since the offer was accepted within the time limit and before withdrawal, the contract became binding upon all parties as it was thereafter supported by the consideration of the mutual promises*." (Emphasis added.)

This statement is generally in accord with the Maryland cases, *supra*.

The chancellor should, therefore, have determined whether or not there was a valid, unrevoked offer to sell the property in dispute and whether or not there was a proper acceptance of that offer sufficient to create a contract specifically enforceable in equity.[1] These issues of offer and acceptance primarily involve factual determinations that initially must be evaluated by the chancellor. As an appellate court, we are limited to a review of the chancellor's findings under the "clearly erroneous" standard. Md. Rule 1086. But our review is dependent upon the existence of factual findings on the issues material to the case. Such findings were not made below.

---

1. We express no opinion concerning the validity of the chancellor's finding that there was no consideration for the option.

It was error for the chancellor to dismiss plaintiff's bill of complaint at the close of his case. A new trial, in accordance with this opinion, is necessitated.

Order reversed; cause remanded for a new trial in accordance with this opinion; costs to abide the final result.

QUESTIONS, NOTES, AND CONNECTIONS

1. Questions about the facts of this case

    1.1. In 1975, when the option was extended for an additional three years, what was each side bargaining for?

    1.2. What was the mistake that Carlton made in 1975? According to the court, when did Carlton's option to purchase the Calvin/Cecelia property expire?

2. Questions about the law

    2.1. What is the specific issue that the chancellor will have to resolve on remand in *Beall*? If you represent Carlton, what evidence will you seek to put forward? How about if you represent Cecelia?

    2.2. Why does the law impose a requirement that the promise of irrevocability be supported by a separate consideration? Would the outcome in *Beall* have been different if, in 1971, the extension of the option had been for eight years instead of five even though the consideration remained $100? How about if, during that eight-year period, but before Carlton exercised the option, Cecelia joined Calvin in the great beyond? Does an option, if enforceable, survive the death of the optionor? Suppose the option had been for eight years, but in year five Carlton told Cecelia that he had decided not to exercise the option. If Carlton changes his mind, can he still enforce the option, or was it terminated by his prior rejection? *See Restatement (Second) of Contracts* § 37. If your answer is "yes," what if Cecelia, having taken Carlton at his word, has already entered into a contract to sell the property to someone else? Is Cecelia just SOL (that's a technical legal term meaning up the creek without a paddle) or is there some other way in which Cecelia might avoid liability under the option?

3. Notes

    3.1. Option contracts can take a variety of different forms, such as an offer with an ancillary contract not to revoke (*"I offer to sell you my land for $50,000 and, in consideration of $50, I agree not to revoke this offer for 30 days"*) or a contract with a condition (*"In consideration of $50, I agree to sell you my land if, within 30 days, you pay me $50,000"*). In either case, it comes down to pretty much the same thing. For some separate consideration, the offeror is bound for a period of time pending a decision by the offeree.

3.2. As a general rule, in civil law systems, the mere statement of irrevocability will be enforced. Indeed, both the *United Nations Convention on Contracts for the International Sale of Goods,* § 16(2)(a), and the *UNIDROIT Principles of International Commercial Contracts, Principle* 2.4(2)(a), effectively provide that an offer cannot be revoked if it states that it is irrevocable, whether by providing a fixed time for acceptance or otherwise. You might wonder why the rule is different in common law jurisdictions. Your answer lies in the common law's general requirement of consideration as a condition for enforcement of promises, a topic that we examine in depth in the next chapter. The next case, however, considers what it takes to satisfy this requirement of consideration in the context of an option contract.

4. Connections

How is this case different, if at all, from *Dickinson v. Dodds*? What does your answer to that question tell you about the relationship between the rules on terminating and preserving the offer? Consider again the rule on termination by death. Would it matter if an offer expressly stated: "This offer shall survive my death and be binding upon my heirs and successors"?

BOARD OF CONTROL OF EASTERN MICHIGAN UNIVERSITY v. BURGESS

Court of Appeals of Michigan
45 Mich.App. 183, 206 N.W.2d 256 (1973)

Opinion by: BURNS

On February 15, 1966, defendant signed a document which purported to grant to plaintiff a 60–day option to purchase defendant's home. That document, which was drafted by plaintiff's agent, acknowledged receipt by defendant of "One and no/100 ($1.00) Dollar and other valuable consideration". Plaintiff concedes that neither the one dollar nor any other consideration was ever paid or even tendered to defendant. On April 14, 1966, plaintiff delivered to defendant written notice of its intention to exercise the option. On the closing date defendant rejected plaintiff's tender of the purchase price. Thereupon, plaintiff commenced this action for specific performance.

At trial defendant claimed that the purported option was void for want of consideration [and] that any underlying offer by defendant had been revoked prior to acceptance by plaintiff. * * * The trial judge * * * held that defendant's acknowledgment of receipt of consideration bars any subsequent contention to the contrary. Accordingly, the trial judge entered judgment for plaintiff.

Defendant appeals. She claims that acknowledgment of receipt of consideration does not bar the defense of failure of consideration. * * *

Options for the purchase of land, if based on valid consideration, are contracts which may be specifically enforced. * * * Conversely, that which purports to be an option, but which is not based on valid consideration, is not a contract and will not be enforced. * * * One dollar is valid consideration for an option to purchase land, provided the dollar is paid or at least tendered. * * * In the instant case defendant received no consideration for the purported option of February 15, 1966.

A written acknowledgment of receipt of consideration merely creates a rebuttable presumption that consideration has, in fact, passed. [Nothing] * * * bars the presentation of evidence to contradict any such acknowledgment. * * *

It is our opinion that the document signed by defendant on February 15, 1966, is not an enforceable option, and that defendant is not barred from so asserting.

The trial court premised its holding to the contrary on *Lawrence v McCalmont*, 43 U.S. (2 How) 426, 452; 11 L Ed 326, 336 (1844). That case is significantly distinguishable from the instant case. Mr. Justice Story held that "[t]he guarantor acknowledged the receipt of one dollar, and is now estopped to deny it." However, in reliance upon the guaranty substantial credit had been extended to the guarantor's sons. The guarantor had received everything she bargained for, save one dollar. * * * In the instant case defendant claims that she never received any of the consideration promised her.

That which purports to be an option for the purchase of land, but which is not based on valid consideration, is a simple offer to sell the same land. * * * An option is a contract collateral to an offer to sell whereby the offer is made irrevocable for a specified period. * * * Ordinarily, an offer is revocable at the will of the offeror. Accordingly, a failure of consideration affects only the collateral contract to keep the offer open, not the underlying offer.

A simple offer may be revoked for any reason or for no reason by the offeror at any time prior to its acceptance by the offeree. * * * Thus, the question in this case becomes, "Did defendant effectively revoke her offer to sell before plaintiff accepted that offer?"

* * *

Defendant testified that within hours of signing the purported option she telephoned plaintiff's agent and informed him that she would not abide by the option unless the purchase price was increased. Defendant also testified that when plaintiff's agent delivered to her on April 14, 1966, plaintiff's notice of its intention to exercise the purported option, she told him that "the option was off".

Plaintiff's agent testified that defendant did not communicate to him any dissatisfaction until sometime in July, 1966.

If defendant is telling the truth, she effectively revoked her offer several weeks before plaintiff accepted that offer, and no contract of sale was created. If plaintiff's agent is telling the truth, defendant's offer was still open when plaintiff accepted that offer, and an enforceable contract was created. The trial judge thought it unnecessary to resolve this particular dispute. In light of our holding the dispute must be resolved.

An appellate court cannot assess the credibility of witnesses. We have neither seen nor heard them testify. * * * Accordingly, we remand this case to the trial court for additional findings of fact based on the record already before the court.

* * *

QUESTIONS, NOTE, AND CONNECTIONS

1. Questions about the facts of this case

    1.1. Why didn't the university just pay the dollar?

    1.2. What was the "other valuable consideration"?

    1.3. Who drafted the February 15, 1966 document? Was that a factor in the case? Should it have been?

    1.4. On February 15, 1966, do you think that the defendant believed that the university had a non-revocable 60–day option to purchase her property? What do you think the university believed?

2. Questions about the law

    2.1. How did the reasoning of the trial court and the court of appeals differ?

    2.2. How is the Michigan Court of Appeals' decision in *Board of Control* distinguishable from the U.S. Supreme Court's holding in *Lawrence v. McCalmont*, the case on which the trial court relied?

    2.3. Is the holding in *Board of Control* consistent with *Beall*?

    2.4. Just what is a "rebuttable presumption"?

3. Note

Not all courts agree with *Board of Control* insofar as the effect of a recital of consideration is concerned. Some courts, for example, treat the recital as a binding acknowledgement of payment. *See Real Estate Co. v. Rudolph*, 301 Pa. 502, 153 A. 438 (1930). The *Restatement (Second) of Contracts* adopts a somewhat different approach in § 87(1)(a). Take a look at that provision now. How would *Board of Control* have been decided if the court of appeals had applied that rule? As a general proposition, most lay people like it when the law conforms to their own intuitive, common sense judgment of what the law ought to be. Which rule—*Board of Control* or *Restatement (Second)* § 87(1)(a)—more closely conforms to what the true intentions of the parties probably are in these cases where the contract recites a consideration?

4. Connections

Is the traditional standard governing when an irrevocable offer will be enforced consistent with the rules discussed in the last section concerning destruction of the offer? Why should the enforceability of an option contract turn on whether something of value has passed from the optionee to the optionor? Or does it? What is required to make an option enforceable?

The brief remaining materials in this section consider whether there are any other circumstances in our legal system where a promise of irrevocability will be enforced despite the absence of consideration. By now you have surely learned in law school that there are few rules without exception, so it will come as no surprise to you to learn that such circumstances do indeed exist.

NOTE ON OPTION CONTRACTS AND FIRM OFFERS

The classical view that a mere promise to hold an offer open for a stated period of time is not itself enforceable is carried forward in the *Restatement (Second) of Contracts* § 25, which provides that: *"An option contract is a promise which meets the requirements for the formation of a contract and limits the promisor's power to revoke an offer."* Of course, the central "requirement for the formation of a contract" is the existence of payment or some other form of consideration given in exchange for the promise of irrevocability, separate and apart from the consideration supporting the underlying offer.*

Thus, today, a typical option contract might take the following form: "In return for payment of $100, A hereby grants B the right through January 5, 2002, to purchase his property for $100,000." The consideration for the promise of irrevocability in this example is the $100, while the consideration for the property, if B elects before the expiry of the option to accept, is $100,000.

Consistent with its philosophy of conforming the governing principles of commercial law with the norms and expectations of the marketplace, the U.C.C. creates an exception to the rule set forth in *Beall* that an offer, even though stated to be irrevocable, may be revoked unless supported by consideration. The exception is in § 2–205 for so-called "firm offers." Under this provision, if a "merchant" (defined in § 2–104(1)) makes an offer, in writing, signed, and which contains an assurance that it will be held open, then it will be regarded as irrevocable in spite of the absence of consideration for either the period stated or, if no period is stated, for a reasonable time, but in no

---

* At common law, a promise not to revoke would also be enforceable if given under seal. Most states no longer attribute any legal significance to the use of a seal—although the seal is still pretty popular, we understand, at Sea World.

event exceeding three months. The theory behind this provision, as stated in the Official Comments, is that when a merchant makes such a promise he understands and intends for it to be binding, and such offers are so understood in the marketplace. Thus, the provision gives effect to this deliberate intention and reasonable expectation. The requirements that the promise be signed and in writing ensures the seriousness of the merchant's promise to effectively create an option contract. A similar form of statutory option contract, applicable to merchants in the non-sale of goods context, can be found in § 5–1109 of the New York General Obligations Law. However, in either case, it is important to bear in mind that there cannot be an enforceable *firm offer* until there is an *offer*, ascertained in the usual way. *See Coastal Aviation, Inc. v. Commander Aircraft Co.*, 937 F.Supp. 1051 (S.D.N.Y. 1996) (holding that the defendant's statement concerning its intent to hold a particular area open for the plaintiff in connection with a proposed exclusive dealership arrangement did not evince an intent to be bound by a promise to do so and, hence, could not be enforced as a "firm offer" within the meaning of U.C.C. § 2–205).

PROBLEM

Epstein owned two four-acre parcels of land on which he grew marijuana that he sold for medicinal use in California. Markell, deciding that this looked like a pretty lucrative business, offered to purchase one of the two parcels for $100,000. As part of the final contract for purchase and sale, Epstein granted Markell a three-year "right of first refusal" in the event of any proposed sale of the second parcel by Epstein. A year later, Epstein solicited an offer from Ponoroff to purchase the second parcel for $125,000. Upon learning of this offer, Markell promptly notified Epstein that he was exercising his first refusal right and that he would send a certified check for $125,000 to Epstein the next day in payment for the other parcel. Epstein turned down Ponoroff's offer and returned Markell's check, claiming that he was going to retain the property.

Incensed, Markell has brought an action against Epstein for specific performance on the basis that he timely exercised his right of first refusal and that Epstein breached this contract both by (1) soliciting Ponoroff's offer, and (2) returning Markell's check. What result in Markell's suit and why?

NOTE ON OPTION CONTRACTS AND RELIANCE

So far, our examination of irrevocability can be boiled down to the following set of rules: All offers are revocable, even when they're stated to be irrevocable (or open for a specified period of time), *unless* the promise of irrevocability is supported by independent consideration (including perhaps the mere recital of consideration) or made enforceable by statute. Are there any other circumstances where an offer will be deemed irrevocable?

Suppose Epstein offers Markell, a recent law school graduate with significant student loans, a job as an associate at Epstein's highly successful law firm in Atlanta. Epstein tells Markell, "this offer is good for one week." At the time, Markell is working for another firm, which although not as prestigious or lucrative as Epstein's, still pays a decent wage. Flush with excitement over the offer, the next day Markell calls his current boss and tells him, in no uncertain terms, to take this job and shove it. Thereupon he calls Epstein to accept the offer, but before Markell can say anything, Epstein says: "Sorry pal, but I must revoke my offer." Markell responds: "You can't do that, I just quit my other job as you had to know I would; this is unfair"! Epstein's rejoinder is short and sweet: "Look, Ace, maybe you should have paid a little more attention in Contracts. My offer could be revoked at any time before acceptance regardless of how long I said it would be good for; if you wanted an option you should have paid for one." Under the traditional rules of contract law does Markell have any recourse? How about under *Restatement (Second) of Contracts* § 87(2)? Does it change your answer at all if Epstein's offer had not been for a stated period of time; *i.e.*, one week? We will return to § 87(2) in the next chapter when we examine "promissory estoppel." For now, however, we shift our attention from "offer" to "acceptance."

SECTION 5: MODES AND METHODS OF ACCEPTANCE

In Section 2 we saw that an offer, so long as it remains open, confers on the offeree the power of acceptance. The acceptance is the other piece of the mutual assent puzzle. But how does an offeree exercise this power of acceptance? What constitutes an acceptance and when is it effective? These are some of the questions we examine in this section.

Restatement (Second) of Contracts § 50(1) provides that *"Acceptance of an offer is a manifestation of assent to the terms thereof made by the offeree in a manner invited or required by the offer."* Is that definition consistent with the objective theory of contract formation? Bear that definition in mind as you consider the next two cases dealing with who controls the permitted form of acceptance.

A. OFFEROR'S CONTROL OVER THE MANNER OF ACCEPTANCE

The plaintiff in the next case is a bank acting in its capacity as a trustee of a trust. A trust is a common law invention whose original purpose was to avoid taxes—in 14th and 15th Century England! Whether from utility or sheer cussedness, trusts survive to this day. Most trusts involve large sums of money entrusted to banks and other moneyed interests to administer for others. In these cases, a trust consists of property (often called the "*res*" from the Latin for "thing") transferred to the trusted individual (the "trustee") who has legal title to the property but holds it for the use or benefit of another (the "beneficiary"). All things considered, it is good to be the beneficiary of a trust. In fact, if we were trust beneficiaries we might not have written this book.

In the next case, however, the common law origins of tax and regulatory avoidance play a role. In Illinois and some other states, land or other real property is often held in a "land trust" in which the legal title holder is the trustee. That trustee holds title for the benefit of the beneficiary. So far, so good; the format is just like regular trusts. But why would the beneficiary not just take title directly? The twist here is that Illinois common law considers beneficial interests in land trusts as *personal* property and not as *real* property, even if the trust *res* is dirt. Thus, in Illinois, those who hold property in a land trust are not listed in the public record as owners. Also, they can transfer their interests quickly without the inherited formality that usually attends a real estate transfer.

Such arrangements, however, involve risk to the bank/trustees. They are on the title, and are in a position to make mistakes. As a consequence, they charge a fee for their services, and they also very carefully specify in the contract creating the trust what they need to do and what they do not need to do. This care usually permeates the formation process, because the bank/trustee certainly doesn't want to sign documents indicating it will buy property if the beneficiary suddenly has a change of heart and refuses to put up the funds to buy the land.* Keep this background in mind when reading the next case.

———————

LA SALLE NATIONAL BANK v. VEGA

Appellate Court of Illinois, Second District
167 Ill.App.3d 154, 117 Ill.Dec. 778, 520 N.E.2d 1129 (1988)

LINDBERG, J.

* * *

Plaintiff's first amended complaint alleged the existence of a contract for the sale of real estate between it and Mel [Vega] and sought specific performance of the alleged contract and damages from defendants for willfully and intentionally breaching it. Borg was permitted to intervene and filed a counterclaim naming plaintiff and defendants as counterdefendants. As finally amended, the counterclaim sought specific performance of a different contract for sale of the same real estate to Borg; a judgment

—————————
* For those curious about Illinois land trusts, see Eric T. Freyfogle, *Land Trusts and the Decline of Mortgage Law*, 1988 U. ILL. L. REV. 67. This is Markell's footnote. Neither Epstein nor Ponoroff has ever had a student, in any of the 20 law schools at which they have taught, who was the least bit curious about Illinois land trusts.

declaring the alleged contract between Mel and plaintiff void and holding it for naught; and, if the alleged contract with plaintiff was "held to be a valid and enforceable contract," damages from defendants for fraud for failure to disclose the contract with plaintiff to Borg.

Borg moved for partial summary judgment * * * requesting a determination by the court that the alleged contract between plaintiff and Mel was unenforceable because it was not "signed in accordance with its terms and provisions" and because plaintiff abandoned it. The trial court granted partial summary judgment on the basis of the first ground argued by Borg.

In its verified first amended complaint, plaintiff alleged, inter alia:

"The Defendant, MEL VEGA, on March 12, 1985, in his own behalf and in behalf of all the owners of record, entered into a Real Estate Sale Contract (herein 'Contract') with the Plaintiff, a true and correct copy of said Contract is attached hereto and incorporated herein as Exhibit A."

Exhibit A is a document, drafted by counsel for plaintiff, entitled "Real Estate Sale Contract." On the first page of this document appears the date March 12, 1985, and the statement that "Attached Rider is part of this Contract." One of the Rider's provisions states:

"This contract has been executed and presented by an authorized agent for the purchaser, the beneficiaries of the La Salle National Bank, under Trust No. 109529, as Trustee aforesaid for the benefit of the Trust only and not personally. Upon execution of this contract by the Seller, this contract shall be presented to the trust for full execution. Upon the trust's execution, this contract will then be in full force and a copy of a fully executed contract along with evidence of the earnest money deposit will be delivered back to Seller."

The document was signed by Bernard Ruekberg as the purchaser's purchasing agent and by Mel Vega (on March 19, 1985, according to the date by his signature on the Rider) as the seller but not by the trustee for the purchaser.

* * *

The trial court held that there was no genuine issue of material fact that no contract was formed because the offer was made by Mel, the offer could only be accepted by execution of the document at issue by the trust, and the document was not executed by the trust. Plaintiff argues that the trial court erred because there were genuine issues of material fact regarding whether the document was ever executed by the trust and whether execution of the document by the trust was necessary to the formation of a contract. Plaintiff is incorrect on both of these points.

[The court first rejected the argument that there was a genuine issue of material fact concerning whether the document was executed by the trust, noting that the exhibit attached to the plaintiff's complaint, which was alleged to be a "true and correct copy" of the written instrument on which the claim of plaintiff was founded, did not show execution by the trust. Therefore, the plaintiff had effectively admitted that the document was never executed by the trust]

* * *

Whether a contract was formed without execution of the document by the trust may now be considered. This requires first an analysis of the events which occurred with respect to the document in terms of offer and acceptance.

The pertinent provision of the document stated:

"This contract has been executed and presented by an authorized agent for the purchaser, the beneficiaries of the La Salle National Bank, under Trust No. 109529, as Trustee aforesaid for the benefit of the Trust only and not personally. Upon execution of this contract by the Seller, this contract shall be presented to the trust for full execution. Upon the trust's execution, this contract will then be in full force and a copy of a fully executed contract along with evidence of the earnest money deposit will be delivered back to Seller."

Thus, a specific order of events was contemplated, after which the contract would be in full force. Ruekberg (the purchasing agent) was to execute the document and present it to Mel (the seller). Then Mel was to execute it. After Mel executed it, the document was to be presented to the trust for execution. Finally, "upon the trust's execution," the contract would be in full force.

An offer is an act on the part of one person giving another person the legal power of creating the obligation called a contract. * * * Where "the so-called offer is not intended to give the so-called offeree the power to make a contract there is no offer." * * * From the provisions contained in the document at bar, particularly the language quoted, it is apparent that there was to be no contract (i.e., the "contract" was not to be in full force) until it was executed by the trust. Thus, Ruekberg's presentation of the document he had executed to Mel was not an offer because it did not give Mel the power to make a contract by accepting it. On the other hand, when Mel executed the document and gave it back to Ruekberg he made an offer which could be accepted by execution of the document by the trust.

An offeror has complete control over an offer and may condition acceptance to the terms of the offer. * * * The language of an offer may moreover govern the mode of acceptance required, and where an offer requires a written acceptance, no other modes may be used. * * * In the case at bar, the document at issue stated clearly that the contract would be in full force upon the trust's execution. This indicates that the only mode by which Mel's offer could be accepted was execution of the document by the trust. The trust not having executed the document, there was no acceptance of the offer, and so there was no contract. * * *

Affirmed.

EVER–TITE ROOFING CORP. v. GREEN

Court of Appeal of Louisiana
83 So.2d 449 (1955)

AYERS, J.

This is an action for damages allegedly sustained by plaintiff as the result of the breach by the defendants of a written contract for the re-roofing of defendants' residence. Defendants denied that their written proposal or offer was ever accepted by plaintiff in the manner stipulated therein for its acceptance, and hence contended no contract was ever entered into. The trial court sustained defendants' defense and rejected plaintiff's demands and dismissed its suit at its costs. From the judgment thus rendered and signed, plaintiff appealed.

Defendants executed and signed an instrument June 10, 1953, for the purpose of obtaining the services of plaintiff in re-roofing their residence situated in Webster Parish, Louisiana. The document set out in detail the work to be done and the price therefor to be paid in monthly installments. This instrument was likewise signed by plaintiff's sale representative, who, however, was without authority to accept the contract for and on behalf of the plaintiff. This alleged contract contained these provisions:

> "This agreement shall become binding only upon written acceptance hereof, by the principal or authorized officer of the Contractor, *or upon commencing performance of the work*. This contract is Not Subject to Cancellation. * * *" (Emphasis supplied.)

Inasmuch as this work was to be performed entirely on credit, it was necessary for plaintiff to obtain credit reports and approval from the lending institution which was to finance said contract. With this procedure defendants were more or less familiar and knew their credit rating would have to be checked and a report made. On receipt of the proposed contract in plaintiff's office on the day following its execution, plaintiff requested a credit report, which was made after investigation and which was received in due course and submitted by plaintiff to the lending agency. Additional information was requested by this institution, which was likewise in due course transmitted to the institution, which then gave its approval.

The day immediately following this approval, which was either June 18 or 19, 1953, plaintiff engaged its workmen and two trucks, loaded the trucks with the necessary roofing materials and proceeded from Shreveport to defendants' residence for the purpose of doing the work and performing the services allegedly contracted for the defendants. Upon their arrival at defendants' residence, the workmen found others in the performance of the work which plaintiff had contracted to do. Defendants notified plaintiff's workmen that the work had been contracted to other parties two days before and forbade them to do the work.

Formal acceptance of the contract was not made under the signature and approval of an agent of plaintiff. It was, however, the intention of plaintiff to accept the contract by commencing the work, which was one of the ways provided for in the instrument for its acceptance, as will be shown by reference to the extract from the contract quoted hereinabove. Prior to this time, however, defendants had determined on a course of abrogating the agreement and engaged other workmen without notice thereof to plaintiff.

The basis of the judgment appealed was that defendants had timely notified plaintiff before 'commencing performance of work'. The trial court held that notice to plaintiff's workmen upon their arrival with the materials that defendants did not desire them to commence the actual work was sufficient and timely to signify their intention to withdraw from the contract. With this conclusion we find ourselves unable to agree.

Defendants' attempt to justify their delay in thus notifying plaintiff for the reason they did not know where or how to contact plaintiff is without merit. The contract itself, a copy of which was left with them, conspicuously displayed plaintiff's name, address and telephone number. Be that as it may, defendants at no time, from June 10, 1953, until plaintiff's workmen arrived for the purpose of commencing the work, notified or attempted to notify plaintiff of their intention to abrogate, terminate or cancel the contract.

Defendants evidently knew this work was to be processed through plaintiff's Shreveport office. The record discloses no unreasonable delay on plaintiff's part in receiving, processing or accepting the contract or in commencing the work contracted to be done. No time limit was specified in the contract within which it was to be accepted or within which the work was to be begun. It was nevertheless understood between the parties that some delay would ensue before the acceptance of the contract and the commencement of the work, due to the necessity of compliance with the requirements relative to financing the job through a lending agency. The evidence as referred to hereinabove shows that plaintiff proceeded with due diligence.

The general rule of law is that an offer proposed may be withdrawn before its acceptance and that no obligation is incurred thereby. This is, however, not without exceptions. For instance, Restatement of the Law of Contracts stated:

Ever-Tite Contract

"(1) The power to create a contract by acceptance of an offer terminates at the time specified in the offer, or, if no time is specified, at the end of a reasonable time.

'What is a reasonable time is a question of fact depending on the nature of the contract proposed, the usages of business and other circumstances of the case which the offeree at the time of his acceptance either knows or has reason to know."

* * *

Therefore, since the contract did not specify the time within which it was to be accepted or within which the work was to have been commenced, a reasonable time must be allowed therefor in accordance with the facts and circumstances and the evident intention of the parties. A reasonable time is contemplated where no time is expressed. What is a reasonable time depends more or less upon the circumstances surrounding each particular case. The delays to process defendants' application were not unusual. The contract was accepted by plaintiff by the commencement of the performance of the work contracted to be done. This commencement began with the loading of the trucks with the necessary materials in Shreveport and transporting such materials and the workmen to defendants' residence. Actual commencement or performance of the work therefore began before any notice of dissent by defendants was given plaintiff. The proposition and its acceptance thus became a completed contract.

By their aforesaid acts defendants breached the contract. They employed others to do the work contracted to be done by plaintiff and forbade plaintiff's workmen to engage upon that undertaking. By this breach defendants are legally bound to respond to plaintiff in damages. * * *

Plaintiff expended the sum of $85.37 in loading the trucks in Shreveport with materials and in transporting them to the site of defendants' residence in Webster Parish and in unloading them on their return, and for wages for the workmen for the time consumed. Plaintiff's Shreveport manager testified that the expected profit on this job was $226. None of this evidence is controverted or contradicted in any manner.

True, as plaintiff alleges, the contract provides for attorney's fees where an attorney is employed to collect under the contract, but this is not an action on the contract or to collect under the contract but is an action for damages for a breach of the contract. The contract in that respect is silent with reference to attorney's fees. In the absence of an agreement for the payment of attorney's fees or of some law authorizing the same, such fees are not allowed.

For the reasons assigned, the judgment appealed is annulled, avoided, reversed and set aside and there is now judgment in favor of plaintiff, Ever–Tite Roofing Corporation, against the defendants, G. T. Green and Mrs. Jessie Fay Green, for the full sum of $311.37, with 5 per cent per annum interest thereon from judicial demand until paid, and for all costs.

Reversed and rendered.

NOTE ON REQUIRED FORM OF ACCEPTANCE

The following statements in *LaSalle National Bank*, *"An offeror has complete control over an offer and may condition acceptance to the terms of the offer. * * * The language of an offer may moreover govern the mode of* *acceptance required, and, where an offer requires a written acceptance, no other mode may be used"* reflect the principle that we encountered earlier; namely, that the offeror is "king". Not only does this principle explain why revocation will terminate an offer, but, as illustrated by *Lasalle* and *Ever–Tite*, it also explains why if an offer prescribes the time, place, and/or manner of assent, the purported acceptance—the manifestation of intent to be bound—in order to be effective *must* comply without variation to the terms of the offer. This notion is, of course, consistent with the core policy of freedom of and *from* contract. The offeror has the unfettered right to determine the terms on which she is willing to deal, such that, if the offer requires as a condition to acceptance that the offeree place a paper bag over his head, dance in circles, and squawk like a chicken, then nothing less than what is bargained for will be sufficient to constitute a valid acceptance of the offer.

Sometimes, however, this rule, which is obviously intended to protect the offeror from liability other than on her terms, will end up frustrating the offeror. Consider again *LaSalle National Bank.* Obviously, Mel intended to sell the property to the bank and certainly the bank wanted the property (why else did it sue?). We are often reminded in the caselaw that contract law is about "effectuating the intention of the parties." And yet, Mel was able to escape liability because, by the bank's own requirement, the proposal could not ripen into a contract until the document had been fully executed by an authorized trust officer of the bank. We think this raises some interesting questions, the answers to which may have a bearing on your advice to a client engaged in contract negotiations and how you draft a proposed agreement for that client.

QUESTIONS ABOUT LASALLE AND EVER-TITE

1. According to the courts' decisions, who were the offerors in *LaSalle National Bank* and *Ever–Tite*? Who drafted the instruments on which the assertion of contractual liability was based? Did that have a bearing on the outcome in either case? Should it have? Is it the *offeror* who controls the terms of the offer or is it more accurate to say that it is the terms of the *offer* that control the deal?

2. In *LaSalle National Bank,* how important was "full execution" to the bank? Who was that provision intended to protect? Suppose it was just a formality? If so, under the guise of protecting the offeror (the sovereign), have we not assisted the offeree in walking on the deal?

3. Why didn't LaSalle National Bank simply have an officer in its trust department execute the Real Estate Sale Contract before the bank filed its complaint against Mel?

4. Returning to *Ever–Tite*, what does the following statement from the Ever-Tite form mean: "written acceptance, hereof, by the principal * * *"? What does the following statement from the *Ever–Tite* opinion mean: "Formal acceptance of the contract was not made under the signature and approval of an agent of the plaintiff"?

5. Suppose that the day before Ever–Tite planned to do the job, the Greens had called and said they were no longer interested. Would there have been a contract? Would it have mattered if, at the time they called, the Greens were aware that their credit had checked out? How could Ever–Tite have protected itself?

6. In *Ever–Tite*, the trial court had concluded that the work did not "commence" until the Ever–Tite workers arrived at the site. Is this a less reasonable construction of the language in the instrument than the appellate court's construction that the work commenced with the loading of the trucks? Even if so, was that a judgment that was appropriate to make on appeal? Accepting, *arguendo*, the trial court's construction of when the work commenced, did that justify the trial court's conclusion that there was no contract? How did the Greens *manifest* their intention to revoke? Does this square with the objective theory of contract formation?

7. What happens when the offer does not stipulate the required manner or method of acceptance? Consider the next case and the material that follows.

Introduction to *Davis v. Jacoby*

This case reflects the attitude of the common law and the first *Restatement of Contracts*, an attitude consistent with the view of offeror as king, that every offer had to be regarded as an offer for a "unilateral" or a "bilateral" contract. The distinction was based on an assessment of whether the offeror was bargaining for, respectively, a specific act by the offeree, or a return promise. Every offer had to be characterized as one or the other, and, as we'll see, this, in turn, affected the manner in which the offer could be accepted; *i.e.*, by performance or return promise.

We know you've already read about offers for unilateral and bilateral contracts in *Gilbert's Law Summaries* and have probably been wondering when we three knuckleheads are going to get around to discussing those concepts. Well, we waited this long because these terms—unilateral and bilateral contract—are not found anywhere in either the *Restatement (Second) of Contracts* or Article 2 of the U.C.C., although the terminology occasionally still does show up in the caselaw. The perspective of the drafters of the *Restatement* and the U.C.C. was to make the law less formal and less rigid so that failure to comply with some legal nicety does not inadvertently frustrate actual contractual intent. The thinking was that in most instances the offeror is indifferent as to what manner of assent, promise or performance, is necessary to accept the offer. If that's so, by construing the offer as requiring one or the other, we run the risk that contractual intent might be defeated because of the failure of the acceptance to comport with the form of the offer. In our judgment, this is almost what happens in *Davis v. Jacoby*. See what you think.

DAVIS v. JACOBY

Supreme Court of California
1 Cal.2d 370, 34 P.2d 1026 (1934)

PER CURIAM

Plaintiffs appeal from a judgment refusing to grant specific performance of an alleged contract to make a will. The facts are not in dispute and are as follows:

The plaintiff Caro M. Davis was the niece of Blanche Whitehead who was married to Rupert Whitehead. Prior to her marriage in 1913 to her coplaintiff Frank M. Davis, Caro lived for a considerable time at the home of the Whiteheads, in Piedmont, California. The Whiteheads were childless and extremely fond of Caro. The record is replete with uncontradicted testimony of the close and loving relationship that existed between Caro and her aunt and uncle. During the period that Caro lived with the Whiteheads she was treated as and often referred to by the Whiteheads as their daughter. In 1913, when Caro was married to Frank Davis the marriage was arranged at the Whitehead home and a reception held there. After the marriage Mr. and Mrs. Davis went to Mr. Davis' home in Canada, where they have resided ever since. During the period 1913 to 1931 Caro made many visits to the Whiteheads, several of them being of long duration. The Whiteheads visited Mr. and Mrs. Davis in Canada on several occasions. After the marriage and continuing down to 1931 the closest and most friendly relationship at all times existed between these two families. They corresponded frequently, the record being replete with letters showing the loving relationship.

By the year 1930 Mrs. Whitehead had become seriously ill. She had suffered several strokes and her mind was failing. Early in 1931 Mr. Whitehead had her removed to a private hospital. The doctors in attendance had informed him that she might die at any time or she might linger for many months. Mr. Whitehead had suffered severe financial reverses. He had had several sieges of sickness and was in poor health. The record shows that during the early part of 1931 he was desperately in need of assistance with his wife, and in his business affairs, and that he did not trust his friends in Piedmont. On March 18, 1931, he wrote to Mrs. Davis telling her of Mrs. Whitehead's condition and added that Mrs. Whitehead was very wistful. "Today I endeavored to find out what she wanted. I finally asked her if she wanted to see you. She burst out crying and we had great difficulty in getting her to stop. Evidently, that is what is on her mind. It is a very difficult matter to decide. If you come it will mean that you will have to leave again, and then things may be serious. I am going to see the doctor, and get his candid opinion and will then write you again. * * * Since writing the above, I have seen the doctor, and he thinks it will help considerably if you come." * * * On March 24, 1931, Mr. Davis, at the request of his wife, telegraphed to Mr. Whitehead as follows: "Your letter received. Sorry to hear Blanche not so well. Hope you are feeling better yourself. If you wish Caro to go to you can arrange for her to leave in about two weeks. Please wire me if you think it advisable for her to go." On March 30, 1931, Mr. Whitehead wrote a long letter to Mr. Davis, in which he explained in detail the condition of Mrs. Whitehead's health and also referred to his own health. He pointed out that he had lost a considerable portion of his cash assets but still owned considerable realty, that he needed someone to help him with his wife and some friend he could trust to help him with his business affairs and suggested that perhaps Mr. Davis might come to California. He then pointed out that all his property was community property; that under his will all the property was to go to Mrs. Whitehead; that he believed that under Mrs. White-head's will practically everything was to go to Caro. Mr. Whitehead again wrote to Mr. Davis under date of April 9, 1931, pointing out how badly he needed someone he could trust to assist him, and giving it as his belief that if properly handled he could still save about $150,000. He then stated: "Having you [Mr. Davis] here to depend on and to help me regain my mind and courage would be a big thing." Three days later, on April 12, 1931, Mr. Whitehead again wrote, addressing his letter to "Dear Frank and Caro", and in this letter made the definite offer, which offer it is claimed was accepted and is the basis of this action. In this letter he first pointed out that Blanche, his wife, was in a private hospital and that "she cannot last much longer * * * my affairs are not as bad as I supposed at first. Cutting everything down I figure 150,000 can be saved from the wreck." He then enumerated the values placed upon his various properties and then continued "my trouble was caused by my friends taking advantage of my illness and my position to skin me

"Now if Frank could come out here and be with me, and look after my affairs, we could easily save the balance I mentioned, provided I dont get into another panic and do some more foolish things.

"The next attack will be my end, I am 65 and my health has been bad for years, so, the Drs. dont give me much longer to live. So if you can come, Caro will inherit everything and you will make our lives happier and see Blanche is provided for to the end

"My eyesight has gone back on me, I cant read only for a few lines at a time. I am at the house alone with Stanley [the chauffeur] who does everything for me and is a fine fellow. Now, what I want is some one who will take charge of my affairs and see I dont lose any more. Frank can do it, if he will and cut out the booze.

"Will you let me hear from you as soon as possible, I know it will be a sacrifice but times are still bad and likely to be, so by settling down you can help me and Blanche and gain in the end. If I had you here my mind would get better and my courage return, and we could work things out."

This letter was received by Mr. Davis at his office in Windsor, Canada, about 9:30 A. M. April 14, 1931. After reading the letter to Mrs. Davis over the telephone, and after getting her belief that they must go to California, Mr. Davis immediately wrote Mr. Whitehead a letter, which, after reading it to his wife, he sent by air mail. This letter was lost, but there is no doubt that it was sent by Davis and received by Whitehead, in fact the trial court expressly so found. Mr. Davis testified in substance as to the contents of this letter. After acknowledging receipt of the letter of April 12, 1931, Mr. Davis unequivocally stated that he and Mrs. Davis accepted the proposition of Mr. Whitehead and both would leave Windsor to go to him on April 25th. This letter of acceptance also contained the information that the reason they could not leave prior to April 25th was that Mr. Davis had to appear in court on April 22d as one of the executors of his mother's estate. The testimony is uncontradicted and ample to support the trial court's finding that this letter was sent by Davis and received by Whitehead. In fact under date of April 15, 1931, Mr. Whitehead again wrote to Mr. Davis and stated "Your letter by air mail received this a. m. Now, I am wondering if I have put you to unnecessary trouble and expense, if you are making any money dont leave it, as things are bad here. * * * You know your business and I dont and I am half crazy in the bargain, but I dont want to hurt you or Caro

"Then on the other hand if I could get some one to trust and keep me straight I can save a good deal, about what I told you in my former letter."

This letter was received by Mr. Davis on April 17, 1931, and the same day Mr. Davis telegraphed to Mr. Whitehead "Cheer up—we will soon be there, we will wire you from the train."

Between April 14, 1931, the date the letter of acceptance was sent by Mr. Davis, and April 22d, Mr. Davis was engaged in closing out his business affairs, and Mrs. Davis in closing up their home and in making other arrangements to leave. On April 22, 1931, Mr. Whitehead committed suicide. Mr. and Mrs. Davis were immediately notified and they at once came to California. From almost the moment of her arrival Mrs. Davis devoted herself to the care and comfort of her aunt, and gave her aunt constant attention and care until Mrs. Whitehead's death on May 30, 1931. * * *

After the death of Mrs. Whitehead, for the first time it was discovered that the information contained in Mr. Whitehead's letter of March 30, 1931, in reference to the contents of his and Mrs. Whitehead's wills was incorrect. By a duly witnessed will dated February 28, 1931, Mr. Whitehead, after making several specific bequests, had bequeathed all of the balance of his estate to his wife for life, and upon her death to respondents Geoff Doubble and Rupert Ross Whitehead, his nephews. Neither appellant was mentioned in his will. * * *

After the discovery of the manner in which the property had been devised was made, this action was commenced upon the theory that Rupert Whitehead had assumed a contractual obligation to make a will whereby "Caro Davis would inherit everything"; that he had failed to do so; that plaintiffs had fully performed their part of the contract; * * *.

It should also be added that the evidence shows that as a result of Frank Davis leaving his business in Canada he forfeited not only all insurance business he might have written if he had remained, but also forfeited all renewal commissions earned on past business. According to his testimony this loss was over $8,000.

The trial court found that the relationship between Mr. and Mrs. Davis and the Whiteheads was substantially as above recounted and that the other facts above stated were true; * * *.

The theory of the trial court and of respondents on this appeal is that the letter of April 12th was an offer to contract, but that such offer could only be accepted by performance and could not be accepted by a promise to perform, and that said offer was revoked by the death of Mr. Whitehead before performance. In other words, it is contended that the offer was an offer to enter into a unilateral contract, and that the purported acceptance of April 14th was of no legal effect.

The distinction between unilateral and bilateral contracts is well settled in the law. It is well stated in section 12 of the American Institute's Restatement of the Law of Contracts as follows:

> "A unilateral contract is one in which no promisor receives a promise as consideration for his promise. A bilateral contract is one in which there are mutual promises between two parties to the contract; each party being both a promisor and a promisee."

This definition is in accord with the law of California. (*Chrisman v. Southern Cal. Edison Co.*, 83 Cal. App. 249[, 256 Pac. 618].)

In the case of unilateral contracts no notice of acceptance by performance is required. Section 1584 of the Civil Code provides, "Performance of the conditions of a proposal, * * * is an acceptance of the proposal." * * *

Although the legal distinction between unilateral and bilateral contracts is thus well settled, the difficulty in any particular case is to determine whether the particular offer is one to enter into a bilateral or unilateral contract. Some cases are quite clear cut. Thus an offer to sell which is accepted is clearly a bilateral contract, while an offer of a reward is a clear-cut offer of a unilateral contract which cannot be accepted by a promise to perform, but only by performance. * * * Between these two extremes is a vague field where the particular contract may be unilateral or bilateral depending upon the intent of the offerer and the facts and circumstances of each case. The offer to contract involved in this case falls within this category. By the provisions of the Restatement of the Law of Contracts it is expressly provided that there is a presumption that the offer is to enter into a bilateral contract. Section 31 provides:

> "In case of doubt it is presumed that an offer invites the formation of a bilateral contract by an acceptance amounting in effect to a promise by the offeree to perform what the offer requests, rather than the formation of one or more unilateral contracts by actual performance on the part of the offeree."

Professor Williston in his Treatise on Contracts, volume 1, section 60, also takes the position that a presumption in favor of bilateral contracts exists.

In the comment following section 31 of the Restatement the reason for such presumption is stated as follows:

"It is not always easy to determine whether an offerer requests an act or a promise to do the act. As a bilateral contract immediately and fully protects both parties, the interpretation is favored that a bilateral contract is proposed."

While the California cases have never expressly held that a presumption in favor of bilateral contracts exists, the cases clearly indicate a tendency to treat offers as offers of bilateral rather than of unilateral contracts. * * *

Keeping these principles in mind we are of the opinion that the offer of April 12th was an offer to enter into a bilateral as distinguished from a unilateral contract. Respondents argue that Mr. Whitehead had the right as offerer to designate his offer as either unilateral or bilateral. That is undoubtedly the law. It is then argued that from all the facts and circumstances it must be implied that what Whitehead wanted was performance and not a mere promise to perform. We think this is a non sequitur, in fact the surrounding circumstances lead to just the opposite conclusion. These parties were not dealing at arm's length. Not only were they related, but a very close and intimate friendship existed between them. The record indisputably demonstrates that Mr. Whitehead had confidence in Mr. and Mrs. Davis, in fact that he had lost all confidence in everyone else. The record amply shows that by an accumulation of occurrences Mr. Whitehead had become desperate, and that what he wanted was the promise of appellants that he could look to them for assistance. He knew from his past relationship with appellants that if they gave their promise to perform he could rely upon them. The correspondence between them indicates how desperately he desired this assurance. Under these circumstances he wrote his offer of April 12th, above quoted, in which he stated, after disclosing his desperate mental and physical condition, and after setting forth the terms of his offer: "Will you let me hear from you as soon as possible—I know it will be a sacrifice but times are still bad and likely to be, so by settling down you can help me and Blanche and gain in the end." By thus specifically requesting an immediate reply Whitehead expressly indicated the nature of the acceptance desired by him—namely, appellants' promise that they would come to California and do the things requested by him. This promise was immediately sent by appellants upon receipt of the offer, and was received by Whitehead. It is elementary that when an offer has indicated the mode and means of acceptance, an acceptance in accordance with that mode or means is binding on the offerer.

* * *

For the foregoing reasons we are of the opinion that the offer of April 12, 1931, was an offer to enter into a bilateral contract which was accepted by the letter of April 14, 1931. * * *

For the foregoing reasons the judgment appealed from is reversed.

QUESTIONS AND NOTES

1. Questions about the facts of this case

    1.1. Did Rupert Whitehead make an offer to Frank and Caro Davis? If so, what was it?

    1.2. Did that offer invite or require acceptance in any particular manner?

    1.3. Did Rupert Whitehead ever revoke that offer? What is the importance of the April 14th letter? Of the February 28th will? Of Rupert's will "maturing"?

    1.4. Who was Jacoby?

2. Questions about the law

    2.1. How did Frank and Caro accept? Can every offer be accepted by a mere promise? How would *Restatement (Second)* § 32 answer that question? *See* Note 3.2 below.

    2.2. What if the letter of March 30th had said, "Caro and you can accept this offer to inherit everything only by moving to California"? What is the difference between that hypothetical language and the language of the April 12th letter—"So if you can come, Caro will inherit everything"?

    2.3. What do you think Mr. Whitehead was *really* bargaining for, the Davis' promise or their performance? Do you think he even thought about it in those terms? If not, should important legal consequences—such as when an acceptance is effective and whether notice of acceptance is required—turn on the distinction between offers for unilateral and bilateral contracts?

3. Notes

    3.1. We will deal more directly with the question of what a party to an agreement was bargaining for when we deal with consideration in Chapter 3. Examination of "incapacity" is deferred until Chapter 4. Professor Monroe Freedman of Hofstra Law School suggests that the lawyers for Davis and Jacoby also decided to defer consideration of incapacity:

    [T]he adversary system will occasionally fail to bring out facts or arguments that might be highly relevant to the court's decision. One illustration is *Davis v. Jacoby*, where the contest was between parties claiming under a will and parties claiming under a contract to make a different will. A material fact was that the testator/contractor was very likely incompetent during the period of time when both instruments were executed. Accordingly, neither party appears to have argued the legal relevance of the testator/contractor's mental condition, one side because they did not want to impeach the will, the other side because they did not want to impeach the contract."

Monroe H. Freedman, *Arguing the Law in the Adversary System*, 16 GA. L. REV. 833, 838 (1982).

3.2. We have seen that the traditional common law view, incorporated into the first *Restatement,* was to use the terms "unilateral contract" and "bilateral contract," and to treat the offeror's designation as to the manner of acceptance as mandatory. Under the first *Restatement,* an offer was either an offer that could only be accepted by performance or one that could only be accepted by a return promise to perform. Sort of binary, if you get our drift.

In contrast to its predecessor, the approach of the *Restatement (Second)* is to presume that the offeror is more flexible (or indifferent) as to the manner of acceptance. That is to say, the *Restatement (Second)* does not use the bilateral/unilateral contract terminology anywhere in the document.

More specifically, § 50(1) provides that *"[a]cceptance of an offer is a manifestation of assent to the terms thereof made by the offeree in a manner invited or required by the offer."* This provision recognizes the principle that the offeror can dictate the permissible manner of assent. However, § 30(2) creates a presumption that, *"unless otherwise indicated by the language or circumstances,"* an offer will be treated as inviting acceptance in any manner that is reasonable under the circumstances. Section 32 then continues that, *"[i]n the case of doubt an offer is interpreted as inviting the offeree to accept either by promising to perform what the offeror requests or by rendering the performance as the offeree chooses."*

The above provisions of the *Restatement (Second)* are consistent with the general approach taken by the U.C.C. concerning acceptance. Specifically, § 2–206(1)(a) provides that "[u]nless otherwise unambiguously indicated by the language or circumstances an offer to make a contract shall be construed as inviting acceptance in any manner and by any medium reasonable in the circumstances."

Both the U.C.C. and the *Restatement (Second)* reflect a belief that, in the vast majority of cases, the offeror is indifferent to the manner in which assent is expressed. Is that a fair assumption?

Would application of the *Restatement (Second)* approach have changed the outcome in *Davis v. Jacoby?* How about the analysis? Consider your answers in light of the following excerpt from *Maryland Supreme Corp. v. The Blake Co.* (the case we examined earlier in connection with what constitutes an offer) addressing acceptance under U.C.C. § 2–206(1).

MARYLAND SUPREME CORP. v. BLAKE CO.

Court of Appeals of Maryland
279 Md. 531, 369 A.2d 1017 (1977)

[Recall that earlier we considered the portion of this decision dealing with whether the Maryland Supreme Corp. made an offer. Now we provide the court's analysis of whether Blake accepted the offer.]

The Acceptance

The mutual assent which is the essential feature of every contract is crystallized when there is a knowing and sufficient acceptance to a certain and definite offer. Supreme urges that even if it made a certain and definite offer, there was no valid acceptance by Blake so as to give rise to a binding contract. It * * * asserts that the judgment of the lower court on the evidence that there was an acceptance was clearly erroneous and should be set aside. We have no difficulty in determining that the lower court was not clearly wrong in ruling that Blake accepted Supreme's offer.

As we have indicated, what is involved here is the sale of goods within the contemplation of the UCC. We start, therefore, with the basic principles that the contract may be made in any manner sufficient to show agreement, including conduct by both parties which recognizes the existence of such a contract, and that an agreement sufficient to constitute a contract for sale may be found even though the moment of its making is undetermined. UCC § 2–204(1) and (2). The Official Comment to subsection (1) states that "appropriate conduct by the parties may be sufficient to establish an agreement." We also note that unless otherwise unambiguously indicated by language or circumstances, "(a)n offer to make a contract shall be construed as inviting acceptance in any manner and by any medium reasonable in the circumstances." UCC § 2–206(1)(a). The Official Comment to § 2–206 observes:

> Any reasonable manner of acceptance is intended to be regarded as available unless the offeror has made quite clear that it will not be acceptable. Former technical rules as to acceptance * * * are rejected and a criterion that the acceptance be 'in any manner and by any medium reasonable under the circumstances,' is substituted.

The trial court found as a fact that Blake "promptly notified Supreme of its successful bid, and verbally accepted Supreme's offer," that Blake "began ordering as concrete was needed, and continued to do so until it received a letter from Supreme dated October 24, 1975 (raising the price)," and that "Supreme and Blake had several times done business before, and * * * that the procedure in this case was as it had always been before." There was credible evidence to support these findings. Applying the applicable statutory provisions of the UCC to these facts leads to the conclusion that the verbal acceptance by Blake of Supreme's offer was reasonable in the circumstances, that Blake did so accept it, and that the conduct of the parties, particularly that of Supreme in delivering concrete and that of Blake in accepting and paying for it, recognized the existence of a contract. There being legally sufficient evidence for the court as the trier of fact to find that Blake accepted Supreme's offer, that judgment on the evidence was not clearly erroneous.

* * *

CONNECTIONS

How do the rules on modes and manner of acceptance, as illustrated in the last several cases cohere* with the rules on what constitutes an offer? What policy objectives do you see as intending to be served by these rules? How well are those objectives actually served by either or both the traditional and more contemporary iterations** of these rules? Why have modern courts, and the *Restatement (Second)* eliminated the sharp distinction between offers for unilateral and bilateral contracts? Does that development mean the distinction is no longer important? Read on.

B. EFFECTIVENESS OF PROMISSORY ACCEPTANCE

Introduction to *Hendricks*

Davis v. Jacoby illustrates that a promise can be effective as an acceptance, at least under most circumstances. The next two cases raise two different questions relating to the *point in time* at which a promise as an acceptance is effective. In the first case, *Hendricks*, we see an attempt to accept and an attempt to revoke an offer. Accordingly, the time at which each becomes effective is going to be critical in determining whether or not there is mutual assent.

HENDRICKS v. BEHEE

Court of Appeals of Missouri, Southern District
786 S.W.2d 610 (1990)

FLANIGAN, J.

Plaintiff Steve L. Hendricks, d/b/a Hendricks Abstract & Title Co., instituted this interpleader action,*** against defendants Eugene Behee,

---

* "Cohere" is a word that Ponoroff recently learned and insisted on using. It is, apparently, the verb form of the noun "coherent" and means "to be logically and aesthetically consistent" or "to be united in principles, relationship, or interest". Epstein and Markell think he might just have said that, but, again, he insisted. * * *

** Yes, we know, there he goes again (Epstein & Markell).

*** This is a procedural device that is available in the following kind of circumstances: Epstein holds certain property which he acknowledges does not belong to him and as to which he asserts

Artice Smith, and Pearl Smith. Plaintiff was the escrowee of $5,000 which had been paid by defendant Behee as a deposit accompanying Behee's offer to purchase real estate owned by defendants Artice and Pearl Smith, husband and wife, in Stockton, Missouri. A dispute between Behee and the Smiths as to whether their dealings resulted in a binding contract prompted the interpleader action. Behee filed a crossclaim against the Smiths.

After a nonjury trial, the trial court awarded plaintiff $997.50 to be paid out of the $5,000 deposit. None of the parties challenges that award. The trial court awarded the balance of $4,002.50 to defendant Behee. Defendants [Smiths] appeal.

In essence the Smiths contend that the dealings between them and Behee ripened into a contract and entitled the Smiths to the balance of $4,002.50, and that the trial court erred in ruling otherwise.

After Behee, as prospective buyer, and the Smiths, as prospective sellers, had engaged in unproductive negotiations, Behee, on March 2, 1987, made a written offer of $42,500 for the real estate and $250 for a dinner bell and flower pots. On March 3 that offer was mailed to the Smiths, who lived in Mississippi, by their real estate agent. There were two real estate agents involved. The trial court found that both were the agents of the Smiths, and that finding has not been disputed by the Smiths in this appeal. For simplicity, the two agents will be considered in this opinion as one agent who acted on behalf of the Smiths.

On March 4 the Smiths signed the proposed agreement in Mississippi. Before Behee was notified that the Smiths had accepted the offer, Behee withdrew the offer by notifying the real estate agent of the withdrawal. That paramount fact is conceded by this statement in the Smiths' brief: "On either March 5, 6 or 7, 1987, Behee contacted [the Smiths' real estate agent] and advised her that he desired to withdraw his offer to purchase the real estate. Prior to this communication, Behee had received no notice that his offer had been accepted by the Smiths."

* * *

An uncommunicated intention to accept an offer is not an acceptance. * * * When an offer calls for a promise, as distinguished from an act, on the part of the offeree, notice of acceptance is always essential. * * * A mere private act of the offeree does not constitute an acceptance. * * * Communication of acceptance of a contract to an agent of the offeree is not sufficient and does not bind the offeror. * * *

no claim. He simply wants to return the property to its rightful owner. The problem is that both Markell and Ponoroff claim that they are entitled to the property and they both demand that Epstein turn it over to them or they will sue! Epstein does not have a dog in that fight He does not really care who is right, he just doesn't want to run the risk of turning it over to the wrong party and then incurring liability to the rightful owner. The solution for Epstein is to bring a lawsuit, naming both Markell and Ponoroff as defendants, in which Epstein *interpleads* the property with the court saying, in effect, "here it is, you decide who gets it, Judge, just leave me out of it, except I think I ought to be reimbursed my costs by the real parties in interest here." Eds.

Unless the offer is supported by consideration, * * * an offeror may withdraw his offer at any time "before acceptance and communication of that fact to him." * * * To be effective, revocation of an offer must be communicated to the offeree before he has accepted. * * *

Notice to the agent, within the scope of the agent's authority, is notice to the principal, and the agent's knowledge is binding on the principal. * * *

Before Behee was notified that the Smiths had accepted his offer, Behee notified the agent of the Smiths that Behee was withdrawing the offer. The notice to the agent, being within the scope of her authority, was binding upon the Smiths. Behee's offer was not supported by consideration and his withdrawal of it was proper. * * *

The judgment is affirmed.

QUESTIONS

1. Questions about the facts of this case

    1.1. What did Mr. Behee indicate to the Smiths concerning the permissible or required manner of acceptance?

    1.2. The court notes that the real estate agents involved in the deal were both agents of the Smiths. Why is that fact important? How would the analysis change if one or both of the agents were agent(s) for Behee?

2. Questions about the law

    2.1. Did the court construe Mr. Behee's offer as an offer for a unilateral contract or an offer for a bilateral contract? How do you construe the offer?

    2.2. Does the holding in *Hendricks* suggest that in *Ever-Tite Roofing, supra,* even if an authorized representative of the Ever–Tite corporation had actually signed the Green's offer as soon as their credit checked out that there would still have been no contract until notice of the signature had been given to the Greens? Why not? By the same token, how could the loading of the truck in *Ever-Tite* have constituted acceptance by commencement of performance if the Greens were not aware that the trucks were being loaded?

    2.3. Is the holding in *Hendricks* consistent with *Restatement (Second) of Contracts* § 50(3)'s language that, **"Acceptance by a promise requires that the offeree complete every act essential to the making of the promise"**?

Introduction to *Adams v. Lindsell*

When, under the terms of the offer, acceptance by return promise is permitted or required, an issue arises if the parties are not face-to-face. *Hendricks* suggests that an uncommunicated intention to accept an offer is not an acceptance; that notice of acceptance is always an essential aspect of a promissory acceptance. Is this consistent with objective theory? In *Hendricks*, there is no indication that the Smiths made any attempt to communicate their acceptance to Behee before Behee withdrew his offer. What about, however, if the offeree does send an acceptance? Unless the parties are face-to-face, inevitably there will be some length of time between the moment the acceptance is actually sent and the moment it is received. If the mail is involved, this could be a matter of days, or, as we all know, even longer. The period of transmission will be much shorter of course if the offeree uses FedEx or another overnight courier, but, even then, there will be some time—a gap—between the offeree's sending and the offeror's receiving the acceptance. Thus, the question arises whether during this period of transmission a contract exists or whether the offeror is still sovereign until the acceptance is actually received. Based on objective theory of contract formation, what would you predict? Of course, you would say that the acceptance is not effective until received by the offeror. However, you may recall that in *Minnesota Linseed Oil Co. v. Collier White Lead Co., supra,* at p. 90, the court suggested that a different rule pertains in these circumstances, citing the next case, *Adams v. Lindsell.* Now we get to see what that case was all about.

Before we do, however, we need to make a disclosure. We admit all three of us are old, although Markell and Ponoroff wish to point out that Epstein is the oldest of the three by far. But that's not the disclosure. Despite our advanced years, we are keenly aware that in a commercial economy increasingly dominated by electronic transactions the rule of *Adams v. Lindsell* is fast becoming something of a relic; a vestigial remnant of an earlier era. Indeed, just to show you how with it we are, we have a section coming up on "electronic acceptances." Nevertheless, we think it is still important to consider *Adams v. Lindsell* and the legal proposition it has come to stand for. We believe this is so for three reasons. First, folks still do business from time to time by mail or other non-electronic means, and letters still get lost in the mail. Second, the rule in *Adams v. Lindsell* provides law professors with an irresistible opportunity to probe both the logic and the limits of the objective theory of contract formation. Finally, three years from now, when you prepare to take a bar exam, you will hear Epstein lecturing about the "mailbox rule" and you should have some vague recollection as to what he is talking about.

ADAMS v. LINDSELL

Court of King's Bench
106 Eng. Rep. 250 (1818)

Action for non-delivery of wool according to agreement. At the trial at the last Lent Assizes for the county of Worcester, before Burrough J. it appeared that the defendants who were dealers in wool, at St. Ives, in the county of Huntingdon, had, on Tuesday the 2d of September 1817, written the following letter to the plaintiffs, who were woolen manufacturers residing in Bromsgrove, Worcestershire. "We now offer you eight hundred tods of wether fleeces, of a good fair quality of our country wool, at 35s. 6d. per tod, to be delivered at Leicester, and to be paid for by two months' bill in two months, and to be weighed up by your agent within fourteen days, receiving your answer in course of post."

This letter was misdirected by the defendants, to Bromsgrove, Leicestershire, in consequence of which it was not received by the plaintiffs in Worcestershire till 7 p.m. on Friday, September 5th. On that evening the plaintiffs wrote an answer, agreeing to accept the wool on the terms proposed. The course of the post between St. Ives and Bromsgrove is through London, and consequently this answer was not received by the defendants till Tuesday, September 9th. On Monday September 8th, the defendants not having, as they expected, received an answer on Sunday September 7th, (which in case their letter had not been misdirected, would have been in the usual course of the post,) sold the wool in question to another person. Under these circumstances, the learned Judge held, that the delay having been occasioned by the neglect of the defendants, the jury must take it, that the answer did come back in due course of post; and that then the defendants were liable for the loss that had been sustained; and the plaintiffs accordingly recovered the verdict.

Jervis having in Easter term obtained a rule nisi for a new trial, on the ground that there was no binding contract between the parties.

Dauncey, Puller, and Richardson, showed cause. They contended, that at the moment of the acceptance of the offer of the defendants by the plaintiffs, the former became bound. And that was on the Friday evening, when there had been no change of circumstances. They were then stopped by the Court, who called upon Jervis and Campbell in support of the rule. They relied on *Payne v Cave* [3 T.R. 148], and more particularly on *Cooke v. Oxley* [Ibid. 653]. In that case, Oxley, who had proposed to sell goods to Cooke, and given him a certain time at his request, to determine whether he would buy them or not, was held not liable to the performance of the contract, even though Cooke, within the specified time, had determined to buy them, and given Oxley notice to that effect. So here the defendants who have proposed by letter to sell this wool are not to be held liable, even though it be now admitted that the answer did come back in due course of post. Till the plaintiffs' answer was actually received, there could be no binding contract between the parties; and before then, the defendants had retracted their offer, by selling the wool to other persons. But—

The Court said, that if that were so, no contract could ever be completed by the post. For if the defendants were not bound by their offer when accepted by the plaintiffs till the answer was received, then the plaintiffs ought not to be bound till after they had received notification that the defendants had received their answer and assented to it. And so it might go on ad infinitum. The defendants must be considered in law as making, during every instant of the time their letter was travelling, the same identical offer to the plaintiffs; and then the contract is completed by the acceptance of it by the latter. Then as to the delay in notifying the acceptance, that arises entirely from the mistake of the defendants, and it therefore must be taken as against them, that the plaintiffs answer was received in course of post.

Rule discharged.

QUESTIONS AND NOTES

1. Questions about the facts of this case

    1.1. *Adams* is celebrated for establishing the so-called "mailbox rule," which holds that an acceptance is effective on *dispatch* rather than *receipt*. This rule continues to the present day. *See Restatement (Second) of Contracts* § 63. Along with automatic termination of an offer on death or disability of the offeror, the dispatch rule represents perhaps the most glaring exception to the objective theory of contract formation. However, the dispatch rule is only operative under certain circumstances. What was the critical fact in *Adams* that convinced the court to employ this rule?

    1.2. In *Adams*, the court invoked the mailbox rule to protect the plaintiffs since the misdirection of the offer letter was the fault of the defendants. However, review the facts closely. Did the court need to resort to the mailbox rule in order to find for the plaintiffs? Also, is it clear that the plaintiffs were entitled to protection? Shouldn't the plaintiffs have been aware that by September 8 the defendants might no longer be interested in selling the fleeces to them? If so, did they still have the power of acceptance?

    1.3. Just how much was at stake in this case? According to Markell, who seems to have this proclivity to traveling to places where there are sheep (Ponoroff doesn't go to any place that does not have Arizona Law alumni, and, Epstein, bless his heart, is of course too old to travel), a "tod" is equivalent to 28 pounds, so the contract involved 22,400 pounds of "wether fleeces" (fleeces from castrated male sheep). At 35S. 6d. per tod, or roughly $15.00, we're talking about $12,000 worth of wool, not an inconsiderable sum in 1818.

1.4. By the way, are you as impressed as we are with the speed of the early nineteenth century English post?

2. Questions about the law

2.1. What justification does the court offer for the "mailbox rule"? How satisfying do you find that rationale?

2.2. If the offeror is truly sovereign and, as such, entitled to dictate the terms on which she is willing to deal, is there some way in which the offeror can protect herself against the mailbox rule; against having legal consequences established based on uncommunicated intent?

2.3. Who is the superior bearer of the risk that a communication will be lost or delayed during transit? Does your answer to this question suggest a more principled justification for the rule than the one offered by the court in *Adams*? *See* A. Corbin, Contracts § 78 (1950).

2.4. Under the rationale of *Adams,* if an offer is made by FedEx, and the acceptance by return post, does the mailbox rule apply? How about the other way around?

2.5. As the pace of technology has made communications between parties almost instantaneous even when those parties are at a distance from one another, e.g., facsimile transmissions and e-mail, does the rationale for the mailbox rule break down? How so? *Cf. Restatement (Second) of Contracts* § 64, cmt. a (*"Where the parties are in each other's presence, the offeree can accept without being in doubt as to whether the offeror has attempted to revoke his offer or whether the offeror has received the acceptance."*)

3. Notes

3.1. What role would you anticipate that the "dispatch rule" will or should play in the legal rules governing so-called "electronic contracts"; that is, contracts formed by means of computer transmissions or over the Internet and stored solely in the form of an electronic record? There is an emerging body of statutory law being developed to deal with electronic contracts. This includes the federal Electronic Signature in Global and National Commerce (E–Sign) Act and the Uniform Electronic Transactions Act, both designed to give legal effect to electronic signatures.

For the most part, the law has treated electronic contracts as tending to raise issues of *form* (*e.g.,* when is an electronic signature effective) rather than involving new substantive rules. Therefore, we discuss electronic contracting again in Part F of this Section, as well as in Chapter 3 as part of our study of the Statute of Frauds.

3.2. In *Dick v. United States,* 82 F.Supp. 326, 113 Ct.Cl. 94 (1949), a contractor received, on March 8, 1945, a purchase order by mail from the Navy for two sets of new propeller equipment consisting of two propellers and a propeller bow each. Believing that the bid was for one set of propellers and a propeller bow (a single "shipset"), the plaintiff mailed its acceptance on March 15, 1945. The following day, plaintiff notified the Navy that he had made a mistake and that the price should be doubled. The plaintiff proceeded with the manufacture and delivery of two shipsets of propellers, but the Navy paid for only one. Thereafter the plaintiff brought an action to recover the value of the second shipset of propeller equipment. In response to the Navy's argument that a binding contract had been formed upon the mailing of plaintiff's acceptance on March 15, the court cited a change in postal regulation permitting anyone who had sent a letter to reclaim it by wiring the postmaster at the destination point. Thus, because the court concluded that the letter of acceptance was not out of the plaintiff's control until it had been delivered, the posting of the letter did not constitute an acceptance. Does this ruling make sense?

PROBLEMS CONCERNING APPLICATION OF THE "MAILBOX RULE"

1. Assume that, on November 26, Ponoroff executes a contract for the purchase and sale of certain real property and mails it to Markell for acceptance. On receipt of the agreement, Markell executes it and sends it, by return mail, to Ponoroff's attorney. Subsequently, Markell changes his mind and calls Ponoroff's attorney to inform her that he is not interested in selling and that she should ignore the agreement when it shows up. The next day, the signed agreement arrives at Ponoroff's attorney's office. What should the attorney advise Ponoroff in terms of whether or not he has a binding contract to buy the property? Would it affect your advice if Markell failed to inform the attorney during their telephone conversation that he had already signed and mailed back the agreement? In that case, suppose, after being informed of the telephone call by his attorney, Ponoroff goes out and enters into a contract to purchase another parcel of property. Thereafter, the signed agreement arrives in Ponoroff's attorney's office and Markell brings an action for specific performance. Is there a contract between Ponoroff and Markell? If so, does Ponoroff have a defense to liability?

2. Assume the same facts as stated at the beginning of Problem 1 above, except that, instead of mailing the agreement to Ponoroff's attorney, Markell mails it to his own lawyer with instructions to deliver to it Ponoroff. Can Markell still change his mind? If so, up to what point in time? Why didn't the mailbox rule protect the sellers in *Hendricks v. Behee, supra*?

3. Suppose that, on Day 1, Epstein sends Markell an offer by mail. The offer does not contain any specification relating to manner of acceptance. On Day 2, Epstein changes his mind and mails a revocation of the offer. On Day 3, Markell receives the offer and immediately mails

an acceptance. On Day 5 the revocation arrives, and on Day 6 the acceptance arrives.

(a) Has a contract been formed? If so, when? *Yes, day 3 under mailbox rule*

(b) Does it change your answer if, on Day 2, right after dropping his letter in the mail, Epstein clutches his chest and dies right there at the mailbox?

(c) How about if Epstein dies on Day 3? Is there anything else you want to know?

(d) How does it affect your answer if, before Epstein dies on Day 3, Markell mails a rejection and then changes his mind and mails an acceptance? *See Restatement (Second) of Contracts* § 40.

(e) Assume the same facts as part (d), except that Epstein doesn't die at all. In analyzing whether a contract is formed, does it matter which communication arrives first?

4. Now assume that, on February 1, Epstein sends Markell an offer by mail agreeing that, in return for $100, he will grant Markell a 60–day option (to expire on April 2) to purchase Epstein's house for $150,000. Markell promptly pays the $100. There are no further communications between the parties until, on March 29, Markell sends a letter to Epstein notifying him that he is exercising the option. The letter reaches Epstein on April 3, whereupon Epstein calls Markell and tells him that it's "too late," and he has already arranged to sell the property to Ponoroff for $155,000. Does Markell have a claim against Epstein? *See Restatement (Second)* § 63, cmt. f. How about against Ponoroff?

C. EFFECTIVENESS OF ACCEPTANCE BY PERFORMANCE

Subject to the mailbox rule, we've seen that an acceptance in the form of a return promise is not effective until communicated to the offeror. However, recall that *"[U]nless otherwise indicated by the language or the circumstances, an offer [is treated as inviting] acceptance in any manner and by any medium reasonable in the circumstances." Restatement (Second) of Contracts* § 30(2). Thus, in most cases, acceptance may occur by performance as well as by promise. If the offeree accepts by performance, when is the acceptance effective? Is it when the act is begun; when it is completed; or when the offeror receives notice that the act has been completed? The next two cases and the material that follow address these questions and the answers may just surprise you.

CARLILL v. CARBOLIC SMOKE BALL CO.

Court of Appeal
1 Q.B. 256 (1893)

[The defendant, a London-based company, ran an advertisement promising to pay a 100£ "reward" to anyone who contracted the flu after inhaling the company's smoke ball three times daily for a two-week period in accordance with the printed directions. The ad noted that, in a gesture of its sincerity, the company had deposited 1,000£ pounds with a local bank. This action was brought by Lilli Carlill who, after seeing the ad, purchased a smoke ball and used it as directed for a period of two months whereupon she contracted influenza.]

LINDLEY, L.J. [The Lord Justice stated the facts, and proceeded:]

£100 REWARD

WILL BE PAID BY THE

CARBOLIC SMOKE BALL CO.

To any person who contracts the increasing Epidemic,

INFLUENZA,

Colds, or any diseases caused by taking cold, AFTER HAVING USED the BALL
3 times daily for two weeks according to the printed directions supplied with each Ball.

£1,000

Is deposited with the ALLIANCE BANK, REGENT-STREET, showing our sincerity in the matter. During the last epidemic of Influenza many thousand CARBOLIC SMOKE BALLS were sold as Preventives against this Disease, and in no ascertained case was the disease contracted by those using the CARBOLIC SMOKE BALL.

One CARBOLIC SMOKE BALL will last a family several months, making it the cheapest remedy in the world at the price—10s., post free. The BALL can be RE-FILLED at a cost of 5s. Address :—

CARBOLIC SMOKE BALL CO.,

27, Princes-street, Hanover-sq., London, W.

Smoke Ball Contract

I will begin by referring to two points which were raised in the Court below. I refer to them simply for the purpose of dismissing them. First, it is said no action will lie upon this contract because it is a policy. You have only to look at the advertisement to dismiss that suggestion. Then it was said that it is a bet. Hawkins, J., came to the conclusion that nobody ever dreamt of a bet, and that the transaction had nothing whatever in common with a bet. I so entirely agree with him that I pass over this contention also as not worth serious attention.

Then, what is left? The first observation I will make is that we are not dealing with any inference of fact. We are dealing with an express promise to pay 100£ in certain events. Read the advertisement how you will, and twist it about as you will, here is a distinct promise expressed in language which is perfectly unmistakable—"100£ reward will be paid by the Carbolic Smoke Ball Company to any person who contracts the influenza after having used the ball three times daily for two weeks according to the printed directions supplied with each ball."

We must first consider whether this was intended to be a promise at all, or whether it was a mere puff which meant nothing. Was it a mere puff? My answer to that question is No, and I base my answer upon this passage: "1000£ is deposited with the Alliance Bank, showing our sincerity in the matter." Now, for what was that money deposited or that statement made except to negative the suggestion that this was a mere puff and meant nothing at all? The deposit is called in aid by the advertiser as proof of his sincerity in the matter—that is, the sincerity of his promise to pay this 100£ in the event which he has specified. I say this for the purpose of giving point to the observation that we are not inferring a promise; there is the promise, as plain as words can make it.

Then it is contended that it is not binding. In the first place, it is said that it is not made with anybody in particular. Now that point is common to the words of this advertisement and to the words of all other advertisements offering rewards. They are offers to anybody who performs the conditions named in the advertisement, and anybody who does perform the condition accepts the offer. In point of law this advertisement is an offer to pay 100£ to anybody who will perform these conditions, and the performance of the conditions is the acceptance of the offer. * * *

But then it is said, "Supposing that the performance of the conditions is an acceptance of the offer, that acceptance ought to have been notified." Unquestionably, as a general proposition, when an offer is made, it is necessary in order to make a binding contract, not only that it should be accepted, but that the acceptance should be notified. But is that so in cases of this kind? I apprehend that they are an exception to that rule, or, if not an exception, they are open to the observation that the notification of the acceptance need not precede the performance. This offer is a continuing offer. It was never revoked, and if notice of acceptance is required—which I doubt very much, for I rather think the true view is that which was expressed and explained by Lord Blackburn in the case of *Brogden v. Metropolitan By Co.*—if notice of acceptance is required, the person who makes the offer gets the notice of acceptance contemporaneously with his notice of the performance of the condition. If he gets notice of the acceptance before his offer is revoked, that in principle is all you want. I, however, think that the true view, in a case of this kind, is that the person who makes the offer shows by his language and from the nature of the transaction that he does not expect and does not require notice of the acceptance apart from notice of the performance.

We, therefore, find here all the elements which are necessary to form a binding contract enforceable in point of law, subject to two observations. First of all it is said that this advertisement is so vague that you cannot really construe it as a promise—that the vagueness of the languages shows that a legal promise was never intended or contemplated. The language is vague and uncertain in some respects, and particularly in this, that the 100£ is to be paid to any person who contracts the increasing epidemic after having used the balls three times daily for two weeks. It is said, When are they to be used? According to the language of the advertisement no time is fixed, and, construing the offer most strongly against the person who has made it, one might infer that any time was meant. I do not think that was meant, and to hold the contrary would be pushing too far the doctrine of taking language most strongly against the person using it. I do not think that business people or reasonable people would understand the words as meaning that if you took a smoke ball and used it three times daily for two weeks you were to be guaranteed against influenza for the rest of your life, and I think it would be pushing the language of the advertisement too far to construe it as meaning that. But if it does not mean that, what does it mean? It is for the defendants to show what it does mean; and it strikes me that there are two, and possibly three reasonable constructions to be put on this advertisement, any one of which will answer the purpose of the plaintiff. Possibly it may be limited to persons catching the "increasing epidemic" (that is, the then prevailing epidemic), or any colds or diseases caused by taking cold, during the prevalence of the increasing epidemic. That is one suggestion; but it does not commend itself to me. Another suggested meaning is that you are warranted free from catching this epidemic, or colds or other diseases caused by taking cold, whilst you are using this remedy after using it for two weeks. If that is the meaning, the plaintiff is right, for she used the remedy for two weeks and went on using it till she got the epidemic. Another meaning, and the one which I rather prefer, is that the reward is offered to any person who contracts the epidemic or other disease within a reasonable time after having used the smoke ball. Then it is asked, What is a reasonable time? It has been suggested that there is no standard of reasonableness; that it depends upon the reasonable time for a germ to develop! I do not feel pressed by that. It strikes me that a reasonable time may be ascertained in a business sense and in a sense satisfactory to a lawyer, in this way; find out from a chemist what the ingredients are; find out from a skilled physician how long the effect of such ingredients on the system could be reasonable expected to endure so as to protect a person from an epidemic or cold, and in that way you will get a standard to be laid before a jury, or a judge without a jury, by which they might exercise their judgement as to what a reasonable time would be. It strikes me, I confess, that the true construction of this advertisement is that 100£ will be paid to anybody who uses this smoke ball three times daily for two weeks according to the printed directions, and who gets the influenza or cold or other diseases caused by taking cold within a reasonable time after so using it; and if that is the true construction, it is enough for the plaintiff.

* * *

It appears to me, therefore, that the defendants must perform their promise, and, if they have been so unwary as to expose themselves to a great many actions, so much the worse for them.

QUESTIONS AND NOTES

1. Questions about the facts of this case

  1.1. The court dismissed "as not worth serious consideration" the argument that the advertisement was a bet. Did the Carbolic Smoke Ball Company really think inhalation of its smoke ball would prevent the flu or was it betting that most users would not contract the flu anyway?

  1.2. What's the difference between a promise and a "puff"? Does that difference depend on what you're "puffing"? [Ok, ignore that last question!] *[handwritten: Degree and language -specificty. What a normal person sees as reasonable]*

  1.3. The court in *Carlill* describes the Carbolic's advertisement as offering a *reward*. Is this a fair analogy? How does Carbolic's advertisement differ from an offer of "$100 for anyone who returns my lost gerbil, Bruce"? From the advertisement in *Leonard, supra*, at p. 47? More on this advertisement/reward distinction below.

  1.4. The court rejected the Carbolic Smoke Ball Company's argument that the offer was too vague to enforce on the basis that the promise was to give the reward to anyone contracting influenza within a *reasonable* time after using the smoke ball for two weeks as directed. Some lay people might suggest that this is an equally vague standard but, as you probably already know from your Torts class, for whatever reasons, lawyers are perfectly content with the "reasonable" answer. So just how long is a reasonable time?

2. Questions about the law

  2.1. According to the court, Ms. Carlill's acceptance was effective when she performed the acts requested by the offer even though the Carbolic Smoke Ball Company had not been notified of this fact. *[handwritten: X]* Why should the rule on notice to the offeror be different when acceptance is by performance rather than promise?

  2.2. Can this rule be reconciled with objective theory? Is there anything the offeror can do to alter this rule?

  2.3. *See Restatement (Second) of Contracts* § 54. Are the *Restatement* rules regarding notice of acceptance by performance consistent with the holding in *Carlill*? If not, how do they differ?

2.4. In distinguishing the situation in *Carlill* from the typical advertisement case, Lord Justice Lindley construed the advertisement as offering a *reward* and noted that "advertisements offering rewards * * * are offers to anybody who performs the conditions named in the advertisement, and anybody who performs the condition accepts the offer." John Leonard tried to make the same argument in *Leonard v. Pepsi Co. supra*, but, in a portion of the opinion we edited out, Judge Wood rejected the argument noting that: "In the present case [unlike *Carlill*], the Harrier Jet commercial did not direct that anyone who appeared at Pepsi headquarters with 7,000,-000 Pepsi Points on the Fourth of July would receive a Harrier Jet. Instead, the commercial urged consumers to accumulate Pepsi Points and to refer to the Catalog to determine how they could redeem their Pepsi Points. The commercial sought a reciprocal promise, expressed through acceptance of, and compliance with, the terms of the Order Form * * * Because the alleged offer in this case was, at most, an advertisement to receive offers rather than an offer of reward, plaintiff cannot show that there was an offer made in the circumstances of this case." Do you agree that *Carlill* and *Leonard* are distinguishable on this basis?

[handwritten margin note: sought reciprocal promise not performance]

2.5. Suppose you were able to get your hands on a Carbolic smoke ball today and snort (er, we mean inhale) it three times daily for two weeks and then, within a reasonable time thereafter, develop the flu. Could you collect the reward? *[handwritten: Reasonable time => lapse of offer]*

3. Notes

3.1. Assume another customer, Mortimer Markell (great, great grandfather of guess who) purchased a Carbolic smoke ball with no knowledge of the company's advertisement. After using the ball as directed for two weeks, Mortimer also contracted the flu. While at the doctor's office, he ran into Lilli Carlill and, upon striking up a conversation, the two discovered the similarity of their circumstances. Carlill told Mortimer that she planned to sue the Carbolic Smoke Ball Co., and he decided he would as well. Should Mortimer also prevail in his suit? *See Broadnax v. Ledbetter*, 100 Tex. 375, 99 S.W. 1111 (1907). Would it change your answer if Mortimer learned of the advertisement *after* he purchased the smoke ball but *before* he finished the two-week regime? *See Restatement (Second) of Contracts* § 51. How about if the offer had been made in a personal letter from the Smoke Ball Company to Ms. Carlill which Mortimer happened to see and, thereupon, went out and purchased a smoke ball, used it properly for two weeks, and then caught the flu? Can he collect?

3.2. Under traditional analysis, an offeree must know of the offer before there can be mutual assent. Is this rule consistent with objective theory? Should it apply in a reward case? If Epstein offered a $100 reward for the return of his lost gerbil, Bruce, and Ponoroff does not learn of the reward until after he's found and returned the gerbil, should Epstein be able to refuse payment of the $100? Hasn't

Epstein gotten what he bargained for, regardless of what Ponoroff knew or didn't know? *See Glover v. Jewish War Veterans*, 68 A.2d 233 (D.C.Mun.App. 1949). What is the situation if, upon reading of the reward, Ponoroff calls Epstein and says, "I accept, I am now off to look for Bruce the gerbil"? If Ponoroff doesn't find the gerbil, is he liable to Epstein? How about if he gets distracted by a wealthy University of Arizona Law College alumna and never even goes out to look for Bruce the gerbil?

In *Carlill,* the offeree had fully performed what was requested by the offer, and the court found that the offeror was bound, notice notwithstanding. Suppose, however, the offeree has only begun performance when the offeror changes his mind and revokes the offer. Is the revocation too late? Is there a contract? If not, are both parties free to walk away without any further liability? Assume that Markell offers Epstein $1,000 to paint Markell's house. Right after Epstein starts painting, Ponoroff tells Markell that he will paint the house for only $600. Can Markell still revoke his offer to Epstein? Or, if Sharon Stone offers Epstein a job as a co-star in her next movie, can Epstein stop painting Markell's house without liability? Does the next case, involving a revocation of an offer to pay commission to a real estate agent, help you answer any of these questions? (Or do you just wish we'd stop asking so many questions!)

MARCHIONDO v. SCHECK

Supreme Court Of New Mexico
78 N.M. 440, 432 P.2d 405 (1967)

WOOD, JUDGE

The issue is whether the offeror had a right to revoke his offer to enter a unilateral contract.

Defendant, in writing, offered to sell real estate to a specified prospective buyer and agreed to pay a percentage of the sales price as a commission to the broker. The offer fixed a six-day time limit for acceptance. Defendant, in writing, revoked the offer. The revocation was received by the broker on the morning of the sixth day. Later that day, the broker obtained the offeree's acceptance.

Plaintiff, the broker, claiming breach of contract, sued defendant for the commission stated in the offer. On the above facts, the trial court dismissed the complaint.

We are not concerned with the revocation of the offer as between the offeror and the prospective purchaser. With certain exceptions, the right of a broker to the agreed compensation, or damages measured thereby, is not defeated by the refusal of the principal to complete or consummate a transaction. * * *

Plaintiff's appeal concerns the revocation of his agency. As to that revocation, the issue between the offeror and his agent is not whether defendant had the power to revoke; rather, it is whether he had the right to revoke. * * *

When defendant made his offer to pay a commission upon sale of the property, he offered to enter a unilateral contract; the offer was for an act to be performed, a sale. * * *

Many courts hold that the principal has the right to revoke the broker's agency at any time before the broker has actually procured a purchaser. * * * The reason given is that until there is performance, the offeror has not received that contemplated by his offer, and there is no contract. Further, the offeror may never receive the requested performance because the offeree is not obligated to perform. Until the offeror receives the requested performance, no consideration has passed from the offeree to the offeror. Thus, until the performance is received, the offeror *usual* may withdraw the offer. * * *

Defendant asserts that the trial court was correct in applying this rule. However, plaintiff contends that the rule is not applicable where there has been part performance of the offer.

Hutchinson v. Dobson–Bainbridge Realty Co., [31 Tenn. App. 490 (1946)], states:

> "A greater number of courts, however, hold that part performance of the consideration may make such an offer irrevocable and that where the offeree or broker manifests his assent to the offer by entering upon performance and spending time and money in his efforts to perform, then the offer becomes irrevocable during the time stated and binding upon the principal according to its terms. * * *"

Defendant contends that the decisions giving effect to a part performance are distinguishable. He asserts that in these cases the offer was of an exclusive right to sell or of an exclusive agency. Because neither factor is present here, he asserts that the "part performance" decisions are not applicable.

Many of the decisions do seem to emphasize the exclusive aspects of the offer. * * *

Defendant's offer did not specifically state that it was exclusive. * * * [However,] [i]t is not the exclusiveness of the offer that deprives the offeror of the right to revoke. It is the action taken by the offeree which deprives the offeror of that right. Until there is action by the offeree—a partial performance pursuant to the offer—the offeror may revoke even if his offer is of an exclusive agency or an exclusive right to sell. * * *

Once partial performance is begun pursuant to the offer made, a contract results. This contract has been termed a contract with conditions or an option contract. This terminology is illustrated as follows:

> "If an offer for a unilateral contract is made, and part of the consideration requested in the offer is given or tendered by the offeree in response thereto, the offeror is bound by a contract, the duty of immediate performance of which is conditional on the full consideration being given or tendered within the time stated in the offer, or, if no time is stated therein, within a reasonable time." Restatement of Contracts, § 45 (1932).

Restatement (Second) of Contracts, § 45, Tent. Draft No. 1, (approved 1964, Tent. Draft No. 2, p. vii) states:

> "(1) Where an offer invites an offeree to accept by rendering a performance and does not invite a promissory acceptance, an option contract is created when the offeree begins the invited performance or tenders part of it.

> "(2) The offeror's duty of performance under any option contract so created is conditional on completion or tender of the invited performance in accordance with the terms of the offer."

Restatement (Second) of Contracts, § 45, Tent. Draft No. 1, comment (g), says:

> "This Section frequently applies to agency arrangements, particularly offers made to real estate brokers. * * *"

See Restatement (Second) of Agency § 446, comment (b).

The reason for finding such a contract is stated in *Hutchinson v. Dobson–Bainbridge Realty Co., supra,* as follows:

> "This rule avoids hardship to the offeree, and yet does not hold the offeror beyond the terms of his promise. It is true by such terms he was to be bound only if the requested act was done; but this implies that he will let it be done, that he will keep his offer open till the offeree who has begun can finish doing it. At least this is so where the doing of it will necessarily require time and expense. In such a case it is but just to hold that the offeree's part performance furnishes the 'acceptance' and the 'consideration' for a binding subsidiary promise not to revoke the offer, or turns the offer into a presently binding contract conditional upon the offeree's full performance."

We hold that part performance by the offeree of an offer of a unilateral contract results in a contract with a condition. The condition is full performance by the offeree. Here, if plaintiff-offeree partially performed prior to receipt of defendant's revocation, such a contract was formed. Thereafter, upon performance being completed by plaintiff, upon defendant's failure to recognize the contract, liability for breach of contract would arise. Thus, defendant's right to revoke his offer depends upon whether plaintiff had partially performed before he received defendant's revocation. * * *

What constitutes partial performance will vary from case to case since what can be done toward performance is limited by what is authorized to be done. Whether plaintiff partially performed is a question of fact to be determined by the trial court.

The trial court denied plaintiff's requested finding concerning his partial performance. It did so on the theory that partial performance was not material. In this the trial court erred.

Because of the failure to find on the issue of partial performance, the case must be remanded to the trial court. * * *

The cause is remanded for findings on the issue of plaintiff's partial performance of the offer prior to its revocation, and for further proceedings consistent with this opinion and the findings so made.

It is so ordered.

QUESTIONS

1. Questions about the facts of this case

    1.1. Did the defendant make one offer or two offers?

    1.2. How, if at all, did the plaintiff perform?

    1.3. Did the specified prospective buyer agree to buy the real property? Was that important?

    1.4. Did the specified prospective buyer agree to buy the real property before the plaintiff received the defendant's revocation? Was that important?

2. Questions about the law

    2.1. What does the court mean by the statement that, "part performance by the offeree of a unilateral contract results in a condition. The condition is full performance by the offeree"?

    2.2. Is there any language that the defendant could have added to its offer to the plaintiff that would have eliminated the possibility of this litigation?

    2.3. The New Mexico Supreme Court looked to what eventually became *Restatement (Second) of Contracts* § 45. Take a look at that section yourself. How can a real estate agent prove that she "begins the invited performance"? How can the real estate agent deal with the "performance/preparation" distinction of *comment f* to § 45 which provides: "What is begun or tendered must be part of the actual performance invited in order to preclude revocation under this Section. Beginning preparations, though they may be essential in carrying out the contract or accepting the offer is not enough"?

2.4.   Assuming, on remand, the trial court does find that the plaintiff partially performed before the defendant's attempted revocation, is there consideration for holding the defendant's offer irrevocable? If not, what is the basis for finding an enforceable option contract?

PROBLEMS ON ACCEPTANCE BY PROMISE, PERFORMANCE, AND PART PERFORMANCE

Consider how the following hypotheticals would be resolved both under classical principles of contract law and under the *Restatement (Second) of Contracts*:

1.   Markell says to Ponoroff, "I'll pay you $20 if you wash and wax my car." Ponoroff says, "I accept." Has a contract been formed? If Ponoroff fails to wash and wax Markell's car is he in breach? How about if Ponoroff says nothing in response, but begins washing Markell's car? Is there a contract? *See Restatement (Second)* §§ 50(2) & 62.

2.   Suppose Markell's offer is phrased, "I'll pay you $20 if you wash and wax my car, and this offer can be accepted only by your doing the job, not by merely promising to do the job." Ponoroff replies, "I accept." Is either party bound at this point? How about if Ponoroff goes out and buys some rags and a can of wax to do the job? What about when he actually begins the job? Suppose Ponoroff is nearly finished, having put in over two hours on the job under a hot sun, when Markell walks up to him and says, "I revoke my offer." Will Ponoroff prevail in a suit for breach of contract? *See Restatement (Second)* § 45. If Markell does not revoke, and instead Ponoroff abandons the job without finishing, can Markell sue for breach?

3.   Now suppose Markell's offer is phrased, "I'll pay you $20 if you will agree to wash and wax my car this weekend, but I want your promise." Ponoroff replies, "I accept." Is either party bound at this point? Suppose Ponoroff says nothing, but that weekend he shows up and begins working on Markell's car. Has a contract been formed? Suppose just prior to Ponoroff's completing the job, Markell shows up and says, "I revoke my offer." Will Ponoroff prevail if he sues Markell for breach? How about if Markell says nothing until after Ponoroff has completed the job and then Markell revokes? *See Restatement (Second)* § 50(3).

4.   Finally, suppose Markell makes the offer, "I'll pay you $20 to wash and wax my car," and then promptly heads off to Monaco to try to win enough money so that he can take a year off from teaching Contracts. Ponoroff locates Markell's car and gives it a first class wash and wax. Two weeks later, Markell, who has lost all his money, e-mails Ponoroff from Monaco to tell him that he is withdrawing his offer. Ponoroff fires back a reply, "Too late, dude, I did the job two weeks ago. Did you forget *Carlill*? You owe me the money." Markell responds with the following message: "Spare me the 19th century case law from merry old England, Bud, go read

§ 54(2) of the *Restatement (Second) of Contracts.*" Was there a contract here? Can Ponoroff recover his $20 fee if he sues?

D. ACCEPTANCE BY SILENCE OR INACTION

LAREDO NATIONAL BANK v. GORDON

United States Court of Appeals, Fifth Circuit
61 F.2d 906 (1932)

BRYAN, CIRCUIT JUDGE.

This is an action at law by an attorney Bernard Gordon, against his client, Laredo National Bank, to recover $12,500 as a fee agreed upon in the settlement of a suit which the attorney had brought for the bank against Abraham Rosenblum, Aaron Rosenblum, and the Abe Rosenblum Corporation. The suit against the Rosenblums was to recover $144,000 which it was alleged they and one Joseph Rosenblum had fraudulently procured from the bank by means of drafts to which were attached fictitious delivery orders falsely purporting to cover actual carload shipments of produce. Gordon brought the suit upon an agreement that he was to receive a contingent fee of 25 per cent. of the amount recovered. While the suit was pending, the bank and its local attorney entered into negotiations with the Rosenblums for a compromise settlement. During the continuance of those negotiations, and on March 4, 1930, the bank wired Gordon that, acting upon his suggestion, it would refuse to accept a proposition of settlement which the Rosenblums had made, but added "in case there should be a counter proposition from them which we may consider acceptable advise what are your minimum fees." On the same day Gordon replied by wire that he felt confident his fee could be adjusted reasonably in the light of prior arrangements and subsequent developments, but that he would welcome the bank's suggestion in regard to his fee. On March 10 the bank wired Gordon, stating that its proposition had not been accepted, but that "we must know immediately what will be your fees in the event we accept settlement offered us. Answer quick"; and Gordon replied, "Answering today's telegram twelve thousand five hundred dollars." Nothing further was said about fees pending negotiations for settlement, which continued until June 16, 1930, when the bank received in settlement of its claim against the Rosenblums about $50,000 in cash, securities of the estimated value of $94,000, and a note of Joseph Rosenblum for $66,000. On June 29 the local attorney for the bank, who lived at Laredo, Tex., addressed a letter to Gordon who lived in New York, advising that a settlement had been effected, directing dismissal of the suit which Gordon had brought in New York and which was still pending, and stating that the bank's president "will write you direct and take up the matter of your fee and its payment." On July 3, 1930, the bank's president wrote Gordon that the bank would pay a reasonable fee, but that the amount mentioned in his telegram of March 10 was beyond

reason. Gordon testified that before he received this last-mentioned letter
he had already dismissed the suit against the Rosenblums, in compliance
with the directions of the bank's local attorney. At the close of the
evidence in this case, both sides moved for a directed verdict; whereupon
the trial court charged the jury to render a verdict in favor of Gordon for
$12,500 with interest. After this charge was given, the bank undertook to
withdraw its motion, and requested the court to submit to the jury the
question whether it had accepted Gordon's offer contained in his telegram
of March 10 to take $12,500 in settlement of his fee.

It is argued that the bank never became bound to pay the $12,500 fee,
because it never replied to or accepted Gordon's offer to take that amount
in settlement for his services. It is true that, generally speaking, an offeree
has a right to make no reply to offers, and hence that his silence is not to
be construed as an acceptance. But, where the relation between the
parties is such that the offeror is justified in expecting a reply, or the
offeree is under a duty to reply, the latter's silence will be regarded as
acceptance. Under such circumstances, "one who keeps silent, knowing
that his silence will be misinterpreted, should not be allowed to deny the
natural interpretation of his conduct," etc. It was upon the bank's
insistence that Gordon agreed to accept the fee he named in his telegram,
in order that the bank might go ahead with its compromise settlement. It
was not until after a settlement had been made, the suit against the
Rosenblums had been dismissed, and Gordon had lost all opportunity of
earning a larger contingent fee, that the bank made any objection or
expressed any dissatisfaction with the amount of the fee Gordon had
agreed to accept in the event of a compromise settlement. Its silence
amounted to conduct which misled its attorney to his detriment, for the
bank could not have failed to know that Gordon was acting in the belief
that the fee which he had agreed to accept would be paid without
question. Under the circumstances, the bank's silence was equivalent to
its acceptance of and assent to Gordon's offer to forego his contingent fee
and receive instead the lump sum payment which he named.

* * *

It is true, of course, that an attorney ought not to take advantage of
his client, or be permitted to drive a hard bargain. But the evidence shows
that Gordon thought a better settlement could be made with the Rosenblums, did not suggest giving up the trial of the case, was reluctant to
accept the bank's suggestion of a compromise and its taking the case out
of his hands, and expressed himself as perfectly willing to let the question
of his fee be postponed until the case in which he was employed was
disposed of. It was only when the bank insisted upon making its own
settlement that he agreed to accept a fee which was less than he would
have been entitled to receive if he had been paid the contingent fee
originally agreed upon. So far as this record shows, his conduct was above
reproach. The duty of fair dealing applies to the client as well as to the
attorney. The record before us leaves no room for reasonable doubt that

Gordon was justly entitled to the verdict which the court directed the jury to render in his favor.

The judgment is affirmed.

QUESTIONS, NOTES, AND CONNECTIONS

1. Questions about the facts of this case

    1.1. Is it just us, or did the Laredo National Bank get a pretty good settlement on its $144,000 case against the Rosenblums?

    1.2. The court states that Gordon thought a better settlement could be obtained and that it was only after the settlement had been arranged and he lost the opportunity for a larger contingency fee that the bank made any objection. But could Gordon really hold up a settlement that his client wanted because of the prospect of earning a larger fee?

2. Questions about the law

    2.1. What is the basis for the general rule that silence or inaction does not constitute an acceptance?

    2.2. Please read *Restatement (Second) of Contracts* § 69; it reflects the general rule that ordinarily acceptance cannot be based on silence or inaction. Note that there are three exceptions. Which exception would have applied in *Gordon*?

    2.3. Who are the exceptions in § 69 intended to benefit, the offeror or the offeree? Are these exceptions consistent with objective theory?

    2.4. What is the relationship between circumstances where silence is considered an acceptance and an implied-in-fact contract?

3. Notes

    3.1. Assume Broker represents a party looking to purchase new warehouse space. Broker is aware of what may be suitable space and shows it to his client, who expresses some interest. Thereupon, Broker sends Owner, with whom Broker has never dealt before, a letter stating that "if you are successful in selling this property to my client, I shall be entitled to a 5% commission at closing." Owner acknowledged receipt of the letter and began negotiations with Broker's client that ultimately culminated in a sale. When Broker demanded his 5% commission, Owner responded that there was no agreement regarding payment of such a commission and, therefore, there is no liability for the commission. Broker claims that if Owner disagreed with Broker's request for the commission, Owner had a duty to let Broker know that she objected to the terms of Broker's letter. Assess the validity of these arguments.

    3.2. In the leading case of *Austin v. Burge,* 156 Mo.App. 286, 137 S.W. 618 (1911), the defendant's subscription for a newspaper expired, but the publisher continued to have it sent to him, even though the defendant ordered the paper stopped. When the publisher sued for the subscription price, the defendant argued that there was no contract. The court disagreed, observing that because the defendant had continued accepting and reading the paper, even after his order to stop delivery, the defendant had accepted the publisher's offer for the price of the paper. In light of this case, what should you do when a merchant continues to send you unordered goods through the mails? Does this open the door to abusive marketing practices? Are the rules of contract law adequate to address the abuse? If not, what should be done? *See United States v. Random Stationers, Inc.,* 1984 U.S. Dist. Lexis 24709 (S.D. Fla. 1984) (applying a federal statute, 39 U.S.C. § 3009, adopted as part of the Postal Reorganization Act of 1970, making it an unfair trade practice in violation of § 5 of the Federal Trade Commission Act to bill a recipient for unsolicited merchandise and permitting such merchandise to be retained by the recipient as a gift).

4. Connections

So, an offer can be accepted by promise, performance, partial performance, and even silence or inaction. In each situation, the corresponding rule on the effectiveness of a purported acceptance is slightly different. Can you articulate the differences? Do these different rules make sense to you? Are they all consistent with the objective theory of contract formation? Are they consistent with one another? If Ponoroff tells Epstein, I offer to purchase your share of next year's royalties from MADD for $250,000,* and will assume this is acceptable to you unless I hear otherwise by Noon on next Tuesday," what are the different ways in which Epstein might accept this offer, and, in each case, when would the acceptance be effective?

E. IMPERFECT ACCEPTANCES

Earlier, we saw that one way in which an offer can be destroyed is express rejection by the offeree. For example, Ponoroff offers to buy Epstein's car for $100 and Epstein replies, "No way dude," the offer is dead and cannot be resuscitated unless Ponoroff chooses to do so.

But, if Ponoroff offers to buy Epstein's car for $100 and Epstein replies, "I want $120," nobody would seriously regard Epstein's reply as an acceptance. However, neither has he unequivocally rejected, as in the first example. Instead, that reply would be treated as a *counteroffer* which is simultaneously an *implied* rejection of the original offer and a new offer over which Ponoroff now has the power of acceptance.

So if Ponoroff offers to buy Epstein's car for $100 and Epstein responds "I want $120," and Ponoroff says: "Okay. I agree to pay $120," then there is a contract for the sale of the car for $120.

---

* Incidentally, based on past experience, the offer in this hypothetical is probably an attractive one from the perspective of the offeree (Eds.).

But remember that a counteroffer is also an implied rejection. And, an implied rejection is still a rejection. Still terminates—kills—the offer. So assume Ponoroff offers to buy Epstein's car for $100 and Epstein responds "I want $120." If Ponoroff says "No," and Epstein replies, "Ok, I'll take $100," there is *no* contract. Epstein is trying to accept a terminated offer—an offer he killed by his implied rejection—and, well, you just can't do that.

A counteroffer—"No, I won't pay X but I will pay Y"—is described not only as an implied rejection, but also as kind of imperfect acceptance. An imperfect acceptance can also take the form of an acceptance with a condition. For example, Ponoroff offers to buy Epstein's car for $100 and Epstein responds, "I'll accept your offer to buy my car for $100, but my acceptance is conditioned on any later disputes about the quality of the car being submitted to arbitration by Tom and Ray." No contract, just a new offer. Such a conditional acceptance is treated just like a counteroffer. Epstein's response is simultaneously an implied rejection of Ponoroff's offer and a new offer to Ponoroff.

Counteroffers and conditional acceptances are not the only forms of implied rejection; not the only forms of imperfect acceptances. Under common law, a third form of imperfect acceptance is a response that merely adds a new or different term, but does not condition acceptance on the new term. For example, Ponoroff offers to buy Epstein's car for $100 and Epstein responds, "I'll accept your offer to buy my car for $100 and I propose that any later disputes about the quality of the car be submitted to arbitration by Tom and Ray."

Do you see any meaningful distinction between the hypotheticals in the preceding two paragraphs? Would the court in the next case distinguish between the two? As you read the next case, also consider the implications of an imperfect acceptance to both the existence of an agreement and the status of the original offer.

GRESSER v. HOTZLER

Court of Appeals of Minnesota
604 N.W.2d 379 (2000)

LANSING, JUDGE.

Michael Gresser sued Calvin and Cheryl Hotzler for specific performance of a purchase agreement for commercial real estate and, alternatively, for breach of contract. On the Hotzlers' motion for partial summary judgment on Gresser's specific-performance claim, the district court held that the purchase agreement was invalid and entered final judgment against Gresser pursuant to Minn. R. Civ. P. 54.02, dismissing both the specific-performance and breach-of-contract claims. Gresser appeals from the judgment.

FACTS

The property in dispute includes five acres of land and a building that formerly housed the Stagecoach Theatre in Shakopee. In early 1998, Michael Gresser, a real estate investor, began negotiating with landowners Calvin and Cheryl Hotzler to purchase the property. In July, Gresser submitted to the Hotzlers an unsigned, proposed purchase agreement that, among other items, required the Hotzlers to deliver a recertified survey on August 10, 1998, and provided for closing on September 1, 1998. The Hotzlers changed several terms, initialed the changes, signed the purchase agreement, and returned it to Gresser's attorney on August 4, 1998.

On August 10, 1998, Gresser initialed the Hotzlers' changes and signed the purchase agreement. Gresser, however, made two additional changes. He changed the survey delivery date to September 10, 1998, and the closing date to October 15, 1998. Gresser initialed both date changes. Gresser made these changes on the advice of his attorney, who had talked to the Hotzlers' realtor. The attorney and the realtor agreed that, because of the time that had elapsed, the original survey and closing dates had become impractical. The attorney knew that the realtor had not consulted the Hotzlers about the changes, and both Gresser and his attorney knew that the realtor did not have the power to bind the Hotzlers.

Gresser's attorney returned the signed purchase agreement to the realtor on August 12, 1998, along with $2,000 earnest money. Gresser and his attorney expected that the Hotzlers would initial the date changes and return the purchase agreement to them. The realtor delivered the purchase agreement to Calvin Hotzler on August 12, 1998, but testified that he did not indicate whether Gresser had signed the counteroffer. Calvin Hotzler assumed the parties had a deal, but he did not read the purchase agreement. Instead, he placed it on the kitchen counter to await the return of Cheryl Hotzler, who was out of town. Later that day, Calvin Hotzler showed Gresser the property and introduced him to tenants as the buyer.

On the afternoon of August 12, 1998, the realtor received another offer for the property, which he forwarded to the Hotzlers. Calvin Hotzler placed this document on the kitchen counter as well. On August 13, the Hotzlers reviewed both documents, decided to accept the new offer, and signed that purchase agreement.

ISSUES

I. Given the undisputed facts in the record, did the district court err by concluding that the purchase agreement between the Hotzlers and Gresser was not legally binding?

II. Did the district court err by refusing to apply equitable estoppel?

ANALYSIS

On appeal from summary judgment, the reviewing court determines whether any genuine issues of material fact exist and whether the district court erred in its application of the law. Whether a contract exists is generally an issue for the factfinder. But when "the record taken as a whole could not lead a rational trier of fact to find for the nonmoving party," summary judgment is proper.

I.

Whether a contract is formed is judged by the objective conduct of the parties and not their subjective intent. Minnesota has followed the "mirror image rule" in analyzing acceptance of offers. Under that rule, "an acceptance must be coextensive with the offer and may not introduce additional terms or conditions." *Podany v. Erickson,* 235 Minn. 36, 39, 49 N.W.2d 193, 194 (1951). When the offer is positively accepted, however, a requested or suggested modification does not prevent contract formation, regardless of whether the modification is accepted. *Podany,* 235 Minn. at 39, 49 N.W.2d at 194; * * *. *See also Restatement (2d) of Contracts* § 61 (1981).

Gresser first argues the district court erred by making findings on disputed facts material to whether the parties formed a contract. We disagree. The district court's function on a summary judgment motion is to determine whether genuine factual issues exist. In making this determination, the court may consider whether reasonable persons could draw only one inference from the evidence. In this case, after reviewing the evidence, the district court listed the facts it found to be uncontroverted. The district court did not exceed the scope of its function on a summary judgment motion in so doing. * * * Even if the court engaged in unwarranted factfinding, however, its error is harmless because its legal conclusion is premised on undisputed facts.

Gresser primarily argues that his changes to the purchase agreement are within the modification exception to the mirror-image rule because he unconditionally accepted the Hotzlers' counteroffer and merely suggested the date changes. According to Gresser, he accepted unconditionally because he would have been willing to comply with the original dates, the realtor encouraged Gresser to make the changes, and Calvin Hotzler introduced Gresser as the owner of the property on August 12.

Viewed objectively, these facts do not demonstrate that Gresser positively accepted the purchase agreement. First, Gresser's uncommunicated subjective intent is not relevant, and, second, these facts do not suggest that the Hotzlers knew or should have known that Gresser offered the change in dates only as a suggestion. To the contrary, the undisputed facts regarding absence of any express communication, the method of initialing the changes, and the prior course of dealings between the parties indicate that the changes were part of the series of counteroffers.

Minnesota has applied the modification exception sparingly and only to those cases in which objective manifestations of acceptance existed separately from the suggestions for modifications. *See Podany,* 235 Minn. at 38, 49 N.W.2d at 195 (offeree's written acceptance clearly stated it had elected to exercise option to purchase property); * * *. Gresser proposed his changes on the face of the purchase agreement and provided no objective indication that his acceptance was not conditioned on them.

Gresser alternatively argues that his changes to the purchase agreement did not preclude contract formation because the changes were immaterial. The mirror-image rule historically has been strictly construed to forbid even minor variations between offer and acceptance. Many modern courts have relaxed the rule, holding that only an acceptance that differs *materially* from the terms of the original offer prevents contract formation.

The corollary to this modern rule is that an immaterial variation in the acceptance does not impede contract formation. For instance, several courts have held that, under this exception, variations implied in the offer do not interfere with the completed contract.

The Minnesota Supreme Court used the language of the immateriality exception in *Markmann v. H.A. Bruntjen Co.*, 249 Minn. 281, 286, 81 N.W.2d 858, 862 (Minn.1957). In *Markmann,* the court held that "an acceptance which differs substantially and materially from the terms of the original offer does not give rise to a completed contract." *Id.* The *Markmann* court did not, however, find an immaterial variation or make clear that it was diverging from its former strict construction of the mirror-image rule. *Id.* (citing *Minar v. Skoog*, 235 Minn. 262, 265, 50 N.W.2d 300, 302 (1951) (holding acceptance must comply *exactly* with terms of the offer)). The Hotzlers argue that Minnesota caselaw has retained the strict mirror-image rule for real estate contracts, while tempering the rule in its application to other types of contracts. Although we note that the Supreme Court and this court have more often applied the strict-construction standard in cases involving real estate, caselaw provides no explicit distinction. *Compare Minar,* 235 Minn. at 265, 50 N.W.2d at 302 (applying strict-construction standard to acceptance of option to purchase real estate), *and Rose v. Guerdon Indus., Inc.,* 374 N.W.2d 282, 284 (Minn.App.1985) (applying strict construction to acceptance of offer to sell real estate), *with Markmann,* 249 Minn. at 286, 81 N.W.2d at 862 (using material-difference standard to analyze contract for sale of product distribution rights). It is, however, unnecessary to define the scope of an immateriality exception unless the changes to the purchase agreement are immaterial.

"Authority on what constitutes a material variation is meager." *Northwest Television Club,* 634 P.2d at 841. Black's Law Dictionary defines "material alteration" as "a change in a legal instrument sufficient to alter the instrument's legal meaning or effect." *Black's Law Dictionary,* 78 (7th ed.1999). Similarly, the Florida Court of Appeals found the addition of "and/or assignees" did not constitute a material variation because it did not "change the legal effect of the contract." *Kitsos v. Stanford,* 291 So.2d 632, 634 (Fla.Dist.Ct.App.1974). We agree that the focus should be on the legal operation of the contract. Thus, only minor changes that do not substantially alter the performance obligations of the parties may be immaterial.

Under this principle, the date changes Gresser made are material. The changes directly affect Gresser's performance obligations under the contract, postponing his duty to perform by almost six weeks. The law of contracts is not advanced by allowing a contracting party to manipulate the finality of an obligation by rejecting an insubstantial change, but few terms are more important to sellers of real estate than the date on which they will receive the purchase money. The purchase agreement's inclusion of a time-is-of-the-essence clause further evidences the materiality of the performance date. As a matter of law, the exception to the mirror-image rule for immaterial variations does not apply to the changes Gresser made to the purchase agreement.

In retrospect, Gresser may have been very willing to expressly note that the changed dates were proposals rather than conditions or to retain the earlier closing date rather than risk the loss of the property. But contract formation proceeds on an objective basis and courts should not reconstruct, much less call back, the written word. The high volume of real estate transactions in Minnesota reinforces the importance of identifying and preserving a bright line in the formation of purchase agreements.

II.

The district court rejected Gresser's argument that the Hotzlers should be equitably estopped from denying the validity of the purchase agreement. * * *

Equitable estoppel arises when "one by his acts or representations, or by his silence when he ought to speak, intentionally or through culpable negligence, induces another to believe certain facts to exist, and such other rightfully acts on the belief so induced in such a matter that if the former is permitted to deny the existence of the facts it will prejudice the latter." *Transamerica Ins. Group v. Paul*, 267 N.W.2d 180, 183 (Minn. 1978). The first element necessary to establish estoppel is a misrepresentation. *Id.* Gresser does not allege the Hotzlers made misrepresentations directly, but contends that the realtor's statements that the changes would not affect the deal are attributable to the Hotzlers under agency theories.

The general rule is that real estate agents have no implied authority to contract on behalf of their principals. *La Plant v. Loveland*, 142 Minn. 89, 92, 170 N.W. 920, 921 (Minn.1919). And apparent authority must be founded on the principal's actions "since no agent by his own act can create evidence of authority." *West Concord Conservation Club, Inc. v. Chilson*, 306 N.W.2d 893, 897 (Minn.1981); *see also Hagedorn v. Aid Ass'n for Lutherans*, 297 Minn. 253, 258, 211 N.W.2d 154, 158 (1973). Gresser has not identified any conduct or statements by the Hotzlers that would support a variance from the general rule on implied authority or a finding of apparent authority.

* * *

Gresser's equitable estoppel claim also fails on the essential element of reasonable reliance. *See Transamerica,* 267 N.W.2d at 183 (listing reasonable reliance as element of equitable estoppel). Both Gresser and his attorney admit that they knew real estate agents are not authorized to contract on behalf of their principals. And Gresser's attorney also knew that the realtor had not contacted the Hotzlers before making the assurances. On these facts, any reliance on the realtor's assurances was unreasonable as a matter of law. *See West Concord Conservation Club,* 306 N.W.2d at 897 (to invoke estoppel doctrine, "truth must have been unknown" to party when he acted).

DECISION

Because the date changes to the purchase agreement precluded contract formation as a matter of law, and because Gresser failed to assert facts sufficient to support an equitable estoppel claim, the district court properly granted summary judgment to the Hotzlers.

Affirmed.

QUESTIONS AND NOTES

1. Questions about the facts of this case
    1.1. Did Calvin Hotzler believe the parties had a deal on August 12 when he showed Gresser the property? Was that relevant to the court? Should it have been?
    1.2. How important to the Hotzlers were Gresser's two changes in dates? Were the two changes the reason that the Hotzlers decided to accept the other offer for the property?
    1.3. How important was it to Gresser that the dates for survey delivery and closing be moved back? Was that relevant to the court? Should it have been?

2. Questions about the law
    2.1. In the note before *Gresser,* we considered counteroffers and conditional acceptances. Does the *Gresser* case involve either a counteroffer or a conditional acceptance? What is the difference, if any, between a response to an offer that triggers the conditional acceptance rule and a response to an offer that triggers the common law mirror image rule?
    2.2. In Section 3.A., *supra,* we noted that when an offeree *expressly* rejects an offer, the offer is terminated and may not be revived unless the offeror elects to renew it. In this case, by signing and returning on August 12 the proposed purchase agreement that the

Hotzlers had submitted on August 4, the court suggests that the offeree, Gresser, has *implicitly* rejected the offer. What is the legal effect of an implied rejection? As of August 12, who had the power of acceptance according to the court?

2.3.   What is the scope of the "modification exception" to the mirror-image rule to which the court refers and how is its applicability determined?

2.4.   What is the scope of the "immateriality exception" to the mirror-image rule in Minnesota? Who determines "materiality"?

2.5.   What is the effect of a counteroffer when the original offer is an irrevocable offer? Suppose on February 1, in exchange for $100, Markell granted Epstein a 60–day option to acquire certain real property owned by Markell for $150,000. Epstein pays the $100 at the time the option is granted. On March 1, Epstein calls Markell and offers to give him $145,000 for the property. Markell refuses. Ten days later Epstein contacts Markell to tell him that he has decided to exercise the option and buy the property for $150,000. Markell, however, citing *Gresser*, contends that it is too late. Does Epstein have a claim for breach against Markell? *See Restatement (Second) of Contracts* § 37. How, if at all, does it affect your answer if, in the March 1 conversation, Epstein also tells Markell that he was simply not interested in the property at the $150,000 price?

3.   Notes

3.1.   *Gresser* introduces the common law "mirror image" rule, which derives from the first principle that the offeror is sovereign. Specifically, that the offeror is not to be required to deal other than on the terms she specified in her offer. Thus, the mirror image rule holds that an acceptance must be a total assent on the terms of the offer. Any variation, request or condition in the acceptance, a so-called "imperfect acceptance," renders it ineffective to form a contract.

What if the reason that the purported acceptance varies or adds to the terms of the offer is that the offeree simply makes a mistake in fashioning her reply, which she is quick to rectify upon having it pointed out to her?

In *Minneapolis & St. Louis Railway Co. v. Columbia Rolling–Mill Co.*, 119 U.S. 149 (1886), the defendant offered iron rails at $54 per gross ton for quantities of between 2,000 and 5,000 tons. The plaintiff responded by ordering 1,200 tons at the quoted price. When the defendant replied that it was impossible to book the order at that price because it was below the minimum quantity, the plaintiff entered an order for 2,000 tons, but the defendant refused to deliver, denying the existence of a contract. What result on plaintiff's claim for breach?

3.2.   *Restatement (Second) of Contracts* §§ 59–61 attempt to draw a distinction between a truly conditional acceptance, which operates as a counteroffer, and an acceptance with suggestions or inquiries, which is still sufficient to form a contract. Is this a break with the common law mirror image rule? Does Minnesota seem to apply the *Restatement* rules? Read those sections and decide whether there is mutual assent in either of these situations. Epstein says to Ponoroff, "I'll sell you my car for $3,000." Ponoroff replies, "I accept; will you take a check?" How about if Ponoroff replies, "I accept, but you fix the brakes?"

—————

Just like the rule that the *manner* of acceptance must abide by the terms of the offer (recall *La Salle National Bank v. Vega, supra,* at 107), the mirror image rule (or what the court in *Gresser* refers to as the "strict" mirror-image rule), which focuses on the *substance* of the acceptance, can work some harsh and unexpectedly restrictive results, both with respect to the aim of protecting the interests of the offeror and in enforcing an arrangement with respect to which the parties indeed intended to be bound. For example, in *Gresser*, after receiving the signed purchase agreement back from Gresser, an argument can be made that Mr. Hotzler considered that the parties had a deal, viewing the changes in dates as either unimportant or details that could be worked out later. However, upon receiving what was a more attractive third-party offer, the Hotzlers changed their minds. Because of the operation of the mirror image rule, they were able to claim no contract existed with Gresser and, effectively, walk on a deal even though there truly had been an agreement reached by the parties on all of the essential terms of the transaction.

The problems of a strict mirror image rule are compounded in an era when so much business is done on the basis of an exchange of standard printed forms between buyer and seller containing lots of detailed and technical language, typically prepared by the parties' lawyers, which neither party may be reading very carefully or capable of understanding. Under the mirror image rule, any divergence in the fine print of these forms prevents formation of a contract on the documents. Nevertheless, if the parties have commenced performance before a dispute occurs or a problem arises, clearly there is a contract of some type, but what are its terms if we can't rely on the documents?

To address both this question and the problem of the offeree being able to use the mirror image rule manipulatively to renege on a deal, the drafters of the U.C.C. came up with § 2–207 applicable in contracts involving the sale of goods. It goes far beyond the reach of the restatement rules.

Section 2–207 has been very controversial and subjected to considerable criticism as flawed in its design and unnecessarily cumbersome in its application. As you read the next three cases, see if you agree with those critics.

—————

DORTON v. COLLINS & AIKMAN CORPORATION

United States Court of Appeals, Sixth Circuit
453 F.2d 1161 (1972)

CELEBREZZE, CIRCUIT JUDGE.

This is an appeal from the District Court's denial of Defendant–Appellant's motion for a stay pending arbitration, pursuant to Section 3 of the United States Arbitration Act of 1925, 9 U.S.C. § 3. The suit arose after a series of over 55 transactions during 1968, 1969, and 1970 in which Plaintiffs–Appellees [hereinafter The Carpet Mart], carpet retailers in Kingsport, Tennessee, purchased carpets from Defendant–Appellant [hereinafter Collins & Aikman], incorporated under the laws of the State of Delaware, with its principal place of business in New York, New York, and owner of a carpet manufacturing plant [formerly the Painter Carpet Mills, Inc.] located in Dalton, Georgia. The Carpet Mart originally brought this action in a Tennessee state trial court, seeking compensatory and punitive damages in the amount of $450,000 from Collins & Aikman for the latter's alleged fraud, deceit, and misrepresentation in the sale of what were supposedly carpets manufactured from 100% Kodel polyester fiber. The Carpet Mart maintains that in May, 1970, in response to a customer complaint, it learned that not all of the carpets were manufactured from 100% Kodel polyester fiber but rather some were composed of a cheaper and inferior carpet fiber. After the cause was removed to the District Court on the basis of diversity of citizenship, Collins & Aikman moved for a stay pending arbitration, asserting that The Carpet Mart was bound to an arbitration agreement which appeared on the reverse side of Collins & Aikman's printed sales acknowledgment forms. Holding that there existed no binding arbitration agreement between the parties, the District Court denied the stay. For the reasons set forth below, we remand the case to the District Court for further findings.

* * *

The primary question before us on appeal is whether the District Court, in denying Collins & Aikman's motion for a stay pending arbitration, erred in holding that The Carpet Mart was not bound by the arbitration agreement appearing on the back of Collins & Aikman's acknowledgment forms. In reviewing the District Court's determination, we must look closely at the procedures which were followed in the sales transactions which gave rise to the present dispute over the arbitration agreement.

In each of the more than 55 transactions, one of the partners in The Carpet Mart, or, on some occasions, Collins & Aikman's visiting salesman, telephoned Collins & Aikman's order department in Dalton, Georgia, and ordered certain quantities of carpets listed in Collins & Aikman's catalogue. There is some dispute as to what, if any, agreements were reached through the telephone calls and through the visits by Collins & Aikman's salesman. After each oral order was placed, the price, if any, quoted by the buyer was checked against Collins & Aikman's price list, and the credit department was consulted to determine if The Carpet Mart had paid for all previous shipments. After it was found that everything was in order, Collins & Aikman's order department typed the information concerning the particular order on one of its printed acknowledgment forms. Each acknowledgment form bore one of three legends: "Acknowledgment," "Customer Acknowledgment," or "Sales Contract." The following provision was printed on the face of the forms bearing the "Acknowledgment" legend:

> "The acceptance of your order is subject to all of the terms and conditions on the face and reverse side hereof, including arbitration, all of which are accepted by buyer; it supersedes buyer's order form, if any. It shall become a contract either (a) when signed and delivered by buyer to seller and accepted in writing by seller, or (b) at Seller's option, when buyer shall have given to seller specification of assortments, delivery dates, shipping instructions, or instructions to bill and hold as to all or any part of the merchandise herein described, or when buyer has received delivery of the whole or any part thereof, or when buyer has otherwise assented to the terms and conditions hereof."

Similarly, on the face of the forms bearing the "Customer Acknowledgment" or "Sales Contract" legends the following provision appeared:

> "This order is given subject to all of the terms and conditions on the face and reverse side hereof, including the provisions for arbitration and the exclusion of warranties, all of which are accepted by Buyer, supersede Buyer's order form, if any, and constitute the entire contract between Buyer and Seller. This order shall become a contract as to the entire quantity specified either (a) when signed and delivered by Buyer to Seller and accepted in writing by Seller or (b) when Buyer has received and retained this order for ten days without objection, or (c) when Buyer has accepted delivery of any part of the merchandise specified herein or has furnished to Seller specifications or assortments, delivery dates, shipping instructions, or instructions to bill and hold, or when Buyer has otherwise indicated acceptance of the terms hereof."

The small print on the reverse side of the forms provided, among other things, that all claims arising out of the contract would be submitted to arbitration in New York City. Each acknowledgment form was signed by an employee of Collins & Aikman's order department and mailed to The Carpet Mart on the day the telephone order was received or, at the latest, on the following day. The carpets were thereafter shipped to The Carpet Mart, with the interval between the mailing of the acknowledgment form and shipment of the carpets varying from a brief interval to a period of several weeks or months. Absent a delay in the mails, however, The Carpet Mart always received the acknowledgment forms prior to receiving the carpets. In all cases The Carpet Mart took delivery of and paid for the carpets without objecting to any terms contained in the acknowledgment form.

In holding that no binding arbitration agreement was created between the parties through the transactions above, the District Court relied on * * * [UCC § 2–207], * * *.

The District Court found that Subsection 2–207(3) controlled the instant case, quoting the following passage from 1 W. Hawkland, A Transactional Guide to the Uniform Commercial Code § 1.090303, at 19–20 (1964):

"If the seller * * * ships the goods and the buyer accepts them, a contract is formed under subsection (3). The terms of this contract are those on which the purchase order and acknowledgment agree, and the additional terms needed for a contract are to be found throughout the U.C.C. * * * [T]he U.C.C. does not impose an arbitration term on the parties where their contract is silent on the matter. Hence, a conflict between an arbitration and an [sic] no-arbitration clause would result in the no arbitration clause becoming effective."

Under this authority alone the District Court concluded that the arbitration clause on the back of Collins & Aikman's sales acknowledgment had not become a binding term in the 50–odd transactions with The Carpet Mart.

In reviewing this determination by the District Court, we are aware of the problems which courts have had in interpreting Section 2–207. This section of the UCC has been described as a "murky bit of prose," Southwest Engineering Co. v. Martin Tractor Co., 205 Kan. 684, 694, 473 P.2d 18, 25 (1970), as "not too happily drafted," Roto–Lith Ltd. v. F. P. Bartlett & Co., 297 F.2d 497, 500 (1st Cir. 1962), and as "one of the most important, subtle, and difficult in the entire Code, and well it may be said that the product as it finally reads is not altogether satisfactory." Duesenberg & King, Sales and Bulk Transfers under the Uniform Commercial Code, (Vol. 3, Bender's Uniform Commercial Code Service) § 3.03, at 3–12 (1969). Despite the lack of clarity in its language, Section 2–207 manifests definite objectives which are significant in the present case.

As Official Comment No. 1 indicates, UCC § 2–207 was intended to apply to two situations:

"The one is where an agreement has been reached either orally or by informal correspondence between the parties and is followed by one or both of the parties sending formal acknowledgments or memoranda embodying the terms so far as agreed upon and adding terms not discussed. The other situation is one in which a wire or letter expressed and intended as the closing or confirmation of an agreement adds further minor suggestions or proposals such as 'ship by Tuesday,' 'rush,' 'ship draft against bill of lading inspection allowed,' or the like." * * *

Although Comment No. 1 is itself somewhat ambiguous, it is clear that Section 2–207, and specifically Subsection 2–207(1), was intended to alter the "ribbon matching" or "mirror" rule of common law, under which the terms of an acceptance or confirmation were required to be identical to the terms of the offer or oral agreement, respectively. * * * Under the common law, an acceptance or a confirmation which contained terms additional to or different from those of the offer or oral agreement constituted a rejection of the offer or agreement and thus became a counter-offer. The terms of the counter-offer were said to have been accepted by the original offeror when he proceeded to perform under the contract without objecting to the counter-offer. Thus, a buyer was deemed to have accepted the seller's counter-offer if he took receipt of the goods and paid for them without objection.

Under Section 2–207 the result is different. This section of the Code recognizes that in current commercial transactions, the terms of the offer and those of the acceptance will seldom be identical. Rather, under the current "battle of the forms," each party typically has a printed form drafted by his attorney and containing as many terms as could be envisioned to favor that party in his sales transactions. Whereas under common law the disparity between the fineprint terms in the parties' forms would have prevented the consummation of a contract when these forms are exchanged, Section 2–207 recognizes that in many, but not all, cases the parties do not impart such significance to the terms on the printed forms. * * *. Subsection 2–207(1) therefore provides that "[a] definite and seasonable expression of acceptance or a written confirmation * * * operates as an acceptance even though it states terms additional to or different from those offered or agreed upon, unless acceptance is expressly made conditional on assent to the additional or different terms." Thus, under Subsection (1), a contract is recognized notwithstanding the fact that an acceptance or confirmation contains terms additional to or different from those of the offer or prior agreement, provided that the offeree's intent to accept the offer is definitely expressed, see Sections 2–204 and 2–206, and provided that the offeree's acceptance is not expressly conditioned on the offeror's assent to the additional or different terms. When a contract is recognized under Subsection (1), the additional terms are treated as "proposals for addition to the contract" under Subsection (2), which contains special provisions under which such additional terms are deemed to have been accepted when the transaction is between merchants. Conversely, when no contract is recognized under Subsection 2–207(1)—either because no definite expression of acceptance exists or, more specifically, because the offeree's acceptance is expressly conditioned on the offeror's assent to the additional or different terms—the entire transaction aborts at this point. If, however, the subsequent conduct of the parties—particularly, performance by both parties under what they apparently believe to be a contract—recognizes the existence of a contract, under Subsection 2–207(3) such conduct by both parties is sufficient to establish a contract, notwithstanding the fact that no contract would have been recognized on the basis of their writings alone. Subsection 2–207(3) further provides how the terms of contracts recognized thereunder shall be determined.

With the above analysis and purposes of Section 2–207 in mind, we turn to their application in the present case. We initially observe that the affidavits and the acknowledgment forms themselves raise the question of whether Collins & Aikman's forms constituted acceptances or confirmations under Section 2–207. The language of some of the acknowledgment forms ("The acceptance of your order is subject to * * *") and the affidavit of Mr. William T. Hester, Collins & Aikman's marketing operations manager, suggest that the forms were the only acceptances issued in response to The Carpet Mart's oral offers. However, in his affidavit Mr. J. A. Castle, a partner in The Carpet Mart, asserted that when he personally called Collins & Aikman to order carpets, someone from the latter's order department would agree to sell the requested carpets, or, alternatively, when Collins & Aikman's visiting salesman took the order, he would agree to the sale, on some occasions after he had used The Carpet Mart's telephone to call Collins & Aikman's order department. Absent the District Court's determination of whether Collins & Aikman's acknowledgment forms were acceptances or, alternatively, confirmations of prior oral agreements, we will consider the application of section 2–207 to both situations for the guidance of the District Court on remand.

Viewing Collins & Aikman's acknowledgment forms as acceptances under Subsection 2–207(1), we are initially faced with the question of whether the arbitration provision in Collins & Aikman's acknowledgment forms were in fact "additional to or different from" the terms of The Carpet Mart's oral offers. In the typical case under Section 2–207, there exist both a written purchase order and a written acknowledgment, and this determination can be readily made by comparing the two forms. In the present case, where the only written forms were Collins & Aikman's sales acknowledgments, we believe that such a comparison must be made between the oral offers and the written acceptances. Although the District Court apparently assumed that The Carpet Mart's oral orders did not include in their terms the arbitration provision which appeared in Collins & Aikman's acknowledgment forms, we believe that a specific finding on this point will be required on remand.

Assuming, for purposes of analysis, that the arbitration provision was an addition to the terms of The Carpet Mart's oral offers, we must next determine whether or not Collins & Aikman's acceptances were "expressly made conditional on assent to the additional * * * terms" therein, within the proviso of Subsection 2–207(1). As set forth in full above, the provision appearing on the face of Collins & Aikman's acknowledgment forms stated that the acceptances (or orders) were "subject to all of the terms and conditions on the face and reverse side hereof, including arbitration, all of which are accepted by buyer." The provision on the "Acknowledgment" forms further stated that Collins & Aikman's terms would become the basis of the contract between the parties * * *.

Although Collins & Aikman's use of the words "subject to" suggests that the acceptances were conditional to some extent, we do not believe the acceptances were "expressly made conditional on [the buyer's] assent to the additional or different terms," as specifically required under the Subsection 2–207(1) proviso. In order to fall within this proviso, it is not enough that an acceptance is expressly conditional on additional or different terms; rather, an acceptance must be expressly conditional on the offeror's assent to those terms. Viewing the Subsection (1) proviso within the context of the rest of that Subsection and within the policies of Section 2–207 itself, we believe that it was intended to apply only to an acceptance which clearly reveals that the offeree is unwilling to proceed with the transaction unless he is assured of the offeror's assent to the additional or different terms therein. * * * That the acceptance is predicated on the offeror's assent must be "directly and distinctly stated or expressed rather than implied or left to inference." * * *

Although the UCC does not provide a definition of "assent," it is significant that Collins & Aikman's printed acknowledgment forms specified at least seven types of action or inaction on the part of the buyer which—sometimes at Collins & Aikman's option—would be deemed to bind the buyer to the terms therein. These ranged from the buyer's signing and delivering the acknowledgment to the seller—which indeed could have been recognized as the buyer's assent to Collins & Aikman's terms—to the buyer's retention of the acknowledgment for ten days without objection—which could never have been recognized as the buyer's assent to the additional or different terms where acceptance is expressly conditional on that assent.

To recognize Collins & Aikman's acceptances as "expressly conditional on [the buyer's] assent to the additional * * * terms" therein, within the proviso of Subsection 2–207(1), would thus require us to ignore the specific language of that provision. Such an interpretation is not justified in view of the fact that Subsection 2–207(1) is clearly designed to give legal recognition to many contracts where the variance between the offer and acceptance would have precluded such recognition at common law.

Because Collins & Aikman's acceptances were not expressly conditional on the buyer's assent to the additional terms within the proviso of Subsection 2–207(1), a contract is recognized under Subsection (1), and the additional terms are treated as "proposals" for addition to the contract under Subsection 2–207(2). Since both Collins & Aikman and The Carpet Mart are clearly "merchants" as that term is defined in Subsection 2–104(1), the arbitration provision will be deemed to have been accepted by The Carpet Mart under Subsection 2–207(2) unless it materially altered the terms of The Carpet Mart's oral offers. * * * [UCC § 2–207(2) (b)]. We believe that the question of whether the arbitration provision materially altered the oral offer under Subsection 2–207(2) (b) is one which can be resolved only by the District Court on further findings of fact in the present case. If the arbitration provision did in fact materially alter The Carpet Mart's offer, it could not become a part of the contract "unless expressly agreed to" by The Carpet Mart. * * * [UCC § 2–207], Official Comment No. 3.

We therefore conclude that if on remand the District Court finds that Collins & Aikman's acknowledgments were in fact acceptances and that the arbitration provision was additional to the terms of The Carpet Mart's oral orders, contracts will be recognized under Subsection 2–207(1). The arbitration clause will then be viewed as a "proposal" under Subsection 2–207(2) which will be deemed to have been accepted by The Carpet Mart unless it materially altered the oral offers.

If the District Court finds that Collins & Aikman's acknowledgment forms were not acceptances but rather were confirmations of prior oral agreements between the parties, an application of Section 2–207 similar to that above will be required. Subsection 2–207(1) will require an initial determination of whether the arbitration provision in the confirmations was "additional to or different from" the terms orally agreed upon. Assuming that the District Court finds that the arbitration provision was not a term of the oral agreements between the parties, the arbitration clause will be treated as a "proposal" for addition to the contract under Subsection 2–207(2), as was the case when Collins & Aikman's acknowledgments were viewed as acceptances above. The provision for arbitration will be deemed to have been accepted by The Carpet Mart unless the District Court finds that it materially altered the prior oral agreements, in which case The Carpet Mart could not become bound thereby absent an express agreement to that effect.

* * *

For the reasons set forth above, the case is remanded to the District Court for further findings consistent with this opinion.

QUESTIONS AND NOTES

1. Questions about the facts of this case

    1.1. U.C.C. § 2–207 is often called the "battle of the forms" provision. Did *Dorton* involve a battle of *forms*?

    1.2. In *Dorton*, when were the contracts for the purchase of carpeting formed? Were these contracts oral or written? When did the district court think the contracts were formed?

    1.3. Why did The Carpet Mart accept and pay for the carpet shipments if it objected to the arbitration provisions contained in the acknowledgements, which were admittedly received prior to delivery of each shipment?

2. Questions about the law

    2.1. How would the *Dorton* case have been decided under the common law mirror image rule? Does U.C.C. § 2–207 change the result?

2.2. In the classic battle of the forms scenario, the buyer's standard form purchase order and the seller's standard form acknowledgement don't match, but the goods are nevertheless shipped by the seller and accepted by the buyer. Section 2–207 was designed to eliminate the unearned "last-shot" advantage that the offeree/seller would enjoy under the common law mirror image rule; *i.e.*, acknowledgment is a counteroffer which buyer accepts by paying for the goods. Did § 2–207 accomplish this objective in *Dorton*?

2.3. If some of the contracts were formed during the telephone conversations between The Carpet Mart and Collins & Aikman, does the court's opinion suggest that § 2–207 can be used to alter the terms of an existing agreement? If so, is this a proper interpretation of the statute? *See* U.C.C. § 2–207, Official Comment 1. As lawyer for the buyer, what steps could you take to prevent this possibility?

2.4. In *Dorton*, the court found that Collins & Aikman's acceptances were *not* expressly conditional on The Carpet Mart's assent to the additional terms. Thus, a contract was deemed to exist under § 2–207(1) and the only issue is, what were its terms under § 2–207(2)? If the acceptances had been made expressly conditional on the offeror's assent to such additional terms, could The Carpet Mart's acceptance of and payment for the goods be recognized as assent?

2.5. Ultimately, what difference would it make under § 2–207 if, on remand, the district court determined that the Collins & Aikman acknowledgements were confirmations of prior oral agreements rather than acceptances?

2.6. How did the district court and the Sixth Circuit's § 2–207 analyses in *Dorton* differ? Did it affect the result? Under the district court's analysis, was there a contract? If so, was arbitration a term of the contract? Was "100% Kodel polyester" a term of the contract?

3. Notes

3.1. Section 2–207(1) makes an "imperfect acceptance" effective as an acceptance rather than as a counteroffer, provided that it constitutes a "definite and seasonable expression of acceptance" but one which is not the mirror image of the offer because it contains terms additional to or different from those specified in the offer. There are, however, a couple of points about the scope of § 2–207 that you need to be aware of.

First, § 2–207(1) does not create a contract in every instance where there are additional or different terms. Remember the hypothetical we started this section with? Ponoroff offered to buy Epstein's car for $100 and Epstein replied that he wanted $120. Would that reply operate as an acceptance under § 2–207(1)? Certainly not, no "seasonable expression of acceptance." Therefore, § 2–207(1) does not apply.

Second, even when the reply would otherwise operate as an acceptance under § 2–207(1), the offeree can prevent the application of § 2–207(1) by expressly making his assent conditional on the offeror's assent to the additional or different terms contained in the reply. This is because of the proviso in the last part of § 2–207(1).

In *Dorton,* however, the court stated, "In order to fall within this proviso, it is not enough that an acceptance is expressly conditional on additional or different terms; rather, an acceptance must be expressly conditional on the offeror's assent to those terms." What does that mean? Do you agree with that interpretation of the language of the statute? How would you draft a conditional acceptance that would satisfy the court in *Dorton?* Assuming you are able to do so, what is the effect of the conditional acceptance?

3.2.   Note that § 2–207(1) deals with "additional or different terms," but § 2–207(2) only deals with "additional terms." Assume in *Dorton* that The Carpet Mart's offers to purchase the carpet had been in the form of written purchase orders containing an explicit provision to the effect that any disputes arising between the parties would be resolved by arbitration. Assume further that the acknowledgment forms from Collins & Aikman contained an express provision to the effect that disputes will *not* be resolved by arbitration. When a disagreement concerning the quality of the carpet breaks out, how should the court go about determining whether there is an obligation to submit the matter to binding arbitration? Based on the caselaw thus far, there are at least three possibilities for dealing with "different" terms. Can you figure out what they are?

3.3.   Many § 2–207 cases involve disputes over warranties. In order to understand these issues it's important for you first to understand a few things about the U.C.C. Article 2 warranty scheme, a topic we take up in much greater depth in Chapter 5. In particular, § 2–314 provides that in every contract for the sale of goods in which the seller is a merchant (i.e., someone in the business of selling goods of that kind) there is an implied warranty of *merchantability.* The implied warranty of merchantability is an assurance that the goods are fit for the ordinary purposes for which such goods are used. Thus, if Epstein were to buy a lawnmower from Sears that didn't cut grass very well, there would probably be a breach of this warranty. However, if Epstein, having grown up in the South where it doesn't snow much, naively purchased a lawn mower to blow snow off of his driveway, there would be no breach of the implied warranty of merchantability even though the lawnmower didn't do a very good job on clearing the driveway. Finally, you need to be aware that § 2–316 allows the seller to exclude any and all warranties from the contract of sale by making an effective *disclaimer* of warranties. Ok, with this brief summary in mind, consider the following:

Ponoroff sends a purchase order for widgets that says nothing about warranties. Markell responds with an acknowledgment that matches all of the terms of the purchase order with respect to price, quantity, shipment terms, etc., but also contains a provision that says: *"Markell hereby disclaims all warranties with respect to these widgets, including the warranty of merchantability. This acknowledgment, if issued in response to an offer, shall only constitute an acceptance of such offer subject to the express condition that Ponoroff assent to any terms herein which vary, add to, or conflict with such offer."* Ponoroff never assents to the disclaimer, but when the goods are shipped Ponoroff accepts and pays for them. Later, it turns out that the widgets are defective. Ponoroff sues for breach of the implied warranty of merchantability. Markell moves to dismiss, pointing to the disclaimer in the acknowledgment form. How would this case be decided under the mirror image rule? Does § 2–207 change the result?

Introduction to *Klocek* and *Hill*

It's a simple story—the plaintiffs in the next two cases bought a computer from Gateway, paying for the computer with a credit card. They were unhappy with the way that the computer performed and sued Gateway. In response to the complaints, Gateway argued that the "Standard Terms and Conditions Agreement" that was in the box in which the computers were shipped prevented the plaintiffs from bringing the law suit. The parts of that Agreement relevant to the cases were:

"This document contains Gateway 2000's Standard Terms and Conditions. By keeping your Gateway 2000 computer system beyond thirty (30) days after the date of delivery, you accept these Terms and Conditions."

"Any dispute or controversy arising out of or relating to this Agreement or its interpretation shall be settled exclusively and finally by arbitration. The arbitration shall be conducted in accordance with the Rules of Conciliation and Arbitration of the International Chamber of Commerce. The arbitration shall be conducted in Chicago, Illinois, U.S.A. before a sole arbitrator. Any award rendered in any such arbitration proceeding shall be final and binding on each of the parties, and judgment may be entered thereon in a court of competent jurisdiction."

KLOCEK v. GATEWAY, INC.

United States District Court for the District of Kansas
104 F. Supp. 2d 1332, order vacated for lack of jurisdiction, 2000
WL 1372886 (D.Kan.), *aff'd,* 2001 WL 1568346 (D.Kan.)

NO. CIV.A. 99–2499–KHV

MEMORANDUM AND ORDER

VRATIL, DISTRICT JUDGE

William S. Klocek brings suit against Gateway, Inc. * * * on claims arising from purchases of a Gateway computer * * *. This matter comes before the Court on the Motion to Dismiss which Gateway filed November 22, 1999 * * * For reasons stated below, the Court overrules Gateway's motion to dismiss. * * *

A.   Gateway's Motion to Dismiss

Plaintiff brings * * * claims against Gateway, alleging that it induced him * * * to purchase [a] computer and special support package by making false promises of technical support. Individually, plaintiff also claims breach of contract and breach of warranty, in that Gateway breached certain warranties that its computer would be compatible with standard peripherals and standard internet services.

Gateway asserts that plaintiff must arbitrate his claims under Gateway's Standard Terms and Conditions Agreement ("Standard Terms"). Whenever it sells a computer, Gateway includes a copy of the Standard Terms in the box which contains the computer battery power cables and instruction manuals. * * *

When deciding whether the parties have agreed to arbitrate, the Court applies ordinary state law principles that govern the formation of contracts. * * * The existence of an arbitration agreement "is simply a matter of contract between the parties; [arbitration] is a way to resolve those disputes-but only those disputes—that the parties have agreed to submit to arbitration." * * * If the parties dispute making an arbitration agreement, a jury trial on the existence of an agreement is warranted if the record reveals genuine issues of material fact regarding the parties' agreement.

* * *

[The court at this point engaged in a discussion of which state law to apply: Missouri, where the plaintiff lived, or Kansas, where plaintiff claimed he purchased the computer at a Gateway store. Ultimately, the court concluded that it did not matter because the issue was one of first impression in both jurisdictions.]

Regardless whether plaintiff purchased the computer in person or placed an order and received shipment of the computer, the parties agree that plaintiff paid for and received a computer from Gateway. This conduct clearly demonstrates a contract for the sale of a computer * * *. Thus the issue is whether the contract of sale includes the Standard Terms as part of the agreement.

State courts in Kansas and Missouri apparently have not decided whether terms received with a product become part of the parties' agreement. Authority from other courts is split. *Compare Step–Saver [Data Sys., Inc. v. Wyse Tech.]*, 939 F.2d 91 (printed terms on computer software package not part of agreement); *Arizona Retail Sys., Inc. v. Software Link, Inc.*, 831 F. Supp. 759 (D. Ariz. 1993) (license agreement shipped with computer software not part of agreement); and *U.S. Surgical Corp. v. Orris, Inc.*, 5 F. Supp. 2d 1201 (D. Kan. 1998) (single use restriction on product package not binding agreement); *with Hill v. Gateway 2000, Inc.*, 105 F.3d 1147 (7th Cir.), cert. denied, 522 U.S. 808 (1997) (arbitration provision shipped with computer binding on buyer); *ProCD, Inc. v. Zeidenberg*, 86 F.3d 1447 (7th Cir. 1996) (shrinkwrap license binding on buyer);[6] and *M.A. Mortenson Co., Inc. v. Timberline Software Corp.*, 140 Wn.2d 568, 998 P.2d 305 (Wash. 2000) (following *Hill* and *ProCD* on license agreement supplied with software).[7] It appears that at least in part, the cases turn on whether the court finds that the parties formed their contract *before* or *after* the vendor communicated its terms to the purchaser. *Compare Step–Saver*, 939 F.2d at 98 (parties' conduct in shipping, receiving and paying for product demonstrates existence of contract; box top license constitutes proposal for additional terms under § 2–207 which requires express agreement by purchaser); *Arizona Retail*, 831 F. Supp. at 765 (vendor entered into contract by agreeing to ship goods, or at latest by shipping goods to buyer; license agreement constitutes proposal to modify agreement under § 2–209 which requires express assent by buyer); and *Orris*, 5 F. Supp. 2d at 1206 (sales contract concluded when vendor received consumer orders; single-use language on product's label was proposed modification under § 2–209 which requires express assent by purchaser); *with ProCD*, 86 F.3d at 1452 (under § 2–204 vendor, as master of offer, may propose limitations on kind of conduct that constitutes acceptance; § 2–207 does not apply in case with only one form); *Hill*, 105 F.3d at 1148–49 (same); and *Mortenson*, 998 P.2d at 311– 314 (where vendor and purchaser utilized license agreement in prior

---

6. The term "shrinkwrap license" gets its name from retail software packages that are covered in plastic or cellophane "shrinkwrap" and contain licenses that purport to become effective as soon as the customer tears the wrapping from the package. *See ProCD*, 86 F.3d at 1449.

7. The *Mortenson* court also found support for its holding in the proposed Uniform Computer Information Transactions Act ("UCITA") (formerly known as proposed UCC Article 2B) (text located at www.law.upenn.edu/library/ulc/ucita/UCITA99.htm), which the National Conference of Commissioners on Uniform State Laws approved and recommended for enactment by the states in July 1999. *See Mortenson*, 998 P.2d at 310 n.6, 313 n.10. The proposed UCITA, however, would not apply to the Court's analysis in this case. The UCITA applies to computer information transactions, which are defined as agreements "to create, modify, transfer, or license computer information or informational rights in computer information." UCITA, §§ 102(11) and 103. In transactions involving the sale of computers, such as our case, the UCITA applies only to the computer programs and copies, not to the sale of the computer itself. *See* UCITA § 103(c)(2).

course of dealing, shrinkwrap license agreement constituted issue of contract formation under § 2–204, not contract alteration under § 2–207).

Gateway urges the Court to follow the Seventh Circuit decision in *Hill*. That case involved the shipment of a Gateway computer with terms similar to the Standard Terms in this case, except that Gateway gave the customer 30 days—instead of 5 days—to return the computer. In enforcing the arbitration clause, the Seventh Circuit relied on its decision in *ProCD*, where it enforced a software license which was contained inside a product box. In *ProCD*, the Seventh Circuit noted that the exchange of money frequently precedes the communication of detailed terms in a commercial transaction. Citing UCC § 2–204, the court reasoned that by including the license with the software, the vendor proposed a contract that the buyer could accept by using the software after having an opportunity to read the license.[8] *ProCD*, 86 F.3d at 1452. Specifically, the court stated:

> A vendor, as master of the offer, may invite acceptance by conduct, and may propose limitations on the kind of conduct that constitutes acceptance. A buyer may accept by performing the acts the vendor proposes to treat as acceptance.

The *Hill* court followed the *ProCD* analysis, noting that "practical considerations support allowing vendors to enclose the full legal terms with their products." *Hill*, 105 F.3d at 1149.[9]

The Court is not persuaded that Kansas or Missouri courts would follow the Seventh Circuit reasoning in *Hill* and *ProCD*. In each case the Seventh Circuit concluded without support that UCC § 2–207 was irrelevant because the cases involved only one written form. *See ProCD,* 86 F.3d at 1452 (citing no authority); *Hill*, 105 F.3d at 1150 (citing *ProCD*). This

---

8. Section 2–204 provides: "A contract for sale of goods may be made in any manner sufficient to show agreement, including conduct by both parties which recognizes the existence of such contract." [U.C.C. § 2–204].

9. Legal commentators have criticized the reasoning of the Seventh Circuit in this regard. *See, e.g.,* Jean R. Sternlight, Gateway Widens Doorway to Imposing Unfair Binding Arbitration on Consumers, Fla. Bar J., Nov. 1997, at 8, 10–12 (outcome in Gateway is questionable on federal statutory, common law and constitutional grounds and as a matter of contract law and is unwise as a matter of policy because it unreasonably shifts to consumers search cost of ascertaining existence of arbitration clause and return cost to avoid such clause); Thomas J. McCarthy et al., Survey: Uniform Commercial Code, 53 Bus. Law. 1461, 1465–66 (Seventh Circuit finding that UCC § 2–207 did not apply is inconsistent with official comment); Batya Goodman, Honey, I Shrink–Wrapped the Consumer: the Shrinkwrap Agreement as an Adhesion Contract, 21 Cardozo L. Rev. 319, 344–352 (Seventh Circuit failed to consider principles of adhesion contracts); Jeremy Senderowicz, Consumer Arbitration and Freedom of Contract: A Proposal to Facilitate Consumers' Informed Consent to Arbitration Clauses in Form Contracts, 32 Colum. J.L. & Soc. Probs. 275, 296–299 (judiciary (in multiple decisions, including Hill) has ignored issue of consumer consent to an arbitration clause). Nonetheless, several courts have followed the Seventh Circuit decisions in *Hill* and *ProCD*. *See, e.g., Mortenson*, 2000 WL 550845 (license agreement supplied with software); Rinaldi v. Iomega Corp., 1999 Del. Super. LEXIS 563, 1999 WL 1442014, Case No. 98C–09–064–RRC (Del. Sept. 3, 1999) (warranty disclaimer included inside computer Zip drive packaging); Westendorf v. Gateway 2000, Inc., 2000 Del. Ch. LEXIS 54, 2000 WL 307369, Case No. 16913 (Del. Ch. March 16, 2000) (arbitration provision shipped with computer); Brower v. Gateway 2000, Inc., 246 A.D.2d 246, 676 N.Y.S.2d 569 (N.Y. App. Div. 1998) (same); Levy v. Gateway 2000, Inc., 1997 WL 823611, 33 U.C.C. Rep. Serv. 2d (Callaghan) 1060 (N.Y. Sup. Ct. August 12, 1997) (same).

conclusion is not supported by the statute or by Kansas or Missouri law. Disputes under § 2–207 often arise in the context of a "battle of forms," * * * but nothing in its language precludes application in a case which involves only one form. The statute provides:

> Additional terms in acceptance or confirmation.

> (1) A definite and seasonable expression of acceptance or a written confirmation which is sent within a reasonable time operates as an acceptance even though it states terms additional to or different from those offered or agreed upon, unless acceptance is expressly made conditional on assent to the additional or different terms.

> (2) The additional terms are to be construed as proposals for addition to the contract [if the contract is not between merchants]. * * *

[U.C.C. § 2–207.] By its terms, § 2–207 applies to an acceptance or written confirmation. It states nothing which requires another form before the provision becomes effective. In fact, the official comment to the section specifically provides that §§ 2–207(1) and (2) apply "where an agreement has been reached orally * * * and is followed by one or both of the parties sending formal memoranda embodying the terms so far agreed and adding terms not discussed." Official Comment 1 of UCC § 2–207. Kansas and Missouri courts have followed this analysis. *See Southwest Engineering Co. v. Martin Tractor Co.*, 205 Kan. 684, 695, 473 P.2d 18, 26 (1970) (stating in dicta that § 2–207 applies where open offer is accepted by expression of acceptance in writing or where oral agreement is later confirmed in writing); *Central Bag Co. v. W. Scott and Co.*, 647 S.W.2d 828, 830 (Mo. App. 1983) (§§ 2–207(1) and (2) govern cases where one or both parties send written confirmation after oral contract). Thus, the Court concludes that Kansas and Missouri courts would apply § 2–207 to the facts in this case. * * *

In addition, the Seventh Circuit provided no explanation for its conclusion that "the vendor is the master of the offer." *See ProCD*, 86 F.3d at 1452 (citing nothing in support of proposition); *Hill*, 105 F.3d at 1149 (citing *ProCD*). In typical consumer transactions, the purchaser is the offeror, and the vendor is the offeree. *See Brown Mach., Div. of John Brown, Inc. v. Hercules, Inc.*, 770 S.W.2d 416, 419 (Mo. App. 1989) (as general rule orders are considered offers to purchase); *Rich Prods. Corp. v. Kemutec Inc.*, 66 F. Supp. 2d 937, 956 (E.D. Wis. 1999) (generally price quotation is invitation to make offer and purchase order is offer). While it is possible for the vendor to be the offeror, see *Brown Machine*, 770 S.W.2d at 419 (price quote can amount to offer if it reasonably appears from quote that assent to quote is all that is needed to ripen offer into contract), Gateway provides no factual evidence which would support such a finding in this case. The Court therefore assumes for purposes of the motion to dismiss that plaintiff offered to purchase the computer (either in person or through catalog order) and that Gateway accepted plaintiff's offer (either by completing the sales transaction in person or by agreeing to ship and/or shipping the computer to plaintiff).[11]

Under § 2–207, the Standard Terms constitute either an expression of acceptance or written confirmation. As an expression of acceptance, the Standard Terms would constitute a counter-offer only if Gateway expressly made its acceptance conditional on plaintiff's assent to the additional or different terms. [U.C.C. § 2–207(1).] "The conditional nature of the acceptance must be clearly expressed in a manner sufficient to notify the offeror that the offeree is unwilling to proceed with the transaction unless the additional or different terms are included in the contract." *Brown Machine*, 770 S.W.2d at 420.[12] Gateway provides no evidence that at the time of the sales transaction, it informed plaintiff that the transaction was conditioned on plaintiff's acceptance of the Standard Terms. Moreover, the mere fact that Gateway shipped the goods with the terms attached did not communicate to plaintiff any unwillingness to proceed without plaintiff's agreement to the Standard Terms. *See, e.g., Arizona Retail*, 831 F. Supp. at 765 (conditional acceptance analysis rarely appropriate where contract formed by performance but goods arrive with conditions attached); *Leighton Indus., Inc. v. Callier Steel Pipe & Tube, Inc.*, 1991 WL 18413, *6, Case No. 89–C–8235 (N.D.Ill. Feb. 6, 1991) (applying Missouri law) (preprinted forms insufficient to notify offeror of conditional nature of acceptance, particularly where form arrives after delivery of goods).

Because plaintiff is not a merchant, additional or different terms contained in the Standard Terms did not become part of the parties' agreement unless plaintiff expressly agreed to them. *See* [U.C.C. § –2–207] Comment 2 (if either party is not a merchant, additional terms are

---

11. UCC § 2–206(b) provides that "an order or other offer to buy goods for prompt or current shipment shall be construed as inviting acceptance either by a prompt promise to ship or by the prompt or current shipment * * *" The official comment states that "either shipment or a prompt promise to ship is made a proper means of acceptance of an offer looking to current shipment." UCC § 2–206, Official Comment 2.

12. Courts are split on the standard for a conditional acceptance under § 2–207. *See Daitom* [*v. Pennwalt Corp.*], 741 F.2d 1569, 1576 (finding that Pennsylvania would most likely adopt "better" view that offeree must explicitly communicate unwillingness to proceed with transaction unless additional terms in response are accepted by offeror). On one extreme of the spectrum, courts hold that the offeree's response stating a materially different term solely to the disadvantage of the offeror constitutes a conditional acceptance. *See Daitom*, 741 F.2d at 1569 (citing *Roto–Lith. Ltd v. F.P. Bartlett & Co.*, 297 F.2d 497 (1st Cir. 1962)). At the other end of the spectrum courts hold that the conditional nature of the acceptance should be so clearly expressed in a manner sufficient to notify the offeror that the offeree is unwilling to proceed without the additional or different terms. *See Daitom*, 741 F.2d at 1569 (citing *Dorton v. Collins & Aikman Corp.*, 453 F.2d 1161 (6th Cir. 1972)). The middle approach requires that the response predicate acceptance on clarification, addition or modification. *See Daitom*, 741 F.2d at 1569 (citing *Construction Aggregates Corp. v. Hewitt–Robins, Inc.*, 404 F.2d 505 (7th Cir. 1968)). The First Circuit has since overruled its decision in *Roto–Lith, see Ionics, Inc. v. Elmwood Sensors, Inc.*, 110 F.3d 184, and the Court finds that neither Kansas nor Missouri would apply the standard set forth therein. *See Boese–Hilburn Co. v. Dean Machinery Co.*, 616 S.W.2d 520, (Mo. App. 1981) (rejecting *Roto–Lith* standard); *Owens–Corning Fiberglas Corp. v. Sonic Dev. Corp.*, 546 F. Supp. 533, 538 (D. Kan. 1982) (acceptance is not counteroffer under Kansas law unless it is made conditional on assent to additional or different terms (citing *Roto–Lith* as comparison)); *Daitom*, 741 F.2d at 1569 (finding that *Dorton* is "better" view). Because Gateway does not satisfy the standard for conditional acceptance under either of the remaining standards (*Dorton* or *Construction Aggregates*), the Court does not decide which of the remaining two standards would apply in Kansas and/or Missouri.

proposals for addition to the contract that do not become part of the contract unless the original offeror expressly agrees). Gateway argues that plaintiff demonstrated acceptance of the arbitration provision by keeping the computer more than five days after the date of delivery. Although the Standard Terms purport to work that result, Gateway has not presented evidence that plaintiff expressly agreed to those Standard Terms. Gateway states only that it enclosed the Standard Terms inside the computer box for plaintiff to read afterwards. It provides no evidence that it informed plaintiff of the five-day review-and-return period as a condition of the sales transaction, or that the parties contemplated additional terms to the agreement.[14] * * * The Court finds that the act of keeping the computer past five days was not sufficient to demonstrate that plaintiff expressly agreed to the Standard Terms. *Accord Brown Machine*, 770 S.W.2d at 421 (express assent cannot be presumed by silence or mere failure to object). Thus, because Gateway has not provided evidence sufficient to support a finding under Kansas or Missouri law that plaintiff agreed to the arbitration provision contained in Gateway's Standard Terms, the Court overrules Gateway's motion to dismiss.

* * *

IT IS THEREFORE ORDERED that the Motion to Dismiss * * * which defendant Gateway filed November 22, 1999 be and hereby is OVERRULED. * * *

———————

QUESTIONS AND NOTES

1. Questions about the facts of this case
    1.1. Does it matter how Klocek bought his computer? Whether by mail order, by phone order, or at a physical "Gateway Country" store?
    1.2. What *Klocek* fact was most important to Judge Vratil?
2. Questions about the law
    2.1. If Gateway had told Klocek that, before he could buy the computer, he would "have to agree to our terms," would that have changed the result? How about if Gateway had made Klocek separately sign the additional terms or recorded his assent to them over the telephone?
    2.2. Under § 2–207(1), does it matter who is the offeror and who is the offeree?
    2.3. In footnote 12 of the case, the court describes the split in the caselaw on what constitutes a "conditional acceptance" for purposes of § 2–207(1). *Dorton*, of course, is cited for the strict view on this

———————

14. The Court is mindful of the practical considerations which are involved in commercial transactions, but it is not unreasonable for a vendor to clearly communicate to a buyer—at the time of sale—either the complete terms of the sale or the fact that the vendor will propose additional terms as a condition of sale, if that be the case.

question, while other courts take a much more expansive view of when an acceptance should be regarded as conditional. Given the purposes of and policies behind § 2–207, which view do you think has the better of it?

2.4. If you were Gateway's counsel, what would you tell Gateway's sales division that it should do to ensure that future purchasers of Gateway computers would be bound to arbitrate their disputes against the company?

3. Notes

3.1. One might have expected that Gateway would take the district court's decision refusing to dismiss Klocek's complaint and compel arbitration up to the Tenth Circuit. As it happened, Gateway had a better idea. Shortly after this opinion was rendered, Gateway filed a motion to dismiss for lack of subject matter jurisdiction alleging that plaintiff had not satisfied his burden of establishing the requisite amount in controversy to invoke the court's diversity jurisdiction. Klocek conceded the point and the case was dismissed. *See* 2000 WL 1372886 (D. Kan. 2000). Left lingering is the precedential value of this decision in light of the subsequent dismissal. Because the court in the order of dismissal did not vacate its earlier opinion, we think *Klocek* continues to have some persuasive force as a source of law and, of course, the subsequent dismissal does not in any way lessen its instructional value, which is important because in our view, this court got it right—even if it ended up not really counting.

3.2. The approach of the *U.N. Convention on Contracts for the International Sales of Goods* to the "battle of the forms" problem is contained in Article 19, which provides:

(1) A reply to an offer which purports to be an acceptance but contains additions, limitations or other modifications is a rejection of the offer and constitutes a counter-offer.

(2) However, a reply to an offer which purports to be an acceptance but contains additional or different terms which do not materially alter the terms of the offer constitutes an acceptance unless the offeror, without undue delay, objects orally to the discrepancy or dispatches a notice to that effect. If he does not so object, the terms of the contract are the terms of the offer with the modifications contained in the acceptance.

(3) Additional or different terms relating, among other things, to the price, payment, quality, or quantity of the goods, place and time of delivery, extent of one party's liability to the other or the settlement of disputes are considered to alter the terms of the offer materially.

How would *Dorton* and *Klocek* have been decided under this provision?

You may have noticed extensive discussion in *Klocek* of an earlier case from the United States Court of Appeals for the Seventh Circuit, *Hill v. Gateway 2000, Inc.* In that case, Judge Easterbrook, writing for the court, took a different approach to delayed terms, both in relation to § 2–207 and otherwise. See what you think.

HILL v. GATEWAY 2000, INC.

United States Court of Appeals, Seventh Circuit
105 F.3d 1147, *cert denied*, 522 U.S. 808 (1997)

EASTERBROOK, CIRCUIT JUDGE

[handwritten margin note: General rules of contract]

A customer picks up the phone, orders a computer, and gives a credit card number. Presently a box arrives, containing the computer and a list of terms, said to govern unless the customer returns the computer within 30 days. Are these terms effective as the parties' contract, or is the contract term-free because the order-taker did not read any terms over the phone and elicit the customer's assent?

One of the terms in the box containing a Gateway 2000 system was an arbitration clause. Rich and Enza Hill, the customers, kept the computer more than 30 days before complaining about its components and performance. They filed suit in federal court arguing, among other things, that the product's shortcomings make Gateway a racketeer (mail and wire fraud are said to be the predicate offenses), leading to treble damages under RICO for the Hills and a class of all other purchasers. Gateway asked the district court to enforce the arbitration clause; the judge refused, writing that "[t]he present record is insufficient to support a finding of a valid arbitration agreement between the parties or that the plaintiffs were given adequate notice of the arbitration clause." Gateway took an immediate appeal, as is its right.

The Hills say that the arbitration clause did not stand out: they concede noticing the statement of terms but deny reading it closely enough to discover the agreement to arbitrate, and they ask us to conclude that they therefore may go to court. * * * A contract need not be read to be effective; people who accept take the risk that the unread terms may in retrospect prove unwelcome. Terms inside Gateway's box stand or fall together. If they constitute the parties' contract because the Hills had an opportunity to return the computer after reading them, then all must be enforced.

ProCD, Inc. v. Zeidenberg, 86 F.3d 1447 (7th Cir. 1996), holds that terms inside a box of software bind consumers who use the software after an opportunity to read the terms and to reject them by returning the product. * * * Gateway shipped computers with the same sort of accept or return offer ProCD made to users of its software. * * *

Plaintiffs ask us to limit *ProCD* to software, but where's the sense in that? *ProCD* is about the law of contract, not the law of software. Payment preceding the revelation of full terms is common for air transportation, insurance, and many other endeavors. Practical considerations support allowing vendors to enclose the full legal terms with their products. Cashiers cannot be expected to read legal documents to customers before ringing up sales. If the staff at the other end of the phone for direct-sales operations such as Gateway's had to read the four-page statement of terms before taking the buyer's credit card number, the droning voice would anesthetize rather than enlighten many potential buyers. Others would hang up in a rage over the waste of their time. And oral recitation would not avoid customers' assertions (whether true or feigned) that the clerk did not read term X to them, or that they did not remember or understand it. Writing provides benefits for both sides of commercial transactions. Customers as a group are better off when vendors skip costly and ineffectual steps such as telephonic recitation, and use instead a simple approve-or-return device. Competent adults are bound by such documents, read or unread. For what little it is worth, we add that the box from Gateway was crammed with software. The computer came with an operating system, without which it was useful only as a boat anchor. * * * So the Hills' effort to limit *ProCD* to software would not avail them factually, even if it were sound legally—which it is not.

For their second sally, the Hills contend that *ProCD* should be limited to executory contracts (to licenses in particular), and therefore does not apply because both parties' performance of this contract was complete when the box arrived at their home. This is legally and factually wrong: legally because the question at hand concerns the *formation* of the contract rather than its *performance*, and factually because both contracts were incompletely performed. *ProCD* did not depend on the fact that the seller characterized the transaction as a license rather than as a contract; we treated it as a contract for the sale of goods and reserved the question whether for other purposes a "license" characterization might be preferable. All debates about characterization to one side, the transaction in *ProCD* was no more executory than the one here: Zeidenberg paid for the software and walked out of the store with a box under his arm, so if arrival of the box with the product ends the time for revelation of contractual terms, then the time ended in *ProCD* before Zeidenberg opened the box. But of course ProCD had not completed performance with delivery of the box, and neither had Gateway. One element of the transaction was the warranty, which obliges sellers to fix defects in their products. The Hills have invoked Gateway's warranty and are not satisfied with its response, so they are not well positioned to say that Gateway's obligations were fulfilled when the motor carrier unloaded the box. What is more, both ProCD and Gateway promised to help customers to use their products. Long-term service and information obligations are common in the computer business, on both hardware and software sides. Gateway offers "lifetime service" and has a round-the-clock telephone hotline to fulfill this promise. Some vendors spend more money helping customers use their products than on developing and manufacturing them. The document in Gateway's box includes promises of future performance that some consumers value highly; these promises bind Gateway just as the arbitration clause binds the Hills.

* * *

Next, the Hills insist that *ProCD* is irrelevant because Zeidenberg was a "merchant" and they are not. Section 2–207(2) of the UCC, the infamous battle-of-the-forms section, states that "additional terms [following acceptance of an offer] are to be construed as proposals for addition to a contract. Between merchants such terms become part of the contract unless. * * *". Plaintiffs tell us that *ProCD* came out as it did only because Zeidenberg was a "merchant" and the terms inside ProCD's box were not excluded by the "unless" clause. This argument pays scant attention to the opinion in *ProCD*, which concluded that, when there is only one form, "§ 2–207 is irrelevant." 86 F.3d at 1452. The question in *ProCD* was not whether terms were added to a contract after its formation, but how and when the contract was formed—in particular, whether a vendor may propose that a contract of sale be formed, not in the store (or over the phone) with the payment of money or a general "send me the product," but after the customer has had a chance to inspect both the item and the terms. *ProCD* answers "yes," for merchants and consumers alike. * * *

At oral argument the Hills propounded still another distinction: the box containing ProCD's software displayed a notice that additional terms were within, while the box containing Gateway's computer did not. The difference is functional, not legal. Consumers browsing the aisles of a store can look at the box, and if they are unwilling to deal with the prospect of additional terms can leave the box alone, avoiding the transactions costs of returning the package after reviewing its contents. Gateway's box, by contrast, is just a shipping carton; it is not on display anywhere. Its function is to protect the product during transit, and the information on its sides is for the use of handlers rather than would-be purchasers.

Perhaps the Hills would have had a better argument if they were first alerted to the bundling of hardware and legal-ware after opening the box and wanted to return the computer in order to avoid disagreeable terms, but were dissuaded by the expense of shipping.

What the remedy would be in such a case—could it exceed the shipping charges?—is an interesting question, but one that need not detain us because the Hills knew before they ordered the computer that the carton would include some important terms, and they did not seek to discover these in advance. Gateway's ads state that their products come with limited warranties and lifetime support. How limited was the warranty—30 days, with service contingent on shipping the computer back, or five years, with free onsite service? What sort of support was offered? Shoppers have three principal ways to discover these things. First, they

can ask the vendor to send a copy before deciding whether to buy. * * *
Concealment would be bad for business, scaring some customers away and
leading to excess returns from others. Second, shoppers can consult public
sources (computer magazines, the Web sites of vendors) that may contain
this information. Third, they may inspect the documents after the product's delivery. Like Zeidenberg, the Hills took the third option. By keeping
the computer beyond 30 days, the Hills accepted Gateway's offer, including the arbitration clause.

The Hills' remaining arguments, including a contention that the
arbitration clause is unenforceable as part of a scheme to defraud, do not
require more than a citation to *Prima Paint Corp. v. Flood & Conklin
Mfg. Co.*, 388 U.S. 395, 87 S. Ct. 1801, 18 L. Ed.2d 1270 (1967). Whatever
may be said pro and con about the cost and efficacy of arbitration (which
the Hills disparage) is for Congress and the contracting parties to consider. * * *

The decision of the district court is vacated, and this case is remanded
with instructions to compel the Hills to submit their dispute to arbitration.

QUESTIONS, NOTES, AND CONNECTIONS

1.   Questions about the facts of this case
    1.1.   From the court's description of the facts, do we know why the Hills
           did not want to settle their dispute with Gateway by arbitration in
           Chicago under the International Chamber of Commerce Rules? Do
           you know what the International Chamber of Commerce Rules are?
           Did the Hills? Did Judge Easterbrook?*

    1.2.   Did the Hills know before they ordered their computer that the
           carton would contain important additional terms? Does that mat-
           ter?

    1.3.   Do we know why the Hills did not return the computer within 30
           days? Did Judge Easterbrook care? Do you care?

    1.4.   Do we know when the Hills first read the Standard Terms and
           Conditions? Did Judge Easterbrook care? Do you care?

---

* Here is an excerpt from a similar case, *Brower v. Gateway 2000, Inc.*, 246 A.D.2d 246, 676
N.Y.S.2d 569 (1998), that perhaps sheds a little light on this question.

In support of their arguments, appellants submitted a copy of the ICC's Rules of Conciliation
and Arbitration and contended that the cost of ICC arbitration was prohibitive, particularly
given the amount of the typical consumer claim involved. For example, a claim of less than
$50,000 required advance fees of $4,000 (more than the cost of most Gateway products), of
which the $2000 registration fee was nonrefundable even if the consumer prevailed at the
arbitration. Consumers would also incur travel expenses disproportionate to the damages
sought, which appellants' counsel estimated would not exceed $1,000 per customer in this
action, as well as bear the cost of Gateway's legal fees if the consumer did not prevail at the
arbitration; in this respect, the ICC rules follow the "loser pays" rule used in England. Also,
although Chicago was designated as the site of the actual arbitration, all correspondence must
be sent to ICC headquarters in France.   *ruled unconscionable*

1.5.   How are the facts of the *Hill* case different from the facts of the *Klocek* case? How would Judge Vratil have decided *Hill*? How would Judge Easterbrook have decided *Klocek?*

2.   Questions about the law

2.1.   What resulted in the "formation of the contract" in this case? The Hills' ordering a computer and giving their credit card number? Gateway's shipping the computer? The Hills' receiving the computer? The Hills' reading the Standard Terms and Conditions? Did Judge Easterbrook's opinion answer this question? How would Judge Vratil answer this question? What does Judge Easterbrook mean by his statement "by keeping the computer beyond 30 days, the Hills accepted Gateway's offer, including the arbitration clause"?

2.2.   Would the Seventh Circuit have decided this case differently if Gateway sent the Hills the Standard Terms and Conditions in a separate envelope that arrived one day after the computer?

2.3.   Recall Hills' attorneys' efforts to distinguish *ProCD*. Convincing to you? To Judge Easterbrook? Would you be surprised to learn that *ProCD* is an Easterbrook opinion? Do you think the Hills' attorneys were pleased when they learned (usually about a week before oral argument) that Easterbrook was one of the three judges hearing their case?

2.4.   What do you think of Judge Easterbrook's conclusion that § 2–207 is "irrelevant to the analysis" because there "was only one form"?* What do you think the *Dorton* court would have thought of that assertion? Would the *Dorton* court have treated the Standard Terms and Conditions as an "expression of acceptance or written confirmation"? How would the analysis in the case have been different if Judge Easterbrook had found § 2–207 to be applicable?

2.5.   Your friend Bill calls. He wants your help with his New York landlord who won't let him keep his dog in the apartment. Bill rented the apartment by telephone outside a bar in Cancun. Bill paid for the first month's rent and the security deposit by credit card. The landlord told Bill that when he arrived, he would give Bill a copy of the apartment rules and regulations. The rules and regulations which Bill received (but did not read) clearly provides "no dogs." What do you tell Bill?

2.6.   Is the holding in this case consistent with the policy objective that contract law should be "fair"? Do you think that "terms in a box" are fair? Assume that Microsoft becomes disenchanted with its present legal counsel and hires your firm. Would you encourage Microsoft to do business different from Gateway and ProCD? Is this

---

* Here's what one commentator had to say about Judge Easterbrook's take on § 2–207: "Even more troublesome is the superficial notion that UCC § 2–207 applies only when there are two conflicting forms, which ignores the UCC's application where a single confirmation containing variant terms follows an oral contract for the sale of goods." John E. Murray, Jr., *Contract Theory and the Rise of Neoformalism*, 71 FORDHAM L. REV. 869, 905 N. 193 (2002).

what Bill Gates had in mind when he talked about "thinking outside the box"?

2.7.   Is the holding in this case consistent with the policy objective of freedom of contract? Could the Hills have bought a Gateway computer without "agreeing" to arbitration of disputes?

3. Notes

3.1.   *Brower v. Gateway 2000, Inc.,* 246 A.D.2d 246, 676 N.Y.S.2d 569 (1998), a case we discuss in chapter 4, involved facts similar to *Hill* and *Klocek*, the court concluded that although a contract had been formed that included the "in-the-box" arbitration provision, the contract was not enforceable on the ground that the arbitration provision was unconscionable due to the unduly burdensome procedure and cost for the individual consumer.* Obviously, the outcome in *Klocek* as to the ultimate enforceability of the delayed term is much more consistent with the outcome in *Brower* than the outcome in *Hill*. Nevertheless, the approaches taken in *Klocek* and *Brower* to reach that outcome are quite different. Can you articulate the difference? Which approach, if either, do you find more satisfying?

3.2.   These are hardly the only reported decisions on shrinkwrap agreements and "terms in the box," nor the only reported decisions on shrinkwrap or delayed form agreements to arbitrate. *See* footnote 9 in *Klocek*. Also, lest you think we're picking on Gateway, in *Defontes v. Dell Computers Corp.*, 52 UCC Rep. Serv.2d 795 (R.I. Super. 2004), the court found Dell's shrinkware arbitration agreement to be unenforceable because 1) the plaintiff's did not "assent" to the provision, and 2) the language of the contract was so one-sided that the provision was unenforceable as an illusory promise; i.e., that it bound the customer but not Dell.

3.3   Cases like *Defontes* send the message that all delayed terms are "rough" on consumers. This may not necessarily be the case. Observing that, "Pay now, terms later, or rolling, contracts are an increasingly important form of commercial contracting," Professor Marotta–Wurgler recently performed an empirical study to "inform the debate about whether rolling contracts impose harsher terms on buyers." She collected and analyzed the terms of several hundred EULAs [end-user licensing agreements] for software packages sold online, involving wide variation in the degree of pre-purchase accessibility of these EULAs. She postulated that "[t]he wide variation in the degree of pre-purchase accessibility of these EULAs enables me to give a fairly rigorous answer to whether rolling contracts offer worse terms to buyers, at least in this particular market setting." Her conclusion was perhaps a bit of a surprise:

---

* Unconscionability was also argued, you will recall, in *R.R. v. M.H*, our very first case. We will study unconscionability further in § 8 of Chapter 3.

"I find that the terms included in rolling contracts are not systematically more pro-seller than those included in contracts disclosed before purchase. In fact, contrary to fears often associated with rolling contracts, I find that contracts displayed pre-purchase are actually slightly more pro-seller than rolling contracts"

Florencia Marotta–Wurgler, *Are "Pay Now, Terms Later" Contracts Worse for Buyers? Evidence From Software Licensing Agreements*, 38 J. LEGAL STUDIES 309, 341 (2009).

4. Connections

Transactions of the sort illustrated in *Klocek* and *Hill* are typical of what have come to be termed "rolling contracts." They are problematic because, as we have seen, classical contract law principles are predicated on the model of "assent". But this model, which works fine when the transaction involves two neighboring farmers negotiating over the price of a chicken, does not reflect the reality of many modern day deals where the seller does not present all the terms of the deal to the customer, or obtain the customer's assent to those terms, before the shipment and delivery of the product. What does this suggest to you about the classic "offer" and "acceptance" model for determining contract formation?

Hill, in particular, has been a very controversial case that has been criticized by many law professors. For example, Professor James J. White of the University of Michigan Law School describes the shrinkwrap contract in cases like *ProCD* and *Hill* as an "autistic contract":

> Parties to modern form contracts sometimes interact with one another in the same way a parent of an autistic child interacts with that child. When a licensor offers a software license with the assertion that it will infer acceptance of all the license terms if the licensee removes the power cord from its plastic wrapper, the licensor is drawing an inference from the licensee's behavior just as doubtful as the inference a hopeful parent draws from an autistic child's apparently knowing response to the parent's statement.

James J. White, *Autistic Contracts*, 45 WAYNE L. REV. 1693 (2000). Why should you care what Jim White, a short, old, bald guy* who teaches at another law school, thinks about the *Hill* decision? Why does your professor care about what you think about the *Hill* decision? What do *Hill* and *Klocek* tell you about how well § 2–207 has worked in practice? What do they tell you about the larger question raised by this Chapter; has your client made a deal?

F. ELECTRONIC ACCEPTANCES

Increasingly, commerce is occurring over the Internet or through other forms of electronic communication where the deal is consummated

---

* White is even older than Epstein! We disagree as to whether White is shorter or balder than Ponoroff.

between computers and without the benefit of written signatures or agreements. Needless to say, these transactions put traditional contract law rules and assumptions (which developed in a very different world) to the test. However, conventional contract law principles nonetheless pertain and are by no means unhelpful, though many questions remain unanswered.

The threshold question of whether wholly electronic contracts are even valid has now been settled by both Federal and State legislation. Specifically, the Uniform Electronic Transactions Act (1999), which has now been adopted in every state, and the Electronic Signatures in Global and National Commerce Act (so-called "E–Sign"), both enable electronic commerce by validating and effectuating electronic records and signatures.

Neither of these laws, however, displaces the common law of contracts, and, thus, neither addresses the substantive questions of what are the terms of an electronic contract and at what point in time does the contract come into existence? The latter issue—"pay now-terms later" is the same one we encountered in *Hill v. Gateway 2000* and *Klocek v. Gateway, Inc.*, even though those transactions occurred by phone. Of course, as we all know, it is just as easy to buy a computer online as it is to order by telephone; indeed, perhaps even easier.

One case that, while far from the final word, is very instructive is *Specht v. Netscape Communications Corp.*, 306 F.3d 17 (2d Cir. 2002). In somewhat simplified form, the issue for the court in *Specht* was whether consumers assented to the terms of an agreement when they downloaded software from an Internet website. In that case, the terms of the licensing agreement were available by a hyperlink at the bottom of the page, below the download button. Such an agreement has become known as a "browsewrap" or "clickwrap" agreement. In this case, it was possible for the plaintiffs to download the software without scrolling down the webpage and seeing the link. Therefore, the plaintiffs, who clicked without scrolling through the whole license agreement (if you could imagine ever doing that!) contended that they downloaded the software without knowing the terms that Netscape insisted applied to the purchase, or without reading those terms.

Netscape, in turn, argued that failing to read a contract is no defense to the contract and that parties are nevertheless bound by its terms, including an arbitration of disputes provision. While acknowledging this general principle, the court nevertheless concluded that consumers did not assent to the terms of this browsewrap agreement because they were not properly notified of the terms. In explanation, the court stated:

> [T]his principle of knowing consent applies with particular force to provisions for arbitration. Clarity and conspicuousness of arbitration terms are important in securing informed assent. If a party wishes to bind in writing another to an agreement to arbitrate future disputes, such purpose should be accomplished in a way that each

party to the arrangement will fully and clearly comprehend that the agreement to arbitrate exists and binds the parties thereto.

In specific response to the argument that a party that fails to read a contract does so at her peril, the court stated: "An exception to this general rule exists when the writing does not appear to be a contract and the terms are not called to the attention of the recipient. In such a case, no contract is formed with respect to the undisclosed term."

Is *Specht* in direct conflict with the holdings in cases like *Hill* which have enforced delayed term arbitration agreements or can they be distinguished?

One final issue of interest in these cases is what law governs when the transaction involves the license of computer software? Although clearly not a "good," within the meaning of Article 2 (at least when not delivered by means of a tangible media), some courts nonetheless apply the U.C.C. by analogy. The *Specht* court ultimately applied common law. To some extent software licenses exist in a legislative void. NCCUSL has tried to fill that void, but without much success. In the 1990's lawmakers began to draft a new Article 2B (licenses) for the U.C.C., which would have complemented Article 2 (sales) and Article 2A (leases). After a few years the effort was abandoned and in 1999 those lawmakers instead promulgated an independent body of law for software licenses, which is known as the Uniform Computer Information Transactions Act ("UCITA"). However, UCITA has only been adopted in two states, Maryland and Virginia, and seems to be something of a legislative dead letter.

SECTION 6:   DEFICIENT AGREEMENTS: INSUFFICIENT, INADEQUATE, AND POSTPONED TERMS

Introduction

So far in this Chapter we have been focused on various dimensions of the issue of when an agreement is formed; *i.e.*, up to what point in time is either party free to walk from the "deal" without liability?

In this final section of the Chapter we consider a related problem or series of problems; namely, what happens when: 1) the parties both believe they have assented to a deal, but each of them has attached a materially different meaning or understanding to their outward manifestations of assent, or 2) the parties have reached some agreement on the proposed exchange, but have not: (i) agreed on all terms, or (ii) expressed their agreement in an indefinite manner, or (iii) deliberately left some terms for future agreement.

Now, in any of these situations, when, if ever, should the law permit one party to withdraw without consequence? In other words, should the law provide that there can be no contract unless the parties have attached the same meaning to all material terms, can be no contract until there is clear and complete agreement on all terms? Or, in the former situation, should the law choose one meaning over the other, and, in the latter case, should we allow the parties to conclude a deal without clear and complete agreement if that's what they intend? If the court does enforce the deal, how does it go about the task of fashioning an appropriate remedy in light of either the misunderstanding or the lack of clarity? What if the parties "agree to agree" on a particular term and do not? Is there a pre-contractual duty to negotiate in good faith? These and others are some of the questions we address in this final section.

In Part A, we will consider the issues surrounding misunderstood terms and indefiniteness. Then, in Part B, we will examine how courts deal with situations where either the parties have made a deal but intentionally decided to defer agreement on a particular term or terms, or have reached agreement on some but less than all of the terms on which the deal hinges. After that, everyone gets 20 minutes of recess to decompress!

<hr>

A. PROBLEMS OF MISUNDERSTOOD, INCOMPLETE, AND INDEFINITE TERMS

Introduction to Mutual Misunderstanding of a Contract Term—*Raffles*

The next case illustrates the problem known as "mutual misunderstanding." One party is contending that even though the parties thought they had a deal, there never was a deal because they later discovered that their respective understandings of what a contract term meant were fundamentally different. In essence, the argument is that there can be no mutual assent if the parties have assented to different things; i.e., there are mutual misunderstandings.

The questions you should be asking yourself as you read *Raffles* are: 1) under what facts should such different understandings of a key term of the deal preclude a finding that a contract was formed; 2) are those facts present in this case; and 3) which of the parties should end up in cases of this sort bearing the risk of different understandings?

<hr>

RAFFLES v. WICHELHAUS

Court of Exchequer
2 H. & C. 906, 159 Eng. Rep. 375 (1864)

Declaration. For that it was agreed between the plaintiff and the defendants, to wit, at Liverpool, that the plaintiff should sell to the defendants, and the defendants buy of the plaintiff, certain goods, to wit, 125 bales of Surat cotton, guaranteed middling fair merchant's Dhollarah, to arrive ex "Peerless" from Bombay; and that the cotton should be taken from the quay, and that the defendants would pay the plaintiff for the same at a certain rate, to wit, at the rate of 17¼ d. per pound, within a certain time then agreed upon after the arrival of said goods in England.

Averments: that the said goods did arrive by the said ship from Bombay in England, to wit, at Liverpool, and the plaintiff was then and there ready and willing and offered to deliver the said goods to the defendants, & c. Breach: that the defendants refused to accept the said goods or pay the plaintiff for them.

Plea. That the said ship mentioned in the said agreement was meant and intended by the defendants to be the ship called the "Peerless," which sailed from Bombay, to wit, in October; and that the plaintiff was not ready and willing, and did not offer to deliver to the defendants any bales of cotton which arrived by the last-mentioned ship, but instead thereof was only ready and willing, and offered to deliver to the defendants 125 bales of Surat cotton which arrived by another and different ship, which was also called the "Peerless," and which sailed from Bombay, to wit, in December.

Demurrer, and joinder therein.

Milward, in support of the demurrer. The contract was for the sale of a number of bales of cotton of a particular description, which the plaintiff was ready to deliver. It is immaterial by what ship the cotton was to arrive, so that it was a ship called the "Peerless." The words "to arrive ex 'Peerless,'" only mean that if the vessel is lost on the voyage, the contract is to be at an end. [Pollock, C.B. It would be a question for the jury whether both parties meant the same ship called the "Peerless."] That would be so if the contract was for the sale of a ship called the "Peerless"; but it is for the sale of cotton on board a ship of that name. [Pollack, C.B. The defendant only bought that cotton which was to arrive by a particular ship. It may as well be said, that if there is a contract for the purchase of certain goods in warehouse A., that is satisfied by the delivery of goods of the same description in warehouse B.] In that case there would be goods in both warehouses; here it does not appear that the plaintiff had any goods on board the other "Peerless." [Martin, B. It is imposing on the defendant a contract different from that which he entered into. Pollack, C.B. It is like a contract for the purchase of wine coming from a particular estate in France or Spain, where there are two estates of that name.] The defendant has no right to contradict by parol evidence a written contract good upon the face of it. He does not impute misrepresentation or fraud, but only says that he fancied the ship was a different one. Intention is of no avail, unless stated at the time of the contract. [Pollock, C.B. One vessel sailed in October and the other in December.] The time of sailing is no part of the contract.

Mellish (Cohen with him), in support of the plea. There is nothing on the face of the contract to shew that any particular ship called the "Peerless" was meant; but the moment it appears that two ships called the "Peerless" were about to sail from Bombay there is a latent ambiguity, and parol evidence may be given for the purpose of shewing that the defendant meant one "Peerless," and the plaintiff another. That being so, there was no consensus ad idem, and therefore no binding contract. He was then stopped by the Court.

PER CURIAM. There must be judgment for the defendants.

Judgment for the defendants.

QUESTIONS

1. Questions about the facts of this case
    1.1. Who sets out the facts of the case? Who were Milward and Mellish?
    1.2. Why did it matter what the parties privately may have intended when they made reference to the ship *Peerless*? And while we're at it, why did it even matter what vessel the cotton was being shipped by? Wasn't the important thing that the plaintiff delivered the proper quantity of the agreed-upon commodity to the defendant? Why then did the parties even specify the ship on which the cotton would be carried? Was it to establish the time of delivery or to protect the seller if the ship went down? Does that make a difference?
    1.3. Why do you suppose that the defendant refused to accept the cotton that arrived on the December *Peerless*? Do you (especially those of you who were history majors) understand why the dates were important? Did the court understand that? Did it care? Presumably, the October *Peerless* arrived in London some weeks or even months before the December *Peerless* and yet there is no indication that defendant raised any inquiry as to why his cotton was not on the October ship.
    1.4. Did the court's decision benefit one party over the other?
2. Questions about the law
    2.1. Is *Raffles* consistent with objective theory? In discussing *Raffles*, Justice Holmes said, "The true ground of the decision was not that each party meant a different thing from the other, as has been implied in the explanation that has been mentioned, but that each said a different thing." O.W. HOLMES, THE COMMON LAW 242 [1881] (Howe ed. 1963). Do you agree with that analysis? Here's what Professor Gilmore had to say about it: "The magician who could 'objectify' *Raffles v. Wichelhaus* * * * could, the need arising, objectify anything. But why bother?" GRANT GILMORE, THE DEATH OF CONTRACT 41 (1974).
    2.2. Did the *Raffles* court go pretty "light" on Mellish compared to Milward? What else might you have asked if you sat on the bench in this case before you were convinced that there was no contract?
    2.3. Read *Restatement (Second) of Contracts* § 20, which deals with the effects of misunderstanding. Is *Restatement (Second) of Contracts* § 20(1) essentially a codification of the Court of Exchequer's deci-

sion in *Raffles*? If not, how does it differ and would its application have changed the result in *Raffles*?

2.4   Notice the five illustrations at the end of *Restatement (Second) of Contracts* § 20. Four of the five use "ex steamer Peerless." Can you illustrate *Restatement (Second) of Contracts* § 20(1) without using the term "Peerless"?

PROBLEM ON MUTUAL MISUNDERSTANDING OF A CONTRACT TERM

Epstein has two prized hunting dogs, a black lab and a golden retriever. Because he was so fond of the name, Epstein named both dogs Goober. Ponoroff has been negotiating with Epstein to purchase one of the dogs, as Epstein has become desperate for money after losing his job due to the commission of certain acts of moral turpitude. After much haggling, Epstein says, "Ok, I'll sell Goober to you for $1,000." Ponoroff promptly replies, "I accept." When Epstein shows up at Ponoroff's house with the retriever and demands his $1,000, Ponoroff refuses to pay, demanding that Epstein turn over the lab "as agreed." Ponoroff knows that Epstein is uncommonly, and perhaps even unnaturally, attached to the black lab and would never part with him for any price. Consult § 20 of *Restatement (Second) of Contracts* and answer the following questions.

- Is there a contract here, and, if so, for which dog? *No*

- How, if at all, does it change your answer if Ponoroff had no reason to know of Epstein's unusual attachment to the lab?

- How, if at all, does it change your answer if the facts were different in that Epstein deliberately showed up with the retriever, a less valuable dog, knowing that Ponoroff meant the lab when Ponoroff agreed to pay the $1,000 price for "Goober."

- Suppose in the last question, Ponoroff was aware of what Epstein was up to, but still accepted, intending to asset a claim for the lab?

Introduction to Indefinite and Incomplete Terms—*Varney*

In *Raffles,* (1) the parties both agreed to term "ex Peerless"; (2) the court held that there was no contract; and (3) we suggested that you look at *Restatement (Second)* § 20. In the next case, *Varney*, (1) the parties agree to the term "fair share of the profits"; and (2) we suggest that you look at *Restatement (Second)* § 33. As you read the next case, think about how *Raffles* and *Varney* are similar and how they differ. When will you discuss *Raffles* on your final exam, and when will you discuss *Varney*?

Analytically, *indefiniteness* can be viewed as a *defense* to liability rather than as an aspect of contract formation. However, it is equally appropriate to conceptualize the requirement of definiteness as an aspect of the bargaining process that must be satisfied, no less than mutual assent, in order for a contract to arise. The purpose of contract enforcement is, as we shall see in Chapter 6, to protect the promisee's *expectation* in the event of breach; that is, to put the non-breaching party in as good a position as performance would have. If the parties have not expressed their agreement with sufficient clarity or completeness to permit the court to fashion an appropriate remedy, than an essential component of contract formation is missing.

As a practical matter, it is impossible for the parties' agreement to speak to every aspect of their relationship. Unquestionably, the requirement of definiteness means something less than specific agreement down to the finest minutiae. The question that forms the basis of contention in the next two cases is when the parties have intended to make a contract but have failed to express their mutual obligations with perfect clarity, how far should the court go in resolving ambiguities and supplying missing terms in order to provide a remedy for nonperformance?

VARNEY v. DITMARS

Court of Appeals of New York
217 N.Y. 223, 111 N.E. 822 (1916)

CHASE, J.

This is an action brought for an alleged wrongful discharge of an employee. The defendant is an architect employing engineers, draftsmen and other assistants. The plaintiff is an architect and draftsman. In October, 1910, he applied to the defendant for employment and when asked what wages he wanted, replied that he would start for $40 per week. He was employed at $35 per week. A short time thereafter he informed the defendant that he had another position offered to him and the defendant said that if he would remain with him and help him through the work in his office he thought he could offer him a better future than anybody else. He continued in the employ of the defendant and became acquainted with a designer in the office and said designer and the plaintiff from time to time prior to the 1st of February, 1911, talked with the defendant about the work in his office. On that day by arrangement the two remained with the defendant after the regular office hours and the defendant said: "I am going to give you $5 more a week; if you boys will go on and continue the way you have been and get me out of this trouble and get these jobs started that were in the office three years, on the first of next January I will close my books and give you a fair share of my profits. That was the result of the conversation. That was all of that conversation." The plaintiff was given charge of the drafting. Thereafter suggestions were made by the plaintiff and said designer about discharging many of the defendant's employees and employing new men and such suggestions were carried out and the two worked in the defendant's office over time and many Sundays and holidays. At least one piece of work that the defendant said had been in his office for three years was completed. The plaintiff on his cross-examination told the story of the employment of himself and said designer as follows: 'And he says at that time 'I am going to give you $5 more a week starting this week.' This was about Thursday. He says 'You boys go on and continue the work you are doing and the first of January next year I will close my books and give you a fair share of my profits.' Those were his exact words."

Thereafter the plaintiff was paid $40 a week. On November 6, 1911, the night before the general election in this state, the defendant requested that all of his employees that could do so, should work on election day. The plaintiff told the defendant that he wanted to remain at home to attend an election in the village where he lived. About four o'clock in the afternoon of election day he was taken ill and remained at his house ill until a time that as nearly as can be stated from the evidence was subsequent to December 1, 1911. On Saturday, November 11, the defendant caused to be delivered to the plaintiff a letter in which he said:

"I am sending you herewith your pay for one day's work of seven hours, performed on Monday, the 6th inst. On Monday night, I made it my special duty to inform you that the office would be open all day Election Day and that I expected you and all the men to report for work. Much to my surprise and indignation, on Tuesday you made no appearance and all the men remained away, in obedience of your instructions to them of the previous evening. An act of this kind I consider one of extreme disloyalty and insubordination and I therefore am obliged to dispense with your services."

After the plaintiff had recovered from his illness and was able to do so he went to the defendant's office (the date does not appear) and told him that he was ready, willing and able to continue his services under the agreement. The defendant denied that he had any agreement with him and refused to permit him to continue in his service. Thereafter and prior to January 1, 1912, the plaintiff received for special work about $50.

The plaintiff seeks to recover in this action for services from November 7, 1911, to December 31, 1911, inclusive, at $40 per week and for a fair and reasonable percentage of the net profits of the defendant's business from February 1, 1911, to January 1, 1912, and demands judgment for $1,680.

At the trial he was the only witness sworn as to the alleged contract and at the close of his case the complaint was dismissed.

The statement alleged to have been made by the defendant about giving the plaintiff and said designer a fair share of his profits is vague, indefinite and uncertain and the amount cannot be computed from anything that was said by the parties or by reference to any document, paper or other transaction. The minds of the parties never met upon any particular share of the defendant's profits to be given the employees or upon any plan by which such share could be computed or determined. The contract so far as it related to the special promise or inducement was never consummated. It was left subject to the will of the defendant or for further negotiation. It is urged that the defendant by the use of the word "fair" in referring to a share of his profits, was as certain and definite as people are in the purchase and sale of a chattel when the price is not expressly agreed upon, and that if the agreement in question is declared to be too indefinite and uncertain to be enforced a similar conclusion must be reached in every case where a chattel is sold without expressly fixing the price therefor.

The question whether the words "fair" and "reasonable" have a definite and enforceable meaning when used in business transactions is dependent upon the intention of the parties in the use of such words and upon the subject-matter to which they refer. In cases of merchandising and in the purchase and sale of chattels the parties may use the words "fair and reasonable value" as synonymous with "market value." A promise to pay the fair market value of goods may be inferred from what is expressly agreed by the parties. The fair, reasonable or market value of goods can be shown by direct testimony of those competent to give such testimony. The competency to speak grows out of experience and knowledge. The testimony of such witnesses does not rest upon conjecture. The opinion of this court in *United Press v. N. Y. Press Co.* (164 N. Y. 406) was not intended to assert that a contract of sale is unenforceable unless the price is expressly mentioned and determined.

In the case of a contract for the sale of goods or for hire without a fixed price or consideration being named it will be presumed that a reasonable price or consideration is intended and the person who enters into such a contract for goods or service is liable therefor as on an implied contract. Such contracts are common, and when there is nothing therein to limit or prevent an implication as to the price, they are, so far as the terms of the contract are concerned, binding obligations.

The contract in question, so far as it relates to a share of the defendant's profits, is not only uncertain but it is necessarily affected by so many other facts that are in themselves indefinite and uncertain that the intention of the parties is pure conjecture. A fair share of the defendant's profits may be any amount from a nominal sum to a material part according to the particular views of the person whose guess is considered. Such an executory contract must rest for performance upon the honor and good faith of the parties making it. The courts cannot aid parties in such a case when they are unable or unwilling to agree upon the terms of their own proposed contract.

It is elementary in the law that, for the validity of a contract, the promise, or the agreement, of the parties to it must be certain and explicit and that their full intention may be ascertained to a reasonable degree of certainty. Their agreement must be neither vague nor indefinite, and, if thus defective, parol proof cannot be resorted to. * * *

The courts in this state, in reliance upon and approval of the rule as stated in the *United Press* case, have decided many cases involving the same rule. Thus, in *Mackintosh v. Thompson,* (58 App. Div. 25), and again in *Mackintosh v. Kimball,* (101 App. Div. 494), the plaintiff sought to recover compensation in addition to a stated salary which he had received and which additional amount rested upon a claim by him that while he was employed by the defendants he informed them that he intended to leave their employ unless he was given an increase in salary, and that one of the defendants said to him that they would make it worth his while if he would stay on, and would increase his salary, and that his idea was to give him an interest in the profits on certain buildings that they were then erecting. The plaintiff further alleges that he asked what would be the amount of the increase and was told, "You can depend upon me; I will see that you get a satisfactory amount." The court held that the arrangement was too indefinite to form the basis of any obligation on the part of the defendants.

In *Bluemner v. Garvin,* (120 App. Div. 29), the plaintiff and defendant were architects, and the plaintiff alleged that he drew plans for a public building in accordance with a contract held by the defendant and pursuant to a special agreement that if the plans were accepted the defendant would give him a fair share of the commissions to be received by him. The court held that a good cause of action was stated on quantum meruit, but that the contract was too vague and indefinite to be enforced.

* * *

The rule stated from the *United Press* case does not prevent a recovery upon quantum meruit in case one party to an alleged contract has performed in reliance upon the terms thereof, vague, indefinite and uncertain though they are. In such case the law will presume a promise to pay the reasonable value of the services. Judge Gray, who wrote the opinion in the *United Press* case, said therein: "I entertain no doubt that, where work has been done, or articles have been furnished, a recovery may be based upon quantum meruit, or quantum valebat; but, where a contract is of an executory character and requires performance over a future period of time, as here, and it is silent as to the price which is to be paid to the plaintiff during its term, I do not think that it possesses binding force. As the parties had omitted to make the price a subject of covenant, in the nature of things, it would have to be the subject of future agreement, or stipulation." (p. 412.)

* * *

So, in this case, while I do not think that the plaintiff can recover anything as extra work, yet if the work actually performed as stated was worth more than $40 per week, he having performed until November 7, 1910, could, on a proper complaint, recover its value less the amount received.

* * *

The plaintiff claims that he at least should have been allowed to go to the jury on the question as to whether he was entitled to recover at the rate of $40 per week from November 7, 1911, to December 31, 1911, inclusive. He did not perform any services for the defendant from November 6 until some time after December 1st, by reason of his illness. He has not shown just when he offered to return. It appears that between the time when he offered to return and January 1st he received $50 for other services.

The amount that the plaintiff could recover, therefore, if any, based upon the agreement to pay $40 per week would be very small, and he did not present to the court facts from which it could be computed. His employment by the defendant was conditional upon his continuing the way he had been working, getting the defendant out of his trouble and getting certain unenumerated jobs that were in the office three years, started. There was nothing in the contract specifying the length of service except as stated. It was not an unqualified agreement to continue the plaintiff in his service until the first of January, and it does not appear whether or not the special conditions upon which the contract was made had been performed. Even apart from the question whether the plaintiff's absence from the defendant's office by reason of his illness would permit the defendant to refuse to take him back into his employ, I do not think that on the testimony as it appears before us it was error to refuse to leave to the jury the question whether the plaintiff was entitled to recover anything at the rate of $40 per week.

The judgment should be affirmed, with costs.

CARDOZO, J. (dissenting).

I do not think it is true that a promise to pay an employee a fair share of the profits in addition to his salary is always and of necessity too vague to be enforced * * *. The promise must, of course, appear to have been made with contractual intent * * *. But if that intent is present, it cannot be said from the mere form of the promise that the estimate of the reward is inherently impossible. The data essential to measurement may be lacking in the particular instance, and yet they may conceivably be supplied. It is possible, for example, that in some occupations an employee would be able to prove a percentage regulated by custom. The difficulty in this case is not so much in the contract as in the evidence. Even if the data required for computation might conceivably have been supplied, the plaintiff did not supply them. He would not have supplied them if all the evidence which he offered, and which the court excluded, had been received. He has not failed because the nature of the contract is such that damages are of necessity incapable of proof. He has failed because he did not prove them.

There is nothing inconsistent with this view in *United Press v. N.Y. Press Co.*, (164 N.Y. 406). The case is often cited as authority for the proposition that an agreement to buy merchandise at a fair and reasonable price is so indefinite that an action may not be maintained for its breach in so far as it is still executory. Nothing of the kind was decided, or with reason could have been. What the court did was to construe a particular agreement, and to hold that the parties intended to reserve the price for future adjustment. If instead of reserving the price for future adjustment, they had manifested an intent on the one hand to pay and on the other to accept a fair price, the case is far from holding that a jury could not determine what such a price would be and assess the damages accordingly. Such an intent, moreover, might be manifested not only through express words, but also through reasonable implication. It was because there was neither an express statement nor a reasonable implication of such an intent that the court held the agreement void to the extent that it had not been executed.

On the ground that the plaintiff failed to supply the data essential to computation, I concur in the conclusion that profits were not to be included as an element of damage. I do not concur, however, in the conclusion that he failed to make out a case of damage to the extent of his loss of salary. The amount may be small, but none the less it belongs to him. The hiring was not at will * * *. The plain implication was that it should continue until the end of the year when the books were to be closed. The evidence would permit the jury to find that the plaintiff was discharged without cause, and he is entitled to damages measured by his salary for the unexpired term.

The judgment should be reversed and a new trial granted, with costs to abide the event.

QUESTIONS

1. Questions about the facts of this case

   1.1. What did the defendant intend when he told plaintiff and the designer that if they would continue the work they had been doing he would give them "a fair share of my profits"? What did the plaintiff understand when the defendant told him and the designer that he would give them "a fair share of my profits"? Were the answers to these questions important to the court? How did the court determine that, "The minds of the parties never met upon any particular share of the defendant's profits to be given the employees"? Why was that important to the court?

   1.2. According to Justice Chase, what was the time duration of the plaintiff's employment contract? According to Justice Cardozo? Was the time duration of the plaintiff's employment contract relevant to the resolution of the plaintiff's contract claim? To the resolution of the plaintiff's quantum meruit claim? By the way, what is "quantum meruit"?

2. Questions about the law

2.1. The majority opinion in *Varney* represents the traditional common law attitude toward issues of definiteness. What is the concern that accounts for this attitude? What is Justice Cardozo's take and how does it differ from the approach adopted by the majority?

2.2. The majority opinion seems concerned that the determination of a "fair share of profits" is inherently more speculative than the determination of a "fair" or "reasonable" price for goods. Do you agree? Does Justice Cardozo agree? What kind of evidence would you try to produce to prove the dollar amount of "fair share of the profits" if given the opportunity?

COMMUNITY DESIGN CORPORATION v. ANTONELL

District Court of Appeal of Florida
459 So.2d 343 (1984)

NESBITT, JUDGE.

Community Design Corporation (CDC) appeals a final judgment against it in a contract case and the award of attorney's fees and costs. * * * We affirm in all respects.

Joseph Antonell was hired by CDC to work as an architectural draftsman on the Brickell Key project. He worked on a weekly basis at $10.00 per hour, with time and one-half for overtime.

Sometime in the fall of 1980, Charles Cheezum, the then-president of CDC, promised a bonus to any employee still working at Christmastime of 1980, if the drawings were complete by that time.[1] The amount each employee was to receive was apparently to be determined by the recommendation of Shirley Wooster, CDC's vice president. Wooster, Antonell's supervisor, promised a one-week paid vacation if the drawings were completed on time. After these promises were made, Antonell worked overtime in an effort to complete the drawings by the specified date.

On December 24, 1980, with Antonell still in CDC's employ, the draftsmen's drawings were collected and blueprints were made. After Christmas, and through much of 1981, changes were made to the drawings, some of which were necessitated by a February 23, 1981 contract which required CDC to coordinate the drawings of various subcontractors. Final acceptance of the drawings for construction purposes occurred by March of 1982.

When Antonell received neither the bonus nor the paid vacation, he sued to recover both. The jury found for him on both claims, finding for CDC on a third claim for a promised raise.

CDC [argues] * * * that the contract is too indefinite and uncertain to be enforced because there was no agreement as to the amount of the

---

1. The amount of the bonus was disputed, but was clearly between $20,000 and $35,000. The degree of completion required was also disputed.

bonus, the degree of completion required and the division among the employees. We disagree.

Courts are reluctant to hold contracts unenforceable on grounds of uncertainty, especially where, as here, one party has received the benefit of the other's performance. When the existence of a contract is clear, the jury may properly determine the exact terms of an oral contract, which often depend on the credibility of the witnesses. While the exact amount of the bonus[2] and the degree of completion required[3] were disputed, there was sufficient evidence for the jury to find an oral contract between the parties with terms which support the award in this case.

CDC asserts that there was no agreement as to exactly how much each employee would receive. While this is true, it is necessarily so because the bonus was to be divided among those still employed at Christmastime and in amounts recommended by Ms. Wooster. Once the drawings were completed, CDC's contractual duty to act in good faith in recommending a bonus for those who qualified arose. It was Wooster's failure to recommend a bonus, and CDC's subsequent failure to pay one, which constituted the breach.[4] It was appropriate for the jury to resolve the compensation question, and the amount awarded is reasonable based on Antonell's efforts in completing the drawings.

* * *

Accordingly, the judgment is, in all respects, affirmed.

QUESTIONS, NOTES, AND CONNECTIONS

1. Questions about the facts of this case

    1.1. What was the bonus promise in *Antonell* and how did it differ from the promise in *Varney*? Did the court in *Antonell* think the two promises were qualitatively different? Do you?

---

2. The parties acknowledge that a particular amount was offered, which distinguishes this case from those in which the amount is indefinite or left for future agreement. *See, e.g., Drake v. Block,* 247 Iowa 517, 74 N.W.2d 577 (1956); *Varney v. Ditmars,* 217 N.Y. 223, 111 N.E. 822 (1916).

3. While there were many changes made to the drawings after the initial blueprinting, there was evidence both that such changes are normal in the industry and that many were required by a February, 1981 contract which called for coordination of the architectural drawings with the electrical and mechanical drawings. Therefore, the jury could have found that the completion contemplated was the initial blueprinting and that the changes made were either those common in the industry, those required by a subsequent contract, or both.

4. We are in no way suggesting that employers are not free to establish bonus plans like that in *Parrish v. General Motors Corp.,* 137 So.2d 255 (Fla. 2d DCA 1962). There, the bonus plan gave the employer, in writing, the discretion to award, or choose not to award, a bonus. Such a writing clearly establishes the employer's intention and does not give rise to a contractual bonus right. Here, the contract is oral and the evidence is reasonably susceptible to the conclusion that once the drawings were complete the duty to recommend and pay a bonus arose. To find otherwise would allow CDC to induce extra efforts from its employees by oral promises and then hide behind a cloak of vagueness resulting from conflicting testimony.

1.2. Why didn't Ms. Wooster make a recommendation about Antonell's bonus amount? If she had, would this court have enforced that recommendation?

2. Questions about the law

2.1. How important was the fact that the Community Design Corp. had received the benefit of Antonell's performance?

2.2. The *Antonell* court says that while the amount of the bonus was not fixed, this is "necessarily so" because it was not known how many employees would still be employed at Christmastime. Does this provide a principled basis for distinguishing the case from *Varney?*

2.3. What role does "good faith" play in the court's analysis? Can the obligation of good faith overcome problems of indefiniteness?

2.4. *Restatement (Second)* § 33(2) suggests that the court may imply a missing term when there is a "reasonable basis" for doing so. Does this refer to a reasonable basis for assuming that the parties *intended* that the court would fill in the omitted or ambiguous item, or just an objectively reasonable basis for supplying or construing that missing or vague term?

2.5. How would the *Varney* court have decided this case? How about Justice Cardozo?

3. Notes

3.1. While *Antonell* and *Restatement (Second) of Contracts* § 33(2) reflect the contemporary attitude of increasing tolerance of indefiniteness, even today some courts still take the definiteness requirement quite seriously. In *Goldstick v. ICM Realty*, 788 F.2d 456, 461 (7th Cir. 1986), for example, Judge Posner, in insisting that the parties must express their agreement with sufficient definiteness to guide the court in determining what they intended, observed: "The parties have a competitive advantage over the court in deciding on what terms a voluntary transaction is value-maximizing; that is the premise of a free enterprise system." Do you agree? Is the concern over inadvertent, judicially-created market inefficiencies sufficient to justify depriving a party of his "fair share of the profits"?

3.2. There is no shortage of litigation over the validity of contracts based on the alleged indefiniteness of terms. If found, does indefiniteness render the contract unenforceable or should the court, as Justice Cardozo suggested in his *Varney* dissent, consider each contested term contextually?

3.3. Should the reason why the parties failed to address some aspect of their relationship with definiteness affect the court's willingness to supply the missing or ambiguous term? For instance, would it make a difference to you if the parties left an item open because they were unable to reach agreement? How about if they left the item open because of the inability to accurately forecast at the time of contracting what the needs of the parties were likely to be over the life of a contract?

3.4.　The shift in attitude and approach from the majority opinion in *Varney* to the decision in *Antonell* is reflective of a more generalized shift in contract law from strict rules to much more flexible standards, such as those set out in *Restatement (Second)* § 33(2) and in U.C.C. § 2–204(3), discussed below in the Note of U.C.C. Gap Fillers. There are many reasons for this shift from "rules to standards," but most notably among them, insofar as the requirement of definiteness is concerned, is the increasing complexity of modern transactions. The traditional theory of mutual assent evolved in an era when simple, one-shot transactions were the norm. As contractual relationships increasingly began to involve multiple performances over an extended period of time, new approaches had to be devised to accommodate the disputes that would inevitably arise in the course of performance and could not possibly have been anticipated by the parties in advance. As discussed in the Note below on long-term agreements and relational contracts, one of the first contract law scholars to examine the impact of long-term relational contracts on traditional doctrine was Professor Ian Macneil. *See* Macneil, *The Many Faces of Contracts,* 47 S. CAL. L. REV. 691 (1974).

4.　Connections

Conceptually, what are the differences between cases involving "indefiniteness," like *Varney* and *Antonell*, and cases dealing with "mutual misunderstanding," like *Raffles*? Are both kinds of cases different as well from the other cases you have read in this chapter on contract formation? Are these cases really about contract formation at all? If not, what are they doing in this chapter titled, "Has Your Client Made a Deal." Did your favorite authors mess up (again)?

NOTE ON LONG-TERM AGREEMENTS AND RELATIONAL CONTRACTS

The basic principles of contract law, including the requirement of definiteness, evolved in simpler economic times. In those simpler economic times, most contractual relations tended to involve discrete, "one-shot" transactions of short duration and limited interpersonal dealings between the parties. Understandably, many of the basic rules of contract law were developed to accommodate this type of transaction.

Now, however, contractual dealings are increasingly characterized by long-term, on-going relations between the contracting parties involving a complex series of performances over time. Of necessity, circumstances will change over the course of this relationship and, because it is impossible to anticipate all of these changes at the inception of the relationship, adjustments inevitably will have to be made by the parties during the course of performance. In a series of articles and an important book, Professor Ian R. Macneil has challenged many of the assumptions upon which both classical and contemporary principles of contract law are based as still misguidedly wedded to the traditional conception of contracts involving discrete transactions rather than long-term *relational* dealings between the parties. *See* MACNEIL, THE NEW SOCIAL CONTRACT (1980). Professor Macneil's work has important implications for the contract formation process, including the traditional demand of classical contract law that all material terms be agreed to at the moment of contracting. He suggests that while this may be possible in the typical one-shot deal, it is unrealistic in the long-term relational contract and is at odds with the needs of the parties to work collaboratively, rather than purely out of self-interest, during the course of their relationship. Ideally, the relational contract will serve more as a private constitution for the parties—setting forth the general standards that will govern their relationship—than an ordinary contract—setting forth in specific detail the terms of performance. In Professor Macneil's view, this should not make the contract any less enforceable in the eyes of the law.

While this is not the place to discuss the full impact of Professor Macneil's work, recognition of the relational character of many modern contracts does help provide perspective on the definiteness requirement and the impracticability of requiring complete projection of the transaction into the future through promises as a condition of meeting the law's demand for certainty. Indeed, while not necessarily reflected in the black-letter rules of contract law, the reality of contract litigation is that the character of the contract and the needs of the parties ultimately affect the degree of indefiniteness that the courts may be willing to allow. This tolerance suggests that the drafter of the long-term contract may be able to preserve some measure of flexibility for the parties in fashioning the agreement without running a serious risk that the agreement will later be declared to be too indefinite to enforce.

NOTE ON *U.C.C. GAP FILLERS*

The Uniform Commercial Code takes a very liberal attitude toward the definiteness requirement once it is established that the parties intended to be bound. Section 2–204(3) makes clear that the fact that one or more terms of a contract are left open does not render the contract too indefinite as long as there is a reasonable basis for affording an appropriate remedy.

This break with the traditional disinclination of common law judges to "make" a contract for the parties is consistent with the general philosophy of the drafters of the U.C.C. to bring the law into line with prevailing commercial practices and expectation. In many business contexts it is desirable, and sometimes even necessary, for the parties to be less than entirely clear in specifying one of the essential terms of the transaction. This can occur for a variety of reasons, ranging from uncertainty about future events to, in the case of agreements involving a series of performances over a lengthy period of time, an inability at the time of contracting to foresee every eventuality. For instance, in connection with the purchase and sale of a particular commodity subject to rapid price fluctuations, neither party may wish today to take the risk of an adverse move in the market. Nevertheless, if it is clear that they intend to be bound to one another at prevailing market prices at the time or times for performance, the thinking of the drafters was that this intention should not be frustrated merely because the parties left the price term open or tied it to an external standard. Similarly, if the parties clearly manifested an intention to be bound and expressed all of the other critical terms of their agreement but for, due to oversight, the place where delivery should occur, a contract for the sale of goods will not fail for indefiniteness.

The Code deals with these "open terms" in two ways. First, as discussed earlier, § 1–201(b)(3) defines "Agreement" as the parties' bargain-in-fact as ascertained not only from the language used but implied from "other circumstances including course of dealing or usage of trade or course of performance as provided in this Act." We will take up each of these concepts in Chapter 4 when we consider what are the terms of the deal? Second, the U.C.C. contains numerous "gap filling" provisions in Article 2. These provisions operate as "default rules" that supply the governing rule as to various aspects of the agreement if the parties, though intending to be bound, have failed to address the particular term.

Be sure that you understand this phrase "default rules." It is a phrase that your professor will use and expect you to use. And, when you graduate, it is a term that older lawyers will use in an effort to intimidate you.

"Default rule" does not mean that someone is in default. A default rule is a rule that applies where the parties have *not* otherwise agreed. Thus, if the parties to a contract governed by Article 2 fail to specify the time for shipment or delivery, the default rules in §§ 2–308 and 2–309(1) provide the missing term. Similarly, even if the parties omit the price term but otherwise intend to conclude a contract, default rule § 2–305(1) applies and "the price is a reasonable price at the time of delivery."

The one term in a sale of goods contract that cannot be supplied by a default rule is quantity; *e.g.,* how many bushels of grits. This is because unlike price, time for shipment, time for delivery, etc., it is impossible to determine a reasonable quantity.

While Article 2 has no default rule to apply where the parties have not agreed on quantity, the parties nonetheless can agree on quantity without using actual numbers. Take a look at the *Black's Law Dictionary* of "outputs" and "requirements" contracts. § 2–306.

If Epstein agrees to buy all of the Viagra he needs from Jim Meyers Pharmacy, that is a requirements contract, and it is valid (enforceable) even though there is no specific quantity stated. If Ponoroff agrees to purchase all of the Voodoo Beer produced by the Voodoo microbrewery, that is an outputs contract and is valid despite the absence of a specific numerical quantity. Why?

In theory, default rules are designed to reflect what the parties *would have* agreed to had they spoken to the issue. In reality, they will sometimes hit their mark and sometimes miss. Moreover, we do not necessarily mean what *these* parties would have agreed to, since they failed to tell us what they wanted, but rather what reasonable persons in the position of these parties would have agreed to assuming that they were bargaining from relatively equal positions of strength. Some commentators have urged that perhaps it would be better in some instances if the default rule was not one that the parties would likely have agreed to had they spoken to the issue. Instead, it has been suggested that if the default rule is an unattractive one—one that neither party would presumably want—then there is more incentive for the parties to express their preference by negotiating more complete agreements. *See* Ian Ayres & Robert Gertner, *Filling Gaps in Incomplete Contracts: An Economics Theory of Default Rules,* 99 Yale L.J. 87 (1989) (distinguishing between "tailored" and "penalty" default rules and urging that in the interests of minimizing the costs of contracting "efficiency-minded courts and legislatures" should move "beyond the received wisdom that default rules should simply be what the majority of contracting parties would have wanted").

B. PROBLEMS OF POSTPONED AGREEMENT

Sometimes during the course of their negotiations, parties will leave a key term of their deal open or vague not because they have failed to reach agreement, but because, although they consider themselves bound, they have deliberately decided to defer agreement on a particular term or aspect of their deal until a later time. This is most often because neither party wishes to make a future commitment until more facts are known or more information is available.

We call such arrangements "agreements to agree." If the parties later reach agreement on the open term everything is copasetic. When, however, the parties fail to come to agreement on that open term, the issue for the courts is whether the agreement as struck is too indefinite to enforce or whether the court should supply the missing term in order to save the deal. The next two cases reveal the approaches taken by courts in this situation.

WALKER v. KEITH

Court of Appeals of Kentucky
382 S.W.2d 198 (1964)

Clay, Commissioner.

In this declaratory judgment proceeding the plaintiff appellee sought an adjudication that he had effectively exercised an option to extend a lease, and a further determination of the amount of rent to be paid. The relief prayed was granted by the Chancellor. The principal issue is whether the option provision in the lease fixed the rent with sufficient certainty to constitute an enforceable contract between the parties.

In July 1951 appellants, the lessors, leased a small lot to appellee, the lessee, for a 10–year term at a rent of $100 per month. The lessee was given an option to extend the lease for an additional 10–year term, under the same terms and conditions except as to rental. The renewal option provided:

> "rental will be fixed in such amount as shall actually be agreed upon by the lessors and the lessee with the monthly rental fixed on the comparative basis of rental values as of the date of the renewal with rental values at this time reflected by the comparative business conditions of the two periods."

The lessee gave the proper notice to renew but the parties were unable to agree upon the rent. Preliminary court proceedings finally culminated in this lawsuit. Based upon the verdict of an advisory jury, the Chancellor fixed the new rent at $125 per month.

The question before us is whether the quoted provision is so indefinite and uncertain that the parties cannot be held to have agreed upon this essential rental term of the lease. There have been many cases from other jurisdictions passing on somewhat similar lease provisions and the decisions are in hopeless conflict. We have no authoritative Kentucky decision.

At the outset two observations may be made. One is that rental in the ordinary lease is a very uncomplicated item. It involves the number of dollars the lessee will pay. It, or a method of ascertaining it, can be so easily fixed with certainty. From the standpoint of stability in business transactions, it should be so fixed.

Secondly, as an original proposition, uncomplicated by subtle rules of law, the provision we have quoted, on its face, is ambiguous and indefinite. The language used is equivocal. It neither fixes the rent nor furnishes a positive key to its establishment. The terminology is not only confusing but inherently unworkable as a formula.

The above observations should resolve the issue. Unfortunately it is not that simple. Many courts have become intrigued with the possible import of similar language and have interpolated into it a binding obligation. The lease renewal option has been treated as something different from an ordinary contract. The law has become woefully complicated. For this reason we consider it necessary and proper to examine this question in depth.

The following basic principles of law are generally accepted:

> "It is a necessary requirement in the nature of things that an agreement in order to be binding must be sufficiently definite to enable a court to give it an exact meaning." Williston on Contracts (3rd Ed.) Vol. 1, section 37 (page 107).

> "Like other contracts or agreements for a lease, the provision for a renewal must be certain in order to render it binding and enforceable. Indefiniteness, vagueness, and uncertainty in the terms of such a provision will render it void unless the parties, by their subsequent conduct or acts supplement the covenant and thus remove an alleged uncertainty. The certainty that is required is such as will enable a

court to determine what has been agreed upon." 32 Am.Jur., Landlord and Tenant, section 958 (page 806).

"The terms of an extension or renewal, under an option therefor in a lease, may be left for future determination by a prescribed method, as by future arbitration or appraisal; but merely leaving the terms for future ascertainment, without providing a method for their determination, renders the agreement unenforceable for uncertainty." 51 C.J.S. Landlord and Tenant 56b (2), page 597. * * *

The degree of certainty is the controlling consideration. An example of an appropriate method by which a non-fixed rental could be determined appears in *Jackson v. Pepper Gasoline Co.*, 280 Ky. 226, 133 S.W.2d 91, 126 A.L.R. 1370. The lessee, who operated an automobile service station, agreed to pay "an amount equal to one cent per gallon of gasoline delivered to said station". Observing that the parties had created a definite objective standard by which the rent could with certainty be computed, the court upheld the lease as against the contention that it was lacking in mutuality. * * *

On the face of the rent provision, the parties had not agreed upon a rent figure. They left the amount to future determination. If they had agreed upon a specific method of making the determination, such as by computation, the application of a formula, or the decision of an arbitrator, they could be said to have agreed upon whatever rent figure emerged from utilization of the method. This was not done.

It will be observed the rent provision expresses two ideas. The first is that the parties agree to agree. The second is that the future agreement will be based on a comparative adjustment in the light of "business conditions". We will examine separately these two concepts and then consider them as a whole.

The lease purports to fix the rent at such an amount as shall "actually be agreed upon." It should be obvious that an agreement to agree cannot constitute a binding contract. Williston on Contracts (3rd Ed.) Vol. 1, section 45 (page 149) * * *

As said in Williston on Contracts (3rd Ed.) Vol. 1, section 45 (page 149):

"Although a promise may be sufficiently definite when it contains an option given to the promisor, yet if an essential element is reserved for the future agreement of both parties, the promise gives rise to no legal obligation until such future agreement. Since either party, by the very terms of the agreement, may refuse to agree to anything the other party will agree to, it is impossible for the law to fix any obligation to such a promise."

We accept this because it is both sensible and basic to the enforcement of a written contract. We applied it in *Johnson v. Lowery, Ky.*, 270 S.W.2d 943, page 946, wherein we said:

"To be enforceable and valid, a contract to enter into a future covenant must specify all material and essential terms and leave nothing to be agreed upon as a result of future negotiations."

This proposition is not universally accepted as it pertains to renewal options in a lease. We have examined the reasons set forth in those opinions and do not find them convincing. The view is taken that the renewal option is for the benefit of the lessee; that the parties intended something; and that the lessee should not be deprived of his right to enforce his contract. This reasoning seems to overlook the fact that a party must have an enforceable contract before he has a right to enforce it. We wonder if these courts would enforce an original lease in which the rent was not fixed, but agreed to be agreed upon.

Surely there are some limits to what equity can or should undertake to compel parties in their private affairs to do what the court thinks they should have done. * * * In any event, we are not persuaded that renewal options in leases are of such an exceptional character as to justify emasculation of one of the basic rules of contract law. An agreement to agree simply does not fix an enforceable obligation.

As noted, however, the language of the renewal option incorporated a secondary stipulation. Reference was made to "comparative business conditions" which were to play some part in adjusting the new rental. It is contended this provides the necessary certainty, and we will examine a leading case which lends support to the argument.

In *Edwards v. Tobin,* 132 Or. 38, 284 P. 562, 68 A.L.R. 152, the court upheld and enforced a lease agreement which provided that the rent should be "determined" at the time of renewal, "said rental to be a *reasonable rental* under the then existing conditions". (Our emphasis) Significance was attached to the last quoted language, the court reasoning that since the parties had agreed upon a reasonable rent, the court would hold the parties to the agreement by fixing it.

All rents tend to be reasonable. When parties are trying to reach an agreement, however, their ideas or claims of reasonableness may widely differ. In addition, they have a right to bargain. They cannot be said to be in agreement about what is a reasonable rent until they specify a figure or an exact method of determining it. The term "reasonable rent" is itself indefinite and uncertain. Would an original lease for a "reasonable rent" be enforceable by either party? The very purpose of a rental stipulation is to remove this item from an abstract area.

It is true courts often must imply such terms in a contract as "reasonable time" or "reasonable price". This is done when the parties fail to deal with such matters in an otherwise enforceable contract. Here the parties were undertaking to fix the terms rather than leave them to implication. Our problem is not what the law would imply if the contract did not purport to cover the subject matter, but whether the parties, in removing this material term from the field of implication, have fixed their mutual obligations.

We are seeking what the agreement actually was. When dealing with such a specific item as rent, to be payable in dollars, the area of possible agreement is quite limited. If the parties did not agree upon such an unequivocal item or upon a definite method of ascertaining it, then there is a clear case of nonagreement. The court, in fixing an obligation under a non-agreement, is not enforcing the contract but is binding the parties to something they were patently unable to agree to when writing the contract.

The opinion in the *Tobin* case, which purportedly was justifying the enforcement of a contractual obligation between the lessor and lessee, shows on its face the court was doing something entirely different. This question was posed in the opinion: "What logical reason is there for equity to refuse to act when the parties themselves *fail to agree* on the rental?" (Our emphasis) The obvious logical answer is that even equity cannot enforce as a contract a nonagreement. No distortion of words can hide the fact that when the court admits the parties "fail to agree," then the contract it enforces is one it makes for the parties.

* * *

We have examined the *Tobin* case at length because it exemplifies lines of reasoning adopted by some courts to dredge certainty from uncertainty. Other courts balk at the process. The majority of cases, passing upon the question of whether a renewal option providing that the future rent shall be dependent upon or proportionate to the valuation of the property at the time of renewal, hold that such provision is not sufficiently certain to constitute an enforceable agreement. * * * The valuation of property and the ascertainment of "comparative business conditions," which we have under consideration, involve similar uncertainties.

* * *

We do not think our problem can be solved by determining which is the "majority" rule and which is the "minority" rule. We are inclined, however, to adhere to a sound basic principle of contract law unless there are impelling reasons to depart from it, particularly so when the practical problems involved in such departure are so manifest. Let us briefly examine those practical problems.

What the law requires is an adequate key to a mutual agreement. If "comparative business conditions" afforded sufficient certainty, we might possibly surmount the obstacle of the unenforceable agreement to agree. This term, however is very broad indeed. Did the parties have in mind local conditions, national conditions, or conditions affecting the lessee's particular business?

* * *

We realize that litigation is oft times inevitable and courts should not shrink from the solution of difficult problems. On the other hand, courts should not expend their powers to establish contract rights which the parties, with an opportunity to do so, have failed to define. As said in *Morrison v. Rossignol,* 5 Cal. 64, quoted in 30 A.L.R. at page 579:

> "A court of equity is always chary of its power to decree specific performance, and will withhold the exercise of its jurisdiction in that respect, unless there is such a degree of certainty in the terms of the contract as will enable it at one view to do complete equity."

That cannot be done in this case.

Stipulations such as the one before us have been the source of interminable litigation. Courts are called upon not to enforce an agreement or to determine what the agreement was, but to write their own concept of what would constitute a proper one. Why this paternalistic task should be undertaken is difficult to understand when the parties could so easily provide any number of workable methods by which rents could be adjusted. As a practical matter, courts sometimes must assert their right not to be imposed upon. This thought was thus summed up in *Slayter v. Pasley, Or.,* 264 P.2d 444, page 449:

> "We should be hesitant about completing an apparently legally incomplete agreement made between persons sui juris enjoying freedom of contract and dealing at arms' length by arbitrarily interpolating into it our concept of the parties' intent merely to validate what would otherwise be an invalid instrument, lest we inadvertently commit them to an ostensible agreement which, in fact, is contrary to the deliberate design of all of them. It is a dangerous doctrine when examined in the light of reason. Judicial paternalism of this character should be as obnoxious to courts as is legislation by judicial fiat. Both import a quality of jural ego and superiority not consonant with long-accepted ideas of legistic propriety under a democratic form of government. If, however, we follow the urgings of the lessee in the instant matter, we will thereby establish a precedent which will open the door to repeated opportunities to do that which, in principle, courts should not do and, in any event, are not adequately equipped to do."

We think the basic principle of contract law that requires substantial certainty as to the material terms upon which the minds of the parties have met is a sound one and should be adhered to. A renewal option stands on the same footing as any other contract right. Rent is a material term of a lease. If the parties do not fix it with reasonable certainty, it is not the business of courts to do so.

The renewal provision before us was fatally defective in failing to specify either an agreed rental or an agreed method by which it could be fixed with certainty. Because of the lack of agreement, the lessee's option right was illusory. The Chancellor erred in undertaking to enforce it.

The judgment is reversed.

QUESTIONS

1. Questions about the facts of this case

     1.1. Why didn't the parties simply fix the rent for the option period in their original lease agreement?

     1.2. The reported decision in *Walker* does not indicate why the parties were unable to reach agreement upon the rent for the option period. Suppose it was because the lessor insisted on an outrageously high figure relative to market value or the lessee demanded an equally outrageous number on the low side. Would those facts have been relevant to the court? Do you think the reason why the parties were unable to reach agreement should matter to a court in deciding whether to imply a "reasonable rate" of rent?

2. Questions about the law

     2.1. If, as the court of appeals, suggests, the determination of rental value is such an uncomplicated affair, why did it set aside the Chancellor's determination of $125 per month?

     2.2. The court in *Walker* indicates that the parties did not in their original agreement specify an objective method or standard for determining rent in the option period. Do you agree with this conclusion? How would you redraft the renewal option provision so as to satisfy the court of appeals?

     2.3. As the court seems to recognize, the effect of its decision in *Walker* is to leave the lessee without the right to enforce the option. Do you think that's what the parties contemplated when the renewal option was negotiated, that the lessee would have an option enforceable only at the pleasure of the lessor?

MOOLENAAR v. CO–BUILD COMPANIES, INC.

District Court of the Virgin Islands
354 F.Supp. 980 (1973)

WARREN H. YOUNG, DISTRICT JUDGE.

This case involves the proper construction of the renewal clause in a lease. Briefly stated, two issues are presented. First, is a valid and specifically enforceable renewal option created by a clause which leaves the rent for this period to be determined by subsequent agreement between the parties? And secondly, if the clause is valid but the parties are unable to agree on the rent, how is this rental figure to be determined? Here I must decide whether the court must look to fair market value at the time when the option is exercised, or whether the court may take a lower figure if it is shown that the parties contemplated that the land would be put to less than its most remunerative use. For the reasons given below, I hold that such a renewal clause contains an implicit term that the new rent shall be fixed at its "reasonable" or "fair market" value. The clause is thus specific enough to be valid and enforceable. I further hold that parol evidence is admissible to explain this implicit term, and to show that the parties intended the rent to be set at the fair market value of the land as if it were subject to certain use restrictions.

The facts of this case are not in dispute. In October of 1967, plaintiff Moolenaar, a sheep and goat farmer, leased 150 acres of land from one Aurea Correa. His leasehold was to run for a period of five years with an option to renew for an additional five. Moolenaar was to pay $375 per month during the initial term, but the rent for the renewal period "shall be renegotiated."[1] Moolenaar took possession under this lease and expanded his sheep and goat farm onto the demised premises. Before the time came to exercise the renewal option, however, Mrs. Correa sold the land to real estate speculators who in turn sold it to West Indies Enterprises, the predecessor corporation to the defendant Co–Build Companies, Inc. ("Co–Build"). The new owners nonetheless took subject to Moolenaar's rights under the pre-existing and duly recorded lease. At this point I should mention that the testimony disclosed, and I so find, that the representatives of Co–Build negotiating the purchase of the land had actual knowledge of the lease and its renewal clause. They discussed its validity or purported lack of validity with their counsel and accepted title insurance with an exception taken by the title insurer to the rights of the tenant in possession, including the lease renewal clause.

In April of 1972, some six months before the first five year term expired, Moolenaar informed Co–Build of his intention to exercise the renewal option. Co–Build expressed its willingness to extend the lease at a "renegotiated" rent of $17,000 per month. Co–Build justified this figure by the high price it had paid for the land, and by its unquestionably great value if put to industrial use. Such a rent, however, is obviously beyond the resources of the less profitable goat husbandry business. Moolenaar therefore proposed a considerably lower figure and indicated his desire to meet for direct negotiations. All such offers were declined. Upon Co–Build's refusal to recede from its initial position, Moolenaar filed the present action for a declaratory judgment setting out the rights of the parties under the lease.

I

The threshold question is, of course, whether Moolenaar possesses a renewal option at all. A number of jurisdictions would hold that he does not, reasoning that a clause which neglects to stipulate the rent is void for uncertainty and indefiniteness. * * * The better view, however, would hold that such a clause intends renewal at a "reasonable" rent, and would

---

1. The renewal clause provides in full as follows:

4. OPTION OF RENEWAL: Provided that Tenant shall not be declared in default at any time during the term hereof, the Tenant shall be entitled to an option to extend the term of this lease for an additional period of FIVE (5) YEARS upon the same terms and conditions except that the rental shall be renegotiated.

find that market conditions are ascertainable with sufficient certainty to make the clause specifically enforceable. A number of policy considerations support this result. First, it will probably effectuate the intent of the parties better than would striking out the clause altogether. A document should be construed where possible to give effect to every term, on the theory that the signatories inserted each for a reason and if one party had agreed to the clause only in the secret belief that it would prove unenforceable, he should be discouraged from such paths. Secondly, a renewal option has a more sympathetic claim to enforcement than do most vague contractual terms, since valuable consideration will often have already been paid for it. The option of renewal is one factor inducing the tenant to enter into the lease, or to pay as high a rent as he did during the initial period. To this extent the landlord benefited from the tenant's reliance on the clause, and so the tenant has a stronger claim to receive the reciprocal benefit of the option. * * *

It then remains to be determined only whether this resolution is within the powers of the Court. In the absence of an applicable statute, the Restatement of Contracts has been designated as positive law in this jurisdiction. Section 32 of the Restatement provides that a contract is valid if it is "so definite in its terms" that the "performances to be rendered by each party are reasonably certain." Under this standard the renewal clause would appear sufficiently definite to be binding. * * *

Even if it were thought that the Restatement is ambiguous or silent on the precise issue *sub judice*, Moolenaar would still recover. In that case we must make our determination under the common law "as generally understood" in courts of other jurisdictions. The rule which I have followed here is admittedly the minority view. * * * But for the reasons which I gave in an earlier opinion, I think it is appropriate to give greater weight to recent decisions rather than weighing the authorities on a strictly numerical basis. * * * Briefly, the common law is in a state of perpetual evolution and recent decisions will more accurately reflect the current understanding on an issue. For the issue at hand the minority view is nonetheless a widely followed one * * * and has been gaining adherents at a rate which indicates that the common law is moving in that direction. * * * And while, of course, not controlling here, the U.C.C. provisions on the Sale of Goods also illustrate the approach of the modern law, with its emphasis on reasonable commercial dealings and its rejection of technical requirements. [U.C.C. § 2–305] provides as follows:

> (1) The parties if they so intend can conclude a contract for sale even though the price is not settled. In such a case the price is a reasonable price at the time for delivery if
>
> (a) nothing is said as to price; or
>
> (b) the price is left to be agreed by the parties and they fail to agree. * * *"

The comments to this section are also informative, and state in part as follows:

This article rejects in these instances the formula that "an agreement to agree is unenforceable" * * * and rejects also defeating such agreements on the grounds of "indefiniteness." Instead this Article recognizes the dominant intention of the parties to have the deal continue to be binding upon both.

For all the above reasons, I hold that the renewal clause is valid and enforceable.

II

Given that the clause is enforceable, there remains the question of what rent Moolenaar should pay during the additional five years. As a general rule the "reasonable rent" will be established at its "fair market value," which is to say, at the highest rent which a responsible bidder is apt to offer. This in turn suggests that the leasehold should be valued at its "highest and best use," for a lessee using the land in the most intensive and remunerative way possible will be able to outbid a person who would use it less efficiently. From this Co–Build asks us to conclude that the rent should be many times higher than it had been, since the 150 acres are now zoned 1–2 and may be subdivided for light industry.

Nonetheless, I believe that Moolenaar is entitled to have the rent established at its fair value for the land as used for agricultural or animal husbandry purposes only. I conclude that this will most accurately reflect the intent of the original signatories to the lease. From the testimony presented at trial, I find that Mrs. Correa intended that Moolenaar be able to use the land for the purpose of raising sheep and goats during the renewal period, and that the rent be set at a fair value for this purpose. It is true that under this arrangement she will lose the possibility of a higher rent if circumstances changed to make a more profitable use practicable. But one purpose of a long-term lease, or of a renewal clause, is precisely to insulate the parties from such changes in circumstances. In any event, I further find that Mrs. Correa was aware of such possibilities but determined that she was willing to see the land remain in an agricultural state for ten years, and so accepted a rent low enough to make this possible.

Co–Build then took title to the land subject to the provisions of the lease as outlined above. In other circumstances, a new owner who has purchased land subject to a lease might defeat the lower agricultural-use rental by arguing lack of notice. The lease states that the land may be used for any legal purpose, and from that a purchaser might reasonably conclude that the rent is to be set according to the "highest and best" such purpose. Nothing in the document indicates the contrary, and a bona fide purchaser charged with constructive notice of the recorded lease ordinarily should not be bound by additional parol understandings which would depart from the basic presumption of fair market valuation.

I believe, however, that Co–Build is fairly chargeable with actual notice of the circumstances here. At the time the company acquired the property in 1970, it was zoned R–10. This classification permitted agricultural use or residential in quarter-acre lots. The latter use is obviously impractical where, as here, the land can be held only for an additional five year term. Thus, it was evident that the landlord and tenant had contemplated continuous agricultural or animal husbandry use. When Co–Build bought the land, it could well have deduced the nature of the underlying understanding in the lease agreement which encumbered the land. It was to this agreement that the company succeeded when it acquired the land. A subsequent change in the zoning laws should not be permitted to defeat that understanding. I find that the "renegotiation" clause was intended to deal only with fluctuations in real estate values and was not intended to permit a response to the major contingency of rezoning. In any event, the clause had a built-in "red flag" to put Co–Build on a duty of inquiry, since execution of the lease under the old zoning law would at least have left the intentions of the parties unclear. This duty would not have been burdensome; those who participated in the drafting of the original lease were available on St. Croix and in San Juan.

Since the parties have been unable to agree on a fair rental value for agricultural purposes, that figure will now be determined by the Court. The testimony at trial indicated that the present rental of $375 per month is, if anything, somewhat high for grazing use. Nonetheless I must take this figure as a freely bargained one, and hence fair. I also feel that I should make a rough adjustment for intervening inflation. A round figure of $400 per month would seem appropriate in the circumstances. Therefore, from the expert testimony given by Mr. Roebuck who has been engaged for many years in St. Croix in the sheep and goat husbandry business, and from the expert testimony of Mr. Hamilton who made an appraisal of the land on a rather novel but nonetheless convincing basis, I find that a reasonable rental would be $400 per month. With all due respect to Mr. Gaztambide, a most learned, respected and highly professional real property appraiser in Puerto Rico and the Virgin Islands, I must reject his appraisal but only for the reason that it was determined on the basis of the land's highest and most productive use—which, for the reasons explained herein—cannot be used in arriving at the reasonable rental for the use contemplated by the original parties to the lease agreement.

* * *

A declaratory judgment will be entered in accordance with this Opinion.

DECLARATORY JUDGMENT

For the reasons set forth in the Memorandum Opinion above, it is hereby adjudged and declared as follows:

1. The renewal clause is valid and enforceable.

2. The clause contemplates a rent for the additional term at a reasonable rate, as calculated by the value of the land for agricultural and animal husbandry purposes.

3. The fair rental in this case is $400 per month, retroactive to the end of the original five-year term.

QUESTIONS AND NOTES

1. Questions about the facts of this case

   1.1. Review the renewal option provisions in both *Walker* and *Moolenaar*. Which provision provided a greater insight into the intention of the parties concerning rent for the option term?

   1.2. Of what significance was the fact in *Moolenaar* that Co–Build refused to meet for direct negotiations?

   1.3. Other than its "roundness," on what factual basis does the court conclude that $400 per month constituted a reasonable rent?

2. Questions about the law

   2.1. In *Walker*, the court dismissed the lessee's equities in the renewal option stating that the lessee is not deprived of the right to enforce the option provision if there is no enforceable contract to begin with. How does the *Moolenaar* court's analysis of the issue differ?

   2.2. Does Co–Build have any claim against the prior owners of the property based on the fact that it will be precluded for five years from putting the land to its highest and best use? Does the answer to that question have any bearing on Moolenaar's right to have rent determined based on the value of the land used for agricultural and animal husbandry, rather than industrial, purposes?

   2.3. Would the case have been decided differently if, after further negotiations, Co–Build had agreed to $1,000 per month in rent during the option term? How about $500 per month? In other words, does the lessee have a claim any time there's a failure to agree?

3. Notes

   3.1. The basis for the traditional reluctance to enforce agreements to agree, even when the parties have manifested an intent to be immediately bound, has been that since there is no assurance that the parties themselves would have reached agreement on the postponed term, the court has no basis for supplying the omitted term in order to enforce the contract. Thus, the courts tended to distinguish cases where the parties simply *neglected* to include a material term—implying a reasonable term—from cases where the parties acknowledged a conscious awareness of the term and deliberately chose to defer agreement. Nevertheless, doubtless influenced by the liberal attitude taken in the Uniform Commercial Code toward enforcing incomplete agreements, decisions like *Moolenaar* represent the trend of modern authority. *Restatement (Second) of Contracts* § 33, illus. 11 offers the following example.

A promises B to construct a building according to stated plans and specification, and B promises to pay A $30,000 therefor. It is also provided that the character of the window fasteners shall be subject to further agreement of the parties. Unless a contrary intention is manifested, the indefiniteness of the agreement with reference to this matter will not prevent the formation of a contract.

3.2. If a particular agreement is too indefinite at its inception to enforce, may that initial indefiniteness as to material terms subsequently be cured by construing those indefinite terms with reference to the parties' performance up to the point that the dispute arises? *See Blackhawk Heating & Plumbing Co. v. Data Lease Financial Corp.*, 302 So.2d 404 (Fla. 1974).

3.3. Obviously, careful drafting of the agreement at the onset can eliminate most of the issues relating to indefiniteness. This is true even when the parties deliberately decide to leave a term open because neither wants to take the risk of adverse market fluctuations or the parties otherwise desire to defer agreement on a particular term until a later time.

In either case, the keys are to indicate clearly somewhere in the writing the parties' intention to be bound and then to point the court toward a mechanism for supplying the missing term. For instance, if the price term is deliberately left open, it behooves the drafter to set forth in the agreement the parties' intention that the price should be set by "fair market value" or some other measurable external standard as of a date certain.

Sometimes, however, particular terms of an agreement will not be addressed because the parties have not really reached agreement on an important issue and perhaps don't want to address it for fear of having the whole deal fall apart over it. If the lawyer who is commissioned to document the deal makes a point of pressing the matter she is likely to receive a chilly reception from her client. On the other hand, if she drafts the agreement without addressing this important term there is a risk that it will not be enforceable, a result also likely to make for an unhappy client. How would you handle this dilemma if you were that lawyer?

3.4. Recall from the Note on U.C.C. gap fillers that particular problems arise when the omitted term relates to quantity. Nevertheless, sometimes a buyer will want to be assured of a specific source of supply and will even be willing to commit to a fixed price, but does not yet know what its needs are and does not wish to be obligated to exclusivity or to purchase more than it needs or to have a commitment for less than is required. Because, unlike the price term, it is virtually impossible for a court to determine what is a *reasonable* quantity, how would you address this problem as a drafting matter from your buyer/client's perspective? Can similar issues arise from the seller's side?

PROBLEM: "LOVE IN THE TIME OF FAXES"

Richard Roth is a movie producer who lives in California and carries out his projects through Richard Roth Productions. Gabriel Garcia Marquez, an internationally renowned author who won the Nobel Prize for Literature in 1982, has written numerous bestselling novels. Garcia Marquez has resided in Mexico City for the last sixteen years. Carmen Balcells is the president of a literary agency headquartered in Barcelona, Spain. A resident of Barcelona, Balcells has been Garcia Marquez's literary agent for more than 25 years.

In late 1986, Roth contacted Garcia Marquez in Mexico City to express his interest in making a film based on *Love in the Time of Cholera*. Roth flew to Havana, Cuba for a meeting with Garcia Marquez on this matter. Garcia Marquez told Roth that he would consider selling film rights under the following three conditions:

1) Roth would agree to pay him a large sum of money (later Balcells specified the sum of five million dollars);

2) Roth would agree to use a Latin American director; and

3) Roth would shoot the film in Colombia.

Garcia Marquez later authorized Balcells to pursue negotiations with Roth.

Negotiations dragged on with disputes both about the price for the option and the identity of the possible director. Roth traveled a number of times to Barcelona and Mexico City to meet with Balcells and Garcia Marquez, and repeated calls, letters, and faxes passed between the parties. Marquez agreed that Roth could shoot the film in Brazil, not Colombia, but he remained firm on the other two terms.

On November 17, 1988, Roth and Garcia Marquez met in Los Angeles. Later that day, Alan Schwartz, Roth's representative, faxed a letter to Balcells in Barcelona. The letter offered Garcia Marquez $200,000 for the grant of an option of two years on the film rights, the right to extend the option for another year for an additional $100,000, these monies to be applied against $1,250,000 to be paid when the option was exercised, $400,000 more on the release of the video, $350,000 more on the release of television showing, and 5% of the net profits of the film. On January 19, 1989, Schwartz faxed another letter, which changed the first sum of $200,000 for the option to $400,000. The letter stated that the first paragraph of the November 17, 1988, letter was changed to the following:

> "A payment of $400,000 for an option of two years to acquire the motion picture and allied rights to this novel. The option shall commence upon signature by Gabriel Garcia Marquez to the formal agreement and the return of said signed agreement to me or Richard Roth, at which time the option payment shall be made to you as agent for Gabriel Garcia Marquez."

The letter also stated: "On behalf of Richard Roth and myself I am very happy to confirm the final agreement between Richard and Gabriel Garcia

Marquez * * *'' and "Please convey to Garcia Marquez the excitement Richard and I feel in being able finally to get this project moving."

Balcells countersigned the letter and faxed back the following the next day:

> Thank you for today's fax and I am happy that this deal is finally concluded. I had no time to tell Gabo [Marquez] about this conclusion. In any case, I am returning your letter duly signed. I shall await the formal agreement at your earliest convenience.

That same day, Roth wrote independently to Balcells thanking her "so much for concluding the deal" and telling her he was "putting the best champagne on ice so we can celebrate and drink it together."

In late February, Schwartz transmitted the twenty-five page formal agreement to Balcells. Balcells objected to a number of points, particularly the omission of clauses about a Latin American director and the site of the shooting. Balcells communicated these objections, and weeks of renewed negotiations failed to produce an agreement. Garcia Marquez never signed the formal agreement, and the money was never paid him.

Roth sues to enforce the option contract. What result? *See Roth v. Marquez*, 942 F.2d 617 (9th Cir. 1991).

We have now seen that if the parties intend to be bound, the courts will endeavor to enforce that intention even if the parties' expression of that agreement is unclear or incomplete. The key is that there must be an intent to be bound to something; *i.e.* mutual assent. Until that point, of course, the traditional view is that either party is free to break off negotiations without fear of being in breach of contract. In the business world, no less than in the flea market, fervent negotiations sometimes lead nowhere and the parties go off in search of other opportunities. Inevitably, time and money are spent during the course of these negotiations in the hope that they will lead to the consummation of a mutually advantageous bargain. If these hopes are not ultimately realized, ordinarily each party absorbs its own out-of-pocket expenses, recognizing them simply as the costs of doing business.

In certain circumstances, however, these costs can be substantial and one party may feel that the other *ought* to be held accountable for these costs—but on what basis?

Common law courts, steeped in the traditional approach to contractual liability, were reluctant to establish an intermediate point after the commencement of negotiations but before the conclusion of the final agreement at which liability might attach. But the traditional "contract/no contract" distinction was a product of a simpler time and simpler transactions. Sophisticated modern business transactions, such as corporate mergers and acquisitions, require multiple points of agreement that must be reached before the deal is final, and because of the number and complexity of issues to be resolved, the agreement tends to come together in stages or pieces over time. These transactions are "heavily lawyered," and at some stage in the process the lawyers will memorialize the points of agreement reached so far, and the matters still subject to negotiation, in a document typically called an "agreement in principle" or "letter of intent." Professor Farnsworth described additional purposes for the letter of intent as follows:

> Usually the parties expect that a record of the understandings that they have reached at a particular stage will facilitate further negotiations. Such a record may prevent misunderstandings, suggest formulas for reaching further agreements, and provide a basis for drafting a definitive text. The parties may also anticipate that it will inform others of the progress of the negotiations. It may be of interest to employees or shareholders of the negotiating parties and to third parties such as prospective lenders and investors. At least one party may hope that it will enhance its position in future negotiations. Thus it may make it harder for the other party to withdraw concessions, especially if they have been made known to prospective lenders and investors, and more disadvantageous for the other party to allow the negotiations to fail, especially if the prospect of success has been made public.

E. Allan Farnsworth, *Precontractual Liability and Preliminary Agreements: Fair Dealing and Failed Negotiations*, 87 COLUM. L. REV. 217, 257–58 (1987).

Because, unlike in the "agreement to agree" cases, neither of the parties is ready at the letter of intent stage to commit to the transaction *in toto*, the letter of intent will also almost always contain a standard "not legally binding" clause indicating that the writing is not intended as a legal agreement or that the understandings expressed in the letter shall not be binding pending, among other things, regulatory approvals, execution of definitive documentation, or further agreement on matters as yet unresolved.

Under the *Restatement (Second) of Contracts* § 21, express manifestations of the parties that their legal relations are not to be affected are generally accorded deference by the courts. In some cases, however, a court may be persuaded that the letter, though denominated "non-binding," nevertheless evidenced the parties' intention to make a binding agreement. *See Borg–Warner Corp. v. Anchor Coupling*, 16 Ill.2d 234, 156 N.E.2d 513 (1958). A less extreme view is to regard the letter of intent as imposing a duty to negotiate in good faith independent of the underlying transaction. Under this view, while neither party is yet bound to the principal transaction, neither may walk away from negotiations without having made every reasonable effort to conclude the deal.

If one party breaches such "contract to bargain," how should the other party's damages be measured? If the parties do not express an undertaking to engage in further good faith negotiations, how far should the court go in implying one? Are there alternative legal theories that a disappointed suitor might pursue when the other party breaks off negotiations before a final agreement can be concluded? One court's answers to some of these questions can be found in the next case.

BUDGET MARKETING, INC. v. CENTRONICS CORPORATION

United States Court of Appeals, Eighth Circuit
927 F.2d 421 (1991)

GIBSON, CIRCUIT JUDGE.

Budget Marketing, Inc. (BMI) and Charles A. Eagle appeal from an order of summary judgment denying their claims against Centronics Corporation for: (1) breach of implied duty to negotiate in good faith; (2) promissory estoppel; and (3) negligent misrepresentation. This suit arises out of the breakdown in negotiations for the purchase of BMI by Centronics. The district court also entered summary judgment against Centronics on its counterclaim of negligent misrepresentation. Both parties appeal. We affirm in part, but reverse on BMI's and Eagle's claim of promissory estoppel and remand for further consideration of this issue.

BMI is a Des Moines-based firm that markets and services magazine subscription agreements. Eagle is the president and principal shareholder of BMI. Centronics is a Delaware corporation based in New Hampshire.

In April 1987, BMI and Centronics executed a letter of intent outlining the basic terms of a proposed acquisition of BMI by Centronics. The letter stated that: (1) initial consideration would be $10 million; (2) additional consideration of up to $7 million would be contingent upon BMI meeting certain cash flow objectives over a 36–month period; (3) Centronics would provide additional capital during the 36–month "earn out" period, but BMI was responsible for cash needs until closing; and (4) BMI was responsible for dealing with any outstanding Federal Trade Commission or Federal Reserve complaints. The letter of intent also stated that completion of the merger depended on four express conditions: (1) satisfactory completion of an accounting, legal, and business review of BMI by Centronics; (2) purchase by BMI of "key man" life insurance coverage for Eagle; (3) avoidance by Centronics of a "significant cash outlay" for taxes because of BMI's planned change in accounting methods; and (4) execution of a definitive and legally binding agreement between BMI and Centronics.

The letter of intent provided that the transaction was subject to approval by the boards of directors of both corporations and by the BMI shareholders. It also contained a specific disclaimer: "This letter shall not be construed as a binding agreement on the part of BMI or Centronics." The letter set a target date for a definitive agreement of May 31, 1987.

Between January and May 1987, Centronics' officials carefully evaluated BMI. On May 21, the parties executed an addendum to the letter of intent that included changes favorable to Centronics. The Centronics' board approved the addendum on May 26, 1987. The addendum changed the target date for the definitive documents to June 30, 1987.

Other steps leading to the proposed merger followed: Centronics' public relations firm issued a press release about the letter of intent, the directors of BMI's parent company and the BMI shareholders approved the proposed merger, and Centronics received all documents necessary to complete the legal, business, and accounting review of BMI.

At the same time, Centronics began considering the acquisition of companies larger than BMI, and, in June 1987, made a formal proposal to acquire the assets of Ecko Group, Inc., for $127 million. In August, Centronics sent its draft of the final agreement to BMI.

Meanwhile, BMI and Eagle began taking the steps necessary to meet the conditions imposed by the letter of intent. Eagle borrowed $750,000 for BMI's use that he personally secured. BMI opened additional branch offices and expanded existing branch operations. BMI also purchased "key man" life insurance coverage for Eagle. Throughout the summer and fall of 1987, Eagle kept Centronics informed of BMI's expansion efforts and the other developments.

During this time, Centronics did not disclose that it might not complete the deal. In August, a Centronics representative confirmed a planned closing date no later than September 30 during a conversation with an official of Norwest Bank, BMI's lender. In mid-September, a Centronics executive participated in a meeting with BMI representatives, an investment banker from R.G. Dickinson, and representatives of Norwest Bank regarding post-closing financing for BMI. All of those present at the meeting proceeded on the assumption that the deal would close, and the Centronics representative said nothing to the contrary. In October, a Centronics representative discussed with a BMI official a necessary SEC filing that would have to be completed after closing. Also in October, Centronics' president and chief executive officer, Robert Stein, told Philip Boesel, an investment banker with R.G. Dickinson who had been involved with the planned merger, that Centronics was ready to move toward closing the deal with BMI.

In November 1987, Centronics abruptly halted preparations for the merger. After evaluating proposed federal tax legislation, Stein sent a letter to Eagle stating that in spite of Centronics' "good faith efforts," conditions beyond its control made the deal "no longer feasible." The letter stated that the merger would lead to a cash outlay for taxes because of BMI's change in accounting methods, thereby triggering one of the negative conditions of the letter of intent.

On appeal, BMI challenges Centronics' stated reason for terminating negotiations as mere "pretext"[3] because the proposed tax legislation did not apply to the proposed merger and the change of accounting methods would not in fact have resulted in Centronics having to make a cash outlay for taxes.

Eagle and BMI brought this action against Centronics, alleging that together they had invested "hundreds of thousands of dollars" to meet the cash flow requirements of the letter of intent. Eagle and BMI originally filed suit in an Iowa district court, but Centronics removed the case to federal court. Centronics filed a counterclaim alleging negligent misrepresentation concerning an FTC investigation of BMI and BMI's financial prospects.

The district court granted Centronics' motion for summary judgment, concluding that: (1) Centronics breached no agreement to acquire BMI: (2) the letter of intent disclaimed a duty to negotiate in good faith; (3) Centronics made no agreement or promise that was sufficiently definite to support recovery under promissory estoppel; and (4) Centronics owed BMI and Eagle no duty to supply the information upon which the negligent misrepresentation claim was based. * * * The court also granted BMI's motion for summary judgment on Centronics' counterclaim. Both parties appeal.

* * *

I.

BMI concedes that the letter of intent did not constitute a binding agreement to merge, but it contends that the letter did establish a duty on the part of both parties to negotiate in good faith. Breach of that duty, it argues, entitles BMI to reliance damages. Specifically, BMI points to language in the letter setting a target date for executing a definitive agreement and stating that the definitive agreement "will contain mutually agreed terms." BMI further points to the extensive efforts devoted by both parties to bring the merger to fruition during the months preceding and following the execution of the letter as confirming the existence of a good faith duty.

Centronics counters by arguing that the specific language in the letter stating that it "shall not be construed as a binding agreement on the part of BMI or Centronics" means that no binding agreement to negotiate in good faith existed between the parties.

The district court found that the language of the letter of intent "plainly disclaimed any such [implied] duty." * * *

BMI relies primarily on three cases, Teachers Insurance & Annuity Association v. Tribune Company, 670 F. Supp. 491 (S.D.N.Y. 1987); Channel Home Centers v. Grossman, 795 F.2d 291 (3d Cir. 1986); Itek Corp. v. Chicago Aerial Industries, Inc., 248 A.2d 625 (Del. 1968), arguing

---

3. BMI alleges that the October 1987 stock market "crash" caused Centronics to be interested in other, more lucrative acquisition opportunities.

that the overall language of the letter, coupled with the parties' conduct, gave rise to an implied duty to negotiate in good faith. The facts of these three cases are plainly distinguishable from the facts before us now.

In *Teachers Insurance & Annuity Association*, the parties had signed a financing commitment letter that, far from disclaiming an intent to be bound, stated that the parties had entered a " 'binding agreement.' " 670 F. Supp. at 491. The court concluded that " 'the intention to create mutually binding contractual obligations is stated with unmistakable clarity. * * *' " *Id.* at 499.

Such an intent is not present here. The letter of intent between BMI and Centronics clearly stated that it should not be construed as a binding agreement "except for the confidentiality obligations set forth in paragraphs 11 and 12." The fact that the parties expressly designated the confidentiality obligations as the sole exception to the general disclaimer lends further support to our conclusion that no binding agreement to negotiate in good faith can be implied from the overall language of the letter. In *Teachers Insurance & Annuity Association*, the court observed that it must determine the intent of the parties "at the time of their entry into the understanding," 670 F. Supp. at 499, and that a party not wanting to be bound by a preliminary letter can "very easily protect itself by not accepting language that indicates a 'firm commitment' or 'binding agreement.' " *Id.* With these observations in mind, we conclude that the parties here evinced no intent to be bound at the time they signed the letter; the letter clearly disclaims that it is a binding agreement.

Similarly, in *Channel Home Centers*, the Third Circuit found that a detailed letter of intent, signed by a property owner and a prospective tenant, gave rise to a duty to negotiate in good faith because the parties intended their promise to be binding. 795 F.2d at 299–300. The court concluded that the agreement contained "an unequivocal promise by [the landlord] to withdraw the store from the rental market and to negotiate the proposed leasing transaction with [the prospective tenant] to completion." *Id.* at 299. No such binding promises are contained in the letter signed by BMI and Centronics. Moreover, *Channel Home Centers* does not suggest that such promises can be implied in the presence of express language disclaiming an intent to be bound.

Finally, *Itek* is equally unpersuasive. The *Itek* court, applying Illinois law, concluded that a jury could find that the parties entered a binding agreement to negotiate in good faith. 248 A.2d at 629. The court relied in part on language in the letter of intent stating that although the parties would have " 'no further obligation' " to each other if they failed to reach ultimate agreement, they would " 'make every reasonable effort' " to agree upon and execute a final contract. *Id.* at 627. The letter signed by BMI and Centronics did not contain similar language. To the contrary, the letter expressly stated that the parties were not bound.

The language of the letter of intent signed by BMI and Centronics is clear, and its interpretation is therefore a matter of law for the court.

* * * *Chariton Feed and Grain, Inc. v. Harder,* 369 N.W.2d 777, 785 (Iowa 1985).

Our conclusion that the letter of intent is not binding and did not give rise to an implied agreement to negotiate in good faith is consistent with Iowa authorities. See *Chariton,* 369 N.W.2d at 785 ("in construction of written contracts, the cardinal principle is that the intent of the parties must control; and except in cases of ambiguity, this is determined by what the contract itself says") * * *.

Courts are reluctant to find implied covenants. * * * They "must arise from the language used or be indispensable to effecting the intention of the parties." [*Pathology Consultants v. Gratton,* 343 N.W.2d 428, 434 (Iowa 1984).] While the court may find an implied term on a point not covered by the express terms of the agreement, "there can be no implied contract on a point fully covered by an express contract and in direct conflict therewith." *Snater v. Walters,* 250 Iowa 1189, 98 N.W.2d 302, 307 (1959). Because the facts here fail to meet the Iowa test for an implied contract and because finding an implied duty would contradict the express disclaimer of the letter of intent, we conclude that the parties did not bind themselves to an obligation to negotiate in good faith, and that the district court did not err in so holding.

II.

BMI next argues that oral promises made by Centronics after the execution of the letter of intent establish a triable claim based on promissory estoppel. BMI contends that Centronics, on numerous occasions, gave oral assurances that the deal would be consummated.[5] Relying on those promises, BMI spent substantial sums of money to comply with the conditions stated in the letter of intent. The record shows that BMI regularly apprised Centronics of its efforts and achievements.

Centronics argues that a promissory estoppel claim is foreclosed by the letter of intent, again relying on the disclaimer language. The district court did not rely on the disclaimer, but rejected BMI's promissory estoppel claim because the statements by Centronics were "vague" rather than "clear and definite." * * *

Under Iowa law, a party claiming recovery under promissory estoppel must establish: (1) a clear and definite agreement; (2) that it acted to its detriment in reasonable reliance on the agreement; and (3) that the equities support enforcement of the agreement. *National Bank of Waterloo*

---

5. BMI specifically points to: (1) an October 1987 telephone conversation between Stein and Boesel, the investment banker from R.G. Dickinson, in which Stein stated that Centronics was ready to move ahead toward closing; (2) an oral confirmation in August of a September 30 closing date during a conversation between a Centronics representative and a Norwest Bank official; (3) a mid-September meeting at Norwest Bank in which all of those present, including the Centronics representative, proceeded on the assumption the deal would close; (4) a statement by Stein in June 1987 that he wanted to defer closing until BMI met July sales projections, which BMI subsequently did; and (5) a statement in October by a Centronics' official to a BMI representative that a certain SEC filing would have to be made after closing, implicitly indicating that the deal would close.

v. Moeller, 434 N.W.2d 887, 889 (Iowa 1989). Moeller further states that while no Iowa case has "squarely defined" the first element of "agreement," that earlier cases of the Iowa Supreme Court demonstrate that agreement can include a "promise" in which the promisor clearly understands that "the promisee was seeking an assurance upon which he could rely and without which he would not act." *Id.* at 889. This approach, Moeller states, adheres to the definition of promissory estoppel found in the Restatement (Second) of Contracts, which states:

> A promise which the promisor should reasonably expect to induce action or forbearance on the part of the promisee or a third person and which does induce such action or forbearance is binding if injustice can be avoided only by enforcement of the promise. The remedy granted for breach may be limited as justice requires.

Restatement (Second) of Contracts § 90(1) (1979). * * *

Our study of the record convinces us that BMI's promissory estoppel claim should be submitted to a jury. Reasonable jurors could find that Centronics provided oral assurances to BMI and others that it would close on the deal. In October 1987, for instance, Stein told the investment banker, Boesel, that Centronics was ready to "move ahead toward a closing" of the deal. Eagle stated in his deposition and in a November 1987 letter to Stein that he and Boesel relied on Stein's "positive assurance" during that conversation to go ahead with the loan that R. G. Dickinson subsequently made to Eagle.[7]

In alleged reliance on Centronics' oral assurances, Eagle and BMI endeavored to meet all of the conditions imposed by the letter of intent. BMI opened new offices, expanded existing operations, hired more dealers and "independents," arranged for necessary credit, and purchased "key man" life insurance coverage for Eagle. BMI contends that it expended considerable effort and incurred substantial expense in doing so. Centronics was promptly apprised of the developments at BMI. We conclude that the evidence of Centronics' oral assurances, coupled with BMI's alleged reliance and Centronics' awareness of BMI's reliance, is substantial enough to establish a triable claim under Iowa's promissory estoppel doctrine. * * *

We also observe that the facts of this case closely resemble those in the Second Circuit case, *Arcadian Phosphates, Inc. v. Arcadian Corp.,* 884 F.2d 69 (2d Cir. 1989). In *Arcadian,* the parties had negotiated under the terms of a letter of intent which stated that a " 'binding sales agreement' " would be completed at a later date. *Id.* at 70. After both sides took numerous steps to consummate the deal, the seller changed its position on what percentage of ownership it wanted to retain, thereby triggering suit

---

7. The conversation between Stein and Boesel and the subsequent loan to Eagle illustrate a necessary element of promissory estoppel, that of detrimental reliance. Logically, the promise must precede the promisee's alleged reliance. *See Moeller,* 434 N.W.2d at 889. In the case before us, BMI alleges a series of assurances, or promises, and a series of actions taken in reliance on those promises. To ultimately prevail on its promissory estoppel claim, BMI will have to establish that it took specific actions in reliance on specific promises.

by the buyer. The Second Circuit reversed summary judgment for the defendant on the plaintiffs' promissory estoppel claim, stating that "Appellants' * * * claim is based on evidence that [the defendant] knew and approved of [the plaintiffs'] expenditures and collateral contracts, but * * * suddenly demanded a majority interest in [the plaintiff corporation] when the phosphate fertilizer business became 'dramatically' profitable." *Id.* at 74. The court concluded that triable issues existed as to whether the seller had made a clear and unambiguous promise to bargain in good faith, whether the buyer had reasonably and foreseeably relied on that promise, and whether the buyer had sustained an injury. *Id.* The court observed that prevailing on a promissory estoppel claim might not entitle the buyer to benefit-of-the-bargain damages. *Id.* at 73. Damages under promissory estoppel are often limited by the extent of the promisee's reliance rather than by the terms of the promise. *Id. See also* Restatement (Second) of Contracts, § 90 comment d; § 349 comment b (1979) (discussion of reliance damages).

* * *

Looking at the facts in the light most favorable to BMI, as we are required to do in determining a motion for summary judgment, we conclude that BMI has established a triable claim of promissory estoppel that would support an award of reliance damages. We therefore reverse the district court's grant of summary judgment on this issue.

III.

BMI finally argues that it also established a triable claim of negligent misrepresentation based on Centronics' oral assurances that the deal would close. We reject this claim under the rule of *Meier v. Alfa–Laval, Inc.*, 454 N.W.2d 576, 580–82 (Iowa 1990), a case recently decided by the Iowa Supreme Court.

Meier states that the tort of negligent misrepresentation applies to "a person in the profession or business of supplying information or opinions" and that such a person "owes a duty of reasonable care to clients or others." *Id.* at 581. The tort does not properly apply to a "vendor of merchandise," *Meier* concludes, citing with approval a Columbia Law Review article that differentiates between those "engaged in the business or profession of supplying guidance to others" and parties dealing at "arm's length" in commercial transactions. *Id.* (citing Hill, *Damages for Innocent Misrepresentation*, 73 Colum. L. Rev. 679, 688 (1973)).

The parties here were not in the business of supplying guidance to others; they were negotiating a commercial transaction at arm's length. The rule of *Meier* bars not only BMI's negligent misrepresentation claim, but also Centronics' counterclaim based on negligent misrepresentation. We therefore affirm the district court's grant of summary judgment on these claims.

For the reasons stated above, we affirm in part the district court's order and remand for further consideration of BMI's promissory estoppel claim.

QUESTIONS, NOTES, AND CONNECTIONS

1. Questions about the facts of this case

    1.1. What was the purpose of the letter of intent between BMI and Centronics?

    1.2. What did BMI and Centronics expressly agree to in the letter of intent?

    1.3. The court distinguished all three cases that BMI invoked to support its contention that the letter of intent established a duty on each party to negotiate in good faith. What were the critical factual distinctions between those cases and the case at hand? Were those differences enough to justify the difference in outcome?

    1.4. What facts will BMI have to establish on remand in order to prevail on its promissory estoppel claim? If BMI is successful, what will it recover from Centronics?

    1.5. Did we make a mistake by including this case in the book? Is this really a "contracts" case at all?

2. Questions about the law

    2.1. Assuming that a court concludes that a binding duty to negotiate in good faith does arise out of a letter of intent, what exactly does that mean? Is it bad faith if one party terminates negotiation for no apparent reason? How about if that party receives a better offer from a third party, or if the reason is that the first party won't yield to that party's demands?

    2.2. Does the duty to negotiate in good faith include a duty to accept all reasonable terms? In stressing that a precontractual duty to negotiate in good faith does not encompass an automatic duty to approve the final deal, consider the following observation from the Seventh Circuit:

> In a business transaction both sides presumably try to get the best of the deal. This is the essence of bargaining and the free market. And in the context of this case, no legal rule bounds the run of business interest. No particular demand in negotiations could be termed dishonest, even if it seemed outrageous to the other party. The proper recourse is to walk away from the bargaining table, not to sue for "bad faith" in negotiations.

> *A/S Apothekernes Laboratorium v. I.M.C. Chemical*, 873 F.2d 155, 159 (7th Cir. 1989).

    2.3. In its summary of the facts giving rise to this lawsuit, the court discusses several events occurring *after* the letter of intent was signed. Should the parties' post-signing conduct be relevant to the determination of whether a duty to negotiate in good faith arose out of the letter? In its analysis of the legal issue, did the court give sufficient weight to that conduct?

2.4.   How do the pre-contract formation liability cases like *Budget Marketing* differ from the "agreement to agree" cases that we examined in Section 6 of this chapter? Ponoroff argues that in the later cases the parties have manifested an intention to be bound at the time of the initial agreement and the only issue is whether the court may imply a reasonable term if the parties fail to subsequently agree or whether the agreement is fatally indefinite from the inception. In cases like *Budget Marketing*, there is clearly no intention to be bound to the terms of the deal in principle, but the question remains whether the parties' negotiations have proceeded to the point where liability may be imposed if one party breaks off negotiations in bad faith. Epstein believes that Ponoroff is splitting hairs (notwithstanding his limited supply of that commodity) and the analytic distinction between the two types of cases is just not all that sharp. Markell thinks Ponoroff and Epstein need to get a life. What do you think?

3.   Notes

3.1.   The clearer the letter of intent is with respect to whether or not it is intending to impose any precontractual obligations on the parties to negotiate in good faith, the more likely it is that this expressed intent will be enforced, although, as *Budget Marketing* suggests, other theories may be available where one party "misbehaves." If a letter of intent is ambiguous, however, the issue of whether a cause of action may lie for breach of the duty to negotiate in good faith must be ascertained from the specificity of the language used by the parties as well as all of the surrounding circumstances.

For example, in *Schwanbeck v. Federal Mogul Corp.*, 31 Mass.App.Ct. 390, 578 N.E.2d 789 (1991), one corporation was negotiating to acquire the assets of another corporation. The parties reached the stage where they had their lawyers draft a letter of intent. The letter contained one provision stating that, "this letter is not intended to create, nor do you or we presently have any binding legal obligation whatsoever in any way relating to such sale and purchase * * *" and a later provision stating that, "it is our intention, and, we understand, your intention immediately to proceed in good faith in the negotiation of * * * a binding definitive agreement." In determining whether the selling corporation had breached its duty of good faith when it arranged a sale of the assets to a third party before attempting to conclude a deal with the first buyer, the court of appeals commented: "To the degree this cordial language [speaking of the second provision] smoothed the hard edge of the 'this is not yet a binding deal' language that had preceded it, the letter soon (on the second page) reverts to a 'keep-your-hands-on-your-wallet' tone." Thus, the court concluded that, "even if given legal effect to some extent, we are of opinion that, in the context of a proposed business acquisition, as to which the parties have agreed not to be bound by their preliminary agreement, and the seller has reserved the right to deal with other buyers, the obligation to proceed in good faith means something less than unremitting efforts to get to 'yes,' with the players at all times playing their cards face up." *Id.* at 795. On further appeal, the Supreme Judicial Court of Massachusetts concurred with the result in the court of appeal, but decided "that it is not necessary to determine what constitutes an obligation to negotiate in good faith or whether [the selling corporation] breached any such obligation, because we conclude that the parties did not bind themselves contractually to any such obligation." 412 Mass. 703, 592 N.E.2d 1289, 1291 (1992).

3.2.   Perhaps the most famous case involving precontractual liability was not a contracts case at all, but a tort case. In 1983, Pennzoil, seeking to acquire control of its substantial oil reserves, negotiated with Getty Oil and its major shareholder for the purchase of 57% of that company's stock at $110 per share. Although awaiting documentation of the transaction, the parties entered into a letter of intent. Subsequently, Texaco offered $128 per share for all of the stock of Getty Oil, which was promptly accepted by Getty Oil's major shareholder. Pennzoil then sued Texaco for the common law tort of inducement of breach of contract. Obviously, central to recovery under this theory was the requirement that the court find a binding obligation under the letter of intent. It did. *Texaco, Inc. v. Pennzoil Co.*, 729 S.W.2d 768 (Tex. App. 1987), *cert. denied*, 485 U.S. 994 (1988). The result was entry of a judgment against Texaco and in favor of Pennzoil for $7.53 *billion* with an additional $1 billion in punitive damages thrown in for good measure. As a result of this judgment, Texaco eventually had to file for reorganization under the federal Bankruptcy Code. Clearly this case serves as a warning to the corporate lawyers negotiating and drafting these sorts of "gentlemen's agreements," and boards of directors properly seeking the best price for the company's shareholders, that the mere fact that *final* documents have not yet been prepared and signed may not prevent the assignment of liability if the circumstances point to the manifestation of assent by the parties.

3.3.   A more recent case involving precontract liability was decided by the California Court of Appeals in 2002. *Copeland v. Baskin Robbins U.S.A.*, 96 Cal.App.4th 1251, 117 Cal.Rptr.2d 875. Copeland purchased one of Baskin Robbins's ice cream manufacturing plants under an agreement that provided for a separate "co-packing" agreement under which Baskin Robbins would purchase a significant portion of Copeland's output from the plant for a three-year period. Baskin Robbins ended negotiations regarding the co-packing agreement and Copeland sued. The trial court granted Baskin Robbins summary judgment finding no agreement for the purchase of the plant's ice cream. The court of appeals, noting that when Baskin Robbins refused to continue negotiating the terms of the co-packing agreement, "many millions of dollars in anticipated profits melted away like so much banana ripple ice cream on a hot summer day," came to a different conclusion. Distinguishing the situation from an unenforceable mere "agreement to agree," the court held that a party can commit itself to negotiate in good faith and that a cause of action may lie for the breach of such agreement. In explaining the policy rationale for its decision, the court noted:

Gone are the days when our ancestors sat around a fire and bargained for the exchange of stone axes. Today the stakes are much higher and negotiations more complex. Deals are rarely made in a single negotiating session. Rather, they are the product of a gradual process in which agreements are reached piecemeal on a variety of issues. * * * For these reasons, the parties should have some assurance that their investments in time and money and effort will not be wiped out by the other party's footdragging or change of heart * * *

Ultimately, however, because Copeland was unable to establish its damages, the court of appeals affirmed the summary judgment in favor of Baskin Robbins. A classic pyrrhic victory for Copeland, but an important precedent.

4. Connections

In an article written probably before most of you were born, Professor Charles Knapp examined several cases where the parties had either: (1) left one or more terms to future agreement (agreements to agree), or (2) had reached agreement on most essential terms, but delayed final agreement pending additional negotiation as to certain unresolved details. He ultimately concluded that in either situation, where the parties concededly considered themselves committed to one another to some extent, neither should be able to walk away from the deal except for a good and sufficient reason. Charles L. Knapp, *Enforcing the Contract to Bargain,* 44 N.Y.U. L. REV. 673 (1969). By contrast, in a more recent analysis, Professors Alan Schwartz and Robert Scott argued that while the courts in these cases can play an important facilitative role by protecting a promisee's reliance when the promisor "strategically delays investment and thus breaches an *ex ante* agreement to pursue a profitable deal," imposing a further duty on the parties to "negotiate in good faith" over the remaining terms is not necessary. Alan Schwartz & Robert E. Scott, *Precontractual Liability and Preliminary Agreements*, 120 HARV. L. REV. 661, 704–05 (2007). What do you think?

———————

Well, now that you know whether your client has made a deal, assuming she has, it's time to find out whether it's a deal that the law will enforce. Are you ready for Chapter 3? Good, because that's where we're going right after recess.

———————

CHAPTER THREE

WHAT IS "CONSIDERATION" AND WHY IS IT STILL AN IMPORTANT PART OF CONTRACT LAW (OR IS CONSIDERATION STILL AN IMPORTANT PART OF CONTRACT LAW?)

■ ■ ■

Consider the following exchange of emails between Pamela Siege Chandler [PSC] of West Academic Publishing and Ponoroff (she likes him best) after completing work on the third edition of this book:

> PSC: "I am so pleased by your work on the third edition. You deserve a reward. Something nice. A car? An SUV? Wouldn't a Hummer be a wonderful reward?"
>
> Ponoroff: "I agree. A Hummer would be a wonderful reward."
>
> PSC: "It's a deal. I will be in Tucson next month to deliver it."

Later Ms. Chandler changes her mind. Is this a deal that the law will enforce?

Recall that in Chapter 2 we learned how to deal with disputes over whether there was an agreement. Here there is no dispute over whether there was an *agreement*: Ms. Chandler and Ponoroff had agreed that he would get a Hummer.

And, recall that at the beginning of Chapter 1, we learned that there are two key elements to the existence of a *contract*:

#1.   A promise or set of promises.

#2.   Enforcement.

From element #1 (and common sense[1]), we see that it is the promise or promises that make up the agreement that the law enforces, not the "agreement." Second, from element #2 (but not necessarily common

---

1. Common sense. You and one of your study buddies agree that this is the best law school casebook ever. Later, when you read some of the stuff in the book that Markell wrote, you change your mind. No obligation for the law to enforce. An agreement, but no promise.

sense[2]) we see that not all promises are legally enforceable. What we will see from this Chapter is that, under these facts, Ms. Chandler's promise of a Hummer for Ponoroff is not a legally enforceable promise because there was no "consideration."

We have already seen the term "consideration" in various cases that we have read in Chapter 2. In this Chapter [and *Restatement (Second) of Contracts* §§ 17 and 71] we will see that:

(1) a promise will be legally enforceable only if there is consideration or a consideration substitute;

(2) consideration for a promise is either some performance or forbearance or promise of performance or forbearance bargained for by the promisor.

Even before reading any more of the consideration material in this Chapter, it should now be obvious to you that there was no "consideration" for Ms. Chandler's promise—she did not ask for (*i.e.*, bargain for) Ponoroff to do anything, forbear from doing anything, promise to do anything or promise to forbear from doing anything. And, it should be equally obvious to you even before reading the consideration material in this Chapter, that there is no issue as to consideration in *R.R. v. M.H.* or *Lucy v. Zehmer* or other cases that we have read.

Regrettably, what we cannot make obvious is (1) why contract law requires consideration or a consideration substitute and (2) why you are required to learn about consideration. The answers to these questions are not obvious to us.

SECTION 1: BARGAIN AND THE LEGAL CONCEPT OF CONSIDERATION

The great English contracts scholar Patrick Atiyah provides the following introduction to consideration:

> The 'doctrine' of consideration is generally seen by lawyers as a set of rules which limits the freedom of individuals to make binding legal promises. Only those promises which are supported by a legal consideration are legally binding; other promises are not binding, even if the promisor *intends* to bind himself by his promise. Thus to many lawyers the central function of the doctrine of consideration is to prevent people from making gratuitous promises, because the typical gratuitous promise is made without any consideration as lawyers understand that term. On this view, the purpose of the law of

------

2. *Cf.* "[N]o legal system makes all promises enforceable. The legal enforcement of promises is costly, and the conception of the sanctity of promises says little about which promises justify this cost of enforcement." E. ALLAN FARNSWORTH, CHANGING YOUR MIND: THE LAW OF REGRETTED DECISIONS 37 (1998).

consideration is to distinguish between gratuitous and non-gratuitous promises. This may, indeed, be one of the chief purposes of the doctrine of consideration, but it is doubtful if it is the only purpose, and certainly this has not traditionally been the only purpose of this doctrine in its very long history. Moreover, to over-emphasize this particular function of the doctrine of consideration is to risk ignoring the relationship between that doctrine and other parts of the law of obligations. Indeed, this has very largely happened in the history of this subject, and for that reason it may be worth stressing at the outset the way in which the doctrine of consideration has roots linking contract law with other parts of the law of obligations. * * *

The doctrine of consideration has traditionally rested on two main legs. The first of these is the idea that a promise is legally binding if it is given in return for some benefit which is rendered, or to be rendered, to the promisor. The second is the notion that a promise becomes binding if the promisee incurs a detriment by reliance upon it, that is, if he changes his position in reliance on the promise in such a way that he would be worse off if the promise were broken than he would have been if the promise had never been made at all. * * *

The doctrine is in a sense a *limitation* on the free power of individuals to bind themselves as they wish. It is, therefore, a paternalistic device. If a promise or a contract is declared not binding even where there has been a clear promise, on the ground of absence of consideration, the law is in effect saying that it is better that individuals should not bind themselves unless they receive some benefit in return, or unless the other party has suffered some detrimental reliance. * * *

In the nineteenth century the doctrine of consideration came to be widely regarded as technical and anomalous, precisely because of its inherent paternalistic tendency. What is much more curious is that in the twentieth century lawyers have continued to regard the doctrine in this critical fashion despite the very paternalistic tendencies of so much modern law. The oddity is even stronger when it is noted that two of the chief trends of modern law have been on the one side, the whittling down of the binding nature of bare promises and on the other side, the great expansion in benefit-based and reliance-based liabilities. These developments were not accompanied by recognition that their obvious corollary ought to have been a renewed faith in the value of the doctrine of consideration. But today, when there is such a resurgence in classical principles, the outlook on many of these matters looks blurred. It seems unlikely that there will be much turning back from the great increase in benefit-based and reliance-based liabilities; but perhaps criticism of the doctrine of consideration will become stronger again, as lawyers once again take their stand on the ability of individuals to make their own judgments.

P.S. ATIYAH, AN INTRODUCTION TO THE LAW OF CONTRACT, 118, 120–21 (5th ed. 1995).

The history of consideration goes back to 13th century England, to a time when the enforceability of an agreement was limited by the common law system of pleading. A case had to fit within a specific form of pleading or writ.

One such early common law writ, covenant, was largely limited to writings with a seal. Today, in England and most states, the absence or existence of a seal does not affect the enforceability of an agreement. Professor Arthur Allen Leff explained seals as follows:

> Seals thus exemplify one of the strongest impulses of legal ordering, to signal formally to people at critical moments that they are about to leave the world of social interaction for the world of compulsion, bureaucracy and impersonality. It is a way of saying "this counts," "this is for keeps," "we're not kidding around any more" and similar things. Seals are not the only mechanism of that kind: the archaic language and ceremony of marriage, the creamy paper and multiple witnesses of a will, even the formal "One dollar in hand paid" recited in a real-estate man's option form has something of the same intent * * * With seals, of course, the modern problem has been that as the form of the seal has been attenuated (down to a preprinted "seal"), its cautionary effect has been vitiated apace. Hence there is a modern trend to render seals powerless to confer legal rights which would not otherwise be conferred.

Arthur Allen Leff, *A Letter from Professor Leff to a Prospective Publisher*, 94 YALE L.J. 1852 (1985).

Assumpsit developed as the primary common law writ for the enforcement of agreements without seals. Assumpsit had a series of requirements that came to be described as "consideration."

Courts and lawyers no longer use the writ of assumpsit, but they continue to use the term "consideration." While courts consistently use the term "consideration," the term is not used consistently and it is not a real issue in many real world problems or cases. In other words,

1. courts, lawyers, and law professors (especially law professors) regularly mention "consideration"; BUT

2. there is not a single, universally accepted definition of consideration; AND

3. it is unusual for an agreement to be unenforceable because of a lack of consideration.

A. CONSIDERATION: "BARGAINED FOR"

The following three definitions of consideration are representative.

First, *Restatement (Second) of Contracts* § 71 defines consideration as follows:

§ 71   Requirement of Exchange; Types of Exchange

(1) To constitute consideration, a performance or a return promise must be bargained for.

(2) A performance or return promise is bargained for if it is sought by the promisor in exchange for his promise and is given by the promisee in exchange for that promise.

(3) The performance may consist of:

   (a) an act other than a promise, or

   (b) a forbearance, or

   (c) the creation, modification, or destruction of a legal relation.

(4) The performance or return promise may be given to the promisor or to some other person. It may be given by the promisee or by some other person.

Second,

CALIFORNIA CIVIL JURY INSTRUCTIONS (BAJI)[4]

January 2005 Edition
The Civil Committee on California Jury Instructions

Part 10.   Contractual Relationships
II.   Contracts (Introduction)

B.   Elements Of A Contract

BAJI 10.61. Consideration

Except in certain situations as to which you will be instructed, a promise without sufficient **consideration** cannot be enforced.

Consideration may be either a benefit conferred or agreed to be conferred upon the person making the promise or some other person, or a detriment suffered or agreed to be suffered by the person to whom the promise is made or some other person. **Consideration** must be bargained for and given in exchange for the promise. In determining whether there was a bargained-for exchange, you must consider only the outward expression of the intention of the parties.

[Promises by the parties bargained for and given in exchange for each other constitute **consideration**.]

To be sufficient, the **consideration** must have some value. Something that is completely worthless cannot constitute sufficient **consideration**.

Third, the North Dakota Code contains the following definition:

---

4. In California, as in most states, a committee of lawyers and judges has prepared model jury instructions which are reviewed and "recommended" by the state supreme court. As the preface to the California model jury instructions explains, "These instructions represent the work of a task force on jury instructions appointed by Chief Justice. * * * The task force's charge was to write instructions that are legally accurate and understandable to the average juror."

9–05–01 Good consideration defined.

(handwritten margin note: benefit conferred or detriment suffered)

Any benefit conferred or agreed to be conferred upon the promisor by any other person to which the promisor is not entitled lawfully, or any prejudice suffered or agreed to be suffered by such person, other than such as he, at the time of consent, is lawfully bound to suffer as an inducement to the promisor, is a good consideration for a promise.

Note that North Dakota defines "good consideration." There is not a North Dakota statute that defines "bad consideration." There is, however, a reported North Dakota case that badly explains how this definition of "good consideration" should be applied.

REED v. UNIVERSITY OF NORTH DAKOTA* AND THE NORTH DAKOTA ASSOCIATION FOR THE DISABLED, INC.

Supreme Court of North Dakota
589 N.W.2d 880 (1999)

[The plaintiff, Jace Reed, was a student at the University of North Dakota (UND) on a hockey scholarship. As part of UND's preseason conditioning program, Reed ran in a ten kilometer race sponsored by the North Dakota Association for the Disabled (NDAD). As a result of the race, Reed himself became "disabled," suffering extensive damage to his kidneys and liver as a result of dehydration. More specifically, Reed required one kidney and two liver transplants.

Reed sued NDAD on a tort theory, alleging that NDAD negligently failed to provide adequate medical services and water at the race site. NDAD defended on a contract theory, alleging that the race registration form that Reed signed was a contract releasing NDAD from any liability. The trial court granted NDAD's motion for summary judgment. Reed appealed.]

MARING, JUSTICE.

Jace Reed appealed a summary judgment dismissing his * * * claims against the North Dakota Association for the Disabled (NDAD). We hold * * * a valid release exonerates NDAD from liability for its alleged negligence * * * We affirm.

    * * *

A

Reed contends a release in a race registration form signed by him does not bar his negligence claim against NDAD. Before the race, Reed signed a registration form which provided, in part:

(handwritten margin note: assumed the risk)

I am entering this event at my own risk and assume all responsibility for injuries I may incur as a direct or indirect result of my participation. For myself and my heirs, I agree not to hold the participating

---

* Reed's suit against the University of North Dakota was dismissed on the ground of "sovereign immunity," a concept that you have discussed, will discuss or should discuss in torts. Eds.

sponsors and their directors, employees, and/or agents responsible for any claims. I also give permission for the free use of my name and/or picture in a broadcast, telecast, or other account of this event.

According to Reed, UND coaches presented the registration form to him before the race, and he had to sign it to run the race, which was a mandatory part of the UND hockey team's preseason conditioning program.

Reed asserts the release is not enforceable, because it was not supported by consideration. Consideration may be any benefit conferred or detriment suffered. See N.D.C.C. § 9–05–01. The forbearance of a legal right is a legal detriment which constitutes good consideration. The existence of consideration is a question of law.

As part of their preseason conditioning program, the UND hockey players were allowed to run on the same course during NDAD's road race. When the hockey players, including Reed, signed the registration form, they agreed not to hold the participating sponsors responsible for any claims arising from their participation in the event and NDAD agreed to let them run on the course during NDAD's road race. Reed's surrender of a legal right in exchange for NDAD allowing him to run the course during the race constitutes consideration for the release. *See Malecha v. St. Croix Valley Skydiving Club*, 392 N.W.2d 727, 731 (Minn. App. 1986) (holding payment of fee and surrender of right to sue for negligence in exchange for skydiving training course constitutes valid consideration for release).

* * *

V

We affirm the summary judgment dismissing Reed's complaint against NDAD. * * *

QUESTIONS

1. Questions about the facts of this case
    1.1. Did either party contend that there was no agreement in this case?
    1.2. What did the plaintiff, Mr. Reed, agree to do or forbear from doing?
    1.3. What did the defendant, North Dakota Association for the Disabled, Inc., agree to do or forbear from doing?
2. Questions about the law
    2.1. Apply the North Dakota statute to the facts of *Reed*. Who is the "promisor"? Was there any "benefit conferred or agreed to be conferred upon the promisor"?
    2.2. Compare the North Dakota statute with *Restatement (Second) of Contracts* § 71. Does the *Restatement (Second)* use the words "benefit" and "prejudice"? Will a "bargained for" "performance" or

"return promise" always be a "benefit" to the promisor or "prejudice" to the promisee?

B. CONSIDERATION AND FAMILY AGREEMENTS

Recall that Professor Atiyah suggested that one purpose of consideration is to distinguish between gratuitous and non-gratuitous promises.
Many, if not most, gratuitous promises are made between members of the
same family. The next three cases, *Kirksey v. Kirksey*, *Hamer v. Sidway*,
and *Schnell v. Nell*, use the concept of consideration to determine whether
an intra-family promise is gratuitous and so unenforceable.

KIRKSEY v. KIRKSEY

Supreme Court of Alabama
8 Ala. 131 (1845)

ASSUMPSIT by the defendant, against the plaintiff in error. The
question is presented in this Court, upon a case agreed, which shows the
following facts:

The plaintiff was the wife of defendant's brother, but had for some
time been a widow, and had several children. In 1840, the plaintiff resided
on public land, under a contract of lease, she had held over, and was
comfortably settled, and would have attempted to secure the land she lived
on. The defendant resided in Talladega county, some sixty, or seventy
miles off. On the 10th October, 1840, he wrote to her the following letter:

> "Dear sister Antillico—Much to my mortification, I heard, that broth-
> er Henry was dead, and one of his children. I know that your
> situation is one of grief, and difficulty. You had a bad chance before,
> but a great deal worse now. I should like to come and see you, but
> cannot with convenience at present. * * * I do not know whether you
> have a preference on the place you live on, or not. If you had, I would
> advise you to obtain your preference, and sell the land and quit the
> country, as I understand it is very unhealthy, and I know society is
> very bad. If you will come down and see me, I will let you have a place
> to raise your family, and I have more open land than I can tend; and
> on the account of your situation, and that of your family, I feel like I
> want you and the children to do well."

Within a month or two after the receipt of this letter, the plaintiff
abandoned her possession, without disposing of it, and removed with her
family, to the residence of the defendant, who put her in comfortable
houses, and gave her land to cultivate for two years, at the end of which
time he notified her to remove, and put her in a house, not comfortable, in
the woods, which he afterwards required her to leave.

A verdict being found for the plaintiff, for two hundred dollars, the
above facts were agreed, and if they will sustain the action, the judgment
is to be affirmed, otherwise it is to be reversed.

ORMOND, J.

The inclination of my mind, is, that the loss and inconvenience, which the plaintiff sustained in breaking up, and moving to the defendant's, a distance of sixty miles, is a sufficient consideration to support the promise, to furnish her with a house, and land to cultivate, until she could raise her family. My brothers, however think, that the promise on the part of the defendant, was a mere gratuity, and that an action will not lie for its breach. The judgment of the Court below must therefore be reversed, pursuant to the agreement of the parties.

QUESTIONS AND NOTES

1. Questions about the facts of this case

    1.1. Did the defendant deny that he made a promise to plaintiff? Did the defendant deny that he did not do what he promised to do?

    1.2. Why did the plaintiff move to Talladega County? Should plaintiff's reason for moving to Talladega County be relevant in deciding whether defendant's promise is enforceable?

    1.3. Do we know the reason that the defendant made a promise to the plaintiff? The reason the defendant changed his mind? Should the defendant's reasons be relevant in deciding whether his promise is enforceable? Professor Gerald Caplan (and Professor William Casto and Professor Val Ricks) provide this explanation:

    "Isaac wanted Angelico to help him acquire title to federal land. The reference in his letter to Angelico to "open land" was to "land open to the public for settlement" under the federal preference acts. The preference laws enacted by Congress throughout the first half of the nineteenth century granted individuals illegally squatting on federal land a preemption right in preference to all others; this permitted them to acquire the land at highly favorable prices. Isaac wanted the land in question for himself, but he could only claim by squatting and this he did not want to do. His letter then was an offer for his sister-in-law to squat on open land and gain a preference that she would then transfer to Isaac. In exchange, Isaac would "let [her] have a place to raise [her] family," most likely as long as she wished. This was the offer that Angelico accepted. Under federal law, this practice was permissible and commonplace.

    [handwritten margin note: real consideration here]

    What then made the deal go sour? A change in the law limited preemption to individuals who owned less than 320 acres and Isaac was a large landowner. But this same enactment law gave Angelico a right to the land on which Isaac placed her at the same attractive, discount price. Had Isaac not evicted her, she could have secured the preference in her own name and Isaac would have lost the benefit of their bargain. Consequently, he moved quickly to evict her and install his twenty-one year old son on the land in hopes his son could secure a preference and keep the land in the family." Gerald Caplan, *Legal Autopsies: Assessing the Performance of Judges and Lawyers Through the Window of Leading Cases*, 73 ALB. L. REV. 1, 42–43 (2009); William R. Casto & Val D. Ricks, *"Dear Sister Antillico * * *": The Story of Kirksey v. Kirksey*, 94 GEO. L.J. 321 (2006)

2. Questions about the law

    2.1. Did Judge Ormond believe that there was "sufficient consideration" to make the defendant's promise legally enforceable? Why/why not?

    2.2. What is "sufficient" consideration? How does "sufficient consideration" differ from "good consideration"? From "consideration"?

    2.3. How would this case have been decided under the California jury instruction on consideration? Under the *Restatement (Second) of Contracts* definition of consideration?

3. Notes

    3.1. Promises, agreements and contracts

    Kirksey, like most cases in which consideration is the issue, asks whether a "promise" is legally enforceable.

    Thinking about the relationship between an "agreement" and a "promise" can be very confusing. If you are going to think about it, keep in mind that:

    (a) Most agreements or deals involve two promises. *E.g.*, (i) P promises to paint H's house and H promises to pay P for her work; and (ii) S promises to sell Blackacre to B and B promises to pay S for Blackacre.

    (b) An agreement can, of course, be based on a promise and conduct. H promises to pay P if P paints her house, and P paints H's house.

    (c) Regardless of whether an agreement is based on one promise or two promises, courts generally are asked to determine the enforceability of a particular promise. P sues D for not doing what she promised to do. D contends that her promise is not enforceable because there is no consideration for her promise. The court is thus asked to determine whether that particular promise is enforceable.

    In review, an agreement may have one or two unperformed promises. If one party to an agreement sues because the other party to the agreement is not performing as promised, a possible legal argument by the defendant is that her promise is not legally enforceable because there was no bargained for benefit to her or detriment to the promisee. *Cf. Restatement (Second) of Contracts* § 1.

    3.2. Judge Ormond's cryptic opinion does not answer the questions: (i) why is a promise not enforceable because it is a "mere gratuity"?; and (ii) how can a court (and, more importantly, a law student) determine whether a promise is supported by consideration or a "mere gratuity"? Does the following excerpt from *Maughs v. Porter*,

157 Va. 415, 418, 161 S.E. 242, 243 (Ct. App. 1931), answer these questions?

A gift is a contract without a consideration, and, to be valid, must be executed. A valid gift is, therefore, a contract executed. It is to be executed by the actual delivery by the donor to the donee, or some one for him, of the thing given, or by delivery of the means of obtaining the subject of the gift, without further act of the donor to enable the donee to reduce it to his own possession. "The intention to give must be accompanied by a delivery, and the delivery must be made with an intention to give." Otherwise there is only an intention or promise to give, which, being gratuitous, would be a mere nullity. Delivery of possession of the thing given or of the means of obtaining it so as to make the disposal of it irrevocable is indispensable to a valid gift.

Clearly then, the plaintiff, under the facts shown here, cannot recover unless defendant is bound by a promise which is supported by a consideration sufficient to support the action. It is often quite difficult to determine in such cases whether or not there is such a consideration. 1 Williston on Contracts, section 112, page 232, thus illustrates the difficulty: "If a benevolent man says to a tramp: 'If you go around the corner to the clothing shop there, you may purchase an overcoat on my credit,' no reasonable person would understand that the short walk was requested as the consideration for the promise, but that in the event of the tramp going to the shop the promisor would make him a gift. Yet the walk to the shop is in its nature capable of being consideration. It is a legal detriment to the tramp to make the walk, and the only reason why the walk is not consideration is because on a reasonable construction it must be held that the walk was not requested as the price of the promise, but was merely a condition of a gratuitous promise. It is often difficult to determine whether words of condition in a promise indicate a request for consideration or state a mere condition in a gratuitous promise. An aid, though not a conclusive test, in determining which construction of the promise is more reasonable is an inquiry whether the happening of the condition will be a benefit to the promisor. If so, it is a fair inference that the happening was requested as a consideration. On the other hand, if, as in the case of the tramp stated above, the happening of the condition will be not only of no benefit to the promisor but is obviously merely for the purpose of enabling the promisee to receive a gift, the happening of the event on which the promise is conditional, though brought about by the promisee in reliance on the promise, will not properly be construed as consideration. In case of doubt where the promisee has incurred a detriment on the faith of the promise, courts will naturally be loath to regard the promise as a mere gratuity and the detriment incurred as merely a condition. But in some cases it is so clear that a conditional gift was intended that even though the promisee has incurred detriment, the promise has been held unenforceable."

3.3. Professor Williston included *Kirksey* in his casebook on contracts and concluded that the result in the case was unjust. *See* Carol Weisbrod, *An Uncertain Trumpet: A Gloss on Kirksey v. Kirksey*, 32 CONN. L. REV. 1699, 1701 (2000). Do you believe that the facts of *Kirksey* are different from the facts of Williston's tramp hypothetical?

3.4. Professor Debora L. Threedy of University of Utah Law School suggests that the outcome of *Kirksey* might have been different if both the Kirkseys had been male:

Not all bargains between family members are excluded from contract law, however. A pair of first year contract law cases illustrates the tensions between "family" and "market." When an uncle promised his nephew $5000 if the nephew would refrain from smoking, drinking and gambling until he turned twenty-one, the court concluded they were bargaining; thus, the nephew's refraining constituted consideration and the parties had contracted. When, however, a brother-in-law promised to give his widowed sister-in-law a place to raise her family if she would give up homesteading and mover closer to him, the court did not perceive them as bargaining; moving was not consideration and the parties had not contracted. One explanation for these divergent outcomes is that in the first case the intrafamilial agreement occurs between two males, while in the latter it occurs between a male and female relation. Bargaining, like beauty, is in the eye of the beholder and judges may be less likely to perceive contract bargaining between the sexes in a family context.

Debora L. Threedy, *Feminists & Contract Doctrine*, 32 IND. L. REV. 1247, 1251 (1999). The case of the uncle's promise to the nephew, that Professor Threedy mentions above is set out below.

HAMER v. SIDWAY
Court of Appeals of New York
124 N.Y. 538, 27 N.E. 256 (1891)

[The facts of this case are somewhat confusing in that none of the parties to the agreement was named either "Hamer" or "Sidway." Both were named "William Story." The older William was the uncle and the promisor to the younger William who was (obviously) the nephew and the promisee.

The trial court found that the promise was legally enforceable; the intermediate appellate court reversed, and then this court reversed the intermediate appellate court and reinstated the decision of the trial court. The intermediate appellate court* provided the following information about the promise:

The testimony introduced by the plaintiff was to the effect that in March, 1869, when the testator and William E. Story were attending the

---
* 11 N.Y. Supp 182 (N.Y. Supreme Court, 4th Dept. 1890). Eds.

golden wedding of the father of the testator, he said to William: "Willie, I am going to make you a proposition." William told him he would like to hear it. That the testator then said: "If you will not drink any liquor, will not smoke, will not play cards or billiards until you are 21, I will give you $5,000 that day. Of course, if you want to play for fun, that I don't consider playing cards." William said he would endeavor to carry it out; that he would do it. When William became 21 years of age he wrote the testator the following letter: "Dear Uncle: I am twenty-one years old to-day, and I am now my own boss, and I believe, according to agreement, that there is due me five thousand dollars. I have lived up to the contract to the letter in every sense of the word." The testator's reply to this letter, so far as material to the questions involved in this case, was as follows: "Buffalo, February 26, 1875. W. E. Story, Jr.—Dear Nephew: Your letter of the 31st ult. came to hand all right, saying you had lived up to the promise made me several years ago. I have no doubt but what you have, for which you shall have $5,000, as I promised you. I had the money in the bank the day you were twenty-one years old that I intended for you, and you shall have the money certain. Now, Willie, I do not intend to interfere with this money in any way until I think you are capable of taking care of it, and the sooner that time comes the better it will please me. I would hate very much to have you start out in some adventure that you thought all right, and lose this money in one year. The first five thousand dollars I got together cost me a heap of hard work. * * * Willie, you are twenty-one, and you have many a thing to learn yet. This money you have earned much easier than I did, besides acquiring good habits at the same time, and you are quite welcome to the money. Hope you will make good use of it. I was ten long years getting this together after I was your age. Now, hoping this will be satisfactory, I stop. * * * P.S. You can consider this money on interest."

Uncle William then died before paying nephew William; the executor of Uncle William's estate refused to pay the promised $5,000 to nephew William and this law suit was filed.]

    * * *

PARKER, J.

The question which provoked the most discussion by counsel on this appeal, and which lies at the foundation of plaintiff's asserted right of recovery, is whether by virtue of a contract defendant's testator, William E. Story, became indebted to his nephew, William E. Story, 2d, on his twenty-first birthday in the sum of $5,000. The trial court found as a fact that "on the 20th day of March, 1869, * * * William E. Story agreed to and with William E. Story, 2d, that if he would refrain from drinking liquor using tobacco, swearing, and playing cards or billiards for money until should become twenty-one years of age, then he, the said William E. Story, would at that time pay him, the said William E. Story, 2d, the sum of $5,000 for such refraining, to which the said William E. Story, 2d, agreed," and that he "in all things fully performed his part of said agreement." The defendant contends that the contract was without consideration to support it, and therefore invalid. He asserts that the promisee, by refraining from the use of liquor and tobacco, was not harmed, but benefitted; that which he did was best for him to do, independently of his uncle's promise,—and insists that it follows that, unless the promisor was benefitted, the contract was without consideration,—a contention which, if well founded, would seem to leave open for controversy in many cases whether that which the promisee did or omitted to do was in fact of such benefit to him as to leave no consideration to support the enforcement of the promisor's agreement. Such a rule could not be tolerated, and is without foundation in the law. The exchequer chamber in 1875 defined "consideration" as follows: "A valuable consideration, in the sense of the law, may consist either in some right, interest, profit, or benefit accruing to the one party, or some forbearance, detriment, loss, or responsibility given, suffered, or undertaken by the other." Courts "will not ask whether the thing which forms the consideration does in fact benefit the promisee or a third party, or is of any substantial value to any one. It is enough that something is promised, done, forborne, or suffered by the party to whom the promise is made as consideration for the promise made to him." Anson, Cont. 63. "In general a waiver of any legal right at the request of another party is a sufficient consideration for a promise." Pars. Cont. "Any damage, or suspension, or forbearance of a right will be sufficient to sustain a promise." 2 Kent, Comm. (12th Ed.) Pollock in his work on Contracts, (page 166,) after citing the definition given by the exchequer chamber, already quoted, says: "The second branch of this judicial description is really the most important one. 'Consideration' means not so much that one party is profiting as that the other abandons some legal right in the present, or limits his legal freedom of action in the future, as an inducement for the promise of the first." Now, applying this rule to the facts before us, the promisee used tobacco, occasionally drank liquor, and he had a legal right to do so. That right he abandoned for a period of years upon the strength of the promise of the testator that for such forbearance he would give him $5,000. We need not speculate on the effort which may have been required to give up the use of those stimulants. It is sufficient that he restricted his lawful freedom of action within certain prescribed limits upon the faith of his uncle's agreement, and now, having fully performed the conditions imposed, it is of no moment whether such performance actually proved a benefit to the promisor, and the court will not inquire into it; but, were it a proper subject of inquiry, we see nothing in this record that would permit a determination that the uncle was not benefitted in a legal sense.

The order appealed from should be reversed, and the judgment of the special term affirmed, with costs payable out of the estate. All concur.

QUESTIONS AND NOTES

1. Questions about the facts of this case

   1.1. Did Sidway, the executor for the estate of William E. Story, contend that Mr. Story did not promise to pay his nephew $5,000 if he refrained from drinking, using tobacco, swearing, and playing cards or billiards for money?

   1.2. Did Sidway contend that the nephew did not so refrain?

2. Questions about the law

   2.1. What was the consideration in *Hamer*?

   2.2. The *Hamer* opinion quotes from an 1875 Exchequer Chamber definition of consideration. Apply the definition to the facts of the *Hamer* case. Was there a "benefit accruing to the one party"? Was there a "forbearance, detriment, loss or responsibility given, suffered or undertaken by the other"?

   2.3. Would *Hamer* have been decided differently under the North Dakota statutory definition of "good consideration"? Under *Restatement (Second) of Contracts* § 71?

   2.4. Would *Hamer* have been decided differently if Uncle William's promise had not been made until after Nephew William turned 21 and Uncle William's promise was "Since you did not drink any liquor or smoke or play cards or billiards for money until you reached the age of 21, I will give you $5,000 at your birthday party next week"? *No, no bargained for exchange*

   2.5. Would *Hamer* have been decided differently if (i) the original conversation between Uncle William and Nephew William had simply been "Willie, you are a fine lad. I will give you $5,000 when you are 21" and (ii) Willie then decided on his own to show his uncle what a fine lad he really was by not drinking liquor, playing cards or billiards, or smoking until he was 21?

   2.6. Would *Hamer* have been decided differently if Uncle William had promised $5,000,000 instead of $5,000? $5 instead of $5,000?

3. Notes

   3.1. Professor Melvin Eisenberg of University of California at Berkeley Law School argues that the world of contracts and the world of donative promises are two different worlds:

   To begin with, the world of contract is a market world, largely driven by relatively impersonal considerations and focused on commodities and prices. The impersonal organs of the state are an appropriate means to enforce promises made in such a world. In contrast, much of the world of gift is driven by affective considerations like love, affection, friendship, gratitude, and comradeship. That world would be impoverished if it were to be collapsed into the world of contract. * * *

Similarly, making simple, affective donative promises enforceable would have the effect of commodifying the gift relationship. Under an enforceability regime, it could never be clear to the promisee, or even to the promisor, whether a donative promise that was made in a spirit of love, friendship, affection, or the like, was also performed for those reasons, or instead was performed to discharge a legal obligation or avoid a lawsuit. Accordingly, gifts made pursuant to simple, affective donative promises would be seriously impoverished, because at the point of the transfer, the promisor's motives would invariably be mixed.

It can now be seen that the principle that simple donative promises are unenforceable does not show that the law fails to value donative promises. Just the opposite is true. The principle that simple donative promises are unenforceable is justified not because simple donative promises are less important than bargain promises, but because they are more important.

Melvin Aron Eisenberg, *The World of Contract and the World of Gift*, 85 CAL. L. REV. 821, 846 (1997).

3.2. Professor Melanie Leslie of Yeshiva Law School studied the cases in which someone attempted to bring a family promise into the world of contracts and concluded:

The scarcity of cases involving breach of promise within intimate relationships reflects two factors: the often indefinite nature of personal agreements and the unwillingness of parties to sue until the relationship is beyond repair.

Even if one family member wanted to sue another for breach of promise, it would be hard to isolate particular promises and acts of reliance within the relationship. Very few cases would display the easy clarity of the rare, but often cited, war horses like *Hamer v. Sidway*, in which a nephew sued his uncle for breaching an express promise to pay the nephew if he forswore drinking and swearing. Agreements within long-term, intimate relationships are most often implicit and multifaceted. The relationships themselves are premised on reciprocity, constructed of a multitude of mutual and simultaneous promises and actions generated, at least in part, by reliance on those promises. The closer and more interdependent the parties, the less likely promises and agreements will be isolated and clearly spelled out, because the parties operate in accordance with implied understandings, and because the value generated by those implied understandings is greatly enhanced if the reciprocal nature of the duties within the relationship is left unspoken. The relationship simply cannot be diagrammed as a series of discrete transactions that fit neatly into the classical contract paradigm of bargained-for exchange, nor should it be.

Of course, indefiniteness alone is not an adequate explanation for family members' reluctance to resort to legal process. After all, courts have become increasingly willing to enforce indefinite agreements in the commercial context. More importantly, family members do not look to the law because doing so would destroy the familial relationship. Personal interdependent relationships are most often characterized by a high degree of trust. When trust disintegrates, it does so slowly, and disappointed parties generally harbor hopes that a disintegrating relationship will improve. In family relationships especially, strong psychological ties often inspire the promisee to hope for reconciliation. Moreover, the promisee would prefer that the promisor's performance be voluntary rather than coerced; the performance is valuable, in large measure, because it is motivated, or appears to be motivated, by love rather than self-interest. The disappointed promisee will abandon hope only when the relationship clearly is beyond repair, and the promisee is sufficiently angered by the promisor's betrayal that she is willing to sever the relationship entirely. Short of that, there will be no lawsuit because the promisee knows that a suit would quickly and finally destroy whatever trust is left. Often, family relationships end only at divorce or death.

Melanie B. Leslie, *Enforcing Family Promises: Reliance, Reciprocity, and Relational Contract*, 77 N.C. L. REV. 551, 555 (1999).

3.3. A later New York Court of Appeals decision, *Weiner v. McGraw–Hill, Inc.*, 57 N.Y.2d 458, 457 N.Y.S.2d 193, 443 N.E.2d 441 (Ct. App. 1982) describes *Hamer* as the "seminal" case on consideration. *Hamer* appears as a principal case in virtually every contracts casebook. *Hamer*, with variations, can be used to illustrate such basic consideration concepts as:

- legal detriment different from actual detriment;
- no inquiry into adequacy of amount of consideration;
- promise as consideration;
- bargained for requirement; and
- past consideration.

In the last case, *Hamer v. Sidway*, the promise looked like a gift, and the court held that it was a contract. In the next case, *Schnell v. Nell*, the agreement looks like a contract, and the court holds that it is a gift. What gives?

SCHNELL v. NELL

Supreme Court of Indiana
17 Ind. 29 (1861)

PERKINS, J.

Action by J.B. Nell against Zacharias Schnell, upon the following instrument:

This agreement, entered into this 13th day of February, 1856, between Zach. Schnell, of Indianapolis, Marion county, State of Indiana,

as party of the first part, and J.B. Nell, of the same place, Wendelin
Lorenz, of Stilesville, Hendricks county, State of Indiana, and Donata
Lorenz, of Frickinger, Grand Duchy of Baden, Germany, as parties of
the second part, witnesseth: The said Zacharias Schnell agrees as
follows: whereas his wife, Theresa Schnell, now deceased, has made a
last will and testament, in which, among other provisions, it was
ordained that every one of the above named second parties, should
receive the sum of $200; and whereas the said provisions of the will
must remain a nullity, for the reason that no property, real or
personal, was in the possession of the said Theresa Schnell, deceased,
in her own name, at the time of her death, and all property held by
Zacharias and Theresa Schnell jointly, therefore reverts to her husband; and whereas the said Theresa Schnell has also been a dutiful
and loving wife to the said Zach. Schnell, and has materially aided
him in the acquisition of all property, real and personal, now possessed by him; for, and in consideration of all this, and the love and
respect he bears to his wife; and, furthermore, in consideration of one
cent, received by him of the second parties, he, the said Zach. Schnell,
agrees to pay the above named sums of money to the parties of the
second part, to wit: $200 to the said J.B. Nell; $200 to the said
Wendelin Lorenz; and $200 to the said Donata Lorenz, in the follow-
ing installments, viz., $200 in one year from the date of these
presents; $200 in two years, and $200 in three years; to be divided
between the parties in equal portions of $66 2/3 each year, or as they
may agree, till each one has received his full sum of $200.

And the said parties of the second part, for, and in consideration of
this, agree to pay the above named sum of money [one cent], and to
deliver up to said Schnell, and abstain from collecting any real or
supposed claims upon him or his estate, arising from the said last will
and testament of the said Theresa Schnell, deceased.

In witness whereof, the said parties have, on this 13th day of
February, 1856, set hereunto their hands and seals.

Zacharias Schnell, [seal.]

J. B. Nell, [seal.]

Wen. Lorenz. [seal.]

The complaint contained no averment of a consideration for the
instrument, outside of those expressed in it; and did not aver that the one
cent agreed to be paid, had been paid or tendered.

A demurrer to the complaint was overruled.

The defendant answered, that the instrument sued on was given for
no consideration whatever.

He further answered, that it was given for no consideration, because
his said wife, Theresa, at the time she made the will mentioned, and at the
time of her death, owned, neither separately, nor jointly with her hus-

band, or any one else (except so far as the law gave her an interest in her husband's property), any property, real or personal, & c.

The will is copied into the record, but need not be into this opinion.

The Court sustained a demurrer to these answers, evidently on the ground that they were regarded as contradicting the instrument sued on, which particularly set out the considerations upon which it was executed. But the instrument is latently ambiguous on this point.

The case turned below, and must turn here, upon the question whether the instrument sued on does express a consideration sufficient to give it legal obligation, as against Zacharias Schnell. It specifies three distinct considerations for his promise to pay $600:

1. A promise, on the part of the plaintiffs, to pay him one cent.

2. The love and affection he bore his deceased wife, and the fact that she had done her part, as his wife, in the acquisition of property.

3. The fact that she had expressed her desire, in the form of an inoperative will, that the persons named therein should have the sums of money specified.

The consideration of one cent will not support the promise of Schnell. It is true, that as a general proposition, inadequacy of consideration will not vitiate an agreement. But this doctrine does not apply to a mere exchange of sums of money, of coin, whose value is exactly fixed, but to the exchange of something of, in itself, indeterminate value, for money, or, perhaps, for some other thing of indeterminate value. In this case, had the one cent mentioned, been some particular one cent, a family piece, or ancient, remarkable coin, possessing an indeterminate value, extrinsic from its simple money value, a different view might be taken. As it is, the mere promise to pay six hundred dollars for one cent, even had the portion of that cent due from the plaintiff been tendered, is an unconscionable contract, void, at first blush, upon its face, if it be regarded as an earnest one. The consideration of one cent is, plainly, in this case, merely nominal, and intended to be so. As the will and testament of Schnell's wife imposed no legal obligation upon him to discharge her bequests out of his property, and as she had none of her own, his promise to discharge them was not legally binding upon him, on that ground. A moral consideration, only, will not support a promise. And for the same reason, a valid consideration for his promise can not be found in the fact of a compromise of a disputed claim; for where such claim is legally groundless, a promise upon a compromise of it, or of a suit upon it, is not legally binding. There was no mistake of law or fact in this case, as the agreement admits the will inoperative and void. The promise was simply one to make a gift. The past services of his wife, and the love and affection he had borne her, are objectionable as legal considerations for Schnell's promise, on two grounds: 1. They are past considerations. * * * 2. The fact that Schnell loved his wife, and that she had been industrious, constituted no consideration for his promise to pay J. B. Nell, and the Lorenzes, a sum of money.

Whether, if his wife, in her lifetime, had made a bargain with Schnell, that, in consideration of his promising to pay, after her death, to the persons named, a sum of money, she would be industrious, and worthy of his affection, such a promise would have been valid and consistent with public policy, we need not decide. Nor is the fact that Schnell now venerates the memory of his deceased wife, a legal consideration for a promise to pay any third person money.

The instrument sued on, interpreted in the light of the facts alleged in the second paragraph of the answer, will not support an action. The demurrer to the answer should have been overruled.

PER CURIAM.—The judgment is reversed, with costs. Cause remanded & c.

QUESTIONS

1. Questions about the facts of this case

    1.1. Did the defendant Mr. Schnell contend that he did not agree to pay the plaintiff J.B. Nell $200?

    1.2. Do you think that Mr. Schnell wrote the agreement himself?

    1.3. Why did the defendant Schnell enter into such an agreement, complete with seal? Was Schnell's reason for making the agreement relevant to the court's reasoning?

    1.4. Was it ethical for Schnell to take the position that his promise to pay was not enforceable? Was it ethical for Schnell's lawyer to take that position? Would it have been ethical for Schnell's lawyer to refuse to take that position? *? / yes / questionable - depends upon the lawyer thinks consideration is a valid defense*

2. Questions about the law

    2.1. Modern concepts of consideration: How would this case be decided under *Restatement (Second) of Contracts* § 71?

    2.2. An even more modern concept: If you were representing the plaintiffs, and the judge deciding your suit against Schnell was Judge Judy, what arguments would you make?

    2.3. A real old concept—seals: Did the court mention that Schnell not only signed the agreement but affixed a seal thereto? Why not?

    2.4. Adequacy of consideration: The court describes the "consideration of one cent" as "nominal." What does "nominal mean"? Will one penny always be "nominal"? What if the consideration recited and actually paid was $10? What if the document had recited consideration of a "mere peppercorn" and the plaintiffs had given Schnell a peppercorn? According to Professor Atiyah, "At one time it was traditional to stipulate a peppercorn as nominal consideration in certain transactions, and this has always been sufficient to satisfy the law's requirements." P.S. ATIYAH, AN INTRODUCTION TO THE LAW OF CONTRACT 127 (5th ed. 1995).

2.5.   Settlement of a claim: Why wasn't the plaintiffs' agreement to "abstain from collecting any real or supposed claims upon him or his estate, arising from the said last will and testament" consideration? Reconsider the court's answer in *Schnell* after considering *Restatement (Second) of Contracts* § 74.

§ 74.   *Settlement of Claims*

(1) Forbearance to assert or the surrender of a claim or defense which proves to be invalid is not consideration unless

(a) the claim or defense is in fact doubtful because of uncertainty as to the facts or the law, or

(b) the forbearing or surrendering party believes *that the claim or defense may be fairly determined to be valid.*

Kirksey v. Kirksey, Hamer v. Sidway, and *Schnell v. Nell* involve "personal" agreements between two individuals. Most cases in which consideration is an issue involve "personal" agreements between two individuals. It is very, very, very unusual for agreements involving two businesses to be unenforceable because of no consideration.

C.   CONSIDERATION: ONE PROMISE AS CONSIDERATION FOR ANOTHER PROMISE

In *Reed*, the consideration took the form of performance: NDAD allowed the promisor, Reed, to run in the race in exchange for this promise not to sue. In *Hamer*, the consideration took the form of forbearance by the promisee: the nephew Willie refrained from drinking etc. until he reached the age of 21.

One promise can be consideration for another promise. See *Restatement (Second) of Contracts* section 75 and comment a thereto. Most business transactions involve an exchange of promises to do something (or not do something) in the future. Consider the following problems involving common business transactions.

PROBLEMS

1.   Faber SPCA (F) contracts with Blutarsky Building Contractors (B) for the construction of a new animal shelter. B promises to complete the building by April 5. F promises to pay $400,000 within 30 days after completion of the building. B never even starts on the building. F hires Stratton

Construction Company (S) which builds the building at a cost of $500,000. Can F sue B for breach of contract? What was the consideration for B's promise? Since F did not yet pay B, what is the detriment to the promisee F or the benefit to promisor B?

2. In October, Mitch McDeere (M), a law student, accepts a job with the law firm of Bandini, Lambert & Locke (BLL) for $150,000 per year starting in August. M later changes his mind and starts his own law firm instead of starting work at BLL law firm. Can BLL sue M for breach of contract? What was the consideration for M's promise? Since BLL did not yet pay M, what is the detriment to the promisee BLL or the benefit to the promisor M?

The above questions should be easy to answer. Obviously, there should be a legal remedy for B's not building the animal house and for M's not working for B. Finding a "legal detriment" is less obvious.

And perhaps, less necessary. Under *Restatement (Second) of Contracts* §§ 71 and 75, a promise can serve as consideration for another promise. Comment a to section 75 explains: "The promise is enforced by fact of bargain, without more."

The *Restatement* comment (and our Faber animal house hypothetical) is taken from the following article on consideration by Professor Lon Fuller who taught contracts at Harvard Law School:

> B promises to build a house for A, and A, in return, promises to pay B $5000 on the completion of the house. B defaults in his promise, and A, without having had occasion to pay anything on the contract, sues B for damages. Judicial intervention in this kind of case apparently began in England toward the end of the sixteenth century. It is now generally assumed that so far as consideration is concerned the executory bilateral contract is on a complete parity with the situation where the plaintiff has already paid the price of the defendant's promised performance. Yet if we examine the executory bilateral contract in terms of the policies underlying consideration, it will become apparent that this assumption is unjustified.

> Where a bilateral contract remains wholly executory the arguments for judicial intervention have been considerably diminished in comparison with the situation of the half-completed exchange. There is here no unjust enrichment. Reliance may or may not exist, but in any event will not be so tangible and direct as where it consists in the rendition of the price of the defendant's performance. On the side of form, we have lost the natural formality involved in the turning over of property or the rendition and acceptance of services. There remains simply the fact that the transaction is an exchange and not a gift.

> In the situation of the half-completed exchange, the element of exchange is only one factor tending toward enforcement. Since that element is there reinforced by reliance, unjust enrichment, and the natural formality involved in the surrender and acceptance of a tangible benefit, it is unnecessary to analyze the concept of exchange closely, and it may properly be left vague. In the executory bilateral contract, on the other

hand, the element of exchange stands largely alone as a basis of liability and its definition becomes crucial. Various definition are possible. We may define exchange vaguely as a transaction from which each participant derives a benefit, or, more restrictively, as a transaction in which the motives of the parties are primarily economic rather than sentimental. The problem of choosing among these varying conceptions may seem remote and unimportant, yet it underlies some of the most familiar problems of contract law. For example, suppose a nephew promises his uncle that he will not smoke until he is twenty-one, and the uncle promises him $5000 as a reward if he will keep his promise. Where the nephew sues after having earned the reward by following the prescribed line of conduct recovery has been permitted. But would such an agreement be enforced as an executory bilateral contract? Could the uncle, for example, sue the nephew for smoking a cigarette? In answering this question it is at once apparent that we are faced with the necessity of defining the particular kind of exchange which is essential to the enforcement of a bilateral contract. A similar problem underlies many of the cases involving "illusory promises."

Like consideration, exchange is a complex concept. To the problem of the executory exchange we may, within a narrower compass, apply the same general approach that we have applied to the problem of consideration as a whole. Here our "archetype" is the business trade of economic values in the form of goods, services, or money. To the degree that a particular case deviates from this archetype, the incentives to judicial intervention decrease, until a point is reached where relief will be denied altogether unless the attenuated element of exchange is reinforced, either on the formal side by some formal or informal satisfaction of the desiderata underlying the use of legal formalities, or on the substantive side by a showing of reliance or unjust enrichment, or of some special need for a regulation of the relations involved by private autonomy.

Lon Fuller, *Consideration and Form*, 41 COLUM. L. REV. 799, 816–18 (1941).

Sometimes, people use words of promise without really promising anything. As comment e to Restatement of Contracts (Second) section (e) states: "Words of promise which by their terms make performance entirely optional with the 'promisor' * * * do not constitute a promise. Although such words are often referred to as forming an illusory promise, they do not fall within the present definition of promise."Are there "such words" of illusory promise in the next case, another case involving legal challenges to an arbitration clause?

In the next case, Phillips argues, inter alia, that her employer Hooters' modification of her employment contract by requiring arbitration is unenforceable because Hooter's promise to arbitrate was illusory and therefore not consideration for her promise to arbitrate. [Another instance of overreaching at Hooters?]

HOOTERS OF AMERICA, INC. v. PHILLIPS

United States District Court, District of South Carolina
39 F. Supp. 2d 582 (1998), affirmed on other grounds, 173 F.3d 933, 935 (4th Cir. 1999).

CURRIE, J.

* * *

I. BACKGROUND

[From 1989 to 1996, Annette Phillips was employed by Hooters of Myrtle Beach (HOMB), a franchisee of Hooters of America, Inc. (HOA). She alleges that in June of 1996, she was sexually harassed by the brother of HOMB's principal owner. After complaining to her manager and being told to "let it go," she instead let her job go and retained an attorney. The attorney contacted HOA, alleging that the sexual harassment and HOMB's failure to address it violated Title VII of the Civil Rights Act of 1964. HOA responded that Ms. Phillips had executed a binding agreement to arbitrate and so was required to submit any claim to arbitration. HOA then initiated this legal proceeding.]

This is a declaratory judgment and Title VII case involving a former "Hooters Girl," who complains of sexual harassment by Hooter's managers and the brother of the company's CEO. * * * Unlike the party alignment in the typical employment discrimination case, the plaintiff here is the former employer, Hooters of America, Inc. ("hereinafter HOA") and the employee, Ms. Phillips, is the defendant (hereinafter "Phillips"). * * *[1]

The matter is before the court on HOA's "Motion for Preliminary Injunction," filed November 8, 1996, treated as a motion to compel arbitration under *9 U.S.C. § 3.* * * * For the reasons given below, the court finds that HOA's motion to compel arbitration * * * should be DENIED.

II. PROCEDURAL HISTORY

This case has a long and convoluted procedural history. * * *

The case commenced when HOA filed a complaint * * *, seeking a declaratory judgment, 28 U.S.C. § 2201, that the November 25, 1994, and April 23, 1995, arbitration agreements signed by Phillips were valid and enforceable. * * *

* * * The answer denied that Phillips had entered into an enforceable arbitration agreement covering her dispute with HOA. Phillips asserted that the agreements were neither knowingly nor voluntarily entered into, and were unconscionable adhesion contracts violative of public policy. Moreover, the answer asserted that the alleged arbitration agreements were not supported by adequate consideration and were illusory. * * *

---

1. Collectively the two defendants, HOA and HOMB, will be referred to as "Hooters."

III. HOA'S § 4 MOTION TO COMPEL ARBITRATION

* * *

Hooters points to the broad language of the arbitration clause executed by Phillips on two occasions:

> In consideration of the Company offering you employment and employing you, you and the company each agrees [sic] that, provided, when appropriate, the employee, complies with the company's open door policy and/or compliance resolution procedure, the employee and the company agree to resolve any claims pursuant to the company's rules and procedures for alternative resolution of employment-related disputes, as promulgated by company from time to time (the "Rules"). Company will make available or provide a copy of the rules upon written request of the employee.

* * *

Fulcher [a Hooters manager] testified (1) that each of his employees was required to hold the arbitration agreement at least five days before signing it in his presence and the presence of another witness; (2) that he told employees, including Phillips, that they should have the arbitration agreement reviewed by a lawyer, if they wished; (3) that he also informed employees they could decline to sign the arbitration agreement, but that they would not be eligible for further promotion; and (4) that he informed employees that the procedural rules to be used in arbitration, while not available at HOMB, were available by request in writing to a Divisional Vice–President. Unquestionably Phillips executed an arbitration agreement, dated November 25, 1994, that expressly covered sexual harassment claims. * * *

Phillips also challenges the arbitration agreement's validity on the separate ground that the agreement and Rules are illusory. Because in the present case no new consideration in tangible benefit (cash, a promotion, etc. * * *) was advanced at the time of execution of the arbitration agreement, the question becomes whether the parties exchanged mutually binding promises that could serve as adequate consideration. It is hornbook contract law that in order for a promise to be enforceable against a promisor, the promisee must have given some consideration for the promise. An illusory contract is also regarded as "an apparent promise which makes performance optional with the promisor * * * is in fact no promise. * * *" Consideration is defined as a bargained for exchange whereby the promisor (here Hooters) receives some benefit or the promisee (here Phillips) suffers a detriment. *Gibson v. Neighborhood Health Clinics, Inc.,* 121 F.3d 1126 (7th Cir. 1997). In order for Phillips' agreement to be enforceable, there must be a detriment to Hooters or benefit to Phillips that was bargained for in exchange for Phillips' promise to arbitrate her statutory claims.

"Often, consideration for one party's promise to arbitrate is the other party's promise to do the same." Thus, in *Gibson* the Seventh Circuit found an arbitration agreement illusory and unenforceable where it was one-sided, and only the employee was bound to submit claims to arbitration. In contrast, in the present case Hooters executed an arbitration agreement that bound it to arbitrate disputes ("you and the company each agrees [sic] that * * * the employee and the company agree to resolve any claims pursuant to the company's rules and procedures for alternative resolution of employment-related disputes, as promulgated by the company from time to time * * *"). However, under the Rules, incorporated into the arbitration agreement, "These Rules and Procedures may be modified, in whole or in part, by the Company from time to time, without notice." Rule 24–1. Moreover, "the Company may cancel the Agreement and Procedure on 30 days written notice," but no termination authority is given to the employee. Rule 23–1.

The question is whether the imperfect mutuality of obligation expressed in the Rules vitiates Hooters' promise to arbitrate set forth in the agreement. The Fourth Circuit has recognized that a promise whereby the promisor "retained an unlimited right to decide later the nature or extent of her performance" is, "in law no promise." The court finds this principle applicable to the present situation. Here, it is clear that the obligations encompassed in the Rules dwarfed whatever promises were contained in the agreement. And even a casual inspection of the Rules yields that the obligations of the two parties are not in equilibrium. For example, under the Rules, an employee's claim would be considered "waived" if arbitration were not commenced within specified time limits, but no similar waiver provision applies to Hooters. Rule 2–3. Similarly, when the employee initiates a claim he must file a detailed "content of notice" settling forth the particulars of his claim, Rule 6–2, but Hooters is under no similar obligation. The employee's witnesses must be sequestered, Rule 13–5, but not Hooters' witnesses. Under the Rules, Hooters retains exclusive authority to compile the record of the proceeding. Rule 18–1. Moreover, although Hooters may vacate under 9 U.S.C. § 10 any award if it proves merely "by the preponderance of the evidence" that the arbitrator exceeded his powers, Rule 21–4, it is not clear under the Rules that employees have any authority to seek a review of any arbitration award. Several additional disparities in obligation are contained in the Rules, but the preceding examples should suffice to illustrate the point.

Upon review of the differing obligations set forth in the Rules, the court concludes that Hooters retained to itself an unfettered "right to decide later the nature or extent of [its] performance" by reserving the authority to modify the Rules, or terminate the agreement, at its choice, while denying the same to Phillips. The court finds the agreement and Rules illusory, and unenforceable under South Carolina law on that basis.

    * * *

VII.   CONCLUSION

IT IS THEREFORE ORDERED that Plaintiff's November 8, 1996, Motion for a Preliminary Injunction, treated by the court as a motion to compel arbitration pursuant to the Federal Arbitration Act, 9 U.S.C. § 4, is DENIED.

* * *

QUESTIONS AND NOTES

1. Questions about the facts of this case

   1.1. Was there a written arbitration agreement?

   1.2. Was Ms. Phillips employed by Hooters before she signed the arbitration agreement? Is that an important fact?

   1.3. Do we know why Ms. Phillips signed the arbitration agreement? Was Hooters' agreeing to arbitrate important to Ms. Phillips? Is determining what is important to Ms. Phillips important in determining whether there was bargained for consideration for her promise to arbitrate?

2. Questions about the law

   2.1. Ms. Phillips had worked for Hooters for five years before she promised to arbitrate. Wasn't the five years of employment a "benefit" to Ms. Phillips? Can benefits already provided by Hooters be consideration for a later promise by Ms. Phillips? Do you agree with the statement by Professor Jean Fleming Powers, who teaches contracts at South Texas College of Law, "Past consideration is an oxymoron"? Jean Fleming Powers, *Rethinking Moral Obligations: A Basis for Contract Recovery*, 54 ME. L. REV. 1, 6 (2002).

   2.2. Can a promise be consideration? If so, can a promise of future employment be consideration? Can a promise to arbitrate be consideration?

   2.3. What is an illusory promise?

   2.4. It is clear from the authorities cited in *Hooters* that an illusory promise is not consideration. *See also Restatement (Second) of Contracts* § 77. It is less clear what made Hooters' promise to arbitrate illusory. Why is Hooters' promise to arbitrate illusory?

   2.5. Assume that Hooters had sued Ms. Phillips in the United States District Court for keeping her tips in violation of company rules. Could Ms. Phillips have compelled Hooters to submit the claim to arbitration? No Yes

   2.6. The *Hooters* opinion states that "even a casual inspection of the Rules yields that the obligations of the two parties are not in equilibrium." What does this statement mean? Is it relevant in determining whether Hooters' promise to arbitrate was an illusory promise?

   2.7. Markell hires Epstein to perform at UNLV's Annual Purim Party. Markell promises to pay $2,700 and Epstein promises "I will show

up and play at the Purim party unless I change my mind." Was
Yes Epstein's promise an illusory promise? Will that be relevant if
Epstein does not show up and Markell sues him for breach of
Yes contract? Will that be relevant if Markell sends Epstein a certified
letter stating that the deal is off and Epstein sues Markell for
breach of contract?

2.8.   Would your answer to question 2.7 change if Epstein's promise is
changed to: "I will play at the Purim Party <u>unless I give you</u>
written notice at least one week before the Purim Party <u>that I have</u>
<u>changed my mind</u>"? *Not illusory. New obligation. The promise is now*
supported by consideration.

3. Notes

3.1.   Reading the *Hooters* case should cause you to care more about the
meaning of "bargained for" in the *Restatement (Second) of Contracts. See Restatement (Second) of Contracts* section 81(1). ("The
fact that what is bargained for does not itself induce the making of
a promise does not prevent it from being consideration for the
promise.") In all likelihood, Ms. Phillips could care less about
whether Hooters agreed to arbitrate any claims it might have
against her. And, in all likelihood, courts could care less about what
Ms. Phillips actually cared about.

3.2.   The agreements recited consideration: "In consideration of the
Company offering you employment * * *" This recital was of
course false—Ms. Phillips was already employed. The district court
opinion did not discuss the question of whether a mere recital of
consideration should be sufficient on the basis that the recital is a
kind of legal formality, like a seal, that evidences an intent to
contract. The *Restatement (Second) of Contracts* does discuss this
question and concludes "a mere pretense of bargain does not
suffice, as where there is a false recital of consideration." *Restatement (Second) of Contracts* § 71, comment b; but cf." *Restatement
(Second) of Contracts* § 87 ("recites a purported consideration").

3.3.   Subsequently, the Sixth Circuit in *Floss v. Ryan's Family Steak
Houses, Inc.*, 211 F.3d 306 (6th Cir. 2000) held that an agreement to
arbitrate between a third-party arbitration services provider (EDSI)
and employee lacked consideration, stating:

Where a promisor retains an unlimited right to decide later the
nature or extent of his performance, the promise is too indefinite for
legal enforcement. The unlimited choice in effect destroys the promise and makes it merely illusory.

EDSI's illusory promise does not create a binding obligation. The
purported arbitration agreement therefore lacks a mutuality of obligation. Without a mutuality of obligation, the agreement lacks consideration and, accordingly, does not constitute an enforceable arbitration agreement.

Ryan's has pursued an acceptable objective in an unacceptable manner. An employer may enter an agreement with employees requiring
the arbitration of all employment disputes, including those involving

federal statutory claims. Yet an employer cannot seek to do so in such a way that leaves employees with no consideration for their promise to submit their disputes to arbitration. Here, we find that Floss and Daniels did not receive any consideration for their promise to arbitrate their disputes. We thus refuse to enforce their promise in favor of Ryan's.

211 F.3d at 315.

3.4.   *Floss* uses the phrase "mutuality of obligation." Great phrase. The kind of combination of words that sounds like "law." The words "mutuality of obligation" just sort of flow together. Kind of like "heartbreak of psoriasis" http://www.psorsite.com/heartbreak.html The Maine Supreme Court in *Zamore v. Whitten*, 395 A.2d 435, 443 n.3 (Me. 1978) questions whether the phrase "mutuality of obligation" is any more helpful in dealing with consideration than Tegrin is in dealing with psoriasis:

> The phrase "mutuality of obligation" has caused much confusion to courts and commentators over the years. Professor Corbin criticizes the expression for its tendency to connote a need for obligations equivalent in terms of detriment and value.

> In fact, mutuality embodies a particularized application of the consideration doctrine in the context of formation of a bilateral contract. In a bilateral contract, one promise is good consideration for another. If the promisee fails to give the required return promise, mutual obligations are not, in fact, created. It is less confusing, and equally accurate, however, to conclude that no contract exists due to the promisee's failure to give legally sufficient consideration.

3.5.   A recent essay by Professor Curtis Bridgeman and Karen Sandrik adds a new term—"bullshit promise": "It is possible to make an insincere yet non-lying promise, what we call a 'bullshit promise.' A party can do so by making an offer on certain specific terms while elsewhere reserving for itself the right to change those terms unilaterally at any time it wishes. * * * Indeed, the promise may end up fulfilling the promised plan. But they are insincere because they misrepresent what the promisor is up to. They are, in a word, bullshit." Curtis Bridgemen & Karen Sandrik, *Bullshit Promises,* 76 TENN. L. REV. 379, 381–382 (2009) Was the promise in the *Hooters* case a "bullshit promise"? Is there any difference between a "bullshit promise" and an "illusory promise"?

D.   CONSIDERATION AND CONTRACT MODIFICATION

Hooters and the next two cases illustrate that consideration questions do sometimes arise in agreements to modify business contracts. Especially employment contracts.

ALASKA PACKERS' ASS'N v. DOMENICO

Circuit Court of Appeals, Ninth Circuit
117 F. 99 (1902)

ROSS, CIRCUIT JUDGE:

[This is a case involving the enforceability of an employer's written agreement to modify an employment agreement by increasing employees' minimum salary. The employer contends that this modification agreement is not enforceable because of lack of consideration. More specifically, the employer, Alaska Packers ("appellant"), owned a salmon packing factor in Alaska. The employees ("libelants"*) were California sailors and fishermen who contracted to work for appellant in Alaska during the salmon season for $50 per sailor or fisherman plus two cents for each red salmon he caught. The libelants arrived in Alaska in April; in late May, the libelants stopped worked and demanded an increase in salary. It was impossible for the appellant to find any replacement workers in Alaska or bring replacement workers from California in time to take full advantage of the short salmon season. The appellant agreed in writing to increased the libelants' fixed salary from $50 to $100. The libelants returned to work. After the catch was in and the libelants returned to California, appellant refused to pay more than the amount originally promised. Libelants sued to enforce the agreement modifying the employment contract.]

* * *

On the trial in the court below, the libelants undertook to show that the fishing nets provided by the respondent were defective, and that it was on that account that they demanded increased wages. On that point, the evidence was substantially conflicting, and the finding of the court was against the libelants the court saying:

> The contention of libelants that the nets provided them were rotten and unserviceable is not sustained by the evidence. The defendants' interest required that libelants should be provided with every facility necessary to their success as fishermen, for on such success depended the profits defendant would be able to realize that season from its packing plant, and the large capital invested therein. In view of this self-evident fact, it is highly improbable that the defendant gave libelants rotten and unserviceable nets with which to fish. It follows from this finding that libelants were not justified in refusing performance of their original contract.'

The evidence being sharply conflicting in respect to these facts, the conclusions of the court, who heard and saw the witnesses, will not be disturbed.

* * * From the foregoing statement of the case, it will have been seen that the libelants agreed in writing, for certain stated compensation, to

---

* A libelant is the admiralty counterpart to a plaintiff. Eds.

render their services to the appellant in remote waters where the season for conducting fishing operations is extremely short, and in which enterprise the appellant had a large amount of money invested; and, after having entered upon the discharge of their contract, and at a time when it was impossible for the appellant to secure other men in their places, the libelants, without any valid cause, absolutely refused to continue the services they were under contract to perform unless the appellant would consent to pay them more money. Consent to such a demand, under such circumstances, if given, was, in our opinion, without consideration, for the reason that it was based solely upon the libelants' agreement to render the exact services, and none other, that they were already under contract to render.

* * * The circumstances of the present case bring it, we think, directly within the sound and just observations of the supreme court of Minnesota in the case of King v. Railway Co., 61 Minn. 482, 63 N.W. 1105:

> No astute reasoning can change the plain fact that the party who refuses to perform, and thereby coerces a promise from the other party to the contract to pay him an increased compensation for doing that which he is legally bound to do, takes an unjustifiable advantage of the necessities of the other party. Surely it would be a travesty on justice to hold that the party so making the promise for extra pay was estopped from asserting that the promise was without consideration. A party cannot lay the foundation of an estoppel by his own wrong, where the promise is simply a repetition of a subsisting legal promise. There can be no consideration for the promise of the other party, and there is no warrant for inferring that the parties have voluntarily rescinded or modified their contract. The promise cannot be legally enforced, although the other party has completed his contract in reliance upon it.

In Lingenfelder v. Brewing Co., 103 Mo. 578, 15 S.W. 844, the court, in holding void a contract by which the owner of a building agreed to pay its architect an additional sum because of his refusal to otherwise proceed with the contract, said:

> It is urged upon us by respondents that this was a new contract. New in what? Jungenfeld was bound by his contract to design and supervise this building. Under the new promise, he was not to do anything more or anything different. What benefit was to accrue to Wainwright? He was to receive the same service from Jungenfeld under the new, that Jungenfeld was bound to tender under the original, contract. What loss, trouble, or inconvenience could result to Jungenfeld that he had not already assumed? No amount of metaphysical reasoning can change the plain fact that Jungenfeld took advantage of Wainwright's necessities, and extorted the promise of five per cent. on the refrigerator plant as the condition of his complying with his contract already entered into. Nor had he even the flimsy pretext that Wainwright had violated any of the conditions of the contract on his

part. Jungenfeld himself put it upon the simple proposition that 'if he, as an architect, put up the brewery, and another company put up the refrigerating machinery, it would be a detriment to the Empire Refrigerating Company,' of which Jungenfeld was president. To permit plaintiff to recover under such circumstances would be to offer a premium upon bad faith, and invite men to violate their most sacred contracts that they may profit by their own wrong. That a promise to pay a man for doing that which he is already under contract to do is without consideration is conceded by respondents. The rule has been so long imbedded in the common law and decisions of the highest courts of the various states that nothing but the most cogent reasons ought to shake it. (Citing a long list of authorities.) But it is 'carrying coals to Newcastle' to add authorities on a proposition so universally accepted, and so inherently just and right in itself. The learned counsel for respondents do not controvert the general proposition. Their contention is, and the circuit court agreed with them, that, when Jungenfeld declined to go further on his contract, the defendant then had the right to sue for damages, and not having elected to sue Jungenfeld, but having acceded to his demand for the additional compensation defendant cannot now be heard to say his promise is without consideration. While it is true Jungenfeld became liable in damages for the obvious breach of his contract, we do not think it follows that defendant is estopped from showing its promise was made without consideration. * * * What we hold is that, when a party merely does what he has already obligated himself to do, he cannot demand an additional compensation therefor; and although, by taking advantage of the necessities of his adversary, he obtains a promise for more, the law will regard it as nudum pactum, and will not lend its process to aid in the wrong.

* * *

It results from the views above expressed that the judgment must be reversed, and the cause remanded, with directions to the court below to enter judgment for the respondent, with costs. It is so ordered.

QUESTIONS AND NOTE

1. Questions about the facts of this case

    1.1. Did the libelants argue that there was consideration for appellant's promise to pay more? If so, what?

    1.2. Do you think that it is "highly improbable" that appellant gave libelants "rotten and unserviceable nets"? Is what you think really happened in Alaska helpful to your understanding the "law" in this case?

2. Questions about the law

2.1. If the court deciding *Alaska Packers* followed the *Restatement (Second)* § 71 definition of consideration—"a performance or return promise must be bargained for," what is appellant's strongest legal argument?

2.2. Consider the following hypothetical based on *Alaska Packers* posed by Professor David Snyder in an article critical of the case: "Say the seamen in Alaska stopped work and said to the boss 'We want our wages doubled. In return, we'll spread the word back in San Fran that you are a great employer.' The boss, with no other labor for thousands of miles, is just as stuck as in the actual *Alaska Packers* case, and he agrees to the sailors' proposal." David V. Snyder, *The Law of Contract and the Concept of Change: Public and Private Attempts to Regulate Modification, Waiver and Estoppel*, 1999 WISC. L. REV. 607, 614. How would Professor Snyder's hypothetical be decided under our definitions of consideration?

3. Note

Professor Debora L. Threedy of University of Utah Law School has explored the historical and social background of the *Alaska Packers* case and concludes: "I confess from my first reading of the case I was skeptical about the reality of the traditional reading, doubting that Alaska Packers was ever at the mercy of the fishermen. Everything that I have since learned about the case has only deepened my skepticism." Debora L. Threedy, *A Fish Story: Alaska Packers' Association v. Domenico*, 2000 UTAH L. REV. 185, 197, n. 78.

————

Notwithstanding Professor Threedy's skepticism about what really happened, courts continue to cite and even rely on *Alaska Packers*. In the next case, the Rhode Island Supreme Court describes *Alaska Packers* as the "classic example of the 'hold-up game.'"

ANGEL v. MURRAY

Supreme Court of Rhode Island
113 R.I. 482, 322 A.2d 630 (1974)

ROBERTS, C.J.

This is a civil action brought by Alfred L. Angel and others against John E. Murray, Jr., Director of Finance of the City of Newport, the city of Newport, and James L. Maher, alleging that Maher had illegally been paid the sum of $20,000 by the Director of Finance and praying that the defendant Maher be ordered to repay the city such sum. The case was heard by a justice of the Superior Court, sitting without a jury, who entered a judgment ordering Maher to repay the sum of $20,000 to the city of Newport. Maher is now before this court prosecuting an appeal.

The record discloses that Maher has provided the city of Newport with a refuse-collection service under a series of five-year contracts beginning in 1946. On March 12, 1964, Maher and the city entered into another such contract for a period of five years commencing on July 1, 1964, and terminating on June 30, 1969. The contract provided, among other things, that Maher would receive $137,000 per year in return for collecting and removing all combustible and noncombustible waste materials generated within the city.

In June of 1967 Maher requested an additional $10,000 per year from the city council because there had been a substantial increase in the cost of collection due to an unexpected and unanticipated increase of 400 new dwelling units. Maher's testimony, which is uncontradicted, indicates the 1964 contract had been predicated on the fact that since 1946 there had been an average increase of 20 to 25 new dwelling units per year. After a public meeting of the city council where Maher explained in detail the reasons for his request and was questioned by members of the city council, the city council agreed to pay him an additional $10,000 for the year ending on June 30, 1968. Maher made a similar request again in June of 1968 for the same reasons, and the city council again agreed to pay an additional $10,000 for the year ending on June 30, 1969.

The trial justice found * * * that Maher was not entitled to extra compensation because the original contract already required him to collect all refuse generated within the city and, therefore, included the 400 additional units. The trial justice further found that these 400 additional units were within the contemplation of the parties when they entered into the contract. It appears that he based this portion of the decision upon the rule that Maher had a preexisting duty to collect the refuse generated by the 400 additional units, and thus there was no consideration for the two additional payments.

* * *

As previously stated, the city council made two $10,000 payments. The first was made in June of 1967 for the year beginning on July 1, 1967, and ending on June 30, 1968. Thus, by the time this action was commenced in October of 1968, the modification was completely executed. That is, the money had been paid by the city council, and Maher had collected all of the refuse. * * *

It is generally held that a modification of a contract is itself a contract, which is unenforceable unless supported by consideration. In *Rose v. Daniels,* 8 R. I. 381 (1866), this court held that an agreement by a debtor with a creditor to discharge a debt for a sum of money less than the amount due is unenforceable because it was not supported by consideration.

Rose is a perfect example of the preexisting duty rule. Under this rule an agreement modifying a contract is not supported by consideration if one of the parties to the agreement does or promises to do something that he is legally obligated to do or refrains or promises to refrain from doing something he is not legally privileged to do. In *Rose* there was no consideration for the new agreement because the debtor was already legally obligated to repay the full amount of the debt.

* * *

The primary purpose of the preexisting duty rule is to prevent what has been referred to as the "hold-up game." A classic example of the "hold-up game" is found in *Alaska Packers' Ass'n v. Domenico*, 117 F. 99 (9th Cir. 1902). There 21 seamen entered into a written contract with Domenico to sail from San Francisco to Pyramid Harbor, Alaska. They were to work as sailors and fishermen out of Pyramid Harbor during the fishing season of 1900. The contract specified that each man would be paid $50 plus two cents for each red salmon he caught. Subsequent to their arrival at Pyramid Harbor, the men stopped work and demanded an additional $50. They threatened to return to San Francisco if Domenico did not agree to their demand. Since it was impossible for Domenico to find other men, he agreed to pay the men an additional $50. After they returned to San Francisco, Domenico refused to pay the men an additional $50. The court found that the subsequent agreement to pay the men an additional $50 was not supported by consideration because the men had a preexisting duty to work on the ship under the original contract, and thus the subsequent agreement was unenforceable.

Another example of the "hold-up game" is found in the area of construction contracts. Frequently, a contractor will refuse to complete work under an unprofitable contract unless he is awarded additional compensation. The courts have generally held that a subsequent agreement to award additional compensation is unenforceable if the contractor is only performing work which would have been required of him under the original contract.

These examples clearly illustrate that the courts will not enforce an agreement that has been procured by coercion or duress and will hold the parties to their original contract regardless of whether it is profitable or unprofitable. However, the courts have been reluctant to apply the preexisting duty rule when a party to a contract encounters unanticipated difficulties and the other party, not influenced by coercion or duress, voluntarily agrees to pay additional compensation for work already required to be performed under the contract.

* * *

Although the preexisting duty rule has served a useful purpose insofar as it deters parties from using coercion and duress to obtain additional compensation, it has been widely criticized as a general rule of law. With regard to the preexisting duty rule, one legal scholar has stated: "There has been a growing doubt as to the soundness of this doctrine as a matter of social policy. * * * In certain classes of cases, this doubt has influenced courts to refuse to apply the rule, or to ignore it, in their actual decisions. Like other legal rules, this rule is in process of growth and change, the process being more active here than in most instances. The result of this is that a court should no longer accept this rule as fully established. It should never use it as the major premise of a decision, at least without giving careful thought to the circumstances of the particular case, to the moral deserts of the parties, and to the social feelings and interests that are involved. It is certain that the rule, stated in general and all-inclusive terms, is no longer so well-settled that a court must apply it though the heavens fall." 1A Corbin, [Contracts] § 171 [(1963)]. * * *

The modern trend appears to recognize the necessity that courts should enforce agreements modifying contracts when unexpected or unanticipated difficulties arise during the course of the performance of a contract, even though there is no consideration for the modification, as long as the parties agree voluntarily.

Under the Uniform Commercial Code, § 2–209(1), which has been adopted by 49 states, "[an] agreement modifying a contract [for the sale of goods] needs no consideration to be binding." Although at first blush this section appears to validate modifications obtained by coercion and duress, the comments to this section indicate that a modification under this section must meet the test of good faith imposed by the Code, and a modification obtained by extortion without a legitimate commercial reason is unenforceable.

The modern trend away from a rigid application of the preexisting duty rule is reflected by § 89D(a) of the American Law Institute's Restatement Second of the Law of Contracts, which provides: "A promise modifying a duty under a contract not fully performed on either side is binding (a) if the modification is fair and equitable in view of circumstances not anticipated by the parties when the contract was made. * * *"

We believe that § 89D(a) is the proper rule of law and find it applicable to the facts of this case. It not only prohibits modifications obtained by coercion, duress, or extortion but also fulfills society's expectation that agreements entered into voluntarily will be enforced by the courts. Section 89D(a), of course, does not compel a modification of an unprofitable or unfair contract; it only enforces a modification if the parties voluntarily agree and if (1) the promise modifying the original contract was made before the contract was fully performed on either side, (2) the underlying circumstances which prompted the modification were unanticipated by the parties, and (3) the modification is fair and equitable.

* * *

The evidence, which is uncontradicted, reveals that in June of 1968 Maher requested the city council to pay him an additional $10,000 for the year beginning on July 1, 1968, and ending on June 30, 1969. This request was made at a public meeting of the city council, where Maher explained in detail his reasons for making the request. Thereafter, the city council voted to authorize the Mayor to sign an amendment to the 1954 contract which provided that Maher would receive an additional $10,000 per year for the duration of the contract. Under such circumstances we have no doubt that the city voluntarily agreed to modify the 1964 contract.

Having determined the voluntariness of this agreement, we turn our attention to the three criteria delineated above. First, the modification was made in June of 1968 at a time when the five-year contract which was made in 1964 had not been fully performed by either party. Second, although the 1964 contract provided that Maher collect all refuse generated within the city, it appears this contract was premised on Maher's past experience that the number of refuse-generating units would increase at a rate of 20 to 25 per year. Furthermore, the evidence is uncontradicted that the 1967–1968 increase of 400 units "went beyond any previous expectation." Clearly, the circumstances which prompted the city council to modify the 1964 contract were unanticipated.[4] Third, although the evidence does not indicate what proportion of the total this increase comprised, the evidence does indicate that it was a "substantial" increase. In light of this, we cannot say that the council's agreement to pay Maher the $10,000 increase was not fair and equitable in the circumstances.

It is clearly a contractual provision requiring the contractor to hold the city harmless and to defend it in any litigation arising out of the performance of his obligations under the contract, whether a result of affirmative action or some omission or neglect on the part of Maher or his agents or employees. We are persuaded that the portion of sec. 2(a) specifically referred to by the court refers to losses resulting to Maher from some action or omission on the part of his own agents or employees. It cannot be disputed, however, that any losses that resulted from an increase in the cost of collecting from the increased number of units generating refuse in no way resulted from any action on the part of either Maher or his employees. Rather, whatever losses he did entail by reason of the requirement of such extra collection resulted from actions completely beyond his control and thus unanticipated.

The judgment appealed from is reversed, and the cause is remanded to the Superior Court for entry of judgment for the defendants.

QUESTIONS AND NOTE

1. Questions about the facts of this case
   1.1. Who agreed to make the additional payments to Maher?
   1.2. Why did the city agree to make the additional payments to Maher? Is that relevant to the court's decision?

---

4. The trial justice found that sec. 2(a) of the 1964 contract precluded Maher from recovering extra compensation for the 400 additional units. Section 2(a) provided: "*The Contractor, having made his proposal after his own examinations and estimates, shall take all responsibility for, and bear, any losses resulting to him in carrying out the contract;* and shall assume the defence of, and hold the City, its agents and employees harmless from all suits and claims arising from the use of any invention, patent, or patent rights, material, labor or implement, by or from any act, omission or neglect of, the Contractor, his agents or employees, in carrying out the contract." (Emphasis added). The trial justice, quoting the italicized portion of sec. 2(a), found that this section required that any losses incurred in the performance of the contract were Maher's responsibility. In our opinion, however, the trial justice overlooked the thrust of sec. 2(a) when read in its entirety.

1.3.   Under the 1964 contract, was Maher legally obligated to collect refuse from the 400 additional units? Should that be relevant to the court's decision?

2.   Questions about the law

2.1.   The *Murray* decision discusses the *Alaska Packers* case and the preexisting duty rule. What was the holding in *Alaska Packers*? Did the court in *Alaska Packers* mention the preexisting duty rule? What is the preexisting duty rule? Is the *Murray* holding consistent with the preexisting duty rule?

2.2.   Is the *Murray* holding consistent with the holding in *Alaska Packers*? Would Chief Justice Roberts of the Rhode Island Supreme Court have decided *Alaska Packers* differently? Would Judge Ross of the United States Court of Appeals for the Ninth Circuit have decided *Murray* differently?

2.3.   The *Murray* case involves a question about the enforceability of a modification to a contract. (Didn't the *Hooters* case and the *Alaska Packers* case also involve a contract modification?) Should courts treat the question of whether a contract modification is legally enforceable differently from the question of whether a "new" agreement is legally enforceable?

2.4.   *Murray* holding: A later decision of the Rhode Island Supreme Court, *Fondedile, S.A. v. C.E. Maguire, Inc.*, 610 A.2d 87, 92 (1992), cites the *Murray* decision for the following proposition: "parties to a contract can mutually assent to modify the contract if the modification does not violate the law or public policy and the modification is supported by adequate consideration." Is that an accurate summary of the *Murray* decision?

2.5.   *Murray* reasoning: The court in *Murray* cites to and relies on the provisions in § 89 of the *Restatement (Second) of Contracts*. *Restatement (Second)* § 89(a) now states "A promise modifying a duty under a contract not fully performed on either side is binding (a) if the modification is fair and equitable in view of the circumstances not anticipated by the parties when the contract was made." Is the Rhode Island Supreme Court obligated to follow the statements in the *Restatement*?

2.6.   More *Murray* reasoning: Note that the court in *Murray* discusses § 2–209 of the Uniform Commercial Code. Is the Rhode Island Supreme Court obligated to follow the sections of the Uniform Commercial Code? Does the *Murray* case involve a sale of goods? If not, why does the court consider § 2–209 of the Uniform Commercial Code?

2.7.   Modification of contracts for sale of goods: How does § 2–209 of the Uniform Commercial Code differ from *Restatement (Second)* § 89(a)? Apply § 2–209 to the following sale of goods problem: Ponoroff contracts to deliver thirty-three pounds of prickly pear cactus pads and fruits to McCain for $400. Ponoroff, who is new to Arizona, then discovers that removing cactus spines and extracting cactus pads and fruits is much harder than he expected. He explains this to McCain and asks McCain to modify the contract by reducing the quantity from thirty-three pounds to twenty-two pounds without reducing the price. McCain agrees. McCain later changes her mind. Is the modification agreement legally enforceable?

2.8.   Modification of debt contracts: D owes C $3,200. The debt is due right now and undisputed. D and C agree that if D pays C $2,000 then C will release the rest of the debt. D pays C $2,000. Is the release agreement legally enforceable? Should it be?

2.9.   Review: Ponoroff (P) contracts with Markell (M) to perform at M's Las Vegas nightclub, The Bottoms Up Review, as the featured "dancer." Under the contract, P is to be paid $3,300. Just before the time advertised for P to perform, as the inebriated and impatient crowd is shouting for P, P tells M that he will not perform unless he is paid $4,000. M agrees to pay $4,000. P performs. M only pays P the original $3,300 contract price. Is M's promise to pay the additional $700 legally enforceable? Is this hypothetical distinguishable from *Alaska Packers*? From *Murphy*? Is consideration [or the lack thereof] the best basis for distinguishing between valid and invalid contract modifications? Reconsider your "answer" after reading Professor Hillman's "answer" below and the materials on duress later in the book.

3.   Note

Professor Robert Hillman of Cornell Law School, the author of an outstanding text on contract law, is critical of the pre-existing duty rule and *Restatement (Second) of Contracts* § 89(a):

The approach of the Restatement (Second) of Contracts to modification enforceability suffers from a lack of clarity and fails to reflect the goals of contract-modification law. The weaknesses of the approach stem both from adherence to the preexisting-duty doctrine—a doctrine which, most commentators agree, has outlived its usefulness—and from failure to apply the doctrine of economic duress directly to the modification problem.

The Restatement (Second) approach suffers from lack of clarity because of the difficulties of defining "unanticipated circumstances" and the broadness of the "fair and equitable," "honesty" and "justice requires" terminology. In addition, in light of the goals of contract modification law, the approach wrongly bars the enforcement of voluntary modification in the absence of consideration, "unanticipated circumstances," or material reliance (unless the promisee reasonably or honestly believes in a defense to performance). The approach is also potentially harmful because the occurrence of "unanticipated circumstances" does not ensure the voluntariness of a modification and because the "fair and equitable" and "pretense of a bargain" language may be insufficient to direct courts to the issue of economic duress.

Proper application of each of the sections of the Restatement Second examined here (sections 73, 74, 89(a), and 89(c)) ultimately requires reference to the issues of duress. Accordingly, to cut through the morass of technical and unclear rules of the past, the duress doctrine should be applied to the problem of contract modification directly. Duress is a superior vehicle for analyzing the voluntariness of a modification because it requires inquiry into all of the factual elements that are probative of the issue. Undoubtedly, courts will face difficult decisions in weighing the various factors involved in the duress inquiry. Nevertheless, even if terms such as "unanticipated circumstances" were capable of clear definition and increased predictability of results, use of such tests would come at the expense of the appropriate broader inquiry—the voluntariness of modifications.

Robert A. Hillman, *Contract Modification Under the Restatement (Second) of Contracts*, 67 CORNELL L. REV. 680, 702–703 (1982).

The pre-existing duty rule is the end of our consideration of the contract law doctrine of consideration. What are the ends served by the contract law doctrine of consideration? Should courts and legislatures consider ending use of the doctrine of consideration? *See generally* James D. Gordon, III, *A Dialogue About the Doctrine of Consideration*, 75 CORNELL L. REV. 987 (1990), a wonderful article which begins by comparing consideration to Elvis* and concludes by quoting Cardozo.**

SECTION 2: PROMISE TO PAY FOR SOME-THING THAT HAPPENED BEFORE THE PROMISE: MORAL OBLIGATIONS

Even though courts and the legislatures have not yet heeded the call of Professor Gordon and others to abolish consideration as a legal requirement for the enforcement of agreements and promises, courts and legislatures have developed concepts that are alternatives to or substitutes for consideration.

Recall that consideration is bargained for: "To constitute consideration, a performance or a return promise must be bargained for." *Restate-*

---

* We would describe Bob's concise hornbook on contracts as "wonderful" if he was not taking food from our childrens' mouths (grandchildren's mouths in the case of Epstein) by co-authoring a "competing" contracts casebook.

** The comparison of consideration to Elvis is in a footnote: "Consideration is to contract law as Elvis is to rock and roll—the King. Revisionists have questioned Elvis's greatness. They have wrestled with one disturbing issue: if Elvis is so great, how come he is buried in his own back yard—like a hamster." *Id.* at 987, n.3.

** Professor Gordon's Cardozo quote is not exactly about either Elvis or consideration: "Benjamin Cardozo observed that the time has come 'when the old forms seem ready to decay and the old rules of action lose their binding force.' Perhaps someday contract law will more closely reflect common sense and modern commercial practice and business people will not have to seek legal advice reflecting irrational rules from centuries long past." *Id.* at 1006.

ment (Second) of Contracts § 71(1). You can't bargain for someone to do something that she has already done—stuff that happened before a promise can't be "bargained for"; can't be consideration. Or, as the *Restatement* more elegantly puts it: " 'Past consideration' is inconsistent with the meaning of consideration stated in section 71." *Restatement (Second) of Contracts* § 86, Comment a.

Assume, for example, that Ms. Chandler's promise to buy a Hummer for Ponoroff was motivated not by his fine work on the third edition of MADD, but rather on the fact that several months earlier Ponoroff wrote a letter to the President of West Academic Publishing praising Ms. Chandler as a superior employee and an exemplary representative of the company. As a direct result, Ms. Chandler got a nice big fat raise. Grateful beyond words, she makes the call to Ponoroff promising him to deliver the Hummer next month—and also to take him to Anthony's In the Catalinas. Again, however, Ms. Chandler later changes her mind. Ponoroff (having once been a real lawyer) decides to sue, and Ms. Chandler contends that her promise should not be enforced because Ponoroff's letter, which was written and sent before her promises about the Hummer and dinner at Anthony's were made, cannot be consideration for those promises. Should the court enforce Ms. Chandler's promises nevertheless? Would the courts that decided the next two cases have enforced those promises?

HARRINGTON v. TAYLOR

Supreme Court of North Carolina
225 N.C. 690, 36 S.E.2d 227 (1945)

PER CURIUM

The plaintiff in this case sought to recover of the defendant upon a promise made by him under the following peculiar circumstances:

The defendant had assaulted his wife, who took refuge in plaintiff's house. The next day the defendant gained access to the house and began another assault upon his wife. The defendant's wife knocked him down with an axe, and was on the point of cutting his head open or decapitating him while he was laying on the floor, and the plaintiff intervened, caught the axe as it was descending, and the blow intended for defendant fell upon her hand, mutilating it badly, but saving defendant's life.

Subsequently, defendant orally promised to pay the plaintiff her damages; but, after paying a small sum, failed to pay anything more. So, substantially, states the complaint.

The defendant demurred to the complaint as not stating a cause of action, and the demurrer was sustained. Plaintiff appealed.

The question presented is whether there was a consideration recognized by our law as sufficient to support the promise. The Court is of the opinion that however much the defendant should be impelled by common gratitude to alleviate the plaintiff's misfortune, a humanitarian act of this kind, voluntarily performed, is not such consideration as would entitle her to recover at law.

The judgment sustaining the demurrer is

Affirmed.

MILLS v. WYMAN

Supreme Judicial Court of Massachusetts
20 Mass. (3 Pick.) 207 (1825)

This was an action of assumpsit brought to recover a compensation for the board, nursing, etc. of Levi Wyman, son of the defendant, from the 5th to the 20th of February 1821. The plaintiff then lived in Hartford, in Connecticut; the defendant, as Shrewsbury, in this county. Levi Wyman, at the time when the services were rendered, was about 25 years of age, and had long ceased to be a member of his father's family. He was on his return from a voyage at sea, and being suddenly taken sick at Hartford, and being poor and in distress, was relieved by the plaintiff in the manner and to the extent above stated. On the 24th of February, after all the expenses had been incurred, the defendant wrote a letter to the plaintiff, promising to pay him such expenses. There was no consideration for this promise, except what grew out of the relation which subsisted between Levi Wyman and the defendant, and Howe J., before whom the cause was tried in the Court of Common Pleas, thinking this not sufficient to support the action, directed a nonsuit. To this direction the plaintiff filed exceptions.

PARKER, CHIEF JUSTICE.

General rules of law established for the protection and security of honest and fair-minded men, who may inconsiderably make promises without any equivalent, will sometimes screen men of a different character from engagements which they are bound in *foro conscientiae* to perform. This is a defect inherent in all human systems of legislation. The rule that a mere verbal promise, without any consideration, cannot be enforced by action, is universal in its application, and cannot be departed from to suit particular cases in which a refusal to perform such a promise may be disgraceful.

The promise declared on in this case appears to have been made without any legal consideration. The kindness and services toward the sick son of the defendant were not bestowed at his request. The son was in no respect under the care of the defendant. He was twenty-five years old, and had long left his father's family. On his return from a foreign country he fell sick among strangers, and the plaintiff acted the part of the good Samaritan, giving him shelter and comfort until he died. The defendant, his father, on being informed of this event, influenced by transient feeling of gratitude, promises in writing to pay the plaintiff for the expenses he had incurred.* But he has determined to break this promise, and is willing

---

* The letter is not reproduced in the opinion. Through some nice detective work, Dr. Watson found the letter and reproduced it in his article on *Mills v. Wyman*:

to have his case appear on record as a strong example of particular injustice sometimes necessarily resulting from the operation of general rules.

It is said a moral obligation is sufficient consideration to support an express promise; and some authorities lay down the rule thus broadly; but upon examination of the case we are satisfied that the universality of the rule cannot be supported, and that there must have been some pre-existing obligation, which has become inoperative by positive law, to form a basis for an effective promise. The cases of debts barred by the statute of limitations, of debts incurred by infants, of debts of bankrupts, are generally put for illustration of the rule. Express promises founded on such pre-existing equitable obligations may be enforced; there is a good consideration for them; they merely remove an impediment created by law to the recovery of debts honestly due, but which public policy protects the debtors from being compelled to pay. In all these cases there was originally a quid pro quo; and according to the principle of natural justice the party receiving ought to pay; but the legislature has said he shall not be coerced; then comes the promise to pay the debt that is barred, the promise of the man to pay the debt of the infant, of the discharged bankrupt to restore to his creditor what by the law he has lost. In all these cases there is a moral obligation founded upon an antecedent valuable consideration. These promises therefore have a sound legal basis. They are not promises to pay something for nothing; not naked pacts; but the voluntary revival or creation of obligation which before existed in natural law, but which had been dispensed with, not for the benefit of the party obliged solely, but principally for the public convenience. If moral obligation, in its fullest sense, is a good substratum for an express promise, it is not easy to perceive why it is not equally good to support an implied promise. What a man ought to do, generally he ought to be made to do, whether he promise or refuse. But the law of society has left most of such obligations to the *interior* forum, as the tribunal of conscience has been aptly called. Is there not a moral obligation upon every son who has become affluent by means of the education and advantages bestowed upon him by his father, to relieve that father from pecuniary embarrassment, to promote his comfort, and happiness, and even to share with him his riches, if thereby he will be made happy? And yet such a son may, with impunity, leave such a father in any degree of penury above that which will expose the community in which he dwells, to the danger of being

Dear Sir:

I received a line from you relating to my Son Levi's sickness and requesting me to come up and see him, but as the going is very bad I cannot come up at the present, but I wish you to take all possible care of him and if you cannot have him at your house I wish you to remove him to some convenient place and if he cannot satisfy you for it I will.

I want that you should write me again immediately how he does and greatly oblige your most obedient servant

Seth Wyman Feb 24th 1821.

Geoffrey R. Watson, *In the Tribunal of Conscience: Mills v. Wyman Reconsidered*, 71 TUL. L. REV. 1749, 1758 (1997). Eds.

obliged to preserve him from absolute want. Is not a wealthy father under strong moral obligation to advance the interest of an obedient, well disposed son, to furnish him with the means of acquiring and maintaining a becoming rank in life, to rescue him from the horrors of debt incurred by misfortune? Yet the law will uphold him in any degree of parsimony, short of that which would reduce his son to the necessity of seeking public charity.

Without doubt there are great interests of society which justify withholding the coercive arm of the law from these duties of imperfect obligation, as they are called; imperfect, not because they are less binding upon the conscience than those which are called perfect, but because the wisdom of the social law does not impose sanctions upon them.

A deliberate promise in writing, made freely and without any mistake, one which may lead the party to whom it is made into contracts and expenses, cannot be broken without a violation of moral duty. But if there was nothing paid or promised for it, the law, perhaps wisely, leaves the execution of it to the conscience of him who makes it. It is only when the party making the promise gains something, or he to whom it is made loses something, that the law gives the promise validity. And in the case of a promise of an adult to pay the debt of the infant, of the debtor discharged by the statute of limitations or bankruptcy, the principle is preserved by looking back to the origin of the transaction, where an equivalent is to be found. An exact equivalent is not required by the law; for there being a consideration, the parties are left to estimate its value; though here the courts of equity will step in to relieve from gross inadequacy between the consideration and the promise.

These principles are deduced from the general current of decided cases upon the subject, as well as from the known maxims of the common law. The general position, that moral obligation is a sufficient consideration for an express promise, is to be limited in its application to cases where at some time or other a good or valuable consideration has existed.

　　　* * *

For the foregoing reasons, we are all of the opinion that the nonsuit directed by the Court of Common Pleas was right, and that judgment be entered thereon for the costs of the defendant.

————————

QUESTIONS AND NOTES

1. Questions about the facts of this case
    1.1. Who is suing whom for what?
    1.2. Why did the plaintiff Mills take care of Levi Wyman? Was he a doctor? Was he expecting to be paid?
    1.3. Why didn't Mills sue Levi Wyman's estate? Why did Mills sue Seth Wyman, Levi's father?

    1.4. Did Mills continue to take care of Levi Wyman after receiving the letter from the defendant? Is that important to the court's decision?

2. Questions about the law

    2.1. Did Chief Justice Parker conclude that Seth Wyman was morally obligated to pay the plaintiff for taking care of his son? What is the basis for any such moral obligation?

    2.2. Should Parker, C.J. have ruled that Seth Wyman's promise to pay Mills for the costs that Mills incurred in taking care of Seth's son was legally enforceable? Could Parker, C.J. have so ruled? Would Judge Judy, T.V. J, have so ruled?

    2.3. Is there a pre-existing duty issue in this case? Why not?

3. Notes

    3.1. Here's one writer's view of *Mills*:

Many lawyers remember great common-law cases more for their facts than their reasoning. Ask a lawyer about the holding of *Mills v. Wyman* and you probably get a blank look. Ask if the lawyer remembers the case about father promising to pay the Good Samaritan for caring for the sick son, and you may get a smile of recognition. * * * Everyone remembers the facts; no one remembers the holding.

For *Mills*, perhaps that is the way it should be. The rule in the case is eminently forgettable: it is as incoherent as it is inefficient. It will be a dead letter in another hundred years. But the facts of the case are memorable. Indeed, the story told by Justice Parker—Seth's hasty promise in a fleeting moment of gratitude, the death of Levi Wyman, Seth's willingness to stand up in court and be counted as a scoundrel—is more compelling than the story told by the surviving documents, in which Seth makes no promise, Levi does not die, and Seth deserves to win. For the law teacher, the reported facts stand as a morality play for lawyers and as a reminder of the limits of the profession. The mythical facts of Mills are an important part of our legal culture.

Geoffrey R. Watson, *In the Tribunal of Conscience:* Mills v. Wyman *Reconsidered*, 71 TUL. L. REV. 1749, 1806 (1997).

    3.2. Lord Mansfield, Lord Chief Justice from 1756 to 1788 of the King's Bench, and a giant figure in the development of the commercial law in England, authored several opinions advancing the view that the moral obligation associated with any *written* agreement ought to serve as a sufficient basis to make that agreement enforceable. *See, e.g., Hawkes v. Saunders*, 1 Cowper 289, 98 Eng. Rep. 1091 (K.B. 1782). He regarded the existence of the writing as a suitable substitute for the evidentiary and cautionary functions purportedly served by the doctrine of consideration or, in early time, the seal. However, by Mansfield's time, the requirement of consideration was too deeply embedded in the common law to be uprooted, although it was not until 1840 that moral obligation alone was eliminated in

England as satisfying the requirement of a good consideration for a promise. *See Eastwood v. Kenyon, 11 Ad. & E. 438, 113 Eng. Rep. 482.* As the decisions in *Harrington* and *Mills* illustrate, courts in this country were also skeptical of accepting moral obligation as a sufficient basis for enforcement of a promise. In *Manwill v. Oyler,* 11 Utah 2d 433, 361 P.2d 177, 178 (1961), the Utah Supreme Court expressed the generally-held sentiment that "if a mere moral, as distinguished from a legal, obligation were recognized as a valid consideration for a contract, that would practically erode to the vanishing point the necessity for finding a consideration" in the first place. Clearly, Chief Justice Parker in *Mills* was bothered by the defendant's abnegation of his promise, indicating his apparent disbelief that Wyman was "willing to have his case appear on record." How much of a deterrent do you suppose this form of shaming is likely to be in the case of persons already inclined to avoid their promises because of the technical absence of consideration?

3.3. The court in *Mills* makes reference to three circumstances in which the law has long recognized exceptions to the rule that past consideration is not good consideration: (1) a promise reviving a previously legally enforceable obligation now barred by an applicable limitations period, (2) a promise to pay an obligation rendered discharged by insolvency, and (3) a promise to pay an obligation incurred by an infant. The enforceability of the first type of promise—reviving an earlier enforceable obligation—is now recognized in *Restatement (Second) of Contracts* § 82, although many states also require a writing as a condition to the enforceability of such promises. *See, e.g., Manwill v. Oyler, supra.* As for the second type of promise, Section 83 of *Restatement (Second) of Contracts* provides that an express promise to pay all or part of a debt discharged in bankruptcy is binding. Since 1978, however, the matter has been preempted by the federal Bankruptcy Code, which expressly makes promises to repay a discharged debt unenforceable. On the other hand, agreements (called "reaffirmations") by a bankruptcy debtor to reinstate personal liability for debts that would otherwise be subject to the discharge may, subject to certain stringent conditions, be binding provided that they are entered into and approved by the court *prior* to the entry of the discharge in bankruptcy. *See Bankruptcy Code* §§ 524(c) & (d). In addition, purely *voluntary* repayment of discharged debts is permitted under the bankruptcy law. *See Bankruptcy Code* § 524(f). Finally, as to the third type of promise, modern courts continue to recognize that a minor with the power to avoid by disaffirmance his contractual obligations may, upon reaching the age of majority and without the requirement of new consideration, make a new enforceable undertaking to perform his duties under the contract. *See generally Restatement (Second) of Contracts* § 85.

3.4. The civil law has a little easier time with these cases, as illustrated by the following decision, bearing remarkable factual similarity to

Mills v. Wyman, but decided under the Louisiana Civil Code rather than the common law.

WEBB v. McGOWIN

Court of Appeals of Alabama
27 Ala.App. 82, 168 So. 196 (1935)

BRICKEN, PRESIDING JUDGE.

This action is in assumpsit. The complaint as originally filed was amended. The demurrers to the complaint as amended were sustained, and because of this adverse ruling by the court the plaintiff took a non-suit, and the assignment of errors on this appeal are predicated upon said action or ruling of the court.

A fair statement of the case presenting the questions for decision is set out in appellant's brief, which we adopt.

"On the 3d day of August, 1925, appellant while in the employ of the W. T. Smith Lumber Company, a corporation, and acting within the scope of his employment, was engaged in clearing the upper floor of mill No. 2 of the company. While so engaged he was in the act of dropping a pine block from the upper floor of the mill to the ground below; this being the usual and ordinary way of clearing the floor, and it being the duty of the plaintiff in the course of his employment to so drop it. The block weighed about 75 pounds.

"As appellant was in the act of dropping the block to the ground below, he was on the edge of the upper floor of the mill. As he started to turn the block loose so that it would drop to the ground, he saw J. Greeley McGowin, testator of the defendants, on the ground below and directly under where the block would have fallen had appellant turned it loose. Had he turned it loose it would have struck McGowin with such force as to have caused him serious bodily harm or death. Appellant could have remained safely on the upper floor of the mill by turning the block loose and allowing it to drop, but had he done this the block would have fallen on McGowin and cause him serious injuries or death. The only safe and reasonable way to prevent this was for appellant to hold to the block and divert its direction in falling from the place where McGowin was standing and the only safe way to divert it so as to prevent its coming into contact with McGowin was for appellant to fall with it to the ground below. Appellant did this, and by holding to the block and falling with it to the ground below, he diverted the course of its fall in such way that McGowin was not injured. In thus preventing the injuries to McGowin appellant himself received serious bodily injuries, resulting in his right leg being broken, the heel of his right foot torn off and his right arm broken. He was badly crippled for life and rendered unable to do physical or mental labor.

"On September 1, 1925, in consideration of appellant having prevented him from sustaining death or serious bodily harm and in consideration of the injuries appellant had received, McGowin agreed with him to care for and maintain him for the remainder of appellant's life at the rate of $15 every two weeks from the time he sustained his injuries to and during the remainder of appellant's life; it being agreed that McGowin would pay this sum to appellant for his maintenance. Under the agreement McGowin paid or caused to be paid to appellant the sum so agreed on up until McGowin's death on January 1, 1934. After his death the payments were continued to and including January 27, 1934, at which time they were discontinued. Thereupon plaintiff brought suit to recover the unpaid installments accruing up to the time of the bringing of the suit.

"The material averments of the different counts of the original complaint and the amended complaint are predicated upon the foregoing statement of facts."

In other words, the complaint as amended averred in substance: (1) That on August 3, 1925, appellant saved J. Greeley McGowin, appellee's testator, from death or grievous bodily harm; (2) that in doing so appellant sustained bodily injury crippling him for life; (3) that in consideration of the services rendered and the injuries received by appellant, McGowin agreed to care for him the remainder of appellant's life, the amount to be paid being $15 every two weeks; (4) that McGowin complied with this agreement until he died on January 1, 1934, and the payments were kept up to January 27, 1934, after which they were discontinued.

The action was for the unpaid installments accruing after January 27, 1934, to the time of the suit.

The principal grounds of demurrer to the original and amended complaint are: (1) It states no cause of action; (2) its averments show the contract was without consideration; (3) it fails to allege that McGowin had, at or before the services were rendered, agreed to pay appellant for them; (4) the contract declared on is void under the statute of frauds.

1. The averments of the complaint show that appellant saved McGowin from death or grievous bodily harm. This was a material benefit to him of infinitely more value than any financial aid he could have received. Receiving this benefit, McGowin became morally bound to compensate appellant for the services rendered. Recognizing his moral obligation, he expressly agreed to pay appellant as alleged in the complaint and complied with this agreement up to the time of his death; a period of more than 8 years.

Had McGowin been accidentally poisoned and a physician, without his knowledge or request, had administered an antidote, thus saving his life, a subsequent promise by McGowin to pay the physician would have been valid. Likewise, McGowin's agreement as disclosed by the complaint to compensate appellant for saving him from death or grievous bodily injury is valid and enforceable.

Where the promisee cares for, improves, and preserves the property of the promisor, though done without his request, it is sufficient consideration for the promisor's subsequent agreement to pay for the service, because of the material benefit received. * * *

In *Boothe v. Fitzpatrick,* 36 Vt. 681, the court held that a promise by defendant to pay for the past keeping of a bull which had escaped from defendant's premises and been cared for by plaintiff was valid, although there was no previous request, because the subsequent promise obviated that objection; it being equivalent to a previous request. On the same principle, had the promisee saved the promisor's life or his body from grievous harm, his subsequent promise to pay for the services rendered would have been valid. Such service would have been far more material than caring for his bull. Any holding that saving a man from death or grievous bodily harm is not a material benefit sufficient to uphold a subsequent promise to pay for the service, necessarily rests on the assumption that saving life and preservation of the body from harm have only a sentimental value. The converse of this is true. Life and preservation of the body have material, pecuniary values, measurable in dollars and cents. Because of this, physicians practice their profession charging for services rendered in saving life and curing the body of its ills, and surgeons perform operations. The same is true as to the law of negligence, authorizing the assessment of damages in personal injury cases based upon the extent of the injuries, earnings, and life expectancies of those injured.

In the business of life insurance, the value of a man's life is measured in dollars and cents according to his expectancy, the soundness of his body, and his ability to pay premiums. The same is true as to health and accident insurance.

It follows that if, as alleged in the complaint, appellant saved J. Greeley McGowin from death or grievous bodily harm, and McGowin subsequently agreed to pay him for the service rendered, it became a valid and enforceable contract.

2. It is well settled that a moral obligation is a sufficient consideration to support a subsequent promise to pay where the promisor has received a material benefit, although there was no original duty or liability resting on the promisor. * * * In the case of *State ex rel. Bayer v. Funk, supra,* [105 Or. 134, 199 P. 592] the court held that a moral obligation is a sufficient consideration to support an executory promise where the promisor has received an actual pecuniary or material benefit for which he subsequently expressly promised to pay.

The case at bar is clearly distinguishable from that class of cases where the consideration is a mere moral obligation or conscientious duty unconnected with receipt by promisor of benefits of a material or pecuniary nature. * * * Here the promisor received a material benefit constituting a valid consideration for his promise.

3.   Some authorities hold that, for a moral obligation to support a subsequent promise to pay, there must have existed a prior legal or equitable obligation, which for some reason had become unenforceable, but for which the promisor was still morally bound. This rule, however, is subject to qualification in those cases where the promisor, having received a material benefit from the promisee, is morally bound to compensate him for the services rendered and in consideration of this obligation promises to pay. In such cases the subsequent promise to pay is an affirmance or ratification of the services rendered carrying with it the presumption that a previous request for the service was made. * * *

Under the decisions above cited, McGowin's express promise to pay appellant for the services rendered was an affirmance or ratification of what appellant had done raising the presumption that the services had been rendered at McGowin's request.

4.   The averments of the complaint show that in saving McGowin from death or grievous bodily harm, appellant was crippled for life. This was part of the consideration of the contract declared on. McGowin was benefited. Appellant was injured. Benefit to the promisor or injury to the promisee is a sufficient legal consideration for the promisor's agreement to pay. * * *

5.   Under the averments of the complaint the services rendered by appellant were not gratuitous. The agreement of McGowin to pay and the acceptance of payment by appellant conclusively shows the contrary.

6.   The contract declared on was not void under the statute of frauds.
* * *

From what has been said, we are of the opinion that the court below erred in the ruling complained of; that is to say, in sustaining the demurrer, and for this error the case is reversed and remanded.

SAMFORD, JUDGE (Concurring)

The questions involved in this case are not free from doubt, and perhaps the strict letter of the rule, as stated by judges, though not always in accord, would bar a recovery by plaintiff, but following the principle announced by Chief Justice Marshall in *Hoffman v. Porter, Fed.Cas. No. 6,577,* 2 Brock. 156, 159, where he says, "I do not think that law ought to be separated from justice, where it is at most doubtful," I concur in the conclusions reached by the court.

WEBB v. McGOWIN

Supreme Court of Alabama
232 Ala. 374, 168 So. 199 (1936)

FOSTER, J

We do not in all cases in which we deny a petition for certiorari to the Court of Appeals approve the reasoning and principles declared in the opinion, even though no opinion is rendered by us. But when the opinion of the Court of Appeals asserts important principles or their application to new situations, and it may be uncertain whether this court agrees with it in all respects, we think it advisable to be specific in that respect when the certiorari is denied. We think such a situation here exists.

Neither this court nor the Court of Appeals has had before it questions similar to those here presented.

The opinion of the Court of Appeals here under consideration recognized and applies the distinction between a supposed moral obligation of the promisor, based upon some refined sense of ethical duty, without material benefit to him, and one in which such a benefit did in fact occur. We agree with that court that if the benefit be material and substantial, and was to the person of the promisor rather than to his estate, it is within the class of material benefits which he has the privilege of recognizing and compensating either by an executed payment or an executory promise to pay. The cases are cited in that opinion. The reason is emphasized when the compensation is not only for the benefits which the promisor received, but also for the injuries either to the property or person of the promisee by reason of the service rendered.

Writ denied.

QUESTIONS, NOTES, AND CONNECTIONS

1. Questions about the facts of this case

    1.1. Was there a written promise in *Webb*?

    1.2. Why was plaintiff paid $15 every two weeks until January 27, 1934? Why did the payments stop on January 27, 1934?

    1.3. Can the facts of *Webb* be distinguished from the facts of *Mills*? Which, if any, of the factual differences explain the different legal result?

    1.4. Recall that in *Webb* the Alabama Court of Appeals reproduced the statement of facts from the appellant/plaintiff's brief. What were the grounds for the defendant's demurrers that were sustained by the trial court?

2. Questions about the law

    2.1. Did the Court of Appeals in *Webb* hold that there was an agreement to pay plaintiff $15 every two weeks? That there was consideration for such a promise?

    2.2. Would a court applying any of our definitions of consideration hold that such a promise was enforceable because of consideration?

    2.3. Both the Alabama Court of Appeals decision and the Alabama Supreme Court decision mention "material benefit." The Reporter to *Restatement (Second) of Contracts* described section 86, set out below, as a "material benefit rule":*

§ 86. *Promise for Benefit Received*

(1) A promise made in recognition of a benefit previously received by the promisor from the promisee is binding to the extent necessary to prevent injustice.

(2) A promise is not binding under Subsection (1):

(a) if the promisee conferred the benefit as a gift or for other reasons the promisor has not unjustly enriched; or

(b) to the extent that its value is disproportionate to the benefit.

How would *Webb* be decided by a court applying this *Restatement* provision? How would *Mills* be decided by a court applying this *Restatement* provision? Is there a difference between *Webb* and *Mills* in terms of the circumstances under which the services were rendered? If so, does this help you reconcile the decisions? Can you reconcile *Webb* and *Harrington* on the same basis?

3. Notes

3.1. Professor Charles Fried, a Harvard law professor, described the Alabama Court of Appeals decision in *Webb* as "a process of reasoning too strained to repeat." CHARLES FRIED, CONTRACT AS PROMISE 33 (1981). Do you agree?

3.2. While moral obligation and past consideration as bases for enforcing a promise have always presented some problems for the common law, the civil law has long recognized the concept of "natural obligation". A natural obligation exists when there is a moral, but not judicially enforceable, duty to render performance where "the law implies a particular moral duty to render a performance." La. Civ. Code Ann. art. 1760. *See also* Thomas v. Bryant, 639 So.2d 378 (La. Ct. App. 1994).

3.3. In his widely-celebrated book, THE DEATH OF CONTRACT, written in 1974, Professor Grant Gilmore, pointing to the general direction being taken in the *Restatement (Second) of Contracts*, concluded that, "we might say that what is happening is that 'contract' is being reabsorbed into the mainstream of 'tort.' " *Id.* at 95. As one of the primary illustrations of this trend, Professor Gilmore pointed to allowing enforcement of a promise made in recognition of a past benefit. He noted: "The principal thing is that *Restatement (Second)* gives overt recognition to an important principle whose existence *Restatement (First)* ignored and, by implication denied. By the time we get to Restatement (Third) it may well be that § 89A* will have flowered like Jack's bean-stalk in the same way that § 90 did between *Restatement (First)* and *Restatement (Second)*." *Id.* at 76.

---

* Robert Braucher, *Freedom of Contract and the Second Restatement*, 78 YALE L. J. 598, 615 (1969).

* Section 89A, to which Professor Gilmore refers, became § 86 in the final draft of the *Restatement (Second)*. Eds.

3.4. Twenty-one years later, Professor Kastely offered the following evaluation of this prediction:

> This prediction has not proved true. Very few reported decisions since 1974 have even mentioned Section 86, and most of those references have been made only in passing, often in reference to contract actions barred by the statute of limitations. I have found only four reported decisions involving Section 86; in two, the courts found that Section 86 would not support enforcement of the promise. Moreover, the two cases holding that Section 86 might support enforcement of the promise involve situations that fit a traditional quasi-contract model**—one involved service rendered by a broker and another care provided by a sister. These cases do not represent movement toward the idea that "to prevent unjust enrichment, any benefit received by a defendant must be paid for unless it was clearly meant as a gift" as Gilmore suggested.
>
> Following some initial expansion, many courts have domesticated the doctrines of promissory estoppel and promise for benefit received, making them compatible with classical contract theory, or at least much less of a threat to it. Most current versions of these doctrines offer little threat to the idea that no one should be liable for anything, at least not anything that she or he has not explicitly agreed to do. It seems that the pressures of contract ideology are so strong that, over time, they have reshaped the rebellious versions of these doctrines, fitting them into line with contract ideology.
>
> Amy H. Kastely, *Cogs or Cyborgs, Blasphemy and Irony in Contract Theories*, 90 NW. U. L. REV. 132, 138–39 (1995).

4. Connections

Think back to the purposes for the doctrine of bargained-for consideration, as discussed in earlier sections of this chapter, as the basic ingredient necessary for an agreement to be legally enforceable. How are those purposes served by enforcement of a promise made in recognition of a benefit previously conferred? How are they done violence? Do you think moral obligation alone should provide a sufficient basis for enforcement?

In the eighteenth century, long after the doctrine of consideration had been firmly rooted in English law, Lord Chief Justice Mansfield attempted to introduce the proposition that any moral obligation arising from a promise should be sufficient to make non-performance of that promise actionable. Eager to break down the barriers between law and equity, and to apply equitable principles in the operation of the common law, Lord Mansfield opined that consideration had only evidentiary value and was not essential to the validity of a contract. But the tradition of the common law was too strong even for Lord Mansfield, whose opinion was overruled by the House of Lords, which reasserted that need for consideration in all contracts.

One of the most famous more contemporary promissory theories is the account put forward by Harvard Law Professor (and former Solicitor

---

** We take up the subject of "quasi contract" in Chapter 7. Eds.

General) Charles Fried in his book, CONTRACT AS PROMISE: A THEORY OF CONTRACTUAL OBLIGATION (1981). In Professor Fried's view, "promising" is seen as a device fashioned by free individuals on the premise of mutual trust, and which gains moral force from that trust. Thus, comparable to lying, the breaking of a promise warrants legal sanction based on the values of individual autonomy and trust, without regard to the existence *vel non* of a bargained for exchange.

What role does moral obligation play in *Mills v. Wyman*? Ask yourself the same question with respect to the cases that follow in the next subsection dealing with another recognized "consideration substitute," reliance.

SECTION 3: RELIANCE AND THE LEGAL CONCEPT OF PROMISSORY ESTOPPEL

A. OVERVIEW

Recall Ms. Chandler and her promise to Ponoroff of a Hummer. When she changed her mind, her promise was not legally enforceable, because there was no consideration.

What if, after Ms. Chandler's promise, Ponoroff, in reliance on Chandler's promise, gave his car to a charity *www.AmericasCars–ForKids.org* and built a new, larger garage to protect the Hummer from Arizona weather. Should her promise of a Hummer now be legally enforceable?

Classical contract law was primarily concerned with protecting the promisee's expectation interest in an exchange transaction. The requirement of consideration, as we have seen, ensures that promises that are part of a bargained-for exchange will be enforceable. By the same token, mere reliance on a promise that was not part of an economic exchange was not cognizable in the eyes of the law; hence, the adage that gift promises are not enforceable. Nonetheless, there are circumstances where leaving a party who detrimentally changed her position in reliance on a promise without a remedy of any sort was perceived as unduly harsh. Accordingly, one of the most important developments in contract law over the course of the twentieth century was the evolution of the principle that, in an appropriate case, unbargained-for reliance may provide a suitable basis for enforcing a promise, even in a non-exchange transaction. This evolution culminated in the *Restatement (Second) of Contracts'* revision of § 90, which now provides:

> *(1) A promise which the promisor should reasonably expect to induce action or forbearance on the part of the promisee or a third person and which does induce such action or forbearance is binding if injustice can be avoided only by enforcement of the promise. The remedy granted for breach may be limited as justice requires.*

Compare this formulation with § 90 of the first <u>Restatement</u> of Contracts

> *A promise which the promisor should reasonably expect to induce action or forbearance of a definite and substantial character on the part of the promisee and which does induce such action or forbearance is binding if injustice can be avoided only by enforcement of the promise.*

Section 90 has been described as "perhaps the most radical and expansive development of this century in the law of promissory liability." *See* Charles L. Knapp, *Reliance in the Revised* Restatement: *The Proliferation of Promissory Estoppel*, 81 COLUM. L. REV. 52, 52 (1981). Reliance, or more properly, compensation for harm suffered as a consequence of reliance on a promise, plays a central role in the *Restatement (Second)*. Section 90 offers a mechanism whereby a purely gratuitous promise might be enforced. In fact, one might not unfairly regard reliance as a substitute for consideration in cases to which § 90 applies. Thus, § 90 has vastly expanded the potential scope of contractual responsibility to the point, at least according to one commentator, that it has "swallowed up the bargain principle" embodied in the doctrine of consideration. GRANT GILMORE, THE DEATH OF CONTRACT 77 (1974).

From where did this seemingly revolutionary doctrine arise? Professor Williston is generally given credit for coining the term "promissory estoppel" in the first edition of his famous Contracts treatise originally published in 1920. 1 WILLISTON ON CONTRACTS § 139 (1st ed. 1920). Not surprisingly, Williston was instrumental in the incorporation of the doctrine of promissory estoppel into the first *Restatement of Contracts* in the form of § 90, quoted above. In Anglo–American jurisprudence, however, the roots of the doctrine go back to at least the nineteenth century, although, as we see in our first case, the courts were not always sure as to the category of the law to which the doctrine belonged.

B. HISTORICAL DEVELOPMENT

RICKETTS v. SCOTHORN

Supreme Court of Nebraska
57 Neb. 51, 77 N.W. 365 (1898)

[handwritten margin note: Enforcement of non-bargain promises based on reliance]

SULLIVAN, J.

In the district court of Lancaster county the plaintiff, Katie Scothorn, recovered judgment against the defendant, Andrew D. Ricketts, as executor of the last will and testament of John C. Ricketts, deceased. The action was based upon a promissory note, of which the following is a copy:

> "May the first, 1891. I promise to pay to Katie Scothorn on demand, $2,000, to be at 6 per cent. per annum. J. C. Ricketts."

In the petition the plaintiff alleges that the consideration for the execution of the note was that she should surrender her employment as bookkeeper for Mayer Bros., and cease to work for a living. She also alleges that the note was given to induce her to abandon her occupation, and that, relying on it, and on the annual interest, as a means of support, she gave up the employment in which she was then engaged. These allegations of the petition are denied by the administrator. The material facts are undisputed. They are as follows: John C. Ricketts, the maker of the note, was the grandfather of the plaintiff. Early in May—presumably on the day the note bears date—he called on her at the store where she was working. What transpired between them is thus described by Mr. Flodene, one of the plaintiff's witnesses:

> "A. Well, the old gentleman came in there one morning about nine o'clock, probably a little before or a little after, but early in the morning, and he unbuttoned his vest, and took out a piece of paper in the shape of a note; that is the way it looked to me; and he says to Miss Scothorn, 'I have fixed out something that you have not got to work any more.' He says, none of my grandchildren work, and you don't have to.
>
> Q.   Where was she?
>
> A.   She took the piece of paper and kissed him, and kissed the old gentleman, and commenced to cry."

It seems Miss Scothorn immediately notified her employer of her intention to quit work, and that she did soon after abandon her occupation. The mother of the plaintiff was a witness, and testified that she had a conversation with her father, Mr. Ricketts, shortly after the note was executed, in which he informed her that he had given the note to the plaintiff to enable her to quit work; that none of his grandchildren worked, and he did not think she ought to. For something more than a year the plaintiff was without an occupation, but in September, 1892, with the consent of her grandfather, and by his assistance, she secured a position as bookkeeper with Messrs. Funke & Ogden. On June 8, 1894, Mr. Ricketts died. He had paid one year's interest on the note, and a short time before his death expressed regret that he had not been able to pay the balance. In the summer or fall of 1892 he stated to his daughter, Mrs. Scothorn, that if he could sell his farm in Ohio he would pay the note out of the proceeds. He at no time repudiated the obligation. We quite agree with counsel for the defendant that upon this evidence there was nothing to submit to the jury, and that a verdict should have been directed peremptorily for one of the parties. The testimony of Flodene and Mrs. Scothorn, taken together, conclusively establishes the fact that the note was not given in consideration of the plaintiff pursuing, or agreeing to pursue, any particular line of conduct. There was no promise on the part of the plaintiff to do, or refrain from doing, anything. Her right to the money promised in the note was not made to depend upon an abandonment of her employment with Mayer Bros., and future abstention from like service. Mr. Ricketts made no condition, requirement, or request. He exacted no quid pro quo. He gave the note as a gratuity, and looked for nothing in return. So far as the evidence discloses, it was his purpose to place the plaintiff in a position of independence, where she could work or remain idle, as she might choose. The abandonment of Miss Scothorn of her position as bookkeeper was altogether voluntary. It was not an act done in fulfillment of any contract obligation assumed when she accepted the note. The instrument in suit, being given without any valuable consideration, was nothing more than a promise to make a gift in the future of the sum of money therein named. Ordinarily, such promises are not enforceable, even when put in the form of a promissory note. * * * But it has often been held that an action on a note given to a church, college, or other like institution, upon the faith of which money has been expended or obligations incurred, could not be successfully defended on the ground of a want of consideration. * * * In this class of cases the note in suit is nearly always spoken of as a gift or donation, but the decision is generally put on the ground that the expenditure of money or assumption of liability by the donee on the faith of the promise constitutes a valuable and sufficient consideration. It seems to us that the true reason is the preclusion of the defendant, under the doctrine of estoppel, to deny the consideration. Such seems to be the view of the matter taken by the supreme court of Iowa in the case of *Simpson Centenary College v. Tuttle,* 71 Iowa, 596, 33 N. W. 74, where Rothrock, J., speaking for the court, said:

> Where a note, however, is based on a promise to give for the support of the objects referred to, it may still be open to this defense [want of consideration], unless it shall appear that the donee has, prior to any revocation, entered into engagements, or made expenditures based on such promise, so that he must suffer loss or injury if the note is not paid. This is based on the equitable principle that, after allowing the donee to incur obligations on the faith that the note would be paid, the donor would be estopped from pleading want of consideration.

And in the case of *Reimensnyder v. Gans,* 110 Pa. St. 17, 2 Atl. 425, which was an action on a note given as a donation to a charitable object, the court said: "The fact is that, as we may see from the case of *Ryerss v. Trustees,* 33 Pa. St. 114, a contract of the kind here involved is enforceable rather by way of estoppel than on the ground of consideration in the original undertaking." It has been held that a note given in expectation of the payee performing certain services, but without any contract binding him to serve, will not support an action. *Hulse v. Hulse,* 84 E. C. L. 709. But when the payee changes his position to his disadvantage in reliance on the promise, a right of action does arise. * * *

Under the circumstances of this case, is there an equitable estoppel which ought to preclude the defendant from alleging that the note in controversy is lacking in one of the essential elements of a valid contract? We think there is. An estoppel in pais is defined to be "a right arising from acts, admissions, or conduct which have induced a change of position in accordance with the real or apparent intention of the party against whom they are alleged." Mr. Pomeroy has formulated the following definition: "Equitable estoppel is the effect of the voluntary conduct of a party whereby he is absolutely precluded, both at law and in equity, from asserting rights which might, perhaps, have otherwise existed, either of property, of contract, or of remedy, as against another person who in good faith relied upon such conduct, and has been led thereby to change his position for the worse, and who on his part acquires some corresponding right, either of property, of contract, or of remedy." 2 Pom. Eq. Jur. 804. According to the undisputed proof, as shown by the record before us, the plaintiff was a working girl, holding a position in which she earned a salary of $10 per week. Her grandfather, desiring to put her in a position of independence, gave her the note, accompanying it with the remark that his other grandchildren did not work, and that she would not be obliged to work any longer. In effect, he suggested that she might abandon her employment, and rely in the future upon the bounty which he promised. He doubtless desired that she should give up her occupation, but, whether he did or not, it is entirely certain that he contemplated such action on her part as a reasonable and probable consequence of his gift. Having intentionally influenced the plaintiff to alter her position for the worse on the faith of the note being paid when due, it would be grossly inequitable to permit the maker, or his executor, to resist payment on the ground that the promise was given without consideration. The petition charges the elements of an equitable estoppel, and the evidence conclusively establishes them. If errors intervened at the trial, they could not have been prejudicial. A verdict for the defendant would be unwarranted. The judgment is right, and is affirmed.

QUESTIONS AND NOTES

1. Questions about the facts of this case
    1.1. Why did Katie's grandfather offer to pay her the $2,000? Did he want her to quit her job?
    1.2. Did Katie quit her job? Do we know whether grandfather's offer was the reason that she quit?
2. Questions about the law
    2.1. Equitable estoppel (estoppel *in pais*) is a doctrine that prohibits one party from asserting the truth of a matter previously misrepresented by that party. The elements of equitable estoppel are "conduct by one party which leads another party, in reliance thereon, to adopt a course of action resulting in detriment or damage if the first party is permitted to repudiate his conduct." *United American Life Insurance Co. v. Zions First National Bank,* 641 P.2d 158 (Utah 1982). In this case, Katie's grandfather's estate was estopped to deny the existence of consideration for the promise to pay her $2,000. But did John Ricketts ever misrepresent that there was consideration for his promise? What's going on here? Is this a

proper application of the doctrine of equitable estoppel? If not, why do you suppose the court invoked the doctrine?

2.2.   Why wasn't Katie's quitting her job consideration for the promise? Is there any less of a bargain here in terms of benefit to the promisor or detriment to the promisee than in *Hamer v. Sidway, supra*?

2.3.   Would Katie have been better off if the court accepted the argument made in the original petition that John Ricketts' execution of the note met the traditional requirements for enforcement, *i.e.*, that it was supported by consideration?

2.4.   Suppose Katie had taken her old job back a week after her grandfather's promise. Would she have been in breach? Even if not, would she have been entitled to recover the whole $2,000? How would the case come out under *Restatement (Second) of Contracts* § 90? What are the similarities between the first and second *Restatements'* versions of § 90? What are the differences?

3.   Notes

3.1.   Until fairly recently, enforcement of non-bargain promises based on reliance was limited to certain categories of cases that existed outside of or on the periphery of the marketplace and where the equities favoring enforcement were unusually compelling. Most notable among these was the willingness of courts to enforce gratuitous promises made to charitable organizations. Sometimes courts would do this by stretching the doctrine of consideration. For example, in *Allegheny College v. National Chautauqua County Bank,* 246 N.Y. 369, 159 N.E. 173 (1927), Justice Cardozo concluded that the donor's desire for posthumous remembrance, coupled with the college's agreement to set up a memorial fund in her name, constituted good consideration to support the donor's pledge to have her estate pay the college $5,000 thirty days after her death. Other courts took a more direct approach to enforcing donative promises by invoking an estoppel in situations where the donee could demonstrate detrimental reliance on the promise. *See, e.g., Gittings v. Mayhew,* 6 Md. 113 (1854). For more than you ever wanted to know about Justice Cardozo's *Allegheny College* opinion, see Markell's summary and analysis on the Internet at http://www2.law.cornell.edu/cgi-bin/foliocgi.exe/Allegheny. Today, in spite of its halting and at times uncertain origins, promissory estoppel is regularly applied in a wide variety of commercial contexts as demonstrated by the cases that follow in this section.

3.2.   Students (and sometimes courts) are often confused by the distinction between a promissory and an equitable estoppel. While doctrinally distinct, the two can sometimes overlap. Consider the following scenario: Suppose Ponoroff signs a promissory note promising to pay Epstein $24,000 in 48 equal monthly installments of $500 each together with interest. The note expressly provides that payments are due on the first of each month and that, in the event of non-payment, Epstein shall have the right to declare the entire debt due and owing in full (*i.e.*, an "acceleration" clause). For the first 18 months, Ponoroff makes all the required payments, but always pays between the 5th and the 10th of the month. Epstein says nothing about this. However, when Epstein fails to receive the 19th monthly payment on the first of the month Epstein immediately declares a default. Even though Ponoroff promptly tenders the past due monthly installment, Epstein brings suit for breach of contract seeking recovery of the entire outstanding balance of the note. In Ponoroff's defense (usually something nobody is much interested in, but then this is a hypothetical), can you successfully raise a defense based on estoppel? Is that an equitable or a promissory estoppel? Are there any other defenses you can think of? What if the contract rate of interest was 6% and the market rate of interest had risen over 18 months to 11%?

C. CONTEMPORARY APPLICATIONS OF THE DOCTRINE

DARGO v. CLEAR CHANNEL COMMUNICATIONS, INCORPORATED

United States District Court for the Northern District of Illinois
2008 WL 2225812 (2008)   *trial court*

VIRGINIA M. KENDALL, UNITED STATES DISTRICT JUDGE.

Plaintiff Kassie Dargo (a/k/a Kassie Banister) ("Dargo") brought suit against Defendant Clear Channel Communications, Incorporated ("Clear Channel") in the Circuit Court of Cook County alleging Promissory Estoppel, Intentional Misrepresentation, Negligent Misrepresentation, and Intentional Infliction of Emotional Distress. Clear Channel removed the case to this Court based on diversity jurisdiction. Clear Channel then moved to dismiss Dargo's Complaint.

STATEMENT OF FACTS

At the time the incidents leading to this suit occurred, Dargo had worked as an on-air radio personality for eight years and was working in a sales position at WLUP–FM in Chicago, Illinois. Rob Morris, Program Director of radio station KDWB in Minneapolis, Minnesota ("Morris") contacted Dargo in March of 2007 and began to recruit her for a morning co-host position.

Dargo and Morris engaged in extensive negotiations in March of 2007. During the negotiations, Dargo told Morris that she would require an increase in compensation to induce her to leave Chicago. Morris repeatedly promised Dargo that Clear Channel would provide her with a two-year employment contract.

In April of 2007, Dargo and Clear Channel agreed upon a two-year contract with a base salary of $60,000 for her first year and a base salary of $63,000 for her second year with the opportunity to earn additional income through promotional appearances. Morris sent an offer letter to Dargo via email on April 18, 2007. Morris stated in that email that the agreed upon two-year employment contract would be forthcoming within a month.

In reliance upon the promise of higher pay and a two-year contract, Dargo resigned her position at WLUP–FM and relocated from Chicago to Minneapolis where she signed a one-year lease for housing. During her employment at KDWB, she received no negative performance feedback but rather was reassured that everything was going well.

Dargo repeatedly inquired about the status of her two-year contract, and Morris repeatedly told her that the contract was being drafted and would be ready shortly. Specifically, after becoming concerned by the fact that she still had not received her contract in June of 2007, Dargo spoke to Morris, who assured her that everything was going well and that the contract would be delivered in a day or two.

However, Morris met with Dargo on June 19, 2007 and terminated her employment effective immediately. At this time, she learned that Clear Channel never intended to enter into a two-year contract with her and that she actually never had a position at KDWB. Defendant actually wanted to audition Dargo for a potential position but knowing that she would not agree to relocate without a guarantee of permanent employment, induced her with the promise of a two-year contract. Morris and Clear Channel had no intention to provide such a contract.

Since Dargo had no contacts in Minneapolis, she relocated to Chicago at her own expense. Clear Channel informed trade publications that she was returning to Chicago for "personal reasons," knowing that this was false. This damaged Dargo's reputation and caused her difficulty in finding a new job.

STANDARD

When considering a motion to dismiss under *Rule 12(b)(6)*, a court must accept as true all facts alleged in the complaint and construe all reasonable inferences in favor of the plaintiff. * * * However, in order to survive a motion to dismiss for failure to state a claim, the claim must be supported by facts that, if taken as true, at least plausibly suggest that the plaintiff is entitled to relief. Such a set of facts must "raise a reasonable expectation that discovery will reveal evidence" of illegality.

DISCUSSION

Promissory Estoppel

In order to establish a claim of promissory estoppel under Illinois law, Dargo must show that 1) the defendant made an unambiguous promise to her; 2) she relied on that promise; 3) her reliance was expected and foreseeable; and 4) to her detriment. *Dumas v. Infinity Broad. Corp., 416*

F.3d 671, 677 (7th Cir. 2005) Under Illinois law, claims of promissory estoppel only succeed where all other elements of a contract exist but consideration is lacking. Under such circumstances, promissory estoppel serves as a substitute for consideration. It follows that there is no gap for promissory estoppel to fill when consideration exists.

Here, Dargo pleads herself out of court by alleging facts establishing consideration for her claimed agreement with Clear Channel. Although simple relinquishment of a prior job is generally insufficient consideration, "being lured away from an existing job with the promise of permanent employment" is generally sufficient. *Kamboj v. Eli Lilly and Co.,* No. 05 C 4023, 2007 WL 178434, at * 8 (N.D.Ill. January 18, 2007)). Notably, in *Kamboj,* the court found consideration where the plaintiff moved from Indianapolis to Chicago in order to accept a job offered by the defendant. Quite similarly, Dargo asserts that in reliance on the promise of a two-year contract with Clear Channel, she resigned her position and relocated from Chicago to Minneapolis. This detriment is enough to establish consideration and thus render promissory estoppel inapplicable. Thus, Count I is dismissed with prejudice.

* * *

So ordered.*

QUESTIONS AND NOTE

1.   Questions about the facts of this case

    1.1.   What exactly did Clear Channel promise Dargo?

    1.2.   The court says of Dargo, "she actually never had a position at KDWB". Is that true? What was the nature of Dargo's employment relationship with Clear Channel?

    1.3.   In what ways did Dargo rely on Clear Channel's promise of a two-year employment contract?

2.   Questions about the law

    2.1.   What are the elements of a claim based on promissory estoppel according to the court? What element(s) was missing in Dargo's complaint?

    2.2.   According to the court, what is the purpose of the doctrine of promissory estoppel?

    2.3.   Was Dargo's moving from Chicago to Minneapolis really consideration for Clear Channel's promise? How would the court in *Kirksey v. Kirksey, supra* p. 232, regard the *Dargo* court's explanation of consideration?

---

* The court similarly granted the defendant's motion to dismiss the negligent misrepresentation and intentional infliction of emotional distress claims. Thus, only the intentional misrepresentation claim survived the Rule 12(b)(6) challenge to the complaint (Eds.).

2.4. If, as the court states, there was never a promise of a two-year contract, then why are we even talking about consideration?

3. Note

It is has been noted that although the doctrine of promissory estoppel in the United States derived from certain English common law concepts, there is still no unified theory of promissory estoppel in English contract law today. *See* Joel M. Ngugi, *Promissory Estoppel: The Life History of and Ideal Legal Transplant,* 41 U. RICH. L. REV. 425 (2007). Promissory estoppel is a creature of the common law, ordinarily thought to be unknown to the civil law. *See* David V. Snyder, *Comparative Law in Action: Promissory Estoppel, The Civil Law, and the Mixed Jurisdiction,* 15 ARIZ. J. INT'L & COMP. LAW 695, 704 (1998) (point out that the flexibility of the doctrine of cause, compared to the stringencies of bargained-for consideration, has arguably lessened the need for promissory estoppel in the civil law).

The court in *Dargo*, stated, "there is no gap for promissory estoppel to fill when consideration exists." Consider that statement in light of the next case.

FORTRESS SYSTEMS, L.L.C. v. BANK OF THE WEST

United States District Court, D. Nebraska   *trial court*
2008 WL 64690 (2008)

BATAILLON, DISTRICT JUDGE:

On February 13, 2006, Fortress Systems, LLC ("Fortress") filed this action against the defendant, Bank of the West, in the District Court of Douglas County, Nebraska and, on March 8, 2006, filed an amended complaint. The First Amended Complaint alleged breach of contract (Count I), promissory estoppel (Count II), and breach of duty of good faith and fair dealing (Count III). The Bank removed the case to this court on March 23, 2006. In response to the Bank's motion, this court granted summary judgment in favor of the Bank as to Fortress's breach of contract (Count I) and breach of duty of good faith and fair dealing (Count II) claims. The court conducted a jury trial in this matter November 26–30, 2007. After four days of evidence, the jury returned answers to Special Interrogatories.

The court has heard all the testimony and has before it all of the evidence presented in the case. Based upon the testimony and evidence presented at trial, the jury responses to the special interrogatories, and arguments of counsel, the court makes the findings of fact and conclusions of law pursuant to Rule 52 of the Federal Rules of Civil Procedure.

FINDINGS OF FACT

Fortress was formed in 1994 by two brothers—Michael and Joseph Carnazzo. Although Fortress initially operated as a marketing consulting company, soon after it was created operations shifted to the development and production of nutritional supplements. As part of Fortress's operations, Joseph Carnazzo invented and patented an effervescent delivery system for creatine, a dietary supplement used primarily by athletes.

In 1998, Fortress began selling the patented Effervescent Creatine to college athletic departments and national professional sports teams including the Arizona Diamondbacks and the Boston Red Socks. Fortress used contract packagers to mix and package the product for the customers and also licensed the product to several companies for private labeling. As Fortress began production of the patented Effervescent Creatine products, the Carnazzos sought investors for Fortress. The Carnazzos approached the Broderick family, who invested $750,000 in Fortress in exchange for 30–32% of the shares of stock and membership on Fortress's board.

By the 2001, Fortress produced a line of products including Creatine Effervescent, Neuro Edge, Vitamin Edge, Joint Edge, Phosphate Edge, Glutamine Edge, Ultra Figora Weight Loss as well as a number of private label products for several companies including their largest client, General Nutrition Company ("GNC"). Fortress began to experience problems with the contract packagers including packaging contaminated with water and packagers who substituted substandard raw product without notice to Fortress.

Fortress decided that to ensure quality control and profitability, it should open its own manufacturing facility that would mix and package its products. However, the Brodericks were not interested in investing further in Fortress and instead wanted to continue operations as is. The Carnazzos's accountant, Jack Lengemann, introduced the Carnazzos to John Houston. Houston attempted to buy out the Brodericks by offering them $300,000 for their interest in Fortress. The Brodericks rejected the offer. The Carnazzos and Houston retained an attorney who assisted with a merger of Fortress into a company owned by John Houston. Houston and the Carnazzos then applied a Nebraska law allowing for the forced buyout of minority shareholders and bought out the Brodericks. The Brodericks were not happy about the forced buyout and the $87,526 that they received for their share of the company. On August 16, 2001, the Brodericks initiated a shareholder lawsuit requesting a temporary restraining order on behalf of themselves and Fortress Systems against Michael and Joseph Carnazzo and John Houston ("the Broderick lawsuit").

After the merger and buyout of the Brodericks was completed, Houston sought to secure financing for the new manufacturing facility. Houston contacted a number of banks in the greater Omaha area, including U.S. Bank. Houston testified that initially, no banks were willing to undertake the financing. In October 2001, a former employee of U.S. Bank, Christy Edwards, who had worked on Fortress's loan application at U.S. Bank, began working for the Bank. On her first day at the Bank, Edwards arranged to have lunch with Houston. At that lunch, Edwards indicated that the Bank was interested in making the loan that Houston requested from U.S. Bank.

Within a few days, Edwards met with Michael and Joseph Carnazzo at the Fortress's office. At that meeting, Joseph and Michael Carnazzo gave Edwards a tour of Fortress's current facility and a product demonstration. Michael Carnazzo testified that he briefed Edwards regarding the market for the patented Effervescent Creatine and other Fortress products. Michael and Joseph Carnazzo testified that at their first meeting with Edwards, they discussed with Edwards how Houston became involved in their business through the forced buyout of the Brodericks. Michael and Joseph Carnazzo further testified that they informed Edwards that the Brodericks were suing them and Houston. Edwards testified that there was no discussion regarding the existence of the Broderick lawsuit.

Edwards next brought her supervisor, Richard Osher, to Fortress's office to meet with Joseph Carnazzo, Michael Carnazzo and John Houston. Michael Carnazzo testified that while he was giving Osher a tour of the manufacturing facility, Osher told him that Edwards had been recruited to join the Bank to expand their commercial business. Joseph Carnazzo testified while Osher and Michael Carnazzo were touring the facility, he and Edwards stayed behind in the conference room and she told him "point blank" that if Michael and he did everything she asked, Fortress would get the loan.

On October 23, 2001, Houston provided to Edwards a letter and booklet regarding Fortress. In the letter, Houston specifically requested an equipment loan in the amount of $2.2 million and a revolving line of credit of $1.5 million. The booklet included product information, financial information on the company, and Fortress's contract with GNC. In response to Edwards's requests, Fortress subsequently provided a breakdown of current purchase orders, explanations of the pro forma financials provided in the informational booklet, and additional financial statements. * * * Additionally, Fortress gave Edwards permission to contact its customers and provided her with names and contact information. Edwards contacted a number of Fortress's clients and confirmed the purchase orders and other supply contracts. At no time did the Bank request, nor did Fortress complete, a formal loan application. In fact, Osher testified that the Bank did not have a formal loan application form for commercial lending.

Michael Carnazzo testified that in late October 2001, Edwards requested that Fortress increase the lease term on the new building from five years to ten years. On November 6, 2001, Fortress entered into an amendment to their lease agreement extending out the leasehold five additional years. * * *

Additionally, Michael Carnazzo testified that Edwards told him that in order to get the loan, Fortress needed to start spending $320,000 of its own money on the new facility because the Bank wanted Fortress to have its own capital already committed. Edwards testified that she didn't remember telling Fortress to start spending money on equipment in order to get the loan.

On October 26, 2001, Edwards prepared what the Bank called a Relationship Approval Presentation ("RAP") requesting approval of the loans to Fortress. On November 30, 2001, the Bank issued a commitment for a credit facility to Fortress consisting of $2.2 million for the build-out and a $1.0 million revolving line of credit (the "Commitment Letter.") Michael Carnazzo signed the Commitment Letter on behalf of Fortress Systems on December 5, 2001. As part of the process for closing, the Bank provided to Fortress a proposed Loan and Security Agreement. The closing was set for December 7, 2001, but was delayed until December 10, 2001, so that Michael Carnazzo, who was traveling out of town, would have time to review the loan documents.

On December 6, 2001, Houston sent a fax outlining issues in the loan documents that to be resolved prior to the closing of the loan. In that fax, Houston indicated that "Page 11, F. Litigation. I don't think the Broderick's lawsuit fits in this category, as it is directed against the current shareholders of [Fortress]." Edwards testified that on that same day she learned from the Bank's legal counsel that it was representing the Brodericks in the Broderick lawsuit.

On December 10, 2001, Edwards and Osher informed the Carnazzos that the loan would not be made because of the Broderick lawsuit. Houston testified that he was shocked when Edwards stated she heard about the Broderick lawsuit for the first time from the Bank's attorneys. Houston testified he spoke to Edwards at least twice regarding the Broderick lawsuit and he was with Michael Carnazzo on another occasion when Michael Carnazzo discussed it with Edwards.

Michael Carnazzo and Houston testified that Edwards told them at the December 10, 2001 meeting that if Fortress could make the Brodericks' lawsuit go away or settle it in a manner that did not adversely impact the company, the Bank would close the loan. Edwards testified that she did not make such a statement because she did not have the authority to do so. Osher testified that while he had not promised Fortress that he would make the loan if the lawsuit was resolved, he did state that he would be willing to reconsider the loan if the lawsuit was resolved.

Nevertheless, Michael Carnazzo and Houston testified that based on Edwards's promise to close the loan if the lawsuit was settled, they entered into intense settlement negotiations with the Brodericks. On or about January 26, 2002, the Carnazzos, Houston and the Brodericks entered into an "Intent to Settle" in which the Brodericks would receive approximately $4 million to be paid out of royalties received by the company over a number of years. Additionally, in order to finance the royalty payments required in the settlement, Fortress negotiated a price increase for their product with GNC. Michael Carnazzo and Houston testified that they agreed to the settlement only because they thought they had no other option or their deal with the Bank wouldn't close. The final settlement agreement was to be signed at the closing of the loan. Because the loan wasn't made, the settlement agreement was never signed. The Broderick lawsuit eventually settled for $17,500.[5]

Houston testified that he believed that the loan would close if the Broderick lawsuit was resolved. He based this on Edwards's promise to close on the loan and on his past experiences. Houston testified that through his prior employment he worked on close to 100 other loans and all of the loans closed once a commitment letter was issued. He testified that with many of the loans there were issues that had to be resolved before the loan would close, including one loan with a legal issue, but once the issues were resolved, the loans closed.

* * *

Between December 10, 2001 and February 20, 2002, Edwards continued to request financial and sales contract information from Fortress. * * * On February 20, 2002, Osher and Edwards advised Fortress that it would not make the original loan.

* * *

Houston testified that after the February 20, 2002 meeting, Fortress attempted to seek new funding but it was too late as the first GNC product was due. Houston testified that if he had known in December that the loan was not going to be made, he could have approached other banks to finance the manufacturing facility build-out. * * *

At trial, Fortress offered the testimony of Luke Northall, a certified public account, as an expert regarding Fortress's damages due to the Bank's failure to make the loan. After his testimony, the court determined Northall's testimony applied only to lost profits, and since "benefit of the bargain" damages are not the proper measure of damages in a promissory estoppel case, the court struck the expert's testimony and it was not considered by the jury. * * *

CONCLUSIONS OF LAW

1. Promissory Estoppel

Recovery on a theory of promissory estoppel is based upon the principle that injustice can be avoided only by enforcement of a promise. *Blinn v. Beatrice Community Hospital and Health Center,* 708 N.W.2d 235, 246 (Neb.2006) (*citing Folgers Architects v. Kerns,* 633 N.W.2d 114 (Neb. 2001)). The Nebraska Supreme Court has adopted the Restatement (Second) of Contracts § 90 at 242 (1981) definition of "promissory estoppel." * * *

Under Nebraska law, the doctrine of promissory estoppel does not require that the promise giving rise to the cause of action must meet the requirements of an offer that would ripen into a contract if accepted by promisee. *Blinn,* 708 N.W.2d at 247. There is no requirement of "definite-

---

5. Fortress filed for Chapter 11 bankruptcy protection on June 2, 2003. The Broderick lawsuit was settled in connection with the bankruptcy action ness" in an action based upon promissory estoppel. Instead of requiring reasonable definiteness, promissory estoppel requires only that reliance be reasonable and foreseeable.

A statement of opinion or future intent is insufficient to give rise to a promise. In addition, promissory estoppel cannot be based on preliminary negotiations and discussions or an agreement to negotiate the terms of a contract. In *168th & Dodge et al. v. Rave Reviews Cinemas, LLC,* 501 F.3d 945, 955 (8th Cir. 2007), the plaintiff entered into a letter of intent regarding the lease of a movie theater to the defendant. The court held that the letter of intent was not a sufficient promise because under Nebraska law "promissory estoppel cannot be based on the parties' agreement to negotiate the terms of the lease agreement."

The Bank argues that the Commitment Letter in this case is analogous to the letter of intent in *168th & Dodge.* While the Commitment Letter is factually similar, this case presents the court with the one element missing in *168th & Dodge*—a promise. The Nebraska Supreme Court has held that a bank can be liable under a promissory estoppel theory for promising to lend money to a customer who begins construction based on the promise that the loan will be made. *Whorley v. First Westside Bank,* 485 N.W.2d 578, 582 (Neb.1992). While the Commitment Letter may not be sufficient under its own terms to constitute a promise under promissory estoppel, there is evidence that at the December 10, 2001 meeting, or at sometime thereafter, Edwards affirmatively promised on behalf of the Bank to close the loan if the Broderick lawsuit was resolved.

Both Michael Carnazzo and Houston testified that Edwards, on behalf of the Bank, promised to close the loan once the Broderick litigation was resolved. Their attempts to quickly resolve the lawsuit, and paying a premium price to do so, corroborate their testimony that they believed the loan would close if the lawsuit was resolved. Edwards testified that she never promised that the loan would be made if the lawsuit was settled. Edwards did testify that she continued to communicate with Fortress trying to get the deal done, however, that Osher had made it clear to her that the Bank would not move forward until either the lawsuit had settled or there was some type of resolution to the issue. Osher testified that he did not promise to close on the loan once the Broderick lawsuit was resolved; he only agreed to reconsider making the loan. This created a genuine issue of fact as to whether a promise was made, and the jury believed Fortress's testimony on this issue.

Promissory estoppel also requires that the promisee's reliance on the promise be reasonable and foreseeable. The Bank argues that as a matter of law Fortress could not rely on Edwards's promise that the Bank would make the loan because Houston is a sophisticated business person who should know that Edwards did not have authority to bind the Bank. However, the evidence presented created a factual question regarding the extent of Edwards's authority. Apparent or ostensible authority "may be conferred if the alleged principal affirmatively, intentionally, or by lack of ordinary care causes third persons to act upon the apparent authority." Michael Carnazzo testified that Edwards introduced herself as a vice-president of the Bank and made statements that if Fortress did everything she asked the loan would close. Edwards testified that she does not remember giving the Carnazzos her title or, if she did, what title she gave them. Michael Carnazzo testified that Osher indicated to Fortress that Edwards, as an agent of the Bank, had the ability to close the loan. Moreover, Osher testified that Edwards had actual authority to sign the Commitment Letter. The jury determined, inherent in their other findings, that Edwards had authority to bind the Bank with her promises. The reasonableness of reliance on the promise and subsequent reassurances is an issue for a jury to determine.

Additionally, the Bank argues that Fortress is a sophisticated business charged with the knowledge of the statutory requirement that contracts that cannot be completed in one year must be in a writing signed by the party to be charged. *168th & Dodge,* 501 F.3d at 957 (holding that sophisticated business entities are charged with the knowledge of the statutory requirement that leases be in writing); *Abboud v. Michals,* 457 N.W.2d 34 (Neb.1992) (finding no reasonable reliance in a claim for fraudulent misrepresentation where licensed real estate agents and brokers knew that contracts for commission must be in writing under state law).

Unlike the parties in *168th & Dodge* and *Abboud,* Fortress provided evidence that negates the presumption that experienced business people are charged with the knowledge of the statutory requirement—namely, testimony of common practice in the industry: that when contingencies arise after loan commitment letters are issued, those loans close as soon as the contingencies are removed. Houston specifically testified that based on his experience that once a commitment letter was issued banks would close the loan as long as the borrower satisfied any issues that arose during the due diligence. Houston indicated he has worked on almost 100 loans where commitment letters were issued, and all these loans closed including one loan where there was a subsequent lawsuit. Houston testified that he believed that if the Broderick lawsuit was resolved, the Bank would close the loan. Additionally, Jack Lengemann, Fortress's outside C.P.A., testified that he told Michael Carnazzo that other loans had closed with lawsuits and that once the Broderick lawsuit was resolved, the loan would close. Further, Fortress's belief that the loan would close was bolstered by Edwards's continued requests for information associated with closing the loan between December 10, 2001 and February 20, 2002.

Moreover, the Bank provided no evidence that the loan failed to close because of another contingency, or because the settlement negatively impacted Fortress's financial situation. Osher's testimony was that the Bank ultimately decided not to fund the loan because the lawsuit had not been disclosed originally. Therefore, the court finds that sufficient evidence existed upon which the jury could base its decision that Fortress reasonably relied on the Bank's promise to close the loan.

Additionally, Fortress's reliance on the Bank's promises was foreseeable. The testimony at trial showed that Edwards knew that Fortress was attempting to settle the Broderick lawsuit. Further, Michael Carnazzo testified that he informed Edwards that construction had begun on the new building. Michael Carnazzo testified that Edwards told him to start spending over $300,000 of Fortress's money on the build-out in order to get the loan. Fortress provided to the Bank copies of the bids to build-out the facilities. Carnazzo testified that while the contracts were dated early November 2001, they did not enter into the contracts until the end of November when Edwards initially informed Fortress that the loan would be made. Michael Carnazzo testified that he informed Edwards that Fortress was starting to build-out the facility when they discussed spending the $300,000. After the loan commitment was issued, Michael Carnazzo committed Fortress to the agreements for the build-out of the facility. Houston testified that he had instructed Carnazzo not to commit Fortress to these loans until the loan closing. However, in later testimony, he opined that he could understand Carnazzo's decision. The jury determined that the Bank expected or should have expected that its course of conduct would induce Fortress Systems to act in reliance on the conduct.

Thus, Fortress presented to the jury sufficient evidence for a finding that the Bank made a promise to Fortress to close the loan if the Broderick lawsuit was resolved without an adverse financial impact, that Fortress reasonably relied on this promise to its detriment, and that this reliance was foreseeable.

2. *Statute of Frauds*

The statute of frauds may bar a plaintiff's claim for promissory estoppel, *168th & Dodge,* 501 F.3d at 955 (*citing Farmland Serv. Coop., Inc. v. Klein,* 244 N.W.2d 86, 89 (Neb.1976)). The Bank argues that pursuant to Neb.Rev.Stat. § 45–1,113,[6] any promise made by Edwards to loan money must be in writing. * * *

On its face, the Commitment Letter, while not a contract, was at the least a memorandum that provided all the relevant terms and conditions to make the loan. "The memorandum required by the statute of frauds must contain the essential terms of the contract." *Reifenrath v. Hansen,* 190 Neb. 58, 206 N.W.2d 42, 44 (1973). * * * Further, equity will not permit the Bank to use the statute of frauds as a shield for their wrongdoing as justice requires compensation for reliance damages reasonably and foreseeably induced by promises made and broken in a business

---

6. "A debtor or a creditor may not maintain an action or assert a defense in an action based on a credit agreement unless the credit agreement is in writing, expresses consideration, sets forth the relevant terms and conditions of the credit agreement, and is signed by the creditor and by the debtor." Neb. Rev. Stat § 45–1,113. Further, Neb.Rev.Stat. § 36–202 provides that oral agreement that, by its terms, is not to be performed within one year from its making, is void. The same analysis applies regardless of which statute is applied; thus, the court will conduct only one analysis.

setting. Thus, the court determines that there was sufficient writing to satisfy of the statute of frauds in this case.

* * *

3.   *Proper Measure of Damages*

Promissory estoppel only provides for damages as justice requires and does not attempt to provide the plaintiff damages based on the benefit of the bargain. *Rosnick,* 457 N.W.2d at 800. The usual measure of damages under a theory of promissory estoppel is the loss incurred by the promisee in reasonable reliance on the promise, or "reliance damages." Reliance damages are relatively easy to determine, whereas the determination of "expectation" or "benefit of the bargain" damages available in a contract action requires more detailed proof of the terms of the contract. *Id.* The correct measure of damages is the amount expended in reasonable reliance of the promise to make a loan, not the damages had the loan been made.

Fortress argues that it had a legal right to look to secure other funding and that it detrimentally altered its position by not seeking other loans from December 10, 2001 until February 20, 2002 based on the Bank's promises. Fortress argues that this reliance and, consequently, failure to secure another loan, entitles it to lost profits. However, as noted above, Fortress did not provide any evidence that it could have received funding from another lending institution if it had sought a loan immediately after the December 10, 2001 meeting. At most, Houston testified that he could have spoken to other lending institutions. This is a complete failure of proof on Fortress's part. Consequently, Fortress is not entitled to recover the $13,326,791 in damages as determined by the jury, as this amount clearly evidences alleged lost profits due to the failure to close the loan, not reliance damages.

* * *

* * * [T]he court determines that the proper measure of damages is the amount spent by Fortress during the time from December 10, 2001 until February 20, 2002 in reliance that the loan would be made. The jury determined those damages based on the evidence to total $2.2 million. The evidence before the jury is that Fortress entered into an agreement with Precision Builders for the build-out on November 29, 2001, after it was verbally notified of the loan approval. Fortress did not pay the first installment payment until December 14, 2001, after Edwards's promise that the Bank would close the loan if the Broderick lawsuit was settled. The jury was presented with an application for payment dated February 28, 2001, which requested $2,167,787. However, as part of the bankruptcy proceedings, Fortress agreed to pay Precision Builders and Thermal Services (a subcontractor to the Precision Builders contract) a reduced amount of $1,321,695.59. Additionally, * * * prior to bankruptcy, Fortress actually paid Precision Builders a total of $326,149.65. Therefore, the total amount paid by Fortress as a result of the Precision Builders Contract was $1,647,845.24.

* * * [T]he court determines that Fortress is entitled to recover on its promissory estoppel claim only the amount actually paid on the Precision Builders Contract in the amount of $1,647,845.24.

IT IS ORDERED:

QUESTIONS AND CONNECTIONS

1. Questions about the facts of this case
   - 1.1. How did Fortress change its position in reliance on the promise of financing from Bank of the West? What would have happened if Fortress hadn't taken this action?
   - 1.2. How might the fact that, apparently, the bank's legal counsel was representing the Brodericks have influenced the outcome?

2. Questions about the law
   - 2.1. What does the court mean when it says that "promissory estoppel does not require that the promise giving rise to the cause of action must meet the requirements of an offer that would ripen into a contract if accepted by promise"?
   - 2.2. Was Edwards' promise on behalf of the bank to close the loan if the Broderick lawsuit was resolved a promise that could ripen into an offer? Why or why not?
   - 2.3. If the Commitment Letter had not been a sufficient memorandum to satisfy the statute of frauds, would the bank have been able to avoid liability based on promissory estoppel?
   - 2.4. Why did the court reject the jury's determination as to Fortress' entitlement to recover lost profits as part of its damage award? More on the remedy for liability based on promissory liability follows in subsection 4, *infra.*

3. Connections:
   Do the courts in *Dargo* and *Fortress Systems* seem to have different views about the role of promissory estoppel? Can you articulate the difference? Which view is more compatible with the *Restatement (Second)'s* formulation of the doctrine? Was it necessary in *Fortress Systems* to invoke promissory estoppel to "do justice," or to "prevent an injustice"? Does it matter whether the test is "do justice" or "prevent an injustice"? And who decides whether non-enforcement would produce an unjust result?

NOTE ON PROMISSORY ESTOPPEL IN EMPLOYMENT AND RETIREMENT AGREEMENTS

Promissory estoppel theory is frequently invoked in connection with employment contracts as a mechanism to convert what is otherwise an "at will" employment. For example, in *Blinn v. Beatrice Community Hospital and Health Center, Inc.*, 270 Neb. 809, 708 N.W.2d 235 (2006), Blinn, a hospital administrator, received an offer from another facility. Beatrice, Blinn's current employer assured him that they wanted him to stay and he could do so until he retired. Seven months later Blinn was asked to resign by Beatrice, and he brought suit. After dismissal on summary judgment, the Nebraska Supreme Court concluded that while the facts did not make out a claim for breach of contract, there was a genuine issue of material fact on Blinn's promissory estoppel claim as to which he was entitled to a trial on the merits.

Several cases have dealt with the promise to pay a lifetime annuity or other benefit on retirement. Generally, where the pension promise is determined to have induced an early retirement, enforcement may be had under § 90 of the *Restatement (Second) of Contracts. See, e.g., Feinberg v. Pfeiffer Co.*, 322 S.W.2d 163 (Mo. App. 1959). By contrast, in *Pitts v. McGraw-Edison Co.*, 329 F.2d 412 (6th Cir. 1964), the employee was informed that he had been retired at the same time that the promise was made to pay a pension. Finding that there was no promise made to Pitts on which he acted to his detriment—that he had not given up anything to which he was legally entitled—the court denied recovery under promissory estoppel.

Some cases fall in-between. In *Katz v. Danny Dare, Inc.*, 610 S.W.2d 121 (Mo. App. 1980), the plaintiff, I.G. Katz, was offered a pension of $13,000 per year, whereupon he retired. Several years later, the company reduced the promised monthly payment and Katz sued. Katz claimed he would not have retired but for the pension, while the company testified that had Katz not retired he would have been terminated. The trial court found for the company on the basis that Katz had not given up anything in reliance on the promise since he could have been discharged at any time. The court of appeals reversed, holding that because Katz voluntarily elected to retire after being promised the annual pension payment, a right to recovery under promissory estoppel was established. Here's what one law professor had to say about the case:

> The *Danny Dare* decision is one that I teach in my class, and it causes no small level of consternation because of the court's distinction between a legal entitlement to employment (which the plaintiff did not have) and an interest in relying on a promise that the promisor may not have been obligated to make (the defendant really could have fired the plaintiff anytime he wanted to). Students catch on to this kind of reasoning and conclude, * * * that what we really have is judicial acrobatics to achieve a desired result.

Craig L. Jackson, *Traditional Contract Theory: Old and New Attacks and Old and New Defenses*, 33 NEW ENG. L. REV. 365, 422 (1998).

Why did the trial court in *Danny Dare* think the fact that Katz faced being fired if he did not accept retirement (with the promise of the pension) made the case distinguishable from *Feinberg v. Pfeiffer*, the case on which the court of appeals placed considerable reliance? Are the cases distinguishable or is the promise in *Danny Dare* actually more like the promise in *Pitts* than in *Feinberg*?

In *Langer v. Superior Steel*, 105 Pa.Super. 579, 161 A. 571 (1932), the president of the defendant/employer sent a letter to the plaintiff, Langer, upon his retirement promising "a pension of $100 per month as long as you live and preserve your present attitude of loyalty to the company and its officers and are not employed in any competitive occupation." After four years, the company ceased the payments and Langer sued. The company defended on the basis that the letter was a gratuitous promise and, as such, unenforceable. The court, however, concluded that there was a sufficient consideration because the company had received a benefit in Langer's not seeking employment with a competitor. Do you think the promise in *Langer* was any less gratuitous than the one in *Danny Dare*? Could you make an argument, based on *Langer*, that Danny Dare's promise was enforceable under traditional bargain theory?

Mr. Katz's victory over Danny Dare may have been even more impressive than he realized. Recently, Professor Robert Hillman published the results of an empirical study he conducted of promissory estoppel cases in the employment context decided during the period from 1994 through 1996. Surprisingly, he found that the employees succeeded *less than five percent* of the time. *See* Robert A. Hillman, *The Unfulfilled Promise of Promissory Estoppel in the Employment Setting*, 31 RUTGERS L. J. 1 (1999). In part, Professor Hillman attributed this low rate of success to an increasing judicial preference for written contracts supported by traditional bargained-for consideration. Indeed, like the rumors of Mark Twain's death, it is possible that Grant Gilmore's fear that promissory estoppel might "swallow up" the bargain principle in contract enforcement was vastly exaggerated!

Historically, enforcement of private employer-sponsored pension plans was handled under state common law theories of breach of contract and promissory estoppel. Much of the litigation over private employer pension promises was abated by the enactment in 1974 of the Employee Retirement Income Security Act (ERISA). ERISA, which was adopted to strengthen and improve pension and welfare security payments for plan participants, establishes a statutory enforcement mechanism that preempts state law. However, the common law contract theories remain viable as to plans that are unfunded or otherwise exempt from ERISA. *See also Schonholz v. Long Island Jewish Medical Center*, 87 F.3d 72 (2d Cir. 1996) (holding that promissory estoppel theory might be applied even in an ERISA case under extraordinary circumstances). The resolution granting Katz's pension likely was not covered by ERISA because it was not a company "plan," but rather a one-time obligation incurred to a single employee.

PROBLEM ON PROMISSORY ESTOPPEL

Let's assume that, in his third year of law school, Epstein accepts a job offer upon graduation from Cornbath, Swine & Moorg, a highly prestigious Wall Street firm with a reputation for paying the highest new associate salaries in the country. Secure in his decision, Epstein turns down other interviews with firms paying well, but not as well as old CS & M. After graduation, Epstein packs up his belongings and moves to New York to begin studying for the bar and working for CS & M. The day before he is to begin work, he receives a call at home from the hiring partner who informs Epstein that CS & M has a policy of only employing new associates who graduated in the top 5% of their law school class. Because, in his last semester of law school, Epstein dropped just below the top 5%, the partner tells him that the firm has filled his slot by hiring someone else. Enraged, Epstein responds by reminding the partner that he had a contract with the firm. The partner replies by telling him, "Ah, but that's where you're wrong. Because this was an employment at will, either party could terminate at any time. This bilateral power of termination means neither of us was committed to performance to the other. Therefore, these mutual so-called promises were illusory and could not give rise to a contract in fact. Perhaps if you studied a little harder, Dave, you would have known that, as well as graduated in the top 5%." Feeling betrayed, lamenting the money he spent to move to New York, and thinking about the other attractive interviews he passed up, Epstein decides to sue. Assuming the partner is right that, under applicable law, no contract arose between Epstein and CS & M, can Epstein successfully bring an action under the theory of promissory estoppel? If so, what damages should he seek?

NOTE ON PROMISSORY ESTOPPEL AND PRE-CONTRACT NEGOTIATIONS

In recent decades, and without any great consistency, courts have sometimes shown a willingness to extend liability under promissory estoppel to situations where one party makes a specific promise in order to entice the other party to enter into negotiations, and then the first party breaks the promise for no apparent reason. Commonly, these cases have involved negotiations over franchise agreements. Typically, the franchisor will offer assurance that a franchise will be forthcoming, and, in reliance on that "promise," the prospective franchisee will make substantial expenditures in order to meet the conditions for receiving the franchise. When the franchisor refuses to go through with the deal, and the negotiations had never ripened into an enforceable agreement, authority exists for the disappointed franchisee to at least recover its expenses in preparing to do business, under promissory estoppel theory. *See, e.g., Midwest Energy, Inc. v. Orion Food Systems, Inc.,* 14 S.W.3d 154 (2000).

In perhaps the most far-reaching application of the doctrine of promissory estoppel to police conduct occurring in the stage of pre-contract negotiations, the Wisconsin Supreme Court, in *Hoffman v. Red Owl Stores, Inc.,* 26 Wis.2d 683, 133 N.W.2d 267 (1965), held that assurances made by a grocery store franchisor to a prospective franchisee concerning the award of a store at a new location could form the basis for recovery of out-of-pocket expenses incurred by the promisee in anticipation of the contract, even though the negotiations of the parties never ripened into a contractually enforceable promise. In justifying its holding, the court stated: "We deem it would be a mistake to regard an action grounded on promissory estoppel as the equivalent of a breach of contract action. As Dean Boyer points out, it is desirable that fluidity in the application of the concept be maintained."

The *Restatement (Second) of Contracts* appears to approve of the holding in *Red Owl*. *See* § 90 cmt. d, illus 10. Nevertheless, the decision represents a significant expansion of the doctrine of promissory estoppel as a basis for enforcing gift promises inducing reliance since there was no actual offer or "promise" in *Red Owl*. In other words, negotiations had not advanced to the point where there was a sufficiently clear and definite agreement that might have supported an action for breach of contract. Instead, recovery of reliance expenditures was based solely on positive assurances made by the franchisor during the course of negotiations that ultimately failed to reach fruition. Failed negotiations are, of course, a fact of life in business. Thus, something else was going on in *Red Owl*. What do you suppose it was? Go back and review *Budget Marketing, Inc. v. Centronics Corp.*, *supra.* at p. 214. Does that offer any hints? Sometimes we begin to wonder whether this class is about contracts or torts. Maybe you're wondering the same thing.

In a recent law review article, very critical of *Red Owl*, here's what the authors had to say: *The conventional wisdom among contemporary scholars is that courts will sometimes impose liability for reliance investments undertaken before any agreement between the parties. * * * Commentators identify as grounds for such enforcement the existence of unjust enrichment, misrepresentations made during negotiation, a specific promise made and relied upon during the negotiation process, and a "general obligation arising out of the negotiations themselves." * * * But even a casual survey of contemporary case law casts significant doubt on the accuracy of this conventional view. Courts actually make some form of agreement a necessary condition to a promisee's recovery. For courts, the real issues are when an agreement will be found and how the nature of the agreement will determine the type of damages a promisee can recover.*

Much of the confusion can be traced to the frequently taught case of Hoffman v. Red Owl Stores, Inc.

* * *

There is scant support in the law of contracts for this legal analysis. To the contrary, the Restatement of Contracts has only one definition of a promise, and that definition applies equally to a promise that is the product of a bargained-for exchange and a promise for which enforcement is sought on the grounds of induced reliance. Thus, if Hoffman stands for the proposition that a commitment can be binding under a theory of promissory estoppel even though it lacks the clarity and certainty required of a bargained-for promise, the case is wrong as a matter of doctrine. More importantly, it is an outlier: the case has not been followed in its own or other jurisdictions. Alan Schwartz & Robert Scott, *Contractual Liability and Preliminary Agreements*, 120 Harv. L. Rev. 661, 668 (2007).

Introduction to *Pavel Enterprises*

We saw in Chapter 2 that all offers, even offers stated to be irrevocable, are in fact revocable at the will of the offeror *unless*: 1) the promise of irrevocability is supported by some consideration, or 2) the promise of irrevocability is made enforceable by statute—thereby, in either case, creating an *option contract*. However, you may recall that we also saw certain situations where the *Restatement (Second) of Contracts* fashions a sort of option contract to protect the offeree's reliance interest. For example, where the offer *requires* acceptance by full performance, and the offeree commences performance, under *Restatement (Second) of Contracts* § 45 the offeree has a reasonable time to complete the performance and, during that time, the offer may not be revoked. In *Marchiondo v. Scheck*, *supra*, at 138, the court concluded that "[w]hat constitutes partial performance will vary from case to case since what can be done toward performance is limited by what is authorized to be done." We also discussed briefly reliance as a basis for creating an option under *Restatement (Second) of Contracts* § 87(2).

A recurring circumstance where the courts have shown some willingness to create an option contract in order to protect the offeree's reliance arises in the construction contract situation. In terms of context, in the conventional scenario (and particularly in government projects), the property owner will seek bids from general contractors for the construction of a building on, or other improvement to, the owner's property. Inevitably, the contractor will plan to perform some portion of its obligations under the prime contract by contracting for services with, and acquiring materials from, an array of subcontractors and suppliers. In order to formulate its bid on the prime contract, therefore, the general contractor often will solicit bids in advance from these subcontractors. These bids, of course, are only *offers*, but the general contractor typically *relies* on these bids in determining what it can bid on the prime contract and still make a profit. Obviously, the general contractor does not want to accept the sub-bids unless and until it knows that its primary bid has been accepted. As you can see, the issue of "fairness" arises when the general contractor, who has been awarded the prime contract having relied on particular subcontractor bids, is faced suddenly with a revocation of a sub-bid before it can accept.

The next case describes the approaches that have been developed over the past seventy years or so to deal with this particular problem. As you read the case, think about what might be done to protect the general contractor's interest *ex ante*, eliminating the need to rely, after the fact and with apologies to Tennessee Williams, on the kindness of judges.

PAVEL ENTERPRISES, INC. v. A. S. JOHNSON COMPANY, INC.

Court of Appeals of Maryland
342 Md. 143, 674 A.2d 521 (1996)

KARWACKI, J.

In this case we are invited to adapt the "modern" contractual theory of detrimental reliance, or promissory estoppel, to the relationship between general contractors and their subcontractors. Although the theory of detrimental reliance is available to general contractors, it is not applicable to the facts of this case. For that reason, and because there was no traditional bilateral contract formed, we shall affirm the trial court.

I

The National Institutes of Health [hereinafter, "NIH"], solicited bids for a renovation project on Building 30 of its Bethesda, Maryland campus. The proposed work entailed some demolition work, but the major component of the job was mechanical, including heating, ventilation and air conditioning ["HVAC"]. Pavel Enterprises Incorporated [hereinafter, "PEI"], a general contractor from Vienna, Virginia and appellant in this action, prepared a bid for the NIH work. In preparing its bid, PEI solicited sub-bids from various mechanical subcontractors. The A. S. Johnson Company [hereinafter, "Johnson"], a mechanical subcontractor located in Clinton, Maryland and the appellee here, responded with a written scope of work proposal on July 27, 1993.[2] On the morning of August 5, 1993, the day NIH opened the general contractors' bids, Johnson verbally submitted a quote of $898,000 for the HVAC component. Neither party disputes that PEI used Johnson's sub-bid in computing its own bid. PEI submitted a bid of $1,585,000 for the entire project.

General contractors' bids were opened on the afternoon of August 5, 1993. PEI's bid was the second lowest bid. The government subsequently disqualified the apparent low bidder, however, and in mid-August, NIH notified PEI that its bid would be accepted.

With the knowledge that PEI was the lowest responsive bidder, Thomas F. Pavel, president of PEI, visited the offices of A. S. Johnson on August 26, 1993, and met with James Kick, Johnson's chief estimator, to discuss Johnson's proposed role in the work. Pavel testified at trial to the purpose of the meeting:

"I met with Mr. Kick. And the reason for me going to their office was to look at their offices, to see their facility, to basically sit down and talk with them, as I had not done, and my company had not performed business with them on a direct relationship, but we had heard

---

2. The scope of work proposal listed all work that Johnson proposed to perform, but omitted the price term. This is a standard practice in the construction industry. The subcontractor's bid price is then filled in immediately before the general contractor submits the general bid to the letting party.

of their reputation. I wanted to go out and see where their facility was, see where they were located, and basically just sit down and talk to them. Because if we were going to use them on a project, I wanted to know who I was dealing with.''

* * *

Following that meeting, PEI sent a fax to all of the mechanical subcontractors from whom it had received sub-bids on the NIH job. The text of that fax is reproduced:

Pavel Enterprises, Inc.

TO: PROSPECTIVE MECHANICAL SUBCONTRACTORS FROM: ESTIMATING DEPARTMENT REFERENCE: NIH, BLDG 30 REN-OVATION

We herewith respectfully request that you review your bid on the above referenced project that was bid on 8/05/93. PEI has been notified that we will be awarded the project as J.J. Kirlin, Inc. [the original low bidder] has been found to be nonresponsive on the solicitation. We anticipate award on or around the first of September and therefor request that you supply the following information.

* * *

On August 30, 1993, PEI informed NIH that Johnson was to be the mechanical subcontractor on the job. On September 1, 1993, PEI mailed and faxed a letter to Johnson formally accepting Johnson's bid. That letter read:

Pavel Enterprises, Inc.

September 1, 1993

Mr. James H. Kick, Estimating Mngr. A.S. Johnson Company 8042 Old Alexandria Ferry Road Clinton, Maryland 20735

Re: NIH Bldg 30 HVAC Modifications IFB #263–93–B (CM)—0422

Subject: Letter of Intent to award Subcontract

Dear Mr. Kick;

We herewith respectfully inform your office of our intent to award a subcontract for the above referenced project per your quote received on 8/05/93 in the amount of $898,000.00. This subcontract will be forwarded upon receipt of our contract from the NIH, which we expect any day. A preconstruction meeting is currently scheduled at the NIH on 9/08/93 at 10 AM which we have been requested that your firm attend.

As discussed with you, a meeting was held between NIH and PEI wherein PEI confirmed our bid to the government, and designated your firm as our HVAC Mechanical subcontractor. This action was taken after several telephonic and face to face discussions with you regarding the above referenced bid submitted by your firm. We look forward to working with your firm on this contract and hope that this will lead to a long and mutually beneficial relationship.

Sincerely,

/s/ Thomas F. Pavel, President

Upon receipt of PEI's fax of September 1, James Kick called and informed PEI that Johnson's bid contained an error, and as a result the price was too low. According to Kick, Johnson had discovered the mistake earlier, but because Johnson believed that PEI had not been awarded the contract, they did not feel compelled to correct the error. Kick sought to withdraw Johnson's bid, both over the telephone and by a letter dated September 2, 1993:

A. S. Johnson Co.

September 2, 1993

PEI Construction 780 West Maples Avenue, Suite 101 Vienna, Virginia 22180

Attention: Thomas Pavel, President

Reference: NIH Building 30 HVAC Modifications

Dear Mr. Pavel,

We respectfully inform you of our intention to withdraw our proposal for the above referenced project due to an error in our bid.

As discussed in our telephone conversation and face to face meeting, the management of A. S. Johnson Company was reviewing this proposal, upon which we were to confirm our pricing to you.

Please contact Mr. Harry Kick, General Manager at [telephone number deleted] for any questions you may have.

Very truly yours,

/s/ James H. Kick Estimating Manager

PEI responded to both the September 1 phone call, and the September 2 letter, expressing its refusal to permit Johnson to withdraw.

On September 28, 1993, NIH formally awarded the construction contract to PEI. PEI found a substitute subcontractor to do the mechanical work, but at a cost of $930,000. PEI brought suit against Johnson in the Circuit Court for Prince George's County to recover the $32,000 difference between Johnson's bid and the cost of the substitute mechanical subcontractor.

The case was heard by the trial court without the aid of a jury. The trial court made several findings of fact, which we summarize:

1. PEI relied upon Johnson's sub-bid in making its bid for the entire project;

2. The fact that PEI was not the low bidder, but was awarded the project only after the apparent low bidder was disqualified, takes this case out of the ordinary;

3. Prior to NIH awarding PEI the contract on September 28, Johnson, on September 2, withdrew its bid; and

✱4. PEI's letter to all potential mechanical subcontractors, dated August 26, 1993, indicates that there was no definite agreement between PEI and Johnson, and that PEI was not relying upon Johnson's bid.

The trial court analyzed the case under both a traditional contract theory and under a detrimental reliance theory. PEI was unable to satisfy the trial judge that under either theory that [sic] a contractual relationship had been formed.

PEI appealed to the Court of Special Appeals, raising both traditional offer and acceptance theory, and "promissory estoppel." Before our intermediate appellate court considered the case, we issued a writ of certiorari on our own motion.

II

The relationships involved in construction contracts have long posed a unique problem in the law of contracts. A brief overview of the mechanics of the construction bid process, as well as our legal system's attempts to regulate the process, is in order.

A. CONSTRUCTION BIDDING.

Our description of the bid process in *Maryland Supreme Corp. v. Blake Co.*, 279 Md. 531, 369 A.2d 1017 (1977) is still accurate:

"In such a building project there are basically three parties involved: the letting party, who calls for bids on its job; the general contractor, who makes a bid on the whole project; and the subcontractors, who bid only on that portion of the whole job which involves the field of its specialty. The usual procedure is that when a project is announced, a subcontractor, on his own initiative or at the general contractor's request, prepares an estimate and submits a bid to one or more of the general contractors interested in the project. The general contractor evaluates the bids made by the subcontractors in each field and uses them to compute its total bid to the letting party. After receiving bids from general contractors, the letting party ordinarily awards the contract to the lowest reputable bidder."

Id. at 533–34, 369 A.2d at 1020–21 (citing The Firm Offer problem).

B. THE CONSTRUCTION BIDDING CASES— AN HISTORICAL OVERVIEW.

The problem the construction bidding process poses is the determination of the precise points on the timeline that the various parties become bound to each other. The early landmark case was *James Baird Co. v. Gimbel Bros., Inc.*, 64 F.2d 344 (2d Cir. 1933). The plaintiff, James Baird Co., ["Baird"] was a general contractor from Washington, D.C., bidding to construct a government building in Harrisburg, Pennsylvania. Gimbel

Bros., Inc., ["Gimbel"], the famous New York department store, sent its bid to supply linoleum to a number of bidding general contractors on December 24, and Baird received Gimbel's bid on December 28. Gimbel realized its bid was based on an incorrect computation and notified Baird of its withdrawal on December 28. The letting authority awarded Baird the job on December 30. Baird formally accepted the Gimbel bid on January 2. When Gimbel refused to perform, Baird sued for the additional cost of a substitute linoleum supplier. The Second Circuit Court of Appeals held that Gimbel's initial bid was an offer to contract and, under traditional contract law, remained open only until accepted or withdrawn. Because the offer was withdrawn before it was accepted there was no contract. Judge Learned Hand, speaking for the court, also rejected two alternative theories of the case: unilateral contract and promissory estoppel. He held that Gimbel's bid was not an offer of a unilateral contract that Baird could accept by performing, i.e., submitting the bid as part of the general bid; and second, he held that the theory of promissory estoppel was limited to cases involving charitable pledges.

Judge Hand's opinion was widely criticized, *see* Note, *Contracts–Promissory Estoppel*, 20 VA. L. REV. 214 (1933) [hereinafter, "Promissory Estoppel"]; Note, *Contracts–Revocation of Offer Before Acceptance–Promissory Estoppel*, 28 ILL. L. REV. 419 (1934), but also widely influential. The effect of the *James Baird* line of cases, however, is an "obvious injustice without relief of any description." *Promissory Estoppel*, at 215. The general contractor is bound to the price submitted to the letting party, but the subcontractors are not bound, and are free to withdraw.

As one commentator described it, "If the subcontractor revokes his bid before it is accepted by the general, any loss which results is a deduction from the general's profit and conceivably may transform overnight a profitable contract into a losing deal." Franklin M. Schultz, *The Firm Offer Puzzle: A Study of Business Practice in the Construction Industry*, 19 U. CHI. L. REV. 237, 239 (1952).

The unfairness of this regime to the general contractor was addressed in *Drennan v. Star Paving*, 333 P.2d 757, 51 Cal. 2d 409 (1958). Like *James Baird*, the *Drennan* case arose in the context of a bid mistake. Justice Traynor, writing for the Supreme Court of California, relied upon § 90 of the *Restatement (First) of Contracts*:

> "A promise which the promisor should reasonably expect to induce action or forbearance of a definite and substantial character on the part of the promisee and which does induce such action or forbearance is binding if injustice can be avoided only by enforcement of the promise."

Restatement (First) of Contracts § 90 (1932).

Justice Traynor reasoned that the subcontractor's bid contained an implied subsidiary promise not to revoke the bid. As the court stated:

"When plaintiff [, a General Contractor,] used defendant's offer in computing his own bid, he bound himself to perform in reliance on defendant's terms. Though defendant did not bargain for the use of its bid neither did defendant make it idly, indifferent to whether it would be used or not. On the contrary it is reasonable to suppose that defendant submitted its bid to obtain the subcontract. It was bound to realize the substantial possibility that its bid would be the lowest, and that it would be included by plaintiff in his bid. It was to its own interest that the contractor be awarded the general contract; the lower the subcontract bid, the lower the general contractor's bid was likely to be and the greater its chance of acceptance and hence the greater defendant's chance of getting the paving subcontract. Defendant had reason not only to expect plaintiff to rely on its bid but to want him to. Clearly defendant had a stake in plaintiff's reliance on its bid. Given this interest and the fact that plaintiff is bound by his own bid, it is only fair that plaintiff should have at least an opportunity to accept defendant's bid after the general contract has been awarded to him."

Drennan, 51 Cal. 2d at 415, 333 P.2d at 760. The *Drennan* court however did not use "promissory estoppel" as a substitute for the entire contract, as is the doctrine's usual function. Instead, the *Drennan* court, applying the principle of § 90, interpreted the subcontractor's bid to be irrevocable. Justice Traynor's analysis used promissory estoppel as consideration for an implied promise to keep the bid open for a reasonable time. Recovery was then predicated on traditional bilateral contract, with the sub-bid as the offer and promissory estoppel serving to replace acceptance.

The *Drennan* decision has been very influential. Many states have adopted the reasoning used by Justice Traynor. * * *

Despite the popularity of the *Drennan* reasoning, the case has subsequently come under some criticism. The criticism centers on the lack of symmetry of detrimental reliance in the bid process, in that subcontractors are bound to the general, but the general is not bound to the subcontractors. The result is that the general is free to bid shop,[13] bid chop,[14] and to encourage bid peddling,[15] to the detriment of the subcontractors. One commentator described the problems that these practices create:

---

13. Bid shopping is the use of the lowest subcontractor's bid as a tool in negotiating lower bids from other subcontractors post-award.

14. "The general contractor, having been awarded the prime contract, may pressure the subcontractor whose bid was used for a particular portion of the work in computing the overall bid on the prime contract to reduce the amount of the bid." Closen & Weiland, at 566 n.6 [13 J. Marshall L. Rev. 565 (1980)].

15. An unscrupulous subcontractor can save estimating costs, and still get the job by not entering a bid or by entering an uncompetitive bid. After bid opening, this unscrupulous subcontractor, knowing the price of the low sub-bid, can then offer to perform the work for less money, precisely because the honest subcontractor has already paid for the estimate and included that cost in the original bid. This practice is called bid peddling.

"Bid shopping and peddling have long been recognized as unethical by construction trade organizations. These 'unethical,' but common practices have several detrimental results. First, as bid shopping becomes common within a particular trade, the subcontractors will pad their initial bids in order to make further reductions during post-award negotiations. This artificial inflation of subcontractor's offers makes the bid process less effective. Second, subcontractors who are forced into post-award negotiations with the general often must reduce their sub-bids in order to avoid losing the award. Thus, they will be faced with a Hobson's choice between doing the job at a loss or doing a less than adequate job. Third, bid shopping and peddling tend to increase the risk of loss of the time and money used in preparing a bid. This occurs because generals and subcontractors who engage in these practices use, without expense, the bid estimates prepared by others. Fourth, it is often impossible for a general to obtain bids far enough in advance to have sufficient time to properly prepare his own bid because of the practice, common among many subcontractors, of holding sub-bids until the last possible moment in order to avoid pre-award bid shopping by the general. Fifth, many subcontractors refuse to submit bids for jobs on which they expect bid shopping. As a result, competition is reduced, and, consequently, construction prices are increased. Sixth, any price reductions gained through the use of post-award bid shopping by the general will be of no benefit to the awarding authority, to whom these price reductions would normally accrue as a result of open competition before the award of the prime contract. Free competition in an open market is therefore perverted because of the use of post-award bid shopping."

Bid Shopping, at 394–96 [18 UCLA L. Rev. 389 (1970)] (citations omitted).

* * *

The doctrine of detrimental reliance has evolved in the time since *Drennan* was decided in 1958. The American Law Institute, responding to *Drennan*, sought to make detrimental reliance more readily applicable to the construction bidding scenario by adding § 87. This new section was intended to make subcontractors' bids binding:

§ 87. Option Contract

* * *

(2) An offer which the offeror should reasonably expect to induce action or forbearance of a substantial character on the part of the offeree before acceptance and which does induce such action or forbearance is binding as an option contract to the extent necessary to avoid injustice.

Restatement (Second) of Contracts § 87 (1979).

Despite the drafter's intention that § 87 of the *Restatement (Second) of Contracts* (1979) should replace *Restatement (First) of Contracts* § 90

(1932) in the construction bidding cases, few courts have availed themselves of the opportunity. * * *

Courts and commentators have also suggested other solutions intended to bind the parties without the use of detrimental reliance theory. The most prevalent suggestion is the use of the firm offer provision of the Uniform Commercial Code. Maryland Code (1992 Repl. Vol.), § 2–205 of the Commercial Law Article. That statute provides:

"An offer by a merchant to buy or sell goods in a signed writing which by its terms gives assurance that it will be held open is not revocable, for lack of consideration, during the time stated or if no time is stated for a reasonable time, but in no event may such period of irrevocability exceed three months; but any such term of assurance on a form supplied by the offeree must be separately signed by the offeror."

In this manner, subcontractor's bids, made in writing and giving some assurance of an intent that the offer be held open, can be found to be irrevocable.

The Supreme Judicial Court of Massachusetts has suggested three other traditional theories that might prove the existence of a contractual relationship between a general contractor and a sub: conditional bilateral contract analysis; unilateral contract analysis; and unrevoked offer analysis. *Loranger Constr. Corp. v. E. F. Hauserman Co.,* 384 N.E.2d 176, 376 Mass. 757 (1978). If the general contractor could prove that there was an exchange of promises binding the parties to each other, and that exchange of promises was made before bid opening, that would constitute a valid bilateral promise conditional upon the general being awarded the job. *Loranger,* 384 N.E.2d at 180, 376 Mass. at 762. This directly contrasts with Judge Hand's analysis in *James Baird,* that a general's use of a sub-bid constitutes acceptance conditional upon the award of the contract to the general. *James Baird,* 64 F.2d at 345–46.

Alternatively, if the subcontractor intended its sub-bid as an offer to a unilateral contract, use of the sub-bid in the general's bid constitutes part performance, which renders the initial offer irrevocable under the *Restatement (Second) of Contracts* § 45 (1979). *Loranger,* 384 N.E.2d at 180, 376 Mass. at 762. This resurrects a second theory dismissed by Judge Learned Hand in *James Baird.*

Finally, the *Loranger* court pointed out that a jury might choose to disbelieve that a subcontractor had withdrawn the winning bid, meaning that acceptance came before withdrawal, and a traditional bilateral contract was formed. *Loranger,* 384 N.E.2d at 180, 376 Mass. at 762–63.

Another alternative solution to the construction bidding problem is no longer seriously considered-revitalizing the common law seal. William Noel Keyes, *Consideration Reconsidered—The Problem of the Withdrawn Bid,* 10 STAN. L. REV. 441, 470 (1958). Because a sealed option contract remains firm without consideration this alternative was proposed as a solution to the construction bidding problem.

It is here that the state of the law rests.

III

If PEI is able to prove by any of the theories described that a contractual relationship existed, but Johnson failed to perform its end of the bargain, then PEI will recover the $32,000 in damages caused by Johnson's breach of contract. Alternatively, if PEI is unable to prove the existence of a contractual relationship, then Johnson has no obligation to PEI. We will test the facts of the case against the theories described to determine if such a relationship existed.

The trial court held, and we agree, that Johnson's sub-bid was an offer to contract and that it was sufficiently clear and definite. We must then determine if PEI made a timely and valid acceptance of that offer and thus created a traditional bilateral contract, or in the absence of a valid acceptance, if PEI's detrimental reliance served to bind Johnson to its sub-bid. We examine each of these alternatives, beginning with traditional contract theory.[22]

A. TRADITIONAL BILATERAL CONTRACT.

The trial judge found that there was not a traditional contract binding Johnson to PEI. A review of the record and the trial judge's findings make it clear that this was a close question. On appeal however, our job is to assure that the trial judge's findings were not clearly erroneous. * * * This is an easier task.

The trial judge rejected PEI's claim of bilateral contract for two separate reasons: 1) that there was no meeting of the minds; and 2) that the offer was withdrawn prior to acceptance. Both need not be proper bases for decision; if either of these two theories is not clearly erroneous, we must affirm.

There is substantial evidence in the record to support the judge's conclusion that there was no meeting of the minds. PEI's letter of August 26, to all potential mechanical subcontractors, reproduced *supra*, indicates, as the trial judge found, that PEI and Johnson "did not have a definite, certain meeting of the minds on a certain price for a certain quantity of goods. * * *" Because this reason is itself sufficient to sustain the trial judge's finding that no contract was formed, we affirm.

---

22. Because they were not raised, either below or in this Court, we need not address the several methods in which a court might interpret a subcontractor's bid as a firm, and thus irrevocable, offer. Nevertheless, for the benefit of bench and bar, we review those theories as applied to this case. First, PEI could have purchased an option, thus supplying consideration for making the offer irrevocable. This did not happen. Second, Johnson could have submitted its bid as a sealed offer. [U.C.C. § 5–102]. An offer under seal supplants the need for consideration to make an offer firm. This did not occur in the instant case. The third method of Johnson's offer becoming irrevocable is by operation of [U.C.C. § 2–205]. We note that Johnson's sub-bid was made in the form of a signed writing, but without further evidence we are unable to determine if the offer "by its terms gives assurance that it will be held open" and if the sub-bid is for "goods" as that term is defined by [U.C.C. §§ 2–105(1)] and by decisions of this Court * * *.

Alternatively, we hold, that the evidence permitted the trial judge to find that Johnson revoked its offer prior to PEI's final acceptance. We review the relevant chronology. Johnson made its offer, in the form of a sub-bid, on August 5. On September 1, PEI accepted. Johnson withdrew its offer by letter dated September 2. On September 28, NIH awarded the contract to PEI. Thus, PEI's apparent acceptance came one day prior to Johnson's withdrawal.

The trial court found, however, "that before there was ever a final agreement reached with the contract awarding authorities, that Johnson made it clear to [PEI] that they were not going to continue to rely on their earlier submitted bid." Implicit in this finding is the judge's understanding of the contract. Johnson's sub-bid constituted an offer of a contingent contract. PEI accepted that offer subject to the condition precedent of PEI's receipt of the award of the contract from NIH. Prior to the occurrence of the condition precedent, Johnson was free to withdraw. See 2 *Williston on Contracts* § 6:14 (4th ed.). On September 2, Johnson exercised that right to revoke.[23] The trial judge's finding that withdrawal proceeded valid final acceptance is therefore logical and supported by substantial evidence in the record. It was not clearly erroneous, so we shall affirm.

B.   DETRIMENTAL RELIANCE

PEI's alternative theory of the case is that PEI's detrimental reliance binds Johnson to its bid. We are asked, as a threshold question, if detrimental reliance applies to the setting of construction bidding. Nothing in our previous cases suggests that the doctrine was intended to be limited to a specific factual setting. The benefits of binding subcontractors outweigh the possible detriments of the doctrine.[24]

This Court has decided cases based on detrimental reliance as early as 1854, and the general contours of the doctrine are well understood by Maryland courts. The historical development of promissory estoppel, or detrimental reliance, in Maryland has mirrored the development nationwide. It was originally a small exception to the general consideration requirement, and found in "cases dealing with such narrow problems as gratuitous agencies and bailments, waivers, and promises of marriage settlement." Jay M. Feinman, Promissory Estoppel and Judicial Method, *97 HARV. L. REV. 678, 680 (1984)*. The early Maryland cases applying

---

23. We have also considered the possibility that Johnson's offer was not to enter into a contingent contract. This is unlikely because there is no incentive for a general contractor to accept a non-contingent contract prior to contract award but it would bind the general to purchase the subcontractor's services even if the general did not receive the award. Moreover, PEI's September 1 letter clearly "accepted" Johnson's offer subject to the award from NIH. If Johnson's bid was for a non-contingent contract, PEI's response substantially varied the offer and was therefore a counter-offer, not an acceptance. * * *

24. General contractors, however, should not assume that we will also adopt the holdings of our sister courts who have refused to find general contractors bound to their subcontractors. *See, e.g., N. Litterio & Co. v. Glassman Constr. Co.,* 115 U.S. App. D.C. 335, 319 F.2d 736 (D.C. Cir. 1963).

"promissory estoppel" or detrimental reliance primarily involve charitable pledges.

* * *

Detrimental reliance doctrine has had a slow evolution from its origins in disputes over charitable pledges, and there remains some uncertainty about its exact dimensions. * * *

To resolve these confusions we now clarify that Maryland courts are to apply the test of the *Restatement (Second) of Contracts* § 90(1) (1979), which we have recast as a four-part test:

1. a clear and definite promise;

2. where the promisor has a reasonable expectation that the offer will induce action or forbearance on the part of the promisee;

3. which does induce actual and reasonable action or forbearance by the promisee; and

4. causes a detriment which can only be avoided by the enforcement of the promise.

In a construction bidding case, where the general contractor seeks to bind the subcontractor to the sub-bid offered, the general must first prove that the subcontractor's sub-bid constituted an offer to perform a job at a given price. We do not express a judgment about how precise a bid must be to constitute an offer, or to what degree a general contractor may request to change the offered scope before an acceptance becomes a counter-offer. That fact-specific judgment is best reached on a case-by-case basis. In the instant case, the trial judge found that the sub-bid was sufficiently clear and definite to constitute an offer, and his finding was not clearly erroneous.

* * *

Second, the general must prove that the subcontractor reasonably expected that the general contractor would rely upon the offer. The subcontractor's expectation that the general contractor will rely upon the sub-bid may dissipate through time.[30]

In this case, the trial court correctly inquired into Johnson's belief that the bid remained open, and that consequently PEI was not relying on the Johnson bid. The judge found that due to the time lapse between bid opening and award, "it would be unreasonable for offers to continue." This is supported by the substantial evidence. James Kick testified that although he knew of his bid mistake, he did not bother to notify PEI because J.J. Kirlin, Inc., and not PEI, was the apparent low bidder. The trial court's finding that Johnson's reasonable expectation had dissipated in the span of a month is not clearly erroneous.

---

30. We expect that evidence of "course of dealing" and "usage of the trade," *see Restatement (Second) of Contracts* § 219–223 (1979), will provide strong indices of the reasonableness of a subcontractor's expectations.

As to the third element, a general contractor must prove that he actually and reasonably relied on the subcontractor's sub-bid. We decline to provide a checklist of potential methods of proving this reliance, but we will make several observations. First, a showing by the subcontractor, that the general contractor engaged in "bid shopping," or actively encouraged "bid chopping," or "bid peddling" is strong evidence that the general did not rely on the sub-bid. Second, prompt notice by the general contractor to the subcontractor that the general intends to use the sub on the job, is weighty evidence that the general did rely on the bid.[31] Third, if a sub-bid is so low that a reasonably prudent general contractor would not rely upon it, the trier of fact may infer that the general contractor did not in fact rely upon the erroneous bid.

In this case, the trial judge did not make a specific finding that PEI failed to prove its reasonable reliance upon Johnson's sub-bid. We must assume, however, that it was his conclusion based on his statement that "the parties did not have a definite, certain meeting of the minds on a certain price for a certain quantity of goods and wanted to renegotiate. * * *" The August 26, 1993, fax from PEI to all prospective mechanical subcontractors, is evidence supporting this conclusion. Although the finding that PEI did not rely on Johnson's bid was indisputably a close call, it was not clearly erroneous.

Finally, as to the fourth prima facie element, the trial court, and not a jury, must determine that binding the subcontractor is necessary to prevent injustice. This element is to be enforced as required by common law equity courts—the general contractor must have "clean hands." This requirement includes, as did the previous element, that the general did not engage in bid shopping, chopping or peddling, but also requires the further determination that justice compels the result. The fourth factor was not specifically mentioned by the trial judge, but we may infer that he did not find this case to merit an equitable remedy.

Because there was sufficient evidence in the record to support the trial judge's conclusion that PEI had not proven its case for detrimental reliance, we must, and hereby do, affirm the trial court's ruling.

V

In conclusion, we emphasize that there are different ways to prove that a contractual relationship exists between a general contractor and its subcontractors. Traditional bilateral contract theory is one. Detrimental reliance can be another. However, under the evidence in this case, the trial judge was not clearly erroneous in deciding that recovery by the general contractor was not justified under either theory.

JUDGMENT AFFIRMED, WITH COSTS.

---

31. Prompt notice and acceptance also significantly dispels the possibility of bid shopping, bid chopping, and bid peddling.

QUESTIONS, NOTES, AND CONNECTIONS

1. Questions about the facts of this case

    1.1.   Try to put together a chronology of events. On what date did Johnson make its offer for the sub-bid? On what date did PEI accept? On what date did Johnson attempt to withdraw its offer? Now look at your chronology of the facts. Does it support the holding in the case?

    1.2.   With respect to PEI's promissory estoppel claim, in its summary of the findings of fact made by the trial court, the court of appeals notes that "PEI relied upon Johnson's sub-bid in making the bid for the entire project." Later in the decision, the court states: "In this case, the trial judge did not make a specific finding that PEI failed to prove its reasonable reliance upon Johnson's sub-bid. * * * Although the finding that PEI did not rely on Johnson's bid was indisputably a close call, it was not clearly erroneous." What's going on here?

    1.3.   See if you can identify the critical factual distinctions between Justice Traynor's holding in *Drennan v. Star Paving*, discussed at length in the *Pavel Enterprises* opinion, and the *Pavel* case itself.

2. Questions about the law

    2.1.   One of the limitations in *Restatement (Second) of Contracts* § 87(2), which expressly adopts the *Drennan* approach, is that the promise is only enforceable "to the extent necessary to prevent injustice." Of course, the same language appears in § 90. What does that language mean in this context? Is it an injustice if, as result of the revocation of the subcontractor's bid, the general contractor will make *less* profit, or is it only an injustice if, because of the price of the next lowest bid, the general contractor will now actually lose money on the job? Who makes that determination?

    2.2.   Despite the different theories under which a general contractor may bind the subcontractor to hold its bid open, as *Pavel Enterprises* illustrates, there is no guarantee that the general contractor will prevail on any of these theories. Therefore, in representing a general contractor who is figuring its costs in reliance on specific subcontractor bids, what advice would you give to ensure protection of your client's interests? Correspondingly, if you represent a subcontractor preparing to make its bid and concerned about application of the rule in *Drennan*, what steps would you advise your client to take?

    2.3.   The court in *Pavel Enterprises* concluded that a traditional bilateral contract had not been formed and that PEI's detrimental reliance would not serve to bind Johnson. Nevertheless, it was undisputed that Pavel used Johnson's sub-bid in computing its own bid. Given this fact, could you construct an argument either for acceptance by performance or, invoking *Restatement (Second) of Contracts* § 45, for irrevocability of the sub-bid based on part performance?

3. Notes

    3.1. In the *Drennan* case, Justice Traynor employed the doctrine of promissory estoppel to find that the subcontractor could not revoke its bid once it had been relied upon by the general contractor. However, as the court in *Pavel Enterprises* noted, this was really an expansion of the doctrine of promissory estoppel since the bid involved an offer for an *exchange* transaction and not a gift promise. Thus, in *Drennan*, the court used promissory estoppel (or detrimental reliance) to *imply* a promise of irrevocability where none actually existed, as well as to *enforce* that promise despite the absence of consideration.

    3.2. Recognizing the one-sided nature of the option contract created by *Drennan*, and the potential for bid-shopping by the general contractor that it creates, in 1963 the California legislature adopted a statute that 1) requires the general contractor in any public project to list the identities of its subcontractors in its bid, and then, 2) proscribes the substitution by the general contractor of any subcontractor listed in the original bid, except upon a showing of exceptional circumstances such as the subcontractor's insolvency or refusal to do the work. Cal. Gov't Code §§ 4100–4108 (Subletting and Subcontractors Fair Practices Act). Does such an approach, which has been followed in other states, level the playing field for general and subcontractors?

4. Connections

    Drennan and *Restatement (Second) of Contracts* § 87(2), discussed in the *Pavel Enterprises* case, demonstrate that courts will sometimes use a promissory estoppel theory as a basis for barring an offeror from revoking an offer on which the offeree has relied. Can you identify other areas where reliance has been invoked by courts as the basis for development of a new rule other than unbargained for reliance as a substitute for consideration?

D.   REMEDIAL CONSIDERATIONS

EDWARD YORIO & STEVE THEL, THE PROMISSORY BASIS OF § 90

101 YALE L.J. 111, 116–17 (1991).

During the 1926 proceedings of the American Law Institute, a member of the audience asked Professor Samuel Williston, the reporter for the First Restatement of Contracts, about the following hypothetical. Uncle, aware that Nephew is thinking about buying a car, promises to give Nephew $1000. Nephew buys a car for $600. If Uncle reneges on his promise and Nephew sues, what does the Nephew recover, $1000 or $600? Williston responded that Uncle would be liable for $1000, the amount of his promise. Although Williston's response satisfied the immediate questioner, Frederic Coudert, the famous New York lawyer, challenged Williston's answer in an exchange that has since become one of the most quoted passages in American contract law:

> MR. COUDERT: Allow me to trespass once more, Mr. Reporter, by asking this question. Please let me see if I understand it rightly. Would you say, Mr. Reporter, in your case of Johnny and the uncle, the uncle promising the $1000 and Johnny buying the car—say, he goes out and buys the car for $500—that uncle would be liable for $1000 or would he be liable for $500?

> MR. WILLISTON: If Johnny had done what he was expected to do, or is acting within the limits of his uncle's expectation, I think the uncle would be liable for $1000; but not otherwise.

> MR. COUDERT: In other words, substantial justice would require that uncle should be penalized in the sum of $500.

> MR. WILLISTON: Why do you say "penalized"?. * * *

> MR. COUDERT: Because substantial justice there would require, it seems to me, that Johnny get his money for his car, but should he get his car and $500 more? I don't see.

Coudert's bewilderment was shared by other members of the audience, who returned repeatedly to the car hypothetical:

> HOMER ALBERS (Massachusetts): I am still not satisfied that Johnny could have the car and $500 both, if he bought a second-hand Buick for $500. * * *

> JUDGE PAGE: To get back to Johnny, how is injustice going to be done Johnny if he is not going to get the other $500; how is he going to be done an injustice, if he only paid $500 for the car?

In the face of this assault, Williston stood his ground:

> MR. WILLISTON: Either the promise is binding or it is not. If the promise is binding it has to be enforced as it is made.

———————

Many commentators have urged that the remedy in promissory estoppel cases should be limited to *reliance* damages—the amount necessary to put the promisee back in the position she would have been had the promise not been made. In fact, however, most cases support Professor Williston's view and award *expectation* damages or even specific performance. Expectation damages are measured by the amount necessary to put the promisee in as good of a position as performance would have. Which measure of damages did the court recommend as appropriate on remand in *Midwest Energy*? How about in *Ricketts*? Can you explain the reasons for the difference?

When we enforce a promise because the promisee detrimentally relied, arguably what we're saying is that we'll hold the promisor liable because it would be wrong to allow him to walk away after foreseeably causing harm or loss to the promisee. In other words, the promisee has been damaged and it is the promisor's fault. Doesn't this suggest that the promisee's recovery should be determined based on the amount necessary to compensate her for her loss, to restore her to the position she would have been in had the promise never been made? How does this rationale differ from the rationale for enforcing exchange promises—those supported by a bargained-for consideration? Should this make a difference in how damages are calculated? What about the language in § 90 that allows courts to limit the remedy "as justice requires"? Consider these questions in light of the discussion which follows about the continued role of reliance in promissory estoppel cases.

E.   THE DIMINISHING IMPORTANCE OF RELIANCE

Oddly, even though the doctrine of promissory estoppel developed in the context of charitable subscription cases, proving reliance in the form of action or forbearance is often most difficult for the promisee in those cases. If you pledge $100 to your alma mater and then stiff the school, how can the institution show that it was *induced* by your pledge to take a particular course of action that it would not otherwise have taken? Chances are, it can't. Thus, courts typically engage in various fictions to find detrimental reliance when none exist in fact. In the next case the court deals with the issue of reliance more honestly. See if you agree with the public policy that the court cites in support of its holding.

SALSBURY v. NORTHWESTERN BELL TELEPHONE COMPANY

Supreme Court of Iowa
221 N.W.2d 609 (1974)

HARRIS, J.

This is the third appeal in which we have considered a claim of charitable subscription following the collapse of an attempt to establish a college in *Charles City. In Pappas v. Hauser,* 197 N.W.2d 607 (Iowa 1972) and *Pappas v. Bever,* 219 N.W.2d 720 (Iowa 1974) we held pledges not legally binding. In this case a letter was sent by the subscriber in lieu of executing the pledge form. The trial court held the letter bound its sender. We affirm.

* * *

John Salsbury (plaintiff) participated in the efforts to establish Charles City College (the college). He was the first and only chairman of the college's board of trustees. The funding project for the college was described in *Pappas v. Hauser, supra.* As part of the funding drive Peter Bruno, a professional fund raiser, solicited a subscription from Northwestern Bell Telephone Company (defendant). Defendant's office manager in Charles City was Daryl V. Winder who was also active in the campaign to raise money for the college. Bruno negotiated a number of times with Winder for the subscription from defendant.

As a fund solicitor Winder had been given a kit which included pledge forms of the type described in *Pappas v. Hauser, supra,* and *Pappas v. Bever, supra.* [These pledge forms or cards were generally given and received with the understanding that they were not binding. Eds.] Winder lacked authority to bind defendant for a pledge but conveyed the request to superiors in defendant corporation. Winder apparently did not have a pledge form available when he received defendant's consent for the subscription. Accordingly he wrote a letter to Bruno as follows:

"This is to advise you that the contribution from Northwestern Bell Telephone Co. to the Charles City College has been approved by Mr. E. A. McDaniel, District Manager, Mason City.

"The $15,000 contribution will be made over a three year period, in three equal payments. Our first $5000 payment will be made in 1968.

"We are very pleased to add our name to the list of contributors to this fine community undertaking.

"If I can be of further assistance, please feel free to contact me."

The college and all others treated the letter exactly as another pledge card. In common with executed pledge cards it was assigned to a material supplier of the college. The letter itself was not transmitted to the supplier. A pledge card form was typed-in to reflect the $15,000 pledge though it was not signed by defendant. If any document reflecting defendant's intended contribution was forwarded in connection with the assignment to the supplier it was a copy of the typed-in pledge card.

Plaintiff executed a personal guaranty in order to gain credit from the supplier. Subscription pledges secured the obligation. The supplier then assigned the pledges to American Acceptance Corporation of Philadelphia, Pennsylvania, and finally, after settling with plaintiff, American Acceptance Corporation assigned them to him. In all assignments no copy of the letter was shown or given. Plaintiff conceded he had no knowledge of the letter. He acted in the belief defendant was obligated in the same manner as those who executed pledge cards.

As we have seen in the earlier cases cited the college failed after a short operation. In this appeal we are faced with the question of whether defendant is bound to pay his subscription by reason of the letter. *Pappas v. Bever, supra,* stands as authority defendant would not be bound had it executed only the pledge card.

I.

The trial court held the letter was a promissory undertaking which constituted a basis for contractual liability. This holding is challenged as being at variance with the understanding of the parties when the letter was given and received.

. . . .

Plaintiff conceded letters, such as defendant's, were sometimes taken "in lieu of" pledge cards and were accepted on the "same basis." Plaintiff also admitted he had not seen defendant's letter until trial and had been unaware of its contents until two months before trial. * * *

The trial court refused to proceed from plaintiff's concession that letters were taken "in lieu of" and on the "same basis" as pledge cards. Defendant assumes it must follow the parties agreed any liabilities and rights under any letter, no matter how it was worded, were fixed by the wording of the pledge cards. The trial court did not agree. It ruled: "* * * A pledge card * * * was never presented to or signed by the defendant, and is irrelevant to any undertaking of the defendant. Any obligation of the defendant must be based on its letter."

We find nothing in plaintiff's concession which rises to an admission all letters were understood to bind the signer in exact accordance with the wording of an unsigned pledge card. The record supports the trial court's determination that defendant's letter set its own terms and was impervious to defenses which might avail against the pledge cards. It follows the trial court was right in excluding as irrelevant the evidence of circumstances surrounding execution of pledge cards.

II.

Defendant separately assigns the claim the trial court failed to apply fundamental contract principles. It is argued there was a failure of consideration because the college failed before any sums were scheduled for payment under the terms of the letter. It is also claimed the trial court should have given the letter the practical construction adopted by the college when it treated it the same as a pledge card. These assignments presuppose a charitable subscription should be viewed by routine contract standards. Many cases, including our own, have considered charitable subscriptions as desirable but enforceable only upon a showing of consideration sufficient for contractual liability.

Cases throughout the country clearly reflect a conflict between the desired goal of enforcing charitable subscriptions and the realities of contract law. The result has been strained reasoning which has been the subject of considerable criticism. This criticism is directed toward efforts by the courts to secure a substitute for consideration in charitable subscriptions. These efforts were thought necessary to bind the subscriber on a contract theory. Yet, in the nature of charitable subscriptions, it is presupposed the promise is made as a gift and not in return for consideration. 1 Williston on Contracts, Third Ed., § 116, page 473.

Consideration sufficient for a binding contract has been found under various criticized theories. *Id.* at 476–479. We have found consideration in the promises of other subscribers. *Brokaw v. McElroy,* 162 Iowa 288, 143 N.W. 1087; *Trustees v. Noyes,* 165 Iowa 601, 146 N.W. 848; *In re Estate of Leigh,* 186 Iowa 931, 173 N.W. 143; *Young Men's Christian Assn. v. Caward,* 213 Iowa 408, 239 N.W. 41. This theory is also criticized:

"* * * The difficulty with this view is its lack of conformity to the facts. It is doubtless possible for two or more persons to make mutual promises that each will give a specified amount to a charity or other object, but in the case of ordinary charitable subscriptions, the promise of each subscriber is made directly to the charity or its trustees, and it is frequently made without any reference to the subscription of others. If induced at all by previous or expected subscriptions, this inducement only affects the motive of the subscriber; it cannot be said that the previous subscriptions were given in exchange for the later one. Indeed the earlier subscriptions would be open to the objection of being past consideration so far as a later subscription was concerned * * *." 1 Williston on Contracts, *supra,* pages 476–477.

In reaction to this widespread criticism a number of courts have turned to promissory estoppel as an alternative for the consideration requirement. 1 Williston on Contracts, Third Ed., § 140. * * *

If promissory estoppel were to be the standard or criterion for enforcement this defendant probably could not be bound on the pledge. * * * Plaintiff relied on defendant's letter but not the form of it. Plaintiff conceded he had not even seen the letter until shortly before trial. And it is the form of the letter that distinguishes it from the pledge cards we have held not to be binding. *Pappas v. Bever, supra.*

We acknowledge as valid the criticism of cases which enforce charitable subscriptions only on a fictional finding of consideration. But we are reluctant to adopt promissory estoppel as the sole alternative basis for such enforcement.

"* * * Wide variation in reasoning indicates the difficulty of enforcing a charitable subscription on grounds of consideration. Yet, the courts have generally striven to find grounds for enforcement, indicating the depth of feeling in this country that private philanthropy serves a highly important function in our society.

"Of late, courts have tended to abandon the attempt to utilize traditional contract doctrines to sustain subscriptions and have placed their decision on grounds of promissory estoppel. Surprisingly, however, if promissory estoppel, in its traditional form, is widely adopted as the grounds upon which such subscriptions are to be tested, fewer subscriptions are likely to be enforced than previously. Under previous holdings, despite the conceptual inadequacy of the reasoning, promises were frequently enforced without regard to detrimental reliance on the promise. It was enough that the promisor had subscribed. If enforcement of charitable subscriptions is a desirable goal, it would seem sounder to view the preponderance of the cases as supporting the proposition that a charitable subscription is enforceable without consideration and without detrimental reliance. This seems to be the position taken in Restatement Second. Recognition of such a rule would also put an end to the flood of needless litigation created by the caution of executors and administrators who, for self-protection against surcharging, will not pay out on a subscription without a court decree." Calamari & Perillo, Law of Contracts, § 103, pages 177–178.

The tentative draft of Restatement of Contracts, Second, includes a new subparagraph 2. Section 90 now reads as follows: * * *

> "(2) A charitable subscription or a marriage settlement is binding under Subsection (1) without proof that the promise induced action or forbearance."

We believe public policy supports this view. It is more logical to bind charitable subscriptions without requiring a showing of consideration or detrimental reliance.

Charitable subscriptions often serve the public interest by making possible projects which otherwise could never come about. It is true some fund raising campaigns are not conducted on a plan which calls for subscriptions to be binding. In such cases we do not hesitate to hold them not binding. *Pappas v. Bever, supra.* However where a subscription is unequivocal the pledgor should be made to keep his word.

AFFIRMED.

QUESTIONS

1. Obviously, the approach to charitable subscriptions adopted in *Salsbury* has found its way into the final version of the *Restatement (Second) of Contracts*. Does this mean if you call and make a $10 pledge to Jerry's Kids on Labor Day but fail to follow-up with the money, that the Muscular Dystrophy Association can sue you and recover? What if your donation was made in an uncontrollable surge of emotion after watching a particularly poignant segment of the telethon, but you cannot really afford to pay the amount you pledged? Speaking of pledges, what exactly was the difference, from a legal standpoint, between the pledge cards and the letter in *Salsbury*?

2. Reliance remains a necessary element of promissory estoppel under § 90 in the commercial context. But what kind of showing is required? Must the reliance result in some form of measurable economic loss? In *Vastoler v. American Can Co.*, 700 F.2d 916 (3d Cir. 1983), the plaintiff brought suit against his former employer to enforce a promise to the effect that his years of service on behalf of the company occurring prior to his promotion would count for purposes of calculating his pension benefits at retirement. The plaintiff's acceptance of the promotion was conditioned on receiving

this credit, so when, at retirement, the employer did not count the years of past service, the plaintiff sued on a promissory estoppel theory alleging the promise induced him to accept the promotion. The trial court granted the employer's summary judgment motion on the basis that the plaintiff had not been disadvantaged by accepting a promotion. The court of appeals reversed and remanded the case for trial, noting that the district court's reasoning contained the following flaw:

The second error in the district court's reasoning involves an even more fundamental deficiency. It failed to consider the human dynamics and anxieties inherent in supervisory positions. All jobs are not the same, and work involves more than one's "daily bread" and the weekly paycheck. Certain jobs have higher levels of stress and anxiety. Often, increased responsibilities torture the mind as well as the body. The different levels of stress associated with different jobs explains why some qualified people do not want to be President of Fortune 500 corporations, nominee for the Presidency of the United States, or foreman of their plants. Some privates do not want the decision-making burdens of majors and generals. Following Justice Frankfurter's admonition that "this Court should not be ignorant as judges of what we know as men [or women]," *Watts v. Indiana,* 338 U.S. 49, 52, 69 S.Ct. 1347, 1349, 93 L.Ed. 1801 (1949), we find that the trial judge erred in failing to recognize that absorption of the stress and anxiety inherent in supervisory positions could be one of the factors that constitutes detrimental reliance.

700 F.2d at 919.

Do you think this is the kind of detrimental reliance the drafters of the *Restatement (Second)* had in mind? Reliance, of course, is very much a tort-based concept. If proof of reliance is becoming less central to recovery under promissory estoppel, does that help explain the trend we discussed in Subsection 4, *supra,* concerning the tendency of the courts to award expectation damages rather than reliance damages in promissory estoppel cases?

CHAPTER FOUR

IS THE AGREEMENT UNENFORCEABLE BECAUSE OF THE FLAWS IN THE AGREEMENT PROCESS OR PROBLEMS WITH THE LANGUAGE OF THE AGREEMENT?

■ ■ ■

This Chapter surveys legal grounds for NOT enforcing an agreement based on either the provisions in the agreement or the agreement process. For example, in the first case in the book, *R.R. v. M.H.*, the agreement was unenforceable because of provisions in the agreement. The court found that an agreement for R.R.'s custody of the baby was unenforceable as against public policy because the agreement provided for payment to M.H. In the very next case we considered, Lucy v. Zehmer, there was an issue of agreement process: whether the Zehmers were drunk. It was important that the court determined that the Zehmers were not intoxicated because a person who is intoxicated lacks capacity to contract

Public policy and lack of capacity are only two of the legal grounds for not enforcing an agreement because of either problems with the language of the agreement or the agreement process. Those are two of the easier grounds to understand.

With the possible exception of the Statute of Frauds, the particulars of, and the policy basis for, the legal grounds for not enforcing an agreement are obvious. So, let's get the Statute of Frauds out of the way, and then we can do easy stuff.

SECTION 1: CONTRACT LAW REASONS FOR NOT ENFORCING AGREEMENTS: STATUTES OF FRAUD

Because of the Statute of Frauds, *some* agreements are not enforceable unless there is *special* proof that the agreement was made. This relatively simple sentence raises five not always simple questions that lawyers and law students need to be able to answer.

1) What is a Statute of Frauds?

2) What are the reasons for a Statute of Frauds?

3) Which agreements are covered by a Statute of Frauds, *i.e.*, "within" the Statute of Frauds?

4) How are the requirements of a Statute of Frauds met, *i.e.*, satisfied?

5) What are the legal consequences of failure to satisfy the Statute of Frauds?

First, what is a Statute of Frauds? The first Statute of Frauds was enacted in England in 1677: "An Act for Prevention of Frauds and Perjuries." It required that certain kinds of agreements must be in writing to be legally enforceable. It remained the law in England until 1954 when most of its provisions were repealed.

While the Statute of Frauds has been virtually eliminated from the law of contracts in England, it remains an important (albeit unpopular) part of the law of contracts in the United States. Virtually every state has enacted one or more statutes of frauds providing that certain kinds of agreements are not legally enforceable unless set out in a signed writing.

Second, what are the reasons for a Statute of Frauds? The title of the first Statute of Frauds sets out the purpose of a Statute of Frauds: "Prevention of Frauds or Perjuries." As the note preceding § 110 of the *Restatement (Second) of Contracts* explains: "In general, the primary purpose of the Statute of Frauds is assumed to be evidentiary, to provide reliable evidence of the existence and terms of the contract, and the classes of contracts covered seem for the most part to have been selected because of importance or complexity."

Third, what kinds of agreements are covered by the Statute of Frauds? Again, Statutes of Frauds vary from state to state. Section 110 of the *Restatement (Second) of Contracts* sets out the kinds of agreements generally covered by a state's Statute of Frauds.

§ 110   *Classes of Contracts Covered*

(1) The following classes of contracts are subject to a statute, commonly called the Statute of Frauds, forbidding enforcement unless there is a written memorandum or an applicable exception;

(a) a contract of an executor or administrator to answer for a duty of his decedent (the executor-administrator provision);

(b) a contract to answer for the duty of another (the suretyship provision);

(c) a contract made upon consideration of marriage (the marriage provision);

d) a contract for the sale of an interest in land (the land contract provision);

(e) a contract that is not to be performed within one year from the making thereof (the one-year provision).

(2) The following classes of contracts, which were traditionally subject to the Statute of Frauds, are now governed by Statute of Frauds provisions of the Uniform Commercial Code:

(a) a contract for the sale of goods for the price of $500 or more (Uniform Commercial Code § 2–201). * * *

* * *

The following three cases illustrate three kinds of contracts that are commonly within a state's Statute of Frauds* (1) land transfer agreements, (2) agreements to buy or sell goods for $500 or more, and (3) agreements that cannot be performed within one year from the date the agreement was made. Additionally, the cases show the answers to question 4—how are the requirements of a Statute of Frauds satisfied, and question 5—what are the consequences of failure to satisfy the Statute of Frauds?

In the first of the cases, *Radke v. Brenon,* the court considers whether a typed letter offering to sell land was sufficient to comply with the Minnesota Statute of Frauds governing land transfers.

RADKE v. BRENON

Supreme Court of Minnesota
271 Minn. 35, 134 N.W.2d 887 (1965)

ROGOSHESKE, JUSTICE.

Defendants appeal from a judgment of the district court decreeing specific performance of a contract for the sale of real estate.

The judgment was entered upon findings made after trial that "subsequent to the Defendant acquiring" the property in question they "did offer to sell the property to the Plaintiff for the sum of Two Hundred Sixty-two ($262.00) Dollars, which offer the Plaintiff did accept"; and that "at all times relevant, the Plaintiff has been ready, willing and able to complete the agreement for the sale of Defendants' property but the Defendants have refused to do so." The court concluded that defendants "have wrongfully and improperly failed and refused" to deliver a deed of the property to plaintiff.

Resolving the conflicts in the evidence in plaintiff's favor, as we must, these appear to be the facts. Plaintiff and defendants are neighbors owning adjoining lots in Wakefield Park addition in Ramsey County. At the times each acquired ownership, their lots and eight neighboring lots did not extend to the west shoreline of Wakefield Lake, located nearby. The strip of land between the shoreline of the lake and the east boundary of the platted lots was owned by Dr. Gulden * * * until December 1, 1959, when defendants acquired ownership of the entire strip. Preston Brenon,

---

* While the *Restatement* capitalizes the Statute of Frauds, Bryan Garner doesn't—at least we think he doesn't. *See* BRYAN A. GARNER, A DICTIONARY OF MODERN LEGAL USAGE 831 (2nd ed. 1995).

hereinafter referred to as defendant, was a licensed real estate agent. Following his purchase, he had the property surveyed, and on June 28, 1960, he sent an identical letter to plaintiff and the eight other neighbors offering to sell them the irregular parcels that separated their lots from the lake. In the letter he explained that since he was interested only in that part of the strip adjoining his property, he had no desire to retain the remainder. He stated he had "no desire to make any profit on this transaction if everyone owning adjoining property is willing to buy their portion" and divide the cost "equally among all 10 including (him)self." He itemized the total cost at $2,120 and offered to sell each lot for $212 on any terms agreeable. This letter was not signed by defendant but his name was typewritten thereon, he having authorized this and considered such to be tantamount to his signature. Previous to the receipt of this letter, plaintiff and defendant had discussed the latter's intent of acquiring the property for the neighborhood on at least two occasions. About [two] weeks after plaintiff received this offer, he orally accepted it. Sometime later, plaintiff learned from a neighbor that two neighbors declined to purchase, and thus the divided cost of each lot was increased to $262. * * * It is clear that plaintiff accepted defendant's offer on May 7, at which time plaintiff knew of the price increase. Defendant testified:

'Q. * * * And did he agree to buy that time?

'A. At that time he did.'

On August 14, plaintiff delivered to his attorney a check for $262 payable to defendants for the purpose of completing the sale. On August 16, plaintiff's attorney wrote defendant informing him that he held the check for payment of the sale price to be delivered on receipt of a deed. Sometime after August 16, plaintiff received a letter from defendant dated August 16 informing him that the offer to sell was revoked.

The question is whether these facts establish a valid and enforceable contract for the sale of land. Defendants contend they do not.

As admitted by defendant, an oral contract to sell the land was made, and the trial court was clearly justified in so finding. There being no formal, integrated, written contract, however, the problem is whether the oral contract is unenforceable because it comes within Minn. St. 513.05[1] of the statute of frauds. Briefly, that provision decrees void any contract for the sale of lands unless the contract or some memorandum of the contract is in writing. The precise issue in this case is whether, under the circumstances, the letter written by defendant offering the land to plaintiff is a memorandum sufficient to satisfy the requirements of the statute.

The statute expresses a public policy of preventing the enforcement by means of fraud and perjury of contracts that were never in fact made.

---

1. Minn. St. 513.05 provides: "Every contract for the leasing for a longer period of than one year or for the sale of any lands, or any interest in lands, shall be void unless the contract, or some note or memorandum thereof, expressing the consideration, is in writing and subscribed by the party by whom the lease or sale is to be made, or by his lawful agent thereunto authorized in writing; and no such contract, when made by an agent, shall be entitled to record unless the authority of such agent be also recorded."

To inhibit perversion of this policy by those who would deny an oral contract actually made, the statute itself permits enforcement of an oral contract if there exists a note or memorandum as evidence of the contract. To the courts, then, is left promotion of the policy of the statute, either by denying enforcement urged by defrauders or by granting enforcement against wrongful repudiators. As an aid in this objective, the statute itself lists some requisites of a memorandum and this court has added others, so that we have some indication of what content a memorandum normally must have in order to be sufficient evidence of the contract.

The statute requires that the writing express the consideration and that it be subscribed by the party by whom the sale is to be made or by his lawful agent authorized in writing. This court has stated that the memorandum is sufficient when, in addition to the above requirements, it states expressly or by necessary implication the parties to the contract, the lands involved, and the general terms and conditions upon which the sale will be made.

These latter elements are clearly present in the letter written by defendant. Plaintiff's name is included in the inside address heading the letter, and Brenon's name is typewritten at the bottom. The land to be sold is positively delineated. The letter offers "their portion" to "everyone owning adjoining property," and the survey map accompanying the letter depicts each tract. Considering the conversation both before the after the letter was sent, it is inconceivable that the parties could be uncertain concerning the land to be sold. As to other terms of the contract, such as manner of payment, Brenon merely held himself ready "to work out any kind of terms" with the purchasers.

The elements expressly required by statute are not so obvious. First, the consideration of $212 stated in the letter is not the same as the $262 tendered in accord with the oral understanding. Despite this discrepancy, we think that the letter sufficiently expresses the consideration because the $212 represented an equal share of the cost divided by all ten interested parties. As Brenon said in the letter, "I feel the only fair way to share the cost is to divide equally among all 10 including myself." There is no dispute that the price was changed from that stated in the letter when two property owners declined to buy. The consideration then was simply a mathematical computation according to the formula specified in the letter. We do not believe this variation in the dollar amount renders the letter's expression of the consideration insufficient, especially since plaintiff paid more under the admitted agreement than he would have paid according to the letter.

The necessity of a subscription presents the final problem. A "subscription" is the same as a "signing," and it is clear that Brenon's typewritten name, which according to his testimony was typed with the intent that it be tantamount to a written signature, is a sufficient subscription. A problem here is that his wife, who owned the property with him in joint tenancy, apparently neither signed the letter nor authorized him in writing to sell her share. But this deficiency was at no time claimed or asserted before the trial court or in defendants' brief to this court. It was suggested for the first time upon oral argument. If it is a fact, it was not a part of the theory upon which the case was tried and submitted. We must therefore adhere to our well-settled rule that an unlitigated issue may not be asserted for the first time on appeal.

We by no means intend to hold that Brenon's letter would be a sufficient memorandum in every case. We will overlook technical requirements only if proof of the oral contract is clear and uncontradicted as in this case where defendant admitted that a contract had been made. But those technical requirements are only aids to discern where the truth lies in a given case, and we will not blindly apply those technicalities if they lead to a conclusion repugnant to common sense. As Professor Williston has said:

> "In brief, the Statute 'was intended to guard against the perils of perjury and error in the spoken word.' Therefore, if after a consideration of the surrounding circumstances, the pertinent facts and all the evidence in a particular case, the court concludes that enforcement of the agreement will not subject the defendant to fraudulent claims, the purpose of the Statute will best be served by holding the note or memorandum sufficient even though it be ambiguous or incomplete."

Most persuasive is defendant's admission during trial that a contract was in fact made between plaintiff and himself. Although we have followed the majority rule that admission of the contract does not preclude assertion of the statute of frauds, an admission that a contract was made certainly cannot be ignored when all other evidence submitted supports the same conclusion. Even though it may be argued that the formal requirements contemplated by the statute are lacking, when all the evidence is taken into account we are of the opinion that the letter should be held a sufficient memorandum in this case. The policy of the statute of frauds would be perverted if the admitted contract were not enforced. The judgment of the trial court is therefore affirmed.

QUESTIONS, NOTES, AND CONNECTIONS

1. Questions about the facts of this case

    1.1. Was the letter from the defendant to the plaintiff a contract or an offer?

    1.2. Did the defendant sign the letter?

    1.3. Was there a writing signed by the plaintiff in which he agreed to buy the land?

    1.4. Did the defendant contend that he did not offer to sell the land? Did the defendant argue that the plaintiff did not accept his offer?

2.   Questions about the law

     2.1.   What was the reason for the court's statement: "We by no means hold that Brenon's letter would be a sufficient memorandum in every case"?

     2.2.   Why was the defendant's admission of an agreement "most persuasive"? Would the court have reached the same result if defendant's June 28 offer to sell was in an e-mail message? In a voice mail message left on plaintiff's answering machine? In some states, statutes of fraud have been revised to answer these questions. California's answers are set out in the footnote.*

     2.3.   Assume that the buyer Radke, not the seller Brenon, changed his mind about the deal and Brenon was suing Radke for $262 for breach of contract. Would the agreement be enforceable against Radke?

3.   Notes

     3.1.   The Minnesota Statute of Frauds seems to contemplate a single writing: "the contract, some note or memorandum thereof." Such language is typical of Statutes of Fraud. Nonetheless, courts generally conclude that several writings can be pieced together to satisfy the Statute of Frauds, even though any one of the writings taken alone would not have been sufficient. *See Restatement (Second) of Contracts* § 132.

     3.2.   The Minnesota Statute of Frauds also requires a writing "expressing the consideration." The requirements for satisfying a Statute of Frauds vary from state to state, and from statute to statute within a state. Compare the requirements of the Minnesota Statute of Frauds set out in the *Radke* case with the requirements of the Uniform Commercial Code's Statute of Frauds for sales of goods for $500 or more set out below. Note the differences in: (i) what the writing must provide (2–201(1)), (ii) who must sign the writing (2–201(2)), and (iii) the significance of an admission that there was an agreement (2–201(3)(b)).

2–201 Formal Requirements; Statute of Frauds

(1) Except as otherwise provided in this section a contract for the sale of goods for the price of $500 or more is not enforceable by way of action or defense unless there is some writing sufficient to indicate that a contract for sale has been made between the parties and

---

* Cal. Civ. Code section 1624:

(3) There is sufficient evidence that a contract has been made in any of the following circumstances:

(A) There is evidence of an electronic communication (including, without limitation, the recording of a telephone call or the tangible written text produced by computer retrieval), admissible in evidence under the laws of this state, sufficient to indicate that in the communication a contract was made between the parties. * * *

(4) For purposes of this subdivision, the tangible written text produced by telex, telefacsimile, computer retrieval, or other process by which electronic signals are transmitted by telephone or otherwise shall constitute a writing, and any symbol executed or adopted by a party with the present intention to authenticate a writing shall constitute a signing.

signed by the party against whom enforcement is sought or by his authorized agent or broker. A writing is not insufficient because it omits or incorrectly states a term agreed upon but the contract is not enforceable under this paragraph beyond the quantity of goods shown in such writing.

(2) Between merchants if within a reasonable time a writing in confirmation of the contract and sufficient against the sender is received and the party receiving it has reason to know its contents, it satisfies the requirements of subsection (1) against such party unless written notice of objection to its contents is given within 10 days after it is received.

(3) A contract which does not satisfy the requirements of subsection (1) but which is valid in other respects is enforceable

alternatives

(a) if the goods are to be specially manufactured for the buyer and are not suitable for sale to others in the ordinary course of the seller's business and the seller, before notice of repudiation is received and under circumstances which reasonably indicate that the goods are for the buyer, has made either a substantial beginning of their manufacture or commitments for their procurement; or

(b) if the party against whom enforcement is sought admits in his pleading, testimony or otherwise in court that a contract for sale was made, but the contract is not enforceable under this provision beyond the quantity of goods admitted; or

(c) with respect to goods for which payment has been made and accepted or which have been received and accepted (Sec. 2–606).

3.3. Reconsider the phrase in section 2–201(1): "signed by the party against whom enforcement is sought." Who is the "party against whom enforcement is sought"? Is that person always the seller? How is section 2–201(2) different from section 2–201(1)? While a writing, or writings, is the most common method of satisfying the Statute of Frauds, note the alternate ways of satisfying the Statute of Frauds set out in section 2–201(3). The next case deals with the "judicial admission" alternative set out in 2–201(3)(b).

4. Connections

Before going forward to the next case on satisfying the Statute of Frauds without a writing under the U.C.C., go back to some of the cases on sales of real estate that we considered earlier:

4.1. How would *Lucy v. Zehmer*, page 37, have been decided if: (i) the farm was in Minnesota, and (ii) the Zehmers had asserted a Statute of Frauds defense?

4.2. How would *Smith v. Boyd*, page 58, have been decided if: (i) the house was in Minnesota, and (ii) the Boyds had asserted a Statute of Frauds defense?

DF ACTIVITIES CORPORATION v. BROWN

United States Court of Appeals, Seventh Circuit
851 F.2d 920 (1988)

POSNER, CIRCUIT JUDGE.

This appeal in a diversity breach of contract case raises an interesting question concerning the statute of frauds, in the context of a dispute over a chair of more than ordinary value. The plaintiff, DF Activities Corporation (owner of the Domino's pizza chain), is controlled by a passionate enthusiast for the work of Frank Lloyd Wright. The defendant, Dorothy [sic] Brown, a resident of Lake Forest (a suburb of Chicago) lived for many years in a house designed by Frank Lloyd Wright—the Willits House—and became the owner of a chair that Wright had designed, the Willits Chair. This is a stark, high-backed, uncomfortable-looking chair of distinguished design that DF wanted to add to its art collection. In September and October 1986, Sarah–Ann Briggs, DF's art director, negotiated with Dorothy Brown to buy the Willits Chair. DF contends—and Mrs. Brown denies—that she agreed in a phone conversation with Briggs on November 26 to sell the chair to DF for $60,000, payable in two equal installments, the first due on December 31 and the second on March 26. On December 3 Briggs wrote Brown a letter confirming the agreement, followed shortly by a check for $30,000.* Two weeks later Brown returned the letter and the check with the following handwritten note at the bottom of the letter: "Since I did not hear from you until December and I spoke with you the middle of November, I have made other arrangements for the chair. It is no longer available for sale to you." Sometime later Brown sold the chair for $198,000, precipitating this suit for the difference between the price at which the chair was sold and the contract price of $60,000. Brown moved under Fed. R. Civ. P. 12(b)(6) to dismiss the suit as barred by the statute of frauds in the Uniform Commercial Code. See UCC § 2–201. * * * Attached to the motion was Brown's affidavit that she had never agreed to sell the chair to DF or its representative, Briggs.* The

---

* The letter stated:

Dear Mrs. Brown:

This letter is to confirm our agreement to purchase from you the high back dining chair from the Ward W. Willits Residence (Highland Park, Illinois, 1901) for $60,000. As agreed to down payment of $30,000 is to be paid in December 1986 and the remaining $30,000 within 90 days. On completion of payment I will contact you to make transportation arrangements for the chair to Domino's Farms.

Domino's Pizza will carry insurance on the chair. Also, we would like to illustrate the chair in future publications. Do you have a transparency we could use?

Sincerely,

Sara–Ann B. Briggs

Director, Archives & Galleries

Eds.

* AFFIDAVIT OF DOROTHEA F. BROWN

I, Dorothea F. Brown, having been first duly deposed and sworn to all states as follows:

i. My name is Dorothea F. Brown and I reside at 671 Beverly Place, Lake Forest, Illinois.

affidavit also denied any recollection of a conversation with Briggs on November 26, and was accompanied by both a letter from Brown to Briggs dated September 20 withdrawing an offer to sell the chair and a letter from Briggs to Brown dated October 29 withdrawing DF's offer to buy the chair.

The district judge granted the motion to dismiss and dismissed the suit. DF appeals, contending that although a contract for a sale of goods at a price of $500 or more is subject to the statute of frauds, the (alleged) oral contract made on November 26 may be within the statutory exception for cases where "the party against whom enforcement is sought admits in his pleading, testimony or otherwise in court that a contract for sale was made." UCC § 2–201(3)(b). * * *

At first glance DF's case may seem quite hopeless. Far from admitting in her pleading, testimony, or otherwise in court that a contract for sale was made, Mrs. Brown denied under oath that a contract had been made. DF argues, however, that if it could depose her, maybe she would admit in her deposition that the affidavit was in error, that she had talked to Briggs on November 26, and that they had agreed to the sale of the chair on the terms contained in Briggs' letter of confirmation to her.

---

    ii.   I am the defendant in the above-captioned case.

   iii.   On August 19, 1986, I drafted a letter to Domino's Pizza Incorporated regarding my Frank Lloyd Wright chair, which is the subject matter of this suit.

   iv.   In response to my letter, Helen M. McNulty drafted her August 26, 1986 correspondence. (exhibit A)

    v.   For a short while thereafter, I negotiated with Sarah Briggs of Domino's Pizza relative to a possible sale of my chair to Domino Farms.

   vi.   I terminated my negotiation with the Plaintiff, herein with my correspondence dated September 20, 1986. (exhibit B)

  vii.   On October 29, 1986, the agent working on behalf of Domino's Farms drafted her letter to terminate further negotiation with respect to the chair, (exhibit C)

 viii.   Thereafter, I was contacted by a person who represented that she was Sarah Briggs and in a November 6, 1986 phone conversation, she further discussed the matter with me, but I did not agree to sell my chair to them.

   ix.   To the best of my recollection, I had no conversation with Sarah Ann Briggs on November 26, 1986.

    x.   I did not accept any offer from Domino's Farms or Sarah Briggs for their purchase of my chair.

   xi.   I did not sign any agreement to sell my chair to DF Activities, Sarah Briggs, or Domino's Farms nor was any person or entity authorized to enter into any alleged agreement in my behalf.

  xii.   I have not accepted any payment whatsoever from Domino's Farms or Sarah Briggs with respect to this matter.

Further deponent saith not.

Eds.

There is remarkably little authority on the precise question raised by this appeal—whether a sworn denial ends the case or the plaintiff may press on, and insist on discovery. In fact we have found no authority at the appellate level, state or federal. Many cases hold, it is true, that the defendant in a suit on an oral contract apparently made unenforceable by the statute of frauds cannot block discovery aimed at extracting an admission that the contract was made, simply by moving to dismiss the suit on the basis of the statute of frauds or by denying in the answer to the complaint that a contract had been made. There is also contrary authority. * * * We need not take sides on the conflict. When there is a bare motion to dismiss, or an answer, with no evidentiary materials, the possibility remains a live one that, if asked under oath whether a contract had been made, the defendant would admit it had been. The only way to test the proposition is for the plaintiff to take the defendant's deposition, or, if there is no discovery, to call the defendant as an adverse witness at trial. But where as in this case the defendant swears in an affidavit that there was no contract, we see no point in keeping the lawsuit alive. Of course the defendant may blurt out an admission in a deposition, but this is hardly likely, especially since by doing so he may be admitting to having perjured himself in his affidavit. Stranger things have happened, but remote possibilities do not warrant subjecting the parties and the judiciary to proceedings almost certain to be futile. * * *

[A]ffidavits in litigation are prepared by lawyers, and merely signed by affiants. Yet to allow an affiant to be deposed by opposing counsel would be to invite the unedifying form of discovery in which the examining lawyer tries to pur words in the witness's mouth and construe them as admissions.

The history of the judicial-admission exception to the statute of frauds reinforces our conclusion. The exception began with common-sense recognition that if the defendant admitted in a pleading that he had made a contract with the plaintiff, the purpose of the statute of frauds—protection against fraudulent or otherwise false contractual claims—was fulfilled. (The situation would be quite otherwise, of course, with an oral admission, for a plaintiff willing to testify falsely to the existence of a contract would be equally willing to testify falsely to the defendant's having admitted the existence of the contract.) Toward the end of the eighteenth century the courts began to reject the exception, fearing that it was an invitation to the defendant to perjure himself. Later the pendulum swung again, and the exception is now firmly established. The concern with perjury that caused the courts in the middle period to reject the exception supports the position taken by Mrs. Brown in this case. She has sworn under oath that she did not agree to sell the Willits Chair to DF. DF wants an opportunity to depose her in the hope that she can be induced to change her testimony. But if she changes her testimony this will be virtually an admission that she perjured herself in her affidavit (for it is hardly likely that her denial was based simply on a faulty recollection). She is not likely to do this. What is possible is that her testimony will be sufficiently ambiguous to enable DF to argue that there should be still further factual investigation—perhaps a full-fledged trial at which Mrs. Brown will be questioned again about the existence of the contract.

With such possibilities for protraction, the statute of frauds becomes a defense of meager value. And yet it seems to us as it did to the framers of the Uniform Commercial Code that the statute of frauds serves an important purpose in a system such as ours that does not require that all contracts be in writing in order to be enforceable and that allows juries of lay persons to decide commercial cases. The methods of judicial factfinding do not distinguish unerringly between true and false testimony, and are in any event very expansive. People deserve some protection against the risks and costs of being hauled into court and accused of owing money on the basis of an unacknowledged promise. And being deposed is scarcely less unpleasant than being cross-examined—indeed, often it is more unpleasant, because the examining lawyer is not inhibited by the presence of a judge or jury who might resent hectoring tactics. The transcripts of depositions are often very ugly documents.

* * * [O]nce the defendant has denied the contract under oath, the safety valve of section 2–201(3)(b) is closed. The chance that at a deposition the defendant might be badgered into withdrawing his denial is too remote to justify prolonging an effort to enforce an oral contract in the teeth of the statute of frauds. If Dorothy [sic] Brown did agree on November 27 to sell the chair to DF at a bargain price, it behooved Briggs to get Brown's signature on the dotted line, posthaste.

Affirmed.

Flaum, Circuit Judge, dissenting.

Because I disagree with the majority's holding that additional discovery is prohibited whenever a defendant raises a statute of frauds defense and submits a sworn denial that he or she formed an oral contract with the plaintiff, I respectfully dissent. Neither would I hold, however, that a plaintiff is automatically entitled to additional discovery in the face of a defendant's sworn denial that an agreement was reached. Rather, in my view district courts should have the authority to exercise their discretion to determine the limits of permissible discovery in these cases. This flexibility is particularly important where, as here, the defendant's affidavit does not contain a conclusive denial of contract formation. * * *

Questions and Notes and Connections

1. Questions about the facts of this case
    1.1. Who is the person "against whom enforcement is sought"? Is there an agreement signed by that person as required by section 2–201(1)?
    1.2. Is there a writing signed by that person that was important to the court's application of 2–201(3)?

1.3. Did the defendant's affidavit "contain a conclusive denial of contract formation"?

2. Questions about the law

   2.1. Writing: Why didn't the December 3rd letter satisfy the Statute of Frauds? Would the writing have satisfied the Statute of Frauds if the defendant was a merchant?

   2.2. Ethics: Would it be ethical for the defendant's attorney to advise her client to file an affidavit denying that she made an oral agreement if she did indeed make an oral agreement? Would it be ethical for defendant's attorney to file a motion to dismiss the suit as barred by the Statute of Frauds if she knew that Mrs. Brown had made such an oral agreement?

   2.3. Part performance: Why didn't the $30,000 payment satisfy the Statute of Frauds? *See* U.C.C. § 2–201(3)(c).

3. Notes

   3.1. Common law judicial admission exception: Notwithstanding the obiter dictum in *DF Activities* that the "judicial admissions exception is firmly established," cases not governed by U.C.C. § 2–201(3) are divided as to whether an oral judicial admission satisfies the Statute of Frauds. Remember the dictum in the *Radke* case.

   3.2. And, remember that England abolished the Statute of Frauds in 1954. More recently, the United Nations Convention on Contracts for the International Sale of Goods, eliminated any statute of frauds. Article 11 of UNCISG provides: "A contract of sale need not be concluded in or evidenced by writing. * * * It may be proved by any means, including witnesses."

4. Connections

   Did the Seventh Circuit discuss the U.C.C. Statute of Frauds in *Hill v. Gateway*, page 172? Should the Seventh Circuit have discussed the U.C.C. Statute of Frauds?

The final Statute of Frauds case involves an employment agreement. Many employment agreements are oral (including many employment agreements between law firms and their lawyers). Does the Hawaiian Statute of Frauds require that an employment agreement be in writing in order to be legally enforceable?

McINTOSH v. MURPHY

Supreme Court of Hawai'i
52 Haw. 29, 469 P.2d 177 (1970)

LEVINSON, JUSTICE.

This case involves an oral employment contract which allegedly violates the provision of the Statute of Frauds requiring "any agreement that is not to be performed within one year from the making thereof" to be in writing in order to be enforceable. HRS § 656–1(5). In this action the plaintiff-employee Dick McIntosh seeks to recover damages from his employer, George Murphy and Murphy Motors, Ltd., for the breach of an alleged one-year oral employment contract.

While the facts are in sharp conflict, it appears that defendant George Murphy was in southern California during March, 1964 interviewing prospective management personnel for his Chevrolet–Oldsmobile dealerships in Hawaii. He interviewed the plaintiff twice during that time. The position of sales manager for one of the dealerships was fully discussed but no contract was entered into. In April, 1964 the plaintiff received a call from the general manager of Murphy Motors informing him of possible employment within thirty days if he was still available. The plaintiff indicated his continued interest and informed the manager that he would be available. Later in April, the plaintiff sent Murphy a telegram to the effect that he would arrive in Honolulu on Sunday, April 26, 1964. Murphy then telephoned McIntosh on Saturday, April 25, 1964, to notify him that the job of assistant sales manager was open and work would begin on the following Monday, April 27, 1964. At that time McIntosh expressed surprise at the change in job title from sales manager to assistant sales manager but reconfirmed the fact that he was arriving in Honolulu the next day, Sunday. McIntosh arrived on Sunday, April 26, 1964, and began work on the following day, Monday, April 27, 1964.

As a consequence of his decision to work for Murphy, McIntosh moved some of his belongings from the mainland to Hawaii, sold other possessions, leased an apartment in Honolulu and obviously forwent any other employment opportunities. In short, the plaintiff did all those things which were incidental to changing one's residence permanently from Los Angeles to Honolulu, a distance of approximately 2,200 miles. McIntosh continued working for Murphy until July 16, 1964, approximately two and one-half months, at which time he was discharged on the grounds that he was unable to close deals with prospective customers and could not train the salesmen.

At the conclusion of the trial, the defense moved for a directed verdict arguing that the oral employment agreement was in violation of the Statute of Frauds, there being no written memorandum or note thereof. The trial court ruled that as a matter of law the contract did not come within the Statute, reasoning that Murphy bargained for acceptance by the actual commencement of performance by McIntosh, so that McIntosh was not bound by a contract until he came to work on Monday, April 27, 1964. Therefore, assuming that the contract was for a year's employment, it was performable within a year exactly to the day and no writing was required for it to be enforceable. Alternatively, the court ruled that if the agreement was made final by the telephone call between the parties on Saturday, April 25, 1964, then that part of the weekend which remained would not be counted in calculating the year, thus taking the contract out of the Statute of Frauds. With commendable candor the trial judge gave as the motivating force for the decision his desire to avoid a mechanical and unjust application of the Statute.[1]

The case went to the jury on the following questions: (1) whether the contract was for a year's duration or was performable on a trial basis, thus making it terminable at the will of either party; (2) whether the plaintiff was discharged for just cause; and (3) if he was not discharged for just cause, what damages were due the plaintiff. The jury returned a verdict for the plaintiff in the sum of $12,103.40. The defendants appeal to this court on four principal grounds, three of which we find to be without merit. The remaining ground of appeal is whether the plaintiff can maintain an action on the alleged oral employment contract in light of the prohibition of the Statute of Frauds making unenforceable an oral contract that is not to be performed within one year.

Appeal

I. TIME OF ACCEPTANCE OF THE EMPLOYMENT AGREEMENT

The defendants contend that the trial court erred in refusing to give an instruction to the jury that if the employment agreement was made more than one day before the plaintiff began performance, there could be no recovery by the plaintiff. The reason given was that a contract not to be performed within one year from its making is unenforceable if not in writing.

The defendants are correct in their argument that the time of acceptance of an offer is a question of fact for the jury to decide. But the trial court alternatively decided that even if the offer was accepted on the Saturday prior to the commencement of performance, the intervening Sunday and part of Saturday would not be counted in computing the year for the purposes of the Statute of Frauds. The judge stated that Sunday was a non-working day and only a fraction of Saturday was left which he would not count. In any event, there is no need to discuss the relative merits of either ruling since we base our decision in this case on the doctrine of equitable estoppel which was properly briefed and argued by both parties before this court, although not presented to the trial court.

II. ENFORCEMENT BY VIRTUE OF ACTION IN RELIANCE ON THE ORAL CONTRACT

In determining whether a rule of law can be fashioned and applied to a situation where an oral contract admittedly violates a strict interpretation of the Statute of Frauds, it is necessary to review the Statute itself together with its historical and modern functions. The Statute of Frauds, which requires that certain contracts be in writing in order to be legally enforceable, had its inception in the days of Charles II of England.

---

1. THE COURT: You make the law look ridiculous, because one day is Sunday and the man does not work on Sunday; the other day is Saturday; he is up in Fresno. He can't work down there. And he is down here Sunday night and shows up for work on Monday. To me that is a contract within a year. I don't want to make the law look ridiculous, Mr. Clause, because it is one day after, one day too much, and that one day is a Sunday, and a non-working day.

Hawaii's version of the Statute is found in HRS § 656–1[5] and is substantially the same as the original English Statute of Frauds.

The first English Statute was enacted almost 300 years ago to prevent "many fraudulent practices, which are commonly endeavored to be upheld by perjury and subornation of perjury." Certainly, there were compelling reasons in those days for such a law. At the time of enactment in England, the jury system was quite unreliable, rules of evidence were few, and the complaining party was disqualified as a witness so he could neither testify on direct-examination nor, more importantly, be cross-examined. The aforementioned structural and evidentiary limitations on our system of justice no longer exist.

Retention of the Statute today has nevertheless been justified on at least three grounds: (1) the Statute still serves an evidentiary function thereby lessening the danger of perjured testimony (the original rationale); (2) the requirement of a writing has a cautionary effect which causes reflection by the parties on the importance of the agreement; and (3) the writing is an easy way to distinguish enforceable contracts from those which are not, thus channeling certain transactions into written form.

In spite of whatever utility the Statute of Frauds may still have, its applicability has been drastically limited by judicial construction over the years in order to mitigate the harshness of a mechanical application. Furthermore, learned writers continue to disparage the Statute regarding it as "a statute for promoting fraud" and a "legal anachronism."

Another method of judicial circumvention of the Statute of Frauds has grown out of the exercise of the equity powers of the courts. Such judicially imposed limitations or exceptions involved the traditional dispensing power of the equity courts to mitigate the "harsh" rule of law. When courts have enforced an oral contract in spite of the Statute, they have utilized the legal labels of "part performance" or "equitable estoppel" in granting relief. Both doctrines are said to be based on the concept of estoppel, which operates to avoid unconscionable injury.

Part performance has long been recognized in Hawaii as an equitable doctrine justifying the enforcement of an oral agreement for the conveyance of an interest in land where there has been substantial reliance by the party seeking to enforce the contract. Other courts have enforced oral contracts (including employment contracts) which failed to satisfy the section of the Statute making unenforceable an agreement not to be performed within a year of its making. This has occurred where the conduct of the parties gave rise to an estoppel to assert the Statute.

---

5. HRS § 656–1 Certain contracts, when actionable.

No action shall be brought and maintained in any of the following cases: * * *

(5) Upon any agreement that is not to be performed within one year from the making thereof; unless the promise, contract, or agreement, upon which the action is brought, or some memorandum or note thereof, is in writing, and is signed by the party to be charged therewith, or by some person thereunto by the party in writing lawfully authorized.

It is appropriate for modern courts to cast aside the raiments of conceptualism which cloak the true policies underlying the reasoning behind the many decisions enforcing contracts that violate the Statute of Frauds. There is certainly no need to resort to legal rubrics or meticulous legal formulas when better explanations are available.

In seeking to frame a workable test which is flexible enough to cover diverse factual situations and also provide some reviewable standards, we find very persuasive section [139] of the Second Restatement of Contracts. That section specifically covers those situations where there has been reliance on an oral contract which falls within the Statute of Frauds. Section [139] states:

> (1) A promise which the promisor should reasonably expect to induce action or forbearance on the part of the promisee or a third person and which does induce the action or forbearance is enforceable not-withstanding the Statute of Frauds if injustice can be avoided only by enforcement of the promise. The remedy granted for breach is to be limited as justice requires.

> (2) In determining whether injustice can be avoided only by enforcement of the promise, the following circumstances are significant: (a) the availability and adequacy of other remedies, particularly cancellation and restitution; (b) the definite and substantial character of the action or forbearance in relation to the remedy sought; (c) the extent to which the action or forbearance corroborates evidence of the making and terms of the promise, or the making and terms are otherwise established by clear and convincing evidence; (d) the reasonableness of the action or forbearance; (e) the extent to which the action or forbearance was forseeable by the promisor.

We think that the approach taken in the Restatement is the proper method of giving the trial court the necessary latitude to relieve a party of the hardships of the Statute of Frauds. This is to be preferred over having the trial court bend over backwards to take the contract out of the Statute of Frauds. In the present case the trial court admitted just this inclination and forthrightly followed it.

There is no dispute that the action of the plaintiff in moving 2200 miles from Los Angeles to Hawaii was foreseeable by the defendant. In fact, it was required to perform his duties. Injustice can only be avoided by the enforcement of the contract and the granting of money damages. No other remedy is adequate. The plaintiff found himself residing in Hawaii without a job.

It is also clear that a contract of some kind did exist. The plaintiff performed the contract for two and one-half months receiving $3,484.60 for his services. The exact length of the contract, whether terminable at will as urged by the defendant, or for a year from the time when the plaintiff started working, was up to the jury to decide.

In sum, the trial court might have found that enforcement of the contract was warranted by virtue of the plaintiff's reliance on the defendant's promise. Naturally, each case turns on its own facts. Certainly there is considerable discretion for a court to implement the true policy behind the Statute of Frauds, which is to prevent fraud or any other type of unconscionable injury. We therefore affirm the judgment of the trial court on the ground that the plaintiff's reliance was such that injustice could only be avoided by enforcement of the contract.

Affirmed.

ABE, JUSTICE (dissenting).

The majority of the court has affirmed the judgment of the trial court; however, I respectfully dissent.

I believe this court is begging the issue by its holding because to reach that conclusion, this court is ruling that the defendant agreed to hire the plaintiff under a one-year employment contract. The defendant has denied that the plaintiff was hired for a period of one year and has introduced into evidence testimony of witnesses that all hiring by the defendant in the past has been on a trial basis. The defendant also testified that he had hired the plaintiff on a trial basis.

Here on one hand the plaintiff claimed that he had a one-year employment contract; on the other hand, the defendant claimed that the plaintiff had not been hired for one year but on a trial basis for so long as his services were satisfactory. I believe the Statute of Frauds was enacted to avoid the consequences this court is forcing upon the defendant. In my opinion, the legislature enacted the Statute of Frauds to negate claims such as has been made by the plaintiff in this case. But this court holds that because the plaintiff in reliance of the one-year employment contract (alleged to have been entered into by the plaintiff, but denied by the defendant) has changed his position, "injustice could only be avoided by enforcement of the contract." Where is the sense of justice?

Now assuming that the defendant had agreed to hire the plaintiff under a one-year employment contract and the contract came within the Statute of Frauds, I cannot agree, as intimated by this court, that we should circumvent the Statute of Frauds by the exercise of the equity powers of courts. As to statutory law, the sole function of the judiciary is to interpret the statute and the judiciary should not usurp legislative power and enter into the legislative field. Thus, if the Statute of Frauds is too harsh as intimated by this court, and it brings about undue hardship, it is for the legislature to amend or repeal the statute and not for this court to legislate.

QUESTIONS, NOTES, AND CONNECTIONS

1. Questions about the facts of this case

   1.1. The Hawaii Statute of Frauds requires that "the promise, contract, or agreement, upon which the action is brought, or some memorandum or note thereof, is in writing, and is signed by the party to be charged therewith." Is there such a writing in this case?

   1.2. Did the defendant admit that he agreed to employ the plaintiff for one year?

2. Questions about the law

   2.1. Not to be performed within one year from the making thereof

       (a) The plaintiff alleged that there was a one year oral employment contract. Can a one year employment contract "be performed within one year from the making thereof"? Is that relevant in this case?

       (b) Epstein hires you to work as his research assistant on the Corpus Juris Thirdundum project—an update and complete rewriting of Corpus Juris Secondum (now 166 books http://west.thomson.com/productdetail/1247/22023000/productdetail.aspx) Epstein and you orally agree that you will be paid $60,000 a year until the treatise is complete. Is the contract "not to be performed within one year from the making"? *capable of being performed in 1 yr. This does not have to \even if possible to go beyond\ be under SOF.*

       (c) Most people work as employees at will, is an employment at will agreement within the Statute of Frauds?

   2.2. McIntosh and the purpose of the Statute of Frauds: The Hawaiian Supreme Court reminds us that the original purpose of the Statute of Frauds was to prevent "many fraudulent practices, which are commonly endeavored to be upheld by perjury and subornation of perjury." Is the holding in this case consistent with this original purpose?

   2.3 Equitable estoppel/promissory estoppel.

       In *McIntosh*, the court states that we "base our decision in this case on equitable estoppel." Later in the opinion, the court refers to two cases decided under the theory of equitable estoppel and a case decided under the theory of promissory estoppel. And then, the court in *McIntosh* finds *Restatement (Second)* § 139 persuasive. Is *Restatement (Second)* § 139 equitable estoppel or promissory estoppel? How does equitable estoppel differ from promissory estoppel?

3. Notes

   Judge Richard Posner is critical of the use of promissory estoppel "to get around" the Statute of Frauds, particularly in employment cases:

   Employment at will (i.e., without a contract of employment) remains the dominant type of employment relationship in this country, and would be seriously undermined if employees could use the doctrine of promissory estoppel to make alleged oral contracts of employment enforceable. Reliance is easily, perhaps too easily, shown in the employment setting. Agreeing to work for a particular employer, thereby giving up alternative opportunities for employment, can easily be described as reliance on the employer's alleged oral promises concerning the terms of employment. Maybe the cases that erode it in the area of promissory estoppel exaggerate the ability of courts to distinguish true oral promises from fabricated promises and language misunderstood as promissory. Maybe they overlook the simple logical point that the promisee should know the promise is unenforceable because of the statute of frauds and therefore shouldn't rely on it. But for what it is worth the logic of such cases is that the element of reliance that is required to make a promise enforceable on grounds of estoppel takes the place of a writing in giving adequate assurance that the promise has not been fabricated, or misunderstood without fault on the part of the promisor. The "promisee" takes a great risk if he gives up something in purported reliance on a nonexistent promise, merely to bolster his claim that there was a promise.

Goldstick v. ICM Realty, 788 F.2d 456, 465 (7th Cir. 1986). Do you agree with Judge Posner? Would Justice Abe of the Hawaii Supreme Court agree?

4. Connections

4.1. Connection between part performance and *Restatement (Second)* § 130. Recall that (1) under section 2–201(3), part performance can satisfy the Statute of Frauds in agreements involving the sale of goods, and (2) the *McIntosh* case mentions (and your property professor will discuss) part performance and the Statute of Frauds in real estate transfer deals. Recall also that the plaintiff worked for the defendant for two and one-half months. According to *Restatement (Second) of Contracts* § 130, comment e: "Part performance not amounting to full performance on one side does not in general take a contract out of the one-year provision." Why?

4.2. Connection between *Restatement (Second)* § 139 and *Restatement (Second)* § 90. How are *Restatement (Second)* § 139 and *Restatement (Second)* § 90 similar? How are *Restatement (Second)* § 139 and *Restatement (Second)* § 90 different? Did Murphy Motors, the defendant in the *McIntosh* case argue that its promise was unenforceable because of no consideration?

Consider some of the ruminations Professor John Kidwell of the University of Wisconsin Law School on teaching the Statute of Frauds:

[A] requirement that a contract be in writing is functionally very like the requirement of a seal. Such a requirement is attractive for the same reasons that the seal requirement is attractive. If everyone knew and followed the forms there would be less conflict, and justice would be speedy and certain. Social order would be enhanced. But we don't care just about social order. We care also about individual justice. And we know that not all people know the rules, and even when they do they might find reasons not to follow them. If we enforce the formal requirement in these cases, we sacrifice individual justice in favor of social order, which always at least makes us pause. And sometimes we yield to the urge to make an exception and soften the formal rule. I then suggest that it can be argued that every formal rule is under relentless pressure from our desire for individual justice. * * * We always are tempted to make exceptions to rules that depend on form because we always care, to some extent, about the injustice, which results when we enforce the formal requirement. Thus, formal requirements tend to decay. Not always, and not perhaps as dramatically as in the case of the seal, but often. Writing requirements, notice requirements, filing requirements, statutes of limitations—all invite exceptions.

John Kidwell, *Ruminations on Teaching the Statute of Frauds*, 44 St. Louis U. L.J. 1427, 1432 (2000).

SECTION 2:   CONTRACT LAW REASONS FOR NOT ENFORCING AGREEMENTS: FRAUD, FRAUDULENT OR MATERIAL MISREPRESENTATIONS AND NONDISCLOSURE

The contract law of misrepresentation is similar to the tort law of fraud and misrepresentation. Both are based in part on common law as it evolved in England and in part on common sense.

First, the old common law part—procedure. Recall that in old England, a writ of assumpsit was the prescribed procedure for enforcement of an agreement. In such assumpsit actions, misrepresentation was not a defense to the enforcement of an agreement. Instead the person who had been a victim of the misrepresentation had to bring a separate tort action in deceit for damages.

While misrepresentation was not a defense in actions at law under assumpsit, courts of equity did allow a person who entered into an agreement because of a misrepresentation to avoid the agreement by means of the equitable remedy of rescission. In rescission, each party returns what she received.

Today, as at early common law, misrepresentation can be the basis for either a tort action or a contract action. The tort action is generally a suit for actual (and possibly punitive damages) for deceit or fraud or misrepresentation. And, the contract action is generally a suit for rescission to make an agreement unenforceable.

Second, the common sense part—the requirements for an action to rescind an agreement because of misrepresentation. In determining whether an agreement should not be enforced or should be rescinded because of one party's misrepresentation, courts generally look to (1) how important (*i.e.*, material) the representation was, (2) whether the other party relied on that misrepresentation, and (3) if that reliance was reasonable. *Cf. Restatement (Second) of Contracts* § 164. Common sense stuff.

Assume, for example, that Markell and Ponoroff agree to do a contract book with Epstein. Should Markell and Ponroff be able to get out of their agreement with Epstein because he told them that he had a masters degree in law from the Harvard Law School, when in reality his LL.M. degree was from the Hahvood Law School, Tanning and Nail Boutique? What if Epstein honestly believes that he went to Harvard (at his age, he gets confused a lot)? What if Markell and Ponoroff could have easily checked on whether Epstein graduated from Harvard?

The next case, *Halpert v. Rosenthal*, involves equally easy facts—a defendant buyer arguing that a court should not enforce an agreement to buy the plaintiff's house because of the plaintiff's misrepresentation as to termites. As you read the case, please notice the court's fairly obvious distinctions between tort actions based on misrepresentations and contract actions based on misrepresentations and the court's (the Restatement's?) more "subtle" distinction between contract actions based on fraudulent misrepresentations and contract actions based on material misrepresentations.

HALPERT v. ROSENTHAL

Supreme Court of Rhode Island
107 R.I. 406, 267 A.2d 730 (1970)

KELLEHER, J.

This is a civil action wherein the plaintiff vendor seeks damages for the breach by the defendant vendee of a contract for the sale of real estate. The defendant filed a counter-claim in which he sought the return of his deposit. A jury trial was held in the Superior Court. The jury found for the defendant and judgment followed. The case is before us on the plaintiff's appeal.

On February 21, 1967, the parties hereto entered into a real estate agreement whereby plaintiff agreed to convey a one-family house located in Providence on the southeasterly corner of Wayland and Upton Avenues to defendant for the sum of $54,000. The defendant paid a deposit of $2,000 to plaintiff. The agreement provided for the delivery of the deed and the payment of the balance of the purchase price by June 30, 1967.

On May 17, 1967, a termite inspection was made of the premises, and it was discovered that the house was inhabited by termites. The defendant then notified plaintiff that, because of the termite infestation, he was not going to purchase the property. The defendant did not appear for the title closing which plaintiff had scheduled for June 30, 1967.

The plaintiff immediately commenced this suit. Her complaint prayed for specific performance or monetary damages. When the case came on for trial, the property had been sold to another buyer for the sum of $35,000. The plaintiff then sought to recover from defendant the $19,000 difference between the selling price called for in the sales agreement and the actual selling price. The defendant in his answer alleged that plaintiff and her agent had, during the preagreement negotiation, intentionally misrepresented the house as being free of termites. The defendant's counterclaim sought the return of the $2,000 deposit.

At the conclusion of the presentation of all the evidence, plaintiff made a motion for a directed verdict on the issue of the alleged fraudulent misrepresentations. The trial justice reserved decision on the motion and submitted the case to the jury. After the jury's verdict, he denied the motion.

This case is unique in that plaintiff made no motion for a new trial. Her appeal is based for the most part on the trial court's refusal to direct a verdict in her favor on the counterclaim. She has also alleged that the trial justice erred in certain portions of his charge to the jury and in failing to adopt some 15 requests to charge submitted by plaintiff.

The absence of a motion for a new trial narrows the scope of an inquiry on appeal. Instead of being concerned with the credibility of witnesses or the weight of the evidence as we would be were we reviewing the usual motion for a new trial, we apply the standards applicable to a motion for a directed verdict. In doing so, it is our duty to consider all of the evidence and reasonable inferences deducible therefrom in the light most favorable to defendant.

Since we consider only the evidence favorable to defendant, we shall set forth defendant's version of three different occasions in 1967 when the alleged misrepresentations relative to absence of any termites were made.

1. In early February, defendant and his wife inspected the Halpert home. They asked the agent about termites and he told them that there was no termite problem and that he had never experienced any termite problem with any of the houses he sold in the East Side section of Providence.

2. Later on in February, defendant, his wife, his sister-in-law and his brother-in-law met plaintiff. The brother-in-law inquired about the presence of termites; plaintiff said that there were no termites in the house.

3. When defendant was about to sign the purchase and sales agreement, he asked plaintiff's real estate agent whether it might not be advisable if the home be inspected for termites before the agreement was

signed. The agent told defendant that such a step was unnecessary because there were no termite problems in the house.

* * *

In contending that she was entitled to a directed verdict, plaintiff contends that to sustain the charge of fraudulent misrepresentation, some evidence had to be produced showing that either she or her agent knew at the time they said there were no termites in the house, that such a statement was untrue. Since the representations made to defendant were made in good faith, she argues that, as a matter of law, defendant could not prevail on his counterclaim.

The defendant concedes that there was no evidence which shows that plaintiff or her agent knowingly made false statements as to the existence of the termites but he maintains that an innocent misrepresentation of a material fact is grounds for rescission of a contract where, as here, a party relies to his detriment on the misrepresentation.

We affirm the denial of the motion for a directed verdict.

The plaintiff, when she made her motion for a directed verdict, stated that her motion was restricted to the issue of "fraud." The word "fraud" is a generic term which embraces a great variety of actionable wrongs. It is a word of many meanings and defies any one all-inclusive definition. Fraud may become important either for the purpose of giving the defrauded person the right to sue for damages in an action for deceit or to enable him to rescind the contract. In this jurisdiction a party who has been induced by fraud to enter into a contract may pursue either one of two remedies. He may elect to rescind the contract to recover what he has paid under it, or he may affirm the contract and sue for damages in an action for deceit.

The distinction between a claim for damages for intentional deceit and a claim for rescission is well defined. Deceit is a tort action, and it requires some degree of culpability on the misrepresenter's part. An individual who sues in an action of deceit based on fraud has the burden of proving that the defendant in making the statements knew they were false and intended to deceive him. On the other hand, a suit to rescind an agreement induced by fraud sounds in contract. It is this latter aspect of fraud that we are concerned with in this case, and the pivotal issue before us is whether an innocent misrepresentation of a material fact warrants the granting of a claim for rescission. We believe that it does.

When he denied plaintiff's motion, the trial justice indicated that a false, though innocent, misrepresentation of a fact made as though of one's knowledge may be the basis for the rescission of a contract. While this issue is one of first impression in this state, it is clear that the trial judge's action finds support in the overwhelming weight of decisional and textual authority which has established the rule that where one induces another to enter into a contract by means of a material misrepresentation, the latter may rescind the contract. It does not matter if the representation was "innocent" or fraudulent.

In 12 Williston, *supra*, § 1500 at 400–01, Professor Jaeger states:

It is not necessary, in order that a contract may be rescinded for fraud or misrepresentation, that the party making the misrepresentation should have known that it was false. Innocent misrepresentation is sufficient, for though the representation may have been made innocently, it would be unjust and inequitable to permit a person who has made false representations, even innocently, to retain the fruits of a bargain induced by such representations.

This statement of law is in accord with Restatement of Contracts, § 476 at 908 which states: "Where a party is induced to enter into a transaction with another party that he was under no duty to enter into by means of the latter's fraud or material misrepresentation, the transaction is voidable as against the latter. * * *" Misrepresentation is defined as "* * * any manifestation by words or other conduct by one person to another that, under the circumstances, amounts to an assertion not in accordance with the facts." Restatement of Contracts, § 470

The comment following this section explains that a misrepresentation may be innocent, negligent or known to be false. A misrepresentation becomes material when it becomes likely to affect the conduct of a reasonable man with reference to a transaction with another person. Restatement of Contracts, § 470 (2) at 891. * * *

A misrepresentation, even though innocently made, may be actionable, if made and relied on as a positive statement of fact. The question to be resolved in determining whether a wrong committed as the result of an innocent misrepresentation may be rectified is succinctly stated in 12 Williston, *supra*, § 1510 at 462 as follows:

"When a defendant has induced another to act by representations false in fact although not dishonestly made, and damage has directly resulted from the action taken, who should bear the loss?"

The question we submit is rhetorical. The answer is obvious. Simple justice demands that the speaker be held responsible. Accordingly, we hold that here defendant vendee could maintain his counterclaim.

* * *

Before leaving this phase of plaintiff's appeal, we think it appropriate that we allude to the tendency of many courts to equate an innocent misrepresentation with some species of fraud. Usually the word "fraud" connotes a conscious dishonest conduct on the part of the misrepresenter. Fraud, however, is not present if the speaker actually believes that what he states as the truth is the truth. We believe that it would be better if an innocent misrepresentation was not described as some specie of fraud. Unqualified statements imply certainty. Reliance is more likely to be placed on a positive statement of fact than a mere expression of opinion or a qualified statement. The speaker who uses the unqualified statement does so at his peril. The risk of falsity is his. If he is to be liable for what he states, the liability is imposed because he is to be held strictly accountable for his words. Responsibility for an innocent misrepresentation should be recognized for what it is—an example of absolute liability rather than as many courts have said, an example of constructive fraud.

* * *

The appeal of the plaintiff is denied and dismissed, and the case is remanded to the Superior Court for entry of judgment thereon.

Motion for reargument denied.

QUESTIONS AND NOTES

1. Questions about the facts of this case
    1.1. Who is suing whom for what?
    1.2. Which of the various statements by the seller or the seller's agent was most favorable to the defendant buyer's position?
    1.3. Did the seller or the seller's agent know that there were termites in the house? Was that important to the court? Should it be important?

2. Questions about the law
    2.1. Would the case have been decided differently if the court had applied *Restatement (Second) of Contracts* § 164, which provides:

    If a party's manifestation of assent is induced by either a fraudulent or a material misrepresentation by the other party upon which the recipient is justified in relying, the contract is voidable by the recipient.

    How is this different from *Restatement of Contracts* § 476 which the court relied on? How is a "fraudulent" misrepresentation different from a "material" misrepresentation? *See also Restatement (Second) of Contracts* §§ 159, 160, 162.

    2.2. Would the case have been decided differently if the seller and the seller's agent had simply and truthfully said "we have not seen any termites" or "I do not believe that there are any termites in the house"?

    2.3. This case uses the terms "deceit," "fraud," and "misrepresentation." How do these terms differ? Which is involved in this case?

    2.4. In negotiating to buy Epstein's 1973 Cadillac, Ponoroff tells Epstein that "$400 is my best offer—it is as much as I am willing to pay for the car." Being an extremely trusting sort of person, Epstein believes Ponoroff and agrees to sell him the car for $400. Shortly thereafter, Epstein learns from Markell that Ponoroff had said that he was willing to pay as much as $1,600 for the car. Can Epstein argue a fraud, deceit, or misrepresentation defense to the enforcement of his agreement to sell the car to Ponoroff based on Pono-roff's statement to him?

3. Notes

   3.1. The facts in *Halpert* (and the facts in the various examples in *Restatement (Second) of Contracts* § 164) involve a statement or representation that is not a part of the contract language.

   It is of course possible to include representations in the contract language. For example, in a typical business acquisition agreement, the seller will make representations about the conditions of the business and the agreement will provide that the buyer can walk away from the deal if any of the "representations" are instead "misrepresentations." *See generally* JAMES C. FREUND, ANATOMY OF A MERGER: STRATEGIES AND TECHNIQUES FOR NEGOTIATING CORPORATE ACQUISITIONS Chapter 7 (1975):

   There are no known statistics on the subject, but I'm willing to bet my briefcase that lawyers spend more time negotiating 'Representations and Warranties of the Seller' than any other single article in the typical acquisition agreement. It is a nit-picker's delight, a forum for expending prodigious amounts of energy in debating the merits of what sometimes seem to be relatively insignificant items.

   Id. at 229.

   3.2. *Halpert* shows the legal consequences of a misstatement that was arguably innocent. In the next two cases, we consider the legal consequences of a "non-statement" that was arguably not so innocent.

SWINTON v. WHITINSVILLE SAVINGS BANK

Supreme Judicial Court of Massachusetts
311 Mass. 677, 42 N.E.2d 808 (1942)

[Plaintiff-appellant Swinton sued defendant-appellee Whitinsville Savings Bank to recover damages for defendant's alleged fraudulent concealment in the sale of a house to plaintiff. Plaintiff appeals an order by the court below which sustained the defendant's demurrer to plaintiff's declaration.]

QUA, J.

The declaration alleges that on or about September 12, 1938, the defendant sold the plaintiff a house in Newton to be occupied by the plaintiff and his family as a dwelling; that at the time of the sale the house "was infested with termites, an insect that is most dangerous and destructive to buildings"; that the defendant knew the house was so infested; that the plaintiff could not readily observe this condition upon inspection; that, "knowing the internal destruction that these insects were creating in said house," the defendant falsely and fraudulently concealed from the plaintiff its true condition; that the plaintiff at the time of his purchase had no knowledge of the termites, exercised due care thereafter, and learned of them about August 30, 1940; and that, because of the destruction that was being done and the dangerous condition that was being created by the termites, the plaintiff was put to great expense for repairs and for the installation of termite control in order to prevent the loss and destruction of said house.

There is no allegation of any false statement or representation, or of the uttering of a half truth which may be tantamount to a falsehood. There is no intimation that the defendant by any means prevented the plaintiff from acquiring information as to the condition of the house. There is nothing to show any fiduciary relation between the parties, or that the plaintiff stood in a position of confidence toward or dependence upon the defendant. So far as appears the parties made a business deal at arm's length. The charge is concealment and nothing more; and it is concealment in the simple sense of mere failure to reveal, with nothing to show any peculiar duty to speak. The characterization of the concealment as false and fraudulent of course adds nothing in the absence of further allegations of fact.

If this defendant is liable on this declaration every seller is liable who fails to disclose any nonapparent defect known to him in the subject of the sale which materially reduces its value and which the buyer fails to discover. Similarly it would seem that every buyer would be liable who fails to disclose any nonapparent virtue known to him in the subject of the purchase which materially enhances its value and of which the seller is ignorant. The law has not yet, we believe, reached the point of imposing upon the frailties of human nature a standard so idealistic as this. That the particular case here stated by the plaintiff possesses a certain appeal to the moral sense is scarcely to be denied. Probably the reason is to be found in the facts that the infestation of buildings by termites has not been common in Massachusetts and constitutes a concealed risk against which buyers are off their guard. But the law cannot provide special rules for termites and can hardly attempt to determine liability according to the varying probabilities of the existence and discovery of different possible defects in the subjects of trade. * * *

The order sustaining the demurrer is affirmed, and judgment is to be entered for the defendant.

So ordered.

QUESTIONS AND NOTES

1. Questions about the facts of this case

    1.1. Did the defendant know that the house was infested with termites?

    Yes, didn't disclose

     1.2.   Did the defendant make any representation to the plaintiff about termites? *No*

     1.3.   Did the plaintiff ask the defendant about termites? *No*

2.   Questions about the law

     2.1.   The court points out that "there is nothing to show any fiduciary relationship between the parties." What is the point of that statement?

     2.2.   Later the court states, "The charge is concealment and nothing more; and it is concealment in the simple sense of mere failure to reveal." Is nondisclosure, i.e., mere failure to reveal, the same thing as concealment?

3.   Notes

     3.1.   "Of the forms of animal life known to modern science, few, if any, classifications other than Homo sapiens have been the subject of as much legal controversy as the members of the order Isoptera. The species involved in this particular lawsuit does not appear in the record, but it is likely it was from the genus Reticulitermes of the family of Rhinotermitidae, known to the nonbiologically oriented as 'termites.' The wooden edifices of man represent nothing more to these despicable insects than an abundant source of cellulose, which is their principal food." *Hughes v. Stusser*, 68 Wash.2d 707, 708, 415 P.2d 89 (1966).

     3.2.   *Swinton* is an old case even older than Epstein. *Swinton* remains "good law" in Massachusetts. The rule of *Swinton*—no defense to enforcement of an agreement based on nondisclosure (silence)—was reaffirmed most recently in *Gossels v. Fleet Nat. Bank*, 69 Mass. App. 797, 806, 876 N.E.2d 872, 881 (Mass. App. 2007).

     3.3.   There are, however, much older cases on nondisclosure. Perhaps the best known such case, the United States Supreme Court decision in *Laidlaw v. Organ*, 15 U.S. 178 (1817),* goes back to the end of the War of 1812. During that war, the British blockade of New Orleans depressed the price of tobacco and other exportable commodities. Organ, a tobacco merchant, obtained advance information that a peace treaty had been signed and bought a large quantity of tobacco from Peter Laidlaw & Co., a New Orleans tobacco broker, without revealing the news of the war's end. When peace was announced, the price of tobacco shot up by almost 50%. The tobacco seller sued to avoid the contract because of Organ's nondisclosure. Chief Justice Marshall wrote: "The question in this case is, whether the intelligence of extrinsic circumstances, which might influence the

---

* Even earlier, Cicero addressed the question of nondisclosure in a hypothetical case of a grain merchant who was the first to visit a town suffering from famine. Cicero's question was whether the merchant should inform the townspeople that other merchants were coming even though this disclosure would lower the price people would pay for his grain. "Holding things back does not always amount to concealment; but it does when you want people, for your own profit, to be kept in the dark about something which you know and would be useful for them to know." *Cicero on Duties III*, in Selected Works 157, 177 (Michael Grant trans. 1971) Cicero then describes a person who would engage in such concealment as "shifty" and "underhanded." *Id.*

price of the commodity, and which was exclusively within the knowledge of the vendee, ought to have been communicated by him to the vendor? The court is of the opinion that he was not bound to communicate it. It would be difficult to circumscribe the contrary doctrine within proper limits, where the means of intelligence are equally accessible to both parties.

WEINTRAUB v. KROBATSCH

Supreme Court of New Jersey
64 N.J. 445, 317 A.2d 68 (1974)

Jacobs, J.

* * *

Mrs. Weintraub owned and occupied a six-year-old English-town home which she placed in the hands of a real estate broker (The Serafin Agency, Inc.) for sale. The Krobatsches were interested in purchasing the home, examined it while it was illuminated and found it suitable. On June 30, 1971 Mrs. Weintraub, as seller, and the Krobatsches, as purchasers, entered into a contract for the sale of the property for $42,500. The contract provided that the purchasers had inspected the property and were fully satisfied with its physical condition, that no representations had been made and that no responsibility was assumed by the seller as to the present or future condition of the premises. A deposit of $4,250 was sent by the purchasers to the broker to be held in escrow pending the closing of the transaction. The purchasers requested that the seller have the house fumigated and that was done. A fire after the signing of the contract caused damage but the purchasers indicated readiness that there be adjustment at closing.

During the evening of August 25, 1971, prior to closing, the purchasers entered the house, then unoccupied, and as they turned the lights on they were, as described in their petition for certification, "astonished to see roaches literally running in all directions, up the walls, drapes, etc." On the following day their attorney wrote a letter to Mrs. Weintraub, care of her New York law firm, advising that on the previous day "it was discovered that the house is infested with vermin despite the fact that an exterminator has only recently serviced the house" and asserting that "the presence of vermin in such great quantities, particularly after the exterminator was done, rendered the house as unfit for human habitation at this time and therefore, the contract is rescinded." On September 2, 1971 an exterminator wrote to Mr. Krobatsch advising that he had examined the premises and that "cockroaches were found to have infested the entire house." He said he could eliminate them for a relatively modest charge by two treatments with a twenty-one day interval but that it would be necessary to remove the carpeting "to properly treat all the infested areas."

Mrs. Weintraub rejected the rescission by the purchasers and filed an action in the Law Division joining them and the broker as defendants. Though she originally sought specific performance she later confined her claim to damages in the sum of $4,250, representing the deposit held in escrow by the broker. * * * There were opposing motions for summary judgment by the purchasers and Mrs. Weintraub. * * * At the argument on the motions it was evident that the purchasers were claiming fraudulent concealment or nondisclosure by the seller as the basis for their rescission. Thus at one point their attorney said: "Your honor, I would point out, and it is in my clients' affidavit, every time that they inspected this house prior to this time every light in the place was illuminated. Now, these insects are nocturnal by nature and that is not a point I think I have to prove through someone. I think Webster's dictionary is sufficient. By keeping the lights on it keeps them out of sight. These sellers had to know they had this problem. You could not live in a house this infested without knowing about it."

The Law Division denied the motion by the purchasers for summary judgment but granted Mrs. Weintraub's motion and directed that the purchasers pay her the sum of $4,250. * * * On appeal, the Appellate Division sustained the summary judgment in Mrs. Weintraub's favor. * * *

Before us the purchasers contend that they were entitled to a trial on the issue of whether there was fraudulent concealment or nondisclosure entitling them to rescind; if there was then clearly they were under no liability to either the seller or the broker and would be entitled to the return of their deposit held by the broker in escrow.

Mrs. Weintraub asserts that she was unaware of the infestation and the Krobatsches acknowledge that, if that was so, then there was no fraudulent concealment or nondisclosure on her part and their claim must fall. But the purchasers allege that she was in fact aware of the infestation and at this stage of the proceedings we must assume that to be true. She contends, however, that even if she were fully aware she would have been under no duty to speak and that consequently no complaint by the purchasers may legally be grounded on her silence. She relies primarily on cases such as *Swinton v. Whitinsville Sav. Bank*, 311 Mass. 677, 42 N.E. 2d 808, 141 A.L.R. 965 (1942). * * * *Swinton* is pertinent but, as Dean Prosser has noted, it is one of a line of "singularly unappetizing cases" which are surely out of tune with our times.

In *Swinton* the plaintiff purchased a house from the defendant and after he occupied it he found it to be infested with termites. The defendant had made no verbal or written representations but the plaintiff, asserting that the defendant knew of the termites and was under a duty to speak, filed a complaint for damages grounded on fraudulent concealment. The Supreme Judicial Court of Massachusetts sustained a demurrer to the complaint and entered judgment for the defendant. In the course of its opinion the court acknowledged that "the plaintiff possesses a certain appeal to the moral sense" but concluded that the law has not "reached the point of imposing upon the frailties of human nature a standard so idealistic as this." 42 N.E. 2d at 808–809. That was written several decades ago and we are far from certain that it represents views held by the current members of the Massachusetts court. In any event we are certain that it does not represent our sense of justice or fair dealing and it has understandably been rejected in persuasive opinions elsewhere. *See Obde v. Schlemeyer,* 56 Wash. 2d 449, 353 P. 2d 672 (1960).

In *Obde v. Schlemeyer,* 353 P. 2d 672, the defendants sold an apartment house to the plaintiffs. The house was termite infested but that fact was not disclosed by the sellers to the purchasers who later sued for damages alleging fraudulent concealment. The sellers contended that they were under no obligation whatever to speak out and they relied heavily on the decision of the Massachusetts court in *Swinton* (311 Mass. 677, 42 N.E. 2d 808, 141 A.L.R. 965). The Supreme Court of Washington flatly rejected their contention, holding that though the parties had dealt at arms length the sellers were under "a duty to inform the plaintiffs of the termite condition" of which they were fully aware. In the course of its opinion the court quoted approvingly from Dean Keeton's article in 15 Tex. L. Rev. 1. There the author first expressed his thought that when Lord Cairns suggested in *Peek v. Gurney,* L.R. 6 H.L. 377 (1873), that there was no duty to disclose facts, no matter how "morally censurable" (at 403), he was expressing nineteenth century law as shaped by an individualistic philosophy based on freedom of contracts and unconcerned with morals. He then made the following comments which fairly embody a currently acceptable principle on which the holding in *Obde* may be said to be grounded:

> In the present stage of the law, the decisions show a drawing away from this idea, and there can be seen an attempt by many courts to reach a just result in so far as possible, but yet maintaining the degree of certainty which the law must have. The statement may often be found that if either party to a contract of sale conceals or suppresses a material fact which he is in good faith bound to disclose then his silence is fraudulent.

> The attitude of the courts toward nondisclosure is undergoing a change and contrary to Lord Cairns' famous remark it would seem that the object of the law in these cases should be to impose on parties to the transaction a duty to speak whenever justice, equity, and fair dealing demand it. This statement is made only with reference to instances where the party to be charged is an actor in the transaction. This duty to speak does not result from an implied representation by silence, but exists because a refusal to speak constitutes unfair conduct.

15 Tex. L. Rev. at 31.

* * *

The purchasers here were entitled to withstand the seller's motion for summary judgment. They should have been permitted to proceed with their efforts to establish by testimony that they were equitably entitled to rescind because the house was extensively infested in the manner described by them, the seller was well aware of the infestation, and the seller deliberately concealed or failed to disclose the condition because of the likelihood that it would defeat the transaction. The seller may of course defend factually as well as legally and since the matter is primarily equitable in nature the factual as well as legal disputes will be for the trial judge alone.

If the trial judge finds such deliberate concealment or nondisclosure of the latent infestation not observable by the purchasers on their inspection, he will still be called upon to determine whether, in the light of the full presentation before him, the concealment or nondisclosure was of such significant nature as to justify rescission. Minor conditions which ordinary sellers and purchasers would reasonably disregard as of little or no materiality in the transaction would clearly not call for judicial intervention. While the described condition may not have been quite as major as in the termite cases which were concerned with structural impairments, to the purchasers here it apparently was of such magnitude and was so repulsive as to cause them to rescind immediately though they had earlier indicated readiness that there be adjustment at closing for damage resulting from a fire which occurred after the contract was signed. We are not prepared at his time to say that on their showing they acted either unreasonably or without equitable justification.

Our courts have come a long way since the days when the judicial emphasis was on formal rules and ancient precedents rather than on modern concepts of justice and fair dealing. While admittedly our law has progressed more slowly in the real property field than in other fields, there have been notable stirrings even there. * * * [W]e are satisfied that current principles grounded on justice and fair dealing, embraced throughout this opinion, clearly call for a full trial below; to that end the judgment entered in the Appellate Division is:

Reversed and remanded.

QUESTIONS

1.   Questions about the facts of this case

    1.1.   Did the contract mention cockroaches?

    1.2.   Did either the seller or the buyer mention cockroaches before the contract was signed?

    1.3.   Did the buyer allege that the seller concealed the cockroaches?

2.   Questions about the law

2.1. Can you distinguish the facts of *Swinton* from the facts of *Weintraub*? Should the Supreme Court of New Jersey have distinguished *Swinton* instead of "dissing" *Swinton* and people in Massachusetts?

2.2 What is the new New Jersey test for determining when an agreement will not be enforced because of a non-disclosure?

2.3. The New Jersey court quotes a Washington court's quote from a law review article by Dean Keeton which (to quote yet again) advocates:

"The attitude of the courts toward non-disclosure is undergoing a change and contrary to Lord Cairns' famous remark it would seem that the object of the law in these cases should be to impose on parties to the transaction a duty to speak whenever justice, equity, and fair dealing demand it." (emphasis added).

What does the underscored language mean? Is the Dean Keeton in this case just as "illusive" as the Dean Keaton in *The Usual Suspects*?

2.4. "Legislation mandating disclosure of residential real property conditions has been enacted by the majority of the states * * * The legislation requires sellers to disclose salient property defects on a mandated form." Gary S. Moore and Gerald Smolen, *Real Estate Disclosure Forms and Information Transfer*, 28 Real Estate Law Journal 319 (2000).

S contracts to sell her house to B. S fails to disclose that cockroaches had infested the entire house. Should the court permit B to rescind the contract if the relevant disclosure law did not expressly require disclosure of cockroach infestation?

2.5. *Weintraub* involved a consumer transaction. Should nondisclosure be a basis for rescission of commercial transactions? B Corp. contracts to buy S Food Processing, Inc. After entering into the contract but before closing on the contract, B Corp. learns that S Food Processing, Inc. had health department licensing problems that it failed to disclose. Should B Corp. be able to rescind the contract? *Cf. Restatement (Second) of Contracts* § 161.

SECTION 3: CONTRACT LAW REASONS FOR NOT ENFORCING AGREEMENTS: DEFENDANT'S LACK OF CAPACITY

Some agreements are enforceable against a person because of who he is. Assume for example that Bruce, a four-year-old child who is a big fan of Tinky–Winky, *http://en.wikipedia.org/wiki/Tinky_Winky*, signs a "contract" to purchase a purple Porsche for $100,000. Should the agreement be legally enforceable?

What if Bruce, the buyer of the $100,000 purple Porsche, is a forty-four year old intoxicated airline pilot who is a big fan of the Minnesota

Vikings? Should that agreement to pay $100,000 for a purple Porsche be legally enforceable against Bruce?

In the Bruce hypotheticals, was there a "meeting of the minds"? Did the Bruces have the capacity to contract?

Common law and then statutes have long recognized categories of individuals who do not have the capacity to contract. At one time, the law of capacity to contract considered a person's sex, color, and even occupation. The present law of capacity in most states resembles *Restatement (Second) of Contracts* § 12:

> (2) *A natural person who manifests assent to a transaction has full legal capacity to incur contractual duties thereby unless he is*
>
> (a) *under guardianship, or*
>
> (b) *an infant, or*
>
> (c) *mentally ill or defective, or*
>
> (d) *intoxicated.*

Today, in most states, the "age of majority" is 18. Historically (and in the next case), an infant or minor was anyone under the age of 21. The case involves a car dealer's efforts to enforce an agreement by a 20–year-old married "infant", who was the father of a real infant, to pay for a used station wagon.

KIEFER v. FRED HOWE MOTORS, INC.

Supreme Court of Wisconsin
39 Wis.2d 20, 158 N.W.2d 288 (1968)

SYLLABUS: On August 9, 1965, the plaintiff, Steven Kiefer, entered into a contract with the defendant, Fred Howe Motors, Inc. ("dealer" hereinafter) for the purchase of a 1960 Willys station wagon. Kiefer paid the contract price of $412 and took possession of the car. At the time of the sale Kiefer was twenty years old, married, and the father of one child.

Kiefer had difficulty with the car which he claimed was caused by a cracked block. Kiefer contacted the dealer and asked it to take the car back. Several other attempts to secure some adjustment with the dealer failed and Kiefer contacted Attorney Paul C. Konnor. The attorney wrote a letter to the dealer advising it that Kiefer was under twenty-one at the time of the sale. The letter declared the contract void, tendered return of the automobile and demanded repayment of the purchase price. There was no response so this action was commenced to recover the $412 purchase price. After a trial to the court, a judgment for the plaintiff was entered and the defendant appeals.

WILKIE, J.

Three issues are presented on this appeal. They are:

1. Should an emancipated minor over the age of eighteen be legally responsible for his contracts?

2. Was the contract effectively disaffirmed?

3. Is the plaintiff liable in tort for misrepresentation?

Legal Responsibility of Emancipated Minor.

The law governing agreements made during infancy reaches back over many centuries. The general rule is that "* * * the contract of a minor, other than for necessaries, is either void or voidable at his option." The only other exceptions to the rule permitting disaffirmance are statutory or involve contracts which deal with duties imposed by law such as a contract of marriage or an agreement to support an illegitimate child. The general rule is not affected by the minor's status as emancipated or unemancipated.

Appellant does not advance any argument that would put this case within one of the exceptions to the general rule, but rather urges that this court, as a matter of public policy, adopt a rule that an emancipated minor over eighteen years of age be made legally responsible for his contracts.

The underpinnings of the general rule allowing the minor to disaffirm his contracts were undoubtedly the protection of the minor. It was thought that the minor was immature in both mind and experience and that, therefore, he should be protected from his own bad judgments as well as from adults who would take advantage of him. The doctrine of the voidability of minors' contracts often seems commendable and just. If the beans that the young naive Jack purchased from the crafty old man in the fairy tale "Jack and the Bean Stalk" had been worthless rather than magical, it would have been only fair to allow Jack to disaffirm the bargain and reclaim his cow. However, in today's modern and sophisticated society the "infancy doctrine" seems to lose some of its gloss.

Paradoxically, we declare the infant mature enough to shoulder arms in the military, but not mature enough to vote; mature enough to marry and be responsible for his torts and crimes, but not mature enough to assume the burden of his own contractual indiscretions. In Wisconsin, the infant is deemed mature enough to use a dangerous instrumentality—a motor vehicle—at sixteen, but not mature enough to purchase it without protection until he is twenty-one.

No one really questions that a line as to age must be drawn somewhere below which a legally defined minor must be able to disaffirm his contracts for nonnecessities. The law over the centuries has considered this age to be twenty-one. Legislatures in other states have lowered the age. We suggest that the appellant might better seek the change it proposes in the legislative halls rather than this court. * * *

Undoubtedly, the infancy doctrine is an obstacle when a major purchase is involved. However, we believe that the reasons for allowing that obstacle to remain viable at this point outweigh those for casting it aside. Minors require some protection from the pitfalls of the marketplace. Reasonable minds will always differ on the extent of the protection that should be afforded. For this court to adopt a rule that the appellant suggests and remove the contractual disabilities from a minor simply because he becomes emancipated, which in most cases would be the result of marriage, would be to suggest that the married minor is somehow vested with more wisdom and maturity than his single counterpart. However, logic would not seem to dictate this result especially when today a youthful marriage is oftentimes indicative of a lack of wisdom and maturity.

Disaffirmance.

The appellant questions whether there has been an effective disaffirmance of the contract in this case.

Williston, while discussing how a minor may disaffirm a contract, states:

> "Any act which clearly shows an intent to disaffirm a contract or sale is sufficient for the purpose. Thus a notice by the infant of his purpose to disaffirm * * * a tender or even an offer to return the consideration or its proceeds to the vendor, * * * is sufficient."

2 Williston, *Contracts* (3d ed.), p. 26, sec. 234.

The testimony of Steven Kiefer and the letter from his attorney to the dealer clearly establish that there was an effective disaffirmance of the contract.

Misrepresentation

Appellant's last argument is that the respondent should be held liable in tort for damages because he misrepresented his age. Appellant would use these damages as a set-off against the contract price sought to be reclaimed by respondent.

The 19th-century view was that a minor's lying about his age was inconsequential because a fraudulent representation of capacity was not the equivalent of actual capacity. This rule has been altered by time. There appear to be two possible methods that now can be employed to bind the defrauding minor: He may be estopped from denying his alleged majority, in which case the contract will be enforced or contract damages will be allowed; or he may be allowed to disaffirm his contract but be liable in tort for damages. Wisconsin follows the latter approach.

* * *

The "motor vehicle purchase contract" signed by Steven Kiefer contained the following language just above the purchaser's signature:

> I represent that I am 21 years of age or over and recognize that the dealer sells the above vehicle upon this representation.

Whether the inclusion of this sentence constitutes a misrepresentation depends on whether elements of the tort have been satisfied. They were not. In [*First Nat. Bank in Oshkosh v. Scieszinski*, 25 Wis. 2d 569, 131 N.W.2d 308 (1964)], it is said:

A party alleging fraud has the burden of proving it by clear and convincing evidence. The elements of fraud are well established:

> To be actionable the false representation must consist, first of a statement of fact which is untrue; second, that it was made with intent to defraud and for the purpose of inducing the other party to act upon it; third, that he did in fact rely on it and was induced thereby to act, to his injury or damage.

No evidence was adduced to show that the plaintiff had an intent to defraud the dealer. To the contrary, it is at least arguable that the majority of minors are, as the plaintiff here might well have been, unaware of the legal consequences of their acts.

Without the element of scienter being satisfied, the plaintiff is not susceptible to an action in misrepresentation. Furthermore, the reliance mentioned in *Scieszinski* must be, as Prosser points out, "justifiable reliance." We fail to see how the dealer could be justified in the mere reliance on the fact that the plaintiff signed a contract containing a sentence that said he was twenty-one or over. The trial court observed that the plaintiff was sufficiently immature looking to arouse suspicion. The appellant never took any affirmative steps to determine whether the plaintiff was in fact over twenty-one. It never asked to see a draft card, identification card, or the most logical indicium of age under the circumstances, a driver's license. Therefore, because there was no intent to deceive, and no justifiable reliance, the appellant's action for misrepresentation must fail.

By the Court: Judgment affirmed.

Hallows, C. J. (dissenting).

The majority opinion on the issue of whether an emancipated minor legally should be responsible for his contracts "doth protest too much." After giving very cogent reasons why the common-law rule should be abandoned, the opinion refrains from reshaping the rule to meet reality. Minors are emancipated by a valid marriage and also by entering military service. If they are mature enough to become parents and assume the responsibility of raising other minors and if they are mature enough to be drafted or volunteer to bear arms and sacrifice their life for their country, then they are mature enough to make binding contracts in the marketplace. The magical age limit of twenty-one years as an indication of contractual maturity no longer has a basis in fact or in public policy.

My second ground of the dissent is that an automobile to this respondent was a necessity and therefore the contract could not be disaffirmed. Here, we have a minor, aged twenty years and seven months, the father of a child, and working. While the record shows there is some public transportation to his present place of work, it also shows he borrowed his mother's car to go to and from work. Automobiles for parents under twenty-one years of age to go to and from work in our current society may well be a necessity and I think in this case the record shows it is. An automobile as a means of transportation to earn a living should not be considered a nonnecessity because the owner is five months too young. I would reverse.

QUESTIONS AND NOTES

1. Questions about the facts of this case

    1.1. Who is suing whom for what?

    1.2. Did the plaintiff deny that he agreed to pay and did not pay $412 for the 5–year–old station wagon?

    1.3. Did the plaintiff deny that he represented to the seller that he was 21?

    1.4. Did the plaintiff contend that he did not understand the contract he signed?

    1.5. Did the plaintiff contend that the agreement was unfair?

    1.6. Did the plaintiff need the car?

    1.7. Was the plaintiff "emancipated"?

    1.8. How much did the car cost? How much did it cost to litigate and appeal this case?

2. Questions about the law

    2.1. In September 1965, Epstein (the only one of your authors who was over 21 in 1965) offers Fred Howe Motors, Inc., $3,000 for a 1960 Willys station wagon. Fred Howe Motors, Inc. wants to get the Willys station wagon back from Steve Kiefer to sell to Epstein. Can Fred Howe Motors, Inc. get the car back from Steve Kiefer on the ground that the sale contract was not effective since Kiefer was a minor?

    2.2. How can you contract with a minor? Your firm represents Jive Records, Inc. which wants to sign Gooberhead, an 11–year–old bluegrass rapper, to a recording contract. What do you advise?

    2.3. Is the discussion of misrepresentation in the *Kiefer* case consistent with the earlier discussion of misrepresentation in *Halpert v. Rosenthal, supra*?

3. Notes

    3.1. "The right of disaffirmance as taught in our law schools has increasingly had little practical import in the billion dollar juvenile marketplace. * * * It [infant incapacity] has been preserved in the cloistered domain of black letter law. In reality, it has been dismantled piece by piece by twin adversaries: the courthouse and the statehouse. The right of disaffirmance has been judicially limited by the creation of an assortment of subdoctrines intended to mollify the harsh effects of the per se rule."

LARRY L. DiMATTEO, CONTRACT THEORY—THE EVOLUTION OF CONTRACTUAL INTENT 103 (1998).

3.2.   The *Kiefer* case illustrates a couple of these limiting judicial "sub-doctrines": (i) infants' liability for "necessaries" and (ii) infants' liability for misrepresentation of age.

3.3.   Another such mollifying subdoctrine is ratification. By her actions or inactions after reaching the age of majority (or otherwise gaining capacity) a person can lose the right of disaffirmance through ratification. For example, ratification prevented Bob Dylan from saying "I'll just say fare thee well, gal" to Columbia Records.

When [CBS/Columbia Records] signed him, Dylan was twenty and a minor under New York state contract law. The folksinger said he had no parent to countersign for him, which was untrue. After his first album bombed, Dylan sent Columbia a letter declaring his contract void. [The letter was] handed over to [Clive] Davis. Clive asked whether Dylan had used the CBS studio since turning twenty-one. Six or seven times [was the response]. In that case, Clive said Dylan had affirmed his contract. Dylan was forced to rescind the letter.

FREDRIC DANNEN, HIT MEN: POWER BROKERS AND FAST MONEY INSIDE THE MUSIC BUSINESS 67–68 (1991).

3.4.   Epstein's sons regularly ask why there is a "bright line" statutory rule to decide who is too young to contract but no similar rule to decide who is too old to contract. *See generally* Comment, *No Protection for the Elderly: The Inadequacy of the Capacity Doctrine in Avoiding Unfair Contracts Involving Seniors*, 78 OR. L. REV. 807, 823–24 (1999) ("setting a strict upper age limit for contracting, similar to the minimum age requirements imposed on minors, would be impractical because the degree of competency among seniors varies. * * * Despite these concerns, states could still set forth a standard that. * * * utilizes factors that, if combined, would create a presumption of incapacity. These factors should include advanced age, medically documented physical or mental illness, knowledge by the other party of such illness or other signs of incapacity, and inadequate consideration or other signs of unfairness.")

SECTION 4: CONTRACT LAW REASONS FOR <u>NOT</u> ENFORCING AGREEMENTS: DURESS AND UNDUE INFLUENCE

In the previous section on capacity, the defense to enforceability of an agreement was based on who happened to make the agreement. In these materials on duress and undue influence, the defense to enforceability of an agreement is based primarily on how the agreement happened.

Obviously, if Epstein agrees to write a book with Markell and Ponoroff only because they have guns pointed at his head, that agreement should not be legally enforceable. Physical duress! *Restatement (Second) of Contracts* § 174 explains duress by physical compulsion.

Restatement (Second) of Contracts § 175 and the following excerpt from Professor Atiyah of Oxford explain duress by threat:

P.S. ATIYAH, AN INTRODUCTION TO THE LAW OF CONTRACT

265–67 (5th ed. 1995)

All persons over the age of 18 and of sound mind are generally treated as of equal capacity for the purpose of contracting, and the law is reluctant to admit the direct plea that the contract is unfair, and that one party was in a position to dictate the terms to the other. But while maintaining the sanctity of contracts as a general principle, the law has, from time to time, stepped in to redress the balance between the strong and the weak.

. . . .

A person who does something under the most severe constraints (such as throwing his cargo overboard to save his ship during a storm), is, said Aristotle, still acting voluntarily, of his own free will. He is choosing between two very unpalatable courses, but he is still making a free choice. Similarly, a person who signs a contract at the point of a gun may be said to be simply choosing between being shot and signing the document. He signs, not because he has no will—indeed, the more strongly he believes in the gunman's threats, the more willing he is likely to be to sign—but because it is the lesser of the two evils open to him.

But this analysis leads to a new difficulty. If even the gunman's victim is acting of his free will, then we must say that all (or anyhow nearly all) contracts are made voluntarily, but we must also admit that all contracts are made under pressure of some sort. Not only is there no such thing as a totally involuntary contract, there is equally no such thing as a totally unconstrained choice. Every contract we make is made under some form of pressure, every contractual offer is made backed by some sort of threat. The pressure and the threats are implicit in the whole concept of exchange, because the offeror is always demanding something in return for his offer, which is only another way of saying that he is threatening not to supply what you want, unless you can give him what he wants in return. This means that some way must be found of distinguishing between the kinds of pressure and the kinds of threats which will be permissible, which will not invalidate a contract, and those pressures and threats which will be ruled out, and which will invalidate a contract. The distinction which the law seeks to draw, therefore, must be that between legitimate and illegitimate pressure, or threats, and has nothing to do with 'overborne wills.'

This excursion into theory is not without practical import, because the questions raised by these two possible approaches are quite different.

If the law were truly concerned with the degree to which a choice was an exercise of free will, the question before the court would presumably be a psychological (or even philosophical) question of no little difficulty, and it would also be a question of fact in each case: has the will been overborne? On the other hand, if the true question concerns the legitimacy of the pressure or threats used, the question must be one of law which has nothing to do with the psychological state of mind of the party in question.

As Professor Atiyah points out, the law of duress is not limited to physical duress. As the next two cases point out, the law of duress is not limited to individuals: businesses can avoid the legal enforcement of an agreement by establishing "illegitimate pressure or threats."

AUSTIN INSTRUMENT, INC. v. LORAL CORPORATION

Court of Appeals of New York
29 N.Y.2d 124, 324 N.Y.S.2d 22, 272 N.E.2d 533 (1971)

Fuld, C.J.

The defendant, Loral Corporation, seeks to recover payment for goods delivered under a contract which it had with plaintiff Austin Instrument, Inc., on the ground that the evidence establishes, as a matter of law, that it was forced to agree to an increase in price on the items in question under circumstances amounting to economic duress.

In July of 1965, Loral was awarded a $6,000,000 contract by the Navy for the production of radar sets. The contract contained a schedule of deliveries, a liquidated damages clause applying to late deliveries and a cancellation clause in case of default by Loral. The latter thereupon solicited bids for some 40 precision gear components needed to produce the radar sets, and awarded Austin a subcontract to supply 23 such parts. That party commenced delivery in early 1966.

In May, 1966, Loral was awarded a second Navy contract for the production of more radar sets and again went about soliciting bids. Austin bid on all 40 gear components but, on July 15, a representative from Loral informed Austin's president, Mr. Krauss, that his company would be awarded the subcontract only for those items on which it was low bidder. The Austin officer refused to accept an order for less than all 40 of the gear parts and on the next day he told Loral that Austin would cease deliveries of the parts due under the existing subcontract unless Loral consented to substantial increases in the prices provided for by that agreement—both retroactively for parts already delivered and prospectively on those not yet shipped—and placed with Austin the order for all 40 parts needed under Loral's second Navy contract. Shortly thereafter, Austin did, indeed, stop delivery. After contacting 10 manufacturers of precision gears and finding none who could produce the parts in time to meet its commitments to the Navy, Loral acceded to Austin's demands; in a letter dated July 22, Loral wrote to Austin that:

> We have feverishly surveyed other sources of supply and find that because of the prevailing military exigencies, were they to start from scratch as would have to be the case, they could not even remotely begin to deliver on time to meet the delivery requirements established by the Government. * * * Accordingly, we are left with no choice or alternative but to meet your conditions.

Loral thereupon consented to the price increases insisted upon by Austin under the first subcontract and the latter was awarded a second subcontract making it the supplier of all 40 gear parts for Loral's second contract with the Navy. Although Austin was granted until September to resume deliveries, Loral did, in fact, receive parts in August and was able to produce the radar sets in time to meet its commitments to the Navy on both contracts. After Austin's last delivery under the second subcontract in July, 1967, Loral notified it of its intention to seek recovery of the price increases.

On September 15, 1967, Austin instituted this action against Loral to recover an amount in excess of $17,750 which was still due on the second subcontract. On the same day, Loral commenced an action against Austin claiming damages of some $22,250—the aggregate of the price increases under the first subcontract—on the ground of economic duress. The two actions were consolidated and, following a trial, Austin was awarded the sum it requested and Loral's complaint against Austin was dismissed on the ground that it was not shown that "it could not have obtained the items in question from other sources in time to meet its commitment to the Navy under the first contract." A closely divided Appellate Division affirmed. * * *

The applicable law is clear and, indeed, is not disputed by the parties. A contract is voidable on the ground of duress when it is established that the party making the claim was forced to agree to it by means of a wrongful threat precluding the exercise of his free will. The existence of economic duress or business compulsion is demonstrated by proof that "immediate possession of needful goods is threatened" or, more particularly, in cases such as the one before us, by proof that one party to a contract has threatened to breach the agreement by withholding goods unless the other party agrees to some further demand. However, a mere threat by one party to breach the contract by not delivering the required items, though wrongful, does not in itself constitute economic duress. It must also appear that the threatened party could not obtain the goods from another source of supply and that the ordinary remedy of an action for breach of contract would not be adequate.

We find without any support in the record the conclusion reached by the courts below that Loral failed to establish that it was the victim of economic duress. On the contrary, the evidence makes out a classic case, as a matter of law, of such duress.

It is manifest that Austin's threat—to stop deliveries unless the prices were increased—deprived Loral of its free will. As bearing on this, Loral's relationship with the Government is most significant. As mentioned above, its contract called for staggered monthly deliveries of the radar sets, with clauses calling for liquidated damages and possible cancellation on default. Because of its production schedule, Loral was, in July, 1966, concerned with meeting its delivery requirements in September, October and November, and it was for the sets to be delivered in those months that the withheld gears were needed. Loral had to plan ahead, and the substantial liquidated damages for which it would be liable, plus the threat of default, were genuine possibilities. Moreover, Loral did a substantial portion of its business with the Government, and it feared that a failure to deliver as agreed upon would jeopardize its chances for future contracts. * * * It was perfectly reasonable for Loral, or any other party similarly placed, to consider itself in an emergency, duress situation.

* * *

Loral, as indicated above, also had the burden of demonstrating that it could not obtain the parts elsewhere within a reasonable time, and there can be no doubt that it met this burden. The 10 manufacturers whom Loral contacted comprised its entire list of "approved vendors" for precision gears, and none was able to commence delivery soon enough. As Loral was producing a highly sophisticated item of military machinery requiring parts made to the strictest engineering standards, it would be unreasonable to hold that Loral should have gone to other vendors, with whom it was either unfamiliar or dissatisfied, to procure the needed parts. * * *

It is hardly necessary to add that Loral's normal legal remedy of accepting Austin's breach of the contract and then suing for damages would have been inadequate under the circumstances, as Loral would still have had to obtain the gears elsewhere with all the concomitant consequences mentioned above. In other words, Loral actually had no choice, when the prices were raised by Austin, except to take the gears at the "coerced" prices and then sue to get the excess back. * * *

In sum, the record before us demonstrates that Loral agreed to the price increases in consequence of the economic duress employed by Austin. Accordingly, the matter should be remanded to the trial court for a computation of its damages.

The order appealed from should be modified, with costs, by reversing so much thereof as affirms the dismissal of defendant Loral Corporation's claim and, except as so modified, affirmed.

* * *

QUESTIONS

1. Questions about the facts of this case

    1.1. Who is suing whom for what?

    1.2. Which company is larger, Austin or Loral? Does size matter? Are Austin's powers relevant?

    1.3. Did Loral agree to Austin's demand for price increases?

    1.4. Do you think that Loral's July 22d letter was written, or at least reviewed, by a lawyer? By a lawyer familiar with the concept of excuse by reason of economic duress?

    1.5. Why did Austin ask for price increases? According to the statement of facts in the Appellate Division opinion:

    Austin claimed that it was losing a substantial sum on the existing job; that it could not afford to do this; and that the prices being paid to it were only a fraction of what it was entitled to. Parenthetically, we note that it is well known that in this time of continual rising of material and manufacturing costs, renegotiation of contract prices does sometimes occur in business and commercial dealings.

    316 N.Y.S. 2d 530. Is that relevant? Was it relevant to the New York Court of Appeals?

2. Questions about the law

    2.1. Is this case covered by Article 2 of the Uniform Commercial Code?

    2.2. Professor Atiyah suggested that the law needs to distinguish between "legitimate and illegitimate pressure." How did the court in the *Austin* case distinguish between the two? What did Austin do that was "illegitimate"?

TOTEM MARINE TUG & BARGE, INC. v. ALYESKA PIPELINE SERVICE COMPANY

Supreme Court of Alaska
584 P.2d 15 (1978)

BURKE, J.

This appeal arises from the superior court's granting of summary judgment in favor of defendants-appellees Alyeska Pipeline Services, et al., in a contract action brought by plaintiffs-appellants Totem Marine Tug & Barge, Inc., Pacific, Inc., and Richard Stair.

The following summary of events is derived from the materials submitted in the summary judgment proceedings below.

Totem is a closely held Alaska corporation which began operations in March of 1975. Richard Stair, at all times relevant to this case, was vice-resident of Totem. In June of 1975, Totem entered into a contract with

Alyeska under which Totem was to transport pipeline construction materials from Houston, Texas, to a designated port in southern Alaska, with the possibility of one or two cargo stops along the way. In order to carry out this contract, which was Totem's first, Totem chartered a barge (The "Marine Flasher") and an ocean-going tug (the "Kirt Chouest"). * * *

By the terms of the contract, Totem was to have completed performance by approximately August 15, 1975. From the start, however, there were numerous problems which impeded Totem's performance of the contract. For example, according to Totem, Alyeska represented that approximately 1,800 to 2,100 tons of regular uncoated pipe were to be loaded in Houston, and that perhaps another 6,000 to 7,000 tons of materials would be put on the barge at later stops along the west coast. Upon the arrival of the tug and barge in Houston, however, Totem found that about 6,700 to 7,200 tons of coated pipe, steel beams and valves, haphazardly and improperly piled, were in the yard to be loaded. This situation called for remodeling of the barge and extra cranes and stevedores, and resulted in the loading taking thirty days rather than the three days which Totem had anticipated it would take to load 2,000 tons. The lengthy loading period was also caused in part by Alyeska's delay in assuring Totem that it would pay for the additional expenses, bad weather and other administrative problems.

The difficulties continued after the tug and barge left Houston. It soon became apparent that the vessels were travelling more slowly than anticipated because of the extra load. In response to Alyeska's complaints and with its verbal consent, on August 13, 1975, Totem chartered a second tug, the "N. Joseph Guidry." When the "Guidry" reached the Panama Canal, however, Alyeska had not yet furnished the written amendment to the parties' contract. Afraid that Alyeska would not agree to cover the cost of the second tug, Stair notified the "Guidry" not to go through the Canal. After some discussions in which Alyeska complained of the delays and accused Totem of lying about the horsepower of the first tug, Alyeska executed the amendment on August 21, 1975.

By this time the "Guidry" had lost its preferred passage through the Canal and had to wait two or three additional days before it could go through. Upon finally meeting, the three vessels encountered the tail of a hurricane which lasted for about eight or nine days and which substantially impeded their progress.

The three vessels finally arrived in the vicinity of San Pedro, California, where Totem planned to change crews and refuel. On Alyeska's orders, however, the vessels instead pulled into port at Long Beach, California. At this point, Alyeska's agents commenced off-loading the barge, without Totem's consent, without the necessary load survey, and without a marine survey, the absence of which voided Totem's insurance. After much wrangling and some concessions by Alyeska, the freight was off-loaded. Thereafter, on or about September 14, 1975, Alyeska terminated the contract. The termination was affirmed a few days later at a meeting at which Alyeska officials refused to give a reason for the termination.

Following termination of the contract, Totem submitted termination invoices to Alyeska and began pressing the latter for payment. The invoices came to something between $260,000 and $300,000. An official from Alyeska told Totem that they would look over the invoices but that they were not sure when payment would be made—perhaps in a day or perhaps in six to eight months. Totem was in urgent need of cash as the invoices represented debts which the company had incurred on 10–30 day payment schedules. Totem's creditors were demanding payment and according to Stair, without immediate cash, Totem would go bankrupt. Totem then turned over the collection to its attorney, Roy Bell, directing him to advise Alyeska of Totem's financial straits. Thereafter, Bell met with Alyeska officials in Seattle, and after some negotiations, Totem received a settlement offer from Alyeska for $97,500. On November 6, 1975, Totem, through its president Stair, signed an agreement releasing Alyeska from all claims by Totem in exchange for $97,500.

On March 26, 1976, Totem, Richard Stair, and Pacific filed a complaint against Alyeska, which was subsequently amended. In the amended complaint, the plaintiffs sought to rescind the settlement and release on the ground of economic duress and to recover the balance allegedly due on the original contract. In addition, they alleged that Alyeska had wrongfully terminated the contract and sought miscellaneous other compensatory and punitive damages.

Before filing an answer, Alyeska moved for summary judgment against the plaintiffs on the ground that Totem had executed a binding release of all claims against Alyeska and that as a matter of law, Totem could not prevail on its claim of economic duress. In opposition, plaintiffs contended that the purported release was executed under duress in that Alyeska wrongfully terminated the contract; that Alyeska knew that Totem was faced with large debts and impending bankruptcy; that Alyeska withheld funds admittedly owed knowing the effect this would have on plaintiffs and that plaintiffs had no alternative but to involuntarily accept the $97,500 in order to avoid bankruptcy. Plaintiffs maintained that they had thus raised genuine issues of material fact such that trial was necessary, and that Alyeska was not entitled to judgment as a matter of law. Alyeska disputed the plaintiffs' assertions.

On November 30, 1976, the superior court granted the defendant's motion for summary judgment. This appeal followed.

* * *

As was noted above, a court's initial task in deciding motions for summary judgment is to determine whether there exist genuine issues of material fact. In order to decide whether such issues exist in this case, we must examine the doctrine allowing avoidance of a release on grounds of economic duress.

This court has not yet decided a case involving a claim of economic duress or what is also called business compulsion. At early common law, a contract could be avoided on the ground of duress only if a party could show that the agreement was entered into for fear of loss of life or limb, mayhem or imprisonment. The threat had to be such as to overcome the will of a person of ordinary firmness and courage. Subsequently, however, the concept has been broadened to include myriad forms of economic coercion which force a person to involuntarily enter into a particular transaction. The test has come to be whether the will of the person induced by the threat was overcome rather than that of a reasonably firm person.

At the outset it is helpful to acknowledge the various policy considerations which are involved in cases involving economic duress. Typically, those claiming such coercion are attempting to avoid the consequences of a modification of an original contract or of a settlement and release agreement. On the one hand, courts are reluctant to set aside agreements because of the notion of freedom of contract and because of the desirability of having private dispute resolutions be final. On the other hand, there is an increasing recognition of the law's role in correcting inequitable or unequal exchanges between parties of disproportionate bargaining power and a greater willingness to not enforce agreements which were entered into under coercive circumstances.

There are various statements of what constitutes economic duress. * * * Section 492(b) of the Restatement of Contracts defines duress as:

> any wrongful threat of one person by words or other conduct that induces another to enter into a transaction under the influence of such fear as precludes him from exercising free will and judgment, if the threat was intended or should reasonably have been expected to operate as an inducement.

Professor Williston states the basic elements of economic duress in the following manner:

1.   The party alleging economic duress must show that he has been the victim of a wrongful or unlawful act or threat, and

2.   Such act or threat must be one which deprives the victim of his unfettered will.

Many courts state the test somewhat differently, eliminating use of the vague term "free will," but retaining the same basic idea. Under this standard, duress exists where: (1) one party involuntarily accepted the terms of another, (2) circumstances permitted no other alternative, and (3) such circumstances were the result of coercive acts of the other party. The third element is further explained as follows:

> In order to substantiate the allegation of economic duress or business compulsion, the plaintiff must go beyond the mere showing of reluctance to accept and of financial embarrassment. There must be a showing of acts on the part of the defendant which produced these

two factors. The assertion of duress must be proven by evidence that the duress resulted from defendant's wrongful and oppressive conduct and not by the plaintiff's necessities.

[*W. R. Grimshaw Co. v. Nevil C. Withrow Co.*, 248 F.2d 896, 904 (1957)].

As the above indicates, one essential element of economic duress is that the plaintiff show that the other party by wrongful acts or threats, intentionally caused him to involuntarily enter into a particular transaction. Courts have not attempted to define exactly what constitutes a wrongful or coercive act, as wrongfulness depends on the particular facts in each case. This requirement may be satisfied where the alleged wrongdoer's conduct is criminal or tortious but an act or threat may also be considered wrongful if it is wrongful in the moral sense.

In many cases, a threat to breach a contract or to withhold payment of an admitted debt has constituted a wrongful act. Implicit in such cases is the additional requirement that the threat to breach the contract or withhold payment be done in bad faith.

Economic duress does not exist, however, merely because a person has been the victim of a wrongful act; in addition, the victim must have no choice but to agree to the other party's terms or face serious financial hardship. Thus, in order to avoid a contract, a party must also show that he had no reasonable alternative to agreeing to the other party's terms, or, as it is often stated, that he had no adequate remedy if the threat were to be carried out. What constitutes a reasonable alternative is a question of fact, depending on the circumstances of each case. An available legal remedy, such as an action for breach of contract, may provide such an alternative. Where one party wrongfully threatens to withhold goods, services or money from another unless certain demands are met, the availability on the market of similar goods and services or of other sources of funds may also provide an alternative to succumbing to the coercing party's demands. * * *

* * * For example, in [*Austin Instrument, Inc. v. Loral Corp.*, 29 N.Y.2d 124 (1971)], duress was found in the following circumstances: A subcontractor threatened to refuse further delivery under a contract unless the contractor agreed to modify the existing contract between the parties. The contractor was unable to obtain the necessary materials elsewhere without delay, and if it did not have the materials promptly, it would have been in default on its main contract with the government. In each case such default would have had grave economic consequences for the contractor and hence it agreed to the modifications. In both, the courts found that the alternatives to agreeing to the modification were inadequate (i.e., suing for breach of contract or obtaining the materials elsewhere) and that modifications therefore were signed under duress and voidable.

     * * *

Turning to the instant case, we believe that Totem's allegations, if proved, would support a finding that it executed a release of its contract claims against Alyeska under economic duress. Totem has alleged that Alyeska deliberately withheld payment of an acknowledged debt, knowing that Totem had no choice but to accept an inadequate sum in settlement of that debt; that Totem was faced with impending bankruptcy; that Totem was unable to meet its pressing debts other than by accepting the immediate cash payment offered by Alyeska; and that through necessity, Totem thus involuntarily accepted an inadequate settlement offer from Alyeska and executed a release of all claims under the contract. If the release was in fact executed under these circumstances,[5] we think that under the legal principles discussed above that this would constitute the type of wrongful conduct and lack of alternatives that would render the release voidable by Totem on the ground of economic duress. We would add that although Totem need not necessarily prove its allegation that Alyeska's termination of the contract was wrongful in order to sustain a claim of economic duress, the events leading to the termination would be probative as to whether Alyeska exerted any wrongful pressure on Totem and whether Alyeska wrongfully withheld payment from Totem.[6]

* * *

Our examination of the materials presented by Totem in opposition to Alyeska's motion for summary judgment leads us to conclude that Totem has made a sufficient factual showing as to each of the elements of economic duress to withstand that motion. There is no doubt that Alyeska disputes many of the factual allegations made by Totem[7] and drawing all inferences in favor of Totem, we believe that genuine issues of material fact exist in this case such that trial is necessary. Admittedly, Totem's showing was somewhat weak in that, for example, it did not produce the testimony of Roy Bell, the attorney who represented Totem in the negotiations leading to the settlement and release. At trial, it will probably be necessary for Totem to produce this evidence if it is to prevail on its claim of duress. However, a party opposing a motion for summary judgment need not produce all of the evidence it may have at its disposal but need only show that issues of material fact exist. Therefore, we hold that the superior court erred in granting summary judgment for appellees and remand the case to the superior court for trial in accordance with the legal principles set forth above.

* * *

---

5. By way of clarification, we would note that Totem would not have to prove that Alyeska admitted to owing the precise sum Totem claimed it was owed upon termination of the contract but only that Alyeska acknowledged that it owed Totem approximately that amount which Totem sought.

6. We make no comment as to whether Alyeska's termination of the contract was wrongful nor as to the truth of Totem's other allegations.

7. For example, Alyeska has denied that it ever admitted to owing any particular sum to Totem and has disputed the truthfulness of Totem's assertions of impending bankruptcy. Other factual issues which remain unresolved include whether or not Alyeska knew of Totem's financial situation after termination of the contract and whether Alyeska did in fact threaten by words or conduct to withhold payment unless Totem agreed to settle.

QUESTIONS, NOTES, AND CONNECTIONS

1. Questions about the facts of this case

    1.1. The opinion mentions two different agreements: (i) the June transport agreement and (ii) the November settlement agreement. Which agreement is involved in this litigation?

    1.2. Does the plaintiff Totem Marine Tug & Barge, Inc. allege a breach of the June transport agreement? Does it allege a breach of the November settlement agreement?

2. Questions about the law

    2.1. According to the first *Restatement's* definition of duress quoted by the Alaska Supreme Court, duress requires a "wrongful" threat or conduct. What "wrongful" threat or conduct does the plaintiff allege?

    2.2. On remand, what does the trial court have to find in order to rescind the November settlement agreement on the ground of economic duress? Will the plaintiff establish economic duress by establishing that the value of its claim was more than $97,500? Significantly more than $97,500? *Cf. Restatement (Second) of Contracts* § 74.

    2.3. The *Totem* decision discusses the *Austin* case. As the attorney for Alyeska, how would you distinguish the *Austin* case?

3. Notes

    3.1. The Alaska Supreme Court discussed the *Totem* decision in *Northern Fabrication Co., Inc. v. Unocal and Star North Services*, 980 P.2d 958 (Alaska 1999), a case with markedly similar facts to *Totem*. There, Northern Fabrication, a company on the brink of bankruptcy, settled its $170,000+ contract cost overruns claim against Unocal and then later sued to rescind the settlement on the ground of economic duress. Unocal moved for summary judgment. In *Northern Fabrication*, unlike *Totem*, the Alaska Supreme Court granted the summary judgment motion distinguishing *Totem*:

    > Herein lies the difference between *Totem* and the case at bar. In *Totem*, it was alleged that the other party deliberately withheld payment of an acknowledged debt. Deliberately withholding payment of an acknowledged debt constitutes an action "wrongful in the moral sense" that satisfies the third prong of the test for economic duress. Here NFC has not produced evidence that UNOCAL ever acknowledged its debt to NFC for the full amount of the cost overruns.

    3.2. While the first *Restatement of Contracts* used the term "wrongful" in defining "duress," the *Restatement (Second) of Contracts* §§ 175 and 176 use the term "improper." The examples of an "improper threat" for this purpose include a threat that is "a breach of the duty of good faith and fair dealing under a contract with the recipient." *Restatement (Second) of Contracts* § 176(d).

3.3.   Professor Grace Giesel provides this summary of the law of duress: "[D]uress can be based on threats of crimes or torts, threats that are criminal or tortuous, threats of criminal prosecution, threats of bad faith use of civil prosecution, and bad faith within an existing contractual relationship. Parties making such threats prove themselves blameworthy. When such blameworthiness creates a contract that is the product of significantly constrained choice, justice is best served by not enforcing the contract. Here the freedom of contract bows to the rightness of not enforcing the contract because the constraint is significant enough to undermine the theories supporting the public policy in favor of freedom of contract. Also, the threatener's blameworthiness robs that party of the legitimate expectation that a court will enforce the contract, or others like it. Also, any attempt to use the duress doctrine as a direct regulator of the substantive fairness of deals should be abandoned. Courts have rejected such a role in general and have rejected such a role for the duress doctrine even in the face of urging by commentators and the Restatement itself." Grace Giesel, *A Realistic Proposal for the Contract Duress Doctrine*, 107 W. Va. L. Rev. 443, 498 (2005).

4.   Connections

Should the *Austin* opinion and the *Totem* opinion have discussed *Alaska Packers' Ass'n v. Domenico, supra* at page 254? What are the similarities of the three cases? The differences?

The next case considers "undue influence." According to the note in the *Restatement (Second) of Contracts,* introducing the sections on duress and undue influence: "Undue influence involves unfair persuasion, a milder form of pressure than duress."

ODORIZZI v. BLOOMFIELD SCHOOL DISTRICT

Court of Appeal of California, Second Appellate District
246 Cal.App.2d 123, 54 Cal.Rptr. 533 (1966)

FLEMING, J.

Appeal from a judgment dismissing plaintiff's amended complaint on demurrer.

Plaintiff Donald Odorizzi was employed during 1964 as an elementary school teacher by defendant Bloomfield School District and was under contract with the district to continue to teach school the following year as a permanent employee. On June 10 he was arrested on criminal charges of homosexual activity, and on June 11 he signed and delivered to his superiors his written resignation as a teacher, a resignation which the district accepted on June 13. In July the criminal charges against Odorizzi were dismissed under Penal Code, section 995, and in September he sought to resume his employment with the district. On the district's refusal to reinstate him he filed suit for declaratory and other relief.

Odorizzi's amended complaint asserts his resignation was invalid because obtained through duress, fraud, mistake, and undue influence and given at a time when he lacked capacity to make a valid contract. Specifically, Odorizzi declares he was under such severe mental and emotional strain at the time he signed his resignation, having just completed the process of arrest, questioning by the police, booking, and release on bail, and having gone for 40 hours without sleep, that he was incapable of rational thought or action. While he was in this condition and unable to think clearly, the superintendent of the district and the principal of his school came to his apartment. They said they were trying to help him and had his best interests at heart, that he should take their advice and immediately resign his position with the district, that there was no time to consult an attorney, that if he did not resign immediately the district would suspend and dismiss him from his position and publicize the proceedings, his "aforedescribed arrest" and cause him "to suffer extreme embarrassment and humiliation"; but that if he resigned at once the incident would not be publicized and would not jeopardize his chances of securing employment as a teacher elsewhere. Odorizzi pleads that because of his faith and confidence in their representations they were able to substitute their will and judgment in place of his own and thus obtain his signature to his purported resignation. A demurrer to his amended complaint was sustained without leave to amend.

By his complaint plaintiff in effect seeks to rescind his resignation pursuant to Civil Code, section 1689,* on the ground that his consent had not been real or free * * *, but had been obtained through duress, menace, fraud, undue influence, or mistake. * * * In our view the facts in the amended complaint are insufficient to state a cause of action for duress, menace, fraud, or mistake, but they do set out sufficient elements to justify rescission of a consent because of undue influence. We summarize our conclusions on each of these points.

1. No duress or menace has been pleaded. Duress consists in unlawful confinement of another's person, or relatives, or property, which causes him to consent to a transaction through fear. Duress is often used interchangeably with menace, but in California menace is technically a threat of duress or a threat of injury to the person, property, or character of another. We agree with respondent's contention that neither duress nor menace was involved in this case, because the action or threat in duress or

---

* § 1689. "(b) A party to a contract may rescind the contract in the following cases: (1) If the consent of the party rescinding, or of any party jointly contracting with him, was given by mistake, or obtained through duress, menace, fraud, or undue influence, exercised by or with the connivance of the party as to whom he rescinds, or of any other party to the contract jointly interested with such party." Eds.

menace must be unlawful, and a threat to take legal action is not unlawful unless the party making the threat knows the falsity of his claim. The amended complaint shows in substance that the school representative announced their intention to initiate suspension and dismissal proceedings under Education Code, section 13403,** 13408,*** et seq. at a time when the filing of such proceedings was not only their legal right but their positive duty as school officials. (Ed.Code, § 13409*). * * *

2. Nor do we find a cause of action for fraud, either actual or constructive.

     * * *

3. As to mistake, the amended complaint fails to disclose any facts which would suggest that consent had been obtained through a mistake of fact or of law. * * *

4. However, the pleading does set out a claim that plaintiff's consent to the transaction had been obtained through the use of undue influence.

Undue influence, in the sense we are concerned with here, is a shorthand legal phrase used to describe persuasion which tends to be coercive in nature, persuasion which overcomes the will without convincing the judgment. The hallmark of such persuasion is high pressure, a pressure which works on mental, moral, or emotional weakness to such an extent that it approaches the boundaries of coercion. In this sense, undue influence has been called overpersuasion. Misrepresentations of law or fact are not essential to the charge, for a person's will may be overborne without misrepresentation. By statutory definition undue influence includes "taking an unfair advantage of another's weakness of mind, or * * * taking a grossly oppressive and unfair advantage of another's necessities or distress." While most reported cases of undue influence involve persons who bear a confidential relationship to one another, a

---

** § 134.03. "Grounds for dismissal of permanent employee. No permanent employee shall be dismissed except for one or more of the following causes: (a) Immoral or unprofessional conduct. * * * (k) Knowing membership by the employee in the Communist Party." Eds.

*** § 13408. "Immediate suspension of permanent employee; hearing upon certain charges. Upon the filing of written charges, duly signed and verified by the person filing them with the governing board of a school district, or upon a written statement of charges formulated by the governing board, charging a permanent employee of the district with immoral conduct, conviction of a felony or of any crime involving moral turpitude, with incompetency due to mental disability, with violation of Section 8455 of this code, with knowing membership by the employee in the Communist Party or with violation of any provision in Sections 12952 to 12958, inclusive, of this code, the governing board may, if it deems such action necessary, immediately suspend the employee from his duties and give notice to him of his suspension, and that 30 days after service of the notice, he will be dismissed, unless he demands a hearing." Eds.

* § 13409. "Compulsory leave of absence on charge of sex offenses and narcotics offenses; effect on salary of acquittal. Whenever any certificated employee of a school district is charged with the commission of any sex offense as defined in Section 12912 by complaint, information or indictment filed in a court of competent jurisdiction, the governing board of the school district shall immediately place the employee upon compulsory leave of absence for a period of time extending for not more than 10 days after the date of the entry of the judgement in the proceedings. The governing board of the school district may extend the compulsory leave of absence of the employee beyond such period by giving notice to the employee within 10 days after the entry of judgment in the proceedings that the employee will be dismissed at the expiration of 30 days from the date of service of the notice, unless the employee demands a hearing as provided in Sections 13313, 13327 and 13338, and Sections 13403 to 13441, inclusive." Eds.

confidential or authoritative relationship between the parties need not be present when the undue influence involves unfair advantage taken of another's weakness or distress.

We paraphrase the summary of undue influence given the jury by Sir James P. Wilde in *Hall v. Hall*, L.R. 1, P. & D. 481, 482 (1868): To make a good contract a man must be a free agent. Pressure of whatever sort which overpowers the will without convincing the judgment is a species of restraint under which no valid contract can be made. Importunity or threats, if carried to the degree in which the free play of a man's will is overborne, constitute undue influence, although no force is used or threatened. A party may be led but not driven, and his acts must be the offspring of his own volition and not the record of someone else's.

In essence undue influence involves the use of excessive pressure to persuade one vulnerable to such pressure, pressure applied by a dominant subject to a servient object. In combination, the elements of undue susceptibility in the servient person and excessive pressure by the dominating person make the latter's influence undue, for it results in the apparent will of the servient person being in fact the will of the dominant person.

Undue susceptibility may consist of total weakness of mind which leaves a person entirely without understanding; or, a lesser weakness which destroys the capacity of a person to make a contract even though he is not totally incapacitated; or, the first element in our equation, a still lesser weakness which provides sufficient grounds to rescind a contract for undue influence. Such lesser weakness need not be longlasting nor wholly incapacitating, but may be merely a lack of full vigor due to age, physical condition, emotional anguish, or a combination of such factors. The reported cases have usually involved elderly, sick, senile persons alleged to have executed wills or deeds under pressure. In some of its aspects this lesser weakness could perhaps be called weakness of spirit. But whatever name we give it, this first element of undue influence resolves itself into a lessened capacity of the object to make a free contract.

In the present case plaintiff has pleaded that such weakness at the time he signed his resignation prevented him from freely and competently applying his judgment to the problem before him. Plaintiff declares he was under severe mental and emotional strain at the time because he had just completed the process of arrest, questioning, booking, and release on bail and had been without sleep for forty hours. It is possible that exhaustion and emotional turmoil may wholly incapacitate a person from exercising his judgment. As an abstract question of pleading, plaintiff has pleaded that possibility and sufficient allegations to state a case for rescission.

Undue influence in its second aspect involves an application of excessive strength by a dominant subject against a servient object. Judicial consideration of this second element in undue influence has been relatively rare, for there are few cases denying persons who persuade but do not misrepresent the benefit of their bargain. Yet logically, the same legal consequences should apply to the results of excessive strength as to the results of undue weakness. Whether from weakness on one side, or strength on the other, or a combination of the two, undue influence occurs whenever there results "that kind of influence or supremacy of one mind over another by which that other is prevented from acting according to his own wish or judgment, and whereby the will of the person is overborne and he is induced to do or forbear to do an act which he would not do, or would do, if left to act freely." *Webb v. Saunders*, 79 Cal. App. 2d 863, 871. Undue influence involves a type of mismatch which our statute calls unfair advantage. Whether a person of subnormal capacities has been subjected to ordinary force or a person of normal capacities subjected to extraordinary force, the match is equally out of balance. If will has been overcome against judgment, consent may be rescinded.

The difficulty, of course, lies in determining when the forces of persuasion have overflowed their normal banks and become oppressive flood waters. There are second thoughts to every bargain, and hindsight is still better than foresight. Undue influence cannot be used as a pretext to avoid bad bargains or escape from bargains which refuse to come up to expectations. A woman who buys a dress on impulse, which on critical inspection by her best friend turns out to be less fashionable than she had thought, is not legally entitled to set aside the sale on the ground that the saleswoman used all her wiles to close the sale. A man who buys a tract of desert land in the expectation that it is in the immediate path of the city's growth and will become another Palm Springs, an expectation cultivated in glowing terms by the seller, cannot rescind his bargain when things turn out differently. If we are temporarily persuaded against our better judgment to do something about which we later have second thoughts, we must abide the consequences of the risks inherent in managing our own affairs.

However, overpersuasion is generally accompanied by certain characteristics which tend to create a pattern. The pattern usually involves several of the following elements: (1) discussion of the transaction at an unusual or inappropriate time, (2) consummation of the transaction in an unusual place, (3) insistent demand that the business be finished at once, (4) extreme emphasis on untoward consequences of delay, (5) the use of multiple persuaders by the dominant side against a single servient party, (6) absence of third-party advisers to the servient party, (7) statements that there is no time to consult financial advisers or attorneys. If a number of these elements are simultaneously present, the persuasion may be characterized as excessive. * * *

The difference between legitimate persuasion and excessive pressure * * * rests to a considerable extent in the manner in which the parties go about their business. For example, if a day or two after Odorizzi's release on bail the superintendent of the school district had called him into his office during business hours and directed his attention to those provisions of the Education Code compelling his leave of absence and authorizing his suspension on the filing of written charges, had told him that the district contemplated filing written charges against him, had pointed out the alternative of resignation available to him, had informed him he was free to consult counsel or any adviser he wished and to consider the matter overnight and return with his decision the next day, it is extremely unlikely that any complaint about the use of excessive pressure could ever have been made against the school district.

But, according to the allegations of the complaint, this is not the way it happened, and if it had happened that way, plaintiff would never have resigned. Rather, the representatives of the school board undertook to achieve their objective by overpersuasion and imposition to secure plaintiff's signature but not his consent to his resignation through a high-pressure carrot-and-stick technique—under which they assured plaintiff they were trying to assist him, he should rely on their advice, there wasn't time to consult an attorney, if he didn't resign at once the school district would suspend and dismiss him from his position and publicize the proceedings, but if he did resign the incident wouldn't jeopardize his chances of securing a teaching post elsewhere.

Plaintiff has thus pleaded both subjective and objective elements entering the undue influence equation and stated sufficient facts to put in issue the question whether his free will had been overborne by defendant's agents at a time when he was unable to function in a normal manner. It was sufficient to pose "* * * the ultimate question * * * whether a free and competent judgment was merely influenced, or whether a mind was so dominated as to prevent the exercise of an independent judgment." (*Williston on Contracts*, § 1625 [rev. ed.]; Rest., Contracts, § 497, com. c.) The question cannot be resolved by an analysis of pleading but requires a finding of fact.

We express no opinion on the merits of plaintiff's case, or the propriety of his continuing to teach school, or the timeliness of his rescission. We do hold that his pleading, liberally construed, states a cause of action for rescission of a transaction to which his apparent consent had been obtained through the use of undue influence.

The judgment is reversed.

QUESTIONS AND NOTES

1. Questions about the facts of this case
    1.1.   There are two Odorizzi/Bloomfield School District agreements: (i) an employment contract for the 1964–65 school year, and (ii) Odorizzi's June resignation. Which is involved in this litigation?
    1.2.   Do we know the grounds for dismissal in the employment contract? Is that relevant? Do we know the grounds for dismissal in the California Education Code? Is that relevant?
    1.3.   Was it important to the California appellate court that the two people who came to Odorizzi's apartment to talk about his resigning

were his superintendent and his principal? Should that be important? What if the two people who had come to Odorizzi's apartment
had been parents of students in his classes?

2. Questions about the law

2.1. The appellate court holds "the facts in the amended complaint are
insufficient to state a cause of action for duress * * * but they do
set out sufficient elements to justify rescission of a consent because
of undue influence." What alleged facts justify rescission because of
undue influence? What additional fact(s) are needed for duress?

2.2. The *Odorizzi* case identifies two elements of undue influence. The
two elements of undue influence are: (i) the susceptibility of the
weaker party, and (ii) the overpersuasion of the stronger party.
Which of these two elements is more important?

2.3. The *Odorizzi* opinion then lists seven elements of the second
element "overpersuasion." Which of the seven elements of overpersuasion were alleged by the plaintiff?

2.4. Why didn't Loral in the *Austin* case allege undue influence?

3. Notes

3.1. Professor Peter Birks of Oxford University and Professor Chin
Nyuk Yin of University of West Australia have suggested that
duress and undue influence be combined: "It is time in this field
that we overcame the old jurisdictional duality. It would be better
that pressure should be litigated as pressure." Peter Birks & Chin
Nyuk Yin, *On the Nature of Undue Influence* in JACK BEASON &
DANIEL FRIEDMANN, GOOD FAITH AND FAULT IN CONTRACT LAW 57, 63
(1995).

3.2. Professor Curtis Nyquist of New England School of Law and two
students active in the Les–Bi–Gay–Trans Caucus at New England
School of Law suggest that the study of the *Odorizzi* case be
combined with the study of LBGT issues: "We think it is impossible
to understand the pressures felt by Odorizzi without considering
LBGT issues in depth. Domination undue influence is fundamentally a claim that a particular person, at the time of the agreement,
suffered from diminished mental capacity. Ruiz (a "heteroqueer
evolved-male") and Smith's (a "gay-white biologically male law
student") participation in the class provided context for students'
understanding of the impact on Odorizzi of the arrest and threat of
public proceedings." Curtis Nyquist, Patrick Ruiz, and Frank
Smith, *Using Students as Discussion Leaders on Sexual Orientation
and Gender Identity Issues in First–Year Courses*, 49 J. LEGAL EDUC.
535 (1999).

SECTION 5: CONTRACT LAW REASONS FOR <u>NOT</u> ENFORCING AGREEMENTS: ILLEGALITY AND PUBLIC POLICY

It is easy to think of agreements that are illegal and understand why an agreement's illegal subject matter makes the agreement unenforceable by either party. For example, Markell hires Frank Falenczyk to kill Epstein. That agreement would be unenforceable by either Markell or Frank. It is against the law to kill someone—even a contracts professor.

The law in question does not have to be a criminal law. We all know and understand that a court will not enforce an agreement to pay interest in excess of the rate set in the usury laws or an agreement to combine businesses that violates the antitrust laws.

A more common illegality problem is the enforceability of an agreement by someone who has failed to comply with a licensing statute. Consider the following illustrative problem.

PROBLEM

Assume that Arizona has statutes that provide (1) "No natural person shall engage in doing the work of a plumber unless he possesses a license or renewal thereof issued by the Arizona Plumbing Board" and (2) "Whoever violates the provisions of this Chapter shall be fined not less than five hundred dollars nor more than five thousand dollars, or imprisoned for not more than ninety days or both."

Ponoroff enters into an agreement with Epstein, who is not a licensed plumber, to pay Epstein $200 to install a urinal in his office. Epstein does the agreed work. Ponoroff refuses to pay. Should Epstein be able to enforce the agreement even though Epstein acted in violation of the state licensing statute? (Board regulations describe the work of a plumber as including the installation of plumbing fixtures.) How would you answer the problem? How would the *Restatement (Second)* answer the problem?

§ 181 Effect of Failure to Comply With Licensing or Similar Requirement

If a party is prohibited from doing an act because of his failure to comply with a licensing, registration or similar requirement, a promise in consideration of his doing that act or of his promise to do it is unenforceable on grounds of public policy if:

(a) the requirement has a regulatory purpose, and

(b) the interest in the enforcement of the promise is clearly outweighed by the public policy <u>behind the requirement</u>.

(Emphasis added).

The defense of public policy is not limited to agreements that directly or even indirectly violate a legislative enactment. *Restatement (Second) of Contracts* § 178 provides:

> *A promise or other term of an agreement is unenforceable on grounds of public policy if legislation provides that it is unenforceable or the interest in its enforcement is clearly outweighed in the circumstances by a public policy against the enforcement of such terms.*

Some of the policies considered in the examples following § 178 and in the following cases are the product of judicial development.

Who decides whether there is a "public policy against the enforcement"? What are the relative roles of legislatures and courts?

The most complicated and controversial cases considering a public policy defense to enforceability of an agreement are cases affecting family relationships such as palimony agreements or surrogacy contracts in which a woman agrees to relinquish any parental rights to the child to whom she gives birth. Attorneys, judges, and professors continue to discuss not only the legal issues, but also the gender, moral, political, and religious issues raised by these contracts. *R.R. v. M.H.*, the first case in the book is illustrative.

In case your professor skipped the first chapter,[6] here is the case again.

R.R. v. M.H.

Supreme Judicial Court of Massachusetts
426 Mass. 501, 689 N.E.2d 790 (1998)

WILKINS, C.J.

On a report by a judge in the Probate and Family Court, we are concerned with the validity of a surrogacy parenting agreement between the plaintiff (father) and the defendant (mother). Both the mother and the father are married but not to each other. A child was conceived through artificial insemination of the mother with the father's sperm, after the mother and father had executed the surrogate parenting agreement. The agreement provided that the father would have custody of the child. During the sixth month of her pregnancy and after she had received funds from the father pursuant to the surrogacy agreement, the mother changed her mind and decided that she wanted to keep the child.

The father thereupon brought this action and obtained a preliminary order awarding him temporary custody of the child. * * * The judge's order granting the preliminary injunction is before us on her report of the propriety of that order which was based in part on her conclusion that the father was likely to prevail on his assertion that the surrogacy agreement is enforceable. On our own motion, we transferred here the appeal and the report, which a single justice of the Appeals Court had consolidated. The question of the enforceability of the surrogacy agreement is before us and,

---

6. Lots of professors do skip the first chapter—Ponoroff wrote most of the first chapter.

although we could defer any ruling until there is a final judgment entered, the issue is one on which we elect to comment because it is fully briefed and is of importance to more than the parties. This court has not previously dealt with the enforceability of a surrogacy agreement.

The Facts

The baby girl who is the subject of this action was born on August 15, 1997, in Leominster. The defendant mother and the plaintiff father are her biological parents. The father and his wife, who live in Rhode Island, were married in June, 1989. The wife is infertile. * * * In April, 1996, responding to a newspaper advertisement for surrogacy services, they consulted a Rhode Island attorney who had drafted surrogacy contracts for both surrogates and couples seeking surrogacy services. On the attorney's advice, the father and his wife consulted the New England Surrogate Parenting Advisors (NESPA), a for-profit corporation that helps infertile couples find women willing to act as surrogate mothers. They entered into a contract with NESPA in September, 1996, and paid a fee of $6,000.

Meanwhile, in the spring of 1996, the mother, who was married and had two children, responded to a NESPA advertisement. She reported to NESPA that her family was complete and that she desired to allow others less fortunate than herself to have children. The mother submitted a surrogacy application to NESPA. The judge found that the mother was motivated to apply to NESPA by a desire to be pregnant, in order to earn money, and to help an infertile couple.

In October, Dr. Angela Figueroa of NESPA brought the mother together with the father and his wife. They had a seemingly informative exchange of information and views. The mother was advised to seek an attorney's advice concerning the surrogacy agreement. Shortly thereafter, the mother, the father, and his wife met again to discuss the surrogacy and other matters. The mother also met with a clinical psychologist as part of NESPA's evaluation of her suitability to act as a surrogate. The psychologist, who also evaluated the father and his wife, advised the mother to consult legal counsel, to give her husband a chance to air his concerns, to discuss arrangements for contact with the child, to consider and discuss her expectations concerning termination of the pregnancy, and to arrange a meeting between her husband and the father and his wife.[2] The psychologist concluded that the mother was solid, thoughtful, and well grounded, that she would have no problem giving the child to the father, and that she was happy to act as a surrogate. The mother told the psychologist that she was not motivated by money, although she did plan to use the funds received for her children's education. The mother's husband told the psychologist by telephone that he supported his wife's decision.

---

2. Her husband had had a vasectomy in 1994 and did not have sexual relations with the mother after October, 1996.

The mother signed the surrogate parenting agreement and her signature was notarized on November 1. The father signed on November 18. The agreement stated that the parties intended that the "Surrogate shall be inseminated with the semen of Natural Father" and "that, on the birth of the child or children so conceived, Natural Father, as the Natural Father, will have the full legal parental rights of a father, and surrogate will permit Natural Father to take the child or children home from the hospital to live with he [sic] and his wife." The agreement acknowledged that the mother's parental rights would not terminate if she permitted the father to take the child home and have custody, that the mother could at any time seek to enforce her parental rights by court order, but that, if she attempted to obtain custody or visitation rights, she would forfeit her rights under the agreement and would be obligated to reimburse the father for all fees and expenses paid to her under it. The agreement provided that its interpretation would be governed by Rhode Island law.

The agreement provided for compensation to the mother in the amount of $10,000 "for services rendered in conceiving, carrying and giving birth to the Child." Payment of the $10,000 was to be made as follows: $500 on verification of the pregnancy; $2,500 at the end of the third month; $3,500 at the end of the sixth month; and $3,500 at the time of birth "and when delivery of child occurs." The agreement stated that no payment was made in connection with adoption of the child, the termination of parental rights, or consent to surrender the child for adoption. The father acknowledged the mother's right to determine whether to carry the pregnancy to term, but the mother agreed to refund all payments if, without the father's consent, she had an abortion that was not necessary for her physical health. The father assumed various expenses of the pregnancy, including tests, and had the right to name the child. The mother would be obliged, however, to repay all expenses and fees for services if tests showed that the father was not the biological father of the child, or if the mother refused to permit the father to take the child home from the hospital. The agreement also provided that the mother would maintain some contact with the child after the birth.

The judge found that the mother entered into the agreement on her own volition after consulting legal counsel. There was no evidence of undue influence, coercion, or duress. The mother fully understood that she was contracting to give custody of the baby to the father. She sought to inseminate herself on November 30 and December 1, 1996. The attempt at conception was successful.

The lawyer for the father sent the mother a check for $500 in December, 1996, and another for $2,500 in February. In May, the father's lawyer sent the mother a check for $3,500. She told the lawyer that she had changed her mind and wanted to keep the child. She returned the check uncashed in the middle of June. The mother has made no attempt to refund the amounts that the father paid her, including $550 that he paid for pregnancy-related expenses.

Procedure

Approximately two weeks after the mother changed her mind and returned the check for $3,500, and before the child was born, the father commenced this action against the mother seeking to establish his paternity, alleging breach of contract, and requesting a declaration of his rights under the surrogacy agreement. Subsequently, the wife's [*sic*. Should be "the mother's." Eds.] husband was added as a defendant. The judge appointed a guardian ad litem to represent the interests of the unborn child. Proceedings were held on aspects of the preliminary injunction request (now resolved) and on the mother's motion to determine whether surrogacy contracts are enforceable in Massachusetts.

On August 4, 1997, the judge entered an order directing the mother to give the child to the father when it was discharged from the hospital and granting the father temporary physical custody of the child. She did so based on her determination that the father's custody claim was likely to prevail on the merits of the contract claim, and, if not on that claim, then on the basis of the best interests of the child. The mother was granted the right to frequent visits.

On August 13, 1997, the judge reported the propriety of her August 1 order which, as we have said, was based in part on her conclusion that the surrogacy contract was enforceable. * * *

Other Jurisdictions

A significant minority of States have legislation addressing surrogacy agreements. Some simply deny enforcement of all such agreements. [Arizona, Indiana, Michigan, New York, North Dakota, Utah.] Others expressly deny enforcement only if the surrogate is to be compensated. [Kentucky, Louisiana, Nebraska, Washington.] Some States have simply exempted surrogacy agreements from provisions making it a crime to sell babies. [Alabama, Iowa, West Virginia.] A few States have explicitly made unpaid surrogacy agreements lawful. [Florida, Nevada, New Hampshire, Virginia.] Florida, New Hampshire, and Virginia require that the intended mother be infertile. New Hampshire and Virginia place restrictions on who may act as a surrogate and require advance judicial approval of the agreement.[6] Last, Arkansas raises a presumption that a child born to a surrogate mother is the child of the intended parents and not the surrogate.

There are few appellate court opinions on the enforceability of traditional surrogacy agreements. * * *

The best known opinion is that of the Supreme Court of New Jersey in *Matter of Baby M.*, 109 N.J. 396, 537 A.2d 1227 (1988), where the court invalidated a compensated surrogacy contract because it conflicted with the law and public policy of the State. The *Baby M* surrogacy agreement

---

6. New Hampshire permits the surrogate to opt out of the agreement to surrender custody at any time up to seventy-two hours after birth. Virginia allows a surrogate who is the child's genetic mother to terminate the agreement within 180 days of the last assisted conception.

involved broader concessions from the mother than the agreement before us because it provided that the mother would surrender her parental rights and would allow the father's wife to adopt the child. The agreement, therefore, directly conflicted with a statute prohibiting the payment of money to obtain an adoption and a statute barring enforcement of an agreement to adoption made prior to the birth of the child. The court acknowledged that an award of custody to the father was in the best interests of the child, but struck down orders terminating the mother's parental rights and authorizing the adoption of the child by the husband's wife. The court added that it found no "legal prohibition against surrogacy when the surrogate mother volunteers, without any payment, to act as a surrogate and is given the right to change her mind and to assert her parental rights."

Discussion

1. *The governing law.* The agreement before us provided that "Rhode Island Law shall govern the interpretation of this agreement." * * * The child was conceived and born in Massachusetts, and the mother is a Massachusetts resident, all as contemplated in the surrogacy arrangement. The significance, if any, of the surrogacy agreement on the relationship of the parties and on the child is appropriately determined by Massachusetts law.

2. *General Laws c. 46, § 4B.* The case before us concerns traditional surrogacy, in which the fertile member of an infertile couple is one of the child's biological parents. Surrogate fatherhood, the insemination of the fertile wife with sperm of a donor, often an anonymous donor, is a recognized and accepted procedure. If the mother's husband consents to the procedure, the resulting child is considered the legitimate child of the mother and her husband.[9] In the case before us, the infertile spouse is the wife. No statute decrees the consequences of the artificial insemination of a surrogate with the sperm of a fertile husband. This situation presents different considerations from surrogate fatherhood because surrogate motherhood is never anonymous and her commitment and contribution is unavoidably much greater than that of a sperm donor.

We must face the possible application of G. L. c. 46, § 4B, to this case. Section 4B tells us that a husband who consents to the artificial insemination of his wife with the sperm of another is considered to be the father of any resulting child. In the case before us, the birth mother was married at the time of her artificial insemination. Despite what he told the psychologist, her husband was not supportive of her desire to become a surrogate parent but acknowledged that it was her decision and her body. The husband, who filed a complaint for divorce on August 8, 1997, may have simply been indifferent because he knew that the marriage was falling apart. The judge found that he was not the biological father of the child.

---

9. General Laws c. 46, § 4B, states: "Any child born to a married woman as a result of artificial insemination with the consent of her husband, shall be considered the legitimate child of the mother and such husband."

His interest might have been vastly greater if he had been informed that § 4B literally says that any child produced by the artificial insemination of his wife with his consent would be his legitimate child whom he would have a duty to support. It is doubtful, however, that the Legislature intended § 4B to apply to the child of a married surrogate mother. Section 4B seems to concern the status of a child born to a fertile mother whose husband, presumably infertile, consented to her artificial insemination with the sperm of another man so that the couple could have a child biologically related to the mother.

3. Adoption statutes. Policies underlying our adoption legislation suggest that a surrogate parenting agreement should be given no effect if the mother's agreement was obtained prior to a reasonable time after the child's birth or if her agreement was induced by the payment of money. Adoption legislation is, of course, not applicable to child custody, but it does provide us with some guidance. Although the agreement makes no reference to adoption and does not concern the termination of parental rights or the adoption of the child by the father's wife, the normal expectation in the case of a surrogacy agreement seems to be that the father's wife will adopt the child with the consent of the mother (and the father). Under G. L. c. 210, § 2, adoption requires the written consent of the father and the mother but, in these circumstances, not the mother's husband. Any such consent, written, witnessed, and notarized, is not to be executed "sooner than the fourth calendar day after the date of birth of the child to be adopted." *Id.* That statutory standard should be interpreted as providing that no mother may effectively agree to surrender her child for adoption earlier than the fourth day after its birth, by which time she better knows the strength of her bond with her child. Although a consent to surrender custody has less permanency than a consent to adoption, the legislative judgment that a mother should have time after a child's birth to reflect on her wishes concerning the child weighs heavily in our consideration whether to give effect to a prenatal custody agreement. No private agreement concerning adoption or custody can be conclusive in any event because a judge, passing on custody of a child, must decide what is in the best interests of the child.

Adoptive parents may pay expenses of a birth parent but may make no direct payment to her. *See* G. L. c. 210, § 11A; 102 Code Mass. Regs. § 5.09 (1997). Even though the agreement seeks to attribute that payment of $10,000, not to custody or adoption, but solely to the mother's services in carrying the child, the father ostensibly was promised more than those services because, as a practical matter, the mother agreed to surrender custody of the child. She could assert custody rights, according to the agreement, only if she repaid the father all amounts that she had received and also reimbursed him for all expenses he had incurred. The statutory prohibition of payment for receiving a child through adoption suggests that, as a matter of policy, a mother's agreement to surrender custody in exchange for money (beyond pregnancy-related expenses) should be given no effect in deciding the custody of the child.

4. Conclusion. The mother's purported consent to custody in the agreement is ineffective because no such consent should be recognized unless given on or after the fourth day following the child's birth. In reaching this conclusion, we apply to consent to custody the same principle which underlies the statutory restriction on when a mother's consent to adoption may be effectively given. Moreover, the payment of money to influence the mother's custody decision makes the agreement as to custody void. Eliminating any financial reward to a surrogate mother is the only way to assure that no economic pressure will cause a woman, who may well be a member of an economically vulnerable class, to act as a surrogate. It is true that a surrogate enters into the agreement before she becomes pregnant and thus is not presented with the desperation that a poor unwed pregnant woman may confront. However, compensated surrogacy arrangements raise the concern that, under financial pressure, a woman will permit her body to be used and her child to be given away.

There is no doubt that compensation was a factor in inducing the mother to enter into the surrogacy agreement and to cede custody to the father. If the payment of $10,000 was really only compensation for the mother's services in carrying the child and giving birth and was unrelated to custody of the child, the agreement would not have provided that the mother must refund all compensation paid (and expenses paid) if she should challenge the father's right to custody. Nor would the agreement have provided that final payment be made only when the child is delivered to the father. We simply decline, on public policy grounds, to apply to a surrogacy agreement of the type involved here the general principle that an agreement between informed, mature adults should be enforced absent proof of duress, fraud, or undue influence.

We recognize that there is nothing inherently unlawful in an arrangement by which an informed woman agrees to attempt to conceive artificially and give birth to a child whose father would be the husband of an infertile wife. We suspect that many such arrangements are made and carried out without disagreement.

If no compensation is paid beyond pregnancy-related expenses and if the mother is not bound by her consent to the father's custody of the child unless she consents after a suitable period has passed following the child's birth, the objections we have identified in this opinion to the enforceability of a surrogate's consent to custody would be overcome. Other conditions might be important in deciding the enforceability of a surrogacy agreement, such as a requirement that (a) the mother's husband give his informed consent to the agreement in advance; (b) the mother be an adult and have had at least one successful pregnancy; (c) the mother, her husband, and the intended parents have been evaluated for the soundness of their judgment and for their capacity to carry out the agreement; (d) the father's wife be incapable of bearing a child without endangering her health; (e) the intended parents be suitable persons to assume custody of the child; and (f) all parties have the advice of counsel. The mother and father may not, however, make a binding best-interests-of-the-child determination by private agreement. Any custody agreement is subject to a judicial determination of custody based on the best interests of the child.

The conditions that we describe are not likely to be satisfactory to an intended father because, following the birth of the child, the mother can refuse to consent to the father's custody even though the father has incurred substantial pregnancy-related expenses. A surrogacy agreement judicially approved before conception may be a better procedure, as is permitted by statutes in Virginia and New Hampshire. A Massachusetts statute concerning surrogacy agreements, pro or con, would provide guidance to judges, lawyers, infertile couples interested in surrogate parenthood, and prospective surrogate mothers.

* * *

A declaration shall be entered that the surrogacy agreement is not enforceable. Such further orders as may be appropriate, consistent with this opinion, may be entered in the Probate and Family Court.

So ordered.

QUESTIONS AND NOTE

1. Questions about the facts of this case
    1.1. Which facts were critical to the court's decision?
    1.2. What is the biological mother's "best" fact?
    1.3. What is the biological father's best fact?
2. Questions about the law
    2.1. Why did the court consider the Massachusetts adoption statutes?
    2.2. According to Professor Gillian Hadfield of the University of Southern California Law School, "contract pregnancy" raises two difficult questions.

The first is a public-law question and is concerned with whether, as a society, we should permit individuals to contract for the conception of a child and the allocation of parental status. This question raises the specter of commodification, and feminists grapple with the implications for children, women and sexuality of the use of market mechanisms to structure childbirth and parenting. The second question is a private-law contract puzzle. It is concerned with whether in a given case in which the birth mother refuses to relinquish her parental status and in the absence of public-law prohibition, contract law should find that the birth mother has a contractual obligation to release the child. Further, the second question asks whether any breach of this obligation should be remedied with an order of specific performance as opposed to an order for compensation.

Gillian K. Hadfield, *An Expressive Theory of Contract: From Feminist Dilemmas to a Reconceptualization of Rational Choice in Contract Law,*

146 U. PA. L. REV. 1235, 1240 (1998). Did the Massachusetts Supreme Judicial Court consider Professor Hadfield's questions? Who should answer Professor Hadfield's questions—the Massachusetts Supreme Judicial Court or the Massachusetts legislature?

3. Note

Arguments that a contract is unenforceable because of public policy arise most often in connection with "exculpatory contracts." We saw an exculpatory contract in the *Reed* case, supra at 230; you will see an exculpatory contract in the next case. You see exculpatory contracts every time you participate in The Burning Man Festival, every time you park your car in a parking garage.

HANKS v. POWER RIDGE RESTAURANT CORP.

Supreme Court of Connecticut
276 Conn. 314, 885 A.2d 734 (2005)

SULLIVAN, C.J.

This appeal arises out of a complaint filed by the plaintiff, Gregory D. Hanks, against the defendants, Powder Ridge Restaurant Corporation and White Water Mountain Resorts of Connecticut, Inc., doing business as Powder Ridge Ski Resort, seeking compensatory damages for injuries the plaintiff sustained while snowtubing at the defendants' facility. The trial court rendered summary judgment in favor of the defendants, concluding that this court's decision in *Hyson v. White Water Mountain Resorts of Connecticut, Inc., 265 Conn. 636, 829 A.2d 827 (2003),* precluded the plaintiff's negligence claim as a matter of law. We reverse the judgment of the trial court.

The record reveals the following factual and procedural history. The defendants operate a facility in Middlefield, known as Powder Ridge, at which the public, in exchange for a fee, is invited to ski, snowboard and snowtube. * * * [I]n order to snowtube at Powder Ridge, patrons were required to sign a "Waiver, Defense, Indemnity and Hold Harmless Agreement, and Release of Liability" (agreement). The plaintiff read and signed the agreement * * * While snowtubing, the plaintiff's right foot became caught between his snowtube and the man-made bank of the snowtubing run, resulting in serious injuries that required multiple surgeries to repair. Thereafter, the plaintiff filed the present negligence action against the defendants. * * * [T]he defendants alleged that the plaintiff's injuries were caused by his own negligence and that the agreement relieved the defendants of liability, "even if the accident was due to the negligence of the defendants." Thereafter, the defendants moved for summary judgment, claiming that the agreement barred the plaintiff's negligence claim as a matter of law. The trial court agreed and rendered summary judgment in favor of the defendants. Specifically, the trial court determined, pursuant to our decision in *Hyson v. White Water Mountain*

Resorts of Connecticut, Inc., supra, 265 Conn. at 640–44, 829 A.2d 827, that the plaintiff, by signing the agreement, unambiguously had released the defendants from liability for their allegedly negligent conduct. * * *

The agreement at issue in the present case provides in relevant part:

> "I understand that there are inherent risks involved in snowtubing, including the risk of serious * physical injury or death and I fully assume all risks associated with [s]nowtubing, even if due to the NEGLIGENCE of [the defendants] * * * including but not limited to: variations in the snow conditions; steepness and terrain; the presence of ice, moguls, bare spots and objects beneath the snowtubing surface such as rocks, debris and tree stumps; collisions with objects both on and off the snowtubing chutes such as hay bales, trees, rocks, snowmaking equipment, barriers, lift cables and equipment, lift towers, lift attendants, employees, volunteers, other patrons and spectators or their property; equipment or lift condition or failure; lack of safety devices or inadequate safety devices; lack of warnings or inadequate warnings; lack of instructions or inadequate instructions; use of any lift; and the like. * * * I * * * agree I will defend, indemnify and hold harmless [the defendants] * * * from any and all claims, suits or demands by anyone arising from my use of the Powder Ridge snowtubing facilities and equipment including claims of NEGLIGENCE on the part of [the defendants]. * * * I * * * hereby release, and agree that I will not sue [the defendants] * * * for money damages for personal injury or property damage sustained by me while using the snowtubing facilities and equipment even if due to the NEGLIGENCE of [the defendants]. * * *" (Emphasis in original.)

We conclude that the agreement expressly and unambiguously purports to release the defendants from prospective liability for negligence. The agreement expressly provides that the snowtuber "fully assume[s] all risks associated with [s]nowtubing, even if due to the NEGLIGENCE" of the defendants. (Emphasis in original.) Moreover, the agreement refers to the negligence of the defendants three times and uses capital letters to emphasize the term "negligence." Accordingly, we conclude that an ordinary person of reasonable intelligence would understand that, by signing the agreement, he or she was releasing the defendants from liability for their future negligence. * * * We conclude that the trial court properly determined that the agreement in the present matter expressly purports to release the defendants from liability for their future negligence and, accordingly, satisfies the standard set forth by this court in *Hyson.*

II

We next address the issue we explicitly left unresolved in *Hyson v. White Water Mountain Resorts of Connecticut, Inc.,* namely, whether the enforcement of a well drafted exculpatory agreement purporting to release a snowtube operator from prospective liability for personal injuries sustained as a result of the operator's negligent conduct violates public policy.

We conclude that it does and, accordingly, reverse the judgment of the trial court.

Although it is well estbablished "that parties are free to contract for whatever terms on which they may agree"; it is equally well established "that contracts that violate public policy are ᵁⁿenforceable." * "[T]he question [of] whether a contract is against public policy is [a] question of law dependent on the circumstances of the particular case, over which an appellate court has unlimited review."

As previously noted, "[t]he law does not favor contract provisions which relieve a person from his own negligence. * * *" This is because exculpatory provisions undermine the policy considerations governing our tort system. Although this court previously has not addressed the enforceability of a release of liability for future negligence, the issue has been addressed by many of our sister states. * * *

Having reviewed the various methods for determining whether exculpatory agreements violate public policy, we conclude, * * * that "[n]o definition of the concept of public interest can be contained within the four corners of a formula." * * * The ultimate determination of what constitutes the public interest must be made considering the totality of the circumstances of any given case against the backdrop of current societal expectations." * * *

We now turn to the merits of the plaintiff's claim. The defendants are in the business of providing snowtubing services to the public generally, regardless of prior snowtubing experience, with the minimal restriction that only persons at least six years old or forty-four inches tall are eligible to participate. Given the virtually unrestricted access of the public to Powder Ridge, a reasonable person would presume that the defendants were offering a recreational activity that the whole family could enjoy safely. Indeed, this presumption is borne out by the plaintiff' own testimony. Specifically, the plaintiff testified that he "trusted that [the defendants] would, within their good conscience, operate a safe ride."

The societal expectation that family oriented recreational activities will be reasonably safe is even more important where, as in the present matter, patrons are under the care and control of the recreational operator as a result of an economic transaction. The plaintiff, in exchange for a fee, was permitted access to the defendants' snowtubing runs and was provided with snowtubing gear. As a result of this transaction, the plaintiff was under the care and control of the defendants and, thus, was subject to the risk of the defendants' carelessness. Specifically, the defendants designed and maintained the snowtubing run and, therefore, controlled the steepness of the incline, the condition of the snow and the method of slowing down or stopping patrons. Further, the defendants provided the plaintiff with the requisite snowtubing supplies and, therefore, controlled the size and quality of the snowtube as well as the provision of any necessary protective gear. Accordingly, the plaintiff voluntarily relinquished control to the defendants with the reasonable expectation of an exciting, but reasonably safe, snowtubing experience.

Moreover, the plaintiff lacked the knowledge, experience and authority to discern whether, much less ensure that, the defendants' snowtubing runs were maintained in a reasonably safe condition. As the Vermont Supreme Court observed, in the context of the sport of skiing, it is consistent with public policy "to place responsibility for maintenance of the land on those who own or control it, with the ultimate goal of keeping accidents to the minimum level. [T]he defendants, not recreational skiers, have the expertise and opportunity to foresee and control hazards, and to guard against the negligence of their agents and employees. They alone can properly maintain and inspect their premises, and train their employees in risk management. They alone can insure against risks and effectively spread the costs of insurance among their thousands of customers. Skiers, on the other hand, are not in a position to discover and correct risks of harm, and they cannot insure against the ski area's negligence.

Further, the agreement at issue was a standardized adhesion contract offered to the plaintiff on a "take it or leave it" basis. The "most salient feature [of adhesion contracts] is that they are not subject to the normal bargaining processes of ordinary contracts. * * * Not only was the plaintiff unable to negotiate the terms of the agreement, but the defendants also did not offer him the option of procuring protection against negligence at an additional reasonable cost. See *Restatement (Third), Torts, Apportionment of Liability § 2*, comment (e), p. 21 (2000) (factor relevant to enforcement of contractual limit on liability is "whether the party seeking exculpation was willing to provide greater protection against tortious conduct for a reasonable, additional fee"). Moreover, the defendants did not inform prospective snowtubers prior to their arrival at Powder Ridge that they would have to waive important common-law rights as a condition of participation. Thus, the plaintiff, who traveled to Powder Ridge in anticipation of snowtubing that day, was faced with the dilemma of either signing the defendants' proffered waiver of prospective liability or forgoing completely the opportunity to snowtube at Powder Ridge. Under the present factual circumstances, it would ignore reality to conclude that the plaintiff wielded the same bargaining power as the defendants. * * *

For the foregoing reasons, we conclude that the agreement in the present matter affects the public interest adversely and, therefore, is unenforceable because it violates public policy.[12] Accordingly, the trial court improperly rendered summary judgment in favor of the defendants.

---

12. We clarify that our conclusion does not extend to the risks inherent in the activity of snowtubing..... As we have explained, inherent risks are those risks that are innate to the activity, "are beyond the control of the [recreational] area operator and cannot be minimized by the operator's exercise of reasonable care." For example, risks inherent in the sport of skiing include, but are not limited to, the risk of collision with another skier or a tree outside the confines of the slope. * * *

The defendants and the dissent point out that our conclusion represents the "distinct minority view" and is inconsistent with the majority of sister state authority upholding exculpatory agreements in similar recreational settings. We acknowledge that most states uphold adhesion contracts releasing recreational operators from prospective liability for personal injuries caused by their own negligent conduct. Put simply, we disagree with these decisions for the reasons already explained in this opinion. * * * The judgment is reversed and the case is remanded for further proceedings according to law.

In this opinion Katz, Vertefeuille and Zarella, Js., concurred.

Norcott, J., with whom Borden and Palmer, Js., join, dissenting.

QUESTIONS AND NOTES

1.   Questions about the facts of this case

    1.1.   Did the plaintiff read the release agreement?

    1.2.   Did you read the release agreement? Did you understand it?

    1.3.   Do you think that the release agreement was prepared by an attorney?

    1.4.   Do you think that the defendant had liability insurance? If so, why did the defendant also have a release agreement?

2.   Questions about the law

    2.1.   What is an exculpatory clause?

    2.2.   Has Connecticut enacted legislation making exculpatory clauses illegal?

    2.3.   Are exculpatory clauses against public policy?

3.   Note

    3.1.   *Hanks* is a case that divided the Connecticut Supreme Court; three judges dissented. And, courts in other states are divided as to whether exculpatory clauses are invalid as against public policy. A law review article on exculpatory clauses on ski lift tickets concluded:

       "Courts are generally reluctant to enforce exculpatory clauses, especially those that include the negligence of the party attempting to enforce the clause. However, these cases show that courts can take very nuanced approaches to deciding whether to enforce such clauses. In the particular area of ski resort liability, the differences between states are primarily based on how the courts view the regulation of seemingly private contracts within a recreational sport and the definition of "inherent risks" of skiing."

       C. Connor Crook, *Validity and Enforceability of Liability Waivers in Ski Lift Tickets*, 28 Campbell L. Rev. 107 (2005).

3.2.   The following law review note argues that you should be seeing an exculpatory contract every time you see your doctor,

The rising cost of healthcare in the United States has prompted many reform proposals pertaining to malpractice. One of the most promising is the reform of medical malpractice rules to allow patients to sacrifice their ability to bring malpractice suits against doctors in exchange for lower fees. If the cost of having the option to bring a malpractice suit truly outweighs the benefit, patients will choose to sign malpractice exculpatory agreements prior to treatment, contracting out of the malpractice system and paying less for healthcare.....

The actual enforceability of medical malpractice exculpatory agreements is an unsettled question, however. Courts treat general exculpatory agreements—like those signed at amusement parks—as they do any other contract, enforcing the contracts as long as they are entered into voluntarily. But medical malpractice exculpatory agreements have been repeatedly invalidated, often under the mysterious "void-for-public-policy" rationale. * * *

This Note argues * * * that a doctor or patient who wants to maximize the chances that an agreement will be enforced should find a way to make sure the patient's choice to sign or not sign remains confidential."

Matthew J.B. Lawrence, Note, *In Search of an Enforceable Medical Malpractice Exculpatory Agreement: Introducing Confidential Contracts as a Solution to the Doctor–Patient Relationship Problem,*, 84 NYU L. REV. 850 (2009).

———————

Covenants not to compete are fairly common in the business world. For example, a buyer of a tavern might want some assurances that her seller is not going to open a competing tavern in the same neighborhood. Or, an employer might want assurances that a key employee will not later work for a competitor.

And law suits challenging the enforceability of covenants not to compete are fairly common in the "legal" world. The holding of a particular case depends in the main on facts relating to the business need for a protective agreement and the reasonableness of the protective agreement; the opinions regularly discuss the public policies of: (i) freedom of contract, (ii) freedom to compete, and (iii) employee mobility.

The next case, involving a covenant not to compete agreement among various doctors, discusses an additional "public policy" as the basis for not enforcing the agreement.

———————

VALLEY MEDICAL SPECIALISTS v. FARBER

Supreme Court of Arizona
194 Ariz. 363, 982 P.2d 1277 (1999)

FELDMAN, J.

We granted review to determine whether the restrictive covenant between Dr. Steven Farber and Valley Medical Specialists is enforceable. We hold that it is not. Public policy concerns in this case outweigh Valley Medical's protectable interests in enforcing the agreement. We thus vacate the court of appeals' opinion, affirm the trial court's judgment, and remand to the court of appeals to resolve any remaining issues. * * *

FACTS AND PROCEDURAL HISTORY

In 1985, Valley Medical Specialists ("VMS"), a professional corporation, hired Steven S. Farber, D.O., an internist and pulmonologist who, among other things, treated AIDS and HIV-positive patients and performed brachytherapy—a procedure that radiates the inside of the lung in lung cancer patients. Brachytherapy can only be performed at certain hospitals that have the necessary equipment. A few years after joining VMS, Dr. Farber became a shareholder and subsequently a minority officer and director. In 1991, the three directors, including Dr. Farber, entered into new stock and employment agreements. The employment agreement contained a restrictive covenant, the scope of which was amended over time.

In 1994, Dr. Farber left VMS and began practicing within the area defined by the restrictive covenant, which at that time read as follows:

> The parties recognize that the duties to be rendered under the terms of this Agreement by the Employee are special, unique and of an extraordinary character. The Employee, in consideration of the compensation to be paid to him pursuant to the terms of this Agreement, expressly agrees to the following restrictive covenants:
>
> (a) The Employee shall not, directly or indirectly:
>
> > (i)   Request any present or future patients of the Employer to curtail or cancel their professional affiliation with the Employer;
> >
> > (ii) Either separately, jointly, or in association with others, establish, engage in, or become interested in, as an employee, owner, partner, shareholder or otherwise, or furnish any information to, work for, or assist in any manner, anyone competing with, or who may compete with the Employer in the practice of medicine.
> >
> >   * * *
> >
> > (iv) Either separately, jointly or in association with others provide medical care or medical assistance for any person or persons who were patients or [sic] Employer during the period that Employee was in the hire of Employer.

* * *

(d) The restrictive covenants set forth herein shall continue during the term of this Agreement and for a period of three (3) years after the date of termination, for any reason, of this Agreement. The restrictive covenants set forth herein shall be binding upon the Employee in that geographical area encompassed within the boundaries measured by a five (5) mile radius of any office maintained or utilized by Employer at the time of execution of the Agreement or at any time thereafter.

(e) The Employee agrees that a violation on his part of any covenant set forth in this Paragraph 17 will cause such damage to the Employer as will be irreparable and for that reason, that Employee further agrees that the Employer shall be entitled, as a matter of right, and upon notice as provided in Paragraph 20 hereof, to an injunction from any court of competent jurisdiction, restraining any further violation of said covenants by Employee, his corporation, employees, partners or agents. Such right to injunctive remedies shall be in addition to and cumulative with any other rights and remedies the Employer may have pursuant to this Agreement or law, including, specifically with regard to the covenants set forth in subparagraph 17(a) above, the recovery of liquidated damages equal to forty percent (40%) of the gross receipts received for medical services provided by the Employee, or any employee, associate, partner, or corporation of the Employee during the term of this Agreement and for a period of three (3) years after the date of termination, for any reason, of this Agreement. The Employee expressly acknowledges and agrees that the covenants and agreement contained in this Paragraph 17 are minimum and reasonable in scope and are necessary to protect the legitimate interest of the Employer and its goodwill.

VMS filed a complaint against Dr. Farber seeking (1) preliminary and permanent injunctions enjoining Dr. Farber from violating the restrictive covenant, (2) liquidated damages for breach of the employment agreement, and (3) damages for breach of fiduciary duty, conversion of patient files and confidential information, and intentional interference with contractual and/or business relations.

Following six days of testimony and argument, the trial court denied VMS's request for a preliminary injunction, finding that the restrictive covenant violated public policy or, alternatively, was unenforceable because it was too broad. Specifically, the court found that: any covenant over six months would be unreasonable; the five-mile radius from each of the three VMS offices was unreasonable because it covered a total of 235 square miles; and the restriction was unreasonable because it did not provide an exception for emergency medical aid and was not limited to pulmonology.

The court of appeals reversed, concluding that a modified covenant was reasonable. The court noted that there were eight hospitals outside the restricted area where Dr. Farber could practice. Although the covenant made no exceptions for emergency medicine, the court held that the severability clause permitted the trial court to modify the covenant so Dr. Farber could provide emergency services within the restricted area. Moreover, VMS was allowed to stipulate that Dr. Farber could perform brachytherapy and treat AIDS and HIV patients within the restricted area, again even though the covenant contained no such exceptions.

The court of appeals found the restriction, when so modified, reasonable as to time and place. Although non-emergency patients might be required to travel further to see Dr. Farber, they could continue to see him if they were willing to drive that far. Three years was reasonable because the record contained testimony that it might take Dr. Farber's replacement three to five years to develop his pulmonary practice referral sources to the level they were when Dr. Farber resigned.

The court found that the restrictive covenant did not violate public policy, believing that courts must not unnecessarily restrict the freedom of contract. Moreover, the record was void of any evidence that the availability of pulmonologists in the restricted area would be inadequate without Dr. Farber.

History of restrictive covenants

A brief reference to basic principles is appropriate. Historically, covenants not to compete were viewed as restraints of trade and were invalid at common law. Eventually, ancillary restraints, such as those incident to employment or partnership agreements, were enforced under the rule of reason. To be enforced, the restriction must do more than simply prohibit fair competition by the employee. In other words, a covenant not to compete is invalid unless it protects some legitimate interest beyond the employer's desire to protect itself from competition.

It is true that in this case, unlike typical employer-employee agreements, Dr. Farber may not have been at a bargaining disadvantage, which is one of the reasons such restrictive covenants are strictly construed. Unequal bargaining power may be a factor to consider when examining the hardship on the departing employee. But in cases involving the professions, public policy concerns may outweigh any protectable interest the remaining firm members may have. Thus, this case does not turn on the hardship to Dr. Farber.

The doctor-patient relationship is special and entitled to unique protection. It cannot be easily or accurately compared to relationships in the commercial context. In light of the great public policy interest involved in covenants not to compete between physicians, each agreement will be strictly construed for reasonableness.

Reasonableness of covenant

Reasonableness is a fact-intensive inquiry that depends on the totality of the circumstances. A restriction is unreasonable and thus will not be enforced: (1) if the restraint is greater than necessary to protect the employer's legitimate interest; or (2) if that interest is outweighed by the hardship to the employee and the likely injury to the public. Thus, in the present case, the reasonableness inquiry requires us to examine the interests of the employer, employee, patients, and public in general. Balancing these competing interests is no easy task and no exact formula can be used.

VMS's protectable interest

VMS contends, and the court of appeals agreed, that it has a protectable interest in its patients and referral sources. In the commercial context, it is clear that employers have a legitimate interest in retaining their customer base. In the medical context, however, the personal relationship between doctor and patient as well as the patient's freedom to see a particular doctor, affects the extent of the employer's interest.

Even in the commercial context, the employer's interest in its customer base is balanced with the employee's right to the customers. Where the employee took an active role and brought customers with him or her to the job, courts are more reluctant to enforce restrictive covenants. Dr. Farber was a pulmonologist. He did not learn his skills from VMS.

Scope of the restrictive covenant

The restriction cannot be greater than necessary to protect VMS's legitimate interests. A restraint's scope is defined by its duration and geographic area. The frequency of contact between doctors and their patients affects the permissible length of the restraint. The idea is to give the employer a reasonable amount of time to overcome the former employee's loss, usually by hiring a replacement and giving that replacement time to establish a working relationship.

In this case, the trial judge found that the three-year period was an unreasonable duration because all of the experts agree that the practice of pulmonology entails treating patients with chronic conditions which require more hospital care than office care and which requires regular contact with the treating physician at least once within each six-month period so that any provision over six months is onerous and unnecessary to protect VMS's economic interests where virtually all of Dr. Farber's VMS patients had an opportunity by late 1994 or early 1995 (Farber left September 12, 1994) to decide which pulmonologist * * * they would consult for their ongoing treatment[.]

On this record, we cannot say this factual finding was clearly erroneous. The three-year duration is unreasonable.

The activity prohibited by the restraint also defines the covenant's scope. The restraint must be limited to the particular specialty of the present employment. On its face, the restriction here is not limited to internal medicine or even pulmonology. It precludes any type of practice, even in fields that do not compete with VMS. Thus, we agree with the trial judge that this restriction is too broad. * * *

Public policy

The court of appeals held that the restrictive covenant does not violate public policy, pointing out that the record contains nothing to suggest there will be a lack of pulmonologists in the restricted area if Dr. Farber is precluded from practicing there. Even if we assume other pulmonologists will be available to cover Dr. Farber's patients, we disagree with this view. It ignores the significant interests of individual patients within the restricted area. * * * A court must evaluate the extent to which enforcing the covenant would foreclose patients from seeing the departing physician if they desire to do so.

Concluding that patients' right to see the doctor of their choice is entitled to substantial protection, VMS's protectable interests here are comparatively minimal. The geographic scope of this covenant encompasses approximately 235 square miles, making it very difficult for Dr. Farber's existing patients to continue treatment with him if they so desire. After six days of testimony, the trial judge concluded that this restrictive covenant was unreasonably broad and against public policy. Specifically, the judge found:

(1) the three year duration was unreasonable because pulmonology patients typically require contact with the treating physician once every six months. Thus, a restriction over six months is unnecessary to protect VMS's economic interests. Patients would have had opportunity within approximately six months to decide which doctor to see for continuing treatment;

(2) the five mile radius was unreasonable because with the three offices, the restriction covered more than 235 square miles;

(3) the restriction was unreasonable because it did not expressly provide for an exception for emergency medical treatment;

(4) the restriction was overly broad because it is not limited to pulmonology;

(5) the covenant violates public policy because of the sensitive and personal nature of the doctor-patient relationship.

Given the facts and the principles discussed, that finding is well supported factually and legally.

Severance—the blue pencil rule

This contract contains a severance clause. The court of appeals accepted a stipulation by VMS that the restriction would not prohibit Dr. Farber from treating HIV-positive and AIDS patients or from performing brachytherapy. On its face, however, the restriction is broader than that, restricting him from providing "medical care or medical assistance for any person or persons who were patients or [sic] Employer during the period that Employee was in the hire of Employer." Arizona courts will "blue pencil" restrictive covenants, eliminating grammatically severable, unreasonable provisions. Here, however, the modifications go further than cutting grammatically severable portions. The court of appeals, in essence, rewrote the agreement in an attempt to make it enforceable. This goes too far. "Where the severability of the agreement is not evident from the contract itself, the court cannot create a new agreement for the parties to uphold the contract."

Even the blue pencil rule has its critics. For every agreement that makes its way to court, many more do not. Thus, the words of the covenant have an in terrorem effect on departing employees. Employers may therefore create ominous covenants, knowing that if the words are challenged, courts will modify the agreement to make it enforceable. *Id.* Although we will tolerate ignoring severable portions of a covenant to make it more reasonable, we will not permit courts to add terms or rewrite provisions.

* * *

CONCLUSION

We hold that the restrictive covenant between Dr. Farber and VMS cannot be enforced. Valley Medical Specialists' interest in enforcing the restriction is outweighed by the likely injury to patients and the public in general. In so holding, we need not reach the question of the hardship imposed on Dr. Farber. The public policy implications here are enough to invalidate this particular agreement. We stop short of holding that restrictive covenants between physicians will never be enforced, but caution that such restrictions will be strictly construed. The burden is on the party wishing to enforce the covenant to demonstrate that the restraint is no greater than necessary to protect the employer's legitimate interest, and that such interest is not outweighed by the hardship to the employee and the likely injury to the public. Here VMS has not met that burden. The restriction fails because its public policy' implications outweigh the legitimate interests of VMS.

* * *

QUESTIONS AND NOTES

1. Questions about the facts of this case
   1.1. Was the defendant an experienced physician when he joined Valley Medical Specialists? How many of his patients were originally patients of other Valley Medical Specialists doctors? Are any of these questions relevant?

1.2. Was there any evidence that there is a shortage of pulmonologists in the Valley of the Sun? Is that relevant?

2. Questions about the law

2.1. Reconsider the first three sentences of the opinion: "We granted review to determine whether the restrictive covenant between Dr. Steven Farber and Valley Medical Specialists is enforceable. We hold that it is not. Public policy concerns in this case outweigh Valley Medical's protectable interests in enforcing this agreement." What are the public policy concerns? What are Valley Medical's protectable interests?

2.2. A is an accountant. Her employment agreement with Valley Accountancy Specialists, Inc., includes a covenant not to compete similar in scope to the covenant not to compete in *Valley Medical Specialists*. A has now decided that she would like to leave Valley Accountancy Specialists, Inc. and start her own accounting practice. Would this court find her covenant not to compete unenforceable because of public policy?

2.3. Would the court have had the same public policy concerns and issued the same ruling if the covenant not to compete had been limited, (i) in time, to one year, and (ii) in place, to five miles from Valley Medical's principal office?

2.4. In discussing the contrary ruling of the court of appeals, the opinion mentions a "severability clause"—"the severability clause permitted the trial court to modify the covenant so Dr. Farber could provide emergency service within the restricted area." What is a severability clause? How is a severability clause connected to the blue pencil rule discussed later in the opinion?

3. Notes

3.1. There are courts that "reform" covenants not to compete that are excessive in time or space. For example, *Ferrofluidics Corp. v. Advanced Vacuum Components, Inc.*, 968 F.2d 1463 (1st Cir. 1992) found that a five year covenant not to compete in an employment agreement was excessive and so enforced it for a three year term.

3.2. Although most states rely on courts and precedent to shape public policy on covenants not to compete, a significant number of states have enacted legislation prohibiting or regulating covenants not to compete. See generally, Kate O'Neill, *Should I Stay or Should I Go?—Covenants Not to Compete in a Down Economy: A Proposal for Better Advocacy and Better Judicial Opinions*, 6 HASTINGS BUS L.J. 83, 96 et seq. (2010). For example, California has enacted legislation prohibiting covenants not to compete in employment contracts, and, in Texas, there is a specific statute regulating physicians' covenants not to compete.

(b) A covenant not to compete relating to the practice of medicine is enforceable against a person licensed as a physician by the Texas Medical Board if such covenant complies with the following requirements:

(1) the covenant must:

(A) not deny the physician access to a list of his patients whom he had seen or treated within one year of termination of the contract or employment;

(B) provide access to medical records of the physician's patients upon authorization of the patient and any copies of medical records for a reasonable fee as established by the Texas Medical Board under Section 159.008, Occupations Code; and

(C) provide that any access to a list of patients or to patients' medical records after termination of the contract or employment shall not require such list or records to be provided in a format different than that by which such records are maintained except by mutual consent of the parties to the contract;

(2) the covenant must provide for a buy out of the covenant by the physician at a reasonable price or, at the option of either party, as determined by a mutually agreed upon arbitrator or, in the case of an inability to agree, an arbitrator of the court whose decision shall be binding on the parties; and

(3) the covenant must provide that the physician will not be prohibited from providing continuing care and treatment to a specific patient or patients during the course of an acute illness even after the contract or employment has been terminated.

V.T.C.A., Bus. & C. § 15.50

SECTION 6: CONTRACT LAW REASONS FOR NOT ENFORCING AN AGREEMENT: UNCONSCIONABILITY

In studying duress and undue influence, misrepresentation, and non-disclosure, we have seen courts refuse to enforce agreements because of problems in the bargaining process. And, in studying illegality and public policy, we have seen courts refuse to enforce agreements because of problems with the substance of the bargain.

Unconscionability, in a sense, is a combination of all that. Unconscionability looks to both the bargaining process and the terms of the bargain.

Scholars trace the concept of unconscionability back to Roman law and find traces of an unconscionability doctrine in basic equity maxims such as ''clean hands.'' The modern American law of unconscionability has its roots in section 2–302 of the Uniform Commercial Code and in the next case, *Williams v. Walker–Thomas Furniture Co.*, a case in which the United States Court of Appeals for the District of Columbia overruled the District of Columbia Court of Appeals in holding that, under common law, a court could refuse to enforce a contract for the sale of consumer goods on credit that provided, "[T]he amount of each periodical installment payment * * * shall be credited pro rata on all outstanding leases, bills and accounts due the Company by (purchaser) at the time each such payment is made."

WILLIAMS v. WALKER–THOMAS FURNITURE COMPANY

Court of Appeals, District of Columbia
198 A.2d 914 (1964)

QUINN, ASSOCIATE JUDGE.

Appellant, a person of limited education separated from her husband, is maintaining herself and her seven children by means of public assistance. During the period 1957–1962 she had a continuous course of dealings with appellee from which she purchased many household articles on the installment plan. These included sheets, curtains, rugs, chairs, a chest of drawers, beds, mattresses, a washing machine, and a stereo set. In 1963 appellee filed a complaint in replevin for possession of all the items purchased by appellant, alleging that her payments were in default and that it retained title to the goods according to the sales contracts. By the writ of replevin appellee obtained a bed, chest of drawers, washing machine, and the stereo set. After hearing testimony and examining the contracts, the trial court entered judgment for appellee.

Appellant's principal contentions on appeal are (1) there was a lack of meeting of the minds, and (2) the contracts were against public policy.

Appellant signed fourteen contracts in all. They were approximately six inches in length and each contained a long paragraph in extremely fine print. One of the sentences in this paragraph provided that payments, after the first purchase, were to be prorated on all purchases then outstanding. Mathematically, this had the effect of keeping a balance due on all items until the time balance was completely eliminated. It meant that title to the first purchase, remained in appellee until the fourteenth purchase, made some five years later, was fully paid.

At trial appellant testified that she understood the agreements to mean that when payments on the running account were sufficient to balance the amount due on an individual item, the item became hers. She testified that most of the purchases were made at her home; that the contracts were signed in blank; that she did not read the instruments; and that she was not provided with a copy. She admitted, however, that she did not ask anyone to read or explain the contracts to her.

We have stated that "one who refrains from reading a contract and in conscious ignorance of its terms voluntarily assents thereto will not be relieved from his bad bargain." "One who signs a contract has a duty to read it and is obligated according to its terms." "It is as much the duty of a person who cannot read the language in which a contract is written to have someone read it to him before he signs it, as it is the duty of one who can read to peruse it himself before signing it."

A careful review of the record shows that appellant's assent was not obtained "by fraud or even misrepresentation falling short of fraud." This is not a case of mutual misunderstanding but a unilateral mistake. Under these circumstances, appellant's first contention is without merit.

Appellant's second argument presents a more serious question. The record reveals that prior to the last purchase appellant had reduced the balance in her account to $164. The last purchase, a stereo set, raised the balance due to $678. Significantly, at the time of this and the preceding purchases, appellee was aware of appellant's financial position. The reverse side of the stereo contract listed the name of appellant's social worker and her $218 monthly stipend from the government. Nevertheless, with full knowledge that appellant had to feed, clothe and support both herself and seven children on this amount, appellee sold her a $514 stereo set.

We cannot condemn too strongly appellee's conduct. It raises serious questions of sharp practice and irresponsible business dealings. A review of the legislation in the District of Columbia affecting retail sales and the pertinent decisions of the highest court in this jurisdiction disclose, however, no ground upon which this court can declare the contracts in question contrary to public policy. We think Congress should consider corrective legislation to protect the public from such exploitive contracts as were utilized in the case at bar.

Affirmed.

WILLIAMS v. WALKER–THOMAS FURNITURE COMPANY

U.S. Court of Appeals, District of Columbia Circuit
350 F.2d 445 (1965)

J. SKELLY WRIGHT, CIRCUIT JUDGE.

* * *

We do not agree that the court lacked the power to refuse enforcement to contracts found to be unconscionable. In other jurisdictions, it has been held as a matter of common law that unconscionable contracts are not enforceable. While no decision of this court so holding has been found, the notion that an unconscionable bargain should not be given full enforcement is by no means novel. In *Scott v. United States*, 79 U.S. (12 Wall.) 443, 445, 20 L.Ed. 438 (1870), the Supreme Court stated:

> "* * * If a contract be unreasonable and unconscionable, but not void for fraud, a court of law will give to the party who sues for its breach damages, not according to its letter, but only such as he is equitably entitled to. * * *"

Since we have never adopted or rejected such a rule, the question here presented is actually one of first impression.

Congress has recently enacted the Uniform Commercial Code, which specifically provides that the court may refuse to enforce a contract which it finds to be unconscionable at the time it was made. The enactment of this section, which occurred subsequent to the contracts here in suit, does not mean that the common law of the District of Columbia was otherwise at the time of enactment, nor does it preclude the court from adopting a similar rule in the exercise of its powers to develop the common law for the District of Columbia. In fact, in view of the absence of prior authority on the point, we consider the congressional adoption of § 2–302 persuasive authority for following the rationale of the cases from which the section is explicitly derived. Accordingly, we hold that where the element of unconscionability is present at the time a contract is made, the contract should not be enforced.

Unconscionability has generally been recognized to include an absence of meaningful choice on the part of one of the parties together with contract terms which are unreasonably favorable to the other party. Whether a meaningful choice is present in a particular case can only be determined by consideration of all the circumstances surrounding the transaction. In many cases the meaningfulness of the choice is negated by a gross inequality of bargaining power. The manner in which the contract was entered is also relevant to this consideration. Did each party to the contract, considering his obvious education or lack of it, have a reasonable opportunity to understand the terms of the contract, or were the important terms hidden in a maze of fine print and minimized by deceptive sales practices? Ordinarily, one who signs an agreement without full knowledge of its terms might be held to assume the risk that he has entered a one-sided bargain. But when a party of little bargaining power, and hence little real choice, signs a commercially unreasonable contract with little or no knowledge of its terms, it is hardly likely that his consent, or even an objective manifestation of his consent, was ever given to all the terms. In such a case the usual rule that the terms of the agreement are not to be questioned should be abandoned and the court should consider whether the terms of the contract are so unfair that enforcement should be withheld.

In determining reasonableness or fairness, the primary concern must be with the terms of the contract considered in light of the circumstances existing when the contract was made. The test is not simple, nor can it be mechanically applied. The terms are to be considered "in the light of the general commercial background and the commercial needs of the particular trade or case." Corbin suggests the test as being whether the terms are "so extreme as to appear unconscionable according to the mores and business practices of the time and place." We think this formulation correctly states the test to be applied in those cases where no meaningful choice was exercised upon entering the contract.

Because the trial court and the appellate court did not feel that enforcement could be refused, no findings were made on the possible unconscionability of the contracts in these cases. Since the record is not sufficient for our deciding the issue as a matter of law, the cases must be remanded to the trial court for further proceedings.

So ordered.

DANAHER, CIRCUIT JUDGE (dissenting):

The District of Columbia Court of Appeals obviously was as unhappy about the situation here presented as any of us can possibly be. Its opinion in the *Williams* case, quoted in the majority text, concludes: "We think Congress should consider corrective legislation to protect the public from such exploitive contracts as were utilized in the case at bar."

My view is thus summed up by an able court which made no finding that there had actually been sharp practice. Rather the appellant seems to have known precisely where she stood.

There are many aspects of public policy here involved. What is a luxury to some may seem an outright necessity to others. Is public oversight to be required of the expenditures of relief funds? A washing machine, e.g., in the hands of a relief client might become a fruitful source of income. Many relief clients may well need credit, and certain business establishments will take long chances on the sale of items, expecting their pricing policies will afford a degree of protection commensurate with the risk. * * *

I mention such matters only to emphasize the desirability of a cautious approach to any such problem, particularly since the law for so long has allowed parties such great latitude in making their own contracts. I dare say there must annually be thousands upon thousands of installment credit transactions in this jurisdiction, and one can only speculate as to the effect the decision in these cases will have.

I join the District of Columbia Court of Appeals in its disposition of the issues.

QUESTIONS AND NOTES

1. Questions about the facts of the case

    1.1. Who is suing whom for what?

    1.2. Was there a written agreement?

    1.3. Was there any dispute over the terms of the agreement?

    1.4. Did the Walker–Thomas Furniture Company do anything that it was not permitted to do under the agreement? Did the Walker–Thomas Furniture Company do anything that it was not permitted to do under then-existing D.C. law?

1.5.   What did the Walker–Thomas Furniture Company do "wrong"?

2.   Questions about the law

2.1.   In the first *Williams* opinion, the intermediate appellate court focused on the contention that the "contracts were against public policy" and concluded that there was "no ground upon which this court can declare the contracts in question contrary to public policy." The appeal of that decision resulted in a remand for further proceedings on unconscionability. What are the differences between Williams' public policy argument and Williams' unconscionability argument?

2.2.   Is unconscionability federal statutory law? State statutory law? Common law?

2.3.   What was unconscionable about the agreement between Ms. Williams and the Walker–Thomas store? What did Judge Wright decide?

2.4.   How would Judge Wright have decided this case if all agreements contained the following warning in bold print: CAUTION. IF YOU DO NOT PAY ON TIME FOR WHAT YOU JUST BOUGHT, WE MAY BE ABLE TO TAKE BACK EVERY–THING WE EVER SOLD YOU? *See generally* Arthur A. Leff, *Contract As Thing*, 19 AM. U. L. REV. 131, 155 (1970).

2.5.   On remand, what evidence would you try to introduce if you represented Ms. Williams? Would it be helpful to show her education and economic situation? Would it be helpful to show why she purchased a $514 stereo? Would it be helpful to show that repossessed "sheets, curtains, rugs" have almost no resale value to Walker–Thomas? Would it be helpful to show that other merchants in the area used similar contracts?

2.6.   On remand, what evidence would you try to find and introduce if you represented Walker–Thomas? Would it be helpful to show that other merchants in the area used similar contracts? Would it be helpful to show that consumer goods lose value so rapidly that the amount owed for consumer goods is generally greater than any resale value? Would it be helpful to show that D.C. law restricted Walker–Thomas to the recovery of the debt owed by Ms. Williams and its collection costs?

3.   Notes

3.1.   According to Professor David Slawson of the University of Southern California Law School, "The theoretical underpinnings of unconscionability * * * are not simple, and to some extent they are self-contradictory. They require one to accept the legitimacy of contracts to which one party did not give meaningful consent but to deny their legitimacy to the extent that they operate unfairly." W. DAVID SLAWSON, BINDING PROMISES, 144 (1996).

3.2.   Professor Richard Epstein* of the University of Chicago Law School and New York University Law School favors a limited use of unconscionability, to police the bargaining process, but not the bargain:

> One of the major conceptual tools used by courts in their assault upon private agreements has been the doctrine of unconscionability. That doctrine has a place in contract law, but it is not the one usually assigned it by its advocates. The doctrine should not, in my view, allow courts to act as roving commissions to set aside those agreements whose substantive terms they find objectionable. Instead, it should be used only to allow courts to police the process whereby private agreements are formed, and in that connection, only to facilitate the setting aside of agreements that are as a matter of probabilities likely to be vitiated by the classical defenses of duress, fraud, or incompetence.

> When the doctrine of unconscionability is used in its substantive dimension, be it in a commercial or consumer context, it serves only to undercut the private right of contract in a manner that is apt to do more social harm than good. The result of the analysis is the same even if we view the question of unconscionability from the lofty perspective of public policy. "[I]f there is one thing which more than another public policy requires, it is that men of full age and competent understanding shall have the utmost liberty of contracting, and that their contracts when entered into freely and voluntarily shall be held sacred and shall be enforced by Courts of justice."

> Richard Epstein, *Unconscionability: A Critical Reappraisal*, 18 J. L. & ECON. 293, 294–5, 314 (1975).

3.3.   Judge Wright was from New Orleans; he served on the D.C. Circuit rather than the Fifth Circuit for "political reasons." Justice William Brennan, Jr. described Judge Wright as "one of the outstanding jurists of the nation's history" and acknowledged Judge Wright's judicial activism:

> It is of course true that some of his most notable decisions were greeted with harsh and bitter invective. The charge was that he was an "activist judge," exceeding his proper role. This, of course, is not an unfamiliar charge. But since our beginnings, lively, even acrimonious, debate about the proper role of judges in a democratic society has been with us. The judge who believes that the judicial power should be made creative and vigorously effective is labeled "activist." The judge inclined to question the propriety of judicial intervention to redress even the most egregious failures of democracy is labeled "neutralist" or "passivist." The labels are not synonymous with "conservative" or "liberal"; where yesterday "activist" was pinned on liberals, today it's on conservatives. As often as not, however, such

---

* Richard consented to our reproducing this excerpt from his article on the conditions that: (i) we make clear that he is not in any way related to David Epstein, and (ii) David Epstein acknowledge that Richard Epstein was a much better basketball player than David Epstein was during the two terms that the University of Chicago let David Epstein teach there.

labels are used merely to express disapproval of a particular judge's decisions. If useful at all, the labels may be more serviceable to distinguish the judge who sees his role as guided by the principle that "justice or righteousness is the source, the substance and the ultimate end of the law," from the judge for whom the guiding principle is that "courts do not sit to administer justice, but to administer the law." Such legendary names as Justice Holmes and Judge Learned Hand have been associated with the latter view. Holmes' imaginary society of Jobbists is limited to judges who hold a tight rein on humanitarian impulse and compassionate action, stoically doing their best to discover and apply already existing rules. But judges acting on the former view, and Skelly Wright was one, believe that the judicial process demands a good deal more than that. Because constitutions, statutes, and precedents rarely speak unambiguously, a just choice between competing alternatives has to be made to decide concrete cases. Skelly Wright would argue that in such cases "the judge's role necessarily is a creative one—he must legislate; there is no help for it; when the critical moment comes and he must say yea or nay, he is on his own; he has nothing to rely on but his own intellect, experience and conscience.

Justice William J. Brennan, Jr., *In Memoriam: J. Skelly Wright*, 102 Harv. L. Rev. 361 (1988).

BROWER v. GATEWAY 2000, INC.

Supreme Court, Appellate Division, First Department
246 A.D.2d 246, 676 N.Y.S.2d 569 (1998)

Milonas, Justice Presiding

Appellants are among the many consumers who purchased computers and software products from defendant Gateway 2000 through a direct-sales system, by mail or telephone order. As of July 3, 1995, it was Gateway's practice to include with the materials shipped to the purchaser along with the merchandise a copy of its "Standard Terms and Conditions Agreement" and any relevant warranties for the products in the shipment. The Agreement begins with a "NOTE TO CUSTOMER," which provides, in slightly larger print than the remainder of the document, in a box that spans the width of the page: "This document contains Gateway 2000's Standard Terms and Conditions. By keeping your Gateway 2000 computer system beyond thirty (30) days after the date of delivery, you accept these Terms and Conditions." The document consists of 16 paragraphs, and, as is relevant to this appeal, paragraph 10 of the agreement, entitled "DISPUTE RESOLUTION," reads as follows:

Any dispute or controversy arising out of or relating to this Agreement or its interpretation shall be settled exclusively and finally by arbitration. The arbitration shall be conducted in accordance with the Rules of Conciliation and Arbitration of the International Chamber of

Commerce [ICC]. The arbitration shall be conducted in Chicago, Illinois, U.S.A. before a sole arbitrator. Any award rendered in any such arbitration proceeding shall be final and binding on each of the parties, and judgment may be entered thereon in a court of competent jurisdiction.

Plaintiffs commenced this action on behalf of themselves and others similarly situated for compensatory and punitive damages, alleging deceptive sales practices in seven causes of action, including breach of warranty, breach of contract, fraud and unfair trade practices.

* * *

Insofar as is relevant to appellants, who purchased their computers after July 3, 1995, Gateway moved to dismiss the complaint based on the arbitration clause in the Agreement. Appellants argued that the arbitration clause is invalid under UCC 2–207, unconscionable under UCC 2–302 and an unenforceable contract of adhesion. Specifically, they claimed that the provision was obscure; that a customer could not reasonably be expected to appreciate or investigate its meaning and effect; that the International Chamber of Commerce ("ICC") was not a forum commonly used for consumer matters; and that because ICC headquarters were in France, it was particularly difficult to locate the organization and its rules. To illustrate just how inaccessible the forum was, appellants advised the court that the ICC was not registered with the Secretary of State, that efforts to locate and contact the ICC had been unsuccessful and that apparently the only way to attempt to contact the ICC was through the United States Council for International Business, with which the ICC maintained some sort of relationship.

In support of their arguments, appellants submitted a copy of the ICC's Rules of Conciliation and Arbitration and contended that the cost of ICC arbitration was prohibitive, particularly given the amount of the typical consumer claim involved. For example, a claim of less than $50,000 required advance fees of $4,000 (more than the cost of most Gateway products), of which the $2000 registration fee was nonrefundable even if the consumer prevailed at the arbitration. Consumers would also incur travel expenses disproportionate to the damages sought, which appellants' counsel estimated would not exceed $1,000 per customer in this action, as well as bear the cost of Gateway's legal fees if the consumer did not prevail at the arbitration; in this respect, the ICC rules follow the "loser pays" rule used in England. Also, although Chicago was designated as the site of the actual arbitration, all correspondence must be sent to ICC headquarters in France.

The IAS[7] court dismissed the complaint as to appellants based on the arbitration clause in the Agreements delivered with their computers. We agree with the court's decision and reasoning in all respects but for the issue of the unconscionability of the designation of the ICC as the arbitration body.

---

7. IAS court means Independent Assignment System court which will mean something to those of you who practice in New York. (Eds.)

First, the court properly rejected appellants' argument that the arbitration clause was invalid under UCC 2–207. Appellants claim that when they placed their order they did not bargain for, much less accept, arbitration of any dispute, and therefore the arbitration clause in the agreement that accompanied the merchandise shipment was a "material alteration" of a preexisting oral agreement. Under UCC 2–207(2), such a material alteration constitutes "proposals for addition to the contract" that become part of the contract only upon appellants' express acceptance. However, as the court correctly concluded, the clause was not a "material alteration" of an oral agreement, but, rather, simply one provision of the sole contract that existed between the parties. That contract, the court explained, was formed and acceptance was manifested not when the order was placed but only with the retention of the merchandise beyond the 30 days specified in the Agreement enclosed in the shipment of merchandise. Accordingly, the contract was outside the scope of UCC 2–207.

In reaching its conclusion, the IAS court took note of the litigation in Federal courts on this very issue, and, indeed, on this very arbitration clause. In *Hill v. Gateway 2000, Inc.*, 105 F.3d 1147, *cert. denied* 522 U.S. 808, 118 S.Ct. 47, 139 L.Ed.2d 13, plaintiffs in a class action contested the identical Gateway contract in dispute before us, including the enforceability of the arbitration clause. As that court framed the issue, the "[t]erms inside Gateway's box stand or fall together. If they constitute the parties contract because the Hills had an opportunity to return the computer after reading them, then all must be enforced" (*id.* at 1148). The court then concluded that the contract was not formed with the placement of a telephone order or with the delivery of the goods. Instead, an enforceable contract was formed only with the consumer's decision to retain the merchandise beyond the 30–day period specified in the agreement. Thus, the agreement as a whole, including the arbitration clause, was enforceable.

* * *

The *Hill* decision, in its examination of the formation of the contract, takes note of the realities of conducting business in today's world. Transactions involving "cash now, terms later" have become commonplace, enabling the consumer to make purchases of sophisticated merchandise such as computers over the phone or by mail-and even by computer. Indeed, the concept of "[p]ayment preceding the revelation of full terms" is particularly common in certain industries, such as air transportation and insurance

While *Hill* and *ProCD*, as the IAS court recognized, are not controlling (although they are decisions of the United States Court of Appeals for the circuit encompassing the forum state designated for arbitration), we agree with their rationale that, in such transactions, there is no agreement or contract upon the placement of the order or even upon the receipt of the goods. By the terms of the Agreement at issue, it is only after the consumer has affirmatively retained the merchandise for more than 30 days-within which the consumer has presumably examined and even used the product(s) and read the agreement-that the contract has been effectuated. In this respect, the case is distinguishable from *S & T Sportswear v. Drake Fabrics,* 190 A.D.2d 598, 593 N.Y.S.2d 799, cited by appellants, where this Court found that an arbitration clause found on the reverse side of defendant's draft sales contract did constitute a "material alteration" where the parties did in fact have a pre-existing oral agreement.

* * * No contract was formed here or in *Hill* until the merchandise was retained beyond the 30–day period. The disputed arbitration clause is simply one provision of the sole contract "proposed" between the parties.

Second, with respect to appellants' claim that the arbitration clause is unenforceable as a contract of adhesion, in that it involved no choice or negotiation on the part of the consumer but was a "take it or leave it" proposition we find that this argument, too, was properly rejected by the IAS court. Although the parties clearly do not possess equal bargaining power, this factor alone does not invalidate the contract as one of adhesion. As the IAS court observed, with the ability to make the purchase elsewhere and the express option to return the goods, the consumer is not in a "take it or leave it" position at all; if any term of the agreement is unacceptable to the consumer, he or she can easily buy a competitor's product instead-either from a retailer or directly from the manufacturer-and reject Gateway's agreement by returning the merchandise The consumer has 30 days to make that decision. Within that time, the consumer can inspect the goods and examine and seek clarification of the terms of the agreement; until those 30 days have elapsed, the consumer has the unqualified right to return the merchandise, because the goods or terms are unsatisfactory or for no reason at all.

While returning the goods to avoid the formation of the contract entails affirmative action on the part of the consumer, and even some expense, this may be seen as a trade-off for the convenience and savings for which the consumer presumably opted when he or she chose to make a purchase of such consequence by phone or mail as an alternative to on-site retail shopping. That a consumer does not read the agreement or thereafter claims he or she failed to understand or appreciate some term therein does not invalidate the contract any more than such claim would undo a contract formed under other circumstances. * * *

Finally, we turn to appellants' argument that the IAS court should have declared the contract unenforceable, pursuant to UCC 2–302, on the ground that the arbitration clause is unconscionable due to the unduly burdensome procedure and for the individual consumer. The IAS court found that while a class-action lawsuit, such as the one herein, may be a less costly alternative to the arbitration (which is generally less costly than litigation), that does not alter the binding effect of the valid arbitration clause contained in the agreement * * *

As a general matter, under New York law, unconscionability requires a showing that a contract is "both procedurally and substantively unconscionable when made" That is, there must be "some showing of 'an absence of meaningful choice on the part of one of the parties together with contract terms which are unreasonably favorable to the other party' [citation omitted]" * * *

As to the procedural element, a court will look to the contract formation process to determine if in fact one party lacked any meaningful choice in entering into the contract, taking into consideration such factors as the setting of the transaction, the experience and education of the party claiming unconscionability, whether the contract contained "fine print," whether the seller used "high-pressured tactics" and any disparity in the parties' bargaining power None of these factors supports appellants' claim here. Any purchaser has 30 days within which to thoroughly examine the contents of their shipment, including the terms of the Agreement, and seek clarification of any term therein The Agreement itself, which is entitled in large print "STANDARD TERMS AND CONDITIONS AGREEMENT," consists of only three pages and 16 paragraphs, all of which appear in the same size print. Moreover, despite appellants' claims to the contrary, the arbitration clause is in no way "hidden" or "tucked away" within a complex document of inordinate length, nor is the option of returning the merchandise,** to avoid the contract, somehow a "precarious" one. We also reject appellants' insinuation that, by using the word "standard," Gateway deliberately meant to convey to the consumer that the terms were standard within the industry, when the document clearly purports to be no more than *Gateway*'s "standard terms and conditions."

With respect to the substantive element, which entails an examination of the substance of the agreement in order to determine whether the terms unreasonably favor one party, we do not find that the possible inconvenience of the chosen site (Chicago) alone rises to the level of unconscionability. We do find, however, that the excessive cost factor that is necessarily entailed in arbitrating before the ICC is unreasonable and surely serves to deter the individual consumer from invoking the process). Barred from resorting to the courts by the arbitration clause in the first instance, the designation of a financially prohibitive forum effectively bars consumers from this forum as well; consumers are thus left with no forum at all in which to resolve a dispute. In this regard, we note that this particular claim is not mentioned in the *Hill* decision, which upheld the clause as part of an enforceable contract.

While it is true that, under New York law, unconscionability is generally predicated on the presence of both the procedural and substantive elements, the substantive element alone may be sufficient to render the terms of the provision at issue unenforceable Excessive fees, such as those incurred under the ICC procedure, have been grounds for finding an arbitration provision unenforceable or commercially unreasonable

* * *

Gateway's brief includes the text of a new arbitration agreement that it claims has been extended to all customers, past, present and future (apparently through publication in a quarterly magazine sent to anyone who has ever purchased a Gateway product). The new arbitration agreement provides for the consumer's choice of the AAA [American Arbitration Association] or the ICC as the arbitral body and the designation of any location for the arbitration by agreement of the parties, which "shall not be unreasonably withheld." It also provides telephone numbers at which the AAA and the ICC may be reached for information regarding the "organizations and their procedures."

As noted, however, appellants complain that the AAA fees are also excessive and thus in no way have they accepted defendant's offer (see, UCC 2–209); because they make the same claim as to the AAA as they did with respect to the ICC, the issue of unconscionability is not rendered moot, as defendant suggests. We cannot determine on this record whether the AAA process and costs would be so "egregiously oppressive" that they, too, would be unconscionable Thus, we modify the order on appeal to the extent of finding that portion of the arbitration provision requiring arbitration before the ICC to be unconscionable and remand to Supreme Court so that the parties have the opportunity to seek appropriate substitution of an arbitrator pursuant to the Federal Arbitration Act (9 U.S.C. § 1 et seq.), which provides for such court designation of an arbitrator upon application of either party, where, for whatever reason, one is not otherwise designated (9 U.S.C. § 5). * * *

Accordingly, the order of Supreme Court, New York County (Beatrice Shainswit, J.), entered October 21, 1997, which, to the extent appealed from, granted defendants' motion to dismiss the complaint as to appellants on the ground that there was a valid agreement to arbitrate between the parties, should be modified, on the law and the facts, to the extent of vacating that portion of the arbitration agreement as requires arbitration before the International Chamber of Commerce, with leave to the parties to seek appointment of an arbitrator pursuant to 9 U.S.C. § 5 and remanding the matter for that purpose, and otherwise affirmed, without costs. * * *

All concur.

QUESTIONS, NOTE, AND CONNECTIONS

1. Questions about the facts of this case

    1.1. What do we know about the appellants? Do we know more about Ms. Williams than we know about the appellants in this case? Is that important?

    1.2. Was it important that "Gateway's brief includes the text of a new arbitration agreement that it claims has been extended to all customers, past, present and future (apparently through publication in a quarterly magazine sent to anyone who has ever purchased a Gateway product)"?

2. Questions about the law

2.1. Procedural/substantive unconscionability: Does section 2–302 use the phrase "procedural unconscionability" or the phrase "substantive unconscionability"?

2.2. Contract of adhesion: While neither the U.C.C. nor the *Restatement (Second) of Contracts* uses the term "adhesion contracts," the term "adhesion contracts" is widely used in cases and adhesion contracts are widely used in the "real world." Have any of the cases we have previously considered in this book involved "adhesion contracts"? Have you ever been party to an "adhesion contract"?

3. Note

As this case illustrates, in the real world, a litigant does not limit herself to a single, contract law concept. For example, in *Hooters v. Phillips, supra,* we considered a successful challenge to an arbitration agreement based on the concept of consideration. That case, like most of the cases in this book, has been aggressively edited; you read only the portion of the opinion on consideration. In the real case, Ms. Phillips also argued, and the court found, that the arbitration agreement was an unconscionable contract of adhesion. A law review article advocates teaching unconscionability through agreements to arbitrate employment claims: "Testing the social utility of these arbitration agreements in the employer-employee context should provoke lively inquiry along with serious analysis, and ultimately provide a most interesting and challenging vehicle for teaching unconscionability." Susan A. Fitzgibbon, *Teaching Unconscionability Through Agreements to Arbitrate Employment Claims,* 44 ST. LOUIS. U. L.J. 1401 (2000).

4. Connections

4.1. With *Hill* and *Klocek*: Are there important factual differences between *Hill* and *Brower*? Between *Klocek* and *Brower*?

4.2. With *Angel v. Murray* and *2–209*: Is this case, like *Angel v. Murray,* a contract modification case?

4.3. With *Valley Medical Specialists v. Farber*: Does this case illustrate the "blue pencil" concept discussed in the *Valley Medical Specialist* case?

SECTION 7: CONTRACT LAW REASONS FOR NOT ENFORCING AGREEMENTS: MISTAKE

All agreements are based on various factual assumptions. Sometimes, these assumptions can be found in the terms of the agreement, and the terms of the agreement sometimes spell out whether a party can cancel the agreement if such an express factual assumption turns out to be erroneous.

It is unlikely, however, that even the most comprehensive commercial agreement sets out all of the factual assumptions of the parties. And, agreements prepared by the parties themselves are likely to omit many if not most factual assumptions. This part of the book focuses on such mistaken, unstated factual assumptions.

Assume that (before Epstein lost his jobs in Dallas) Epstein, Markell, and Ponoroff agreed that they will spend two summers in Dallas working on the contracts book. Subsequently, Markell and Ponoroff try to get out of the agreement to work in Dallas, alleging that they erroneously believed that the women in Dallas would all be like the woman in their favorite movie, "Debbie Does Dallas"—*i.e.*, that all women would have "big hair."[1]

What factual issues and legal questions are presented by this hypothetical? The hypothetical and the cases in this section raise three core problems for courts and lawyers.

First, there is the problem of proof. How can a lawyer prove what her client was thinking about but did not say when he entered into the agreement?

Second, there is problem of policy. Why should courts excuse a person from doing what she agreed to do because of a mistaken, unstated factual assumption? Is the concern conceptual—mistake somehow prevents mutual assent, *i.e.*, no meeting of the minds? Is the concern ethical—it is somehow unfair for one party to benefit from mistaken, factual assumptions? Is the concern economic—the law should reward efficient bargaining behavior, whatever that is?

Third, there is the related problem of "rules." Once the courts have decided what the relevant policy consideration(s) is (are), what rule with respect to relief for unstated factual assumptions advances that policy? Should it matter whether the mistake relates to "quality" or "nature"? Whether the mistake is a mistake of judgment or a clerical error? Whether the mistake relates to facts of law? Whether both parties have made the same mistake?

SHERWOOD v. WALKER

Supreme Court of Michigan
66 Mich. 568, 33 N.W. 919 (1887)

MORSE, J.

Replevin for a cow. Suit commenced in justice's court; Judgment for plaintiff; Appealed to circuit court of Wayne county, and verdict and judgment for plaintiff in that court. The defendants bring error, and set out 25 assignments of the same.

     * * *

---

1. In a July 14, 2005, DALLAS MORNING NEWS article about Dallas' new plan to attract tourists to Dallas because of museums and the arts, Dallas's Mayor, Laura Miller, said: "Dallas and Fort Worth are no longer just about big hair, shopping, football and J.R. [Ewing]." 2005 WLNR 11031451.

The Walkers are importers and breeders of polled Angus cattle.

The plaintiff is a banker living at Plymouth, in Wayne county. He called upon the defendants at Walkerville for the purchase of some of their stock, but found none there that suited him. Meeting one of the defendants afterwards, he was informed that they had a few head upon this Greenfield farm. He was asked to go out and look at them, with the statement at the time that they were probably barren, and would not breed.

May 5, 1886, plaintiff went out to Greenfield and saw the cattle. A few days thereafter, he called upon one of the defendants with the view of purchasing a cow, known as "Rose 2d of Aberlone." After considerable talk, it was agreed that defendants would telephone Sherwood at his home in Plymouth in reference to the price. The second morning after this talk he was called up by telephone, and the terms of the sale were finally agreed upon. He was to pay five and one-half cents per pound, live weight, fifty pounds shrinkage. He was asked how he intended to take the cow home, and replied that he might ship her from King's cattle-yard. He requested defendants to confirm the sale in writing, which they did by sending him the following letter:

Walkerville, May 15, 1886.

T. C. Sherwood,

President, etc.,—

Dear Sir: We confirm sale to you of the cow Rose 2d of Aberlone, lot 56 of our catalogue, at five and a half cents per pound, less fifty pounds shrink. We inclose herewith order on Mr. Graham for the cow. You might leave check with him, or mail to us here, as you prefer.

Yours truly,

Hiram Walker & Sons.

The order upon Graham inclosed in the letter read as follows:

Walkerville, May 15, 1886.

George Graham: You will please deliver at King's cattle-yard to Mr. T. C. Sherwood, Plymouth, the cow Rose 2d of Aberlone, lot 56 of our catalogue. Send halter with cow, and have her weighed.

Yours truly,

Hiram Walker & Sons.

On the twenty-first of the same month the plaintiff went to defendants' farm at Greenfield, and presented the order and letter to Graham, who informed him that the defendants had instructed him not to deliver the cow. Soon after, the plaintiff tendered to Hiram Walker, one of the defendants, $80, and demanded the cow. Walker refused to take the money or deliver the cow. The plaintiff then instituted this suit.

* * *

It appears from the record that both parties supposed this cow was barren and would not breed, and she was sold by the pound for an insignificant sum as compared with her real value if a breeder. She was evidently sold and purchased on the relation of her value for beef, unless the plaintiff had learned of her true condition, and concealed such knowledge from the defendants. Before the plaintiff secured possession of the animal, the defendants learned that she was with calf, and therefore of great value, and undertook to rescind the sale by refusing to deliver her. The question arises whether they had a right to do so.

The circuit judge ruled that this fact did not avoid the sale, and it made no difference whether she was barren or not. I am of the opinion that the court erred in this holding. I know that this is a close question, and the dividing line between the adjudicated cases is not easily discerned. But it must be considered as well settled that a party who has given an apparent consent to a contract of sale may refuse to execute it, or he may avoid it after it has been completed, if the assent was founded, or the contract made, upon the mistake of a material fact,—such as the subject-matter of the sale, the price, or some collateral fact materially inducing the agreement; and this can be done when the mistake is mutual.

If there is a difference or misapprehension as to the substance of the thing bargained for; if the thing actually delivered or received is different in substance from the thing bargained for and intended to be sold,—then there is no contract; but if it be only a difference in some quality or accident, even though the mistake may have been the actuating motive to the purchaser or seller, or both of them, yet the contract remains binding.

The difficulty in every case is to determine whether the mistake or misapprehension is as to the substance of the whole contract, going, as it were, to the root of the matter, or only to some point, even though a material point, an error as to which does not affect the substance of the whole consideration.

It has been held, in accordance with the principles above stated, that where a horse is bought under the belief that he is sound, and both vendor and vendee honestly believe him to be sound, the purchaser must stand by his bargain, and pay the full price, unless there was a warranty.

It seems to me, however, in the case made by this record, that the mistake or misapprehension of the parties went to the whole substance of the agreement. If the cow was a breeder, she was worth at least $750; if barren, she was worth not over $80. The parties would not have made the contract of sale except upon the understanding and belief that she was incapable of breeding, and of no use as a cow. It is true she is now the identical animal that they thought her to be when the contract was made; there is no mistake as to the identity of the creature. Yet the mistake was not of the mere quality of the animal, but went to the very nature of the thing. A barren cow is substantially a different creature than a breeding one. There is as much difference between them for all purposes of use as there is between an ox and a cow that is capable of breeding and giving milk. If the mutual mistake had simply related to the fact whether she was with calf or not for one season, then it might have been a good sale; but the mistake affected the character of the animal for all time, and for her present and ultimate use. She was not in fact the animal, or the kind of animal, the defendants intended to sell or the plaintiff to buy. She was not a barren cow, and, if this fact had been known, there would have been no contract. The mistake affected the substance of the whole consideration, and it must be considered that there was no contract to sell or sale of the cow as she actually was. The thing sold and bought had in fact no existence. She was sold as a beef creature would be sold; she is in fact a breeding cow, and a valuable one.

The court should have instructed the jury that if they found that the cow was sold, or contracted to be sold, upon the understanding of both parties that she was barren, and useless for the purpose of breeding, and that in fact she was not barren, but capable of breeding, then the defendants had a right to rescind, and to refuse to deliver, and the verdict should be in their favor.

The judgment of the court below must be reversed, and a new trial granted, with costs of this Court to defendants.

Sherwood, J., (dissenting.)

I do not concur in the opinion given by my brethren in this case. I think the judgments before the justice and at the circuit were right. * * *

As has already been stated by my brethren, the record shows that the plaintiff is a banker and farmer as well, carrying on a farm, and raising the best breeds of stock, and lived in Plymouth, in the county of Wayne, 23 miles from Detroit; that the defendants lived in Detroit, and were also dealers in stock of the higher grades; that they had a farm at Walkerville, in Canada, and also one in Greenfield in said county of Wayne, and upon these farms the defendants kept their stock. The Greenfield farm was about 15 miles from the plaintiff's. In the spring of 1886 the plaintiff, learning that the defendants had some "polled Angus cattle" for sale, was desirous of purchasing some of that breed, and meeting the defendants, or some of them, at Walkerville, inquired about them, and was informed that they had none at Walkerville, "but had a few head left on their farm in Greenfield, and asked the plaintiff to go and see them, stating that in all probability they were sterile and would not breed." In accordance with said request, the plaintiff, on the fifth day of May, went out and looked at the defendants' cattle at Greenfield, and found one called "Rose, Second," which he wished to purchase, and the terms were finally agreed upon at five and a half cents per pound, live weight, 50 pounds to be deducted for shrinkage. The sale was in writing, and the defendants gave an order to the plaintiff directing the man in charge of the Greenfield farm to deliver the cow to plaintiff. This was done on the fifteenth of May. On the twenty-first of May plaintiff went to get his cow, and the defendants refused to let him have her; claiming at the time that the man in charge at the farm thought the cow was with calf, and, if such was the case, they would not sell her for the price agreed upon. The record further shows that the defendants, when they sold the cow, believed the cow was not with calf, and barren; that from what the plaintiff had been told by defendants (for it does not appear he had any other knowledge or facts from which he could form an opinion) he believed the cow was farrow, but still thought she could be made to breed. The foregoing shows the entire interview and treaty between the parties as to the sterility and qualities of the cow sold to the plaintiff. The cow had a calf in the month of October.

There is no question but that the defendants sold the cow representing her of the breed and quality they believed the cow to be, and that the purchaser so understood it. And the buyer purchased her believing her to be of the breed represented by the sellers, and possessing all the qualities stated, and even more. He believed she would breed. There is no pretense that the plaintiff bought the cow for beef, and there is nothing in the record indicating that he would have bought her at all only that he thought she might be made to breed. Under the foregoing facts,—and these are all that are contained in the record material to the contract,—it is held that because it turned out that the plaintiff was more correct in his judgment as to one quality of the cow than the defendants, and a quality, too, which could not by any possibility be positively known at the time by either party to exist, the contract may be annulled by the defendants at their pleasure. I know of no law, and have not been referred to any, which will justify any such holding, and I think the circuit judge was right in his construction of the contract between the parties.

It is claimed that a mutual mistake of a material fact was made by the parties when the contract of sale was made. There was no warranty in the case of the quality of the animal. When a mistaken fact is relied upon as ground for rescinding, such fact must not only exist at the time the contract is made, but must have been known to one or both of the parties. Where there is no warranty, there can be no mistake of fact when no such fact exists, or, if in existence, neither party knew of it, or could know of it; and that is precisely this case. If the owner of a Hambletonian horse had speeded him, and was only able to make him go a mile in three minutes, and should sell him to another, believing that was his greatest speed, for $300, when the purchaser believed he could go much faster, and made the purchase for that sum, and a few days thereafter, under more favorable circumstances, the horse was driven a mile in 2 min. 16 sec., and was found to be worth $20,000, I hardly think it would be held, either at law or in equity, by any one, that the seller in such case could rescind the contract. The same legal principles apply in each case.

In this case neither party knew the actual quality and condition of this cow at the time of the sale. The defendants say, or rather said, to the plaintiff, "they had a few head left on their farm in Greenfield, and asked plaintiff to go and see them, stating to plaintiff that in all probability they were sterile and would not breed." Plaintiff did go as requested, and found there these cows, including the one purchased, with a bull. The cow had been exposed, but neither knew she was with calf or whether she would breed. The defendants thought she would not, but the plaintiff says that he thought she could be made to breed, but believed she was not with calf. The defendants sold the cow for what they believed her to be, and the plaintiff bought her as he believed she was, after the statements made by the defendants. No conditions whatever were attached to the terms of sale by either party. It was in fact as absolute as it could well be made, and I know of no precedent as authority by which this court can alter the contract thus made by these parties in writing,—interpolate in it a condition by which, if the defendants should be mistaken in their belief that the cow was barren, she could be returned to them and their contract should be annulled. It is not the duty of courts to destroy contracts when called upon to enforce them, after they have been legally made. There was no mistake of any material fact by either of the parties in the case as would license the vendors to rescind. There was no difference between the parties, nor misapprehension, as to the substance of the thing bargained for, which was a cow supposed to be barren by one party, and believed not to be by the other. As to the quality of the animal, subsequently developed, both parties were equally ignorant, and as to this each party took his chances. If this were not the law, there would be no safety in purchasing this kind of stock.

I entirely agree with my brethren that the right to rescind occurs whenever "the thing actually delivered or received is different in substance from the thing bargained for, and intended to be sold; but if it be only a difference in some quality or accident, even though the misapprehension may have been the actuating motive" of the parties in making the contract, yet it will remain binding. In this case the cow sold was the one delivered. What might or might not happen to her after the sale formed no element in the contract. * * * The judgment should be affirmed.

———————

QUESTIONS AND NOTES

1. Questions about the facts of this case

    1.1.   Who sued whom for what?

    1.2.   What is "replevin"?

    1.3.   Was Sherwood in the cattle business? Was Walker? Did that matter to the court? Should it have?

    1.4.   Could the parties have determined at the time of their agreement whether Rose was barren (or merely somewhat shy)?

    1.5.   Did either party sustain a loss because the court refused to enforce the sale agreement? Would either party have sustained a loss if the court had enforced the agreement?

    1.6.   The Michigan Supreme Court ordered a new trial with the following direction to the trial court: "the court should have instructed the jury that if they found that the cow was sold, or contracted to be sold, upon the understanding of both parties that she was barren * * * then the defendant has the right to rescind." If you were the attorney for the plaintiff/buyer, would you give up and dismiss? If not, what known facts would you emphasize at this new trial?

2. Questions about the law

    2.1. How is this case different from *Raffles*? How is the use of the contract term "Rose 2d" in this case different from the use of the contract term "Peerless" in *Raffles*?

    2.2. What is the *Sherwood v. Walker* test for determining whether a mistake is a defense to enforcement of an agreement?

    2.3. Apply that test to the following problem: Markell buys a painting from Ponoroff for $23,000. Both believe that it is a major work by Warhol. Markell later learns that while the painting is by Warhol, it is one of his minor works and is worth no more than $1,000. Markell wants out of the agreement, and he wants his money back.

    2.4. Is it possible to distinguish mistakes "running to the value," from mistakes "touching the substance of the consideration" in agreements with a subject matter other than the sale of goods? For example:

        (a) A and B agree that A will pay $240 to support C, B's child. At the time of the agreement, both A and B mistakenly assume that A is the father of C. When A later learns that D is C's father, A asserts mutual mistake of fact as a defense to enforcement of the child support agreement.

        (b) P is injured in an automobile accident caused by D. P agrees to release D from any liability for injuries from the accident for $24. At the time of the agreement, both P and D mistakenly assume that P is not seriously injured. When P later learns that she has suffered serious internal injuries, P asserts mutual mistake of fact as a defense to enforcement of the release agreement.

    2.5. Ninety-five years after *Sherwood v. Walker*, the Michigan Supreme Court, in *Lenawee County Board of Health v. Messerly*, 417 Mich. 17, 331 N.W.2d 203 (1982), described the test in *Sherwood* as "inexact and confusing," stated that *Sherwood* should be "limited to [its] facts," and adopted the rule stated in the *Restatement (Second) of Contracts*:

        We think that the better-reasoned approach is a case-by-case analysis whereby rescission is indicated when the mistaken belief relates to a basic assumption of the parties upon which the contract is made, and which materially affects the agreed performance of the parties. [Restatement (Second) of Contracts § 152.] * * * Rescission is not available, however, to relieve a party who has assumed the risk of loss, in connection with a mistake. [Restatement (Second) of Contracts §§ 152, 154.]

        More recently, the Michigan Supreme Court cited to *Sherwood v. Walker*, approvingly, *Briggs Tax Service, LLC v. Detroit Public*

Schools, 485 Mich. 69 780 N.W.2d 753, 758–9 (2010) ("seminal case"). More important, is the *Restatement (Second)* test less "inexact and confusing" than the *Sherwood* test?

3. Notes

3.1. A substantial body of case law supports an important but unacknowledged rule of contract doctrine: the proper legal response to certain problems resulting from contracts that are "incomplete" or "not fully specified" is to leave the parties alone. * * *

* * * The party who balked at performing will not be forced to proceed, but the completed exchange will not be recalled. * * *

* * * [I]f the parties have not allocated the risk of a particular windfall or casualty to one of them, neither have they allocated it to the other.

Andrew Kull, *Mistake, Frustration and the Windfall Principle of Contracts Remedies*, 43 HASTINGS L. J. 1, 5–6 (1991).

3.2. "[I]t is plain that contract law needs a rule or principle that affords relief in cases involving clerical mistakes, arithmetical blunders, misidentification of persons or property and the like. The rule, however, needs to be confined to cases of just that sort * * *—one roughly speaking that separates inadvertent errors from misjudgments." MARVIN A. CHIRELSTEIN, CONCEPTS AND CASE ANALYSIS IN THE LAW OF CONTRACTS 162 (5th 2006).

3.3 One of the reasons that many if not most contracts casebooks include this case is that, almost 60 years ago, a famous law professor, Brainerd Currie, wrote a lengthy poem in rhymed verse about the case. See Brainerd Currie, *Rose of Aberlone*, 1 Green Bag 2d 445 (1998).

ESTATE OF NELSON v. RICE

Court of Appeals of Arizona
198 Ariz. 563, 12 P.3d 238 (2000)

ESPINOSA, CHIEF JUDGE.

Plaintiff/appellant the Estate of Martha Nelson, through its copersonal representatives Edward Franz and Kenneth Newman, appeals from a summary judgment in favor of defendants/appellees Carl and Anne Rice in the Estate's action seeking rescission or reformation of the sale of two paintings to the Rices. The Estate argues that these remedies are required because the sale was based upon a mutual mistake. The Estate also contends that enforcing the sale "contract" would be unconscionable. We affirm.

Facts and Procedural History

After Martha Nelson died in February 1996, Newman and Franz, the copersonal representatives of her estate, employed Judith McKenzie–

Larson to appraise the Estate's personal property in preparation for an estate sale. McKenzie–Larson told them that she did not appraise fine art and that, if she saw any, they would need to hire an additional appraiser. McKenzie–Larson did not report finding any fine art, and relying on her silence and her appraisal, Newman and Franz priced and sold the Estate's personal property.

Responding to a newspaper advertisement, Carl Rice attended the public estate sale and paid the asking price of $60 for two oil paintings. Although Carl had bought and sold some art, he was not an educated purchaser, had never made more than $55 on any single piece, and had bought many pieces that had "turned out to be frauds, forgeries or * * * to have been [created] by less popular artists." He assumed the paintings were not originals given their price and the fact that the Estate was managed by professionals, but was attracted to the subject matter of one of the paintings and the frame of the other. At home, he compared the signatures on the paintings to those in a book of artists' signatures, noticing they "appeared to be similar" to that of Martin Johnson Heade. As they had done in the past, the Rices sent pictures of the paintings to Christie's in New York, hoping they might be Heade's work. Christie's authenticated the paintings, Magnolia Blossoms on Blue Velvet and Cherokee Roses, as paintings by Heade and offered to sell them on consignment. Christie's subsequently sold the paintings at auction for $1,072,000. After subtracting the buyer's premium and the commission, the Rices realized $911,780 from the sale.

Newman and Franz learned about the sale in February 1997 and thereafter sued McKenzie–Larson on behalf of the Estate, believing she was entirely responsible for the Estate's loss. The following November, they settled the lawsuit because McKenzie–Larson had no assets with which to pay damages. During 1997, the Rices paid income taxes of $337,000 on the profit from the sale of the paintings, purchased a home, created a family trust, and spent some of the funds on living expenses.

The Estate sued the Rices in late January 1998, alleging the sale contract should be rescinded or reformed on grounds of mutual mistake and unconscionability. In its subsequent motion for summary judgment, the Estate argued the parties were not aware the transaction had involved fine art, believing instead that the items exchanged were "relatively valueless, wall decorations." In their opposition and cross-motion, the Rices argued the Estate bore the risk of mistake, the doctrine of laches precluded reformation of the contract, and unconscionability was not a basis for rescission. The trial court concluded that, although the parties had been mistaken about the value of the paintings, the Estate bore the risk of that mistake. The court ruled the contract was not unconscionable, finding the parties had not negotiated Carl's paying the prices the Estate had set. Accordingly, the court denied the Estate's motion for summary judgment and granted the Rices' cross-motion. The Estate's motion for new trial was denied, and this appeal followed. * * *

The Estate first argues that it established a mutual mistake sufficient to permit the reformation or rescission of the sale of the paintings to the Rices.[1] A party seeking to rescind a contract on the basis of mutual mistake must show by clear and convincing evidence that the agreement should be set aside. A contract may be rescinded on the ground of a mutual mistake as to a " 'basic assumption on which both parties made the contract.' " Renner v. Kehl, 150 Ariz. 94, 97, 722 P.2d 262, 265 (1986), quoting Restatement (Second) of Contracts § 152 cmt. b (1979). Furthermore, the parties' mutual mistake must have had " 'such a material effect on the agreed exchange of performances as to upset the very bases of the contract.' " Id., quoting Restatement § 152 cmt. a. However, the mistake must not be one on which the party seeking relief bears the risk under the rules stated in § 154(b) of the Restatement.

In concluding that the Estate was not entitled to rescind the sale, the trial court found that, although a mistake had existed as to the value of the paintings, the Estate bore the risk of that mistake under § 154(b) of the Restatement, citing the example in comment a. Section 154(b) states that a party bears the risk of mistake when "he is aware, at the time the contract is made, that he has only limited knowledge with respect to the facts to which the mistake relates but treats his limited knowledge as sufficient." In explaining that provision, the Washington Supreme Court stated, "In such a situation there is no mistake. Instead, there is an awareness of uncertainty or conscious ignorance of the future.".

The Estate contends neither party bore the risk of mistake, arguing that § 154 and comment a are not applicable to these facts. In the example in comment a, the risk of mistake is allocated to the seller when the buyer discovers valuable mineral deposits on property priced and purchased as farmland. Even were we to accept the Estate's argument that this example is not analogous, comment c clearly applies here and states:

Conscious ignorance. Even though the mistaken party did not agree to bear the risk, he may have been aware when he made the contract that his knowledge with respect to the facts to which the mistake relates was limited. If he was not only so aware that his knowledge was limited but undertook to perform in the face of that awareness, he bears the risk of the mistake. It is sometimes said in such a situation that, in a sense, there was not mistake but "conscious ignorance."

Through its personal representatives, the Estate hired two appraisers, McKenzie–Larson and an Indian art expert, to evaluate the Estate's collection of Indian art and artifacts. McKenzie–Larson specifically told Newman that she did not appraise fine art. In his deposition, Newman testified that he had not been concerned that McKenzie–Larson had no expertise in fine art, believing the Estate contained nothing of "significant

---

1. Reformation is not an available remedy under these facts. It is a remedy to correct a written instrument that fails to express the terms agreed upon by the parties and "is not intended to enforce the terms of an agreement the parties never made value" except the house and the Indian art collection. Despite the knowledge that the Estate contained framed art other than the Indian art, and that McKenzie–Larson was not qualified to appraise fine art, the personal representatives relied on her to notify them of any fine art or whether a fine arts appraiser was needed. Because McKenzie–Larson did not say they needed an additional appraiser, Newman and Franz did not hire anyone qualified to appraise fine art. By relying on the opinion of someone who was admittedly unqualified to appraise fine art to determine its existence, the personal representatives consciously ignored the possibility that the Estate's assets might include fine art, thus assuming that risk. See Klas v. Van Wagoner, 829 P.2d 135, 141 n. 8 (Utah App.1992) (real estate buyers not entitled to rescind sale contract because they bore risk of mistake as to property's value; by hiring architects, decorators, and electricians to examine realty, but failing to have it appraised, purchasers executed sale contract knowing they "had only 'limited knowledge' with respect to the value of the home"). Accordingly, the trial court correctly found that the Estate bore the risk of mistake as to the paintings' value.[2]

The Estate asserts that the facts here are similar to those in Renner, in which real estate buyers sued to rescind a contract for acreage upon which they wished to commercially grow jojoba after discovering the water supply was inadequate for that purpose. The Arizona Supreme court concluded that the buyers could rescind the contract based upon mutual mistake because both the buyers and the sellers had believed there was an adequate water supply, a basic assumption underlying formation of the contract. The parties' failure to thoroughly investigate the water supply did not preclude rescission when "the risk of mistake was not allocated among the parties." 150 Ariz. at 97 n. 2, 722 P.2d at 265 n. 2. The Estate's reliance on Renner is unavailing because, as stated above, the Estate bore the risk of mistake based on its own conscious ignorance.

Furthermore, under Restatement § 154(c), the court may allocate the risk of mistake to one party "on the ground that it is reasonable in the circumstances to do so." In making this determination, "the court will consider the purposes of the parties and will have recourse to its own general knowledge of human behavior in bargain transactions." Restatement § 154 cmt. d. Here, the Estate had had ample opportunity to discover what it was selling and failed to do so; instead, it ignored the possibility that the paintings were valuable and attempted to take action only after learning of their worth as a result of the efforts of the Rices. Under these circumstances, the Estate was a victim of its own folly and it was reasonable for the court to allocate to it the burden of its mistake. * * *

The Estate also argues that enforcement of the "contract" to sell the paintings is unconscionable. The determination of a contract's unconscionability is for the trial court as a matter of law. We review that ruling de

---

2. In view of our conclusion that the Estate bore the risk of any mistake in the paintings' value, we need not address the remainder of its mutual mistake arguments.

novo. * * * 'Unconscionability includes both procedural unconscionability, i.e., something wrong in the bargaining process, and substantive unconscionability, i.e., the contract terms per se.' * * *''

[T]the Estate contends this is a case of substantive unconscionability, which concerns the actual terms of the contract and the relative fairness of the parties' obligations. Indicia of substantive unconscionability include one-sided terms that oppress or unfairly surprise an innocent party, an overall imbalance in the obligations and rights imposed by the bargain, and significant cost-price disparity. Maxwell. Unconscionability is determined as of the time the parties entered into the contract.

In refusing to rescind the sale on the basis of unconscionability, the trial court stated that, "[w]hile the results of the transaction may seem unconscionable to the [Estate] in hindsight, the terms of the contract certainly were not." We agree. The transaction involved no negotiation, the Estate dictated the terms of the contract by naming a price for each painting, and Carl paid the asking prices. " 'Courts should not assume an overly paternalistic attitude toward the parties to a contract by relieving one or another of them of the consequences of what is at worst a bad bargain * * * and in declaring the [contract] at issue here unconscionable, we would be doing exactly that.'

Affirmed.

QUESTIONS

1. Questions about the facts

     1.1.   Who made a "mistake"? Did the Estate make a "mistake"? Did the Estate's appraiser, Judith McKenzie–Larson, make a "mistake"?

     1.2.   Is it relevant that the Estate settled with Judith McKenzie–Larson because she had no assets?

     1.3.   Do we know that the Rices were mistaken as to the value of the paintings?

2. Questions about law

     2.1.   How would the court that decided *Sherwood v. Walker* decide this case?

     2.2.   What is a "mistake" as the term is used in the Restatement? What language in the Restatement was important to the Arizona Court of Appeals in deciding this case?

In *Sherwood* and *Estate of Nelson*, the courts considered the argument that a mutual mistake should be a defense to enforcement of an agreement. Unilateral mistake occurs when only one party to the agreement has an erroneous assumption concerning an important aspect of the deal that makes the deal far less favorable to him than he had assumed. Because, in these cases, only one party is mistaken and the other is "innocent," courts have traditionally been more reluctant to grant relief based on unilateral mistake.

GRENALL v. UNITED OF OMAHA LIFE INSURANCE COMPANY

Court of Appeals of California, First District
165 Cal.App.4th 188, 80 Cal.Rptr.3d 609 (2008)

[Jean M. Simes (Simes) died of cancer less than four months after purchasing an annuity that provided for monthly benefit payments as long as she lived. On October 2, 2001, Simes paid a single premium of $321,131. United then issued a policy for a single premium immediate annuity, effective the date of Simes' application. On January 25, 2002, after receiving three benefit payments, Simes was diagnosed with ovarian cancer. She died less than a week later on January 30, 2002.

The administrators of her estate (the Estate), sued to rescind the annuity, alleging a mistake of fact, namely, that Simes was unaware at the time of the contract that she was terminally ill. The trial court granted summary judgment in favor of the issuing company, defendant United of Omaha Life Insurance Company (United). The Estate appealed. United filed a motion for sanctions with its respondent's brief.]

STEIN, J.:

The facts on which the Estate relied below purport to show the following: (1) Simes did not know at the time of her application and during the statutory rescission period that she had terminal ovarian cancer that would result in her death four months later; (2) Simes's illness affected her ability to make decisions; and (3) Simes did not receive a copy of the annuity policy until mid-November 2001. The sole issue argued by the Estate on appeal is whether these facts provide a legal basis for rescission of the life annuity contract based on a mistake of fact. We hold, as a matter of law, that they do not, for the following reasons.

California law permits rescission of a contract when a party's consent is given by mistake. On this basis, the Estate asserts a right to rescind the annuity policy, alleging that Simes would not have entered the contract but for a mistake of fact, specifically, the terminal illness she did not know she had. A mistake of fact may consist of a "[b]elief in the present existence of a thing material to the contract, which does not exist." (Civ. Code, § 1577.) The alleged mistake therefore may be characterized as Simes's erroneous belief at the time of the contract that she was in good health and had a reasonable life expectancy.

A mistake of this nature does not support a claim for rescission. The Estate asserts a unilateral mistake and offers no evidence that United had reason to know of or caused the mistake. Accordingly, to prevail at trial, the Estate would have been required to prove the following: (1) Simes was mistaken regarding a basic assumption upon which she made the contract; (2) the mistake materially affected the agreed exchange of performances in a way that was adverse to Simes; (3) Simes did not bear the risk of the mistake; and (4) the effect of the mistake was such that enforcement of the contract would be unconscionable. The facts on which the Estate relies demonstrate that it cannot establish the third of these elements.

We conclude, based on the nature of the contract and the alleged mistake, that Simes bore the risk of the mistake, as a matter of law. A contracting party bears the risk of a mistake when the agreement so provides or when the party is aware of having only limited knowledge of the facts relating to the mistake but treats this limited knowledge as sufficient. Additionally, the court may allocate the risk to a party because it is reasonable under the circumstances to do so. The contract in this case does not expressly assign the risk of the alleged mistake. Nonetheless, parties who contract for "life contingent" benefits necessarily do so based on limited knowledge of the very facts about which Simes was mistaken. We cannot fix the length of our lives or even the state of our health with certainty, and the parties knew that their expectations in this regard were at best an educated guess.

The allocation of this risk to Simes is reasonable because such risks are an inherent part of life annuity contracts, which reflect, at their essence, a longevity wager measured by average life expectancy. (See Rest.2d Contracts, § 154, illus. 3: reasonable allocation of risk that annuitant has incurable disease and will live no more than a year.) Annuitants who survive the average life expectancy receive benefits beyond the premium; those who die earlier do not recoup their investments. Both risks are contemplated by the parties and, indeed, are an integral part of their bargain.

* * *

Our sister states recognize that allocation of the risk to the annuitant in these circumstances is not only reasonable but a practical necessity. * * * In light of these authorities, we hold that Simes bore the risk of the alleged mistake regarding her health and life expectancy at the time of the annuity contract. Because the Estate cannot establish an essential element of its rescission claim, summary judgment is proper. Accordingly, we need not discuss the other elements of this claim or decide the additional grounds for affirmance urged by United in its respondent's brief and its related motion to dismiss.

Finally, although we reject the Estate's arguments, because there is no California authority directly on point, we do not find them so wholly devoid of merit as to warrant the imposition of sanctions.

Questions, Note and Connections

1. Question about the facts

   1.1. What was the Estate's "best" fact?

   1.2. Did we know whether United knew, at the time of contract, that Simes was terminally ill? Was that relevant?

2. Question about the law

   2.1. The opinion refers to an illustration to *Restatement (Second) Contracts* section 154. That section addresses when a party bears the risk of a mistake, mutual or unilateral. Section 153 is entitled, "When a Mistake of One Party Makes a Contract Voidable". It provides:

   > **Where a mistake of one party at the time a contract was made as to a basic assumption on which he made the contract has a material effect on the agreed exchange of performances that is adverse to him, the contract is voidable by him if he does not bear the risk of the mistake under the rule stated in § 154, and**

   > **(a) the effect of the mistake is such that enforcement of the contract would be unconscionable, or**

   > **(b) the other party had reason to know of the mistake or his fault caused the mistake.**

   Why didn't the California court rule for the Estate on the ground that the "effect of the mistake is such that enforcement of the contract would be unconscionable"?

3. Note

   When a contractor submits a bid in which the owner has reason to know that a mistake has been made, courts consistently hold that such a unilateral mistake prevents contract formation. Professor Kull explains such cases on the basis that "the owner cannot form a contract on terms he knows the contractor does not intend." Andrew Kull, *Unilateral Mistake: The Baseball Card Case,* 70 Wash. U. L.Q. 57, 70 (1992). Professor Corbin offered a different explanation for the same result:

   Suppose * * * a bidding contractor makes an offer to supply specified goods or to do specified work for a definitely named price, and that he was caused to name this price by an antecedent error of computation. If, before acceptance, the offeree knows, or has reason to know, that a material error has been made, he is seldom mean enough to accept; and if he does accept, the courts have no difficulty in throwing him out. He is not permitted 'to snap up' such an offer and profit thereby. If, without knowledge of the mistake and before any revocation, he has accepted the offer, it is natural for him to feel a sense of disappointment at not getting a good bargain, when the offeror insists on withdrawal; but a just and reasonable man will not insist upon profiting by the other's mistake. There are now many decisions to the effect that if the error was a substantial one and notice is given before the other party has made such a change of position that he cannot be put substantially in status quo, the bargain is voidable and rescission will be decreed.

3 ARTHUR LINTON CORBIN, CORBIN ON CONTRACTS § 609, at 680–82 (1960).

4. Connections

   4.1. Mutual mistake and unilateral mistake. Why is *Grenall* a "unilateral mistake" case and *Estate of Nelson* a "mutual mistake" case? Would the holding of Estate of Nelson have been different if the court had treated the facts as unilateral mistake and applied *Restatement (Second) Contracts* section 153?

   4.2. Unilateral mistake and unconscionability

   How is the law of unilateral mistake similar to and different from the law of unconscionability? The California Supreme Court provides this possible, partial answer:

   The standards of unconscionability warranting rescission for mistake are similar to those for unconscionability * * * An unconscionable contract ordinarily involves both a procedural and a substantive element: (1) oppression or surprise due to unequal bargaining power, and (2) overly harsh or one-sided results) Nevertheless, " 'a sliding scale is invoked which disregards the regularity of the procedural process of the contract formation, that creates the terms, in proportion to the greater harshness or unreasonableness of the substantive terms themselves.' [Citations.]" *(Ibid.)* For example, the Restatement Second of Contracts states that "[i]nadequacy of consideration does not of itself invalidate a bargain, but gross disparity in the values exchanged may be an important factor in a determination that a contract is unconscionable and may be sufficient ground, without more, for denying specific performance." *(Rest.2d Contracts, § 208*, com. c, p. 108.) In ascertaining whether rescission is warranted for a unilateral mistake of fact, substantive unconscionability often will constitute the determinative factor, because the oppression and surprise ordinarily results from the mistake—not from inequality in bargaining power. Accordingly, even though defendant is not the weaker party to the contract and its mistake did not result from unequal bargaining power, defendant was surprised by the mistake, and in these circumstances overly harsh or one-sided results are sufficient to establish unconscionability entitling defendant to rescission. Donovan, v. RRL Corp, 27 P.3d 702, 723 (2001).

   4.3. Reason to know unilateral mistake and nondisclosure (and *Hadley v Baxendale*). If B is making an agreement with A, and B realizes that A is making a mistake, does B have a duty to disclose the mistake to A? How is a fact pattern involving a known unilateral mistake different from a fact pattern involving nondisclosure? Professor Michael Borden discusses these questions in a recent law review article: "This paper will examine some theoretical aspects of contractual non-disclosure and the related doctrine of unilateral mistake. These two legal rubrics are conceptually similar; each is concerned with the degree to which parties must communicate their understandings about the nature of the contract into which they are about to enter. If one party fails to reveal enough information, the other party may enter into the agreement under a misunderstanding and consequently may attempt to avoid contractual liability on the basis of mistake or on a theory of nondisclosure. The law of contracts clearly attaches a great deal of importance to ensuring that contracting parties have a mutual understanding about their agreement—a meeting of the minds—for that is the cornerstone of mutual assent. Indeed, one of the foundational theoretical goals of contract doctrine is to establish rules of law that will induce parties to reveal information that will reduce the cost of contracting and minimize the negative effects of breach. This "information forcing" concept * * * [is] the animating principle behind the rule of *Hadley v Baxendale*, which limits consequential damages to those that are foreseeable (i.e., those that have been communicated by the party seeking damages)." Michael J. Borden, *Mistake and Nondisclosure in a Model of Two–Sided Informational Inputs*, 73 Mo. L. Rev. 667 (2007).

CHAPTER FIVE

WHAT ARE THE TERMS OF THE DEAL?

■ ■ ■

Up to this point, this book has focused on whether there is a contract. From here on, we, for the most part, assume that a contract exists.

In this chapter we shift our focus to the content of the contract. More specifically to the questions of (1) what are the terms of the contract, and (2) what do the contract terms mean.

Lawyers deal with these terms and questions much more frequently than they deal with the question of whether there was a contract. For the deal lawyer, his daily focus is the task of drafting language so that a court or jury will construe the contract in the way his client intended. For the trial lawyer, the parallel focus is the devising of strategies that will lead to a court or jury accepting her client's position with respect to the terms of a contract drafted long ago by another lawyer. To accomplish either of these goals, the deft lawyer will know and understand how courts will approach and answer the questions of (1) what are the terms of the contract and (2) what do those terms mean.

SECTION 1: TERMS OF THE CONTRACT THAT ARE NOT WORDS OF THE PARTIES: TRADE CUSTOMS AND USAGE

As stated on the first page of this casebook, there is a tendency to confuse the written paper signed by the parties with the contract that binds them. It is an easy mistake to make; everyone calls the signed paper "the contract." But that paper is, at best, only *evidence* of the contract. That is, the contract is represented by that paper; it is not that paper. Otherwise, if you tore the paper up (or spilled coffee on it) you would also tear up or water down the parties' obligations. While that may be the case with some types of obligations (such as checks or other negotiable instruments), that is not the case with regular, everyday contracts.

So what is a contract? To go back again to the beginning of this book, according to the *Restatement (Second) of Contracts*, it is "a promise or set of promises for the breach of which the law gives a remedy, or the

performance of which the law in some way recognizes as a duty."
Restatement (Second) of Contracts § 1.

Where do we find the promises recognized as the contract? There are many sources. The most important, but not exclusive, source of contract terms is the words of the parties, be they written words or oral words.

We'll have lots more to say about the words of the parties as a source of terms later on. In particular, Section 2 of this chapter looks at the parol evidence rule, which governs the relationship between the written paper signed by the parties and earlier written or oral words of the parties

Initially, our focus will be on what seems to be an oxymoron: promises that are a part of the contract (and thus enforceable) which are not derived from the words of the parties. The term at issue in the next case was one which the parties never actually uttered. In reading the case, ask yourself, "Self, why did the court make 'risk of probe loss is on the driller' a contract term, instead of a rule of law applicable to all contracts for drilling test holes?"

THREADGILL v. PEABODY COAL CO.

Court of Appeals of Colorado
34 Colo.App. 203, 526 P.2d 676 (1974)

PIERCE, JUDGE.

Defendant, Peabody Coal Company (Peabody), appeals from a judgment holding it liable for damages for the loss of certain equipment owned by the plaintiff which was lost in the process of probing test holes drilled by Peabody. Plaintiff was an independent contractor hired by Peabody to probe the test holes for the purpose of locating coal deposits. After the test holes were sunk to the appropriate depth by Peabody, plaintiff's employees lowered a probing device to the bottom of each hole and proceeded to "log" the hole as the probe was retrieved. "Logging" consists of gathering soil samples and other data. During the probing of one of the test holes by the employees of the plaintiff, the probing device became stuck in the hole. Employees of Peabody then commenced recovery operations which were unsuccessful.

Plaintiff's complaint alleged two claims for relief: (1) that the loss of the probe was due to defendant's negligence in attempting to recover the probe, and (2) that the defendant was obligated under a contract between the parties to pay the value of any equipment owned by the plaintiff lost in the course of the probing operation. Defendant filed an answer containing several defenses and pleaded a counterclaim for expenses incurred in the recovery attempt based on the alleged negligence of plaintiff's employees.

Upon trial to the court, the court found that an oral contract for the services of the plaintiff did exist, but that there had been no express agreement, oral or otherwise, upon the placement of the risk of loss of the probing device. The court then found that the plaintiff had satisfactorily established "a certain practice or custom in the drilling industry which places the risk of probe loss on the driller (here the defendant) where, as here, there is no agreement otherwise." Furthermore, the court found that Peabody's employees had not been negligent in conducting the recovery operation but made no finding as to any negligence on the part of the plaintiff, or his employees. However, the court ruled that the negligence was immaterial under the trade practice, and thus, in effect, placed a duty of strict liability upon Peabody. The court then entered judgment in favor of the plaintiff and dismissed Peabody's counterclaim.

I

Peabody's first allegation of error is that the evidence is not sufficient to support the trial court's finding that a custom or trade usage existed that was binding on defendant.

In order to bind a party by a usage in the trade, it must be shown either that the party had actual knowledge of the existence of the trade usage or that the usage is so well established as to justify a finding of constructive knowledge. * * * The issue of knowledge of the trade usage, whether actual or constructive, is generally a question to be decided by the trier of fact. * * * Peabody's representatives testified that they had no knowledge of the alleged custom, and Peabody argues that, to show constructive knowledge, the custom or usage must be demonstrated to be "universal" and "notorious." Such terms have been used where the evidence was insufficient to support a finding that the alleged custom even existed. * * * However, these requirements are only applicable to the English law of custom by which accepted practices have developed into substantive rules of law. They do not apply to a trade usage which is offered only as evidence as to the intent of the parties. * * *

The proper test applicable to this issue is stated in the more recent case of *Ryan v. Fitzpatrick Drilling Co.*, 139 Colo. 471, 342 P.2d 1040. That is, to be binding upon a party, a trade usage must be "sufficiently general so that the parties could be said to have contracted with reference to it." *See Lorraine Mfg. Co. v. Allen Mfg. Co., supra.*[1]

Although contradicted on some points by Peabody's evidence, each of the plaintiff's witnesses testified as to his experience in the trade within the geographical locale of the instant operation and to the existence, within that locale, of the alleged trade usage. These witnesses further explained the usage by pointing out that the driller has primary control over the drilling of the hole and that since the prober has no connection with the operation until he begins the "logging" process, he must rely on the driller's judgment as to the readiness of the hole to receive the probe.

---

1. While the Uniform Commercial Code does not govern this case, we think it significant to note that the drafters of the Code in defining a trade usage have adopted a similar standard focusing on the likelihood that the parties contracted with reference to the usage. *See* Uniform Commercial Code § 1–205(2) (C.R.S.1963, 155–1–205(2)). They have also rejected the "universal" and "notorious" language. Uniform Commercial Code § 1–205(2) (Comment 5). [These provisions are now found in Section 1–303 of the Uniform Commercial Code. Eds.]

Furthermore, once a probe becomes lodged in the hole, the prober must rely on the driller's equipment for recovery operations. The testimony of these witnesses also indicated that the loss of equipment was generally considered to be a cost to the owner of the land being probed; in this case, Peabody.

Finally, as pointed out by the trial court, the actions of the parties with regard to the recovery operation were consistent with the alleged usage. Such actions tending to demonstrate the intent of the parties are proper considerations for the fact finder. * * *

We hold that the evidence produced at trial was sufficient to support a finding of a general trade usage which permitted the inference that the parties must have contracted with reference to it.

Peabody also argues, however, that the evidence failed to establish that the alleged trade usage was sufficiently certain to permit its application to the facts before the court. It cites testimony to the effect that, in some cases, the driller is obligated only to provide a certain number of "rig hours" for the purpose of recovering lost tools and that the obligation of the driller does not extend to liability for the value of unrecoverable tools. However, this testimony referred to cases in which the parties expressly agreed with respect to the obligations of the parties regarding the loss of the contractor's tools. Other witnesses testified that in the majority of logging jobs, as was the case here, no written agreement is actually entered into by the parties. Furthermore, the alleged trade usage which plaintiff sought to establish, and which the trial court found, provided a rule in cases in which no express agreement was reached by the parties.

The evidence in the record was sufficient to support the finding of the trial court that, in the absence of other factors, the trade usage would place on the driller the responsibility for the loss of the probing device in addition to the cost of the recovery attempt. That finding will not be disturbed upon review.

II

Peabody, however, also asserts that even though the trial court found the trade usage, the issue of plaintiff's negligence is not removed from the case. We agree with this contention.

In order for a trade custom or usage to be binding upon a person who has not expressly agreed to be bound by it, it must be reasonable. * * * This requirement in the law of trade usage generally specifies only that the usage not be illegal or in violation of public policy. * * *

The public policy of our state dictates that, generally, parties cannot contract away their potential liability for their own negligence. * * * If, under most circumstances, one cannot by express contract, immunize himself from the consequences of his own negligence, then an implied agreement to that effect arising out of a general custom or trade usage will not be given effect. * * * Only where such agreement is entered into by parties of equal bargaining power and where the agreement is express and unequivocal, have such clauses been held enforceable. * * * Here, there is no evidence in the record of such circumstances and the trial court erred in ruling that the trade usage applied regardless of the negligence of the parties. To the extent that the trade usage before us purports to relieve the contractor of the consequences of his own negligence, it is in conflict with the express public policy of this state.

Therefore, we hold that the findings of the trial court regarding the existence and generality of a trade usage placing the risk of loss upon the driller or owner in the absence of an express agreement are affirmed. The finding that negligence was made irrelevant by such usage is rejected, as a matter of law, and the case is remanded for further proceedings not inconsistent with this opinion.

COYTE and SMITH, JJ., concur.

Judgment affirmed in part, reversed in part, and cause remanded with directions.

QUESTIONS AND NOTE

1. Questions about the facts of this case
    1.1. Was it important that the trial court found that, while there was an oral contract, the oral contract did not address the risk of loss of Threadgill's gear?
    1.2. Did the court find that Peabody had no knowledge of the alleged custom?

2. Questions about the law
    2.1. The court makes a distinction between "accepted practices [that] have developed into substantive rules of law" and "trade usage which is offered only as evidence as to the intent of the parties." What is the difference?
    2.2. If on remand the court finds that the trade practice did contemplate indemnity against Threadgill's negligence, what result? Does your answer change if the trial court also finds that Threadgill, although protected by the trade usage, was not negligent with respect to the probe stuck in Peabody's hole?
    2.3. If you were Threadgill's lawyer, what type of defense would you prepare on remand?

3. Note

    The *UNIDROIT Principles of International Commercial Contracts*, finalized in 1994, state that the "contractual obligations of the parties may be express or implied" (Article 5.1), and that implied obligations "stem from: (a) the nature and purpose of the contract; (b) practices established between the parties and usages; (c) good faith and fair dealing; (d) reasonableness." (Article 5.2). Given that such principles are meant to cover international contracts involving large sums of money, don't these principles seem to undercut certainty in commercial matters? Or do you suppose that they are just a reflection of actual practice?

———

Once you become accustomed to the baseline assumption that contracts need not be in writing (unless there are Statute of Frauds considerations), and that courts hold that customs, practices and past dealings form the basis of contract terms, even if they are not discussed, it is a short hop to thinking that determining contract terms is not much different from nailing jelly to a wall.

Resist that thought. There is *a measure* of order.

SECTION 2:   WORDS OF THE PARTIES THAT ARE NOT IN THE FINAL WRITTEN VERSION OF THE DEAL: THE PAROL EVIDENCE RULE

Where, unlike *Threadgill*, there is a final written version of the deal, contract law affords a great deal of deference to that final writing. The court's determining that there is final written version of the deal triggers a body of law with the misleading name, "parol evidence rule." We will use this "parol evidence rule" to answer questions similar to (but more difficult than) the following:

1. S and B enter into a written contract that provides that each week in 2011, S will deliver 100 chickens to B, and B will pay S $3 for each chicken. B later initiates litigation to reform the contract contending that S told her before the contract was entered into that S would deliver as many chickens as B wants for $3 a chicken. Should the court grant S's motion to dismiss B's suit on the ground that the terms in the written contract should be conclusive and exclusive?

2. S and B enter into a written contract that provides that each week in 2011, S will deliver 100 chickens to B, and B will pay S $3 for each chicken. The written contract is silent as to how the chickens are to be wrapped. B later sues to reform the contract contending that S told her before the contract was entered into that S would deliver the chickens wrapped for freezing. Should the court grant S's motion to dismiss B's suit on the ground the contract terms are limited to the terms in the written contract?

3. Same facts as 2 except that the written contract provides: "This is the complete and final agreement between the parties and super-

sedes any previous understandings and agreements between the parties, written or oral.''

The parol evidence rule is a rule of venerable heritage, as illustrated by the following explanation of its purpose, written by Chief Justice Popham almost four hundred years ago, but still relevant today:

> It would be inconvenient that matters in writing made by advice and on consideration, and which finally import the certain truth of the agreement of the parties should be controlled by averment of the parties to be proved by the uncertain testimony of slippery memory. And it would be dangerous to purchasers and farmers, and all others in such cases, if such averments against matter in writing should be admitted.

The Countess of Rutland's Case, 5 Co. 26a, 77 Eng. Rep. 89 (K.B. 1604).

Regardless of this salutary purpose, the effect of the parol evidence rule is to exclude evidence that you or I might think relevant to the interpretation of a contract. It is also full of (some might say riddled with) exceptions and shadings. Before stating the rule, however, it is wise to keep in mind the following statement about the rule by Professor James Thayer, as true now as it was when it was written over one hundred years ago: "Few things are darker than this, or fuller of subtle difficulties." JAMES B. THAYER, A PRELIMINARY TREATISE ON EVIDENCE AT THE COMMON LAW 390 (1898).

A. COMMON LAW

For starters, the name "parol evidence rule" is a misnomer. As we will see, there is more than one rule, and it is not limited to parol statements. Moreover, it is more than just a rule of evidence. As Comment a to Section 213 of the *Restatement (Second) of Contracts* states:

> *[T]he parol evidence rule * * * is not a rule of evidence but a rule of substantive law. Nor is it a rule of interpretation; it defines the subject matter of interpretation. It renders inoperative prior written agreements as well as prior oral agreements. Where writings relating to the same subject matter are assented to as parts of one transaction, both form part of the integrated agreement. Where an agreement is partly oral and partly written, the writing is at most a partially integrated agreement.*

So what is this substantive rule of law? As with most rules in this course, there is no definitive statement of the parol evidence rule—it is a rule of common law origin, which means that it must be derived from cases applying it. For purposes of our study, however, we can start with the *Restatement (Second)*, as it provides a workable statement of the general rule:

§ 213 Effect of Integrated Agreement on Prior Agreements (Parol Evidence Rule)

(1) A binding integrated agreement discharges prior agreements to the extent that it is inconsistent with them.

(2) A binding completely integrated agreement discharges prior agreements to the extent that they are within its scope.

This text seems fine, but mentions an "integrated agreement." Indeed, the statement of the rule in Section 213 makes the presence of a "completely" or "partially" integrated agreement critical to the application of the parol evidence rule.

So what's an integrated agreement? This next case explores that concept in the context of an agreement signed by a Super Bowl quarterback—someone who obviously can afford good legal talent.

When reading this case, keep in mind some practices often followed in large acquisitions. First, the parties will often sign a binding contract to acquire a business well ahead of the time that they anticipate the actual change of ownership will occur. You may have seen this in buying a house—first you sign the contract, and then later on you "close" by actually transferring title. The interim period allows the parties to finalize their financing, take care of obtaining permissions that may be necessary to effectuate the transfer and other tasks.

Second, many businesses borrow money. When ownership changes, the borrowers may be a better or worse credit risk, and thus it is an event that lenders care deeply about. Accordingly, lenders customarily draft their loan documents to require payment in full whenever ownership changes. In actual practice, however, the lender may be persuaded by the buyer to "rollover" the loan, or agree to let the new owners assume the debt outstanding. The lender may agree if it is comfortable in the expertise of the new owners, or if it is comfortable that it, as a lender, will be paid in full before or at the same time the exiting owners are paid anything.

In this case, both of these assumptions come into play. As in most matters financial, it is a good idea to "follow the money" when reading this case; keep in mind not just who is making contracts, but who is benefitting, and when, from the contracts made.

NELSON v. ELWAY

Supreme Court of Colorado
908 P.2d 102 (1995)

CHIEF JUSTICE VOLLACK delivered the Opinion of the Court.

We granted certiorari to review the decision by the court of appeals in *Nelson v. Elway*, No. 93CA0629 (Colo. App. May 26, 1994), affirming in part and reversing in part the trial court's grant of summary judgment in favor of the respondents. The court of appeals affirmed the trial court's entry of summary judgment in the respondents' favor as to the petitioners' allegations of breach of contract. * * * We * * * affirm. * * *

I.

Mel T. Nelson (Nelson) was the president and sole shareholder of two car dealerships, Metro Auto and Metro Toyota, Inc. General Motors Acceptance Corporation (GMAC) provided all the financing for both dealerships. In the first half of 1990, both dealerships were experiencing financial difficulties. In July of 1990, Nelson retained John J. Pico and the Aspen Brokerage Company (Pico) to represent him in the selling or refinancing of one or both of the dealerships.

In early 1991, Pico, acting on behalf of Nelson and Metro Toyota, began negotiations with John A. Elway, Jr. (Elway) and Rodney L. Buscher (Buscher) regarding the sale of Metro Toyota and the property upon which it was situated. On March 14, 1991, pursuant to those negotiations, Elway and Buscher signed a "Buy–Sell Agreement" and a separate real estate contract to purchase Metro Toyota. The closing was scheduled for April 15, 1991.

Soon after the signing of these documents, Pico asked Nelson if he would be willing to sell both Metro Auto and Metro Toyota to Elway. Nelson stated that he would be willing to sell both dealerships along with the land upon which they were located if he received sufficient personal remuneration. Pico then began negotiating with Elway and Buscher regarding the sale of both dealerships. Through these negotiations it became apparent that Elway and Buscher were unwilling or unable to pay the full purchase price for the dealerships and the land upon which they were located.

In order to consummate the transaction, Pico suggested to Nelson that Elway and Buscher reimburse Nelson for his interest in Metro Toyota by paying Nelson $50 per vehicle sold by both dealerships for a period of seven years commencing on May 1, 1991. In exchange for this compensation arrangement, Elway and Buscher would purchase Metro Auto from Nelson at a greatly reduced purchase price. These terms, referred to by the parties as the "Service Agreement," were reduced to writing but never signed by the parties. Subsequently, on March 16, 1991, the parties signed a "Buy–Sell Agreement" and a separate real estate contract for the purchase of Metro Auto. This written, signed agreement did not incorporate the terms of the Service Agreement.

By early 1991, the dealerships owed GMAC over $3 million. In order to protect its security interests, on April 3, 1991, GMAC required Nelson to execute agreements referred to as "keeper letters," allowing GMAC significant control over the dealerships. GMAC imposed this requirement as consideration for its agreement to pay [sic. Instead of "pay," this probably should read "finance for Elway" or "rollover and charge to

Elway." Eds.] in excess of $890,000 in debt owed by Metro Auto and Metro Toyota at the closing of the sale of the dealerships to Elway and Buscher. Nelson knew that execution of these letters would preclude his ability to file for bankruptcy protection and proceed through re-organization. He alleges that he thus sought and received assurances from Elway and Buscher that the orally agreed upon, but as yet unsigned, Service Agreement would be honored.

On April 8, 1991, after the execution of the keeper letters, Pico, Elway, and Buscher met at Pico's office. During this meeting, GMAC telephoned Pico's office and informed Pico, Elway, and Buscher that as a condition to its agreement to finance the acquisition of the land and assets of the dealerships by Elway and Buscher, Nelson was not to receive any proceeds from the sale of the dealerships. The respondents then informed Nelson they would not be able to enter into the Service Agreement with him, and the Service Agreement was therefore not executed at the closing on April 12, 1991. After closing, Nelson demanded that the respondents honor the Service Agreement. When the respondents refused, Nelson filed the instant action.

In his complaint, Nelson sought damages from Elway and Buscher for breach of contract. * * * [Elway and Buscher] moved the trial court for summary judgment, which the court granted as to all counts.

    * * *

IV.

The * * * issue is whether the court of appeals erred in upholding the trial court's entry of summary judgment on the petitioners' claim of breach of contract. The petitioners' claim for breach of contract is based on the alleged March 15, 1991, Service Agreement orally agreed upon by Nelson, Elway and Buscher.

A.

The first issue with regard to the breach of contract claim is whether the merger clauses in the Buy–Sell Agreements precluded the consideration of evidence that the parties intended the Service Agreement to be part of the overall agreement to sell the dealerships.[1] The petitioners argue that the court of appeals erred by ruling that the merger clauses precluded the consideration of the intent of the contracting parties. The respondents assert that the merger clauses wholly manifest the intention of the parties that only those terms of the transaction reduced to writing and signed at the closing would be enforceable terms of the agreement.

---

1. Paragraph 14 of both of the Buy–Sell Agreements (the "Merger Clauses") for Metro Toyota and Metro Auto, both signed on March 16, 1991, by Nelson, Elway, and Buscher, states:

This Agreement constitutes the entire Agreement between the parties pertaining to the subject matter contained herein, and supersedes all prior agreements, representations and understandings of the parties. No modification or amendment of this Agreement shall be binding unless in writing and signed by the parties. * * *

We agree with the court of appeals that the merger clauses preclude consideration of extrinsic evidence to ascertain the intent of the parties. Integration clauses generally allow contracting parties to limit future contractual disputes to issues relating to the express provisions of the contract. * * * Therefore, the terms of a contract intended to represent a final and complete integration of the agreement between the parties are enforceable, and extrinsic evidence offered to prove the existence of prior agreements is inadmissible. * * * Even when extrinsic evidence is admissible to ascertain the intent of the parties, such evidence may not be used to demonstrate an intent that contradicts or adds to the intent expressed in the writing. * * *

In this case, the merger clauses plainly and unambiguously manifest the intent of the parties that the Buy–Sell Agreements executed on March 16, 1991 constitute the entire agreement between the parties pertaining to the subject matter contained therein. Where, as here, sophisticated parties who are represented by counsel have consummated a complex transaction and embodied the terms of that transaction in a detailed written document, it would be improper for this court to rewrite that transaction by looking to evidence outside the four corners of the contract to determine the intent of the parties.

The petitioners and respondents signed the March 16, 1991 Buy–Sell Agreements after extensive negotiation and numerous drafts of documents. By doing so, all parties expressly agreed, pursuant to the merger clauses, that the terms of those Buy–Sell Agreements would control the transaction and that all other agreements, oral or written, would be void. We will not step into a commercial transaction after the fact and attempt to ascertain the intent of the parties when that intent is clearly manifested by an express term in a written document. We thus conclude that the merger clauses in the March 16, 1991, Buy–Sell Agreements are dispositive as to the intent of the parties in this case. As there is no dispute as to any material fact with regard to this issue, the court of appeals correctly affirmed the trial court's order of summary judgment in favor of the respondents on this issue.

* * *

VI.

[The Court affirmed the summary judgment]

LOHR, J., dissents, and KIRSHBAUM and SCOTT, JJ., join in the dissent.

JUSTICE LOHR dissenting:

Petitioners Mel T. Nelson and Metro Auto, Inc. (collectively "Nelson") appealed a trial court ruling dismissing their claims on summary judgment grounds. * * * On certiorari review in this court, the majority holds that Nelson's * * * breach of contract * * * claims were all properly dismissed by the trial court on summary judgment.

I respectfully dissent. Summary judgment is a severe remedy. As the majority notes, in summary judgment proceedings courts must resolve all doubts as to the existence of genuine issues of material fact against the moving party. Maj. op. at 105. In view of the record and the procedural posture of this case, I would hold that Nelson's * * * breach of contract * * * claims were improperly dismissed. I would therefore reverse the judgment of the court of appeals upholding [the] breach of contract claims. * * *

I.

The following facts are derived from the record in this case, resolving all doubts against the party moving for summary judgment, as we must. * * * Mel T. Nelson was the president and sole shareholder of both Metro Toyota, Inc. ("Metro Toyota") and Metro Auto, Inc. ("Metro Auto"). Nelson also owned the land upon which the dealerships were located. Although Metro Auto was historically profitable, Metro Toyota was less successful. After hiring John J. Pico and Aspen Brokerage Co. (collectively "Pico") to serve as his agent and negotiator, Nelson agreed to sell Metro Toyota to John A. Elway, Jr., Rodney L. Buscher, J.R. Motors Company, and J.R. Motors Company South (collectively "Elway"). * * * The parties signed buy-sell and real estate contracts for the Metro Toyota concern on March 14, 1991, and set a closing date in April of 1991.

Soon after the Metro Toyota contracts were executed, Pico approached Nelson with the idea of selling Metro Auto to Elway as well. The parties agreed that any successful deal would have to meet two conditions: John A. Elway's total cash contribution would have to be limited to approximately $1.2 million dollars, and Nelson would have to receive enough personal compensation to make a sale of the historically profitable Metro Auto worthwhile. On March 15, 1991, Elway and Nelson agreed that if Nelson made the up-front concessions envisioned by Elway regarding the sale price for the real estate and dealership assets, Nelson would receive deferred personal compensation through a side agreement ("service agreement") providing that Nelson was to receive $50.00 for every new or used vehicle sold by the dealerships for the next seven years. Both buy-sell agreements noted that sale of the dealerships was contingent on GMAC approval. The parties subsequently signed buy-sell and real estate contracts for Metro Auto on March 16, 1991.

Anticipating the pending sale of the dealerships, GMAC insisted that Nelson relinquish control over the dealerships on April 3, 1991. Since Nelson and Elway had yet to sign the service agreement, Nelson contacted Rodney L. Buscher and received assurances that the service agreement would be honored before relinquishing control to GMAC.

On April 8 or 9, 1991, Pico and Elway met at the Landmark Hotel to discuss the sale of Nelson's dealerships. During the meeting, GMAC called Pico and told Elway that they would not finance the deal if Elway signed a side agreement with Nelson. Despite Nelson's understanding that Elway would honor the service agreement, Elway informed Nelson on April 8 or 9, 1991, that the service agreement would not be signed.

The parties disagree as to why Elway did not sign the service agreement. Elway contends that GMAC refused to approve the sale if the service agreement was executed. Nelson, on the other hand, alleges that Pico and Elway prompted GMAC to impose such conditions. Nelson suggests that Pico was interested in sabotaging the service agreement because of a fee dispute between Pico and Nelson. Nelson further contends that Elway realized that even if a portion of the money earmarked for the service agreement was diverted to pay Pico a commission, the total payout under any side agreements would be less if Nelson's compensation under the service agreement was eliminated. Nevertheless, Nelson proceeded with the sale of the dealerships because he already had turned control over to GMAC and thereby eliminated a bankruptcy reorganization alternative that was previously under consideration.

The parties' present dispute revolves around the enforceability of the service agreement. The district court dismissed Nelson's claims in a summary judgment proceeding. * * * Nelson then petitioned this court for certiorari review of the court of appeals' affirmance of the trial court's summary judgment ruling regarding his * * * breach of contract claims. * * *

     * * *

IV.

Nelson * * * contends that Elway is liable for breach of contract in failing to honor the service agreement. The majority affirms the dismissal of Nelson's breach of contract claim on summary judgment, holding * * * that the merger clauses in the buy-sell agreements preclude consideration of the alleged service agreement. * * * I disagree with the majority * * *

First, merger clauses preclude consideration of extrinsic evidence only where the parties intend that the document containing the merger is exclusive. * * * The very essence of this case is a dispute regarding whether the parties intended the service agreement to be part and parcel of the overall deal. Because Nelson's position is adequately supported in the record, the intention of the parties regarding the exclusivity of the document containing the merger agreement is a disputed issue of material fact. As a result, this case is inappropriate for summary judgment disposition. * * *

     * * *

A.

Nelson and Elway disagree regarding their intent to honor the alleged service agreement. The majority contends that the merger clauses in the buy-sell agreements affirmatively preclude consideration of extrinsic evidence such as the alleged oral service agreement, and refuses to look at "evidence outside the four corners of the contract to determine the intent of the parties." * * * Maj. op. at 107. However, the "four corners" approach to contract interpretation is in decline. * * * The "modern trend" * * * is that merger and integration clauses are to be afforded varying weight depending on the circumstances of the case. *Franklin v. White*, 493 N.E.2d 161, 166 (Ind.1986); *see also ARB*, 663 F.2d at 199 (court must consider "the circumstances surrounding the making of the contract" to ascertain whether an integration clause serves to "express the genuine intention of the parties to make the written contract the complete and exclusive statement of their agreement"); *Darner*, 140 Ariz. at 393, 682 P.2d at 398 ("Evidence on surrounding circumstances, including negotiation, prior understandings, subsequent conduct and the like, is taken to determine the parties' intent with regard to integration of the agreement. * * * This method obtains even though the parties have bargained for and written the actual words found in the instrument."); *Anderson*, 100 Idaho at 180, 595 P.2d at 714 (courts "should consider not only the language of the agreement but all extrinsic evidence relevant to the issue of whether the parties intended the written agreement to be a complete integration"); *Restatement (Second) of Contracts* § 209(2) (1979) ("Whether there is an integrated agreement is to be determined by the court as a question preliminary to determination of a question of interpretation or to application of the parol evidence rule."); *Restatement (Second) of Contracts* § 210 cmt. b (1979) (for purposes of proving a complete integration, "a writing cannot of itself prove its own completeness, and wide latitude must be allowed for inquiry into circumstances bearing on the intention of the parties"). * * *

Although I believe that merger and integration clauses are presumptively valid, in keeping with the honored tenets of contract law there is an exception such that "[w]here giving effect to the merger clause would frustrate and distort the parties' true intentions and understanding regarding the contract, the clause will not be enforced." * * * In particular, where the parties intend that both a written contract and an alleged oral agreement constitute components of an overall agreement, a merger clause does not preclude consideration of extrinsic evidence. * * *

The parties' intention that the buy-sell agreements constituted entire contracts, allegedly evidenced by the merger clauses within, was by no means clearly manifested. * * * In this case, despite the disclaimer in both merger clauses that each buy-sell agreement constituted the entire agreement, the overall deal involved two buy-sell agreements and two real estate contracts. Furthermore, each buy-sell agreement made reference to the real estate contracts despite the exclusivity disclaimer. Regardless of the standard merger and integration language in the buy-sell agreements, it is clear that the parties intended their ultimate bargain to encompass other agreements, although the substantive weight of the alleged service agreement remains unclear. * * *

When the parties disagree as to whether a document expresses the complete agreement of the parties, and a court subsequently finds that the evidence is conflicting or admits of more than one inference, the resolution of the parties' dispute requires a factual determination. * * *

VI.

In short, this case is singularly inappropriate for resolution in a summary judgment proceeding. * * * [T]he merger clauses in the parties' buy-sell agreements [do not] preclude[] Nelson's breach of contract claim for summary judgment purposes. At base, the parties are embroiled in a dispute regarding whether they intended the buy-sell agreements to be fully integrated and whether they intended the service agreement to be enforced. Nelson again supported his factual construction in the record, and as a result the parties' disagreement over the factual issues of integration * * * cannot properly be resolved by summary judgment.
* * *

For the aforementioned reasons, I respectfully dissent. I would reverse the judgment of the court of appeals upholding dismissal of Nelson's * * * breach of contract claim[ ]. * * *

KIRSHBAUM and SCOTT, JJ., join in this dissent.

———————

QUESTIONS AND NOTE

1. Questions about the facts of this case
    1.1. What was the parol evidence that the majority thought ought not to be considered by the trier of fact?
    1.2. Did the parties contest that there was a side agreement negotiated and agreed to?
2. Questions about the law
    2.1. Did the court find as a matter of law that both Nelson and Elway intended the Buy–Sell Agreements to be the "final and complete integration of the agreement"? If so, what was the basis for such a finding?
    2.2. If the dissent is correct about the trend of the law (and it is), did the majority reach the correct result? In hindsight, what should Nelson's litigation attorneys have done differently to at least get the case to trial? What should Nelson's lawyers have done at the time of the 1991 closing?
    2.3. Again, assuming that the dissent is correct on the law, under the modern trend, what are the advantages of a merger clause?
3. Note

    Elway later sold these two dealerships, along with four others that he owned in the Denver area, for $82.5 million. *Huizenga Has Big Ideas about Selling Automobiles*, THE DENVER POST, June 11, 1998, p. C–01.

———————

Parol evidence does not just apply to acquisitions and other intensely-lawyered deals. It applies to all contracts, including the $3000 promissory note in the following case (and which you'll find quoted in the dissent).

ROGERS v. JACKSON

Supreme Judicial Court of Maine
804 A.2d 379, 48 UCC Rep. Serv. 2d 643, 2002 Me. 140 (2002)

CALKINS, J.

[¶ 1][1] Glenn Jackson appeals from a summary judgment entered in the District Court (Belfast, *Worth, J.*) in favor of Paul and Pamela Rogers on their claim for enforcement of a promissory note. Jackson contends that a genuine issue of material fact exists as to whether his payment obligation under the note was subject to an unfulfilled oral condition. We agree and vacate the judgment.

I.

[¶ 2] On December 21, 1994, Jackson signed and delivered to the Rogers a promissory note in which he promised to pay them $3000, plus seven percent interest, with half the principal payable in one year and the remaining principal and interest payable in two years. Jackson did not pay any of the amount due under the note. In November 1998, the Rogers brought an action on the note in District Court. In his answer, Jackson denied liability, alleging that the agreement between the parties was that he would pay only if and when he was able, and he had not been able.

[¶ 3] The Rogers filed a motion for summary judgment. Jackson filed an opposition to the motion including a statement of material facts that admitted or qualified the facts stated in the Rogers' statement by reference to Jackson's accompanying affidavit. In his affidavit, Jackson stated that the note was part of a larger oral agreement: instead of foreclosing on a mortgage he held on real property the Rogers had bought from him, he would pay them $10,000 to buy back the property, they would pay any attorney fees, and he "would issue them a note for $3,000 to be paid if and when I was able."

[¶ 4] The court granted the Rogers' motion and entered summary judgment against Jackson. Jackson then brought this appeal.

II.

* * *

[¶ 6] Jackson's statement of material facts and supporting affidavit raise factual issues of whether the parties' agreement included a condition

---

1. [Eds.: The paragraph designations are actually part of the official opinion. In 1997, Maine adopted the following rule regarding citation form in its opinions: "The sequential decision number shall be included in each opinion at the time it is made available to the public and the paragraphs in the opinion shall be numbered. The official publication of each opinion issued on or after January 1, 1997 shall include the sequential number in the caption of the opinion and the paragraph numbers assigned by the Court." Order, § 4, Maine Supreme Judicial Court, Docket No. SJC–216 (Aug. 26, 1996).]

that Jackson was not obligated to pay unless he was able and, if so, whether he was able to pay. Neither the courts' order nor the Rogers' brief on appeal explain why these factual issues do not preclude summary judgment.

    * * *

[¶ 9] Another possible explanation for the grant of summary judgment is that proof of the oral condition of ability to pay could be barred by the parol evidence rule. "The parol evidence rule operates to exclude from judicial consideration extrinsic evidence offered to alter or vary unambiguous contractual language. This proposition, however, presupposes the existence of an integrated contract." *Astor v. Boulos Co.,* 451 A.2d 903, 905 (Me.1982) (footnote omitted). Accepting the allegations of Jackson's affidavit, as we must in reviewing a summary judgment, the agreement between Jackson and the Rogers was only partially integrated. "Where the parties to a written agreement agree orally that performance of the agreement is subject to the occurrence of a stated condition," the agreement is not integrated with respect to the oral condition. *Paine v. Paine,* 458 A.2d 420, 421 (Me.1983) (quoting RESTATEMENT (SECOND) OF CONTRACTS § 217 (1981)). Even apart from the oral condition, the agreement was not completely integrated; the only writing, the promissory note, could not have been the entire agreement of the parties because it was merely a promise by Jackson that imposed no contractual duties on the Rogers.

[¶ 10] As a general rule parol evidence of additional terms is admissible to supplement a partially integrated written agreement if the additional terms are consistent with the writing. *Astor,* 451 A.2d at 905–06; RESTATEMENT (SECOND) §§ 215, 216. We have previously stated that this rule applies to proof of oral conditions. *Burrowes Corp. v. Read,* 151 Me. 92, 96–97, 116 A.2d 127, 129 (1955) (citing RESTATEMENT OF CONTRACTS § 241 (1932)). The Second Restatement, however, takes a somewhat different approach with respect to conditions, providing that inconsistency is merely one factor to be considered in determining whether and to what degree an agreement is integrated and does not *per se* bar proof of an oral condition. RESTATEMENT (SECOND) § 217 cmt. B We need not decide whether to adopt this approach because the oral condition alleged by Jackson is not inconsistent with the written promissory note.

[¶ 11] In deciding whether an oral condition is consistent with a writing, courts have observed that

> [a] certain disparity is inevitable, of course, whenever a written promise is, by oral agreement of the parties, made conditional upon an event not expressed in the writing. Quite obviously, though, the parol evidence rule does not bar proof of every orally established condition precedent, but only of those which in a real sense contradict the terms of the written agreement.

Intercont'l Monetary Corp. v. Performance Guars., Inc., 705 F.Supp. 144, 149 (S.D.N.Y.1989). The ability-to-pay condition alleged by Jackson is not repugnant to the terms of the note and does not in a real sense contradict them. Instead, the condition, as a term of the larger agreement of which the promissory note is but one part, prevents Jackson's payment obligation under the note from coming into effect until such time as he can afford to pay.

[¶ 12] In sum, because the oral condition supplements but does not contradict the writing, proof of it is not barred by the parol evidence rule. The existence of the oral condition is thus a question of fact; Jackson is entitled to present his evidence on that question even though the fact-finder may receive it with skepticism. *See* 3 ARTHUR L. CORBIN, CORBIN ON CONTRACTS § 592, at 554–55 (1960) (although it is "highly improbable" that parties to written contract would orally agree to condition on promise to pay, "[t]he 'parol evidence rule' should not be allowed to close the door" to proof of such condition).

* * *

[¶ 14] We see no basis for concluding that Jackson did not raise genuine issues of material fact as to whether there was an oral condition to his obligation to pay the Rogers and, if so, whether the condition was satisfied. Accordingly, the District Court erred in granting summary judgment in favor of the Rogers.

The entry is:

Judgment vacated. Remanded for further proceedings consistent with this opinion.

SAUFLEY, C.J., dissenting.

[¶ 15] In defending against the Rogers's action to collect on the promissory note, Jackson asserts that the note he signed and delivered to the Rogers was not intended to be binding unless he was able to pay. The Court concludes that this assertion, based entirely on Jackson's proposed testimony of an oral agreement, raises the factual issue of whether a condition precedent was a part of the contract, thereby precluding summary judgment. Because this conclusion represents a misapplication of contract principles, I must respectfully dissent.

[¶ 16] A promissory note is a contract to which basic principles of contract law apply. A promissory note may also qualify as a negotiable instrument pursuant to 11 M.R.S.A. § 3–1104 (1995). When interpreting a contract, courts effectuate " 'the parties' intentions as reflected in the written instrument, construed with regard for the subject matter, motive, and purpose of the agreement, as well as the object to be accomplished. When an agreement is reduced to writing, extrinsic evidence may be considered only in limited circumstances. *See Gagne v. Stevens*, 1997 ME 88, ¶ 9 n. 5, 696 A.2d 411, 415 n.5 (indicating that, once it is determined that the statute of frauds is satisfied, "parol evidence may be employed for limited purposes").

[¶ 17] If, for example, there is an ambiguity in the written agreement, the court may consider extrinsic evidence in order to ascertain the intent of the parties. * * * A contract term is ambiguous if it is reasonably susceptible to more than one interpretation. * * * When the language of an agreement is unambiguous, however, it must be given its plain meaning. * * * The interpretation of an unambiguous contract is a question of law. * * *

[¶ 18] If the parties allege that the unambiguous written instrument reflects only part of their agreement, extrinsic evidence may be presented to assist the court in determining the extent to which the written document represents an integration of their agreement. * * * RESTATE-MENT (SECOND) OF CONTRACTS § 214 (1981). A writing is integrated if it represents the final expression of any term of the agreement. *Id.* § 209(1) ("An integrated agreement is a writing or writings constituting a final expression of one or more terms of an agreement."). The extent to which an agreement is integrated is also a question of law. * * *

[¶ 19] When an agreement is integrated, the parol evidence rule applies. * * * If the written document embodies all the terms of the agreement, it is completely integrated and parol evidence may not be introduced. RESTATEMENT (SECOND) OF CONTRACTS § 213 (1981). If, however, there is a supplemental term not contained in the writing, the agreement is only partially integrated. * * * In a partially integrated agreement, extrinsic evidence can be offered to support the existence of a supplemental term *if it does not contradict* the written terms of the agreement. *Loe v. Town of Thomaston,* 600 A.2d 1090, 1092 (Me.1991) ("Under the parol evidence rule a binding partially integrated agreement discharges prior agreements to the extent that it is inconsistent with them."); *Karnofsky v. Elliott,* 570 A.2d 1223, 1224 (Me.1990) ("Consistent with the Restatement analysis, we conclude that the * * * letter superseded the prior oral agreement to the extent they were inconsistent because the letter need not be a completely integrated agreement to be binding. * * *"); *see also* RESTATEMENT (SECOND) OF CONTRACTS § 213. Therefore, evidence of a condition precedent may be considered, but only if the condition is not inconsistent with the language in the written agreement. *Burrowes Corp. v. Read,* 151 Me. 92, 96–97, 116 A.2d 127, 129 (1955) (quoting 3 WILLISTON ON CONTRACTS § 634 (rev. ed. 1936)) (" '[I]t may be shown * * * that the parties agreed by parol that the writing in question should not become effective until some future day or the happening of some contingency, if this is not inconsistent with the express terms of the writing.' ").

* * *

[¶ 21] Here, the promissory note is an unambiguous written agreement. Jackson does not dispute the existence or validity of the promissory note, but rather argues that there is a supplemental term. He concedes, therefore, that the promissory note represents at least a partial integration of their agreement. Because the agreement is partially integrated, the parol evidence rule applies and permits the introduction of an orally agreed upon supplemental term only if it does not contradict the written terms of the promissory note.

[¶ 22] The supplemental term proffered by Jackson directly contradicts the specifics of his written payment obligation. Jackson alleges that the parties agreed that he was not required to honor the promissory note unless he was "able" to do so. Jackson stated in the affidavit he submitted to the District Court: "Part of our oral agreement was that [the Rogers] pay any attorney fees and that I would issue them a note for $3,000 to be paid if and when I was able." The terms of the promissory note, however, explicitly state not only that Jackson agrees to pay the Rogers, but also how much he will pay, when he will pay, and the consequences of failing to pay. The promissory note states, in relevant part:

> FOR VALUABLE CONSIDERATION RECEIVED, I, Glenn L. Jackson * * * promise to pay to the order of Paul E. Rogers and Pamela J. Rogers * * * the principal sum of THREE THOUSAND DOLLARS ($3,000.00) with interest at the rate of SEVEN PER CENT (7%) per annum, one half the principal amount due and payable one year from the date of this promissory note; the remaining one-half of the principal and interest due and payable on or before two years from the date of this promissory note.
>
> * * *
>
> Failure to pay principal and interest as aforesaid, shall constitute a default which shall render the full amount of the unpaid balance, both principal and interest, immediately due and payable at the option of the holder.

Jackson's alleged oral condition thus contradicts the express language in the agreement and the District Court, therefore, properly disregarded it. By its holding today, the Court risks opening every contract, except those whose drafters are savvy enough to include an ironclad integration clause, to a factual dispute over the agreement to pay, even when that agreement is specifically and unambiguously included in the written contract. This holding represents an error of law.

[¶ 23] Because the proffered evidence is barred by the parol evidence rule, and there are no disputed issues of material fact, the District Court properly granted a summary judgment in favor of the Rogers. I would affirm the judgment.

QUESTIONS

1. Questions about the facts of this case
    1.1. What was the contract? Did it have an integration clause? What is an integration clause? Does an integration clause have to use the word "integration"? Could you recognize an integration clause if you saw it?

1.2. What was the oral condition? Is it the type of condition that you would expect the parties to reduce to writing? Do you agree that it doesn't contradict the writing?

1.3. So Jackson escapes summary judgment. How do you think he will fare at trial? Were you his counsel, would you initiate settlement discussions? If so, for how much? If you were brought in as Rogers' trial counsel, what questions would you ask and what facts would you like to know that are not in the opinion?

2. Questions about the law

2.1. Is it so bad, as the dissent laments, that Maine residents will have to "include an ironclad integration clause" in order to enforce agreements? Shouldn't every agreement contain each and every term so that people know what their obligations are?

2.2 Is this case in the majority or the minority according to *Nelson v. Elway*?

B.   UNIFORM COMMERCIAL CODE

According to *Elway* and *Rogers*, the key to the applicability of the parol evidence rule is whether the document is "integrated." The Uniform Commercial Code has its own version of the parol evidence rule, which is reprinted below. Note that nowhere in the following section is the term "integrated" used. Nevertheless, does it appear that the U.C.C. also has an "integration" concept?

§ 2–202.   Final Expression in a Record: Parol or Extrinsic Evidence.

(1) Terms with respect to which the confirmatory records of the parties agree or which are otherwise set forth in a record intended by the parties as a final expression of their agreement with respect to such terms as are included therein may not be contradicted by evidence of any prior agreement or of a contemporaneous oral agreement but may be supplemented by evidence of:

(a) course of performance, course of dealing, or usage of trade (Section 1–303); and

(b) consistent additional terms unless the court finds the record to have been intended also as a complete and exclusive statement of the terms of the agreement.

(2) Terms in a record may be explained by evidence of course of performance, course of dealing, or usage of trade without a preliminary determination by the court that the language used is ambiguous.

Does this language change the common law parol evidence rule? In reading the next case, focus on how the Eighth Circuit Court of Appeals views or tries to determine the "final expression of their agreement" language in Section 2–202.

SIMMONS FOODS, INC. v. HILL'S PET NUTRITION, INC.

United States Court of Appeals, Eighth Circuit
270 F.3d 723, 45 UCC Rep. Serv. 2d 1055 (2001)

Before BOWMAN, HEANEY, and BYE, CIRCUIT JUDGES.

BYE, CIRCUIT JUDGE.

Simmons Foods, Inc., (Simmons) an Arkansas corporation that produces pet food poultry meal, sued Hill's Pet Nutrition, Inc., (HPN) a Kansas corporation that produces and markets pet foods, for breach of contract and promissory estoppel. Simmons claimed that HPN breached the last two years of an alleged three-year contract for the sale and purchase of poultry meal. Simmons also claimed that HPN orally promised a long-term business relationship. Simmons sought to recover the value of business improvements made in reliance on that promise. The district court granted summary judgment in favor of HPN on both claims. We affirm.

BACKGROUND

Poultry by-product meal is the main ingredient in HPN's Science Diet® and Prescription Diet® pet foods. HPN started buying poultry meal from Simmons in 1986; at that time HPN obtained poultry meal from a number of suppliers under short-term (monthly or bimonthly) contracts. By 1988 or 1989, Simmons had modified its processing for "regular ash" poultry meal in accordance with HPN's specifications, and became one of HPN's regular suppliers. About the same time, HPN began negotiating longer-term contracts with fewer suppliers, one of which was Simmons. In early 1990, HPN and Simmons entered their first long-term written contract, a two-year agreement.

The first long-term contract was an "output" contract whereby HPN agreed to purchase all poultry meal produced by Simmons at its facility in Southwest City, Missouri. After the first contract expired in 1992, the parties entered into a series of one-year contracts through 1997. Some were "output" contracts like the first; at least one was a "requirements" contract whereby Simmons agreed to supply the needs of HPN's Los Angeles plant.

In 1995, Simmons began expanding its operation to produce "low ash" poultry meal. "Low ash" is a higher, more expensive grade poultry meal than "regular ash," and requires machines called "classifiers" to remove ash from the poultry meal during the production process. Simmons expanded its operation because HPN needed "low ash" meal and wanted Simmons to produce it. At the time of these additional investments, Simmons contemplated asking HPN for a long-term contract to recoup money spent on improvements, but decided against it. Simmons's

Chairman, Mark Simmons, when asked if Simmons requested a long-term supply agreement from HPN, answered, "I know we talked about the pros and cons of it internally, a little bit. I don't think that we actually asked them for a long term contract, no." * * * Simmons's Chief Operating Officer, Gene Woods, admitted that Simmons continued to negotiate one-year agreements following the expansion project:

Q: * * * And you made your investments in the expansion and in the classification during 1995 and 1996; true?

A: We made expenditures for those items, yes.

Q: And when you came around to negotiating the contract for 1997, you once again negotiated a one year contract; correct?

A: Yes. * * *

In the fall of 1997, the parties met to discuss the 1998 contract. HPN had just recently hired a new buyer, Rhett Butler, who brought with him a new purchasing philosophy. HPN had initiated "Focus 75," a program under which HPN hoped to reduce the cost of doing business by $75 million over a three-year period. HPN asked its principal suppliers, including Simmons, to reduce supply costs to meet that goal. In November 1997, after the contract meetings, Simmons sent HPN a fax that stated:

Below are the general terms of our agreement, as we understand it, for the purchase of Poultry By–Product Meal from Simmons Foods, in Southwest City, Mo for the next three (3) years:

1.   Both Simmons and Hills have agreed to join together in a (sic) effort to find at least 3% cost saving per year over the next three (3) years in the production, handling and usage of Poultry By–Product Meal.

2.   It is the intent of both parties to have products that are more economical through cost saving and to share in that cost saving.

3.   Cost saving for 1999 and 2000 will be explored by representatives from both companies working together in an organized "team effort." This team should be formed ASAP and certainly before the end of January 1998.

4.   The 3% cost saving for 1998 will be expressed by each company absorbing 1.5%. Simmons will reduce prices by 1.5% of the 3% cost saving for 1998.

5.   Volumes for 1998 will be 36.6 million pounds of Low Ash Poultry Meal for Richmond and 14 Million pounds of Regular Ash Poultry Meal for Bolling (sic) Green. Please forward a copy of your PO at your convenience.

Based on the above information, Simmons will price 1998 Low Ash at $591.00 per ton and Regular Ash at $522.00.

We look forward to working with you on this project. * * *

HPN responded with two purchase orders for the 1998 contract year. Unlike the parties' previous contracts, the terms of these purchase orders did not refer to Simmons's "output" or HPN's "requirements." Instead, one purchase order referred to the specific quantity of low ash meal set forth in the November 1997 fax (36.6 million pounds) and the other referred to the specific quantity of regular ash meal set forth therein (14 million pounds). Both parties fully performed the 1998 contract.

In the fall of 1998, when the parties met to discuss prices for the year 1999, the relationship became estranged. HPN's buyer, and buying philosophy, had changed again. Bill Ziehm now represented HPN. Ziehm wanted more than a 3% reduction from the prices set forth in Simmons's November 1997 fax and HPN's 1998 purchase orders. Ziehm indicated that Simmons would have to agree to a substantial price reduction, or risk termination of its relationship with HPN. On December 4, 1998, Simmons wrote to HPN to confirm a six-month agreement from January 1 through June 30, 1999. Instead of fixed prices, the parties agreed that pricing would be based on the Chicago Board of Trade index prices. This contract resulted in prices substantially less than the 3% reduction per year that Simmons set forth in the November 1997 fax.

When the parties were unable to reach an agreement for the sale and purchase of poultry meal beyond June 30, 1999, Simmons sued HPN alleging breach of contract for the years 1999 and 2000. Simmons alleged that the November 1997 fax set forth a three-year deal, and claimed damages for 1999 and 2000 in an amount equal to the difference between sales to other customers, and the prices set forth in the November 1997 fax. Simmons also alleged a promissory estoppel claim, seeking to recover the cost of improvements made in 1995 and 1996 to produce "low ash" poultry meal.

HPN moved for summary judgment on both claims, which the district court granted. With respect to the breach of contract claim, the district court held that the November 1997 fax failed to satisfy the Uniform Commercial Code's (UCC) statute of frauds because the fax did not refer to quantities for the years 1999 and 2000. With respect to the promissory estoppel claim, the district court held that evidence of HPN's alleged oral promise of a long-term relationship was barred by the UCC's parol evidence rule because Simmons subsequently entered into one-year written contracts with HPN.

DISCUSSION

* * *

I.   The Breach of Contract Claim

Simmons contends that the November 1997 fax sets forth a three-year contract and that HPN did not perform the last two years of that contract. The district court held that the November 1997 fax did not set forth an enforceable contract for the years 1999 and 2000 because it contained no quantities for those years. We agree. The UCC's statute of frauds provides that a "writing * * * is not enforceable under this paragraph beyond the quantity of goods shown in such writing." UCC § 2–201(1). The November 1997 fax sets forth "Volumes for 1998" in the amount of "36.6 million pounds of Low Ash Poultry Meal" and "14 Million pounds of Regular Ash," but contains no quantities for the years 1999 and 2000.

Simmons relies upon an exception for contracts that include "term[s] which measure[ ] the quantity by the output of the seller or the requirements of the buyer * * *" UCC § 2–306(1). Simmons contends that the November 1997 fax should be construed as an output or requirements contract because of the parties prior course of dealing—every previous contract between the parties had been an output or requirements contract. The district court held that § 2–306(1) did not apply because, to the extent the November 1997 fax set forth an agreement for the year 1998, the fax indicated an express quantity rather than an output or requirements term like the parties' previous contracts. More significantly, the fax was silent as to any quantity terms (output, requirements, or otherwise) for the years 1999 and 2000. As a result, the district court declined Simmons's invitation to consider parol evidence of the parties' course of dealing to supply the missing quantity term. So must we. "[W]here the writing relied upon to form the contract of sale is totally silent as to quantity, parol evidence cannot be used to supply the missing quantity term." *Thomas J. Kline, Inc. v. Lorillard, Inc.,* 878 F.2d 791, 794 (4th Cir.1989) (quotation omitted) (applying UCC § 2–201).

II.   The Promissory Estoppel Claim

Simmons contends that HPN orally promised a long-term business relationship on more than one occasion, and that Simmons relied upon those promises when it expanded its facilities in 1995 and 1996 to produce "low ash" poultry meal. The district court held that the alleged oral promises of a long-term relationship were barred by the parol evidence rule, UCC § 2–202, because Simmons had subsequently entered into written one-year contracts with HPN. *See, e.g., Shelton v. Valmac Indus., Inc.,* 539 F.Supp. 328, 333 (W.D.Ark.1982) (interpreting UCC § 2–202 under Arkansas law and holding that a plaintiff who entered into a series of written one-year contracts after improving his company, was barred by the parol evidence rule from claiming that the defendant had made representations about a long-term contract). We agree.

Simmons contends that its annual written contracts with HPN were not fully-integrated contracts, and that its contractual relationship with HPN went far beyond the terms of the annual purchase orders the two parties negotiated. Simmons argues that the parol evidence rule does not bar the alleged oral promises because the rule allows a party to explain or supplement written agreements with evidence of the parties' performance, usage, and prior dealings, so long as the evidence does not actually *contradict* the written terms. Simmons contends that the alleged oral promises do not contradict the terms of the written agreements. We disagree. Even if we accept Simmons's contention that the annual contracts were not fully-integrated agreements, the fact remains that one of the express terms included in the written contracts were their length of time, i.e., one year. Simmons wants to introduce parol evidence to prove the parties had a contract with a longer term. But the parol evidence rules clearly provides that a written agreement "may not be contradicted by evidence of any prior agreement or of a contemporaneous oral agreement * * * with respect to *such terms as are included* [within the written agreement]." UCC § 2–202 (emphasis added).

CONCLUSION

We affirm the district court's grant of summary judgment in all respects.

QUESTIONS AND NOTE

1. Questions about the facts of this case

   1.1. Was there a contract? If so, what were its terms?

   1.2. Why did Simmons want the court to look to prior practice in determining what the contract meant?

2. Questions about the law

   2.1. Do you think the Eighth Circuit and the Supreme Judicial Court of Maine use different definitions of "contradictory"?

   2.2. Under the U.C.C., does the parol evidence rule as set forth in Section 2–202 bar admission of prior dealings to determine the meaning of a contract? Does it matter if (a) the contract contains an integration clause; or (b) the contract does not contain an integration clause?

3. Note

   Note the structure of Section 2–202. It permits the introduction of parol evidence to "supplement" the terms of the agreement by showing a "course of performance, course of dealing or usage of trade (Section 1–303)." Under the Uniform Commercial Code, however, the "contract" is the enforceable agreement of the parties, § 1–201(a)(12), and the agreement is the "bargain of the parties in fact as found in their language or by inferred from other circumstances including course of performance, course of dealing or usage of trade" § 1–201(a)(3). Thus, harkening back to *Threadgill*, the U.C.C. incorporates trade usage, course of dealing and usage of trade into each agreement within its scope. We'll see more of this later in Section 3, Subsection B.

C. EXCEPTIONS

As we have seen above, the finding that there is an integrated agreement (a/k/a "final expression of agreement") carries with it significant consequences. It deprives the parties from introducing other terms that are inconsistent with the level of integration found: that is, if the agreement is *partially* integrated, the parol evidence rule bars evidence of terms inconsistent with the integrated terms (usually the ones written down); if *fully* integrated, the parol evidence rule bars introduction of any evidence of terms that may supplement or contradict the agreement.

There are, of course, cases to which these blanket statements don't apply. Although not an exception, note that the rule does not apply to evidence relating to terms discussed or agreed to *after* the execution of the agreement. Technically, under the *Restatement*, the rule applies only to acts to "discharge[ ] *prior* agreements." *Restatement (Second) of Contracts* § 213(1) (emphasis added). This is a sensible result; if the rule acted prospectively, it would effectively eliminate any possibility of amendment or individual waiver of provisions of an integrated agreement. Contracts are typically not that static or rigid.

It would also be the height (or nadir) of formalism to deny a party the ability to introduce parol evidence to demonstrate that the contract was procured by fraud, or through mistake or some other affirmative defense. A species of such fraud, stemming from the common practice of signing documents in advance of their effectiveness would be to take an otherwise complete document and assert its validity before such validity was intended. This is often done when purchasing a home to facilitate the closing (the seller will sign the deed ahead of time, and give it to her attorney or escrow company), and in large corporate transactions given the sheer complexity and number of documents that attend such transactions. Thus, there is another exception that allows parties to show that there was an oral condition to the effectiveness of documents. *See Restatement (Second) of Contracts* § 217.

PROBLEMS ON PAROL EVIDENCE

Try to synthesize your understanding thus far with the following problems based on the facts set out below:

Ponoroff and Epstein are negotiating for the purchase of a cow. They reach agreement on a purchase price of $600, after several back and forth negotiations over the price involving other terms such as delivery date, veterinarian inspections and the like. At the end of negotiations, Ponoroff and Epstein sign the following document:

Ponoroff agrees to sell to Epstein, and Epstein agrees to buy, for $600, Ponoroff's cow known as Bossie without any veterinarian's certificate. Payment to be by cashier's check.

1. One week after the signing, Epstein shows up at Ponoroff's barn and tries to give Ponoroff a cashier's check for $600. Ponoroff tells Epstein to leave. When Epstein sues Ponoroff for breach, can Epstein introduce evidence of discussions between them that tends to indicate that Ponoroff and Epstein had a side agreement to deliver the cow on the date Epstein showed up?

2. If Epstein shows up with a personal check instead of a cashier's check, and Ponoroff refuses to accept it, may Epstein defend Ponoroff's lawsuit by offering evidence that, prior to signing the document, Ponoroff had indicated that a personal check from Epstein would be acceptable?

3. Does the result in Problem 2 above change if Epstein's evidence is that instead of before the signing, Ponoroff's assent to a personal check occurred *after* the signing?

4. Same facts as in Problem 1, except now the written agreement has an additional clause that states:

   This agreement, though short, contains all of the agreements of the parties on this subject, and is intended as a complete and final expression of all of the terms the parties deem relevant to this transaction.

5. Same facts as in Problem 4, except assume that, after signing, Epstein asked Ponoroff to hold the document "in escrow" until Epstein checked the cost of obtaining a cashier's check. When he found that the bank would charge him $25 for the check, Epstein asked Ponoroff to reduce the price to $575. Ponoroff said no. Later, Ponoroff sues Epstein for nonpayment of the $600. When Epstein tries to introduce evidence of their understanding about holding the agreement, Ponoroff asserts that, in light of the integration clause, Epstein is barred from doing so by the parol evidence rule. Who's right? How does this differ from the facts in *Rogers v. Jackson, supra,* at page 449?

6. Same facts as in Problem 4, except that when Epstein appears, he demands a veterinarian's certificate attesting to the health of Bossie. Ponoroff points to the contractual term negating such a duty, but Epstein claims that such a certificate is customary in the cattle industry. In litigation over the point, it turns out that neither Epstein nor Ponoroff (both experienced cattle merchants) have ever heard of a cattle transaction in which a veterinarian's certificate was not a precondition to payment.

D. A WORLD WITHOUT PAROL EVIDENCE—*THE CONVENTION ON THE INTERNATIONAL SALE OF GOODS*

Before we leave direct consideration of the parol evidence rule, it is helpful to step back and wonder about its value. Would Western civilization as we know it collapse if the parol evidence rule were not part of our jurisprudence? The next case presents that issue. When reading it, check your statutory supplement for the *Convention on the International Sale of Goods*. It is the law of the United States, and potentially applicable to transactions in which you may be involved in the future.

MCC–MARBLE CERAMIC CENTER, INC. v. CERAMICA NUOVA D'AGOSTINO, S.P.A.

U.S. Court of Appeals, Eleventh Circuit
144 F.3d 1384 (1998)

Appeal from the United States District Court for the Southern District of Florida.

Before EDMONDSON and BIRCH, CIRCUIT JUDGES, and FAY, SENIOR CIRCUIT JUDGE.

BIRCH, CIRCUIT JUDGE:

This case requires us to determine whether a court must consider parol evidence in a contract dispute governed by the United Nations Convention on Contracts for the International Sale of Goods ("CISG").[1] The district court granted summary judgment on behalf of the defendant-appellee, relying on certain terms and provisions that appeared on the reverse of a pre-printed form contract for the sale of ceramic tiles. The plaintiff-appellant sought to rely on a number of affidavits that tended to show both that the parties had arrived at an oral contract before memorializing their agreement in writing and that they subjectively intended not to apply the terms on the reverse of the contract to their agreements. The magistrate judge held that the affidavits did not raise an issue of material fact and recommended that the district court grant summary judgment based on the terms of the contract. The district court agreed with the magistrate judge's reasoning and entered summary judgment in the defendant-appellee's favor. We REVERSE.

BACKGROUND

The plaintiff-appellant, MCC–Marble Ceramic, Inc. ("MCC"), is a Florida corporation engaged in the retail sale of tiles, and the defendant-appellee, Ceramica Nuova d'Agostino S.p.A. ("D'Agostino") is an Italian corporation engaged in the manufacture of ceramic tiles. In October 1990, MCC's president, Juan Carlos Mozon, met representatives of D'Agostino at a trade fair in Bologna, Italy and negotiated an agreement to purchase ceramic tiles from D'Agostino based on samples he examined at the trade fair. Monzon, who spoke no Italian, communicated with Gianni Silingardi, then D'Agostino's commercial director, through a translator, Gianfranco Copelli, who was himself an agent of D'Agostino. The parties apparently arrived at an oral agreement on the crucial terms of price, quality, quantity, delivery and payment. The parties then recorded these terms on one of D'Agostino's standard, pre-printed order forms and Monzon signed

---

1. United Nations Convention on Contracts for the International Sale of Goods, opened for signature April 11, 1980, S. Treaty Doc. No. 9, 98th Cong., 1st Sess. 22 (1983), 19 I.L.M. 671, reprinted at, 15 U.S.C. app. 52 (1997).

the contract on MCC's behalf. According to MCC, the parties also entered into a requirements contract in February 1991, subject to which D'Agostino agreed to supply MCC with high grade ceramic tile at specific discounts as long as MCC purchased sufficient quantities of tile. MCC completed a number of additional order forms requesting tile deliveries pursuant to that agreement.

MCC brought suit against D'Agostino claiming a breach of the February 1991 requirements contract when D'Agostino failed to satisfy orders in April, May, and August of 1991. In addition to other defenses, D'Agostino responded that it was under no obligation to fill MCC's orders because MCC had defaulted on payment for previous shipments. In support of its position, D'Agostino relied on the pre-printed terms of the contracts that MCC had executed. The executed forms were printed in Italian and contained terms and conditions on both the front and reverse. According to an English translation of the October 1990 contract, the front of the order form contained the following language directly beneath Monzon's signature:

> [T]he buyer hereby states that he is aware of the sales conditions stated on the reverse and that he expressly approves of them with special reference to those numbered 1–2–3–4–5–6–7–8.

R2–126, Exh. 3 ¶ 5 ("Maselli Aff."). Clause 6(b), printed on the back of the form states:

> [D]efault or delay in payment within the time agreed upon gives D'Agostino the right to * * * suspend or cancel the contract itself and to cancel possible other pending contracts and the buyer does not have the right to indemnification or damages.

Id. ¶ 6.

D'Agostino also brought a number of counterclaims against MCC, seeking damages for MCC's alleged nonpayment for deliveries of tile that D'Agostino had made between February 28, 1991 and July 4, 1991. MCC responded that the tile it had received was of a lower quality than contracted for, and that, pursuant to the CISG, MCC was entitled to reduce payment in proportion to the defects.[4] D'Agostino, however, noted that clause 4 on the reverse of the contract states, in pertinent part:

> Possible complaints for defects of the merchandise must be made in writing by means of a certified letter within and not later than 10 days after receipt of the merchandise. * * *

Maselli Aff. ¶ 6. Although there is evidence to support MCC's claims that it complained about the quality of the deliveries it received, MCC never submitted any written complaints.

MCC did not dispute these underlying facts before the district court, but argued that the parties never intended the terms and conditions printed on the reverse of the order form to apply to their agreements. As evidence for this assertion, MCC submitted Monzon's affidavit, which

---

4. Article 50 of the CISG permits a buyer to reduce payment for nonconforming goods in proportion to the nonconformity under certain conditions. See CISG, art. 50.

claims that MCC had no subjective intent to be bound by those terms and that D'Agostino was aware of this intent. MCC also filed affidavits from Silingardi and Copelli, D'Agostino's representatives at the trade fair, which support Monzon's claim that the parties subjectively intended not to be bound by the terms on the reverse of the order form. The magistrate judge held that the affidavits, even if true, did not raise an issue of material fact regarding the interpretation or applicability of the terms of the written contracts and the district court accepted his recommendation to award summary judgment in D'Agostino's favor. MCC then filed this timely appeal.

DISCUSSION

* * *

The parties to this case agree that the CISG governs their dispute because the United States, where MCC has its place of business, and Italy, where D'Agostino has its place of business, are both States party to the Convention.[5] See CISG, art. 1.[6] Article 8 of the CISG governs the interpretation of international contracts for the sale of goods and forms the basis of MCC's appeal from the district court's grant of summary judgment in D'Agostino's favor.[7] MCC argues that the magistrate judge and the district court improperly ignored evidence that MCC submitted regarding the parties' subjective intent when they memorialized the terms of their agreement on D'Agostino's pre-printed form contract, and that the magistrate judge erred by applying the parol evidence rule in derogation of the CISG.

I. Subjective Intent Under the CISG

Contrary to what is familiar practice in United States courts, the CISG appears to permit a substantial inquiry into the parties' subjective

---

5. The United States Senate ratified the CISG in 1986, and the United States deposited its instrument of ratification at the United Nations Headquarters in New York on December 11, 1986. See Preface to Convention, reprinted at 15 U.S.C. App. 52 (1997). The Convention entered into force between the United States and the other States Parties, including Italy, on January 1, 1988. See id.; Filanto S.p.A. v. Chilewich Int'l Corp., 789 F. Supp. 1229, 1237 (S.D. N.Y.1992).

6. Article 1 of the CISG states in relevant part:

(1) This Convention applies to contracts of sale of goods between parties whose places of business are in different States:

(a) When the States are Contracting States. * * *

CISG, art. 1.

7. Article 8 provides:

(1) For the purposes of this Convention statements made by and other conduct of a party are to be interpreted according to his intent where the other party knew or could not have been unaware what that intent was.

(2) If the preceding paragraph is not applicable, statements made by and conduct of a party are to be interpreted according to the understanding a reasonable person of the same kind as the other party would have had in the same circumstances.

(3) In determining the intent of a party or the understanding a reasonable person would have had, due consideration is to be given to all relevant circumstances of the case including the negotiations, any practices which the parties have established between themselves, usages and any subsequent conduct of the parties.

CISG, art. 8.

intent, even if the parties did not engage in any objectively ascertainable means of registering this intent.[8] Article 8(1) of the CISG instructs courts to interpret the "statements * * * and other conduct of a party * * * according to his intent" as long as the other party "knew or could not have been unaware" of that intent. The plain language of the Convention, therefore, requires an inquiry into a party's subjective intent as long as the other party to the contract was aware of that intent.

In this case, MCC has submitted three affidavits that discuss the purported subjective intent of the parties to the initial agreement concluded between MCC and D'Agostino in October 1990. All three affidavits discuss the preliminary negotiations and report that the parties arrived at an oral agreement for D'Agostino to supply quantities of a specific grade of ceramic tile to MCC at an agreed upon price. The affidavits state that the "oral agreement established the essential terms of quality, quantity, description of goods, delivery, price and payment." * * * The affidavits also note that the parties memorialized the terms of their oral agreement on a standard D'Agostino order form, but all three affiants contend that the parties subjectively intended not to be bound by the terms on the reverse of that form despite a provision directly below the signature line that expressly and specifically incorporated those terms.[9]

The terms on the reverse of the contract give D'Agostino the right to suspend or cancel all contracts in the event of a buyer's non-payment and require a buyer to make a written report of all defects within ten days. As the magistrate judge's report and recommendation makes clear, if these terms applied to the agreements between MCC and D'Agostino, summary judgment would be appropriate because MCC failed to make any written complaints about the quality of tile it received and D'Agostino has

---

8. In the United States, the legislatures, courts, and the legal academy have voiced a preference for relying on objective manifestations of the parties' intentions. For example, Article Two of the Uniform Commercial Code, which most states have enacted in some form or another to govern contracts for the sale of goods, is replete with references to standards of commercial reasonableness. *See e.g.*, U.C.C. § 2–206 (referring to reasonable means of accepting an offer); *see also Lucy v. Zehmer*, 196 Va. 493, 503, 84 S.E.2d 516, 522 (1954) ("Whether the writing signed * * * was the result of a serious offer * * * and a serious acceptance * * *, or was a serious offer * * * and an acceptance in secret jest * * *, in either event it constituted a binding contract of sale between the parties."). Justice Holmes expressed the philosophy behind this focus on the objective in forceful terms: "The law has nothing to do with the actual state of the parties' minds. In contract, as elsewhere, it must go by externals, and judge parties by their conduct." Oliver W. Holmes, *The Common Law* 242 (Howe ed. 1963) quoted in JOHN O. HONNOLD, UNIFORM LAW FOR INTERNATIONAL SALES UNDER THE 1980 UNITED NATIONS CONVENTION § 107 at 164 (2nd ed. 1991) (hereinafter Honnold, Uniform Law).

9. MCC makes much of the fact that the written order form is entirely in Italian and that Monzon, who signed the contract on MCC's behalf directly below this provision incorporating the terms on the reverse of the form, neither spoke nor read Italian. This fact is of no assistance to MCC's position. We find it nothing short of astounding that an individual, purportedly experienced in commercial matters, would sign a contract in a foreign language and expect not to be bound simply because he could not comprehend its terms. We find nothing in the CISG that might counsel this type of reckless behavior and nothing that signals any retreat from the proposition that parties who sign contracts will be bound by them regardless of whether they have read them or understood them. *See e.g., Samson Plastic Conduit and Pipe Corp. v. Battenfeld Extrusionstechnik GMBH*, 718 F. Supp. 886, 890 (M.D. Ala.1989) ("A good and recurring illustration of the problem * * * involves a person who is * * * unfamiliar with the language in which a contract is written and who has signed a document which was not read to him. There is all but unanimous agreement that he is bound. * * *")

established MCC's non-payment of a number of invoices amounting to $108,389.40 and 102,053,846.00 Italian lira.

Article 8(1) of the CISG requires a court to consider this evidence of the parties' subjective intent. Contrary to the magistrate judge's report, which the district court endorsed and adopted, article 8(1) does not focus on interpreting the parties' statements alone. Although we agree with the magistrate judge's conclusion that no "interpretation" of the contract's terms could support MCC's position, article 8(1) also requires a court to consider subjective intent while interpreting the conduct of the parties. The CISG's language, therefore, requires courts to consider evidence of a party's subjective intent when signing a contract if the other party to the contract was aware of that intent at the time. This is precisely the type of evidence that MCC has provided through the Silingardi, Copelli, and Monzon affidavits, which discuss not only Monzon's intent as MCC's representative but also discuss the intent of D'Agostino's representatives and their knowledge that Monzon did not intend to agree to the terms on the reverse of the form contract. This acknowledgment that D'Agostino's representatives were aware of Monzon's subjective intent puts this case squarely within article 8(1) of the CISG, and therefore requires the court to consider MCC's evidence as it interprets the parties' conduct.

II. Parol Evidence and the CISG

Given our determination that the magistrate judge and the district court should have considered MCC's affidavits regarding the parties' subjective intentions, we must address a question of first impression in this circuit: whether the parol evidence rule, which bars evidence of an earlier oral contract that contradicts or varies the terms of a subsequent or contemporaneous written contract, plays any role in cases involving the CISG. We begin by observing that the parol evidence rule, contrary to its title, is a substantive rule of law, not a rule of evidence. See II E. Allen Farnsworth, Farnsworth on Contracts, § 7.2 at 194 (1990). The rule does not purport to exclude a particular type of evidence as an "untrustworthy or undesirable" way of proving a fact, but prevents a litigant from attempting to show "the fact itself—he fact that the terms of the agreement are other than those in the writing." Id. As such, a federal district court cannot simply apply the parol evidence rule as a procedural matter—as it might if excluding a particular type of evidence under the Federal Rules of Evidence, which apply in federal court regardless of the source of the substantive rule of decision. *Cf. id.* § 7.2 at 196.[13]

The CISG itself contains no express statement on the role of parol evidence. See Honnold, Uniform Law § 110 at 170. It is clear, however,

---

13. An example demonstrates this point. The CISG provides that a contract for the sale of goods need not be in writing and that the parties may prove the contract "by any means, including witnesses." CISG, art. 11. Nevertheless, a party seeking to prove a contract in such a manner in federal court could not do so in a way that violated in the rule against hearsay. See Fed.R.Evid. 802 (barring hearsay evidence). A federal district court applies the Federal Rules of Evidence because these rules are considered procedural, regardless of the source of the law that governs the substantive decision. Cf. Farnsworth on Contracts § 7.2 at 196 & n. 16 (citing cases).

that the drafters of the CISG were comfortable with the concept of permitting parties to rely on oral contracts because they eschewed any statutes of fraud provision and expressly provided for the enforcement of oral contracts. Compare CISG, art. 11 (a contract of sale need not be concluded or evidenced in writing) with U.C.C. § 2–201 (precluding the enforcement of oral contracts for the sale of goods involving more than $500). Moreover, article 8(3) of the CISG expressly directs courts to give "due consideration * * * to all relevant circumstances of the case including the negotiations * * *." to determine the intent of the parties. Given article 8(1)'s directive to use the intent of the parties to interpret their statements and conduct, article 8(3) is a clear instruction to admit and consider parol evidence regarding the negotiations to the extent they reveal the parties' subjective intent.

        * * *

Our reading of article 8(3) as a rejection of the parol evidence rule, however, is in accordance with the great weight of academic commentary on the issue. As one scholar has explained:

> [T]he language of Article 8(3) that "due consideration is to be given to all relevant circumstances of the case" seems adequate to override any domestic rule that would bar a tribunal from considering the relevance of other agreements. * * * Article 8(3) relieves tribunals from domestic rules that might bar them from "considering" any evidence between the parties that is relevant. This added flexibility for interpretation is consistent with a growing body of opinion that the "parol evidence rule" has been an embarrassment for the administration of modern transactions.

Honnold, Uniform Law § 110 at 170–71.[17] * * * One of the primary factors motivating the negotiation and adoption of the CISG was to provide parties to international contracts for the sale of goods with some degree of certainty as to the principles of law that would govern potential disputes and remove the previous doubt regarding which party's legal system might otherwise apply. See Letter of Transmittal from Ronald Reagan, President of the United States, to the United States Senate, reprinted at 15 U.S.C. app. 70, 71 (1997). Courts applying the CISG

---

[17]. *See also* LOUIS F. DEL DUCA, ET AL., SALES UNDER THE UNIFORM COMMERCIAL CODE AND THE CONVENTION ON INTERNATIONAL SALE OF GOODS, 173–74 (1993); Henry D. Gabriel, *A Primer on the United Nations Convention on the International Sale of Goods: From the Perspective of the Uniform Commercial Code*, 7 Ind. Int'l & Comp. L.Rev. 279, 281 (1997) ("Subjective intent is given primary consideration. * * * [Article 8] allows open-ended reliance on parol evidence. * * *"); HERBERT BERSTEIN & JOSEPH LOOKOFSKY, UNDERSTANDING THE CISG IN EUROPE 29 (1997) ("[T]he CISG has dispensed with the parol evidence rule which might otherwise operate to exclude extrinsic evidence under the law of certain Common Law countries."); Harry M. Fletchner, *Recent Developments: CISG*, 14 J.L. & Com. 153, 157 (1995) (criticizing the Beijing Metals opinion and noting that "[c]ommentators generally agree that article 8(3) rejects the approach to the parol evidence questions taken by U.S. domestic law.") (collecting authority); John E. Murray, Jr., *An Essay on the Formation of Contracts and Related Matters Under the United Nations Convention on Contracts for the International Sale of Goods*, 8 J.L. & Com. 11, 12 (1988) ("We are struck by a new world where there is * * * no parol evidence rule, among other differences."); Peter Winship, *Domesticating International Commercial Law: Revising U.C.C. Article 2 in Light of the United Nations Sales Convention*, 37 Loy. L.Rev. 43, 57 (1991).

cannot, therefore, upset the parties' reliance on the Convention by substituting familiar principles of domestic law when the Convention requires a different result. We may only achieve the directives of good faith and uniformity in contracts under the CISG by interpreting and applying the plain language of article 8(3) as written and obeying its directive to consider this type of parol evidence.

This is not to say that parties to an international contract for the sale of goods cannot depend on written contracts or that parol evidence regarding subjective contractual intent need always prevent a party relying on a written agreement from securing summary judgment. To the contrary, most cases will not present a situation (as exists in this case) in which both parties to the contract acknowledge a subjective intent not to be bound by the terms of a pre-printed writing. In most cases, therefore, article 8(2) of the CISG will apply, and objective evidence will provide the basis for the court's decision. See Honnold, Uniform Law § 107 at 164–65. Consequently, a party to a contract governed by the CISG will not be able to avoid the terms of a contract and force a jury trial simply by submitting an affidavit which states that he or she did not have the subjective intent to be bound by the contract's terms. * * * Moreover, to the extent parties wish to avoid parol evidence problems they can do so by including a merger clause in their agreement that extinguishes any and all prior agreements and understandings not expressed in the writing.[19]

Considering MCC's affidavits in this case, however, we conclude that the magistrate judge and the district court improperly granted summary judgment in favor of D'Agostino. Although the affidavits are, as D'Agostino observes, relatively conclusory and unsupported by facts that would objectively establish MCC's intent not to be bound by the conditions on the reverse of the form, article 8(1) requires a court to consider evidence of a party's subjective intent when the other party was aware of it, and the Silingardi and Copelli affidavits provide that evidence. This is not to say that the affidavits are conclusive proof of what the parties intended. A reasonable finder of fact, for example, could disregard testimony that purportedly sophisticated international merchants signed a contract without intending to be bound as simply too incredible to believe and hold MCC to the conditions printed on the reverse of the contract. Nevertheless, the affidavits raise an issue of material fact regarding the parties' intent to incorporate the provisions on the reverse of the form contract. If the finder of fact determines that the parties did not intend to rely on those provisions, then the more general provisions of the CISG will govern the outcome of the dispute.

---

19. *See* Ronald A. Brand & Harry M. Fletchner, *Arbitration and Contract Formation in International Trade: First Interpretations of the U.N. Sales Convention*, 12 J.L. & Com. 239, 252 (1993) (arguing that article 8(3) of the CISG will not permit the consideration of parol evidence when the parties have expressly excluded oral modifications of the contract pursuant to article 29); *see also* I ALBERT KRITZER, GUIDE TO PRACTICAL APPLICATIONS OF THE UNITED NATIONS CONVENTION ON CONTRACTS FOR THE INTERNATIONAL SALE OF GOODS 125 (1989) (counseling the use of a merger clause to compensate for the absence of a parol evidence rule in the CISG).

MCC's affidavits, however, do not discuss all of the transactions and orders that MCC placed with D'Agostino. Each of the affidavits discusses the parties' subjective intent surrounding the initial order MCC placed with D'Agostino in October 1990. The Copelli affidavit also discusses a February 1991 requirements contract between the parties and reports that the parties subjectively did not intend the terms on the reverse of the D'Agostino order form to apply to that contract either. * * * D'Agostino, however, submitted the affidavit of its chairman, Vincenzo Maselli, which describes at least three other orders from MCC on form contracts dated January 15, 1991, April 27, 1991, and May 4, 1991, in addition to the October 1990 contract. * * * MCC's affidavits do not discuss the subjective intent of the parties to be bound by language in those contracts, and D'Agostino, therefore, argues that we should affirm summary judgment to the extent damages can be traced to those order forms. It is unclear from the record, however, whether all of these contracts contained the terms that appeared in the October 1990 contract. Moreover, because article 8 requires a court to consider any "practices which the parties have established between themselves, usages and any subsequent conduct of the parties" in interpreting contracts, CISG, art. 8(3), whether the parties intended to adhere to the ten day limit for complaints, as stated on the reverse of the initial contract, will have an impact on whether MCC was bound to adhere to the limit on subsequent deliveries. Since material issues of fact remain regarding the interpretation of the remaining contracts between MCC and D'Agostino, we cannot affirm any portion of the district court's summary judgment in D'Agostino's favor.

CONCLUSION

MCC asks us to reverse the district court's grant of summary judgment in favor of D'Agostino. The district court's decision rests on preprinted contractual terms and conditions incorporated on the reverse of a standard order form that MCC's president signed on the company's behalf. Nevertheless, we conclude that the CISG, which governs international contracts for the sale of goods, precludes summary judgment in this case because MCC has raised an issue of material fact concerning the parties' subjective intent to be bound by the terms on the reverse of the pre-printed contract. The CISG also precludes the application of the parol evidence rule, which would otherwise bar the consideration of evidence concerning a prior or contemporaneously negotiated oral agreement. Accordingly, we REVERSE the district court's grant of summary judgment and REMAND this case for further proceedings consistent with this opinion.

QUESTIONS

1. Questions about the facts of this case

1.1. Let's get this straight. Monzon goes to Italy speaking no Italian, attends an Italian trade show, signs a document completely in Italian and then gets to say he really didn't mean to be bound by the acknowledged terms of that agreement? If that is the case, why didn't the court just say that he was not bound by the terms because he couldn't read them (see note 9 to the court's opinion)?

1.2. If D'Agostino had insisted on a merger clause, would the result have been different? Would it have mattered if D'Agostino wrote the merger clause in English on the front of the order form?

2. Questions about the law

2.1. As the Court indicates, the *CISG* is yet another source of law that must be consulted in this era of increasing globalization. Lazy lawyers, however, are assisted by Article 6 of the Convention, which states:

The parties may exclude the application of this Convention or, subject to Article 12 [related to writing requirements], derogate from or vary the effect of any of its provisions.

If Monzon had gone to Italy with a stamp (provided by his lawyers) that said (in English): "The provisions of the *Convention on the International Sales of Goods* do not apply to this contract," and had stamped it on D'Agostino's form, would the result have changed? What more would you need to know to answer this question?

How about if the stamp had said: "This contract is to be governed by the Uniform Commercial Code as in force in Florida, USA, on the date of this contract"?

2.2. It is clear that the *CISG* adopts a different view than Chief Judge Popham in the *Countess of Rutland's* case, quoted above at 509. Does this mean that international transactions will be more litigation-prone in the future?

SECTION 3: USING PAROL EVIDENCE AND OTHER EXTRINSIC EVIDENCE TO DISCOVER THE MEANING OF THE TERMS USED IN THE WRITTEN CONTRACT

Words are the stock in trade of a lawyer—especially a deal lawyer. He has to make the words of the deal work for his client.

Sometimes, however, words betray. When time comes for performance, the dispute isn't over what words are to be used (the primary province of the parol evidence rule), but over the meaning of the words that both sides agree are part of the contract.

Another exception to the parol evidence rule is that parol evidence may be admitted to interpret the agreement to establish "the meaning of the writing, whether or not it is integrated." *Restatement (Second) of Contracts* § 214(c).

If unchecked, this could be the loophole that swallows the parol evidence rule. As Oliver Wendell Holmes stated:

> [Y]ou cannot prove a mere private convention between the two parties to give language a different meaning from its common one. It would open too great risks if evidence were admissible to show that when they said five hundred feet they agreed it should mean one hundred inches, or that Bunker Hill Monument should signify the Old South Church.

Goode v. Riley, 153 Mass. 585, 586, 28 N.E. 228 (1891).

Accordingly, we need to know not only (1) how courts use parol evidence and other extrinsic evidence to find the meaning of the words in the written contract but also (2) when it is appropriate for courts to look to parol evidence and other extrinsic evidence to interpret the meaning of the words in the written contract. The next case, a classic, shows the tangles that can come from failing to anticipate that a word as common as "chicken" might be the basis for disagreement.

FRIGALIMENT IMPORTING CO., LTD. v. B.N.S. INTERNATIONAL SALES CORP.

U.S. District Court, Southern District of New York
190 F.Supp. 116 (1960)

FRIENDLY, J.:

OPINION:

The issue is, what is chicken? Plaintiff says 'chicken' means a young chicken, suitable for broiling and frying. Defendant says 'chicken' means any bird of that genus that meets contract specifications on weight and quality, including what it calls 'stewing chicken' and plaintiff pejoratively terms 'fowl'. Dictionaries give both meanings, as well as some others not relevant here. To support its [sic. The word "meaning" should probably be inserted here. Eds.], plaintiff sends a number of volleys over the net; defendant essays to return them and adds a few serves of its own. Assuming that both parties were acting in good faith, the case nicely illustrates Holmes' remark 'that the making of a contract depends not on the agreement of two minds in one intention, but on the agreement of two sets of external signs—not on the parties' having meant the same thing but on their having said the same thing.' The Path of the Law, in Collected Legal Papers, p. 178. I have concluded that plaintiff has not sustained its burden of persuasion that the contract used 'chicken' in the narrower sense.

The action is for breach of the warranty that goods sold shall correspond to the description, New York Personal Property Law, McKinney's Consol. Laws, c. 41, § 95. Two contracts are in suit. In the first, dated May 2, 1957, defendant, a New York sales corporation, confirmed the sale to plaintiff, a Swiss corporation, of

> 'US Fresh Frozen Chicken, Grade A, Government Inspected, Eviscerated 2 ½–3 lbs. and 1 ½–2 lbs. each all chicken individually wrapped in cryovac, packed in secured fiber cartons or wooden boxes, suitable for export
>
> 75,000 lbs. 2 ½–3 lbs. * * * @ $33.00
>
> 25,000 lbs. 1 ½–2 lbs. * * * @ $36.50
>
> per 100 lbs. FAS New York
>
> scheduled May 10, 1957 pursuant to instructions from Penson & Co., New York.'

The second contract, also dated May 2, 1957, was identical save that only 50,000 lbs. of the heavier 'chicken' were called for, the price of the smaller birds was $37 per 100 lbs., and shipment was scheduled for May 30. The initial shipment under the first contract was short but the balance was shipped on May 17. When the initial shipment arrived in Switzerland, plaintiff found, on May 28, that the 2 ½–3 lbs. birds were not young chicken suitable for broiling and frying but stewing chicken or 'fowl'; indeed, many of the cartons and bags plainly so indicated. Protests ensued. Nevertheless, shipment under the second contract was made on May 29, the 2 ½–3 lbs. birds again being stewing chicken. Defendant stopped the transportation of these at Rotterdam.

This action followed. Plaintiff says that, notwithstanding that its acceptance was in Switzerland, New York law controls under the principle of Rubin v. Irving Trust Co., 1953, 305 N.Y. 288, 305, 113 N.E.2d 424, 431; defendant does not dispute this, and relies on New York decisions. I shall follow the apparent agreement of the parties as to the applicable law.

Since the word 'chicken' standing alone is ambiguous, I turn first to see whether the contract itself offers any aid to its interpretation. Plaintiff says the 1 ½–2 lbs. birds necessarily had to be young chicken since the older birds do not come in that size, hence the 2 ½–3 lbs. birds must likewise be young. This is unpersuasive—a contract for 'apples' of two different sizes could be filled with different kinds of apples even though only one species came in both sizes. Defendant notes that the contract called not simply for chicken but for 'US Fresh Frozen Chicken, Grade A, Government Inspected.' It says the contract thereby incorporated by reference the Department of Agriculture's regulations, which favor its interpretation; I shall return to this after reviewing plaintiff's other contentions.

The first hinges on an exchange of cablegrams which preceded execution of the formal contracts. The negotiations leading up to the contracts were conducted in New York between defendant's secretary, Ernest R. Bauer, and a Mr. Stovicek, who was in New York for the Czechoslovak government at the World Trade Fair. A few days after meeting Bauer at the fair, Stovicek telephoned and inquired whether defendant would be interested in exporting poultry to Switzerland. Bauer then met with Stovicek, who showed him a cable from plaintiff dated April 26, 1957, announcing that they 'are buyer' of 25,000 lbs. of chicken 2 ½–3 lbs. weight, Cryovac packed, grade A Government inspected, at a price up to 33 cents per pound, for shipment on May 10, to be confirmed by the following morning, and were interested in further offerings. After testing the market for price, Bauer accepted, and Stovicek sent a confirmation that evening. Plaintiff stresses that, although these and subsequent cables between plaintiff and defendant, which laid the basis for the additional quantities under the first and for all of the second contract, were predominantly in German, they used the English word 'chicken'; it claims this was done because it understood 'chicken' meant young chicken whereas the German word, 'Huhn,' included both 'Brathuhn' (broilers) and 'Suppenhuhn' (stewing chicken), and that defendant, whose officers were thoroughly conversant with German, should have realized this. Whatever force this argument might otherwise have is largely drained away by Bauer's testimony that he asked Stovicek what kind of chickens were wanted, received the answer 'any kind of chickens,' and then, in German, asked whether the cable meant 'Huhn' and received an affirmative response. Plaintiff attacks this as contrary to what Bauer testified on his deposition in March, 1959, and also on the ground that Stovicek had no authority to interpret the meaning of the cable. The first contention would be persuasive if sustained by the record, since Bauer was free at the trial from the threat of contradiction by Stovicek as he was not at the time of the deposition; however, review of the deposition does not convince me of the claimed inconsistency. As to the second contention, it may well be that Stovicek lacked authority to commit plaintiff for prices or delivery dates other than those specified in the cable; but plaintiff cannot at the same time rely on its cable to Stovicek as its dictionary to the meaning of the contract and repudiate the interpretation given the dictionary by the man in whose hands it was put. * * * Plaintiff's reliance on the fact that the contract forms contain the words 'through the intermediary of: _____', with the blank not filled, as negating agency, is wholly unpersuasive; the purpose of this clause was to permit filling in the name of an intermediary to whom a commission would be payable, not to blot out what had been the fact.

Plaintiff's next contention is that there was a definite trade usage that 'chicken' meant 'young chicken.' Defendant showed that it was only beginning in the poultry trade in 1957, thereby bringing itself within the principle that 'when one of the parties is not a member of the trade or other circle, his acceptance of the standard must be made to appear' by proving either that he had actual knowledge of the usage or that the usage is 'so generally known in the community that his actual individual knowledge of it may be inferred.' * * * Here there was no proof of actual knowledge of the alleged usage; indeed, it is quite plain that defendant's belief was to the contrary. In order to meet the alternative requirement, the law of New York demands a showing that 'the usage is of so long continuance, so well established, so notorious, so universal and so reasonable in itself, as that the presumption is violent that the parties contracted with reference to it, and made it a part of their agreement.' * * *

Plaintiff endeavored to establish such a usage by the testimony of three witnesses and certain other evidence. Strasser, resident buyer in New York for a large chain of Swiss cooperatives, testified that 'on chicken I would definitely understand a broiler.' However, the force of this testimony was considerably weakened by the fact that in his own transactions the witness, a careful businessman, protected himself by using 'broiler' when that was what he wanted and 'fowl' when he wished older birds. Indeed, there are some indications, dating back to a remark of Lord Mansfield, Edie v. East India Co., 2 Burr. 1216, 1222 (1761), that no credit should be given 'witnesses to usage, who could not adduce instances in verification.' * * * While Wigmore thinks this goes too far, a witness' consistent failure to rely on the alleged usage deprives his opinion testimony of much of its effect. Niesielowski, an officer of one of the companies that had furnished the stewing chicken to defendant, testified that 'chicken' meant 'the male species of the poultry industry. That could be a broiler, a fryer or a roaster', but not a stewing chicken; however, he also testified that upon receiving defendant's inquiry for 'chickens', he asked whether the desire was for 'fowl or frying chickens' and, in fact, supplied fowl, although taking the precaution of asking defendant, a day or two after plaintiff's acceptance of the contracts in suit, to change its confirmation of its order from 'chickens,' as defendant had originally prepared it, to 'stewing chickens.' Dates, an employee of Urner–Barry Company, which publishes a daily market report on the poultry trade, gave it as his view that the trade meaning of 'chicken' was 'broilers and fryers.' In addition to this opinion testimony, plaintiff relied on the fact that the Urner–Barry service, the Journal of Commerce, and Weinberg Bros. & Co. of Chicago, a large supplier of poultry, published quotations in a manner which, in one way or another, distinguish between 'chicken,' comprising broilers, fryers and certain other categories, and 'fowl,' which, Bauer acknowledged, included stewing chickens. This material would be impressive if there were nothing to the contrary. However, there was, as will now be seen.

Defendant's witness Weininger, who operates a chicken eviscerating plant in New Jersey, testified 'Chicken is everything except a goose, a duck, and a turkey. Everything is a chicken, but then you have to say, you have to specify which category you want or that you are talking about.' Its witness Fox said that in the trade 'chicken' would encompass all the various classifications. Sadina, who conducts a food inspection service, testified that he would consider any bird coming within the classes of 'chicken' in the Department of Agriculture's regulations to be a chicken. The specifications approved by the General Services Administration include fowl as well as broilers and fryers under the classification 'chickens.' Statistics of the Institute of American Poultry Industries use the phrases

'Young chickens' and 'Mature chickens,' under the general heading 'Total chickens' and the Department of Agriculture's daily and weekly price reports avoid use of the word 'chicken' without specification.

Defendant advances several other points which it claims affirmatively support its construction. Primary among these is the regulation of the Department of Agriculture, 7 C.F.R. § 70.300–70.370, entitled, 'Grading and Inspection of Poultry and Edible Products Thereof.' and in particular 70.301 which recited:

Chickens. The following are the various classes of chickens:

(a) Broiler or fryer * * *

(b) Roaster * * *

(c) Capon * * *

(d) Stag * * *

(e) Hen or stewing chicken or fowl * * *

(f) Cock or old rooster * * *

Defendant argues, as previously noted, that the contract incorporated these regulations by reference. Plaintiff answers that the contract provision related simply to grade and Government inspection and did not incorporate the Government definition of 'chicken,' and also that the definition in the Regulations is ignored in the trade. However, the latter contention was contradicted by Weininger and Sadina; and there is force in defendant's argument that the contract made the regulations a dictionary, particularly since the reference to Government grading was already in plaintiff's initial cable to Stovicek.

Defendant makes a further argument based on the impossibility of its obtaining broilers and fryers at the 33 cents price offered by plaintiff for the 2 ½–3 lbs. birds. There is no substantial dispute that, in late April, 1957, the price for 2 ½–3 lbs. broilers was between 35 and 37 cents per pound, and that when defendant entered into the contracts, it was well aware of this and intended to fill them by supplying fowl in these weights. It claims that plaintiff must likewise have known the market since plaintiff had reserved shipping space on April 23, three days before plaintiff's cable to Stovicek, or, at least, that Stovicek was chargeable with such knowledge. It is scarcely an answer to say, as plaintiff does in its brief, that the 33 cents price offered by the 2 ½–3 lbs. 'chickens' was closer to the prevailing 35 cents price for broilers than to the 30 cents at which defendant procured fowl. Plaintiff must have expected defendant to make some profit—certainly it could not have expected defendant deliberately to incur a loss.

Finally, defendant relies on conduct by the plaintiff after the first shipment had been received. On May 28 plaintiff sent two cables complaining that the larger birds in the first shipment constituted 'fowl.' Defendant answered with a cable refusing to recognize plaintiff's objection and announcing 'We have today ready for shipment 50,000 lbs. chicken 2

½–3 lbs. 25,000 lbs. broilers 1 ½–2 lbs.,' these being the goods procured for shipment under the second contract, and asked immediate answer 'whether we are to ship this merchandise to you and whether you will accept the merchandise.' After several other cable exchanges, plaintiff replied on May 29 'Confirm again that merchandise is to be shipped since resold by us if not enough pursuant to contract chickens are shipped the missing quantity is to be shipped within ten days stop we resold to our customers pursuant to your contract chickens grade A you have to deliver us said merchandise we again state that we shall make you fully responsible for all resulting costs.'[2] Defendant argues that if plaintiff was sincere in thinking it was entitled to young chickens, plaintiff would not have allowed the shipment under the second contract to go forward, since the distinction between broilers and chickens drawn in defendant's cablegram must have made it clear that the larger birds would not be broilers. However, plaintiff answers that the cables show plaintiff was insisting on delivery of young chickens and that defendant shipped old ones at its peril. Defendant's point would be highly relevant on another disputed issue— whether if liability were established, the measure of damages should be the difference in market value of broilers and stewing chicken in New York or the larger difference in Europe, but I cannot give it weight on the issue of interpretation. Defendant points out also that plaintiff proceeded to deliver some of the larger birds in Europe, describing them as 'poulets'; defendant argues that it was only when plaintiff's customers complained about this that plaintiff developed the idea that 'chicken' meant 'young chicken.' There is little force in this in view of plaintiff's immediate and consistent protests.

When all the evidence is reviewed, it is clear that defendant believed it could comply with the contracts by delivering stewing chicken in the 2 ½ –3 lbs. size. Defendant's subjective intent would not be significant if this did not coincide with an objective meaning of 'chicken.' Here it did coincide with one of the dictionary meanings, with the definition in the Department of Agriculture Regulations to which the contract made at least oblique reference, with at least some usage in the trade, with the realities of the market, and with what plaintiff's spokesman had said. Plaintiff asserts it to be equally plain that plaintiff's own subjective intent was to obtain broilers and fryers; the only evidence against this is the material as to market prices and this may not have been sufficiently brought home. In any event it is unnecessary to determine that issue. For plaintiff has the burden of showing that 'chicken' was used in the narrower rather than in the broader sense, and this it has not sustained.

This opinion constitutes the Court's findings of fact and conclusions of law. Judgment shall be entered dismissing the complaint with costs.

---

2. These cables were in German; 'chicken', 'broilers' and, on some occasions, 'fowl,' were in English.

QUESTIONS, NOTE, AND CONNECTION

1. Questions about the facts of this case

    1.1. What was Frigaliment suing for? Put another way, why does Frigaliment think that BNS breached the contract?

    1.2. This is a trick question: Does the court hold that BNS did not breach the contract?

    1.3. Given the result and the Court's reason for its ruling, and the likely cost of procuring all the various experts and testimony about the meaning of chicken, what more could Frigaliment's lawyers done to persuade the Court that its definition of chicken was the intended one?

2. Questions about the law

    2.1. According to Judge Friendly, the "word 'chicken' standing alone is ambiguous." Do you agree? Was this finding of ambiguity important? Reconsider that question after considering the next two cases in this chapter.

    2.2. Did Judge Friendly consider parol evidence in interpreting the word "chicken"? Did Judge Friendly even consider the parol evidence rule?

    2.3. Change the facts somewhat. Instead of stopping the shipment at Rotterdam, and suing BNS for breach, assume that Frigaliment had accepted the second shipment of chickens, but paid BNS an amount equal to the contract price less its damages. If BNS was thereby forced to sue Frigaliment for the difference, does BNS win on the facts as alleged and proved at trial?

    2.4. Change the facts even more. BNS shipped alligator. When sued by Frigaliment for breach of contract, BNS argues that the contract term "chicken" includes alligator because alligator tastes like chicken http://cherokeetribune.com/view/full_story/4009317/art icle-Tastes-like-chicken—Processing-plant-gets-alligator-ready-for-the-dinner-table Would Judge Friendly decide this case differently?

3. Note

    Judge Henry Friendly was one of the best federal judges in our nation's history. He not only wrote well-crafted opinions, but also contributed to the legal literature with numerous law review articles on many subjects. As noted by Judge Richard Posner:

    He was the greatest federal appellate judge of his time—in analytic power, memory, and application perhaps of any time. His opinions have exhibited greater staying power than that of any of his contemporaries on the federal courts of appeals. In addition, his extrajudicial scholarship has been extraordinarily influential, more so, perhaps, than any judge's since Cardozo.

    Richard Posner, *In Memoriam: Henry J. Friendly*, 99 HARV. L. REV. 1724, 1724 (1986).

Before appointment to the federal Second Circuit Court of Appeals, Judge Friendly had been a successful business practitioner in New York City. As recalled by one of the attorneys involved in *Frigaliment*, "Judge Friendly [who had been appointed from practice directly to the Second Circuit without any trial experience] felt that he needed trial court experience in order to be able to perform his function as a appellate court judge and requested a case to be assigned to him as a trial judge. The *Frigaliment* case was assigned." One wonders if the parties knew then what lay in store for the reported opinion, which is a staple in all major contracts casebooks.

4. Connection

Think back to *Raffles v. Wichelhaus* and the cases regarding mistake in formation. Why doesn't the court rule that since neither party had the same conception of chicken, then no contract was formed? *See Restatement (Second) of Contracts* § 20. A year after issuing the *Frigaliment* decision, Judge Friendly acknowledged that the case might better have been decided on other grounds. *Dadourian Exp. Corp. v. United States*, 291 F.2d 178, 187 n.4 (2d Cir. 1961)

A. COURSE OF PERFORMANCE, COURSE OF DEALING AND TRADE USAGE (AGAIN)

Frigaliment was decided before the Uniform Commercial Code, or the *Convention on the International Sale of Goods*, was in effect. The types of evidence adduced in *Frigaliment* would today come under the heading of "usage of trade" and would be admissible under section 2–202(a) to explain the term "chicken."

Section 1–303 set out below explains the term "usage of trade" as well as the terms "course of performance" and "course of dealing".

§ 1–303. Course of Performance, Course of Dealing, and Usage of Trade.

(a) A "course of performance" is a sequence of conduct between the parties to a particular transaction that exists if:

(1) the agreement of the parties with respect to the transaction involves repeated occasions for performance by a party; and

(2) the other party, with knowledge of the nature of the performance and opportunity for objection to it, accepts the performance or acquiesces in it without objection.

(b) A "course of dealing" is a sequence of conduct concerning previous transactions between the parties to a particular transaction that is fairly to be regarded as establishing a common basis of understanding for interpreting their expressions and other conduct.

(c) A "usage of trade" is any practice or method of dealing having such regularity of observance in a place, vocation, or trade as to justify an expectation that it will be observed with respect to the transaction in question. The existence and scope of such a usage must be proved as facts. If it is established that such a usage is embodied in a trade code or similar record, the interpretation of the record is a question of law.

(d) A course of performance or course of dealing between the parties, or usage of trade in the vocation, or trade in which they are engaged or of which they are, or should be, aware is relevant in ascertaining the meaning of the parties' agreement, may give particular meaning to specific terms of the agreement, and may supplement or qualify the terms of the agreement. * * *

(e) Except as otherwise provided in subsection (f), the express terms of an agreement and any applicable course of performance, course of dealing, or usage of trade must be construed whenever reasonable as consistent with each other. If such a construction is unreasonable: (1) express terms prevail over course of performance, course of dealing, and usage of trade; (2) course of performance prevails over course of dealing and usage of trade; and (3) course of dealing prevails over usage of trade. * * *

The *CISG* also makes references to such practices, as shown below:

Article 9, *Convention on the International Sale of Goods*

(1) The parties are bound by any usages to which they have agreed and by any practices which they have established between themselves.

(2) The parties are considered, unless otherwise agreed, to have impliedly made applicable to their contract or its formation a usage of which the parties knew, or ought to have known, and which in international trade is widely known to, and regularly observed by, parties to contracts of the type involved in the particular trade concerned.

PROBLEMS ON TRADE USAGE AND COURSE OF DEALING

1. Under the U.C.C., what is the difference between a course of dealing and a course of performance? Can you ever have a course of performance in a contract to sell just one item (such as a car)?

2. Under either the U.C.C. or the *CISG*,* do you have to be a merchant to be bound by a usage of trade? If not, how do you protect yourself as a novice when buying something for which there is a recognized market and recognized practices of trade?

---
* The *CISG* does not apply to sales of goods bought for personal, family or household use, Article 2(a), but the U.C.C. does not have a similar limitation. So for this problem, assume that you are a entrepreneur seeking to buy goods for your business.

3. Note that under the U.C.C., a usage of trade may arise with respect to a "place, vocation, or trade." What is the difference among these three items? Does the *CISG* have a similar broad application?

Note that Section 1–303(e) of the U.C.C. tries to prioritize conflicts as among course of performance, course of dealing, trade usage and express terms. Is this a satisfactory ordering?

B. AMBIGUITY IN CONTRACT TERMS— IS IT IMPORTANT, AND, IF SO, WHEN DOES IT EXIST?

Judge Friendly's *Frigaliment* opinion helps us see the tools a court uses in interpreting a contract term the court has found to be ambiguous. The *Frigaliment* opinion does not, however, help us answer the questions (1) can a court use these interpretative tools only if the contract term is ambiguous, and, if so (2) how does a court determine whether a term is ambiguous.

In the next case, the question involves whether words used at one time can encompass actions or developments that occur later on. Is such a situation one in which ambiguity is created?

RANDOM HOUSE, INC. v. ROSETTA BOOKS LLC

U.S. District Court, Southern District of New York
150 F. Supp. 2d 613 (2001)

SIDNEY H. STEIN, U.S. DISTRICT JUDGE.

In this copyright infringement action, Random House, Inc. seeks to enjoin Rosetta Books LLC and its Chief Executive Officer from selling in digital format eight specific works on the grounds that the authors of the works had previously granted Random House—not Rosetta Books—the right to "print, publish and sell the work[s] in book form." Rosetta Books, on the other hand, claims it is not infringing upon the rights those authors gave Random House because the licensing agreements between the publisher and the author do not include a grant of digital or electronic rights. Relying on the language of the contracts and basic principles of contract interpretation, this Court finds that the right to "print, publish and sell the work[s] in book form" in the contracts at issue does not include the right to publish the works in the format that has come to be known as the "ebook." Accordingly, Random House's motion for a preliminary injunction is denied.

BACKGROUND

In the year 2000 and the beginning of 2001, Rosetta Books contracted with several authors to publish certain of their works—including The Confessions of Nat Turner and Sophie's Choice by William Styron;

Slaughterhouse–Five, Breakfast of Champions, The Sirens of Titan, Cat's Cradle, and Player Piano by Kurt Vonnegut; and Promised Land by Robert B. Parker—in digital format over the Internet. * * * On February 26, 2001 Rosetta Books launched its ebook business, offering those titles and others for sale in digital format. * * * The next day, Random House filed this complaint accusing Rosetta Books of committing copyright infringement and tortiously interfering with the contracts Random House had with Messrs. Parker, Styron and Vonnegut by selling its ebooks. It simultaneously moved for a preliminary injunction prohibiting Rosetta from infringing plaintiff's copyrights.

A. Ebooks

Ebooks are "digital book[s] that you can read on a computer screen or an electronic device." (Hrg. at 13; http://www.rosettabooks.com/pages/about_ebooks.html) Ebooks are created by converting digitized text into a format readable by computer software. The text can be viewed on a desktop or laptop computer, personal digital assistant or handheld dedicated ebook reading device. * * * Rosetta's ebooks can only be read after they are downloaded into a computer that contains either Microsoft Reader, Adobe Acrobat Reader, or Adobe Acrobat eBook Reader software.

Included in a Rosetta ebook is a book cover, title page, copyright page and "eforward" all created by Rosetta Books. Although the text of the ebook is exactly the same as the text of the original work, the ebook contains various features that take advantage of its digital format. For example, ebook users can search the work electronically to find specific words and phrases. They can electronically "highlight" and "bookmark" certain text, which can then be automatically indexed and accessed through hyperlinks. They can use hyperlinks in the table of contents to jump to specific chapters.

Users can also type electronic notes which are stored with the related text. These notes can be automatically indexed, sorted and filed. Users can also change the font size and style of the text to accommodate personal preferences; thus, an electronic screen of text may contain more words, fewer words, or the same number of words as a page of the original published book. In addition, users can have displayed the definition of any word in the text. * * * In one version of the software, the word can also be pronounced aloud.

Rosetta's ebooks contain certain security features to prevent users from printing, emailing or otherwise distributing the text. Although it is technologically possible to foil these security features, anyone who does so would be violating the licensing agreement accompanying the software. * * *

B. Random House's licensing agreements

While each agreement between the author and Random House differs in some respects, each uses the phrase "print, publish and sell the work in book form" to convey rights from the author to the publisher. * * *

1. Styron Agreements

Forty years ago, in 1961, William Styron granted Random House the right to publish The Confessions of Nat Turner. Besides granting Random House an exclusive license to "print, publish and sell the work in book form," Styron also gave it the right to "license publication of the work by book clubs," "license publication of a reprint edition," "license after book publication the publication of the work, in whole or in part, in anthologies, school books," and other shortened forms, "license without charge publication of the work in Braille, or photographing, recording, and microfilming the work for the physically handicapped," and "publish or permit others to publish or broadcast by radio or television * * * selections from the work, for publicity purposes. * * *" * * * Styron demonstrated that he was not granting Random House the rights to license publication in the British Commonwealth or in foreign languages by crossing out these clauses on the form contract supplied by Random House. * * *

The publisher agreed in the contract to "publish the work at its own expense and in such style and manner and at such a price as it deems suitable." * * * The contract also contains a non-compete clause that provides, in relevant part, that "the Author agrees that during the term of this agreement he will not, without the written permission of the Publisher, publish or permit to be published any material in book or pamphlet form, based on the material in the work, or which is reasonably likely to injure its sale." * * * Styron's contract with Random House for the right to publish Sophie's Choice, executed in 1977, is virtually identical to his 1961 contract to publish The Confessions of Nat Turner. * * *

2. Vonnegut Agreements

Kurt Vonnegut's 1967 contract granting Random House's predecessor-in-interest Dell Publishing Co., Inc. the license to publish Slaughterhouse–Five and Breakfast of Champions follows a similar structure to the Styron agreements. Paragraph #1 is captioned "grant of rights" and contains those rights the author is granting to the book publisher. Certain rights on the publisher's form contract are crossed out, indicating that the author reserved them for himself. * * *One of the rights granted by the author includes the "exclusive right to publish and to license the Work for publication, after book publication * * * in anthologies, selections, digests, abridgements, magazine condensations, serialization, newspaper syndication, picture book versions, microfilming, Xerox and other forms of copying, either now in use or hereafter developed." * * *

Vonnegut specifically reserved for himself the "dramatic * * * motion picture (silent and sound) * * * radio broadcasting (including mechanical renditions and/or recordings of the text) * * * [and] television" rights. * * * Unlike the Styron agreements, this contract does not contain a non-compete clause.

Vonnegut's 1970 contract granting Dell the license to publish The Sirens of Titan, Cat's Cradle, and Player Piano contains virtually identical grants and reservations of rights as his 1967 contract. However, it does contain a non-compete clause, which provides that "the Author * * * will not publish or permit to be published any edition, adaptation or abridgment of the Work by any party other than Dell without Dell's prior written consent." * * *

3.   Parker Agreement

Robert B. Parker's 1982 contract granting Dell the license to publish Promised Land is similar to the 1970 Vonnegut contract. * * * Paragraph #1 contains the "grant of rights," certain of which have been crossed out by the author. The contract does grant Random House the right to "Xerox and other forms of copying of the printed page, either now in use or hereafter developed." * * * Parker also reserved the rights to the "dramatic * * * motion picture (silent and sound) * * * radio broadcasting * * * television * * * mechanical or electronic recordings of the text. * * *" * * * There is also a non-compete clause that provides, in relevant part, that "the Author * * * will not, without the written permission of Dell, publish or permit to be published any material based on the material in the Work, or which is reasonably likely to injure its sale." * * *

DISCUSSION

* * *

B.   Ownership of a Valid Copyright

* * * It is well settled that although the authors own the copyrights to their works, "the legal or beneficial owner of an exclusive right under a copyright is entitled * * * to institute an action for any infringement of that particular right committed while he or she is the owner of it." * * * The question for resolution, therefore, is whether Random House is the beneficial owner of the right to publish these works as ebooks.

1.   Contract Interpretation of Licensing Agreements—Legal Standards

Random House claims to own the rights in question through its licensing agreements with the authors. Interpretation of an agreement purporting to grant a copyright license is a matter of state contract law. * * *

In New York, a written contract is to be interpreted so as to give effect to the intention of the parties as expressed in the contract's language. * * * The court must consider the entire contract and reconcile all parts, if possible, to avoid an inconsistency. * * *

Determining whether a contract provision is ambiguous is a question of law to be decided by the court. * * * Pursuant to New York law, "contract language is ambiguous if it is capable of more than one meaning when viewed objectively by a reasonably intelligent person who has examined the context of the entire integrated agreement and who is cognizant of the customs, practices, usages and terminology as generally understood in the particular trade or business." * * * "No ambiguity exists when contract language has a 'definite and precise meaning, unattended by danger of misconception in the purport of the [contract] itself, and concerning which there is no reasonable basis for a difference of opinion.' "

rule

If the language of a contract is ambiguous, interpretation of the contract becomes a question of fact for the finder of fact and extrinsic evidence is admissible. * * *

These principles are in accord with the approach the U.S. Court of Appeals for the Second Circuit uses in analyzing contractual language in disputes, such as this one, "about whether licensees may exploit licensed works through new marketing channels made possible by technologies developed after the licensing contract—often called 'new use' problems." * * * The two leading cases in this Circuit on how to determine whether "new uses" come within prior grants of rights are Boosey [& Hawkes Music Publishers, Ltd v. Walt Disney Co., 145 F.3d 481 (2d Cir. 1998)] and Bartsch v. Metro–Goldwyn–Mayer, Inc., 391 F.2d 150 (2d Cir. 1968), decided three decades apart.

In *Bartsch*, the author of the play "Maytime" granted Harry Bartsch in 1930 "the motion picture rights [to 'Maytime'] throughout the world," including the right to "copyright, vend, license and exhibit such motion picture photoplays throughout the world; together with the further sole and exclusive rights by mechanical and/or electrical means to record, reproduce and transmit sound, including spoken words. * * *" 391 F.2d at 150. He in turn assigned those rights to Warner Bros. Pictures, which transferred them to MGM. In 1958 MGM licensed its motion picture "Maytime" for viewing on television. Bartsch sued, claiming the right to transmit the play over television had not been given to MGM.

Judge Henry Friendly, for the Second Circuit, wrote in 1968 that "any effort to reconstruct what the parties actually intended nearly forty years ago is doomed to failure." * * * He added that the words of the grant by Bartsch "were well designed to give the assignee [*i.e.*, MGM] the broadest rights with respect to its copyrighted property." * * * The words of the grant were broad enough to cover the new use—i.e. viewing on television—and Judge Friendly interpreted them to do so. This interpretation, he wrote, permitted the licensee to "properly pursue any uses which may reasonably be said to fall within the medium as described in the license." * * * That interpretation also avoided the risk "that a deadlock between the grantor and the grantee might prevent the work's being shown over the new medium at all." * * *

In *Boosey*, the plaintiff was the assignee of Igor Stravinsky's copyrights in the musical composition, "The Rite of Spring." In 1939, Stravinsky had licensed Disney's use of "The Rite of Spring" in the motion picture "Fantasia." Fifty-two years later, in 1991, Disney released "Fantasia" in video format and Boosey brought an action seeking, among other relief, a declaration that the grant of rights did not include the right to use the Stravinsky work in video format. In *Boosey*, just as in *Bartsch*, the language of the grant was broad, enabling the licensee "to record in any manner, medium or form, and to license the performance of, the musical composition [for use] in a motion picture." * * *

At the Second Circuit, a unanimous panel focused on "neutral principles of contract interpretation rather than solicitude for either party." * * * "What governs," Judge Pierre Leval wrote, "is the language of the contract. If the contract is more reasonably read to convey one meaning, the party benefitted by that reading should be able to rely on it; the party seeking exception or deviation from the meaning reasonably conveyed by the words of the contract should bear the burden of negotiating for language that would express the limitation or deviation. This principle favors neither licensors nor licensees. It follows simply from the words of the contract." * * *

The Second Circuit's neutral approach was specifically influenced by policy considerations on both sides. On the one hand, the approach seeks to encourage licensees—here, the publishers—to develop new technologies that will enable all to enjoy the creative work in a new way. On the other hand, it seeks to fulfill the purpose underlying federal copyright law—to encourage authors to create literary works. * * *

2. Application of Legal Standards

Relying on "the language of the license contract and basic principles of interpretation," * * * as instructed to do so by *Boosey* and *Bartsch*, this Court finds that the most reasonable interpretation of the grant in the contracts at issue to "print, publish and sell the work in book form" does not include the right to publish the work as an ebook. At the outset, the phrase itself distinguishes between the pure content—i.e. "the work"—and the format of display—"in book form." The Random House Webster's Unabridged Dictionary defines a "book" as "a written or printed work of fiction or nonfiction, usually on sheets of paper fastened or bound together within covers" and defines "form" as "external appearance of a clearly defined area, as distinguished from color or material; the shape of a thing or person." Random House Webster's Unabridged Dictionary (2001), available in searchable form at http://www.allwords.com.

Manifestly, paragraph #1 of each contract—entitled either "grant of rights" or "exclusive publication right"—conveys certain rights from the author to the publisher. * * * In that paragraph, separate grant language is used to convey the rights to publish book club editions, reprint editions, abridged forms, and editions in Braille. This language would not be necessary if the phrase "in book form" encompassed all types of books. That paragraph specifies exactly which rights were being granted by the author to the publisher. Indeed, many of the rights set forth in the publisher's form contracts were in fact not granted to the publisher, but rather were reserved by the authors to themselves. For example, each of the authors specifically reserved certain rights for themselves by striking out phrases, sentences, and paragraphs of the publisher's form contract.

This evidences an intent by these authors not to grant the publisher the broadest rights in their works.

Random House contends that the phrase "in book form" means to faithfully reproduce the author's text in its complete form as a reading experience and that, since ebooks concededly contain the complete text of the work, Rosetta cannot also possess those rights. * * * While Random House's definition distinguishes "book form" from other formats that require separate contractual language—such as audio books and serialization rights—it does not distinguish other formats specifically mentioned in paragraph #1 of the contracts, such as book club editions and reprint editions. Because the Court must, if possible, give effect to all contractual language in order to "safeguard against adopting an interpretation that would render any individual provision superfluous," * * * Random House's definition cannot be adopted.

Random House points specifically to the clause requiring it to "publish the work at its own expense and in such a style and manner and at such a price as [Random House] deems suitable" as support for its position. * * * However, plaintiff takes this clause out of context. It appears in paragraph #2, captioned "Style, Price and Date of Publication," not paragraph #1, which includes all the grants of rights. In context, the phrase simply means that Random House has control over the appearance of the formats granted to Random House in the first paragraph; i.e., control over the style of the book.

Random House also cites the non-compete clauses as evidence that the authors granted it broad, exclusive rights in their work. Random House reasons that because the authors could not permit any material that would injure the sale of the work to be published without Random House's consent, the authors must have granted the right to publish ebooks to Random House. This reasoning turns the analysis on its head. First, the grant of rights follows from the grant language alone. * * * Second, non-compete clauses must be limited in scope in order to be enforceable in New York. * * * Third, even if the authors did violate this provision of their Random House agreements by contracting with Rosetta Books—a point on which this Court does not opine—the remedy is a breach of contract action against the authors, not a copyright infringement action against Rosetta Books. * * *

The photocopy clause—giving Random House the right to "Xerox and other forms of copying, either now in use or hereafter developed"—similarly does not bolster Random House's position. Although the clause does appear in the grant language paragraph, taken in context, it clearly refers only to new developments in xerography and other forms of photocopying. Stretching it to include new forms of publishing, such as ebooks, would make the rest of the contract superfluous because there would be no reason for authors to reserve rights to forms of publishing "now in use." This interpretation also comports with the publishing industry's trade usage of the phrase. * * *

Not only does the language of the contract itself lead almost ineluctably to the conclusion that Random House does not own the right to publish the works as ebooks, but also a reasonable person "cognizant of the customs, practices, usages and terminology as generally understood in the particular trade or business," * * *, would conclude that the grant language does not include ebooks.[7] "To print, publish and sell the work in book form" is understood in the publishing industry to be a "limited" grant. * * *

In *Field v. True Comics*, the court held that "the sole and exclusive right to publish, print and market in book form"—especially when the author had specifically reserved rights for himself—was "much more limited" than "the sole and exclusive right to publish, print and market the book." * * * In fact, the publishing industry generally interprets the phrase "in book form" as granting the publisher "the exclusive right to publish a hardcover trade book in English for distribution in North America." * * *

III.   CONCLUSION

Employing the most important tool in the armamentarium of contract interpretation—the language of the contract itself—this Court has concluded that Random House is not the beneficial owner of the right to publish the eight works at issue as ebooks. This is neither a victory for technophiles nor a defeat for Luddites. It is merely a determination, relying on neutral principles of contract interpretation, that because Random House is not likely to succeed on the merits of its copyright infringement claim and cannot demonstrate irreparable harm, its motion for a preliminary injunction should be denied.

QUESTIONS AND NOTES

1.   Questions about the facts of this case

　　1.1.   In the first paragraph of the opinion, Judge Stein states that his holding is based on "the language of the contracts and basic principles of contract interpretation." What contract language does he focus on? Who are the parties to the contracts? Do they include Rosetta Books, the defendant in the lawsuit? Why not?

　　1.2.   Why does Judge Stein treat all five contracts the same? Do any of the contracts contain language that would have warranted different treatment?

---

7. Although *Boosey* recognizes that extrinsic evidence of industry custom is not likely to be helpful in analyzing the intent of the parties, it does not prohibit considering trade usage in understanding specific terms of the contract. * * *

Even were this Court to find the contracts ambiguous, thus allowing consideration of extrinsic evidence other than trade usage to determine whether Random House has a likelihood of success on the merits, a review of that evidence leads to the conclusion that it is unhelpful to either party.

1.3.   Did the authors breach their contracts with Random House?

2.   Questions about the law

2.1. What's a preliminary injunction? What does it have to do with contract law?

2.2.   Were any of the contracts ambiguous? Did the court think so? Does it matter?

2.3.   What if Random House had released the authors' works in ebook format and the authors sued, claiming that Random House did not have the right to release their books in ebook format? Would the court have interpreted the contracts the same way?

2.4.   Is there any way Random House's attorneys could have drafted the contracts differently to avoid this problem?

3.   Notes

3.1.   Strangely enough, in the brief of one of the parties that appeared as *amicus curiae* (a so-called "friend of the court") it was stated that two of Rosetta Books' exclusive distributors, Microsoft and Adobe, market the ebook format as being nearly identical to a hardcover book. *See* Brief of Amici Curiae Penguin Putnam, Inc., et al. at 8.

3.2.   Still confused over the difference between a book and an ebook? You are not alone. The following is an excerpt from the deposition of Rosetta Books' CEO and co-founder, Arthur Klebanoff:

Q: Is an electronic book a book?

A: Is an electronic book a book. I guess—if I—my answer, to me, that would be I don't know.

Q: You never thought about that?

A: Well, in—an electronic book is not a book in the sense in which a physical book is a book.

Q: I think you testified to that earlier. My question was meant to be slightly broader * * * is the conception of a book broad enough in your estimation to include for the purpose of books other than physical books?

A: Electronic book incorporates the contents—can incorporate the contents of a physical book.

Q: But you're unprepared sitting here to state, in your view, that an e-book or * * * electronic book is a book.

A: Well, I would answer it this way. They call, it an ebook because it's an e-book.

Q: Who is they?

A: I mean people. The name e-book has come about I mean I would argue because it is actually a different form of a book.

Q: In what sense is it a different form of a book?

A: In the sense that it moves in a digital environment, that it's received in a digital environment, that it's read on a screen, that it's not on paper.

Klebanoff Dep. at 9, lines 4–25, to 10, lines 2–17. Note: we omitted the numerous objections of Mr. Klebanoff's attorney. He was not too happy with this line of questioning.

3.3. Two of the three co-founders of Rosetta Books, including Mr. Klebanoff, received law degrees from Harvard Law School and were editors of the Harvard Law Review. Do you think they knew what they were getting into when they founded Rosetta Books? Should Harvard be looking for a new Contracts Professor?

Rosetta Books takes a sensible—but expansive—view of what courts will consider when construing what a contract requires the parties to do. Maybe that's appropriate given its factual setting. When all is said and done, however, certainty of obligation and reduction of litigation may not be served by such an expansive rule.

In the next case, a federal judge applies similar state law, but in a widely different factual setting. The judge, Alex Kozinski of the Ninth Circuit Court of Appeals, is applying California law. And he doesn't like it.* When reading this opinion, keep in mind that Judge Kozinski and Judge Ideman (the trial court judge) both had the same texts relating to California law at their disposal, but came to diametrically opposite views. Has Judge Kozinski overplayed his hand? Or was Judge Ideman just trying to clear his trial docket?

TRIDENT CENTER v. CONNECTICUT GENERAL LIFE INS. CO.

U.S. Court of Appeals, Ninth Circuit
847 F.2d 564 (1988)

KOZINSKI, CIRCUIT JUDGE:

The parties to this transaction are, by any standard, highly sophisticated business people: Plaintiff is a partnership consisting of an insurance company and two of Los Angeles' largest and most prestigious law firms; defendant is another insurance company. Dealing at arm's length and from positions of roughly equal bargaining strength, they negotiated a commercial loan amounting to more than $56 million. The contract documents are lengthy and detailed; they squarely address the precise issue that is the subject of this dispute; to all who read English, they appear to resolve the issue fully and conclusively.

---

* He may not like it, but he has to apply California law. Federal law requires application of state law when the parties have invoked the federal court's diversity jurisdiction; that is, when both parties are citizens of different states. Thus, federal judges, who have no ability to extend or limit California law, must determine it and apply it (or some estimate of what it is in case of a lacuna) as it stands.

Plaintiff nevertheless argues here, as it did below, that it is entitled to introduce extrinsic evidence that the contract means something other than what it says. This case therefore presents the question whether parties in California can ever draft a contract that is proof to parol evidence. Somewhat surprisingly, the answer is no.

Facts

The facts are rather simple. Sometime in 1983 Security First Life Insurance Company and the law firms of Mitchell, Silberberg & Knupp and Manatt, Phelps, Rothenberg & Tunney formed a limited partnership for the purpose of constructing an office building complex on Olympic Boulevard in West Los Angeles. The partnership, Trident Center, the plaintiff herein, sought and obtained financing for the project from defendant, Connecticut General Life Insurance Company. The loan documents provide for a loan of $56,500,000 at 12 ¼ percent interest for a term of 15 years, secured by a deed of trust on the project. The promissory note provides that "maker shall not have the right to prepay the principal amount hereof in whole or in part" for the first 12 years. Note at 6. In years 13–15, the loan may be prepaid, subject to a sliding prepayment fee. The note also provides that in case of a default during years 1–12, Connecticut General has the option of accelerating the note and adding a 10 percent prepayment fee.

Everything was copacetic for a few years until interest rates began to drop. The 12 1/4 percent rate that had seemed reasonable in 1983 compared unfavorably with 1987 market rates and Trident started looking for ways of refinancing the loan to take advantage of the lower rates. Connecticut General was unwilling to oblige, insisting that the loan could not be prepaid for the first 12 years of its life, that is, until January 1996.

Trident then brought suit in state court seeking a declaration that it was entitled to prepay the loan now, subject only to a 10 percent prepayment fee. Connecticut General promptly removed to federal court and brought a motion to dismiss, claiming that the loan documents clearly and unambiguously precluded prepayment during the first 12 years. The district court agreed and dismissed Trident's complaint. The court also "*sua sponte*, sanction[ed] the plaintiff for the filing of a frivolous lawsuit.". * * * Trident appeals both aspects of the district court's ruling.

Discussion

I

Trident makes two arguments as to why the district court's ruling is wrong. First, it contends that the language of the contract is ambiguous and proffers a construction that it believes supports its position. Second, Trident argues that, under California law, even seemingly unambiguous contracts are subject to modification by parol or extrinsic evidence. Trident faults the district court for denying it the opportunity to present evidence that the contract language did not accurately reflect the parties' intentions.

A.   The Contract

As noted earlier, the promissory note provides that Trident "shall not have the right to prepay the principal amount hereof in whole or in part before January 1996." Note at 6. It is difficult to imagine language that more clearly or unambiguously expresses the idea that Trident may not unilaterally prepay the loan during its first 12 years. Trident, however, argues that there is an ambiguity because another clause of the note provides that "in the event of a prepayment resulting from a default hereunder or the Deed of Trust prior to January 10, 1996 the prepayment fee will be ten percent (10%)." Note at 6–7. Trident interprets this clause as giving it the option of prepaying the loan if only it is willing to incur the prepayment fee.

We reject Trident's argument out of hand. In the first place, its proffered interpretation would result in a contradiction between two clauses of the contract; the default clause would swallow up the clause prohibiting Trident from prepaying during the first 12 years of the contract. The normal rule of construction, of course, is that courts must interpret contracts, if possible, so as to avoid internal conflict. * * *

In any event, the clause on which Trident relies is not on its face reasonably susceptible to Trident's proffered interpretation. Whether to accelerate repayment of the loan in the event of default is entirely Connecticut General's decision. The contract makes this clear at several points. *See* Note at 4 ("in each such event [of default], the entire principal indebtedness, or so much thereof as may remain unpaid at the time, shall, *at the option of Holder*, become due and payable immediately" (emphasis added)); *id.* at 7 ("in the event Holder exercises its *option to accelerate* the maturity hereof * * *" (emphasis added)); Deed of Trust para. 2.01, at 25 ("in each such event [of default], Beneficiary *may* declare all sums secured hereby immediately due and payable * * *" (emphasis added)). Even if Connecticut General decides to declare a default and accelerate, it "may rescind any notice of breach or default." *Id.* para. 2.02, at 26. Finally, Connecticut General has the option of doing nothing at all: "Beneficiary reserves the right at its sole option to waive noncompliance by Trustor with any of the conditions or covenants to be performed by Trustor hereunder." *Id.* para. 3.02, at 29.

Once again, it is difficult to imagine language that could more clearly assign to Connecticut General the exclusive right to decide whether to declare a default, whether and when to accelerate, and whether, having chosen to take advantage of any of its remedies, to rescind the process before its completion.

Trident nevertheless argues that it is entitled to precipitate a default and insist on acceleration by tendering the balance due on the note plus the 10 percent prepayment fee.[1] The contract language, cited above, leaves no room for this construction. It is true, of course, that Trident is free to stop making payments, which may then cause Connecticut General to declare a default and accelerate. But that is not to say that Connecticut General would be required to so respond. The contract quite clearly gives Connecticut General other options: It may choose to waive the default, or to take advantage of some other remedy such as the right to collect "all the income, rents, royalties, revenue, issues, profits, and proceeds of the Property." Deed of Trust para. 1.18, at 22. By interpreting the contract as Trident suggests, we would ignore those provisions giving Connecticut General, not Trident, the exclusive right to decide how, when and whether the contract will be terminated upon default during the first 12 years.

In effect, Trident is attempting to obtain judicial sterilization of its intended default. But defaults are messy things; they are supposed to be. Once the maker of a note secured by a deed of trust defaults, its credit rating may deteriorate; attempts at favorable refinancing may be thwarted by the need to meet the trustee's sale schedule; its cash flow may be impaired if the beneficiary takes advantage of the assignment of rents remedy; default provisions in its loan agreements with other lenders may be triggered. Fear of these repercussions is strong medicine that keeps debtors from shirking their obligations when interest rates go down and they become disenchanted with their loans.[4] That Trident is willing to suffer the cost and delay of a lawsuit, rather than simply defaulting, shows far better than anything we might say that these provisions are having their intended effect. We decline Trident's invitation to truncate the lender's remedies and deprive Connecticut General of its bargained-for protection.

B. Extrinsic Evidence

Trident argues in the alternative that, even if the language of the contract appears to be unambiguous, the deal the parties actually struck is

---

1. Trident's position is that the prepayment fee must either be a fee imposed as part of an "alternative method of performance" or "a liquidated damages provision specifying the amount of damages payable by Trident in the event that it defaults by prepaying the * * * loan." Appellant's Reply Brief at 12–13. Trident contends that if the prepayment fee is instead read as a provision for liquidated damages triggered by any default whatsoever, it would be invalid as a penalty because it would not be a reasonable estimate of the likely injury to Connecticut General resulting from most types of default: "If, for example, Trident were to default on the payment of a single installment, a fee of 10% of the outstanding balance of the loan would not qualify as a valid liquidated damages payment." *Id.* at 8.

California law is unsettled on this point and it may be that Connecticut General could not enforce the 10 percent fee in the event of certain defaults by Trident. *See generally* 1 H. Miller & M. Starr, *Current Law of California Real Estate* § 3:71 n.12 (Supp. 1987). But the contract assigns to Connecticut General alone the right to decide whether and under what circumstances to seek the prepayment fee. Connecticut General may well attempt to enforce the fee only in circumstances where it is valid. What the contract clearly does not provide is what Trident suggests. If the parties had wanted to give Trident the option of prepaying with a 10 percent fee, they certainly could have done so expressly.

4. This provides a symmetry with the situation where interest rates go up and it is the lender who is stuck with a loan it would prefer to turn over at market rates. In an economy where interest rates fluctuate, it is all but certain that one side or the other will be dissatisfied with a long-term loan at some time. Mutuality calls for enforcing the contract as written no matter whose ox is being gored.

in fact quite different. It wishes to offer extrinsic evidence that the parties had agreed Trident could prepay at any time within the first 12 years by tendering the full amount plus a 10 percent prepayment fee. As discussed above, this is an interpretation to which the contract, as written, is not reasonably susceptible. Under traditional contract principles, extrinsic evidence is inadmissible to interpret, vary or add to the terms of an unambiguous integrated written instrument. * * *

Trident points out, however, that California does not follow the traditional rule. Two decades ago the California Supreme Court in *Pacific Gas & Electric Co. v. G. W. Thomas Drayage & Rigging Co.*, 69 Cal. 2d 33, 442 P.2d 641, 69 Cal. Rptr. 561 (1968), turned its back on the notion that a contract can ever have a plain meaning discernible by a court without resort to extrinsic evidence. The court reasoned that contractual obligations flow not from the words of the contract, but from the intention of the parties. "Accordingly," the court stated, "the exclusion of relevant, extrinsic, evidence to explain the meaning of a written instrument could be justified only if it were feasible to determine the meaning the parties gave to the words from the instrument alone." 69 Cal. 2d at 38, 442 P.2d 641. This, the California Supreme Court concluded, is impossible: "If words had absolute and constant referents, it might be possible to discover contractual intention in the words themselves and in the manner in which they were arranged. Words, however, do not have absolute and constant referents." *Id.* In the same vein, the court noted that "the exclusion of testimony that might contradict the linguistic background of the judge reflects a judicial belief in the possibility of perfect verbal expression. This belief is a remnant of a primitive faith in the inherent potency and inherent meaning of words." *Id.* at 37 (citation and footnotes omitted).[5]

Under *Pacific Gas*, it matters not how clearly a contract is written, nor how completely it is integrated, nor how carefully it is negotiated, nor how squarely it addresses the issue before the court: the contract cannot be rendered impervious to attack by parol evidence. If one side is willing to claim that the parties intended one thing but the agreement provides for another, the court must consider extrinsic evidence of possible ambiguity. If that evidence raises the specter of ambiguity where there was none before, the contract language is displaced and the intention of the parties must be divined from self-serving testimony offered by partisan witnesses whose recollection is hazy from passage of time and colored by their conflicting interests. * * * We question whether this approach is more likely to divulge the original intention of the parties than reliance on the seemingly clear words they agreed upon at the time. * * *

Pacific Gas casts a long shadow of uncertainty over all transactions negotiated and executed under the law of California. As this case illus-

---

5. In an unusual footnote, the court compared the belief in the immutable meaning of words with " 'the elaborate system of taboo and verbal prohibitions in primitive groups * * * [such as] the Swedish peasant custom of curing sick cattle smitten by witchcraft, by making them swallow a page torn out of the psalter and put in dough. * * *' " *Id.* n.2 (quoting Ullman, *The Principles of Semantics* 43 (1963)).

trates, even when the transaction is very sizeable, even if it involves only sophisticated parties, even if it was negotiated with the aid of counsel, even if it results in contract language that is devoid of ambiguity, costly and protracted litigation cannot be avoided if one party has a strong enough motive for challenging the contract. While this rule creates much business for lawyers and an occasional windfall to some clients, it leads only to frustration and delay for most litigants and clogs already overburdened courts.

It also chips away at the foundation of our legal system. By giving credence to the idea that words are inadequate to express concepts, *Pacific Gas* undermines the basic principle that language provides a meaningful constraint on public and private conduct. If we are unwilling to say that parties, dealing face to face, can come up with language that binds them, how can we send anyone to jail for violating statutes consisting of mere words lacking "absolute and constant referents"? How can courts ever enforce decrees, not written in language understandable to all, but encoded in a dialect reflecting only the "linguistic background of the judge"? Can lower courts ever be faulted for failing to carry out the mandate of higher courts when "perfect verbal expression" is impossible? Are all attempts to develop the law in a reasoned and principled fashion doomed to failure as "remnant[s] of a primitive faith in the inherent potency and inherent meaning of words"?

Be that as it may. While we have our doubts about the wisdom of *Pacific Gas*, we have no difficulty understanding its meaning, even without extrinsic evidence to guide us. As we read the rule in California, we must reverse and remand to the district court in order to give plaintiff an opportunity to present extrinsic evidence as to the intention of the parties in drafting the contract.[6] It may not be a wise rule we are applying, but it is a rule that binds us. *Erie R.R. Co. v. Tompkins*, 304 U.S. 64, 78, 82 L. Ed. 1188, 58 S. Ct. 817 (1938).

II

In imposing sanctions on plaintiff, the district court stated:

> Pursuant to Fed. R. Civ. P. 11, the Court, *sua sponte*, sanctions the plaintiff for the filing of a frivolous lawsuit. The Court concludes that the language in the note and deed of trust is plain and clear. No reasonable person, much less firms of able attorneys, could possibly misunderstand this crystal-clear language. Therefore, this action was brought in bad faith.

Order of Dismissal at 3. Having reversed the district court on its substantive ruling, we must, of course, also reverse it as to the award of sanctions. While we share the district judge's impatience with this litigation, we

---

6. Nothing we say should be construed as foreclosing Connecticut General from moving for summary judgment after completion of discovery; given the unambiguous language of the contract itself, such a motion would succeed unless Trident were to come forward with extrinsic evidence sufficient to render the contract reasonably susceptible to Trident's alternate interpretation, thereby creating a genuine issue of fact resolvable only at trial.

would suggest that his irritation may have been misdirected. It is difficult to blame plaintiff and its lawyers for bringing this lawsuit. With this much money at stake, they would have been foolish not to pursue all remedies available to them under the applicable law. At fault, it seems to us, are not the parties and their lawyers but the legal system that encourages this kind of lawsuit. By holding that language has no objective meaning, and that contracts mean only what courts ultimately say they do, *Pacific Gas* invites precisely this type of lawsuit.[9] With the benefit of 20 years of hindsight, the California Supreme Court may wish to revisit the issue. If it does so, we commend to it the facts of this case as a paradigmatic example of why the traditional rule, based on centuries of experience, reflects the far wiser approach.

Conclusion

The judgment of the district court is REVERSED. The case is RE-MANDED for reinstatement of the complaint and further proceedings in accordance with this opinion. The parties shall bear their own costs on appeal.

QUESTIONS, NOTE, AND CONNECTIONS

1. Questions about the facts of this case

   1.1. Why do the law firms wish to prepay the loan? Where are they likely to get the money to make the payment?

   1.2. Do the law firms contend that the provisions regarding inability to prepay the loan for the first twelve years of the loan are ambiguous? How do the law firms interpret these provisions?

   1.3. What possible extrinsic evidence could the law firms offer to support their position? And if the evidence supports what the law firms are contending—a unilateral prepayment right—what answer do the law firms have as to why that wasn't spelled out more clearly in the contract?

2. Questions about the law

   2.1. Do you agree with the following statement by Judge Kozinski? Why or why not?

   Under *Pacific Gas*, it matters not how clearly a contract is written, nor how completely it is integrated, nor how carefully it is negotiated, nor how squarely it addresses the issue before the court: the contract cannot be rendered impervious to attack by parol evidence.

---

9. This is not to say, of course, that all lawsuits seeking to challenge the interpretation of facially unambiguous contracts are necessarily immune from imposition of sanctions. Even under *Pacific Gas*, a party urging an interpretation lacking any objectively reasonable basis in fact might well be subject to sanctions for bringing a frivolous lawsuit.

2.2. Trident's second argument was that "under California law, even seemingly unambiguous contracts are subject to modification by parol or extrinsic evidence." Does either this case (or what you can discern from this case) or *Pacific Gas* so hold?

2.3. Is California law consistent with the statement of New York law set forth in *Rosetta Books*? How would Judge Kozinski, if freed from the restraining influence of state law, decide *Rosetta Books*? If Judge Kozinski were the trial court judge in *Trident*, how would he rule on remand?

2.4. Did you read the footnotes? Footnote 6? Is footnote 6 important? We of course think it is—that is why we included it in the book. The Ninth Circuit also thinks footnote 6 is important; in *A. Kemp Fisheries, Inc. v. Castle & Cooke, Inc., Bumble Bee Seafoods Division*, 852 F.2d 493, 497 n.2 (9th Cir. 1988), the Ninth Circuit explained: "The broad language in *Trident* suggests that under California law courts must always admit extrinsic evidence to determine the meaning of disputed contract language. *Trident* held only that courts may not dismiss on the pleadings when one party contends that extrinsic evidence renders the contract ambiguous. The case must proceed beyond the pleadings so that the court may consider the evidence. If, after considering the evidence, the court determines that the contract is not susceptible to the interpretation advanced, the parol evidence rule operates to exclude the evidence. The court may then decide the case on a motion for summary judgment. See *Trident* at 570 n.6."

3. Note

Judge Alex Kozinski is a judge on the federal Ninth Circuit Court of Appeals. Widely considered to be bright, engaging, and conservative (or libertarian, depending on how the label is defined), he is a Romanian emigre, who arrived in this country at the age of twelve barely able to speak English. His moving account of his journey to the west can be read at *Freedom's Scents: A Romanian Remembers*, WALL ST. J., Nov. 28, 1989.

He learned quickly, however, and ultimately graduated first in his class at UCLA. He was one of the first clerks to Justice Anthony Kennedy (when the Justice sat on the Ninth Circuit), and then went on to clerk for Chief Justice Warren Burger. Appointed to the Ninth Circuit at the young age of 35 (after serving as Chief Judge for the Court of Claims), he is the author of many solid appellate opinions and a frequent speaker at Federalist Society events.

He also has an "adventurous" side. He has been filmed bungee jumping http://www.youtube.com/watch?v= and was on the television show, *The Dating Game*—twice, http://www.youtube.com/watch?v=OdjCdbGucCU&NR=1

He also tweaks casebook authors from time to time:

How important do I think casebooks are? So important that, once in a while, I write an opinion precisely for the purpose of getting into one. Mind you, it doesn't change the outcome of the case, but it does change the way I write the opinion. The classic example happened about ten years ago. I had grown tired of law clerks who thought California Chief Justice Traynor was the cat's pajamas because he didn't believe that any contract could be interpreted without the use of extrinsic evidence. Whenever I would get a case where I thought the contract language was clear, they would quote me back some idiot line from Traynor about how this merely reflected the effete linguistic prejudices of judges. It turns out this came from Traynor's opinion in *Pacific Gas and Electric Co. v. G.W. Thomas Drayage & Rigging Co.*, which had found its way into every contracts casebook in the country. What the casebooks seemed to lack were cases responding to Traynor's argument.

So I decided to write one. The case [was] Trident Center v. Connecticut General Life Insurance. * * *

Alex Kozinski, *Who Gives a Hoot About Legal Scholarship*, 37 HOUSTON L. REV. 295, 298–99 (2000).

4. Connections

Remember in *Frigaliment*, the reasonbleness of the litigants' contract interpretation was important to Judge Friendly: "Defendant's subjective intent would not be significant if this did not coincide with an objective meaning of 'chicken.'" Does Judge Kozinski think that the reasonableness of the litigants' contract interpretation was important to Judge Traynor?

C. THE USE OF RULES, MAXIMS AND EXTRINSIC EVIDENCE TO CONSTRUE CONTRACT LANGUAGE

Once ambiguity exists, counsel for the parties can introduce extrinsic evidence to show what the parties meant by the words they used. Sometimes, as in the cases above, the extrinsic evidence can take the form of testimony of the parties who negotiated the contract.

Other times, however, the extrinsic evidence may be guides or manuals on style, or guides prepared by experts. In *In re Envirodyne Industries, Inc.*, 29 F.3d 301 (7th Cir. 1994), Chief Judge Posner had this to say about such extrinsic aids to interpretation:

If the written contract is clear without extrinsic evidence, then such evidence could have no office other than to contradict the writing, and is therefore excluded. The object in excluding such evidence is to prevent parties from trying to slip out of their clearly stated, explicitly assumed contractual obligations through self-serving testimony or documents—which, though self-serving, might impress a jury—purporting to show that the parties didn't mean what they said in the written contract. Contractual obligations would be too uncertain if such evidence were allowed. But dictionaries, treatises, articles, and other published materials created by strangers to the dispute, like evidence of trade usage, which is also admissible because it is also evidence created by strangers rather than by a party trying to slip out of a contractual bind, do not present a similar danger of manufactured doubts and are therefore entirely appropriate for use in contract cases as interpretive aids. Appropriate, and sometimes indispensable. It would be passing odd to forbid people to look up words in dictionaries, or to consult explanatory commentaries that, like trade usage, are in the nature of specialized dictionaries.

Contract law has also developed common law rules for interpretation in doubtful cases. The *Restatement (Second) of Contracts* lists the following:

> § 203   *Standards of Preference in Interpretation*
>
> *In the interpretation of a promise or agreement or a term thereof, the following standards of preference are generally applicable:*
>
> (a) *an interpretation which gives a reasonable, lawful, and effective meaning to all the terms is preferred to an interpretation which leaves a part unreasonable, unlawful, or of no effect;*
>
> (b) *express terms are given greater weight than course of performance, course of dealing, and usage of trade, course of performance is given greater weight than course of dealing or usage of trade, and course of dealing is given greater weight than usage of trade;*
>
> (c) *specific terms and exact terms are given greater weight than general language;*
>
> (d) *separately negotiated or added terms are given greater weight than standardized terms or other terms not separately negotiated.*

In addition, the *Restatement* adopts a rebuttable presumption that may trouble those who think that they should draft everything on behalf of their clients:

> § 206   *Interpretation Against the Draftsman*
>
> *In choosing among the reasonable meanings of a promise or agreement or a term thereof, that meaning is generally preferred which operates against the party who supplies the words or from whom a writing otherwise proceeds.*

Finally, over 40 years ago, Professor Edwin Patterson set forth ten general maxims of interpretation, some of which are in Latin. An edited version of those ten maxims appears below.

EDWIN W. PATTERSON, *THE INTERPRETATION AND CONSTRUCTION OF CONTRACTS*

64 COLUM. L. REV. 833, 852–54 (1964)

In this brief treatment we can only quote a list of standard maxims, which may not be complete. The ones most often phrased in Latin are given first.

1. *Noscitur a sociis.* The meaning of a word in a series is affected by others in the same series; or, a word may be affected by its immediate context. The example for the next maxim may be taken to illustrate this one.

2. *Ejusdem generis.* A general term joined with a specific one will be deemed to include only things that are like (of the same genus as) the specific one. This one if applied usually leads to a restrictive interpretation. *E.g.*, S contracts to sell R his farm together with the "cattle, hogs, and other animals." This would probably not include S's favorite house-dog, but might include a few sheep that S was raising for the market.

3. *Expressio unius exclusio alterius.* If one or more specific items are listed, without any more general or inclusive terms, other items although similar in kind are excluded. *E.g.*, S contracts to sell R his farm together with "the cattle and hogs on the farm." This language would be interpreted to exclude the sheep and S's favorite house-dog.

4. *Ut magis valeat quam pereat.* By this maxim, an interpretation that makes the contract valid is preferred to one that makes it invalid.

5. *Omnia praesumuntur contra proferentem.* This maxim states that if a written contract contains a word or phrase which is capable of two reasonable meanings, one of which favors one party and the other of which favors the other, that interpretation will be preferred which is less favorable to the one by whom the contract was drafted. This maxim favors the party of lesser bargaining power, who has little or no opportunity to choose the terms of the contract, and perforce accepts one drawn by the stronger party. * * * [T]he maxim is commonly invoked in cases that do not reveal any disparity of bargaining power between the parties.

6. *Interpret contract as a whole.* A writing or writings that form part of the same transaction should be interpreted together as a whole, that is, every term should be interpreted as a part of the whole and not as if isolated from it. This maxim expresses the contextual theory of meaning, which is, perhaps, a truism.

7. *"Purpose of the parties."* "The principal apparent purpose of the parties is given great weight in determining the meaning to be given to manifestations of intention or to any part thereof." This maxim must be used with caution. In fact, the two parties to a (bargain) contract necessarily have different purposes, and if these are apparent, then the court can construe a principal or common purpose from the two as a guide to the interpretation of language or the filling of gaps. Thus a contract to sell, buy, and export scrap copper was construed to make the buyer's obtaining of an export license a condition of the seller's promise to deliver.

However, if the purposes of the parties are obscure the court may well fall back upon "plain meaning."

8. *Specific provision is exception to a general one.* If two provisions of a contract are inconsistent with each other and if one is "general" enough to include the specific situation to which the other is confined, the specific provision will be deemed to qualify the more general one, that is, to state an exception to it. A lease of a truck-trailer provided that the lessee should be absolutely liable for loss or damage to the vehicle, yet another clause stated that no party's liability should be increased by this contract. It was held that the former was more specific and therefore controlled the general provision, hence the lessee was liable. A careful draftsman would have stated the former as an exception to the latter, and the court in effect does it for him.

9. *Handwritten or typed provisions control printed provisions.* Where a written contract contains both printed provisions and handwritten or typed provisions, and the two are inconsistent, the handwritten or typed provisions are preferred. This maxim is based on the inference that the language inserted by handwriting or by typewriter for this particular contract is a more recent and more reliable expression of their intentions than is the language of a printed form. While this maxim is used in interpreting insurance contracts and other contracts of adhesion, it is also applicable to all contracts drawn up on a printed form.

10. *Public interest preferred.* If a public interest is affected by a contract, that interpretation or construction is preferred which favors the public interest. The proper scope of application of this rule seems doubtful. It may have some appropriate uses in construing contracts between private parties. However, as applied to government contracts it would, if applied, be used to save the taxpayers' money as against those contracting with the government. But this is not, it is believed, a standard of interpretation or construction uniformly applied to government contracts.

PROBLEMS ON CONSTRUCTION OF CONTRACTS

1. James wants to buy a sailboat at Sears. He seeks to use his Sears credit card to complete the purchase. On the credit card slip to be signed, right above where his signature is to be placed, are the words "By signing this, the Cardholder agrees to grant to Sears a security interest in the goods purchased hereby, as set forth in more detail in the most recent Cardholder agreement between Sears and the undersigned."

   a. James has no idea what a "security interest" is, but he signs anyway. He finds out what a security interest is when he doesn't pay his credit card bill, and Sears sends some of its workers over to "repossess" the sailboat, which they accomplish by sailing the boat away without any fuss. Assume for now (and you'll confirm this later in your Article 9 course) that Sears could do this only if they had been contractually granted a "security interest." Based on your reading so far, have they been? What maxims or rules would help you here?

b. Now assume that James sees the language above his signature, and then crosses it out before signing. The clerk at the register makes no complaint, and lets James drive off with his new boat. If James doesn't pay, can Sears repossess the boat? What maxims or rules would help you here?

2. A contract to sell land states that the buyer is reserving all rights to "all coal and other minerals." Who gets the subsurface oil and gas? *See McCormick v. Union Pac. R.R. Co.*, 983 P.2d 84 (Colo. Ct. App. 1998).

3. Fred is a book collector. He advertises the following on eBay:

For sale: One first edition Trollope, *circa* 1860. Signed by author. Excellent condition.

Lucinda enters the auction, ultimately entering the highest bid of $500. When she receives the book, she notices that it is written and signed by Thomas Adolphus Trollope, the brother of Anthony Trollope. Thomas wrote travel books; Anthony was more in the literary vein. Both she and Fred believe they have a contract. Questions of mistake aside, what are the best arguments you can muster using the maxims that Lucinda should have received an Anthony Trollope book?

D. SPECIAL INTERPRETIVE RULES FOR CONTRACTS OF ADHESION

How often have you wanted to rent a car or obtain some other good or service, and were then presented with a pre-printed form to sign (and no opportunity to negotiate anything)? Are these types of contracts just as valid as fully-negotiated, specially-prepared custom contracts? Are they subject to the same interpretive rules? The next two cases examine this issue.

MEYER v. STATE FARM FIRE & CAS. CO.

Court of Special Appeals of Maryland
85 Md.App. 83, 582 A.2d 275 (1990)

OPINION:

For over 100 years, it has been common—indeed standard—for fire insurance policies to contain a clause requiring disputes concerning the amount of a covered loss suffered by the insured to be resolved through an appraisal process. Such a clause is at issue here. It provides, in relevant part, that, if the company and the insured are unable to agree on the amount of loss, either one can demand that the amount be determined by appraisal. Upon such a demand, each party is obliged to select an appraiser; the two appraisers so selected then "select a competent, impartial umpire." If the two appointed appraisers agree on an amount, that amount "shall be the amount of loss." If they are unable to agree, they submit their differences to the umpire. Written agreement signed by any two of the three then will constitute the amount of loss. The policy further provides that "[n]o action shall be brought unless there has been compliance with the policy provisions."

Appellants purchased a policy of fire insurance containing that clause from appellee. A fire occurred at their home, but, unfortunately, they and the company were unable to agree on the amount of loss. Although it is not entirely clear from the Agreed Statement of the Case that constitutes the record in this appeal, it appears that the company, at some point, sought to invoke the appraisal process. Appellants instead filed suit for damages in the Circuit Court for Wicomico County, contending that the appraisal provisions were invalid. The basis of their claim was that [among other things,] because the policy was a contract of adhesion and because they were actually unaware that it contained the appraisal provision, there was no effective waiver of their Constitutional right.

The company moved to dismiss the action. Though conceding the factual averments of appellants' complaint for purpose of the motion, it contended that the dispute resolution clause was not invalid and that, by omitting to allege compliance with it, appellants had failed to state a claim upon which relief could be granted. The court found merit in that defense and dismissed the action. Hence, this expedited appeal. * * *

.   .   .   .

[W]e are not dealing here with a statute mandating this form of dispute resolution. It is a contractual provision. The issue is whether appellants can escape its effect because the policy was a contract of adhesion and, as they were allegedly (and for purposes of this case concededly) unaware that such a provision was in the policy, they did not knowingly, voluntarily, and intelligently waive their right to try the issue of the amount of their loss before a jury. In urging their position, we think that the appellants give too expansive a meaning to both the requirements for waiving their right to a judicial resolution of the controversy and the effect of a contract of adhesion.

A contract of adhesion has been defined as one "that is drafted unilaterally by the dominant party and then presented on a 'take-it-or-leave-it' basis to the weaker party who has no real opportunity to bargain about its terms." *Restatement (Second) of Conflict of Laws* § 187, Comment b. The comment goes on to note that such contracts "are usually prepared in printed form, and frequently at least some of their provisions are in extremely small print." It is generally recognized that insurance policies qualify as contracts of adhesion, and so we shall assume that the policy at issue here is such a contract.

The fact that a contract is one of adhesion does not mean that either it or any of its terms are invalid or unenforceable. A court will, to be sure, look at the contract and its terms with some special care. As in most cases, it will refuse to enforce terms that it finds unconscionable and will construe ambiguities against the draftsman; but it will not simply excise or ignore terms merely because, in the given case, they may operate to the perceived detriment of the weaker party. *See,* in general, *Restatement (Second) of Contracts* § 211, Comment c; also *Corbin on Contracts* §§ 559, 1376.

There is no asserted ambiguity in the appraisal provision; indeed, in *Aetna Cas. & Sur., supra,* 293 Md. at 420, 445 A.2d 14, the Court declared such a provision "plain and unambiguous." Nor do we see anything unconscionable about it. The appraisal process has generally been regarded by the courts as a fair method of resolving disputes over the amount of loss. As Appleman notes, rather than being stricken down as unconscionable, appraisal provisions are usually *upheld* on grounds of public policy "since they tend to fair dealing and the prevention of litigation." J. Appleman, *Insurance Law and Practice* § 3921. Moreover, although certainly standard language in the policy, the appraisal provision at issue here is by no means "buried" or enunciated in the proverbial "fine print." It is worded in plain, colloquial English as part of the stated Conditions of the policy and, except for headings, is in the same size and type print as the other provisions of the policy.

It is true, of course, that a waiver of basic Constitutional rights is not ordinarily valid unless it is knowing and voluntary. * * * It is also true that where such a waiver is founded upon a provision in a contract of adhesion, the court will, as noted above, be especially careful to protect against an unconscionable result. * * *

These precepts, however, must be weighed against the equally well-established view that favors and enforces agreements to arbitrate disputes, including disputes over insured losses. An agreement to arbitrate either future or existing disputes involves more than just the waiver of a right to jury trial, although that is certainly implicit in such an agreement. It constitutes an election to use an alternative dispute resolution mechanism that the law not only recognizes but encourages. If appellants' position were correct, the whole foundation of the Federal and uniform arbitration acts could be placed in jeopardy. Arbitration clauses are standard not only in insurance contracts but in construction contracts, employment agreements, and a variety of other contracts that may, in some instances, be regarded as being of adhesion. If the "weaker" party to such contracts were able to escape the duty to arbitrate on the premise that he was unaware of the arbitration clause and therefore had not validly waived his Federal or State Constitutional right to a jury trial, the viability of this favored method of dispute resolution would be significantly circumscribed.

We recognize that if the insertion of an arbitration clause in a contract is induced by *fraud*, the clause will not be enforced. * * * But that is not the case here. On the record before us, we hold that the appraisal clause is not invalid and that the procedure required by it must be used in good faith.

Judgment Affirmed; Appellants to Pay the Costs.

QUESTIONS

1. Questions about the facts of this case
    1.1. Did the insurance company refuse to pay anything on the policy?
    1.2. Why did Meyer pay money to State Farm if she had never read the contract under which State Farm provided her fire insurance?
2. Questions about the law
    2.1. In Maryland, are parties always bound to contract language in adhesion contracts they don't read or understand? What exceptions would this court recognize?
    2.2. Would it have made any difference to this court if the practice contained in the adhesion contract had not been "standard", that is, if the insurance company defendant had language different from all other insurance companies?

LAUVETZ v. ALASKA SALES AND SERVICE D/B/A NATIONAL CAR RENTAL

Supreme Court of Alaska
828 P.2d 162 (1991)

Opinion

BURKE, JUSTICE.

This matter is before the court on petition for review. By previous order, we agreed to examine the superior court's grant of partial summary judgment against the operator of a rental vehicle in an action against the operator for collision damage to the vehicle. The issue that we address is whether the operator is entitled to the coverage afforded by a collision damage waiver found in the vehicle rental agreement if the operator is intoxicated while operating the vehicle.

I

Vacationers John Osborne and Thomas Lauvetz arrived in Alaska on August 26, 1988. Before leaving Anchorage International Airport, they rented a previously reserved van from Alaska Sales and Service, doing business as National Car Rental (National). Although Osborne rented the vehicle, he listed Lauvetz as an authorized driver. While at the rental desk, Osborne was offered an optional collision damage waiver (CDW), which he accepted, and optional personal accident insurance, which he declined. The CDW added $8.95 per day to the basic daily rate of $70.00.

On the face of the Rental Agreement there is no indication of the scope of the CDW. Directly above the CDW box, in bold face and in the same size type as "Collision Damage Waiver Option," are the words "See Terms and Conditions." The National agent did not inform Osborne and Lauvetz where the terms and conditions could be found. The agent apparently made no representations about the scope of the CDW, nor did the agent indicate that the terms and conditions contained specific exclusions to the CDW.

The terms and conditions of the Rental Agreement were, in fact, on the inside of the travel folder in which the agent placed the Rental Agreement. The right flap of the travel folder opened into three panels containing the terms and conditions. The terms and conditions were printed in black on a white background and were legible. Lauvetz and Osborne did not read the terms and conditions.

Paragraph seven of the terms and conditions concerns the CDW option:

> If I [the renter] am involved in an accident or the car sustains collision damage, even from unknown causes, I am responsible for the resulting damages including loss of use, claims processing fees, and administrative charges regardless of fault. This financial responsibility is eliminated if I accept the CDW Option, pay for it, and comply with the Agreement, including all Terms and Conditions.

> I UNDERSTAND THAT CDW IS NOT INSURANCE. I understand that some automobile insurance policies cover loss and damages to the rental vehicle; that National cannot interpret the terms of my insurance policies; and that it is my responsibility to check with my insurance company and my insurance agent.

> If I accept the CDW Option, I agree to pay the charge per day shown on the Rental document for each full or partial day. I understand that CDW does not apply to interior or exterior damage to the Vehicle caused by negligent loading or unloading of baggage or equipment.

The Terms and Conditions also included a paragraph on prohibited uses:

> I agree that the Vehicle shall NOT be used by or for any of the following PROHIBITED USES:

> a. by an unauthorized driver;

> b. by any driver under the influence of intoxicants, drugs, or any other substance known to impair driving ability;

c. for any illegal purpose;

d. by anyone who gives the Company a false name, address, age or other false or misleading information;

e. in any abusive or reckless manner;

f. to carry persons or property for hire;

g. to tow or push anything;

h. in any race, test, contest, or training activity;

i. for any use in Mexico without the prior written permission of the renting location. All protection is void in Mexico. Your written permission must be obtained and special insurance must be purchased before entering Mexico.

I UNDERSTAND THAT IF THE VEHICLE IS OBTAINED OR USED FOR ANY PROHIBITED USE OR IN VIOLATION OF THIS AGREEMENT, THEN THE CDW OPTION SHALL BE VOID AND, WHERE PERMITTED BY THE LAW, THE LIABILITY AND COMPREHENSIVE PROTECTION, PAI, PEC, AND SLI INSURANCE SHALL BE VOID.

On August 29, 1988, the van was damaged while Lauvetz was driving. As a result of the accident, Lauvetz was charged with and pled no contest to reckless driving. AS 28.35.040.

National subsequently filed suit against Lauvetz and Osborne, seeking compensatory and punitive damages for the wreck of the van. The complaint alleged that Lauvetz was intoxicated at the time of the accident and that this intoxication was a causal factor of the accident. The complaint further claimed that the CDW did not apply, because Osborne and Lauvetz remained liable for any damage resulting from a prohibited use of the vehicle, specifically, use by an intoxicated driver or use in a reckless manner.

During preliminary proceedings, National sought and obtained partial summary judgment on the validity and enforceability of the exclusions to the CDW option. The superior court ruled that the "terms and provisions of the collision damage waiver in the car rental agreement governing drunk and reckless driving are valid, binding, and enforceable, and the Court rejects Defendants' position that the CDW is insurance." This court accepted Lauvetz's petition to review the grant of partial summary judgment.

II

Lauvetz argues that the exclusions were beyond the reasonable expectations of lessees accepting National's standardized contract. Before considering the parties' specific arguments, it is necessary to discuss the applicable law.

A

Section 211 of the Restatement Second of Contracts addresses the question of interpreting standardized form agreements:

(1) Except as stated in Subsection (3), where a party to an agreement signs or otherwise manifests assent to a writing and has reason to believe that like writings are regularly used to embody terms of agreements of the same type, he adopts the writing as an integrated agreement with respect to the terms included in the writing.

* * *

(3) Where the other party has reason to believe that the party manifesting such assent would not do so if he knew that the writing contained a particular term, the term is not part of the agreement.

Restatement (Second) of Contracts § 211 (1981). Thus, this section establishes the general enforceability of the terms of standardized forms, without regard for whether the customer reads or understands those terms. Id. at comment b. This general enforceability, however, is subject to limitations of reasonableness: Customers "are not bound to unknown terms which are beyond the range of reasonable expectation." Id. at comment f.

Although we have never explicitly endorsed Section 211 as the appropriate analysis for standardized agreements, we have invoked a doctrine of reasonable expectations in analogous situations. * * * [T]hose cases involved insurance contracts. The operative fact * * *, however, was that the policy was a contract of adhesion, rather than a negotiated agreement. * * * As a consequence, the agreements were "construed according to the principle of reasonable expectations." * * *

These cases suggest that "reasonable expectations" are those expectations a consumer would have after reading the form. For example, we noted that an "insurance policy may be considered a contract of adhesion, and as such, should be construed to provide the coverage which a layperson would have reasonably expected, given a lay interpretation of the policy language." * * * Thus, this principle of reasonable expectations is somewhat different from the principle embodied in Section 211, which actually presumes that the customer does not read the contract. Restatement (Second) of Contracts § 211 comment b (1981) ("Customers do not in fact ordinarily understand or even read the standard terms.").

The distinction is significant in this case. Given the clarity of the terms and conditions, there is little room for argument that a Stordahl-type "lay interpretation" of the terms would differ from a legal interpretation. The Stordahl approach is inadequate, however, in cases where consumers probably will not read adhesive contracts and will not have any choice in the terms even if they do read them. * * * Section 211, on the other hand, emphasizes the reasonableness of the term or condition, no matter how clear its meaning might be to the layman if he happened to read it. The Arizona Supreme Court justified its endorsement of Section 211 by noting that

> to acknowledge standardized contracts for what they are—rules written by commercial enterprises—and to enforce them as written, subject to those reasonable limitations provided by law, is to recognize the reality of the marketplace as it now exists, while imposing just limits on business practice.

Darner Motor Sales v. Universal Underwriters Insurance Co., 140 Ariz. 383, 682 P.2d 388, 399 (Ariz. 1984). We agree and adopt the analysis of Section 211 with regard to standardized form agreements outside the insurance context.

B

National emphasizes that reasonableness is an objective concept, and adds that "no person who drives a car that does not belong to him can have any reasonable expectation that he can drive that car recklessly or while intoxicated." It argues that Lauvetz's claimed reasonable expectations are nothing more than "subjective and self-serving statements of [his] intent concerning the meaning of the CDW." Such subjective intent, National asserts, has no probative value, citing Peterson v. Wirum, 625 P.2d 866, 870 (Alaska 1981).

National notes that the doctrine of reasonable expectations is nothing more than a judicial construct for imposing community standards of reasonable behavior on the private law of contracts. National argues that under modern community standards, drunk driving is viewed as a serious threat to public safety. * * * Thus, National contends that Lauvetz's position that a prohibition against drunk and reckless driving is an unconscionable or unreasonable limit on the CDW is absurd.

National mischaracterizes the relevant question. It is not whether a prohibition against drunk driving is unreasonable; any renter would certainly know that the law prohibits drunk driving on pain of severe penalties. See AS 28.35.030(c) (mandating incarceration, a fine, and revocation of driver's license even for first conviction). Rather, the relevant question here is whether the purchaser of the damage waiver reasonably expected the waiver to be subject to any exclusions. We conclude that a consumer would not reasonably expect the damage waiver to be less than complete.

The common law rule is that bailees are not responsible "for damages unattributable to their fault." * * * This rule may be altered by contract. Id. The standardized form used by National did in fact purport to alter that common law rule by making the bailee responsible for any damage, however caused. The CDW then offered the bailee protection from National's unilateral alteration of the common law rule, ostensibly subject to the exclusions.

We think that the common law rule aptly expresses a bailee's reasonable expectation: He will be responsible for any damage caused by his fault. The average car renter would not parse that "fault" into the fine legal categories of "negligence," "recklessness" or "volitional conduct." When offered the CDW, the bailee would reasonably expect this option, at the not inconsiderable rate of $8.95 per day, to relieve him of responsibility even if the damage were caused by his fault. Again, the average car renter would not parse that fault into fine legal categories.

As the Colorado Supreme Court commented in a case similar to the present one, "lessors should know that the simple, highly readable summary of the collision responsibility alternatives will lead an average customer to reasonably conclude that he is protected against most, if not all, risks." * * * In this case, there was not even a summary of the responsibility alternatives. Lauvetz merely had the choice between a damage waiver and no waiver, protection against damaging the car or no protection. In deciding today that a consumer would reasonably expect that the rental company's waiver is complete, we join the large number of courts who have refused to enforce damage waiver exclusions under a variety of circumstances. * * *

The superior court's grant of partial summary judgment in favor of National on the enforceability of the CDW exclusions is REVERSED and this case REMANDED for further proceedings consistent with this opinion.

QUESTIONS AND NOTE

1. Questions about the facts of this case
    1.1. What did Lauvetz contend the CDW provision meant? In other words, what did it appear that he believed his $8.95 per day bought?
    1.2. Is the court saying that Lauvetz in any way relied on his reasonable expectation of the CDW provision in making the decision to purchase it?
2. Questions about the law
    2.1. In Alaska, can people now rent cars, get drunk, and not worry about what happens to the car when they wreck it? If you don't think so, what in the opinion would you point to that would exclude such an interpretation?
    2.2. Can you apply *Lauvetz* to an individually-negotiated contract to buy land? Even if it was documented by use of a standardized form?
    2.3. After *Lauvetz*, what evidence would a consumer introduce to establish reasonable expectations? What evidence would the purveyor of form contracts use?
    2.4. Which court has the better view of how to handle standard form contracts, *Lauvetz* or *Meyers*? Before answering that question, think about how companies offering goods or services through standard form contracts are going to react to decisions such as *Lauvetz*.

3. Note

The Alaska Supreme Court more recently had another opportunity to review standard language in insurance contracts. In *Kim v. National Indemnity Co.*, 6 P.3d 264 (Alaska 2000), a taxicab driver, Kim, had sexually abused a minor passenger. After Kim's criminal conviction, the minor's parents sued Kim and his insurance company for the injuries suffered. The insurance contract Kim had purchased for his taxi operations provided up to $300,000 in coverage for injuries "caused by an accident and resulting from the ownership, maintenance or use of a covered auto." The insurance contract also had an exclusion from personal injury "expected or intended from the standpoint of the insured."

Without even mentioning *Lauvetz*, the Alaska Supreme Court found for Kim, and dismissed the lawsuit. They said that the contractual language required coverage only for accidents, and not for intentional injuries. Should the parties have cited *Lauvetz*? Should the court have distinguished it?*

SECTION 4: TERMS ADDED BY THE COURTS

Rarely do parties enter into an agreement that spells everything out with perfect clarity. Sometimes, there are gaps—problems arise not covered by the agreement. This section of the book considers the questions of (1) whether courts should imply terms to fill these gaps, and if so, (2) how courts should fill the gaps.

A. TERMS IMPLIED BY COURTS TO EFFECTUATE ASSUMED INTENT

According to Professor Victor Goldberg of the Columbia University Law School, "Everyone knows about *Wood v. Lucy, Lady Duff Gordon.*" VICTOR GOLDBERG, FRAMING CONTRACT LAW 43 (2006) What? You don't know? Best read the case then.

WOOD v. LUCY, LADY DUFF–GORDON

Court of Appeals of New York
222 N.Y. 88, 118 N.E. 214 (1917)

CARDOZO, J:

The defendant styles herself "a creator of fashions." Her favor helps a sale. Manufacturers of dresses, millinery and like articles are glad to pay

---

* The Alaska Supreme Court partially overruled *Kim* in *Shaw v. State Farm Mut. Auto. Ins. Cos.*, 19 P.3d 588 (Alaska 2001) on the grounds that the minor was the "insured" under the uninsured motorist coverage, and the minor's acts were certainly not "intentional". The court let stand, however, the holding that the primary coverage's exclusion of non-accidental actions covered Kim's case. *Shaw* also did not cite or mention *Lauvetz*.

for a certificate of her approval. The things which she designs, fabrics, parasols and what not, have a new value in the public mind when issued in her name. She employed the plaintiff to help her to turn this vogue into money. He was to have the exclusive right, subject always to her approval, to place her indorsements on the designs of others. He was also to have the exclusive right to place her own designs on sale, or to license others to market them. In return, she was to have one-half of "all profits and revenues" derived from any contracts he might make. The exclusive right was to last at least one year from April 1, 1915, and thereafter from year to year unless terminated by notice of ninety days. The plaintiff says that he kept the contract on his part, and that the defendant broke it. She placed her indorsement on fabrics, dresses and millinery without his knowledge, and withheld the profits. He sues her for the damages, and the case comes here on demurrer.

The agreement of employment is signed by both parties. It has a wealth of recitals. The defendant insists, however, that it lacks the elements of a contract. She says that the plaintiff does not bind himself to anything. It is true that he does not promise in so many words that he will use reasonable efforts to place the defendant's indorsements and market her designs. We think, however, that such a promise is fairly to be implied. The law has outgrown its primitive stage of formalism when the precise word was the sovereign talisman, and every slip was fatal. It takes a broader view to-day. A promise may be lacking, and yet the whole writing may be "instinct with an obligation," imperfectly expressed. * * * If that is so, there is a contract.

The implication of a promise here finds support in many circumstances. The defendant gave an *exclusive* privilege. She was to have no right for at least a year to place her own indorsements or market her own designs except through the agency of the plaintiff. The acceptance of the exclusive agency was an assumption of its duties. * * * We are not to suppose that one party was to be placed at the mercy of the other. * * * Many other terms of the agreement point the same way. We are told at the outset by way of recital that "the said Otis F. Wood possesses a business organization adapted to the placing of such indorsements as the said Lucy, Lady Duff–Gordon has approved." The implication is that the plaintiff's business organization will be used for the purpose for which it is adapted. But the terms of the defendant's compensation are even more significant. Her sole compensation for the grant of an exclusive agency is to be one-half of all the profits resulting from the plaintiff's efforts. Unless he gave his efforts, she could never get anything. Without an implied promise, the transaction cannot have such business "efficacy as both parties must have intended that at all events it should have" (Bowen, L. J., in *The Moorcock*, 14 P. D. 64, 68). But the contract does not stop there. The plaintiff goes on to promise that he will account monthly for all moneys received by him, and that he will take out all such patents and copyrights and trademarks as may in his judgment be necessary to protect the rights and articles affected by the agreement. It is true, of course, as the Appellate Division has said, that if he was under no duty to try to market designs or to place certificates of indorsement, his promise to account for profits or take out copyrights would be valueless. But in determining the intention of the parties, the promise *has* a value. It helps to enforce the conclusion that the plaintiff *had* some duties. His promise to pay the defendant one-half of the profits and revenues resulting from the exclusive agency and to render accounts monthly, was a promise to use reasonable efforts to bring profits and revenues into existence. For this conclusion, the authorities are ample * * *.

The judgment of the Appellate Division should be reversed, and the order of the Special Term affirmed, with costs in the Appellate Division and in this court.

QUESTIONS, NOTE, AND CONNECTIONS

1. Questions about the facts of this case

    1.1. Why do you think the contract lacked any express obligation on the part of Wood to market the designs?

    1.2. Note that Wood brought this lawsuit. Why do you think Lady Duff–Gordon gave her endorsement to others without Wood's knowledge? Didn't she know that Wood would find out?

2. Questions about the law

    2.1. What is Lucy's argument as to why she was entitled to break her promise without liability to Wood?

    2.2. Assume that Lady Duff–Gordon had not made another deal, and the case is instead Lady Duff–Gordon suing Wood for breach of contract because Wood hadn't done a darn thing to market Lucy's fashions. What result?

    2.3. How is *Wood v. Lucy* similar to *Threadgill, supra*, at [435]? How is it different?

    2.4. Would Cardozo have reached a different result if the agreement between Lucy and Wood had a merger clause?

3. Note

    In *Wood v. Lucy*, Cardozo states: "The law has outgrown its primitive stage of formalism when the precise word was the sovereign talisman, and every slip was fatal. It takes a broader view to-day." This is a hallmark of Cardozo; catchy language describing a common situation. But think about what it says. Is it true? Think back to our earlier materials about the required level of definiteness for a communication to be an offer. Have your views changed since then?

Lady Duff–Gordon had a curious career, as indicated by the following excerpt:*

DANIEL WM. FESSLER, TEACHING NOTES FOR FES-SLER & LOISEAUX'S CONTRACTS: MORALITY, ECONOMICS AND THE MARKETPLACE

47–48 (1982)

For some reason I have become fascinated by Lady Duff–Gordon and over the years have collected a good deal of trivia concerning her exploits. The most famous affair involving Lady Duff grew out of her status as a passenger on the Titanic.** It seems that she was traveling with her husband, Sir Cosmo Duff–Gordon, and her maid. In the midst of history's greatest marine disaster, Lady Duff, Sir Cosmo, the maid and two other passengers managed to appropriate a life boat with a capacity of 34. They were accompanied by seven members of the crew! As they were rowed to safety amidst the heroism and the death of the men who volunteered to remain on board Lady Duff is said to have declared to her maid: "Oh look, there goes my beautiful dressing gown." Later an Admiralty Court was to examine formal charges that Sir Cosmo had bribed members of the crew. It was established that Sir Cosmo had given £5 checks to the members of the crew on the life boat and had objected when one of the crew suggested that they go back in the attempt to pick up people who were in the sea and crying for help. Notwithstanding, the court acquitted Sir Cosmo of the charge of bribery. This acquittal shocked the press, perhaps because—or in spite of—Lady Duff's appearance in the court as a witness. In a special dispatch to the New York Times on May 21, 1912, we find the following description of a dramatic figure: "[She was] dressed entirely in black except for a white lace collar." Harold Spencer reported that her second day on the stand gave quite a different impression from that of the first:

> * * * she is a fair creation, daintily chiseled, graceful in movement, arresting in speech. Her voice is tuned to the siren's note, her little face is pale and plaintive, and her whole being is braced to the edge of victory over her accusers. The white aigrette of Friday last, erect and challenging, had given place to the sweep of a large black picture hat, shading her eyes to the left and drooping with hint of tears over the right shoulder. A collar of exquisite lace ripples down from the shapely neck to the waist, very white and vivid against the black dress.

My colleague, Jack Ayer, supplied some further information respecting her business activities:

---

* For those who can't get enough of Lady Duff–Gordon, or who just want to see a picture of her, you can go to *Encyclopedia Titanica: First Class Passenger: Lady Duff–Gordon (Lucy Christiana Sutherland)* (http://www.encyclopedia-titanica.org/biography/ 101/). Eds.

** For the sharp-eyed, Lady Duff–Gordon is introduced to Leonardo DeCaprio's character in the movie, *Titanic*, in the scene in which Leonardo bluffs his way into the first class dining room. Eds.

It was big. When she died in 1935 at the age of 72, the New York Times described her as a 'pioneer in bringing freedom and grace back to women's dress after the Victorian era'. She was a Canadian, daughter of one Douglas Sutherland, sister of Elinor Glyn, the sexy novelist, widow of one James S. Wallace. She married Sir Cosmo in 1900; but before that she had undertaken the dressmaking business which later spanned the hemispheres. At her peak, she operated in London, Paris, Chicago and New York. Her name became synonymous with glamour and high style. Among her injunctions:

> A girl should never dress so that the dress subjects her personality.

> One should never make 'sex appeal' on the street. Wear black by all means.

> One should never wear skirts so short as to allow a bit of leg above the top of the boots.

Her eye for fashion apparently did not translate into business sense. She went bankrupt in New York in 1922, and in London in 1924. At a bankruptcy inquiry in London, an examiner asked: "Can you give me some particulars on your shareholders?" To which she replied: "It is all Greek to me. I don't know what a share is."

Her success as a glamour girl seems to have been coupled with something of a sullen contempt for society at large. Her New York troubles began with an accusation that she engaged in conspiracy to defraud customs laws. In 1919, she gained notoriety of a small sort by answering a creditor's inquiry for non-payment of a $1,500 breach of contract judgment (not Woods!) in person. She wore a pearl necklace with an estimated worth of $5,000, and testified that she drew $365 per week from her firm, Lucille, Inc., and another $100 per week from International Features Services. What did she do for the $100? "Nothing" she replied. Her examiner asked if she ever bought Liberty Bonds. She replied: "Why should I buy any? This country means nothing to me. I have nothing but trouble over here. It is an awful country." She did add: "I believe I have one that my maid bought for me."

The plaintiff, Otis Wood, is almost as interesting. He was the son of Fernando Wood, the first Mayor of New York elected by the Tammany Hall machine.

Fernando Wood was a member of Congress during the Civil War and was a supporter of slavery. More relevant to this case, Fernando Wood played an important role in the appointment of Albert Cardozo, Benjamin Cardozo's father, to the New York Supreme Court and Albert Cardozo's later resignation from the bench after being confronted with impeachment for a ruling in favor of Fernando Wood in a fraud case.

More relevant still, before contracting with Lady Duff Gordon, Otis Wood had entered into an exclusive promotion agreement with Rose O'Neil, the inventor of the Kewpie Doll. That contract contained an explicit best efforts clause. See generally Victor Goldberg, FRAMING CONTRACT LAW: AN ECONOMIC PERSPECTIVE 43–73 (2006).

BILLMAN v. HENSEL

Court of Appeals of Indiana, Third District
181 Ind.App. 272, 391 N.E.2d 671 (1979)

GARRAD, PRESIDING JUDGE.

The Hensels, as sellers, entered into a contract to sell their home to the Billmans (the buyers) for $54,000 cash. A condition of the contract was the ability of the buyers to secure a conventional mortgage on the property for not less than $35,000 within thirty (30) days. When the buyers did not complete the purchase, the sellers commenced this suit to secure a thousand dollars ($1,000) earnest money/liquidated damage deposit required by the contract. The buyers defended upon the basis that they were relieved from performing. The case was tried by the court and judgment was entered in favor of the sellers. The sole question raised on appeal is whether the court properly determined that the buyers were not excused from performance. We affirm.

The parties do not dispute, nor do we, that the "subject to financing" clause constituted a condition precedent in the contract. It is also undisputed that the buyers did not, in fact, secure a mortgage loan commitment within the contractual period.

The evidence at trial disclosed that on September 30, the day following execution of the contract, Mr. Billman met with an agent of the Lincoln National Bank and Trust Company of Fort Wayne. Billman was told that he could not obtain a mortgage loan of $35,000 unless he could show he had the difference between the purchase price and the amount of the mortgage. After totaling his available resources, including a 90 day short term note for $10,000 representing the proceeds from the sale of his present home, Billman was $6,500 short of the required $19,000 balance. On October 1st, the Hensels deposited the earnest money check into their account. Billman called Mr. Hensel to tell him that he was close on the financing and requested permission to show the home to his parents on October 3rd.

The Billmans and Mr. Billman's parents went through the house by themselves. The Hensels overheard Mr. Billman's father tell Mr. Billman that "I think I'd be careful with this * * * I'm afraid of it." The Billmans returned without the parents later that same day. Mr. Billman told the Hensels that the deal was off because his parents were unable to loan him the $5,000 needed to complete his financing. The next day, Mr. Hensel told Mr. Billman that he would reduce the price of the home by $5,000.

Mr. Billman refused to consider such a reduction, stating that he still needed another $1,500. The Billmans did not deposit funds to cover the check given as earnest money, and Mrs. Billman stopped payment on the check on October 4th.

The Billmans contacted only one financial institution concerning a mortgage loan, and made no formal loan application whatever. They limited discussion to a loan of $35,000 although they subsequently claimed to have required more. When Billman told Hensels he was cancelling the sale, he stated the reason was that his parents would not give him $5,000 for the purchase. However, prior to that time he had not mentioned relying upon any assistance and had instead assured Hensels they had all the money needed to complete the sale. Then when Hensels offered to reduce the price by the figure Billman had mentioned, he stated he needed yet an additional $1,500.

We believe the better view to be that such subject to financing clauses impose upon the buyers an implied obligation to make a reasonable and good faith effort to satisfy the condition.

Such an interpretation not only comports with the reasonable expectations of the parties, but is a logical extension of the sound rule of contract law that a promisor cannot rely upon the existence of a condition precedent to excuse his performance where the promisor, himself, prevents performance of the condition.

We recognize that the First District's decision in *Blakley v. Currence (1977), Ind. App., 361 N.E.2d 921* refused to impose such an obligation where the condition was not expressed in terms of the *ability* of the buyers to secure financing. We need not reach that question on the facts before us, although we believe the rule in *Blakley* should be limited to the facts there present.

Here the condition imposed was that the buyers be Able to secure a conventional mortgage of not less than $35,000. From the evidence recited above the court was justified in concluding that the sellers had carried their burden of proof by establishing that the buyers did not make a reasonable and good faith effort to secure the necessary financing,* and therefore could not rely upon the condition to relieve their duty to perform.

Affirmed.

QUESTIONS AND CONNECTIONS

1. Questions about the facts of this case
    1.1. Do we know if the Billmans have the ability to obtain a $35,000 mortgage? Did the court know? Does it matter?

---

* Note that ordinarily this burden will fall upon the buyer who must bring suit seeking return of his earnest money.

    1.2. Of what significance is the fact that Mr. Billman refused Mr. Hensel's offer on October 4 to reduce the purchase price by $5,000?

2. Questions about the law

    2.1. What's the difference between the duty to use "reasonable efforts," imposed by the court in *Wood v. Lucy*, and the obligation to use a "reasonable and good faith effort," imposed by the court in *Billman*?

    2.2. The *Billman* court distinguished an earlier decision from another district of the same court on the basis that the condition in that case was not expressed in terms of the *ability* of the buyers to secure financing. Why should that make a difference? Or should it?

3. Connections

The previous two cases are related to two areas of Contract law that we've previously explored: Deficient Agreements (Chap. 2, § 6) and Consideration (Chap. 3, § 1). The first connection entails the inclination of courts and legislatures not to let an agreement fail for indefiniteness or incompleteness if the parties intended to enter into a legally binding agreement and there is a reasonably certain basis for enforcement. The technique of supplying (or implying) a term or terms to save contractual intent inevitably also has consequences in the performance stage of the contract as the last two cases have shown.

The second connection may be a bit more obscure at first. You'll recall that, in *Lucy*, Lady Duff–Gordon argued in response to Wood's suit against her that Wood did "not bind himself to do anything," and that, therefore, their agreement lacked "the elements of a contract." What elements were missing? Well, if Wood did not really commit to do anything, then there was no real promise from him; or, put in other terms, his promise was *illusory*. Ok, but so what? Well, if she was receiving nothing back from Wood in return for her promise to give him exclusive endorsement rights, then her promise was not supported by—yes, now you see it—*consideration*. The court's implication of the "best efforts" undertaking not only prevented the agreement from being too indefinite to enforce, it also provided the *mutuality of obligation* essential to enforcement.

Next, think about what Hensels' defense would have been in *Billman* if the Billmans had secured financing and then the Hensels refused to go forward with the deal. Surely, the Hensels would have contended that if the Billmans reserved unfettered discretion over the satisfaction of the condition to their obligation to buy, then there was no consideration for the Hensels' promise to sell because the Billmans' promise was *illusory*.

In the introduction to this chapter, we suggested that perspective is necessary to appreciate the law relating to contract terms. We now need to add to that statement. A certain amount of cynicism is also necessary.

We are certain that not all lawsuits regarding contract terms are bona fide disputes. That is, if courts and juries could examine the hearts and minds of the litigants, we think in many cases they would find that the terms proffered were manufactured, or at least refined, only after some problem with the economics of the transaction surfaced. But courts and juries don't have that power. They must start from the terms being argued by the parties, and work backwards to reach the best interpretation of the parties' original intent.

B. TERMS IMPLIED BY COURTS TO EFFECTU-ATE PUBLIC POLICY—THE IMPLIED DUTY OF GOOD FAITH AND FAIR DEALING

In *Lucy* and *Billman,* the courts' justification for implying terms was supplying what the parties surely forgot. In the cases in this part of the book, we find courts' implying terms and conditions in contracts to achieve substantial justice, whatever that may ultimately mean, or supplying terms that the parties would have agreed to had they thought about the matter at all. When assessing either of these types of terms, ask yourself whether the implication of such terms is based on pure public policy—that is, whether they represent society's collective judgment as to what ought to be in every contract. Also ask yourself to what extent such implication is based on rough empiricism—that is, do they represent society's collective judgment as to what parties in similar transactions would usually insert if they thought about it?*

Early on in our studies, and as recently as the last case, we encountered assertions that contract law, or at least the enforcement of contracts, is infused and imbued with notions of good faith. The next few cases examine that concept in several different contexts.

LOCKE v. WARNER BROS., INC.

Court of Appeals of California, Second District
57 Cal.App.4th 354, 66 Cal.Rptr.2d 921 (1997)

KLEIN, P. J.

Plaintiffs and appellants Sondra Locke (Locke) and Caritas Films, a California corporation (Caritas) (sometimes collectively referred to as Locke) appeal a judgment following a grant of summary judgment in favor of defendant and respondent Warner Bros., Inc. (Warner). * * *

We conclude triable issues are present with respect to whether Warner breached its development deal with Locke by categorically refusing to work with her. * * * The judgment therefore is reversed. * * *

---

* You also might ask yourself if you (or the judges deciding these cases) are in the best position to make that empirical call.

FACTUAL AND PROCEDURAL BACKGROUND

1. Locke's dispute with Eastwood.

In 1975, Locke came to Warner to appear with Clint Eastwood in *The Outlaw Josey Wales* (Warner Bros. 1976). During the filming of the movie, Locke and Eastwood began a personal and romantic relationship. For the next dozen years, they lived in Eastwood's Los Angeles and Northern California homes. Locke also appeared in a number of Eastwood's films. In 1986, Locke made her directorial debut in *Ratboy* (Warner Bros. 1986).

In 1988, the relationship deteriorated, and in 1989 Eastwood terminated it. Locke then brought suit against Eastwood, alleging numerous causes of action. That action was resolved by a November 21, 1990, settlement agreement and mutual general release. Under said agreement, Eastwood agreed to pay Locke additional compensation in the sum of $450,000 "on account of past employment and Locke's contentions" and to convey certain real property to her.

2. Locke's development deal with Warner.

According to Locke, Eastwood secured a development deal for Locke with Warner in exchange for Locke's dropping her case against him. Contemporaneously with the Locke/Eastwood settlement agreement, Locke entered into a written agreement with Warner, dated November 27, 1990. It is the Locke/Warner agreement which is the subject of the instant controversy.

The Locke/Warner agreement had two basic components. The first element states Locke would receive $250,000 per year for three years for a "non-exclusive first look deal." It required Locke to submit to Warner any picture she was interested in developing before submitting it to any other studio. Warner then had 30 days either to approve or reject a submission.

The second element of the contract was a $750,000 "pay or play" directing deal. The provision is called "pay or play" because it gives the studio a choice: It can either "play" the director by using the director's services, or pay the director his or her fee.

Unbeknownst to Locke at the time, Eastwood had agreed to reimburse Warner for the cost of her contract if she did not succeed in getting projects produced and developed. Early in the second year of the three-year contract, Warner charged $975,000 to an Eastwood film, *Unforgiven* (Warner Bros. 1992).

Warner paid Locke the guaranteed compensation of $1.5 million under the agreement. In accordance with the agreement, Warner also provided Locke with an office on the studio lot and an administrative assistant. However, Warner did not develop any of Locke's proposed projects or hire her to direct any films. Locke contends the development deal was a sham, that Warner never intended to make any films with her, and that Warner's sole motivation in entering into the agreement was to assist Eastwood in settling his litigation with Locke.

3. Locke's action against Warner.

On March 10, 1994, Locke filed suit against Warner, alleging four causes of action.

* * *

The second cause of action alleged that Warner breached the contract by refusing to consider Locke's proposed projects and thereby deprived her of the benefit of the bargain of the Warner/Locke agreement.

* * *

Warner answered, denied each and every allegation and asserted various affirmative defenses.

4. Warner's motion for summary judgment and opposition thereto.

On January 6, 1995, Warner filed a motion for summary judgment. Warner contended it did not breach its contract with Locke because it did consider all the projects she presented, and the studio's decision not to put any of those projects into active development or "hand" Locke a script which it already owned was not a breach of any express or implied contractual duty. Warner asserted the odds are slim a producer can get a project into development and even slimmer a director will be hired to direct a film. During the term of Locke's deal, Warner had similar deals with numerous other producers and directors, who fared no better than Locke.

* * *

In opposing summary judgment, Locke contended Warner breached the agreement in that it had no intention of accepting any project regardless of its merits. Locke also asserted Warner committed fraud by entering into the agreement without any intention of approving any project with Locke or allowing Locke to direct another film.

Locke's opposition papers cited the deposition testimony of Joseph Terry, who recounted a conversation he had with Bob Brassel, a Warner executive, regarding Locke's projects. Terry had stated to Brassel: " 'Well, Bob, this woman has a deal on the lot. She's a director that you want to work with. You have a deal with her. * * * I've got five here that she's interested in.' [¶] And then I would get nothing. [¶] * * * [¶] I was told [by Brassel], 'Joe, we're not going to work with her,' and then, 'That's Clint's deal.' And that's something I just completely did not understand."

Similarly, the declaration of Mary Wellnitz stated: She worked with Locke to set up projects at Warner, without success. Shortly after she began her association with Locke, Wellnitz submitted a script to Lance Young, who at the time was a senior vice-president of production at Warner. After discussing the script, Young told Wellnitz, "Mary, I want you to know that I think Sondra is a wonderful woman and very talented, but, if you think I can go down the hall and tell Bob Daly that I have a movie I want to make with her he would tell me to forget it. They are not going to make a movie with her here."

5. Trial court's ruling.

On February 17, 1995, the trial court granted summary judgment in favor of Warner. Thereafter, the trial court signed an extensive order granting summary judgment. The order stated:

> Under the contract, Warner had no obligation either to put into development any of the projects submitted to the studio for its consideration, or to 'hand off' to Locke any scripts for her to direct that it previously had acquired from someone else. The implied covenant of good faith and fair dealing cannot be imposed to create a contract different from the one the parties negotiated for themselves. Warner had the option to pass on each project Locke submitted. Warner was not required to have a 'good faith' or 'fair' basis for declining to exercise its right to develop her material. Such a requirement would be improper and unworkable. A judge or jury cannot and should not substitute its judgment for a film studio's when the studio is making the creative decision of whether to develop or produce a proposed motion picture. Such highly subjective artistic and business decisions are not proper subjects for judicial review. Moreover, Warner had legitimate commercial and artistic reasons for declining to develop the projects Locke submitted.

* * *

Locke filed a timely notice of appeal from the judgment.

CONTENTIONS

Locke contends: The trial court erred by granting Warner's motion for summary judgment based on its conclusion there were no disputed issues of material fact; the trial court erred in weighing the evidence, resolving doubts against Locke, the nonmoving party, and adopting only those inferences favorable to Warner where the evidence supported contrary inferences; and the trial court committed reversible error first by failing to make any findings or evidentiary rulings and then by adopting Warner's defective ruling.

DISCUSSION

* * *

2. *A triable issue exists as to whether Warner breached its contract with Locke by failing to evaluate Locke's proposals on their merits.*

As indicated, the second cause of action alleged Warner breached the contract by "refusing to consider the projects prepared by [Locke] and depriving [Locke] of the benefit of the bargain of the Warner–Locke agreement."[3]

In granting summary judgment on this claim, the trial court ruled "[a] judge or jury cannot and should not substitute its own judgment for a film studio's when the studio is making the creative decision of whether to develop or produce a proposed motion picture. Such highly-subjective artistic and business decisions are not proper subjects for judicial review."

The trial court's ruling missed the mark by failing to distinguish between Warner's right to make a subjective creative decision, which is not reviewable for reasonableness, and the requirement the dissatisfaction be bona fide or genuine.

a.   General principles.

" '[W]here a contract confers on one party a discretionary power affecting the rights of the other, a duty is imposed to exercise that discretion in good faith and in accordance with fair dealing.' [Citations.]" * * * It is settled that in " 'every contract there is an implied covenant that neither party shall do anything which will have the effect of destroying or injuring the right of the other party to receive the fruits of the contract. * * *   * * *

Therefore, when it is a condition of an obligor's duty that he or she be subjectively satisfied with respect to the obligee's performance, the subjective standard of *honest satisfaction* is applicable. * * * "Where the contract involves matters of fancy, taste or judgment, the promisor is the sole judge of his satisfaction. If he asserts *in good faith* that he is not satisfied, there can be no inquiry into the reasonableness of his attitude. Traditional examples are employment contracts * * * and agreements to paint a portrait, write a literary or scientific article, or produce a play or vaudeville act. [Citations.]" * * * In such cases, "the promisor's determination that he is not satisfied, *when made in good faith*, has been held to be a defense to an action on the contract. [Citations.]" * * *

Therefore, the trial court erred in deferring entirely to what it characterized as Warner's "creative decision" in the handling of the development deal. If Warner acted in bad faith by categorically rejecting Locke's work and refusing to work with her, irrespective of the merits of her proposals, such conduct is not beyond the reach of the law.

---

3.   Contrary to Warner's contention Locke is raising an unpled claim for breach of the implied covenant of good faith and fair dealing, the second cause of action for breach of contract adequately alleges Warner deprived Locke of the benefit of the bargain of the development deal by refusing to consider her projects. Such conduct by Warner, if proven, would amount to a breach of the covenant, implied "in every contract that neither party will do anything which will injure the right of the other to receive the benefits of the agreement. [Citation.]" (*Comunale v. Traders & General Ins. Co.* (1958) 50 Cal. 2d 654, 658[, 328 P.2d 198, 68 A.L.R.2d 883]; accord, *Waller v. Truck Ins. Exchange, Inc.* (1995) 11 Cal. 4th 1, 36[, 44 Cal. Rptr. 2d 370, 900 P.2d 619].)

    *b.   Locke presented evidence from which a trier of fact reasonably
could infer Warner breached the agreement by refusing to
consider her proposals in good faith.*

Merely because Warner paid Locke the guaranteed compensation
under the agreement does not establish Warner fulfilled its contractual
obligation. As pointed out by Locke, the value in the subject development
deal was not merely the guaranteed payments under the agreement, but
also the opportunity to direct and produce films and earn additional sums,
and most importantly, the opportunity to promote and enhance a career.

Unquestionably, Warner was entitled to reject Locke's work based on
its subjective judgment, and its creative decision in that regard is not
subject to being second-guessed by a court. However, bearing in mind the
requirement that subjective dissatisfaction must be an honestly held
dissatisfaction, the evidence raises a triable issue as to whether Warner
breached its agreement with Locke by not considering her proposals on
their merits.

As indicated, the deposition testimony of Joseph Terry recounted a
conversation he had with Bob Brassel, a Warner executive, regarding
Locke's projects. In that conversation, Brassel stated " 'Joe, we're not
going to work with her,' and then, 'That's Clint's deal.' "

Similarly, the declaration of Mary Wellnitz recalled a conversation she
had with Lance Young, a senior vice-president of production at Warner.
After discussing the script with Wellnitz, Young told her: "Mary, I want
you to know that I think Sondra is a wonderful woman and very talented,
but, if you think I can go down the hall and tell Bob Daly that I have a
movie I want to make with her he would tell me to forget it. They are not
going to make a movie with her here."

The above evidence raises a triable issue of material fact as to
whether Warner breached its contract with Locke by categorically refusing
to work with her, irrespective of the merits of her proposals. While
Warner was entitled to reject Locke's proposals based on its subjective
dissatisfaction, the evidence calls into question whether Warner had an
honest or good faith dissatisfaction with Locke's proposals, or whether it
merely went through the motions of purporting to "consider" her projects.

    *c.   No merit to Warner's contention Locke seeks to rewrite the
instant agreement to limit Warner's discretionary power.*

Warner argues that while the implied covenant of good faith and fair
dealing is implied in all contracts, it is limited to assuring compliance with
the express terms of the contract and cannot be extended to create
obligations not contemplated in the contract. * * *

This principle is illustrated in *Carma Developers (Cal.), Inc. v. Marathon Development California, Inc.* (1992) 2 Cal. 4th 342, 351–352 [6 Cal.
Rptr. 2d 467, 826 P.2d 710], wherein the parties entered into a lease
agreement which stated that if the tenant procured a potential sublessee
and asked the landlord for consent to sublease, the landlord had the right

to terminate the lease, enter into negotiations with the prospective sublessee, and appropriate for itself all profits from the new arrangement. *Carma* recognized "[t]he covenant of good faith finds particular application in situations where one party is invested with a discretionary power affecting the rights of another." (*Id.*, at p. 372.) The court expressed the view that "[s]uch power must be exercised in good faith." (*Ibid.*) At the same time, *Carma* upheld the right of the landlord under the express terms of the lease to freely exercise its discretion to terminate the lease in order to claim for itself—and deprive the tenant of—the appreciated rental value of the premises. (*Id.*, at p. 376.)

In this regard, *Carma* stated: "We are aware of no reported case in which a court has held the covenant of good faith may be read to prohibit a party from doing that which is expressly permitted by an agreement. On the contrary, as a general matter, implied terms should never be read to vary express terms. [Citations.] 'The general rule [regarding the covenant of good faith] is plainly subject to the exception that the parties may, by express provisions of the contract, grant the right to engage in the very acts and conduct which would otherwise have been forbidden by an implied covenant of good faith and fair dealing. * * * [¶] This is in accord with the general principle that, in interpreting a contract "an implication * * * should not be made when the contrary is indicated in clear and express words." 3 Corbin, Contracts, § 564, p. 298 (1960). * * * [¶] *As to acts and conduct authorized by the express provisions of the contract*, no covenant of good faith and fair dealing can be implied which forbids such acts and conduct. And if defendants were given the right to do what they did by the express provisions of the contract there can be no breach.' [Citation.]" * * *

In *Third Story Music, Inc. v. Waits* (1995) 41 Cal. App. 4th 798, 801 [48 Cal. Rptr. 2d 747], the issue presented was "whether a promise to market music, or to refrain from doing so, at the election of the promisor is subject to the implied covenant of good faith and fair dealing where substantial consideration has been paid by the promisor."

In that case, Warner Communications obtained from Third Story Music (TSM) the worldwide right to manufacture, sell, distribute and advertise the musical output of singer/songwriter Tom Waits. * * * The agreement also specifically stated that Warner Communications " 'may at our election refrain from any or all of the foregoing.' " * * * TSM sued Warner Communications for contract damages based on breach of the implied covenant of good faith and fair dealing, claiming Warner Communications had impeded TSM's receiving the benefit of the agreement. * * * Warner Communications demurred to the complaint, alleging the clause in the agreement permitting it to " 'at [its] election refrain' from doing anything to profitably exploit the music is controlling and precludes application of any implied covenant." * * * The demurrer was sustained on those grounds. * * *

The reviewing court affirmed, holding the implied covenant was unavailing to the plaintiff. * * * Because the agreement *expressly* provided Warner Communications had the right to *refrain* from marketing the Waits recordings, the implied covenant of good faith and fair dealing did not limit the discretion given to Warner Communications in that regard. * * *

Warner's reliance herein on *Third Story Music, Inc.*, is misplaced. The Locke/Warner agreement did not give Warner the express right to refrain from working with Locke. Rather, the agreement gave Warner *discretion* with respect to developing Locke's projects. The implied covenant of good faith and fair dealing obligated Warner to exercise that discretion honestly and in good faith.

In sum, the Warner/Locke agreement contained an implied covenant of good faith and fair dealing, that neither party would frustrate the other party's right to receive the benefits of the contract. * * * Whether Warner violated the implied covenant and breached the contract by categorically refusing to work with Locke is a question for the trier of fact.

* * *

DISPOSITION

The judgment is reversed * * * Locke to recover costs on appeal.

QUESTIONS AND NOTES

1. Questions about the facts of this case

    1.1. Was the contract term Ms. Locke claimed Warner Bros. violated an express term of the contract? If not, how do the parties know what the term requires of them in their efforts to perform as promised?

    1.2. Did Ms. Locke not receive the compensation she was promised under the contract with Warner? If she did, what remedy does she want?

    1.3. Of what relevance is Clint Eastwood's relationship with Ms. Locke and his business dealings with Warner?

2. Questions about the law

    2.1. Can you succinctly state the implied term of good faith that California (and indeed almost every other state) inserts into every contract?

    2.2. Section 205 of the *Restatement (Second) of Contracts* states:

    Every contract imposes upon each party a duty of good faith and fair dealing in its performance and its enforcement.

    Comment d adds:

WHAT ARE THE TERMS OF THE DEAL?

Subterfuges and evasions violate the obligation of good faith in performance even though the actor believes his conduct to be justified. But the obligation goes further: bad faith may be overt or may consist of inaction, and fair dealing may require more than honesty. A complete catalogue of types of bad faith is impossible, but the following types are among those which have been recognized in judicial decisions: evasion of the spirit of the bargain, lack of diligence and slacking off, willful rendering of imperfect performance, abuse of a power to specify terms, and interference with or failure to cooperate in the other party's performance.

The Uniform Commercial Code also imposes such a duty:

Every contract or duty within [the Uniform Commercial Code] imposes an obligation of good faith in its performance and enforcement.

U.C.C. § 1–304.

In turn, the U.C.C. defines good faith by stating that "good faith" means:

honesty in fact and the observance of reasonable commercial standards of fair dealing.

U.C.C. § 1–201(a)(20).

Is California law, as set forth in *Locke*, consistent with these statements, or is it aberrational?

2.3.   Would it be a valid defense on remand if Warner Bros. asserted that each idea that Ms. Locke pitched was silly or non-commercial?

2.4.   What if Warner Bros. had given serious consideration to Ms. Locke's first 10 projects, but had found them all wanting and then just internally decided not to consider any more projects? What if its refusal came after only one project?

3. Notes

3.1.   *Hey, That's Hollywood* * * * According to the *Los Angeles Times*, here's how the suit was resolved on remand:

Actress' Settlement Ends Long Legal Saga

LOS ANGELES TIMES, Part B, May 27, 1999, at 2

They said she'd never work in this town again, but all is forgiven between Sondra Locke and Warner Bros.

The actress is going back to work for the studio under terms of a legal settlement. The agreement came at the start of a trial on her lawsuit accusing Warner Bros. of harming her career by going along with a sham movie directing deal allegedly engineered by Locke's former lover and co-star, Clint Eastwood.

The last-minute settlement gives Locke a new lease on her career behind the camera, said her attorney, Neil Papiano.

The lawyer acknowledged that at times the three hours of settlement talks Monday more closely resembled a Hollywood pitch session as Locke discussed projects that caught her interest.

Asked how it felt to be back in business with a studio that a few years ago had rejected all her ideas, a beaming Locke quipped, "Hey, that's Hollywood."

The settlement came as jury selection was about to begin in a case that had been dismissed by a Los Angeles judge, then reinstated by a state appeals court.

The lawyers would not discuss the financial terms. But as he left the Burbank courthouse, Papiano said the agreement reaches beyond money considerations to create writing and directing opportunities for Locke, who had been all but blacklisted by the major studios for a decade.

"It involves a business arrangement beneficial to Ms. Locke," Papiano said. "She's going to be paid for her services—we believe handsomely."

Locke said, "This is my best day in a long, long time." She said she felt vindicated as a professional.

"We're happy too," said Warner Bros. attorney Robert Schwartz, who declined to discuss the matter further.

The case was the second installment in Locke's legal fight to regain her professional viability after the acrimonious split with Eastwood, a popular box office draw and Academy Award-winning director.

The lanky, laconic star settled with Locke for an undisclosed sum of money 2 ½ years ago, just as a jury was about to return a verdict in her favor. Testimony during that trial showed that he had paid $1.5 million under the table to subsidize her development deal with Warner Bros.

Eastwood acknowledged on the witness stand that he never told Locke about his role in subsidizing her development deal, struck as partial settlement of her palimony case against him.

Locke testified at the previous trial that she would never accept such a deal because it gave Eastwood too much control and sent a signal that she wasn't to be taken seriously.

Indeed, she pitched more than 30 ideas to the studio over three years, and none was accepted.

Monday's settlement finally lays to rest a long legal saga that began when Eastwood packed up Locke's belongings and changed the locks to their Brentwood home after the New Year's holiday in 1989.

Discovered in Nashville, Tenn., during a national talent search, Locke won a Golden Globe and an Academy Award nomination for her first film, "The Heart Is a Lonely Hunter."

She was in her 20s when she became romantically involved with Eastwood, and soon was his constant companion and co-star, even sharing billing with Clyde the orangutan in his "Every Which Way" films. The couple split after spending 14 years together.

3.2.   All readers of this note will no doubt recall the joys of the SAT and LSAT exams. Did you ever wonder what would happen if, after getting 170 on the LSAT, you then got a letter from the Educational Testing Service questioning your performance, and refusing to forward your score to the schools of your choice? If you did wonder, you might well ask what contract law has to do with any answer.

That's where *Dalton v. Educational Testing Service*, 87 N.Y.2d 384, 663 N.E.2d 289, 639 N.Y.S.2d 977 (1995) would come in. In that case, Brian Dalton took the SAT test twice, improving his score by 410 points on the second try. After finding what it thought was different handwriting on each test, the test administrator, Educational Testing Service (ETS) canceled Dalton's second score. It believed it could do this because Dalton had signed a form agreement upon registering for the test allowing ETS to take such an action if it found any unexplained discrepancies.

But the form, held to be a contract by the New York Court of Appeals, also obligated ETS to "notif[y] the test taker of the reasons for questioning the score" and offer the test-taker the * * * five options: (1) the opportunity to provide additional information, (2) confirmation of the score by taking a free retest, (3) authorization for ETS to cancel the score and refund all fees, (4) third-party review by any institution receiving the test score or (5) arbitration.

Dalton took the first option and supplied ETS with additional information (he had been ill during the first exam, and other tests indicated that his second score was a better indicator of his abilities). ETS promptly ignored this information, since they did not deem it relevant to whether Dalton had used a "ringer" in the second test.

This refusal, the court said, was a breach of the duty of good faith inherent in all contracts. "Where * * * ETS refuses to exercise its discretion * * * by declining even to consider relevant material submitted by the test-taker, the legal question is whether this refusal breached an express or implied term of the contract,. * * * Here, the courts below agreed that ETS did not consider the relevant information furnished by Dalton. By doing so, ETS failed to comply in good faith with its own test security procedures, thereby breaching its contract with Dalton."

So Dalton won the battle. Did he win the war and obtain an order forcing ETS to release his scores? No. "Dalton is entitled to relief that comports with ETS' contractual promise—good-faith consideration of the material he submitted to ETS. We cannot agree with Dalton's assumption that ETS will merely rubber-stamp its prior determination without good-faith attention to his documentation and that reconsideration by ETS will be an empty exercise. Our conclusion that the contract affords Dalton a meaningful remedy rests also on the provision in the Procedures for Questioned Scores [contained in the contract] allowing Dalton to utilize one or more of the remaining four options in combination with renewed consideration by the Board of Review. Those options—including third-party review by any institution receiving the test score as well as arbitration— remain available should ETS determine that the information submitted fails to resolve its concerns about the validity of the [second test] score."

Based on *Dalton*, how satisfying is it to prevail on a claim that someone did not consider information in good faith before making a decision related to a contract?

HOBIN v. COLDWELL BANKER RESIDENTIAL AFFILIATES, INC.

Supreme Court of New Hampshire
144 N.H. 626, 744 A.2d 1134 (2000)

HORTON, J.

The plaintiff, Ross T. Hobin, the owner of a Coldwell Banker franchise, appeals from an order of the Superior Court (Gray, J.) dismissing his claims against the defendant, Coldwell Banker Residential Affiliates, Inc. (Coldwell Banker), relating to Coldwell Banker's alleged placement of additional franchises in Hobin's territory. The trial court dismissed the claims of breach of the implied covenant of good faith and fair dealing [and] breach of contract * * * for failure to state a claim. We affirm.

Upon review of the rulings on this motion to dismiss, we assume the following facts alleged by Hobin to be true for purposes of this appeal. * * * In 1994, Hobin, who operated a real estate office in Rye, contacted Coldwell Banker about becoming one of its franchisees. At the time, the nearest Coldwell Banker office was Marple Associates (Marple), located 5.5 miles away in Portsmouth. Marple maintained a Rye telephone number, but no office in Rye.

Although the real estate market was depressed and Coldwell Banker was having difficulty selling new franchises in the area, Hobin thought he could make a franchise successful if Marple did not expand into Rye. Hobin raised the issue of Marple's potential expansion in his discussions with a Coldwell Banker recruiter, who told him that Coldwell Banker treated Rye as a "small market" area for which it charged a reduced franchise fee, implying that it could not support a second franchise and that the probability of a second franchise in Rye would be unthinkable. Throughout discussions of other Coldwell Banker franchisees, including its largest, Hunneman Real Estate Corporation (Hunneman), the recruiter did not mention the possibility of any franchisee opening an office in Rye. The recruiter did, however, suggest that Coldwell Banker's internal policies and procedures for awarding franchises would not permit the placement of a second franchise in such proximity to an existing franchise as to jeopardize that franchisee's business. As a result of these representations,

Hobin executed a franchise agreement effective July 25, 1994, and entered Coldwell Banker's Small Market Program.

Throughout the next two years, Hobin competed with the Joycelyn Caulfield Agency (Caulfield), which maintained two locations—the first in Rye, within 300 feet of Hobin's office, and the second in North Hampton, 3.2 miles away. Sometime around January 1997, Hunneman, which had purchased Marple in late 1995, also purchased Caulfield, resulting in its ownership of three offices within 5.5 miles of Hobin.

As represented to Hobin by the recruiter, Coldwell Banker maintains procedures for approving the placement of one franchise near or in another franchisee's territory. During Hobin's discussions with Coldwell Banker executives regarding his dissatisfaction with the additional Coldwell Banker offices in his territory, he discovered that those procedures include review of the proposed placement by a committee of ten to fifteen individuals and an opportunity for the existing franchisee to comment upon the placement. He also learned that, as Coldwell Banker's largest franchisee, Hunneman is given special preference and does not have to follow normal franchise-placement procedures. Coldwell Banker did not follow its procedures in permitting Hunneman to locate in Rye and North Hampton, but rather granted approval on a single telephone call from Hunneman's owner to Coldwell Banker's Franchise Development department.

Hobin brought a petition for injunctive relief against Coldwell Banker [seeking to enjoin the continued grant of a franchise to Hunneman]. * * * He appeals the dismissal of his claims against Coldwell Banker for breach of implied covenant of good faith and fair dealing [and] breach of contract

* * *

As a preliminary matter, we note that in the franchise agreement, which was appended to the petition, the parties chose the law of California, the State of Coldwell Banker's incorporation, to govern the agreement and their "legal relationships." * * * We will * * * honor the parties' selection of California law.

Hobin's first issue is whether the trial court erred in dismissing his claim of breach of the implied covenant of good faith and fair dealing. The court dismissed the claim because the action of which Hobin complains, the grant of another franchise in Hobin's marketing area, is expressly permitted in the franchise agreement.

Hobin argues that although the agreement expressly reserved Coldwell Banker's right to place additional franchisees in Hobin's territory, Coldwell Banker had the duty to exercise its discretion in accordance with the covenant of good faith and fair dealing implied in all contracts. According to Hobin, allowing Coldwell Banker's largest franchisee to open two locations in his small-market territory, one within 300 feet of his office, was a breach of that duty.

Coldwell Banker counters that, under California law, the express terms of a contract always limit any implied covenants, and a party may not pursue a cause of action for breach of an implied covenant where the supposed covenant contradicts the express term.

The franchise agreement provided, in pertinent part:

1.02   Grant of Franchise

(a) Franchisor hereby grants to Franchisee, and Franchisee hereby accepts, a non-exclusive franchise. * * * Nothing contained herein shall be deemed to grant Franchisee an exclusive territory and Franchisor * * * may * * * franchise or license others to locate and operate additional residential real estate brokerage businesses within the market area within which Franchisee conducts and operates the Franchised Business.

Although the parties agree that the agreement expressly provided that Coldwell Banker may place additional franchises in Hobin's market area, they disagree as to whether the implied covenant of good faith and fair dealing implied in every contract * * * operated to limit the extent of its discretion to do so.

In determining that a tenant had not breached the implied covenant of good faith and fair dealing against its landlord when the actions complained of were expressly allowed in the lease, * * * *Carma* [*Developers v. Marathon Dev. Cal.*, 2 Cal. 4th 342, 826 P.2d 710, 726 (Cal. 1992)] discussed two apparently inconsistent principles: that the covenant of good faith and fair dealing should be implied to limit the exercise of a discretionary power, and that express terms of a contract cannot be varied by an implied covenant. *Carma*, 826 P.2d at 726–28.

On one hand, as argued by Hobin, "the covenant of good faith finds particular application in situations where one party is invested with a discretionary power affecting the rights of another. Such power must be exercised in good faith." * * *

On the other hand, supporting Coldwell Banker's contentions, the court stated that it was

> aware of no reported case in which a court has held the covenant of good faith may be read to prohibit a party from doing that which is expressly permitted by an agreement. On the contrary, as a general matter, implied terms should never be read to vary express terms. The general rule regarding the covenant of good faith is plainly subject to the exception that the parties may, by express provisions of the contract, grant the right to engage in the very acts and conduct which would otherwise have been forbidden by an implied covenant of good faith and fair dealing. * * * As to acts and conduct authorized by the express provisions of the contract, no covenant of good faith and fair dealing can be implied which forbids such acts and conduct. And if defendants were given the right to do what they did by the express provisions of the contract there can be no breach.

Carma, 826 P.2d at 728 (quotation, citations, and brackets omitted).

A subsequent California Court of Appeal opinion reconciled these seemingly inconsistent principles. *Third Story Music, Inc. v. Waits*, 41 Cal. App. 4th 798, 48 Cal. Rptr. 2d 747 (Ct. App. 1995) (holding that the plaintiff music company had not stated a claim for breach of implied covenant of good faith and fair dealing when its contract with the defendant, to which it had sold certain music rights, expressly allowed the defendant to refrain from marketing the music). The *Third Story Music* court distinguished between the proper implication of a covenant of good faith and fair dealing "to contradict an express contractual grant of discretion when necessary to protect an agreement which otherwise would be rendered illusory and unenforceable," and situations in which a court may not imply such a covenant because "regardless of how such [discretionary] power [is] exercised, the agreement [is] supported by adequate consideration." * * *

The case before us is of the latter type. In consideration of Hobin's agreement to purchase and operate a Coldwell Banker franchise, his business accrued numerous benefits stemming from its association with a nationally recognized real estate marketing organization, including those resulting from chain identification, participation in a uniform system to promote and assist the business, training, and centralized programs for its use. Specifically, it received rights to the Coldwell Banker trademarks and trade names and the goodwill associated therewith, benefits accruing from Coldwell Banker's national and regional advertising, public relations and promotional campaigns, orientation and on-going training, operating advice and assistance, operational techniques and service concepts, on-site visits by Coldwell Banker field representatives, business-planning tools, sales and informational material, and available staff-recruitment, training, and advertising materials. Hobin was also eligible for cash awards based on his franchise's performance. Regardless of the extent of Coldwell Banker's exercise of its discretion—whether it chose to place competing franchises next door to Hobin or to leave the territory free of competitors—Hobin retained the right to the contractual benefits set forth above. Importantly, Coldwell Banker also incurred costs in providing its programs and assistance to Hobin. Even were we to adjudge the benefits accruing to Hobin to be worthless, the detriment Coldwell Banker incurred in providing its programs and assistance to Hobin was "sufficient to constitute consideration." * * * In sum, the consideration provided was "more than the peppercorn of consideration the law requires" to save the contract from unenforceability. * * *

The next issue presented is whether Hobin has stated a claim for breach of contract. Hobin concedes that Coldwell Banker did not breach an express term of the agreement. Given our holding that Hobin has not alleged a breach of the implied covenant of good faith and fair dealing, we conclude that Hobin has not alleged a breach of an implied term of the agreement. Therefore, we hold that he has failed to state a claim for breach of contract. * * *

Affirmed.

___

QUESTIONS AND NOTE

1. Questions about the facts of this case

   1.1. Why can't Hobin rely on the representations and discussions with Coldwell Banker's recruiter to make out a case for breach of contract?

   1.2. Did Coldwell Banker exercise its discretion with respect to Hunneman in good faith? Why would Coldwell Banker favor one broker over another?

   1.3. Does Coldwell Banker's profit motive come into play here? Would you want to know the termination provisions in Hobin's contract before taking his case? Why?

2. Questions about the law

   2.1. The court in *Coldwell Banker* applies California law. Is this case consistent with *Locke* which also applied California law? Are *Coldwell Banker* and *Locke* consistent with the statement found in cases from California and other states that you cannot rely on an implied good faith term to expand or otherwise contradict the express terms of a contract by claiming that some additional obligations existed?

   2.2. Does this decision mean that Coldwell Banker could intentionally drive Hobin out of business by packing his market area indiscriminately with other, newer, brokers? Why, or why not?

   2.3. If a client wished to have "total" discretion in making decisions under a contract, can you, after the last two cases, give her assurances that such a term will be honored? If you believe that you can, how would you go about drafting such a clause?

3. Note

   The implied duty of good faith and fair dealing has had particular application in connection with insurance contracts where courts have for many years entertained actions for bad faith failure to settle or satisfy a claim brought by third parties. More recently, however, this action has been expanded in some jurisdictions to cover actions brought directly by the insured. While these actions technically originate in tort, in the first instance they hinge on the courts' willingness to impose by implication, and then find a breach of, the duty of good faith and fair dealing in the underlying contract of insurance. *Cf. Harris v. Provident Life & Accident Ins. Co.*, 310 F.3d 73, 80 n.3 (2d Cir. 2002) (holding that New York does not recognize a "separate cause of action for breach of the implied covenant of good faith and fair dealing when a breach of contract claim based on the same facts is also pled).

___

SECTION 5: TERMS ADDED
BY LEGISLATURES

Courts are not alone in implying terms into contracts. Legislatures write provisions that are to be a part of every contract made within their jurisdiction. We have seen this in the Uniform Commercial Code with good faith (§ 1–304).

More often though, legislation adds terms to fill gaps—default terms that apply when the parties have not otherwise agreed Consider the following examples from Article 2 of the Uniform Commercial Code.

§ 2–305. Open Price Term.

(1) The parties if they so intend may conclude a contract for sale even though the price is not settled. In such a case the price is a reasonable price at the time for delivery if:

(a) nothing is said as to price;

(b) the price is left to be agreed by the parties and they fail to agree; or

(c) the price is to be fixed in terms of some agreed market or other standard as set or recorded by a third person or agency and it is not so set or recorded. * * *

§ 2–308. Absence of Specified Place for Delivery.

Unless otherwise agreed:

(a) the place for delivery of goods is the seller's place of business or if none, the seller's residence; but

(b) in a contract for sale of identified goods that to the knowledge of the parties at the time of contracting are in some other place, that place is the place for their delivery. * * *

§ 2–309. Absence of Specific Time Provisions. * * *

(1) The time for shipment or delivery or any other action under a contract if not provided in this Article or agreed upon shall be a reasonable time. * * *

Connections

We have discussed the U.C.C. gap fillers before. We first encountered them in Chapter 2 in connection with incomplete agreements. That's the same place where we encountered a related U.C.C. provision; namely, § 2–306 dealing with outputs and requirements contracts. Section 2–306's imposition of "good faith" limitation to insulate outputs and requirements contracts from vulnerability on grounds of both indefiniteness and lack of mutuality. *See* Official Comment 2 to § 2–306.

Now consider the U.C.C. gap fillers, or implied terms, in connection with the following problems.

PROBLEMS ON TERMS IMPLIED BY THE U.C.C.

1. Epstein and Markell meet and agree that Markell will sell, and Epstein will buy, Markell's 1965 Cadillac convertible, painted fire engine red.

    Two months later, after calling Markell several times and getting no response, Epstein sues Markell for breach of contract. Issues of damages aside, who will prevail?

2. Markell and Ponoroff see each other at a Star Trek convention in Wawautosa, Wisconsin, and Markell agrees that he will purchase, and Ponoroff agrees he will sell, Ponoroff's prize pair of plastic Vulcan ears.

    Two weeks later, Markell shows up on Ponoroff's doorstep, flashes a crisp $100 bill at Ponoroff, and demands the ears. Ponoroff yawns and slams the door on Markell's face.

    Markell sues for breach. Issues of damages aside, who will prevail?

3. Ponoroff places an order for a Galaxy 950 computer over the telephone with Galaxy Computers, Inc. The price agreed upon is $999, but no delivery date is discussed. The next day, Galaxy sends a confirming invoice stating the computer will arrive in three weeks, and indicating a price of $1,099. There is no explanation for the increase.

    When the computer arrives in three weeks as indicated, Ponoroff refuses delivery, stating that it is late. Issues of damages aside, what result if Galaxy sues Ponoroff for breach?

4. Epstein sells asphalt; Ponoroff uses it to pave roads. Ponoroff and Epstein have a contract under which Epstein agrees to sell Ponoroff all of Ponoroff's requirements of asphalt for a period of five years, with the price to be the "posted price" at Tucson for Grade A asphalt. Epstein gets a bigger contract to supply asphalt, and doesn't want to supply Ponoroff's puny needs anymore. When Ponoroff orders some asphalt he needs for a job, Epstein tells him that they have no contract, because there is no agreement on price. What result?

SECTION 6:   WARRANTIES AND THE U.C.C.

A.   INTRODUCTION

As we have seen, contract liability is promise-based. An alternative theory of obligation that may or may not be based on agreement of the parties is "warranty" liability. At its most basic level, a warranty is, in essence, an allocation of risk. That is to say, a party who makes a warranty accepts the risk of the untruth of the subject matter of that warranty. For instance, a seller of a business might warrant to the buyer that the assets of the company are free and clear of liens and encumbrances. If it should later turn out that some third party, perhaps a creditor or even the IRS, does have a claim against the assets of the business, then the seller must make it good to the buyer by satisfying the amount of the third party's claim. It makes no difference whether the seller-warrantor was aware of the claim, whether he intended to mislead the buyer, or even whether the buyer relied on the warranty in agreeing to buy the business. Unlike an action for fraud, which requires proof of bad intent, breach of warranty is a "strict liability" kind of offense.

The law recognizes several kinds of warranties concerning the nature or quality of one party's performance to the other. For instance, you may have learned in your property law class that many states recognize an implied "warrant of habitability" with respect to residential leases. If the premises are not habitable, the tenant has a defense to liability under the lease. Our focus in this section is on the statutory warranty scheme contained in Article 2 of the U.C.C. relating to contracts for the sale of goods. While you will probably receive more in-depth instruction on warranty theory in your upper-level commercial law courses, we think it is useful to briefly introduce warranty liability here for two reasons. First, it will allow you to contrast warranty liability with traditional contract liability. Second, it will give you an opportunity to engage in close statutory analysis which, as you will see, is very different from caselaw analysis.

The U.C.C. warranties come in two flavors: (1) "express warranties," which are statements made or assurances given by the seller concerning the quality or characteristics of the goods subject to the contract, and (2) "implied warranties," which are assurances concerning the seller's title to the goods and their basic quality. While express warranties arise from overt manifestations from the seller to the buyer, implied warranties are supplied by operation of law. That is to say, implied warranties are deemed to automatically become part of the contract *unless* they are excluded from the contract by affirmative agreement of the parties. Thus, warranties are "in" unless they are consciously taken "out." This is just the opposite from ordinary contract terms which are "out" unless they're deliberately put "in." Confused? Well, the U.C.C.'s warranty scheme is contained in § 2–312 through § 2–316. Review those provisions now before reading on to the next case, but bear in mind that we are only introducing warranty liability in this section. In most law schools, as we mentioned, the subject is treated in much more detail in one of the upper-level commercial law courses.

B.   EXPRESS WARRANTIES

We begin our examination of warranty liability by considering express warranties. Unlike the other terms considered in this section, these are not implied terms. However, we think it will help you to understand the

U.C.C. implied warranties if you first understand how the U.C.C. handles express warranties.

U.C.C. § 2–313(1) provides that an express warranty may be created by (a) any affirmation of fact or promise that relates to the goods, (b) any description of the goods, or (c) any sample or model. In each case, however, the affirmation, description, or sample must be made part of the *basis of the bargain*. What does that language mean?

DAUGHTREY v. ASHE

Supreme Court of Virginia
243 Va. 73, 413 S.E.2d 336 (1992)

WHITING, JUSTICE.

In this dispute between the buyers and the sellers of a diamond bracelet, the principal issues arise under the Uniform Commercial Code—Sales. [Article 2]. Specifically, they are: (1) whether the sellers' appraisal statement of the grade of diamonds on the bracelet is a description of the goods under Code § 8.2–313(1)(b), and therefore an express warranty; and (2) whether such a statement made the description "a part of the bargain" under Code § 8.2–313(1)(b), and therefore an express warranty, when the buyers did not know of the warranty until some time after the purchase price was paid and the bracelet was delivered. * * *

In October 1985, W. Hayes Daughtrey consulted Sidney Ashe (Ashe), a jeweler, about the purchase of a diamond bracelet as a Christmas gift for his wife, Fenton C. Daughtrey. Ashe exhibited, and offered to sell, a diamond bracelet to Daughtrey for $15,000. Although Ashe "knew" and "classified" the bracelet diamonds as v.v.s. grade (v.v.s. is one of the highest ratings in a quality classification system employed by gemologists and jewelers), he merely described the diamonds as "nice" in his conversation with Daughtrey. Ashe told Daughtrey that if he was later dissatisfied with the bracelet, he would refund the purchase price upon its return.

When Daughtrey later telephoned Ashe and told him he would buy the bracelet, Ashe had Adele Ashe, his business associate, complete an appraisal form which he signed. The form contained the following pertinent language:

> The following represents our estimate *for insurance purposes only, of the present retail replacement cost of identical items*, and not necessarily the amounts that might be obtained if the articles were offered for sale. * * *

DESCRIPTION	APPRAISED VALUE
platinum diamond bracelet, set with 28 brilliant full ct diamonds weighing a total of 10 carats. H color and v.v.s. quality.	$25,000.00

(emphasis added).

When Daughtrey came with his daughter to close the sale, he showed the bracelet to his daughter and then paid Ashe for it. As Ashe was counting the money, Daughtrey handed the bracelet to Adele Ashe, who put it in a box together with the appraisal and delivered the box to Daughtrey. Daughtrey later gave the bracelet to his wife as a Christmas present.

In February 1989, Daughtrey discovered that the diamonds were not of v.v.s. quality when another jeweler looked at the bracelet. Shortly thereafter, Daughtrey complained to Ashe, who refused to replace the bracelet with one mounted with diamonds of v.v.s. quality but offered to refund the purchase price upon return of the bracelet. Because the value of diamonds generally had increased in the meantime, Daughtrey declined Ashe's offer.

On May 8, 1989, Daughtrey and his wife filed this specific performance suit against Sidney Ashe and Adele Ashe t/a Ashe Jewelers (the Ashes) to compel them to replace the bracelet with one mounted with v.v.s. diamonds or pay appropriate damages. After hearing the evidence, the trial court found that the diamonds "were of substantially lesser grade" than v.v.s. Nevertheless, because it concluded that the Daughtreys had not proven that "the appraisal was a term or condition of the sale nor a warranty upon which [they] relied in the purchase of the bracelet," the court denied relief for breach of warranty.* The Daughtreys appeal.

First, we consider whether Ashe's statement of the grade of the diamonds was an express warranty. Code § 2–313 provides in pertinent part:

(1) Express warranties by the seller are created as follows:

* * *

(b) any description of the goods which is made part of the basis of the bargain creates an express warranty that the goods shall conform to the description.

The Ashes argue that the statement in the appraisal form is not an express warranty for two reasons.

First, they say the "appraisal on its face stated that it was 'for insurance purposes only.'" However, we think that the balance of the emphasized language in the appraisal form demonstrates that the limiting language relates *only* to the statement of the *appraised value*. Therefore, Ashe's description of the grade of the diamonds should be treated as any other statement he may have made about them.

---

* In conformity with the court's order, the Ashes refunded the purchase price without interest to the Daughtreys upon their return of the bracelet. However, the refund of the purchase price did not satisfy the Daughtreys' claim for the cost of replacing the bracelet with one with diamonds of v.v.s. quality.

Second, the Ashes contend that Ashe's statement of the grade of the diamonds is a mere opinion and, thus, cannot qualify as an express warranty under Code § 2–313(2). Code § 2–313(2) provides:

It is not necessary to the creation of an express warranty that the seller use formal words such as "warrant" or "guarantee" or that he have a specific intention to make a warranty, but an affirmation merely of the value of the goods or a statement purporting to be merely the seller's opinion or commendation of the goods does not create a warranty.

The Ashes rely principally upon a North Carolina case construing the identical code section from the North Carolina Uniform Commercial Code. *Hall v. T.L. Kemp Jewelry, Inc.,* 71 N.C. App. 101, 104, 322 S.E.2d 7, 10 (1984) (jeweler's assurance of value of jewels mere opinion under N.C. Gen. Stat. § 25–2–313, not warranty). However, here, Ashe did more than give a mere opinion of the value of the goods; he specifically described them as diamonds of "H color and v.v.s. quality."

Ashe did not qualify his statement as a mere opinion. And, if one who has superior knowledge makes a statement about the goods sold and does not qualify the statement as his opinion, the statement will be treated as a statement of fact. * * *

Nor does it matter that the opinions of other jewelers varied in minor respects. All of them said, and the trial judge found, that the diamonds were of a grade substantially less than v.v.s.

Clearly, Ashe intended to sell Daughtrey v.v.s. diamonds. He testified that he used only the term "nice" diamonds but "[n]ever mentioned vvs because [Daughtrey] didn't know anything about vvs." Later, Ashe testified that "I know when I sold the bracelet and I classified it as vvs, I knew it was vvs."

Given these considerations, we conclude that Ashe's description of the goods was more than his opinion; rather, he intended it to be a statement of a fact. Therefore, the court erred in holding that the description was not an express warranty under Code § 2–313(2).

Next, the Ashes maintain that because the description of the diamonds as v.v.s. quality was not discussed, Daughtrey could not have relied upon Ashe's warranty and, thus, it cannot be treated as "a part of the basis of the bargain."

In our opinion, the "part of the basis of the bargain" language of Code § 2–313(1)(b) does not establish a buyer's reliance requirement. Instead, this language makes a seller's description of the goods that is not his mere opinion a representation that defines his obligation. * * *

Our construction of [Virginia's version of] § 2–313, containing language identical to § 2–313 of the Uniform Commercial Code, is supported by a consideration of the following pertinent portions of the Official Comment to the Uniform Commercial Code section:

The present section deals with affirmations of fact by the seller, descriptions of the goods * * * exactly as any other part of a negotiation which ends in a contract is dealt with. No specific intention to make a warranty is necessary if any of these factors is made part of the basis of the bargain. In actual practice affirmations of fact made by the seller about the goods during a bargain are regarded as a part of the description of those goods; hence *no particular reliance* on such statements need be shown in order to weave them into the fabric of the agreement. Rather, any fact which is to take such affirmations, once made, out of the agreement requires clear affirmative proof. The issue normally is one of fact. Official Comment 3 (emphasis added).

In view of the principle that *the whole purpose of the law of warranty is to determine what it is that the seller has in essence agreed to sell*, the policy is adopted of those cases which refuse except in unusual circumstances to recognize a material deletion of the seller's obligation. Thus, a contract is normally a contract for a sale of something describable and described. Official Comment 4 (emphasis added).

Paragraph (1)(b) makes specific some of the principles set forth above when a description of the goods is given by the seller. * * * Official Comment 5.

The precise time when words of description or affirmation are made * * * is not material. The sole question is whether the language [is] fairly to be regarded as part of the contract. If language is used after the closing of the deal (as when the buyer when taking delivery asks and receives an additional assurance), the warranty becomes a modification, and need not be supported by consideration, if it is otherwise reasonable and in order (Section 2–209). Official Comment 7.

Concerning affirmations of value or a seller's opinion or commendation under subsection (2), the basic question remains the same: What statements of the seller have in the circumstances and in objective judgment become part of the basis of the bargain? As indicated above, all of the statements of the seller do so unless good reason is shown to the contrary. The provisions of subsection (2) are included, however, since common experience discloses that some statements or predictions cannot fairly be viewed as entering into the bargain. Official Comment 8 (emphasis added).

We conclude from the language used in Code § 2–313 and the Official Comment thereto that the drafters of the Uniform Commercial Code intended to modify the traditional requirement of buyer reliance on express warranties. Such a requirement was contained in the following pertinent language of the earlier Uniform Sales Act § 12: "[a]ny affirmation of fact or any promise by the seller relating to the goods is an express warranty if the natural tendency of such affirmation or promise is to *induce* the buyer to purchase the goods, and if the buyer purchases the goods *relying thereon*." (Emphasis added.) We note that "induce" and "reliance" appear nowhere in Code § 2–313, as contrasted with the reference to buyer reliance in the subsequent section, Code § 2–315, dealing with an implied warranty of fitness for a particular purpose.

Hence, the seller's representation need only be "a part of the basis of the bargain," as set forth in Code § 2–313(1)(b). The term "bargain" is not defined in the Code, but it is used in the following definition of "agreement" as

> the bargain of the parties in fact as found in their language or by implication from other circumstances. * * * Whether an agreement has legal consequences is determined by the provisions of this act, if applicable; otherwise by the law of contracts as provided in Code § 1–103. (Compare 'Contract'). Code § 1–201(3). The word " 'Contract' means the total legal obligation which results from the parties' agreement as affected by this act and any other applicable rules of law. (Compare 'Agreement')." Code § 1–201(11).

Ashe introduced no evidence of any factor that would take his affirmation of the quality of the diamonds out of the agreement. Therefore, his affirmation was "a part of the basis of the bargain." Accordingly, we hold that the Daughtreys are entitled to recover for their loss of bargain, and that the court erred in ruling to the contrary.

Therefore, we will reverse the judgment of the trial court and remand the case for further proceedings to ascertain the Daughtreys' damages.

Reversed and remanded.

QUESTIONS, NOTES, AND CONNECTIONS

1. Questions about the facts of this case

    1.1. How important to Mr. Daughtrey's purchase of the bracelet was the fact that the diamonds were of v.v.s. quality? Does that matter?

    1.2. Was the representation concerning the grade of the diamonds a contractual term of the sale?

    1.3. Should the fact that the appraisal was for "insurance purposes only" make a difference in determining whether the seller's statement was part of the "basis of the bargain"? Why wasn't it an important factor for the court in this case?

    1.4. Another issue raised by *Daughtrey* is whether the representation concerning the grade of the diamonds was a statement of fact or a "mere opinion." What is the distinction between the two? Would the outcome in the case have been different if the appraisal had not referred to "v.v.s. quality" but it turned out that, unrelated to changes in the market price for diamonds, the bracelet was worth considerably less than $25,000?

2. Questions about the law

2.1.   The view in *Daughtrey* that the buyer need not prove that she *relied* on the seller's representation is widely followed. Thus, unlike proof of specific contract terms, the buyer does not have to establish that the statement or description was consciously *bargained for*. Does it affect the analysis, however, if the buyer *knows* prior to consummation of the sale that the goods are *not* as represented by the seller?

2.2.   The court in *Daughtrey* specifically refers to the seller's *superior knowledge* about the goods. Does this suggest a different outcome if the Daughtreys knew only that the grade of the diamonds was less than v.v.s.? Or does it mean they must have known the actual grade of the diamonds? Whatever level of knowledge is required, should access to that knowledge be sufficient or must the buyer have actual knowledge? What are the practical consequences from a litigation standpoint of having the "basis of the bargain" requirement depend on the buyer's knowledge or access to knowledge? In *Rogath v. Siebenmann,* 129 F.3d 261 (2d Cir. 1997), the court observed that the issue was not whether the buyer believed the truth of the seller's statement, but rather whether he was purchasing the seller's promise. Does that make sense?

2.3.   In addition to determining (by virtue of factors such as superior knowledge) which party is best placed to bear the risk if the goods fail to conform to a specific statement or description, are there economic considerations that bear on the issue as well? Are you willing to pay more for goods with a warranty than without? If so, what does that tell you about how broadly the "basis of the bargain" language in § 2–313(1)(a) (Rev. § 2–313(2)(a)) should be construed?

2.4.   Should the Ashes have argued that the alleged representation concerning the quality of the diamonds was barred by the parol evidence rule? By the same token, why didn't the Daughtreys argue misrepresentation in addition to breach of warranty?

2.5.   What was Ashe prepared to give the Daughtreys when they found out the diamonds were not v.v.s. grade? What will they likely receive after remand as a result of the court's holding in this case?

3. Notes

3.1.   Official Comment 7 to U.C.C. § 2–313, cited by the court in *Daughtrey,* makes clear that a statement or description made after the deal closes does not preclude that statement or description from constituting an express warranty as long as it is part of the basis for the bargain. The post-closing statement is simply considered a *modification* of the original agreement and, of course, under the U.C.C. modifications require no separate consideration. *See* U.C.C. § 2–209. However, if the buyer is completely unaware of the seller's affirmation of fact, arguably that statement did not become part of the basis of the bargain. This possible limitation played a key role in the well-known case of *Cipollone v. Liggett Group,* 893 F.2d 541 (3d Cir. 1990), *aff'd in part, rev'd in part,* 505 U.S. 504 (1992). In that case, the plaintiff brought suit against a cigarette manufacturer for breach of express warranty based on the company's general advertisements relating to its product. The court of appeals rejected the lower court's holding that an express warranty may be created by statements to the public at large *regardless* of whether the buyer heard or could remember hearing or seeing those advertisements. Instead, the court ruled that the "basis of the bargain" limitation requires the buyer to establish that she saw, heard, or was otherwise aware of the statements. Upon making this showing, there is a presumption that the statements did become part of the basis of the bargain. According to the court, however, the seller can rebut this presumption by "clear and affirmative" proof that the buyer *knew* the statements to be untrue, at which point, the plaintiff may still make out a claim by proving *reliance* despite the non-belief. You got all that? Is it any surprise that plaintiffs' lawyers in subsequent tobacco litigation turned their attention from warranty to tort theories of liability? *See also In re Bridgestone/Firestone Inc. Tires Products Liability Litigation*, 205 F.R.D. 503 (S.D. Ind. 2001) (advertising-related warranty claims cannot form the basis of a class action).

Suppose you purchase an appliance which is accompanied by a manual containing certain affirmations of fact about the product, but you're one of those people who never reads the manual. If the appliance doesn't comply with one of those affirmations are you just out of luck? How the heck is anyone going to know whether you read it or not? Also, can merchant-sellers have it both ways? Remember *Hill v. Gateway 2000, Inc., supra* p. 142? If sellers can add the terms they want to the contract by materials included inside of the box, should they also be able to claim that warranties contained in the box were not part of the basis of the bargain?

3.2. What the courts in cases like *Cipollone* and *Bridgestone, supra*, have struggled with is warranties (and sometimes remedial promises; *i.e.*, assurances to repair or replace defective products) made to "remote purchasers." This situation arises because more often than not the product will pass from the manufacturer to one or more wholesalers and then eventually to a retailer who will sell to the ultimate purchaser. Thus, there is no contract or direct bargain between the manufacturer and the buyer who will actually use or consume the product. Nevertheless, the manufacturer may have made certain factual affirmations or promises packaged with the goods, fully intending that they would pass through the various intermediaries in the distribution chain to the remote purchaser. Likewise, as in *Cipollone*, the manufacturer may make certain promises or assurances regarding the goods in public advertisements designed to induce parties to buy the product from a seller other than the manufacturer.

3.3. All courts recognize that there is some room for sellers to "talk up" their products without subsequently being held accountable under warranty theory. The terminology generally used to refer to these communications is "sales puffery." The next problem provides an opportunity to consider the fact/opinion (puffery) distinction further.

4. Connections

> What is the difference between a claim for breach of contract and a claim for breach of an express warranty? Are "affirmations of fact" promises? Why is "an affirmation merely of the value of the goods" not an express warranty? What does the use of the term "merely" in this context mean?

PROBLEM ON EXPRESS WARRANTY

Markell is in the market for a new car. As it happens, Epstein happens to have the make and model car that Markell is looking for and Epstein is interested in selling. Although Markell never specifically asked, during the course of their discussions over price and other terms, Epstein volunteered that the car was "a sweet runner" and that "you won't have any problems with her; I even had the carburetor rebuilt just last month." Eventually, the two agree on price and close the deal. Markell drives off with the car of his dreams, only to have things turn into a nightmare. Over the course of the next month, the car breaks down several times, and it is anything but a "sweet runner." During one of his visits to the repair shop, Markell's mechanic informs him the carburetor is in bad shape and was never rebuilt. Does Markell have any claims against Epstein based on breach of express warranty. *Compare Crothers v. Cohen*, 384 N.W.2d 562 (Minn. App. 1986) *with Performance Motors, Inc. v. Allen*, 280 N.C. 385, 186 S.E.2d 161 (1972). Are there any other facts you'd like to know before reaching a final conclusion? How, if at all, would it change your analysis if Epstein were a used car dealer and this was one of the cars on Epstein's lot?

C. IMPLIED WARRANTIES GENERALLY

Article 2 contains two *implied* warranties relating to the quality of the goods forming the subject matter of the contract: an implied warranty of merchantability, provided that the seller is a merchant with respect to goods of that kind (§ 2–314), and, under certain circumstances, an implied warranty that the goods are fit for the particular purpose to which the buyer intends to put them (§ 2–315). We will briefly examine both of those warranties here. In addition, you will recall from our discussion in Section A, *supra*, of this Chapter that the U.C.C. also provides implied warranties relating to the seller's *title* to the goods. Specifically, that the goods are free and clear of any third party claims, including liens, encumbrances, and claims arising by way of infringement or the like (§ 2–312, reprinted in the section immediately above). Bear in mind that implied warranties do not depend on anything the seller says or does. Recall as well that, unlike normal contract terms, an implied warranty becomes part of the contract without any affirmative undertaking by the seller. As we will see in Subsection 6, *infra*, however, a seller can, by taking affirmative steps under the Code, eliminate the warranty from the contract by way of an express disclaimer. First, however, let's look at each of these implied warranties.

D. IMPLIED WARRANTY OF MERCHANTABILITY

WEBSTER v. BLUE SHIP TEA ROOM, INC.

Supreme Judicial Court of Massachusetts
347 Mass. 421, 198 N.E.2d 309 (1964)

REARDON, JJ.

This is a case which by its nature evokes earnest study not only of the law but also of the culinary traditions of the Commonwealth which bear so heavily upon its outcome. It is an action to recover damages for personal injuries sustained by reason of a breach of implied warranty of food served by the defendant in its restaurant. An auditor, whose findings of fact were not to be final, found for the plaintiff. On a retrial in the Superior Court before a judge and jury, in which the plaintiff testified, the jury returned a verdict for her. The defendant is here on exceptions to the refusal of the judge (1) to strike certain portions of the auditor's report, (2) to direct a verdict for the defendant, and (3) to allow the defendant's motion for the entry of a verdict in its favor under leave reserved.

The jury could have found the following facts: On Saturday, April 25, 1959, about 1 p.m., the plaintiff, accompanied by her sister and her aunt, entered the Blue Ship Tea Room operated by the defendant. The group was seated at a table and supplied with menus.

This restaurant, which the plaintiff characterized as "quaint," was located in Boston "on the third floor of an old building on T Wharf which overlooks the ocean."

The plaintiff, who had been born and brought up in New England (a fact of some consequence), ordered clam chowder and crabmeat salad. Within a few minutes she received tidings to the effect that "there was no more clam chowder," whereupon she ordered a cup of fish chowder. Presently, there was set before her "a small bowl of fish chowder." She had previously enjoyed a breakfast about 9 a.m. which had given her no difficulty. "The fish chowder contained haddock, potatoes, milk, water and seasoning. The chowder was milky in color and not clear. The haddock and potatoes were in chunks" (also a fact of consequence). "She agitated it a little with the spoon and observed that it was a fairly full bowl. * * * It was hot when she got it, but she did not tip it with her spoon because it was hot * * * but stirred it in an up and under motion. She denied that she did this because she was looking for something, but it was rather because she wanted an even distribution of fish and potatoes." "She started to eat it, alternating between the chowder and crackers which were on the table with * * * [some] rolls. She ate about 3 or 4 spoonfuls then stopped. She looked at the spoonfuls as she was eating. She saw equal parts of liquid, potato and fish as she spooned it into her mouth. She did not see anything unusual about it. After 3 or 4 spoonfuls she was aware that something had lodged in her throat because she couldn't swallow and couldn't clear her throat by gulping and she could feel it." This misadventure led to two esophagoscopies at the Massachusetts General Hospital, in the second of which, on April 27, 1959, a fish bone was found and removed. The sequence of events produced injury to the plaintiff which was not insubstantial.

We must decide whether a fish bone lurking in a fish chowder, about the ingredients of which there is no other complaint, constitutes a breach of implied warranty under applicable provisions of the Uniform Commercial Code,[1] the annotations to which are not helpful on this point. As the judge put it in his charge, "Was the fish chowder fit to be eaten and wholesome? * * * [N]obody is claiming that the fish itself wasn't wholesome. * * * But the bone of contention here—I don't mean that for a pun—but was this fish bone a foreign substance that made the fish chowder unwholesome or not fit to be eaten?"

The plaintiff has vigorously reminded us of the high standards imposed by this court where the sale of food is involved (see *Flynn v. First Natl. Stores Inc.*, 296 Mass. 521, 523) and has made reference to cases involving stones in beans (*Friend v. Childs Dining Hall Co.*, 231 Mass. 65), trichinae in pork (*Holt v. Mann*, 294 Mass. 21, 22), and to certain other cases, here and elsewhere, serving to bolster her contention of breach of warranty.

The defendant asserts that here was a native New Englander eating fish chowder in a "quaint" Boston dining place where she had been before; that "[f]ish chowder, as it is served and enjoyed by New Englanders, is a hearty dish, originally designed to satisfy the appetites of our seamen and fishermen"; that "[t]his court knows well that we are not talking of some insipid broth as is customarily served to convalescents." We are asked to rule in such fashion that no chef is forced "to reduce the pieces of fish in the chowder to minuscule size in an effort to ascertain if they contained any pieces of bone." "In so ruling," we are told (in the

---

1. "(1) Unless excluded or modified by section 2–316, a warranty that the goods shall be merchantable is implied in a contract for their sale if the seller is a merchant with respect to goods of that kind. Under this section the serving for value of food or drink to be consumed either on the premises or elsewhere is a sale. (2) Goods to be merchantable must at least be such as * * * (c) are fit for the ordinary purposes for which such goods are used. * * *" G. L. c. 106, § 2–314.

"* * * (3) (b) [W]hen the buyer before entering into the contract has examined the goods or the sample or model as fully as he desired or has refused to examine the goods there is no implied warranty with regard to defects which an examination ought in the circumstances to have revealed to him. * * *" G. L. c. 106, § 2–316.

defendant's brief), "the court will not only uphold its reputation for legal knowledge and acumen, but will, as loyal sons of Massachusetts, save our world-renowned fish chowder from degenerating into an insipid broth containing the mere essence of its former stature as a culinary master-piece." Notwithstanding these passionate entreaties we are bound to examine with detachment the nature of fish chowder and what might happen to it under varying interpretations of the Uniform Commercial Code.

Chowder is an ancient dish preexisting even "the appetites of our seamen and fishermen." It was perhaps the common ancestor of the "more refined cream soups, purees, and bisques." *Berolzheimer, The American Woman's Cook Book* (Publisher's Guild Inc., New York, 1941) p. 176. The word "chowder" comes from the French "chaudiere," meaning a "cauldron" or "pot." "In the fishing villages of Brittany * * * 'faire la chaudiere' means to supply a cauldron in which is cooked a mess of fish and biscuit with some savoury condiments, a hodgepodge contributed by the fishermen themselves, each of whom in return receives his share of the prepared dish. The Breton fishermen probably carried the custom to Newfoundland, long famous for its chowder, whence it has spread to Nova Scotia, New Brunswick, and New England." *A New English Dictionary* (MacMillan and Co., 1893) p. 386. Our literature over the years abounds in references not only to the delights of chowder but also to its manufacture. A namesake of the plaintiff, Daniel Webster, had a recipe for fish chowder which has survived into a number of modern cookbooks[2] and in which the removal of fish bones is not mentioned at all. One old time recipe recited in the New English Dictionary study defines chowder as "A dish made of fresh fish (esp. cod) or clams, stewed with slices of pork or bacon, onions, and biscuit. 'Cider and champagne are sometimes added.' " Hawthorne, in *The House of the Seven Gables* (Allyn and Bacon, Boston, 1957) p. 8, speaks of "[a] codfish of sixty pounds, caught in the bay, [which] had been dissolved into the rich liquid of a chowder." A chowder variant, cod "Muddle," was made in Plymouth in the 1890s by taking "a three or four pound codfish, head added. Season with salt and pepper and boil in just enough water to keep from burning. When cooked, add milk and piece of butter."[3] The recitation of these ancient formulae suffices to indicate that in the construction of chowders in these parts in other years, worries about fish bones played no role whatsoever. This broad outlook on

---

2. "Take a cod of ten pounds, well cleaned, leaving on the skin. Cut into pieces one and a half pounds thick, preserving the head whole. Take one and a half pounds of clear, fat salt pork, cut in thin slices. Do the same with twelve potatoes. Take the largest pot you have. Try out the pork first, then take out the pieces of pork, leaving in the drippings. Add to that three parts of water, a layer of fish, so as to cover the bottom of the pot; next a layer of potatoes, then two tablespoons of salt, 1 teaspoon of pepper, then the pork, another layer of fish, and the remainder of the potatoes. Fill the pot with water to cover the ingredients. Put over a good fire. Let the chowder boil twenty-five minutes. When this is done have a quart of boiling milk ready, and ten hard crackers split and dipped in cold water. Add milk and crackers. Let the whole boil five minutes. The chowder is then ready to be first-rate if you have followed the directions. An onion may be added if you like the flavor." "This chowder," he adds, "is suitable for a large fishing party." Wolcott, *The Yankee Cook Book* (Coward–McCann, Inc., New York City, 1939) p. 9.

3. Atwood, Receipts for Cooking Fish (Avery & Doten, Plymouth, 1896) p. 8.

chowders has persisted in more modern cookbooks. "The chowder of today is much the same as the old chowder. * * *" *The American Woman's Cook Book*, supra, p. 176. The all embracing Fannie Farmer states in a portion of her recipe, fish chowder is made with a "fish skinned, but head and tail left on. Cut off head and tail and remove fish from backbone. Cut fish in 2–inch pieces and set aside. Put head, tail, and backbone broken in pieces, in stewpan; add 2 cups cold water and bring slowly to boiling point. * * *" The liquor thus produced from the bones is added to the balance of the chowder. Farmer, *The Boston Cooking School Cook Book* (Little Brown Co., 1937) p. 166.

Thus, we consider a dish which for many long years, if well made, has been made generally as outlined above. It is not too much to say that a person sitting down in New England to consume a good New England fish chowder embarks on a gustatory adventure which may entail the removal of some fish bones from his bowl as he proceeds. We are not inclined to tamper with age old recipes by any amendment reflecting the plaintiff's view of the effect of the Uniform Commercial Code upon them. We are aware of the heavy body of case law involving foreign substances in food, but we sense a strong distinction between them and those relative to unwholesomeness of the food itself, e.g., tainted mackerel (*Smith v. Gerrish,* 256 Mass. 183), and a fish bone in a fish chowder. Certain Massachusetts cooks might cavil at the ingredients contained in the chowder in this case in that it lacked the heartening lift of salt pork. In any event, we consider that the joys of life in New England include the ready availability of fresh fish chowder. We should be prepared to cope with the hazards of fish bones, the occasional presence of which in chowders is, it seems to us, to be anticipated, and which, in the light of a hallowed tradition, do not impair their fitness or merchantability. While we are buoyed up in this conclusion by *Shapiro v. Hotel Statler Corp.,* 132 F. Supp. 891 (S. D. Cal.), in which the bone which afflicted the plaintiff appeared in "Hot Barquette of Seafood Mornay," we know that the United States District Court of Southern California, situated as are we upon a coast, might be expected to share our views. We are most impressed, however, by *Allen v. Grafton,* 170 Ohio St. 249, where in Ohio, the Midwest, in a case where the plaintiff was injured by a piece of oyster shell in an order of friend [sic] oysters, Mr. Justice Taft (now Chief Justice) in a majority opinion held that "the possible presence of a piece of oyster shell in or attached to an oyster is so well known to anyone who eats oysters that we can say as a matter of law that one who eats oysters can reasonably anticipate and guard against eating such a piece of shell. * * *" (P. 259.)

Thus, while we sympathize with the plaintiff who has suffered a peculiarly New England injury, the order must be

Exceptions sustained. Judgment for the defendant.

QUESTIONS AND NOTES

1. Questions about the facts of this case

     1.1. Just how important was it to the court's decision in *Webster* that the plaintiff had been born and brought up in New England? Would the result have been different if the plaintiff was from Wyoming visiting Boston on vacation? And while we're at it, did the court conclude the chowder was merchantable because it contained no foreign substances or no *unexpected* foreign substances? If you find yourself intrigued by this question, you might want to take a look at *Green v. American Tobacco Co.,* 304 F.2d 70 (5th Cir. 1962), one of the early cigarette cases, where the court, in denying the claim, noted, "We are not dealing with an obvious, harmful foreign body in a product. * * * They (the cigarettes) are exactly like all others of the particular brand and virtually the same as all other brands on the market."

     1.2. Goods are "merchantable" if they *would pass in the trade* without objection or they are *fit for the ordinary purposes* for which such goods are used. But what does this mean? Obviously, the presence of a large fish bone did not render the chowder in *Webster* unmerchantable, but what if the facts had been that the bone was in a cup of cream of broccoli soup?

2. Questions about the law

     2.1. Should it make a difference in terms of warranty liability if the defect was latent and, therefore, not readily ascertainable to the buyer *or* the seller? In *Willis Mining, Inc. v. Noggle,* 235 Ga.App. 747, 509 S.E.2d 731 (1998), the seller made just that argument with respect to granite blocks to be used by the buyer as gravestone monuments. About 18 months after sale of the blocks, they became discolored and had to be replaced. How would you expect the court to respond? Suppose the defect had been patent, rather than latent, and discoverable to the buyer upon exercise of reasonable diligence; how would that alter your analysis under § 2–314?

     2.2. Note that, unlike the provisions of § 2–313 relating to express warranties, the implied warranty of merchantability applies only if *the seller is a merchant with respect to goods of that kind.* What do you suppose is the reason for this limitation? How do you tell whether a seller is or is not a merchant? *See* U.C.C. § 2–104(1).

     2.3. In *Bayliner Marine Corp. v. Crow,* 257 Va. 121, 509 S.E.2d 499 (1999), the court suggested that the first phrase—would pass without objection in the trade—concerns whether a significant segment of the buying public would object to buying the goods, while the second phrase—fit for the ordinary purpose—concerns whether the goods are capable of performing their ordinary functions. The claim in *Crow* was that a certain fishing boat was unmerchantable because of its inability to reach a maximum speed of 30 miles per hour. How would you resolve that question under each of these tests of merchantability? What kind of evidence would be relevant to your determination? Would a significant segment of the public object to a creamy chowder that might mask the existence of a nasty fish bone? What is the ordinary function of a bowl of chowder?

3. Notes

3.1. Although most of the merchantability cases are litigated under the "fitness for the ordinary purpose" or the "would pass without objection in the trade" standard, to be merchantable for purposes of § 2–314(1) the good must also, among other things, conform with any promises or representations made on the container or label. U.C.C. § 2–314(2)(f). Wouldn't such a promise or representation ordinarily constitute an express warranty? If so, what, if anything, does § 2–314(2)(f) add from the buyer's perspective?

3.2. Article 35(2)(a) of the *U.N. Convention on Contracts for the International Sale of Goods* has its own implied warranty of merchantability that requires that the goods be "fit for the purposes for which goods of the same description would ordinarily be used." How does this language compare with U.C.C. § 2–314(2)(c)?

3.3. Obviously, Justice Reardon, the author of the opinion in *Webster*, had a lot of fun with this case. Some people, however, think the term "judicial humor" is an oxymoron. Here's what Professor William Prosser (of tort law fame) had to say on the subject:

Judicial humor is a dreadful thing. In the first place, the jokes are usually bad; * * * There seems to be something about the judicial ermine which puts its wearer in the same general class with the radio comedian. He is just not funny. In the second place, the bench is not an appropriate place for levity. The litigant has vital interests at stake. His entire future, or even his life, may be trembling in the balance, and the robed buffoon who makes merry at his expense should be chocked with his own wig.

THE JUDICIAL HUMORIST: A COLLECTION OF JUDICIAL OPINIONS AND OTHER FRIVOLITIES (1952) vii–viii. We suspect Ms. Webster might be inclined to agree with Professor Prosser.

NOTE ON CAUSATION

Official Comment 13 to § 2–314 states that "it is of course necessary to show not only the existence of the warranty but the fact that the warranty was broken and that the breach was the *proximate cause* of the loss sustained" (emphasis added). In many cases, the trickiest element for the buyer in a claim for breach of the implied warranty of merchantability is establishing a causal link between the breach and the loss for which recovery is sought. And you thought causation issues only came up in torts? Sorry.

In *Reybold Group, Inc. v. Chemprobe Technologies, Inc.*, 721 A.2d 1267 (Del. 1998), the court suggested that proof of causation must "tend to negate other reasonable causes of the injury sustained." Thus, a buyer could presumably show that the defect in the seller's product was the cause in fact of her injury and still not prevail if she was unable to eliminate other intervening or supervening events. How can that be? Consider a buyer who purchases a chainsaw from a hardware store. On assembling the product, buyer notices that the blade is not seated firmly in the housing. Nevertheless, buyer fires up the chain saw and proceeds to mangle his arm when the blade comes loose. Was the chain saw unmerchantable? Presumably so; this product would hardly pass muster in the trade. Was the defect in the chainsaw the cause in fact for buyer's injury? Sure, but for the defect the injury would never have occurred. But was the defect the proximate cause of buyer's injuries? Maybe not. Does it matter whether the instructions contained a warning not to use the chainsaw unless the blade is seated firmly in the housing?

The court in *Reybold* also stated that typically expert testimony is required to prove causation in a claim for breach of the implied warranty of merchantability. Why should this be so? Are there circumstances when the connection between the defect and the injury are so obvious that expert proof would be superfluous? Suppose the housing in which the chainsaw blade was seated was enclosed in a casing and not visible to the naked eye? If the buyer is injured when the blade comes loose is expert testimony really necessary to prove causation between the defect and the loss? And by the way, who are these experts? Do they work for free? Of course not, they're retained and paid for by the parties. Doesn't that tend to color their judgment? How can their testimony be taken seriously? Put another way, what safeguards exist to ensure that the expert will not just give the opinion that the party paying him or her wants? Are these safeguards adequate?

PROBLEMS ON MERCHANTABILITY

1. You all remember the "Clapper" don't you? That was the little device, marketed through television ads, which allowed you to turn an appliance on and off by clapping twice. Well it seems Edna Hubbs, an 80–year old woman suffering from arthritis and osteoporosis, purchased a Clapper. Alas, upon installing the Clapper, she found that her claps were not activating the device. Determined to make it work, Edna thereupon attempted one last, extra hard clap. Lamentably, however, the effort was too much and Edna sustained injuries to her hand and wrist. Edna proceeded to file suit against the manufacturer and the retailer of the device for breach of the warranty of merchantability. How should Edna's case be resolved? Lest you think we're making this up, see *Hubbs v. Joseph Enterprises*, 198 A.D.2d 757, 604 N.Y.S.2d 292 (1993).

2. Bruce Markell, Jr., a first year law student with a rare blood type, received a call from the local Red Cross office telling him that there was a critical shortage of his blood type and asking him to consider donating. The Red Cross official explained that a bloodmobile would be on campus the next week. Being a compassionate soul, Bruce showed up at the bloodmobile and donated a pint of his blood. Afterwards, a nurse insisted

that he have a glass of orange juice and some cookies supplied by the Red Cross to help him regain his strength and prevent light-headedness or even fainting. Bruce, never one to pass on freebies, had about six cookies along with his juice. As a goodwill gesture, Briesckes Bakery had donated the cookies to the Red Cross. Later that afternoon, Bruce became violently ill and had to be hospitalized. Tests revealed a form of food poisoning typically associated with bacteria that germinate in processed flour. Bruce is convinced that the cookies were the source of his woes. As a result of his illness, which came toward the end of the semester, Bruce was unable to take his final exams. Therefore, he will now have to spend an extra semester in law school in order to graduate. Bruce has brought a suit against both the Red Cross and Briesckes seeking to recover the additional education costs he will now incur and the wages he has lost by having to delay accepting full-time employment. What result in Bruce's case and why? *See, inter alia*, U.C.C. § 2–318.

E.   IMPLIED WARRANTY OF FITNESS FOR PARTICULAR PURPOSE

In many instances a buyer will have purchased goods for a particular purpose or with a particular objective in mind. In some of these cases the goods will not be fit for the particular purpose the buyer had in mind. If the seller affirmed that the goods would serve that purpose, the buyer will have a claim for breach of express warranty. In other situations, the goods will not accomplish the purpose because they are unmerchantable, *i.e.* not fit for the purposes for which such goods are ordinarily used. In still other cases, however, there will be no express warranty concerning the suitability of the goods to the purpose for which they were acquired *and* the failure to satisfy the buyer's purpose will not be attributable to a defect that renders the goods unmerchantable. What recourse does the buyer have in these situations? Sometimes, for example when the buyer was relying on her own judgment about the adequacy of the goods, there will be no recourse. In these cases, the hard lesson learned would be that the buyer should have done a more careful investigation into the suitability of the goods to the purpose for which they were acquired before purchasing. In other circumstances, however, the buyer may have recourse against the seller for breach of the implied warranty of fitness for a particular purpose under U.C.C. § 2–315. Nevertheless, establishing a breach of the fitness warranty when the goods fail to do what the buyer wanted them to do is a little trickier than establishing breach of the merchantability warranty when the goods are simply defective. The next case and the material that follow, are intended to help you to flesh out what the buyer must prove to make out a case under § 2–315.

LEAL v. HOLTVOGT

Court of Appeals of Ohio
123 Ohio App.3d 51, 702 N.E.2d 1246 (1998)

FAIN, J.

* * *

Joseph and Claudia Holtvogt owned and operated Shady Glen Arabians, a horse barn in Miami County, Ohio. They were experienced in Arabian horse training, breeding, boarding, selling, and showing. In 1992, the Leals, novices in the equine industry, decided to begin raising horses. In April, 1993, Ferdinand Leal began visiting Shady Glen Arabians regularly to learn how to ride and handle horses. Before long, a friendship developed between the Holtvogts and Leals, and Ferdinand Leal began spending three to four days each week at the Holtvogts' barn helping Joseph Holtvogt with the horses.

In late 1993, the Leals decided they wanted to start a breeding program by purchasing a stallion to breed with a mare they owned. At first, they were interested in purchasing Procale, a stallion owned by John Bowman. After talking to Mr. Holtvogt about Procale, the Leals decided not to buy him. The Holtvogts then offered the Leals a one-half interest in Mc Que Jabask, an Arabian stallion that the Holtvogts owned. At trial, the Leals testified that before they agreed to invest in Mc Que Jabask, Mr. Holtvogt made a number of statements regarding the stallion, such as: Mc Que Jabask was a national top ten champion in three categories; he was an all-around winning stallion; he earns $20,000.00 per year in stud fees; he is capable of attaining national show titles again; and his foals were selling for $6,000 to $10,000 each [these statements will be referred to hereinafter as "the five contested statements"].

In January, 1994, the Leals and Holtvogts entered into a contract of sale for a one-half interest in Mc Que Jabask for $16,000. The contract also established a partnership agreement, which called for the parties to share equally in the expenses and profits arising from their joint ownership of Mc Que Jabask.

There was expert testimony that prior to January, 1994, Mc Que Jabask had been treated for lameness and was suffering a chronic lameness condition in his right rear and fore fetlocks. Mr. Holtvogt testified that he had taken the stallion for lameness treatments numerous times. He also stated that he did not disclose this information to the Leals.

By July, 1994, the Leals were dissatisfied with the partnership and indicated to the Holtvogts that they wanted either a refund of their money or a remedy for their concerns. In March, 1995, the mortality insurance on Mc Que Jabask lapsed when neither the Leals nor the Holtvogts paid the insurance premium.

* * *

On January 17, 1996, Mc Que Jabask died from stomach ulcer complications. Since neither party had renewed the stallion's mortality insurance, Mc Que Jabask was uninsured.

In February, 1995, the Leals filed suit against the Holtvogts, who then brought counterclaims against the Leals. The Miami Country Common Pleas Court found that the Holtvogts had negligently misrepresented the stallion's condition and that they had breached an "express warranty on the condition of the horse for the purposes intended" and awarded the Leals $16,000 in compensatory damages. * * *

II

The Holtvogts' Second Assignment of Error is as follows:

THE TRIAL COURT COMMITTED REVERSIBLE ERROR WHEN IT HELD THAT DEFENDANTS' ACTIONS CONSTITUTED NEGLIGENT MISREPRESENTATION BECAUSE PLAINTIFFS FAILED TO PRESENT ANY FACTUAL EVIDENCE WHATSOEVER WHICH WOULD LEAD A REASONABLE PERSON TO BELIEVE THAT MC QUE JABASK WAS LAME AT THE TIME THE PARTIES ENTERED INTO THE PARTNERSHIP AGREEMENT OR THAT MC QUE JABASK WAS NOT FIT TO BE SHOWN.

* * *

Negligent misrepresentation is defined as follows:

[One] who, in the course of his business, profession or employment, or in any other transaction in which he has a pecuniary interest, *supplies false information* for the guidance of others in their business transactions, is subject to liability for pecuniary loss caused to them by their justifiable reliance upon the information, if he fails to exercise reasonable care or competence in communicating the information. *Textron Financial Corp. v. Nationwide Mut. Ins. Co. (1996),* 115 Ohio App. 3d 137, 149, 684 N.E.2d 1261, *cert. denied,* 78 Ohio St. 3d 1425, 1425, 676 N.E.2d 531. (Emphasis in original.)

[The court ruled that the concealment of Mc Que Jabask's lameness did not support a claim of negligent misrepresentation since it was not an *affirmative* false statement. However, the court concluded that the record did support the trial court's finding that the Holtvogts negligently misrepresented to the Leals that Mc Que Jabask was fit to be shown, and thus overruled the Holtvogts' second assignment of error.]

III

The Holtvogts' First Assignment of Error is as follows:

THE TRIAL COURT COMMITTED REVERSIBLE ERROR WHEN IT FOUND THAT DEFENDANTS' ACTIONS CONSTITUTED A BREACH OF AN EXPRESSED WARRANTY BECAUSE THE TRANSACTION BETWEEN THE PARTIES DOES NOT MEET THE DEFINITIONAL REQUIREMENTS UNDER OHIO EXPRESSED

WARRANTY LAW; DEFENDANTS' CONDUCT DOES NOT RISE
TO THE LEVEL OF AN EXPRESSED WARRANTY; AND THE
INTEGRATION CLAUSE IN THE PARTNERSHIP AGREEMENT
PRECLUDES THE COURT'S CONSIDERATION OF ANY AND ALL
PRIOR ORAL REPRESENTATIONS.

The Holtvogts' argument that there was no breach of an express
warranty is three-fold. First, they argue that Ohio's express warranty law
is not applicable to their transaction. Second, they argue that their
conduct was not sufficient to constitute an express warranty. Third, they
argue that there was a clause in the parties' agreement precluding
consideration of any oral representations.

We begin with the Holtvogts' argument that Ohio's express warranty
law does not apply to the transaction that occurred between the parties.
The Holtvogts contend that an express warranty can arise only if there
has been a "sale" between the parties and that their transaction with the
Leals created a "partnership agreement," not a "sale."

We first address this argument by noting that Ohio warranty law is
governed by the Uniform Commercial Code, Sales, R.C. [Article 2]. The
scope of [Article 2] is set forth in [§ 2–102], which provides in part that
"sections [§§ 2–101 to 2–725], inclusive, of the Revised Code, apply to
transactions in goods." Goods are defined as "all things * * * which are
moveable at the time of identification to the contract for sale * * * [and]
must be both existing and identified before any interest in them can
pass." [§ 2–105(1), (2)]. The Arabian stallion, Mc Que Jabask, was moveable, existing, and could be identified at the time of the contract. Thus, he
would qualify as a "good" under [§ 2–102].

As for the Holtvogts' contention that the transaction was not a
"sale," they correctly argue that a "sale" is defined as "the passing of title
from the seller to the buyer for a price." [§ 2–106(1)]. There is no
statutory requirement, however, that full title to the good must pass from
the buyer to the seller. In fact, [Article 2] explicitly states, in its definition
of "goods," "there may be a sale of a part interest in existing identified
goods." [§ 2–103(3)]. Thus, although the transaction involved the sale of
only a half-interest in Mc Que Jabask, the transaction was within the
definitional requirements of [Article 2] and thus is governed by Ohio
warranty law. Therefore, the first part of the Holtvogts' argument is not
well-taken.

We next address the Holtvogts' argument that their conduct did not
amount to an express warranty. The trial court found that "* * * the
[Holtvogts] engaged in 'puffing' at the time of the sale of the one-half
interest in the horse but did not fraudulently misrepresent a material
fact." Although the trial court did not enlighten us as to what part of the
Holtvogts' conduct it believed to be "puffing," our review of the record
leads us to believe that the trial court was talking about the five contested
statements that the Leals claim the Holtvogts made. The Holtvogts
contend that the trial court's finding that they engaged in "puffing" is

inconsistent with the trial court's conclusion that they gave the Leals an express warranty.

* * *

"Puffing," or merely stating the seller's opinion, cannot amount to an express warranty. * * * The five contested statements were the subject of extensive testimony during the trial. Mr. Holtvogt denied making any of these statements and the Leals repeatedly testified that Mr. Holtvogt did make these statements. The trial court seems to have found the five contested statements to be "puffing." Our review of the record shows that there is credible and competent evidence that these five contested statements were no more than "puffing." The Holtvogts correctly argue that when statements are mere "puffing," they cannot constitute an express warranty.

We cannot sustain this Assignment of Error, however, because we find that the Holtvogts breached an implied warranty of fitness for a particular purpose.

In its entry, the trial court found the following:

"* * * the information the [Holtvogts] failed to apprise the [Leals] was the lameness of the horse at the time the contract was executed in January 1994.

The [Leals] suffered damages in the amount of $16,000.00 as a result of this negligent misrepresentation.

The *same set of facts* establish a cause of action for breach of express warranty *on the condition of the horse for the purposes intended* * * *" (emphasis added).

In its entry, the trial court did not just say an express warranty was breached, but rather said that an "express warranty on the condition of the horse for the purposes intended" was breached. We conclude that the trial court intended to say that an implied warranty of fitness for a particular purpose was breached. Our conclusion is supported by the trial court's statement that the same set of facts establishes claims for both a breach of express warranty on the condition of the horse for the purposes intended and negligent misrepresentation. We note that the elements of a claim for negligent misrepresentation and breach of an implied warranty of fitness for a particular purpose are quite similar, while the elements of negligent misrepresentation and breach of an express warranty are not similar. Thus, we conclude that the trial court, in its conclusions of law, intended to say that an implied warranty of fitness for a particular purpose was given and breached by the Holtvogts when they failed to disclose Mc Que Jabask's lameness to the Leals.

An implied warranty of fitness for a particular purpose is covered by the Uniform Commercial Code, Sales, [§ 2–315], which provides:

"Where the seller at the time of contracting has reason to know any particular purpose for which the goods are required and that the buyer is relying on the seller's skill or judgment to select or furnish suitable goods, there is unless excluded or modified under section [2–316] of the Revised Code an implied warranty that the goods shall be fit for such purpose."

Ohio courts have set forth the following test to determine whether an implied warranty of fitness for a particular purpose has been created: (1) the seller must have reason to know of the buyer's particular purpose; (2) the seller must have reason to know that the buyer is relying on the seller's skill or judgment to furnish or select appropriate goods; and (3) the buyer must, in fact, rely upon the seller's skill or judgment. * * *

The first element requires that Mr. Holtvogt knew why the Leals decided to buy an interest in Mc Que Jabask. From our review of the record, we see that Mr. Holtvogt clearly knew that the Leals wanted to buy an interest in the stallion to start a breeding program. Mr. Holtvogt testified:

> "* * * [The Leals] had explained what type of horse they were looking for [and] it seemed to me that [Mc Que] Jabask fit the bill [of] what they were looking for and that's why I mentioned to them, uh, to Ferdinand that there might be a possibility that we would be interested in selling part interest in him.

> * * * The things that they were saying, * * * those things were, were present in, in [Mc Que] Jabask. * * *

> * * * It just, it made sense that, you know, in the fact that the Leals could breed to [Mc Que] Jabask. * * * * * * Um, we could, uh, with the experience and the reputation that we had we could help market their foals, um, it was, I really felt that it was something that could work."

Thus, evidence of the first element of an implied warranty of fitness for a particular purpose was presented at trial.

The second element requires that Mr. Holtvogt had reason to know that the Leals were relying on his skill and judgment to select or furnish the appropriate goods. Evidence presented at trial shows that Mr. Holtvogt knew, or at least should have known, that the Leals were relying on his judgment when they purchased an interest in the stallion. The relationship between Mr. Holtvogt and Mr. Leal was like that of a teacher and student. Mr. Leal spent a great deal of time at the Holtvogts' barn, helping Mr. Holtvogt with the horses and learning from Mr. Holtvogt. Mr. Holtvogt testified that he was an expert trainer and breeder with Arabian horses, and the evidence shows that he knew Mr. Leal knew very little about horses. Furthermore, the Leals testified that they were interested in purchasing another horse, Procale, but that Mr. Holtvogt steered them away from that horse, saying that horse was not the type of horse that the Leals wanted to buy. Mr. Holtvogt even testified that he mentioned Mc Que Jabask to the Leals because the stallion was the type of horse that they were looking for. Thus, evidence of the second element of an implied warranty of fitness for a particular purpose was presented at trial.

The third element requires that the Leals actually did rely upon Mr. Holtvogt's skill and judgment when they purchased an interest in the stallion. The trial court found that the Leals justifiably relied upon the Holtvogts' representations regarding the stallion. This finding is not against the manifest weight of the evidence. As stated earlier, there was competent and credible evidence presented at trial to support this finding as both Leals were novices in the horse industry and they testified that they trusted Mr. Holtvogt and considered him to be the expert. Thus, evidence of the third element was presented at trial.

Because all three elements were proven at trial, we conclude that an implied warranty of fitness for a particular purpose was given by the Holtvogts to the Leals at the time of the sale. There must be evidence that the warranty was breached if the Leals are to recover. *Delorise Brown, M.D., Inc.,* 86 Ohio App. 3d at 363. "Whether a warranty has failed to fulfill its essential purpose is ordinarily a determination for the factfinder." *Id.*

The trial court found that a warranty was breached by the Holtvogts because the horse was lame. As stated above, competent and credible evidence was presented to support the trial court's finding that Mc Que Jabask suffered from chronic lameness at the time of the sale. At trial, Dixie Gansmiller testified that even though a lame stallion could stand for stud, its lameness would affect her decision whether to breed her mares with it. Thus, we conclude that competent and credible evidence in the record does demonstrate that Mc Que Jabask was not fit for the particular purpose intended by the Leals when they invested in him.

* * *

Judgment accordingly.

QUESTIONS

1. Questions about the facts of this case

    1.1. Presumably, the court came up with the $16,000 in "compensatory damages" based upon the amount the Leals had paid for a one-half interest in Mc Que Jabask. Did that award really give the Leals the "benefit of their bargain"?

    1.2. What was the "purpose" for which the Leals acquired an interest in Mc Que Jabask? Did the horse's lameness make him no longer fit for that purpose?

    1.3. The court describes the relationship between Mr. Holtvogt and Mr. Leal as "like that of teacher and student." Why was that fact important?

2.   Questions about the law

   2.1.   The court of appeals in *Leal* agreed with the trial court that the "five contested statements" were no more than mere puffing. Do you agree? How do you think the court in *Daughtrey, supra,* at 568, would have characterized those statements? Should evidence relating to those statements have been excluded under the parol evidence rule?

   2.2.   The court of appeals also concluded that the failure to disclose Mc Que Jabask's lameness could not support a negligent misrepresentation claim because it was not an *affirmative* false statement. Isn't deliberate concealment of a material fact tantamount to an affirmative misstatement of fact? Why didn't the Leals make a non-disclosure argument along the lines of *Weintraub v. Krobatsch, supra,* at 371?

   2.3.   The court of appeals concludes that when the trial court in its entry of judgment stated not just that an express warranty was breached, but that an "express warranty on the condition of the horse for the purposes intended" was breached, it really meant to say that the sellers breached the implied warranty of fitness for a particular purpose. Do you think the trial court really just misspoke? If not, how should the court of appeals have disposed of the case?

   2.4.   Obviously, the Leals did not bring a claim for breach of the warranty of merchantability. Why do you suppose their lawyer made that judgment? What would you have done? Is there an upside to including alternative causes of action in a complaint even though you know they may be weak? Is there a downside? How does a court deal with multiple warranties? As for the last question, we offer you the next case.

SINGER COMPANY v. E.I. DU PONT DE NEMOURS AND COMPANY

United States Court of Appeals, Eighth Circuit
579 F.2d 433 (1978)

HANSON, SENIOR DISTRICT JUDGE.

In this diversity contract action, the Singer Company sued to recover losses incurred when the E.I. du Pont de Nemours and Company allegedly breached both an express warranty and an implied warranty of fitness in failing to provide plaintiff with suitable industrial paint for its plant operations at Red Bud, Illinois. The case was submitted to a jury only on the implied warranty theory, and judgment was returned for Singer in the amount of $108,367.00. Defendant was awarded no recovery on either of its two attendant counterclaims. Du Pont unsuccessfully moved for judgments notwithstanding the verdict and for new trial, contending that the trial court improperly instructed the jury and that there was insufficient evidence to support the jury verdicts. Du Pont appeals from those rulings. We affirm.

Singer became interested during late 1972 in obtaining an electrodeposition paint system for its Red Bud, Illinois plant, where until this time the metal, or ware, used in the manufacture of air-conditioners and furnaces had been painted in a spray system. Electrodeposition is a method of painting by which pretreated ware is conveyed through an electrically charged paint tank and the ware, serving as an anode, is coated with paint in an electroplating type of process. After a period of negotiation between representatives from the two parties, Du Pont, in September and October of 1972, was contracted to provide Singer with paint for its approximately 22,000 gallon tank. Three additional companies were contracted to provide other interrelated steps in the overall finishing process, steps such as pretreatment of the ware and conveyance of the ware through the entire system.

From the beginning, in October of 1973, Singer experienced problems with the electrodeposition system. Ware frequently emerged from the paint tank with "blotches" and "streaks." Repainting was necessary. Du Pont, which supervised the installation and starting up of this electrodeposition system, tried unsuccessfully for six months to correct this problem. Finally, in April of 1974, the Du Pont paint was removed from the tank and replaced with paint supplied by the Sherwin–Williams Company. This lawsuit was filed the following year.

The nub of the factual controversy in the trial court was the cause for the blotches and streaks on the painted ware. Du Pont maintained that the problem was with the substrate, pretreated ware; Singer, however, insisted that the paint was at fault. In countering Singer's claim, Du Pont argued that the paint provided to plaintiff met contract specifications until the substrate was altered in February of 1974, at which time Du Pont could no longer be held to have expressly warranted its product. Singer contends that even if the specifications of this express warranty were met, Du Pont had given an implied warranty of fitness for a particular purpose by representing throughout the period in question that its paint would satisfy plaintiff's needs. Over Du Pont's objection, the trial court instructed the jury on implied warranty for a particular purpose. The issue of express warranty was not submitted.

I. The Uniform Commercial Code

While disagreeing on whether the trial court should have instructed as to an implied warranty of fitness for a particular purpose, the parties are properly in accord that the Illinois adoption of the Uniform Commercial Code governs the disposition of this case. * * * There is also no dispute that the "all tests" provision of the contract, which specified such set standards as color and texture that the paint was to satisfy upon pretreated laboratory test panels, was an express warranty pursuant to Section 2–313(1)(b) of the U.C.C. But Singer claims that the contract further preserved an implied warranty of fitness, a warranty that pursuant to Section 2–315 assured plaintiff the paint supplied would satisfactorily cover its substrate. A paragraph in the contract provided:

> None of the provisions or remedies herein are in lieu of any claims for damages Buyer may have at law or equity under the Uniform Commercial Code or otherwise, for the breach of any contracts or warranties with Buyer, which rights are specifically reserved by Buyer.

Du Pont contends that parties who have an express warranty regarding a contracted for item cannot also have an implied warranty of fitness for that same item. The warranty of fitness for a specific purpose is alleged to have been limited by expressly defining it in a set of specifications, and Du Pont claims that to find otherwise would permit Singer to escape the parties' true contractual bargain.

> * * *

Pertinent sections of the U.C.C., and the comments pursuant thereto, lend inferential support to Singer's position that the implied warranty of fitness was cumulative to and not excluded by the express warranty. Section 2–316(2), with regard to the exclusion or modification of such warranties, states:

> * * * To exclude or modify any implied warranty of fitness the exclusion must be a writing and *conspicuous*. (Emphasis added.)

Comment 9 to that section provides in part:

> The situation in which the buyer gives precise and complete *specifications to the seller* is not explicitly covered in this section, but this is a frequent circumstance by which the implied warranties may be excluded. The warranty of fitness for a particular purpose would not normally arise since in such a situation there is usually *no reliance on the seller by the buyer*. (Emphasis added.)

See also U.C.C. § 2–315, comment 2. Because the evidence in this case fully indicates that it was not the buyer but the seller who in fact recommended and supplied the paint specifications, and remained in control of the paint tank, it would appear that the trial court did not err in its determination that an implied warranty of fitness was at issue. This is especially so in view of the purported exclusion of this warranty, which could be scarcely termed "conspicuous."

A reading of the U.C.C. to suggest that an express warranty and an implied warranty of fitness are not necessarily mutually exclusive, as Singer has argued, receives support from Code authority.

> The fact that a warranty of fitness for a particular purpose does or does not exist has no bearing on any other warranty or theory of product liability. Conversely, the fact that there may be some other basis for liability of the defendant does not preclude the existence of a warranty for a particular purpose. *Thus the fact that there is a warranty of conformity to sample [an express warranty] does not*

preclude the existence of a warranty for a particular purpose. (Emphasis added.) Anderson, Uniform Commercial Code § 2–315:5 (1970).

* * * Relevant case law, in the balance, further indicates that an express warranty would not control under the circumstances of this case.

Cases can be found prior to the adoption of the U.C.C. to support Du Pont's argument of mutual exclusiveness. This Court, without specific adoption of the position, recognized in *Hercules Powder Co. v. Rich,* 3 F.2d 12 (8th Cir. 1924) that there was law to the effect that an implied warranty of fitness could not prevail in the presence of an express warranty on the same item or subject.

An express warranty excludes an implied warranty relating to the same subject or of the same general nature, on the theory that no warranty should be implied where the parties with relation to the very same subject have expressed by words the warranty by which they will be bound. *Id.* at 18.

There was also case law to the contrary. * * * But while there may have once been a split of authority, we fail to find since the general adoption of the above-quoted sections of the U.C.C. any case holding directly in favor of Du Pont's mutual exclusivity agreement. In fact unless the exclusion of the implied warranty of fitness is specifically and conspicuously excluded, courts, often relying upon Section 2–317,[4] have found that such implied and express warranties can be cumulative and co-exist within the same agreement. * * *

Du Pont, in arguing the law upon appeal, relies principally upon two types of cases that have arisen under the U.C.C.: those in which there has been a showing that the buyer, in possession or control of the item, failed to follow the express warranty specifications; and those where an enforceable disclaimer of an implied warranty has been established. With respect to the first type of case, it is clear that the trial court did not confront a situation where a buyer in possession or control of an item failed to follow seller's specifications, used the item in a manner for which it was not intended, lost that for which he had contracted, and then erroneously claimed a breach of an implied warranty for fitness. * * * Here, Du Pont, as the seller, was in control of the disputed item. No one denies that Du Pont was throughout this time in control of Singer's paint tank, directing its operation and determining its contents.

The disclaimer cases are likewise inapplicable. Even without a paragraph in the contract reserving all further warranties under the U.C.C., Du Pont would have difficulty in arguing that an express warranty of the paint effected a disclaimer of any further warranty. It is clear from these cases that disclaimers under the Code are not favored and are limited whenever possible. * * *

---

4. Section 2–317 of the U.C.C. provides in part:

Warranties whether express or implied shall be construed as consistent with each other and as cumulative. * * *

Du Pont also argues in general that to permit Singer to assert an implied warranty of fitness would be to allow utilization of the U.C.C. in avoidance of the parties' true bargain. The true bargain, though, is less than apparent from the face of the contract. This was not a situation where a buyer ordered according to specifications and then claimed an implied warranty of fitness when the product failed to measure up to expectations. In this instance, the buyer approached the seller describing the results desired and the seller professed to be able to supply it, thereby inducing a reliance that created the possibility of an implied warranty of fitness. Notwithstanding the express warranty contained within the specifications particularly defining and describing the item to be supplied, there may have been a further warranty that an item with those specifications would accomplish certain results or be adequate for the specified purpose. That is, the accomplishment of the purpose might be viewed as the essence of the contractual undertaking, and not the mere furnishing of the specified item. Nothing within this contract, or in writings or statements subsequent to it, indicate whether the end of the agreement was the specified item or the use for which the item was intended. * * *

Du Pont simply failed to negotiate a contract that clearly delineated and limited allocation of risk. This case would never have arisen had defendant, as a party to and a scrivener of the contract, either inserted a specific disclaimer or demanded that the warranty savings clause be deleted.

Having left the contract ambiguous, the question as to whether use rather than supply of the product was intended to be of the essence, as well as questions regarding buyer's reliance and seller's knowledge of that reliance, are for jury determination. Such were submitted to the jury in this case under the trial court's following instruction.

Your verdict on the plaintiff's claim must be for the plaintiff if you believe:

First: The defendant sold paint to the plaintiff.

Second: The defendant knew the use for which plaintiff purchased the paint, and

Third: Plaintiff reasonably relied upon defendant's judgment for the suitability of the paint for such use, and,

Fourth: The paint was not suitable for such use, and

Fifth: As a direct result plaintiff was damaged.

Du Pont contends on appeal, as it did below, that the trial court was in error giving an instruction which allowed the jury to determine the construction of the contract. The question regarding the presence of an implied warranty, defendant maintains, constituted a question of law that should have been determined by the trial judge. Moreover, it is claimed that the jury should have been instructed with respect to the express warranty.

The better rule, when there remains an issue of contractual intent, is to submit the issue to the jury unless the evidence is so clear that no reasonable person would determine the issue but one way. * * * Du Pont fails to offer any sustaining reason as to why the construction of an ambiguous contract, which involves the existence or nonexistence of an implied warranty of fitness under the U.C.C., should also not be left to a jury determination. * * * The question of buyer's reliance and seller's knowledge of that reliance is a factual inquiry particularly well-suited for jury deliberation. U.C.C. §§ 2–316, 2–317 * * *

There was no prejudicial error in refusing to instruct the jury with respect to the express warranty. As concluded above, the law is that an implied warranty of fitness is not necessarily excluded by the presence of an express warranty. Thus, satisfaction of the express warranty, a factual issue that could be and was argued to the jury, would not preclude the jury from further consideration of the alleged implied warranty. We note that defendant, in presenting its appeal, did indicate that its primary purpose in requesting the express warranty instruction was to implement this mistaken contention that no implied warranty could be present by the fact that it had been specified and those specifications met. Plaintiff, while not conceding that the express warranty had been satisfied, agreed to go to the jury on the issue of implied warranty alone.

II. Substantial Evidence

Once having determined that the issue of implied warranty was properly submitted to the jury, sufficiency of the evidence becomes the controlling inquiry. We review the evidence to determine whether there was sufficient evidence for the jury to find that Singer reasonably relied upon Du Pont's judgment regarding the suitability of the paint, that Du Pont knew the use for which Singer purchased the paint, and that the paint was not suitable for such use. On appeal, Du Pont does not appear to contest the interrelated issues of buyer's "reliance" and seller's "knowledge." In view of the extensive negotiations prior to the contract, Du Pont's supervision of the installation of the paint tank, and the continuing presence of Du Pont in a supervisory capacity throughout the period in question, defendant's reason for not pursuing these lines of argument is apparent. Du Pont does contend, however, that there is insufficient proof to show that the paint was not suitable for Singer's use and was the cause of the blotches and streaks on the painted ware. It insists that an uneven pretreatment, with resulting un-uniform substrate, was the source of the problem.

[The court proceeded to review the evidence put on by Singer at trial concerning the cause for the blotches and streaks on painted ware. This consisted of expert scientific testimony to the effect that impurities and non-uniformity of elements within the paint tank were the source of the problem as well as evidence that after the Du Pont paint was removed and replaced with a different manufacturer's paint the problem was resolved.]

III. Conclusion

In reviewing the evidence pursuant to the judgment n.o.v. standards, we cannot conclude that Singer failed to offer the necessary evidence to sustain a jury verdict against Du Pont for a breach of an implied warranty of fitness. Clearly, Du Pont, which reviewed the entire finishing system, knew at the time of contracting the particularized use for which plaintiff purchased the paint, and Singer reasonably relied upon Du Pont's judgment that its paint was suitable for the electrodeposition system. Du Pont makes some argument that the change in substrate affected the suitability, but it was an argument not pressed upon appeal. In any event, if defendant did not consider itself bound by warranty to do anything more than furnish a paint of particular specifications, we find it difficult to explain not only why Du Pont supervised the installation of the system, but worked to alleviate the problems during the entire period its paint was in the tank.

Finally, in satisfaction of the last element necessary to an implied warranty of fitness, the evidence was sufficient to show that Du Pont's paint was not suitable for Singer's use. The evidence here presents a close question. Yet giving the "jury verdict the benefit of all reasonable inferences to be drawn from the evidence," this Court, though we might have cast our verdict otherwise, cannot say there was no more than a scintilla of evidence to support the jury verdict. The testimony of Singer employees and [plaintiff's expert] De Vittorio, and such evidence as the unexplained blotches and streaks upon the laboratory test panels, sufficiently takes this case from the undeterminative equipoise for which defendant argues. * * *

With respect to damages, which were reasonably assessed, we find the trial court did not err in denying a judgment n.o.v. on Du Pont's counterclaim for paint sold and delivered or further counterclaim for value of services rendered. Nor did the trial court abuse its discretion in denying defendant's motions for new trial.

The judgment appealed from is affirmed.

QUESTIONS, NOTES, AND CONNECTIONS

1. Questions about the facts of this case

    1.1. What specific facts were most favorable to Singer? What facts tended to support Du Pont's argument?

    1.2. What did Du Pont *expressly* warrant? Why do you suppose the issue of express warranty was not submitted to the jury? Why did Du Pont think it was prejudicial error not to submit the issue of express warranty to the jury?

    1.3. Of what significance was the fact that the Sherman–Williams paint apparently performed without any of the problems experienced with the Du Pont paint? Why does the court refer to the evidence regarding breach of the fitness warranty as presenting a close call? What other facts would you like to know about the Sherwin–Williams paint?

2. Questions about the law

    2.1. The decision in *Singer* is a good example of how a court goes about analyzing issues arising under a statute, but why did the court relegate its discussion of § 2–317 to a footnote? That curiosity aside, note how the court used the specific provisions of Article 2 and the Official Comments to dismantle each of Du Pont's contentions. Sometimes, however, the statute does not address every issue that arises in a case. For example, in *Singer*, Du Pont contended that the issue regarding the presence of a warranty is a question of law for the court and not one of fact for the jury. Article 2 simply does not offer any guidance as to whether the question should be regarded as one of law or fact. What should a court do in that situation? What did the *Singer* court do? *See* U.C.C. § 1–103.

    2.2. In deciding that the issue of contractual intent was properly submitted to the jury, was the court saying that the issue of the presence of a fitness warranty was not a question of law?

    2.3. According to the court in *Singer,* for there to be a breach of the fitness warranty the buyer must show that the seller *knew* both the buyer's purpose in acquiring the goods and that the buyer was relying on the seller's expertise in selecting suitable goods. Is that consistent with the *Leal* court's view of the elements of an action under § 2–315?

    2.4. If you represent Du Pont, after the case is decided, what changes would you recommend that the company make in supply contracts of this type?

3. Notes

    3.1. Article 35(2)(b) of the *U.N. Convention on Contracts for the International Sale of Goods* provides that goods will not be deemed as conforming to the contract unless they "are fit for any particular purpose expressly or impliedly made known to the seller at the time of the conclusion of the contract, except where the circumstances show that the buyer did not rely, or that it was unreasonable for him to rely, on the seller's skill and judgment." How does this provision differ from the comparable U.C.C. warranty? Can you construct a situation where there would be a breach of warranty under domestic law but not under *CISG*?

    3.2. As the facts in *Singer* illustrate, sometimes warranties can conflict. Du Pont's argument that its express warranty negated the implied warranty of fitness was directly contradicted by § 2–317(c). However, the exception in that provision for the fitness warranty does not apply to other implied warranties, including an implied warranty of merchantability. Thus, if the two warranties cannot be construed consistently with one another, under the terms of § 2–317(c), the express warranty displaces the merchantability warranty. Is this an invitation to crafty sellers to deprive their buyers of a merchantability warranty with an express warranty that is not as broad? Suppose a seller warrants that her product is free from defects in workmanship and materials for three months. In the middle of the fourth month, the product breaks down because of a serious, latent manufacturing defect. Does the buyer have a valid breach of implied warranty claim? *See Koellmer v. Chrysler Motors Corp.*, 6 Conn.Cir. Ct. 478, 276 A.2d 807 (1970). If so, what does the language in § 2–317(c) mean? If not, hasn't the seller effectively disclaimed the merchantability warranty without going thorough the required statutory procedure? To answer these questions, perhaps we better also take a look at the Code's provisions relating to warranty disclaimers.

4. Connections

In what manner is the implied warranty of merchantability broader than the implied warranty of fitness for a particular purpose? In what way is it narrower? How does the concept of an "implied warranty" differ from the basic scheme of contract liability? Have you encountered implied warranties in other contexts? What do these implied warranties all have in common?

F. DISCLAIMERS OF WARRANTIES

The court in *Singer* obviously considered it relevant that Du Pont had not followed the regular statutory procedure for excluding an implied warranty of fitness for particular purpose. This implies, of course, that, had Du Pont been more conscientious, it could have disclaimed the warranty. But why should this ever be permitted? As we have discussed, the purpose for warranty theory is to allocate to the seller the risk that the goods do not conform to general or specific expectations. After all, usually the seller, and particularly a professional seller, is in the best position to know whether there is a problem with the goods and, in any event, the seller can pass the risk along via insurance, higher prices, etc. But this is not always the case. Sometimes the seller is in no better position than the buyer to avoid the loss. Moreover, sometimes the buyer is willing to accept the risk, typically because it means a better price. If warranties were absolute, the parties would lose the flexibility to negotiate over this term and the buyer would always pay the higher price. Have you purchased a computer, a television, or perhaps a stereo system lately? Did the cashier offer you an extended warranty? Did you take it? We bet you didn't. Why not?

The U.C.C.'s rules governing effective warranty disclaimers are set forth in U.C.C. § 2–316. Take a look at that statute right now. You'll see that the procedures differ depending on which warranty is at issue and that some warranties are harder to get rid of than others. It should also be apparent that the subject is a technical one. Therefore, an extended discussion of warranty disclaimers, and the related topic of seller efforts to limit liability for breach of warranty, must await the upper-level commercial law courses. However, we think it might be instructional, and perhaps even helpful in your personal life, to examine the basic framework right now.

OFFICE SUPPLY CO., INC. v. BASIC/FOUR CORPORATION

United States District Court, Eastern District of Wisconsin
538 F.Supp. 776 (1982)

REYNOLDS, CHIEF JUDGE.

This is an action for damages brought pursuant to 28 U.S.C. § 1332. The plaintiff Office Supply Co., Inc. ("Office Supply") is a corporation located in Racine, Wisconsin, which sells office supplies. The defendant Basic/Four Corporation ("Basic/Four") is a California corporation which manufactures and sells computer hardware and software. In 1975, Office Supply purchased computer hardware and leased computer software from Basic/Four. Office Supply claims that the system was defective and caused it to suffer substantial losses. It seeks compensation for "lost customers, income, good will and executive time and incurred additional hardware and software expense, office form expense, personnel expense and maintenance expense, all to its damage in the sum of $186,000 plus reasonable interest since April, 1975."

* * *

On January 31, 1975, the plaintiff's president, James F. Bruno, signed a contract for the purchase of computer hardware from the defendant and of computer software which was intended to control order processing, inventory control, sales analysis, and accounts receivable. Mr. Bruno mailed the contract to the defendant, and it was accepted by the defendant's assistant treasurer, R. C. Trost, on February 7, 1975. On April 1, 1975, the hardware was installed. In a letter dated May 22, 1975, the defendant advised the plaintiff that the warranty on the hardware would expire on July 1, 1975. The input of data on the software programs took longer to complete, and for a period of time the plaintiff ran parallel operations on the computer and manually as a check on the accuracy of the software applications. In a letter dated October 6, 1975, Mr. Bruno advised Basic/Four:

> "All of the applications anticipated by our company in agreeing to acquire our BASIC/FOUR System are complete and the system appears to be satisfactory. This fulfills your contractual obligation.

"Although the applications programs appear to be operating satisfactorily, some 'defects' might become apparent [sic] later. (Defects might comprise misinterpretation of data, mishandling of a keyboarding error, or a confusing operator instruction—but would not include anything beyond the scope of the system design specification.) It is my understanding that you warrant your programs, when used in accordance with Basic/Four operating instructions, to be free from 'defects' for a period of ninety days, and that you will correct such 'defects' promptly when they are brought to your attention." (Exhibit E to defendant's memorandum in support of motion for summary judgment, filed December 15, 1981.)

Basic/Four took the position that its warranty on the software expired on January 6, 1976. As to complaints received after that date from Office Supply, it did continue to work with Office Supply in an effort to correct any claimed defects in the computer system. Office Supply also hired Ted Templeton, an independent programmer with a company called Computer Methods, Inc., who was recommended by Basic/Four, to work on its Basic/Four system starting some time after Basic/Four advised that the warranty period was over. The record established that Mr. Templeton made some modifications in the Basic/Four software. He also added at least one new program, the ABC program which involved inventory control, to the system. Starting in January 1978, Office Supply also hired a programmer, Marc Jerome, as a fulltime employee. He found what he claims were three major defects in the software system. The record establishes that two of those defects were in programs which Basic/Four did not supply to the plaintiff. The third defect was in the UJ portion of the Basic/Four accounts receivable program, but there is no evidence that the defect arose in the UJ program until after July 1976, which was after the end of the ninety-day period during which Basic/Four continued to warrant its software applications to be free from defects.

The plaintiff's vice president, David Carlson, testified during his deposition that starting at the end of October 1975 and continuing through early 1978, approximately 20% of the customer accounts were out of balance and the Basic/Four system performed up to 78% of expectation for Office Supply. Since February 1978, when Marc Jerome finished correcting the defects in the system, Carlson testified that it has performed up to 100% of expectation. The plaintiff's president, James Bruno, testified that the system only performed up to 50% of expectation prior to 1978, that the accounts receivable first went out of balance on the October 1975 monthly statement printed during the first week of November 1975, that it printed through for the first time in February 1976, but that thereafter the accounts receivable problem continued on an intermittent basis until it was corrected by Marc Jerome in early 1978. Both men testified that there were also problems with the hardware but that those problems were always corrected by Sorbus, a service corporation related to Basic/Four with which Office Supply had a hardware maintenance contract, with only a very few minimal extra charges not covered by the monthly maintenance charges.

On June 17, 1980, Office Supply commenced its action against Basic/Four.

The portion of the Office Supply–Basic/Four contract dealing with the purchase of the hardware is a straightforward document. It describes on the front of the document the computer model and features and the purchase price. Additional terms and conditions of sale are set forth on the reverse. In relevant part it provides on the reverse that it constitutes the entire agreement and understanding between the parties, that it shall be governed by the law of California, and as to warranties and remedies for breach of warranty:

> "3.   For ninety (90) days after the Equipment is installed * * * the Seller warrants the Equipment to be free from defects in material, workmanship, and operating failure from ordinary use, and the Seller's liability is limited solely to correcting any such defect or failure without charge. * * *"

In italic print paragraph 3 also states:

> "The warranties contained in this Agreement are in lieu of all other warranties, express or implied, including any regarding merchantability or fitness for a particular purpose, arising out of or in connection with any Equipment (or the delivery, use or performance thereof). The Seller will not be liable * * * (b) for loss of profits or other incidental or consequential damages. * * *"

The portion of the contract dealing with the lease of the software is not as clearly drafted. On its first page, which is page 3 of the contract, it states:

> "This Addendum to the Agreement for the Purchase of BASIC/FOUR Equipment, dated as of the 31 day of January 1975, between Basic/Four Corporation and Office Supply Inc. is hereby incorporated therein and made a part thereof."

Page 3 describes the program applications and their price. Additional terms and conditions are set forth on the reverse side. As to warranties and limitation of remedies, paragraph 3 provides:

> "The Seller believes that the programming being furnished hereunder is accurate and reliable and when programming accomplishes the results set forth in the 'Design Specifications,' to be agreed to by the Seller and the Purchaser, such programming will be considered completed."

Paragraph 3 continues in italics:

> "However, the amounts to be paid to the Seller under this Agreement and this Addendum do not include any assumption of risk, and the Seller disclaims any and all liability for incidental or consequential damages arising out of the delivery, use or operation of the programs provided herein.

"If the purchaser, without the written consent of the Seller, makes any modification to the programming or any deviations from the operating instructions or violates the provisions of paragraph 2, all warranties set forth herein cease immediately.

"All warranties set forth herein are in lieu of all other warranties, express or implied, including any regarding merchantability or fitness for a particular purpose, arising out of or in connection with any program (or the delivery, use or performance thereof)."

The contract also contains a fourteen-page description of the program applications.

The parties agree that the contract is a sales contract, that the choice of law provision which it contains is valid, and consequently that the parties' rights and liabilities are governed by the Uniform Commercial Code ("UCC") as adopted in California. They agree about very little else.

The defendant contends in its motion for summary judgment that * * * the warranty disclaimer and damage limitation provisions in the contact are valid and binding and therefore the plaintiff is entitled to no relief, * * * The plaintiff's summary judgment motion consists of a denial of each of those contentions and arguments favoring the application of contrary rules of law at the ultimate trial of this action.

Each of the defendant's contentions, along with the arguments as to the applicable legal principles raised by the plaintiff in opposing defendant's summary judgment motion, is discussed separately below.

* * *

(2) Disclaimer of Warranties

The Office Supply–Basic/Four contract specifically provides that it constitutes the entire agreement and understanding between the parties. That being so, parol evidence is not admissible under California law to vary the terms of the agreement. * * * The language of the contract must be interpreted in an effort to determine the intent of the contracting parties. * * *

If there are no exclusions or modifications in the contract, every sales contract governed by the UCC contains an implied warranty of merchantability and, if the seller has reason to know of a particular purpose for which the goods are required, an implied warranty of fitness for a particular purpose. Section 2315, Cal. Comm. Code [UCC § 2–315]. Express warranties are created if the seller makes an affirmation of fact or promise to the buyer and the affirmation becomes part of the bargain between the parties. Section 2313, Cal. Comm. Code [UCC § 2–313]. Thus, any express warranties must be found in the language of the contract. Implied warranties, in contrast, will be held to exist unless they are specifically excluded.

With regard to the computer hardware, the contract expressly warrants the hardware to be free from defects in material, workmanship, and operating failure from ordinary use for ninety days after installation.

With regard to the computer software, the most reasonable interpretation of the contract is that the same ninety-day warranty of material, workmanship, and operating failure applies, dating from the time when the "programming accomplishes the results set forth in the 'Design Specifications,'" which in this case was on October 6, 1975, when plaintiff's president so advised the defendant.

The plaintiff contends that the language just quoted is a warranty of future performance, and that in fact the programming did not accomplish the desired results until 1978. Courts have been parsimonious in finding warranties of future performance where there is no explicit language in the contract creating such a warranty. *Standard Alliance Industries, Inc. v. Black Clawson Company,* 587 F.2d 813, 820 (6th Cir. 1978). For example, a representation as to the performance ability of an existing product will not be construed as an explicit warranty of future performance ability of the product. *Jones & Laughlin Steel Corporation v. Johns–Manville Sales Corporation,* 626 F.2d 280, 291 (3d Cir. 1980) (interpreting California law). Section 2316(1), Cal. Comm. Code [UCC § 2–316(1)], provides in part:

> "(1) Words or conduct relevant to the creation of an express warranty and words or conduct tending to negate or limit warranty shall be construed wherever reasonable as consistent with each other,. * * *"

The first page of the software addendum (page 3 of the contract) provides that it is incorporated within and made a part of the hardware purchase agreement. That agreement contains the ninety-day express warranty provision which, as a result of the incorporation, also applies to the software purchase. In light of the ninety-day express warranty, the most reasonable construction of the software addendum language regarding the results to be accomplished by the programming is that the completion of the programming and installation of all of the bargained-for applications starts the running of the ninety-day warranty period, and not that the applications are warranted to run perfectly once their installation is apparently successfully completed.

The UCC allows contracting parties to exclude or modify all implied warranties. There is no correlative requirement that if implied warranties are excluded, express warranties must be given. Thus it is permissible, for example, to exclude all implied warranties and to provide for a ninety-day express warranty limited to repair or replacement of defective goods. * * *

In order to make an effective waiver of implied warranties, the provisions of § 2316(2), Cal. Comm. Code [UCC § 2–316(2)], must be followed:

> "* * * to exclude or modify the implied warranty of merchantability or any part of it the language must mention merchantability and in

case of a writing must be conspicuous, and to exclude or modify any implied warranty of fitness the exclusion must be by a writing and conspicuous. * * *"

There is no dispute that the language contained in the contract was in this case sufficient to waive all implied warranties. The issue is whether the disclaimer was "conspicuous." Section 1201(1), Cal. Comm. Code, [UCC § 1–201(1)] provides:

"(10) 'Conspicuous.' A term or clause is conspicuous when it is so written that a reasonable person against whom it is to operate ought to have noticed it. A printed heading in capitals (as: NONNEGOTIABLE BILL OF LADING) is conspicuous. Language in the body of a form is 'conspicuous' if it is in larger or other contrasting type or color. But in a telegram any stated term is 'conspicuous.' Whether a term or clause is 'conspicuous' or not is for decision by the court."

Basic/Four points out that it disclaimed the implied warranties not once but twice, and that the disclaimers were written in italicized print, in contrast to the regular print used on the rest of the contract. Nevertheless, the disclaimers are not conspicuous. In *Dorman v. International Harvester Company,* 46 Cal. App. 3d 11, 120 Cal. Rptr. 516 (Cal. App. 1975), the California court of appeals noted that under pre-Code California law, disclaimers of warranty are strictly construed, and, applying the code, it found that an attempted disclaimer written in only slightly contrasting print and without a heading adequate to call the buyer's attention to the disclaimer clause was not effective. That decision controls in this case. The two disclaimers in the Office Supply–Basic/Four contract are on the reverse sides of the first two pages of the contract. They are not positioned close to the buyer's signature line. The contracts are printed on pale green paper and the disclaimers are set forth in print which, although italicized, is only slightly contrasting with the remainder of the contract. There are no headings noting the disclaimers of warranty. Since there is only " 'some slight contrasting set-off' " and there is " 'only a slight contrast with the balance of the instrument,' " *Dorman, supra,* 120 Cal. Rptr. at 522, *quoting Woodruff v. Clark County Farm Bureau Coop. Ass'n.,* (Ind. App. 1972), 153 Ind. App. 31, 286 N.E.2d 188, 198, *quoting* in turn *Greenspun v. American Adhesives, Inc.,* 320 F. Supp. 442 (E.D. Pa. 1970), therefore, the disclaimers are not conspicuous.

Discussion of the effectiveness of the disclaimer provisions in the contract does not end with the finding of lack of conspicuousness. In their treatise Uniform Commercial Code § 12–5 at 444 (2d ed. 1980), Messrs. White and Summers note "with apprehension" the growing number of cases which hold that if a buyer is actually aware of a warranty disclaimer, then the disclaimer is effective even if not conspicuous. * * * The Official Comment to UCC § 2–316 states that the section is designed "to protect a buyer from unexpected and unbargained language of disclaimer." Pointing to that language, the Court in *Dorman, supra, at 521–522,* indicated that California will follow the trend:

"* * * [W]e must rely predominantly on the official comments to sections 2–316 and 1–201, subdivision (1), and to foreign law. The official comment to subdivision (10) of section 1201 states that the 'test [of conspicuousness] is whether attention can reasonably be expected to be called to [the disclaimer provision].' * * * We must examine this comment in the light of the official comment to section 2–316, which states: 'This section is designed principally to deal with those frequent clauses in sales contracts which seek to exclude "all warranties, express or implied." It seeks to protect a buyer from unexpected and unbargained language of disclaimer by denying effect to such language when inconsistent with language of express warranty and permitting the exclusion of implied warranties only by conspicuous language or other circumstances which protect the buyer from surprise.' In other words, section 2–316 seeks to protect the buyer from the situation where the salesman's 'pitch,' advertising brochures, or large print in the contract, giveth, and the disclaimer clause—in fine print—taketh away."

The *Dorman* Court also noted that under pre-Code California law as well, a provision disclaiming implied warranties "was ineffectual unless the buyer assented to the provision or was charged with notice of the disclaimer before the bargain was completed." *Id.* at 521.

James Bruno testified during his deposition taken on November 3, 1980, that before he purchased the Basic/Four system, he spent approximately two months comparing it with other systems, and that he drew up a written comparison of the Basic/Four and Qantel systems, including their guarantees. Basic/Four, 90 days; and Qantel had one year." He read the back of the contract before he signed it, when he received the contract from Basic/Four he made out a list of questions to ask Basic/Four before signing and one subject on his list was the ninety-day guarantee, and before he signed he showed the warranty provision in the contract to someone he knew in the data processing filed. He discussed the warranties with Basic/Four before signing and tried to have them modified:

"Q Did you read the provisions of the warranty?

"A Yes.

"Q And did you discuss those provisions with Basic/Four, or with someone from Basic/Four?

"A Yes.

"Q And what was said to you about those provisions?

"A That that was the condition that I had to accept.

"Q All right. And was that discussion before or after the contract as signed?

"A I would say before.

"Q * * * did you call up Darryl Bannister, for example, and say I want to buy this system but I refuse to agree to the warranty provisions in the contract?

"A Well, I argued with him, but it was to no avail. Nothing."

He also was aware of the warranty limitations before he signed the contract:

"Q Well, were you aware of the provisions of that warranty before you signed the contract?

"A That there were limitations?

"Q That there are limitations to the warranty? Were you aware of that?

"A Certainly.

"Q You were?

"A Yes."

That testimony establishes that the warranty disclaimers were neither unexpected nor unbargained for, and that, consequently, under *Dorman*, they should be enforced.

* * *

ORDER

For the foregoing reasons.

IT IS ORDERED that the plaintiff's motions to compel discovery and for partial summary judgment are denied.

IT IS FURTHER ORDERED that the defendant's motion for summary judgment is granted, and that judgment be entered dismissing this action with prejudice and awarding costs to the defendant.

QUESTIONS, NOTES, AND CONNECTIONS

1. Questions about the facts of this case

   1.1. What exactly did Basic/Four warrant with respect to the performance of its software programs and for how long?

   1.2. What facts did the court consider most important in making its finding that the Basic/Four warranty began to run on October 6, 1975?

   1.3. Were the Basic/Four software applications merchantable? Did that matter to the court?

   1.4. The court states at one point in its opinion that "the plaintiff is also an established commercial operation of significant size, and the plaintiff's president testified during his deposition that he is accustomed to engaging in contract negotiation on behalf of Office Supply." To what issue were those factual findings relevant?

2.   Questions about the law

   2.1.   Most courts that have spoken to the issue agree with *Office Supply* that a non-conspicuous warranty disclaimer may be effective where it can be shown that the buyer had actual knowledge of the disclaimer. *See, e.g., Cate v. Dover Corp.*, 790 S.W.2d 559 (Tex. 1990). However, in a separate opinion in *Cate*, Justice Ray offered the following rationale against permitting this exception to the conspicuousness requirement:

   The statute, on its face, provides for no actual knowledge exception. There is no room for judicial crafting of those omitted by the legislature. I would hold that the extent of a buyer's knowledge of a disclaimer is irrelevant to a determination of enforceability under § 2–316(b) of the UCC.

   The effect of actual knowledge is subject to debate among leading commentators on commercial law. The purpose of the objective standard of conspicuousness adopted by the court today reflects the view that "The drafters intended rigid adherence to the conspicuousness requirement in order to avoid arguments concerning what the parties said about the warranties at the time of sale." J. WHITE AND R. SUMMERS, Uniform Commercial Code § 12–5 (2d ed. 1980). An absolute rule that an inconspicuous disclaimer is invalid, despite the buyer's actual knowledge, encourages sellers to make their disclaimers conspicuous, thereby reducing the need for courts to evaluate swearing matches as to actual awareness in particular cases. * * * Today's decision condemns our court to a parade of such cases.

   Do you agree with this argument? Does it make a difference if the transaction involves a consumer rather than a commercial sale? If actual knowledge is irrelevant, does that also mean that a conspicuous disclaimer is effective regardless of whether the buyer had actual knowledge of it? *See* U.C.C. § 1–201(10). How many buyers seeking to establish a claim for breach of warranty do you think admit that they had knowledge of the disclaimer? No, we're not suggesting anyone would perjure themselves, we just think maybe it's not as big of a problem as some courts seem to have made it out to be.

   2.2.   We understand why the court applied Article 2 to the sales of the computer hardware, but should Article 2 have been applied to the *lease* of the software? Also, Article 2 applies to "transactions in goods." U.C.C. § 2–102. Is software a "good"?

   2.3.   In the course of its opinion, the court in *Office Supply* states that, "If there are no exclusions or modifications in the contract, *every* sale contract governed by the U.C.C. contains an implied warranty of merchantability * * *" (emphasis ours). What statute was Judge Reynolds reading? Not one we're acquainted with!

   2.4.   While the enforceability of disclaimers of implied warranties focuses on the conspicuousness of the language of disclaimer, § 2–316(1) adopts a different standard for attempts to disclaim express warranties. As noted in *Office Supply*, contractual language attempting to negate or limit an express warranty is required to be construed consistently with the language creating the warranty and, if that cannot be done, the negation or limitation is inoperative. In short, it's more difficult for a seller to get rid of an express warranty than an implied warranty. Is this as it should be? Why? Even if you agree with the judgment of the drafters on this point, there is one fly in the ointment. Look closely at the language in § 2–316(1). The negation of words of limitation that are inconsistent with an express warranty is made *subject* to § 2–202, the parol evidence rule for Article 2 contracts. Does this mean that a seller can effectively eliminate an express warranty made during the course of contract negotiations by including an expansive merger or integration clause into the final writing, thereby excluding introduction of the contradictory oral warranty? Technically it would seem so, but courts, not surprisingly, tend to have limited tolerance for that sort of elevation of form over substance. Thus, Professors White and Summers suggest that to be effective the merger clause needs to be: 1) conspicuous, and 2) explicit that it is intended to exclude prior oral assurances made by the seller or its sales staff. *See* J. WHITE & R. SUMMERS, UNIFORM COMMERCIAL CODE, § 12–5, at p. 421 (4th ed. 1995). Is this a satisfactory resolution of the problem?

3. Notes

　3.1. Note that in *Office Supply* the court was dealing not only with the effectiveness of Basic/Four's disclaimer under § 2–316, but also the enforceability of Basic/Four's attempt to: (1) limit the remedy (to repair or replace) for breach of the express warranty that was given, and (2) exclude liability for consequential damages. In Article 2, the enforceability of remedy limitations and exclusions is governed by § 2–719. We omitted the portion of the opinion dealing with that provision because we cover limitations on damage remedies in Chapter 6. Suffice it to say for now that the relationship between § 2–719 and § 2–716 is subtle, but important. An effective disclaimer eliminates any cause of action for breach of warranty. A remedy limitation, by contrast, restricts the buyer's access to the remedy provisions of Article 2, or substitutes an entirely different remedy in their place, in the event of a breach. As we said, more on that to come.

　3.2. The approach used by Basic/Four in *Office Supply* to include a limited express warranty that at the same time disclaims the broader Code warranties is not uncommon. In effect, the warranty "takes much and gives little." Recognizing that these provisions can be a trap for the unwary or the unsophisticated consumer, in 1975 Congress enacted the Magnuson–Moss Warranty—Federal Trade Commission Improvement Act (15 U.S.C. § 2301 *et seq.*). The Act, which only applies to the sale of goods used primarily for personal, family, and household purposes, is primarily a disclosure statute. This is consistent with the general approach taken in federal consumer protection legislation. Specifically, Magnuson–Moss requires manufacturers that elect to make written warranties do so in a manner that is least likely to mislead or confuse consumers. For example, § 103 of Magnuson–Moss requires sellers to designate their warranties as "full," meeting specified federal minimum standards in § 104, or "limited," not meeting those federal minimum standards. In addition, § 108 of the Act precludes a seller that makes any written warranty to a consumer from simultaneously attempting to disclaim or modify any implied warranty, except as to duration. Congress' hope was that many, if not most, manufacturers would feel competitive pressures to offer consumers full warranties. Alas, this hope has not been realized as will become obvious to you if you start reading the warranties that accompany the products you buy. Nevertheless, Magnuson–Moss, with its restrictions on disclaimers, has enlarged the scope of warranty protection for consumer buyers and, perhaps just as importantly, has provided an effective mechanism for enforcement of warranty obligations by allowing recovery of attorneys' fees by a consumer who is damaged by a seller's failure to comply with any obligation under the Act or under any written or implied warranty. *See* Magnuson–Moss § 110(d)(2).

4. Connections

The implied warranties of Article 2 are said to be "default terms". What does that mean? Can other terms of a contract be disclaimed? What about express warranties? What does this suggest about the difference between promissory liability and liability based on breach of an implied warranty? Where else, quite recently, have you observed a court addressing the extent to which an implied undertaking can be negated (or limited) by contractual agreement?

CHAPTER SIX

WHEN IS SOMEONE WHO MADE AN ENFORCEABLE DEAL EXCUSED FROM DOING WHAT SHE AGREED TO DO?

■ ■ ■

Sometimes a person who made an enforceable deal, i.e., a contract, is discharged or excused from doing what she contracted to do because of something that happens (or does not happen) after the contract. This chapter then focuses on such post-contract happenings.

SECTION 1: CONDITIONS: NON–OCCURRENCE OF SOMETHING THAT CONTRACT EXPRESSLY PROVIDED MUST OCCUR AS AN EXCUSE FOR NOT DOING WHAT YOU AGREED TO DO

Earlier, when we considered "imperfect acceptances" in Chapter 2, we encountered language of condition in a response to an offer. For example, S offers to sell his house to B for $100,000. B responds that she accepts "on the condition that the house appraises at $100,000." No contract.

That is the effect of language of condition in a response to an offer. Words such as "on condition that," "if," "provided that, or so long as" in a response to an offer operate as a rejection and counter offer so that there is not yet a contract.

These same words of condition have a very different effect when they appear in a contract, rather than in a response to an offer. For example, S and B enter into a contract that provides for the sale of S's house to B for $100,000 "on the condition that the house appraises at $100,000." Such language of condition in a contract does not affect whether there is a contract, but rather whether there is a legal obligation to perform that contract. If the house does not appraise for $100,000 or more, then B does not have to buy the house. Saying the same thing another way, the non-

579

occurrence of an express condition in a contract can provide an excuse to any legal obligation to perform that contract.

The *Restatement (Second) of Contracts* says the same thing in yet a third way:

> § 224   *Condition Defined*
>
> *A condition is an event, not certain to occur, which must occur, unless its nonoccurrence is excused, before performance is due.*

Saying the same thing yet one more time: non-occurrence of condition excuses performance. Indeed the *Restatement (Second) of Contracts* says the same thing in another section.

> § 225(1): *Performance of a duty subject to a condition cannot become due unless the condition occurs or its non-occurrence is excused.*

The non-occurrence of a condition is not, however, a breach. Language of condition in a contract, unlike other language in a contract, does not create a new obligation. Instead, contract language of condition modifies or limits obligations created by other contract language. B cannot sue S because the house did not appraise at $100,000. The contract language "on the condition that the house appraises at $100,000" is not a promise by S that the house will so appraise; it instead modifies B's promise to buy the house.

A.   OCCURRENCE OF EXPRESS CONDITIONS AND STRICT COMPLIANCE

If non-occurrence of an express condition can excuse performance of a contract, then determining whether an express condition has "occurred" can be important. As the late Professor E. Allan Farnsworth explained, "If the occurrence of a condition is required by the agreement of the parties * * * a rule of strict compliance traditionally applies. * * * Just as the event that is made a condition need not be of great moment, the respect in which the event has failed to occur need not be of great moment." E. ALLAN FARNSWORTH, Contracts 510 (4th ed. 2004).

What does that mean? Should the Connecticut Supreme Court have made a similar statement in the next case?

LUTTINGER v. ROSEN

Supreme Court of Connecticut
164 Conn. 45, 316 A.2d 757 (1972)

LOISELLE, ASSOCIATE JUSTICE.

The plaintiffs contracted to purchase for $85,000 premises in the city of Stamford owned by the defendants and paid a deposit of $8,500. The contract was 'subject to and conditional upon the buyers obtaining first mortgage financing on said premises from a bank or other lending institution in an amount of $45,000 for a term of not less than twenty (20) years and at an interest rate which does not exceed 8 1/2 per cent per annum.' The plaintiffs agreed to use due diligence in attempting to obtain such financing. The parties further agreed that if the plaintiffs were unsuccessful in obtaining financing as provided in the contract, and notified the seller within a specific time, all sums paid on the contract would be refunded and the contract terminated without further obligation of either party.

In applying for a mortgage which would satisfy the contingency clause in the contract, the plaintiffs relied on their attorney who applied at a New Haven lending institution for a $45,000 loan at 8 1/4 percent per annum interest over a period of twenty-five years. The plaintiffs' attorney knew that this lending institution was the only one which at that time would lend as much as $45,000 on a mortgage for a single-family dwelling. A mortgage commitment was obtained for $45,000 with 'interest at the prevailing rate at the time of closing but not less that 8 3/4%.' Since this commitment failed to meet the contract requirement, timely notice was given to the defendants and demand was made for the return of the down payment. The defendants' counsel thereafter offered to make up the difference between the interest rate offered by the bank and the 8 1/2 percent rate provided in the contract for the entire twenty-five years by a funding arrangement, the exact terms of which were not defined. The plaintiffs did not accept this offer and on the defendants' refusal to return the deposit an action was brought. From a judgment rendered in favor of the plaintiffs the defendants have appealed.

The defendants claim that the plaintiffs did not use due diligence in seeking a mortgage within the terms specified in the contract. The unattacked findings by the court establish that the plaintiffs' attorney was fully informed as to the conditions and terms of mortgages being granted by various banks and lending institutions in and out of the area and that the application was made to the only bank which might satisfy the mortgage conditions of the contingency clause at that time. These findings adequately support the court's conclusion that due diligence was used in seeking mortgage financing in accordance with the contract provisions. The defendants assert that notwithstanding the plaintiffs' reliance on their counsel's knowledge of lending practices, applications should have been made to other lending institutions. This claim is not well taken. The law does not require the performance of a futile act.

The remaining assignment of error briefed by the defendants is that the court erred in concluding that the mortgage contingency clause of the contract, a condition precedent, was not met and, therefore, the plaintiffs were entitled to recover their deposit. 'A condition precedent is a fact or event which the parties intend must exist or take place before there is a right to performance. If the condition precedent is not fulfilled the contract is not enforceable. In this case the language of the contract is unambiguous and clearly indicates that the parties intended that the purchase of the defendants' premises be conditioned on the obtaining by the plaintiffs of a mortgage as specified in the contract. From the subordinate facts found the court could reasonably conclude that since the plaintiffs were unable to obtain a $45,000 mortgage at no more than 8 1/2 percent per annum interest 'from a bank or other lending institution' the condition precedent to performance of the contract was not met and the plaintiffs were entitled to the refund of their deposit. Any additional offer by the defendants to fund the difference in interest payments could be rejected by the plaintiffs. There was no error in the court's exclusion of testimony relating to the additional offer since the offer was obviously irrelevant. There is no error.

QUESTIONS AND CONNECTIONS

1. Questions about the facts of this case

    1.1. Who is suing whom for what? What result if the sellers had sued the buyer for breach of contract for not paying the balance of the purchase price?

    1.2. Was the following fact important to the court: "The defendants' counsel thereafter offered to make up the difference between the interest rate offered by the bank and the 8 1/2 percent rate provided in the contract for the entire twenty-five years by a funding arrangement"? Should it have been?

    1.3. Do we know whether the buyers bought another house and, if so, whether the rate of interest on financing for that house exceeded 8.5%? Would that information be helpful in deciding this case?

2. Questions about the law

    2.1. B contracts to buy a house from S on the condition that it is appraised at $200,000 or more. The house is only appraised at $190,000. Is B excused from buying the house? Can B sue S for breach of contract?

    2.2. George Kent (GK) contracts with a plumber Jake Young (JY) to replace some pipes in his house. The contract provides in pertinent part, "Payment by GK is conditioned on JY's using Cohoe Pipe and only Cohoe pipe." In doing the work, JY inadvertently uses Reading Pipe, instead of Cohoe Pipe. Even though the manufacturers of Cohoe Pipe concede that Reading Pipe is at least comparable in quality to Cohoe Pipe, GK refuses to pay. JY sues for breach of contract. Is GK's contract obligation to perform excused by the non-occurrence of the condition? Can GK sue JY for breach of contract?

    2.3. Is it important that the contract expressly required the buyers to use due diligence in attempting to obtain financing? What if:

    — there was no such language in the contract, and

    — buyers decided that they did not want the house and made no effort to obtain financing?

2.4. The court uses the phrase "condition precedent." What does the word "precedent" mean in the context of "condition precedent"? What does the word "precedent" add? Can there be language of condition in a contract that is a "condition" but not a "condition precedent"? Assume, for example, that Ponoroff contracts with Bison Witches Bar for his students' exclusive use of its patio for $100 an hour *until the temperature rises to above 105 degrees.*" Is the italicized contract language a condition? A condition precedent? Who can sue whom when the Tucson temperature exceeds 105 degrees?

3. Connections

3.1. Does *Billman v. Henson,* supra at page 515, help you answer 2.3?

3.2. Reconsider question 2.2 when we consider *Restatement (Second)* section 229, infra at page 601 and again when we consider *Jacob & Youngs v. Kent*, infra at page 660.

B. RECOGNIZING LANGUAGE OF EXPRESS CONDITION

The three consequences of an express condition language in a contract are "straightforward" and "easy."

First, excuse of performance. Non-occurrence of a condition excuses any duty to perform.

Second, strict compliance. Occurrence of a condition requires strict compliance with the contract language of condition.

Third, no breach. The non-occurrence of a condition is not a breach of contract.

To illustrate yet again: Ponoroff contracts to rent Markell's house for $5,000 for the last week of January 2015, on the condition that the 2015 Super Bowl is held in Las Vegas. After the Ponoroff/Markell contract, the NFL awards the 2015 Super Bowl to Richmond. Ponoroff is excused from renting Markell's house, and neither can sue the other for breach of contract.

As the next case illustrates, recognizing language of express condition is not always "straightforward" and "easy."

PEACOCK CONST. CO., INC. v. MODERN AIR CONDITIONING, INC.

Supreme Court of Florida
353 So.2d 840 (1977)

BOYD, ACTING C.J.:

* * *

Peacock Construction was the builder of a condominium project. Modern Air Conditioning subcontracted with Peacock to do the heating and air conditioning work and Overly Manufacturing subcontracted with Peacock to do the "rooftop swimming pool" work. Both written subcontracts provided that Peacock would make final payment to the subcontractors,

> "within 30 days after the completion of the work included in this subcontract, written acceptance by the Architect and full payment therefor by the Owner."

Modern Air Conditioning and Overly Manufacturing completed the work specified in their contracts and requested final payment. When Peacock refused to make the final payments the two subcontractors separately brought actions in the Lee County Circuit Court for breach of contract. In both actions it was established that no deficiencies had been found in the completed work.[3] But Peacock established that it had not received from the owner[4] full payment for the subcontractors' work. And it defended on the basis that such payment was a condition which, by express term of the final payment provision, had to be fulfilled before it was obligated to perform under the contract. On motions by the plaintiffs, the trial judges granted summary judgments in their favor. The orders of judgment implicitly interpreted the contract not to require payment by the owner as a condition precedent to Peacock's duty to perform.

The Second District Court of Appeal affirmed the lower court's judgment in the appeal brought by Modern Air Conditioning. In so doing it adopted the view of the majority of jurisdictions in this country that provisions of the kind disputed here do not set conditions precedent but rather constitute absolute promises to pay, fixing payment by the owner as a reasonable time for when payment to the subcontractor is to be made. When the judgment in the *Overly Manufacturing* case reached the Second District Court, *Modern Air Conditioning* had been decided and the judgment, therefore, was affirmed on the authority of the latter decision. These two decisions plainly conflict with [*Edward J. Gerrits, Inc. v. Astor Electric Service, Inc.*, 328 So. 2d 522 (Fla. 3d DCA 1976).]

In *Gerrits*, the Court had summarily ordered judgment for the plaintiff/subcontractor against the defendant/general contractor on a contractual provision for payment to the subcontractor which read,

> "The money to be paid in current funds and at such times as the General Contractor receives it from the Owner." * * *

In its review of the judgment, the Third District Court of Appeal referred to the fundamental rule of interpretation of contracts that it be done in accordance with the intention of the parties. Since the defendant had introduced below the issue of intention, a material issue, and since the

---

3. In fact, in the Modern Air Conditioning case the Architect stated in a sworn deposition that he felt the heating and air conditioning equipment, although not yet operated, was complete per the plans and specifications. Original Record, p. 37. Sup. Ct. Case No. 50,758.

4. The owner, a corporation, had entered proceedings in bankruptcy.

issue was one that could be resolved through a factual determination by the jury, the Third District reversed the summary judgment and remanded for trial.

Peacock urges us to adopt *Gerrits* as the controlling law in this State. It concedes that the Second District's decisions are backed by the weight of authority. But it argues that they are incorrect because the issue of intention is a factual one which should be resolved after the parties have had an opportunity to present evidence on it. *Peacock* urges, therefore, that the causes be remanded for trial. If there is produced no evidence that the parties intended there be condition precedents, only then, says *Peacock*, should the judge, by way of a directed verdict for the subcontractors, be allowed to take the issue of intention from the jury.

The contractual provisions in dispute here are susceptible to two interpretations. They may be interpreted as setting a condition precedent or as fixing a reasonable time for payment. The provision disputed in *Gerrits* is susceptible to the same two interpretations. The questions presented by the conflict between these decisions, then, are whether ambiguous contractual provisions of the kind disputed here may be interpreted only by the factfinder, usually the jury, or if they should be interpreted as a matter of law by the court, and if so what interpretation they should be given.

Although it must be admitted that the meaning of language is a factual question, the general rule is that interpretation of a document is a question of law rather than of fact. * * * If an issue of contract interpretation concerns the intention of parties, that intention may be determined from the written contract, as a matter of law, when the nature of the transaction lends itself to judicial interpretation. A number of courts, with whom we agree, have recognized that contracts between small subcontractors and general contractors on large construction projects are such transactions. * * * The reason is that the relationship between the parties is a common one and usually their intent will not differ from transaction to transaction, although it may be differently expressed.

That intent in most cases is that payment by the owner to the general contractor is not a condition precedent to the general contractor's duty to pay the subcontractors. This is because small subcontractors, who must have payment for their work in order to remain in business, will not ordinarily assume the risk of the owner's failure to pay the general contractor. And this is the reason for the majority view in this country, which we now join.

Our decision to require judicial interpretation of ambiguous provisions for final payment in subcontracts in favor of subcontractors should not be regarded as anti-general contractor. It is simply a recognition that this is the fairest way to deal with the problem. There is nothing in this opinion, however, to prevent parties to these contracts from shifting the risk of payment failure by the owner to the subcontractor. But in order to make such a shift the contract must unambiguously express that intention. And the burden of clear expression is on the general contractor.

The decisions of the Second District Court of Appeal to affirm the summary judgments were correct. We adopt, therefore, these two decisions as the controlling law in Florida and we overrule *Gerrits*, to the extent it is inconsistent with this opinion.

The orders allowing certiorari in these two causes are discharged. It is so ordered.

QUESTIONS AND CONNECTIONS

1. Questions on the facts of this case

    1.1. What are the "contractual provisions in dispute" in this case?

    1.2. Which party has "deeper pockets": Peacock or Modern Air? Was that relevant to the court?

2. Questions about the law

    2.1. Do you understand the court's statement: "The contractual provisions in dispute here are susceptible to two interpretations. They may be interpreted as setting a condition precedent or as fixing a reasonable time for payment." Do you agree with this statement? If so, how could the provisions have been worded to avoid two interpretations? What if the contract had provided: "It is specifically understood and agreed that the payment to Modern is dependent as a condition precedent upon Peacock's receiving payment from the Owner?" *Cf. Richard F. Kline, Inc. v. Shook Excavating & Hauling, Inc.*, 165 Md.App. 262, 274–274, 885 A.3d 381, 388 (2005).

    2.2. Is the *Peacock* decision consistent with *Restatement (Second) of Contracts* § 227 set out below:

    § 227.   Standards of Preference With Regard to Conditions

    (1) In resolving doubts as to whether an event is made a condition of an obligor's duty, and as to the nature of such an event, an interpretation is preferred that will reduce the obligee's risk of forfeiture, unless the event is within the obligee's control or the circumstances indicate that he has assumed the risk.

    * * *

    Comment:

    * * *

    b.   Condition or not. The non-occurrence of a condition of an obligor's duty may cause the obligee to lose his right to the agreed exchange after he has relied substantially on the expectation of that exchange, as by preparation or performance. The word "forfeiture" is used in this Restatement to refer to the denial of compensation that results in such a case. The policy favoring freedom of contract requires that, within broad limits (see § 229), the agreement of the parties should be honored even though forfeiture results. When, however, it is doubtful whether or not the agreement makes an event a condition of an obligor's duty, an interpretation is preferred that will reduce the risk of forfeiture.

Illustrations:

1. A, a general contractor, contracts with B, a sub-contractor, for the plumbing work on a construction project. B is to receive $100,000, "no part of which shall be due until five days after Owner shall have paid Contractor therefor." B does the plumbing work, but the owner becomes insolvent and fails to pay A. A is under a duty to pay B after a reasonable time.

3. Connections

    3.1. Contract interpretation: Do any of the "interpretive maxims" set forth above help in resolving this question? Or does this case (and the *Restatement* section quoted below) simply create another maxim?

    3.2. Parol evidence: Is this a parol evidence case? What evidence did each party offer to persuade the court to adopt its interpretation?

C. EXCUSING CONDITIONS (*i.e.*, ELIMINATES THE EXCUSE)

Just as the non-occurrence of a condition excuses (*i.e.*, eliminates) an obligation to perform, (1) "avoidance of forfeiture," or (2) prevention excuses (*i.e.*, extinguishes) the requirement of occurrence of a condition, making the obligation to perform unconditional. In other words, (1) "avoidance of forfeiture," or (2) "prevention" excuses/extinguishes the excuse for doing what you agreed to do so that you are obligated to do what you agreed to do.

1. Avoidance of Forfeiture as a Reason for Eliminating a Condition

We have already seen that avoiding a forfeiture is a reason for interpreting language as not imposing a condition. Sometimes, the language can only be interpreted as a condition—*e.g.*, "This is language of condition. We really mean it. Cross our hearts and hope to die."

Even where the contract language can only be interpreted as language of condition, there is authority for excusing that condition to avoid a forfeiture. For example, section 229 of the *Restatement (Second) of Contracts* provides:

§ 229. Excuse of a Condition to Avoid Forfeiture

To the extent that the non-occurrence of a condition would cause disproportionate forfeiture, a court may excuse the non-occurrence of

588 WHEN IS SOMEONE WHO MADE AN ENFORCEABLE DEAL? CH. 6

that condition unless its occurrence was a material part of the agreed exchange.

The *Restatement (Second) of Contracts* also provides this illustration of excuse of a condition to avoid forfeiture:

Illustrations:

1. A contracts to build a house for B, using pipe of Reading manufacture.

In return, B agrees to pay $75,000 in progress payments, each payment to be made "on condition that no pipe other than that of Reading manufacture has been used." Without A's knowledge, a subcontractor mistakenly uses pipe of Cohoes manufacture which is identical in quality and is distinguishable only by the name of the manufacturer which is stamped on it. The mistake is not discovered until the house is completed, when replacement of the pipe will require destruction of substantial parts of the house. B refuses to pay the unpaid balance of $10,000. A court may conclude that the use of Reading rather than Cohoes pipe is so relatively unimportant to B that the forfeiture that would result from denying A the entire balance would be disproportionate, and may allow recovery by A subject to any claim for damages for A's breach of his duty to use Reading pipe.

The next case provides another illustration.

ACME MARKETS, INC. v. FEDERAL ARMORED EXPRESS, INC.

Superior Court of Pennsylvania
437 Pa.Super. 41, 648 A.2d 1218 (1994)

Opinion by HESTER, J:

Acme Markets, Inc., appeals from the order entered in the Court of Common Pleas of Montgomery County on December 21, 1993, which granted Federal Armored Express, Inc. ("Federal") summary judgment. For the reasons set forth below, we reverse that order and remand the matter for further proceedings.

The procedural history of this case may be summarized as follows. On November 20, 1990, appellant filed a breach of contract complaint against Federal. In that complaint, appellant alleged that the parties had entered into a contract for armored car service and that the agreement later was amended to provide for the timely reimbursement of service-related losses. In addition, appellant averred that a Federal employee was robbed on May 19, 1990, after accepting possession of one of appellant's cashbags. Finally, appellant asserted that even though it had notified Federal promptly of the $62,544.32 loss, Federal had not made the reimbursement required by the agreement. Consequently, appellant requested, among other things, an award of damages equivalent to the amount of the loss.

On September 26, 1991, following the effectuation of service, appellant filed an answer and new matter. In connection with one of the defenses asserted in that document, Federal relied upon the fifth paragraph of the agreement which provides, "Responsibility of Federal under this contract shall begin when said [cash]bags or packages have been accepted and receipted for by Federal or its authorized employees, and shall terminate upon delivery to consignee or upon return to shipper." See Complaint at exhibit A. Specifically, Federal claimed that it bore no responsibility for the loss since neither it nor any of its employees had accepted the bag or provided the necessary receipt prior to the robbery.

On June 30, 1993, claiming that discovery was complete and that an examination of the record revealed no genuine issue of material fact, appellant moved for summary judgment. Federal responded by filing a cross-motion for summary judgment in which it acknowledged that one of its employees possessed appellant's cashbag at the time of the robbery. In addition, Federal noted that neither party disputed the fact that the employee in question had not provided a receipt for the bag prior to its loss. Consequently, relying upon both the fifth paragraph of the agreement and an affidavit demonstrating that the receipt requirement conformed with the custom of the armored car industry, Federal requested the entrance of judgment in its favor. On December 21, 1993, the trial court concluded that the fifth paragraph constituted a condition precedent to Federal's liability under the agreement. Thus, the court denied appellant's summary judgment motion and granted Federal relief. This timely appeal followed.

* * *

Appellant asserts that the trial court erroneously concluded that the fifth paragraph of the agreement constituted a condition precedent to Federal's liability for the lost bag. Specifically, appellant argues that since the paragraph was not labelled a condition precedent and does not contain other language normally associated with such a condition, "there is no means by which to state with the certainty required by Pennsylvania law that it creates a condition precedent." Appellant's brief at 13. We find appellant's claim devoid of merit.

Initially, we note that a condition precedent may be defined as a condition which must occur before a duty to perform under a contract arises. * * * While the parties to a contract need not utilize any particular words to create a condition precedent, an act or event designated in a contract will not be construed as constituting one unless that clearly appears to have been the parties' intention. * * * In addition, we note that the purpose of any condition set forth in a contract must be determined in accordance with the general rules of contractual interpretation. * * * Those rules may be summarized as follows.

When construing agreements involving clear and unambiguous terms, this Court need only examine the writing itself to give effect to the parties['] understanding. * * * The court must construe the contract only as written and may not modify the plain meaning of the words under the guise of interpretation. * * * When the terms of a written contract are clear, this Court will not re-write it to give it a construction in conflict with the accepted and plain meaning of the language used. * * * Conversely, when the language is ambiguous and the intention of the parties cannot be reasonably ascertained from the language of the writing alone, the parol evidence rule does not apply to the admission of oral testimony to show both the intent of the parties and the circumstances attending the execution of the contract. * * *

Creeks v. Creeks, 422 Pa.Super. 432, 435, 619 A.2d 754, 756 (1993).

In the present case, the contested paragraph indicates that Federal's responsibility under the contract "shall begin when bags or packages have been accepted and receipted for by Federal or its employees. * * *" Complaint at exhibit A. Our reading of this plain language demonstrates that it clearly and unambiguously conditions Federal's performance under the contract upon both the acceptance of bags or packages and the granting of a receipt for them. Thus, it unquestionably delineates a condition precedent involving those requirements.

Since we have found that Federal's liability under the contract was subject to a condition precedent and neither party disputes that the receipt portion of the condition remained unfulfilled at the time of the robbery, we must determine whether satisfaction of that requirement may be excused. Apparently arguing that strict application of the condition would be unfair, appellant asserts that the receipt requirement was immaterial and could only be seen as incidental to the far more significant satisfied requirement of possession and acceptance by Federal's employee of appellant's property. See Appellant's brief at 15.

Restatement (Second) of Contracts § 229 discusses the excuse of a condition to avoid unfairness in connection with its strict enforcement. More specifically, that section relates to the excuse of a condition leading to a forfeiture, a term referring to "the denial of compensation that results when the obligee loses his right to the agreed exchange after he has relied substantially, as by preparation or performance on the expectation of that exchange." Restatement (Second) of Contracts § 229, comment b. Section 229 provides, "To the extent that the non-occurrence of a condition would cause disproportionate forfeiture, a court may excuse the non-occurrence of that condition unless its occurrence was a material part of the agreed exchange." Restatement (Second) of Contracts § 229. Since Pennsylvania law "abhors forfeitures and penalties and enforces them with the greatest reluctance when a proper case is presented[,]" * * * section 229 is consistent with the law of this Commonwealth. * * * Consequently, we will apply it in the present case.

There can be little doubt that the operation of the condition in question will lead to a forfeiture since the condition's nonoccurrence results in the denial of compensation for the loss of a cashbag possessed by

Federal for transportation in accordance with the contract. Thus, the question becomes whether the forfeiture would be disproportionate.

> In determining whether the forfeiture is "disproportionate," [the] court must weigh the extent of the forfeiture by the obligee against the importance to the obligor of the risk from which he sought to be protected and the degree to which that protection will be lost if the nonoccurrence of the condition is excused to the extent required to prevent forfeiture.

Restatement (Second) of Contracts § 229, comment b.

In the present case, appellant obviously entered into the armored car service contract so that it would have a secure method of transporting cash and checks to the bank. Strict application of the condition precedent would result in the loss of appellant's ability to recover from Federal for the theft of the bag entrusted to Federal's care. Moreover, we believe that the receipting requirement was intended to provide Federal with proof that it accepted, at a specific time, a certain number of cashbags for shipment. Thus, in our opinion, the requirement probably was little more than an accounting device designed to track bags picked up in accordance with the agreement. Under such circumstances, the receipt primarily would serve to protect Federal rather than Acme from, among other things, theft by its own employees and disputes regarding the number of bags accepted. Those are two risks not at issue herein.

While we believe that the receipt requirement probably was an accounting device which had little impact upon the situation presently at issue, our examination of the certified record reveals that it is devoid of any evidence demonstrating the requirement's actual purpose. Thus, even though we have speculated on the matter, the record is inadequate to determine whether our speculation is accurate. In view of the inadequate record, we may not conduct the critical weighing analysis required by the Restatement or determine whether fulfillment of the condition may be excused. Indeed, we note that the trial court erroneously believed that its analysis ended upon concluding that a receipt was required to fulfill the condition precedent. Thus, the court did not consider whether the forfeiture would be disproportionate, decide if the receipt requirement constituted a material part of the exchange, or require the parties to provide an adequate record either for resolving those issues or deciding whether summary judgment in favor of Federal would be appropriate. Accordingly, we must reverse the trial court's grant of summary judgment and remand the matter for further proceedings.

On remand, the trial court should conduct an evidentiary hearing to determine the purpose of the receipt requirement and engage in the necessary weighing analysis. In addition, the court should determine whether the contested requirement constituted a material part of the agreement.[6] While this determination rests to a large extent on the

---

6. We note that the form on which the requirement appears is pre-printed and does not contain any alterations. Thus, while not dispositive, our examination of that document suggests that the requirement was not specifically bargained-for.

analysis of the requirement's purpose, it also involves a consideration of the negotiations of the parties along with all other circumstances relevant to the formation of the contract or to the requirement itself, including the circumstances surrounding the theft.[7]

Order reversed. Case remanded for further proceedings. Jurisdiction relinquished.

QUESTIONS

1. Questions about the facts of this case
    1.1. When did the robbery occur? Was it as the cashbags were being loaded? Is this clear, or even relevant?
    1.2. Do you think Acme thought about the order of performance when it signed the agreement? Should it have?
    1.3. Does the contract between Acme and Federal use the word "condition"? What is the "plain language" that "clearly and unambiguously conditions Federal's performance"?
    1.4. The court also tells us: "There can be little doubt that the operation of the condition in question will lead to a forfeiture." What is the "forfeiture"?
2. Questions about the law
    2.1. You represent Federal on remand. What evidence do you introduce? Whom do you interview to get this evidence?
    2.2. If the court is correct about the nature of the contract in note 6, would this case be better decided as a contract of adhesion?

---

2. Prevention as a Reason for Eliminating an Express Condition

This is how the *Gilbert Law Summary on Contracts* explains prevention as an excuse of a condition:

> A condition will be excused if the party favored by the condition wrongfully prevents or hinders the fulfillment of the condition.

MELVIN A. EISENBERG, CONTRACTS: GILBERT LAW SUMMARIES 233 (14th ed. 2002). That makes sense. (Professor Eisenberg always does.)

Here is an easy example of prevention: Markell contracts to buy Ponoroff's house on January 15th. The contract provides "Payment or other performance by Markell is expressly conditioned on Markell's receiv-

---

7. In light of our determination, we do not address appellant's two remaining claims which relate to whether Federal assumed liability for the bag immediately upon obtaining possession of it and whether satisfaction of the condition precedent may be excused since the failure of the condition resulted from the conduct of Federal's own employee.

ing a loan from a financial institution of at least $1,000,000." Notwithstanding his immense wealth from sales of this book, Markell is unable to obtain a loan because each time he visits a financial institution, he is wearing his Spider–Man suit. Prevention, right?

Let's be sure that we (you) understand the legal significance of "prevention" of the occurrence of a condition—of elimination of the excuse of non-occurrence of the condition. If Markell does not perform—does not pay Ponoroff $1,000,000 for his house on January 15th—Ponoroff could recover from Markell for breach of contract. Markell has no excuse—his excuse based on non-occurrence of the loan condition has been extinguished because the loan condition has been extinguished by Markell's "prevention."

The next case is a more realistic example of prevention (albeit less memorable and much longer than my Markell in a Spider–Man suit example).

MOORE BROTHERS CO. v. BROWN & ROOT, INC.

U.S. Court of Appeals, Fourth Circuit
207 F.3d 717 (2000)

MURNAGHAN, CIRCUIT JUDGE:

This case arises out of the construction of the Dulles Toll Road Extension, a privately owned and operated toll road connecting Dulles Airport and Leesburg, Virginia. [The issue on appeal is] whether a general contractor may rely on the non-occurrence of a valid "pay when paid" condition precedent in the subcontract as a defense to liability where the general contractor was partly responsible for the failure of the condition precedent. [W]e answer [the] question[] in the negative. * * *

I.

The Dulles Toll Road Extension ("DTRE") is a fourteen mile long private toll road between Dulles Airport and Leesburg, Virginia. It was built and is operated by the Toll Road Investors Partnership II ("TRIP"). In 1993, TRIP (the "Owners") awarded the general construction contract to Brown & Root, Inc. In addition to its role as general contractor, Brown & Root was also an equity partner in TRIP.

Brown & Root in turn entered into subcontracts with Moore Brothers Co., Inc. and The Lane Construction Corp., the plaintiffs, to build parts of the road. * * *

The subcontracts between Brown & Root and plaintiffs contain a general "pay when paid" clause:

Notwithstanding any other provision hereof, payment by Owner to General Contractor is a condition precedent to any obligation of General Contractor to make payment hereunder; General Contractor shall have no obligation to make payment to Subcontractor for any portion of the Sublet Work for which General Contractor has not received payment from the Owner.

* * *

The prime construction contract contains provisions for additional payment if the Owners order substantial design changes that constitute a "change in scope" of the project, including a provision for binding arbitration. The early drafts of the contract also contained several specific design change illustrations to clarify the type of situation in which Brown & Root would be entitled to additional payment from the Owners.

Changing the thickness of the pavement sub-base material was included in the examples of design changes that would warrant additional payment. Changing the thickness of the pavement sub-base is a common and costly design change in highway construction, and throughout the development of the DTRE project there was some uncertainty about the adequacy of the initial pavement design and the thickness of the sub-base material that would be required by the Virginia Department of Transportation. As early as 1991 the Brown & Root project manager knew that the initial pavement design for the DTRE was on the "marginal end."

The lenders who were financing the highway project, however, wanted to contain the costs of the project and insisted on a "high degree of certainty" in assessing the total project costs. They were hesitant to agree to a contract that contained specific illustrations of design changes that would warrant additional payment. The Owners and Brown & Root, therefore, agreed in July of 1993 to delete the specific illustrations of design changes from the prime contract to placate the lenders. At the same time, the Owners and Brown & Root assured the lenders that no substantial changes in the work, as defined in the base contract, were anticipated.

After deleting the design change illustrations from the prime contract, the Owners and Brown & Root incorporated the illustrations into a "Policy and Procedures" letter, the existence of which was not revealed to the lenders. In essence, the Owners and Brown & Root reached a side agreement concerning additional "change in scope" illustrations and then concealed that agreement from the lenders by placing it in a side letter, while leaving it out of the prime contract. Brown & Root did not tell the subcontractors that the design change illustrations and the potential need for additional "change in scope" work were hidden from, and therefore not adequately funded by, the lenders.

When the need for a thicker pavement sub-base became apparent, Brown & Root ordered the subcontractors to proceed with the additional work. Under the terms of the "pay when paid" condition precedent in the subcontract, Brown & Root knew that if payment for the additional work were not forthcoming from TRIP, it was the subcontractors who would assume the bulk of the loss.

After the additional work was completed, both Brown & Root and the subcontractors sought arbitration of their claim for additional payment from the Owners. The arbitrator concluded that the additional work did constitute a "change in scope" and therefore ordered the Owners to make payments beyond the base contract price. The arbitrator ordered TRIP to pay Brown & Root, who was subsequently required to pay the subcontractors.

Because the lenders were not made aware of the significant likelihood that additional work would be necessary, financing was never arranged to cover payment for additional "change in scope" work. TRIP, therefore, did not have the funds to pay Brown & Root the amount of the arbitration award. Brown & Root, as a result, claims that it is not obligated to pay the subcontractors for the additional work because of the "pay when paid" clause contained in the subcontracts.

* * *

Plaintiffs filed separate complaints against Brown & Root and its payment bond surety, Highlands, in the U.S. District Court for the Eastern District of Virginia in December of 1996. * * * On December 30, 1998, the district court issued extensive findings of fact and conclusions of law after a bench trial on the plaintiffs' claims against Brown & Root. The court held that Brown & Root is liable (1) to Lane for $1.4 million plus prejudgment interest for the additional "change in scope" work, (2) to Lane for $2.4 million for the early completion bonus, (3) to Moore for $2.1 million for the additional "change in scope" work, and (4) to Moore for $2.4 million for the early completion bonus.

Defendants appeal the * * * judgment against Brown & Root. * * *

* * *

III.

We next consider whether the district court properly found that Brown & Root is liable to the plaintiffs for payment for the additional "change in scope" work. * * *

A. Findings of fact

The district court found that Brown & Root's own actions in connection with the prime contract and the arrangements for financing additional "change in scope" work contributed to the non-occurrence of the condition precedent. The court found that Brown & Root knew that additional "change in scope" work on the DTRE project would likely be necessary to accommodate design changes regarding the thickness of the pavement sub-base material. Brown & Root nonetheless assured the lenders that no additional work would be necessary. Brown & Root then acquiesced in the decision to remove the "change in scope" illustrations from the contract to accommodate the lenders' interest in capping costs, while at the same time protecting themselves with the Policy and Procedures Letter which memorialized the change illustrations as a "side agreement."

In short, the district court found that Brown & Root agreed to remove the design change illustrations from the prime construction contract to placate the lenders, placed those illustrations in a side agreement (the existence of which was not revealed to the lenders), and assured the lenders that no additional work or design changes would be necessary. In finding these facts, the district court weighed the credibility of witnesses, the testimony offered during the prior arbitration, and various documents entered into evidence during the trial. Because the district court's findings of fact are consistent with the evidence contained in the record before this court, those findings are not clearly erroneous.

B.   Conclusions of law

The subcontracts between Brown & Root and the plaintiffs contain a valid "pay when paid" condition precedent. * * * Because the Owners have not paid Brown & Root for the arbitration judgment regarding the additional "change in scope" work, Brown & Root can, as an initial matter, assert the nonoccurrence of the condition precedent as a valid defense to plaintiffs' claims.

Having found that by its own actions Brown & Root contributed to the non-occurrence of the condition precedent, however, the district court applied the "prevention doctrine" to waive the condition precedent and held that Brown & Root is liable to the plaintiffs for payment for the additional "change in scope" work notwithstanding the "pay when paid" clause in the subcontract.

The prevention doctrine is a generally recognized principle of contract law according to which if a promisor prevents or hinders fulfillment of a condition to his performance, the condition may be waived or excused. * * *

The prevention doctrine does not require proof that the condition would have occurred "but for" the wrongful conduct of the promisor; instead it only requires that the conduct have "contributed materially" to the non-occurrence of the condition. * * * The Supreme Court of Virginia does not require the plaintiff to prove "but for" causation. Rather, as that court specifically noted, "it is as effective an excuse of performance of a condition that the promisor has hindered performance as that he has actually prevented it." * * *

The district court found that Brown & Root misled the lenders regarding its expectations that potentially costly design changes would occur. By misleading the lenders in this way, Brown & Root made it less likely that the lenders would arrange additional financing to cover the cost of anticipated design changes. We therefore agree with the district court's conclusion that Brown & Root's conduct "hindered" the fulfillment of the condition precedent.

Brown & Root offers an alternative explanation for the failure of the condition precedent. The failure, they contend, was caused by the financial insolvency of the DTRE project, which was a result of lower than projected traffic flow on the DTRE. According to TRIP's Chief Financial Officer, because of the project's financial distress, sometime in December of 1995 the lenders halted all payments to Brown & Root since it was a partner in the DTRE project. Brown & Root concludes, therefore, that the May 1996 arbitration award would not have been paid regardless of whether additional contingency funding had been arranged by the lenders.

We are not persuaded by Brown & Root's argument. The fact that the lenders halted payments to Brown & Root under the circumstances as they existed in December of 1995 is not proof that the lenders would have forbidden TRIP to draw on some other source of funds to pay Brown & Root for the additional work after the arbitration award in May of 1996 under different circumstances. Had the lenders been apprised early on of the strong possibility that the pavement design would change, it is reasonable to infer that appropriate funding would have been arranged and made available for payment to Brown & Root.

The question is essentially a factual inquiry: why did TRIP fail to pay Brown & Root for the additional "change in scope" work? The district court found that TRIP failed to pay, at least in part, because of Brown & Root's misconduct. Because the district court's findings of fact are not clearly erroneous, and given the speculative nature of Brown & Root's alternative explanation, we do not find reversible error in the conclusions reached below as to the additional work claims. We agree that Brown & Root's misrepresentations "contributed materially" to TRIP's failure to pay for the additional "change in scope" work.

Having so concluded, we hold that the prevention doctrine was properly invoked and the performance of the condition precedent was correctly waived as to the additional "change in scope" work. Without the condition precedent as a defense, Brown & Root is liable to the plaintiffs for payment for the additional work.

* * *

VI.

For the reasons discussed above, we affirm the orders of the district court in part, reverse in part, and remand for further proceedings consistent with this opinion.

Affirmed in Part, Reversed in Part, and Remanded

QUESTIONS AND CONNECTIONS

1. Questions about the facts of this case
   1.1. What was the condition in this case?

    1.2.   How did Brown & Root prevent the occurrence of the condition?

    1.3.   Did Brown & Root break any law? Breach any contract provision?

2.   Questions about the law

    2.1.   What is being "excused" here? Is it the obligation to perform? Or is it the satisfaction of a condition precedent to some other duty?

    2.2.   Does this case in effect hold that Brown & Root has to pay the subcontractors even though it bargained for the right to not have to pay subcontractors until it was paid?

3.   Connections

    3.1.   How does the "pay when paid" clause in this case differ from the "pay when paid" provision in *Peacock Construction*? Is the holding in this case consistent with the holding in the *Peacock Construction*?

    3.2.   What does the "prevention" doctrine add to the "good faith" doctrine that good faith is implied into every contract performance obligation?

----

3. Waiver as a Reason for Eliminating a Condition

As Chancellor John Edward Murray, Jr. states in his excellent hornbook on contracts:

> By language or conduct, a promisor may manifest his intention to forego the benefit of ("waive) a condition. * * * Where a party manifests an intention to perform his promise notwithstanding the non-occurrence of a condition to his duty * * * the condition will be excused if it is not a material part of the agreed exchange."

JOHN EDWARD MURRAY, JR., MURRAY ON CONTRACTS 719, 721 (4th ed. 2001).

For example, B promises to buy S's house on the condition that the house is appraised by A to have a market value of at least $100,000. A appraises the value of the house at $80,000.

Obviously, B can "forego the benefit of" the condition and buy the house. S cannot use the non-occurrence of the appraisal condition to refuse to sell the house to B—that condition has been excused by B's waiver.

And, it is obvious that only B can excuse the "benefit of" the appraisal condition by waiver because only B benefits from that condition. S could not simply compel B to buy the house.

Not much else is obvious or simple. Is the appraisal condition "a material part of the agreed exchange"? What if B promises to buy the house notwithstanding the low appraisal but later changes his mind? Should B's promise be enforceable notwithstanding the absence of consideration or a consideration substitute such as promissory estoppel?

The Comment to *Restatement (Second) of Contracts* § 84 provides an answer to these questions: Comment d says the following about "Conditions which may be waived": "may be thought of as procedural or technical or to instances in which the non-occurrence of the condition is comparatively minor." And Comment f says the following about "reinstatement after waiver": "where the requirement of a condition is waived in advance, the promisor may reinstate the requirement by giving notice to the other party before the latter has materially changed his position."

Reconsider these questions (and answers) after considering the next three cases in the section which deals with modification and waiver as excuses for performance of promises as well as causes for non-occurrence of conditions.

SECTION 2: MODIFICATION, WAIVER, OR ESTOPPEL AS AN EXCUSE FOR NOT DOING WHAT YOU AGREED TO DO

People sometimes change their minds and want to change their deals. If both of the people who made the deal agree to change the deal, they are excused from performing the original deal because of modification.

We have talked about modification before. In considering "consideration" we considered *Angel v. Murray*, in which the Rhode Island Supreme Court told us "modification of a contract is itself a contract." And like any contract, modification is based on agreement—mutual manifestations of assent.

In the next case, the Massachusetts Supreme Court tells us the differences between an excuse for not doing what you agreed to do based on a modification and an excuse for not doing what you agreed to do based on waiver:

DYNAMIC MACHINE WORKS, INC. v. MACHINE & ELECTRICAL CONSULTANTS, INC.

Supreme Judicial Court of Massachusetts
444 Mass. 768, 831 N.E.2d 875 (2005)

CORDY, J.

A judge of the United States District Court for the District of Massachusetts has certified the following question: "Under the Massachusetts version of the Uniform Commercial Code, does a buyer have a right to retract a written extension allowing more time for the seller to cure defects in a delivered product absent reliance on the extension by the seller?" We answer the certified question as follows: If the written extension constitutes a modification of the agreement to purchase the product, then the buyer may not retract it unilaterally. If, on the other hand, the written extension constitutes a waiver of an executory portion of the agreement, the buyer may retract it "by reasonable notification received by the [seller] that strict performance will be required * * * unless the retraction would be unjust in view of a material change of position in reliance on the waiver.

Background. The undisputed facts and relevant procedural history are as follows. Dynamic Machine Works, Inc. (Dynamic), is a Massachusetts manufacturer of precision components for the aerospace, chemical, military, and oil industries. Machine & Electrical Consultants, Inc. (Machine), located in Biddeford, Maine, distributes heavy machinery and turning equipment. In January, 2003, Dynamic agreed to purchase from Machine a Johnford lathe (lathe) for $355,000.

The lathe was to be manufactured in Taiwan by Roundtop Machinery Industries, Co., Ltd. Under the terms of Dynamic's purchase order, Machine would receive a down payment of $29,500, a second payment of $148,000 on delivery, which was scheduled for May 15, 2003, and a final payment of $177,500 on acceptance. In the interim, Dynamic rented a Johnford ST–60B lathe (rental lathe) from Machine. In February, 2003, Dynamic informed Machine that it was experiencing problems with the rental lathe and that if these problems were not addressed and remedied in the new lathe, Dynamic would reject it.

Sometime before June, 2003, production of the lathe in Taiwan was delayed due to the "SARS" epidemic and other events beyond the control of Machine. In letters dated June 26 and July 8 (collectively the July agreement), Machine and Dynamic confirmed an oral agreement to, among other things, extend the deadline for the installation and commissioning of the lathe to September 19, 2003. The parties further agreed that any further delay would result in a $500 per day penalty assessed against Machine. On October 9, Machine delivered the lathe to Dynamic. It was subsequently installed and, throughout the month of November, the lathe was tested and readjusted in connection with its final commissioning.

On December 9, Dynamic's president, Ven Fonte, wrote a letter to the vice-president of Machine, Norman Crepeau, which advised in relevant part: "As I stated to you early this morning on the telephone, we will grant you one last and final deadline for the machine to be fully and unconditionally commissioned by the close of business day, Friday December 19, 2003." On the following day, Fonte received additional information regarding the lathe that led him to conclude that it would not be able to meet the required specifications. Dynamic promptly notified Machine that it intended to retract the deadline extension. In a letter dated December 11, counsel for Dynamic advised Machine that Dynamic was revoking acceptance of the lathe, demanded return of Dynamic's down payment and the payment of the penalty fees, and requested instructions concerning disposition of the lathe. Machine had not relied on the deadline extension granted in Fonte's letter of December 9 in any material way prior to Dynamic's written revocation of it on December 11.

On February 20, 2004, Dynamic filed this action * * * seeking a declaratory judgment concerning its rights and remedies under the Uniform Commercial Code, and alleging breach of warranty, breach of contract, and unfair business practices. * * * The judge certified the above question to this court because "the resolution of the determinative issue in this case depends on a question of Massachusetts law as to which there are no clearly controlling precedents in the decisions of the Supreme Judicial Court of Massachusetts."

2.   Discussion. The contract in this case is one for the sale of goods. Consequently, it is governed by the Commonwealth's version of art. 2 of the Uniform Commercial Code (UCC). Section 2–209 of the UCC provides:

"(1) An agreement modifying a contract within this Article needs no consideration to be binding.

"(2) A signed agreement which excludes modification or rescission except by a signed writing cannot be otherwise modified or rescinded, but except as between merchants such a requirement on a form supplied by the merchant must be separately signed by the other party.

"(3) The requirements of the Statute of Frauds section of this Article (section 2–201) must be satisfied if the contract as modified is within its provisions.

"(4) Although an attempt at modification or rescission does not satisfy the requirements of subsection (2) or (3) it can operate as a waiver.

"(5) A party who has made a waiver affecting an executory portion of the contract may retract the waiver by reasonable notification received by the other party that strict performance will be required of any term waived, unless the retraction would be unjust in view of a material change of position in reliance on the waiver."

The UCC does not define "waiver" or "modification," but they "are distinct concepts." Massachusetts common law defines waiver as the "intentional relinquishment of a known right," or, as one commentator has explained, "the excuse of the nonoccurrence of or a delay in the occurrence of a condition or a duty." A modification is the changing of the terms of the agreement which may diminish or increase the duty of either party. While a waiver may be effectuated by one party, a modification "is the result of the bilateral action of both parties to the sales transaction.Under Massachusetts law, the parties to a contract must agree to a modification. By the plain terms of § 2–209(5), a waiver is retractable in the absence of reliance. A modification, in contrast, cannot be retracted unilaterally. * * *

Dynamic contends that its letter of December 9, 2003, is a waiver (or at least a partial waiver) of the time by which Machine had a duty to perform, and not a mutual agreement to change the terms of the contract. In support of this position, it points out that the letter does not expressly state that both parties "agreed" to the "last and final deadline" of Friday, December 19, 2003, and reflects only what Dynamic's president "stated" in that regard, without any reference to Machine's position on the matter. Moreover, it argues that the use of the word "grant," as opposed to "agree," is dispositive. Machine, on the other hand, argues that Dynamic's extension of the commissioning deadline constitutes a modification because (1) the extension satisfies the Statute of Frauds; (2) the extension was granted in a letter written and signed by Dynamic's president; (3) the letter granting the extension "clearly demonstrates that both parties had discussed and agreed to the new commissioning deadline"; and (4) the terms of the letter are sufficiently definite.

Determining whether Dynamic's letter of December 9 (or the conversation to which it refers) constitutes a waiver or a modification is in large measure a question of fact. As applied to this case, the answer turns on whether Dynamic and Machine mutually agreed to extend the commissioning deadline to December 19, 2003. The fact that the extension was granted in a signed writing does not of itself establish that the extension was intended to be a modification, and not a waiver. A waiver "can be inferred from a party's conduct and the surrounding circumstances," but it can also be "express," And there is no reason why it cannot be in writing. Conversely, the absence of consideration for the extension of the time of performance does not preclude a finding that the extension was the product of a mutual agreement to modify the contract terms, as the UCC explicitly states that "[a]n agreement modifying a contract * * * needs no consideration to be binding." § 2–209(1)

We answer only the certified question, and the judge has not asked us to determine whether the December 9 letter extending the time for performance constitutes a modification of the July agreement or a waiver of Machine's duty to perform by a particular date.

QUESTIONS

1. Questions about the facts of the case

    1.1. Which party is arguing that it is excused from doing what it agreed to do?

    1.2. Which party is arguing Dynamic's December 9th letter was a waiver?

    1.3. What facts most strongly support that argument?

2. Questions about the law

    2.1. Can waiver excuse a party to a contract from doing what it agreed to do? If so, why is it necessary in this case to determine whether the December 9th letter was waiver or modification?

2.2. Was there "consideration" for Dynamics' December 9th deadline extension? Was that important? Would it be important if the subject matter of the contract was land and not a lathe?

2.3. Was it important that the December 9th extension was in a signed writing? Can modification or waiver be based on conduct?

MAY CENTERS, INC. v. PARIS CROISSANT OF ENFIELD SQUARE, INC., ET AL.

Superior Court of Connecticut
42 Conn.Supp. 77, 599 A.2d 407 (1991)

Satter, Judge.

The plaintiff is suing the corporate defendant, Paris Croissant of Enfield Square, Inc., (Paris) to recover unpaid rent, common assessments and attorney's fees pursuant to a lease, and is also suing the individual defendants* as guarantors of Paris' liability under the lease.

The facts are as follows. On February 4, 1986, the plaintiff as landlord and Paris as tenant entered into a ten year lease (prepared by the plaintiff) of commercial space at the Enfield Mall, commencing April 15, 1986. The lease provided for a minimum rent, to be paid in advance on the first day of each calendar month, the first month's minimum rent to be paid at the time of execution of the lease, a percentage rent and various assessments. If Paris failed "to remedy any default in the payment of any sum due under this lease for ten (10) days after notice" the plaintiff could reenter the premises and sublet them, or declare the lease at an end, evict Paris and collect the rent due over the balance of the term of the lease. Paris' failure to pay rent also entitled the plaintiff to charge interest at twelve percent on the unpaid balance, plus attorney's fees incurred to collect back rent. The lease also provided that "[n]o waiver of any default hereunder shall be implied from any omission by either party to take any action on account of such default if such default persists or is repeated. * * * The acceptance by landlord of rent with knowledge of the breach of any of the covenants of this lease by tenant shall not be a waiver or any such breach."

The individual defendants executed a guaranty (prepared by the plaintiff) of the obligations of Paris under the lease. The guaranty provided that the guarantors "absolutely, unconditionally and irrevocably" guarantee to the plaintiff to be liable for full payment of all rent and other charges payable by Paris under the lease, and if Paris defaults, forthwith to pay such rent and charges to the plaintiff, without the necessity of any notice to the guarantors, which they expressly waive. The guaranty was to remain in effect during the first two years of the term of the lease. It further provided: "In the event [Paris] is in default or has failed to *condition precedent*

---

* Those individuals are represented by the "et al." in the case caption. Eds.

perform any of the terms and conditions of the lease as of the expiration of the second (2nd) year of the term of the lease, this [guaranty] shall remain in full force and effect during the entire term of the lease."

Paris, having paid the first month's minimum rent at the time the lease was executed on February 4, 1986, continued to pay the rent around the middle of each month. Thus, in 1986, the June rent was posted by the plaintiff as having been paid on June 13, the July rent on July 21, the August rent on August 14, the September rent on September 16, the October rent on October 13, the November rent on November 17, and, the December rent on December 11, 1986. Similar patterns persisted through 1987, although in some instances the rent was paid later. In 1988, the January rent was posted as having been paid on January 29, the February rent on February 22, the March rent on March 24, and the April rent on April 25. The two year period of the guaranty expired on April 14, 1988.

The procedure established by the plaintiff was that the tenants of Enfield Mall mailed their rent checks to a lock box in a St. Louis, Missouri bank. Bank employees deposited checks to the plaintiff's account and the next day posted the payment to the plaintiff. The evidence is that Paris' April, 1988 rent was posted to the plaintiff's account on April 25, 1988. That day was a Monday. The court infers the check was received in St. Louis on the previous Friday, or April 22, 1988. The defendant William Summers testified that he could not recall when he mailed the April rent check in Connecticut. It could possibly have been prior to April 15, although he regularly mailed such checks after the fifteenth of the month. This court, taking judicial notice of the mails between Enfield and St. Louis; *Lloyd & Elliott, Inc. v. Parke*, 114 Conn. 12, 14, 157 A. 272 (1931); concludes, from all the evidence, that Paris' April rent check was more probably than not mailed on April 20, 1988.

In June, 1987, the defendant Anthony Scussel sold his interest in Paris to Summers; Scussel thereafter ceased to be involved in Paris' business.

In July, 1988, Paris became erratic in its rent payments and the plaintiff started sending notices of default. Notices were sent in July, 1988, September, 1988, February, 1989, and April, 1989.

In May, 1989, Paris ceased paying rent and gave up its key to the plaintiff. The plaintiff boarded up the premises and eventually relet them in May, 1990. The unpaid rent, charges and assessments under the lease as of May, 1990, amount to $43,945. Interest on the arrearage to the date of trial amounts to $5799.35. Attorney's fees and costs of collection through the trial amount to $6223.70, totaling $55,968.05, which the plaintiff claims as damages.

On the first count against Paris, the plaintiff has proven its claim and is entitled to recover $55,968.05.

On the second count against the individual defendants as guarantors, the question is whether the plaintiff proved the existence of the condition precedent that triggered the extension of the guaranty beyond the initial two years. * * * More specifically, did the plaintiff prove Paris was in default in its rent (the only default the plaintiff claims) as of April 14, 1988? This court concludes that the plaintiff did not.

The lease term commenced on April 15, 1986. Paris paid the first month's minimum rent in February, 1986. The plaintiff's records are unclear whether this payment covered the period from April 15 to May 15, 1986, and the plaintiff produced no evidence to clarify this point. What is clear is that starting in June, 1986, Paris paid the rent each month around the fifteenth and the plaintiff accepted it without complaint. Although the lease provided for rent payments on the first of the month, it is a form lease and does not specifically take into account that the lease term started in the middle of the month.

A course of conduct may not only indicate the intent of the parties for the purpose of interpreting ambiguous language in a contract; * * * but also evince a subsequent modification of a contract or an abrogation of specific contract terms. * * * Proof that a contract has been modified is established by a showing of mutual consent; * * * which, in turn, " 'may be inferred from the attendant circumstances and conduct of the parties.' " * * *

In the present case, the court concludes from the starting date of the lease on April 15, 1986, and from the rent being regularly sent by Paris and accepted by the plaintiff without protest around the fifteenth of each month, that the parties indicated by their conduct their mutual consent to substitute the fifteenth as the due date for the rent. 2 Restatement (Second), Contracts § 279, comment (a).

The lease provides the tenant has ten days to remedy a default in rent payment before the plaintiff can take action. * * * The court interprets the lease as giving Paris a ten day grace period.

In the present case, Paris mailed the April, 1988 rent on April 20, 1988, and since the plaintiff directed that the rent be sent that way, that is the date the April rent was paid. * * * Since the court finds the April, 1988 rent was due on April 15, 1988, Paris was not in default in payment of that month's rent.

Even assuming the due date of the rent was April 1, 1988, and the April rent check was sent on April 20, 1988, while Paris technically may have been in default on April 14, 1988, it was not in default "as of" April 14, 1988, as required by the guaranty for the guaranty to be extended. When the plaintiff received the April rent check, it had several alternatives: (1) refuse the check because it was late and hold Paris in default; (2) return the check and declare it was holding it not as rent but as use and occupancy; (3) accept the check as payment of the April rent. The third is the alternative the plaintiff selected. The plaintiff could not both accept the check and claim a default. The law is clearly stated in the Restatement (Second) of Contracts § 278(1): "If an obligee accepts in satisfaction of the obligator's duty a performance by the obligor that differs from what is due, the duty is discharged." See also comment (a). Section 47a–19 of the General Statutes provides that "[a]cceptance of rent with the knowledge that such rent is overdue constitutes a waiver of the landlord's right to terminate the rental agreement for the tenant's failure to pay such rent when it was due." While the statute is not directly applicable, it reveals the general rule that a landlord cannot simultaneously accept a month's rent and claim a default because of late payment.

Particularly, the plaintiff cannot accept the April, 1988 rent, claim no default, (although in subsequent months in 1988 and 1989 the plaintiff sent out notices of default), then initiate this case in November, 1989, a year and a half later, and demand that this court find Paris in default in April, 1988, so that the guaranty was extended and the individual defendants are obligated for $55,968.05. Rather, this court finds that by the plaintiff's acceptance of the April, 1988 rent on April 20, 1988, any consequence of the late payment for April was cured. Paris was not in default as of April 14, 1988, and the guaranty was not extended.

The plaintiff argues that the nonwaiver provisions of the lease allow a claim of default despite payment. This court disagrees. The court interprets the language that no waiver of any default shall be implied from omission to take action "if such default persists or is repeated," to mean that a prior default, such as late payment, did not require the plaintiff to excuse and to accept a subsequent late payment, but when the plaintiff accepted the late payment, the default as to that payment was cured. The court interprets the language that acceptance by the landlord of rent with knowledge of the breach of any of the covenants of the lease "shall not be a waiver of any such breach" to mean breaches of covenants other than relating to rent.

In essence, the plaintiff wants this court to construe the lease so that the failure by Paris to pay the April rent exactly on April 1, 1988, constitutes a default, which the plaintiff did not waive by accepting the rent, and which extended the guaranty. The established standards of preference in interpreting contracts favor interpretations that are reasonable rather than unreasonable; * * * practical; * * * and consistent with common sense. The plaintiff's desired construction is unconscionable because it creates a lease and guaranty " 'no man in his right senses * * * would make * * * and * * * no honest and fair man would accept.' " 2 Restatement (Second), Contracts § 208, comment (b). This court exercises its prerogative to "limit the application of any unconscionable term [of a contract so] as to avoid any unconscionable result." 2 Restatement (Second), Contracts § 208.

Judgment may enter on the first count for the plaintiff against Paris for $55,968.05. Judgment may enter on the second count for the individual defendants.

QUESTIONS

1. Questions about the facts of the case

    1.1. Did the court find that the tenant, Paris, was liable for all of the rent? In making that determination, did the date the rent was due matter?

    1.2. If the court found that Paris was fully liable, why is May Centers pursuing the individual guarantors?

    1.3. How many contracts are involved in this case? Upon which of those contracts are the individual defendants liable? If the guarantors are not directly liable on the lease (they did not sign that document), then why is the question of whether the parties amended their obligations to change the due date for the rent payment relevant?

2. Questions about the law

    2.1. Where does this court find the consent necessary for the modification of the lease? Where does the court find the consideration necessary for the modification?

    2.2. If you represented May Centers, and wanted to hold the guarantors to their obligations, what would you advise May Centers to do with the rent check that showed up in late April?

    2.3. The court finds a "discharge" of the obligation to pay rent from "acceptance" of the check. Is there anything that you might want to put in leases drafted in Connecticut after this case that could help your landlord clients?

    2.4. How does the court deal with the anti-waiver provision in the lease?

    2.5. Again, what are the differences between modification and waiver? And, again, consider this question again after reading the next case.

CLARK v. WEST

Court of Appeals of New York
193 N.Y. 349, 86 N.E. 1 (1908)

WERNER, J:

The contract before us, stripped of all superfluous verbiage, binds the plaintiff to total abstention from the use of intoxicating liquors during the continuance of the work which he was employed to do. The stipulations relating to the plaintiff's compensation provide that if he does not observe this condition he is to be paid at the rate of $2 per page, and if he does comply therewith he is to receive $6 per page.* The plaintiff has written one book under the contract known as "Clark & Marshall on Corpora-

---

* The actual language was:

"In consideration of the above promises," the defendant agrees to pay the plaintiff $2 per page on each book prepared by him, and if he "abstains from the use of intoxicating liquor and tions," which has been accepted, published and copies sold in large numbers by the defendant. The plaintiff admits that while he was at work on this book he did not entirely abstain from the use of intoxicating liquors. He has been paid only $2 per page for the work he has done. He claims that, despite his breach of this condition, he is entitled to the full compensation of $6 per page because the defendant, with full knowledge of plaintiff's non-observance of this stipulation as to total abstinence, has waived the breach thereof and cannot now insist upon strict performance in this regard. This plea of waiver presents the underlying question which determines the answers to the questions certified.

Briefly stated, the defendant's position is that the stipulation as to plaintiff's total abstinence is the consideration for the payment of the difference between $2 and $6 per page and therefore could not be waived except by a new agreement to that effect based upon a good consideration; that the so-called waiver alleged by the plaintiff is not a waiver but a modification of the contract in respect of its consideration. The plaintiff on the other hand argues that the stipulation for his total abstinence was merely a condition precedent intended to work a forfeiture of the additional compensation in case of a breach and that it could be waived without any formal agreement to that effect based upon a new consideration. * * *

The subject-matter of the contract was the writing of books by the plaintiff for the defendant. The duration of the contract was the time necessary to complete them all. The work was to be done to the satisfaction of the defendant, and the plaintiff was not to write any other books except those covered by the contract unless requested so to do by the defendant, in which latter event he was to be paid for that particular work by the year. The compensation for the work specified in the contract was to be $6 per page, unless the plaintiff failed to totally abstain from the use of intoxicating liquors during the continuance of the contract, in which event he was to receive only $2 per page. That is the obvious import of the contract construed in the light of the purpose for which it was made, and in accordance with the ordinary meaning of plain language. It is not a contract to write books in order that the plaintiff shall keep sober, but a contract containing a stipulation that he shall keep sober so that he may write satisfactory books. When we view the contract from this standpoint it will readily be perceived that the particular stipulation is not the consideration for the contract, but simply one of its conditions which fits in with those relating to time and method of delivery of manuscript, revision of proof, citation of cases, assignment of copyrights, keeping track of new cases and citations for new editions, and other details which might be waived by the defendant, if he saw fit to do so. * * *

It is obvious that the parties thought that the plaintiff's normal work was worth $6 per page. That was the sum to be paid for the work done by the plaintiff and not for total abstinence. If the plaintiff did not keep to

---

otherwise fulfills his agreements as hereinbefore set forth, he shall be paid an additional $4 per page in manner hereinbefore stated." Eds.

the condition as to total abstinence, he was to lose part of that sum. Precisely the same situation would have risen if the plaintiff had disregarded any of the other essential conditions of the contract. The fact that the particular stipulation was emphasized did not change its character. It was still a condition which the defendant could have insisted upon, as he has apparently done in regard to some others, and one which he could waive just as he might have waived those relating to the amount of the advance payments, or the number of pages to be written each month. A breach of any of the substantial conditions of the contract would have entailed a loss or forfeiture similar to that consequent upon a breach of the one relating to total abstinence, in case of the defendant's insistence upon his right to take advantage of them. This, we think, is the fair interpretation of the contract, and it follows that the stipulation as to the plaintiff's total abstinence was nothing more nor less than a condition precedent. If that conclusion is well founded there can be no escape from the corollary that this condition could be waived; and if it was waived the defendant is clearly not in a position to insist upon the forfeiture which his waiver was intended to annihilate. The forfeiture must stand or fall with the condition. If the latter was waived, the former is no longer a part of the contract. Defendant still has the right to counterclaim for any damages which he may have sustained in consequence of the plaintiff's breach, but he cannot insist upon strict performance. * * *

This whole discussion is predicated of course upon the theory of an express waiver. We assume that no waiver could be implied from the defendant's mere acceptance of the books and his payment of the sum of $2 per page without objection. It was the defendant's duty to pay that amount in any event after acceptance of the work. The plaintiff must stand upon his allegation of an express waiver and if he fails to establish that he cannot maintain his action.

The theory upon which the defendant's attitude seems to be based is that even if he has represented to the plaintiff that he would not insist upon the condition that the latter should observe total abstinence from intoxicants, he can still refuse to pay the full contract price for his work. The inequity of this position becomes apparent when we consider that this contract was to run for a period of years, during a large portion of which the plaintiff was to be entitled only to the advance payment of $2 per page, the balance being contingent, among other things, upon publication of the books and returns from sales. Upon this theory the defendant might have waived the condition while the first book was in process of production, and yet when the whole work was completed, he would still be in a position to insist upon the forfeiture because there had not been strict performance. Such a situation is possible in a case where the subject of the waiver is the very consideration of a contract * * *, but not where the waiver relates to something that can be waived. In the case at bar, as we have seen, the waiver is not of the consideration or subject-matter, but of an incident to the method of performance. The consideration remains the same. The defendant has had the work he bargained for, and it is alleged that he has waived one of the conditions as to the manner in which it was to have been done. He might have insisted upon literal performance and then he could have stood upon the letter of his contract. If, however, he has waived that incidental condition, he has created a situation to which the doctrine of waiver very precisely applies.

The cases which present the most familiar phases of the doctrine of waiver are those which have arisen out of litigation over insurance policies where the defendants have claimed a forfeiture because of the breach of some condition in the contract * * *, but it is a doctrine of general application which is confined to no particular class of cases. A waiver has been defined to be the intentional relinquishment of a known right. It is voluntary and implies an election to dispense with something of value, or forego some advantage which the party waiving it might at its option have demanded or insisted upon * * * and this definition is supported by many cases in this and other states. In the recent case of *Draper v. Oswego Co. Fire R. Assn.* (190 N. Y. 12, 16) Chief Judge Cullen, in speaking for the court upon this subject, said: "While that doctrine and the doctrine of equitable estoppel are often confused in insurance litigation, there is a clear distinction between the two. A waiver is the voluntary abandonment or relinquishment by a party of some right or advantage. As said by my brother Vann in the Kiernan Case (150 N. Y. 190): 'The law of waiver seems to be a technical doctrine, introduced and applied by the court for the purpose of defeating forfeitures. * * * While the principle may not be easily classified, it is well established that if the words and acts of the insurer reasonably justify the conclusion that with full knowledge of all the facts it intended to abandon or not to insist upon the particular defense afterwards relied upon, a verdict or finding to that effect establishes a waiver, which, if it once exists, can never be revoked.' The doctrine of equitable estoppel, or estoppel in pais, is that a party may be precluded by his acts and conduct from asserting a right to the detriment of another party who, entitled to rely on such conduct, has acted upon it. * * * As already said, the doctrine of waiver is to relieve against forfeiture; it requires no consideration for a waiver, nor any prejudice or injury to the other party." * * *

It remains to be determined whether the plaintiff has alleged facts which, if proven, will be sufficient to establish his claim of an express waiver by the defendant of the plaintiff's breach of the condition to observe total abstinence. In the 12th paragraph of the complaint, the plaintiff alleges facts and circumstances which we think, if established, would prove defendant's waiver of plaintiff's performance of that contract stipulation. These facts and circumstances are that long before the plaintiff had completed the manuscript of the first book undertaken under the contract, the defendant had full knowledge of the plaintiff's non-observance of that stipulation, and that with such knowledge he not only accepted the completed manuscript without objection, but "repeatedly avowed and represented to the plaintiff that he was entitled to and would receive said royalty payments (i.e., the additional $4 per page), and plaintiff believed and relied upon such representations * * * and at all times during the writing of said treatise on corporations, and after as well as before publication thereof as aforesaid, it was mutually understood, agreed and intended by the parties hereto that notwithstanding plaintiff's said use of intoxicating liquors, he was nevertheless entitled to receive and would receive said royalty as the same accrued under said contract."

* * *

The three questions certified should be answered in the affirmative, the order of the Appellate Division reversed, the interlocutory judgment of the Special Term affirmed, with costs in both courts, and the defendant be permitted to answer the complaint within twenty days upon payment of costs.

QUESTIONS

1. Questions about the facts of this case

    1.1. Who is suing whom for what? Did Clark agree not to drink liquor? Why isn't West suing Clark for breach of contract?

    1.2. What facts on remand does Clark need to prove to show a waiver? Would one instance of West saying that it was all right for Clark to drink and write be enough? What if a West representative, upon receiving the first draft and being told that West drank while writing it, said "If you do stuff this good while shikker, where can we buy you more liquor?"

2. Questions about the law

    2.1. Why did Clark want the court to find a waiver instead of a modification?

    2.2. Was the contract provision regarding abstinence a "condition" or a "promise"? Did the court's answer to that question affect its analysis of waiver as an excuse?

    2.3. Note the court's use of the phrase "breach of this condition." Can a condition be breached?

    2.4. What is the difference between waiver and estoppel? Recall that West had contracted with Clark to produce a series of books. If Clark later writes another of the books in the series while intoxicated, is West legally obligated to pay him $6 a page?

    2.5. If you were West's lawyer, and wanted to protect West from the effect of statements made after the conclusion of the contract that waive various provisions of the contract, what language would you add to West's contracts?

SECTION 3: IMPOSSIBILITY, IMPRACTICABILITY, FRUSTRATION OF PURPOSE: OCCURRENCE OF SOMETHING NOT PROVIDED FOR IN THE CONTRACT AS AN EXCUSE FOR NOT DOING WHAT YOU AGREED TO DO

To borrow from the movie Forrest Gump and the bumper sticker the movie borrowed, "shit happens." And, sometimes it: (1) happens after a contract has been entered into but before the contract has been fully performed, (2) affects the ability to perform or the purpose of the performance, and (3) it is not provided for in the contract.

In section 1 on express conditions, we dealt primarily with the effect of something not happening that the contract expressly contemplated happening. Remember the Ponoroff/Markell home rental contract conditioned on the 2015 Super Bowl being awarded to Las Vegas?

In this section, we will be dealing primarily with the effect of something happening that the contract does not expressly contemplate. Assume for example that after the 2015 Super Bowl was awarded to Richmond that Ponoroff entered into a contract with Epstein to rent Epstein's house the last week in January 2015. Then, in the third week of January, after the Ponoroff/Epstein contract but before the time of performance, an unprecedented flood of the James River destroys Epstein's house. Should Epstein be excused from performing? Or instead, the Commonwealth of Virginia enacts a statute requiring that a person be over 5 feet 7 inches tall in order to attend the Super Bowl. Or instead, a twisted Arizona alum gives Ponoroff two tickets to the ballet the same night as the Super Bowl and "the missus" tells Ponoroff that he cannot possibly go to the Super Bowl instead of the ballet? Should Ponoroff be excused from performing? What later occurrences will excuse a person from doing what he contracted?

The materials in this section address these questions and begin with the case that courts and commentators describe as the first case to recognize "impossibility" as an excuse, *Taylor v. Caldwell.*

✳ TAYLOR v. CALDWELL
Court of King's Bench
122 Eng.Rep. 309 (1863)

BLACKBURN, J. In this case the plaintiffs and defendants had, on the 27th May, 1861, entered into a contract by which the defendants agreed to let the plaintiffs have the use of The Surrey Gardens and Music Hall on four days then to come, viz., the 17th June, 15th July, 5th August and 19th August, for the purpose of giving a series of four grand concerts, and day and night fetes at the Gardens and Hall on those days respectively;

and the plaintiffs agreed to take the Gardens and Hall on those days, and pay £100 for each day.

The parties inaccurately call this a "letting," and the money to be paid a "rent"; but the whole agreement is such as to shew that the defendants were to retain the possession of the Hall and Gardens so that there was to be no demise of them, and that the contract was merely to give the plaintiffs the use of them on those days. Nothing however, in our opinion, depends on this. The agreement then proceeds to set out various stipulations between the parties as to what each was to supply for these concerts and entertainments, and as to the manner in which they should be carried on. The effect of the whole is to shew that the existence of the Music Hall in the Surrey Gardens in a state fit for a concert was essential for the fulfilment of the contract,-such entertainment as the parties contemplated in their agreement could not be given without it.

After the making of the agreement, and before the first day on which a concert was to be given, the Hall was destroyed by fire. This destruction, we must take it on the evidence, was without the fault of either party, and was so complete that in consequence the concerts could not be given as intended. And the question we have to decide is whether, under these circumstances, the loss which the plaintiffs have sustained is to fall upon the defendants. The parties when framing their agreement evidently had not present to their minds the possibility of such a disaster, and have made no express stipulation with reference to it, so that the answer to the question must depend upon the general rules of law applicable to such a contract.

There seems no doubt that where there is a positive contract to do a thing, not in itself unlawful, the contractor must perform it or pay damages for not doing it, although in consequence of unforeseen accidents, the performance of his contract has become unexpectedly burdensome or even impossible. * * * But this rule is only applicable when the contract is positive and absolute, and not subject to any condition either express or implied; and there are authorities which, as we think, establish the principle that where, from the nature of the contract, it appears that the parties must from the beginning have known that it could not be fulfilled unless when the time for the fulfilment of the contract arrived some particular specified thing continued to exist, so that, when entering into the contract, they must have contemplated such continuing existence as the foundation of what was to be done; there, in the absence of any express or implied warranty that the thing shall exist, the contract is not to be construed as a positive contract, but as subject to an implied condition that the parties shall be excused in case, before breach, performance becomes impossible from the perishing of the thing without default of the contractor.

There seems little doubt that this implication tends to further the great object of making the legal construction such as to fulfill the intention of those who entered into the contract. For in the course of affairs men in making such contracts in general would, if it were brought to their minds, say that there should be such a condition.

* * *

There is a class of contracts in which a person binds himself to do something which requires to be performed by him in person; and such promises, e.g. promises to marry, or promises to serve for a certain time, are never in practice qualified by an express exception of the death of the party; and therefore in such cases the contract is in terms broken if the promisor dies before fulfilment. Yet it was very early determined that, if the performance is personal, the executors are not liable; Hyde v. The Dean of Windsor (Cro.Eliz. 552, 553). See 2 Wms.Exors. 1560, 5th ed., where a very apt illustration is given. "Thus," says the learned author, "if an author undertakes to compose a work, and dies before completing it, his executors are discharged from this contract: for the undertaking is merely personal in its nature, and, by the intervention of the contractor's death, has become impossible to be performed." For this he cites a dictum of Lord Lyndhurst in Marshall v. Broadhurst (1 Tyr. 348, 349), and a case mentioned by Patteson J. in Wentworth v. Cock (10 A. & E. 42, 45–46). In Hall v. Wright (E.B. & E. 746, 749), Crompton J., in his judgment, puts another case. "Where a contract depends upon personal skill, and the act of God renders it impossible, as, for instance, in the case of a painter employed to paint a picture who is struck blind, it may be that the performance might be excused."

It seems that in those cases the only ground on which the parties or their executors, can be excused from the consequences of the breach of the contract is, that from the nature of the contract there is an implied condition of the continued existence of the life of the contractor, and, perhaps in the case of the painter of his eyesight. In the instances just given, the person, the continued existence of whose life is necessary to the fulfilment of the contract, is himself the contractor, but that does not seem in itself to be necessary to the application of the principle; as is illustrated by the following example. In the ordinary form of an apprentice deed the apprentice binds himself in unqualified terms to "serve until the full end and term of seven years to be fully complete and ended," during which term it is covenanted that the apprentice his master "faithfully shall serve," and the father of the apprentice in equally unqualified terms binds himself for the performance by the apprentice of all and every covenant on his part. It is undeniable that if the apprentice dies within the seven years, the covenant of the father that he shall perform his covenant to serve for seven years is not fulfilled, yet surely it cannot be that an action lie against the father? Yet the only reason why it would not is that he is excused because of the apprentice's death.

These are instances where the implied condition is of the life of a human being, but there are others in which the same implication is made as to the continued existence of a thing. For example, where a contract of sale is made amounting to a bargain and sale, transferring presently the property in specific chattels, which are to be delivered by the vendor at a future day; there, if the chattels, without fault of the vendor, perish in the interval, the purchaser must pay the price and the vendor is excused from performing his contract to deliver, which has thus become impossible.

It may, we think, be safely asserted to be now English law, that in all contracts of loan of chattels or bailments if the performance of the promise of the borrower or bailee to return the things lent or bailed, becomes impossible because it has perished, this impossibility (if not arising upon the fault of the borrower or bailee from some risk which he has taken upon himself) excuses the borrower or bailee from the performance of his promise to redeliver the chattel.

* * *

In none of these cases is the promise in words other than positive, nor is there any express stipulation that the destruction of the person or thing shall excuse the performance; but that excuse is by law implied, because from the nature of the contract it is apparent that the parties contracted on the basis of the continued existence of the particular person or chattel. In the present case, looking at the whole contract, we find that the parties contracted on the basis of the continued existence of the Music Hall at the time when the concerts were to be given; that being essential to their performance.

We think, therefore, that the Music Hall having ceased to exist, without fault of either party, both parties are excused, the plaintiffs from taking the gardens and paying the money, the defendants from performing their promise to give the use of the Hall and Gardens and other things. Consequently the rule must be absolute to enter the verdict for the defendants.

Rule absolute.

QUESTIONS AND NOTES

1. Questions about the facts of this case
    1.1. Was there any contract language that was relevant to the decision?
    1.2. How was the concert hall destroyed? Was that relevant to the decision?
    1.3. Could Caldwell build a new concert hall before June 17? Would that be relevant to the decision?
2. Questions about the law
    2.1. What legal device ("fiction") did the court use to find that both parties are excused from performing?
    2.2. Today, insurance companies sell not only fire insurance that covers the cost of rebuilding but also "business interruption" insurance that covers losses due to any business interruption resulting from

the fire. What result in *Taylor v. Caldwell* if Caldwell had bought such a policy?

2.3.   Caldwell later contracts with Epstein Construction Co. (ECC) to build a new concert hall. After ECC begins work but before the concert hall construction is complete, lightning strikes again and fire destroys the construction. ECC has other more rewarding construction contracts that it would prefer to do. Does destruction of the concert hall excuse ECC's performance?

3.   Notes

In a recent law review article, Professor Nancy Kim provides the following analysis of *Taylor v. Caldwell*:

The court decided that the continued existence of the music hall was an implied condition of the contract and because the music hall was destroyed, Caldwell's performance was excused. The "implied condition" was a tacit assumption of the parties. The invalidity of the parties' tacit assumption reveals an absence of cognitive intent for both Taylor and Caldwell. Caldwell would not have agreed to rent out the music hall, and Taylor would not have agreed to rent it, if either had known the hall would be destroyed by fire. Furthermore, each party lacked contextual purposive intent to enter into the actual contract because the fire destroyed both parties' ability to perform. In other words, Caldwell never had the intent to enter into an agreement that required him to deliver possession of a non-existent structure, or one that needed to be entirely rebuilt. Similarly, Taylor lacked contextual purposive intent to enter into the contract because he wanted to rent the premises to stage music performances—something he could no longer do after the fire. He lacked contextual purposive intent because an event subsequent to the formation of the contract—the fire—destroyed his reason for renting the premises. The same circumstances—the fire and the subsequent destruction of the music hall—defeated the contractual intent of both parties.

Nancy Kim, *Mistakes, Changed Circumstances and Intent*, 56 U. Kan. L. Rev. 473 (2008). Do you agree with Professor Kim's analysis of *Taylor v. Caldwell*? Does Judge Posner use a similar analysis in the next case.

WISCONSIN ELECTRIC POWER CO. v. UNION PACIFIC RAILROAD CO.

United States Court of Appeals, Seventh Circuit
557 F.3d 504 (2009)

POSNER, CIRCUIT JUDGE.

WEPCO, an electric utility that is the plaintiff in this diversity suit for breach of contract (governed by Wisconsin law), appeals from the grant of summary judgment to the defendant, the Union Pacific railroad. The contract was for the transportation of coal to WEPCO from coal mines in Colorado between the beginning of 1999 and the end of 2005. The appeal presents two issues: whether a force majeure clause in the contract authorized the railroad to increase its rate for shipping the coal, and whether the railroad breached its duty of good-faith performance of its contractual obligations by failing to ship the tonnage requested by WEP-CO on railcars supplied by the railroad.

The doctrine of impossibility in the common law of contracts excuses performance when it would be unreasonably costly (and sometimes downright impossible) for a party to carry out its contractual obligations. If the doctrine is successfully invoked, the contract is rescinded without liability. The standard explanation for the doctrine is that nonperformance is not a breach if it is caused by a circumstance "the non-occurrence of which was a 'basic assumption on which the contract was made.'" Restatement (Second) of Contracts, introductory note to ch. 11, preceding § 261 (1981), quoting UCC § 2–615. But this explanation leaves unexplained why parties to a contract would have assumed that a condition would not occur that has occurred. Was it just a lack of foresight? Or is the idea behind the doctrine, rather, that the parties, had they negotiated with reference to the contingency that has come to pass and has made performance infeasible or fearfully burdensome, would have excused performance? The latter is the more promising line of inquiry, and is the line we took in Northern Indiana Public Service Co. v. Carbon County Coal Co., 799 F.2d 265, 276–78 (7th Cir.1986), where we said that "the proper question in an 'impossibility' case is * * * whether [the promisor's] nonperformance should be excused because the parties, if they had thought about the matter, would have wanted to assign the risk of the contingency that made performance impossible or uneconomical to the promisor or to the promisee; if to the latter, the promisor is excused." "Impossibility" is thus a doctrine "for shifting risk to the party better able to bear it, either because he is in a better position to prevent the risk from materializing or because he can better reduce the disutility of the risk (as by insuring) if the risk does occur."

Liability for breach of contract is strict, Globe Refining Co. v. Landa Cotton Oil Co., 190 U.S. 540, 543–44, 23 S.Ct. 754, 47 L.Ed. 1171 (1903) (Holmes, J.); Restatement, supra, introductory note to ch. 11, preceding § 261, which makes the performing party an insurer against the consequences of his failing to perform, even if the failure is not his fault. But formal insurance contracts contain limits of coverage, and the impossibility doctrine in effect caps the "insurance" coverage that strict liability for breach of contract provides. The analogy is to a provision in a fire insurance contract that excepts from coverage a fire caused by an act of war. So it is no surprise that in Allanwilde Transport Corp. v. Vacuum Oil Co., 248 U.S. 377, 385–86, 39 S.Ct. 147, 63 L.Ed. 312 (1919), the doctrine of impossibility was successfully invoked when a wartime embargo prevented the performance of a shipping contract because the ship could not complete its voyage.

Parties can, however, contract around the doctrine, because it is just a gap filler, a guess at what the parties would have provided in their contract had they thought about the contingency that has arisen and has prevented performance or made it much more costly. As Holmes explained, "the consequences of a binding promise at common law are not affected by the degree of power which the promisor possesses over the promised event. * * * In the case of a binding promise that it shall rain to-morrow, the immediate legal effect of what the promisor does is, that he takes the risk of the event, within certain defined limits, as between himself and the promisee. He does no more when he promises to deliver a bale of cotton." O.W. Holmes, Jr., The Common Law 299–300 (1881); The key is binding promise. To defeat the application of the doctrine of impossibility the contract must state that the promisor must pay damages even if he commits a breach that could not have been prevented at a reasonable cost.

Modern contracting parties often do contract around the doctrine, though not by making the promisor liable for any and every failure to perform-rather by specifying the failures that will excuse performance. The clauses in which they do this are called force majeure ("superior force") clauses. The name suggests a purpose similar to that of the impossibility doctrine. But it is essential to an understanding of this case that a force majeure clause must always be interpreted in accordance with its language and context, like any other provision in a written contract, rather than with reference to its name. It is not enough to say that the parties must have meant that performance would be excused if it would be "impossible" within the meaning that the word has been given in cases interpreting the common law doctrine.

The provision at issue in this case does not specify circumstances that would make performance impossible or infeasible in any sense, and does not excuse the performing party (the railroad) from performing the contract. The provision is part of Article XI of the contract, and some of the other provisions in the article do specify contingencies that would excuse performance, including certain "acts of God." But the provision at issue merely provides that if the railroad is prevented by "an event of Force Majeure" from reloading its empty cars (after it has delivered coal to WEPCO) with iron ore destined for Geneva, Utah, it can charge the higher rate that the contract makes applicable to shipments that do not involve backhauling * * * For example, the rate for coal shipped from one of the Colorado mines to WEPCO was specified as $13.20 per ton if there was a backhaul shipment but $15.63 if there was not. The reason for the higher rate, obviously, was that if the railroad's cars were empty on the trip back to Colorado, the railroad would obtain no revenue on that trip; it would be underutilizing the cars.

The iron ore that the railroad's freight train would have picked up in Minnesota on its way back was intended for a steel mill in Utah owned by the Geneva Steel company. (The mill had been built during World War II well inland because of fear that the Japanese might attack the West Coast.) The company was bankrupt when the parties signed the contract. It was still operating, but obviously might cease to do so; hence the provision. Why the parties used the term "force majeure," rather than simply providing that the railroad could charge the higher rate if the steel company stopped buying iron ore, has not been explained. More careful drafting might have averted this lawsuit.

In November 2001 the steel mill shut down, never to reopen. It was closed for good in February 2004. A couple of months after that final closing the railroad wrote WEPCO to declare "an event of Force Majeure" and that henceforth it would be charging WEPCO the higher rate applicable to shipments without a backhaul. It did not attempt to make the rate change retroactive. Had it invoked the force majeure clause when the steel mill first shut down, WEPCO would have incurred an extra $7 million in shipping charges between then and the belated declaration of force majeure.

Despite this windfall, WEPCO argues that the railroad broke the contract by invoking the force majeure clause when it did. The fact that the railroad didn't invoke the clause earlier shows that the shutting down of the steel mill did not prevent the railroad from charging the low, backhaul rate. Well of course not; it is never "impossible" to offer a discount. But what the contract says is that the railroad may charge the higher rate if it is prevented from reloading its cars, rather than if it is prevented from charging a lower rate.

WEPCO points out that Article XI requires prompt notification of an event of force majeure and also requires the invoker to make reasonable efforts to eliminate or abate the force majeure. It argues that the railroad violated its duty of prompt notice and by doing so waived its right to declare a force majeure. But another clause in the contract provides that a failure of a party to insist on a right that the contract confers on it shall not be deemed a waiver. That scotches WEPCO's argument except insofar as it wishes to complain not about the declaration of force majeure as such but simply about the breach of the duty of prompt notice.

A "no waiver" clause is appropriate in a complex multiyear contract that imposes (as we will see) duties of performance on both parties, as distinct from a simple sales contract in which one party performs and the other pays. If a party lost a contract right through waiver by failing to assert it as soon as it was violated, the process of amicable adjustment of contingencies bound to arise in the course of performing the contract would be impeded by premature assertion of legal claims. When the parties were getting along and there was some possibility that Geneva Steel would not be liquidated, the railroad was disinclined to stand on its rights. But at about the same time that the steel mill closed irrevocably, WEPCO threatened the railroad with a lawsuit over alleged poor service. Since WEPCO was standing on its claimed rights, the railroad decided to stand on its own. We cannot see anything wrong in that. * * *

WEPCO argues that the railroad made no reasonable effort to abate the force majeure, as the contract required. The railroad did not explore the possibility of finding some other commodity, besides iron ore, to ship west. (It couldn't be iron ore, because Geneva Steel was the only buyer of iron ore served by the railroad.) But that is not what the duty of abatement contemplated. The event of force majeure—the event that the railroad was required to exert reasonable efforts to abate—was an event that prevented the railroad from reloading its cars with iron ore for the trip back west.

Had Geneva Steel owed the railroad some small amount of money and begged it to forbear to sue to collect because that would force the company into bankruptcy, forbearance to sue might conceivably be a reasonable effort to avoid the railroad's having to send its trains west without a backhaul, and therefore an effort that the railroad was obligated to undertake. But there is no suggestion of that. WEPCO's argument, rather, is that the railroad should have looked for something else to carry back in its trains. But that would have placed on the railroad a burdensome open-ended duty to explore the possibility of reconfiguring its operations, which would have required searching for, finding, and making contracts with other shippers and perhaps purchasing or renting railcars optimized to carry those shippers' commodities. Disputes over the adequacy of the railroad's efforts would present unmanageable issues for litigation. This cannot*510 have been what the abatement clause envisaged.

The point about unmanageability goes far to resolve the other issue presented by the appeal. Article VI of the contract required WEPCO to notify the railroad monthly of how many tons of coal (within the maximum tonnage specified by the contract) it wanted shipped the next month, and "the parties agree to make good faith reasonable efforts to meet the Monthly Shipping Schedule." Nowhere did the contract require the railroad to comply with the schedule; it merely had to make, in good faith, a reasonable effort to do so. Article VII did require the railroad to transport tonnages specified by WEPCO, but only if WEPCO supplied the railcars for the shipment, and it did not; the railroad did; during the period in which WEPCO charges that the railroad was acting in bad faith, the railroad transported in its own cars 84 percent of the total shipments of coal requested by WEPCO.

Not enough, argues WEPCO. Without specifying the minimum percentage that would have demonstrated good faith, it argues that it would have exceeded 90 percent. It says that the railroad shipped less because it had other customers who paid higher rates. WEPCO invokes the legal duty of good faith in the performance of a contract. The duty entails the avoidance of conduct such as "evasion of the spirit of the bargain, lack of diligence and slacking off, willful rendering of imperfect performance, abuse of a power to specify terms, and interference with or failure to cooperate in the other party's performance." Foseid v. State Bank, 197 Wis.2d 772, 541 N.W.2d 203, 213 (App.1995).

But the duty of good faith does not require your putting one of your customers ahead of the others, even if the others are paying you more. "Parties are not prevented from protecting their respective economic interests." John Edward Murray, Jr., Murray on Contracts § 90, p. 501 (4th ed.2001). As we explained, interpreting Wisconsin law in Market Street Associates Ltd. Partnership v. Frey, 941 F.2d 588, 594 (7th Cir. 1991), "even after you have signed a contract, you are not obliged to become an altruist toward the other party and relax the terms if he gets into trouble in performing his side of the bargain."

Another customer of the railroad might be paying a very high rate because it had an urgent need for service-so could it charge the railroad with bad faith if it had a contract similar to the railroad's contract with WEPCO and the railroad told it, very sorry, but we cannot serve you; it is not that we love you less, but that we love WEPCO more? "A duty of good faith does not mean that a party vested with a clear right is obligated to exercise that right to its own detriment for the purpose of benefiting another party to the contract." Rio Algom Corp. v. Jimco Ltd., 618 P.2d 497, 505 (Utah 1980). And it certainly doesn't mean exercising that right to the detriment of another party with which it has a contract. Again WEPCO invites the court to undertake an unmanageable judicial task-that of working out an equitable allocation of Union Pacific's railcars among its various customers.

Affirmed.

QUESTIONS, AND CONNECTIONS

1. Questions about the facts of the case
    1.1. Who is suing whom for what? Who is invoking the doctrine of impossibility?
    1.2. Is Union Pacific still delivering coal?
    1.3. Is it impossible for Union Pacific to be delivering coal at the original contract rates?
2. Questions about the law
    2.1. What is a force majeure clause?
    2.2. Would this case have been decided differently if the contract did not have the force majeure clause?
    2.3. What is the relationship between a force majeure clause and impossibility? If a contract has a force majeure clause, can a party to that contract still invoke impossibility?
    2.4. Like Professor Kim (and unlike *Taylor v. Caldwell*), Judge Posner uses the term "impossibility." Judge Posner also makes use of the *Restatement (Second) of Contracts* which uses the term "impracticable" instead of "impossible."

261. Discharge By Supervening Impracticability

Where, after a contract is made, a party's performance is made impracticable without his fault by the occurrence of an

event the non-occurrence of which was a basic assumption on which the contract was made, his duty to render that performance is discharged, unless the language or the circumstances indicate the contrary.

Restatement 261 comment d explains: "Although the rule stated in this Section is sometimes phrased in terms of "impossibility," it has long been recognized that it may operate to discharge a party's duty even though the event has not made performance absolutely impossible. This Section, therefore, uses "impracticable," the term employed by Uniform Commercial Code § 2–615(a), to describe the required extent of the impediment to performance. Performance may be impracticable because extreme and unreasonable difficulty, expense, injury, or loss to one of the parties will be involved. . . . . However, "impracticability" means more than "impracticality." A mere change in the degree of difficulty or expense due to such causes as increased wages, prices of raw materials, or costs of construction, unless well beyond the normal range, does not amount to impracticability since it is this sort of risk that a fixed-price contract is intended to cover. Furthermore, a party is expected to use reasonable efforts to surmount obstacles to performance (see § 205), and a performance is impracticable only if it is so in spite of such efforts.

> Did you ever use the word "impracticable" before this? Can you use it now? Was performance in *Taylor v. Caldwell* "impossible" or merely "impracticable"? Was performance in this case "impossible" or merely "impracticable"?

2.5.   Should the parties in *Taylor v. Caldwell* have foreseen that the concert hall would be destroyed? Under the *Restatement* provision set out above, is it necessary that the occurrence be unforeseen?

3.   Connections

3.1.   Impracticability and mistake: Professor Mark Gergen has stated "The doctrines on impracticability [and] mistake share a feature that is unusual in contract law. They give courts the power to excuse or modify terms in contracts between sophisticated parties who bargained over the terms of the contract with equal power and information." Mark Gergen, *A Defense of Judicial Reconstruction of Contracts*, 71 Ind. L.J. 45, 45 (1995). Do you agree? Do sophisticated parties have better abilities to predict and account for the future than unsophisticated people? Or is that the wrong question to ask?

3.2.   *Wisconsin Electric Power* and *Locke*: Is the discussion of "good faith" in this case consistent with the discussion of "good faith" in the *Locke* case?

3.3.   *Wisconsin Electric Power* and *May Center*: Is the discussion of nonwaiver clauses in this case consistent with the discussion in the *May Center* case?

The previous two cases involved changes in circumstances that affected the defendant's ability to perform. The next case, *Krell v. Henry*, involves a change in circumstances that affects the value of the performance to the plaintiff.

✶KRELL v. HENRY

Frustration of Purpose

Court of Appeal
2 K.B. 740 [1903]

Appeal from a decision of DARLING, J. The plaintiff, Paul Krell, sued the defendant, C.S. Henry for £50, being the balance of a sum of £75, for which the defendant had agreed to hire a flat at 56A, Pall Mall on the days of June 26 and 27, for the purpose of viewing the processions to be held in connection with the coronation of His Majesty [Edward VII]. The defendant denied his liability, and counterclaimed for the return of the sum of £25, which had been paid as a deposit, on the ground that, the processions not having taken place owing to the serious illness of the King, there had been a total failure of consideration for the contract entered into by him.

The facts [were undisputed]. The plaintiff on leaving the country in March, 1902, left instructions with his solicitor to let his suite of chambers at 56A, Pall Mall on such terms and for such period (not exceeding six months) as he thought proper. On June 17, 1902, the defendant noticed an announcement in the windows of the plaintiff's flat to the effect that windows to view the coronation processions were to be let. The defendant interviewed the housekeeper on the subject, when it was pointed out to him what a good view of the processions could be obtained from the premises, and he eventually agreed with the housekeeper to take the suite for the two days in question for a sum of £75.

On June 20, the defendant wrote the following letter to the plaintiff's solicitor:

"I am in receipt of yours of the 18th instant, inclosing form of agreement for the suite of chambers on the third floor at 56A, Pall Mall, which I have agreed to take for the two days the 26th and 27th instant, for the sum of £75. For reasons given you I cannot enter into the agreement, but as arranged over the telephone I inclose herewith cheque for £25, as deposit, and will thank you to confirm to me that I shall have the entire use of these rooms during the days (not the nights) of the 26th and 27th instant. You may rely that every care will be taken of the premises and their contents. On the 24th inst. I will pay the balance, viz., £50, to complete the £75 agreed upon."

On the same day the defendant received the following reply from the plaintiff's solicitor:

"I am in receipt of your letter of to-day's date inclosing cheque for £25 deposit on your agreeing to take Mr. Krell's chambers on the third floor at 56A, Pall Mall for the two days, the 26th and 27th June, and I confirm the agreement that you are to have the entire use of these rooms during the days (but not the nights), the balance, £50, to be paid to me on Tuesday next the 24th instant."

The processions not having taken place [on] June 26 and 27, the defendant declined to pay the balance of £50 alleged to be due from him under the contract in writing of June 20 constituted by the above two letters. Hence the present action. Darling J., on August 11, 1902, held, upon the authority of Taylor v. Caldwell, 3 B. & S. 826, and The Moorcock, (1889) 14 P.D. 64, that there was an implied condition in the contract that the procession should take place, and gave judgment for the defendant on the claim and counter-claim. The plaintiff appealed.

Vaughan Williams, L.J. The real question in this case is the extent of the application in English law of the principle of the Roman law which has been adopted and acted on in many English decisions, and notably in the case of Taylor v. Caldwell, 3 B. & S. 826. That case at least makes it clear that "where, from the nature of the contract, it appears that the parties must from the beginning have known that it could not be fulfilled unless, when the time for the fulfillment of the contract arrived, some particular specified thing continued to exist, so that when entering into the contract they must have contemplated such continued existence as the foundation of what was to be done; there, in the absence of any express or implied warranty that the thing shall exist, the contract is not to be considered a positive contract, but as subject to an implied condition that the parties shall be excused in case, before breach, performance becomes impossible from the perishing of the thing without default of the contractor."

* * *

I do not think that [the principle] is limited to cases in which the event causing the impossibility of performance is the destruction or nonexistence of some thing which is the subject-matter of the contract or of some condition or state of things expressly specified as a condition of it. I think that you first have to ascertain, not necessarily from the terms of the contract, but, if required, from necessary inferences, drawn from surrounding circumstances recognized by both contracting parties, what is the substance of the contract, and then to ask the question whether that substantial contract needs for its foundation the assumption of the existence of a particular state of things. If it does, this will limit the operation of the general words, and in such case, if the contract becomes impossible of performance by reason of the nonexistence of the state of things assumed by both contracting parties as the foundation of the contract, there will be no breach of the contract thus limited.

Now what are the facts of the present case? The contract is contained in [the] two letters of June 20. * * * These letters do not mention the coronation, but speak merely of the taking of Mr. Krell's chambers, or, rather, of the use of them. * * * [T]he plaintiff [had] exhibited on his premises, third floor, 56A, Pall Mall, an announcement to the effect that windows to view the Royal coronation procession were to be let, and [defendant] was induced by that announcement to apply to the housekeeper on the premises, who said that the owner was willing to let the suite of rooms for the purpose of seeing the Royal procession for both days, but not nights, of June 26 and 27. In my judgment the use of the rooms was let and taken for the purpose of seeing the Royal procession. It was not a demise of the rooms, or even an agreement to let and take the rooms. It is a license to use rooms for a particular purpose and none other. And in my judgment the taking place of those processions on the days proclaimed along the proclaimed route, which passed 56A, Pall Mall, was regarded by both contracting parties as the foundation of the contract; and I think that it cannot reasonably be supposed to have been in the contemplation of the contracting parties, when the contract was made, that the coronation would not be held on the proclaimed days, or the processions not take place on those days along the proclaimed route. * * *

It was suggested in the course of the argument that if the occurrence, on the proclaimed days, of the coronation and the procession in this case were the foundation of the contract, and if the general words are thereby limited or qualified, so that in the event of the nonoccurrence of the coronation and procession along the proclaimed route they would discharge both parties from further performance of the contract, it would follow that if a cabman was engaged to take some one to Epsom on Derby Day at a suitable enhanced price for such a journey, say £10, both parties to the contract would be discharged in the contingency of the race at Epsom for some reason becoming impossible; but I do not think this follows, for I do not think that in the cab case the happening of the race would be the foundation of the contract. No doubt the purpose of the engager would be to go to see the Derby, and the price would be proportionately high; but the cab had no special qualifications for the purpose which led to the selection of the cab for this particular occasion. Any other cab would have done as well. Moreover, I think that, under the cab contract, the hirer, even if the race went off, could have said, "Drive me to Epsom; I will pay you the agreed sum; you have nothing to do with the purpose for which I hired the cab," and that if the cabman refused he would have been guilty of a breach of contract, there being nothing to qualify his promise to drive the hirer to Epsom on a particular day. Whereas in the case of the coronation, there is not merely the purpose of the hirer to see the coronation procession, but it is the coronation procession and the relative position of the rooms which is the basis of the contract as much for the lessor as the hirer; and I think that if the King, before the coronation day and after the contract, had died, the hirer could not have insisted on having the rooms on the days named. It could not in the cab case be reasonably said that seeing the Derby race was the foundation of the contract. * * * Whereas in the present case, where the rooms were offered and taken, by reason of their peculiar suitability from the position of the rooms for a view of the coronation procession, surely the view of the coronation procession was the foundation of the contract, which is a very different thing from the purpose of the man who engaged the cab—namely, to see the race—being held to be the foundation of the contract. Each case must be judged by its own circumstances. In each case one must ask oneself first, what, having regard to all the circumstances, was the foundation of the contract? Secondly, was the performance of the contract prevented? Thirdly, was the event which prevented the performance of the contract of such a character that it cannot reasonably be said to have been in the contemplation of the parties at the date of the contract? If all these questions are answered in the affirmative (as I think they should be in this case), I think both parties are discharged from further performance of the contract. I think that the coronation procession was the foundation of this contract, and that the non-happening of it prevented the performance of the contract. * * * The test seems to be whether the event which causes the impossibility was or might have been anticipated and guarded against. It seems difficult to say, in a case where both parties anticipate the happening of an event, which anticipation is the foundation of the contract, that either party must be taken to have anticipated, and ought to have guarded against, the event which prevented the performance of the contract. * * *

I myself am clearly of opinion that in this case, where we have to ask ourselves whether the object of the contract was frustrated by the nonhappening of the coronation and its procession on the days proclaimed, parol evidence is admissible to shew that the subject of the contract was rooms to view the coronation procession, and was so to the knowledge of both parties. When once this is established, I see no difficulty whatever in the case. It is not essential to the application of the principle of Taylor v. Caldwell that the direct subject of the contract should perish or fail to be in existence at the date of performance of the contract. It is sufficient if a state of things or condition expressed in the contract and essential to its performance perishes or fails to be in existence at that time. In the present case the condition which fails and prevents the achievement of that which was, in the contemplation of both parties, the foundation of the contract, is not expressly mentioned either as a condition of the contract or the purpose of it; but I think for the reasons which I have given that the principle of Taylor v. Caldwell ought to be applied. This disposes of the plaintiff's claim for £50 unpaid balance of the price agreed to be paid for the use of the rooms. The defendant at one time set up a cross-claim for the return of the £25 he paid at the date of the contract. As that claim is now withdrawn it is unnecessary to say anything about it. I have only to add that the facts of this case do not bring it within the principle laid down in Stubbs v. Holywell Ry. Co., L.R., 2 Ex. 311, that in the case of contracts falling directly within the rule of Taylor v. Caldwell the subsequent impossibility does not affect rights already acquired, because the defendant had the whole of June 24 to pay the balance, and the public announcement that the coronation and processions would not take place on the proclaimed days was made early on the morning of the 24th, and no cause of action could accrue till the end of that day. * * *

Appeal dismissed.

———————

QUESTIONS AND NOTE

1. Questions about the facts of this case

    1.1. At the time of the contract, why did Henry want to hire the flat (English for rent an apartment)? Did Krell know Henry's purpose?

    1.2. Why did Henry later decide he did not want the use of the flat, but wanted instead to be excused from performing?

    1.3. Who gets the £25 that Henry paid? What if Henry had paid the full £75 up front?

2. Questions about the law

    2.1. Just as *Taylor v. Caldwell* is viewed as the first "impossibility" case even though it never uses the word "impossibility," *Krell* is regarded as the first frustration of purpose case even though it never uses the phrase "frustration of purpose." How is frustration of purpose similar to impossibility and impracticability? How is it different?

    2.2. Does this court read *Taylor* correctly?

    2.3. What makes the Epsom Derby hypothetical in the *Krell* opinion different from the facts in *Krell*?

    2.4. In Charlottesville, Virginia, all the hotels jack up their room rates around graduation time, and require a minimum two-day, non-refundable deposit. Six months before graduation, Ponoroff reserves a room in Charlottesville around graduation since he wants to use the UVA law school dean's graduation speech at the University of Arizona College of Law graduation ceremonies the following week. Ponoroff pays the two-day minimum. The day before graduation, a tornado sweeps through the town, leaving a trail of desolation and some disconsolate students—the school cancels graduation. Can Ponoroff get his money back? What if he was traveling to Charlottesville not to attend graduation, but rather to eat at Eppie's, http://eppiesrestaurant.com/, the wonderful restaurant in the Downtown Mall in Charlottesville that belongs to Epstein's sons, and was not affected by the tornado?

3. Note

    "The doctrine of frustration of purpose is nearly identical to the doctrine of impossibility and has been referred to as its "companion rule." The difference is that with the frustration of purpose doctrine, "performance remains possible but the expected value of the performance to the party seeking to be excused has been destroyed" by the supervening event. The third changed circumstances doctrine, *506 impracticability, has been referred to as a "catch-all" for situations where performance is physically possible but would entail a much higher cost than originally expected. As Richard Posner and Andrew Rosenfield have noted, "[t]here is thus no functional distinction between impossibility and frustration cases on the one hand and impracticability cases on the other." With all three doctrines, the central issue concerns the allocation of risk, independent of fault, of the event giving rise to the claim of impossibility, frustration of purpose, or impracticability. The allocation of risk, however, is not always readily determinable."

Nancy Kim, *Mistakes, Changed Circumstances and Intent*, 56 U. KAN. L. REV. 473 (2008). Consider Professor Kim's comments as you read the next case in which the court considered both impossibility and frustration of purpose arguments.

MEL FRANK TOOL & SUPPLY, INC. v. DI–CHEM CO.

Supreme Court of Iowa
580 N.W.2d 802 (1998)

LAVORATO, JUSTICE.

City authorities informed a lessee, a chemical distributor, that it could no longer use its leased premises to store its hazardous chemicals because of a recently enacted ordinance. The lessee vacated the premises, and the lessor sued for breach of the lease and for damages to the premises. The district court awarded the lessor judgment for unpaid rent and for damages to the premises. The lessee appeals, contending that the district court should have found that the city's actions constituted extraordinary circumstances rendering the performance of the lease impossible. * * * We affirm.

I.   Facts.

Di–Chem Company is a chemical distributor. In May 1994, Di–Chem began negotiating with Mel Frank Tool & Supply, Inc. to lease a storage and distribution facility in Council Bluffs, Iowa. Mel Frank's real estate agent handled the negotiations so there were no actual face-to-face negotiations between the parties. However, a day before the lease was executed, Mel Frank's owner, Dennis Frank, talked with Di–Chem representatives who were touring the premises. Frank asked them what Di–Chem was going to be selling and was told chemicals. The agent brought the lease to Frank for his signature.

The lease appears to be an Iowa State Bar Association form. *See* Iowa State Bar Association Official Form No. 164. The lease was to start June 1, 1994 and end May 31, 1997. The lease limited Di–Chem's use of the premises to "storage and distribution."

Some of the chemicals Di–Chem distributes are considered "hazardous material." There was no testimony that Dennis Frank was aware of this at the time the lease was executed. A Di–Chem representative, who was present during the earlier-mentioned conversation with Dennis Frank, testified that hazardous materials did not come up in the conversation.

The lease contained several provisions that bear on the issues in this appeal. One requires Di–Chem to "make no unlawful use of the premises and * * * to comply with all * * * City Ordinances." There is also a destruction-of-premises provision that allows either party to terminate the lease under certain circumstances.

On July 21, 1995, the city's fire chief and several other city authorities inspected the premises. Following the inspection, the city's fire marshal wrote Di–Chem, stating:

> At the time of the inspection the building was occupied as Hazardous Materials Storage. I have given you a copy of 1994 Uniform Fire Code, which the City has adopted, covering Hazardous Material Storage. As you can see the building does not comply with the Code requirements which creates Health and Life Safety Hazards. The Hazardous Materials must be removed within seven (7) days to eliminate the hazard.

* * * Both Frank and Di–Chem representatives testified they understood the letter to mean that if these deficiencies were eliminated, Di–Chem could continue to store hazardous material. There was testimony that the changes in the code occurred after Di–Chem took occupancy of the premises. * * *

Thereafter Dennis Frank and Di–Chem representatives met with city officials about what it would take to correct the various code deficiencies to allow Di–Chem to continue storing hazardous materials. Di–Chem representatives and Dennis Frank briefly considered bringing the building up to code. There was talk about the possibility of Di–Chem splitting the costs with Mel Frank, but Dennis Frank felt the cost was prohibitive.

On October 23 Di–Chem notified Mel Frank by letter of its intention to vacate the premises by the end of October. The letter in part stated: "The city's position that we cannot legally store all of our inventory at this site prior to extensive alteration of the building makes the structure useless to us as a chemical warehouse." True to its word, Di–Chem vacated the premises.

II. Proceedings.

Later, Mel Frank sued for breach of the lease and for damages to the property. Di–Chem asserted several affirmative defenses: mutual mistake, * * * and impossibility. * * *

The court found for Mel Frank. The court found that Mel Frank had "no reason to believe or [know] that chemicals classified as hazardous would be stored in the warehouse." The court relied on the testimony of Norm Wirtala, an officer of Di–Chem:

> Mr. Wirtala testified he would be in a "superior position of knowledge" concerning the items to be stored in the building and that he had a general understanding of fire code requirements for the storage of hazardous materials due to his experience in the business although [neither] he nor his agents claimed to have examined the Council

Bluffs' fire codes as they may have related to hazardous materials and building specifications for storage of hazardous materials.

With this the court concluded that there was:

> clear and conclusive [evidence] that the plaintiff made no representations to the defendant that the warehouse was suitable for any specific purpose, nor were any discussions or representations made concerning the character of the products to be stored by the defendant. Consequently, this Court concludes the lease was breached by the defendants for vacating the premises and failing to pay the balance of the lease term as required by its terms and conditions and the defendants owe the sum of $55,913.77 for rent [and $2,357.00 for damage to the property].

> * * *

IV.   Impossibility of Performance.

A.   The law. The introduction to the Restatement (Second) of Contracts covers impossibility of performance but with a different title: impracticability of performance and frustration of purpose. *See* Restatement (Second) of Contracts ch. 11, at 309 (1981) [hereinafter Restatement]. According to the Restatement,

> Contract liability is strict liability. * * * The obligor is therefore liable in damages for breach of contract even if he is without fault and even if circumstances have made the contract more burdensome or less desirable than he had anticipated. * * * The obligor who does not wish to undertake so extensive an obligation may contract for a lesser one by using one of a variety of common clauses: * * * he may reserve a right to cancel the contract. * * * The extent of his obligation then depends on the application of the rules of interpretation. * * *

Id.

Even though the obligor has not restricted his or her obligation by agreement, a court may still grant relief: "An extraordinary circumstance may make performance so vitally different from what was reasonably to be expected as to alter the essential nature of that performance." *Id.* In these circumstances, "the court must determine whether justice requires a departure from the general rule that the obligor bear the risk that the contract may become more burdensome or less desirable." Restatement (Second) of Contracts ch. 11, at 310 (1981). Whether extraordinary circumstances exist justifying discharge is a question of law for the court. *Id.*

The Restatement recognizes three distinct grounds for the discharge of the obligor's contractual duty:

> First, the obligor may claim that some circumstance has made his own performance impracticable. * * * Second, the obligor may claim that some circumstance has so destroyed the value to him of the other party's performance as to frustrate his own purpose in making the

contract. * * * Third, the obligor may claim that he will not receive the agreed exchange for the obligee's duty to render that agreed exchange, on the ground of either impracticability or frustration.

Id.

The rationale behind the doctrines of impracticability and frustration is whether the nonoccurrence of the circumstance was a basic assumption on which the contract was made. Restatement (Second) of Contracts ch. 11, at 310–311 (1981). The parties need not have been conscious of alternatives for them to have had a "basic assumption." Restatement (Second) of Contracts ch. 11, at 311 (1981). The Restatement gives an example: Where an artist contracts to paint a painting and dies, the artist's death is an "event the nonoccurrence of which was a basic assumption on which the contract was made, even though the parties never consciously addressed themselves to that possibility." *Id.* * * *

B. Discharge by supervening frustration. For reasons that follow, we think the facts of this case fall within the parameters of section 265 of the Restatement. Section 265 provides:

> Where, after a contract is made, a party's principal purpose is substantially frustrated without his fault by the occurrence of an event the nonoccurrence of which was a basic assumption on which the contract was made, his remaining duties to render performance are discharged, *unless the language or the circumstances indicate the contrary.*

(Emphasis added.) As mentioned, this is one of the three grounds the Restatement recognizes for discharging the obligor's contractual duty. *See id.* ch. 11, at 310.

The rule deals with the problem that arises when a change in circumstances makes one party's performance virtually worthless to the other, frustrating the purpose in making the contract. *Id.* § 265 cmt. a, at 335. The obligor's contractual obligation is discharged only if three conditions are met:

> First, the purpose that is frustrated must have been a principal purpose of that party in making the contract. It is not enough that he had in mind some specific object without which he would not have made the contract. The object must be so completely the basis of the contract that, as both parties understand, without it the transaction would make little sense. Second, the frustration must be substantial. It is not enough that the transaction has become less profitable for the affected party or even that he will sustain a loss. The frustration must be so severe that it is not fairly to be regarded as within the risks that he assumed under the contract. Third, the non-occurrence of the frustrating event must have been a basic assumption on which the contract was made. * * * The foreseeability of the event is * * * a factor in that determination, but the mere fact that the event was

foreseeable does not compel the conclusion that its non-occurrence was not such a basic assumption.

Id. * * *

Based on the foregoing authorities, we reach the following conclusions. A subsequent governmental regulation like a statute or ordinance may prohibit a tenant from legally using the premises for its originally intended purpose. In these circumstances, the tenant's purpose is substantially frustrated thereby relieving the tenant from any further obligation to pay rent. The tenant is not relieved from the obligation to pay rent if there is a serviceable use still available consistent with the use provision in the lease. The fact that the use is less valuable or less profitable or even unprofitable does not mean the tenant's use has been substantially frustrated.

C. The merits. It is clear from the pleadings and testimony that Di–Chem was asserting a defense of frustration of purpose. Di–Chem had the burden of persuasion to prove that defense. * * * The district court's decision in favor of Mel Frank is a determination that Di–Chem did not carry its burden on this defense.

Di–Chem produced no evidence that *all* of its inventory of chemicals consisted of hazardous material. In fact, its own correspondence to Mel Frank indicates otherwise. For example, Di–Chem's October 23 letter to Mel Frank stated: "The city's position that we cannot legally store *all* of our inventory at this site prior to extensive alteration of the building makes the structure useless to us as a chemical warehouse." (Emphasis added.) A reasonable inference from this statement is that not all of Di–Chem's inventory consisted of hazardous material. * * * Another Di–Chem representative testified that Di–Chem's product line included industrial chemicals and *food additives*. Presumably, food additives are not hazardous materials.

Given the posture of this appeal, Di–Chem has to establish as a matter of law that its principal purpose for leasing the facility—storing and distributing chemicals—was substantially frustrated by the city's actions. Di–Chem presented no evidence as to the nature of its inventory and what percentage of the inventory consisted of hazardous chemicals. The company also failed to show what its lost profits, if any, would be without the hazardous chemicals. Thus, there is no evidence from which the district court could have found the city's actions substantially frustrated Di–Chem's principal purpose of storing and distributing chemicals. Put another way, there is insufficient evidence that the city's action deprived Di–Chem of the beneficial enjoyment of the property for other uses, *i.e.*, storing and distributing nonhazardous chemicals.

Simply put, Di–Chem failed to establish its affirmative defense of what it has termed impossibility. We must therefore affirm the district court's decision as to this issue.

* * *

VII.   Disposition.

In sum, we conclude Di–Chem has failed to establish—as a matter of law—that it is entitled to relief via its impossibility defense or the terms of the lease. The district court's erroneous finding that the real estate agent represented Di–Chem was harmless. We affirm.

AFFIRMED.

QUESTIONS AND NOTE

1.   Questions about the facts of this case

 1.1.   The court found that the local ordinance was enacted after the lease was signed. Was that significant?

 1.2.   The court said: "The lease appears to be an Iowa State Bar Association form." What does that mean? Did the court rely on any language in the lease contract in deciding this case?

 1.3.   Did the court make a finding that continued storage of Di–Chem's hazardous materials would have been a violation of the local ordinances? Did it have to make such a finding?

2.   Questions about the law

 2.1.   What if the contract had provided that Di–Chem is leasing the building for the sole purpose of storing hazardous materials??

 2.2.   Is this case more like *Taylor*, or more like *Krell*?

 2.3.   If Markell inserts the following clause into a contract with Epstein will he never, ever worry about impracticability or frustration of purpose?

 "Markell and Epstein agree that Epstein hereby assumes all risks, known or unknown, which relate to this contract, and agrees to perform 'come hell or high water', no matter what may happen between the time this agreement is signed and the time this agreement requires Epstein to perform."

3.   Note

 Impracticability vs. Frustration. In *7200 Scottsdale Road General Partners v. Kuhn Farm Machinery, Inc.*, 184 Ariz. 341, 909 P.2d 408 (Ariz. Ct. App. 1995), Kuhn, a United States subsidiary of a French manufacturer of farm machinery, booked a block of rooms at a Phoenix resort. Unfortunately, after formation and before performance, the Gulf War of 1991 broke out, bringing with it enhanced fears of terrorism against international air travel, especially travel to the United States. After a drop in attendance caused by the fact that representatives from the French parent would likely not travel by air to the conference, Kuhn sought to cancel and avoid damages on the ground of "apprehension of impossibility." The trial court agreed, but the appellate court reversed, analyzing the problem as follows:

The trial court held that the contract was discharged under the doctrines of impracticability of performance and frustration of purpose. These are similar but distinct doctrines. *See* Restatement (Second) of Contracts ("Restatement") § 265 cmt. a (1981) (discussing the differences between impracticability of performance and frustration of purpose). Impracticability of performance is, according to the Restatement, utilized when certain events occurring after a contract is made constitute an impediment to performance by either party. *See* Restatement § 261. Traditionally, the doctrine has been applied to three categories of supervening events: (1) death or incapacity of a person necessary for performance, (2) destruction of a specific thing necessary for performance, and (3) prohibition or prevention by law. *Id.* cmt. a.

On the other hand, frustration of purpose deals with "the problem that arises when a change in circumstances makes one party's performance virtually worthless to the other. * * *" Restatement § 265 cmt. a. "Performance remains possible but the expected value of performance to the party seeking to be excused has been destroyed by a fortuitous event, which supervenes to cause an actual but not literal failure of consideration." * * * While the impact on the party adversely affected is the same regardless of which doctrine is applied, frustration of purpose, unlike the doctrine of impracticability, involves no true failure of performance by either party.

Notwithstanding, some cases speak of a contract as "frustrated" when performance has become impossible or impracticable. * * * This usage is inaccurate. "Frustration is not a form of impossibility even under the modern definition of that term, which includes not only cases of physical impossibility but also cases of extreme impracticability of performance." * * *

Turning to the contract between Kuhn and the resort, Kuhn clearly has no claim for impossibility or impracticability. The contract required the resort to reserve and provide guest rooms, meeting rooms, and food and services. In return, Kuhn was required to pay the monies specified in the contract. Kuhn does not allege that it was impossible or impracticable to perform its contractual duty to make payment for the reserved facilities. Rather, it contends that the value of the resort's counter-performance—the furnishing of convention facilities—was rendered worthless because of the Gulf War's effect on convention attendance. This is a claim of frustration of purpose. 184 Ariz. at 345–46.

In applying the standards of frustration of purpose, the court cited *Krell* and previous Arizona frustration cases. After that summary, it noted:

We begin our analysis on this point with the proposition that substantial frustration means frustration "so severe that it is not fairly to be regarded as within the risks * * * assumed under the contract." Restatement § 265 cmt. a. Furthermore, "it is not enough that the transaction has become less profitable for the affected party or even that he will sustain a loss." *Id.* The value of the counter-performance to be rendered by the promisee must be "totally or nearly totally destroyed" by the occurrence of the event. * * *

Here, the conduct of Kuhn and its dealers clearly demonstrates that the value of the resort's counter-performance—the furnishing of its facilities for Kuhn's convention—was not totally or nearly totally destroyed by terrorist threats. In late January, after the United States attacked Iraq and when the threat of terrorism was at its highest level, Kuhn implicitly confirmed the convention date by reducing the reserved room block from 190 to 140. Furthermore, although several dealers canceled in early February, the uncontroverted record demonstrates that over one hundred dealers registered for the convention after the commencement of Operation Desert Storm on January 16, 1991. Thus, the frustration was not so severe that it cannot fairly be regarded as one of the risks assumed by Kuhn under the contract.

* * *

We conclude that Kuhn's cancellation of the convention because of the perceived threat of terrorism was not an objectively reasonable response to an extraordinary and specific threat. The slight risk to domestic air travel by vague threats of terrorism does not equate with the actual and substantial danger of running a naval blockade in time of war. Consequently, Kuhn gains nothing by recasting its frustration of purpose argument as one of "apprehension of impossibility."

Finally, we consider whether Kuhn is entitled to relief on the ground that fear of terrorist activities resulted in less than expected attendance, which in turn made the convention uneconomical. Although economic return may be characterized as the "principal purpose" of virtually all commercial contracts, mere economic impracticality is no defense to performance of a contract. *See* Restatement § 265 cmt. a. ("it is not enough that transaction has become less profitable for affected party or even that he will sustain a loss"). * * * Thus, although the Gulf War's effect on the expected level of attendance may have rendered the convention uneconomical, Kuhn was not on this ground relieved of its contractual obligation.

Id. at 349–51.

Would the Arizona court have ruled the same as the English court in *Krell* if presented with the same facts?

The Arizona Supreme Court and the *Restatement* tell us "Traditionally, the doctrine has been applied to three categories of supervening events: death or incapacity of a person necessary for performance, destruction of a specific thing necessary for performance, and prohibition or prevention by law." In *Taylor v. Caldwell*, we considered "destruction of a specific thing necessary for performance" and in *Mel Frank*, we considered "prohibition or prevention by law." Now let's consider what happens when people die after making, but before performing, a contract.

Under *Restatement (Second) of Contracts* § 262, death or incapacity of a person "necessary for the performance of a duty" excuses the nonperformance. What does "necessary for the performance of a duty" mean? Consider the following three problems:

(1) Before dying, Epstein had borrowed $30,000 from Markell. Although Epstein signed a contract agreeing to repay the loan, he had not repaid the loan at the time of his death. Markell sues Epstein's estate. Again, should Epstein's nonperformance be excused because of the later unforeseen occurrence? If a person's contractual obligations to pay debts disappear when he dies, will lenders and vendors extend credit to really old people like Epstein?

(2) Markell contracts with Epstein to paint his house for $10,000. Epstein dies before painting Markell's house. Markell hires Ponoroff who charges Markell $15,000. Markell sues Epstein's estate for breach of contracts. Should Epstein's nonperformance be executed because of the later unforeseen occurrence?

(3) HBO contracts with Owen Wilson to star in a made-for-television movie, "Law School Legend—The David Epstein Story." Wilson dies before the movie is finished. HBO sues Wilson's estate. Should Wilson's nonperformance be excused?

SECTION 4: "ANTICIPATORY REPUDIATION": OTHER GUY'S UNAMBIGUOUS INDICATION OF AN UNWILLINGNESS OR INABILITY TO PERFORM AS AN EXCUSE FOR NOT DOING WHAT YOU AGREED TO DO

A. STATEMENT AS ANTICIPATORY REPUDIATION

Ponoroff contracts to paint Epstein's house for $5,000. The contract provides that Epstein is to pay Ponoroff within 15 days after Ponoroff finishes work.

Ponoroff is painting his little heart out,[1] more than halfway finished, when Epstein tells him: "Son, you are doing a great job. Best paint work I have ever seen—painting is what you ought to be doing instead of writing a contracts book. Damn shame that I am one of these people who makes a deal and does not do what he agreed to do. I am not going to pay you anything for your work15 days after you finish or ever."

Do you think Ponoroff is going to keep on painting? Shouldn't Epstein's statement—his anticipatory repudiation—excuse Ponoroff from

---

1. *Cf.* AC/DC "Rock Your Heart Out" ("Rock your little heart out"), http://www.sing365.com/music/lyric.nsf/ROCK–YOUR–HEART–OUT-lyrics-AC–DC/90–E1918BBDF702344825686B000DA4CA.

doing what he agreed to do and give Ponoroff the right to sue Epstein for breach of contract without waiting 15 days?

Easy questions. And, *Restatement (Second) of Contracts* § 253 answers both questions "yes," using the word "repudiation" which is defined in *Restatement (Second) of Contracts* § 250. Similarly, section 2–610 answers both questions "yes," using the term "anticipatory repudiation" in both the title and the Official Comment.

The next case, *Hochster v. De La Tour*, provides a similar answer, without using the term "anticipatory repudiation" or the word "repudiation" (even though *Hochster v. De La Tour* is generally regarded as the seminal case on anticipatory repudiation).

HOCHSTER v. DE LA TOUR

Anticipatory Repudiation

Court of Queen's Bench
118 Eng. Rep. 922 (1853)

On the trial, before Erle, J., at the London sittings in last Easter Term, it appeared that plaintiff was a courier, who, in April, 1852, was engaged by defendant to accompany him on a tour, to commence on 1st June 1852, on the terms mentioned in the declaration. On the 11th May 1852, defendant wrote to plaintiff that he had changed his mind, and declined his services. He refused to make him any compensation. The action was commenced on 22d May. The plaintiff, between the commencement of the action and the 1st June, obtained an engagement with Lord Ashburton, on equally good terms, but not commencing till 4th July. The defendant's counsel objected that there could be no breach of the contract before the 1st of June. The learned judge was of a contrary opinion, but reserved leave to enter a nonsuit on this objection. The other questions were left to the jury, who found for plaintiff.

Hugh Hill, in the same Term, obtained a rule Nisi to enter a nonsuit, or arrest the judgment. * * *

LORD CAMPBELL, C.J., now delivered the judgment of the Court.

On this motion in arrest of judgment, the question arises, Whether, if there be an agreement between A. and B., whereby B. engages to employ A. on and from a future day for a given period of time, to travel with him into a foreign country as a courier, and to start with him in that capacity on that day, A. being to receive a monthly salary during the continuance of such service, B. may, before the day, refuse to perform the agreement and break and renounce it, so as to entitle A. before the day to commence an action against B. to recover damages for breach of the agreement; A. having been ready and willing to perform it, till it was broken and renounced by B. The defendant's counsel very powerfully contended that, if the plaintiff was not contented to dissolve the contract, and to abandon all remedy upon it, he was bound to remain ready and willing to perform it till the day when the actual employment as courier in the service of the defendant was to begin; and that there could be no breach of the agreement, before that day, to give a right of action. But it cannot be laid down as a universal rule that, where by agreement an act is to be done on a future day, no action can be brought for a breach of the agreement till the day for doing the act has arrived. If a man promises to marry a woman on a future day, and before that day marries another woman, he is instantly liable to an action for breach of promise of marriage; Short v. Stone, (8 Q.B. 358). If a man contracts to execute a lease on and from a future day for a certain term, and, before that day, executes a lease to another for the same term, he may be immediately sued for breaking the contract; Ford v: Tiley, (6 B. & C. 325). So, if a man contracts to sell and deliver specific goods on a future day, and before the day he sells and delivers them to another, he is immediately liable to an action at the suit of the person with whom he first contracted to sell and deliver them; Bowdef v. Parsons, (10 East, 359). One reason alleged in support of such an action is, that the defendant has, before the day, rendered it impossible for him to perform the contract at the day; but this does not necessarily follow; for, prior to the day fixed for doing the act, the first wife may have died, a surrender of the lease executed might be obtained, and the defendant might have repurchased the goods so as to be in a situation to sell and deliver them to the plaintiff. Another reason may be, that, where there is a contract to do an act on a future day, there is a relation constituted between the parties in the meantime by the contract, and that they impliedly promise that in the meantime neither will do anything to the prejudice of the other inconsistent with that relation. As an example, a man and woman engaged to marry are affianced to one another during the period between the time of the engagement and the celebration of the marriage. In this very case, of traveller and courier, from the day of the hiring till the day when the employment was to begin, they were engaged to each other; and it seems to be a breach of an implied contract if either of them renounces the engagement. This reasoning seems in accordance with the unanimous decision of the Exchequer Chamber in Edlerton v. Emmens, [6 Com. B. 160], which we have followed in subsequent cases in this Court. The declaration in the present case, in alleging a breach, states a great deal more than a passing intention on the part of the defendant which he may repent of, and could only be proved by evidence that he had utterly renounced the contract, or done some act which rendered it impossible for him to perform it. If the plaintiff has no remedy for breach of the contract unless he treats the contract as in force, and acts upon it down to the 1st June 1852, it follows that, till then, he must enter into no employment which will interfere with his promise "to start with the defendant on such travels on the day and year," and that he must then be properly equipped in all aspects as a courier for a three months' tour on the continent of Europe. But it is surely much more rational, and more for the benefit of both parties, that, after the renunciation of the agreement by the defendant, the plaintiff should be at liberty to consider himself absolved from any future performance of it, retaining his right to sue for any damage he has suffered from the breach of it. Thus, instead of remaining idle and laying out money in preparations which must be useless, he is at liberty to seek service under another employer; which would go in mitigation of the damages to which he would otherwise be for a breach of the contract. It seems strange that the defendant, after renouncing the contract, and absolutely declaring that he will never act under it, should be permitted to object that faith is given to his assertion, and that an opportunity is not left to him of changing his mind. If the plaintiff is barred of any remedy by entering into an engagement inconsistent with starting as a courier with the defendant on the 1st June, he is prejudiced by putting faith in the defendant's assertion: and it would be more consonant with principle, if the defendant were precluded from saying that he had not broken the contract when he declared that he entirely renounced it. Suppose that the defendant, at the time of his renunciation, had embarked on a voyage for Australia, so as to render it physically impossible for him to employ the plaintiff as a courier on the continent of Europe in the months of June, July, and August 1852: according to decided cases, the action might have been brought before the 1st June; but the renunciation may have been founded on other facts, to be given in evidence, which would equally have rendered the defendant's performance of the contract impossible. The man who wrongfully renounces a contract into which he has deliberately entered cannot justly complain if he is immediately sued for a compensation in damages by the man whom he has injured: and it seems reasonable to allow an option to the injured party, either to sue immediately; or to wait till the time when the act was to be done, still holding it as prospectively binding for the exercise of this option, which may be advantageous to the innocent party, and cannot be prejudicial to the wrongdoer. An argument against the action before the 1st of June, is urged from the difficulty of calculating the damages: but this argument is equally strong against an action before the 1st of September, when the three months would expire. In either case, the jury in assessing the damages would be justified in looking to all that had happened, or was likely to happen, to increase or mitigate the loss of the plaintiff down to the day of trial. We do not find any decision contrary to the view we are taking of this case. * * *

If it should be held that, upon a contract to do an act on a future day, a renunciation of the contract by one party dispenses with a condition to be performed in the meantime by the other, there seems no reason for requiring that other to wait till the day arrives before seeking his remedy by action: and the only ground on which the condition can be dispensed with seems to be, that the renunciation may be treated as a breach of the contract.

Upon the whole, we think that the declaration in this case is sufficient. It gives us great satisfaction to reflect that, the question being on the record, our opinion may be reviewed in a Court of Error. In the meantime we must give judgment for the plaintiff.

Judgment for Plaintiff.

QUESTIONS

1. Questions about the facts of this case

    1.1. What was Hochster hired to do? Why couldn't he do it?

    1.2. What were De La Tour's duties under the contract? Had they yet matured when De La Tour indicated that he would not need Hochster's services?

2. Questions about the law

    2.1. What is a "motion to arrest the judgment"? Sheriffs aren't taking involuntary possession of pieces of paper, are they?

    2.2. If De La Tour's obligations under the contract had not yet matured (he didn't yet owe Hochster anything, right?), how can he be held in breach?

    2.3. Suppose that, on the day after Hochster files his lawsuit, De La Tour changes his mind again, and tells Hochster that he wants Hochster to work as promised. One small problem, though: Hochster has contracted to travel with Lord Ashburton? So if De La Tour retracts his repudiation, isn't Hochster immediately in breach with either De La Tour or Lord Ashburton?

    2.4. On April 1, you are hired by Hewes & Associates to work for the summer after your first year of law school, and agree to show up on May 15. Hewes & Associates agree to pay you $3,000 per week. On April 1, the law firm calls you and says "Sorry. We hired too many summer associates and you no longer have a job." What is your legal position?

B. REPUDIATION BASED ON CONDUCT

In the Ponoroff/Epstein house painting story, Epstein's words clearly indicated his intent not to perform. His words were definite and unequivocal. Similarly, in *Hochster v. De La Tour*, De La Tour's words of repudiation were definite and unequivocal.

As the United States Court of Appeals for the Seventh Circuit stated in *Carnes Co. v. Stone Mechanical, Inc.*, 412 F.3d 845, 854 (7th Cir. 2005):

> In order to constitute an anticipatory repudiation of a contract, there must be a definite and unequivocal manifestation of intention on the part of the repudiator that he will not render the promised performance when the time fixed for it in the contract arrives.

Note the Seventh Circuit's use of the term "manifestation of intention." An intent to repudiate can be manifested by conduct as well as words. The Restatement provides the following easy example: "On April 1, A contracts to sell, and B to buy land, delivery of the deed and payment of the price to be on July 29. A says nothing to B on May 1, but on that date he contracts to sell the land to C. A's making of the contract with C is a repudiation." Illustration 5 to *Restatement (Second)* section 250.

How unequivocal does the conduct have to be? In *Wholesale Sand & Gravel, Inc. v. Decker*, 630 A.2d 710 (Me. 1993), Decker, a Maine resident, contracted with Wholesale to replace Decker's dirt driveway with a gravel one. The contract was signed on June 12, about the end of winter in Maine. Payment was to be made within 90 days of the date the contract was signed.

> Wholesale began work on the driveway on the weekend after the contract was executed and immediately experienced difficulty because of the wetness of the ground. In fact, Wholesale's bulldozer became stuck in the mud and had to be removed with a backhoe. Wholesale returned to the site the following weekend, when it attempted to stabilize the driveway site by hauling out mud and hauling in gravel. Because the ground was too wet to allow Wholesale to perform the work without substantially exceeding the contract price. Goodenow [Wholesale's president] decided to wait for the ground to dry out before proceeding further.
>
> On July 12, 1989, Decker contacted Goodenow concerning the lack of activity at the site and his urgent need to have the driveway completed. Goodenow responded that he would "get right on it." On July 19, Decker telephoned Goodenow to inquire again about the lack of activity and gave him one week in which to finish the driveway. Again, Goodenow said that he would "get right on it." On July 28, Decker called Goodenow for the purpose of terminating the contract. When Goodenow stated that he would be at the site the next day, Decker decided to give him one more chance. Goodenow, however, did not appear at the site and Decker subsequently terminated the contract.
>
> 630 A.2d at 711.

When Decker sues Wholesale for breach, who wins—Decker, because of Wholesale's repudiation through inaction, or Wholesale, because of Decker's termination?

C. FAILURE TO GIVE ADEQUATE ASSURANCE OF FUTURE PERFORMANCE AS LIKE UNTO REPUDIATION

Given the strong requirements in repudiation doctrine for a definite and unambiguous statement, what is a party to a contract to do if the other side is "just making noises" about not performing? Is there anything that can be done?

The next case tries to answer this in a common law setting. In doing so, it borrows from the U.C.C. How does the court accomplish its result? How does the U.C.C.?

NORCON POWER PARTNERS, L.P. v. NIAGARA MOHAWK POWER CORP.

Court of Appeals of New York
92 N.Y.2d 458, 705 N.E.2d 656, 682 N.Y.S.2d 664 (1998)

BELLACOSA, J.

The doctrine, known as demand for adequate assurance of future performance, is at the heart of a Federal lawsuit that stems from a 1989 contract between Norcon Power Partners, L.P., an independent power producer, and Niagara Mohawk Power Corporation, a public utility provider. Niagara Mohawk undertook to purchase electricity generated at Norcon's Pennsylvania facility. The contract was for 25 years, but the differences emerged during the early years of the arrangement.

The case arrives on this Court's docket by certification of the substantive law question from the United States Court of Appeals for the Second Circuit. Our Court is presented with an open issue that should be settled within the framework of New York's common-law development. We accepted the responsibility to address this question involving New York contract law:

"Does a party have the right to demand adequate assurance of future performance when reasonable grounds arise to believe that the other party will commit a breach by non-performance of a contract governed by New York law, where the other party is solvent and the contract is not governed by the U.C.C.?" (*Norcon Power Partners v. Niagara Mohawk Power Corp.*, 110 F.3d 6, 9.)

As framed by the particular dispute, we answer the law question in the affirmative with an appreciation of this Court's traditional common-law developmental method, and as proportioned to the precedential sweep of our rulings.

I.

The Second Circuit Court of Appeals describes the three pricing periods, structure and details as follows:

"In the first period, Niagara Mohawk pays Norcon six cents per kilowatt-hour for electricity. In the second and third periods, the price paid by Niagara Mohawk is based on its 'avoided cost.' The avoided cost reflects the cost that Niagara Mohawk would incur to generate electricity itself or purchase it from other sources. In the second period, if the avoided cost falls below a certain floor price (calculated according to a formula), Niagara Mohawk is obligated to pay the floor price. By the same token, if the avoided cost rises above a certain amount (calculated according to a formula), Niagara Mohawk's payments are capped by a ceiling price. An 'adjustment account' tracks the difference between payments actually made by Niagara Mohawk in the second period and what those payments would have been if based solely on Niagara Mohawk's avoided cost.

"In the third period, the price paid by Niagara Mohawk is based on its avoided cost without any ceiling or floor price. Payments made by Niagara Mohawk in the third period are adjusted to account for any balance existing in the adjustment account that operated in the second period. If the adjustment account contains a balance in favor of Niagara Mohawk—that is, the payments actually made by Niagara Mohawk in the second period exceeded what those payments would have been if based solely on Niagara Mohawk's avoided cost—then the rate paid by Niagara Mohawk will be reduced to reflect the credit. If the adjustment account contains a balance in favor of Norcon, Niagara Mohawk must make increased payments to Norcon. If a balance exists in the adjustment account at the end of the third period, the party owing the balance must pay the balance in full within thirty days of the termination of the third period" (*Norcon Power Partners v. Niagara Mohawk Power Corp.*, 110 F.3d 6, 7, supra).

In February 1994, Niagara Mohawk presented Norcon with a letter stating its belief, based on revised avoided cost estimates, that substantial credits in Niagara Mohawk's favor would accrue in the adjustment account during the second pricing period. "[A]nalysis shows that the Cumulative Avoided Cost Account * * * will reach over $610 million by the end of the second period." Anticipating that Norcon would not be able to satisfy the daily escalating credits in the third period, Niagara Mohawk demanded that "Norcon provide adequate assurance to Niagara Mohawk that Norcon will duly perform all of its future repayment obligations."

Norcon promptly sued Niagara Mohawk in the United States District Court, Southern District of New York. It sought a declaration that Niagara Mohawk had no contractual right under New York State law to demand adequate assurance, beyond security provisions negotiated and expressed in the agreement. Norcon also sought a permanent injunction to stop Niagara Mohawk from anticipatorily terminating the contract based on the reasons described in the demand letter. Niagara Mohawk counterclaimed. It sought a counter declaration that it properly invoked a right to demand adequate assurance of Norcon's future payment performance of the contract.

The District Court granted Norcon's motion for summary judgment. It reasoned that New York common law recognizes the exceptional doctrine of demand for adequate assurance only when a promisor becomes insolvent, and also when the statutory sale of goods provision under UCC 2–609, is involved. Thus, the District Court ruled in Norcon's favor because neither exception applied, in fact or by analogy to the particular dispute (decided sub nom. *Encogen Four Partners v. Niagara Mohawk Power Corp.*, 914 F. Supp. 57).

The Second Circuit Court of Appeals preliminarily agrees (110 F.3d 6, supra) with the District Court that, except in the case of insolvency, no common-law or statutory right to demand adequate assurance exists under New York law which would affect non-UCC contracts, like the instant one. Because of the uncertainty concerning this substantive law question the Second Circuit certified the question to our Court as an aid to its correct application of New York law, and with an eye toward settlement of the important precedential impact on existing and future non-UCC commercial law matters and disputes.

II.

Our analysis should reference a brief review of the evolution of the doctrine of demands for adequate assurance. Its roots spring from the doctrine of anticipatory repudiation (*see,* Garvin, *Adequate Assurance of Performance: Of Risk, Duress, and Cognition,* 69 U. Colo. L. Rev. 71, 77 [1998]). Under that familiar precept, when a party repudiates contractual duties "prior to the time designated for performance and before" all of the consideration has been fulfilled, the "repudiation entitles the nonrepudiating party to claim damages for total breach" * * * A repudiation can be either "a statement by the obligor to the obligee indicating that the obligor will commit a breach that would of itself give the obligee a claim for damages for total breach" or "a voluntary affirmative act which renders the obligor unable or apparently unable to perform without such a breach". * * *

That switch in performance expectation and burden is readily available, applied and justified when a breaching party's words or deeds are unequivocal. Such a discernible line in the sand clears the way for the nonbreaching party to broach some responsive action. When, however, the apparently breaching party's actions are equivocal or less certain, then the nonbreaching party who senses an approaching storm cloud, affecting the contractual performance, is presented with a dilemma, and must weigh hard choices and serious consequences. One commentator has described the forecast options in this way:

> "If the promisee regards the apparent repudiation as an anticipatory repudiation, terminates his or her own performance and sues for breach, the promisee is placed in jeopardy of being found to have breached if the court determines that the apparent repudiation was not sufficiently clear and unequivocal to constitute an anticipatory repudiation justifying nonperformance. If, on the other hand, the promisee continues to perform after perceiving an apparent repudiation, and it is subsequently determined that an anticipatory repudiation took place, the promisee may be denied recovery for post-repudiation expenditures because of his or her failure to avoid those expenses as part of a reasonable effort to mitigate damages after the repudiation" * * *.

III.

The Uniform Commercial Code settled on a mechanism for relieving some of this uncertainty. It allows a party to a contract for the sale of goods to demand assurance of future performance from the other party when reasonable grounds for insecurity exist (*see*, UCC 2–609; II Farnsworth, Contracts § 8.23). When adequate assurance is not forthcoming, repudiation is deemed confirmed, and the nonbreaching party is allowed to take reasonable actions as though a repudiation had occurred (see, 4 Anderson, Uniform Commercial Code § 2–609:3 [3rd ed. 1997 rev.]).

UCC 2–609 provides, in relevant part:

"(1) A contract for sale imposes an obligation on each party that the other's expectation of receiving due performance will not be impaired. When reasonable grounds for insecurity arise with respect to the performance of either party the other may in writing demand adequate assurance of due performance and until he receives such assurance may if commercially reasonable suspend any performance for which he has not already received the agreed return. * * *

"(4) After receipt of a justified demand failure to provide within a reasonable time not exceeding thirty days such assurance of due performance as is adequate under the circumstances of the particular case is a repudiation of the contract."

In theory, this UCC relief valve recognizes that "the essential purpose of a contract between commercial [parties] is actual performance * * * and that a continuing sense of reliance and security that the promised performance will be forthcoming when due, is an important feature of the bargain" (UCC 2–609, Comment 1). In application, section 2–609 successfully implements the laudatory objectives of quieting the doubt a party fearing repudiation may have, mitigating the dilemma flowing from that doubt, and offering the nonbreaching party the opportunity to interpose timely action to deal with the unusual development. * * *

Indeed, UCC 2–609 has been considered so effective in bridging the doctrinal, exceptional and operational gap related to the doctrine of anticipatory breach that some States have imported the complementary regimen of demand for adequate assurance to common-law categories of contract law, using UCC 2–609 as the synapse (*see, e.g., Lo Re v. Tel–Air Communications*, 200 N.J. Super. 59, 490 A.2d 344 [finding support in U.C.C. 2–609 and *Restatement (Second) of Contracts* § 251 for applying doctrine of adequate assurance to contract to purchase radio station]; *Conference Ctr. v. TRC—The Research Corp. of New England*, 189 Conn. 212, 455 A.2d 857 [analogizing to U.C.C. 2–609, as supported by *Restatement (Second) of Contracts* § 251, in context of constructive eviction]).

Commentators have helped nudge this development along. They have noted that the problems redressed by UCC 2–609 are not unique to contracts for sale of goods, regulated under a purely statutory regime. Thus, they have cogently identified the need for the doctrine to be available in exceptional and qualifying common-law contractual settings and disputes because of similar practical, theoretical and salutary objectives (e.g., predictability, definiteness, and stability in commercial dealings and expectations) * * *.

The American Law Institute through its Restatement (Second) of Contracts has also recognized and collected the authorities supporting this modern development. Its process and work settled upon this black letter language:

> "(1) Where reasonable grounds arise to believe that the obligor will commit a breach by non-performance that would of itself give the obligee a claim for damages for total breach under § 243, the obligee may demand adequate assurance of due performance and may, if reasonable, suspend any performance for which he has not already received the agreed exchange until he receives such assurance.

> "(2) The obligee may treat as a repudiation the obligor's failure to provide within a reasonable time such assurance of due performance as is adequate in the circumstances of the particular case"

(Restatement [Second] of Contracts § 251).

Modeled on UCC 2–609, Restatement § 251 tracks "the principle that the parties to a contract look to actual performance 'and that a continuing sense of reliance and security that the promised performance will be forthcoming when due, is an important feature of the bargain' " (Restatement [Second] of Contracts § 251, comment a, quoting UCC 2–609, Comment 1). The duty of good faith and fair dealing in the performance of the contract is also reflected in section 251 (*see*, Restatement [Second] of Contracts § 251, comment a).

Some States have adopted Restatement § 251 as their common law of contracts, in varying degrees and classifications. * * *

IV.

New York, up to now, has refrained from expanding the right to demand adequate assurance of performance beyond the Uniform Commercial Code. * * * Hence, the need for this certified question emerged so this Court could provide guidance towards a correct resolution of the Federal lawsuit by settling New York law with a modern pronouncement governing this kind of contract and dispute.

Niagara Mohawk, before our Court through the certified question from the Federal court, urges a comprehensive adaptation of the exceptional demand tool. This wholesale approach has also been advocated by the commentators (*see generally, Dowling, op. cit.; Campbell, op. cit.*). Indeed, it is even reflected in the breadth of the wording of the certified question.

This Court's jurisprudence, however, usually evolves by deciding cases and settling the law more modestly. * * * The twin purposes and functions of this Court's work require significant professional discipline and judicious circumspection.

We conclude, therefore, that it is unnecessary, while fulfilling the important and useful certification role, to promulgate so sweeping a change and proposition in contract law, as has been sought, in one dramatic promulgation. That approach might clash with our customary incremental common-law developmental process, rooted in particular fact patterns and keener wisdom acquired through observations of empirical application of a proportioned, less than absolute, rule in future cases.

It is well to note the axiom that deciding a specific case, even with the precedential comet's tail its rationale illuminates, is very different from enacting a statute of general and universal application. * * *

Experience and patience thus offer a more secure and realistic path to a better and fairer rule, in theory and in practical application. Therefore, this Court chooses to take the traditionally subtler approach, consistent with the proven benefits of the maturation process of the common law, including in the very area of anticipatory repudiation which spawns this relatively newer demand for assurance corollary. * * *

This Court is now persuaded that the policies underlying the UCC 2–609 counterpart should apply with similar cogency for the resolution of this kind of controversy. A useful analogy can be drawn between the contract at issue and a contract for the sale of goods. If the contract here was in all respects the same, except that it was for the sale of oil or some other tangible commodity instead of the sale of electricity, the parties would unquestionably be governed by the demand for adequate assurance of performance factors in UCC 2–609. We are convinced to take this prudent step because it puts commercial parties in these kinds of disputes at relatively arm's length equilibrium in terms of reliability and uniformity of governing legal rubrics. The availability of the doctrine may even provide an incentive and tool for parties to resolve their own differences, perhaps without the necessity of judicial intervention. Open, serious renegotiation of dramatic developments and changes in unusual contractual expectations and qualifying circumstances would occur because of and with an eye to the doctrine's application.

The various authorities, factors and concerns, in sum, prompt the prudence and awareness of the usefulness of recognizing the extension of the doctrine of demand for adequate assurance, as a common-law analogue. It should apply to the type of long-term commercial contract between corporate entities entered into by Norcon and Niagara Mohawk here, which is complex and not reasonably susceptible of all security features being anticipated, bargained for and incorporated in the original contract. Norcon's performance, in terms of reimbursing Niagara Mohawk for credits, is still years away. In the meantime, potential quantifiable damages are accumulating and Niagara Mohawk must weigh the hard choices and serious consequences that the doctrine of demand for adequate assurance is designed to mitigate. This Court needs to go no further in its promulgation of the legal standard as this suffices to declare a dispositive and proportioned answer to the certified question.

Accordingly, the certified question should be answered in the affirmative.

CHIEF JUDGE KAYE and JUDGES SMITH, LEVINE, CIPARICK and WESLEY concur.

Following certification of a question by the United States Court of Appeals for the Second Circuit and acceptance of the question by this Court pursuant to section 500.17 of the Rules of the Court of Appeals (22 NYCRR 500.17), and after hearing argument by counsel for the parties and consideration of the briefs and the record submitted, certified question answered in the affirmative.

QUESTIONS AND NOTES

1. Questions about the facts of this case

   1.1. Was Norcon in breach of any relevant contract term at any time relevant for this opinion? Was that relevant to the court? Should that have been relevant?

   1.2. What was Niagara Mohawk's concern? Could that concern have been addressed with a contract term when Niagra Mohawk and Norcon were negotiating and drafting a contract?

2. Questions about the law

   2.1. Does the U.C.C. apply in this case? If not, why does the court cite U.C.C. § 2–609?

   2.2. It seems as if *Niagara Mohawk* can turn a case of no breach into a case of breach. Why is that? If the day after the contract was signed, and before there was any balance in the Cumulative Avoided Cost Account, Niagara Mohawk had sent the same letter, would the court order the same result?

   2.3. If you represented Norcon, and your client indicated that it wished to respond to the letter sent, how would you respond? What response would satisfy Niagara Mohawk? Just a letter saying, "We intend to perform"?

3. Notes

   3.1. Article 72 of the *Convention for the International Sale of Goods*, which has been adopted by the United States, states as follows:

   (1) If prior to the date for performance of the contract it is clear that one of the parties will commit a fundamental breach of contract, the other party may declare the contract avoided.

   (2) If time allows, the party intending to declare the contract avoided must give reasonable notice to the other party in order to permit him to provide adequate assurance of his performance.

Is this superior or inferior to the U.C.C. § 2–609? In thinking about this, consider Article 7.3.4 of the *UNIDROIT* principles which states:

A party who reasonably believes that there will be a fundamental nonperformance by the other party may demand adequate assurance of due performance and may meanwhile withhold its own performance. Where this assurance is not provided within a reasonable time the party demanding it may terminate the contract.

3.2.   In referring this case to the New York Court of Appeals, the Second Circuit had this to say about the possible effects of U.C.C. § 2–609:

[S]ome authorities argue that the right to demand adequate assurance may not mitigate many of the problems faced by a party who has substantial concerns about the ability of the other party to perform the contract. A party, and eventually a court, may have to determine what constitutes "reasonable grounds for insecurity" or "adequate" assurance. "Partly as a result of the uncertain application of the concepts involved, section 2–609 sometimes does little more than extend the minuet between the weaseling party and the contractual counterpart and add a couple of new moves." 1 James J. White & Robert S. Summers, Uniform Commercial Code § 6–2 (4th ed. 1995); cf. Mollohan v. Black Rock Contracting, Inc., 160 W.Va. 446, 235 S.E.2d 813, 816 n.1 (W. Va. 1977) (declining to adopt Restatement position "except to the extent that a demand for assurances and failure to give them may be evidence of repudiation to present to a jury with other evidence to prove * * * positive repudiation and anticipatory breach"). But see 4 Ronald A. Anderson, Anderson on the Uniform Commercial Code § 2–609:6 (3d ed. 1983) ("courts * * * will undoubtedly expand the application of U.C.C. § 2–609 to transactions that do not come within the * * * Code").

Norcon Power Partners, L.P. v. Niagara Mohawk Power Corp., 110 F.3d 6, 8–9 (2d Cir. 1997).

SECTION 5: MATERIAL BREACH: OTHER GUY'S IMPROPER PERFORMANCE AS AN EXCUSE FOR NOT DOING WHAT YOU AGREED TO DO UNDER A COMMON LAW CONTRACT

A. THE MATERIAL BREACH CONCEPT

This last category of excuse may seem strange. It is the excuse provided by the other party's material breach of its obligations. Many think that such a result—you don't have to perform if the other party breaches—is so self-evident as to not require much thought.

For starters, we need to distinguish between the situations in which the other party never even starts to perform and situations in which the other party's nonperformance is incomplete or imperfect. Consider the following situations:

(1) Epstein contracts to paint Markell's office white on Saturday for $1,000. Epstein once again does not perform—once again does not do what he contracted to do. Does Markell still have to peform under the contract—still have to pay Epstein—or is Markell excused from performing because of Epstein's nonperformance?

(2) Same facts as (1) except that Epstein paints Markell's office but paints it purple[2] instead of white as required by the contract. Everything is purple: walls, floor, ceiling, windows. Does Markell still have to peform under the contract—still have to pay Epstein—or is Markell excused from performing because of Epstein's improper performance?

(3) Same facts as (1) except that Epstein does paint Markell's office white and does an incredibly fine job except that he fails to paint the back of one of the doors. Markell pays another painter $25 to do that. Does Markell still have to peform under the contract—still have to pay Epstein—or is Markell excused from performing because of Epstein's improper performance?

The common law rule with respect to a party's ability to suspend performance or terminate the contract when the other party breaches is relatively easy to state. Under common law, you are excused from performing because of the other guy's breach only when the other guy's breach is a "material breach." That much is backed up by the following section of the *Restatement*:

> *§ 237   Effect on Other Party's Duties of a Failure to Render Performance*
>
> *[I]t is a condition of each party's remaining duties to render performances to be exchanged under an exchange of promises that there be no uncured material failure by the other party to render any such performance due at an earlier time.*

Note the legal device used to implement the material breach rule: conditions. Under contract law, the duty to tender performance is conditioned upon the other party's not being in "material breach."

The conditions referenced in the above *Restatement* provision are different from the express conditions that we considered earlier in this Chapter. The express conditions we learned about in Section 1 of this Chapter were "real", based on the real words of the contract. The conditions that are a part of the material breach are not "real", not based on the words of the contract. Instead, the conditions are "constructive."

---

2. Epstein is Gogol Bordello's oldest groupie. http://www.roxwel.com/player/gogolbordellostart wearingpurple.html?1=1&detect_bitrate=_2000

B. "MATERIAL BREACH" AND "CONSTRUCTIVE CONDITIONS" AND "SUBSTANTIAL PERFORMANCE"; THE CONCEPTUAL BASIS FOR THE MATERIAL BREACH DOCTRINE

Professor Perillo explains "constructive" conditions in his outstanding hornbook:

> Constructive conditions are created by courts in order to do justice. * * * In a bilateral contract, the parties often neglect to state the order in which their promises are to be performed. Constructive conditions fill these gaps. * * * The first and simplest rule is that, unless otherwise agreed, a party who is to perform work over an extended period of time must substantially perform before becoming entitled to payment. Performance of the work is a constructive condition precedent to the duty to pay.

JOSEPH PERILLO, CALAMARI AND PERILLO ON CONTRACTS 428–29 (5th ed. 2003).

Check whether you understand what Professor Perillo is saying. Do you see the relationship between express conditions and strict compliance? Between constructive conditions and substantial performance? Between substantial performance and material breach?

1. A Short[2] History of Constructive Conditions

As we have seen, in every contract there are usually at least two obligations. In the typical bilateral contract, each party makes a promise to the other; if Epstein and Ponoroff agree that Epstein will sell Ponoroff his prized collection of road-kill recipes, Epstein has an obligation to transfer the recipes and Ponoroff has the duty to pay for them.

What's the timing of each party's performance? Does Epstein hold his recipes in one hand high in the air over Ponoroff's head (Epstein's taller, at least in physical stature) while extending the palm of his other hand towards Ponoroff to accept the payment? Does Ponoroff adopt a like stature? In short, who has to perform first and take the risk that the other will not honor his promise?

Conditions are a nice way to order things. They would seem to be tailor-made for regulating this type of exchange. A short detour into the common law, however, shows that it took some time for the common law to embrace this concept. Let's start with the state of the law in the early seventeenth century.

NICHOLS v. RAYNBRED
Court of King's Bench
Hobart 88, 80 Eng. Rep. 238 (1615)

Nichols brought an assumpsit against Raynbred, declaring that in consideration that Nichols promised to deliver the defendant to his own

---

2. "Short" is the adjective chosen by Ponoroff, the primary author (and user) of these materials on constructive conditions.

use a cow, the defendant promised to deliver him 50 shillings: adjudged for the plaintiff in both Courts, that the plaintiff need not to aver the delivery of the cow, because it is promise for promise. Note here the promises must be at one instant, for else they will be both nuda pacta.

- - - - - - -

That's all there is. What's going on here? What was the contract in this case? If you were Nichols, and could do it all over again, what would you put in the contract? In the complaint? As things stand, is Nichols out one cow?

The law evolved after *Nichols*. By 1772 (158 years later), the following case proved to be a turning point in the law of conditions.

KINGSTON v. PRESTON

Court of King's Bench
2 Douglas 689, 99 Eng. Rep. 437 (1773)

"It was an action of debt, for non-performance of covenants contained in certain articles of agreement between the plaintiff and the defendant. The declaration stated:—That, by articles made the 24th of March, 1770, the plaintiff, for the considerations thereinafter mentioned, covenanted, with the defendant, to serve him for one year and a quarter next ensuing, as a covenant-servant, in his trade of a silk-mercer, at £200 a year, and in consideration of the premises, the defendant covenanted, that at the end of the year and a quarter, he would give up his business of a mercer to the plaintiff, and a nephew of the defendant, or some other person to be nominated by the defendant, and give up to them his stock in trade, at a fair valuation; and that, between the young traders, deeds of partnership should be executed for 14 years, and from and immediately after the execution of the said deeds, the defendant would permit the said young traders to carry on the said business in the defendant's house. Then the declaration stated a covenant by the plaintiff, that he would accept the business and stock in trade, at a fair valuation, with the defendant's nephew, or such other person, & c., and execute such deeds of partnership, and, further, that the plaintiff should, and would, at, and before the sealing and delivery of the deeds, cause and procure good and sufficient security to be given to the defendant, to be approved of by the defendant, for the payment of £250 monthly, to the defendant, in lieu of a moiety of the monthly produce of the stock in trade, until the value of the stock should be reduced to £4,000.—Then the plaintiff averred, that he had performed, and been ready to perform, his covenants, and assigned for breach on the part of the defendant, that he had refused to surrender and give up his business, at the end of the said year and quarter.—The defendant pleaded, 1. That the plaintiff did not offer sufficient security;

and, 2. That he did not give sufficient security for the payment of the £250, & c.—And the plaintiff demurred generally to both pleas.—On the part of the plaintiff, the case was argued by Mr. Buller, who contended, that the covenants were mutual and independent, and, therefore, a plea of the breach of one of the covenants to be performed by the plaintiff was no bar to an action for a breach by the defendant of one of which he had bound himself to perform, but that the defendant might have his remedy for the breach by the plaintiff, in a separate action. On the other side, Mr. Grose insisted, that the covenants were dependent in their nature, and, therefore, performance must be alleged: the security to be given for the money, was manifestly the chief object of the transaction, and it would be highly unreasonable to construe the agreement, so as to oblige the defendant to give up a beneficial business, and valuable stock in trade, and trust to the plaintiff's personal security, (who might, and, indeed, was admitted to be worth nothing,) for the performance of his part.—In delivering the judgment of the Court, Lord Mansfield expressed himself to the following effect: There are three kinds of covenants: 1. Such as are called mutual and independent, where either party may recover damages from the other, for the injury he may have received by a breach of the covenants in his favour, and where it is no excuse for the defendant, to allege a breach of the covenants on the part of the plaintiff. 2. There are covenants, which are conditions and dependent, in which the performance of one depends on the prior performance of another, and therefore, till this prior condition is performed, the other party is not liable to an action on his covenant. 3. There is also a third sort of covenants, which are mutual conditions to be performed at the same time; and, in these, if one party was ready, and offered, to perform his part, and the other neglected, or refused, to perform his, he who was ready, and offered, has fulfilled his engagement, and may maintain an action for the default of the other; though it is not certain that either is obliged to do the first act.—His Lordship then proceeded to say, that the dependence, or independence, of covenants, was to be collected from the evident sense and meaning of the parties, and, that, however transposed they might be in the deed, their precedency must depend on the order of time in which the intent of the transaction requires their performance. That, in the case before the Court, it would be the greatest injustice if the plaintiff should prevail: the essence of the agreement was, that the defendant should not trust to the personal security of the plaintiff, but before he delivered up his stock and business, should have good security for the payment of the money. The giving such security, therefore, must necessarily be a condition precedent.—Judgment was accordingly given for the defendant because the part to be performed by the plaintiff was clearly a condition precedent."*

---

* The reason this case is reported within quotation marks is that it is not reported under its title, but is reported as part of the oral argument in another case, that being Jones v. Barkley, 2 Douglas 684, 99 Eng. Rep. 434 (1781). In 17th Century England there were no official reports of

Is Lord Mansfield finding something that isn't there? Did the parties insert a condition of concurrent exchange in their contract? Could they have? Is the rationale for implying a condition (in essence, writing it in when it isn't there) the same rationale Judge Cardozo would use 143 years later in *Wood v. Lucy, Lady Duff–Gordon* (*see supra*, at page 510)?

———————

Thus, promises of payment by the buyer and of delivery by the seller came to be dependent upon each other through the use of court-supplied assumptions called conditions. These assumptions are played out in the next case.

2. Constructive Conditions of Exchange in Current Practice

PULLMAN, COMLEY, BRADLEY AND REEVES v. TUCK-IT-AWAY, BRIDGEPORT, INC.

Appellate Court of Connecticut
28 Conn.App. 460, 611 A.2d 435 (1992)

FREEDMAN, J:

In this interpleader action,* the defendant, Vestpro Corporation, appeals from the judgment of the trial court awarding the other defendant, Tuck-it-away, Bridgeport, Inc., $100,000 as liquidated damages for Vestpro's default under the terms of a contract for the sale of real property.[2] Vestpro claims that the trial court improperly found that Tuck-it-away was entitled to the $100,000 as liquidated damages for Vestpro's default in performance of the contract of sale. We affirm the judgment of the trial court.

The parties stipulated to the following facts. On or about April 13, 1988, Tuck-it-away, as seller, and Vestpro, as buyer, signed a contract for

———————

court decisions, and often the same case received several differing treatments. Indeed, in another report of this case, at 98 Eng. Rep. 606, Lord Mansfield is reported to have said:

> It would be the most monstrous case in the world, if the argument on the side of Mr. Buller's client was to prevail. It's of the very essence of the agreement, that the defendant will not trust the personal security of the plaintiff. A Court of Justice is to say, that by operation of law he shall, against his teeth. He is to let him into his house to squander every thing there, without any thing to rely on but what he has absolutely refused to trust. This payment, therefore, was a precedent condition before the covenant of putting into possession was to be performed on the part of the defendant.

Eds.

* This action was commenced by the plaintiff, Pullman, Comley, Bradley and Reeves, as the holder of a $100,000 escrow deposit made by Vestpro in connection with the underlying real estate transaction here in dispute. The plaintiff sought and was granted an interlocutory judgment requiring the defendants to interplead concerning their claims to the funds so that the court could order the plaintiff to give the funds to the proper party and be released of any further obligations or liabilities to Vestpro.

2. Paragraph 15 of the contract provided in pertinent part: "If the buyer fails to perform the terms of this contract, seller shall be entitled to retain all sums theretofore paid as provided in Sections 2 and 8 hereof which sums, to the extent held in escrow hereunder, shall be released from escrow and thereupon paid to the seller together with any accrued and unpaid interest thereon, as liquidated damages for loss of a bargain and not as a penalty. * * *"

the sale of real property located in Bridgeport. Pursuant to the contract, Vestpro deposited $100,000 in escrow with Tuck-it-away's attorneys, Pullman, Comley, Bradley and Reeves. This is the money presently in dispute between the parties. By correspondence dated October 14, 1988, Tuck-it-away and Vestpro agreed in writing to extend the closing date until December 10, 1988.

On December 10, 1988, a Saturday, no closing took place. On or about December 14, 1988, Tuck-it-away received from Vestpro a letter purporting to cancel the contract on the basis of three alleged title defects: (1) a lis pendens dated August 9, 1983, (2) a certificate of attachment dated June 27, 1988, and (3) a three foot nonconformity in one of the lengths in the legal description of the property as referenced in the contract.

Before December 10, 1988, Tuck-it-away's attorneys had in their possession a release of the August 9, 1983 lis pendens and a release of the June 27, 1988 attachment. At the time of execution of the contract, neither Tuck-it-away nor Vestpro was aware that the legal description contained an incorrect length. On or about September 16, 1988, attorneys for both Tuck-it-away and Vestpro received a survey from Preferred Land Title Services, Inc., showing a correct legal description of the property. At no time prior to the December 12, 1988 letter did Vestpro ever advise Tuck-it-away or complain to Tuck-it-away about the error in the legal description of the property contained in the contract.

In addition to these stipulated facts, other facts necessary to a resolution of this matter can be summarized as follows. The total purchase price due under the contract was $1,900,000. The contract provided that the closing date would be 120 days from the date of execution of the contract, but that Vestpro could obtain four extensions of time upon payment to Tuck-it-away of $15,000 for each extension. Because Vestpro exercised all four rights of adjournment, the actual closing date was December 10, 1988. The contract provided that time was of the essence.

As December 10 approached, Vestpro was short of the total funds necessary to complete the deal. On December 7, 1988, Alan Goldman, one of Vestpro's principals, met with Gerald Sprayragen, Tuck-it-away's president, to discuss the situation. At that meeting, Goldman indicated that Vestpro did not yet have the total funds necessary, but that it was close to attaining its goal, and optimistic that it would reach its goal, but that a further extension of time was needed. Although the express contractual language did not permit another extension, Sprayragen indicated that he would permit another extension if Vestpro would pay a fee for the extension. Vestpro refused to pay for a further extension, and as a result no agreement for an extension came from this meeting. Sprayragen also spoke with Stephen Hochman, a partner in Vestpro whose job was to solicit investors. He too indicated to Sprayragen that Vestpro was unable to close on December 10 and needed an extension of the closing date.

During that week, Michael Proctor, an attorney who represented Tuck-it-away in this deal, spoke with Gary Kleinman, an attorney who represented Vestpro in its negotiations and dealings with Tuck-it-away. Kleinman told Proctor that Vestpro would not be able to close on December 10 and needed another two weeks to secure the remaining funds. It thus was clear to Tuck-it-away that Vestpro would not be able to close the deal on December 10, 1988.

On December 9, 1988, Vestpro representatives met with their prospective investors to discuss the situation. During the meeting, the group received a call from Kleinman, who told the group "You got lucky" because he had discovered a discrepancy in one of the courses in the property description. As a result of this information, Vestpro decided to send a letter to Tuck-it-away electing to cancel the contract under its provisions because of Tuck-it-away's inability to convey title to the premises in accordance with the terms of the contract.[5] The letter represented to Tuck-it-away that Vestpro elected to cancel the contract because of the three alleged defects in title previously discussed. The letter was not mailed to Tuck-it-away until the end of the day on December 12, 1988, and Tuck-it-away did not receive the letter until December 14, 1988. * * *

Vestpro * * * argues that the trial court improperly found Vestpro in default for failing to appear for the closing on December 10, 1988. Vestpro claims that this finding was improper because Tuck-it-away also failed to appear for the closing and tender title to the property.

* * *

The trial court * * * found that Vestpro breached its duty to perform by not showing up at the closing on December 10 and tendering full payment of the purchase price, and that such a breach excused Tuck-it-away from its obligation to perform.

With respect to the time for performance of obligations contained in a contract, the general rule is: "Where all or part of the performances to be exchanged under an exchange of promises can be rendered simultaneously, they are to that extent due simultaneously, unless the language of [*sic.* Should be "or." Eds.] the circumstances indicate the contrary." 2 Restatement (Second), Contracts § 234(1). Here, paragraph 4 of the contract provided: "At the closing, *on payment of the purchase price as provided above,* the seller shall deliver and the buyer shall accept, a full covenant Warranty deed * * *" This language indicates that the parties agreed that the performances would not be rendered simultaneously, but rather that Vestpro's duty to perform would be a condition precedent to Tuck-it-away's obligation to tender and convey title.

"A condition precedent is a fact or event which the parties intend must exist or take place before there is a right to performance." * * * " 'Whether the performance of a certain act by a party to a contract is a condition precedent to the duty of the other party to act depends on the

___

5. Paragraph 11 of the contract provided in pertinent part: "If the seller shall be unable to convey title to the buyer at the closing, or adjourned closing, in accordance with the terms of this contract, the buyer shall have the option of * * * (b) canceling this contract. * * *"

intent of the parties as expressed in the contract and read in light of the circumstances surrounding the execution of the instrument.' * * *'' * * *

The express language of paragraph 4 of the contract evidences the parties' intent that Vestpro's duty to tender full payment of the purchase price is a condition precedent of Tuck-it-away's obligation to convey title to Vestpro. Because Vestpro failed on December 10, 1988, to tender the $1,800,000 balance due on the purchase price, Tuck-it-away was excused of its obligation to perform under the contract.

Vestpro argues, however, that Tuck-it-away's failure to go through the act of tendering a deed to the nonappearing buyer placed it in default and thus precluded it from recovering the $100,000 as liquidated damages. The law, however, does not require a party to undertake a futile act. * * * Because Vestpro failed to appear at the closing and perform its obligation, which was a condition precedent to Tuck-it-away's obligation to perform, it would have been an act in futility for Tuck-it-away to tender a deed to Vestpro. We will not require the seller in this situation to perform such a futile act.

We conclude that the trial court's factual findings were adequately supported by the record. The trial court, therefore, correctly awarded the $100,000 deposit to Tuck-it-away.

The judgment is affirmed.

QUESTIONS

1. Questions about the facts of this case

   1.1. What is the seller's law firm doing holding the $100,000? Would you do this for your client?

   1.2. Why did the buyer keep extending (or as the argot goes, "adjourning") the closing?

   1.3. Under the court's reasoning, who was obligated to perform first? Is that the same answer the old common law gave in *Nichols*? That Judge Mansfield gave in *Kingston*?

2. Questions about the law

   2.1. Why wasn't the contract terminated as of the December 7th meeting?

   2.2. Knowing what you know now, what would you have told the investors at the December 9th meeting when the call from Kleinman came in?

   2.3. Would it have made a difference if the December 12th letter had been hand delivered to the seller on December 9th?

   2.4. If you represented the seller, and received the December 12th letter on December 9th, what do you advise your client to do?

2.5.   The Appellate Court of Connecticut quotes from *Restatement (Second) of Contracts* § 234. Is the court's finding of Vestpro's tender a constructive condition precedent consistent with that *Restatement* provision? Is the following dictum from *Kaufman v. Byers*, 159 Ohio App.3d 238, 823 N.E.2d 530, 537 (Ohio App. 11 Dist. 2004) consistent with either the *Restatement* or this case? "Where possible, courts should construe promises in a bilateral contract as mutually dependent and concurrent, rather than one promise as a condition precedent to the other."

Now that you have a better sense of constructive conditions, let's revisit the interplay between constructive and express conditions.

3.   The Interplay Between Constructive and Express Conditions

The interplay between implied conditions, which regulates the order of performance and express conditions, which attempt to do the same, was analyzed in *MXL Indust., Inc. v. Mulder*, 252 Ill.App.3d 18, 623 N.E.2d 369, 191 Ill.Dec. 124 (1993). There, a lease had an early termination clause; the tenant could leave early upon the condition that it pays "all sums then due" plus four months' rent. This is the clause:

(a) The term of this Lease shall be for a period of five (5) years commencing on the 1st day of March, 1987 and ending on the 29th day of February, 1992 (hereinafter referred to as 'the term of this Lease'). Notwithstanding the foregoing provisions of this Subsection 1 (a), at any time after the 29th day of February, 1988, Lessee may terminate this Lease by paying to Lessor all sums then due pursuant to the provisions of this Lease and an additional sum equal to four (4) months' rent specified in Section 2 hereof. If Lessee exercises such right, the term of this Lease shall end on the date on which Lessor receives such payment from Lessor [*sic*].

The tenant tried to exercise this option on February 28, 1988, by tendering $11,400, the amount of four months' rent (less a credit for a security deposit), and by vacating the premises. The landlord, however, correctly pointed out that one of the obligations of the lease was that, upon vacating the premises, the tenant was to repair certain damage. The exact amount of this obligation was debated for two months, and finally agreed to be $2,000. When the tenant sent a check for that amount along with a check for four months' rent, the landlord rejected it, contending that the tenant owed rent for the two months during which the parties negotiated the settlement. The tenant disagreed, and contended that it had met the condition, or at least substantially met the condition, allowing it to terminate early by its February 28 tender. In response, the court said:

Illinois courts define a condition precedent as one which must be performed either before a contract becomes effective or which is to be performed by one party to an existing contract before the other party is obligated to perform. * * * The satisfaction of a condition is generally subject to the rule of strict compliance. * * * Professor Williston explains, " 'since an express condition * * * depends for its validity on the manifested intention of the parties, it has the same sanctity as the promise itself. Though the court may regret the harshness of such a condition, as it may regret the harshness of a promise, it must, nevertheless, generally enforce the will of the parties.' " * * * A party seeking the benefit of a condition precedent, however, may waive strict compliance by conduct indicating that strict compliance with the provision will not be required. * * *

Distinctly different, although analogous to the concept of a condition, are constructive conditions of exchange. The concept of constructive conditions of exchange was developed by the courts in order to allow the court to supply terms under which a party's duties to perform are conditioned on the performance to be given in return. * * * The purpose of constructive conditions of exchange is to play an integral role in assuring the parties to a bilateral contract that they will actually receive the performance that they have been promised. * * * A common application of the concept occurs when one party seeks to justify its own refusal to perform on the ground that the other party has committed a breach of the contract. In sum, the doctrine serves the salutary purpose of assuring each party to a bilateral contract that it will receive the promised return performance, and it expresses a judicial preference for dependent promises. * * *

Because constructive conditions of exchange invoked the concept that one party's duty to perform was conditioned on the other party's performance, the need arose to ameliorate the rule of strict compliance ordinarily applied to express conditions. As explained by Professor Farnsworth, "the doctrine evolved that if one party's performance is a constructive condition of the other party's duty, only 'substantial performance' is required of the first party before that party can recover under the contract." (E. Farnsworth, Farnsworth on Contracts § 12, at 415 (1990).) Farnsworth further notes, however, that "the flexible requirement of substantial performance stands in sharp contrast to the requirement of strict compliance that protects a party that has taken the precaution of making its duty expressly conditional." (E. Farnsworth, Farnsworth on Contracts § 12, at 415 (1990).) Stated differently, the doctrine does not address substantial performance of a condition; rather, it focuses on substantial performance by one party of its obligations arising out of an agreed exchange of performances. * * * Accordingly, an express condition precedent, unless otherwise excused, operates by agreement of the parties to define the satisfaction of a necessary antecedent to a party's performance under the contract and is subject to the rule of strict compliance, unless such compliance is waived. In contrast, constructive or implied conditions of exchange operate to regulate the parties' course of performance and are subject to the rule of substantial performance.

The court found that the clause, being drafted by the parties, required strict compliance, and held that the tenant's $11,400 tender did not effectively terminate the lease. It was thus not only liable for the extra two months' rent, but also for the total amount of contract damages for the rest of the term (since it vacated and treated the lease as terminated, when it in fact was not); an amount claimed to be in excess of $230,000. And that was not all—because the tenant litigated the case and lost, it also wound up paying the landlord's attorneys' fees under the lease's attorneys' fees clause, and those fees were alleged to be in excess of $65,000.

C.   WHAT CONSTITUTES A MATERIAL BREACH

Now that we know that (1) whether a breach is "material" matters, (2) what a "constructive condition" is, (3) why the law requires only "substantial performance" of "constructive conditions", and (4) if there has been "substantial performance" of a "constructive condition", there is no "material breach" and thus no excuse from performing because of the other party's improper performance, we need to learn more about whether the performance was substantial or whether, instead, there was a material breach,

Let's start with another classic, Cardozo opinion.

JACOB & YOUNGS, INCORPORATED v. KENT

Court of Appeals of New York
230 N.Y. 239, 129 N.E. 889 (1921)

CARDOZO, J:

The plaintiff built a country residence for the defendant at a cost of upwards of $77,000, and now sues to recover a balance of $3,483.46, remaining unpaid. The work of construction ceased in June, 1914, and the defendant then began to occupy the dwelling. There was no complaint of defective performance until March, 1915. One of the specifications for the plumbing work provides that "all wrought iron pipe must be well galvanized, lap welded pipe of the grade known as 'standard pipe' of Reading manufacture." The defendant learned in March, 1915, that some of the pipe, instead of being made in Reading, was the product of other factories. The plaintiff was accordingly directed by the architect to do the work anew. The plumbing was then encased within the walls except in a few places where it had to be exposed. Obedience to the order meant more than the substitution of other pipe. It meant the demolition at great expense of substantial parts of the completed structure. The plaintiff left the work untouched, and asked for a certificate that the final payment was due. Refusal of the certificate was followed by this suit.

The evidence sustains a finding that the omission of the prescribed brand of pipe was neither fraudulent nor willful. It was the result of the oversight and inattention of the plaintiff's subcontractor. Reading pipe is distinguished from Cohoes pipe and other brands only by the name of the manufacturer stamped upon it at intervals of between six and seven feet. Even the defendant's architect, though he inspected the pipe upon arrival, failed to notice the discrepancy. The plaintiff tried to show that the brands installed, though made by other manufacturers, were the same in quality, in appearance, in market value and in cost as the brand stated in the contract—that they were, indeed, the same thing, though manufactured in another place. The evidence was excluded, and a verdict directed for the defendant. The Appellate Division reversed, and granted a new trial.

We think the evidence, if admitted, would have supplied some basis for the inference that the defect was insignificant in its relation to the project. The courts never say that one who makes a contract fills the measure of his duty by less than full performance. They do say, however, that an omission, both trivial and innocent, will sometimes be atoned for by allowance of the resulting damage, and will not always be the breach of a condition to be followed by a forfeiture * * *. The distinction is akin to that between dependent and independent promises, or between promises and conditions * * * Some promises are so plainly independent that they can never by fair construction be conditions of one another. * * * Others are so plainly dependent that they must always be conditions. Others, though dependent and thus conditions when there is departure in point of substance, will be viewed as independent and collateral when the departure is insignificant * * * Considerations partly of justice and partly of presumable intention are to tell us whether this or that promise shall be placed in one class or in another. The simple and the uniform will call for different remedies from the multifarious and the intricate. The margin of departure within the range of normal expectation upon a sale of common chattels will vary from the margin to be expected upon a contract for the construction of a mansion or a "skyscraper." There will be harshness sometimes and oppression in the implication of a condition when the thing upon which labor has been expended is incapable of surrender because united to the land, and equity and reason in the implication of a like condition when the subject-matter, if defective, is in shape to be returned. From the conclusion that promises may not be treated as dependent to the extent of their uttermost minutiae without a sacrifice of justice, the progress is a short one to the conclusion that they may not be so treated without a perversion of intention. Intention not otherwise revealed may be presumed to hold in contemplation the reasonable and probable. If something else is in view, it must not be left to implication. There will be no assumption of a purpose to visit venial faults with oppressive retribution.

Those who think more of symmetry and logic in the development of legal rules than of practical adaptation to the attainment of a just result will be troubled by a classification where the lines of division are so wavering and blurred. Something, doubtless, may be said on the score of consistency and certainty in favor of a stricter standard. The courts have balanced such considerations against those of equity and fairness, and found the latter to be the weightier. The decisions in this state commit us to the liberal view, which is making its way, nowadays, in jurisdictions slow to welcome it * * * Where the line is to be drawn between the important and the trivial cannot be settled by a formula. "In the nature of the case precise boundaries are impossible". * * * The same omission may take on one aspect or another according to its setting. Substitution of equivalents may not have the same significance in fields of art on the one side and in those of mere utility on the other. Nowhere will change be tolerated, however, if it is so dominant or pervasive as in any real or substantial measure to frustrate the purpose of the contract. * * * There is no general license to install whatever, in the builder's judgment, may be regarded as "just as good". * * * The question is one of degree, to be answered, if there is doubt, by the triers of the facts * * * and, if the inferences are certain, by the judges of the law. * * * We must weigh the purpose to be served, the desire to be gratified, the excuse for deviation from the letter, the cruelty of enforced adherence. Then only can we tell whether literal fulfilment is to be implied by law as a condition. This is not to say that the parties are not free by apt and certain words to effectuate a purpose that performance of every term shall be a condition of recovery. That question is not here. This is merely to say that the law will be slow to impute the purpose, in the silence of the parties, where the significance of the default is grievously out of proportion to the oppression of the forfeiture. The willful transgressor must accept the penalty of his transgression. * * * For him there is no occasion to mitigate the rigor of implied conditions. The transgressor whose default is unintentional and trivial may hope for mercy if he will offer atonement for his wrong * * *

In the circumstances of this case, we think the measure of the allowance is not the cost of replacement, which would be great, but the difference in value, which would be either nominal or nothing. Some of the exposed sections might perhaps have been replaced at moderate expense. The defendant did not limit his demand to them, but treated the plumbing as a unit to be corrected from cellar to roof. In point of fact, the plaintiff never reached the stage at which evidence of the extent of the allowance became necessary. The trial court had excluded evidence that the defect was unsubstantial, and in view of that ruling there was no occasion for the plaintiff to go farther with an offer of proof. We think, however, that the offer, if it had been made, would not of necessity have been defective because directed to difference in value. It is true that in most cases the cost of replacement is the measure. * * * The owner is entitled to the money which will permit him to complete, unless the cost of completion is grossly and unfairly out of proportion to the good to be attained. When that is true, the measure is the difference in value. Specifications call, let us say, for a foundation built of granite quarried in

Vermont. On the completion of the building, the owner learns that through the blunder of a subcontractor part of the foundation has been built of granite of the same quality quarried in New Hampshire. The measure of allowance is not the cost of reconstruction. "There may be missions of that which could not afterwards be supplied exactly as called for by the contract without taking down the building to its foundations, and at the same time the omission may not affect the value of the building for use or otherwise, except so slightly as to be hardly appreciable". * * * The rule that gives a remedy in cases of substantial performance with compensation for defects of trivial or inappreciable importance, has been developed by the courts as an instrument of justice. The measure of the allowance must be shaped to the same end.

The order should be affirmed, and judgment absolute directed in favor of the plaintiff upon the stipulation, with costs in all courts.

McLaughlin, J. (dissenting). I dissent. The plaintiff did not perform its contract. Its failure to do so was either intentional or due to gross neglect which, under the uncontradicted facts, amounted to the same thing, nor did it make any proof of the cost of compliance, where compliance was possible.

Under its contract it obligated itself to use in the plumbing only pipe (between 2,000 and 2,500 feet) made by the Reading Manufacturing Company. The first pipe delivered was about 1,000 feet and the plaintiff's superintendent then called the attention of the foreman of the subcontractor, who was doing the plumbing, to the fact that the specifications annexed to the contract required all pipe used in the plumbing to be of the Reading Manufacturing Company. They then examined it for the purpose of ascertaining whether this delivery was of that manufacture and found it was. Thereafter, as pipe was required in the progress of the work, the foreman of the subcontractor would leave word at its shop that he wanted a specified number of feet of pipe, without in any way indicating of what manufacture. Pipe would thereafter be delivered and installed in the building, without any examination whatever. Indeed, no examination, so far as appears, was made by the plaintiff, the subcontractor, defendant's architect, or any one else, of any of the pipe except the first delivery, until after the building had been completed. Plaintiff's architect then refused to give the certificate of completion, upon which the final payment depended, because all of the pipe used in the plumbing was not of the kind called for by the contract. After such refusal, the subcontractor removed the covering or insulation from about 900 feet of pipe which was exposed in the basement, cellar and attic, and all but 70 feet was found to have been manufactured, not by the Reading Company, but by other manufacturers, some by the Cohoes Rolling Mill Company, some by the National Steel Works, some by the South Chester Tubing Company, and some which bore no manufacturer's mark at all. The balance of the pipe had been so installed in the building that an inspection of it could not be had without demolishing, in part at least, the building itself.

I am of the opinion the trial court was right in directing a verdict for the defendant. The plaintiff agreed that all the pipe used should be of the Reading Manufacturing Company. Only about two-fifths of it, so far as appears, was of that kind. If more were used, then the burden of proving that fact was upon the plaintiff, which it could easily have done, since it knew where the pipe was obtained. The question of substantial performance of a contract of the character of the one under consideration depends in no small degree upon the good faith of the contractor. If the plaintiff had intended to, and had complied with the terms of the contract except as to minor omissions, due to inadvertence, then he might be allowed to recover the contract price, less the amount necessary to fully compensate the defendant for damages caused by such omissions. * * * But that is not this case. It installed between 2,000 and 2,500 feet of pipe, of which only 1,000 feet at most complied with the contract. No explanation was given why pipe called for by the contract was not used, nor was any effort made to show what it would cost to remove the pipe of other manufacturers and install that of the Reading Manufacturing Company. The defendant had a right to contract for what he wanted. He had a right before making payment to get what the contract called for. It is no answer to this suggestion to say that the pipe put in was just as good as that made by the Reading Manufacturing Company, or that the difference in value between such pipe and the pipe made by the Reading Manufacturing Company would be either "nominal or nothing." Defendant contracted for pipe made by the Reading Manufacturing Company. What his reason was for requiring this kind of pipe is of no importance. He wanted that and was entitled to it. It may have been a mere whim on his part, but even so, he had a right to this kind of pipe, regardless of whether some other kind, according to the opinion of the contractor or experts, would have been "just as good, better, or done just as well." He agreed to pay only upon condition that the pipe installed were made by that company and he ought not to be compelled to pay unless that condition be performed. * * * The rule, therefore, of substantial performance, with damages for unsubstantial omissions, has no application. * * *

What was said by this court in *Smith* v. *Brady* * * * is quite applicable here: "I suppose it will be conceded that everyone has a right to build his house, his cottage or his store after such a model and in such style as shall best accord with his notions of utility or be most agreeable to his fancy. The specifications of the contract become the law between the parties until voluntarily changed. If the owner prefers a plain and simple Doric column, and has so provided in the agreement, the contractor has no right to put in its place the more costly and elegant Corinthian. If the owner, having regard to strength and durability, has contracted for walls of specified materials to be laid in a particular manner, or for a given number of joists and beams, the builder has no right to substitute his own judgment or that of others. Having departed from the agreement, if performance has not been waived by the other party, the law will not allow him to allege that he has made as good a building as the one he engaged to erect. He can demand payment only upon and according to the terms of his contract, and if the conditions on which payment is due have not been performed, then the right to demand it does not exist. To hold a different doctrine would be simply to make another contract, and would be giving to parties an encouragement to violate their engagements, which the just policy of the law does not permit." (p. 186.)

I am of the opinion the trial court did not err in ruling on the admission of evidence or in directing a verdict for the defendant.

For the foregoing reasons I think the judgment of the Appellate Division should be reversed and the judgment of the Trial Term affirmed.

QUESTIONS AND NOTES

1. Questions about the facts of this case

    1.1. Do we know why the contract specified pipe of "Reading manufacture"? Should we know? Should that be relevant?

    1.2. Do we know whether the contract contained an express condition? Should that be relevant?

    1.3. As far as you can tell from the opinion, what is the difference between Reading pipe and Cohoes pipe? Is this difference what is driving the lawsuit? If not, what do you think is?

    1.4. Was Jacob & Youngs in breach?

    1.5. Was Jacob & Youngs' breach unintentional?

2. Questions about the law

    2.1. Does either the majority opinion or the dissenting opinion use the term "material breach"? The dissenting opinion refers to "substantial performance." What is the relationship between substantial performance and material breach?

    2.2. Would the result be different if Jacob & Youngs had used neither Reading nor Cohoes but had instead used the vastly inferior Drek paper mache pipe?

    2.3. Would the result have been different if Kent had sued Jacob & Youngs for damages for breach of contract?

    2.4. According to Judge Cardozo, "This is not to say that the parties are not free by apt and certain words to effectuate a purpose that performance of every term shall be a condition of recovery." Have we seen such "apt and certain words" earlier in this Chapter?

3. Notes

    3.1. The requirement of Reading pipe was found in General Condition 225 of the contract. General Condition 22 of the same contract stated:

(22) Where any particular brand of manufactured article is specified, it is to be considered as a standard. Contractors desiring to use another shall first make application in writing to the Architect, stating the difference in cost, and obtain their written approval of the change.

Does examination of this clause make the result reached more or less palatable? *See* RICHARD DANZIG, THE CAPABILITY PROBLEM IN CONTRACT LAW: FURTHER READINGS ON WELL-KNOWN CASES 111–12 (1978).

3.2.   Almost 75 years after *Jacob & Youngs*, the New York Court of Appeals had the occasion to review part of that opinion. In *Oppenheimer & Co., Inc. v. Oppenheim, Appel, Dixon & Co.*, 86 N.Y.2d 685, 660 N.E.2d 415, 636 N.Y.S.2d 734 (1995), two parties signed a sub-lease of New York office space, but made the effectiveness of the lease expressly conditional on obtaining the landlord's consent to making certain tenant improvements necessary for the sub-leasee's business. In particular, the relevant language required the sub-tenant to obtain:

'the Prime Landlord's written notice of confirmation, substantially to the effect that [defendant] is a subtenant of the Premises reasonably acceptable to Prime Landlord.' If such written notice of confirmation were not obtained 'on or before December 30, 1986, then this letter agreement and the Sublease * * * shall be deemed null and void and of no further force and effect and neither party shall have any rights against nor obligations to the other.'

The deadline was mutually extended to February 25, 1987, but still the sub-tenant could not comply. As noted by the court:

However, plaintiff never delivered the prime landlord's written consent to the proposed tenant work on or before the modified final deadline of February 25, 1987. Rather, plaintiff's attorney telephoned defendant's attorney on February 25 and informed defendant that the prime landlord's consent had been secured. On February 26, defendant, through its attorney, informed plaintiff's attorney that the letter agreement and sublease were invalid for failure to timely deliver the prime landlord's written consent and that it would not agree to an extension of the deadline. The document embodying the prime landlord's written consent was eventually received by plaintiff on March 20, 1987, 23 days after expiration of paragraph 4(c)'s modified final deadline.

Okay, so they had only oral consent, not written consent, by the deadline. That's substantial performance within *Jacob & Youngs*, isn't it?

No. As phrased by the New York Court of Appeals:

Plaintiff's reliance on the well-known case of *Jacob & Youngs v. Kent*, is misplaced. There, a contractor built a summer residence and the buyer refused to pay the remaining balance of the contract price on the ground that the contractor used a different type of pipe than was specified in the contract. The buyer sought to enforce the contract as written. This would have involved the demolition of large parts of the structure at great expense and loss to the seller. This Court, in an opinion by then-Judge Cardozo, ruled for the contractor on the ground that "an omission, both trivial and innocent, will sometimes be atoned for by allowance of the resulting damage, and will not always be the breach of a condition to be followed by a forfeiture." But Judge Cardozo was careful to note that the situation would be different in the case of an express condition:

> 'This is not to say that the parties are not free by apt and certain words to effectuate a purpose that performance of every term shall be a condition of recovery. That question is not here. This is merely to say that the law will be slow to impute the purpose, in the silence of the parties, where the significance of the default is grievously out of proportion to the oppression of the forfeiture.'

So there is no lease; just read the "apt and certain" words of the contract. As the New York appeals court concluded in the *Oppenheimer* case: "Freedom of contract prevails in an arm's length transaction between sophisticated parties such as these, and in the absence of countervailing public policy concerns there is no reason to relieve them of the consequences of their bargain. If they are dissatisfied with the consequences of their agreement, 'the time to say so [was] at the bargaining table.' "

The next case does not rely on *Jacob & Youngs*—does not even mention *Jacob & Youngs*. Should it have?

O. W. GRUN ROOFING & CONSTRUCTION CO. v. COPE
Court of Civil Appeals of Texas
529 S.W.2d 258 (1975)

CADENA, J:

Plaintiff, Mrs. Fred M. Cope, sued defendant, O. W. Grun Roofing & Construction Co., to set aside a mechanic's lien filed by defendant and for damages in the sum of $1,500.00 suffered by plaintiff as a result of the alleged failure of defendant to perform a contract calling for the installation of a new roof on plaintiff's home. Defendant, in addition to a general denial, filed a cross-claim for $648.00, the amount which plaintiff agreed to pay defendant for installing the roof, and for foreclosure of the mechanic's lien on plaintiff's home.

Following trial to a jury, the court below entered judgment awarding plaintiff $122.60 as damages for defendant's failure to perform the contract; setting aside the mechanic's lien; and denying defendant recovery on its cross-claim. It is from this judgment that defendant appeals.

The jury found * * * defendant did not substantially perform the contract [and that] * * * the reasonable cost of performing the contract in a good and workmanlike manner would be $777.60. Although the verdict shows the cost of proper performance to be $777.60, the judgment describes this finding as being in the amount of $770.60, and the award of $122.60 to plaintiff is based on the difference between $770.60 and the contract price of $648.00.

* * *

The written contract required defendant to install a new roof on plaintiff's home for $648.00. The contract describes the color of the shingles to be used as "russet glow," which defendant defined as a "brown varied color." Defendant acknowledges that it was his obligation to install a roof of uniform color.

After defendant had installed the new roof, plaintiff noticed that it had streaks which she described as yellow, due to a difference in color or shade of some of the shingles. Defendant agreed to remedy the situation and he removed the nonconforming shingles. However, the replacement shingles do not match the remainder, and photographs introduced in evidence clearly show that the roof is not of a uniform color. Plaintiff testified that her roof has the appearance of having been patched, rather than having been completely replaced. According to plaintiff's testimony, the yellow streaks appeared on the northern, eastern and southern sides of the roof, and defendant only replaced the non-matching shingles on the northern and eastern sides, leaving the southern side with the yellow streaks still apparent. The result is that only the western portion of the roof is of uniform color.

When defendant originally installed the complete new roof, it used 24 "squares" of shingles. In an effort to achieve a roof of uniform color, five squares were ripped off and replaced. There is no testimony as to the number of squares which would have to be replaced on the southern, or rear, side of the house in order to eliminate the original yellow streaks. Although there is expert testimony to the effect that the disparity in color would not be noticeable after the shingles have been on the roof for about a year, there is testimony to the effect that, although some nine or ten months have elapsed since defendant attempted to achieve a uniform coloration, the roof is still "streaky" on three sides. One of defendant's experts testified that if the shingles are properly applied the result will be a "blended" roof rather than a streaked roof.

In view of the fact that the disparity in color has not disappeared in nine or ten months, and in view of the fact that there is testimony to the effect that it would be impossible to secure matching shingles to replace the nonconforming ones, it can reasonably be inferred that a roof of uniform coloration can be achieved only by installing a completely new roof.

The evidence is undisputed that the roof is a substantial roof and will give plaintiff protection against the elements.

The principle which allows recovery for part performance in cases involving dependent promises may be expressed by saying that a material breach or a breach which goes to the root of the matter or essence of the contract defeats the promisor's claim despite his part performance, or it may be expressed by saying that a promisor who has substantially performed is entitled to recover, although he has failed in some particular to comply with his agreement. The latter mode of expressing the rule is generally referred to as the doctrine of substantial performance and is especially common in cases involving building contracts, although its application is not restricted to such contracts.

It is difficult to formulate definitive rule [*sic*] for determining whether the contractor's performance, less than complete, amounts to "substantial performance," since the question is one of fact and of degree, and the answer depends on the particular facts of each case. But, although the decisions furnish no rule of thumb, they are helpful in suggesting guidelines. One of the most obvious factors to be considered is the extent of the nonperformance. The deficiency will not be tolerated if it is so pervasive as to frustrate the purpose of the contract in any real or substantial sense. The doctrine does not bestow on a contractor a license to install whatever is, in his judgment, "just as good." The answer is arrived at by weighing the purpose to be served, the desire to be gratified, the excuse for deviating from the letter of the contract and the cruelty of enforcing strict adherence or of compelling the promisee to receive something less than for which he bargained. Also influential in many cases is the ratio of money value of the tendered performance and of the promised performance. In most cases the contract itself at least is an indication of the value of the promised performance, and courts should have little difficulty in determining the cost of curing the deficiency. But the rule cannot be expressed in terms of a fraction, since complete reliance on a mathematical formula would result in ignoring other important factors, such as the purpose which the promised performance was intended to serve and the extent to which the nonperformance would defeat such purpose, or would defeat it if not corrected.

Although definitions of "substantial performance" are not always couched in the same terminology and, because of the facts involved in a particular case, sometimes vary in the recital of the factors to be considered, the following definition by the Commission of Appeals in *Atkinson v. Jackson Bros.*, 270 S.W. 848, 849 (Tex. Com. App. 1925), is a typical recital of the constituent elements of the doctrine:

> To constitute substantial compliance the contractor must have in good faith intended to comply with the contract, and shall have substantially done so in the sense that the defects are not pervasive, do not constitute a deviation from the general plan contemplated for the work, and are not so essential that the object of the parties in making the contract and its purpose cannot, without difficulty, be accomplished by remedying them. Such performance permits only such omissions or deviations from the contract as are inadvertent and

unintentional, are not due to bad faith, do not impair the structure as a whole, and are remediable without doing material damage to other parts of the building in tearing down and reconstructing.

* * *

What was the general plan contemplated for the work in this case? What was the object and purpose of the parties? It is clear that, despite the frequency with which the courts speak of defects that are not "pervasive," which do not constitute a "deviation from the general plan," and which are "not so essential that the object of the parties in making the contract and its purpose cannot, without difficulty, be accomplished by remedying them," when an attempt is made to apply the general principles to a particular case difficulties are encountered at the outset. Was the general plan to install a substantial roof which would serve the purpose which roofs are designed to serve? Or, rather, was the general plan to install a substantial roof of uniform color? Was the object and purpose of the contract merely to furnish such a roof, or was it to furnish such a roof which would be of a uniform color? It should not come as a shock to anyone to adopt a rule to the effect that a person has, particularly with respect to his home, to choose for himself and to contract for something which exactly satisfies that choice, and not to be compelled to accept something else. In the matter of homes and their decoration, as much as, if not more than, in many other fields, mere taste or preference, almost approaching whimsy, may be controlling with the homeowner, so that variations which might, under other circumstances, be considered trifling, may be inconsistent with that "substantial performance" on which liability to pay must be predicated. Of mere incompleteness or deviations which may be easily supplied or remedied after the contractor has finished his work, and the cost of which to the owner is not excessive and readily ascertainable, present less cause for hesitation in concluding that the performance tendered constitutes substantial performance, since in such cases the owner can obtain complete satisfaction by merely spending some money and deducting the amount of such expenditure from the contract price.

In the case before us there is evidence to support the conclusion that plaintiff can secure a roof of uniform coloring only by installing a completely new roof. We cannot say, as a matter of law, that the evidence establishes that in this case that a roof which so lacks uniformity in color as to give the appearance of a patch job serves essentially the same purpose as a roof of uniform color which has the appearance of being a new roof. We are not prepared to hold that a contractor who tenders a performance so deficient that it can be remedied only by completely redoing the work for which the contract called has established, as a matter of law, that he has substantially performed his contractual obligation.

. . . .

The judgment of the trial court is affirmed.

QUESTIONS AND NOTE

1. Questions about the facts of this case

    1.1.   How much was Grun Roofing paid for its work on the roof?

    1.2.   Did the roof leak? Did the roof "serve the purpose for which roofs are designed to serve"?

    1.3.   Did the contract provide that the roof was to be a uniform color?

2. Questions about the law

    2.1.   How did the court define "substantial performance"?

    2.2.   What was the basis for the court's determination that the uniformity of the color of the roof was important to the Copes? Would the Texas Court of Civil Appeals have reversed the trial court if the trial court had concluded that Grun Roofing's breach was "trivial and innocent"?

    2.3.   Is the court's statement that "It should not come as a shock to anyone to adopt a rule to the effect a person has, particularly with respect to his home, to choose for himself and to contract for something which exactly satisfies his choice, and not to be compelled to accept something else" a shock to anyone who has read *Jacob & Youngs v. Kent*?

3. Note

In *RW Power Partners, L.P. v. Virginia Electric and Power Co.*, 899 F.Supp. 1490 (E.D. Va. 1995), two power companies had entered into a contract for the provision of power over a long-term period. The relationship soured, with Virginia Electric and Power Co. wishing to get out of the contract any legal way it could. Virginia Electric and Power Co. tried to terminate the contract when RW Power breached by failure to keep in place a letter of credit (a financial device akin to a bank guaranty) for a seven to ten-day period. The contract required continuous coverage by the letter of credit; the letter of credit lapse therefore was an incurable breach.

But was the breach material, allowing Virginia Electric to consider its obligations discharged and permitting it to terminate the agreement? Applying the factors set forth in Section 241 of the *Restatement (Second) of Contracts*, quoted in footnote 7 above, the court held that:

Application of these basic principles in this action leads to the inevitable conclusion that the failure to have in place a letter of credit for a period of at most 10 days, during which time no injury befell Virginia Power, was not a material breach of contract. Consequently, Virginia Power was not entitled to terminate the Agreement. It would be entitled to damages for partial breach, but it has shown none.

899 F.Supp. at 1498.

Virginia Electric, however, was not without backup arguments. Pointing to a clause that stated that "If Operator [RW Power] fails to perform any of its obligations pursuant to this Agreement, then Virginia Power may cancel this Agreement," Virginia Electric then argued that the contract of the parties had superceded the common law of material breach, and thus clauses which allow termination for "partial" or "immaterial" breaches are enforceable. The court, while agreeing that parties to a contract may agree to cancellation for any reason, even immaterial breach, did not agree that the contract before it permitted such a cancellation. In trying to give effect to the above language the parties had agreed up for cancellation, the court noted that:

Where the breach is not material and the contract does not explicitly state that an immaterial breach will excuse further performance, termination of the contract is improper, and the injured party is limited to damages for the breach.

Id. at 1502.

Without the explicit notation that an immaterial breach would be grounds for termination, the court declined to permit Virginia Power to terminate the agreement.

Which leads one to wonder how you should draft clauses in which the parties actually agree that immaterial breaches can permit termination. Do you have to put "AND WE REALLY MEAN IT" after every clause in the contract?

———

D. DIVISIBLE CONTRACTS

As *Grun Roofing* illustrates, the rule that a "material breach * * * defeats the promisor's claim" can lead to harsh consequences—Grun Roofing received nothing for its work. There is a tendency on the part of judges, lawyers, law professors and law students to look for ways to avoid or mitigate harsh consequences.

The concept of "divisible" contract is a mitigating doctrine that reduces the harsh consequences in a class of cases. The California Court of Appeals explained the concept of divisible contracts in *Filet Menu, Inc. v. C.C.L. & G., Inc.*, 79 Cal.App.4th 852, 94 Cal.Rptr.2d 438 (Cal. Ct. App. 2000):

A "divisible" contract is one "under which the whole performance is divided into two sets of partial performances, each part of each set being the agreed exchange for a corresponding part of the set of performances to be rendered by the other promisor. * * * * * * It is one in which two or more separate partial performances on each side are agreed to be exchanged for partial performances on the other side. The failure to perform one part does not bar recovery for performance of another. The "performance of each division of the service will be impliedly a condition precedent to the recovery of a corresponding portion of the price."

Once a contract is determined to be divisible, various consequences ensue. "If the performances to be exchanged under an exchange of promises can be apportioned into corresponding pairs of part performances so that the parts of each pair are properly regarded as agreed equivalents, *a party's performance of his part of such a pair has the same effect on the other's duties to render performance of the agreed equivalent as it would have if only that pair of performances had been promised.*" (Rest.2d Contracts, § 240, italics added.) Comment a to section 240, states: "This Section embodies another mitigating doctrine which reduces the risk of forfeiture in that important class of cases in which it is proper to regard corresponding parts of the performances of each party as agreed equivalents. Its effect is to give a party who has performed one of these parts the right to its agreed equivalent just as if the parties had made a separate contract with regard to that pair of corresponding parts." (Rest.2d Contracts, § 240, com. a.) Thus, if a party has breached one part of a divisible contract, he or she is not precluded from obtaining the consideration that was allocated to that portion of the contract that he or she performed.

79 Cal.App.4th at 860.

Apply this concept of divisible contract from *Filet Menu* and *Restatement (Second) of Contracts* § 240 to the following problems:

PROBLEMS ON DIVISIBLE CONTRACTS

1. Ponoroff entered into four separate contracts to develop four different video games for EA for $1,000 a game. Ponoroff again falls short and only develops one of the games, the game covered by the third of the four contracts. Should Ponoroff be able to recover $1,000 from EA under the third contract?

2. Same facts as problem 1 except that Ponoroff and EA sign one contract that provides for payment of $1,000 at the time each of the four games is delivered, instead of four separate contracts. Again, Ponoroff only develops one of the games. Should Ponoroff be able to recover $1,000 from EA under the contract?

3. Same facts as problem 1 except that Ponoroff and EA sign one contract that provides for the payment of $4,000 at the time the four games are delivered, instead of four separate contracts. Again, Ponoroff only develops one of the four games. Should Ponoroff be able to recover from EA under the contract?

E. "PERFECT TENDER"

"Material breach" is a common law concept. Under common law, in contracts such as services contracts only a breach by one of the parties to the contract excuses the performance of the other party to the contract and only if the breach is a "material breach."

This material breach concept is not a part of the law governing sales of goods. The comparable Article 2 concept is "perfect tender." In sale of goods contracts, any breach by a seller will excuse the buyer from performing.

In reading U.C.C. section 2–601 set out below, consider why section 2–601 is called the "perfect tender rule" and whether section 2–601 supports our statement that, "In sale of goods contracts, any breach by the seller will excuse the buyer from performing."

§ 2–601. Buyer's Rights on Improper Delivery.

Subject to the provisions of this Article on breach in installment contracts (Section 2–612) and unless otherwise agreed under the sections on contractual limitations of remedy (Sections 2–718 and 2–719), if the goods or the tender of delivery fail *in any respect* to conform to the contract, the buyer may:

(a) reject the whole; or

(b) accept the whole; or

(c) accept any commercial unit or units and reject the rest.

ALASKA PACIFIC TRADING COMPANY v. EAGON FOREST PRODUCTS, INC.

Court of Appeals of Washington
85 Wn. App. 354, 933 P.2d 417 (1997).

AGID, JUDGE

Alaska Pacific Trading Company (ALPAC) and Eagon Forest Products, Inc. (Eagon) contracted to sell and buy raw logs. After months of communications between the parties, the delivery date passed with no shipment. Eagon canceled the contract, alleging that ALPAC had breached. ALPAC brought an action for breach. The trial court found that ALPAC breached the contract by failing to timely deliver the logs and that there was no modification of the delivery date and Eagon did not repudiate. It granted Eagon's motion for summary judgment. ALPAC contends that failure to timely deliver the goods is not a material breach. * * * We affirm the trial court because ALPAC's failure to timely deliver goods is a material breach * * *

ALPAC and Eagon are both corporations engaged in importing and exporting raw logs. In April 1993, Setsuo Kimura, ALPAC's president, and

C.K. Ahn, Eagon's vice president, entered into a contract under which ALPAC would ship about 15,000 cubic meters of logs from Argentina to Korea between the end of July and the end of August 1993. Eagon agreed to purchase the logs. In the next few months, the market for logs began to soften, making the contract less attractive to Eagon. ALPAC became concerned that Eagon would try to cancel the contract. * * *

The logs were not loaded or shipped by August 31, 1993. * * * ALPAC's first contention is that it did not breach the contract by failing to timely deliver the logs because time of delivery was not a material term of the contract. ALPAC relies on common law contract cases to support its position that, when the parties have not indicated that time is of the essence, late delivery is not a material breach which excuses the buyer's duty to accept the goods. However, as a contract for the sale of goods, this contract is governed by the Uniform Commercial Code, Article II (UCC II) which replaced the common law doctrine of material breach, on which ALPAC relies, with the "perfect tender" rule. Under this rule, "if the goods or the tender of delivery fail in any respect to conform to the contract, the buyer may * * * reject the whole." RCW 62A.2–601(a). Both the plain language of the rule and the official comments clearly state that, if the tender of the goods differs from the terms of the contract in any way, the seller breaches the contract and the buyer is released from its duty to accept the goods * * * ALPAC does not dispute that the contract specified a date for shipment or that the logs were not shipped by that date. Thus, under the applicable "perfect tender" rule, ALPAC breached its duty under the contract and released Eagon from its duty to accept the logs. * * *

QUESTIONS AND CONNECTIONS

1. Questions about the facts

    1.1. Did ALPAC breach the contract?

    1.2. Does ALPAC contend that it did not breach the contract?

        The contract contemplated shipment of logs from Argentina to Korea. A long way. Do you think the distance separating Argentina and Korea was important to Judge Agid in reaching a legal decision? Important to the parties in reaching their decisions?

    1.3. Do we know why Eagon refused late delivery of the logs?

    1.4. Do we know why ALPAC did not timely ship the logs?

2. Questions about the law

    2.1. Why did the appellate court say "We affirm the trial court because ALPAC's failure to timely deliver goods is a material breach"?

    2.2. Why did Article 2 replace the common law material breach rule with its own perfect tender standard?

3. Connections

Good faith: Should Judge Agid's law clerk have seen a connection between this case and the Locke case?

Adequate assurance of future performance: Should ALPAC's attorneys have made a connection to section 2–609 and Norcon?

Epstein contracts to sell his 1973 Cadillac to Markell for $1,000. The contract provides that Epstein shall deliver the car no later than the end of August. Epstein does not deliver the car until September 9. Does Epstein's breach enable Markell to elect not to perform, i.e., not to take and pay for the car? Can Markell elect instead to take the car, pay for it, and sue Epstein for damages for breach of contract? The next case considers election of remedies where there has been a breach of a common law contract.

F. MATERIAL BREACH AND ELECTION OF REMEDIES

ESPN, INC. v. OFFICE OF THE COMMISSIONER OF BASEBALL

U.S. District Court, Southern District of New York
76 F. Supp. 2d 383 (1999)

Opinion and Order

SCHEINDLIN, J.

Introduction

This is a contract dispute between ESPN, Inc. ("ESPN"), an all-sports cable television network, and The Office of Major League Baseball ("Baseball"), which acts on behalf of the Major League Baseball clubs. In 1996, the parties entered into a telecasting agreement (the "1996 Agreement") pursuant to which Baseball granted ESPN the right to telecast regular season major league baseball games on its primary cable service. In exchange, ESPN agreed, among other things, to pay Baseball yearly rights fees and to produce baseball game telecasts on Wednesday and Sunday nights during the regular season.

A. Background

The 1996 Agreement includes two provisions that are the primary focus of this litigation. The first is a representation by ESPN that "it has not made nor will it make any contractual or other commitments that conflict with or will prevent full performance [of the 1996 Agreement]." 1996 Agreement, Ex. O to 10/15/99 Affidavit of Robert J. Kheel, attorney for Baseball ("Kheel Aff."), at 60. The second provision permits ESPN to preempt up to ten baseball games a season with Baseball's prior written approval, which may not be unreasonably withheld. The preemption provision states:

> With the prior written approval of Baseball, which shall not be unreasonably withheld or delayed, ESPN may * * * preempt any [Baseball game telecast] hereunder, up to a maximum of ten [Baseball game telecasts] per year, for an event of significant viewer interest.

Pursuant to this provision, Baseball may telecast the preempted baseball games on its secondary cable service, ESPN2.

On January 13, 1998, ESPN entered into a telecasting contract with the National Football League ("NFL") whereby ESPN obtained the rights to broadcast regular season NFL games on Sunday nights. On January 30, 1998, ESPN requested Baseball's approval to telecast NFL games in place of baseball games on three Sunday nights in September 1998. Baseball declined to approve ESPN's request. Despite Baseball's disapproval, however, ESPN substituted NFL games for baseball games on the three Sunday nights in question. Baseball refused to allow ESPN to broadcast the preempted baseball games on ESPN2.

This exact series of events repeated itself in January 1999, when ESPN again sought Baseball's approval to replace three baseball games scheduled for Sunday nights in September 1999 with football games. Baseball denied ESPN's preemption request; ESPN preempted the three September 1999 baseball games in favor of football games; and Baseball refused to allow ESPN to broadcast the preempted games on ESPN2.

B. Contentions of the Parties

In April 1999, Baseball terminated the 1996 Agreement contending that ESPN had materially breached the contract. In response, ESPN commenced the instant litigation in which it alleges that Baseball materially breached the contract by (i) unreasonably withholding its approval of ESPN's preemption requests in 1998 and 1999; (ii) precluding ESPN from broadcasting the preempted baseball games on ESPN2; and (iii) improperly terminating the parties' agreement. ESPN seeks damages and declaratory and injunctive relief.

Baseball has asserted counterclaims against ESPN in which it alleges that ESPN materially breached the 1996 Agreement by (i) entering into a "conflicting" contract with the NFL; (ii) preempting Baseball games in 1998 and 1999 without ESPN's prior written approval; and (iii) utilizing highlight footage of baseball games in excess of the amount authorized by the 1996 Agreement. Baseball also seeks damages and declaratory and injunctive relief.

. . . . .

I.   Baseball's Motion * * * to Strike the Affirmative Defense of Election of Remedies or in the Alternative for Summary Judgment

In its Amended Answer to Baseball's counterclaim, ESPN asserts the affirmative defense of "election of remedies." By this motion, Baseball seeks to preclude ESPN from asserting such a defense.

A.   Election of Remedies

The doctrine of "election of remedies" provides as follows:

> When a party materially breaches a contract, the non-breaching party must choose between two remedies—[it] can elect to terminate the contract and recover liquidated damages or [it] can continue the contract and recover damages solely for the breach. A party can indicate that [it] has chosen to continue the contract by continuing to perform under the contract or by accepting the performance of the breaching party. Once a party elects to continue the contract, [it] can never thereafter elect to terminate the contract based on that breach, although [it] retains the option of terminating the contract based on other, subsequent breaches.

Bigda v. Fischbach Corp., 898 F.Supp. 1004, 1011–12 (S.D.N.Y. 1995) (citations omitted). * * *

ESPN contends that because Baseball accepted full performance by ESPN for the 1998 and 1999 seasons, it elected to continue the 1996 Agreement and therefore cannot seek termination of the contract based on any alleged breaches by ESPN during those years. According to ESPN, Baseball can only seek damages for ESPN's alleged breaches of the 1996 Agreement.

B.   Ability to Terminate for Alleged 1998 Breaches

To the extent Baseball seeks termination based solely on ESPN's 1998 contract with the NFL or its preemption of three baseball games in 1998—assuming that those acts constitute material breaches of the 1996 Agreement—the election of remedies defense bars such relief. That is, with respect to both of the alleged 1998 breaches, Baseball continued to perform and continued to accept performance under the 1996 Agreement for more than a year, and thus it lost its right to terminate for those breaches. * * *

Baseball concedes that it "continued performance of the 1996 Agreement after ESPN's 1998 breach" but claims that its ability to terminate the agreement based on those breaches is preserved by the contract's broadly worded "no waiver" provision. Essentially, Baseball argues that a contractual "no waiver" provision trumps the common law contract principle of election of remedies. Although Baseball's contention is legally without merit, it raises interesting and seldom addressed issues regarding the relationship between the doctrines of waiver and election and thus merits a more detailed analysis.[3]

1. Waiver Versus Election of Remedies

The doctrines of waiver and election of remedies are complementary rather than competing common law contract principles. Under the doctrine of waiver, "a party may, by words or conduct, waive a provision in a contract or eliminate a condition in a contract which was inserted for [its] benefit." * * * Suppose, for example, that under the 1996 Agreement ESPN is obligated to make bi-weekly payments of $100,000 to Baseball. Suppose further that after several months of making the required bi-weekly payments, ESPN begins to tender monthly payments of $100,000 to Baseball. If Baseball accepts and/or fails to object to ESPN's deficient payments, then Baseball has eliminated or "waived" its contractual right to bi-weekly payments of $100,000 under the 1996 Agreement.[4]

In contrast to a waiver of contractual rights, an election is simply a choice among remedies by the party; it is a decision by that party as to how it should proceed in the wake of the breaching party's nonperformance. In other words, "an election is not a waiver of any rights under the contract but rather a choice between two inconsistent remedies for breach of the contract." * * *

Returning to the hypothetical, suppose that Baseball had, in fact, objected when ESPN began to tender monthly rather than bi-weekly payments. Under these facts, Baseball has preserved its contractual right to bi-weekly payments of $100,000, and thus there is no waiver of that provision. However, Baseball must still decide how to proceed in light of ESPN's hypothetical nonperformance. Assuming that ESPN's hypothetical failure to make timely and sufficient payment is a material breach, Baseball has two choices. It can terminate the parties' contract and claim damages for total breach. Or, it can continue the contract and sue for partial breach. The election of remedies simply requires that Baseball choose or "elect" a single course of action. Thus, if Baseball terminates the contract, then it has elected termination, and it cannot continue to perform or expect performance under the contract. If Baseball chooses to continue the contract, then it has elected to continue, and it cannot later decide to terminate based on the same breach. In essence, the election of remedies doctrine is implicated only in the absence of waiver. That is, if a party waives her right to performance under a contract, then she has no remedies to elect because she has waived her ability to enforce the relevant provision. If a party has not waived her right to enforce a provision in the event of breach, then she can elect the appropriate and

---

3. Baseball also argues that ESPN must demonstrate that it "changed its position to its detriment in reliance on [Baseball's] indication that [it] elected to treat the contract as valid" in order to establish an election of remedies defense. BB MIL at 4. However, the Second Circuit has clearly held that detrimental reliance is not an essential element of an election of remedies defense. * * *

4. Note that a party's waiver of a contract provision is not absolute. That is, a previously waived provision may be restored " 'by a reasonable notice demanding performance and stating that the contract will be rescinded if the notice is not complied with.' " * * *

desired remedy. The key is that once a party has elected a remedy for a particular breach, her choice is binding with respect to that breach.

* * *

The remedy of termination—or, more accurately, the "right" to terminate—is available only where one party has materially breached the contract. A breach is material if it defeats the object of the parties in making the contract and "deprive[s] the injured party of the benefit that it justifiably expected." Farnsworth, Contracts § 8.16 (3d ed.1999). Where a breach is material, the party is justified in refusing to go on, and thus the law provides that party with the right to terminate. And, a party who terminates in response to a material breach presumably does so because it can no longer derive a worthwhile benefit from its contractual relationship.

On the other hand, where a party with the right to terminate chooses instead to continue, the only inference to be drawn is that the party will derive a worthwhile benefit from its contractual relationship. Therefore, the party's election to continue rather than end the contract essentially moots its legal justification for termination. Once a party recognizes contractual benefits in the wake of a material breach, that particular breach can no longer be considered the antithesis of the contract, and it can no longer serve as the basis for termination. Of course, if a party chooses to continue with the contract and the other party subsequently commits another material breach, the party has the right to terminate based on the new breach. This is the scenario to which I now turn.[7]

C.   Termination for Alleged 1999 Breach

Baseball elected to continue the 1996 Agreement despite ESPN's alleged material breaches in 1998. As a result, Baseball can no longer terminate the parties' contract based on those breaches. However, to the extent Baseball seeks termination based upon ESPN's preemption of three baseball games in 1999—assuming arguendo that the 1999 preemptions constitute material breaches of the parties' agreement—the election of remedies doctrine does not bar such relief.

In January 1999, ESPN sought permission to preempt baseball games on three Sunday nights in September 1999. On February 11, Baseball declined to approve the requested preemption. On March 1, ESPN advised Baseball that it would preempt the September games notwithstanding Baseball's denial of its request. In response, on April 21, 1999, Baseball terminated the parties' agreement effective at the end of the Baseball season in October. Baseball's notice of termination stated: "As outlined above, ESPN has materially breached the [1996] Agreement. Therefore,

---

7. For all of the reasons discussed in the preceding section, I reject Baseball's similar argument that the doctrine of election is inapplicable because "in its written correspondence with ESPN on this matter, [Baseball] in addition, reserved specifically all its rights." BB MIL at 6. Regardless of how many times Baseball "reserved its rights" in written correspondence regarding the alleged 1998 breaches, Baseball cannot avoid the fact that once it elected to continue the contract, it lost its ability to terminate based on the 1998 breaches. * * *

Baseball hereby terminates the Agreement pursuant to Paragraph XX.B. thereof effective immediately following the last game of the 1999 regular season." See 5/21/99 letter from Paul Beeston, President and CEO of Baseball, to various officers of ESPN * * *

It is useful to compare Baseball's actions in connection with the alleged 1998 breaches to its actions in connection with the alleged 1998 breaches. In 1998, Baseball clearly elected to continue its contract with ESPN. Although Baseball informed ESPN that it considered the NFL contract and the 1998 preemptions to be material breaches, * * *, and although it "reserved" its right to terminate, * * *, there is no question that Baseball elected to continue and did continue the agreement throughout 1998 and into the 1999 season. In 1999, however, Baseball did not merely mention or reserve its right to terminate, it in fact terminated the agreement.

Despite Baseball's purported election to terminate in April 1999, ESPN maintains that Baseball cannot seek termination based on the 1999 preemptions

> because even while the parties were litigating their claims and counterclaims about the propriety of termination, in which Baseball was insisting that ESPN's actions threatened not just 1998 or 1999 but all five remaining years on the contract, the parties both continued performing under the contract for the full remainder of the 1999 season, with Baseball again receiving from ESPN the full 1999 rights fee of $3.4 million and the national cable telecasting of over 80 of its games.

According to ESPN, "Baseball plainly made a choice. It elected to continue the contract in the face of the claimed breaches and anticipatory breaches as to five years of the contract that it now cites as the basis for termination, and elected to obtain substantial benefits under the contract from ESPN by so doing." In particular, ESPN argues that because Baseball purported to terminate in April 1999 but continued to accept performance under the contract for nearly six more months, it was pursuing two inconsistent courses of action, the very behavior election of remedies disdains.

In response, Baseball asserts that its method of delayed termination was the most reasonable way to sever the parties' contractual relationship. Baseball argues:

> ESPN has cited no cases, nor, we submit, could they, to suggest that Baseball's termination notice was defective because it was not immediately effective at the time the notice was given. Baseball gave ESPN reasonable notice to wind down its relationship with Baseball once Baseball determined that it had no choice but to terminate the 1996 Agreement in view of ESPN's breaches and anticipatory breaches in 1999.

BB Reply at 7. Baseball also states that "the effective date of termination was chosen out of fairness to ESPN and its scheduling arrangements." Id. at 6.

As Baseball notes, there is little guidance regarding whether a party can give present notice of future termination without running afoul of election of remedies. Again, it is helpful to look at the policy underlying that doctrine. To begin, "the doctrine of election permits parties to wait a 'reasonable time' after learning of the alleged breaches before terminating the contract. * * * [H]ow much time is reasonable depends on the nature of the performance to be rendered under the contract." * * * The critical factor is not the passage of time but "whether the non-breaching party has taken an action (or failed to take an action) that indicated to the breaching party that [it] had made an election." * * *

In the instant case, the issue is not whether Baseball rendered or accepted performance during the time between breach and election but whether Baseball rendered or accepted performance during the time between its election of termination and the effective date of that termination.[8] On the one hand, both Baseball and ESPN tendered and accepted dozens of performances during the six months between April and October 1999. Indeed, ESPN telecast approximately eighty baseball games during the 1999 season. However, those individual performances were part of a more global performance. Stated somewhat differently, the 1996 Agreement, in keeping with its subject matter, is seasonal in nature. As a result, it calls for seasonal performance. For example, the baseball games that are ultimately telecast on ESPN are organized and scheduled months in advance. Indeed, under the 1996 Agreement, Baseball must provide ESPN with a regular season schedule of games "no later than August 15th of the calendar year preceding each Baseball season." * * * By the time the baseball season commences each spring, the parties' global performance for that season is already well under way. Games and other programming have been scheduled and those schedules have been published to, and relied upon by, third parties including sponsors, advertisers, the media and the public. Of course, performance continues throughout the summer and fall as baseball games are telecast and payment is made, but it is clearly all part of the same seasonal undertaking.

---

8. There is no question that Baseball's April 1999 termination was timely. Pursuant to the doctrine of anticipatory repudiation, Baseball had no duty to "elect its remedies" prior to ESPN's actual breach of the contract in September 1999. Under New York law, where an anticipatory breach has occurred the party may either sue immediately or wait until there has been actual breach:

When a promisor repudiates a contract, the injured party faces an election of remedies; [it] can treat the repudiation as an anticipatory breach and immediately seek damages for breach of contract, thereby terminating the contractual relation between parties, or [it] can treat the repudiation as an empty threat, wait until the time for performance arrives and exercise [its] remedies for actual breach if a breach does in fact occur at such time.

Silver Air v. Aeronautic Dev. Corp. Ltd., 656 F.Supp. 170, 178 (S.D.N.Y.1987) (internal quotations omitted). Accordingly, Baseball could have waited until ESPN actually preempted the September 1999 baseball games to seek termination of the contract.

This difference is critical because it demonstrates that Baseball did not act inconsistently when it terminated effective at the end of the season. Instead, Baseball's method of termination merely mirrored the nature of the 1996 Agreement. At the time Baseball elected to terminate the contract in April 1999, the 1999 season and performance for that season was well underway. Thus, rather than stop the agreement mid-performance at a high cost to both parties and nonparties, Baseball simply notified ESPN that it would render and accept no "new" performance under the contract; it would not go forward with the 2000 season.[9]

Not only do I find that Baseball's approach did not violate the doctrine of election, I also find that it was eminently reasonable under the circumstances. Had Baseball terminated effective immediately, not only would both parties have suffered enormous hardship, an immeasurable number of third parties including sponsors, advertisers and the public would have been affected. In an industry where so much time and energy is expended in advance preparation, it makes little sense to treat the fruits of those efforts as a wholly separate "performance" for purposes of the election of remedies defense. I suspect that if ESPN were not Baseball's adversary in this litigation, it would appreciate rather than complain of Baseball's considerate approach to termination.

Accordingly, I find as a matter of law that if the 1999 preemptions by themselves or in connection with other alleged breaches constitute a material breach, Baseball has a right to terminate the 1996 Agreement.

     * * *

E. Conclusion

As a matter of law, Baseball cannot terminate the 1996 Agreement based on ESPN's 1998 contract with the NFL or its 1998 preemptions of baseball games, regardless of whether those actions constitute material breaches of the 1996 Agreement. However, if the 1999 preemptions constitute a material breach of the parties' agreement then Baseball can terminate the contract.

QUESTIONS

1. Questions about the facts of this case

    1.1. Did ESPN breach? How many times? What were the breaches in 1998? What were the breaches in 1999? Were the breaches "material"?

    1.2. Did Baseball make an election of remedies? How many times? The same election each time?

---

9. This is markedly different than Baseball's response to the alleged 1998 breaches. In 1998, Baseball not only completed performance of the 1998 season, but it started and continued performance for the new 1999 season.

1.3. Were there explicit contract provisions governing termination of the contract?

1.4. What facts lead the court to conclude that the 1999 termination was "eminently reasonable"?

2. Questions about the law

2.1. What does the court mean by "election of remedies"? What is the relationship between "material breach" and "election of remedies"?

2.2. Did the *Alaska Pacific Trading* case involve an election of remedies? A material breach?

2.3. Is the court right that Baseball can terminate for reasons other than the ones it states? Recall that Baseball based its termination on the 1998 *and* 1999 breaches by ESPN; the court disallowed termination based on the 1998 breaches.

2.4. Epstein contracts with Markell to provide ten lessons on case book writing. If Epstein is a no-show for the first tutoring session, advise Markell based upon *ESPN* what to do if Markell wants to be done with Epstein and hire Ponoroff, a cheaper and more energetic tutor than the aged Epstein. Assume that Markell doesn't really want to pursue any remedies against Epstein (being quit of him is sufficient, thank you), but Markell sure doesn't want Epstein suing him for breach.

ONE MORE NOTE ON "SUBSTANTIAL PERFORMANCE" (A/K/A "PARTIAL BREACH") AND "MATERIAL BREACH" (A/K/A "TOTAL BREACH")

As *ESPN* notes, remedies often turn on whether the breach is "material." To expand upon *ESPN*, there is an essential link between a material breach and how much you can sue for in damages. As stated in section 243(1) of the *Restatement (Second) of Contracts*, "With respect to performances to be exchanged under an exchange of promises, a breach by non-performance gives rise to a claim for damages for total breach only if it discharges the injured party's remaining duties to render such performance. * * *"

What is the difference between a total and partial breach? Again, the *Restatement*:

  b. Total and partial breach distinguished. *Although every breach gives rise to a claim for damages, not every claim for damages is one for damages based on all of the injured party's remaining rights to performance under the contract. Such a claim is said to be one for damages for total breach. * * * If the injured party elects to or is required to await the balance of the other party's performance under the contract, his claim is said instead to be one for damages for partial breach. For example, an injured party who claims damages in addition to specific performance claims damages for partial breach. Rules for determining whether a particular breach gives rise to a claim for damages for partial breach, for total breach, or for either partial or* *total breach at the election of the injured party are stated in §§ 243 [relating to material breach] and 253 [relating to repudiation].*

Restatement (Second) of Contracts § 236, com. b.

Thus, if the breach is material, then the non-breaching party is not only justified in suspending its performance and, if it is sufficiently serious, canceling the contract (thus preventing any executory duties it has from maturing), but it may also then sue for damages measured by the breaching party's failure to perform now, *and* in the future. As indicated above, this is sometimes referred to as suing for "total" breach, and the remedies examined in Chapter Seven will often assume that such a total breach exists (that is, the breacher's conduct constitutes a material breach).

But what if the breach is not material, or as in *ESPN*, there is an argument that the other side "accepted" the material breach and continued performance? There still is a breach, and there still is a remedy in damages— but only for the present breach, not for a cessation of all future obligations. This is often referred to as "partial" breach.

Whether the breach is "material" or "partial", the nonbreaching party to the contract still has a right to a legal remedy. The next chapter addresses the question of what is the appropriate remedy for a breach of contract.

CHAPTER SEVEN

HOW DOES THE LAW ENFORCE A DEAL?

■ ■ ■

SECTION 1:   THE PROBLEM EXAMINED

So what's a young lawyer to do when a senior lawyer hands him (as happened to one of your casebook authors on his first day as a lawyer) a contract with a scribbled notation "Get our client out of this"? You know from Chapter 4 that some agreements are unenforceable because of problems with the agreement process or the language of the agreement. And you know from Chapter 6 that contract performance is sometimes excused because of something that happens (or does not happen) after the agreement. More important, you know that the cases in Chapters 4 and 6 are outliers. How should you advise a client who wants out of a legally enforceable agreement?

For example, assume that your client Ponoroff has contracted to wash Markell's car for $10 on Monday, and Ponoroff wants out of the contract. No Chapter 4 defenses, no Chapter 6 excuses. What advice should you give Ponoroff?

Is it "bad" to advise the client to breach? Many judges and professors have said "no", with one of the earliest being Oliver Wendell Holmes, Jr. In his classic series of lectures, *The Common Law,* Holmes said this in 1881:

> The only universal consequence of a legally binding promise is, that the law makes the promisor pay damages if the promised event does not come to pass. In every case it leaves him free from interference until the time for fulfillment has gone by, and therefore free to break his contract if he chooses.

OLIVER WENDELL HOLMES, JR., THE COMMON LAW 236 (Mark DeWolfe Howe ed., 1963).

Holmes said it more forcefully some sixteen years later, in his article *The Path of the Law:*

> Nowhere is the confusion between legal and moral ideas more manifest than in the law of contract. Among other things, here again the so-called primary rights and duties are invested with a mystic signifi-

cance beyond what can be assigned and explained. The duty to keep a contact at common law means a prediction that you must pay damages if you do not keep it—and nothing else. * * * But such a mode of looking at the matter stinks in the nostrils of those who think it advantageous to get as much ethics into the law as they can. * * *

Oliver Wendell Holmes, Jr., *The Path of the Law*, 10 HARV. L. REV. 457 (1897).

So, according to Holmes, there is no moral component to the law of contracts.

Should there be a moral component to the law of contracts? And, if so, should the law enforce that moral component?

Some might say that if we were really serious about people keeping their promises, we would simply put contract breachers in jail. Or we could just brand the breacher's forehead with a scarlet "B." Of course, we don't do any of these things.

You might take this as an indication of a lack of societal interest in having people honor their contracts, but that would be too hasty a conclusion. While punishment of the breaching party might discourage or deter future breaches of other contracts, it does not accomplish "diddly-squat"[1] for the party who was expecting performance. For that party (sometimes referred to as the "aggrieved party," sometimes referred to as the "non-breaching party", sometimes referred to as the "injured party") society does provide courts with enforcement mechanisms to allow a chance for redress.

But what form does this redress take? While we don't throw contract breachers in jail, should we make them do what they promised they would do? Put another way, if Markell has a valid contract with Ponoroff to wash Markell's car for $10 on Monday, and Ponoroff hasn't washed it by lunch, can Markell run to court on his lunch hour and get a court to sign an order directing Ponoroff to wash the car that afternoon?

The next series of cases looks at the issues raised by having courts order people to perform specific tasks that they have promised to perform. This form of redress, or relief, is called "specific performance" and the following case looks at when a court will order that type of relief.

SECTION 2: SPECIFIC PERFORMANCE

You can't always get what you want,
You can't always get what you want,
You can't always get what you want,
But if you try sometimes, you just might find
You'll get what you need.

---

1. Two of your co-authors have spent a substantial portion of their lives in the Midwest. The other author requires constant translations.

Keith Richards & Mick Jagger of the *Rolling Stones*
You Can't Always Get What You Want,
on Let It Bleed (ABKCO Records 1969)

VAN WAGNER ADVERTISING CORP.
v. S & M ENTERPRISES

Court of Appeals of New York
67 N.Y.2d 186, 501 N.Y.S.2d 628, 492 N.E.2d 756 (1986)

Kaye, Judge.

* * *

By agreement dated December 16, 1981, Barbara Michaels leased to plaintiff, Van Wagner Advertising, for an initial period of three years plus option periods totaling seven additional years space on the eastern exterior wall of a building on East 36th Street in Manhattan. Van Wagner was in the business of erecting and leasing billboards, and the parties anticipated that Van Wagner would erect a sign on the leased space, which faced an exit ramp of the Midtown Tunnel and was therefore visible to vehicles entering Manhattan from that tunnel.

In early 1982 Van Wagner erected an illuminated sign and leased it to Asch Advertising, Inc. for a three-year period commencing March 1, 1982. However, by agreement dated January 22, 1982, Michaels sold the building to defendant S & M Enterprises. Michaels informed Van Wagner of the sale in early August 1982, and on August 19, 1982 S & M sent Van Wagner a letter purporting to cancel the lease as of October 18 pursuant to section 1.05. [As the lower court found, and as this court affirmed, that letter constituted a breach of the lease. The trial court then] declared the lease valid and subsisting and found that the demised space is unique as to location for the particular advertising purpose intended by Van Wagner and Michaels, the original parties to the Lease. However, the court declined to order specific performance in light of its finding that Van Wagner "has an adequate remedy at law for damages. Moreover, the court noted that specific performance would be inequitable in that its effect would be disproportionate in its harm to the defendant and its assistance to plaintiff. Concluding that [t]he value of the unique qualities of the demised space has been fixed by the contract Van Wagner has with its advertising client, Asch for the period of the contract, the court awarded Van Wagner the lost revenues on the Asch sublease for the period through trial, * * *

Given defendant's unexcused failure to perform its contract, we * * * turn to a consideration of remedy for the breach: Van Wagner seeks specific performance of the contract, S & M urges that money damages are adequate but that the amount of the award was improper.[1]

---

1. We note that the parties' contentions regarding the remedy of specific performance in general, mirror a scholarly debate that has persisted throughout our judicial history. While the

Whether or not to award specific performance is a decision that rests in the sound discretion of the trial court, and here that discretion was not abused. Considering first the nature of the transaction, specific performance has been imposed as the remedy for breach of contracts for the sale of real property * * *, but the contract here is to lease rather than sell an interest in real property. While specific performance is available, in appropriate circumstances, for breach of a commercial or residential lease, specific performance of real property leases is not in this State awarded as a matter of course.

Van Wagner argues that specific performance must be granted in light of the trial court's finding that the "demised space is unique as to location for the particular advertising purpose intended. The word "uniqueness" is not, however, a magic door to specific performance. A distinction must be drawn between physical difference and economic interchangeability. The trial court found that the leased property is physically unique, but so is every parcel of real property and so are many consumer goods. Putting aside contracts for the sale of real property, where specific performance has traditionally been the remedy for breach, uniqueness in the sense of physical difference does not itself dictate the propriety of equitable relief.

By the same token, at some level all property may be interchangeable with money. Economic theory is concerned with the degree to which consumers are willing to substitute the use of one good for another, the underlying assumption being that "every good has substitutes, even if only very poor ones", and that "all goods are ultimately commensurable" (*id.*). Such a view, however, could strip all meaning from uniqueness, for if all goods are ultimately exchangeable for a price, then all goods may be valued. Even a rare manuscript has an economic substitute in that there is a price for which any purchaser would likely agree to give up a right to buy it, but a court would in all probability order specific performance of such a contract on the ground that the subject matter of the contract is unique.

The point at which breach of a contract will be redressable by specific performance thus must lie not in any inherent physical uniqueness of the property but instead in the uncertainty of valuing it: "What matters, in measuring money damages, is the volume, refinement, and reliability of the available information about substitutes for the subject matter of the breached contract. When the relevant information is thin and unreliable, there is a substantial risk that an award of money damages will either exceed or fall short of the promisee's actual loss. Of course this risk can always be reduced-but only at great cost when reliable information is difficult to obtain. Conversely, when there is a great deal of consumer behavior generating abundant and highly dependable information about substitutes, the risk of error in measuring the promisee's loss may be reduced at much smaller cost. In asserting that the subject matter of a

---

usual remedy in Anglo–American law has been money damages, rather than specific performance, there are prominent law professors who have argued for increased use of specific performance.

particular contract is unique and has no established market value, a court is really saying that it cannot obtain, at reasonable cost, enough information about substitutes to permit it to calculate an award of money damages without imposing an unacceptably high risk of undercompensation on the injured promisee. Conceived in this way, the uniqueness test seems economically sound." (45 U Chi L Rev, at 362.) This principle is reflected in the case law and is essentially the position of the Restatement (Second) of Contracts, which lists "the difficulty of proving damages with reasonable certainty" as the first factor affecting adequacy of damages (Restatement [Second] of Contracts § 360[a]).

Thus, the fact that the subject of the contract may be "unique as to location for the particular advertising purpose intended" by the parties does not entitle a plaintiff to the remedy of specific performance.

Here, the trial court correctly concluded that the value of the "unique qualities" of the demised space could be fixed with reasonable certainty and without imposing an unacceptably high risk of undercompensating the injured tenant. Both parties complain: Van Wagner asserts that while lost revenues on the Asch contract may be adequate compensation, that contract expired February 28, 1985, its lease with S & M continues until 1992, and the value of the demised space cannot reasonably be fixed for the balance of the term. S & M urges that future rents and continuing damages are necessarily conjectural, both during and after the Asch contract, and that Van Wagners damages must be limited to 60 days-the period during which Van Wagner could cancel Asch's contract without consequence in the event Van Wagner lost the demised space. S & M points out that Van Wagner's lease could remain in effect for the full 10–year term, or it could legitimately be extinguished immediately, either in conjunction with a bona fide sale of the property by S & M, or by a reletting of the building if the new tenant required use of the billboard space for its own purposes. Both parties' contentions were properly rejected.

First, it is hardly novel in the law for damages to be projected into the future. Particularly where the value of commercial billboard space can be readily determined by comparisons with similar uses—Van Wagner itself has more than 400 leases—the value of this property between 1985 and 1992 cannot be regarded as speculative. Second, S & M having successfully resisted specific performance on the ground that there is an adequate remedy at law, cannot at the same time be heard to contend that damages beyond 60 days must be denied because they are conjectural. If damages for breach of this lease are indeed conjectural, and cannot be calculated with reasonable certainty, then S & M should be compelled to perform its contractual obligation by restoring Van Wagner to the premises. Moreover, the contingencies to which S & M points do not, as a practical matter, render the calculation of damages speculative. While S & M could terminate the Van Wagner lease in the event of a sale of the building, this building has been sold only once in 40 years; S & M paid several million dollars, and purchased the building in connection with its plan for major development of the block. The theoretical termination right of a future tenant of the existing building also must be viewed in light of these circumstances. If any uncertainty is generated by the two contingencies, then the benefit of that doubt must go to Van Wagner and not the contract violator. Neither contingency allegedly affecting Van Wagner's continued contractual right to the space for the balance of the lease term is within its own control; on the contrary, both are in the interest of S & M * * * Thus, neither the need to project into the future nor the contingencies allegedly affecting the length of Van Wagner's term render inadequate the remedy of damages for S & M's breach of its lease with Van Wagner.

The trial court, additionally, correctly concluded that specific performance should be denied on the ground that such relief "would be inequitable in that its effect would be disproportionate in its harm to defendant and its assistance to plaintiff" (see Restatement [Second] of Contracts § 364[1] [b]). It is well settled that the imposition of an equitable remedy must not itself work an inequity, and that specific performance should not be an undue hardship. Here, * * * the finding that specific performance would disproportionately harm S & M and benefit Van Wagner has been affirmed by the Appellate Division and has support in the proof regarding S & M's projected development of the property. [As a consequence,] specific performance was properly denied * * *

QUESTIONS AND NOTES

1. Questions about the facts of this case
    1.1. Did Michaels' sale of the building to S & M Enterprises terminate Michaels' lease to Van Wagner?
    1.2. What is the "demised space"? Was the "demised space" unique?
    1.3. What is plaintiff Van Wagner losing because of S & M's breach? Is there anything unique about what Van Wagner is losing because of S & M's breach?
    1.4. Why did the trial court find that "specific performance would disproportionately harm S & M and benefit Van Wagner"? Was that finding important? Outcome determinative?

2. Questions about the law in this case
    2.1. The court indicates that under New York law (which, on this issue, is reflective of American common law generally), specific performance "rests in the discretion of the trial court." Why bother with precedent if ultimately the court is guided by its own discretion?
    2.2. The court also distinguishes between real estate sales contracts ("specific performance * * * the remedy") and real estate leases ("specific performance is available, in appropriate circumstances.") Is there a policy basis for the distinction?

2.3 The court also states: " 'uniqueness' is not, however, a magic door to specific performance." Is this statement consistent with the Uniform Commercial Code section 2–716(1) which governs specific performance of a contract to sell goods? Here is what section 2–716(1) says:

> (1) Specific performance may be decreed if the goods are unique or in other proper circumstances. * * *

3. Notes

3.1. The preference for damages over specific performance tends to be limited to Anglo–American systems. The *UNIDROIT Principles of International Commercial Contracts*, for example, states that "[w]here a party who owes an obligation other than one to pay money does not perform, the other party may require performance," subject to certain restrictions such as impossible or unreasonably burdensome performance. Art. 7.2.2.

Similarly, the *Convention on the International Sales of Goods* says, in Article 46(1), that the buyer of goods "may require performance by the seller of his obligations." If the seller delivers goods that do not meet contract specifications, "the buyer may require delivery of substitute goods" if the goods that were delivered would have represented a fundamental breach of contract (defined in Article 25 of the *CISG*). Finally, if a seller under the *CISG* delivers goods that do not comply with the contract, "the buyer may require the seller to remedy the lack of conformity by repair, unless this is unreasonable having regard to all the circumstances."

3.2. As indicated in the footnote in *Van Wagner*, there is significant debate as to whether the adequacy of remedy rule retains any true vitality. In *The Death of the Irreparable Injury Rule*, 103 HARV. L. REV. 687 (1990), Professor Douglas Laycock argued at length that courts have essentially vitiated the rule that money damages are an adequate substitute for actual performance. His words: "Courts have escaped the rule by defining adequacy in such a way that damages are never an adequate substitute for plaintiff's loss. Thus, our law embodies a preference for specific relief if plaintiff wants it." *Id.* at 691.

3.3. Is the difficulty to quantify damages exactly the only basis for the inadequacy of the law remedy? Perhaps not. In *Miller v. LeSea Broadcasting, Inc.*, 87 F.3d 224 (7th Cir. 1996), a television station manager had bargained for the right of first refusal regarding the sale of the television station. When the station owner breached that duty, the manager sued for specific performance. The court, speaking through Chief Judge Posner, first noted that:

> The normal remedy for breach of contract is an award of damages. Specific performance is exceptional, for reasons unnecessary to get into here. * * * The exception comes into play when damages are an inadequate remedy, whether because of

the defendant's lack of solvency or because of the difficulty of quantifying the injury to the victim of the breach. * * *

The *Restatement (Second) of Contracts* deals with specific performance in section 357(1) and with injunctive relief in section 357(2) and uses the phrases "granted in the discretion of the court" in both. What are the differences between "specific performance" and an "injunction"? If H, the head chef at the Capital City Club, breaches her two-year employment contract so that she can work at the Piedmont Driving Club, is the court more likely to grant specific performance or injunctive relief?

Is the next case a "specific performance case" or an "injunction case"? Was the answer to that question important to Judge Posner? (Regardless of whether that question was important to Judge Posner [or you], it still might be important to your contracts professor.)

WALGREEN CO. v. SARA CREEK PROPERTY CO., B.V.

United States Court of Appeals, Seventh Circuit
966 F.2d 273 (1992)

POSNER, CIRCUIT JUDGE.

This appeal from the grant of a permanent injunction raises fundamental issues concerning the propriety of injunctive relief. * * * The essential facts are simple. Walgreen has operated a pharmacy in the Southgate Mall in Milwaukee since its opening in 1951. Its current lease, signed in 1971 and carrying a 30–year, 6–month term, contains, as had the only previous lease, a clause in which the landlord, Sara Creek, promises not to lease space in the mall to anyone else who wants to operate a pharmacy or a store containing a pharmacy. * * *

In 1990, fearful that its largest tenant-what in real estate parlance is called the "anchor tenant"–having gone broke was about to close its store, Sara Creek informed Walgreen that it intended to buy out the anchor tenant and install in its place a discount store operated by Phar–Mor Corporation, a "deep discount" chain, rather than, like Walgreen, just a "discount" chain. Phar–Mor's store would occupy 100,000 square feet, of which 12,000 would be occupied by a pharmacy the same size as Walgreen's. The entrances to the two stores would be within a couple of hundred feet of each other.

Walgreen filed this diversity suit for breach of contract against Sara Creek and Phar–Mor and asked for an injunction against Sara Creek's letting the anchor premises to Phar–Mor. After an evidentiary hearing, the judge found a breach of Walgreen's lease and entered a permanent injunction against Sara Creek's letting the anchor tenant premises to Phar–Mor until the expiration of Walgreen's lease. He did this over the defendants' objection that Walgreen had failed to show that its remedy at law-damages-for the breach of the exclusivity clause was inadequate. Sara

Creek had put on an expert witness who testified that Walgreen's damages could be readily estimated, and Walgreen had countered with evidence from its employees that its damages would be very difficult to compute, among other reasons because they included intangibles such as loss of goodwill.

Sara Creek reminds us that damages are the norm in breach of contract as in other cases. Many breaches, it points out, are "efficient" in the sense that they allow resources to be moved into a more valuable use. Perhaps this is one-the value of Phar–Mor's occupancy of the anchor premises may exceed the cost to Walgreen of facing increased competition. If so, society will be better off if Walgreen is paid its damages, equal to that cost, and Phar–Mor is allowed to move in rather than being kept out by an injunction. That is why injunctions are not granted as a matter of course, but only when the plaintiff's damages remedy is inadequate. Walgreen's is not. Sara Creek argues; the projection of business losses due to increased competition is a routine exercise in calculation. Damages representing either the present value of lost future profits or the diminution in the value of the leasehold have either been awarded or deemed the proper remedy in a number of reported cases for breach of an exclusivity clause in a shopping-center lease. * * * Why, Sara Creek asks, should they not be adequate here?

Sara Creek makes a beguiling argument that contains much truth, but we do not think it should carry the day. For if, as just noted, damages have been awarded in some cases of breach of an exclusivity clause in a shopping-center lease, injunctions have been issued in others. * * * The choice between remedies requires a balancing of the costs and benefits of the alternatives. * * * The task of striking the balance is for the trial judge, subject to deferential appellate review in recognition of its particularistic, judgmental, fact-bound character. * * *

The plaintiff who seeks an injunction has the burden of persuasion-damages are the norm, so the plaintiff must show why his case is abnormal. But when, as in this case, the issue is whether to grant a permanent injunction, not whether to grant a temporary one, the burden is to show that damages are inadequate * * *

The benefits of substituting an injunction for damages are twofold. First, it shifts the burden of determining the cost of the defendant's conduct from the court to the parties. If it is true that Walgreen's damages are smaller than the gain to Sara Creek from allowing a second pharmacy into the shopping mall, then there must be a price for dissolving the injunction that will make both parties better off. Thus, the effect of upholding the injunction would be to substitute for the costly processes of forensic fact determination the less costly processes of private negotiation. Second, a premise of our free-market system, and the lesson of experience here and abroad as well, is that prices and costs are more accurately determined by the market than by government. A battle of experts is a less reliable method of determining the actual cost to Walgreen of facing new competition than negotiations between Walgreen and Sara Creek over the price at which Walgreen would feel adequately compensated for having to face that competition.

That is the benefit side of injunctive relief but there is a cost side as well. Many injunctions require continuing supervision by the court, and that is costly. * * * A request for specific performance (a form of mandatory injunction) of a franchise agreement was refused on this ground in *North American Financial Group, Ltd. v. S.M.R. Enterprises, Inc.*, 583 F.Supp. 691, 699 (N.D.Ill.1984). * * * Some injunctions are problematic because they impose costs on third parties.

The determination of Walgreen's damages would have been costly in forensic resources and inescapably inaccurate. * * * The lease had ten years to run. So Walgreen would have had to project its sales revenues and costs over the next ten years, and then project the impact on those figures of Phar–Mor's competition, and then discount that impact to present value. All but the last step would have been fraught with uncertainty. * * *

It is difficult to forecast the profitability of a retail store over a decade, let alone to assess the impact of a particular competitor on that profitability over that period. Of course one can hire an expert to make such predictions, * * * and if injunctive relief is infeasible the expert's testimony may provide a tolerable basis for an award of damages. We cited cases in which damages have been awarded for the breach of an exclusivity clause in a shopping-center lease. But they are awarded in such circumstances not because anyone thinks them a clairvoyant forecast but because it is better to give a wronged person a crude remedy than none at all. * * * Sara Creek presented evidence of what happened (very little) to Walgreen when Phar–Mor moved into other shopping malls in which Walgreen has a pharmacy, and it was on the right track in putting in comparative evidence. But there was a serious question whether the other malls were actually comparable to the Southgate Mall, so we cannot conclude, in the face of the district judge's contrary conclusion, that the existence of comparative evidence dissolved the difficulties of computing damages in this case. Sara Creek complains that the judge refused to compel Walgreen to produce all the data that Sara Creek needed to demonstrate the feasibility of forecasting Walgreen's damages. Walgreen resisted, on grounds of the confidentiality of the data and the cost of producing the massive data that Sara Creek sought. Those are legitimate grounds; and the cost (broadly conceived) they expose of pretrial discovery, in turn presaging complexity at trial, is itself a cost of the damages remedy that injunctive relief saves.

Damages are not always costly to compute, or difficult to compute accurately. In the standard case of a seller's breach of a contract for the sale of goods where the buyer covers by purchasing the same product in the market, damages are readily calculable by subtracting the contract price from the market price and multiplying by the quantity specified in the contract. But this is not such a case and here damages would be a costly and inaccurate remedy; and on the other side of the balance some of the costs of an injunction are absent and the cost that is present seems low. The injunction here, like one enforcing a covenant not to compete (standardly enforced by injunction) * * * is a simple negative injunction-Sara Creek is not to lease space in the Southgate Mall to Phar–Mor during the term of Walgreens lease-and the costs of judicial supervision and enforcement should be negligible. * * *

To summarize, the judge did not exceed the bounds of reasonable judgment in concluding that the costs (including forgone benefits) of the damages remedy would exceed the costs (including forgone benefits) of an injunction. We need not consider whether, as intimated by Walgreen, exclusivity clauses in shopping-center leases should be considered presumptively enforceable by injunctions. Although we have described the choice between legal and equitable remedies as one for case-by-case determination, the courts have sometimes picked out categories of case in which injunctive relief is made the norm. The best-known example is specific performance of contracts for the sale of real property. * * * The rule that specific performance will be ordered in such cases as a matter of course is a generalization of the considerations discussed above. Because of the absence of a fully liquid market in real property and the frequent presence of subjective values (many a homeowner, for example, would not sell his house for its market value), the calculation of damages is difficult; and since an order of specific performance to convey a piece of property does not create a continuing relation between the parties, the costs of supervision and enforcement if specific performance is ordered are slight. The exclusivity clause in Walgreen's lease relates to real estate, but we hesitate to suggest that every contract involving real estate should be enforceable as a matter of course by injunctions. Suppose Sara Creek had covenanted to keep the entrance to Walgreen's store free of ice and snow, and breached the covenant. An injunction would require continuing supervision, and it would be easy enough if the injunction were denied for Walgreen to hire its own ice and snow remover and charge the cost to Sara Creek. * * * On the other hand, injunctions to enforce exclusivity clauses are quite likely to be justifiable by just the considerations present here-damages are difficult to estimate with any accuracy and the injunction is a one-shot remedy requiring no continuing judicial involvement. So there is an argument for making injunctive relief presumptively appropriate in such cases, but we need not decide in this case how strong an argument.

Questions and Note

1. Questions about the facts of the case
    1.1. Who sued whom for what? Who won at the trial court level?

1.2. Do you think that there were more than two stores in the South-gate Mall in Milwaukee? http://www.labelscar.com/wisconsin/southgate-mall Should that be relevant in this litigation between the landlord and one tenant?

2. Questions about the law

2.1. Do you agree with Judge Posner's statement that "a battle of experts is a less reliable method of determining the actual cost to Walgreen of facing new competition than negotiations between Walgreen and Sara Creek"? Do you think negotiations between Walgreen and Sara Creek after Posner affirmed the injunctive relief focused on the "actual cost to Walgreen of facing new competition"?

2.2. How would Judge Posner have decided this case if the trial court had ruled for Sara Creek and denied injunctive relief?

2.3. Does Judge Posner distinguish between a trial court's discretion to order specific performance and a trial court's discretion to order an injunction?

2.4. How would Judge Posner have decided the appeal of the trial court's denial of specific performance in the *Van Wagner* case?

2.5. Covenants not to compete: According to Judge Posner, covenants not to compete "are standardly enforceable by injunction." What is a covenant to compete? Why wasn't the covenant not to compete in the *Valley Medical* case enforceable by injunction?

3. Note

In the third paragraph of the opinion, Judge Posner discusses the concept of "efficient breach", a concept discussed much more often by law professors than by judges not named "Posner." A Westlaw search for 2009 cases shows that only the Seventh Circuit and courts in California, Delaware, and Massachusetts used the term "efficient breach."

Efficient breach is used not only to explain the denial of specific performance but also to explain the denial of punitive damages. Again, Judge Posner: "Even if the breach is deliberate, it is not necessarily blameworthy. The promisor may simply have discovered that his performance is worth more to someone else. If so, efficiency is promoted by allowing him to break his promise, provided he makes good the promisee's actual losses. If he is forced to pay more than that, an efficient breach may be deterred, and the law doesn't want to bring about such a result. * * * Not all breaches of contract are involuntary or otherwise efficient. Some are opportunistic; the promisor wants the benefit of the bargain without bearing the agreed-upon cost, and exploits the inadequacies of purely compensatory remedies (the major inadequacies being that pre-and post-judgment interest rates are frequently below market levels when the risk of nonpayment is taken into account and that the winning party cannot recover his attorney's fees). * * * [T]he breach did little, perhaps no, damage to either plaintiff, and it is therefore quite possible that it was an efficient breach in the sense that it increased Mid–Continent's profits by more than it caused anyone losses." *Patton v. Mid–Continental Sys.*, 841 F.2d 742, 750 (7th Cir. 1988).

Professor William S. Dodge, who teaches contracts at the Hastings Law School, provides this distinction between opportunistic and efficient breaches. "An opportunistic breach does not increase the size of the economic pie; the breaching party gains simply by capturing a larger share of the pie at the expense of the nonbreaching party. An efficient breach, on the other hand, increases the size of the pie, allowing the breaching party more without decreasing the amount that the nonbreaching party receives." William S. Dodge, *The Case for Punitive Damages in Contracts*, 48 Duke L. J. 629 (1999).

We'll see more about efficient breach, opportunistic breach and punishment in the next section on the ability to contract for a particular dollar amount of damages.

Consider the following hypothetical: Ponoroff agreed to wash Markell's car for $10 on Monday. It is now Tuesday, and Markell's car is still dirty. Epstein's Car Wash will do a nice job for $15—$5 more than Ponoroff agreed to take for the exact same job. Can Markell get a court order requiring Ponoroff to wash the car? Note that, due to the passage of time, it is now impossible for Markell to get exactly what he bargained for—a car wash on Monday. And given the easy quantification of the value of a car wash (thanks to Epstein), Markell probably will have an adequate remedy at law that even Professor Laycock would acknowledge.

But it pains Markell that Ponoroff doesn't have to get wet and messy cleaning his car. And money damages don't seem to cover the excruciating pain Markell will have to go through listening to Epstein babbling about how his parts of the Contracts casebook are the best while Markell waits for the car to be washed. Is there a way that Markell can ensure that Ponoroff feels his pain?

Recall this is contracts, the study of consensual obligations. Can Ponoroff and Markell agree ahead of time what Ponoroff will pay if Ponoroff doesn't do what he promised to do? What if Ponoroff and Markell agree that if the car isn't washed by Monday, and there's no excuse, Ponoroff will pay Markell $500? Can Markell go into court Tuesday, get an order directing Ponoroff to pay him $500 smackers,[3] and then brave the hot air at Epstein's and pocket the extra $485? Whether Markell can do that is the subject of the next section.

SECTION 3: AGREED REMEDIES

You can't always win what you want,
You can't always win what you want,

---

3. "Smackers" is Markell's word and shows how living in Las Vegas can affect you. DGE/LP

You can't always win what you want,
But if you try sometimes, you just might find
You'll get what you agreed.

> David "Rockabilly" Epstein & Bruce "Vegas" Markell
> *You Can't Always Win What You Want*,
> on LET THEM READ (Ponoroff Records 2001)

A. LIQUIDATED DAMAGES

O'BRIAN v. LANGLEY SCHOOL

Supreme Court of Virginia
256 Va. 547, 507 S.E.2d 363 (1998)

KINSER, JUSTICE:

This appeal concerns a liquidated damages clause requiring parents to pay tuition for an entire academic year to a school for failure to give timely notice of their decision to withdraw their daughter from the school. Because the circuit court entered summary judgment for the school before permitting the parents to conduct discovery with regard to their defense that the clause is an unenforceable penalty, we will reverse the judgment of the circuit court.

I.

William E. O'Brian, Jr., and Fern P. O'Brian (the O'Brians) enrolled their daughter as a student at Langley School (Langley) for the 1995–96 academic year. On February 29, 1996, the O'Brians executed the "Langley School 1996–97 Membership Agreement" (the Agreement) to enroll their daughter in the second grade for the ensuing academic year. Pursuant to the Agreement, they paid a deposit in the amount of $1,055 to Langley. The O'Brians subsequently decided to withdraw their daughter from Langley, and, in a letter dated June 13, 1996, they notified Langley of their decision.

In response, Langley informed the O'Brians in two separate letters dated June 18 and June 20, 1996, that they were obligated to pay the entire amount of the 1996–97 tuition because they had not timely notified Langley of their decision to withdraw their daughter. Langley based its demand on paragraphs D(1) and (4) of the Agreement. These paragraphs state:

D. WITHDRAWALS AND REFUNDS:

1. All withdrawals MUST BE made by June 1, 1996, as follows:

a. The withdrawal must be made in writing stating the name and grade of the children to be withdrawn.

b. This notice must be received by an authorized administrative employee of the School no later than 4:30 p.m. on June 1, 1996.

* * *

4. IT IS UNDERSTOOD THAT THERE SHALL BE NO REFUND OF OR RELIEF FROM ANY PORTION OF THE FULL TUITION OR ANY OTHER OBLIGATION ACCEPTED HEREIN FOR ANY REASON IF WRITTEN NOTICE OF WITHDRAWAL OF ANY CHILD IS NOT RECEIVED IN ACCORDANCE WITH THE ABOVE PROCEDURE. SINCE DAMAGE TO THE SCHOOL DUE TO SUCH A WITHDRAWAL WOULD BE DIFFICULT TO DETERMINE, MEMBER AGREES TO PAY AGREED–UPON TUITION AS LIQUIDATED DAMAGES, TOGETHER WITH ANY COURT COSTS AND/OR LEGAL FEES THE SCHOOL MAY BE OBLIGED TO INCUR IN THE COLLECTION OF SUCH LIQUIDATED DAMAGES IN THE EVENT OF WITHDRAWAL AFTER JUNE 1, 1996.

The O'Brians refused to pay the agreed-upon tuition as liquidated damages. Consequently, Langley filed a motion for judgment on September 4, 1996, alleging that the O'Brians had breached the terms of the Agreement. Langley sought judgment against the O'Brians for the tuition that was due under the Agreement, plus late fees and attorney's fees.

During pretrial proceedings, the O'Brians submitted written interrogatories to Langley. In one of the interrogatories, the O'Brians asked Langley whether it had made reasonable efforts to fill the spot made available by the withdrawal of the O'Brians' daughter. In response, Langley stated that it "does not so contend because it has no obligation to do so by virtue of" the Agreement. Langley either partially answered or objected to the remaining interrogatories. The O'Brians then filed a motion to compel discovery, which the circuit court denied. Thereafter, Langley moved for summary judgment. After considering memorandum and oral argument from both parties, the circuit court granted Langley's motion and entered judgment on October 3, 1997, against the O'Brians in the amount of $9,745, plus late payment fees from June 1, 1996, and an attorney's fee in the amount of $8,900. The O'Brians appeal.

II.

The dispositive issue in this case is whether the circuit court erred by awarding summary judgment before permitting the O'Brians to conduct discovery with regard to their defense that paragraph D(4) of the Agreement is not a valid liquidated damages clause. Langley asserts that the circuit court did not err because the O'Brians were asserting a defense that is not legally cognizable. We do not agree.

We have previously enunciated the test for determining the validity of a liquidated damages clause:

[P]arties to a contract may agree in advance about the amount to be paid as compensation for loss or injury which may result from a breach of the contract "[w]hen the actual damages contemplated at the time of the agreement are uncertain and difficult to determine with exactness and when the amount fixed is not out of all proportion to the probable loss.

301 Dahlgren Ltd. Partnership v. Bd. of Supervisors King George County. * * *

The fact that a party enters into a contract containing a liquidated damages clause does not prevent that party from later litigating the validity of the clause. The party opposing the imposition of liquidated damages is entitled to conduct discovery and present relevant evidence that the damages resulting from breach of the contract are susceptible of definite measurement or that the stipulated damages are grossly in excess of the actual damages suffered by the nonbreaching party. Upon proof of either of these elements, a liquidated damages clause becomes an unenforceable penalty.

As the party challenging the validity of paragraph D(4) of the Agreement, the O'Brians bear the burden of proof on that issue. [Citations omitted] We believe this allocation of the burden of proof is appropriate since the O'Brians initially assented to the clause when they signed the Agreement. Moreover, the purpose of a liquidated damages provision is to obviate the need for the nonbreaching party to prove actual damages. This purpose would not be served if the nonbreaching party, instead of proving actual damages, had to show that "the damage resulting from a breach of contract is [not] susceptible of definite measurement" and that "the stipulated amount [is not] grossly in excess of actual damages. However, if the O'Brians are successful in proving that paragraph D(4) is an unenforceable penalty, Langley must then prove its actual damages as in any breach of contract action where the contract does not contain a liquidated damages provision. * * *

In the present case, the circuit court precluded any inquiry into the validity of the liquidated damages clause by denying the O'Brians' motion to compel and subsequently awarding summary judgment before hearing any relevant evidence on the issue. Generally, the granting or denying of discovery is a matter within the discretion of the trial court and will not be reversed on appeal unless "the action taken was improvident and affected substantial rights.". However, the court's actions here substantially affected the O'Brians' ability and right to litigate the validity of the liquidated damages clause.

For these reasons, we will reverse the judgment of the circuit court and remand this case for further proceedings consistent with this opinion.

Reversed and remanded.

QUESTIONS

1. Questions about the facts of this case
    1.1. Was there a contract in this case? A breach of contract?
    1.2. Do you think that the Langely School admitted another student after the O'Brians notified the Langley School of their decision to withdraw their daughter? Should that be relevant?

1.3. Do you think that the Langley School was in any way damaged by the O'Brians' withdrawing their daughter from the Langley School?

1.4. Do we know whether the O'Brian's breach was an "efficient breach"? An "opportunistic breach"? Should we care?

1.5. Is it relevant that the O'Brian's were "Big Law" partners? Surprising?

2. Questions about the law

2.1. What is the test for liquidated damages in *O'Brian*?

2.2. Do you see any inconsistency between the court's quotation from *301 Dahlgren* and the court's own statements in the very next paragraph? Which is more consistent with the *Restatement*? Section 356 of the *Restatement (Second) of Contracts* states the general test for liquidated damages as follows:

§ 356 Liquidated Damages and Penalties

(1) Damages for breach by either party may be liquidated in the agreement but only at an amount that is reasonable in light of the anticipated or actual loss caused by the breach and the difficulties of proof of loss. A term fixing unreasonably large liquidated damages is unenforceable on grounds of public policy as a penalty.

2.3. In litigation as to the validity of a liquidated damages provision, who has the burden of pleading and proving what?

2.4. Does it seem strange that the law does not let the parties attack the reasonableness or adequacy of consideration in determining whether there is an enforceable agreement but does let them litigate the issue of the reasonableness of liquidated damage clauses in determining how to enforce that agreement?

The next case is governed by the Uniform Commercial Code. When reading it, ask yourself if the U.C.C. adopts the same rule for liquidated damages as *O'Brian* and the *Restatement*.

KVASSAY v. MURRAY

Court of Appeals of Kansas
15 Kan.App.2d 426, 808 P.2d 896 (1991)

Walker, District Judge, Assigned:

Plaintiff Michael Kvassay, d/b/a Kvassay Exotic Food, appeals the trial court's finding that a liquidated damages clause was unenforceable and from the court's finding that damages for lost profits were not recoverable. Kvassay contends these damages occurred when Great American Foods, Inc., (Great American) breached a contract for the purchase of baklava. * * *

On February 22, 1984, Kvassay, who had been an independent insurance adjuster, contracted to sell 24,000 cases of baklava to Great American at $19.00 per case. Under the contract, the sales were to occur over a one-year period and Great American was to be Kvassay's only customer. The contract included a clause which provided: "If Buyer refuses to accept or repudiates delivery of the goods sold to him, under this Agreement, Seller shall be entitled to damages, at the rate of $5.00 per case, for each case remaining to be delivered under this Contract."

Problems arose early in this contractual relationship with checks issued by Great American being dishonored for insufficient funds. Frequently one of the Murrays issued a personal check for the amount due. After producing approximately 3,000 cases, Kvassay stopped producing the baklava because the Murrays refused to purchase any more of the product. * * *

In April 1985, Kvassay filed suit for damages arising from the collapse of his baklava baking business. Great American counterclaimed and, in May 1988, the trial court sustained a defense motion to bifurcate the case. The court conducted bench hearings on the validity of the liquidated damages clause. * * * The trial court ruled that liquidated damages could not be recovered. * * * The court also held "as a matter of law" that Kvassay would not be able to recover damages for lost profits in the action because they were too "speculative and conjectural."

      * * *

Kvassay first attacks the trial court's ruling that the amount of liquidated damages sought by him was unreasonable and therefore the liquidated damages clause was unenforceable.

Kvassay claimed $105,000 in losses under the liquidated damages clause of the contract, representing $5 per case for the approximately 21,000 cases of baklava which he was not able to deliver. The trial court determined that Kvassay's use of expected profits to formulate liquidated damages was improper because the business enterprise lacked duration, permanency, and recognition. The court then compared Kvassay's previous yearly income (about $20,000) with the claim for liquidated damages ($105,000) and found "the disparity becomes so great as to make the clause unenforceable."

Since the contract involved the sale of goods between merchants,* the Uniform Commercial Code governs. See K.S.A. 84–2–102 [U.C.C. 2–102]. "The Code does not change the pre-Code rule that the question of the propriety of liquidated damages is a question of law for the court." 4 Anderson, Uniform Commercial Code § 2–718:6, p. 572 (3d ed. 1983). Thus, this court's scope of review of the trial court's ruling is unlimited.

---

* Okay. We can't let this wait until the *Questions and Notes.* Does a transaction have to be "between merchants" to be within the U.C.C.? *OF COURSE NOT!* If you don't believe us, reread § 2–102. Your purchase of this casebook was governed by the U.C.C., as was your purchase of the highlighter you're using to note this sentence. Those trained in the classics will have heard the phrase, "Even Homer nods," but here we're not even sure the judge qualifies as a Homer of the prairie. Despite this goof, don't discount the rest of the case. Perhaps the judge took the test from the trial court, who *really* made a hash of § 2–718. And hash and baklava don't mix; trust us. Eds.

Liquidated damages clauses in sales contracts are governed by K.S.A. 84–2–718, which reads in part:

> (1) Damages for breach by either party may be liquidated in the agreement but only at an amount which is reasonable in the light of the anticipated or actual harm caused by the breach, the difficulties of proof of loss, and the inconvenience or nonfeasibility of otherwise obtaining an adequate remedy. A term fixing unreasonably large liquidated damages is void as a penalty.

To date, the appellate courts have not interpreted this section of the UCC in light of facts similar to those presented in this case. In ruling on this issue, the trial court relied on rules governing liquidated damages as expressed in *U.S.D. No. 315 v. DeWerff*, 6 Kan. App.2d 77, 626 P.2d 1206 (1981). *DeWerff*, however, involved a teacher's breach of an employment contract and was not governed by the UCC. Thus, the rules expressed in that case should be given no effect if they differ from the rules expressed in 84–2–718.

In *DeWerff*, this court held a "stipulation for damages upon a future breach of contract is valid as a liquidated damages clause if the set amount is determined to be reasonable and the amount of damages is difficult to ascertain." 6 Kan.App.2d at 78, 626 P.2d 1206. This is clearly a two-step test: Damages must be reasonable and they must be difficult to ascertain. Under the UCC, however, reasonableness is the only test. K.S.A. 84–2–718. K.S.A. 84–2–718 provides three criteria by which to measure reasonableness of liquidated damages clauses: (1) anticipated or actual harm caused by breach; (2) difficulty of proving loss; and (3) difficulty of obtaining an adequate remedy.

In its ruling, the trial court found the liquidated damages clause was unreasonable in light of Kvassay's income before he entered into the manufacturing contract with Great American. There is no basis in 84–2–718 for contrasting income under a previous unrelated employment arrangement with liquidated damages sought under a manufacturing contract. Indeed, the traditional goal of the law in cases where a buyer breaches a manufacturing contract is to place the seller "in the same position he would have occupied if the vendee had performed his contract." *Outcault Adv. Co. v. Citizens' Nat'l Bank*, 118 Kan. 328, 330–31, 234 P. 988 (1925). Thus, liquidated damages under the contract in this case must be measured against the anticipated or actual loss under the baklava contract as required by 84–2–718. The trial court erred in using Kvassay's previous income as a yardstick.

Was the trial court correct when it invalidated the liquidated damages clause, notwithstanding the use of an incorrect test? If so, we must uphold the decision even though the trial court relied on a wrong ground or assigned an erroneous reason for its decision. To answer this question, we must look closer at the first criteria for reasonableness under 84–2–718, anticipated or actual harm done by the breach.

Kvassay produced evidence of anticipated damages at the bench trial showing that, before the contract was signed between Kvassay and Great American, Kvassay's accountant had calculated the baklava production costs. The resulting figure showed that, if each case sold for $19, Kvassay would earn a net profit of $3.55 per case after paying himself for time and labor. If he did not pay himself, the projected profit was $4.29 per case. Nevertheless, the parties set the liquidated damages figure at $5 per case. In comparing the anticipated damages of $3.55 per case in lost net profit with the liquidated damages of $5 per case, it is evident that Kvassay would collect $1.45 per case or about 41 percent over projected profits if Great American breached the contract. If the $4.29 profit figure is used, a $5 liquidated damages award would allow Kvassay to collect 71 cents per case or about 16½% percent over projected profits if Great American breached the contract.

An examination of these pre-contract comparisons alone might well lead to the conclusion that the $5 liquidated damages clause is unreasonable because enforcing it would result in a windfall for Kvassay and serve as a penalty for Great American. A term fixing unreasonably large liquidated damages is void as a penalty under 84–2–718.

A better measure of the validity of the liquidated damages clause in this case would be obtained if the actual lost profits caused by the breach were compared to the $5 per case amount set by the clause. However, no attempt was made by Kvassay during the bench trial to prove actual profits or actual costs of production. Thus, the trial court could not compare the $5 liquidated damages clause in the contract with the actual profits lost by the breach. It was not until the jury trial that Kvassay attempted to prove his actual profits lost as part of his damages. Given the trial court's ruling that lost profits were not recoverable and could not be presented to the jury, it is questionable whether the court would have permitted evidence concerning lost profits at the bench trial.

The trial court utilized an impermissible factor to issue its ruling on the liquidated damages clause and the correct statutory factors were not directly addressed. We reverse the trial court on this issue and remand for further consideration of the reasonableness of the liquidated damages clause in light of the three criteria set out in 84–2–718 and our ruling on recoverability of lost profits which follows.

* * *

The trial court's decisions with respect to liquidated damages and lost profits are reversed and the case is remanded for a new trial on those issues. * * *

Questions and Note

1. Questions about the facts of this case

    1.1. What is baklava?

    1.2. What evidence did Kvassay introduce? At the new trial, what additional evidence should Kvassay introduce?

2. Questions about the law

    2.1. What are the differences between: (i) the law of liquidated damages under common law as set forth in the *Restatement* and in *O'Brian,* and (ii) the law of liquidated damages set forth in U.C.C. § 2–718 and *Kvassay?*

    2.2. Who measures reasonableness? The court or the jury? Do you think the $5 per case was unreasonable?

    2.3 In a bar journal "how to" article, a Missouri lawyer discusses burden of proof in liquidated damages clause litigation: "The majority of courts in other jurisdictions impose the burden of invalidating a liquidated damages clause on the party challenging its validity. One such court reasoned that placing the burden on the party seeking to invalidate a liquidated damages provision was appropriate because that party had initially agreed to it. Moreover, requiring the non-breaching party to bear the burden of proving the provision's enforceability would defeat one of the provision's primary benefits, *i.e.,* that of dispensing with the need to prove actual damages at trial. By defeating the primary benefit of a liquidated damages clause, such a holding would likewise defeat the parties' intent in agreeing to the clause." Henry F. Luepke, III, *How to Draft and Enforce a Liquidated Damages Clause,* 61 Mo. B.J. 324 (2005) Is that advice consistent with what you have learned from reading *O'Brian, Kvassay,* the *Restatement* and the U.C.C.?

    2.4. In that same article, Mr. Luepke offers the following suggestion for drafting liquidated damages clauses:

    "The law governing liquidated damages clauses has developed so as to make clear that the question of enforceability is, essentially, a question of intent. At the time they agreed to the liquidated damages clause, did the parties intend to compensate for a breach or to punish for a breach? By demonstrating that, **at the time of contracting**, the intent was compensatory rather than punitive, counsel will ensure that a provision for liquidated damages will be upheld in the courts and enforced according to its terms." *Id.* (emphasis added). Note Mr. Luepke's focus on the "time of contracting." Is that the time focus in *Kavassy?* In *Restatement (Second) of Contracts* section 356? In U.C.C. § 2–718?

3. Note

Another look at liquidated damages, penalties and efficient breach. In *Lake River Corp. v. Carborundum Co.,* 769 F.2d 1284 (7th Cir. 1985), Judge

Richard Posner had the following to say about the liquidated damages/penalty distinction:

> Deep as the hostility to penalty clauses runs in the common law, see Loyd, *Penalties and Forfeitures*, 29 Harv. L. Rev. 117 (1915), we still might be inclined to question, if we thought ourselves free to do so, whether a modern court should refuse to enforce a penalty clause where the signator is a substantial corporation, well able to avoid improvident commitments. Penalty clauses provide an earnest of performance. The clause here enhanced Carborundum's credibility in promising to ship the minimum amount guaranteed by showing that it was willing to pay the full contract price even if it failed to ship anything. On the other side it can be pointed out that by raising the cost of a breach of contract to the contract breaker, a penalty clause increases the risk to his other creditors; increases (what is the same thing and more, because bankruptcy imposes "deadweight" social costs) the risk of bankruptcy; and could amplify the business cycle by increasing the number of bankruptcies in bad times, which is when contracts are most likely to be broken. But since little effort is made to prevent businessmen from assuming risks, these reasons are no better than makeweights.
>
> A better argument is that a penalty clause may discourage efficient as well as inefficient breaches of contract. Suppose a breach would cost the promisee $12,000 in actual damages but would yield the promisor $20,000 in additional profits. Then there would be a net social gain from breach. After being fully compensated for his loss the promisee would be no worse off than if the contract had been performed, while the promisor would be better off by $8,000. But now suppose the contract contains a penalty clause under which the promisor if he breaks his promise must pay the promisee $25,000. The promisor will be discouraged from breaking the contract, since $25,000, the penalty, is greater than $20,000, the profits of the breach; and a transaction that would have increased value will be forgone.
>
> On this view, since compensatory damages should be sufficient to deter inefficient breaches (that is, breaches that cost the victim more than the gain to the contract breaker), penal damages could have no effect other than to deter some efficient breaches. But this overlooks the earlier point that the willingness to agree to a penalty clause is a way of making the promisor and his promise credible and may therefore be essential to inducing some value-maximizing contracts to be made. It also overlooks the more important point that the parties (always assuming they are fully competent) will, in deciding whether to include a penalty clause in their contract, weigh the gains against the costs—costs that include the possibility of discouraging an efficient breach somewhere down the road—and will include the clause only if the benefits exceed those costs as well as all other costs.
>
> On this view the refusal to enforce penalty clauses is (at best) paternalistic—and it seems odd that courts should display parental solicitude for large corporations. But however this may be, we must be on guard to avoid importing our own ideas of sound public policy into an area where

our proper judicial role is more than usually deferential. The responsibility for making innovations in the common law of Illinois rests with the courts of Illinois, and not with the federal courts in Illinois. And like every other state, Illinois, untroubled by academic skepticism of the wisdom of refusing to enforce penalty clauses against sophisticated promisors, see, e.g., Goetz & Scott, Liquidated Damages, Penalties and the Just Compensation Principle, 77 Colum. L. Rev. 554 (1977), continues steadfastly to insist on the distinction between penalties and liquidated damages. * * * To be valid under Illinois law a liquidation of damages must be a reasonable estimate at the time of contracting of the likely damages from breach, and the need for estimation at that time must be shown by reference to the likely difficulty of measuring the actual damages from a breach of contract after the breach occurs. If damages would be easy to determine then, or if the estimate greatly exceeds a reasonable upper estimate of what the damages are likely to be, it is a penalty. * * *

Id. at 1288–90.

PROBLEMS ON LIQUIDATED DAMAGES

1. *Liquidated Damages and Specific Performance*

   Despite all advice to the contrary, Epstein, Markell and Ponoroff form a law partnership. Being crafty devils, they place in their partnership agreement a non-compete clause, and set liquidated damages for breach of that non-compete clause at $50,000, a sum everyone agrees is on the high side of reasonable given the nature of the proposed practice.

   Unfortunately, a year later, to everyone's surprise, Epstein wins a huge case. His name and picture (with a big, toothy grin) is plastered all over the papers. When Markell and Ponoroff refuse to amend the formula used to allocate partnership profits to give Epstein more of a share, Epstein is silent for a second, checks the partnership agreement, and then says, "G'bye, y'all."

   Epstein then sets up shop next door to Markell and Ponoroff and begins competing in direct violation of the non-compete clause. Markell and Ponoroff sue to enjoin Epstein. What result?

   If an injunction is not granted, may Markell and Ponoroff show that their real damages from Epstein's blatant violation of the non-compete clause are closer to $200,000, given that Epstein is now sucking all of the legal work in town to his new boutique? Why, or why not?

2. *Scare Tactics*

   Many retail stores have signs above the counter that say "$25 charge on returned checks." Putting aside for now the question as to whether this sign becomes part of the contract, if it is, do you think such a term is enforceable? Would you advise a retailer client to rely on such a sign?

3. *Final Problem*

   Most construction contracts call for a per day "penalty" or "fee" to be paid if a job is not completed within the agreed time. Assume that Markell Construction Co. agrees with Epstein to build an addition to

Epstein's house for $10,000. The contract says that Markell will pay $100 a day for each day he is late in finishing past the agreed due date of July 1. True to form, Markell (as his mother would say) is "slower than molasses running uphill in the month of January." He finishes thirty days late. Can he successfully contest the $3,000 in liquidated damages as a penalty? What more would you want to know before answering? What if Markell is 100 days late? Are Epstein's damages then $10,000 on this $10,000 contract? What if Markell never finishes?

B. LIMITATION OF REMEDIES TO REPAIR, REPLACEMENT, OR RETURN OF MONEY PAID

As we have seen with liquidated damages, parties often try to anticipate the effect of breach and specify its consequences. With the sale of goods, especially goods produced on a mass scale, the parties (or at least the seller) know that a breach to a least some buyers is inevitable. Sellers often attempt to control their costs by providing in contracts governing the sales of their goods that damages are not available as a remedy—that the seller's efforts to repair or replace the defective goods or return of the purchase price will be the only remedies available to an aggrieved buyer. Such provisions in contracts for the sale of goods are governed by U.C.C. section 2–719, entitled "Contractual Modification or Limitation of Remedy":

(1) Subject to the provisions of subsections (2) and (3) of this section and of the preceding section on liquidation and limitation of damages,

    (a) the agreement may provide for remedies in addition to or in substitution for those provided in this Article and may limit or alter the measure of damages recoverable under this Article, as by limiting the buyer's remedies to return of the goods and repayment of the price or to repair and replacement of non-conforming goods or parts; and

    (b) resort to a remedy as provided is optional unless the remedy is expressly agreed to be exclusive, in which case it is the sole remedy.

(2) Where circumstances cause an exclusive or limited remedy to fail of its essential purpose, remedy may be had as provided in this Act.

One of the recurring problems in determining if and when a "repair and replacement" remedy has failed its essential purpose within the meaning of § 2–719(2) occurs when the seller fails to effect repairs despite several attempts to do so, or, while individual defects are repaired, unrelated defects keep cropping up. Eventually, the frustrated buyer wants to return the goods or sue for damages. The seller, however, is perfectly happy to continue to offer repair opportunities. Clearly, at some point the remedy has failed, but just how many repair efforts, or how many defects, must the buyer endure?

The reported cases offer very little consistent guidance on this question, so we have not included a case applying section 2–719. Moreover, the federal government and state governments have addressed this problem for consumer buyers through consumer protection statutes which are addressed in second and third year courses in consumer protection.

For this contracts course, it is valuable to distinguish between clauses that limit or modify remedies (as in the last case) and clauses that attempt to disclaim liability. We encountered an example of the latter in Chapter 5 in contracts for the sale of goods where the seller attempts to disclaim liability for breach of warranty. A disclaimer, if effective, eliminates a cause of action altogether and, therefore, eliminates the need to worry about limiting damages. The final sentences of Official Comment 2 to § 2–316 (the warranty disclaimer provision) makes this clear: "If no warranty exists, there is of course no problem of limiting remedies for breach of warranty."

It is also important to see the relationship between remedy limitations and agreed remedies, the topic of the previous subsection.

In "theory", § 2–719 governs when enforceability of a provision under which the parties have agreed to limit or exclude, but not actually fix, damages, while § 2–718 applies where the parties have actually specified what the damaged upon breach will be. As we have seen, the principle concern in liquidated damage cases is that the stipulated sum will be unreasonably large. See § 2–718(1). By contrast, the rationale underlying the "essential-purpose" doctrine in § 2–719 is that a seller will use the remedy limitation provision to deprive the buyer of a "minimum adequate remedy." See Off. Cmt. 1 to § 2–719.

In practice, a "clever" lawyer can draft a liquidated damage clause that has the effect of virtually always excluding or limiting the buyer's recovery in the event of a breach. Likewise, a "clever" lawyer can craft a clause stipulating an exclusive remedy to just as easily over-compensate a party as opposed to deprive the other party of an adequate remedy. Because the rules and standards governing enforceability under §§ 2–718 and 2–719 differ, it can make an important difference which section of Article 2 a court chooses to employ in reviewing either or both kinds of remedy provisions.

SECTION 4: JUDICIAL DETERMINATION OF MONEY DAMAGES

You can't always win what you want,
You can't always win what you want,
You can't always win what you want,
But if you try sometimes, you just might find
You'll get wads of green.

> David "Rockabilly" Epstein & Bruce "Vegas" Markell
> *You Can't Always Win What You Want,*
> on LET THEM READ (Ponoroff Records 2010)

A. THE GENERAL MEASURE OF MONEY DAMAGES: "EXPECTATION INTEREST" (RECEIPT OF THE BENEFIT OF THE BARGAIN)

Let's go back to the contract for car washing between Markell and Ponoroff, *supra,* at 698. Ponoroff was to wash Markell's car on Monday for $10. And recall that Markell could get the same car wash from Epstein for $15. We have seen that Markell cannot compel Ponoroff to wash the car through a decree of specific performance. And, it is safe to assume that Markell wasn't smart enough to put in a liquidated damages clause.

What's left? Money damages. That is, Markell will seek an order from a court (called a judgment) that Ponoroff owes Markell some money. If Ponoroff, does not pay the amount ordered by the court (and does not appeal) Markell will then be able to take that judgment to the local sheriff who will seize and sell Ponoroff's property until Markell is paid the amount listed in the judgment.

But what amount will the court insert in its judgment? In short, what amount will compensate Markell? Should the amount of the award to Markell be $15, the amount Markell will have to pay to Epstein? No. Ponoroff will argue successfully that Markell was already going to spend $10 for his service, thus, giving Markell $15 would be the same as giving Markell a free car wash, which is not what the deal was. $15 overcompensates Markell, something contract law is loathe to do.

What would Markell get? The *Restatement* has an answer. According to section 345 of the *Restatement (Second) of Contracts*: "the injured party has a right to damages based on his expectation interest. * * *"

What does "expectation interest" mean? How do you measure someone's "expectation interest"? The *Restatement* has an answer to that too. It states that the expectation interest is measured as:

> *(a) the loss in value to [the injured party] of the other party's performance caused by its failure or deficiency, plus*

(b) *any other loss, including incidental[4] or consequential[5] loss, caused by the breach, less*

(c) *any cost or other loss that [the injured party] has avoided by not having to perform.*

Restatement (Second) of Contracts § 347 (1981).

We also have an answer to what "expectation interest" means, and our answer is easier to understand. When a person makes a contract, she expects that the other person will not breach. Accordingly, protection of that expectation means damages should put the nonbreaching party in the same dollar position as if the contract had been performed without breach.

If, in our car washing story, damages were based on Markell's expectation interest, what would Markell get for Ponoroff's breach of the car wash contract? $5. Markell was expecting no breach, i.e., Markell was expecting that his car would be washed for the contract price of $10. Instead, because of Ponoroff's breach, Markell has to pay $5 more than the contract price. Accordingly, Ponoroff's paying Markell breach of contract damages of $5 protects that expectation—puts Markell in the same economic position he would have been in had the contract been performed without breach.

––––––––

Some Other Easy Expectation Damages Problems:

1. P hired D to paint his house for $10,000. D breaches. What are P's expectation damages if D breaches and P is unable to hire another painter for less than $12,000?

2. B contracts to buy a machine from S. As required by the contract, B pays S the $400,000 as soon as the contract is signed and before the machine is delivered. S breaches and never delivers the machine. What are B's expectation damages if B is unable to buy a comparable machine for less than $430,000?

3. B buys a machine from S for $600,000. The contract provides that the machine will produce 100 widgets an hour. The machine as

––––––––

4. Incidental damages are: (1) easy to understand, and (2) generally insignificant in amount. Restatement (Second) section 347 gives the following helpful explanation and example: "Incidental losses include costs incurred in a reasonable effort, whether successful or not, to avoid loss, as where a party pays brokerage fees in arranging or attempting to arrange a substitute transaction." See Illustration 3.

Illustrations:

3. A contracts to employ B for $10,000 to supervise the production of A's crop, but breaks his contract by firing B at the beginning of the season. B reasonably spends $200 in fees attempting to find other suitable employment through appropriate agencies. B can recover the $200 incidental loss in addition to any other loss suffered, whether or not he succeeds in finding other employment. Incidental damages are always recoverable.

5. Consequential damages are: (1) NOT easy to understand, and (2) can be very significant in amount. Moreover, the *Restatement (Second)*'s explanation and examples of consequential damages are not particularly helpful. And, consequential damages are not always recoverable. We will cover consequential damages later in this chapter.

delivered only produces 60 widgets an hour. If B decides to keep the machine and sue for money damages, what result?

The next case would answer (3) above "As a general rule, the measure of the vendee's damages is the difference between the value of the goods as they would have been if the warranty as to quality had been true, and the actual value at the time of the sale." As you read the next case, think about whether you agree with the court's application of that rule to George Hawkins.

HAWKINS v. McGEE

Supreme Court of New Hampshire
84 N.H. 114, 146 A. 641 (1929)

Assumpsit against a surgeon for breach of an alleged warranty of the success of an operation. Trial by jury. [A $3,000] Verdict for the plaintiff. The writ also contained a count in negligence upon which a nonsuit was ordered, without exception.

Defendant's motions for a nonsuit and for a directed verdict on the count in assumpsit were denied, and the defendant excepted. During the argument of plaintiff's counsel to the jury, the defendant claimed certain exceptions, and also excepted to the denial of his requests for instructions and to the charge of the court upon the question of damages, as more fully appears in the opinion. The defendant seasonably moved to set aside the verdict upon the grounds that it was (1) contrary to the evidence; (2) against the weight of the evidence; (3) against the weight of the law and evidence; and (4) because the damages awarded by the jury were excessive. The court denied the motion upon the first three grounds, but found that the damages were excessive, and made an order that the verdict be set aside, unless the plaintiff elected to remit all in excess of $500. The plaintiff having refused to remit, the verdict was set aside "as excessive and against the weight of the evidence," and the plaintiff excepted.

BRANCH, J.

The operation in question consisted in the removal of a considerable quantity of scar tissue from the palm of the plaintiff's right hand and the grafting of skin taken from the plaintiff's chest in place thereof. The scar tissue was the result of a severe burn caused by contact with an electric wire, which the plaintiff received about nine years before the time of the transactions here involved. There was evidence to the effect that before the operation was performed the plaintiff and his father went to the defendant's office, and that the defendant, in answer to the question, "How long will the boy be in the hospital?" replied, "Three or four days, not over four; then the boy can go home and it will be just a few days when he will go back to work with a good hand." Clearly this and other testimony to the same effect would not justify a finding that the doctor contracted to complete the hospital treatment in three or four days or that the plaintiff would be able to go back to work within a few days thereafter. The above statements could only be construed as expressions of opinion or predictions as to the probable duration of the treatment and plaintiff's resulting disability, and the fact that these estimates were exceeded would impose no contractual liability upon the defendant. The only substantial basis for the plaintiff's claim is the testimony that the defendant also said before the operation was decided upon, "I will guarantee to make the hand a hundred per cent perfect hand or a hundred per cent good hand." The plaintiff was present when these words were alleged to have been spoken, and, if they are to be taken at their face value, it seems obvious that proof of their utterance would establish the giving of a warranty in accordance with his contention.

The defendant argues, however, that, even if these words were uttered by him, no reasonable man would understand that they were used with the intention of entering "into any contractual relation whatever," and that they could reasonably be understood only "as his expression in strong language that he believed and expected that as a result of the operation he would give the plaintiff a very good hand." It may be conceded, as the defendant contends, that, before the question of the making of a contract should be submitted to a jury, there is a preliminary question of law for the trial court to pass upon, i.e. "whether the words could possibly have the meaning imputed to them by the party who founds his case upon a certain interpretation," but it cannot be held that the trial court decided this question erroneously in the present case. It is unnecessary to determine at this time whether the argument of the defendant, based upon "common knowledge of the uncertainty which attends all surgical operations," and the improbability that a surgeon would ever contract to make a damaged part of the human body "one hundred per cent perfect" would, in the absence of countervailing considerations, be regarded as conclusive, for there were other factors in the present case which tended to support the contention of the plaintiff. There was evidence that the defendant repeatedly solicited from the plaintiff's father the opportunity to perform this operation, and the theory was advanced by plaintiff's counsel in cross examination of defendant that he sought an opportunity to "experiment on skin grafting," in which he had little previous experience. If the jury accepted this part of plaintiff's contention, there would be a reasonable basis for the further conclusion that, if defendant spoke the words attributed to him, he did so with the intention that they should be accepted at their face value, as an inducement for the granting of consent to the operation by the plaintiff and his father, and there was ample evidence that they were so accepted by them. The question of the making of the alleged contract was properly submitted to the jury.

The substance of the charge to the jury on the question of damages appears in the following quotation: "If you find the plaintiff entitled to anything, he is entitled to recover for what pain and suffering he has been made to endure and for what injury he has sustained over and above what injury he had before." To this instruction the defendant seasonably excepted. By it, the jury was permitted to consider two elements of damage: (1) Pain and suffering due to the operation; and (2) positive ill effects of the operation upon the plaintiff's hand. Authority for any specific rule of damages in cases of this kind seems to be lacking, but, when tested by general principle and by analogy, it appears that the foregoing instruction was erroneous.

"By 'damages,' as that term is used in the law of contracts, is intended compensation for a breach, measured in the terms of the contract." Davis v. New England Cotton Yarn Co., 77 N.H. 403, 92 A. 732. The purpose of the law is "to put the plaintiff in as good a position as he would have been in had the defendant kept his contract." 3 Williston Cont. § 1338. The measure of recovery "is based upon what the defendant should have given the plaintiff, not what the plaintiff has given the defendant or otherwise expended." 3 Williston Cont. § 1341 * * *

The present case is closely analogous to one in which a machine is built for a certain purpose and warranted to do certain work. In such cases, the usual rule of damages for breach of warranty in the sale of chattels is applied, and it is held that the measure of damages is the difference between the value of the machine, if it had corresponded with the warranty and its actual value, together with such incidental losses as the parties knew, or ought to have known, would probably result from a failure to comply with its terms. * * *

The rule thus applied is well settled in this state. "As a general rule, the measure of the vendee's damages is the difference between the value of the goods as they would have been if the warranty as to quality had been true, and the actual value at the time of the sale, including gains prevented and losses sustained, and such other damages as could be reasonably anticipated by the parties as likely to be caused by the vendor's failure to keep his agreement, and could not by reasonable care on the part of the vendee have been avoided." Union Bank v. Blanchard, 65 N.H. 21, 18 A. 90; * * * P.L. ch. 166, § 69, subd. 7. We therefore conclude that the true measure of the plaintiff's damage in the present case is the difference between the value to him of a perfect hand or a good hand, such as the jury found the defendant promised him, and the value of his hand in its present condition, including any incidental consequences fairly within the contemplation of the parties when they made their contract. Damages not thus limited, although naturally resulting, are not to be given.

The extent of the plaintiff's suffering does not measure this difference in value. The pain necessarily incident to a serious surgical operation was a part of the contribution which the plaintiff was willing to make to his joint undertaking with the defendant to produce a good hand. It was a legal detriment suffered by him which constituted a part of the consideration given by him for the contract. It represented a part of the price which he was willing to pay for a good hand, but it furnished no test of the value of a good hand or the difference between the value of the hand which the defendant promised and the one which resulted from the operation.

It was also erroneous and misleading to submit to the jury as a separate element of damage any change for the worse in the condition of the plaintiff's hand resulting from the operation, although this error was probably more prejudicial to the plaintiff than to the defendant. Any such ill effect of the operation would be included under the true rule of damages set forth above, but damages might properly be assessed for the defendant's failure to improve the condition of the hand, even if there were no evidence that its condition was made worse as a result of the operation.

It must be assumed that the trial court, in setting aside the verdict, undertook to apply the same rule of damages which he had previously given to the jury, and, since this rule was erroneous, it is unnecessary for us to consider whether there was any evidence to justify his finding that all damages awarded by the jury above $500 were excessive.

* * *

New trial.

QUESTIONS AND NOTES

1. Questions about the facts of this case
    1.1. Do you agree with Professor Charles Kingsfield's summary of the facts of this case? http://www.youtube.com/watch?v=cZJEhlIefxA
    1.2. Why was Dr. McGee liable to Hawkins under contract law? What exactly was the promise made by Dr. McGee to Hawkins?
    1.3. Do we know the contract price, i.e. how much the Hawkins family paid Dr. McGee? Do we need to know the contract price to determine the measure of damages for breach of contract?
    1.4. Do we know the cost of fixing George Hawkins' hand so that it is "a hundred per cent perfect hand"? Do we know whether George's hand can be fixed so that it is a hundred per cent perfect hand?
    1.5. What additional facts would Hawkins have to establish in order to recover from Dr. McGee under tort?
2. Questions about the law
    2.1. Rule
        a. What is the measure of damages adopted by this court?
        b. Did Mr. Hart correctly answer Professor Kingfield's question: "What should the doctor pay?" http://www.youtube.com/watch?v=cZJEhlIefxA
        c. Is *Hawkins v. McGee* consistent with *Restatement (Second)* sections 345 and 347? With our more helpful explanation of expectation interest?

2.2.   Remand.

    a. On remand, would evidence about the contract price be relevant? Why?

    b. What about evidence that Hawkins had been apprenticing as a watchmaker, but he lost that position because he no longer had the necessary manual dexterity?

    c. What about evidence that Hawkins' pain and suffering lasted far longer than the usual recovery period for such surgeries?

2.3.   Does this court seriously believe that a hand is like a "chattel"? By the way, what is a chattel?

2.4.   Comparison of contract damages with tort damages. If Dr. McGee was found to have been negligent, what would the measure of George Hawkins' damages be?

3.   Notes

3.1.   Subsequent research into the facts of this case indicated that before the new trial Dr. McGee settled the lawsuit for $1,400. We know this because Dr. McGee then sued his insurance carrier to recover that sum and an additional $2,850 in expenses, mostly attorneys' fees. Dr. McGee lost, because the insurance policy only covered liability "in consequence of any malpractice, error, or mistake." *McGee v. United States Fidelity & Guaranty Co.*, 53 F.2d 953 (1st Cir. 1931).

3.2.   The same appellate case tells us what the main case does not: the condition of Hawkins' hand. In the words of the appellate court, after three months of hospitalization, "the new tissue grafted upon said hand became matted, unsightly, and so healed and attached to said hand as to practically fill the hand with an unsightly growth, restricting the motion of the plaintiff's hand so that said hand has become useless to the plaintiff. * * *"

3.3.   Cases such as this inspire doggerel:

> A terrible need for a fee
> Brought great grief to Doctor McGee.
> And his promises airy
> Led a patient unwary
> To a hand that no mortal should see.

Douglass G. Boshkoff, *Selected Poems on The Law of Contracts: Raintree County Memorial Library Occasional Paper No. 1*, 66 N.Y.U. L. REV. 1533, 1542 (1991).

3.4.   While *Hawkins v. McGee*, a 1929 case, does not use the term "expectation interest," many, more modern cases do. In an uncommonly influential law review article, Lon L. Fuller & William R. Perdue, Jr., *The Reliance Interest in Contract Damages*, 46 YALE L.J. 52 (1936), Professor Fuller and his student, William Perdue, suggested the use of the term "expectation interest".

[W]e may seek to give the promisee the value of the expectancy which the promise created. We may in a suit for specific performance actually compel the defendant to render the promised performance to the plaintiff, or, in a suit for damages, we may make the defendant pay the money value of this performance. Here our object is to put the plaintiff in as good a position as he would have occupied had the defendant performed his promise The interest protected in this case we may call the expectation interest.

Id. at 53–55.

The *Restatement (Second) of Contracts* paid Fuller and Perdue the ultimate compliment of adopting their terminology. See *Restatement (Second) of Contracts* § 344 (1981). And, remember, section 347 of the *Restatement (Second) of Contracts* tells us that protection of the expectation interest is the general rule: "the injured party has a right to damages based on his expectation interest. * * *".

In *Hawkins v. McGee*, expectation damages were based on diminution in the value of the contract performance resulting from the breach of contract—the difference between the value of the hand that was promised and the hand after Dr. McGee's breach of that promise. There was no alternative method of determining expectation damages in *Hawkins v. McGee*. We could not look to the cost of remedying the defects because George's scarred and hairy hand could not be fixed.

In the next case involving breach of a roofing contract, we do know the cost of fixing the roof and the plaintiff's measure of damages is based on that cost.

PANORAMA VILLAGE HOMEOWNERS ASS'N v. GOLDEN RULE ROOFING, INC.

Court of Appeals of Washington
102 Wash.App. 422, 10 P.3d 417 (2000)

Coleman, J.

Panorama Village Homeowners Association sued Golden Rule Roofing, claiming that Golden Rule breached its contracts to install roofs on four of its buildings and to provide Panorama with 10–year manufacturers' warranties. The trial court ruled that the roofs were defective, that the roofing materials were not installed in accordance with the contract and manufacturers' specifications, and that Golden Rule did not provide Panorama with valid manufacturers' warranties. The trial court entered a judgment for Panorama and awarded the association a portion of the cost of replacing the roofs. On appeal, Golden Rule contends that the trial court erred in finding that it had breached its contracts with Panorama and in awarding damages. We conclude that the record supports the trial court's rulings, and we affirm.

FACTS

From 1991 to 1995, Golden Rule contracted to install nine roofs for the Panorama Village Homeowners Association. Five of the contracts involved the installation of U.S. Intec materials and included U.S. Intec's 10–year material warranty. A sixth contract was for the installation of a Firestone membrane and included the manufacturer's 10–year labor and material warranty. In 1997, Panorama discovered that neither U.S. Intec nor Firestone had a record of any warranties issued for its roofs. Panorama sued Golden Rule, claiming that the construction was defective and that they had not received manufacturers' warranties for the materials. Golden Rule responded by issuing Panorama backdated U.S. Intec warranties. The company further provided its own 10–year labor and material warranty as a substitute for the Firestone warranty and agreed to complete some items that had not been performed in accordance with the contracts' specifications. Panorama, however, maintained that the repairs would not cure the deficiencies in the roofs. It further argued that the U.S. Intec warranties were not valid because Golden Rule lacked authority to issue them on behalf of the manufacturer and because the materials had not been installed in accordance with the manufacturer's specifications. The trial court awarded Panorama $28,612 in damages. The award included a portion of the cost to replace the roofs, prorated to reflect the existing roofs' performance prior to the suit, and incidental and consequential losses.

DISCUSSION

* * *

Damages

Golden Rule * * * challenges the trial court's decision to award damages based on the cost of replacing the roofs. Contract damages are ordinarily based on the injured party's expectation interest and are intended to give the injured party the benefit of its bargain. *Eastlake Constr. Co., Inc. v. Hess,* 102 Wash.2d 30, 46, 686 P.2d 465 (1984) (quoting Restatement (Second) of Contracts § 347 cmt. *a* (1981)). In cases involving breach of a construction contract, the injured party may recover the reasonable cost of completing performance or remedying defects in the construction if the cost is not clearly disproportionate to the probable loss in value to the party. *Eastlake,* 102 Wash.2d at 47, 686 P.2d 465 (adopting Restatement (Second) of Contracts § 348 (1981)). The comments to the rule indicate that this alternative basis for damages applies when it is difficult to determine the value of performance to the injured party with sufficient certainty.

> Sometimes, especially if the performance is defective as distinguished from incomplete, it may not be possible to prove the loss in value to the injured party with reasonable certainty. In that case he can usually recover damages based on the cost to remedy the defects. Even if this gives him a recovery somewhat in excess of the loss in

value to him, it is better that he receive a small windfall than that he be undercompensated by being limited to the resulting diminution in the market price of his property.

Eastlake, 102 Wash.2d at 47–48, 686 P.2d 465 (quoting Restatement (Second) of Contracts § 348 cmt. *c* (1981)); *see also* Restatement (Second) of Contracts § 347 cmt. *b* (1981).

Here, Panorama sought damages based on the cost of remedying the defects and submitted evidence indicating that it would be cheaper to replace the roofs than to attempt a labor-intensive repair. The testimony also indicated that a repair of the roofs would not completely cure the defects or provide Panorama with valid manufacturer warranties. Golden Rule, however, argues that the award was inappropriate in the absence of any evidence of the cost of repair or the diminution in the buildings' market value because of the breach * * *

The Restatement proportionality rule adopted in *Eastlake* does not require the trial court to measure the loss in value caused by the breach, but only to determine whether the cost to remedy the defect is clearly disproportionate to the owner's loss.). Once the injured party has established the cost to remedy the defects, the contractor bears the burden of challenging this evidence in order to reduce the award, including providing the trial court with evidence to support an alternative award. Here, Golden Rule provided no evidence of the buildings' diminution in value or the cost to repair the defects and did not challenge the reasonableness of Panorama's estimate for the work.

Golden Rule further contends that any award of damages is inappropriate because there was no evidence that Panorama was harmed by the breach. But as discussed above, the trial court found that all of the roofs installed by Golden Rule exhibited poor workmanship and contained numerous deficiencies. The record indicates that the roofs were substantially inferior to what Golden Rule had contracted to provide and that the installation defects directly affected the performance and life of the roofs, which clearly reduced their value. In addition, Golden Rule failed to provide valid manufacturer warranties for the roofing materials. We conclude the trial court did not err in including Panorama's repair costs in the award. * * *

For the reasons discussed above, we affirm the judgment and award of damages below. * * *

Questions and Connection

1. Questions about the facts of this case
   1.1. In the portion of the opinion entitled "FACTS," what facts were important to the court's decision on damages?
   1.2. What fact, if any, supported Golden Rule's position on measure of damages?

    1.3. Do we know whether Panorama used the $28,612 in damages to replace the roofs? Should that be relevant?

2. Questions about the law

    2.1. What should we learn from this case about burden of proof?

    2.2. $28,612 apparently reflects the cost to replace the roofs "prorated to reflect the existing roofs' performance prior to the suits." Do you agree with this reduction? Does the *Restatement*?

3. Connection

Is the measure of damages in *Panorama Village* consistent with the measure of damages in *O.W. Grun Roofing & Construction Co. v. Cope*, supra at page 721?

In *Panorama*, the court did not have evidence as to the diminution in value resulting from defendant's breach, and awarded damages equal to the replacement cost. What if unlike *Hawkins* and unlike *Panorama* we have information about both the replacement costs, i.e., the defendant's cost of fixing her breach, and diminution in value, i.e., the plaintiff's loss in value that results from the breach, and the former is much larger than the latter?

In such a case, should the expectation damages be based on the lower diminution in value or the much higher cost of fixing the breach? Fortunately, the next two cases are "such" cases—cases that raise the question of whether expectation damages should be based on diminution in value of the performance or cost of fixing the breach. Unfortunately, the next two cases provide different answers to this question of whether expectation damages should be based on the lower diminution in value or the much higher cost of fixing the breach

GROVES v. JOHN WUNDER CO.

Supreme Court of Minnesota
205 Minn. 163, 286 N.W. 235 (1939)

STONE, JUSTICE:

Action for breach of contract. Plaintiff got judgment for a little over $15,000. Sorely disappointed by that sum, he appeals.

In August, 1927, S. J. Groves & Sons Company, a corporation (hereinafter mentioned simply as Groves), owned a tract of 24 acres of Minneapolis suburban real estate. It was served or easily could be reached by railroad trackage. It is zoned as heavy industrial property. But for lack of development of the neighborhood its principal value thus far may have been in the deposit of sand and gravel which it carried. The Groves company had a plant on the premises for excavating and screening the gravel. Near by defendant owned and was operating a similar plant.

In August, 1927, Groves and defendant made the involved contract. For the most part it was a lease from Groves, as lessor, to defendant, as lessee; its term seven years. Defendant agreed to remove the sand and gravel and to leave the property "at a uniform grade, substantially the same as the grade now existing at the roadway * * * on said premises, and that in stripping the overburden * * * it will use said overburden for the purpose of maintaining and establishing said grade."

Under the contract defendant got the Groves screening plant. The transfer thereof and the right to remove the sand and gravel made the consideration moving from Groves to defendant, except that defendant incidentally got rid of Groves as a competitor. On defendant's part it paid Groves $105,000. So that from the outset, on Groves' part the contract was executed except for defendant's right to continue using the property for the stated term. (Defendant had a right to renewal which it did not exercise.)

Defendant breached the contract deliberately. It removed from the premises only "the richest and best of the gravel" and wholly failed, according to the findings, "to perform and comply with the terms, conditions, and provisions of said lease * * * with respect to the condition in which the surface of the demised premises was required to be left." Defendant surrendered the premises, not substantially at the grade required by the contract "nor at any uniform grade." Instead, the ground was "broken, rugged, and uneven." Plaintiff sues as assignee and successor in right of Groves.

As the contract was construed below, the finding is that to complete its performance 288,495 cubic yards of overburden would need to be excavated, taken from the premises, and deposited elsewhere. The reasonable cost of doing that was found to be upwards of $60,000. But, if defendant had left the premises at the uniform grade required by the lease, the reasonable value of the property on the determinative date would have been only $12,160. The judgment was for that sum, including interest, thereby nullifying plaintiff's claim that cost of completing the contract rather than difference in value of the land was the measure of damages. The gauge of damage adopted by the decision was the difference between the market value of plaintiff's land in the condition it was when the contract was made and what it would have been if defendant had performed. The one question for us arises upon plaintiff's assertion that he was entitled, not to that difference in value, but to the reasonable cost to him of doing the work called for by the contract which defendant left undone.

Defendant's breach of contract was wilful. There was nothing of good faith about it. Hence, that the decision below handsomely rewards bad faith and deliberate breach of contract is obvious. That is not allowable. Here the rule is well settled * * * that where the contractor wilfully and fraudulently varies from the terms of a construction contract he cannot sue thereon and have the benefit of the equitable doctrine of substantial performance. That is the rule generally.

Jacob & Youngs, Inc. v. Kent, 230 N.Y. 239, 243, 244, 129 N.E. 889, 891, 23 A.L.R. 1429, is typical. It was a case of substantial performance of a building contract. (This case is distinctly the opposite.) Mr. Justice Cardozo, in the course of his opinion, stressed the distinguishing features. "Nowhere," he said, "will change be tolerated, however, if it is so dominant or pervasive as in any real or substantial measure to frustrate the purpose of the contract." Again, "the willful transgressor must accept the penalty of his transgression."

In reckoning damages for breach of a building or construction contract, the law aims to give the disappointed promisee, so far as money will do it, what he was promised. It is so ruled by a long line of decisions in this state, beginning with Carli v. Seymour, Sabin & Co. 26 Minn. 276, 3 N.W. 348, where the contract was for building a road. There was a breach. Plaintiff was held entitled to recover what it would cost to complete the grading as contemplated by the contract.

Never before, so far as our decisions show, has it even been suggested that lack of value in the land furnished to the contractor who had bound himself to improve it any escape from the ordinary consequences of a breach of the contract. * * *

Even in case of substantial performance in good faith, the resulting defects being remediable, it is error to instruct that the measure of damage is "the difference in value between the house as it was and as it would have been if constructed according to contract." The "correct doctrine" is that the cost of remedying the defect is the "proper" measure of damages.

Value of the land (as distinguished from the value of the intended product of the contract, which ordinarily will be equivalent to its reasonable cost) is no proper part of any measure of damages for wilful breach of a building contract. The reason is plain.

The summit from which to reckon damages from trespass to real estate is its actual value at the moment. The owner's only right is to be compensated for the deterioration in value caused by the tort. That is all he has lost. But not so if a contract to improve the same land has been breached by the contractor who refuses to do the work, especially where, as here, he has been paid in advance. The summit from which to reckon damages for that wrong is the hypothetical peak of accomplishment (not value) which would have been reached had the work been done as demanded by the contract.

* * *

Suppose a contractor were suing the owner for breach of a grading contract such as this. Would any element of value, or lack of it, in the land have any relevance in reckoning damages? Of course not. The contractor would be compensated for what he had lost, i.e., his profit. Conversely, in such a case as this, the owner is entitled to compensation for what he has lost, that is, the work or structure which he has been promised, for which he has paid, and of which he has been deprived by the contractor's breach.

To diminish damages recoverable against him in proportion as there is presently small value in the land would favor the faithless contractor. It would also ignore and so defeat plaintiff's right to contract and build for the future. To justify such a course would require more of the prophetic vision than judges possess. This factor is important when the subject matter is trackage property in the margin of such an area of population and industry as that of the Twin Cities.

     * * *

The objective of this contract of present importance was the improvement of real estate. That makes irrelevant the rules peculiar to damages to chattels, arising from tort or breach of contract. *Crowley v. Burns Boiler & Mfg. Co.*, 100 Minn. 178, 187, 110 N.W. 969, 973, dealt with a breach of contract for the sale of a steam boiler. The court observed:

> "If the application of a particular rule for measuring damages to given facts results in more than compensation, it is at once apparent that the wrong rule has been adopted."

That is unquestioned law, but for its correct application there must be ascertainment of the loss for which compensation is to be reckoned. In tort, the thing lost is money value, nothing more. But under a construction contract, the thing lost by a breach such as we have here is a physical structure or accomplishment, a promised and paid for alteration in land. That is the "injury" for which the law gives him compensation. Its only appropriate measure is the cost of performance.

It is suggested that because of little or no value in his land the owner may be unconscionably enriched by such a reckoning. The answer is that there can be no unconscionable enrichment, no advantage upon which the law will frown, when the result is but to give one party to a contract only what the other has promised; particularly where, as here, the delinquent has had full payment for the promised performance.

It is said by the Restatement, Contracts, § 346, Comment b:

> "Sometimes defects in a completed structure cannot be physically remedied without tearing down and rebuilding, at a cost that would be imprudent and unreasonable. The law does not require damages to be measured by a method requiring such economic waste. If no such waste is involved, the cost of remedying the defect is the amount awarded as compensation for failure to render the promised performance."

The "economic waste" declaimed against by the decisions applying that rule has nothing to do with the value in money of the real estate, or even with the product of the contract. The waste avoided is only that which would come from wrecking a physical structure completed, or nearly so, under the contract. The cases applying that rule go no further. Absent such waste, as it is in this case, the rule of the Restatement, Contracts, § 346, is that "the cost of remedying the defect is the amount awarded as compensation for failure to render the promised performance." That means that defendants here are liable to plaintiff for the reasonable cost of doing what defendants promised to do and have wilfully declined to do.

It follows that there must be a new trial. The initial question will be as to the proper construction of the contract. Thus far the case has been considered from the standpoint of the construction adopted by plaintiff and acquiesced in, very likely for strategic reasons, by defendants. The question has not been argued here, so we intimate no opinion concerning it, but we put the question whether the contract required removal from the premises of any overburden. The requirement in that respect was that the overburden should be used for the purpose of "establishing and maintaining" the grade. A uniform slope and grade were doubtless required. But whether, if it could not be accomplished without removal and deposit elsewhere of large amounts of overburden, the contract required as a condition that the grade everywhere should be as low as the one recited as "now existing at the roadway" is a question for initial consideration below.

The judgment must be reversed with a new trial to follow.

So ordered.

QUESTIONS

1. Questions about the facts of this case
    1.1. Which of the following facts were relevant?
        — Defendant paid Groves $105,000
        — "Defendant breached the contract deliberately"
        — Cost of leveling the property would be $60,000
        — Value of the land after leveling would be $12,160
        — "Plaintiff sues as assignee and successor in right of Groves"
    1.2. Are there any other relevant facts?
2. Questions about the law
    2.1. According to the Minnesota Supreme Court, at the trial court, "the gauge of damages * * * was the difference between the market value of plaintiff's land in the condition it was when the contract was made and what it would have been if the defendant had performed." Is that "gauge of damages" consistent with *Hawkins v. McGee*?
    2.2. The court started off by noting that the breach was wilful. So? Are damages increased just because of the mental state of the contract

breacher? If not, then why are the intentions of the breacher relevant?

2.3. Do you think the court would reach a different result if the cost of repair were $1,000,000 (such as is often the case with environmental cleanups of dumping sites), but the value after repair was still only $12,000? Why or why not?

2.4. Why does the court mention *Jacob & Youngs, supra,* at 660? How are the cases similar? How are they different? Is the breaching party in this case the plaintiff or the defendant? Was the breaching party in *Jacob & Youngs* the plaintiff or the defendant? Does that matter?

2.5. Recall that the court noted that this contract involves the "improvement of real estate." Why does the court then say that rules for damages for breach of contracts relating to chattels are "irrelevant"?

2.6. Recall the court's discussion of "economic waste." Does the court understand the concept of economic waste? What is the defendant's economic waste argument in this case?

2.7. What is the relationship between "economic waste" and "efficient breach"? Was the breach in this case an "efficient breach"? An "opportunistic breach"? Was whether the breach was an "efficient breach" or an "opportunistic breach" relevant to the court? Should it have been?

PEEVYHOUSE v. GARLAND COAL & MINING CO.

Supreme Court of Oklahoma
382 P.2d 109 (1962)

Jackson, Justice.

In the trial court, plaintiffs Willie and Lucille Peevyhouse sued the defendant, Garland Coal and Mining Company, for damages for breach of contract. Judgment was for plaintiffs in an amount considerably less than was sued for. Plaintiffs appeal and defendant cross-appeals.

In the briefs on appeal, the parties present their argument and contentions under several propositions; however, they all stem from the basic question of whether the trial court properly instructed the jury on the measure of damages.

Briefly stated, the facts are as follows: plaintiffs owned a farm containing coal deposits, and in November, 1954, leased the premises to defendant for a period of five years for coal mining purposes. A 'strip-mining' operation was contemplated in which the coal would be taken from pits on the surface of the ground, instead of from underground mine shafts. In addition to the usual covenants found in a coal mining lease, defendant specifically agreed to perform certain restorative and remedial work at the end of the lease period. It is unnecessary to set out the details of the work to be done, other than to say that it would involve the moving of many thousands of cubic yards of dirt, at a cost estimated by expert witnesses at about $29,000.00. However, plaintiffs sued for only $25,000.00.

During the trial, it was stipulated that all covenants and agreements in the lease contract had been fully carried out by both parties, except the remedial work mentioned above; defendant conceded that this work had not been done.

Plaintiffs introduced expert testimony as to the amount and nature of the work to be done, and its estimated cost. Over plaintiffs' objections, defendant thereafter introduced expert testimony as to the 'diminution in value' of plaintiffs' farm resulting from the failure of defendant to render performance as agreed in the contract—that is, the difference between the present value of the farm, and what its value would have been if defendant had done what it agreed to do.

At the conclusion of the trial, the court instructed the jury that it must return a verdict for plaintiffs, and left the amount of damages for jury determination. On the measure of damages, the court instructed the jury that it might consider the cost of performance of the work defendant agreed to do, 'together with all of the evidence offered on behalf of either party'.

It thus appears that the jury was at liberty to consider the 'diminution in value' of plaintiffs' farm as well as the cost of 'repair work' in determining the amount of damages.

It returned a verdict for plaintiffs for $5000.00—only a fraction of the 'cost of performance', but more than the total value of the farm even after the remedial work is done.

On appeal, the issue is sharply drawn. Plaintiffs contend that the true measure of damages in this case is what it will cost plaintiffs to obtain performance of the work that was not done because of defendant's default. Defendant argues that the measure of damages is the cost of performance 'limited, however, to the total difference in the market value before and after the work was performed'.

It appears that this precise question has not heretofore been presented to this court. In Ardizonne v. Archer, 72 Okl. 70, 178 P. 263, this court held that the measure of damages for breach of a contract to drill an oil well was the reasonable cost of drilling the well, but here a slightly different factual situation exists. The drilling of an oil well will yield valuable geological information, even if no oil or gas is found, and of course if the well is a producer, the value of the premises increases. In the case before us, it is argued by defendant with some force that the performance of the remedial work defendant agreed to do will add at the most only a few hundred dollars to the value of plaintiffs' farm, and that the damages should be limited to that amount because that is all plaintiffs have lost.

Plaintiffs rely on Groves v. John Wunder Co., 205 Minn. 163, 286 N.W. 235, 123 A.L.R. 502. In that case, the Minnesota court, in a substantially similar situation, adopted the 'cost of performance' rule as-opposed to the 'value' rule. The result was to authorize a jury to give plaintiff damages in the amount of $60,000, where the real estate concerned would have been worth only $12,160, even if the work contracted for had been done.

It may be observed that Groves v. John Wunder Co., supra, is the only case which has come to our attention in which the cost of performance rule has been followed under circumstances where the cost of performance greatly exceeded the diminution in value resulting from the breach of contract. Incidentally, it appears that this case was decided by a plurality rather than a majority of the members of the court.

Defendant relies principally upon Sandy Valley & E. R. Co., v. Hughes, 175 Ky. 320, 194 S.W. 344; Bigham v. Wabash–Pittsburg Terminal Ry. Co., 223 Pa. 106, 72 A. 318; and Sweeney v. Lewis Const. Co., 66 Wash. 490, 119 P. 1108. These were all cases in which, under similar circumstances, the appellate courts followed the 'value' rule instead of the 'cost of performance' rule. Plaintiff points out that in the earliest of these cases (Bigham) the court cites as authority on the measure of damages an earlier Pennsylvania tort case, and that the other two cases follow the first, with no explanation as to why a measure of damages ordinarily followed in cases sounding in tort should be used in contract cases. Nevertheless, it is of some significance that three out of four appellate courts have followed the diminution in value rule under circumstances where, as here, the cost of performance greatly exceeds the diminution in value.

The explanation may be found in the fact that the situations presented are artificial ones. It is highly unlikely that the ordinary property owner would agree to pay $29,000 (or its equivalent) for the construction of 'improvements' upon his property that would increase its value only about ($300) three hundred dollars. The result is that we are called upon to apply principles of law theoretically based upon reason and reality to a situation which is basically unreasonable and unrealistic.

In Groves v. John Wunder Co., supra, in arriving at its conclusions, the Minnesota court apparently considered the contract involved to be analogous to a building and construction contract, and cited authority for the proposition that the cost of performance or completion of the building as contracted is ordinarily the measure of damages in actions for damages for the breach of such a contract. * * *

Even in the case of contracts that are unquestionably building and construction contracts, the authorities are not in agreement as to the factors to be considered in determining whether the cost of performance rule or the value rule should be applied. The American Law Institute's

Restatement of the Law, Contracts, Volume 1, Sections 346(1)(a)(i) and (ii) submits the proposition that the cost of performance is the proper measure of damages 'if this is possible and does not involve unreasonable economic waste'; and that the diminution in value caused by the breach is the proper measure 'if construction and completion in accordance with the contract would involve *unreasonable economic waste*'. (Emphasis supplied.) In an explanatory comment immediately following the text, the Restatement makes it clear that the 'economic waste' referred to consists of the destruction of a substantially completed building or other structure. Of course no such destruction is involved in the case now before us.

On the other hand, in McCormick, Damages, Section 168, it is said with regard to building and construction contracts that '* * * in cases where the defect is one that can be repaired or cured without undue expense' the cost of performance is the proper measure of damages, but where '* * * the defect in material or construction is one that cannot be remedied without *an expenditure for reconstruction disproportionate to the end to be attained*' (emphasis supplied) the value rule should be followed. The same idea was expressed in Jacob & Youngs, Inc. v. Kent, 230 N.Y. 239, 129 N.E. 889, 23 A.L.R. 1429, as follows:

'The owner is entitled to the money which will permit him to complete, unless the cost of completion is grossly and unfairly out of proportion to the good to be attained. When that is true, the measure is the difference in value.'

It thus appears that the prime consideration in the Restatement was 'economic waste'; and that the prime consideration in McCormick, Damages, and in Jacob & Youngs, Inc. v. Kent, supra, was the relationship between the expense involved and the 'end to be attained'—in other words, the 'relative economic benefit'.

In view of the unrealistic fact situation in the instant case, and certain Oklahoma statutes to be hereinafter noted, we are of the opinion that the 'relative economic benefit' is a proper consideration here. This is in accord with the recent case of Mann v. Clowser, 190 Va. 887, 59 S.E.2d 78, where, in applying the cost rule, the Virginia court specifically noted that '* * * the defects are remediable from a practical standpoint and the costs *are not grossly disproportionate to the results to be obtained*' (Emphasis supplied).

* * *

We therefore hold that where, in a coal mining lease, lessee agrees to perform certain remedial work on the premises concerned at the end of the lease period, and thereafter the contract is fully performed by both parties except that the remedial work is not done, the measure of damages in an action by lessor against lessee for damages for breach of contract is ordinarily the reasonable cost of performance of the work; however, where the contract provision breached was merely incidental to the main purpose in view, and where the economic benefit which would result to lessor by full performance of the work is grossly disproportionate to the cost of performance, the damages which lessor may recover are limited to the diminution in value resulting to the premises because of the non-performance.

We believe the above holding is in conformity with the intention of the Legislature as expressed in the statutes mentioned, and in harmony with the better-reasoned cases from the other jurisdictions where analogous fact situations have been considered. It should be noted that the rule as stated does not interfere with the property owner's right to 'do what he will with his own' Chamberlain v. Parker, 45 N.Y. 569), or his right, if he chooses, to contract for 'improvements' which will actually have the effect of reducing his property's value. Where such result is in fact contemplated by the parties, and is a main or principal purpose of those contracting, it would seem that the measure of damages for breach would ordinarily be the cost of performance.

The above holding disposes of all of the arguments raised by the parties on appeal.

Under the most liberal view of the evidence herein, the diminution in value resulting to the premises because of non-performance of the remedial work was $300.00. After a careful search of the record, we have found no evidence of a higher figure, and plaintiffs do not argue in their briefs that a greater diminution in value was sustained. It thus appears that the judgment was clearly excessive, and that the amount for which judgment should have been rendered is definitely and satisfactorily shown by the record.

We are asked by each party to modify the judgment in accordance with the respective theories advanced, and it is conceded that we have authority to do so. * * *

We are of the opinion that the judgment of the trial court for plaintiffs should be, and it is hereby, modified and reduced to the sum of $300.00, and as so modified it is affirmed.

WELCH, DAVISON, HALLEY, and JOHNSON, JJ., concur.

WILLIAMS, C. J., BLACKBIRD, V. C. J., and IRWIN and BERRY, JJ., dissent.

IRWIN, JUSTICE (dissenting). By the specific provisions in the coal mining lease under consideration, the defendant agreed as follows:

'. . . 7b Lessee agrees to make fills in the pits dug on said premises on the property line in such manner that fences can be placed thereon and access had to opposite sides of the pits.

'7c Lessee agrees to smooth off the top of the spoil banks on the above premises.

'7d Lessee agrees to leave the creek crossing the above premises in such a condition that it will not interfere with the crossings to be made in pits as set out in 7b.

'7f Lessee further agrees to leave no shale or dirt on the high wall of said pits. * * *'

Following the expiration of the lease, plaintiffs made demand upon defendant that it carry out the provisions of the contract and to perform those covenants contained therein.

Defendant admits that it failed to perform its obligations that it agreed and contracted to perform under the lease contract and there is nothing in the record which indicates that defendant could not perform its obligations. Therefore, in my opinion defendant's breach of the contract was wilful and not in good faith.

Although the contract speaks for itself, there were several negotiations between the plaintiffs and defendant before the contract was executed. Defendant admitted in the trial of the action, that plaintiffs insisted that the above provisions be included in the contract and that they would not agree to the coal mining lease unless the above provisions were included.

In consideration for the lease contract, plaintiffs were to receive a certain amount as royalty for the coal produced and marketed and in addition thereto their land was to be restored as provided in the contract.

Defendant received as consideration for the contract, its proportionate share of the coal produced and marketed and in addition thereto, the right to use plaintiffs' land in the furtherance of its mining operations.

The cost for performing the contract in question could have been reasonably approximated when the contract was negotiated and executed and there are no conditions now existing which could not have been reasonably anticipated by the parties. Therefore, defendant had knowledge, when it prevailed upon the plaintiffs to execute the lease, that the cost of performance might be disproportionate to the value or benefits received by plaintiff for the performance.

Defendant has received its benefits under the contract and now urges, in substance, that plaintiffs' measure of damages for its failure to perform should be the economic value of performance to the plaintiffs and not the cost of performance.

If a peculiar set of facts should exist where the above rule should be applied as the proper measure of damages, (and in my judgment those facts do not exist in the instant case) before such rule should be applied, consideration should be given to the benefits received or contracted for by the party who asserts the application of the rule.

Defendant did not have the right to mine plaintiffs' coal or to use plaintiffs' property for its mining operations without the consent of plaintiffs. Defendant had knowledge of the benefits that it would receive under the contract and the approximate cost of performing the contract. With this knowledge, it must be presumed that defendant thought that it would be to its economic advantage to enter into the contract with plaintiffs and that it would reap benefits from the contract, or it would have not entered into the contract.

Therefore, if the value of the performance of a contract should be considered in determining the measure of damages for breach of a contract, the value of the benefits received under the contract by a party who breaches a contract should also be considered. However, in my judgment, to give consideration to either in the instant action, completely rescinds and holds for naught the solemnity of the contract before us and makes an entirely new contract for the parties.

* * *

In my judgment, we should follow the case of Groves v. John Wunder Company, 205 Minn. 163, 286 N.W. 235, 123 A.L.R. 502, which defendant agrees 'that the fact situation is apparently similar to the one in the case at bar', and where the Supreme Court of Minnesota held:

> 'The owner's or employer's damages for such a breach (i. e. breach hypothesized in 2d syllabus) are to be measured, not in respect to the value of the land to be improved, but by the reasonable cost of doing that which the contractor promised to do and which he left undone.'

The hypothesized breach referred to states that where the contractor's breach of a contract is wilful, that is, in bad faith, he is not entitled to any benefit of the equitable doctrine of substantial performance.

In the instant action defendant has made no attempt to even substantially perform. The contract in question is not immoral, is not tainted with fraud, and was not entered into through mistake or accident and is not contrary to public policy. It is clear and unambiguous and the parties understood the terms thereof, and the approximate cost of fulfilling the obligations could have been approximately ascertained. There are no conditions existing now which could not have been reasonably anticipated when the contract was negotiated and executed. The defendant could have performed the contract if it desired. It has accepted and reaped the benefits of its contract and now urges that plaintiffs' benefits under the contract be denied. If plaintiffs' benefits are denied, such benefits would inure to the direct benefit of the defendant.

Therefore, in my opinion, the plaintiffs were entitled to specific performance of the contract and since defendant has failed to perform, the proper measure of damages should be the cost of performance. Any other measure of damage would be holding for naught the express provisions of the contract; would be taking from the plaintiffs the benefits of the contract and placing those benefits in defendant which has failed to perform its obligations; would be granting benefits to defendant without a resulting obligation; and would be completely rescinding the solemn obligation of the contract for the benefit of the defendant to the detriment of the plaintiffs by making an entirely new contract for the parties.

I therefore respectfully dissent to the opinion promulgated by a majority of my associates.

QUESTIONS AND NOTE

1. Questions about the facts of this case

    1.1. Can you distinguish the facts of this case from the facts of *Groves?*

    1.2. Is there an allegation of intentional breach here? Does it matter?

    1.3. Does the dissenting opinion disagree with the majority opinion's "briefly stated" facts in the third paragraph of the majority opinion? Does the dissenting opinion believe that the majority states the facts too "briefly"?

    1.4. Would it be helpful to see the Peevyhouse's farm? http://law professors.typepad.com/contractsprof_blog/2009/08/alan-white-teach ing-peevyhouse-first.html#comments To see a documentary about the Peevyhouse's farm? Professor Judith Maute had produced such a documentary and provided a complimentary copy to law school libraries.

2. Questions about the law

    2.1. What does the court mean by the statement "In view of the unrealistic fact situation in the instant case * * * we are of the opinion that 'relative economic benefit' is a proper consideration here"? What makes this fact situation "unrealistic"? What is the "relative economic benefit"? What would be the waste in forcing Garland to do what it said it would do?

    2.2. Both *Peevyhouse* and *Groves* cite Judge Cardozo's opinion in *Jacob & Youngs v. Kent, supra,* at [660]. Which case is more consistent with the holding in *Jacob & Youngs v. Kent*? Which case is more consistent with the language in *Jacob & Youngs v. Kent*?

    2.3. Remember Cardozo's indicating that Kent could have changed the result in *Jacob & Youngs v. Kent* by "apt and certain words." Could the Peevyhouses have changed the result in this case with "apt and certain words" in their contract with Garland ? What if the lease had provided "performance of every term shall be a condition of recovery"? What if the lease provided "Regardless of the economic waste that might be involved, Garland hereby promises to restore the land to its original state upon completion of the strip mining" and included a liquidated damages clause of $29,000 upon non-performance of the restoration obligation?

    2.4. Which decision—*Groves* or *Peevyhouse*—is more consistent with the protection of expectation approach to contracts damages? Which decision is more consistent with Section 348 of the *Restatement (Second) of Contracts*?

3. Note

    Great cases, great doggerel:

    > We picked a fine time to strip mine, Lucille.
    > It sure looks to me like we got a raw deal.
    > That smooth city-slicker said we'd all get rich quicker

> I should have known it warn't real.
> We picked a fine time to strip mine, Lucille.
>
>   . . .
>
> We picked a fine time to strip mine, Lucille.
> Make no mistake, hon, we got a raw deal,
> I never went to law school,
> I didn't know the value rule,
> I thought sure we'd win our appeal,
> The Supreme Court done gyped us, Lucille.

Sung to the tune of "You Picked a Fine Time to Leave Me Lucille," as sung by Kenny Rogers. *See* Judith Maute, *Peevyhouse v. Garland Coal & Mining Co. Revisited: The Ballad of Willie and Lucille*, 89 Nᴡ. U. L. Rᴇᴠ. 1341, 1345 (1995), for the full text of the tune, and for a fascinating examination of the case.

B.   MONEY DAMAGES UNDER THE U.C.C.

Recall that *Hawkins v. McGee* is based on a sale of goods damages rule: "the measure of damages is the difference between the value of the machine, if it had corresponded with the warranty and its actual value." That rule is premised on putting the nonbreaching party in the same position as if the contract had been performed without breach. In other words, that rule protects the expectation interest.

Hawkins v. McGee was decided before: (i) the Fuller and Perdue article which suggested the term "expectation interest", (ii) the *Restatement of Contracts* which adopted the term, and (iii) Article 2 of the Uniform Commercial Code which now governs sale of goods contracts. Article 2 devotes 25 sections to "Remedies."

In section 2–703, sellers' remedies are catalogued. Section 2–711 does the same for buyers' remedies. These various sections on money damages are consistent with protection of the expectation interest.

Full examination of these sections awaits you in a Sales course. For now, we will look at some basic problems (and if your professor is so inclined a couple of more challenging cases).

Bᴀsɪᴄ Pʀᴏʙʟᴇᴍs ᴏɴ Bᴜʏᴇʀ's Dᴀᴍᴀɢᴇs Uɴᴅᴇʀ ᴛʜᴇ *U.C.C.*

What are the damages in each of these cases? (Assume good faith, reasonable purchases in each case.).

1. Contract for sale of a machine for $1,000. Seller breaches. Buyer pays $800 for a replacement machine.

2. Same facts as problem 1 except Buyer pays $1,400 for replacement machine.

3. Same facts as problem 1 except now Buyer does not replace the machine. He establishes that the market price for a replacement machine is $1,400. (Question: How can the buyer who does not replace prove market price?)

4. A harder problem: Same facts as problem 1 except Buyer replaces at $800 through her "connections." She establishes that the market price for a replacement machine is $1,400.

Does the next case help you answer #4?

KGM HARVESTING CO. v. FRESH NETWORK

Court of Appeal of California, Sixth Appellate District
36 Cal.App.4th 376, 42 Cal.Rptr.2d 286 (1995)

COTTLE, P. J.

California lettuce grower and distributor KGM Harvesting Company (hereafter seller) had a contract to deliver 14 loads of lettuce each week to Ohio lettuce broker Fresh Network (hereafter buyer). When the price of lettuce rose dramatically in May and June 1991, seller refused to deliver the required quantity of lettuce to buyer. Buyer then purchased lettuce on the open market in order to fulfill its contractual obligations to third parties. After a trial, the jury awarded buyer damages in an amount equal to the difference between the contract price and the price buyer was forced to pay for substitute lettuce on the open market. On appeal, seller argues that the damage award is excessive. We disagree and shall affirm the judgment. * * *

FACTS

In July 1989 buyer and seller entered into an agreement for the sale and purchase of lettuce. Over the years, the terms of the agreement were modified. By May 1991 the terms were that seller would sell to buyer 14 loads of lettuce each week and that buyer would pay seller 9 cents a pound for the lettuce. (A load of lettuce consists of 40 bins, each of which weighs 1,000 to 1,200 pounds. Assuming an average bin weight of 1,100 pounds, 1 load would equal 44,000 pounds, and the 14 loads called for in the contract would weigh 616,000 pounds. At 9 cents per pound, the cost would approximate $55,440 per week.)

Buyer sold all of the lettuce it received from seller to a lettuce broker named Castellini Company who in turn sold it to Club Chef, a company that chops and shreds lettuce for the fast food industry (specifically, Burger King, Taco Bell, and Pizza Hut). Castellini Company bought lettuce from buyer on a "cost plus" basis, meaning it would pay buyer its actual cost plus a small commission. Club Chef, in turn, bought lettuce from Castellini Company on a cost plus basis.

Seller had numerous lettuce customers other than buyer, including seller's subsidiaries Coronet East and West. Coronet East supplied all the lettuce for the McDonald's fast food chain.

In May and June 1991, when the price of lettuce went up dramatically, seller refused to supply buyer with lettuce at the contract price of 9 cents per pound. Instead, it sold the lettuce to others at a profit of between $800,000 and $1.1 million. Buyer, angry at seller's breach, refused to pay seller for lettuce it had already received. Buyer then went out on the open market and purchased lettuce to satisfy its obligations to Castellini Company. Castellini covered all of buyer's extra expense except for $70,000. Castellini in turn passed on its extra costs to Club Chef which passed on at least part of its additional costs to its fast food customers.

* * *

Subsequently, seller filed suit for the balance due on its invoices, and buyer cross-complained for the additional cost it incurred to obtain substitute lettuce after seller's breach. At trial, the parties stipulated that seller was entitled to a directed verdict on its complaint for $233,000, the amount owing on the invoices. Accordingly, only the cross-complaint went to the jury, whose task was to determine whether buyer was entitled to damages from seller for the cost of obtaining substitute lettuce and, if so, in what amount. The jury determined that seller breached the contract, that its performance was not excused, and that buyer was entitled to $655,960.22, which represented the difference between the contract price of nine cents a pound and what it cost buyer to cover by purchasing lettuce in substitution in May and June 1991. It also determined that such an award would not result in a windfall to buyer and that buyer was obligated to the Castellini Company for the additional costs. The court subtracted from buyer's award of $655,960.22 the $233,000 buyer owed to seller on its invoices, leaving a net award in favor of buyer in the amount of $422,960.22. * * *

DISCUSSION

A. Seller's Appeal

Section 2711 of the California Uniform Commercial Code provides a buyer with several alternative remedies for a seller's breach of contract. The buyer can " 'cover' by making in good faith and without unreasonable delay any reasonable purchase of * * * goods in substitution for those due from the seller." (§ 2712, subd. (1).) In that case, the buyer "may recover from the seller as damages the difference between the cost of cover and the contract price. * * *" (§ 2712, subd. (2).) If the buyer is unable to cover or chooses not to cover, the measure of damages is the difference between the market price and the contract price. (§ 2713.) Under either alternative, the buyer may also recover incidental and consequential damages. (§ 2711, 2715.) In addition, in certain cases the buyer may secure specific performance or replevin "where the goods are unique" (§ 2716) or may recover goods identified to a contract (§ 2502).

In the instant case, buyer "covered" as defined in section 2712 in order to fulfill its own contractual obligations to the Castellini Company. Accordingly, it was awarded the damages called for in cover cases—the difference between the contract price and the cover price. (§ 2712.)

In appeals from judgments rendered pursuant to section 2712, the dispute typically centers on whether the buyer acted in "good faith," whether the "goods in substitution" differed substantially from the contracted for goods, whether the buyer unreasonably delayed in purchasing substitute goods in the mistaken belief that the price would go down, or whether the buyer paid too much for the substitute goods. * * *

In this case, however, none of these typical issues is in dispute. Seller does not contend that buyer paid too much for the substitute lettuce or that buyer was guilty of "unreasonable delay" or a lack of "good faith" in its attempt to obtain substitute lettuce. Nor does seller contend that the lettuce purchased was of a higher quality or grade and therefore not a reasonable substitute.

Instead, seller takes issue with section 2712 itself, contending that despite the unequivocal language of section 2712, a buyer who covers should not necessarily recover the difference between the cover price and the contract price. Seller points out that because of buyer's "cost plus" contract with Castellini Company, buyer was eventually able to pass on the extra expenses (except for $70,000) occasioned by seller's breach and buyer's consequent purchase of substitute lettuce on the open market. It urges this court under these circumstances not to allow buyer to obtain a "windfall."[2]

The basic premise of contract law is to effectuate the expectations of the parties to the agreement, to give them the "benefit of the bargain" they struck when they entered into the agreement. In its basic premise, contract law therefore differs significantly from tort law. As the California Supreme Court explained in *Foley v. Interactive Data Corp.* (1988) 47 Cal. 3d 654 [254 Cal. Rptr. 211, 765 P.2d 373], "* * * contract actions are created to enforce the intentions of the parties to the agreement [while] tort law is primarily designed to vindicate 'social policy.' " * * *

" 'The basic object of damages is compensation, and in the law of contracts the theory is that the party injured by breach should receive as nearly as possible the equivalent of the benefits of performance.' " * * * A compensation system that gives the aggrieved party the benefit of the bargain, and no more, furthers the goal of "predictability about the cost of contractual relationships * * * in our commercial system." * * *

With these rules in mind, we examine the contract at issue in this case to ascertain the reasonable expectations of the parties. The contract recited that its purpose was "to supply [buyer] with a consistent quality

---

2. In answering special interrogatories, the jury found (1) that if buyer were awarded the difference between the contract price and the cost of cover, it would not result in a windfall to buyer, and (2) that buyer had an obligation to pay Castellini Company for the amount Castellini Company paid buyer to acquire the substitute lettuce. * * *

raw product at a fair price to [seller], which also allows [buyer] profitability for his finished product.' Seller promised to supply the designated quantity even if the price of lettuce went up ("We agree to supply said product and amount at stated price regardless of the market price or conditions") and buyer promised to purchase the designated quantity even if the price went down ("[Buyer] agrees to purchase said product and amounts at stated price regardless of the market price or conditions, provided quality requirements are met"). The possibility that the price of lettuce would fluctuate was consequently foreseeable to both parties.

Although the contract does not recite this fact, seller was aware of buyer's contract with the Castellini Company and with the Castellini Company's contract with Club Chef. This knowledge was admitted at trial and can be inferred from the fact that seller shipped the contracted for 14 loads of lettuce directly to Club Chef each week. Thus, seller was well aware that if it failed to provide buyer with the required 14 loads of lettuce, buyer would have to obtain replacement lettuce elsewhere or would itself be in breach of contract. This was within the contemplation of the parties when they entered into their agreement.

As noted earlier, the object of contract damages is to give the aggrieved party " 'as nearly as possible the equivalent of the benefits of performance.' " * * * In the instant case, buyer contracted for 14 loads of lettuce each week at 9 cents per pound. When seller breached its contract to provide that lettuce, buyer went out on the open market and purchased substitute lettuce to fulfill its contractual obligations to third parties. However, purchasing replacement lettuce to continue its business did not place buyer "in as good a position as if the other party had fully performed." This was because buyer paid more than 9 cents per pound for the replacement lettuce. Only by reimbursing buyer for the additional costs above 9 cents a pound could buyer truly receive the benefit of the bargain. This is the measure of damages set forth in section 2712.

As White and Summers point out, "Since 2712 measures buyer's damages by the difference between his actual cover purchase and the contract price, the formula will often put buyer in the identical economic position that performance would have." (White & Summers, *supra*, Buyer's Remedies, Cover, § 6–3, p. 285.) Therefore, "[i]n the typical case a timely 'cover' purchase by an aggrieved buyer will preclude any 2715 [incidental and consequential] damages.' (*Ibid.*) "Not only does the damage formula in 2712 come close to putting the aggrieved buyer in the same economic position as actual performance would have," White and Summers conclude, "but it also enables him to achieve his prime objective, namely that of acquiring his needed goods." (*Id.* at p. 292.)

In this case, the damage formula of section 2712 put buyer in the identical position performance would have: it gave buyer the contracted for 14 loads of lettuce with which to carry on its business at the contracted for price of 9 cents per pound.

Despite the obvious applicability and appropriateness of section 2712, seller argues in this appeal that the contract-cover differential of section 2712 is inappropriate in cases, as here, where the aggrieved buyer is ultimately able to pass on its additional costs to other parties. Seller contends that section 1106's remedial injunction to put the aggrieved party "in as good a position as if the other party had fully performed' demands that all subsequent events impacting on buyer's ultimate profit or loss be taken into consideration (specifically, that buyer passed on all but $70,000 of its loss to Castellini Company, which passed on all of its loss to Club Chef, which passed on most of its loss to its fast food customers).

     * * *

As noted earlier, section 2712 "will often put buyer in the identical economic position that performance would have." (White & Summers, *supra*, Buyer's Remedies, Cover, § 6–3, p. 285.) In contrast, the contract-market differential of section 2713 "bears no necessary relation to the change in the buyer's economic status that the breach causes. It is possible that this differential might yield the buyer a handsome sum even though the breach actually saved him money in the long run (as for example when a middleman buyer's resale markets dry up after the breach). It is also quite possible that the buyer's lost profit from resale or consumption would be greater than the contract-market difference." (*Id.,* § 6–4, at p. 294.)

White and Summers argue that the drafters of section 2713 could not have intended to put the buyer in the same position as performance since "[p]erformance would have given the buyer certain goods for consumption or resale" (White & Summers, *supra*, Buyer's Remedies, Cover, § 6–4, at p. 294) which would have resulted in "either a net economic gain for the buyer or a net economic loss." (*Ibid.*) The best explanation of section 2713, they suggest, is that it is a "statutory liquidated damage clause, a breach inhibitor the payout of which need bear no close relation to the plaintiff's actual loss." * * * In discussing the "problem of a buyer who has covered but who seeks to ignore 2712 and sue for a larger contract-market differential under 2713," the authors suggest: "If the Code's goal is to put the buyer in the same position as though there had been no breach, and if 2712 will accomplish that goal but 2713 will do so only by coincidence, why not force the covering buyer to use 2712?" (White & Summers, *supra*, at p. 304.) Professor Robert Childres has actually called for the repeal of section 2713 and the requirement of compulsory cover. (Childres, *Buyer's Remedies: The Danger of Section 2–713* (1978) 72 Nw. U. L.Rev. 837.)

With these prefatory comments in mind, we look to the *Allied Canners* case. In *Allied Canners*, [Victor Packing, a] raisin supplier breached another contract to sell raisins in 1976. The buyer, Allied Canners, had contracts to resell the raisins it bought from Victor to two Japanese companies for its cost plus 4 percent. Such a resale would have resulted in a profit of $4,462.50 to Allied. When Victor breached the contract, Allied sued for the difference between the market price and the contract price as authorized by section 2713. As the market price of raisins had soared due to the disastrous 1976 rains, the market-contract price formula would have yielded damages of approximately $150,000. Allied did not purchase substitute raisins and did not make any deliveries under its resale contracts to the Japanese buyers. One of the Japanese buyers simply released Allied from its contract because of the general unavailability of raisins. The other buyer did not release Allied, but it did not sue Allied either. By the time Allied's case against Victor went to trial, the statute of limitations on the Japanese buyer's claim had run.

Under these circumstances, the court held that the policy of section 1106 (that the aggrieved party be put in as good a position as if the other party had performed) required that the award of damages to Allied be limited to its actual loss. It noted that for this limitation to apply, three conditions must be met: (1) "the seller knew that the buyer had a resale contract'; (2) "the buyer has not been able to show that it will be liable in damages to the buyer on its forward contract"; and (3) "there has been no finding of bad faith on the part of the seller. * * *" (*Allied Canners & Packers, Inc. v. Victor Packing Co.*, *supra*, 162 Cal. App. 3d at p. 915.)

The result in *Allied Canners* seems to have derived in large part from the court's finding that Victor had not acted in bad faith in breaching the contract. The court noted, "It does appear clear, however, that, as the trial court found, the rains caused a severe problem, and Victor made substantial efforts [to procure the raisins for Allied]. We do not deem this record one to support an inference that windfall damages must be awarded the buyer to prevent unjust enrichment to a deliberately breaching seller. (Compare *Sun–Maid Raisin Growers v. Victor Packing Co.*, *supra*, 146 Cal. App. 3d 787 [where, in a case coincidentally involving Victor, Victor was expressly found by the trial court to have engaged in bad faith by gambling on the market price of raisins in deciding whether to perform its contracts to sell raisins to Sun Maid].)" (162 Cal. App. 3d at p. 916.)[7]

We believe that this focus on the good or bad faith of the breaching party is inappropriate in a commercial sales case. As our California Supreme Court recently explained, courts should not differentiate between good and bad motives for breaching a contract in assessing the measure of

---

7. In view of Allied Canners' three-part test, we assume the results would have been different here if the court had found Victor was "a deliberately breaching seller." Perhaps in that case, the court would not have focused on what the aggrieved buyer ultimately would have received on resale but might have focused on what benefits the seller reaped from breaching. In Allied Canners, the price of raisins went up from 30 cents a pound to 87 cents a pound. If seller had not breached, it would have had to go out on the market and buy raisins for Allied at considerably more than it was contracted to sell them for to Allied. By breaching, it avoided a loss that might have been more in the $150,000 range (market-contract differential) than the $4,000 range (Allied's lost profits). Thus, the court prevented a windfall to Allied at the cost of providing a windfall to Victor. Such a result is curious if the intent of contract damages is to effectuate the expectations of the parties to the contract. Here, the parties clearly contemplated when they entered into their fixed price agreement that the price of raisins would fluctuate and that sometimes buyer would receive a price better than the market price and that other times it would have to pay more than the market price.

the nonbreaching party's damages. (*Applied Equipment Corp. v. Litton Saudi Arabia Ltd.* (1994) 7 Cal. 4th 503, 513–515 [28 Cal.Rptr.2d 475, 869 P.2d 454].) Such a focus is inconsistent with the policy "to encourage contractual relations and commercial activity by enabling parties to estimate in advance the financial risks of their enterprise." (*Id.* at p. 515.) " 'Courts traditionally have awarded damages for breach of contract to compensate the aggrieved party rather than to punish the breaching party.' [Citations.]" (*Foley v. Interactive Data Corp.*, *supra*, 47 Cal. 3d at p. 683.) * * *

As the foregoing discussion makes clear, we have serious reservations about whether the result in *Allied Canners*, with its emphasis on the good faith of the breaching party, is appropriate in an action seeking damages under section 2713. We have no reservations, however, in not extending the *Allied Canners* rationale to a section 2712 case. As noted earlier, no section 2712 case, including *Sun–Maid Growers v. Victor Packing Co.*, *supra*, 146 Cal. App. 3d 787, has ever held that cover damages must be limited by section 1106. The obvious reason is that the cover-contract differential puts a buyer who covers in the exact same position as performance would have done. This is the precisely what is called for in section 1106. In this respect, the cover/contract differential of section 2712 is very different than the market/contract differential of section 2713, which "need bear no close relation to the plaintiff's actual loss." (White & Summers, *supra*, Buyer's Remedies, Cover, at p. 295.)

In summary, we hold that where a buyer " 'cover[s]" by making in good faith and without unreasonable delay any reasonable purchase of * * * goods in substitution for those due from the seller, * * * [that buyer] may recover from the seller as damages the difference between the cost of cover and the contract price. * * *" (§ 2712.) This gives the buyer the benefit of its bargain. What the buyer chooses to do with that bargain is not relevant to the determination of damages under section 2712.

    * * *

DISPOSITION

* * * [The] judgment is affirmed. Costs on appeal to buyer.

Questions and Note

1. Questions about the facts of this case

    1.1. Did the buyer cover? Is that relevant? Would the buyer have recovered less from the seller if it had not covered?

    1.2. Was the buyer's contract with the Castellini Company relevant in determining the amount that the buyer could recover from the seller?

1.3.   Why does the court tell us "seller was aware of the buyer's contract with the Castellini Company"? Was that fact relevant to a determination of the amount that the buyer could recover from the seller?

1.4.   Was the seller's breach an efficient breach? Did the seller in this case, like the seller in the *Allied Canners* case, "not acted in bad faith in breaching the contract"? Was that fact relevant in determining the amount that the buyer could recover from the seller?

1.5.   Why did the seller allege that recovery in this case would result in a windfall?

2.   Questions about the law

2.1.   Do you agree with the statement in the penultimate (next to last) paragraph of the edited opinion: "[T]he cover-contract differential puts a buyer who covers in the exact same position as performance would have done"? Do you understand the statement?

2.2.   That same paragraph twice refers to section 1–106 (found in Revised Article 1 at section 1–305): "The remedies provided by this Act shall be liberally administered to the end that the aggrieved party may be put in as good a position as if the other party had fully performed." Was this provision relevant to the *KGM Harvesting* holding? Should it have been?

2.3.   Is *KGM Harvesting* helpful in answering the last problem preceding *KGM Harvesting*: "Contract for sale of goods for $1,000. Buyer replaces at $800 through her "connections." Buyer establishes that the market price for the replacement is $1,400. How much, if anything, can the buyer recover from the seller?" Is the following statement by Professor Roy Anderson of the Dedman School of Law helpful to answering this problem: "There is no persuasive argument in favor of allowing market damages to a buyer who has covered unless the premise is that an injured party should be allowed to recover damages in excess of those actually caused and regardless of whether those damages could have been reasonably avoided"[6]?

2.4.   The court said: "We believe that this focus on the good or bad faith of the breaching party is inappropriate in a commercial sales case." Does this mean that Cardozo was wrong in *Jacob & Youngs v. Kent, supra*, at 660 when he said "The willful transgressor must accept the penalty of his transgression. * * * For him there is no occasion to mitigate the rigor of implied conditions." Or is that "different"?

3.   Note

     The U.C.C. does not make cover [replacement purchases] mandatory. As indicated in *KGM*, a buyer may use market-based damages if she does not cover. U.C.C. § 2–713.

---

6. Roy Ryden Anderson, *Of Hidden Agendas, Naked Emperors, and a Few Good Soldiers: The Conference's Breach of Promise * * * Regarding Article 2 Damage Remedies*, 54 SMU L. Rev. 795, 829 (2001).

Similarly, the U.C.C. does not make resale [replacement sales] mandatory. A seller may use market-based damages or resale-based damages. U.C.C. § 2–703.

***

BASIC PROBLEMS ON SELLER'S DAMAGES UNDER THE U.C.C.

What are the damages in each of these basic problems on seller's damages? (Assume good faith, reasonable resales in each problem.).

1. Sales contract for $1,000. Seller delivers the goods. Buyer does not pay. U.C.C. § 2–709(1)(a).

2. Sales contract for $1,000. Buyer breaches before Seller delivers the goods. Seller is unable to sell the goods. U.C.C. § 2–709(1)(b).

3. Sales contract for $1,000. Buyer breaches before Seller delivers the goods. Seller is able to sell the goods for $800. U.C.C. § 2–706.

4. Sales contract for $1,000. Buyer breaches before Seller delivers the goods. Seller is able to resell the goods for $1,000. *Id.* Do you need more information? What if the seller is Epstein and the goods is Epstein's one and only 1973 Cadillac? What if the seller is Markell Mega–Metro Honda Superstore Inc., Nevada's largest Honda dealer, and the goods is a new, white Honda Accord? U.C.C. § 2–708(2).

What happens if, as is often the case with retail sellers, all the breach does is force the seller to resell the goods to someone else—in short, all that happens is that the seller is just "out of a sale." The next case explores this lost volume sale question in the context of whether a liquidated damages clause provides a reasonable estimate of damages, a question we first considered in *O'Brian* and *Kvassay*.

RODRIGUEZ v. LEARJET, INC.

Court of Appeals of Kansas
24 Kan.App.2d 461, 946 P.2d 1010 (1997)

MARQUARDT, PRESIDING JUDGE:

Miguel A. Diaz Rodriguez (Diaz) appeals from the district court's decision that a liquidated damages clause in his contract with Learjet, Inc., (Learjet) was reasonable and enforceable.

On August 21, 1992, Diaz executed a contract with Learjet to purchase a model 60 jet aircraft. The contract called for a $250,000 deposit to be made upon execution of the contract; a $750,000 payment to be made on September 18, 1992; a $1,000,000 payment to be made 180 days before the delivery date of July 30, 1993; and the balance of the purchase price to be paid upon delivery.

Diaz paid Learjet $250,000 on the day that he executed the contract, but made no other payment.

At the time of the purchase, Diaz worked for Televisa. Diaz was purchasing the aircraft at the request of Alejandro Burillo, his supervisor at Televisa. Near the end of September 1992, Burillo told Diaz that he no longer wanted the aircraft. Diaz testified that he called Alberto Castaneda at Learjet and told him that he was not going to buy the aircraft and that he wanted Learjet to return his $250,000 deposit.

On September 30, 1992, Castaneda sent Diaz a fax, requesting payment. On October 6, 1992, Castaneda wrote Diaz a letter, which stated, in part: "Unless we receive payment from you or your company by October 9, 1992, [Learjet, Inc.,] will consider this agreement terminated and will retain all payments as liquidation damages in accordance with Paragraph C * * * of Section VII * * * of said agreement." By letter dated October 20, 1992, Learjet informed Diaz that it considered their contract terminated and that the $250,000 deposit was being retained as liquidated damages.

The contract provides, in part:

> Learjet may terminate this Agreement as a result of the Buyer's * * * failure to make any progress payment when due. * * * If this Agreement is terminated by Learjet for any reason stipulated in the previous sentence Learjet shall retain all payments theretofore made by the Buyer as liquidated damages and not as a penalty and the parties shall thenceforth be released from all further obligations hereunder. Such damages include, but are not limited to, loss of profit on this sale, direct and indirect costs incurred as a result of disruption in production, training expense advance and selling expenses in effecting resale of the Airplane.

After Diaz had breached the parties' contract, Circus Circus Enterprises, Inc., (Circus) contracted with Learjet to buy the aircraft. Circus requested that changes be made to the aircraft, which cost $1,326. Learjet realized a $1,887,464 profit on the sale of the aircraft to Circus, which was a larger profit than Learjet had originally budgeted.

Diaz filed suit against Learjet, seeking to recover the $250,000 deposit. Diaz' petition alleged, in part, that the actual amount of Learjet's liquidated damages was not $250,000 and that Learjet's retention of the $250,000 deposit was unreasonable and an unenforceable penalty.

The district court initially granted Learjet's motion for summary judgment, holding that the liquidated damages provision of the contract was reasonable. Diaz appealed that decision. On appeal, this court held that the district court had erred in using the wrong standard to evaluate the liquidated damages clause and in not examining all of the necessary factors and remanded the case to the district court for further consideration of the reasonableness of the liquidated damages clause.

On remand, a bench trial was held. Following the presentation of evidence, the district court found that Learjet was a lost volume seller and that its actual damages included lost profits. The district court held that $250,000 in liquidated damages was reasonable and upheld the liquidated damages clause.

Diaz argues that the district court erred in holding that the liquidated damages clause was reasonable and enforceable. Diaz reasons that the liquidated damages clause was unreasonably large and, therefore, void as a penalty.

A determination concerning the reasonableness and enforceability of a liquidated damages clause is a question of law subject to unlimited review by this court. *Kvassay v. Murray*, 15 Kan.App.2d 426, 429, 808 P.2d 896, *rev. denied* 248 Kan. 996 (1991).

K.S.A. 84–2–718 [UCC § 2–718] governs liquidated damages in contracts for the sale of goods and provides, in part:

"(1) Damages for breach by either party may be liquidated in the agreement but only at an amount which is reasonable in the light of the anticipated or actual harm caused by the breach, the difficulties of proof of loss, and the inconvenience or nonfeasibility of otherwise obtaining an adequate remedy. A term fixing unreasonably large liquidated damages is void as a penalty."

In Kvassay, 15 Kan.App.2d at 430, 808 P.2d 896, this court noted that "reasonableness is the only test" for liquidated damages under the Uniform Commercial Code. This court paraphrased the three criteria for measuring the reasonableness of a liquidated damages clause provided in K.S.A. 84–2–718: "(1) anticipated or actual harm caused by breach; (2) difficulty of proving loss; and (3) difficulty of obtaining an adequate remedy." 15 Kan.App.2d at 430, 808 P.2d 896.

A liquidated damages clause that " 'fixes damages in an amount grossly disproportionate to the harm actually sustained or likely to be sustained' " is considered a penalty and will not be enforced by the courts. * * * If a liquidated damages clause is invalidated as a penalty, then the nonbreaching party may recover actual damages instead. * * * The burden of proving that a liquidated damages clause is unenforceable rests with the party challenging its enforcement. * * *

Diaz' challenge to the reasonableness of the liquidated damages clause focuses on the first factor of K.S.A. 84–2–718—the anticipated or actual harm caused by the breach. The question of whether a seller qualifies as a lost volume seller is relevant when evaluating whether a liquidated damages clause is reasonable in light of the anticipated or actual harm caused by the breach.

Diaz argues that the district court erred in concluding that Learjet qualifies as a lost volume seller. As a lost volume seller, Learjet's actual damages would include lost profits, notwithstanding that Circus purchased the aircraft which Diaz had contracted to buy and that Learjet made a profit on the Circus sale. The two contracts contained identical base prices, and both contracts had escalation clauses. The evidence indicates that the lost profit from the Diaz contract would have been approximately $1.8 million.

Whether a seller is a lost volume seller is a question of fact. * * * An appellate court reviews factual findings to determine if they are supported by substantial competent evidence. * * *

Courts have "unanimously" held that a lost volume seller can recover lost profits under § 2–708(2) of the Uniform Commercial Code. * * * The Kansas Legislature has enacted this statute as K.S.A. 84–2–708(2). * * *

Similarly, Restatement (Second) of Contracts § 350, Comment d (1979) notes that if a seller would have entered into both transactions but for the breach, then the seller has lost volume as a result of the breach. Thus, lost profits are awarded to a lost volume seller, notwithstanding that the seller resells the item that a buyer contracted to buy, based on the principle that the seller was deprived of an additional sale and the corresponding profit by the buyer's breach. * * *

Awarding lost profits to a lost volume seller serves the general principle that the purpose of awarding damages is to make a party whole by restoring the nonbreaching party to the position that that party occupied prior to the breach—to place a seller in as good a position as if a buyer had performed. K.S.A. 84–1–106. * * *

The issue in *Jetz* was whether the plaintiff qualified as a lost volume lessor, and this court did not expressly state the specific requirements for qualifying as a lost volume seller. The Jetz court held that lost volume status is available to businesses providing services and identified the following evidence as sufficient to affirm the trial court's finding that the plaintiff was a lost volume lessor:

> "[J]etz Service is in the business of supplying coin-operated laundry equipment; it has several warehouses in which it has available for lease about 1,500 used washers and dryers; it continually looks for new locations in which to install laundry equipment; it would have been able to fulfill the Kansas City lease without using the machines from Salina Properties; and it is uncontroverted Jetz Service would have been able to enter into both transactions irrespective of the breach by Salina Properties." 19 Kan.App.2d at 152, 865 P.2d 1051.

In *Diasonics*, 826 F.2d at 685, the court held that in order to qualify as a lost volume seller and recover for lost profits, a seller must establish three factors: (1) that it possessed the capacity to make an additional sale, (2) that it would have been profitable for it to make an additional sale, and (3) that it probably would have made an additional sale absent the buyer's breach. See also *R.E. Davis Chemical Corp. v. Diasonics*, 924 F.2d 709, 711 (7th Cir.1991) (restating rule formulated in prior appeal of case); Kansas Comment 2 to 84–2–708 (citing first Diasonics case).

Here, in finding that Learjet qualified as a lost volume seller, the district court referred to *Jetz*, 19 Kan.App.2d 144, Syl. & 2, 865 P.2d 1051.

Applying the more specific criteria established in *Diasonics*, 826 F.2d at 684–85, there is adequate evidence to support the district court's finding. The master scheduler for Learjet testified that Learjet was operating at 60 percent capacity during the relevant time period and that Learjet was able to accelerate its production schedule to produce more of the model 60 planes in any given year. Learjet also presented testimony about its accounting system which indicated that an additional sale would have been profitable to Learjet. Learjet's profit from the Circus transaction and the similarity between the Diaz contract price and the Circus contract price also indicate that the additional sale would have been profitable.

We agree with the district court that Learjet qualifies as a lost volume seller and that the $250,000 in liquidated damages was reasonable in light of the anticipated or actual harm caused by the breach. See K.S.A. 84-2-718(2).

Even if we were to conclude that Learjet was not a lost volume seller, there is authority to support the holding that the liquidated damages clause was reasonable. In *Aero Consulting Corp. v. Cessna Aircraft Co.*, 867 F.Supp. 1480, 1493-94 (D.Kan.1994), the court held that a liquidated damages clause in an aircraft purchase agreement was reasonable under Kansas law. The *Aero* court did not consider the lost volume theory. The base price of the aircraft was $3,995,000. The liquidated damages, which were in the form of a deposit that was retained by Cessna after Aero breached, equaled $425,000. The court found that the liquidated damages clause "was reasonable in light of the damages that Cessna could reasonably anticipate would flow from such a cancellation of the contract." 867 F.Supp. at 1494. The court also noted that "in light of the nature of the production of aircraft and the costs associated with maintaining production, it would not be feasible for Cessna to otherwise obtain an adequate remedy for breach." 867 F.Supp. at 1494. Under both analyses, the liquidated damages claimed by Learjet were reasonable.

Affirmed.

QUESTIONS AND CONNECTION

1. Questions about the facts of this case
    1.1. Do we know the contract price in the sale of goods contract between Learjet and Diaz? Was that contract price relevant to the court's decision?
    1.2. Do we know the contract price in the sale of goods contract between Learjet and Circus Circus? Was that contract price relevant to the court's decision?
    1.3. We know "The evidence indicates that the lost profit from the Diaz contract would have been approximately $1.8 million." Is $1.8 million the amount that Learjet recovered from Diaz?
    1.4. We also know "Learjet was operating at 60 percent capacity during the relevant time period"? Was that fact relevant to the court's decision?

2. Questions about the law

    2.1. What is a "lost volume seller"? Is Markell Mega–Metro Honda Inc. a "lost volume seller"? Is Learjet?

    2.2. According to the court in this case: "The question of whether a seller qualifies as a lost volume seller is relevant when evaluating whether a liquidated damages clause is reasonable in light of the anticipated or actual harm caused by the breach." Do you agree with this statement? Why?

    2.3. Again, playing everyone's favorite law school game, "Change the Facts", how much could Learjet have recovered from Diaz if their sale of goods contract did not have a liquidated damages clause?

    2.4. Recall that it was Diaz who challenged the validity of the liquidated damages clause: "Diaz argues that the district court erred in holding that the liquidated damages clause was reasonable and enforceable. Diaz reasons that the liquidated damages clause was unreasonably large, and therefore, void as a penalty" Why didn't Learjet argue that the liquidated damages clause was unenforceable because it was unreasonably small?

    2.5. How can the seller prove that not only could it have produced the additional item, but that it also would have been *profitable* to produce and sell both items? See if this explanation of the "lost volume" concept helps you to answer the question:

> In passing, we observe that this lost volume situation can be described in several ways. Focusing on the breached unit, one can say that due to a market in which supply meets demand, the lost volume seller cannot resell the breached unit without sacrificing the additional sale. Focusing on the additional unit, one can say but for the buyer's breach, the lost volume seller would have made an additional sale. Focusing on both units, one can say that but for the buyer's breach, the lost volume seller would have sold two units. Each statement is equivalent to the others.

> *Kenco Homes, Inc. v. Williams*, 94 Wash.App. 219, 972 P.2d 125, 129 (1999). Can one supplier actually "out supply" the entire market?

3. Connection

Recall we considered the *Kvassay* case and liquidated damages generally earlier in this chapter. To borrow from the second President Bush, does the treatment of liquidated damages in *Rodriguez* "resonate" with what you remember from that earlier consideration of liquidated damages.

PROBLEM: ANOTHER LOST PROFITS RECOVERY SCENARIO

Another class of sellers to which § 2–708(2) might apply are what are sometimes referred to as "component sellers." The term refers to sellers who, for example, manufacture the contract goods and are faced with a breach after manufacture has begun but before it is completed. Although the seller in this position who, under § 2–704(2) elects to "cease manufacture in the exercise of reasonable commercial judgment," will, like the lost volume seller, also have lost one sale of completed goods. Consider how the seller's damages would be calculated under the formula § 2–708(2) in the following situation:

Ponoroff, a widgets' manufacturer, enters into a contract to sell 10 widgets to Epstein at a price of $1,000 ($100 per widget). While Ponoroff is in the middle of manufacturing the widgets, Epstein repudiates. Because the market for widgets has declined sharply since the contract was entered (perhaps explaining Epstein's repudiation), Ponoroff ceases work on the widgets, at which point in time:

- Ponoroff has incurred costs of $300 for labor and materials, and would have incurred an additional $350 to finish the widgets.

- Ponoroff's accountant will testify that overhead (indirect) costs allocable to this contract were $100 (or $10 per widget).

- The materials on hand that Ponoroff purchased for the job can be sold for scrap at a price of $25.

- Under the contract, but for Epstein's breach, Ponoroff would have incurred a cost of $50 to ship the widgets to Epstein.

C. LIMITATIONS ON MONEY DAMAGES AWARDS

1. First Limitation on Money Damages: Avoided Costs

According to Comment d to *Restatement (Second) of Contracts* section 347: "**Sometimes** the breach itself results in a saving of some cost that the injured party would have incurred if he had had to perform. * * * The cost avoided is to be subtracted from the loss in value covered by the breach in calculating his damages." (emphasis added).

For example, Mike[7] Holmes' contracts to repair Epstein's basement for $20,000. After Holmes begins work, Epstein repudiates the contract and Holmes stops working. Holmes would have to spend $7,000 more to finish the basement repair. The $7,000 cost avoided is subtracted from the $20,000 contract price in determining Holmes' damages.

Both the "law" and "math" in the above Holmes hypothetical are easy. What is hard in the real world and the next case are the facts. More specifically, the factual basis for fixing the amount of cost avoided by not having to perform.

LEINGANG v. MANDAN WEED BOARD

Supreme Court of North Dakota
468 N.W.2d 397 (1991)

EVINE, JUSTICE.

Robert Leingang appeals from an award of damages for breach of contract. The issue is whether the trial court used the appropriate measure of damages. We hold it did not, and reverse and remand.

---

7. Not to be confused with Oliver Wendell Holmes, Jr. Unlike his great-grand Uncle Oliver, Mike does not believe that contractors can morally walk away from their contracts.

The City of Mandan Weed Board awarded Leingang a contract to cut weeds on lots with an area greater than 10,000 square feet. Another contractor received the contract for smaller lots. During 1987, Leingang discovered that the Weed Board's agent was improperly assigning large lots to the small-lot contractor. Leingang complained and the weed board assigned some substitute lots to him.

Leingang brought a breach of contract action in small claims court and the City removed the action to county court. The City admitted that it had prevented Leingang's performance under the contract and that the contract price for the lost work was $1,933.78. A bench trial was held to assess the damages suffered by Leingang.

At trial, Leingang argued that the applicable measure of damages was the contract price less the costs of performance he avoided due to the breach. Leingang testified that the total gas, oil, repair and replacement blade expenses saved when he was prevented from cutting the erroneously assigned lots was $211.18.

The City argued that to identify Leingang's damages for net profits, some of Leingang's overhead expenses should be attributed to the weed cutting contract and deducted from the contract price. The City offered testimony about the profitability of businesses in Mandan and testimony from Leingang's competitor about the profitability of a weed cutting business in Mandan. The City also offered Leingang's 1986 and 1987 federal tax returns. Based on the Schedule C—"Profit or Loss From Business"—in those returns, the City argued that Leingang attributed considerably more expenses to the business of cutting weeds than he had testified he had avoided.

The trial court adopted what it called a "modified net profit" approach as the measure of damages. It derived a profit margin of 20% by subtracting four categories of expenses reported on Leingang's Schedule C, and attributed to the weed-cutting business, from the weed-cutting income reported to the IRS. The trial court selected insurance, repairs, supplies, and car and truck expenses as costs attributed to the weed-cutting business. Applying the profit margin of 20% to the contract price, the trial court deducted 80% from the contract price as expenses and awarded Leingang $368.59 plus interest. Leingang appeals.

Leingang contends that the method used by the trial court to derive net profits was improper because it did not restrict the expenses that are deductible from the contract price to those which would have been incurred but for the breach of the contract, i.e., those expenses Leingang did not have to pay because the City kept him from doing the work. We agree.

For a breach of contract, the injured party is entitled to compensation for the loss suffered, but can recover no more than would have been gained by full performance. NDCC §§ 32–03–09, 32–03–36. Our law thus incorporates the notion that contract damages should give the nonbreaching party the benefit of the bargain by awarding a sum of money that will put that person in as good a position as if the contract had been performed. * * * Where the contract is for service and the breach prevents the performance of that service, the value of the contract consists of two items: (1) the party's reasonable expenditures toward performance, including costs paid, material wasted, and time and services spent on the contract, and (2) the anticipated profits. Thus, a party is entitled to recover for the detriment caused by the defendant's breach, including lost profits if they are reasonable and not speculative. Id. * * *

Where a plaintiff offers evidence estimating anticipated profits with reasonable certainty, they may be awarded. See King Features Synd. v. Courrier, 241 Iowa 870, 43 N.W.2d 718 (1950). In *King Features*, the plaintiff proved the value of its anticipated profits by reducing the contract price by the amount it would have spent to perform. The court held that this proof was reasonably certain. In quantifying the costs of performance, the plaintiff did not deduct "overhead" expenses because the evidence established that those expenses were constant whether or not the contract was performed. 43 N.W.2d at 725–26.

The *King Features* approach fulfills the requirement that a plaintiff be compensated for all the detriment caused by the breach. *Under King Features,* constant overhead expenses are not deducted from the contract price because they are expenses the plaintiff had to pay whether or not the contract was breached. The *King Features* approach compensates plaintiff for constant overhead expenses by allowing an award of the contract price, reduced only by expenses actually saved because the contract did not have to be performed. The remaining contract proceeds are available to pay constant expenses. See also Buono Sales, Inc. v. Chrysler Motors Corp., 449 F.2d 715, 720 (3d Cir.1971) [because fixed expenses must be paid from the sum remaining after costs of performance are deducted, further reducing contract price by fixed expenses would not fully, or fairly, compensate plaintiff].

Neither side argues that lost profits are not calculable here. Instead, each urges a different method for computing lost profits. In measuring Leingang's anticipated profits, the trial court erroneously calculated a "net profit" margin by deducting general costs of doing business including insurance, repairs, supplies, and car and truck expenses, without determining whether these costs remained constant regardless of the City's breach and whether they were, therefore, not to be deducted from the contract price. King Features, 43 N.W.2d at 726. The reduction from the contract price of a portion of the "fixed," or constant expenses, effectively required Leingang to pay that portion twice. See Buono Sales, Inc., 449 F.2d at 720.

We reverse the judgment and remand for a new trial on the issue of damages.

ERICKSTAD, C.J., and VANDE WALLE, GIERKE and MESCHKE, JJ., concur.

QUESTIONS AND NOTE

1. Questions about the facts of this case

    1.1. Was the contract price a relevant fact in this case?

    1.2. What facts did Leingang contend were relevant?

    1.3. What facts did the City contend were relevant?

    1.4. What, if any, additional facts would be relevant to the trial court on remand?

2. Questions about the law

    2.1. North Dakota has enacted legislation governing the measure of damages for breach of contract. Are the North Dakota statutory provisions on damages for breach of contract, as explained in *Leingang*, consistent with protection of the expectation interest?

    2.2. Do you agree with the court's statement: "The reduction from the contract price of a portion of the 'fixed' or constant expenses, effectively required Leingang to pay the portion twice"? Do you understand the statement?

3. Note

    For those of you who are culturally limited and not familiar with North Dakota, weed control is a big thing in North Dakota. According to the April 2009, Mandan Messenger: "At a minimum, all noxious weeds, tall grasses, and any other unhealthy vegetation within Mandan city limits must be sprayed or cut by the first of May, June, July, August and September. If property owners do not comply with the requirement within 7 days of receipt of notice, the City weed officer will arrange to have the property mowed or sprayed. Costs will be assessed to the property owner." http://www.cityofmandan.com/vertical/Sites/% 7B258F AE31–4B8B–4CFF–8DC0–96BBE36183FB% 7D/uploads/% 7BE03E4AE4– 6A4D–4E2D–8AEC–DE3263F7EBD7% 7D.PDF

---

2. Second Limitation on Money Damages: Avoidable Loss

In avoided costs cases such as *Leingang*, the focus is on the savings the non-breaching party actually realized by not having to perform after the other party's breach. Remember Epstein's contract with Mike Holmes to repair Epstein's basement for $20,000. Epstein repudiates when the work is partly done—when it would cost Holmes $7,000 more to finish the work. Holmes' damages are reduced by costs he actually saved.

Now let's think about reducing damages by the costs that the non-breaching party did not actually save but could have, and should have, saved. What if Holmes continued work after being told unequivocally that Epstein was breaching? Should Holmes then be able to recover the full $20,000 contract price?

Holmes should not be able to recover damages based on work done after Epstein's repudiation. Holmes, the non-breaching party, cannot simply continue to perform after being told Epstein breaches and then charge Epstein the full contract price. "[T]he plaintiff has no right, by obstinately persisting in the work, to make the penalty upon the defendant greater than it would otherwise have been." *Rockingham County v. Luten Bridge Co.*, 35 F.2d 301, 308 (4th Cir. 1929).

The question of whether Holmes should stop working on Epstein's basement after being told unequivocally that Epstein was breaching is an easy question. The harder question is whether Holmes should accept other work to minimize his loss from Epstein's breach of contract. What if Ponoroff offers Holmes $6,000 to build a closet—a job that Holmes could complete in the time that he would have spent working Epstein's basement? If Holmes does not accept Ponoroff's offer, should that limit the amount of damages that Holmes can recover from Epstein for breach of contract? Is the following statement from *United States Bank Nat. Ass'n v. Ables & Hall Builders*, 696 F.Supp.2d 428 (S.D.N.Y. 2010), helpful in answering this question?

> In a breach of contract action, a plaintiff ordinarily has a duty to mitigate the damages that he incurs. If the plaintiff fails to mitigate his damages, the defendant cannot be charged with them. This duty applies to those damages that the plaintiff could have avoided with reasonable effort and without undue risk, burden, or expense. *See* Restatement (Second) of Contracts § 350(1)). The duty to mitigate damages, also called the doctrine of avoidable consequences, requires only reasonable, practical care and diligence, not extraordinary measures.

Is the statement from *U.S. Bank* helpful to understanding the next case?

PARKER v. TWENTIETH CENTURY–FOX FILM CORP.

Supreme Court of California
3 Cal.3d 176, 89 Cal.Rptr. 737, 474 P.2d 689 (1970)

BURKE, J:

Defendant Twentieth Century–Fox Film Corporation appeals from a summary judgment granting to plaintiff the recovery of agreed compensation under a written contract for her services as an actress in a motion picture. As will appear, we have concluded that the trial court correctly ruled in plaintiff's favor and that the judgment should be affirmed.

Plaintiff is well known as an actress,* and in the contract between plaintiff and defendant is sometimes referred to as the "Artist." Under the contract, dated August 6, 1965, plaintiff was to play the female lead in defendant's contemplated production of a motion picture entitled "Bloomer Girl." The contract provided that defendant would pay plaintiff a minimum "guaranteed compensation" of $53,571.42 per week for 14 weeks commencing May 23, 1966, for a total of $750,000. Prior to May 1966 defendant decided not to produce the picture and by a letter dated April 4, 1966, it notified plaintiff of that decision and that it would not "comply with our obligations to you under" the written contract.

By the same letter and with the professed purpose "to avoid any damage to you," defendant instead offered to employ plaintiff as the leading actress in another film tentatively entitled "Big Country, Big Man" (hereinafter, "Big Country"). The compensation offered was identical, as were 31 of the 34 numbered provisions or articles of the original contract.[1] Unlike "Bloomer Girl," however, which was to have been a musical production, "Big Country" was a dramatic "western type" movie. "Bloomer Girl" was to have been filmed in California; "Big Country" was to be produced in Australia. Also, certain terms in the proffered contract varied from those of the original.[2] Plaintiff was given one week within which to accept; she did not and the offer lapsed. Plaintiff then commenced this action seeking recovery of the agreed guaranteed compensation.

---

* The plaintiff is more commonly known as Shirley MacLaine. Actually, more commonly know as Warren Beatty's sister. Eds.

1. Among the identical provisions was the following found in the last paragraph of Article 2 of the original contract: "We [defendant] shall not be obligated to utilize your [plaintiff's] services in or in connection with the Photoplay hereunder, our sole obligation, subject to the terms and conditions of this Agreement, being to pay you the guaranteed compensation herein provided for."

2. Article 29 of the original contract specified that plaintiff approved the director already chosen for "Bloomer Girl" and that in case he failed to act as director plaintiff was to have approval rights of any substitute director. Article 31 provided that plaintiff was to have the right of approval of the "Bloomer Girl" dance director, and Article 32 gave her the right of approval of the screenplay.

Defendant's letter of April 4 to plaintiff, which contained both defendant's notice of breach of the "Bloomer Girl" contract and offer of the lead in "Big Country," eliminated or impaired each of those rights. It read in part as follows: "The terms and conditions of our offer of employment are identical to those set forth in the 'BLOOMER GIRL' Agreement, Articles 1 through 34 and Exhibit A to the Agreement, except as follows:

    "1. Article 31 of said Agreement will not be included in any contract of employment regarding 'BIG COUNTRY, BIG MAN' as it is not a musical and it thus will not need a dance director.

    "2. In the 'BLOOMER GIRL' agreement, in Articles 29 and 32, you were given certain director and screenplay approvals and you had preapproved certain matters. Since there simply is insufficient time to negotiate with you regarding your choice of director and regarding the screenplay and since you already expressed an interest in performing the role in 'BIG COUNTRY, BIG MAN,' we must exclude from our offer of employment in 'BIG COUNTRY, BIG MAN' any approval rights as are contained in said Articles 29 and 32; however, we shall consult with you respecting the director to be selected to direct the photoplay and will further consult with you with respect to the screenplay and any revisions or changes therein, provided, however, that if we fail to agree * * * the decision of * * * [defendant] with respect to the selection of a director and to revisions and changes in the said screenplay shall be binding upon the parties to said agreement."

The complaint sets forth two causes of action. The first is for money due under the contract; the second, based upon the same allegations as the first, is for damages resulting from defendant's breach of contract. Defendant in its answer admits the existence and validity of the contract, that plaintiff complied with all the conditions, covenants and promises and stood ready to complete the performance, and that defendant breached and "anticipatorily repudiated" the contract. It denies, however, that any money is due to plaintiff either under the contract or as a result of its breach, and pleads as an affirmative defense to both causes of action plaintiff's allegedly deliberate failure to mitigate damages, asserting that she unreasonably refused to accept its offer of the leading role in "Big Country."

Plaintiff moved for summary judgment under Code of Civil Procedure section 437c, the motion was granted, and summary judgment for $750,000 plus interest was entered in plaintiff's favor. This appeal by defendant followed.

The familiar rules are that the matter to be determined by the trial court on a motion for summary judgment is whether facts have been presented which give rise to a triable factual issue. The court may not pass upon the issue itself. Summary judgment is proper only if the affidavits or declarations in support of the moving party would be sufficient to sustain a judgment in his favor and his opponent does not by affidavit show facts sufficient to present a triable issue of fact. The affidavits of the moving party are strictly construed, and doubts as to the propriety of summary judgment should be resolved against granting the motion. Such summary procedure is drastic and should be used with caution so that it does not become a substitute for the open trial method of determining facts. * * *

As stated, defendant's sole defense to this action which resulted from its deliberate breach of contract is that in rejecting defendant's substitute offer of employment plaintiff unreasonably refused to mitigate damages.

The general rule is that the measure of recovery by a wrongfully discharged employee is the amount of salary agreed upon for the period of service, less the amount which the employer affirmatively proves the employee has earned or with reasonable effort might have earned from other employment. * * *[4] However, before projected earnings from other employment opportunities not sought or accepted by the discharged employee can be applied in mitigation, the employer must show that the other employment was comparable, or substantially similar, to that of which the employee has been deprived; the employee's rejection of or failure to seek other available employment of a different or inferior kind may not be resorted to in order to mitigate damages. * * *

---

4. Although it would appear that plaintiff was not discharged by defendant in the customary sense of the term, as she was not permitted by defendant to enter upon performance of the "Bloomer Girl" contract, nevertheless the motion for summary judgment was submitted for decision upon a stipulation by the parties that "plaintiff Parker was discharged."

In the present case defendant has raised no issue of reasonableness of efforts by plaintiffs to obtain other employment; the sole issue is whether plaintiff's refusal of defendant's substitute offer of "Big Country" may be used in mitigation. Nor, if the "Big Country" offer was of employment different or inferior when compared with the original "Bloomer Girl" employment, is there an issue as to whether or not plaintiff acted reasonably in refusing the substitute offer. Despite defendant's arguments to the contrary, no case cited or which our research has discovered holds or suggests that reasonableness is an element of a wrongfully discharged employee's option to reject, or fail to seek, different or inferior employment lest the possible earnings therefrom be charged against him in mitigation of damages.

Applying the foregoing rules to the record in the present case, with all intendments in favor of the party opposing the summary judgment motion—here, defendant—it is clear that the trial court correctly ruled that plaintiff's failure to accept defendant's tendered substitute employment could not be applied in mitigation of damages because the offer of the "Big Country" lead was of employment both different and inferior, and that no factual dispute was presented on that issue. The mere circumstance that "Bloomer Girl" was to be a musical review calling upon plaintiff's talents as a dancer as well as an actress, and was to be produced in the City of Los Angeles, whereas "Big Country" was a straight dramatic role in a "Western Type" story taking place in an opal mine in Australia, demonstrates the difference in kind between the two employments; the female lead as a dramatic actress in a western style motion picture can by no stretch of imagination be considered the equivalent of or substantially similar to the lead in a song-and-dance production.

Additionally, the substitute "Big Country" offer proposed to eliminate or impair the director and screenplay approvals accorded to plaintiff under the original "Bloomer Girl" contract (see fn. 2, *ante*), and thus constituted an offer of inferior employment. No expertise or judicial notice is required in order to hold that the deprivation or infringement of an employee's rights held under an original employment contract converts the available "other employment" relied upon by the employer to mitigate damages, into inferior employment which the employee need not seek or accept
* * *

Statements found in affidavits submitted by defendant in opposition to plaintiff's summary judgment motion, to the effect that the "Big County" offer was not of employment different from or inferior to that under the "Bloomer Girl" contract, merely repeat the allegations of defendant's answer to the complaint in this action, constitute only conclusionary assertions with respect to undisputed facts, and do not give rise to a triable factual issue so as to defeat the motion for summary judgment.
* * *

In view of the determination that defendant failed to present any facts showing the existence of a factual issue with respect to its sole defense—plaintiff's rejection of its substitute employment offer in mitigation of damages—we need not consider plaintiff's further contention that for various reasons, including the provisions of the original contract set forth in footnote 1, *ante*, plaintiff was excused from attempting to mitigate damages.

The judgment is affirmed.

McCOMB, J., PETERS, J., TOBRINER, J., KAUS, J., and ROTH, J., concurred.

Dissent: SULLIVAN, ACTING C. J.

The basic question in this case is whether or not plaintiff acted reasonably in rejecting defendant's offer of alternate employment. The answer depends upon whether that offer (starring in "Big Country, Big Man") was an offer of work that was substantially similar to her former employment (starring in "Bloomer Girl") or of work that was of a different or inferior kind. To my mind this is a factual issue, which the trial court should not have determined on a motion for summary judgment. The majority have not only repeated this error but have compounded it by applying the rules governing mitigation of damages in the employer-employee context in a misleading fashion. Accordingly, I respectfully dissent.

The familiar rule requiring a plaintiff in a tort or contract action to mitigate damages embodies notions of fairness and socially responsible behavior which are fundamental to our jurisprudence. Most broadly stated, it precludes the recovery of damages which, through the exercise of due diligence, could have been avoided. Thus, in essence, it is a rule requiring reasonable conduct in commercial affairs. This general principle governs the obligations of an employee after his employer has wrongfully repudiated or terminated the employment contract. Rather than permitting the employee simply to remain idle during the balance of the contract period, the law requires him to make a reasonable effort to secure other employment.[1] He is not obliged, however, to seek or accept any and all types of work which may be available. Only work which is in the same field and which is of the same quality need be accepted.[2]

Over the years the courts have employed various phrases to define the type of employment which the employee, upon his wrongful discharge, is under an obligation to accept. Thus in California alone it has been held

---

1. The issue is generally discussed in terms of a duty on the part of the employee to minimize loss. The practice is long-established and there is little reason to change despite Judge Cardozo's observation of its subtle inaccuracy. "The servant is free to accept employment or reject it according to his uncensored pleasure. What is meant by the supposed duty is merely this, that if he unreasonably reject, he will not be heard to say that the loss of wages from then on shall be deemed the jural consequence of the earlier discharge. He has broken the chain of causation, and loss resulting to him thereafter is suffered through his own act." (*McClelland v. Climax Hosiery Mills* (1930) 252 N.Y. 347, 359 [169 N.E. 605, 609], concurring opinion.).

2. This qualification of the rule seems to reflect the simple and humane attitude that it is too severe to demand of a person that he attempt to find and perform work for which he has no training or experience. Many of the older cases hold that one need not accept work in an inferior rank or position nor work which is more menial or arduous. This suggests that the rule may have had its origin in the bourgeois fear of resubmergence in lower economic classes.

that he must accept employment which is "substantially similar" * * * employment "in the same general line of the first employment". * * *

It has never been the law that the mere existence of differences between two jobs in the same field is sufficient, as a matter of law, to excuse an employee wrongfully discharged from one from accepting the other in order to mitigate damages. Such an approach would effectively eliminate any obligation of an employee to attempt to minimize damage arising from a wrongful discharge. The only alternative job offer an employee would be required to accept would be an offer of his former job by his former employer.

Although the majority appear to hold that there was a difference "in kind" between the employment offered plaintiff in "Bloomer Girl" and that offered in "Big Country" * * *, an examination of the opinion makes crystal clear that the majority merely point out differences between the two films (an obvious circumstance) and then apodically [sic] assert that these constitute a difference in the kind of employment. The entire rationale of the majority boils down to this; that the "mere circumstances" that "Bloomer Girl" was to be a musical review while "Big Country" was a straight drama "demonstrates the difference in kind" since a female lead in a western is not "the equivalent of or substantially similar to" a lead in a musical. This is merely attempting to prove the proposition by repeating it. It shows that the vehicles for the display of the star's talents are different but it does not prove that her employment as a star in such vehicles is of necessity different in kind and either inferior or superior. * * *

Resolving whether or not one job is substantially similar to another or whether, on the other hand, it is of a different or inferior kind, will often (as here) require a critical appraisal of the similarities and differences between them in light of the importance of these differences to the employee. This necessitates a weighing of the evidence, and it is precisely this undertaking which is forbidden on summary judgment. * * *

It is not intuitively obvious, to me at least, that the leading female role in a dramatic motion picture is a radically different endeavor from the leading female role in a musical comedy film

I believe that the judgment should be reversed so that the issue of whether or not the offer of the lead role in "Big Country, Big Man" was of employment comparable to that of the lead role in "Bloomer Girl" may be determined at trial.

Appellant's petition for a rehearing was denied October 28, 1970. Mosk, J., did not participate therein. Sullivan, J., was of the opinion that the petition should be granted.

QUESTIONS AND NOTES

1. Questions about the facts of this case

    1.1. What facts are most favorable to the plaintiff? Most favorable to the defendant?

    1.2. Do the plaintiff and the defendant disagree as to what the facts are? Do the majority and dissent disagree as to what the facts are?

    1.3. Recall from footnote 1 that the contract at issue provided: "We [defendant] shall not be obligated to utilize your [plaintiff's] services in or in connection with the Photoplay hereunder; our sole obligation, subject to the terms and conditions of this Agreement, being to pay you the guaranteed compensation herein provided for." Was this provision relevant to the decision of the Supreme Court of California? Should it have been relevant?

    1.4. Should it be relevant that the contract repeatedly referred to the specific film "Bloomer Girl", instead of "a Photoplay to be selected at the sole discretion of the defendant"?

2. Questions about the law

    2.1. Recall that the excerpt from *U.S. Bank Nat. Ass'n* which preceded *Parker* suggests that the nonbreaching party to a contract has a duty to mitigate her damages. In the *Parker* case, do the majority and the dissent differ as to whether there is such a duty to mitigate?

    2.2. Is the relevant test a "substantially similar" test or a "not of a different or inferior kind" test? Is there any substantive difference between the two phrases?

    2.3. Note the procedural context in this case: the matter comes up after denial of summary judgment. If "the issue of whether or not the offer of the lead role in "Big Country, Big Man" was of employment comparable to that of the lead role in "Bloomer Girl" had been determined at a trial, what evidence would you proffer as attorney for the defendant?

    2.4. If the plaintiff had accepted the lead role in "Big Country, Big Man," could she still have recovered from defendant for breach of contract? If so, how should her expectation damages be measured?

3. Notes

    3.1. Subsequent commentary on this case has brought out other facts. "Bloomer Girl" was based on the life of Amelia Jenks Bloomer, a champion for women's rights in the 19th Century. Its literary antecedent, a Broadway musical comedy, had strong strains of what we would identify today as feminism and the promotion of racial justice. Shirley MacLaine had publicly identified with both of these themes at or before the time of the contract. Should these facts have mattered? If so, why? *See* Mary Jo Frug, *Re–Reading Con-*

tracts: A Feminist Analysis of a Contracts Casebook, 34 Am. U. L. Rev. 1065, 1113–1123 (1985).

3.2.   More doggerel:

> There once was a lawsuit by Shirley
> Who thought the defendant quite surly.
> Re the movie she missed,
> The defense was dismissed
> And the judgment for Shirley came early.

Douglass G. Boshkoff, *Selected Poems on The Law of Contracts: Raintree County Memorial Library Occasional Paper No. 1*, 66 N.Y.U. L. Rev. 1533, 1542 (1991).

R. R. DONNELLEY & SONS CO. v. VANGUARD TRANSP. SYSTEMS, INC.

United States District Court, N.D. Illinois
641 F. Supp. 2d 707 (2009)

Jeffrey Cole, United States Magistrate Judge

[Donnelley is a commercial printer; Vanguard is a interstate motor carrier. Donnelley contracted with Vanguard to pay Vanguard $750 to transport brochures for Macy's post-Christmas sale brochures from a Kentucky printer to Donnelly's Atlanta distribution Center by December 16. Vanguard breached. While the Vanguard tractor trailer carrying the materials arrived in Atlanta on December 16, the trailer was left at Vanguard's Atlanta facility. In calls after December 16, Vanguard told Donnelley variously that it would "attempt" to deliver the load, that it was having difficulty getting a driver, and that its computers were down. The brochures were not delivered to Donnelley's distribution center in Atlanta until December 27, 2005—eleven days after the promised date of delivery. By then it was too late to mail the brochures to Macy's customers, and so Macy's did not pay Donnelley for the brochures. Donnelley sued Vanguard for breach of contract, and, at the bench trial, Donnelley sought to recover the cost of the brochures, $81,650. Vanguard contends that Donnelley can not recover because it failed to mitigate damages."]

* * *

Failure to mitigate is an affirmative defense on which Vanguard has the burden of proof. Cates v. Morgan Portable Bldg., 780 F.2d 683, 687 (7th Cir. 1985) * * * The so-called duty to mitigate damages, which is often referred to as a general contractual duty, is a principle of ancient vintage. Referring to mitigation of damages—or as it is called in tort law "avoidable consequences"—in terms of a "duty" is somewhat misleading, because a plaintiff incurs no liability for failing to act. See Restatement (Second) of Contracts § 350, Comment b. (1981). Rather the amount of loss that could reasonably have been avoided by stopping performance or making substitute arrangements is simply subtracted from the amount that would otherwise have been recoverable as damages * * *

The victim of the breach must " 'exercise reasonable diligence and ordinary care in attempting to minimize the damages after injury has been inflicted.' " And while he must act with "reasonable dispatch," *Cates*, 780 F.2d at 687, the injured party is not required to take steps that involve "undue risk or burden." But there are instances where the victim of th breach might be lulled by the breaching party into inaction because of assurances that all will be well. "[T]o put this differently, the [breaching party] may not insist on mitigation when by its words or deeds it has led the [non-breaching party] to believe that it has assumed what would otherwise be the buyer's burden of mitigation." *Cates*, 780 F.2d at 687.[8] While that is going on, the duty to mitigate is suspended.

Donnelley contends that is what occurred here, * * * Donnelley is adamant that it could and would have mitigated its damages by retaining a "local cartage company" to deliver the load if only Vanguard had told the truth about not having a driver to redeliver the load and not have misled it on a daily basis. "Think about what mitigation would have occurred it that had happened," Donnelley laments. But Donnelley's claim is unsupportable and is indeed contradicted by not only the evidence at trial, but by the judicial admissions in the Complaint * * * Paragraph 31 charges that Donnelley was trying to "persuade" Vanguard to reschedule, but Vanguard was unresponsive, "claim[ing] variously that its compute was down and that it did not have trucks or divers available to effect delivery." * * *

Donnelley could not indefinitely operate on the assumption or on the further assumption that the load would be delivered by the 21st. There comes a point at which even unequivocal promises by the breaching party—and there were no such promises by Vanguard—cannot be uncritically relied on. Judge Posner made the point in *Cates* with the tale of the host waiting for the late dinner guest: "If you invite someone to dinner, and hours after he was due he still hasn't arrived, you had better infer that he isn't coming, and start eating. You can't let yourself and your other guests starve merely because there is a slight chance that he will show up days later." *Cates*, 780 F.2d at 687. * * *

Donnelley was perhaps entitled to wait until Tuesday the 20th.It was not, however, entitled to wait beyond that since the brochures would be of no valued unless delivered to Donnelley by Wednesday the 21st. * * * By the 20th, it should have been clear to any reasonable and commercially sophisticated person in the industry—and Donnelley was an exceedingly sophisticated consume or cartage services—that Vanguard's equivocal statement that it would "attempt" delivery on the 21st could not be

---

8. *This is an application of the broader principle that a party cannot complain about the consequences of his actions. Cf. R.H. Stearns Co. v. United States,* 291 U.S. 54, 61–62, 54 S.Ct. 325, 78 L.Ed. 647 (1934) (Cardozo, J.) ("He who prevents a thing from being done may not avail himself of the non-performance which he has himself occasioned, for the law says to him in effect 'this is your own act, and therefore you are not damnified. * * *' ").

relied. On the morning of the 21st—which Mr. Janiak described at trial a the "drop dead" date for delivery—the best Vanguard could say was that it "will attempt delivery this AM." At 2:23 p.m. that afternoon, Donnelley was told that the load would not be delivered until the 22nd at 1:00 p.m. * * *

Normally "[i]t is a nice question, however, just when the [non-breaching party] should have awakened to the fact that [the breaching party]" can no longer be relied on. *Cates*, 780 F.2d at 687. In most cases, there will be no precise time that can be pointed to that marks when the plaintiff's duty to mitigate can no longer be held in suspension. It is often a guess and "no more than a guess [will be] possible." *Id.* In *Cates*, waiting a month to see if the defendant would make the promised repairs was reasonable. In the instant case, there is no guess work involved, and the precise time can be pointed to that marks when the plaintiff's duty to mitigate can no longer be held in suspension. For Donnelley to have allowed December 20th to have passed without having taken remedial steps its Reply Brief amists were cheap and easy was unreasonable. To return to Judge Posner's parable, by December 20th—and surely by the morning of the 21st—Donnelly should have "infer[red] that [Vanguard] [wa]sn't coming," *Cates*, 780 F. 2d at 687, and if it continued to wait for Vanguard to arrive, the soufflé would fall, the candles would go out, and the guest would all be gone. * * *

Donnelley's inaction is mystifying, especially in light of what its post-trial Reply Brief concedes was the minimal time and effort needed for Donnelley to have eliminated any damage. As the Reply Brief acknowledges, all that would have been entailed was the minimal cost of renting a truck from a local cartage company and driving the half hour to the Vanguard lot to pick up the load and delivering it to the Atlanta facility. Mr. Menne, of Vanguard, estimated that the cost would have been about $250. Even if the estimate is low, the cost would have been less than the $750 it cost to haul the load several hundred miles from Kentucky to Georgia.

The fact that Vanguard could have rented another truck or hired a local cartage company does not resolve the question of the whether Donnelley was required to mitigate its damages by making the alternative arrangements it insists Vanguard should have made. "Contract law seeks to preserve the [the non-breaching party's] incentive to consider a wide range of possible methods of mitigation of damages, by imposing a duty to mitigate even if some of the possibilities are equally within the [breaching party's] power." *Cates*, 780 F. 2d at 689. Phrased differently, the breaching party's ability to cure the breach does not excuse the victim of the breach from its duty to mitigate. *Id.*

Beyond pointing out how easy it would have been for Vanguard to have rented a truck from a local company and delivered the brochures, Donnelley's post trial briefs have effectively nothing to say about its own duty to mitigate damages. Its Memorandum of Points and Authorities in

Support of Closing Arguments does not mention mitigation at all, even though it was an issue in the pretrial order (Contested Issues of Law, ¶ H), was a significant issue at trial, and was a prominent feature of Vanguard's closing argument.

The Reply Brief * * * merely emphasized how easy and cheap it would have been for Vanguard to have hired a truck from a local cartage company and delivered the load, and how Donnelley could and would have mitigated its damages if it had only known Vanguard was lying when it promised that it would deliver the load. (Reply, at 6–8). However, as already discussed, Vanguard merely told Donnelley that it would *attempt* to deliver the load, and it was apparent certainly by the morning of the 21st, if by not the afternoon of the 20th, that it was unlikely that the load would be delivered in time. The specific time-sensitivity of the load and Vanguard's repeated failures to have made good on its "attempts" to deliver it made Donnelley's duty to mitigate all the more obvious and urgent * * *

That one cannot rely indefinitely on promises of performance no matter what the accompanying circumstances is a common-sense concept that is not confined to the law of contracts or to questions of mitigation of damages * * * if you can easily get out of the way of that forklift at work, you can't shut your eyes and hope to take your company for enough money to retire early.

All that stood between Donnelley and the fulfillment of this obligations to Continental Web Press and the complete mitigation of its certain damages of $81,000 was about and hour of either its time or that of a local cartage company and a few hundred dollars. Donnelly chose to do nothing, as it had the right to do. But in law as in life, choices have consequences. The consequence here is that the avoidable loss of more than $80,000 cannot be taxed to Vanguard * * *

QUESTIONS

1. Questions about the facts of this case

    1.1. Vanguard had the burden of proof. What fact was most important to Vanguard's meeting its burden?

    1.2. Would the court have reached a different decision if, at noon on December 20th, Vanguard had unequivocally promised delivery by 5 p.m. that day?

2. Questions of law

    2.1. If on December 19, Donnelley had spent $400 to rent a truck and transport the brochures from Vanguard's Atlanta facility to Donnelley's Atlanta distribution center, would Donnelley have recovered the $400 from Vanguard?

2.2. Is Judge Posner's dinner party analogy helpful? In light of the quality and quantity of his writings, were you surprised that Judge Posner knows anything about dinner parties and souffles? Cf. http:// www.law.uchicago.edu/node/79/publications.

---

3. Third Limitation on Money Damages: Foreseeability

Remember the Markell/Ponoroff car wash contract: Ponoroff contracted to wash Markell's car for $10. Markell's expectation was that Ponoroff would perform the contract without breach, that his car would be washed for $10. Damages are generally measured by the expectation interest. Markell gets the amount of damages that which would have put him in the same dollar position as he would have been had Ponoroff not breached. So if Epstein is willing to wash Markell's car for $15, it would seem that Markell's damages award should be $5.

But what if the breach relates to the acquisition of a good or service that the non-breaching party was going to use to make money elsewhere? What if Ponoroff was to wash Markell's car by seven on Monday evening; and Ponoroff breached;

— Markell had a contract with Epstein, to drive Epstein in a clean car starting at 7:30 that night for $1,000 plus expenses. It was imperative that the car be clean because Epstein was planning to wear his white leather Evel Knievel jumpsuit. http://www.eurostar leather.com/evel-knievel-white-leather-jumpsuit-new.htmlt;

— Markell was unable to find anyone else who can wash his car in time for him to pick up Epstein at 7:30. Epstein saw Markell's dirty car and cancelled the contract, so Markell lost the $1,000 he would have legitimately made had Ponoroff not breached.

Under these facts, can Markell still recover the $5 more that it will cost him to have the car washed the next day? Under these facts, can Markell also recover the $1,000 he lost because of Ponoroff's breach so that Markell will be in the same dollar position as he would have been had Ponoroff not breached?

We need more facts to answer the question of whether Markell can recover the $1,000. As Justice Souter (when he was a Justice on the New Hampshire Supreme Court) explained: "*Hadley v. Baxendale*, 156 Eng. Rep. 145 (1854) thus limits damages to those reasonably foreseeable at the time of the contract. To satisfy the foreseeability requirement, the injury for which damages are sought "must follow the breach in the natural course of events, or the evidence must specifically show that the breaching party had reason to foresee the injury." *Salem Engineering & Const. Corp. v. Londonderry School Dist.*, 122 N.H. 379, 384, 445 A.2d 1091, 1094 (1982). Thus, peculiar circumstances and particular needs must be made known to the [breaching party] if they are to be considered in determining the forseeability of damages." *Hydraform Products Corp. v. American Steel & Aluminum Corp.*, 127 N.H. 187, 197, 498 A.2d 339, 345 (1985).

Hadley v. Baxendale, a 19th century case, is an important case, even to men and women of the 21st century.[9] Indeed, *Hadley v. Baxendale* may be the most famous contracts case. *Hadley v. Baxendale* has inspired not only law review articles but a character in a "classic" porn movie "Behind the Green Door."[10]

We think that *Hadley v. Baxendale* is such an important case that we have included the entire case report—including the reporter's misleading statement of facts. Notice, unlike Justice Souter, neither the reporter nor Baron Alderson uses the word "foreseeable" or the word "foreseeability."

HADLEY v. BAXENDALE

Court of the Exchequer
9 Exch. 341, 156 Eng.Rep. 145 (1854)

At the trial before Crompton, J., at the last Gloucester Assizes, it appeared that the plaintiffs carried on an extensive business as millers at Gloucester; and that, on the 11th of May, their mill was stopped by a breakage of the crank shaft by which the mill was worked. The steam-engine was manufactured by Messrs. Joyce & Co., the engineers, at Greenwich, and it became necessary to send the shaft as a pattern for a new one to Greenwich. The fracture was discovered on the 12th, and on the 13th the plaintiffs sent one of their servants to the office of the defendants, who are the well known carriers trading under the name of Pickford & Co., for the purpose of having the shaft carried to Greenwich. The plaintiffs' servant told the clerk that the mill was stopped, and that the shaft must be sent immediately; and in answer to the inquiry when the shaft would be taken, the answer was, that if it was sent up by twelve o'clock any day, it would be delivered at Greenwich on the following day. On the following day the shaft was taken by the defendants, before noon, for the purpose of being conveyed to Greenwich, and the sum of 2£. 4s. was paid for its carriage for the whole distance; at the same time the defendants' clerk was told that a special entry, if required, should be made to hasten its delivery. The delivery of the shaft at Greenwich was delayed by some neglect; and the consequence was, that the plaintiffs did not receive the new shaft for several days after they would otherwise have done, and the working of their mill was thereby delayed, and they thereby lost the profits they would otherwise have received.

On the part of the defendants, it was objected that these damages were too remote, and that the defendants were not liable with respect to

---

9. "Justice Souter is often described as a man of the 18th or 19th century." http://www.law. harvard.edu/news/bulletin/2010/winter/feature_5.php.

10. http://www.imdb.com/title/tt0068260/ [Markell and Ponoroff want to make clear that Marilyn Chambers' "Behind the Green Door" is Epstein's "cultural allusion", Epstein's footnote. BAM, LP]

them. The learned Judge left the case generally to the jury, who found a verdict with 25£. damages beyond the amount paid into Court.

Whateley, in last Michaelmas Term, obtained a rule nisi for a new trial, on the ground of misdirection.

Keating and Dowdeswell showed cause.

Alderson, B. We think that there ought to be a new trial in this case; but, in so doing, we deem it to be expedient and necessary to state explicitly the rule which the Judge, at the next trial, ought, in our opinion, to direct the jury to be governed by when they estimate the damages.

It is, indeed, of the last importance that we should do this; for if the jury are left without any definite rule to guide them, it will, in such cases as these, manifestly lead to the greatest injustice. The Courts have done this on several occasions; and, in Blake v. Midland Railway Company (18 Q.B. 93), the Court granted a new trial on this very ground, and the rule had not been definitely laid down to the jury by the learned Judge at Nisi Prius.

"There are certain established rules," this Court says, in Alder v. Keighley, 15 M. & W. 117, "according to which the jury ought to find." And the Court, in that case, adds: "and here there is a clear rule, that the amount which would have been received if the contract had been kept, is the measure of damages if the contract is broken."

Now we think the proper rule in such a case as the present is this:— Where two parties have made a contract which one of them has broken, the damages which the other party ought to receive in respect of such breach of contract should be such as may fairly and reasonably be considered either arising naturally, i.e., according to the usual course of things, from such breach of contract itself, or such as may reasonably be supposed to have been in the contemplation of both parties, at the time they made the contract, as the probable result of the breach of it. Now, if the special circumstances under which the contract was actually made were communicated by the plaintiffs to the defendants, and thus known to both parties, the damages resulting from the breach of such a contract, which they would reasonably contemplate, would be the amount of injury which would ordinarily follow from a breach of contract under these special circumstances so known and communicated. But, on the other hand, if these special circumstances were wholly unknown to the party breaking the contract, he, at the most, could only be supposed to have had in his contemplation the amount of injury which would arise generally, and in the great multitude of cases not affected by any special circumstances, from such a breach of contract. For, had the special circumstances been known, the parties might have specially provided for the breach of contract by special terms as to the damages in that case; and of this advantage it would be very unjust to deprive them. Now the above principles are those by which we think the jury ought to be guided in estimating the damages arising out of any breach of contract. It is said, that other cases, such as breaches of contract in the nonpayment of money, or in the not making a good title to land, are to be treated as exceptions from this, and as governed by a conventional rule. But as, in such cases, both parties must be supposed to be cognisant of that well-known rule, these cases may, we think, be more properly classed under the rule above enunciated as to cases under known special circumstances, because there both parties may reasonably be presumed to contemplate the estimation of the amount of damages according to the conventional rule. Now, in the present case, if we are to apply the principles above laid down, we find that the only circumstances here communicated by the plaintiffs to the defendants at the time the contract was made, were, that the article to be carried was the broken shaft of a mill, and that the plaintiffs were the millers of that mill. But how do these circumstances show reasonably that the profits of the mill must be stopped by an unreasonable delay in the delivery of the broken shaft by the carrier to the third person? Suppose the plaintiffs had another shaft in their possession put up or putting up at the time, and that they only wished to send back the broken shaft to the engineer who made it; it is clear that this would be quite consistent with the above circumstances, and yet the unreasonable delay in the delivery would have no effect upon the intermediate profits of the mill. Or, again, suppose, that, at the time of the delivery to the carrier, the machinery of the mill had been in other respects defective, then, also, the same results would follow. Here it is true that the shaft was actually sent back to serve as a model for a new one, and that the want of a new one was the only cause of the stoppage of the mill, and that the loss of profits really arose from not sending down the new shaft in proper time, and that this arose from the delay in delivering the broken one to serve as a model. But it is obvious that, in the great multitude of cases of millers sending off broken shafts to third persons by a carrier under ordinary circumstances, such consequences would not, in all probability, have occurred; and these special circumstances were here never communicated by the plaintiffs to the defendants. It follows, therefore, that the loss of profits here cannot reasonably be considered such a consequence of the breach of contract as could have been fairly and reasonably contemplated by both the parties when they made this contract. For such loss would neither have flowed naturally from the breach of this contract in the great multitude of such cases occurring under ordinary circumstances, nor were the special circumstances, which, perhaps, would have made it a reasonable and natural consequence of such breach of contract, communicated to or known by the defendants. The Judge ought, therefore to have told the jury that, upon the facts then before them, they ought not to take the loss of profits into consideration at all in estimating the damages. There must therefore be a new trial in this case.

Rule absolute.

QUESTIONS AND NOTES

1. Questions about the facts of this case

    1.1. Where is the dramatis personae? Who are the players here, and what are their roles? Who, for example, is "Alderson, B."? Who are Whateley, Keating and Dowdeswell? For that matter, who is Hadley? Where is Baxendale?

    "Alderson, B." is Baron Alderson, a law lord of the Court of the Exchequer. He was one of only fifteen judges with general jurisdiction in all of England at the time of the decision. He is hearing an appeal from a county court, where the case was heard in Assize session.

    Whateley, Keating and Dowdeswell are counsel for the respective parties; the style of English reports from this time period was to include a summary of the arguments of counsel in the opinion; you can see this in early editions of the reports of the United States Supreme Court as well.

    Joseph and Jonah Hadley were the proprietors of City Steam Mills, the flour mill that engaged Pickford & Co. to transport the mill shaft.

    Joseph Baxendale was one of the managing directors of Pickford & Co.; under the rules of agency and company law then-existing in England, managing directors were personally liable for the unpaid debts of their unincorporated businesses. It was not until 1855 that England extended limited liability to companies not chartered by Parliament.

    1.2. What is the relevant time? When must the "special circumstances under which the contract was actually made [be] * * * communicated by the plaintiffs to the defendants, and thus known to both parties"?

    1.3. What were the "special circumstances" in this case?

    1.4. Were these special circumstances communicated by the plaintiffs to the defendants? *Victoria Laundry (Windsor) Ltd. v. Newman Industries, Ltd.* [1949] 2 K.B. 528, 537, 1 All E.R. 997 expressed the opinion that the headnote to *Hadley* is "definitely misleading insofar as it says that the defendants' clerk, who attended at the office, was told that the mill was stopped and that the shaft must be delivered immediately."

2. Questions about the law

    2.1. What is the rule of this case according to Baron Alderson? Do you agree with Baron Alderson's application of his rule to the facts of *Hadley v. Baxendale* as stated by Baron Alderson?

2.2.   Illustration 1 to *Restatement (Second) of Contracts* section 351 restates the facts of *Hadley v. Baxendale*.[11] Does Restatement (Second) Section 351, set out in pertinent part below, restate the law of *Hadley v. Baxendale*?

§ 351   *Unforseeability and Related Limitations on Damages*

(1) *Damages are not recoverable for loss that the party in breach did not have reason to foresee as a probable result of the breach when the contract was made.*

(2) *Loss may be foreseeable as a probable result of a breach because it follows from the breach:*

(a) *in the ordinary course of events, or*

(b) *as a result of special circumstances, or beyond the ordinary course of events, that the party in breach had reason to know.*

2.3.   Do you agree with the following, more recent "restatement" of the law of *Hadley v. Baxendale* by the Seventh Circuit: "Hadley v. Baxendale, 9 Ex. 341, 156 Eng. Rep. 145 (1854), which bars the recovery of consequential damages in a suit for breach of contract unless the defendant was on notice of what the consequences of a breach would be and agreed to compensate the plaintiff for them if there was a breach"? *Leister v. Dovetail, Inc.* 546 F.3d 875, 883 (7th Cir. 2008). Would you agree with the *Leister* restatement of *Hadley* if you knew what "consequential damages are"?[12] If we told you that *Leister* is a Judge Posner opinion?

2.4.   Do you need an actual agreement that one party will be liable for consequential damages of a particular sort, or do you just need notice of that fact? Evaluate the following clauses:

a.   Seller acknowledges that Buyer needs the widgets being sold hereunder to meet its obligations under a contract with Bamco.

b.   Seller agrees and understands that Buyer will use the widgets hereunder to meet its obligations hereunder in Buyer's contract with Bamco. Time is of the essence under the Bamco contract, so any failure by seller to make timely delivery of widgets under this contract will result in default under the Bamco contract.

c.   Time is of the essence for all performance due under this contract.

---

11.   Illustrations:

1.   A, a carrier, contracts with B, a miller, to carry B's broken crankshaft to its manufacturer for repair. B tells A when they make the contract that the crankshaft is part of B's milling machine and that it must be sent at once, but not that the mill is stopped because B has no replacement. Because A delays in carrying the crankshaft, B loses profit during an additional period while the mill is stopped because of the delay. A is not liable for B's loss of profit. That loss was not foreseeable by A as a probable result of the breach at the time the contract was made because A did not know that the broken crankshaft was necessary for the operation of the mill.

12.   "Consequential damages are those which arise from the intervention of 'special circumstances' not ordinarily predictable." *Roanoke Hosp. Ass'n v. Doyle & Russell, Inc.*, 215 Va. 796, 214 S.E.2d 155, 160 (1975). Consequential damages are also referred to as "special damages" and contrasted with "general damages."

d. Seller agrees that should it default, Buyer's damages will include any and all lost profits under Buyer's contract with Bamco, and Seller agrees to assume that risk and responsibility.

Which clause is more likely to result in an award of consequential damages? Which clause is more likely to be agreed to by the parties during their negotiations? If you represented the Seller, and the Buyer presented the language found in item (d), what would you advise your client to do? If you represented the Buyer and requested the language in item (d), would you be surprised if the Seller countered with a price increase request?

3. Notes

3.1. The "Terms and Conditions" for Federal Express' contract with its customers state the following:

[Federal Express] will not be liable for any damage, whether direct, incidental, special or consequential in excess of the declared value of a shipment, whether or not Federal Express had knowledge that such damage might be incurred including but not limited to loss of income or profits.

3.2. *Hadley*'s history is unearthed in Richard Danzig, *Hadley v Baxendale A Study in the Industrialization of the Law*, 4 J. LEGAL STUD. 249 (1975). Professor Danzig's article was then substantially incorporated in his excellent book THE CAPABILITY PROBLEM IN CONTRACT LAW 95 et seq (2d ed. 2004).

3.3. The concept of small acts leading to large consequences is common and venerable. See the following from Benjamin Franklin:

> For want of a nail the shoe was lost;
> For want of a shoe the horse was lost;
> And for want of a horse the rider was lost;
> For the want of a rider the battle was lost;
> For the want of the battle the kingdom was lost;
> And all for the want of a horseshoe-nail.

Benjamin Franklin, *Preface: Note to Courteous Readers*, POOR RICHARD'S ALMANACK (1758). The poem, in some form, is attributed to George Herbert (1651), quoted in JOHN BARTLETT, FAMILIAR QUOTATIONS 270 (15th ed. 1980).

3.4. Again, more doggerel:

> There once was a young man named Hadley
> Whose contract of transport went badly.
> "My mill shaft is gone,
> All my goods are in pawn,
> And my business is closed, he said sadly.

Douglass G. Boshkoff, *Selected Poems on The Law of Contracts: Raintree County Memorial Library Occasional Paper No. 1*, 66 N.Y.U. L. REV. 1533, 1542 (1991).

4. Fourth Limitation on Money Damages: Certainty

"As a general rule of limitation, damages for breach are recoverable only to the extent that the injured party's loss can be established with reasonable certainty. The issue has arisen most frequently in connection with lost profits claims, presumably for the reason that determining the injured party's 'profits' entails projections and predictions that are sometimes speculative and conjectural and are almost always open to debate." Marvin A. Chirelstein, CONCEPTS AND CASE ANALYSIS IN THE LAW OF CONTRACTS, 197 (5th ed. 2006) (great book).

MANOUCHEHRI v. HEIM

Court of Appeals of New Mexico
123 N.M. 439, 941 P.2d 978 (1997)

HARTZ, CHIEF JUDGE.

Jeff Heim sold Dr. A. H. Manouchehri a used x-ray machine. Manouchehri sued for breach of warranty and was awarded $4400 in damages after a bench trial. Heim appeals, claiming the following errors: * * * (2) direct damages based on the cost of repair should not have been awarded because there was no evidence of such cost; and (3) consequential damages should not have been awarded because (a) Manouchehri could have avoided them by obtaining a replacement machine; (b) they were not foreseeable, and (c) they were not proved with the required certainty. We affirm.

I. BACKGROUND

Manouchehri was the sole witness at trial. Heim presented no evidence other than through cross-examination of Manouchehri. We summarize Manouchehri's testimony.

Manouchehri is a physician in Cedar Crest, New Mexico. Heim, a sales representative of a medical supply company, had previously sold various items to Manouchehri. In December 1991 Heim learned that Manouchehri wanted to buy a used 100/100 x-ray machine. The two numbers refer to the rating of the machine in kilovolts and milliamps, respectively. The rating of the machine affects the quality of the image obtained. A weak machine often will not be able to produce adequate images.

On December 9 Manouchehri purchased a machine from Heim. He paid with a check for $1900 on which he wrote at the top "guaranteed to work (install Continental 100–100 x-ray) without limitation" and wrote on the memo line "purchase and installation of Continental 100–100 x-ray." Heim signed his name on the front of the check after Manouchehri read the notations to him.

During the following weeks Manouchehri realized that the machine was performing as a 100/60 machine. The power was sufficient only for x-rays of small children and thin people. Manouchehri notified Heim and asked him to repair it, offering to pay half the repair costs. Although Heim sent someone to inspect the machine, no repairs were made. Manouchehri continued to talk regularly with Heim about the problem until the lawsuit was filed in September 1994. Heim at first denied knowing that the x-ray machine was a 100/60 machine but later admitted that he knew. At that time he indicated that it was the sort of machine one can buy for only $1900.

Manouchehri initially obtained a default judgment, but it was later set aside. After trial on April 4, 1996 Manouchehri obtained judgment in the amount of $4400. Of the total, $1900 was for direct contract damages and $2500 was for consequential damages. The district court denied Heim's motion for reconsideration and Heim appealed.

* * *

III. DAMAGES

Heim does not dispute the district court's finding that he breached a warranty to provide Manouchehri with a 100/100 x-ray machine. His appeal focuses on the propriety of the award of damages. The decretal language of the court's judgment was as follows:

> IT IS, THEREFORE, ORDERED, ADJUDGED AND DECREED that [Manouchehri] is entitled to judgment against [Heim] in the amount of $1,900.00, for the cost of repair of the X-ray machine and the amount of $2,500.00 for incidental damages for a total of $4,400.00.

A contract for the sale of merchandise is governed by Article 2 of the Uniform Commercial Code. See NMSA 1978, §§ 55–2–102 and –105(1) (Repl. Pamp. 1993). For breach of warranty the buyer may recover direct, incidental, and consequential damages. The statutory provisions applicable to this appeal are NMSA 1978, §§ 55–2–714 and –715 (Repl. Pamp. 1993). The pertinent portions of Section 55–2–714 state:

> (2) The measure of damages for breach of warranty is the difference at the time and place of acceptance between the value of the goods accepted and the value they would have had if they had been as warranted, unless special circumstances show proximate damages of a different amount.

> (3) In a proper case any incidental and consequential damages under the next section may also be recovered.

Section 55–2–715 states:

> (1) Incidental damages resulting from the seller's breach include expenses reasonably incurred in inspection, receipt, transportation and care and custody of goods rightfully rejected, any commercially reasonable charges, expenses or commissions in connection with effecting cover and any other reasonable expense incident to the delay or other breach.

> (2) Consequential damages resulting from the seller's breach include:

(a) any loss resulting from general or particular requirements and needs of which the seller at the time of contracting had reason to know and which could not reasonably be prevented by cover or otherwise; and

(b) injury to person or property proximately resulting from any breach of warranty.

Of the $4400 awarded by the district court, $1900 is for direct damages under Section 55–2–714 and $2500 is for damages under Section 55–2–715. Heim challenges both figures. We first discuss direct damages.

A. Direct Damages

The judgment awarded Manouchehri $1900 for the cost to repair the x-ray machine. The cost of repair can be an appropriate measure of direct damages. Although Section 55–2–714(2) sets the measure of direct damages for breach of warranty as the difference between the value of the goods as warranted and the value of the goods as accepted, often that difference can be approximated by the cost to repair the goods so that they conform to the warranty. For example, if it costs $200 to fix the x-ray machine so that it performed as a 100/100 machine, then one could assume that the unrepaired machine (the "goods accepted") was worth $200 less than the repaired machine (the goods "as warranted"). Thus, the cost of repair is commonly awarded as the direct damages. * * *

As pointed out by Heim, however, there was no evidence at trial of the cost to repair the x-ray machine. On the contrary, the evidence at trial was that the machine could not be transformed into a 100/100 machine. Consequently, Manouchehri could not be awarded direct damages based on a cost of repair. As stated in a leading treatise:

> There are many cases in which the goods will be irreparable or not replaceable and therefore the costs of repair or replacement cannot serve as a yardstick of the buyer's damages. In those cases, the court will have to find some other way to measure the difference between the value of the goods as warranted and the value of the goods as accepted.

1 White & Summers, supra, § 10–2, at 557.

Nevertheless, we affirm the award of $1900 as direct damages. When to do so would not be unfair to the appellant, we can affirm a ruling by the trial court on a ground other than what was expressed by that court. * * * Such a course is particularly appropriate in this case because our review of the record indicates that the district court in fact computed the direct damages on a proper ground even though the judgment does not state that ground.

At the hearing on Heim's motion for reconsideration, Heim's attorney properly stated the law, arguing that Manouchehri's direct damages should be limited to the difference between the value of the x-ray machine as warranted and the value of the machine as it was delivered to

Manouchehri. He sought to set aside the award of $1900 on the basis that there was insufficient evidence to support it. Acknowledging that the sales price constituted sufficient evidence of the value of the machine as warranted, see 1 White & Summers, supra, § 10–2, at 557 ("The purchase price of the damaged goods may be the best evidence of the value of the goods as warranted."), he focused his argument on the alleged absence of evidence to support a finding regarding the value of the machine delivered to Manouchehri.

The district court did not dispute the contentions of Heim's attorney as to the proper measure of damages, but it rejected the claim that there was insufficient evidence regarding the value of the machine delivered to Manouchehri. Indeed, Finding No. 5 in the district court's decision states: "Any value to [Manouchehri] of the X–Ray machine 'as is' is offset by the cost to [Manouchehri] of having the machine removed from his premises." On appeal Heim has not challenged this finding. As we understand Finding No. 5, the court determined that Manouchehri could not recover any money for the machine; at the conclusion of trial the court had said, "I presume that someone will be willing to remove the machine for its residual value." * * * Hence, we do not find it unfair to affirm the district court's award of $1900 in direct damages as the difference between the value of the x-ray machine as warranted and the value of the machine actually delivered to Manouchehri.

B. Consequential Damages

The district court's judgment awarded "$2500 for incidental damages." Again, the judgment was not prepared with sufficient care. The damage award was clearly for consequential damages, not incidental damages. See § 55–2–715 (defining "incidental" and "consequential" damages). Finding No. 6 of the district court's decision states: "[Manouchehri] has suffered consequential damages in the form of loss of business of at least $2,500.00 during the time [Manouchehri] reasonably waited for [Heim] to repair the X–Ray machine or otherwise perform under the guarantee."

Manouchehri's testimony with respect to consequential damages was straightforward. He said that taking an x-ray would cost him from three to six dollars and he would charge "about $85 to $88" for taking and reading an x-ray. He also claimed that the inadequacy of the machine prevented him from taking at least 30 x-rays a month, although he had no documentation to support his estimate. Using the lowest possible profit per x-ray, Manouchehri contended in closing argument that the monthly loss would be $2370—computed by multiplying $79 net income per x-ray times 30 x-rays a month.

Heim contends that the award is improper for three reasons. First, he contends that Manouchehri failed to present evidence that he could not avoid the damages by renting or buying a substitute machine. Second, he contends that any lost profits were not reasonably foreseeable. Third, he contends that the proof of damages was too indefinite. Each of Heim's arguments has some force. But they must be examined in light of the district court's award of only $2500. It appears that the district court considered the three matters raised by Heim and adjusted the award accordingly. We now examine each of Heim's arguments.

1. Failure to Obtain Replacement Machine

Consequential damages are not recoverable if they could "reasonably be prevented by cover or otherwise." Section 55–2–715(2)(a). Heim argues that Manouchehri needed to present evidence that he could not avoid the damages by renting or buying a substitute machine. On the record before us, we reject the argument.

Manouchehri testified that he asked Heim to have someone repair the machine and that Heim responded that he would have someone come to the office for that purpose. Manouchehri further testified that he talked to Heim on a monthly basis regarding the problem and that until about a month before he filed the lawsuit he believed that Heim would fix the problem.

The UCC requirement to take reasonable steps to prevent consequential damages derives from standard contract law. In particular, guidance in interpreting Section 55–2–715(2)(a) can be found in the Restatement (Second) of Contracts § 350 (1981). See 1 White & Summers, supra, § 10–4, at 577 ("Restatement [§ 350] may be regarded as an articulation of the rules embodied in the adverb 'reasonably' in 2–715."). Restatement, supra, Section 350 reads:

Avoidability as a Limitation on Damages

(1) Except as stated in Subsection (2), damages are not recoverable for loss that the injured party could have avoided without undue risk, burden or humiliation.

(2) The injured party is not precluded from recovery by the rule stated in Subsection (1) to the extent that he has made reasonable but unsuccessful efforts to avoid loss.

The comment to this section states that it may be reasonable to rely on a breaching party's assurances that the breach will be remedied. See id. cmt. g and illus. 19. * * *

We cannot say that it was unreasonable as a matter of law for Manouchehri to delay seeking a replacement machine for a few months. The district court found that Manouchehri "suffered consequential damages in the form of loss of business of at least $2,500.00 during the time [he] reasonably waited for [Heim] to repair the X–Ray machine or otherwise perform under the guarantee." The district court did not state how long it was reasonable for Manouchehri to wait, nor did it state how much business Manouchehri lost in any particular month. Nevertheless, we see no need for mathematical precision in the circumstances of this case. The question is only whether it was rational for the district court to find, on the basis of the evidence presented, that by the time Manouchehri should have stopped relying on Heim's promises, he had lost at least $2500 in profits. Our answer is yes.

2. Foreseeability

Heim next argues that the lost profits cannot be awarded because Manouchehri failed to present any evidence on the issue of foreseeability. He relies on the language in Section 55–2–715(2)(a) that restricts recovery for consequential damages to losses "resulting from general or particular requirements * * * of which the seller at the time of contracting had reason to know. * * *" We are not persuaded.

This was not a sale of a mass-produced item to an anonymous buyer. Heim knew his customer and knew how the x-ray machine was to be used. Any reasonable person in his position would assume that a doctor using such a machine would charge more for its use than the cost of operation and would earn income from it. Moreover, Manouchehri testified to conversations with Heim that at least touched on the economics of the machine. For example, Manouchehri related one occasion when parts from an old failed x-ray machine were in front of his office:

> [Heim] asked that I had that x-ray and what to do with them and how come it was still sitting there. And I told him that this was a failed x-ray and I am stuck with the loss of this much money. And at that time he promised me, quoting from him, that "I know a doctor that has just [the] x-ray that you want. X-ray 100/100 is what you want, and I can get it for you and install in your office for this much money.

On the evidence at trial the district court could properly find that lost income would be a foreseeable consequence of an underpowered x-ray machine. * * * Although Manouchehri did not tell Heim how much income he would earn from use of the machine, he did not need to do so in order to recover consequential damages so long as the consequence of lost income was reasonably foreseeable. The law does not require those who enter into contracts to disclose to other parties the profits they expect to make from the contracts. See Richard A. Posner, Economic Analysis of Law 115 (3d ed. 1986) ("Any other rule would make it difficult for a good bargainer to collect damages unless before the contract was signed he had made disclosures that would reduce the advantage of being a good bargainer—disclosures that would prevent the buyer from appropriating the gains from his efforts to identify a resource that was undervalued in its present use.");* * * Perhaps some limit could be placed on recovery for particularly large lost profits, cf. Restatement, supra, § 351(3) (court may limit damages for foreseeable loss "in order to avoid disproportionate compensation"), but the award of $2500 in this case was within proper bounds.

3. Certainty of Proof of Damages

Finally, Heim argues that the evidence of lost profits was not certain enough. We disagree. We recognize that "when it is possible to present accurate evidence on the amount of damages, the party upon whom the burden rests to prove damages must present such evidence." * * * This requirement must be understood, however, in the context of the amount at stake. What it is "possible" to present in a suit for a million dollars may be an excessive burden for a small claim. Although Manouchehri's evidence was minimal, it was adequate in the circumstances. The absence of detail and documentary corroboration detracted from the weight of the testimony, but the district court could still find it sufficiently credible to support the $2500 award.

IV. CONCLUSION

We affirm the judgment below.

QUESTIONS

1. Questions about the facts of this case

    1.1. What value did the court place on the X-ray machine as delivered?

    1.2. Why do you suppose that Heim put on no evidence? If you were Heim's counsel, what evidence would you have introduced?

    1.3. What evidence did Dr. Manouchehri put on? If you were Manouchehri's counsel, what evidence would you have introduced?

2. Questions about the law

    2.1. The cost of the X-ray machine was $1,900. Why did the court award more than the purchase price?

    2.2. Did this court really suggest that Dr. Manouchehri would have needed more proof if the amount at issue had been more? Why? Is that discriminatory justice?

In the next case, the amount at issue was more—"exceed millions of dollars." It's just that no one seemed to know how many "millions of dollars."

ESPN, INC. v. OFFICE OF THE COMMISSIONER OF BASEBALL

U.S. District Court, Southern District of New York
76 F. Supp. 2d 416 (1999)

SHIRA A. SCHEINDLIN, U.S.D.J.:

On October 15, 1999, ESPN, Inc. ("ESPN") and the Office of the Commissioner of Baseball ("Baseball") moved in limine to preclude the admission of certain evidence and argument at their forthcoming trial. Ten separate motions—five by ESPN and five by Baseball—were fully submitted on October 29, 1999. Six of the motions were resolved by opinion dated November 22, 1999 [which is reprinted above, at 804]. Three of the motions were resolved from the bench during a hearing on November 23, 1999. The final motion, ESPN's motion in limine to preclude damages evidence, is the subject of this Opinion and Order.

I. ESPN's Motion in Limine to Preclude Damages Evidence

In my November 22 opinion, I ruled that ESPN breached its 1996 telecasting agreement ("1996 Agreement") with Baseball when it preempted six baseball games scheduled for Sunday nights in September 1998 and September 1999 without the prior written approval of Baseball. See ESPN, Inc. v. Office of the Commissioner of Baseball, 76 F. Supp. 2d 383 (S.D.N.Y. 1999). ESPN broadcast NFL football games rather than the previously scheduled baseball games on those six nights.

Baseball claims that it has been damaged in an amount "believed to exceed millions of dollars" as a result of ESPN's breach of the 1996 Agreement. * * * Baseball attributes its damages to an alleged loss of:

(1) national television exposure;

(2) promotional opportunities and ratings;

(3) value of the "Sunday Night Baseball" television package;

(4) prestige;

(5) potential sponsorships; and

(6) the future value of all of Baseball's national telecast packages

* * * Because Baseball received full payment from ESPN under the contract, it may only seek extra-contractual damages stemming from the six preemptions.

By its motion, ESPN seeks to preclude Baseball from introducing testimony or other evidence of its alleged monetary damages. ESPN contends that "there is no factual basis to support any claim for monetary damages arising from these perceived injuries, and that such claims are the product of speculation and guesswork." * * * Baseball argues that it has made the "requisite showing of damage" and therefore it is "entitled to have the opportunity to prove its damages at trial." * * *

II. Legal Standard

It is well-settled under New York law that

[a] plaintiff seeking compensatory damages has the burden of proof and should present to the court a proper basis for ascertaining the damages [it] seeks to recover. They must be susceptible of ascertainment in some manner other than by mere conjecture or guesswork.

Dunkel v. McDonald, 272 A.D. 267, 70 N.Y.S.2d 653, 656 (1st Dep't 1947), aff'd, 298 N.Y. 586, 81 N.E.2d 323 (1948). * * * Although it is true that "when the existence of damage is certain, and the only uncertainty is as to its amount, the plaintiff will not be denied recovery of substantial damages," but even then the plaintiff must show "a stable foundation for a reasonable estimate" of damages. * * *

With respect to damages for loss of goodwill, business reputation or future profits, the proof requirements are much more stringent. * * * Not only must the claimant prove the fact of loss with certainty, but the "loss must be 'reasonably certain in amount.'" * * * "In other words, the damages may not be merely possible speculative or imaginary but must be reasonably certain and directly traceable to the breach, not remote or the result of other intervening causes." * * *

III. Baseball's Proffered Damages Evidence

During discovery, ESPN served Baseball with interrogatories regarding its claims for monetary damages. Among other things, ESPN asked Baseball to "state the amount of monetary damages you seek in this action and explain the basis for the computation of your claim." ESPN Interrogatory No. 6, Ex. A to Lobenfeld Aff. at 7. Baseball responded as follows:

> Baseball has not quantified the amount of damages it has sustained by reason of ESPN's willful refusal to carry [baseball] games as required by the 1996 Agreement. A quantification of those damages, however real, is extremely complex and for that reason Baseball insisted, and ESPN agreed, in the 1996 Agreement that ESPN would produce and distribute the telecasts and that its failure to do so could be specifically enforced, without regard to the need for Baseball to prove irreparable harm. At its essence the damages, believed to exceed millions of dollars, are attributable to [loss of national television exposure; promotional opportunities and ratings; value of the "Sunday Night Baseball" television package; prestige; potential sponsorships; and the future value of all of Baseball's national telecast packages].

Id. at 7–8.[2] Nowhere in its response does Baseball set forth any specific dollar amount of monetary damages other than its estimate that damages are "believed to exceed millions of dollars." Nor does Baseball set forth any method of calculating its alleged damages.

As the following excerpts demonstrate, Baseball's [designated] witness on the topic of damages, Baseball's President Paul Beeston, was equally speculative and vague regarding the alleged harm caused by ESPN's breach.

---

2. Baseball's interrogatory response is quite revealing. Baseball concedes that it had agreed that in the event of a breach it would seek "specific[] enforcement" without the need to prove "irreparable harm." Baseball's failure to seek that specific enforcement is puzzling and leads one to question whether it really wanted the games aired, or whether it really wanted an excuse to renegotiate a contract which it no longer found sufficiently lucrative. On the other hand, ESPN's behavior is also suspect. In the November 22 opinion, I held that ESPN should not have engaged in self-help but should have sought judicial intervention as to whether Baseball's failure to grant permission to broadcast football in place of baseball games was unreasonable. ESPN's failure leads one to question whether the fear of an adverse ruling, and the accompanying loss of millions of dollars in revenues, caused ESPN to choose the option of intentionally breaching its contract.

Q: Has Baseball quantified any of the damages it alleges in this case?

A: No, we have not quantified it to the extent of a specific dollar, no.

Q: Has Baseball made any calculations as to any specific element of its alleged damages?

A: We have not.

Q: Is there a reason why Baseball has not done any calculation of its damages in this case?

A: No. We just believe it's significant. We believe that the case speaks for itself at the present time, and we have not worked out what the dollars are of the damages.

9/27/99 Deposition of Paul Beeston ("Beeston Dep.") at 6–7.

* * *

Q: What's the basis for your belief that Baseball's alleged damages exceed millions of dollars?

A: Based on what we have right here and what we've said what we've got here going forward. I don't have anything specific, as I said.

Q: If somebody suggested to you that they believed you're right, Baseball was damaged but it's only a hundred thousand dollars, would you be able to point me to anything to say it's not a hundred thousand dollars, it's a million dollars?

A: Specifically I won't be able to say this is what it is, try this calculation and that's the way it works out, no.

Id. at 28.

* * *

Q: Can you point to anything specific as evidence that ESPN's [breach] has made Baseball less valuable in any way?

A: "Specifically, no if you're asking for one example that I could give you. * * *"

Q: You say you think it probably hurt you. Are you able to point to us specifically—

A: No, I said I cannot.

Id. at 10–11. Not once during his deposition did Beeston offer a concrete example of harm or monetary loss stemming from Baseball's breach. Baseball's expert witness, Robert J. Wussler,[13] was similarly unable to cite specific examples of loss. During his deposition, Wussler testified as follows:

Q: Are you aware of any money that Baseball lost as a result of those three games?

---

13. [Mr. Wussler had been President of CBS Sports and then President of CBS Television Network. Eds]

A: No I'm not.

Q: And the same thing is true in '99, same question with respect to '99?

A: They've lost in perception. It's very hard to evaluate dollars and perception.

Q: I'm not going to ask you about perception. You are not aware of any dollars lost, correct?

A: I'm not.

10/15/99 Deposition of Robert J. Wussler at 92–93.

* * *

Q: Again, just so I'm clear, are you aware of 5 cents of advertising revenue that Baseball lost as a result of the three games being [not shown on ESPN]—

A: No I'm not.

Id. at 107.

* * *

Q: I take it you are not aware of any lost sponsors or lost advertisers; is that correct?

A: That is correct.

Id. at 108.

Finally, on November 23, this Court held oral argument on ESPN's motion to preclude damages evidence. During that argument, this Court specifically asked counsel for Baseball whether Baseball had any "concrete proof of monetary harm.". * * * In response, counsel for Baseball merely reiterated the entirely subjective and speculative assertion that Baseball "feel[s] this was very dilatory [sic] to our position and denigrated our product and cost us in the marketplace and otherwise." * * * Counsel for Baseball was unable to show "any loss of sponsorship, any loss of advertising, [or] any loss of ancillary sales or ticket sales." * * * As counsel for Baseball conceded: "We have not shown specific losses your Honor, we agree with you there. What we have said is we believe it did affect us."[3]

IV.   Discussion

As the above-quoted testimony and answers to ESPN's interrogatories demonstrate, there can be no question that Baseball has failed to adequately demonstrate either the fact of damages or the amount of damages.

---

3. At the end of oral argument, counsel for Baseball set forth, for the very first time, an alternate theory of damages. Baseball proposed that damages be calculated according to the amount it would have sought had ESPN asked Baseball to "sell the right to dump [Baseball] onto [another channel]." 11/23/99 Tr. at 30. In other words, Baseball seeks to calculate damages based on a hypothetical negotiation or sale of the six preempted games.

Regardless of the merits of Baseball's alternate theory, I reject it as a basis for the calculation of damages. Baseball's failure to mention this alternate theory of damages until six days before trial—months after the close of discovery and weeks after the submission of pre-trial motions—bars it from presenting such a theory at trial.

Put simply, Baseball's subjective belief that the amount of damages is "significant"—no matter how fervent—does not meet any of the required proofs set forth under New York law. Baseball has not cited a single lost promotional opportunity, sponsor or advertising dollar stemming from ESPN's breach. Nor has Baseball set forth any evidence of a decrease in ratings or box office ticket sales. Although damage to Baseball's prestige and future value are difficult to prove, such difficulty does not allow Baseball to proceed with speculative claims of damages. To the contrary, under New York law, a claim of damages for loss of reputation and future profits must be "reasonably certain." * * *

Baseball's damages claim is based on nothing more than its own vague assertions that it was "hurt." Baseball cites no specific examples of monetary damage, nor does it proffer a method for calculating such damages. The proffered unsupported allegations are simply inadequate to sustain a claim for damages under New York law, and therefore ESPN's motion to preclude damages evidence is granted.

V. Nominal Damages and Materiality

Although Baseball is not entitled to an award of money damages, it may still receive nominal damages. "It is a well-settled tenet of contract law that even if the breach of contract caused no loss or if the amount of the loss cannot be proven with sufficient certainty, the injured party is entitled to recover as nominal damages a small sum fixed without regard to the amount of the loss, if any." * * *[4] Accordingly, I will instruct the jury that if Baseball proves its breach of damages claim, it is entitled to an award of nominal damages.

Baseball's ability to recover only nominal damages does not impede its ability to present testimony and evidence regarding the materiality of ESPN's breach. Materiality goes to the essence of the contract. That is, a breach is material if it defeats the object of the parties in making the contract and "deprive[s] the injured party of the benefit that it justifiably expected." Farnsworth, Contracts § 8.16 (3d ed. 1999). Materiality does not depend upon the amount of provable money damages, it depends upon whether the nonbreaching party lost the benefit of its bargain. Thus, although Baseball is only entitled to nominal damages, it may still present evidence and argument to the effect that ESPN's breach was material. * * *

VII. Conclusion

For the reasons set forth above, Baseball is precluded from presenting damages evidence at trial and is only entitled to seek an award of nominal damages.

----

4. Although unable to prove monetary damage, there is no question that Baseball was harmed by virtue of ESPN's breach. Baseball was entitled to the broadcast of six baseball games during September 1998 and September 1999. When ESPN failed to broadcast those games, ESPN was harmed regardless of whether it can prove any monetary damage.

QUESTIONS

1. Questions about the facts of this case

    1.1. Did ESPN make all payments to Baseball required under the contract?

    1.2. Did ESPN breach the contract?

    1.3. Do you believe that Baseball was harmed by ESPN's showing NFL games in September instead of baseball games? If so, was the damage to Baseball "nominal"?

2. Questions about the law

    2.1. The court states, "Because Baseball received full payment from ESPN, it may only seek extra-contractual damages." What does the court mean by the phrase "extra-contractual damages"? Are "extra-contractual damages" the same thing as "consequential damages"?

    2.2. What are the merits and "demerits" of Baseball's alternate theory set out in footnote 3?

    2.3. What does "nominal damages" mean? What should be the amount of "nominal" damages in this case? Why do nominal damages even exist? Why not just dismiss the case for failure of proof of an essential element of a breach of contract cause of action; that is, damages?

    2.4. Do you agree with the statement in footnote 2 that "Baseball's failure to seek specific enforcement is puzzling"? If Baseball had timely filed a lawsuit seeking specific performance, would the court have ordered ESPN to show baseball games on Sunday nights in September?

    2.5. Should this contract have provided for liquidated damages? If so, how would you set them, and how would you draft that clause in the contract?

    2.6. If you were counsel for Baseball, wouldn't you be embarrassed if your bill exceeded the "nominal" damages awarded? Doesn't Baseball have the resources to hire counsel who should have seen this result coming? What do you think really happened?

D. THE RELIANCE INTEREST AS AN ALTERNATIVE MEASURE OF DAMAGES

The *Restatement (Second) of Contracts* and case law also recognize damages based on reliance interest as an alternative.

§ 349. Damages Based On Reliance Interest.[14]

As an alternative to the expectation measure of damages stated in § 347, the injured party has a right to damages based on his reliance interest, including expenditures made in preparation for performance or in performance, less any loss that the party in breach can prove with reasonable certainty the injured party would have suffered had the contract been performed."

You should now be asking yourself two questions. Just in case you are not, we will ask the two questions: "Self, (1) how do you compute damages using the reliance interest as the measure of damages? and (2) when do you compute damages based on the reliance interest instead of damages based on the expectation interest?"

HOLLYWOOD FANTASY CORPORATION v. GABOR

U.S. Court of Appeals, Fifth Circuit
151 F.3d 203 (1998)

Before King and Wiener, Circuit Judges, and Rosenthal,* District Judge

Rosenthal, District Judge:

Appellee Hollywood Fantasy Corporation was briefly in the business of providing "fantasy vacation" packages that would allow participants to "make a movie" with a Hollywood personality and imagine themselves movie stars, for one week, for a fee. In May 1991, Hollywood Fantasy planned to offer its second fantasy vacation package, in San Antonio, Texas. Hollywood Fantasy arranged to have Zsa Zsa Gabor as one of two celebrities at the event. Two weeks before the fantasy vacation event, Ms. Gabor canceled her appearance. A short time later, Hollywood Fantasy canceled the vacation event, to which it had sold only two tickets. A short time after that, Hollywood Fantasy went out of business.

Hollywood Fantasy sued Ms. Gabor for breach of contract and fraud. After the trial judge found that Ms. Gabor and Hollywood Fantasy had reached a contract, the jury found that Ms. Gabor had breached that contract. The jury awarded Hollywood Fantasy $100,000 for the breach, as well as $100,000 for fraud. The district court set aside the jury's fraud verdict for lack of evidence and entered judgment in favor of Hollywood Fantasy for $100,000 on the breach of contract claim, plus attorneys' fees

---

14. The *Restatement*:"borrowed" not only the term "expectation interest" from Fuller and Perdue but also the term "reliance interest." Fuller and Perdue provide the following explanation of "reliance interest": We may award damages to the plaintiff for the purpose of undoing the harm which his reliance on the defendant's promise has caused. Our object is to put him in as good a position as he was in before the promise was made. The interest protected in this case may be called the reliance interest." Lon L. Fuller & William R. Perdue, Jr., *The Reliance Interest in Contract Damages*, 46 Yale L. J. 52, 54 (1937).

* District Judge of the Southern District of Texas, sitting by designation.

and post-judgment interest. Ms. Gabor appealed. We affirm the district court's judgment as to liability; reverse the district court's damages award; and render judgment for a lesser amount of damages.

I. The Facts as to Hollywood Fantasy

Leonard Saffir created Hollywood Fantasy and served as its chief executive officer. The company Mr. Saffir created charged each vacation "client" $7,500 for a week of "pampering," instruction on making movies, rehearsals, and a "starring" role in a short videotaped film with a "nationally known" television or movie star. Mr. Saffir hoped that "bloopers" and "outtakes" from the videotapes would ultimately become the basis for a television series. A new venture, Hollywood Fantasy had conducted only one vacation event before the package scheduled to take place in San Antonio in May 1991. The first event, held in Palm Springs, California, had received some media coverage, but had lost money. * * *

This case began with a letter Hollywood Fantasy sent Zsa Zsa Gabor dated March 4, 1991. The letter opened with the following language:

> This will confirm our agreement whereby Hollywood Fantasy Corporation (HFC) will employ you under the following terms and conditions: * * *

The letter set out the terms and conditions of Ms. Gabor's appearance in fourteen numbered paragraphs. The terms and conditions specified the dates of employment; the hours of work; the duties required; the payment; and certain perquisites to be provided. The letter stated that Ms. Gabor was to be employed from May 2–4, 1991, in San Antonio, Texas; was to be "on call" from after breakfast until before dinner each day; was to act in videotaped "movie" scenes with the clients, using scripts and direction provided by Hollywood Fantasy, and was to join the clients for lunch and dinner; was to allow Hollywood Fantasy to use her name and photograph for publicity; and was to provide media interviews "as appropriate" during her stay in San Antonio. Hollywood Fantasy was to pay Ms. Gabor a $10,000 appearance fee and $1,000 for miscellaneous expenses. Hollywood Fantasy would also provide Ms. Gabor two first-class round-trip plane fares from Los Angeles; transportation to the Los Angeles airport and in San Antonio; hair and makeup services; meals; hotel expenses, excluding long distance telephone calls; and a hotel suite with "two bath rooms if available." * * *

Ms. Gabor sent Mr. Saffir a telegram dated April 15, 1991, [terminating the contract.] * * *

Hollywood Fantasy unsuccessfully attempted to replace Ms. Gabor for the San Antonio event. The San Antonio event was canceled; the two ticket purchasers received their money back; Hollywood Fantasy went out of business; and this litigation began. * * *

[T]the jury awarded Hollywood Fantasy $100,000 on its breach of contract claim and $100,000 on its fraud claim. * * * The district court * * * upheld the jury's finding that Ms. Gabor's cancellation was not based on "a significant acting opportunity in a film," as the contract permitted. The district court entered judgment in favor of Hollywood Fantasy for $100,000, plus attorneys' fees and post-judgment interest. Ms. Gabor timely appealed.

* * *

At trial, Ms. Gabor moved for judgment as a matter of law that there was insufficient evidence to support the jury's award of $100,000 for breach of contract. The district court denied Ms. Gabor's motion. Ms. Gabor renews her objection here.

* * *

"It is a general rule that the victim of a breach of contract should be restored to the position he would have been in had the contract been performed." * * * "However, an injured party may, if he so chooses, ignore the element of profits and recover as damages his expenditures in reliance." * * *

The $100,000 damages award cannot be supported as the recovery of lost profits. Mr. Saffir testified that Hollywood Fantasy lost $250,000 in profits from future fantasy vacation events and at least $1,000,000 in future profits from the creation of a television series based on "bloopers" and "outtakes" from the videotapes of clients "acting" with Hollywood personalities. Although "[r]ecovery of lost profits does not require that the loss be susceptible to exact calculation," * * *, lost profits must be proved with "reasonable certainty." * * * "[A] party claiming injury from lost profits need not produce in court the documents that support his opinions or estimates." * * * A witness may testify "from personal knowledge as to what profits would have been." * * * However, "[a]t a minimum, opinions or estimates of lost profits must be based on objective facts, figures or data from which the amount of lost profits may be ascertained." * * * "Mere speculation" of the amount of lost profits is insufficient. * * *

Leonard Saffir's testimony that Hollywood Fantasy lost $250,000 in future profits was based on his estimate that Hollywood Fantasy would make a $25,000 profit from each of ten future events. Hollywood Fantasy was a new venture. It had put on one event, in which nine people participated, and in which it had lost money. Two weeks before the San Antonio event, only two people had bought tickets for the event. Hollywood Fantasy had no commitments to, or arrangements for, specific future events. "Profits which are largely speculative, as from an activity dependent on uncertain or changing market conditions, or on chancy business opportunities, * * * or on the success of a new and unproven enterprise, cannot be recovered." * * * "The mere hope for success of an untried enterprise, even when that hope is realistic, is not enough for recovery of lost profits." * * * In Texas Instruments, the Texas Supreme Court made it clear that the relevant "enterprise" in the lost profits inquiry is "not the business entity, but the activity which is alleged to have been damaged." * * * There was no evidence at trial that the "movie fantasy vacation" enterprise promoted by Hollywood Fantasy had been a successful enterprise in any context. There was no evidence that the Hollywood Fantasy management had ever been involved in any prior fantasy vacation enterprise, let alone a successful one. * * *

In Texas Instruments, the Texas Supreme Court stated that even a new enterprise may attempt to recover lost profits when there are "firmer reasons" to "expect [the] business to yield a profit." * * * There was no evidence at trial that Hollywood Fantasy had "firm" reasons to expect a profit. Nine participants attended the [earlier] Palm Springs event; not all of those participants paid the full $7,500 price of admission and only "some" of the Hollywood Fantasy employees were paid for their work. As of April 15, 1991, two weeks before the San Antonio event, only two tickets had been sold. Mr. Saffir's testimony that he still expected twenty participants was based on the optimistic but unsupported assertion that people generally "don't send in their money right away."

Hollywood Fantasy's claim for loss of television revenue is even more speculative. Mr. Saffir admitted that he had not sold a television pilot, let alone a series, based on the fantasy vacation videotapes. Mr. Saffir testified that the actors appearing in the videotapes could have unilaterally declined to permit Hollywood Fantasy to use the tapes in a television pilot. Mr. Saffir testified that unidentified producers and others were enthusiastic about the "concept" of such a television series, but he had difficulty even estimating what the profits from a series might be. No "objective facts, figures, or data" substantiated the estimate of lost profits.

Hollywood Fantasy's claims for lost profits also fail because there was no evidence of how Hollywood Fantasy estimated the profits or what data it used to do so. * * *

Hollywood Fantasy also seeks to support the damages awarded as based on evidence of lost investment in the corporation. Mr. Saffir testified that Hollywood Fantasy lost $200,000 that had been invested in the corporation. Under Texas law, "actual damages may be recovered when loss is the natural, probable, and foreseeable consequence of the defendant's conduct." * * * The record must contain evidence that permits the jury "to assess with reasonable certainty the * * * degree of causation of the damage by the breach or interference relative to other factors." * * * It is pure speculation that but for Ms. Gabor's breach, Hollywood Fantasy would not have gone out of business. Hollywood Fantasy had lost money on the Palm Springs event despite the fact that it had not charged the full fee to several participants and had not paid all of its employees. Hollywood Fantasy had sold only two tickets to the San Antonio event. Hollywood Fantasy is not entitled to an award of damages representing a return of $200,000 invested in the corporation.

Although Hollywood Fantasy did not present evidence to base an award of compensatory damages on either lost profits or lost investment, it did present sufficient evidence as to certain out-of-pocket expenses to justify their recovery. Mr. Saffir testified that Hollywood Fantasy incurred the following out-of-pocket expenses for the San Antonio event: (1) $8,500 in printing costs for color brochures and press releases; (2) $12,000 in marketing costs for mailings and advertising; (3) $22,000 in personnel and miscellaneous expenses, including air fares, staff accommodations, script-writing costs, telephone calls, and logo t-shirts; (4) $9,000 in travel expenses for Mr. Saffir and members of the Hollywood Fantasy "staff," including Margo Mayor, Hollywood Fantasy's president; and (5) $6,000 in expenses relating to preparations to film the San Antonio event for a possible television pilot. These expenses total $57,500. * * *

Ms. Gabor presented no evidence controverting Mr. Saffir's testimony as to Hollywood Fantasy's lost out-of-pocket expenses for the San Antonio event. Mr. Saffir's testimony as to Hollywood Fantasy's out-of-pocket expenses is sufficient to support an award of $57,500 for breach of contract, but not to support an award of $100,000.[5] The award of $100,000 is reversed in part on the basis that the evidence disclosed in the record does not support compensatory damages beyond $57,500.

* * *

VI.   Conclusion

We affirm the district court's judgment with respect to Ms. Gabor's liability for breach of contract. We reverse the district court's award of $100,000 for breach of contract and render judgment in the amount of $57,500, with post-judgment interest from the date of the district court's judgment to the date it is paid, at the rate previously set by the district court, and the attorneys' fees awarded by the district court.

Affirmed in Part and Reversed and Rendered in Part.

QUESTIONS AND NOTES

1.   Questions about the facts of this case

   1.1.   Do you know who Zsa Zsa Gabor is? Unlike Epstein who fantasized about Ms. Gabor before his current Sharon Stone fixation,[15] you may not be familiar with Ms. Gabor and so * * * http://www.imdb. com/name/nm0001248/bio. Mr. Saffir's past is almost as interesting:

      "In his nearly 68 years, the Brooklyn-born Saffir has been a Marine in the Korean War, a foreign press correspondent, a friend of Ferdinand Marcos in his pre-dictator days, a four-time newspaper publisher, a husband three times, a father three times, a Republican U.S. senator's chief of staff, a smuggler of

---

5. Hollywood Fantasy cannot recover the $15,000 it refunded to the two individuals who had bought tickets to the San Antonio event before it was cancelled. The ticket price refund was not an out-of-pocket expense. Hollywood Fantasy presented no testimony as to what portion, if any, of this amount it would have kept as profit had the event gone forward with Ms. Gabor's participation.

15. Epstein still regularly watches his Betamax video of "Queen of Outer Space."

Hebrew Bibles into Communist Russia, a top New York City public relations executive, an author, a television producer, a past president of a foreign press club, a president of a New Jersey-based Internet company, a successful player in The Palm Beach Post's stock market game, and, let the record show, an adversary of Zsa Zsa Gabor."

Palm Beach Post, March 16, 1998, Page 1A.

1.2. If you had represented Ms Gabor, what fact would you have emphasized?

1.3. If you had represented Mr. Saffir, what fact would you have emphasized?

2. Questions about the law

2.1. In requiring certainty for admitted losses, aren't we knowingly setting up a system that will systematically undercompensate aggrieved parties? Are "reliance" damages a way of giving at least something but which we know is less than full compensation?

2.2. Will damages based on protection of the nonbreaching party's reliance interest always be less than damages based on protection of the nonbreaching party's expectation interest?

2.3. Does the requirement that damages must be proved with "reasonable certainty" apply to damages based on protection of the nonbreaching party's reliance interest?

2.4. If Ms. Gabor could prove that Saffir would have incurred even more significant losses if she had performed, should the court award any damages, even for costs incurred in reliance on the contract? Cf. *Restatement (Second) of Contracts* § 349: "a plaintiff may recover damages based on his reliance interest, including expenditures made in preparation for performance or in performance, less any loss that the party in breach can prove with reasonable certainty the injured party would have suffered had the contract been performed."

3. Notes

Here's what the popular press had to say about this case.

Court: Failed Fantasy Worth Only $57,500
Janet McConnaughey

NEW ORLEANS—Would you pay $7,500 to spend a week pretending to be a Hollywood star, being videotaped with and dining with Zsa Zsa Gabor in San Antonio, Texas?

Two people sent in their money before Gabor pulled out, two weeks before the "fantasy vacation" was to start.

Leonard Saffir, who set it all up, said her cancellation forced his Hollywood Fantasy Corp. out of business and cost him millions of dollars.

Most of that was pure speculation, a federal appeals court ruled Wednesday. However, it did order Gabor to pay $57,500—Hollywood Fantasy's actual expenses—for breaking her 1991 contract. * * *

The 5th Circuit is the third court to rule in the case.

Gabor was a no-show at her first trial, and a federal District Court jury in San Antonio ordered her to pay the full $3 million Saffir wanted. Another judge threw out the verdict and heard the case after attorney Melvin Belli said that Gabor had never been told of the trial date in San Antonio.

The second jury ruled that Gabor owed Saffir $200,000, half for breach of contract and half for fraud. The judge threw out the fraud verdict, but accepted the breach of contract claim.

After the 5th Circuit heard arguments in the case, Gabor, under court order to pay Elke Sommers $3.3 million for calling her a haggard Hollywood has-been,[16] asked a bankruptcy court for protection from her creditors.

That stopped Saffir's case until the California bankruptcy court agreed in March 1997 that it could go forward.

The $3 million he claimed in damages included $250,000 in profits from 10 future fantasy vacations and at least $1 million from a planned television series of "bloopers" from the videotapes.

However, the 5th Circuit noted, Hollywood Fantasy had lost money on its only previous fantasy vacation, which attracted nine paying customers; it had sold only two tickets to Gabor's week; and it had no arrangements for any future events.

Nor had Saffir sold a television pilot, and he acknowledged that the actors could have refused to let Hollywood Fantasy use the tapes, the appeals court said.

However it said he did provide enough evidence about his out-of-pocket expenses, including $6,000 to prepare to film the San Antonio event for a possible TV pilot, to add up to the $57,500 award.

The Baton Rouge Advocate, Aug. 14, 1998, Page 7B.

E. RESTITUTION INTEREST AS AN ALTERNATIVE MEASURE OF DAMAGES

As yet another alternative to the expectation measure of damages stated in § 347, the injured party has a right to damages based on the restitution interest,[17] "which is his interest in having restored to him

---

16. http://www.imdb.com/media/rm586319872/nm0813961 [In fairness, which is rarely our concern, this is a 2009 photo of Ms. Sommer. Eds.].

17. You guessed it! "Restitution interest" is another Fuller and Perdue term: "The court may force the defendant to disgorge the value he received from the plaintiff. The object here may be any benefit that he has conferred on the other party." *Restatement (Second) Contracts.* § 344(c).

Addie v. Kjaer. 2009 WL 2584833 (D. Virgin Islands 2009) is the only 2009 case on Westlaw that uses the term "restitution interest." Embarrassingly easy facts: "Here, the uncontroverted evidence at trial establishes that the Buyers deposited $1,500,000 into an escrow account in compliance with the parties' escrow agreement. Indeed, the escrow agreement, which was admitted into evidence at trial, clearly states that the Buyers were obligated to make that deposit in two installments: one for $1,000,000 and another for $500,000. * * * Given the Sellers' breach, the appropriate amount of restitution damages necessary and payable to restore the Buyers to their original position is $1,500,000. See Restatement (Second) of Contracts § 344 (1981) (explaining that a party asserting a breach of contract claim may seek to protect his " 'restitution interest,' which is his interest in having restored to him any benefit that he has conferred on the other party"); id. § 345 (noting that a court making a restitution award may "award[ ] a sum of money to prevent unjust enrichment"); see also ATACS Corp. v. Trans World Communications, 155 F.3d 659, 669 (3d Cir.1998) ("[R]estitution damages will require the party in breach to disgorge the benefit received by returning it to the party who conferred it.")

In *Addide*, the nonbreaching party performed by paying money. Restitution damages become more challenging where, as in the next two cases, the nonbreaching party performed by providing a service.

UNITED STATES v. ALGERNON BLAIR, INCORPORATED

U.S. Court of Appeals, Fourth Circuit
479 F.2d 638 (1973)

CRAVEN, CIRCUIT JUDGE:

May a subcontractor, who justifiably ceases work under a contract because of the prime contractor's breach, recover in quantum meruit the value of labor and equipment already furnished pursuant to the contract irrespective of whether he would have been entitled to recover in a suit on the contract? We think so, and, for reasons to be stated, the decision of the district court will be reversed.

The subcontractor, Coastal Steel Erectors, Inc., brought this action under the provisions of the Miller Act, 40 U.S.C.A. § 270a et seq., in the name of the United States against Algernon Blair, Inc., and its surety, United States Fidelity and Guaranty Company. Blair had entered a contract with the United States for the construction of a naval hospital in

termed the prevention of gain by the defaulting promisor at the expense of the promise; more briefly, the prevention of unjust enrichment. The interest protected may be called the restitution interest." Lon L. Fuller & William R. Perdue, Jr., *The Reliance Interest in Contract Damages*, 46 Yale L. J. 52, 53 (1937).

Charleston County, South Carolina. Blair had then contracted with Coastal to perform certain steel erection and supply certain equipment in conjunction with Blair's contract with the United States. Coastal commenced performance of its obligations, supplying its own cranes for handling and placing steel. Blair refused to pay for crane rental, maintaining that it was not obligated to do so under the subcontract. Because of Blair's failure to make payments for crane rental, and after completion of approximately 28 percent of the subcontract, Coastal terminated its performance. Blair then proceeded to complete the job with a new subcontractor. Coastal brought this action to recover for labor and equipment furnished.

The district court found that the subcontract required Blair to pay for crane use and that Blair's refusal to do so was such a material breach as to justify Coastal's terminating performance. This finding is not questioned on appeal. The court then found that under the contract the amount due Coastal, less what had already been paid, totaled approximately $37,000. Additionally, the court found Coastal would have lost more than $37,000 if it had completed performance. Holding that any amount due Coastal must be reduced by any loss it would have incurred by complete performance of the contract, the court denied recovery to Coastal. While the district court correctly stated the " 'normal' rule of contract damages,"[1] we think Coastal is entitled to recover in quantum meruit.

In United States for Use of Susi Contracting Co. v. Zara Contracting Co., 146 F.2d 606 (2d Cir. 1944), a Miller Act action, the court was faced with a situation similar to that involved here—the prime contractor had unjustifiably breached a subcontract after partial performance by the subcontractor. The court stated:

> For it is an accepted principle of contract law, often applied in the case of construction contracts, that the promisee upon breach has the option to forego any suit on the contract and claim only the reasonable value of his performance.

146 F.2d at 610. The Tenth Circuit has also stated that the right to seek recovery under quantum meruit in a Miller Act case is clear. Quantum meruit recovery is not limited to an action against the prime contractor but may also be brought against the Miller Act surety, as in this case. Further, that the complaint is not clear in regard to the theory of a plaintiff's recovery does not preclude recovery under quantum meruit. Narragansett Improvement Co. v. United States, 290 F.2d 577 (1st Cir. 1961). A plaintiff may join a claim for quantum meruit with a claim for damages from breach of contract.

In the present case, Coastal has, at its own expense, provided Blair with labor and the use of equipment. Blair, who breached the subcontract,

---

1. Fuller & Perdue, *The Reliance Interest in Contract Damages*, 46 Yale L. J. 52 (1937); *Restatement of Contracts* § 333 (1932).

has retained these benefits without having fully paid for them. On these facts, Coastal is entitled to restitution in quantum merit.

> The "restitution interest," involving a combination of unjust impoverishment with unjust gain, presents the strongest case for relief. If, following Aristotle, we regard the purpose of justice as the maintenance of an equilibrium of goods among members of society, the restitution interest presents twice as strong a claim to judicial intervention as the reliance interest, since if A not only causes B to lose one unit but appropriates that unit to himself, the resulting discrepancy between A and B is not one unit but two.

Fuller & Perdue, *The Reliance Interest in Contract Damages*, 46 *Yale L. J.* 52, 56 (1937).[6]

The impact of quantum meruit is to allow a promisee to recover the value of services he gave to the defendant irrespective of whether he would have lost money on the contract and been unable to recover in a suit on the contract. *Scaduto v. Orlando,* 381 F.2d 587, 595 (2d Cir. 1967). The measure of recovery for quantum meruit is the reasonable value of the performance, Restatement of Contracts § 347 (1932); and recovery is undiminished by any loss which would have been incurred by complete performance. 12 Williston on Contracts § 1485, at 312 (3d ed. 1970). While the contract price may be evidence of reasonable value of the services, it does not measure the value of the performance or limit recovery.

It should be noted, however, that in suits for restitution there are many cases permitting the plaintiff to recover the value of benefits conferred on the defendant, even though this value exceeds that of the return performance promised by the defendant. In these cases it is no doubt felt that the defendant's breach should work a forfeiture of his right to retain the benefits of an advantageous bargain. Fuller & Perdue, *supra* at 77. Rather, the standard for measuring the reasonable value of the services rendered is the amount for which such services could have been purchased from one in the plaintiff's position at the time and place the services were rendered.

Since the district court has not yet accurately determined the reasonable value of the labor and equipment use furnished by Coastal to Blair, the case must be remanded for those findings. When the amount has been determined, judgment will be entered in favor of Coastal, less payments already made under the contract. Accordingly, for the reasons stated above, the decision of the district court is

Reversed and remanded with instructions.

---

6. This case also comes within the requirements of the *Restatements* for recovery in quantum meruit. *Restatement of Restitution* § 107 (1937); *Restatement of Contracts* §§ 347–357 (1932).

QUESTIONS AND NOTES

1. Questions about the facts of this case

    1.1. Who won in the district court? Who is bringing this appeal?

    1.2. What makes cases like this somewhat unusual? Think about it in these terms. If we have a contract under which one party made a bad deal and is going to lose money, which of the two parties would you guess is most likely to commit a breach?

2. Questions about the law

    2.1. If the contract to Coastal would not return a profit, why should it be awarded anything? Doesn't that undermine the expectancy basis of contract damages?

    2.2. What amount is the court on remand supposed to calculate? What will it do then?

    2.3. So Coastal gets damages even though it would have lost money on the contract? What is to stop the Coastals of this world, every time they enter into a losing contract, from goading the other side into breach so that it can get out of the contract with its costs? Take a look at *Restatement (Second) of Contracts* § 349 and, in particular, the last clause in that section, beginning with ''* * * less any loss the party in breach * * *'' In what circumstance might that clause apply?

3. Notes

    3.1. Section 373(1) of the *Restatement (Second)* expressly provides that ''on breach for nonperformance * * * the injured party is entitled to restitution. * * *'' This is certainly consistent with the holding in *Algernon Blair*. However, that provision is also made ''[s]ubject to the rule stated in Subsection (2).'' That rule carves out an exception to the option of the injured party to seek restitution in lieu of enforcement of her claim under the contract. Look at subsection (2) and see if you can figure out what the justification might be for this exception.

    3.2. Restitution measures the value of the benefit conferred on the other party, which may or may not be the same as the costs incurred by the non-breaching party—that's the difference between a restitutionary recovery and a reliance recovery; *i.e.*, the former excludes recovery of non-beneficial reliance expenditures. But can recovery based on restitution actually exceed the direct expenditures incurred by the injured party? Epstein agrees to build a house for Ponoroff at a price of $100,000. After Epstein has incurred $70,000 of costs, and would have had to incur an additional $40,000 to complete the construction, Ponoroff repudiates. If Epstein puts on evidence at trial in the form of expert testimony from Markell, another local contractor, that Markell would have charged $75,000 to do just the work that Epstein did up to the point of Ponoroff's breach, can Epstein recover $75,000, and thereby turn what would have been a losing contract into a winner? The answer is that there is authority for both views. So, it is up to you to figure out which is the *right* view!

3.3.   What if Coastal were in breach instead of Blair? The fact that a person is in breach does not affect the value of the services that he has rendered, does it? Section 373(1) of the *Restatement (Second)*, however, talks about the right of the *injured party* to seek restitution in lieu of suing under the contract. So, if Coastal were in breach, does that mean it would just be out of luck even though it conferred a benefit on Blair for which it was not compensated? Consider that question as you read, and try to make sense of, the next case.

BRITTON v. TURNER

Supreme Court of New Hampshire
6 N.H. 481 (1834)

Syllabus:

Assumpsit for work and labour, performed by the plaintiff, in the service of the defendant, from March 9th, 1831, to December 27, 1831.

The declaration contained the common counts, and among them a count in quantum meruit, for the labor, averring it to be worth one hundred dollars.

At the trial in the C. C. Pleas, the plaintiff proved the performance of the labor as set forth in the declaration.

The defence was that it was performed under a special contract—that the plaintiff agreed to work one year, from some time in March, 1831, to March 1832, and that the defendant was to pay him for said year's labor the sum of one hundred and twenty dollars; and the defendant offered evidence tending to show that such was the contract under which the work was done.

Evidence was also offered to show that the plaintiff left the defendant's service without his consent, and it was contended by the defendant that the plaintiff had no good cause for not continuing in his employment.

There was no evidence offered of any damage arising from the plaintiffs departure, farther than was to be inferred from his non fulfillment of the entire contract.

The court instructed the jury, that if they were satisfied from the evidence that the labor was performed, under a contract to labor a year, for the sum of one hundred and twenty dollars, and if they were satisfied that the plaintiff labored only the time specified in the declaration, and then left the defendant's service, against his consent, and without any good cause, yet the plaintiff was entitled to recover, under his quantum meruit count, as much as the labor he performed was reasonably worth, and under this direction the jury gave a verdict for the plaintiff for the sum of $95.

The defendant excepted to the instructions thus given to the jury.

Parker, J.

It may be assumed, that the labor performed by the plaintiff, and for which he seeks to recover a compensation in this action, was commenced under a special contract to labor for the defendant the term of one year, for the sum of one hundred and twenty dollars, and that the plaintiff has labored but a portion of that time, and has voluntarily failed to complete the entire contract.

It is clear, then, that he is not entitled to recover upon the contract itself, because the service, which was to entitle him to the sum agreed upon, has never been performed.

But the question arises, can the plaintiff, under these circumstances, recover a reasonable sum for the service he has actually performed, under the count in quantum meruit.

* * *

That such rule in its operation may be very unequal, not to say unjust, is apparent * * *.

The case before us presents an illustration. Had the plaintiff in this case never entered upon the performance of his contract, the damage could not probably have been greater than some small expense and trouble incurred in procuring another to do the labor which he had contracted to perform. But having entered upon the performance, and labored nine and a half months, the value of which labor to the defendant as found by the jury is $95, if the defendant can succeed in this defence, he in fact receives nearly five sixths of the value of a whole year's labor, by reason of the breach of contract by the plaintiff a sum not only utterly disproportionate to any probable, not to say possible damage which could have resulted from the neglect of the plaintiff to continue the remaining two and an half months, but altogether beyond any damage which could have been recovered by the defendant, had the plaintiff done nothing towards the fulfillment of his contract.

* * *

We hold then, that where a party undertakes to pay upon a special contract for the performance of labor, or the furnishing of materials, he is not to be charged upon such special agreement until the money is earned according to the terms of it, and where the parties have made an express contract the law will not imply and raise a contract different from that which the parties have entered into, except upon some farther transaction between the parties.

In case of a failure to perform such special contract, by the default of the party contracting to do the service, if the money is not due by the terms of the special agreement he is not entitled to recover for his labor, or for the materials furnished, unless the other party receives what has been done, or furnished, and upon the whole case derives a benefit from it. * * *

But if, where a contract is made of such a character, a party actually receives labor, or materials, and thereby derives a benefit and advantage, over and above the damage which has resulted from the breach of the contract by the other party, the labor actually done, and the value received, furnish a new consideration, and the law thereupon raises a promise to pay to the extent of the reasonable worth of such excess. This may be considered as making a new case, one not within the original agreement, and the party is entitled to "recover on his new case, for the work done, not as agreed, but yet accepted by the defendant." 1 Dane's Abr. 224.

If on such failure to perform the whole, the nature of the contract be such that the employer can reject what has been done, and refuse to receive any benefit from the part performance, he is entitled so to do, and in such case is not liable to be charged, unless he has before assented to and accepted of what has been done, however much the other party may have done towards the performance. He has in such case received nothing, and having contracted to receive nothing but the entire matter contracted for, he is not bound to pay, because his express promise was only to pay on receiving the whole, and having actually received nothing the law cannot and ought not to raise an implied promise to pay. But where the party receives value—takes and uses the materials, or has advantage from the labor, he is liable to pay the reasonable worth of what he has received. * * * And the rule is the same whether it was received and accepted by the assent of the party prior to the breach, under a contract by which, from its nature, he was to receive labor, from time to time until the completion of the whole contract; or whether it was received and accepted by an assent subsequent to the performance of all which was in fact done. If he received it under such circumstances as precluded him from rejecting it afterwards, that does not alter the case—it has still been received by his assent.

* * *

It is easy, if parties so choose, to provide by an express agreement that nothing shall be earned, if the laborer leaves his employer without having performed the whole service contemplated, and then there can be no pretence [sic] for a recovery if he voluntarily deserts the service before the expiration of the time.

The amount, however, for which the employer ought to be charged, where the laborer abandons his contract, is only the reasonable worth, or the amount of advantage he receives upon the whole transaction, and, in estimating the value of the labor, the contract price for the service cannot be exceeded. * * *

If a person makes a contract fairly he is entitled to have it fully performed, and if this is not done he is entitled to damages. He may maintain a suit to recover the amount of damage sustained by the non performance.

The benefit and advantage which the party takes by the labor, therefore, is the amount of value which he receives, if any, after deducting the amount of damage; and if he elects to put this in defence he is entitled so to do, and the implied promise which the law will raise, in such case, is to pay such amount of the stipulated price for the whole labor, as remains after deducting what it would cost to procure a completion of the residue of the service, and also any damage which has been sustained by reason of the non fulfillment of the contract.

If in such case it be found that the damages are equal to, or greater than the amount of the labor performed, so that the employer, having a right to the full performance of the contract, has not upon the whole case received a beneficial service, the plaintiff cannot recover.

This rule, by binding the employer to pay the value of the service he actually receives, and the laborer to answer in damages where he does not complete the entire contract, will leave no temptation to the former to drive the laborer from his service, near the close of his term, by ill treatment in order to escape from payment; not to the latter to desert his service before the stipulated time, without a sufficient reason; and it will in most instances settle the whole controversy in one action and prevent a multiplicity of suits and cross actions.

* * *

The defendant sets up a mere breach of contract in defense of the action, but this cannot avail him. He does not appear to have offered evidence to show that he was damnified by such breach, or to have asked that a deduction should be made on that account. The direction to the jury was therefore correct, that the plaintiff was entitled to recover as much as the labor performed was reasonably worth, and the jury appear to have allowed a pro rata compensation, for the time which the plaintiff labored in the defendant's service.

As the defendant has not claimed or had any adjustment of damages, for the breach of the contract, in this action, if he has actually sustained damage he is still entitled to a suit to recover the amount.

* * *

Judgment on the verdict.

_____

Questions and Note

1. Questions about the facts of this case

    1.1. Why do you think Turner failed to offer any evidence of damages arising from Britton's breach of his employment contract?

    1.2. Was the court concerned with the reasons why Britton left Turner's employ before the end of the one-year? Is that fact relevant to the legal issue in the case?

2. Questions about the law

    2.1. Look at the trial court's instruction to the jury. Did the court permit Britton to recover under the contract?

    2.2. Could you argue that Britton "substantially performed"? How would the analysis and/or the outcome have been different if the court had concluded that there had been substantial performance?

    2.3. What, if anything, would Turner have had to pay to Britton if Turner had been able to show that it cost him $50 to hire someone else to perform Britton's duties for the balance of the contract term? Suppose the cost was only $15?

    2.4. Suppose Turner had been able to show that the contract price was above market rates for similar services or that Britton performed his job in a sloppy manner. Would either of these facts affect the amount Britton should be able to recover in a *quantum meruit* claim?

    2.5. What are the policy issues with which the court was concerned? Does the rule devised by the court in this case advance those policies? How is the rule different from the rule advanced in *Algernon Blair*?

3. Note

Today, in virtually all jurisdictions, employers are required by statute to pay their employees periodically (*i.e.*, bi-weekly or monthly) without regard to either the quality of the employee's work or whether the employee has substantially performed the contract. In effect, employment contracts are made divisible by statute. However, the "net benefit rule" established in *Britton v. Turner* still has enormous viability in other contexts, including construction services and independent contractor arrangements.

CHAPTER EIGHT

WHAT ARE THE ALTERNATIVES TO CONTRACTS AND CONTRACT LAW? (QUASI-CONTRACT AND RESTITUTION)

■ ■ ■

SECTION 1: NATURE AND ORIGINS OF QUASI-CONTRACT

As we discussed way back in Chapter 1, contract liability is distinguished from other forms of liability in that it is *consensual*. That is to say, a contractual obligation exists because it is voluntarily undertaken by the promisor rather than, as in the case of tort or criminal liability, imposed as a matter of societal judgment about what forms of behavior will be deemed culpable. Our legal regime has, however, devised another form of liability which is neither purely fault-based nor truly promise-based, although, for historical reasons discussed more fully below, the terminology used to describe this type of liability sounds eerily like the terminology used to describe conventional contract liability. In fact, this form of liability has come to bear the appellation of *Quasi-Contract*.

A quasi-contractual claim, which exists somewhere in-between classic contract and classic tort liability, is based neither on an express agreement nor an agreement implied-in-fact. Instead, it is a legal fiction, or an *implied-in-law* agreement, that rests on the proposition or general theory of obligation that one party should not be permitted to be enriched unjustly at the expense of a second party unless the first party makes compensation to the second party for the value of the benefit conferred. In effect, then, the cause of action for quasi-contract is based on the doctrine of *unjust enrichment*. It is a separate theory of liability (distinct from ordinary contract liability) that provides a remedy, namely, *restitution*, in circumstances where no true contract exists.

Restitution is its own area of law, with its own history, its own jurisprudence, and even its own *Restatement*. You will recall that when we considered how the law enforces a deal in Chapter 6, we looked at "restitutionary" recovery as an alternative to recovery under the contract based on either the expectation or reliance interests. Indeed, the law of restitution pertains to situations wholly unrelated to contract, such as cases involving fraud and conversion, as well as cases that arise in the more typical contractual or quasi-contractual contexts. Thus, the term restitution really has two meanings: it refers to both the substantive legal rules that embody the right of an innocent party to recover for unjust enrichment and the remedy, at law or equity, that is available to redress an unjust enrichment. For present purposes, however, what is critical is that you understand two things: (1) the formal distinction between a genuine contract (whether express or implied-in-fact) and a quasi or implied-in-law contract; and (2) the fundamentally different purposes served by these separate areas of law. To this end, consider the following explanation offered more than a hundred years ago by Professor Maine.

HENRY SUMNER MAINE, ANCIENT LAW

3rd American Ed. 332–33 (1888)

The part of Roman law which has had most extensive influence on foreign subjects of inquiry has been the law of Obligation, or, what comes nearly to the same thing, of Contract and Delict. The Romans themselves were not unaware of the offices which the copious and malleable terminology belonging to this part of their system might be made to discharge, and this is proved by their employment of the peculiar adjunct *quasi* in such expressions as Quasi–Contract and Quasi–Delict. 'Quasi,' so used, is exclusively a term of classification. It has been usual with English critics to identify the quasi-contracts with implied contracts; but this is an error, for implied contracts are true contracts, which quasi-contracts are not. In implied contracts, acts and circumstances are the symbols of the same ingredients which are symbolized, in express contracts, by words; and whether a man employs one set of symbols or the other must be a matter of indifference so far as concerns the theory of agreement. But a quasi-contract is not a contract at all. The commonest sample of the class is the relation subsisting between two persons, one of whom has paid money to the other through mistake. The law, consulting the interests of morality, imposes an obligation on the receiver to refund; but the very nature of the transaction indicates that it is not a contract, inasmuch as the convention, the most essential ingredient of contract, is wanting. This word 'quasi,' prefixed to a term of Roman law, implies that the conception to which it serves as an index is connected with the conception with which the comparison is instituted by a strong superficial analogy or resemblance. It does not denote that the two conceptions are the same, or that they belong to the same genus. On the contrary, it negatives the notion of an identity between them; but it points out that they are sufficiently similar for one to be classed as the sequel to the other, and that the phraseology taken from one department of law may be transferred to the other, and employed without violent straining, in the statement of rules which would otherwise be imperfectly expressed.

———————

In order to understand how claims for unjust enrichment came to be based on a fictional contract, it must be emphasized that early common law lawyers in seeking redress for a particular kind of action thought not in terms of *rights*, as modern lawyers tend to do, but in terms of *remedies*. This was because, in medieval England, a plaintiff seeking relief against a particular defendant was required to fit his claim into a recognized form of action or *writ*. For example, the modern law of contracts was developed through extension of the form of trespass on the case known as *special assumpsit* (literally that the defendant undertook or promised to perform a particular act).* Early on, however, assumpsit, which was really a tort-based remedy, was not available if the action of *Debt*—to recover a sum certain—more neatly fit the facts. But the older action of Debt was still subject to the ancient procedure known as "wager of law," pursuant to which a defendant could avoid liability by producing a number of professional "oath-sayers" who would swear that the defendant was telling the truth. This made the action of Debt easy for the defendant to manipulate in order to avoid a just debt. Therefore, ingenious common law judges,** desirous of providing a remedy in deserving cases, gradually began to permit actions for payment of a sum certain to be brought in assumpsit. However, to circumvent the cumbersome action of Debt, this action was known as *general assumpsit* and, unlike special assumpsit, it did not depend on the existence of a real promise or an actual contract. Instead, it rested on a promise implied in law where one party had already performed but received nothing in return from the party benefitted by that performance. For this reason, in addition to an alternative to either an action of Debt or special assumpsit, this action proved useful when the defendant had received a clear benefit from the plaintiff, but no express promise could be proved or established. In effect, general assumpsit would lie where one party had been unjustly enriched at the expense of another party because the court would indulge the fiction that the benefit was conferred by the plaintiff *at the request* of the defendant and with the attendant obligation to compensate the plaintiff for the value of the benefit conferred. In the parlance of the common law at the time, such claims were said to arise *quasi ex contractu,* and the enduring link between contract law and unjust enrichment was forged.

———————

_____

* For more on the history of the development of the writ of assumpsit, *see* A.W.B. SIMPSON, A HISTORY OF THE COMMON LAW OF CONTRACT: THE RISE OF THE ACTION OF ASSUMPSIT (1975); KEVIN M. TEEVEN, A HISTORY OF THE ANGLO-AMERICAN COMMON LAW OF CONTRACT, 27–50 (1990); James Barr Ames, *The History of Assumpsit,* 2 HARV. L. REV. 1 (1888).

** Lord Mansfield is generally credited with bringing quasi-contract into the mainstream of English common law. *See* Moses v. Macferlan, 2 Burr. 1005, 97 Eng. Rep. 676 (K.B. 1760). ("In one word, the gist of this kind of action is, that the defendant, upon the circumstances of the case, is obliged by the ties of natural justice and equity to refund the money" [paid by mistake]).

SECTION 2:   ELEMENTS OF A QUASI-CONTRACTUAL CLAIM

A.   IN GENERAL

JOHN W. WADE, *RESTITUTION FOR BENEFITS CONFERRED WITHOUT REQUEST*

19 VAND. L. REV. 1183, 1183–84, 1211–12 (1966)

I.   Introduction

The principle is now fully recognized in this country that a "person who has been unjustly enriched at the expense of another is required to make restitution to the other." This is the language of the first section of the *Restatement of Restitution*. When one person confers a benefit upon another without the latter's solicitation, the benefit received constitutes an enrichment—a windfall, so to speak. This benefit may take one of several forms. It may involve (1) transferring property to the defendant, (2) saving, preserving or improving his property, (3) rendering personal services for him, or (4) performing for him a duty imposed directly by law by his own contractual arrangements. In any of these situations there is an enrichment, and the principle quoted above comes into play if the enrichment is "unjust." When is it unjust? Obviously, it would not be so characterized if it were intended as a gift; just as obviously, the opposite is true if the plaintiff acted under legal compulsion and against his will. In making the determination, considerable weight is given to the circumstances that the benefit was not requested by the defendant.

The common law has long had a pronounced policy that benefits may not be forced upon a party against his will, so as to require him to pay for them. This idea has been forcefully expressed on a number of occasions. Said the court in the leading English case, "Liabilities are not to be forced upon people behind their backs any more than you can confer a benefit upon a man against his will." Most of the time this idea has been indicated by applying an epithet to the plaintiff. The term most frequently used is that of "volunteer." Applied to the plaintiff, particularly if it carries the adjective "mere," it has played the "kiss of death" and the sure indication that he will not be allowed to recover. Other derogatory terms used include meddler, intermeddler, interloper, mere stranger, mere impertinence. The Restatement uses the adjective "officious," which carries a somewhat more restricted connotation.[1] All of these terms embody the policy that one should not be required to pay for benefits which he did not solicit and does not desire.

. . . .

---

1.   "A person who officiously confers a benefit upon another is not entitled to restitution therefor." *Restatement, Restitution* § 2 (1937). "Officiousness means interference in the affairs of others not justified by the circumstances under which the interference takes place." *Id.*, comment a.

IV. Conclusion

The restrictions on recovery which have been spelled out at considerable length have all been presented from a negative standpoint.

It may now be possible to summarize them and present a general principle stated in a positive fashion.

Perhaps the following two sentences will prove helpful in this regard:

One who without intent to act gratuitously, confers a measurable benefit upon another, is entitled to restitution, if he affords the other an opportunity to decline the benefit or else has a reasonable excuse for failing to do so. If the other refuses to receive the benefit, he is not required to make restitution unless the actor justifiably performs for the other a duty imposed upon him by law.

QUESTIONS, NOTE, AND CONNECTIONS

Dean Wade's definition suggests that a mere volunteer, one who confers a benefit gratuitously, is not entitled to restitution under this doctrine. Why not? Can you think of some examples where this limitation would preclude a quasi-contractual recovery? Suppose, without being asked, Markell rushes out and washes Epstein's filthy car. Does Markell have a claim against Epstein for payment? Does it matter if Markell can show that the rear window was so dirty that it was becoming a safety hazard?

PATTERSON v. PATTERSON

Court of Appeals of New York
59 N.Y. 574 (1875)

[This case was filed by the executrix of the estate of William Patterson to foreclose a mortgage executed by the defendant and given to the testator to secure the payment of $1,200 due upon William Patterson's death. By way of counterclaim, the defendant raised his right to set off against this claim, among other amounts, the sum of $180.30, representing the amount paid by the defendant to the undertakers to defray the cost of the testator's funeral expenses. The trial court held in favor of the plaintiff on the basis that, under applicable statutes, the defendant could not setoff a debt arising after the death of the testator against a debt due from the defendant arising during the life of the testator. The defendant appealed].

FOLGER, JUSTICE.

* * *

I have no doubt but that the reasonable and necessary expenses of the interment of the dead body of one deceased, are a charge against his estate, though not strictly a debt due from him. The ground of this is the general right of every one to have decent burial after death; which implies the right to have his body carried, decently covered, from the place where it lies to a cemetery or other proper inclosure, and there put under ground. (*Regina v. Stewart*, 12 Ad. & Ell., 773, citing *Gilbert v. Buzzard*, 2 Hagg. Consist. R., 333; see, also, *Chapple v. Coope*, 13 M. & W., 252.) In the last case, in which an infant, a widow, was held liable on her contract for the funeral expenses of the burial of her deceased husband, it was said, that "there are many authorities which lay it down that decent Christian burial is a part of a man's own rights; and we think it not great extension of the rule to say, that it may be classed as a personal advantage and reasonably necessary to him." This right existing, the law casts upon some one the duty of seeing that it is accorded. So it would seem, at common law, that if a poor person of no estate dies, it is the duty of him under whose roof his body lies, to carry it, decently covered, to the place of burial. The husband surviving is bound to bury the corpse of his wife; and in his absence, another, a relative, with whom she has lived up to her death, having directed the funeral and paid the expense, may recover it of the husband. * * * And where the owner of some estate dies, the duty of the burial is upon the executor. * * * And our Revised Statutes (2 R. S., 71 § 16) recognize this duty, in that the executor is prohibited from any interference with the estate until after probate, except that he may discharge the funeral expenses. From this duty springs a legal obligation, and from the obligation the law implies a promise to him who, in the absence or neglect of the executor, not officiously, but in the necessity of the case, directs a burial and incurs and pays such expense thereof as is reasonable. * * * It is analogous to the duty and obligation of a father to furnish necessaries to a child, and of a husband to a wife, from which the law implies a promise to pay him who does what the father or the husband, in that respect, omits. * * *

No statutory provisions are now in mind which interpose an obstacle. Though our statute of payment of debts and legacies (2 R.S., p. 87 § 27) gives the order in which the executor shall make payment of debts against the estate, and though there is no provision there for a priority of payment of funeral expenses, it is not to be held therefrom that the common-law rule is abrogate. Those expenses are not to be treated as a debt against the estate, but as a charge upon the estate, the same as the necessary expenses of administration. * * * The expenses of probate of will precede the formal authority to the executor, but are allowed to him on an accounting. So should funeral expenses be. The decent burial of the dead is a matter in which the public have concern. It is against the public health if it do not take place at all, and against a proper public sentiment, that it should not take place with decency. * * *

Can the defendant set off these expenses in this action? His cause of action is against the plaintiff on a promise implied by law from her. He had no cause of action therefor, against the testator. As the cause of action against the defendant, arose after the death of the testator, and to the plaintiff, it appears that the two demands are mutual debts respectively due to and from defendant, and to and from the plaintiff in the same capacity. This demand may therefore be set off.

The judgment appealed from, must be modified so as to allow to the defendant, in diminution of the amount of the claim established against him, the sum of $180.30. He is also entitled to the interest thereon.

The judgment so modified, should be affirmed, without costs to either party in this court.

QUESTIONS

1. Questions about the facts of this case

   1.1. What was the relationship between William Patterson and the defendant?

   1.2. The court concludes that William Patterson's estate is liable for the costs incurred by defendant in arranging for the burial of the testator. Did William Patterson, during his life, agree to reimburse the defendant for the costs of paying Mr. Patterson's funeral expenses? Did the executrix agree to reimburse those expenses? If the answer to both questions is "no," then what were the key facts from which this obligation could be said to arise?

2. Questions about the law

   2.1. The court also concludes that the set-off sought by the defendant for funeral expenses was proper because "the two demands are mutual debts respectively due to and from the defendant, and to and from the plaintiff in the same capacity." What does this mean? If mutuality of obligation is a requirement to the right of set-off, did the court properly apply it in this case? Wasn't the defendant's debt owed to William Patterson and his claim against the estate?

   2.2. Under the trial court's reasoning, would the defendant have been able to recover for the $180.30 paid to defray funeral expenses?

B. AT THE REQUEST OF THE DEFENDANT

SCHOTT v. WESTINGHOUSE ELECTRIC CORPORATION

Supreme Court of Pennsylvania
436 Pa. 279, 259 A.2d 443 (1969)

POMEROY, J.

During the period 1962 to 1965 (the relevant times for the purpose of this case), there was in effect at Westinghouse Electric Corporation (hereinafter "Company") a formalized suggestion program under which its employees were invited to submit to the Company any suggestions they might have for increasing production and reducing costs. The question in this case is whether the Company may have become contractually obligated to one of its employees, appellant herein, by virtue of the actions of both parties pursuant to the program. This appeal is from the sustaining of preliminary objections by the Company in the nature of a demurrer. Consequently, the facts before us are confined to the appellant's complaint, as amended, and the demurrer admits for present purposes every well pleaded material fact set forth in the pleading to which it is addressed, as well as the inferences reasonably deducible therefrom. * * *

The terms of the suggestion program are set forth in the documentary exhibits attached to the complaint. In pertinent part, the basic form of the suggestion system provides as follows:

> "With a view toward increasing production and reducing costs, thereby promoting employment, the Westinghouse Electric Corporation encourages practical suggestions from employees.

> "Cash awards ranging from a minimum of $5.00 to a maximum of $15,000 will be paid for each suggestion adopted. * * *

> "Suggestions must be submitted on this form. * * * All suggestions will be passed upon as soon as possible, and suggesters will be notified as to the action taken. * * *"

Space was provided for the statement of the employee's suggestion. Beneath that space and immediately above the signature line where the employee-suggester was to sign was the following stipulation:

> "In submitting this suggestion, I agree that the decision of the local Suggestion Committee on all matters pertaining to this suggestion, my eligibility for an award, and the amount of award, if any, will be final. I further understand that if this suggestion is rejected, I have the right to reopen it within 12 months from the date of rejection, or to re-submit it as a new suggestion at any time thereafter.

> "Note: If adopted; Minimum Award—$5.00

> Maximum Award—$15,000"

In May, 1962, the appellant, an employee of the Company, submitted a suggestion that certain panels used on circuit breakers manufactured by the Company be made from fabricated heavy gauge steel rather than the material then used, cast aluminum. Appellant submitted the suggestion, as required, on the standard form with its stipulation that the decision of the Suggestion Committee should be determinative as to all matters. Thereafter, the Suggestion Committee informed the appellant in writing that his suggestion had been rejected (Exhibit C to the complaint). This communication stated that a change of the panels would necessitate large expenditures for design work, the building of models, and laboratory tests, and that these costs would more than offset any savings which might be realized from the proposed change. Appellant was informed that "If breaker re-design is started for other reasons in the future, this idea will be considered." He was also advised, in the same communication, that his suggestion could be reopened within a year or resubmitted after a year.

In September, 1963, appellant resubmitted his suggestion, again using the Company's prescribed form for his submission; in January, 1964, he was informed that the suggestion had again been rejected. In explaining its action, the Suggestion Committee cited its original reasons, adverted to further problems in the design of the panels resulting from the need to use nonmagnetic materials in the panel, and mentioned that redesign of the panels to include partial nonmagnetic materials was being undertaken as part of an independent cost reduction study.

At this point in the narrative, resort must be had to the complaint itself, as distinguished from the documentary exhibits. The complaint averred, in paragraph 8, that thereafter, probably in 1964, the Company "did adopt and utilize" the recommendations advanced by the suggestion, and the plaintiff (appellant) thereupon requested reconsideration of his suggestion. The Company apparently made such a review and communicated the results thereof to appellant in a letter of May, 1965 (Exhibit F to the complaint). This letter adverts to the Company's "application of the same basic idea [as that contained in appellant's suggestion] in a redesign" and confirms the Company's view that the reason given for the initial rejection of the suggestion in 1962 had been valid at that time. It further states the opinion of the writer (General Manager of the Switchgear Division) that "the action taken [by the Company] in 1964 changing the back plate was the result of independent action taken without knowledge of your [appellant's] suggestion," and reaffirmed the Company's refusal to make an award to appellant.

In November, 1966, appellant filed a complaint which averred that the Company had adopted the appellant's suggestion and prayed for an accounting as to the Company's savings therefrom, and damages equal to 20% thereof. The Company filed preliminary objections, on the ground that the complaint did not set forth a valid claim against the Company on which relief could be granted. In support of this conclusion the objections cited the stipulation that "the decision of the Local Suggestion Committee on all matters pertaining to this suggestion * * * will be final." The lower court in sustaining the Company's objections, found that the suggestion program of the Company was an invitation to its employees to make an offer; that the offer of the appellant was by its terms subject to acceptance or rejection by the Company through its Committees; and that the offer had been duly and consistently rejected by the Company. The court further held: "Plaintiff is bound by the statement to which he agreed that the decision of the Suggestion Committee will be final on all matters pertaining to his suggestion and his eligibility for an award unless there is fraud or deceit practiced by or an unjust enrichment inuring to the defendant and no such allegations are made in this case." Finding that no enforceable contract had been pleaded by appellant, the court sustained defendant's preliminary objections and granted plaintiff leave to amend his complaint.

Thereafter, appellant filed an amended complaint seeking damages both under a theory of contract and under a theory sounding in unjust enrichment, properly set forth in a separate count. The amended complaint alleged no new facts but charged appropriation of plaintiff's valuable idea.

The Company again filed preliminary objections, renewing its position that appellant had failed to state a cause of action sounding in contract and further asserting that no cause of action based on unjust enrichment had been set forth. The lower court (McKenna, Jr., J.) found that the amended complaint added no substantial allegation to the original complaint. Holding that appellant was bound by the adverse determinations of the Suggestion Committee, the court below sustained the objections and dismissed the amended complaint. * * *

The present appeal is from the order of the lower court dismissing appellant's amended complaint. Appellant argues that he was entitled to recover the value of his suggestion, either under a theory of performance of a unilateral contract or under a theory of unjust enrichment.

We agree with the lower court that the appellant cannot recover under a contract theory, but under the facts averred we believe the appellant has stated a cause of action in unjust enrichment. Accordingly, we are obliged to reverse and remand.

I

As we view the first cause of action, we need not decide whether the purported contract was unilateral or bilateral in nature. Whichever interpretation is adopted, it is clear that appellant agreed to abide by the decision of the Suggestion Committee on "all matters" (including the acceptableness of the suggestion itself). The Committee rejected the suggestion, and that rejection bars the appellant's recovery under his first cause of action, not because appellant was thereby made ineligible for an award under a valid contract with the Company, but rather because, in view of the Committee's action, no contract existed between the parties.
* * *

II

Appellant's alternative position is that, relying on the Company's promise in the suggestion invitation, he submitted a valuable idea to the Company in hope of securing a monetary award therefor; that the Company "adopted" or appropriated the idea to its own use and benefit; that the Company has refused to make payment to appellant therefor in accordance with the terms of the suggestion system; that in consequence appellant is entitled to the full value of the saving realized by the Company from its use of his idea. The Company responds that these are but conclusory averments and that no cause of action is set forth. * * *

Returning to the applicable law, we note that this Court has found the quasi-contractual doctrine of unjust enrichment inapplicable when the relationship between parties is founded on a written agreement or express contract. * * * But in the present case, having found that no legal contract bound the parties, it would be manifestly unjust to fail to consider appellant's claim on the ground that there might have been a contract or that the parties had attempted to enter into a contract.

Quasi-contracts, or contracts implied in law, are to be distinguished from express contracts or contracts implied in fact. "[U]nlike true contracts, quasi-contracts are not based on the apparent intention of the parties to undertake the performances in question, nor are they promises. They are obligations created by law for reasons of justice." Restatement (Second) of Contracts, § 5, comment b at 24 (Tent. Draft No. 1, 1964). See also Corbin, Contracts, § 19 (1950); * * * Quasi-contracts may be found in the absence of any expression of assent by the party to be charged and may indeed be found in spite of the party's contrary intention. * * * Consequently, the failure of the Company's Suggestion Committee to accept the appellant's suggestion is not determinative of appellant's quasi-contractual cause of action.

* * *

MR. JUSTICE ROBERTS (concurring):

I agree that appellee's preliminary objections should be dismissed and this case should be permitted to go to trial, but I do so because, in my view, appellant's complaint alleges facts which if established would prove that appellee's actions have created a contract.

* * *

I cannot accept, however, the majority's conclusion that appellant can withstand appellee's preliminary objections on an "unjust enrichment" theory. When appellant submitted his suggestion on appellee's form, in accordance with appellee's procedure, in my view he gave up any claim he might have had to unjust enrichment damages. If appellant is to recover at all, it must be within the limitations of appellee's procedure for offering suggestions. I do not believe that it is wise to become entangled in metaphysical notions of whether appellee extended an offer or an invitation to deal, and whether appellant thus tendered an acceptance or an offer. In my view it is enough to say that appellant cannot, under these circumstances, recover outside of appellee's established procedure, a procedure appellant accepted when tendering his suggestion, and thus unjust enrichment in my judgment is not appropriate.

* * *

MR. CHIEF JUSTICE BELL (dissenting):

The Majority admits there was no fraud or deceit by defendant. I am strongly opposed to the doctrine of unjust enrichment. Furthermore, even if the doctrine be judicially adopted by this Court, it cannot be applied in this case in view of the written contract which so clearly prescribes and defines, and thus limits, the rights of the parties.

————————

QUESTIONS AND NOTE

1. Questions about the facts of this case

     1.1. Did the court believe that the company's redesign of the panels was "independent action" taken without knowledge of Schott's earlier suggestion? Does it matter?

     1.2. If the reasons for the company's rejection of Schott's suggestion were valid when made, is it unjust for the company to later use that suggestion, after circumstances change, without compensating Schott?

     1.3. What is the significance of the fact that, at the time of the resubmittal of Schott's suggestion, the company acknowledged that it was undertaking an effort to redesign the panels to include partial nonmagnetic materials?

     1.4. What do you suppose Chief Justice Bell has against the doctrine of unjust enrichment?

2. Questions about the law

     2.1. Why was the dismissal of the plaintiff's breach of contract claim affirmed on appeal?

     2.2. Do you agree with Chief Justice Bell that the parties can, by their contract, preclude the possibility of a claim for restitution?

     2.3. Justice Roberts seems to believe that the existence of a valid contract would preclude a claim for restitution. Do you agree? If Justice Roberts' view had prevailed, what would Schott's argument be on remand to establish the existence of a contract?

     2.4. Note that Schott's complaint prayed for damages equal to 20 percent of the savings realized by the company for use of his suggestion, as determined by an accounting. Was that proper in view of the fact that the suggestion program promised cash awards ranging from $5 to $15,000?

3. Note

The aim of restitution is to make the defendant account for the value of the benefit conferred on the defendant. Suppose, however, that during the course of contractual negotiations, one party performs work at the request of the other, but those negotiations never ripen into an enforceable contract. If those services do not *benefit* the requesting party, can the person providing the services nevertheless bring a claim for unjust enrichment? *See Earhart v. William Low Co.*, 25 Cal.3d 503, 158 Cal. Rptr. 887, 600 P.2d 1344 (1979).

————————

C. NOT AT THE REQUEST OF THE DEFENDANT

CABLEVISION OF BRECKENRIDGE, INC. v. TANNHAUSER CONDOMINIUM ASSOCIATION

Supreme Court of Colorado
649 P.2d 1093 (1982)

LOHR, J.

We granted certiorari to review the decision of the Colorado Court of Appeals in *Cablevision of Breckenridge, Inc. v. Tannhauser Condominium Association,* * * * which reversed the judgment of the Summit County District Court awarding the plaintiff, Cablevision of Breckenridge, Inc. (Cablevision), damages for the wrongful conversion of its subscription cable service. We reverse the decision of the court of appeals and remand for reinstatement of the district court judgment.

I.

This case was tried to the district court under a stipulated set of facts which included those that follow. Cablevision is a corporation engaged in providing cable television and FM radio to its subscribers in areas where the television signals are weak or nonexistent. This is a frequently encountered problem in the vicinity of Breckenridge, Colorado, because the topography of the community and its distance from the originating broadcast stations generally result in an inability to receive a useful broadcast signal when using only the traditional antennas normally employed by individual households.

In order to provide its service, Cablevision constructed several antennas on a mountain peak near Breckenridge, by which it receives six television stations as well as FM radio. At the point of reception, the television signals are strong enough to reproduce a black and white picture, but are too weak to allow color reproduction. Consequently, the signals are fed into a "pre-amp," which magnifies their strength. The signals are then transmitted to a "head-end" building, located near the receiving antennas, where they are passed through a channel processor and mixer for the purpose of improving the clarity of the picture produced by the transmission. From this building, the signals are sent by coaxial cable to the "hub" facility in Breckenridge, and thence through distribution lines to the individual subscribers. Additional amplification of the signals is necessary as they are transmitted through the system, so amplifiers are installed along the distribution lines. Cablevision's capital investment in the transmission system is approximately $450,000.

The stipulated facts further establish that in October 1972 Cablevision entered into an oral agreement for the provision of subscription cable services with Judy Keller, who was acting on behalf of the owners of the condominium units comprising the Tannhauser I development in Breckenridge. The Tannhauser I building consisted of 33 condominium units, and each was to receive the Cablevision service. Pursuant to this agreement Cablevision installed the equipment necessary to provide its service to each of the units. This was accomplished by running a connecting line from the distribution system to an amplifier located inside Tannhauser I. The signals were then transmitted from this amplifier to individual wall plates serving each of the units. From January 1, 1972, through March 1974, Tannhauser I paid for the service to these 33 units at a specified rate per unit.

Effective May 1974, Cablevision ceased billing for service to 33 units and began billing for service to only three units. This was done at the request of Jerry White, whose status is not described in the stipulation but who apparently acted as a representative for the Tannhauser I owners. The stipulation reflects disagreement over the exact events leading to this change in service, but it is undisputed that the Cablevision amplifier inside Tannhauser I was removed; that White then substituted his own amplifier and connected it to the Cablevision line; and that, following May 1, television and FM radio service was still provided to all 33 units of Tannhauser I despite the payment to Cablevision for service to only three of those units. This state of affairs continued from May 1, 1974, to approximately December 1, 1976.

In the fall of 1974 a second building, known as Tannhauser II and comprised of 25 condominium units, was constructed near Tannhauser I. Cablevision was never requested to supply service to Tannhauser II. However, the new building was wired internally for cable television and FM radio, and in November 1974 White supervised and assisted in the installation of a cable between Tannhauser I and Tannhauser II enabling extension of the Cablevision service to each of the 25 units in Tannhauser II. Tannhauser II began receiving the Cablevision transmission approximately November 30, 1974. Cablevision subsequently discovered the unauthorized use of its transmission by Tannhauser I and II and terminated all service to the condominiums about December 1, 1976.

Thereafter, Cablevision brought the present action, naming the condominium associations for Tannhausers I and II and the owners of the individual condominium units as defendants. Cablevision's amended complaint contained eight claims for relief, including breach of contract, concealment, conversion, various claims of unjust enrichment, and a request for injunctive relief.

However, as part of the pre-trial stipulation of facts summarized above, the parties submitted for judicial resolution the following single stipulated issue:

> Have the Defendants, or any of them, breached any contract with Plaintiff, written or oral, in fact or implied, for which Plaintiff is entitled for damages, actual or punitive?

After a hearing, the trial court entered an oral ruling incorporating the parties' stipulated facts, and holding that the defendants were liable for conversion of Cablevision's service. The parties had originally provided in their stipulation that, in the event of recovery, the damages would be $12,195, plus appropriate interest. However, the defendants advised the court subsequent to entry of the stipulation that they objected to this figure, so a further hearing was held on the question of damages. The court then entered its written judgment. The court again adopted the stipulation of the parties as its findings of fact and concluded:

> The plaintiff's property and services in the furnishing of cable television is a legally protected interest for which it is entitled to charge an appropriate and lawful rate to its subscribers. The defendants, through the actions stated in the Stipulation, have converted those protected interests without fully paying for them.

Based upon the damages hearing, the court entered judgment for actual damages of $11,597.50 plus statutory interest and court costs, and denied the prayer for punitive damages. The defendants then appealed.

The court of appeals reversed. It held that the trial court erred in ruling that the defendants were liable on the basis that they converted Cablevision's property interests because, pursuant to the parties' stipulation, "the only issue before the trial court was whether any defendant breached any contract with [Cablevision]." It further held that, because the stipulation did not establish the essential elements of a contract, Cablevision had not proved its breach of contract claim. Therefore, it directed the trial court to enter judgment for the defendants.

We accepted certiorari to review the court of appeals' decision. * * * [W]e do not address these arguments because we conclude that the judgment of the trial court is supported by an alternative basis of liability raised by the stipulated issue submitted by the parties.

II.

As stipulated by the parties, the issue for decision was whether "the Defendants, or any of them, *breached any contract* with Plaintiff, written or oral, in fact or implied." (Emphasis added.) We read the mention of "implied" contracts as a reference to the doctrine of quasi-contract or unjust enrichment, under which courts imply a contract as a matter of law where necessary to avoid unjust enrichment. This interpretation is based in part upon the apparent intent of parties in distinguishing "implied contracts" and contracts "in fact," and draws further support from the inclusion of unjust enrichment claims in the complaint.

In addressing only the issue of whether the stipulated evidence established a contract in fact, the court of appeals did not consider this alternative basis of liability. We conclude that the facts of this case present an appropriate basis for application of the doctrine of unjust enrichment, and reverse the decision of the court of appeals for that reason.

To recover under a theory of quasi-contract or unjust enrichment, a plaintiff must show (1) that a benefit was conferred on the defendant by the plaintiff, (2) that the benefit was appreciated by the defendant, and (3) that the benefit was accepted by the defendant under such circumstances that it would be inequitable for it to be retained without payment of its value. * * * Application of the doctrine does not depend upon the existence of a contract, express or implied in fact, but on the need to avoid unjust enrichment of the defendant notwithstanding the absence of an actual agreement to pay for the benefit conferred. * * * The scope of this remedy is broad, cutting across both contract and tort law, with its application guided by the underlying principle of avoiding the unjust enrichment of one party at the expense of another. 1 G. Palmer, *The Law of Restitution* § 1.1 (1978); 66 *Am. Jur. 2d Restitution and Implied Contracts*, *supra*, § 11.

In the present case, we conclude that a benefit was conferred upon the defendants by Cablevision and that the defendants appreciated this benefit. The defendants' initial payment for this service in connection with the 33 Tannhauser I condominium units and their continued payment for service to three of those units amply demonstrate both the beneficial service provided by Cablevision and the appreciation of that service by the defendants. Instructive in this regard is the broad definition of benefit contained in the *Restatement of Restitution* § 1, comment b (1937):

> A person confers a benefit upon another if he gives to the other possession of or some other interest in money, land, chattels, or choses in action, performs services beneficial to or at the request of the other, satisfies a debt or a duty of the other, or in any way adds to the other's security or advantage. He confers a benefit not only where he adds to the property of another, but also where he saves the other from expense or loss. The word "benefit," therefore, denotes any form of advantage.

We also conclude that the defendants have retained this service under such circumstances that it would be inequitable to allow its use without payment for its value. The stipulated facts demonstrate that Cablevision never intended to provide its service to all of Tannhausers I and II in exchange for payment in connection with only three units. Indeed, upon discovery of the unauthorized use of its signals, Cablevision terminated all service to the defendants. Further, the defendants were not innocent or unwilling recipients of this benefit, but actively facilitated its provision.

    * * *

The defendants have accepted a service from Cablevision that is customarily paid for and, in fact, was initially paid for by these defendants. The defendants were active participants in obtaining this benefit from Cablevision, and, based on the initial agreement to serve Tannhauser I, their representatives must have acted with the knowledge that Cablevision expected compensation for each Tannhauser unit receiving the Cablevision transmission. Under these facts, restitution is appropriate to avoid unjust enrichment to the defendants. * * *

The damages awarded were based upon the rate prescribed in Cablevision's franchise from Breckenridge, which correspond to the rate paid for the three Tannhauser I units during the period of unauthorized use of the Cablevision signals. This was an appropriate measure of the benefit conferred upon the defendants and the amount of restitution due.

* * *

We reverse the decision of the court of appeals and return the case to that court for remand to the trial court with directions to enter judgment in accordance with the views expressed in this opinion.

QUESTIONS

1. Questions about the facts of this case
   1.1. Why did Cablevision's lawyer agree in the pre-trial stipulation that the only issue to be resolved at trial was the issue of breach of contract? Was that a mistake? Was it malpractice?
   1.2. Did the residents of the Tannhauser units know they were getting for free a service that other people pay for? Was that fact important to the court? Should it matter? If an ATM malfunctions and gives you twice as much cash as you requested, without charging your account, is it a good defense to the bank's unjust enrichment claim if you can show that you were unaware of the error?
   1.3. How important was the fact that the Tannhauser I units had received and paid for cable service for over two years?
2. Questions about the law
   2.1. What was the key difference in the interpretation given to the parties' pre-trial stipulation by the Colorado Court of Appeals and the Colorado Supreme Court? Did the Colorado Supreme Court conclude that there had been a breach of contract in the traditional sense?
   2.2. The court awarded damages based on the rate prescribed in Cablevision's franchise from the City of Breckenridge* during the period of the unauthorized use. Was that appropriate? If you represented the defendants, what kind of evidence would you have sought to introduce to justify a lesser recovery?

WATTS v. WATTS

Supreme Court of Wisconsin
137 Wis.2d 506, 405 N.W.2d 303 (1987)

ABRAHAMSON, J.

This is an appeal from a judgment of the circuit court for Dane County, William D. Byrne, Judge, dismissing Sue Ann Watts' amended

---

* Actually, Breckenridge fancies itself (even if unofficially) a "kingdom," not a city, and, as far as we know, the only such governmental entity in the country. But that's another story.

complaint, pursuant to sec. 802.06(2)(f), Stats. 1985–86, for failure to state a claim upon which relief may be granted. * * *

The case involves a dispute between Sue Ann Evans Watts, the plaintiff, and James Watts, the defendant, over their respective interests in property accumulated during their nonmarital cohabitation relationship which spanned 12 years and produced two children. The case presents an issue of first impression and comes to this court at the pleading stage of the case, before trial and before the facts have been determined.

* * *

We test the sufficiency of the plaintiff's amended complaint by first setting forth the facts asserted in the complaint and then analyzing each of the five legal theories upon which the plaintiff rests her claim for relief.

I.

The plaintiff commenced this action in 1982. The plaintiff's amended complaint alleges the following facts, which for purposes of this appeal must be accepted as true. The plaintiff and the defendant met in 1967, when she was 19 years old, was living with her parents and was working full time as a nurse's aide in preparation for a nursing career. Shortly after the parties met, the defendant persuaded the plaintiff to move into an apartment paid for by him and to quit her job. According to the amended complaint, the defendant "indicated" to the plaintiff that he would provide for her.

Early in 1969, the parties began living together in a "marriage-like" relationship, holding themselves out to the public as husband and wife. The plaintiff assumed the defendant's surname as her own. Subsequently, she gave birth to two children who were also given the defendant's surname. The parties filed joint income tax returns and maintained joint bank accounts asserting that they were husband and wife. The defendant insured the plaintiff as his wife on his medical insurance policy. He also took out a life insurance policy on her as his wife, naming himself as the beneficiary. The parties purchased real and personal property as husband and wife. The plaintiff executed documents and obligated herself on promissory notes to lending institutions as the defendant's wife.

During their relationship, the plaintiff contributed childcare and homemaking services, including cleaning, cooking, laundering, shopping, running errands, and maintaining the grounds surrounding the parties' home. Additionally, the plaintiff contributed personal property to the relationship which she owned at the beginning of the relationship or acquired through gifts or purchases during the relationship. She served as hostess for the defendant for social and business-related events. The amended complaint further asserts that periodically, between 1969 and

1975, the plaintiff cooked and cleaned for the defendant and his employees while his business, a landscaping service, was building and landscaping a golf course.

From 1973 to 1976, the plaintiff worked 20–25 hours per week at the defendant's office, performing duties as a receptionist, typist, and assistant book-keeper. From 1976 to 1981, the plaintiff worked 40–60 hours per week at a business she started with the defendant's sister-in-law, then continued and managed herself after the dissolution of that partnership. The plaintiff further alleges that in 1981 the defendant made their relationship so intolerable that she was forced to move from their home and their relationship was irretrievably broken. Subsequently, the defendant barred the plaintiff from returning to her business.

The plaintiff alleges that during the parties' relationship, and because of her domestic and business contributions, the business and personal wealth of the couple increased. Furthermore, the plaintiff alleges that she never received any compensation for these contributions to the relationship and that the defendant indicated to the plaintiff both orally and through his conduct that he considered her to be his wife and that she would share equally in the increased wealth.

The plaintiff asserts that since the breakdown of the relationship the defendant has refused to share equally with her the wealth accumulated through their joint efforts or to compensate her in any way for her contributions to the relationship.

* * *

The plaintiff's fourth theory of recovery involves unjust enrichment. Essentially, she alleges that the defendant accepted and retained the benefit of services she provided knowing that she expected to share equally in the wealth accumulated during their relationship. She argues that it is unfair for the defendant to retain all the assets they accumulated under these circumstances and that a constructive trust should be imposed on the property as a result of the defendant's unjust enrichment. In his brief, the defendant does not attack specifically either the legal theory or the factual allegations made by the plaintiff.

Unlike claims for breach of an express or implied in fact contract, a claim of unjust enrichment does not arise out of an agreement entered into by the parties. Rather, an action for recovery based upon unjust enrichment is grounded on the moral principle that one who has received a benefit has a duty to make restitution where retaining such a benefit would be unjust. * * *

Because no express or implied in fact agreement exists between the parties, recovery based upon unjust enrichment is sometimes referred to as "quasi contract," or contract "implied in law" rather than "implied in fact." Quasi contracts are obligations created by law to prevent injustice.
* * *

In Wisconsin, an action for unjust enrichment, or quasi contract, is based upon proof of three elements: (1) a benefit conferred on the defendant by the plaintiff, (2) appreciation or knowledge by the defendant of the benefit, and (3) acceptance or retention of the benefit by the defendant under circumstances making it inequitable for the defendant to retain the benefit. * * *

The plaintiff has cited no cases directly supporting actions in unjust enrichment by unmarried cohabitants, and the defendant provides no authority against it. * * *

As part of his general argument, the defendant claims that the court should leave the parties to an illicit relationship such as the one in this case essentially as they are found, providing no relief at all to either party. * * *

As we have discussed previously, allowing no relief at all to one party in a so-called "illicit" relationship effectively provides total relief to the other, by leaving that party owner of all the assets acquired through the efforts of both. Yet it cannot seriously be argued that the party retaining all the assets is less "guilty" than the other. Such a result is contrary to the principles of equity. Many courts have held, and we now so hold, that unmarried cohabitants may raise claims based upon unjust enrichment following the termination of their relationships where one of the parties attempts to retain an unreasonable amount of the property acquired through the efforts of both.

In this case, the plaintiff alleges that she contributed both property and services to the parties' relationship. She claims that because of these contributions the parties' assets increased, but that she was never compensated for her contributions. She further alleges that the defendant, knowing that the plaintiff expected to share in the property accumulated, "accepted the services rendered to him by the plaintiff" and that it would be unfair under the circumstances to allow him to retain everything while she receives nothing. We conclude that the facts alleged are sufficient to state a claim for recovery based upon unjust enrichment.

As part of the plaintiff's unjust enrichment claim, she has asked that a constructive trust be imposed on the assets that the defendant acquired during their relationship. A constructive trust is an equitable device created by law to prevent unjust enrichment. * * * To state a claim on the theory of constructive trust the complaint must state facts sufficient to show (1) unjust enrichment and (2) abuse of a confidential relationship or some other form of unconscionable conduct. The latter element can be inferred from allegations in the complaint which show, for example, a family relationship, a close personal relationship, or the parties' mutual trust. These facts are alleged in this complaint or may be inferred. * * * Therefore, we hold that if the plaintiff can prove the elements of unjust enrichment to the satisfaction of the circuit court, she will be entitled to demonstrate further that a constructive trust should be imposed as a remedy.

* * *

PROBLEM: *THE GOOD SAMARITAN AND THE GREEDY DOCTOR*

One day, Epstein, an elderly man, was crossing the street when he was hit by a car. Markell, an attorney who had dropped out of medical school several years earlier, witnessed the accident and rushed to Epstein's aid. Able to draw on his prior medical training, Markell saved Epstein's life. Thereafter, he submitted a bill to Epstein for the reasonable value of his services. Epstein balked at paying, so Markell now brought his legal training to bear and filed suit. Should Markell recover? Would it make a difference if Epstein had not survived the accident? How about if Markell were a real doctor? How about if the basis for Epstein's refusal to pay is his strong religious convictions against seeking medical intervention under any circumstances? *See In re Crisan's Estate*, 362 Mich. 569, 107 N.W.2d 907 (1961).

D.   AT THE REQUEST OF A THIRD PARTY

FLOORING SYSTEMS, INC. v. RADISSON GROUP, INC.

Supreme Court of Arizona
160 Ariz. 224, 772 P.2d 578 (1989)

CORCORAN, JUSTICE.

Plaintiff Flooring Systems, Inc. appeals from summary judgment entered in favor of defendants Radisson Group, Inc. and CSA, Inc. We granted review to consider whether summary judgment was properly granted on Flooring's unjust enrichment claim. * * *

Facts

In July 1985, CSA, as Radisson's agent, invited Flooring to bid on carpeting work for the Scottsdale Radisson Resort. Flooring submitted a bid, which CSA accepted in August 1985.

In October 1985, Radisson chose Five Star Services, Inc. as the general contractor for the renovations and an agreement was executed. Five Star then entered into a subcontract agreement with Flooring for the same carpeting work included in Flooring's bid that CSA accepted. Neither Radisson nor CSA was a party to this subcontract agreement. During renovation, Flooring submitted all payment requests to Five Star, not Radisson.

Although Flooring completed its work, Five Star failed to pay Flooring the full amount due under the subcontract. Because of Five Star's default,

Radisson withheld approximately $25,000 due under its general contract with Five Star. Section 6.2 of Radisson's general contract with Five Star permitted Radisson to withhold final payment until Five Star satisfied "all known indebtedness" connected with the work.

Flooring sued Radisson, CSA and Five Star to recover the amount due. Five Star later filed for bankruptcy and was dismissed as a party.

Procedure and Issue

In its complaint, Flooring alleged breach of contract and unjust enrichment. Radisson and CSA moved for summary judgment, arguing that, * * * the existence of a subcontract agreement between Five Star and Flooring precluded any recovery from Radisson and CSA under an unjust enrichment theory. The trial court granted summary judgment against Flooring. The court of appeals affirmed. * * *

Discussion

Flooring contends that it is entitled to recover on its unjust enrichment claim because it has sold and installed $59,000 worth of carpet, and Radisson has paid no one for at least $25,000 of it. In response, Radisson and CSA rely on *Stratton v. Inspiration Consol. Copper Co.*, 140 Ariz. 528, 683 P.2d 327 (App.1984), and *Advance Leasing & Crane Co. v. Del E. Webb Corp.*, 117 Ariz. 451, 573 P.2d 525 (App.1977).

In *Stratton*, the defendant hired a general contractor to do remodeling. The general contractor subcontracted the painting work to the plaintiff. Defendant approved the general contractor's hiring of plaintiff and inspected the work from time to time, but no contract existed between defendant and plaintiff. Defendant fully paid the general contractor pursuant to the contract and later changed orders, but the general contractor did not pay plaintiff. Attempting to recover from defendant, plaintiff filed a mechanic's lien and sued to foreclose on defendant's property. The complaint also alleged unjust enrichment.

The trial court granted summary judgment in defendant's favor. The court of appeals affirmed, stating that "the doctrine of unjust enrichment has no application to the owner where an explicit contract exists between the subcontractor and the prime contractor." 140 Ariz. at 531, 683 P.2d at 330.

The *Stratton* court relied on *Advance Leasing*, in which the court of appeals also held that a contract between a general contractor and a subcontractor precluded recovery by the subcontractor against the owner. 117 Ariz. at 452, 573 P.2d at 526. In so holding, the court indicated its agreement with *Restatement of Restitution* § 110 (1937), which states:

§ 110 Restitution from Beneficiary of a Contract with Third Person Who Has Failed to Perform.

A person who has conferred a benefit upon another as the performance of a contract with a third person is not entitled to restitution from the other merely because of the failure of performance by the third person.

The facts in *Advance Leasing* were similar to those in *Stratton*: no contract existed between the owner and the subcontractor and, although the owner fully paid the general contractor, the general contractor failed to pay the subcontractor.

In support of its position, Flooring relies on *Commercial Cornice & Millwork, Inc. v. Camel Constr. Serv. Corp.,* 154 Ariz. 34, 739 P.2d 1351 (App.1987), and *Costanzo v. Stewart,* 9 Ariz. App. 430, 453 P.2d 526 (1969). The plaintiff in *Commercial Cornice,* a subcontractor, alleged that the owner had agreed to pay the full amount due under the contract between plaintiff and the general contractor. In fact, the owner had paid a portion of the amount due, but neither the owner nor the general contractor paid the remainder. The trial court granted the owner's motion to dismiss for failure to state a claim because of plaintiff's contract with the general contractor.

The court of appeals held that dismissal was inappropriate, despite the existence of the contract between the subcontractor and the general contractor. The court distinguished *Stratton* and *Advance Leasing* by noting that in both cases the owner had fully paid the general contractor, and thus was not unjustly enriched.

The owner in *Costanzo* had assured the subcontractor that "the money for the job was in escrow and that he would write a check to him and [the general contractor] when the job was finished. * * *" 9 Ariz. App. at 431, 453 P.2d at 527. The subcontractor completed the job, but the bank did not honor the general contractor's check to him. In permitting the subcontractor to recover from the owner on an unjust enrichment claim, the court of appeals commented, "Costanzo [the owner] has paid no one anything for the work done." 9 Ariz. App. at 431, 453 P.2d at 527, citing *Restatement of Restitution* § 40, comment d (1937),[1] the court stated:

> The trial court found, and the testimony shows, that defendant [the owner] knew plaintiff [the subcontractor] was concerned about his payment and he assured him escrow arrangements had been made. These facts establish a good case for restitution. 9 Ariz. App. at 432–33, 453 P.2d at 528–29.

Neither party cites our decision in *Murdock–Bryant Constr., Inc. v. Pearson,* 146 Ariz. 48, 703 P.2d 1197 (1985). In that case, we held that a general contractor's joint venturers were liable for benefits received from a subcontractor, even though they became joint venturers after the general contractor had contracted with the subcontractor. We stated that

---

1. Restatement of Restitution § 40, comment d (1937) provides:

[W]here a person accepts services from another, having reason to know that the other is under a belief that the recipient or a third person has promised compensation or is otherwise under a duty to pay for them * * * the recipient is liable for the reasonable value of the services irrespective of their value to him.

"a party may be liable to make restitution for benefits received, even though he has committed no tort and is not contractually obligated to the plaintiff." 146 Ariz. at 53, 703 P.2d at 1202. We set forth the following analysis to be used in deciding unjust enrichment claims:

> In determining whether it would be unjust to allow the retention of benefits without compensation, a court need not find that the defendant intended to compensate the plaintiff for the services rendered or that the plaintiff intended that the defendant be the party to make compensation. This is because the duty to compensate for unjust enrichment is an obligation implied by law without reference to the intention of the parties. 1 S. Williston, Contracts § 3A at 13 (3rd ed. 1957). What is important is that it be shown that it was not intended or expected that the services be rendered or the benefit conferred gratuitously, and that the benefit was not "conferred officiously."

146 Ariz. at 54, 703 P.2d at 1203, *quoting Pyeatte v. Pyeatte,* 135 Ariz. 346, 353, 661 P.2d 196, 203 (App.1982). We explained that the subcontractor's contract with the general contractor

> has importance in considering [the] claim for unjust enrichment because it both evidences [plaintiff's] expectation of compensation and the circumstances which make it unjust to allow [defendant] to retain the benefits.

Id.

Using the above analysis, we find that Radisson and CSA were not entitled as a matter of law to prevail on Flooring's unjust enrichment claim. Flooring clearly did not intend to provide carpeting work gratuitously or officiously; its contract with Five Star evinces its intent to be paid for its services. Although Flooring has completed its work, it has not been paid fully for its services. CSA invited Flooring to bid on the job and accepted Flooring's bid. Radisson obviously knew that Flooring had not been paid and on that basis Radisson withheld final payment from Five Star. Under these circumstances, to permit Radisson and CSA to retain the full benefit of Flooring's work at Flooring's expense may be unjust. We therefore hold that summary judgment in favor of Radisson and CSA on this issue was improper.

Radisson argues that it is merely protecting itself from having to pay an amount in excess of that contracted for, should other subcontractors on the remodeling job also seek payment, and that it will pay the approximately $25,000 retained to Five Star and/or its creditors after the court enters a final, non-appealable judgment in its favor. Radisson may have a remedy through interpleader, requiring all parties with potential claims to the retained funds to bring their claims before a single court for resolution. However, Radisson may not merely retain the money, making promises of disbursement at some future time.

CONCLUSION

We hold that summary judgment was improperly granted on Flooring's unjust enrichment claim and therefore reverse the trial court's judgment on that issue, as well as the trial court's award of attorneys' fees to Radisson and CSA. * * * We vacate that portion of the opinion that is inconsistent with this opinion, including the award of attorneys' fees to Radisson and CSA, and remand the case to the trial court for proceedings consistent with this opinion.

* * *

QUESTIONS AND NOTE

1. Questions about the facts of this case

    1.1. How important in this case was the fact that CSA had solicited Flooring Systems' original bid for the carpeting work?

    1.2. How important was it to the decision in *Flooring Systems* that Radisson had withheld a portion of the contract price due to the general contractor, Five Star Services?

2. Questions about the law

    2.1. Is the court saying that it is always unjust for an owner to retain the benefits of a subcontractor's work without paying?

    2.2. On remand, should Flooring Systems' recovery be limited to the amount withheld ($25,000), even though its claim was for a greater amount ($59,000)? If so, what about other unpaid subcontractors who come along later; are they just out of luck? If not, what should Radisson do? Will the interpleader technique suggested by the court be a viable approach?

3. Note

    In most states, subcontractors, suppliers, and laborers who work on a construction project are protected by statutory mechanic's liens. These statutes differ considerably from state to state in terms of scope and procedure. Generally speaking, however, they allow unpaid suppliers of goods and services on the project to file a *lien* against the owner's property for the amount they are owed by the general contractor. A lien is a charge against the property rather than an *in personam* claim against the owner. Ultimately, the lien must be satisfied through a judicial foreclosure proceeding in which the property is auctioned to the highest bidder and the lienholder is paid with the proceeds. In the typical situation, the owner will already have paid the general contractor the full contract price. However, if the general contractor is dishonest or insolvent, it will not always make payment under its subcontracts with laborers and suppliers, thus giving rise to their lien claims. To avoid the loss of her property, obviously the owner will have to pay the lien. This means the owner will end up having paid twice for the same work and will be left only with what often amounts to a worthless claim against the general contractor. Knowing how these mechanic's liens work, why didn't Flooring Systems seek to enforce a lien against Radisson rather than suing for breach of contract and unjust enrichment? If you are contract-ing for a major renovation on your house, what steps might you take to ensure that the property does not later become subject to such liens?

PROBLEM ON THIRD PARTY BENEFITS

Ponoroff retained Epstein, attorney-at-law, to pursue a claim against the Great South Health Network, Ponoroff's health insurer, for failing to pay expenses incurred by Ponoroff at the Tulane Medical Center ("TMC"). As a result of Epstein's adroit lawyering skills, Great South finally capitulated and agreed to pay the disputed charges. Thereupon, Epstein sued TMC claiming that the latter benefited from his services by virtue of receiving a payment for services from Ponoroff's insurer that Ponoroff never would have paid out of his own pocket. What result? *See generally Lynch v. Deaconess Medical Center,* 113 Wash.2d 162, 776 P.2d 681 (1989).

E. BREACH OF FIDUCIARY DUTY

GEORGE E. PALMER, LAW OF RESTITUTION
§ 1 at 2 (1978)

Restitution based upon unjust enrichment cuts across many branches of the law, including contract, tort, and fiduciary relationship, but it also occupies much territory that is its sole preserve.

WIENER v. LAZARD FRERES & CO.

Supreme Court of New York, Appellate Division
241 A.D.2d 114, 672 N.Y.S.2d 8 (1998)

Milonas, J. P.

At issue in this action is the nature of the relationship between plaintiffs and the Lazard defendants (hereinafter collectively referred to as Lazard) in the context of plaintiffs' efforts to repurchase from the mort-gagee bank a building on whose mortgage plaintiffs had defaulted. Plain-tiffs are partners of 1500 Realty, which owned an office building at 1500 Broadway. In the spring of 1994, the partnership defaulted on the build-ing's mortgage held by Crossland Federal Savings Bank and filed for bankruptcy pursuant to chapter 11 of the Bankruptcy Code (11 USC). In April 1995, plaintiffs and Crossland entered into an agreement by which Crossland would release plaintiffs from the limited personal guaranty executed in connection with the mortgage in exchange for certain pay-ments as well as plaintiffs' cooperation in transferring the property to the bank. Two months later, a reorganization plan was approved in the bankruptcy proceeding, whereby the property was to be transferred to Crossland or its designee.

However, both prior to and after defaulting on the mortgage, plaintiffs were engaged in an effort to raise sufficient funds to enable them to settle with Crossland and retain ownership of the building. Their intent was to secure Crossland's consent to a transfer of the building to a new entity under plaintiffs' ownership and control, free and clear of the original $75 million mortgage, for a price in the $40 million to $60 million range. To this end, plaintiffs made preliminary arrangements with Credit Lyonnais for a first mortgage in the amount of up to $30 million; they then initiated contact with Lazard to secure a second mortgage for the balance of the purchase price. By letter dated December 22, 1993, Lazard proposed extending an interim first mortgage loan in the amount of $50 million to $55 million, to be replaced within a year by financing from an outside lender in the $35 million to $50 million range, with Lazard retaining a subordinated mortgage of $15 million to $17 million.

Plaintiffs decided to proceed with Lazard's proposal and to work with Lazard in dealing with Crossland. Plaintiffs and Lazard executed a commitment letter dated September 16, 1994, pursuant to which Lazard, as lender, agreed to provide $45 million as interim financing for the purchase or refinancing of the Crossland mortgage, in return for a $300,000 application fee. Lazard was given the exclusive right to provide the financing during an "exclusive period," as defined in the letter, unless it elected earlier not to proceed with the loan.

In connection with Lazard's due diligence under this commitment letter, plaintiffs were to provide Lazard with information regarding the financial history, physical condition and all other relevant data in their possession as owners of the property. Plaintiffs considered this information highly confidential and refused to disclose it until after a formal agreement was executed. It was, and remains, plaintiffs' contention that, as owner of the property, their detailed knowledge of every aspect of the building's operation—from the specifics of its construction and safety-related conditions to negotiations with tenants and labor unions—placed them in a uniquely advantageous position in terms of making the best (i.e., the highest) offer to Crossland. Once the commitment letter was executed, plaintiffs provided this information to Lazard, which reviewed it and arranged for the necessary financial and environmental audits of the property.

By letter dated November 16, 1994, Lazard indicated that it was prepared to go ahead with the interim financing described and asked plaintiffs to sign an "agreement to proceed" under which they would pay a $400,000 deposit by December 1, 1994. This agreement was never signed, however, because Crossland would not agree to a transaction at the price specified in the commitment letter; Crossland also insisted that any agreement be made within the context of the then-pending bankruptcy proceeding, whereby Crossland would become the owner. At this point, according to plaintiffs, the parties agreed that Anthony Meyer, a Lazard executive, would take over the negotiations with Crossland on behalf of plaintiffs, while the latter would attempt to finalize a reorganization plan and resolve their obligations under the personal guaranty executed in conjunction with the Crossland mortgage.

Thus, according to plaintiffs, as of December 1994 through August 1995, they believed that Lazard was actively negotiating with Crossland on their behalf to effect the purchase of the property, with the financing to be provided by a Lazard affiliate and/or Credit Lyonnais. Pursuant to their understanding to this effect, plaintiffs went ahead and reached an agreement with Crossland on the reorganization plan, by which 1500 Realty would transfer the property to Crossland or its designee in exchange for the settlement of plaintiffs' personal guaranty.

Apparently, however, unbeknownst to plaintiffs and contrary to the agreements just described, Lazard decided not to proceed with the plan contemplated in the commitment letter and instead entered into a relationship with defendant Zapco that culminated in Zapco's acquisition of the property from Crossland on terms similar to those Lazard was ostensibly negotiating on behalf of plaintiffs. Zapco's August 1995 contract to purchase the property for $55 million under the reorganization plan was based on financing provided by Lazard and Credit Lyonnais on terms similar to those proposed for plaintiffs.

According to plaintiffs, Lazard not only worked with Zapco to this end while Lazard was supposedly working on plaintiffs' behalf, but also shared with Zapco the confidential information plaintiffs had provided regarding the property's operation, thus enabling Zapco to make an offer that would be acceptable to Crossland—and one that was comparable to plaintiffs' intended offer. Plaintiffs claim that Lazard's dealings with Zapco constituted a gross violation of ethical standards applicable to investment bankers and advisors as well as a clear breach of fiduciary duty.

Plaintiffs' original complaint alleged causes of action for unjust enrichment and breach of fiduciary duty. Defendants moved to dismiss on the grounds that a defense was based on documentary evidence that plaintiffs had failed to state a cause of action and that the complaint failed to set forth in sufficient detail the alleged breach of fiduciary duty. Plaintiffs thereafter served an amended complaint, amplifying the factual allegations underlying their claims and adding the claim of unfair competition based on the misappropriation of plaintiffs' trade secrets, the building's operating data. Construing the dismissal motions as against the amended complaint at defendants' request, the court concluded that plaintiffs had failed to state a cause of action against the Lazard defendants or Zapco and dismissed the complaint. We disagree. Accepting the allegations as true and according them every favorable inference, we find that plaintiffs have sufficiently stated causes of action against the Lazard defendants for breach of fiduciary duty and for unjust enrichment as to the $300,000 application fee.

The Unjust Enrichment Claims

A cause of action for unjust enrichment is stated where "plaintiffs have properly asserted that a benefit was bestowed * * * by plaintiffs and that defendants will obtain such benefit without adequately compensating plaintiffs therefor" (*Tarrytown House Condominiums v. Hainje,* 161 AD2d 310, 313). Where defendants have reaped such benefit, equity and good conscience require that they make restitution. In dismissing the unjust enrichment claims, the court found that plaintiffs had failed to show how defendants had been enriched or that any enrichment had been at plaintiffs' expense. According to the court, plaintiffs did no more than allege that Lazard received a benefit from them (the application fee) as well as benefits from Zapco (fees, equity interest and future profits). The court further found that the Zapco deal was not made "at plaintiffs' expense" because Crossland would never have concluded a deal with plaintiffs under any circumstances; thus, plaintiffs were never in a position to have made such a deal for themselves.

As plaintiffs correctly argue in the first instance, the court, in reaching these conclusions on motions to dismiss, made improper findings of fact. It is well established that, on such a motion, the pleadings must be liberally construed and the facts alleged accepted as true; the court must determine "only whether the facts as alleged fit within any cognizable legal theory" * * *

Here, while the court determined that Crossland would never have sold the property to plaintiffs, the pleadings only refer to Crossland's unwillingness to sell to plaintiffs at the $45 million price specified in the commitment letter. According to plaintiffs' allegations, once it became clear that this price was not acceptable, Crossland continued to negotiate with plaintiffs, with Meyer now conducting the negotiations on plaintiffs' behalf. Thus, the court erred in dismissing the unjust enrichment claims on this ground.

With respect to the benefit bestowed on defendants, the receipt of a benefit alone, pursuant to the standard set forth above, is insufficient to establish a cause of action for unjust enrichment * * * Here, having been paid $300,000, defendants did not fulfill the terms of their agreement to work to secure a deal for plaintiffs but instead secured a deal for Zapco, using plaintiffs' confidential information. Defendants argue that, as to the $300,000 fee, plaintiffs are precluded from asserting that their payment of this fee constituted unjust enrichment when, in the commitment letter, plaintiffs specifically agreed that the fee "shall be deemed fully earned by us [Lazard]." According to Lazard, plaintiffs thereby acknowledged that the fee had been earned—that Lazard had an absolute right to it—and therefore cannot now claim to the contrary. In making this argument, defendants insist on too literal a reading of the phrase. Indeed, the language establishes to the contrary that the fee has not actually been earned at all; it is "deemed" earned, i.e., it is a nonrefundable sum paid pursuant to the parties' understanding as to what Lazard will do on plaintiffs' behalf. Thus, plaintiffs may claim that a benefit ($300,000) was bestowed upon Lazard, for which Lazard has not adequately compensated plaintiffs (in that it abandoned its efforts on plaintiffs' behalf and secured a deal for Zapco instead). As to this benefit, the cause of action for unjust enrichment should not have been dismissed.

The remaining benefits alleged by plaintiffs, consisting of whatever flowed from the Crossland–Zapco deal to Lazard—fees paid and any equity interest or profits to be paid in the future—cannot be said to be benefits bestowed on defendants for which plaintiffs should have been compensated or to which plaintiffs were entitled. Thus, to the extent the unjust enrichment claims were based on these benefits, they were properly dismissed.

The Breach of Fiduciary Duty Claim

[The court also reinstated the plaintiffs' breach of fiduciary duty claim against the Lazard defendants.]

* * *

SECTION 3: PROMISSORY RESTITUTION

Webb v. McGowin

In *Webb, supra,* at 274, the Alabama Court of Appeals recognized, and the Alabama Supreme Court affirmed that an exception to the general rule that past consideration is not good consideration exists when the promise is made in recognition of an antecedent benefit conferred on the defendant by the plaintiff. As we saw, the so-called "material benefit rule" is now codified in § 86 of the *Restatement (Second) of Contracts.* Take a moment to review § 86 again. It sets forth the elements that must be established in order for a party to recover on a promise even though the benefit which induced the promise occurred before it was made. Do these elements sound familiar? In fact, do they even sound a little bit like the elements for recovery under quasi-contract? The similarity is no accident. There is unquestionably a relationship between the material benefit rule and the doctrine of unjust enrichment. Consider whether, if McGowin had not made the promise to pay Webb $15 every two weeks, Webb could have succeeded in an action for unjust enrichment? Clearly, the benefit conferred was material; McGowin's life, and the exigency of the situation would excuse Webb's failure to give McGowin the opportunity to deny the benefit. So far so good. But was there really an expectation of compensation on Webb's part? Probably not; the act was gratuitous. However, when you add to the mix McGowin's subsequent decision to agree to pay a reasonable amount in recognition of the benefit conferred, the case for enforcement becomes sufficiently compelling, or so the argument goes, to justify the case for enforcement. Professor (later, Judge) Robert Braucher, the first Reporter for the *Restatement (Second) of Contracts*, in commenting on an earlier draft of § 86, stated that the section fairly "bristles with nonspecific concepts." Do you agree? At the same time, however, he also noted that the provision "seeks to draw a distinction between the cases involving moral obligation based on gratitude and sentiment and those cases which are on the borderline of quasi-contract. * * *" Braucher, *Freedom of Contract and the Second Restatement*, 78 YALE L.J. 598, 605 (1969).

Recall in Chapter 3 we examined two other cases (*Harrington v. Taylor*, *supra*, at 278, and *Mills v. Wyman*, *supra*, at 279), in both of which the court rejected the argument that past consideration creates a moral obligation sufficient to support enforcement of a subsequent promise of payment. Instead of asserting the enforceability of the actual promises made by the defendants in *Harrington* and *Mills*, what if the plaintiffs in those cases had brought a claim for restitution based on unjust enrichment? Would either or both of them have prevailed? Why did the court in *Mills* stress the age of the defendant's son? If the son had been a minor or a dependent how would that have helped the case for recovery for breach of contract? For unjust enrichment?

Look again at the elements of § 86, specifically subsection (2), which provides that the promise is *not* binding if (a) the promisee conferred the benefit as a *gift*, or (b) the promisor has not been unjustly enriched. Can an act be gratuitous and still not intended as a gift? We think so. Was Webb making a gift when he decided to fall with the 75–pound pine block? The other limitation in § 86(2) is that the promise will not be enforced to the extent that its value is disproportionate to the benefit. Is there a link to the doctrine of unjust enrichment here, too? In answering that question for yourself, consider the material from Chapter 6 dealing with how to measure the value of the restituionary interest.

SECTION 4:   OTHER REMEDIES
FOR UNJUST ENRICHMENT

The idea behind quasi-contract is to prevent the inequitable enrichment of one party at the expense of the other. Thus, the benefit conferred must be restored if equity is to be done. That is to say, the defendant must make *restitution*. But sometimes that can be easier said than done, particularly when the benefit is not an object or commodity that is capable of being physically returned to the plaintiff. Also, as we observed in § 7 of Chapter 6, when the basis of the plaintiff's claim is an action for unjust enrichment, then, unlike in a conventional breach of contract action where the object is to enforce a broken promise, it is not necessarily appropriate to award the plaintiff her "expectation" (*i.e.*, what she would have received had an actual promise been made by the defendant). Instead, in many cases, the court will have to determine the *reasonable value* of the benefit conferred in order to fashion an appropriate remedy. But often value, like beauty, is in the eye of the beholder.

In the next case, the plaintiffs have no contractual claim against the defendants—no claim in law. The plaintiffs do, however, assert the right to recover in equity. Pay particular attention to the way in which the claim is cast by the plaintiffs affects the remedy that the court awards.

PULL v. BARNES

Supreme Court of Colorado
142 Colo. 272, 350 P.2d 828 (1960)

PER CURIAM:

The parties appear here in the same order they appeared in the trial court, namely Burnard T. and Margaret H. Pull as plaintiffs, and Margaret Barnes and Mary E. Moffat as defendants. * * *

The action was brought by the plaintiffs in September of 1956 in the district court of Jefferson County to determine the boundary line between properties owned by the plaintiffs and the defendants, for damages and other relief.

In June of 1953 the plaintiffs located a parcel of land about one acre in size in Jefferson County, upon which they desired to build a mountain home and began to search out the owners of it. Just west of the piece of land selected was a line of an old fence which had upon it "No Trespassing" signs. Plaintiffs proceeded to negotiate with and buy from the parties who, in good faith, asserted the title to the land now in question. It later was determined by a survey that the defendants Barnes and Moffat, who owned the land west of the fence line, actually owned most of the land east of the fence line which the plaintiffs believed they had purchased, and upon which they had constructed their cabin.

Prior to constructing their cabin the plaintiffs hired a licensed surveyor to stake out the corners of the cabin site, but did not ask him to survey the land itself to determine the boundary lines between their property and that of the defendants'. Construction of the cabin upon the site, with a concrete slab floor and foundation, was begun in August 1953 and substantially completed by the fall of 1953.

During the construction the defendants several times were on the scene and acted as neighbors-about-to-be. The evidence clearly discloses that neither party knew or even suspected at the time of the construction of the cabin that it was being built upon land belonging to defendants.

After the cabin was completed the defendant Barnes negotiated with plaintiffs for a right-of-way through the land upon which the plaintiffs had built their cabin, and upon being refused hired a surveyor, and for the first time learned that the cabin which the plaintiffs had erected was solely upon her and the defendant Moffatt's land. Thereupon defendants erected a fence excluding the plaintiffs from the cabin and the land until a preliminary injunction was entered in this case some two years later.

Defendants now assert dominion over the cabin, contending that the plaintiffs had no rights therein, it having been built on defendants' land and as a result became a part of the land by operation of law.

Plaintiffs contend that the principles laid down by *Golden Press v. Rylands,* 124 Colo. 122, 235 P. (2d) 592, which permitted relief to a party who had encroached to a small extent on his neighbor's land, should apply. Plaintiffs further contend that the defendants are estopped by reason of their conduct from asserting title to the house.

On the other hand defendants urged that the facts in the present case do not bring it within the rule of *Golden Press, supra,* and further in the light of *Jacobs v. Perry,* 135 Colo. 550, 313 P. (2d) 1008, the doctrine of estoppel cannot apply here.

The trial court held that the boundary line of the property was the line surveyed east of the old fence line, thereby placing the cabin entirely within the land owned by the defendants, and held that the doctrine announced in *Golden Press, supra,* did not apply and that *Jacobs, supra,* forbade the application of the doctrine of estoppel. Judgment was entered for the defendants. In the course of its findings the court said:

"We would be inclined to grant some relief with reference to this building if it were within our power to do so. However, the only suggestion that has been made to us would be relief under the principle as laid down in the case of *Golden Press v. Rylands,* 124 Colo. 122, and we believe that the principle of encroachment set forth in that case is not applicable."

The trial court was correct in determining that *Golden Press, supra,* presented a different fact situation than is presented here; however, it is clear from the trial court's finding that it was searching for an equitable remedy which it could apply and which would prevent the harshness of the ruling.

As an abstract principle of law it is true that the moment a house is built upon land, it belongs to the owner of the land by mere operation of law and he may possess and enjoy it as his own. But this is merely stating the technical rule of law by which the owner seeks to hold what, in a just sense, he never had the slightest title to; that is, the house if it were not attached to the realty. It is not answering the objection by merely and dryly stating that the law so holds; for admitting this to be so, in law, such a situation furnishes a strong ground why equity should and does interpose and grant relief in proper cases.

Here the powers of the trial court were invoked to settle a boundary dispute and the problems arising from the situation in which the plaintiffs and the defendants found themselves without bad faith on the part of any of the parties. The matter having been presented to the court, it was the court's duty to grant the relief in equity which the situation demanded.

We think the applicable rule is stated in *Johnson v. Dunkel (1955)*, 132 Colo. 383, 288 P. (2d) 343, and is peculiarly applicable to the situation before us. In that case the adjoining owner who had in good faith erected improvements on adjoining land, believing it to be his own, was granted the right to remove same if feasible and if not, then was given an equitable lien on the property for the value thereof.

The judgment is accordingly reversed with directions to the trial court to hold a further hearing to determine whether it would be practical and feasible for Pull to remove the improvements from the land in question, and if so to specify the conditions under which it shall be done. If removal of the cabin is not feasible, then the value thereof should be determined and the land subjected to a lien in favor of plaintiffs in an amount equal to the value so determined.

QUESTIONS AND NOTES

1. Questions about the facts of this case

    1.1. What facts are most helpful to the plaintiffs' case?

    1.2. What facts are most helpful to support the defendants' contentions?

2. Questions about the law

    2.1. What do you understand the court to be saying in this case about the relationship between law and equity?

    2.2. On remand, if the trial court in *Pull* determines that removal is not feasible and, therefore, decides to impose an equitable lien on the defendants' property for the value of the cabin constructed on the defendants' land, how should "value" be determined under these circumstances? *See Restatement (Second) of Contracts* § 371. What if the defendants didn't really like the design of the cabin and planned to tear it down because they considered it an eyesore?

    2.3. If removal of the cabin were practicable, can plaintiffs recover the costs associated with doing so?

3. Notes

    3.1. In *Watts v. Watts, supra*, the plaintiff requested that a *constructive trust* be imposed on the defendant's assets acquired during the course of the relationship. In *Pull v. Barnes*, the Colorado Supreme Court directed that if removing the cabin was not feasible, the defendants' land should be subjected to an *equitable lien* in favor of the plaintiffs for the value of the improvements made on the land. As we noted earlier, a lien creates a charge against the property for the amount owed to the lienholder such that good title to the land cannot be conveyed until the lien is discharged by payment to the lienholder. Most liens, like most trusts, are created by agreement between the parties. In *Pull*, however, the court imposed the lien as a matter of law, rather than as a matter of contract, hence the term *equitable lien*. Similarly, a constructive trust is not a real trust in the conventional sense of the term, but instead is a remedy whereby the party with legal title to certain assets is deemed to hold title for the benefit of the party with a superior claim to such assets. Both constructive trusts and equitable liens are restitutionary remedies that may be employed by the court to prevent unjust enrichment. How would you describe the difference between the two? Why would the constructive trust not have been an appropriate remedy in *Pull*?

3.2. As we have seen, sometimes a court may simply award damages based on the monetary value of what the defendant has unjustly received from the plaintiff. Indeed, this is the traditional remedy at common law for recovery in a quasi-contract action. Historically, an action in quasi-contract was sometimes referred to as a count (cause of action) of *quantum meruit* (literally, "as much as it deserves"), and that terminology still shows up in cases today. We have also seen that such a recovery differs from a recovery under the contract and that, when the benefit conferred consists of something other than money, for example property or services, measuring the value of the restitutionary interest can get tricky. In case you forgot, let the cross-reference to our last case serve as a reminder.

BRITTON v. TURNER

Supreme Court of New Hampshire
6 N.H. 481 (1834)

Supra p. 795

CHAPTER NINE

WHEN DO YOU HAVE RIGHTS AND/OR DUTIES UNDER A CONTRACT THAT YOU DID NOT MAKE?

■ ■ ■

We have now covered the story of a contract from beginning to end. We have considered the questions:

- is there a contract, *i.e.*, an agreement that is legally enforceable?
- if so, what are its terms?
- have the two contracting parties performed pursuant to those terms?
- if not, is the nonperformance excused?
- and, if not, what are the legal remedies?

While we have covered the entire story, it has been a two-character or a two-party story. We now need to consider when third parties have rights or duties under a contract that they did not enter into themselves. More specifically, we need to consider third party beneficiaries, assignees of contract rights, and delegatees of contract duties.

SECTION 1: THIRD PARTY BENEFICIARIES

Issues of third party beneficiary law arise in situations in which a person who is not a party to a contract and who did not provide the consideration for that contract claims that she can enforce the contract because the parties intended for her to benefit from performance of the contract.

The most obvious example of a third party beneficiary contract is a life insurance contract. For example, Epstein enters into a life insurance contract with the Allstate Insurance Company in which Epstein agrees to make annual premium payments of $1,000, and Allstate agrees to pay $25,000 in policy benefits to Sharon Stone on Epstein's death. When Epstein dies, Allstate refuses to pay Sharon Stone, contending that it never contracted with her and never received consideration from her.

Even though Sharon Stone was not a party to the Epstein–Allstate contract and provided no consideration to Allstate, she can enforce that life insurance contract. She is a third party beneficiary.

It is important to understand that example and to understand that it is an example based on general contract law rather than special life insurance law. The legal basis for Sharon Stone's rights against Allstate is the general contract law concept of third party beneficiary rather than some special life insurance law rule.

Consider a third party beneficiary example unrelated to life insurance. Ponoroff owed Markell $300. Ponoroff later entered into a contract whereby Ponoroff loaned Epstein $300 and Epstein promised to repay that $300 to Markell, thus satisfying Ponoroff's debt to Markell.

Under these facts, Markell is not a party to the contract between Ponoroff and Epstein. Under these facts, Markell did not provide the consideration to Epstein in exchange for Epstein's promise to pay him $300. Nonetheless, Markell as a "third party beneficiary" can enforce the promise of the "promisor," Epstein.

This Ponoroff–Markell hypothetical is similar to *Lawrence v. Fox*, which is generally regarded as the seminal case recognizing rights of certain third party beneficiaries.

LAWRENCE v. FOX

Court of Appeals of New York
20 N.Y. 268 (1859)

APPEAL from the Superior Court of the city of Buffalo. On the trial before Mr. Justice MASTEN, it appeared by the evidence of a bystander, that one Holly, in November, 1857, at the request of the defendant, loaned and advanced to him $300, stating at the time that he owed that sum to the plaintiff for money borrowed of him, and had agreed to pay it to him the then next day; that the defendant in consideration thereof, at the time of receiving the money, promised to pay it to the plaintiff the then next day. Upon this state of facts the defendant moved for a nonsuit, upon three several grounds, viz.: That there was no proof tending to show that Holly was indebted to the plaintiff; that the agreement by the defendant with Holly to pay the plaintiff was void for want of consideration, and that there was no privity between the plaintiff and defendant. The court overruled the motion, and the counsel for the defendant excepted. The cause was then submitted to the jury, and they found a verdict for the plaintiff for the amount of the loan and interest, $344.66, upon which judgment was entered; from which the defendant appealed to the Superior Court, at general term, where the judgment was affirmed, and the defendant appealed to this court.

H. GRAY, J.

The first objection raised on the trial amounts to this: That the evidence of the person present, who heard the declarations of Holly giving directions as to the payment of the money he was then advancing to the defendant, was mere hearsay and therefore not competent. Had the plaintiff sued Holly for this sum of money no objection to the competency of this evidence would have been thought of; and if the defendant had performed his promise by paying the sum loaned to him to the plaintiff, and Holly had afterwards sued him for its recovery, and this evidence had been offered by the defendant, it would doubtless have been received without an objection from any source. All the defendant had the right to demand in this case was evidence which, as between Holly and the plaintiff, was competent to establish the relation between them of debtor and creditor. For that purpose the evidence was clearly competent; it covered the whole ground and warranted the verdict of the jury.

But it is claimed that notwithstanding this promise was established by competent evidence, it was void for the want of consideration. It is now more than a quarter of a century since it was settled by the Supreme Court of this State—in an able and pains-taking opinion by the late Chief Justice SAVAGE, in which the authorities were fully examined and carefully analysed—that a promise in all material respects like the one under consideration was valid; and the judgment of that court was unanimously affirmed by the Court for the Correction of Errors. (Farley v. Cleveland, 4 Cow., 432; same case in error, 9 id., 639.) In that case one Moon owed Farley and sold to Cleaveland a quantity of hay, in consideration of which Cleaveland promised to pay Moon's debt to Farley; and the decision in favor of Farley's right to recover was placed upon the ground that the hay received by Cleaveland from Moon was a valid consideration for Cleaveland's promise to pay Farley, and that the subsisting liability of Moon to pay Farley was no objection to the recovery. The fact that the money advanced by Holly to the defendant was a loan to him for a day, and that it thereby became the property of the defendant, seemed to impress the defendant's counsel with the idea that because the defendant's promise was not a trust fund placed by the plaintiff in the defendant's hands, out of which he was to realize money as from the sale of a chattel or the collection of a debt, the promise although made for the benefit of the plaintiff could not enure to his benefit. The hay which Cleaveland delivered to Moon was not to be paid to Farley, but the debt incurred by Cleaveland for the purchase of the hay, like the debt incurred by the defendant for money borrowed, was what was to be paid.

That case has been often referred to by the courts of this State, and has never been doubted as sound authority for the principle upheld by it. It puts to rest the objection that the defendant's promise was void for want of consideration. The report of that case shows that the promise was not only made to Moon but to the plaintiff Farley. In this case the promise was made to Holly and not expressly to the plaintiff; and this difference between the two cases presents the question, raised by the defendant's objection, as to the want of privity between the plaintiff and defendant.

But it is urged that because the defendant was not in any sense a trustee of the property of Holly for the benefit of the plaintiff, the law will not imply a promise. I agree that many of the cases where a promise was implied were cases of trusts, created for the benefit of the promiser. The duty of the trustee to pay the cestuis que trust, according to the terms of the trust, implies his promise to the latter to do so. In this case the defendant, upon ample consideration received from Holly, promised Holly to pay his debt to the plaintiff; the consideration received and the promise to Holly made it as plainly his duty to pay the plaintiff as if the money had been remitted to him for that purpose, and as well implied a promise to do so as if he had been made a trustee of property to be converted into cash with which to pay. The fact that a breach of the duty imposed in the one case may be visited, and justly, with more serious consequences than in the other, by no means disproves the payment to be a duty in both. The principle illustrated by the example so frequently quoted (which concisely states the case in hand) "that a promise made to one for the benefit of another, he for whose benefit it is made may bring an action for its breach," has been applied to trust cases, not because it was exclusively applicable to those cases, but because it was a principle of law, and as such applicable to those cases.

It was also insisted that Holly could have discharged the defendant from his promise, though it was intended by both parties for the benefit of the plaintiff, and therefore the plaintiff was not entitled to maintain this suit for the recovery of a demand over which he had no control. It is enough that the plaintiff did not release the defendant from his promise, and whether he could or not is a question not now necessarily involved; but if it was, I think it would be found difficult to maintain the right of Holly to discharge a judgment recovered by the plaintiff upon confession or otherwise, for the breach of the defendant's promise; and if he could not, how could he discharge the suit before judgment, or the promise before suit, made as it was for the plaintiff's benefit and in accordance with legal presumption accepted by him until his dissent was shown. Suppose the defendant had given his note in which, for value received of Holly, he had promised to pay the plaintiff and the plaintiff had accepted the promise, retaining Holly's liability. Very clearly Holly could not have discharged that promise, be the right to release the defendant as it may.

No one can doubt that he owes the sum of money demanded of him, or that in accordance with his promise it was his duty to have paid it to the plaintiff; nor can it be doubted that whatever may be the diversity of opinion elsewhere, the adjudications in this State, from a very early period, approved by experience, have established the defendant's liability; if, therefore, it could be shown that a more strict and technically accurate application of the rules applied, would lead to a different result (which I by no means concede), the effort should not be made in the face of manifest justice.

The judgment should be affirmed.

COMSTOCK, J. (Dissenting.)

The plaintiff had nothing to do with the promise on which he brought this action. It was not made to him, nor did the consideration proceed from him. If he can maintain the suit, it is because an anomaly has found its way into the law on this subject. In general, there must be privity of contract. The party who sues upon a promise must be the promisee, or he must have some legal interest in the undertaking. In this case, it is plain that Holly, who loaned the money to the defendant, and to whom the promise in question was made, could at any time have claimed that it should be performed to himself personally. He had lent the money to the defendant, and at the same time directed the latter to pay the sum to the plaintiff. This direction he could countermand, and if he had done so, manifestly the defendant's promise to pay according to the direction would have ceased to exist. The plaintiff would receive a benefit by a complete execution of the arrangement, but the arrangement itself was between other parties, and was under their exclusive control. If the defendant had paid the money to Holly, his debt would have been discharged thereby. So Holly might have released the demand or assigned it to another person, or the parties might have annulled the promise now in question, and designated some other creditor of Holly as the party to whom the money should be paid. It has never been claimed, that in a case thus situated, the right of a third person to sue upon the promise rested on any sound principle of law. We are to inquire whether the rule has been so established by positive authority.

The cases in which some trust was involved are also frequently referred to as authority for the doctrine now in question, but they do not sustain it. If A delivers money or property to B, which the latter accepts upon a trust for the benefit of C, the latter can enforce the trust by an appropriate action for that purpose.

A fund received under such an agreement does not belong to the person who receives it. He must account for it specifically; and perhaps there is no gross violation of principle in permitting the equitable owner of it to sue upon an express promise to pay it over. Having a specific interest in the thing, the undertaking to account for it may be regarded as in some sense made with him through the author of the trust. But further than this we cannot go without violating plain rules of law. In the case before us there was nothing in the nature of a trust or agency. The defendant borrowed the money of Holly and received it as his own. The plaintiff had no right in the fund, legal or equitable. The promise to repay the money created an obligation in favor of the lender to whom it was made and not in favor of any one else.

The judgment of the court below should therefore be reversed, and a new trial granted.

————————

QUESTIONS AND NOTE

1. Questions about the facts of this case

    1.1. To whom did the plaintiff loan money?

    1.2. From whom is the plaintiff trying to collect that debt?

    1.3. Why is the plaintiff trying to collect his debt from the defendant instead of his borrower? Does the court answer that question? Should it?

2. Questions about the law

    2.1. Why is the court considering consideration?

    2.2. Is there any question as to whether the defendant received consideration for its promise to pay the plaintiff $300?

    2.3. Did the defendant receive consideration from the plaintiff?

    2.4. What is the purpose of requiring consideration?

    2.5. What is "privity"? Are the plaintiff and the defendant in privity? Didn't the defendant promise to pay the plaintiff? Why is the court discussing implied promises?

    2.6. Who could have sued whom? Could the plaintiff have sued Holly for $300? Could the plaintiff have collected the $300 from Holly and still sued the defendant?

    2.7. If the plaintiff sued Holly because the defendant refused to pay the plaintiff, could Holly have then sued the defendant for breach of contract?

    2.8. Have you studied garnishment in procedure? Could Lawrence have used garnishment to recover from Fox? How is third party beneficiary law different from garnishment?

3. Note

    For a more complete understanding of why Lawrence sued Fox instead of Lawrence suing Holly or Holly suing Fox, *see* Anthony Jon Waters, *The Property in the Promise: A Study of the Third Party Beneficiary Rule*, 98 HARV. L. REV. 1109 (1985).

    Professor Waters' article provides not only an understanding of what happened in *Lawrence v. Fox* but also what happened after *Lawrence v. Fox*:

    The second Part of this Article deals impressionistically with the question of how this new rule, quite at odds with received wisdom, became all but universally accepted in American jurisdictions, state and federal. This inquiry centers on the work of Arthur Corbin, Professor of Law at Yale Law School, author of six articles on the subject of third party contract rights, and highly influential in the formulation of both Restatements of Contracts. Between the years 1918 and 1930, Corbin managed nothing less than a campaign on behalf of the third party beneficiary rule, singling out for a special brand of jurisprudential hounding those jurisdictions that denied or tightly limited third party recovery and basing much of his work on flagrant misrepresentation of the law of those states. It is an extraordinary story of how one well-placed academic influenced the development of the common law.

* * *

During the sixty years or so between the New York Court of Appeals decision in *Lawrence v. Fox* and the beginning of Arthur Corbin's activity in this area, the third party beneficiary rule enjoyed a fitful existence. In 1918, Corbin launched what became a campaign on behalf of the third party beneficiary rule, a campaign that would last about fifty years and would culminate in the "Corbinized," "intended beneficiary" rule of the Second Restatement.

Arthur Linton Corbin was born in 1874, fifteen years after the New York Court of Appeals decided *Lawrence v. Fox*. He died in 1967, the same year that the American Law Institute unveiled the 'intended beneficiary' formulation. During his life he became the most influential academic figure in American contract law, achieving a preeminence that no one since has matched. * * *

When Arthur Corbin first published on the subject of third party beneficiary doctrine, the courts had been struggling with the doctrinal repercussions of this judicial innovation for more than half a century. The rule of *Lawrence v. Fox* had quickly generated difficult questions that could not be answered by the logical application of doctrine, for there was, as yet, no doctrine to apply. By 1918, when Corbin published the first of his six articles on the subject, there was enough case law, enough controversy, and enough chaos to have warranted several attempts, by various people, to set things straight. Williston, for example, began his 1902 article "Contracts for the Benefit of a Third Person," with this quote:

"In no department of the law has a more obstinate and persistent battle between practice and theory been waged than in regard to the answer to the question: Whether a right of action accrues to a third person from a contract made by others for his benefit? Nor is the strife ended; for if it be granted that the scale inclines in favor of practice, yet the advocates of this result are continually endeavoring to extend the territory which they have conquered and to apply the doctrines thereby established to cases which should be governed by other principles."

From the outset of his lengthy crusade on behalf of the third party beneficiary, Corbin was resolute in his belief that the rule was supported by many practical considerations and opposed only by empty formalism. Here, as elsewhere, Williston and Corbin disagreed. Williston took the position that a beneficiary's recovery on the contract, while theoretically anomalous, was sometimes justified by the equities of the case. By contrast, Corbin pushed for the recognition of third party enforcement as the general rule rather than the exception.

98 HARV. L. REV. at 1148–51.

The debate Corbin and Williston conducted in contracts law treatises and law review articles and *Restatements* was not, in the main, a debate over whether traditional contracts concepts such as consideration or privity precluded a third party from ever enforcing a contract. Rather the focus of the debate was on when third parties could enforce contracts. This debate continues today not only in contract law treatises and law review articles but also in cases such as the following two cases: *Ex parte Stamey* and *Midwest Grain Products of Illinois, Inc. v. Productization, Inc. and CMI Corp.*

To participate in this debate, we need to understand the terms and how the debaters—courts and commentators—are defining the terms.[1] For starters, we need to know who the "third party beneficiary" is, who the "promisor" is, and who the "promisee" is. The *Restatement (Second) of Contracts* provides these definitions:

§ 2. Promise; Promisor; Promisee; Beneficiary

(1) A promise is a manifestation of intention to act or refrain from acting in a specified way, so made as to justify a promisee in understanding that a commitment has been made.

(2) The person manifesting the intention is the promisor.

(3) The person to whom the manifestation is addressed is the promisee.

(4) Where performance will benefit a person other than the promisee, that person is a beneficiary.

Are these definitions helpful? Obviously, Lawrence was the beneficiary in *Lawrence v. Fox.* Is it equally obvious that Fox was the promissor and Holly the promisee? Try again in *Stamey.*

A. WHEN A THIRD PARTY IS A "THIRD PARTY BENEFICIARY"

EX PARTE STAMEY

Supreme Court of Alabama
776 So.2d 85 (2000)

HOUSTON, JUSTICE.

Gary Stamey and Deborah Stamey, third-party plaintiffs in an action currently pending in the Mobile Circuit Court, petition for a writ of mandamus directing the trial court to vacate its order compelling arbitration of the Stameys' claims against Green Tree Financial Corporation, Hallmont Homes, Inc., and Hallmont employees Jarod Hall and Gaylon Hall. We deny the writ.

---

1. Cf Austin J, Freely & David Steinberg, Argumentation and Debate: Critical Thinking for Reasoned Decisions 61 (2009).

http://books.google.com/books?id=ZR6RxPGlOgQC&pg=PA61&lpg=PA61&dq=debate+and+importance+of+defining+the+terms&source=bl&ots=vYaMJV1zIN&sig=rz3D-cTRSUd RJVA_aQqenWg8Kss&hl=en&ei=DKTZS8G6D5P49AST0dFQ&sa=X&oi=book_result& ct=result&resnum=1&ved=0CAYQ6AEwAA#v=onepage&q=d%20and%20importance% 20of%20defining%20the%20terms&f=false

In December 1996, the Stameys contracted with Hallmont Homes, Inc., to purchase land and a mobile home. The contract also included assurances that Hallmont would prepare a foundation for the mobile home and would install a septic system and a light pole. The Stameys claim that the septic system and the light pole were never installed. The Stameys had borrowed money from Green Tree to pay for these purchases and installations. Included in the financing agreement between Green Tree and the Stameys was this arbitration provision:

"ARBITRATION: ALL DISPUTES, CLAIMS OR CONTROVERSIES ARISING FROM OR RELATING TO THIS CONTRACT OR THE PARTIES THERETO SHALL BE RESOLVED BY BINDING ARBITRATION BY ONE ARBITRATOR SELECTED BY YOU WITH MY CONSENT. THIS AGREEMENT IS MADE PURSUANT TO A TRANSACTION IN INTERSTATE COMMERCE AND SHALL BE GOVERNED BY THE FEDERAL ARBITRATION ACT AT 9 U.S.C. SECTION 1. JUDGMENT UPON THE AWARD RENDERED MAY BE ENTERED IN ANY COURT HAVING JURISDICTION. THE PARTIES AGREE AND UNDERSTAND THAT THEY CHOOSE ARBITRATION INSTEAD OF LITIGATION TO RESOLVE DISPUTES. THE PARTIES UNDERSTAND THAT THEY HAVE A RIGHT OR OPPORTUNITY TO LITIGATE DISPUTES IN COURT, BUT THAT THEY PREFER TO RESOLVE THEIR DISPUTES THROUGH ARBITRATION, EXCEPT AS PROVIDED HEREIN. THE PARTIES VOLUNTARILY AND KNOWINGLY WAIVE ANY RIGHT THEY HAVE TO A JURY TRIAL, EITHER PURSUANT TO ARBITRATION UNDER THIS CLAUSE OR PURSUANT TO A COURT ACTION BY YOU (AS PROVIDED HEREIN). THE PARTIES AGREE AND UNDERSTAND THAT ALL DISPUTES ARISING UNDER CASE LAW, STATUTORY LAW AND ALL OTHER LAWS INCLUDING, BUT NOT LIMITED TO, ALL CONTRACT, TORT AND PROPERTY DISPUTES WILL BE SUBJECT TO BINDING ARBITRATION IN ACCORD WITH THIS CONTRACT.

Dr. Bernard Eichold II, in his capacity as health officer of Mobile County, sued for injunctive relief against the Stameys, alleging that their property was in violation of state health laws—specifically, his complaint alleged a violation concerning the septic system on the Stameys' property. The Stameys filed an answer, along with a third-party complaint against Hallmont and Green Tree, alleging conversion, fraud, and breach of contract. The Stameys contend that Hallmont and/or Green Tree caused the problem with the septic system for which the Stameys were sued. Hallmont and Green Tree both moved the trial court to compel arbitration of the claims asserted against them. Hallmont was not a signatory to the arbitration agreement. The trial court granted the motions to compel. * * *

While the Stameys' contract with Green Tree contains an arbitration agreement, neither the sale contract between the Stameys and Hallmont nor any other document to which Hallmont was a signatory contained an arbitration agreement. Hallmont's motion to compel arbitration was based on the arbitration provision in the contract between Green Tree and the Stameys.

Normally, in order to have a valid arbitration provision, there must be an agreement to arbitrate, and if no agreement exists, then a party cannot be forced to submit a dispute to arbitration. The question whether one has assented to an arbitration provision is governed by ordinary principles of a state's common law and statutory law governing the formation of contracts. Assent to arbitrate is usually to be manifested through a party's signature on the contract containing the arbitration provision. However, both Federal courts and Alabama courts have enforced exceptions to this rule, so as to allow a nonsignatory, and even one who is not a party, as to a particular contract, to enforce an arbitration provision within that same contract. * * * If Hallmont is a third-party beneficiary, then it should be able to enforce the arbitration provision included in the contract between the Stameys and Green Tree. Thus, we must determine whether Hallmont is a third-party beneficiary of that contract.

A party claiming to be a third-party beneficiary, "must establish that the contracting parties intended, upon execution of the contract, to bestow a direct, as opposed to an incidental, benefit upon the third party." Weathers Auto Glass, Inc. v. Alfa Mut. Ins. Co., 619 So.2d 1328, 1329 (Ala.1993). In other words, Hallmont must show that the Stameys and Green Tree intended for Hallmont to receive a direct benefit from the financing contract. This issue will be determined with the intent of the parties as indicated by the language used. [W]e look to the language of the entire financing contract between the Stameys and Green Tree. We conclude that they did intend for Hallmont to receive a direct benefit.

The financing contract is a standard contract that provides for a secured transaction in which Green Tree received a security interest in the manufactured home and in which Green Tree would pay Hallmont for the manufactured home on behalf of the Stameys. In other words, this contract allows Green Tree to pay the obligation of the Stameys to Hallmont. The section of the contract entitled "ITEMIZATION OF THE AMOUNT FINANCED" sets out the amounts that were to be "paid on [the Stameys'] behalf." Included in this chart are the amounts that were paid on behalf of the Stameys to Hallmont for the cost of the manufactured home, the cost of the land, and the cost of the installations.

Furthermore, the language of the contract clearly shows that the parties contemplated Hallmont as a third-party beneficiary. The last section of the contract states:

"WAIVER OF JURY TRIAL: I HEREBY WAIVE ANY RIGHT TO A TRIAL BY JURY THAT I HAVE IN ANY SUBSEQUENT LITIGATION BETWEEN ME AND THE SELLER, OR ME AND ANY ASSIGNEE OF THE SELLER, WHERE SUCH LITIGATION ARISES OUT OF, IS RELATED TO, OR IS IN CONNECTION WITH ANY PROVISION OF THIS AGREEMENT, WHETHER THE

AGREEMENT IS ASSERTED AS RELATED TO, OR IS IN CON-NECTION WITH ANY PROVISION OF THIS AGREEMENT, WHETHER THE AGREEMENT IS ASSERTED AS THE BASIS FOR A CLAIM, COUNTERCLAIM OR CROSS CLAIM, OR A DEFENSE TO A CLAIM, COUNTERCLAIM OR CROSS CLAIM."

(Emphasis added.) By this section, the Stameys clearly waived the right to a jury trial, not against Green Tree, but against Hallmont—"the seller."

The language of the two sections mentioned in the two preceding paragraphs clearly indicates an intent on behalf of the Stameys and Green Tree to benefit Hallmont through the financing contract. Therefore, we conclude that Hallmont is a third-party beneficiary of the financing contract and that it has all the rights that exist under that contract. As a result, Hallmont can enforce the arbitration agreement set out in that contract. * * *

QUESTIONS

1. Questions about the facts of this case

    1.1. Did the contract between the Stameys and Hallmont have an arbitration clause?

    1.2. Who is alleging that it is a third-party beneficiary? Who is the promisor?

    1.3. Why did the Stameys and Green Tree enter into a contract? Would there have been a Stamey/Green Tree contract if the Stameys had not purchased land and a mobile home from Hallmont?

2. Questions about the law

    2.1. According to the Alabama Supreme Court, "the language of the contract clearly shows that the parties contemplated Hallmont as a third party beneficiary." (emphasis added) What language?

    2.2. Should the question be whether "the parties contemplated Hallmont as a third-party beneficiary" of the contract or whether "the parties contemplated Hallmont as a third-party beneficiary" of the arbitration clause in the contract?

    2.3. How would this case have been decided by the judge in the next case?[2]

---

2. Justice Houston was undoubtedly a neat guy http://news.google.com/newspapers?nid= 1891&dat=19880605&id=RmUfAAAAIBAJ&sjid=vNQEAAAAIBAJ&pg=4464,527965 (and his son was a Methodist minister http://www.lagniappemobile.com/articles/3120–pastor-gorman-houston-resigns-from-post-at-dauphin-way-united-methodist-church), BUT, as best we can tell, he was never on President Bush's short list for Supreme Court nominees (a list, which you may remember, included Harriet Miers http://topics.nytimes.com/topics/reference/timestopics/people/m/ harriet_e_miers/index.html). Judge Wood, who authored the next opinion, was on President

MIDWEST GRAIN PRODUCTS OF ILLINOIS, INC. v. PRODUCTIZATION, INC. AND CMI CORP.

U.S. Court of Appeals, Seventh Circuit
228 F.3d 784 (2000)

DIANE P. WOOD, CIRCUIT JUDGE.

This case presents a classic contract dispute: A orders a product from B, and B turns to C to manufacture it. When A receives the product, it is not satisfied, and it wants to hold C responsible for the alleged flaws. We must decide whether there is enough evidence of some kind of warranty, either express or as a matter of law, to allow Midwest Grain Products (Company A) to move beyond summary judgment in its action against CMI Corporation (Company C). (Midwest settled its claims against Productization, Inc. (PI) (Company B), and so that actor has not been part of this case for some time.) The district court concluded that Midwest's evidence was lacking and that CMI was entitled to judgment as a matter of law. It also ruled that CMI was not entitled to its attorneys' fees. Each company has appealed from the part of the judgment adverse to it, but, finding no error in the district court's disposition of the action, we affirm.

I.

On January 12, 1993, Midwest Vice President Anthony Petricola sent a letter to PI President Andrew Livingston requesting a quote on grain dryers to be used in Midwest's expansion of its facility in Pekin, Illinois. Livingston responded on January 26 with an offer on PI's behalf to provide two dryers for a total price of $1,515,800. Midwest accepted PI's offer on February 25, through a purchase order sent to Livingston.

With the deal in hand, PI then turned to CMI to manufacture the dryers. On April 29, 1993, it sent CMI a set of specifications for the dryers Midwest wanted. CMI replied with a fax giving price terms and stating that "[a]cceptance of the order will be subject to receipt by CMI of a letter from Midwest Grain agreeing to make payment, with checks made payable jointly to CMI and Productization." * * *

On May 10, Midwest's Petricola sent the requested letter directly to CMI. The letter commits Midwest to "make payment for equipment purchased by Productization, Inc. from CMI Corporation for its [*i.e.*, Midwest's] project in Pekin, Illinois, with check(s) payable jointly to Productization, Inc. and CMI Corporation." It also mentions the shipment, price, and storage terms of the PI/CMI agreement and states that CMI will issue waivers of liens to Midwest upon CMI's receipt of payment.

This was Midwest's only direct appearance into the dealings between PI and CMI. The latter two companies continued to work out the details of their contract. * * *

Obama's short list (and even more important, she was a student in Epstein's contracts class at the University of Texas Law School a long, long time ago)

* * * Paragraph 8 addressed warranties, and said in pertinent part:

CMI warrants such equipment, accessories, parts and other goods covered by this order and as are manufactured by CMI against defective material or workmanship for a period of six (6) months after date of first delivery or for one thousand (1,000) hours of use, whichever comes first; * * * THIS WARRANTY IS EXPRESSLY IN LIEU OF AND EXCLUDES ALL OTHER WARRANTIES, EX-PRESSED OR IMPLIED (INCLUDING ANY WARRANTY OF MER-CHANTABILITY AND FITNESS OF ANY PRODUCT OR GOODS FOR A PARTICULAR PURPOSE), AND ALL OTHER OBLI-GATIONS OR LIABILITIES ON CMI'S PART, AND CMI NEITHER ASSUMES NOR AUTHORIZES ANY OTHER PERSON TO AS-SUME FOR CMI ANY OTHER LIABILITY IN CONNECTION WITH THE SALE OF CMI'S PRODUCTS. THERE ARE NOT ANY WAR-RANTIES WHICH EXTEND BEYOND THE DESCRIPTION ON THE FACE OF THIS ORDER.

* * *

The first dryer reached Midwest in February 1994, but it was not put into service until 1995. The other dryer was delivered in April 1994 and was put into service two months later. Midwest experienced a variety of problems with both units. Initially, CMI and PI serviced them. Later, still unhappy with PI and CMI, it filed this action.

* * *

We begin with the question whether, under Oklahoma law, Midwest has any claim to third-party beneficiary status to the agreement between CMI and PI.

* * *

Under Oklahoma law, a party may be a third-party beneficiary to an agreement only if the contracting parties intended the benefits of the contract to run to the third party. * * * "[I]t is not necessary that third-party beneficiaries be specifically identified at the time of contracting, but it must appear that the contract was expressly made for the benefit of a class of persons to which the party seeking enforcement belongs."

There are only two pieces of evidence in this record that link the CMI/PI contract to Midwest: first, the fact that CMI knew that PI wanted the dryers so that it could then sell them to Midwest, and second, the fact that CMI insisted that it be paid by checks that Midwest made payable jointly to PI and to itself. Nothing in Oklahoma law the parties have cited, and nothing in Oklahoma law that we have been able to find ourselves, comes close to holding that an ultimate buyer is a third-party beneficiary of every contract its seller enters into with suppliers in order to fulfill the contract. Nor are we referred to, or can we find, any Oklahoma decision indicating that the kind of financial arrangement CMI secured here is enough to give the ultimate buyer third-party beneficiary status. That step was enough to make Midwest a surety for PI, and in that sense it allowed

CMI to look not only to PI for payment (a right it had under the basic contract) but also to Midwest. But it did not indicate that the contract was expressly for Midwest's benefit. From CMI's point of view, it was a contract for the sale of goods, and it was not CMI's problem in the final analysis what PI wanted to do with the dryers once it received them.

Indeed, in the section of Midwest's brief entitled "Plaintiff's third-party beneficiary status was ignored or improperly addressed," it cites not a single decision of an Oklahoma court. It refers instead to one Illinois case, *Olson v. Etheridge*, 177 Ill.2d 396, 226 Ill.Dec. 780, 686 N.E.2d 563 (Ill.1997), and one decision from this court in a diversity case governed by Illinois law. States vary in their approach to rules like those governing the recognition and rights of third-party beneficiaries, and we would at least need some reason to conclude that Oklahoma and Illinois take the same approach before these authorities would be persuasive.

If Midwest was not a third-party beneficiary of the CMI/PI contract, which is our best predication of what an Oklahoma court would find, then it has no case. * * *

In the final analysis, the party that Midwest needed to pursue was its seller, PI. Indeed, it did include PI in this action at the outset. The terms of its settlement with PI are not pertinent to its case against CMI and are not in any event a matter of record. We hold only that, under the facts as presented and the governing law, the district court correctly granted summary judgment in the case Midwest wanted to bring against CMI.

QUESTIONS

1. Questions about the facts of this case

    1.1. Who bought what from whom?

    1.2. Why is the buyer, Midwest, suing CMI instead of PI?

    1.3. What facts support Midwest's contention that it is a third-party beneficiary of the CMI/PI contract?

2. Questions about the law

    2.1. Why is Midwest arguing that it is a third-party beneficiary of the contract between PI and CMI?

    2.2. In omitted dictum, Judge Wood stated: "Indeed, as a general matter, the Oklahoma courts do not seem to be inclined to adopt rules from the Contracts *Restatement*, perhaps because Title 15 of the Oklahoma Code is a comprehensive legislative statement of the law of contracts in that state." 238 F.3d at 790. Would Judge Wood have reached a different decision if Oklahoma had been "inclined to adopt rules from the Contracts restatement" such as section 304? A promise in a contract creates a duty in the promisor to any intended beneficiary to perform the promise, and the intended beneficiary may enforce the duty?

 2.3. There is no omitted dicta regarding U.C.C. section 2–318[3]. The opinion does not mention U.C.C. section 2–318. Is the contract in this case within the scope of Article 2? Should Judge Wood have discussed 2–318? Is U.C.C. section 2–318 relevant to understanding this case? Is U.C.C. section 2–318 relevant to a more general understanding of third party beneficiary law?

B. CANCELLATION AND MODIFICATION OF THE RIGHTS OF THE THIRD PARTY BENEFICIARY AND DEFENSES AGAINST THE THIRD PARTY BENEFICIARY

The previous three cases focused on the question of whether a third party has any right to enforce a contract entered into by others. That is the primary focus of most of the reported third party beneficiary cases.

The next case deals with: (i) the related question of when the rights of a third party beneficiary can be cancelled or modified—a question raised but not considered in *Lawrence v. Fox,* and (ii) the question of what defenses can be asserted against a third-party beneficiary.

OLSON v. ETHERIDGE
Supreme Court of Illinois
177 Ill.2d 396, 226 Ill.Dec. 780, 686 N.E.2d 563 (1997)

[Plaintiffs (the third party beneficiaries) sold their John Deere dealership to Etheridge (the promisee) pursuant to Agreement I with annual payments to be made by Etheridge to Plaintiffs pursuant to Note I. Subsequently, in 1983, Etheridge sold one-half of the business to Engelhaupt (the promisor) pursuant to Agreement II with annual payments to be made pursuant to Note II. Agreement II and Note II provided that Engelhaupt's payments were to be made to Plaintiffs to reduce Etheridge's obligation to Plaintiffs under Note 1. In 1986, Etheridge and

---

 3. As adopted in Oklahoma, section 2–318 provides: § 2–318. Third Party Beneficiaries of Warranties Express or Implied Third Party Beneficiaries of Warranties Express or Implied.

 (1) A seller's warranty whether express or implied extends to any natural person who is in the family or household of his buyer or who is a guest in his home if it is reasonable to expect that such person may use, consume or be affected by the goods and who is injured in person by breach of the warranty.

 (2) This section does not displace principles of law and equity that extend a warranty to or for the benefit of a buyer to other persons.

 (3) The operation of this section may not be excluded, modified, or limited by a seller, but an exclusion, modification, or limitation of the warranty, including any with respect to rights and remedies, effective against the buyer is also effective against any beneficiary designated under this section.

Engelhaupt and Princeton Bank entered into Agreement III which provided for Engelhaupt to pay the remaining balance of Note II to Princeton Bank to satisfy one of Etheridge's other debts. Engelhaupt made such a payment. Etheridge defaulted on its obligations under Agreement I and Note I. Plaintiffs sued both Etheridge and Engelhaupt for the unpaid balance of Note I.]

JUSTICE BILANDIC delivered the opinion of the court:

Bay v. Williams, 112 Ill. 91, 1 N.E. 340 (1884), established the rule in Illinois that the rights of a third-party beneficiary in a contract are subject to immediate vesting and, once vested, cannot be altered or extinguished through a later agreement of the contracting parties without the assent of the beneficiary. We are here called upon to determine the continued validity of the *Bay* rule.

The four plaintiffs in this case are third-party beneficiaries of a promise contained in a contract entered into by the appellant and another party. The circuit court of Bureau County awarded summary judgment to the plaintiffs based on *Bay*. The appellate court affirmed. We now reverse this award of summary judgment and remand for further proceedings, for the reasons set forth below.

* * *

Engelhaupt's appeal focuses on the appellate court's rejection of his claim that he is not subject to liability to the plaintiffs because all his obligations under Agreement II and Note II were discharged by the actions taken between him, Etheridge, and Princeton Bank on February 10, 1986. The actions pointed to by Engelhaupt are his $83,385 payment to Princeton Bank on Note II, and Princeton Bank's agreement that this constituted full payment; and his $100 payment to Princeton Bank for Agreement II, and Princeton Bank's and Etheridge's assignments of all their interests in Agreement II over to Engelhaupt. Engelhaupt concedes that the vesting rule in Bay commands a contrary conclusion, but argues that the *Bay* rule should be replaced with the vesting rule set forth in section 311 of the Restatement (Second) of Contracts (1981). According to Engelhaupt, if section 311 is applied, the summary judgment entered in favor of the plaintiffs was improper because questions of material fact remain to be determined.

* * *

Before addressing the parties' arguments, we briefly summarize third-party beneficiary law. The well-established rule in Illinois is that if a contract is entered into for the direct benefit of a third person, the third person may sue for a breach of the contract in his or her own name, even though the third person is a stranger to the contract and the consideration. This principle of law is widely accepted throughout the United States, because allowing a third-party beneficiary to sue the promisor directly is said to be manifestly just and practical. In cases such as this one, it increases judicial efficiency by removing the privity requirement, under which the beneficiary must sue the promisee, who then in turn must sue the promisor.

An important corollary to this principle is that the promisor may assert against the beneficiary any defense that the promisor could assert against the promisee if the promisee were suing on the contract. This is because the third-party beneficiary's rights stem from a contract to which the beneficiary is not a party. Accordingly, the promisor in this case, Engelhaupt, may assert against the plaintiffs-beneficiaries any defense that he could assert against the promisee, Etheridge, if Etheridge were suing him on Agreement II. Engelhaupt here asserts the defense that all his obligations under Agreement II and Note II were discharged when he made full payment to Princeton Bank on Note II and obtained assignments of both Princeton Bank's and Etheridge's interests in Agreement II.

The plaintiffs maintain, however, that Engelhaupt is not entitled to assert this defense against them because their rights as third-party beneficiaries had "vested." The vesting doctrine is an exception to the above rule that the promisor may assert against the beneficiary any defense that the promisor could assert against the promisee. Under this doctrine, once a third-party beneficiary's rights vest, the original contracting parties cannot modify or discharge those rights without the beneficiary's assent. The "question of vesting arises only where the promisor and the promisee purport to vary or discharge the rights of the beneficiary"; otherwise, "the topic of vesting is irrelevant." Before proceeding, then, we must determine in this case what rights the plaintiffs are asserting under Agreement II, and whether Engelhaupt and Etheridge attempted to vary or discharge those rights.

The plaintiffs here are asserting third-party beneficiary rights in Agreement II. In particular, they claim that they are the beneficiaries of Engelhaupt's promise in Agreement II "to assume" one-half of Etheridge's obligation to pay the plaintiffs under Agreement I and Note I. This assumption by Engelhaupt of one-half of Etheridge's obligation to pay is a classic example of a delegation. Unlike an assignment, which involves only a transfer of rights, a delegation involves the appointment of another to perform one's duties. ("Rights are assigned; duties are delegated"); J. Calamari & J. Perillo, Contracts § 18–1, at 722 (3d ed.1987). When a duty is delegated, the delegating party continues to remain liable for performance. The effects of this delegation are as follows: Etheridge remains liable to the plaintiffs under Agreement I and Note I, while Engelhaupt is liable to the plaintiffs under the third-party beneficiary theory. The plaintiffs therefore have a claim against both Etheridge and Engelhaupt, but are entitled to only one satisfaction. Thus, in count V, the plaintiffs are asserting their rights as third-party beneficiaries to payment from Engelhaupt, as provided for in Agreement II.

* * *

We now turn to the primary issue in this case: how vesting should be defined in this context. The plaintiffs urge application of the vesting rule declared in *Bay*. Engelhaupt, on the other hand, asks us to apply the vesting rule set forth in section 311 of the Second Restatement of Contracts.

In *Bay*, 112 Ill. 91, 1 N.E. 340, Williams sold land to Newman and Sissons in exchange for a down payment and promissory notes payable in installments. Newman and Sissons then sold the land to Bay. The deed tendered to Bay contained an express promise by Bay to pay the balance due on the promissory notes executed by Williams and Newman and Sissons. Bay later obtained a release of his obligation to pay Williams from Sissons. Newman went bankrupt without giving Bay a release. Williams exercised her power of foreclosure and sold the land, but was left being owed $3,559 on the notes. She sued Bay for that amount as third-party beneficiary of the deed between Newman and Sissons and Bay.

Bay argued that he was absolved from his promise to pay the promissory notes by Sissons' release. He proposed three different theories: (1) that third-party beneficiary rights do not vest until suit is brought; (2) that third-party beneficiary rights do not vest until the beneficiary relies upon or accepts the promisor's promise; and (3) that the promisor's promise to pay is a mere indemnity, which cannot be reached until the promisee is insolvent or on some other equitable ground. This court in *Bay* rejected these views, holding:

> "[The promisor's] promise invests the person for whose use it is made with an immediate interest and right, as though the promise had been made to him. This being true, the person who procures the promise has no legal right to release or discharge the person who made the promise, from his liability to the beneficiary. Having the right, it is under the sole control of the person for whose benefit it is made,—as much so as if made directly to him."

Consequently, *Bay* established the rule in Illinois that third-party beneficiary rights vest immediately and cannot be altered or extinguished through a later agreement of the original parties to the contract, unless the beneficiary assents.

Engelhaupt urges us to replace the *Bay* rule with the "modern view" as set forth in section 311 of the Second Restatement. Section 311, entitled "Variation of a Duty to a Beneficiary," stands in direct contrast to *Bay*. It provides that, in the absence of language in a contract making the rights of a third-party beneficiary irrevocable, the parties to the contract "retain power to discharge or modify the duty by subsequent agreement," without the third-party beneficiary's assent, at any time until the third-party beneficiary, without notice of the discharge or modification, materially changes position in justifiable reliance on the promise, brings suit on the promise or manifests assent to the promise at the request of the promisor or promisee. Restatement (Second) of Contracts § 311 (1981).

Section 311 now represents the majority view on the subject of vesting. In contrast, the immediate vesting rule as set forth in *Bay* represents the minority view, followed by only a handful of states.

Engelhaupt maintains that we should adopt section 311. He asserts that section 311 represents the majority rule on vesting because it better conforms to modern commercial practices and general principles of contract law. According to Engelhaupt, parties should remain free to modify or discharge their contracts as they see fit, without the assent of a third-party beneficiary, subject only to the three exceptions provided for in section 311. Section 311 makes sense, Engelhaupt contends, because third-party beneficiaries should not be able to enforce contracts for which they do not give any consideration, unless they demonstrate some detriment or act of faith in reliance on the contract.

Engelhaupt asserts that the superiority of the Restatement approach over the *Bay* rule is demonstrated by the facts present in this case. As he explains, the plaintiffs here freely chose to extend credit to Etheridge, who was then bound to pay them under Agreement I and Note I. Etheridge and Engelhaupt then freely contracted with each other that Engelhaupt would make one-half of Etheridge's payments to the plaintiffs, in Agreement II and Note II. The plaintiffs, however, were not bound to accept Engelhaupt's promise to pay in Agreement II and Note II in replacement of Etheridge's promise to pay in Agreement I and Note I, and did not do so. Consequently, the plaintiffs' contractual remedies against Etheridge in the event of Etheridge's nonpayment under Agreement I remained intact. Engelhaupt asserts that, in this situation, he and Etheridge should not be forever barred from modifying or discharging their agreement without the plaintiffs' assent, which is precisely what *Bay* mandates. Rather, Engelhaupt asserts, the third-party beneficiary plaintiffs should be found to have obtained vested rights in his and Etheridge's contract only if they meet one of the circumstances set forth in section 311.

Finding Engelhaupt's arguments persuasive, we hereby adopt the vesting rule set forth in section 311 of the Second Restatement. The rationale underlying section 311's vesting rule is that "parties to a contract should remain free to amend or rescind their agreement so long as there is no detriment to a third party who has provided no consideration for the benefit received." This rationale is compelling. Moreover, we find this rationale to be consistent with the general principles running throughout contract law. Contract law generally favors the freedom to contract. Contract law also allows for equitable remedies where the facts compel such a result.

In contrast, the immediate vesting rule of *Bay* curtails the freedom to contract. It provides, in essence, that every promise which benefits a third-party beneficiary carries with it another term, implied at law, that the parties to the contract are prohibited from modifying or discharging the promise that benefits the beneficiary, without the beneficiary's assent. We do not believe that the modern law of contracts should always imply such a term. To do so can work a great injustice upon the parties involved in a particular case. Although, as the plaintiffs contend, the *Bay* rule is clear and easy to apply, this does not persuade us to retain it. Our concern is that the rule of law we expound best serves the pursuit of justice, not that it is the easiest rule of law for courts to apply.

We note, moreover, that the plaintiffs' argument against adoption of the Restatement rule is not persuasive. They maintain that the Restatement position has fluctuated so much over the past century that it is not stable. We do not agree with this characterization. In fact, the Restatement position regarding creditor beneficiaries, such as the plaintiffs, is essentially the same as it has always been. Under the original Restatement, the rights of creditor beneficiaries vested once the beneficiary brought suit or otherwise materially changed position in reliance on the promise. Restatement of Contracts §§ 142, 143 (1932). Today, creditor beneficiaries are called intended beneficiaries, and their rights vest once the beneficiary brings suit on the promise, materially changes position in justifiable reliance on the promise or manifests assent to the promise at the request of the promisor or promisee. Restatement (Second) of Contracts §§ 302, 311 (1981). As to donee beneficiaries, the original Restatement provided that their rights vested immediately. Restatement of Contracts §§ 142, 143 (1932). This was changed after substantial criticism. Now donee beneficiaries are also classified as intended beneficiaries, and their rights vest as in the same manner stated above. Restatement (Second) of Contracts §§ 302, 311 (1981). Even were we to agree with the plaintiffs' characterization of the Restatement view as unstable, however, this would not impact our decision. We find the current Restatement position on vesting to be consistent with general principles underlying contract law. This court is free to reject any later revisions of the Restatement.

In conclusion, we adopt the vesting rule set forth in section 311 of the Second Restatement. *Bay* is hereby overruled. The circuit court awarded summary judgment to the plaintiffs based on the *Bay* rule. The circuit court did not consider the plaintiffs' motion for summary judgment in the context of the vesting rule of section 311. We therefore reverse this award of summary judgment for the plaintiffs and remand to the circuit court for further proceedings, consistent with section 311's vesting rule. * * *

QUESTIONS

1. Questions about the facts of this case

    1.1. At the time the plaintiffs agreed to sell their business to Etheridge and entered into Agreement I and Note 1, was Engelhaupt legally obligated to make payments to the plaintiffs?

    1.2. Do we know whether Note 1 is in default? Should that be relevant?

1.3.   Who is the third party beneficiary of Agreement II?

1.4.   Who is the promisor in Agreement II?

1.5.   Has the promisor paid all amounts that he promised to pay in Agreement II?

2.   Questions about the law

2.1.   At trial, Engelhaupt argued that the plaintiffs were not intended third-party beneficiaries of Agreement II. The trial court held that the plaintiffs were intended third-party beneficiaries and Engelhaupt did not challenge that holding on appeal. Do you agree with that decision? Would Judge Wood agree? Recall that this case, *Olson v. Etheridge*, was the one case referred to in the *Midwest Grain Products* case.

2.2.   Would this case have been decided differently if Etheridge was in default under Agreement I after 1985 but plaintiffs had not foreclosed because of the promised payments from Engelhaupt under Agreement II?

2.3.   What is the practical significance, if any, of the court's statement in this case that "the promisor may assert against the beneficiary any defense that the promisor could assert against the promisee if the promisee were suing on the contract"? What if in *Lawrence v. Fox*, the $300 that Holly "loaned and advanced" to the defendant was counterfeit funds?

2.4.   On January 15, 2011, Batman contracts to provide protection to Gotham for the remainder of 2011 in exchange for Gotham's promise to pay Robin $20,000 on December 31, 2011. Notwithstanding this contract, Batman fails to provide any protection to Gotham. Does Gotham still have to pay Robin $20,000 on December 31, 2011?

2.5.   Do you agree with the statement in *Olson* that "the vesting doctrine is an exception to the * * * rule that the promisor may assert against the beneficiary any defense that the promisor could assert against the promisee"?

2.6.   Do you understand the statement in *Olson* that "the assumption by Engelhaupt of one half of Etheridge's obligation to pay is a classic example of a delegation"? Was *Lawrence v. Fox* also a "classic example of a delegation"? What is the difference between a delegation and a third-party beneficiary transaction? Between a delegation and an assignment?

SECTION 2: ASSIGNMENT AND DELEGATION

A. INTRODUCTION TO ASSIGNMENT AND DELEGATION: WHAT ARE THEY?

A contract creates both rights and duties. If for example, Markell contracts to buy Epstein's car for $400, Markell has a right to obtain Epstein's car and a duty to pay $400. Epstein has a right to be paid $400 and a duty to deliver his car.

Similarly, if Epstein contracts with BARBRI to do contracts bar review lectures in California for $10 a lecture, Epstein has a right to be paid $10 and a duty to deliver contracts lectures. BARBRI has a right to Epstein's lectures and a duty to pay $10.

A contracting party's later transfer of his contract rights to a third party is generally referred to as assignment. If, for example, Markell transfers his right to obtain Epstein's car to Ponoroff, that is an "assignment" and, Markell is an assignor, and Ponoroff is an assignee. The *Olson* case above provides another example of an assignment. Recall that in *Olson*, Etheridge assigned the right to payment from Engelhaupt under Agreement II to Princeton Bank. Etheridge is the assignor; Princeton Bank is the assignee; and Engelhaupt is the obligor.

A contracting party's later transfer of his contract duties to a third party is generally referred to as a delegation. If, for example, Epstein gets Ponoroff to do the BARBRI contracts bar review lectures in California, that is a delegation, Epstein is a delegator, and Ponoroff is a delegatee. Again, the *Olson* case provides another example of a delegation. Recall that in Agreement II in *Olson*, Etheridge got Engelhaupt to agree to pay one-half of what Etheridge owed to Plaintiffs, *i.e.*, Etheridge delegated that duty to Engelhaupt. Etheridge is the delegator; Emgelhaupt is the delegate; and the Plaintiff Olson is the obligee

As the *Olson* case illustrates, a contracting party can both assign his contract rights and delegate his contract duties. Another example of both assignment and delegation: Epstein and Ponoroff agree that Ponoroff will do the California BARBRI lectures and collect the $10 from BARBRI as provided for in Epstein's earlier contract with BARBRI.

There are three questions about contract assignments and delegations that lawyers and first year law students need to be able to answer:

1. How is an assignment of rights under a contract factually different from a contract intended to benefit a third party? (In other words, when do you look to the law regarding third party beneficiaries and when do you look to the law regarding assignments?)

2. What are the legal consequences of an assignment and/or a delegation?

3. What are the limitations on the making of an assignment and/or a delegation?

You should be able to answer the first question from the previous material in this Chapter, and you should be able to answer the next two questions from the remaining materials in this Chapter.

B. CONSEQUENCES OF AN ASSIGNMENT AND DELEGATION: WHO CAN SUE WHOM?

1. Assignee Can Sue Obligor

Illustration 1 to *Restatement (Second) Contracts* § 317 illustrates that the assignee can sue the obligor:

> 1. *A has a right to $100 against B. A assigns his right to C. A's right is thereby extinguished, and C acquires a right against B to receive $100.*

PROBLEMS

1. Markell enters into a contract with Epstein to purchase Epstein's 1973 Cadillac for $400. The contract provides that Markell will pay Epstein for the car within ten days after delivery. Epstein delivers the car to Markell. Epstein then assigns his right to the $400 payment under the Markell contract to Ponoroff. Markell refuses to pay Ponoroff. Can Ponoroff sue Markell for breach of the Cadillac contract even though Ponoroff was not a party to that contract?

2. Under the facts in question 1 above, can Epstein sue Markell for breach of contract?

3. In questions 1 and 2, should it matter whether Ponoroff paid Epstein or Epstein simply made a gift to Ponoroff?

4. Epstein's klezmer band, The Alter Kochers, signs a contract with Bad Boy Records to record "Bubba's Bar Mitzvah." The contract provides for the payment of royalties to Epstein based on sales. Subsequently, Epstein assigns his right to "Bubba's Bar Mitzvah" royalty payments to Markell. To whom should Bad Boy make the royalty payments? What if Bad Boy makes a royalty payment to Epstein after the assignment but before it had been notified of the assignment?

---

2. Obligee Can Sue Delegator

The *Restatement* restates the law with respect to who can sue whom after a delegation of duties to perform under a contract. Please read section 318 of the *Restatement (Second) of Contracts* set out below and apply it in the questions below.

§ 318   Delegation of Performance of Duty

(1) An obligor can properly delegate the performance of his duty to another unless the delegation is contrary to public policy or the terms of his promise.

(2) Unless otherwise agreed, a promise requires performance by a particular person only to the extent that the obligee has a substantial interest in having that person perform or control the acts promised.

(3) Unless the obligee agrees otherwise, neither delegation of performance nor a contract to assume the duty made with the obligor by the person delegated discharges any duty or liability of the delegating obligor.

Comments & Illustrations:

1.   A owes B $100, and asks C to pay B. Payment or tender to B by C has the effect of payment or tender by A.

2.   A contracts to deliver to B coal of specified kind and quality. A delegates the performance of this duty to C, who tenders to B coal of the specified kind and quality. The tender has the effect of a tender by A.

3.   A contracts to build a building for B in accordance with specifications, and delegates the plumbing work to C. Performance by C has the effect of performance by A.

. . . .

d.   Delegation and novation. *An obligor is discharged by the substitution of a new obligor only if the contract so provides or if the obligee makes a binding manifestation of assent, forming a novation. See §§ 280, 328 and 329. Otherwise, the obligee retains his original right against the obligor, even though the obligor manifests an intention to substitute another obligor in his place and the other purports to assume the duty. The obligee may, however, have rights against the other as an intended beneficiary of the promise to assume the duty.*

Illustrations:

9.   A borrows $50,000 from B and contracts to repay it. The contract provides that, if a corporation C is organized and assumes the debt under described conditions, A will be under no further obligation. C is organized and in good faith assumes the debt as provided. A is discharged.

10.   A contracts with B to cut the grass on B's meadow. A delegates performance to C, who contracts with A to assume A's duty and perform the work. C begins performance with B's assent, but later breaks the contract. C is liable to B, but A is not discharged.

PROBLEMS

1. Epstein contracts with BARBRI to do bar review lectures in California for $10. Being the kind of friend that he is, Ponoroff agrees to do the lectures for Epstein without charge. And, being the kind of friend that he is, notwithstanding this agreement, Ponoroff does not do the lectures. Can BARBRI sue Epstein for breach of contract?

2. Same facts as question 1. Can BARBRI sue Ponoroff for breach of contract?

3. Would your answers to questions 1 and/or 2 change if Epstein paid Ponoroff $30 to do the lectures?

4. Would your answers change if BARBRI and Epstein and Ponoroff had agreed that Ponoroff could do the lectures instead of Epstein? (Hint: you do not have to be a Catholic to know what a "novation" is.)

5. H enters into a contract with M under which M loans H $50,000 and H grants M a mortgage on H's house. Subsequently, H sells the house to T who assumes the mortgage. If T misses a mortgage payment, can M still sue H? Can M sue T? What, if any, needed facts are missing?

6. Is the following statement doctrine as well as doggerel: "A delegation for consideration results in a third party beneficiary obligation"?

C. LIMITATIONS ON ASSIGNMENT AND DELEGATION

It should be obvious that there are limitations on a contracting party's ability to assign her contract rights and/or delegate her contract duties. If not, consider the following easy questions:

1. Shirley MacLaine enters into a contract with Ponoroff Pictures, Inc. in which she promises to star in a musical to be filmed in the United States. Can Ponoroff Pictures, Inc. assign its rights under this contract to Markell Movies Ltd. which wants Ms. MacLaine to star in a Western to be filmed in Australia?

2. Ron Jeremy contracts with Markell Mature Movies LLC, to star in "A Star is Porn II." Can Jeremy delegate his duty to perform to Epstein?

As the first question illustrates, there is a common law prohibition on assignments that "materially change the duty of the obligor." *See Restatement (Second) of Contracts* § 317(2)(a). And, as should be obvious from the second illustration, delegation is not permitted if "the obligee has a substantial interest in having that person perform or control the acts promised." *See Restatement (Second)* § 318(2).

The final three cases illustrate less obvious limitations on assignment and delegation.

MACKE CO. v. PIZZA OF GAITHERSBURG, INC.

Court of Appeals of Maryland
259 Md. 479, 270 A.2d 645 (1970)

SINGLEY, JUDGE.

The appellees and defendants below, Pizza of Gaithersburg, Inc.; Pizzeria, Inc.; The Pizza Pie Corp., Inc. and Pizza Oven, Inc. * * * operated at six locations in Montgomery and Prince George's Counties. The appellees had arranged to have installed in each of their locations cold drink vending machines owned by Virginia Coffee Service, Inc., and on 30 December 1966, this arrangement was formalized at five of the locations, by contracts for terms of one year, automatically renewable for a like term in the absence of 30 days' written notice. A similar contract for the sixth location was entered into on 25 July 1967.

On 30 December 1967, Virginia's assets were purchased by The Macke Company (Macke) and the six contracts were assigned to Macke by Virginia. In January, 1968, the Pizza Shops attempted to terminate the five contracts having the December anniversary date, and in February, the contract which had the July anniversary date.

Macke brought suit in the Circuit Court for Montgomery County against each of the Pizza Shops for damages for breach of contract. From judgments for the defendants, Macke has appealed.

The lower court based the result which it reached on two grounds: first, that the Pizza Shops, when they contracted with Virginia, relied on its skill, judgment and reputation, which made impossible a delegation of Virginia's duties to Macke; and second, that the damages claimed could not be shown with reasonable certainty. These conclusions are challenged by Macke.

In the absence of a contrary provision—and there was none here—rights and duties under an executory bilateral contract may be assigned and delegated, subject to the exception that duties under a contract to provide personal services may never be delegated, nor rights be assigned under a contract where delectus personae was an ingredient of the bargain.[1] * * *

The six machines were placed on the appellees' premises under a printed 'Agreement–Contract' which identified the 'customer,' gave its place of business, described the vending machine, and then provided:

"TERMS

"1. The Company will install on the Customer's premises the above listed equipment and will maintain the equipment in good operating order and stocked with merchandise.

---

1. Like all generalizations, this one is subject to an important exception. Uniform Commercial Code § 9–318 makes ineffective a term in any contract prohibiting the assignment of a contract right: *i.e.*, a right to payment. Compare Restatement, *Contracts* § 151(c) (1932).

"2. The location of this equipment will be such as to permit accessibility to persons desiring use of same. This equipment shall remain the property of the Company and shall not be moved from the location at which installed, except by the Company.

"3. For equipment requiring electricity and water, the Customer is responsible for electrical receptacle and water outlet within ten (10) feet of the equipment location. The Customer is also responsible to supply the Electrical Power and Water needed.

"4. The Customer will exercise every effort to protect this equipment from abuse or damage.

"5. The Company will be responsible for all licenses and taxes on the equipment and sale of products.

"6. This Agreement–Contract is for a term of one (1) year from the date indicated herein and will be automatically renewed for a like period, unless thirty (30) day written notice is given by either party to terminate service.

"7. Commission on monthly sales will be paid by the Company to the Customer at the following rate: * * *"

The rate provided in each of the agreements was '30% of Gross Receipts to $300.00 monthly[,] 35% over [$]300.00,' except for the agreement with Pizza of Gaithersburg, Inc., which called for '40% of Gross Receipts.'

We cannot regard the agreements as contracts for personal services. They were either a license or concession granted Virginia by the appellees, or a lease of a portion of the appellees' premises, with Virginia agreeing to pay a percentage of gross sales as a license or concession fee or as rent * * * and were assignable by Virginia unless they imposed on Virginia duties of a personal or unique character which could not be delegated. * * *

The appellees earnestly argue that they had dealt with Macke before and had chosen Virginia because they preferred the way it conducted its business. Specifically, they say that service was more personalized, since the president of Virginia kept the machines in working order, that commissions were paid in cash, and that Virginia permitted them to keep keys to the machines so that minor adjustments could be made when needed. Even if we assume all this to be true, the agreements with Virginia were silent as to the details of the working arrangements and contained only a provision requiring Virginia to 'install * * * the above listed equipment and * * * maintain the equipment in good operating order and stocked with merchandise.' We think the Supreme Court of California put the problem of personal service in proper focus a century ago when it upheld the assignment of a contract to grade a San Francisco street:

'All painters do not paint portraits like Sir Joshua Reynolds, nor landscapes like Claude Lorraine, nor do all writers write dramas like Shakespeare or fiction like Dickens. Rare genius and extraordinary skill are not transferable, and contracts for their employment are therefore personal, and cannot be assigned. But rare genius and extraordinary skill are not indispensable to the workmanlike digging down of a sand hill or the filling up of a depression to a given level, or the construction of brick sewers with manholes and covers, and contracts for such work are not personal, and may be assigned.' *Taylor v. Palmer*, 31 Cal. 240 at 247–248 (1866).

* * * Moreover, the difference between the service the Pizza Shops happened to be getting from Virginia and what they expected to get from Macke did not mount up to such a material change in the performance of obligations under the agreements as would justify the appellees' refusal to recognize the assignment.

* * *

Restatement, *Contracts* § 160(3) (1932) reads, in part:

'Performance or offer of performance by a person delegated has the same legal effect as performance or offer of performance by the person named in the contract, unless,

(a) performance by the person delegated varies or would vary materially from performance by the person named in the contract as the one to perform, and there has been no * * * assent to the delegation * * *'

In cases involving the sale of goods, the Restatement rule respecting delegation of duties has been amplified by Uniform Commercial Code § 2–210(5), which permits a promisee to demand assurances from the party to whom duties have been delegated.

As we see it, the delegation of duty by Virginia to Macke was entirely permissible under the terms of the agreements. * * *

QUESTIONS

1. Questions about the facts of the case
    1.1. Who is suing whom for what? Which contract was breached?
    1.2. What if any facts were important to the trial court's ruling for Pizza Shops? For the appellate court's ruling for Macke?
    1.3. What, if any, contract language was important to the appellate court in making its decision?
2. Questions about the law
    2.1. The court stated, "We cannot regard the agreements as contracts for personal services." Which agreements? Did the trial court regard the "agreements as contracts for personal services"?
    2.2. Do you understand the "delectus personae rule," *i.e.*, "duties under a personal services contract may never be delegated * * * where

delectus personae was an ingredient of the bargain"? Did you find the court's mention of Joshua Reynolds and Claude Lorraine helpful or, like Epstein, do you have no clue who they are? Would Ron Jeremy be a more helpful cultural allusion? Was Ron Jeremy's contract with Markell Mature Movies LLC, to star in "A Star is Porn II" a personal services contract?

2.3. Was this case about the validity of Virginia's assignment of contract rights to Macke or the validity of Virginia's delegation of contract duties to Macke?

2.4. What result if the contract had provided "the President of Virginia Coffee Service, Inc. shall personally keep the machines in working order"? Dean James Nehf suggests:

The general rule is that contracts are assignable unless the assignment will materially alter the rights or obligations of the nonassigning party. In deciding whether the assignment will change the contract materially, contract language can be critical.

The typical scenario involves the nonassigning party complaining that the assignment will substitute an inferior actor for the original contracting party, now the assignor. In one often-cited case, an owner of several pizza shops contracted with a vending machine company to stock and service its vending machines. This particular vending company was chosen because its president personally tended to the maintenance, paid commissions in cash, and allowed the shops to keep a key to the machines, making minor adjustments fast and easy. When the vending company sold its assets and assigned all its contracts, the pizza shops terminated the agreement. The court held that the contract was assignable. There would not be a material change in service even though the new company did not pay cash commissions or allow the shops to keep a key on hand. A deciding factor was that the contract did not mention these benefits which the non-assigning party now claimed were so important. The lesson for contract drafters is that all important expectations should be spelled out in the contract; otherwise, it may be difficult to contend later that they were material parts of the bargain that would be altered through an assignment.

James P. Nehf, *Writing Contracts in the Client's Interest*, 51 S.C. L. REV. 153, 179 (1999). Dean Nehf teaches contracts at Indiana University–Indianapolis. If he asked a student to state the holding in the *Macke* case, would he be satisfied with the statement "The court held that the contract was assignable"?

2.5. What result if the contract had provided: "This contract may not be assigned"? The next case involves a contract provision prohibiting assignment and, unlike *Macke*, is about the validity of the assignment.

RUMBIN v. UTICA MUTUAL INSURANCE CO.

Supreme Court of Connecticut
254 Conn. 259, 757 A.2d 526 (2000)

VERTEFEUILLE, J.

The defendant Safeco Life Insurance Company (Safeco), appeals from the judgment of the trial court approving the transfer by the plaintiff, Marco Rumbin, of payments due to him under an annuity issued pursuant to a structured settlement agreement between the plaintiff and the named defendant, Utica Mutual Insurance Company (Utica Mutual).[1] The plaintiff proposes to sell the remaining payments to the intervening plaintiff, J.G. Wentworth.[2] The principal issues in this appeal are: (1) whether General Statutes § 52–225f invalidates antiassignment provisions that are included in structured settlement agreements and annuities issued pursuant to such agreements; and (2) whether the antiassignment clause contained in the annuity issued by Safeco for the plaintiff beneficiary invalidates his assignment to Wentworth. We conclude that § 52–225f does not invalidate such antiassignment provisions. We further conclude that, under Connecticut common law, the antiassignment provision in the annuity contract does not invalidate the plaintiff's assignment of his right to payments under the annuity to Wentworth. In accordance with case law and § 322 of the Restatement (Second) of Contracts, an antiassignment provision that does not limit the power to assign or expressly invalidate the assignment does not render the assignment of the annuity ineffective. Safeco, however, has the right to recover damages for the plaintiff's breach of the antiassignment provision. We therefore affirm the judgment of the trial court.

The record reveals the following facts. In April, 1998, the plaintiff and Utica Mutual entered into a structured settlement agreement to resolve a personal injury claim. Pursuant to that settlement agreement, the plaintiff was to receive from Utica Mutual a lump sum payment, followed by a series of periodic payments over the next fifteen years.[5] The structured portion of the settlement was funded by the annuity contract issued by Safeco. The annuity contract provided under its "Assignment" provision that "[n]o payment under this annuity contract may be * * * assigned * * * in any manner by the [plaintiff]. * * *"[6]

---

1. The only party objecting to the sale of the annuity contract is Safeco, the issuer of the annuity contract. Utica Mutual is not a party to this appeal.

2. For the remainder of this opinion, we use the term "plaintiff" to refer to Rumbin and the term "plaintiffs" to refer to both the named plaintiff, Rumbin, and the intervening plaintiff, Wentworth.

5. Under the terms of the settlement agreement, the plaintiff was entitled to receive $52,000 within thirty days of its execution, thirty semiannual payments of $1323.09 beginning on March 6, 1999, and a final lump sum payment of $44,000 on March 6, 2014.

6. The plaintiff has not claimed that the annuity contract is a contract of adhesion. Typically, "life insurance contracts are [considered] contracts of adhesion because [t]he contract is drawn up by the insurer and the insured, who merely adheres to it, has little choice as to its terms. * * * Standardized contracts of insurance continue to be prime examples of contracts of adhesion,

Approximately six months after the execution of the settlement agreement and the issuance of the annuity, the plaintiff had become unemployed and faced a mortgage foreclosure action against his home, where he lived with his family. In order to resolve his financial troubles, the plaintiff decided to sell his right to the annuity payments. In November, 1998, he filed a declaratory judgment action seeking court approval to transfer his right to the remaining annuity payments to Wentworth in exchange for a lump sum payment and other consideration. * * *

The primary issue raised by this case is whether, under Connecticut common law, an antiassignment provision in an annuity contract invalidates the plaintiff payee's transfer of his right to future payments under the annuity to a third party. We conclude, in accordance with case law and § 322 of the Restatement (Second) of Contracts, that the antiassignment provision at issue here does not render the assignment of the annuity ineffective, but, instead, gives the annuity issuer, Safeco, the right to recover damages for breach of the antiassignment provision.

Although we previously have addressed the issue of the validity of contractual provisions prohibiting the assignment of contractual rights; *see Lewin & Sons, Inc. v. Herman*, 143 Conn. 146, 149, 120 A.2d 423 (1956) (upholding validity of contractual provision that prohibited assignment without consent); the law of contracts has changed considerably since our earlier decision. Accordingly, we now reexamine the basic legal principles regarding contractual antiassignment provisions.

* * * Common-law restrictions on assignment were abandoned when courts recognized the necessity of permitting the transfer of contract rights. * * *

The parties to a contract can include express language to limit assignment and courts generally uphold these contractual antiassignment clauses. Given the importance of free assignability, however, antiassignment clauses are construed narrowly whenever possible.

In interpreting antiassignment clauses, the majority of jurisdictions now distinguish between the assignor's "right" to assign and the "power" to assign (modern approach). For example, in *Bel–Ray Co. v. Chemrite (Pty.) Ltd.*, 181 F.3d 435, 442 (3d Cir.1999), the United States Court of Appeals for the Third Circuit recognized that numerous jurisdictions followed the general rule "that contractual provisions limiting or prohibiting assignments operate only to limit [the] parties' *right* to assign the contract, but not their *power* to do so, unless the parties manifest an intent to the contrary with specificity." (Emphasis added.) The court concluded, however, that the "assignment clauses [did] not contain the requisite clear language to limit [the] 'power' to assign" and, therefore, held the assignment valid and enforceable. The court acknowledged that

---

whose most salient feature is that they are not subject to the normal bargaining processes of ordinary contracts." *Aetna Casualty & Surety Co. v. Murphy*, 206 Conn. 409, 416, 538 A.2d 219 (1988). A review of the annuity contract in the present case reveals that it is a preprinted, standardized insurance contract in which the plaintiff was the named annuitant. It was not a contract arrived at by actual negotiation between the parties. * * *

contracting parties could limit the *power* to assign by including an "assignment provision [that] generally states that nonconforming assignments (i) shall be 'void' or 'invalid,' or (ii) that the assignee shall acquire no rights or the nonassigning party shall not recognize any such assignment." Without such express contractual language, however, "the provision limiting or prohibiting assignments will be interpreted merely as a covenant not to assign. * * * Breach of such a covenant may render the assigning party liable in damages to the non-assigning party. The assignment, however, remains valid and enforceable against both the assignor and the assignee."

* * *

The modern approach offers the advantage of free assignability together with full protection for any obligor who actually suffers damages as a result of an assignment. An assignor who breaches a contractual provision limiting his or her right to assign will be liable for any damages that result from that assignment. * * *

This approach is also adopted in the Restatement (Second) of Contracts. Section 322(2)(b) of the Restatement (Second), supra, provides that the general rule is "[a] contract term prohibiting assignment of rights under the contract, unless a different intention is manifested * * * (b) gives the obligor a right to damages for breach of the terms forbidding assignment but does not render the assignment ineffective. * * *"

In the present case, the annuity contract provided that "[n]o payment under this annuity contract may be * * * assigned" by the plaintiff. This antiassignment provision limited the plaintiff's *right* to assign, but not his *power* to do so. The provision did not contain any express language to limit the power to assign or to void the assignment itself. Therefore, in accordance with the modern approach, we conclude that the plaintiff's assignment to Wentworth is valid and enforceable despite the plaintiff's breach of the contract's antiassignment provision. We further conclude, however, that Safeco is free to sue for any damages that it might sustain as a result of the assignment by bringing an action for breach of contract against the plaintiff as assignor. Alternatively, Safeco may pursue damages from Wentworth, who, as the assignee, " 'stands in the shoes of the assignor.' " * * * Safeco, therefore, is fully protected against any actual damages that it might sustain as a result of the plaintiff's breach of the antiassignment provision.[11] The modern approach thus serves the dual

---

11. At the trial court hearing, Safeco did not show any actual damages resulting from the assignment. It argues, however, that upholding the assignment increases the risk of losing certain purported favorable federal tax treatment afforded to both the insurance company and the annuitant. More specifically, an insurer can fund its liability under a structured settlement agreement by purchasing an annuity that grows tax free while the annuitant receives tax free payments from that annuity. Safeco argues that allowing a party to assign his rights to payments frustrates the public policy of ensuring a steady source of income to that party and creates a risk that the favorable tax treatment will be lost. We agree with the trial court's findings that "[Safeco] * * * has not offered evidence of danger of suffering adverse tax effects as a result of the transfer nor is there other evidence of any detriment to it by virtue of the transfer." Although Safeco has raised the specter of a risk of losing its favorable tax treatment, it has not provided objectives of free assignability of contracts together with full compensation for any actual damages that might result from an assignment made in breach of an antiassignment provision.

    The judgment is affirmed.

QUESTIONS AND NOTE

1. Questions about the facts of this case

    1.1. Which contract is the subject matter of this litigation? Was the plaintiff, Marco Rumbin, a party to the annuity contract? Do we know? Do we need to know?

    1.2. Who was the assignor? The assignee? The obligor? The delegator? The delegatee? The obligee? The third party beneficiary? The promisor? The promisee?

    1.3. Was there an "antiassignment" provision in the annuity contract? Why?

2. Questions about the law

    2.1. Is this decision consistent with the language of the contract? With the intention of the parties to the contract?

    2.2. Would this court have reached a different decision if the contract had added the words "and any assignments will be void"?

    2.3. Would the court have reached a different decision if Safeco produced evidence that it was damaged by the assignment? If you were representing Safeco, what evidence could you offer to show damage from the assignment? If Safeco was not damaged by the assignment, why is Safeco objecting to the sale of the annuity contract by Rumbin and paying for an appeal to the Supreme Court of Connecticut?

3. Note

    Professor Gregory Scott Crespi, who teaches contracts at the Dedman School of Law of Southern Methodist University, wrote an article on the *Rumbin* case and the assignability of structured settlement contracts. He concludes: "Courts should start their analyses with Restatement section 322(2), and first determine whether the anti-assignment provision at issue demonstrates the parties' intent to preclude assignment, rather than the intent to merely confer a right to seek damages upon the obligor. They should not, however, follow the Rumbin II approach and make this determination solely on the basis of fine verbal distinctions concerning the language of the anti-assignment clause. These clauses generally appear to be standard "boilerplate" provisions drawn from a form book and not individually tailored to the parties, particular circumstances, or concerns to any meaningful extent. Instead, courts should consider the

---

any evidence that there will be an actual adverse effect if this court were to uphold the assignment.

entire conduct of the settlement negotiations and the extent to which the obligor has evidenced a concern with adverse tax or other implications of an assignment." Gregory Scott Crespi, *Selling Structured Settlements: The Uncertain Effect of Anti–Assignment Clauses*, 28 PEPPERDINE L REV. 787, 817 (2001).

The next case, our last case, is a great last case. A great case for your:

— reflecting on the concepts that you have learned in this chapter and elsewhere in the book;

— comparing the skills you have acquired in distinguishing cases and reading statutes with the skills of the judges on the Seventh Circuit and their law clerks;

— appreciating the importance of a deal lawyer's knowing contract law;

— understanding, that notwithstanding the incredible amount that you have learned from this wonderful contracts course, there is a need for more law school courses.

SALLY BEAUTY CO., INC. v. NEXXUS PRODUCTS CO., INC.

U.S. Court of Appeals, Seventh Circuit
801 F.2d 1001 (1986)

CUDAHY, CIRCUIT JUDGE.

Nexxus Products Company ("Nexxus") entered into a contract with Best Barber & Beauty Supply Company, Inc. ("Best"), under which Best would be the exclusive distributor of Nexxus hair care products to barbers and hair stylists throughout most of Texas. When Best was acquired by and merged into Sally Beauty Company, Inc. ("Sally Beauty"), Nexxus cancelled the agreement. Sally Beauty is a wholly-owned subsidiary of Alberto–Culver Company ("Alberto–Culver"), a major manufacturer of hair care products and a competitor of Nexxus'. Sally Beauty claims that Nexxus breached the contract by cancelling; Nexxus asserts by way of defense that the contract was not assignable or, in the alternative, not assignable to Sally Beauty. The district court granted Nexxus' motion for summary judgment, ruling that the contract was one for personal services and therefore not assignable. We affirm on a different theory—that this contract could not be assigned to the wholly-owned subsidiary of a direct competitor under section 2–210 of the Uniform Commercial Code.

I.

Only the basic facts are undisputed and they are as follows. Prior to its merger with Sally Beauty, Best was a Texas corporation in the business of distributing beauty and hair care products to retail stores, barber shops and beauty salons throughout Texas. Between March and July 1979, Mark Reichek, Best's president, negotiated with Stephen Redding, Nexxus' vice-president, over a possible distribution agreement between Best and Nexxus. Nexxus, founded in 1979, is a California corporation that formulates and markets hair care products. Nexxus does not market its products to retail stores, preferring to sell them to independent distributors for resale to barbers and beauticians. On August 2, 1979, Nexxus executed a distributorship agreement with Best, in the form of a July 24, 1979 letter from Reichek, for Best, to Redding, for Nexxus:

Dear Steve:

It was a pleasure meeting with you and discussing the distribution of Nexus Products. The line is very exciting and we feel we can do a substantial job with it—especially as the exclusive distributor in Texas (except El Paso).

If I understand the pricing structure correctly, we would pay $1.50 for an item that retails for $5.00 (less 50%, less 40% off retail), and Nexus will pay the freight charges regardless of order size. This approach to pricing will enable us to price the items in the line in such a way that they will be attractive and profitable to the salons.

* * *

While we feel confident that we can do an outstanding job with the Nexus line and that the volume we generate will adequately compensate you for your continued support, it is usually best to have an understanding should we no longer be distributing Nexus Products—either by our desire or your request. Based on our discussions, cancellation or termination of Best Barber & Beauty Supply Co., Inc. as a distributor can only take place on the anniversary date of our original appointment as a distributor—and then only with 120 days prior notice. If Nexus terminates us, Nexus will buy back all of our inventory at cost and will pay the freight charges on the returned merchandise.

Steve, we feel that the Nexus line is exciting and very promotable. With the program outlined in this letter, we feel it can be mutually profitable and look forward to a long and successful business relationship. If you agree that this letter contains the details of our understanding regarding the distribution of Nexus Products, please sign the acknowledgment below and return one copy of this letter to me.

Very truly yours,
/s/ Mark E. Reichek
President

Acknowledged /s/ Stephen Redding Date 8/2/79. Appellant's Appendix at 2–3.

In July 1981, Sally Beauty acquired Best in a stock purchase transaction and Best was merged into Sally Beauty, which succeeded to Best's rights and interests in all of Best's contracts. Sally Beauty, a Delaware corporation with its principal place of business in Texas, is a wholly-owned subsidiary of Alberto–Culver. Sally Beauty, like Best, is a distributor of hair care and beauty products to retail stores and hair styling salons. Alberto–Culver is a major manufacturer of hair care products and, thus, is a direct competitor of Nexxus in the hair care market.

Shortly after the merger, Redding met with Michael Renzulli, president of Sally Beauty, to discuss the Nexxus distribution agreement. After the meeting, Redding wrote Renzulli a letter stating that Nexxus would not allow Sally Beauty, a wholly-owned subsidiary of a direct competitor, to distribute Nexxus products:

> "As we discussed in New Orleans, we have great reservations about allowing our NEXXUS Products to be distributed by a company which is, in essence, a direct competitor. We appreciate your argument of autonomy for your business, but the fact remains that you are totally owned by Alberto–Culver.
>
> Since we see no way of justifying this conflict, we cannot allow our products to be distributed by Sally Beauty Company."

In August 1983, Sally Beauty commenced this action by filing a complaint in the Northern District of Illinois, claiming that Nexxus had breached the distribution agreement. * * * Nexxus filed a motion for summary judgment on the breach of contract claim the next day.

The district court granted Nexxus' motion for summary judgment. * * *

In ruling on this motion, the district court framed the issue before it as "whether the contract at issue here between Best and Nexxus was of a personal nature such that it was not assignable without Nexxus' consent." It ruled:

> The court is convinced, based upon the nature of the contract and the circumstances surrounding its formation, that the contract at issue here was of such a nature that it was not assignable without Nexxus's consent. First, the very nature of the contract itself suggests its personal character. A distribution agreement is a contract whereby a manufacturer gives another party the right to distribute its products. It is clearly a contract for the performance of a service. In the court's view, the mere selection by a manufacturer of a party to distribute its goods presupposes a reliance and confidence by the manufacturer on the integrity and abilities of the other party. * * * In addition, in this case the circumstances surrounding the contract's formation support the conclusion that the agreement was not simply an ordinary commercial contract but was one which was based upon a relationship of personal trust and confidence between the parties. Specifically, Stephen Redding, Nexxus's vice-president, travelled to Texas and met with Best's president personally for several days before making the decision to award the Texas distributorship to Best. Best itself had

been in the hair care business for 40 years and its president Mark Reichek had extensive experience in the industry. It is reasonable to conclude that Stephen Redding and Nexxus would want its distributor to be experienced and knowledgeable in the hair care field and that the selection of Best was based upon personal factors such as these.

* * *

We cannot affirm this summary judgment on the grounds relied on by the district court. * * * Although it might be "reasonable to conclude" that Best and Nexxus had based their agreement on "a relationship of personal trust and confidence," and that Reichek's participation was considered essential to Best's performance, this is a finding of fact. Since the parties submitted conflicting affidavits on this question,[3] the district court erred in relying on Nexxus' view as representing undisputed fact in ruling on this summary judgment motion.

We may affirm this summary judgment, however, on a different ground if it finds support in the record. Sally Beauty contends that the distribution agreement is freely assignable because it is governed by the provisions of the Uniform Commercial Code (the "UCC" or the "Code"), as adopted in Texas. Appellants' Brief at 46–47. We agree with Sally that the provisions of the UCC govern this contract and for that reason hold that the assignment of the contract by Best to Sally Beauty was barred by the UCC rules on delegation of performance, UCC § 2–210(1).

* * * Texas applies the "dominant factor" test to determine whether the UCC applies to a given contract or transaction: was the essence of or dominant factor in the formation of the contract the provision of goods or services? No Texas case addresses whether a distribution agreement is a contract for the sale of goods, but the rule in the majority of jurisdictions is that distributorships (both exclusive and non-exclusive) are to be treated as sale of goods contracts under the UCC.

Several of these courts note that "a distributorship agreement is more involved than a typical sales contract." This is true of the contract at issue here (as embodied in the July 24, 1979 letter from Reichek to Redding). Most of the agreed-to terms deal with Nexxus' sale of its hair care products to Best. We are confident that a Texas court would find the sales

3. Reichek stated the following in an affidavit submitted in support of Sally Beauty's Memorandum in Opposition to Nexxus' Motion for Summary Judgment:

At no time prior to the execution of the Distribution Agreement did Steve Redding tell me that he was relying upon my personal peculiar tastes and ability in making his decision to award a Nexxus distributorship to Best. Moreover, I never understood that Steve Redding was relying upon my skill and ability in particular in choosing Best as a distributor. I never considered the Distribution Agreement to be a personal service contract between me and Nexxus or Stephen Redding. I always considered the Distribution Agreement to be between Best and Nexxus as expressly provided in the Distribution Agreement which was written by my brother and me. At all times I conducted business with Nexxus on behalf of Best and not on my own behalf. In that connection, when I sent correspondence to Nexxus, I invariably signed it as president of Best. Neither Stephen Redding nor any other Nexxus employee ever told me that Nexxus was relying on my personal financial integrity on executing the Distribution Agreement or in shipping Nexxus products to Best * * *

aspect of this contract dominant and apply the majority rule that such a distributorship is a contract for "goods" under the UCC.

The fact that this contract is considered a contract for the sale of goods and not for the provision of a service does not, as Sally Beauty suggests, mean that it is freely assignable in all circumstances. The delegation of performance under a sales contract (whether in conjunction with an assignment of rights, as here, or not) is governed by UCC section 2–210(1). The UCC recognizes that in many cases an obligor will find it convenient or even necessary to relieve himself of the duty of performance under a contract, *see* Official Comment 1, UCC § 2–210 ("[T]his section recognizes both delegation of performance and assignability as normal and permissible incidents of a contract for the sale of goods."). The Code therefore sanctions delegation except where the delegated performance would be unsatisfactory to the obligee: "A party may perform his duty through a delegate unless otherwise agreed to or unless the other party has a substantial interest in having his original promisor perform or control the acts required by the contract." UCC § 2–210(1). Consideration is given to balancing the policies of free alienability of commercial contracts and protecting the obligee from having to accept a bargain he did not contract for.

We are concerned here with the delegation of Best's duty of performance under the distribution agreement, as Nexxus terminated the agreement because it did not wish to accept Sally Beauty's substituted performance.[6] Only one Texas case has construed section 2–210 in the context of a party's delegation of performance under an executory contract. In *McKinnie v. Milford*, 597 S.W.2d 953 (Tex.Civ.App.1980, writ ref'd, n.r.e.), the court held that nothing in the Texas Business and Commercial Code prevented the seller of a horse from delegating to the buyer a pre-existing contractual duty to make the horse available to a third party for breeding. "[I]t is clear that Milford [the third party] had no particular interest in not allowing Stewart [the seller] to delegate the duties required by the contract. Milford was only interested in getting his two breedings per year, and such performance could only be obtained from McKinnie [the buyer] after he bought the horse from Stewart." *Id.* at 957. In McKinnie, the Texas court recognized and applied the UCC rule that bars delegation of duties if there is some reason why the non-assigning party would find performance by a delegate a substantially different thing than what he had bargained for.

In the exclusive distribution agreement before us, Nexxus had contracted for Best's "best efforts" in promoting the sale of Nexxus products

---

6. If this contract is assignable, Sally Beauty would also, of course, succeed to Best's rights under the distribution agreement. But the fact situation before us must be distinguished from the assignment of contract rights that are no longer executory (*e.g.*, the right to damages for breach or the right to payment of an account), which is considered in UCC section 2–210(2), Tex.Bus. & Com.Code Ann. S 2–210(b) (Vernon 1968), and in several of the authorities relied on by appellants. The policies underlying these two situations are different and, generally, the UCC favors assignment more strongly in the latter. *See* UCC § 2–210(2) (non-executory rights assignable even if agreement states otherwise).

in Texas. UCC § 2–306(2), states that "[a] lawful agreement by either buyer or seller for exclusive dealing in the kind of goods concerned imposes unless otherwise agreed an obligation by the seller to use best efforts to supply the goods and by the buyer to use best efforts to promote their sale." This implied promise on Best's part was the consideration for Nexxus' promise to refrain from supplying any other distributors within Best's exclusive area. *See* Official Comment 5, UCC S 2–306. It was this contractual undertaking which Nexxus refused to see performed by Sally.

In ruling on Nexxus' motion for summary judgment, the district court noted: "Unlike Best, Sally Beauty is a subsidiary of one of Nexxus' direct competitors. This is a significant distinction and in the court's view, it raises serious questions regarding Sally Beauty's ability to perform the distribution agreement in the same manner as Best." We agree with these assessments and hold that Sally Beauty's position as a wholly-owned subsidiary of Alberto–Culver is sufficient to bar the delegation of Best's duties under the agreement.

We do not believe that our holding will work the mischief with our national economy that the appellants predict. We hold merely that the duty of performance under an exclusive distributorship may not be delegated to a competitor in the market place—or the wholly-owned subsidiary of a competitor—without the obligee's consent. We believe that such a rule is consonant with the policies behind section 2–210, which is concerned with preserving the bargain the obligee has struck. Nexxus should not be required to accept the "best efforts" of Sally Beauty when those efforts are subject to the control of Alberto–Culver. It is entirely reasonable that Nexxus should conclude that this performance would be a different thing than what it had bargained for. At oral argument, Sally Beauty argued that the case should go to trial to allow it to demonstrate that it could and would perform the contract as impartially as Best. It stressed that Sally Beauty is a "multi-line" distributor, which means that it distributes many brands and is not just a conduit for Alberto–Culver products. But we do not think that this creates a material question of fact in this case. When performance of personal services is delegated, the trier merely determines that it is a personal services contract. If so, the duty is *per se* nondelegable. There is no inquiry into whether the delegate is as skilled or worthy of trust and confidence as the original obligor: the delegate was not bargained for and the obligee need not consent to the substitution. And so here: it is undisputed that Sally Beauty is wholly owned by Alberto–Culver, which means that Sally Beauty's "impartial" sales policy is at least acquiesced in by Alberto–Culver—but could change whenever Alberto–Culver's needs changed. Sally Beauty may be totally sincere in its belief that it can operate "impartially" as a distributor, but who can guarantee the outcome when there is a clear choice between the demands of the parent-manufacturer, Alberto–Culver, and the competing needs of Nexxus? The risk of an unfavorable outcome is not one which the law can force Nexxus to take. Nexxus has a substantial interest in not seeing this contract performed by Sally Beauty, which is sufficient to bar the delegation under section 2–210. Because Nexxus should not be forced to accept performance of the distributorship agreement by Sally, we hold that the contract was not assignable without Nexxus' consent.

The judgment of the district court is AFFIRMED.

POSNER, CIRCUIT JUDGE, dissenting.

My brethren have decided, with no better foundation than judicial intuition about what businessmen consider reasonable, that the Uniform Commercial Code gives a supplier an absolute right to cancel an exclusive-dealing contract if the dealer is acquired, directly or indirectly, by a competitor of the supplier. I interpret the Code differently.

Nexxus makes products for the hair and sells them through distributors to hair salons and barbershops. It gave a contract to Best, cancellable on any anniversary of the contract with 120 days' notice, to be its exclusive distributor in Texas. Two years later Best was acquired by and merged into Sally Beauty, a distributor of beauty supplies and wholly owned subsidiary of Alberto–Culver. Alberto–Culver makes "hair care" products, too, though they mostly are cheaper than Nexxus's, and are sold to the public primarily through grocery stores and drugstores. * * *

* * * So far as appears, the same people who distributed Nexxus's products for Best (except for Best's president) continued to do so for Sally Beauty. Best was acquired, and continues, as a going concern; the corporation was dissolved, but the business wasn't. Whether there was a delegation of performance in any sense may be doubted. The general rule is that a change of corporate form—including a merger—does not in and of itself affect contractual rights and obligations.

The fact that Best's president has quit cannot be decisive on the issue whether the merger resulted in a delegation of performance. The contract between Nexxus and Best was not a personal-services contract conditioned on a particular individual's remaining with Best. If Best had not been acquired, but its president had left anyway, as of course he might have done, Nexxus could not have repudiated the contract.

    * * *

Steel companies both make fabricated steel and sell raw steel to competing fabricators. General Motors sells cars manufactured by a competitor, Isuzu.

    * * *

Suppose there had been no merger, but the only child of Best's president had gone to work for Alberto–Culver as a chemist. Could Nexxus have canceled the contract, fearing that Best (perhaps unconsciously) would favor Alberto–Culver products over Nexxus products? That would be an absurd ground for cancellation, and so is Nexxus's actual ground. At most, so far as the record shows, Nexxus may have had grounds for "insecurity" regarding the performance by Sally Beauty of its obligation to use its best efforts to promote Nexxus products, but if so its remedy was not to cancel the contract but to demand assurances of due performance. *See* UCC § 2–609; Official Comment 5 to § 2–306. No such demand was made. An anticipatory repudiation by conduct requires conduct that makes the repudiating party unable to perform. The merger did not do this. At least there is no evidence it did. The judgment should be reversed and the case remanded for a trial on whether the merger so altered the conditions of performance that Nexxus is entitled to declare the contract broken.

<hr />

QUESTIONS AND CONNECTION

1. Questions about the facts of this case

   1.1. What fact did the court treat as the most important fact in the case? Do you agree?

   1.2. What facts do you think should be important?

      (a) Was there language in the contract between Nexxus and Best regarding assignment and delegation of the contract? Is that important?

      (b) Is it important that the contract made Best the exclusive distributor for Nexxus' products for most of the State of Texas?

      (c) Is it important that Texas is sometimes referred to as the "Big Hair State"?

2. Questions about the law

   2.1. Why did the court apply Article 2? Which contract was a contract for the sale of goods—the distributorship contract between Nexxus and Best or the contract between Best and Sally transferring the distributorship contract? If Article 2 applies in this case, should the court in *Macke* also have applied Article 2?

   2.2. Why did the court look to section 2–210(1) instead of section 2–210(2)? Under section 2–210(1), which of the parties in this case is the "party"? The "original promisor"? The "other party"? In this case, what is the "substantial interest in having his original promisor perform"?

   2.3. What is the court's holding? Is it that the contract could not be delegated, or that the contract could not be delegated to a competitor of the obligee? Would the Seventh Circuit have decided this case differently if Sally Beauty had been owned by Alberto Markell, Bruce Markell's South American cousin, instead of Alberto–Culver, a competitor of Nexxus? Should a court applying section 2–210(1) decide the two cases differently?

   2.4. If the contract between Nexxus and Best had stated "This contract is not assignable," would Sally have filed this law suit? *Cf.* section 2–210(3). Would Sally have still given the same amount of consideration to the prior owners of Best in order to acquire Best?

3. Connection
   3.1 Exclusive agency: Recall that Wood was the exclusive agent for Lucy, Lady Duff Gordon. Should the Seventh Circuit have recalled *Wood v, Lucy, Lady Duff Gordon* in deciding the *Nexus* case?
   3.2. Insecurity: Recall that in the *Norcon* case, Niagara Mohawk was concerned about Norcon's future performance under the contract. Should the Seventh Circuit have recalled *Norcon Power Partners, L.P. v. Niagara Mohawk Power Corp* in deciding the *Nexxus* case? Did Judge Posner once again get it right—should this case have been decided under U.C.C. section 2–609 instead of 2–210?

The *Nexxus* case involves not only the transfer of contract rights but also a stock purchase transaction and a merger—stuff covered in second and third year courses on business associations. (And stuff covered by a casebook that Epstein has co-authored on business structures (a/k/a "B.S.")). Increasingly, the transfer of contract rights are governed by statutes. Articles 3 and 4 of the Uniform Commercial Code deal with the transfer of rights under contracts that are negotiable instruments; Article 9 of the Uniform Commercial Code deals with transferring rights under accounts receivable and other contracts as security for loans courses on the U.C.C. (And stuff covered by a casebook that Markell and Ponoroff have co-authored.) The Bankruptcy Code provides special rules for transfers of contract rights by or to a person who is a debtor in a bankruptcy case—stuff covered in second and third year courses in bankruptcy. (And stuff covered by a casebook that Epstein and Markell have co-authored.) Take these courses and use our books!

FINAL NOTE FROM THE AUTHORS

We hope you enjoyed reading *Making and Doing Deals* as much as we enjoyed writing it. In fact, we hope you enjoyed it so much that you decide to keep it rather than to sell it back to the bookstore! Either way, we wish you the best of luck throughout the remainder of your law school career—and beyond!

DGE, BAM, LP

INDEX

References are to Pages

A

ACCEPTANCE
Generally 106
"Battle of the forms" 154–178
Control over form or manner of acceptance by offeror 106–115
Electronic acceptance 178–180
Imperfect acceptances 180–195
Lapse or delay in acceptance 90–94
Mailbox or dispatch rule 128–132
Method or form of acceptance, conditions for 106–195
Mirror image rule of offer and acceptance 180–195
Performance, acceptance through 132–142
Promissory acceptance 124–132
Sale of goods 155–195
Silence or inaction to solicitations or offers 143–146
Termination of power of acceptance 83–106
Time of acceptance
General rule 125–128
Mailbox rule 128–132

ADVERTISEMENTS
False and misleading advertising 81
Offers made through 78–82
Revocation 90

AMENDMENT OR MODIFICATION OF CONTRACT
Generally 253–264
Preexisting duty rule and 257–263
Sale of goods 601–603
Waiver distinguished 601

ANTICIPATORY REPUDIATION
Adequate assurance and 641–649
Conditions for 636–641
Generally 636–649
History 636–640
Retraction 601–602

ARBITRATION
Battle of forms 155–178
Consideration 248–253
Generally 32–35
Shrink-wrap contracts 155–178
Unconscionable 410–416

ASSIGNMENT AND DELEGATION
Generally 856–859
Assignee's right to sue obligor 857–859

ASSIGNMENT AND DELEGATION
—Cont'd
Limitations on 859–868
Obligee's right to sue delegator 842–845

ASSUMPSIT
History 6–9

AVOIDABLE DAMAGES (See DAMAGES)

B

"BATTLE OF THE FORMS" (See ACCEPTANCE)

BENEFIT OR DETRIMENT
Consideration 229–230, 236–241

BREACH OF CONTRACT
Anticipatory breach of contract 636–649
Material breach (See MATERIAL BREACH OF CONTRACT)

C

CAPACITY OR INCAPACITY TO CONTRACT
Generally 94–96
Death or incapacity of offeror 95–96
Mentally ill or intoxicated persons 44, 357
Minors 356–362

CHICKEN CASE
Interpretation 471–478

CONCEALMENT
Fraudulent concealment 349–352
Nondisclosure of material facts 352–356

CONDITIONS
Generally 579–580
Conditional acceptance distinguished 579
Constructive (implied) conditions of exchange 650–660
Covenants and promises, compared to conditions 583–586
Express and constructive conditions compared 658–660
Express conditions 580–583
Forfeiture 587–592
Prevention or hindrance of condition by one party 592–597
Standard of interpretation as to establishing existence of condition 583–586
Waiver of conditions 598

CONSEQUENTIAL DAMAGES (See DAM-AGES)

CONSIDERATION
Benefit or detriment 229
Definition of 228–229
Family agreements 241–252
Forbearance as consideration 245
History of 7–9, 226–228
Illusory promises, lack of consideration due to 248–253
Modification of contracts
    Preexisting duty rule and 253–264
    Sale of goods 262–263
Moral duty as sufficient consideration 264–278
Mutuality of obligation doctrine 253
Option contracts, consideration required for 85, 97, 101–104
Past claims, promises made for settlement of 245
Past consideration, enforcement of promises made under 253
Preexisting duty rule 253–264
Promissory estoppel doctrine (See PROMISSO-RY ESTOPPEL)
Sufficient or adequate consideration 241–245

CONSTRUCTION (See INTERPRETATION OF CONTRACTS)

COUNTEROFFERS
UCC provision for sale of goods 152–154

COURSE OF DEALING OR PERFORM-ANCE
    Generally 478–480
Parol evidence and 459, 478–480

COVENANTS NOT TO COMPETE
Enforcement of 395–403

D

DAMAGES
    Generally 711–800
Consequential or special damages 712, 769–770
Economic Waste 721–734
Efficient breach of contract theory 697–698, 706–708
Incidental damages 712, 772
Limitation on damages
    Avoided Costs 749–752
    Avoidable Loss 752–764
    Certainty 770–783
    Foreseeability 764–770
    Mitigation 752–764
Liquidated damages 698–708
Money damages
    Cost of completion 718–721
    Diminution in value 713–718
    Expectation interest 711–713
    General Measure 711–713
    Incidental damages 712, 772
    Lost profits 764–790
    Reliance interest 783–784

DAMAGES—Cont'd
Promissory estoppel doctrine, claiming damages under (See PROMISSORY ESTOP-PEL)
Proof of damages
    Certainty 770–783
    Foreseeability 764–770
    Reliance, damages based on 783–790
    Restitution, damages based on 790–800
    UCC 734–749

DEATH
Offeror, death of 94–96

DECEIT OR FRAUD
Damages or rescission of contract for 355–356

DELEGATION (See ASSIGNMENT AND DELEGATION)

DISCLAIMER
Warranty 163–164, 567–578

DISPATCH RULE
Acceptance under 128–132

DIVISIBLE CONTRACTS
Performance under 672–673

DURESS
Generally 362–374

E

ELECTION OF REMEDIES
Material breach 649–672, 684–685

ESTOPPEL (See also PROMISSORY ESTOP-PEL)
Excuse for breach 599–611

EXCULPATORY CLAUSES
Public policy against enforcement of 382–395

EXCUSE FROM LIABILITY OR PER-FORMANCE
Anticipatory repudiation 636–649
Condition precedent and 636–640
    Constructive (implied) conditions of ex-change 651–660
    Covenants or promises compared to condi-tions 583–586
    Excusing conditions
        Forfeiture resulting from strict interpre-tation or enforcement 587–592
        Prevention or hindrance of conditions by one party 592–597
        Waiver of condition 598
Failure to give adequate assurance of future performance 641–649
Impossibility, impracticability and frustration of purpose 612–636
Material breach (See MATERIAL BREACH OF CONTRACT)
Waivers 598

F

FAIR DEALING
Duty to bargain in good faith and 211–214
Implied, duty of good faith and 518–533

FIRM OFFERS
UCC 104–105

FRAUD OR CONCEALMENT
Damages or rescission of contract for 355–356
Generally 343–356
Statute of frauds (See STATUTE OF FRAUDS)

FRUSTRATION OF PURPOSE
Performance/non-performance of contract and 612–636

G

GIFT
Promise to make gifts, enforcement of
Generally 235, 276–279
Promissory estoppel doctrine (See PROMISSORY ESTOPPEL)

GOOD FAITH
Duty to bargain and negotiate in good faith 211–214

H

HAIRY HAND CASE
Damages, and 713–718

HOLD–HARMLESS CLAUSES
Public policy against 382–395

I

ILLEGAL CONTRACTS AND AGREE-MENTS
Generally 381–403
Licensing 381–382

IMPLIED–IN–LAW CONTRACTS (See QUASI–CONTRACTS AND RESTITUTION)

IMPOSSIBILITY OR IMPRACTICABILITY OF PERFORMANCE
Common law 612–636
UCC 617, 622

INACTION (See SILENCE OR INCAPACITY TO CONTRACT)

INDEFINITENESS
Agreements to agree 198–212
Fair and reasonable terms, settlement by 185–195

INDEFINITENESS—Cont'd
Sale of goods, additional or different terms to contract 154–178
UCC gap fillers 196–198, 534–535

INFANTS (See MINORS)

INSTALLMENT CONTRACT
UCC 672–673

INTERPRETATION OF CONTRACTS
Adhesion 501–510
Course of dealing or performance 478–480
Parol evidence and 459, 478–488
Rules and maxims of interpretation 497–501
Standardized forms and clauses, use of 501–510

L

LAPSE (See ACCEPTANCE)

LETTER OF INTENT
Defined 212–213
Enforceability 212–224

LIMITATION OF REMEDIES
UCC 709–710

LIQUIDATED DAMAGES
Agreements for 699–709

M

MAILBOX RULE
Acceptance under 128–132

MATERIAL BREACH OF CONTRACT
Categories of breaches 684–685
Damages (See DAMAGES)
Divisible contracts 672–672
Election of remedies doctrine 676–684
Partial breach 684–685
Perfect tender rule under UCC 674–678
Remedies for 684–685
Substantial performance doctrine 660–671, 684–685

MATERIAL MISREPRESENTATION
Damages and rescission of contract for 355–356

MENTAL INCOMPETENCE
Incapacity to contract 44, 357

MINORS
Capacity to contract 356–362
Enforcement of contracts at age of majority 360–362
Reaffirmation 361–362

MIRROR IMAGE RULE
Offer and acceptance under 180–195

MISREPRESENTATION
Fraudulent misrepresentation 343–356
Material misrepresentation 344–348

MISSING TERMS (See INDEFINITENESS)

MISTAKE
Formation of agreement or contract, mistake in 417–420
Generally 416–433
Mutual 417–428
Unilateral 429–433

MISUNDERSTANDING
Agreement or contract, misunderstanding terms of 182–185

MODIFICATION OF CONTRACT (See AMENDMENT OR MODIFICATION OF CONTRACT)

MORAL DUTY
Legal obligation under 264–278

N

NEGOTIATIONS
Letter of intent 212–224
Price quotations 70–77

NONDISCLOSURE OF MATERIAL FACTS
Rescission of contract for 344–348

O

OFFER
Generally 66–83
Advertisements, offers made through 78–82
Counteroffer (See COUNTEROFFERS)
Death or incapacity of offeror 94–96
Firm offers under UCC 105
Irrevocable offers 104
Lapse of offer 90–94
Option contracts 96–104
Price quotations 70–77
Rejection of offer 84
Revocation of offer 84–90
UCC 77, 104

OMITTED TERMS (See INDEFNITENESS)

OPTION CONTRACTS
Consideration required for 85, 97, 101–104
Firm offers and 105
Reliance 105–106

ORAL AGREEMENTS AND CONTRACTS
Enforcement, generally 434–439
Parol evidence rule (See PAROL EVIDENCE RULE)
Statute of Frauds (See STATUTE OF FRAUDS)

P

PAROL EVIDENCE RULE
Generally 439–455

PAROL EVIDENCE RULE—Cont'd
Common law 440–454
Exceptions 460–461
Uniform Commercial Code 454–455

PEERLESS, SHIP
Ambiguity 182–185

PEPPERCORN
Consideration 244–245

PERFECT TENDER RULE
Generally 672–673
Installment contract exception 672

PERFORMANCE
Acceptance of offer through performance 132–142
Adequate assurance of future performance under UCC 641–649
Conditions for performance (See CONDITIONS)
Divisible contracts 672–673
Excuse from performance (See EXCUSE FROM LIABILITY OR PERFORMANCE)
Good faith, duty to perform in 211–214
Impossibility or impracticability of performance 612–636

PRICE QUOTATIONS
As offers 70–77

PROMISSORY ESTOPPEL
Generally 278–322
Charitable Subscriptions. enforcement of 321–322
Equitable estoppel 283–284
General contractors reliance on subcontractors' bids, relief for 301–315
Historical development 279–284
Pre-contract negotiations, application to 299–300
Remedies available under 287–296, 305–317
Statute of frauds 287–296

PUBLIC POLICY
Generally 381–403
Covenants not to compete 396
Exculpatory clauses, public policy against 389–396
Hold-harmless clauses, public policy against 389–396
Licensing requirements, compliance with 381–382
Restrictive covenants 396–403
Surrogacy parenting agreements 382–389

Q

QUASI–CONTRACTS AND RESTITUTION
Generally 790–800, 803–834

QUOTATIONS (See PRICE QUOTATIONS)

R

RELATIONAL CONTRACT
Generally 64–65

RELIANCE
Damages and 315–317, 783–790
Detrimental reliance
  Promissory estoppel doctrine (See PROMIS-
    SORY ESTOPPEL)
Option contracts 105–106

REPUDIATION
Anticipatory repudiation 636–649
Repudiation 636–637

RESCISSION
Fraud, due to 355–356
Incapacity to contract, due to (See CAPACITY
    OR INCAPACITY TO CONTRACT)
Misrepresentation, due to 355–356
Mistake of fact or law, due to 416–433
Non-disclosure of material facts, due to
    344–348
Unconscionability, due to 248–253

RESTITUTION (See QUASI–CONTRACTS
    AND RESTITUTION)

RESTRICTIVE COVENANTS
Enforcement of 395–403

REVOCATION
Promissory estoppel doctrine (See PROMISSO-
    RY ESTOPPEL)
Rescission (See RESCISSION)

ROSE THE COW
Mistake 417–420

S

SEALS
Consideration alternative 104, 269–270

SILENCE OR INACTION
Acceptance 143–146
Concealment or non-disclosure of material
    facts 351–356

SPECIFIC PERFORMANCE
Generally 687–698
Real estate 688–698
Sale of goods 692

STATUTE OF FRAUDS
Generally 323–343
Classes of contracts covered under 324–325
Employment agreements 335–343
Estoppel 335–343
Judicial admission exceptions to 335
Real estate 325–329
Sale of goods 329–335

**SURROGACY PARENTING AGREE-
MENTS**
Enforcement of 382–389

T

THIRD–PARTY BENEFICIARIES
Generally 835–855
Cancellation or modification of rights of third
    party 849–856
Defenses against third party 849–855
History 836–842
Intended 842–849

TRADE USAGE
Generally 435–439, 478–480
Contractual liability under 435–439

U

UCC (See UNIFORM COMMERCIAL CODE
    (UCC))

UNCONSCIONABILITY
Common law 403–416
Mistake, and 431–432
UCC 410–416

UNDUE INFLUENCE
Generally 374–380

UNIFORM COMMERCIAL CODE (UCC)
Acceptance of goods 123–124
Adequate assurance of future performance
    642–649
Disclaimers 163–164, 567–578
Firm offers 105
Gap fillers 196–198, 534–535
Installment contracts, breach of 672–673
Limitation of remedies 709–710
Open terms 478–488
Parol evidence rule and 454–459
Perfect tender rule 674–678
Warranties (See WARRANTIES)

UNJUST ENRICHMENT
Quasi-contractual claims or restitution for (See
    QUASI–CONTRACTS AND RESTITU-
    TION)

V

VALUE
Expectation interest 711–713
Reliance interest 783–784
Restitution interest 790–791

W

WAIVER
Generally 598
Modification distinguished 599–611

WARRANTIES

Generally 535–578
Disclaimers 567–578
Express warranties 536–545

WARRANTIES—Cont'd
Implied warranties
Fitness for a particular purpose 552–567
Merchantability 545–552
Repair or replacement as exclusive remedy for
breach of warranty 709–710

†